the
bentlens

2nd Edition

the
bentlens
2ND EDITION

a world guide to gay & lesbian film

Lisa Daniel & Claire Jackson

alyson books
los angeles

© 2003 by Lisa Daniel and Claire Jackson. All rights reserved.

Printed in Singapore   .

This trade paperback is published by Alyson Publications
P.O. Box 4371, Los Angeles, California 90078-4371

Second edition (first U.S. edition): April 2003

Simultaneouly published in Australia by Allen & Unwin

03 04 05 06 07 a 10 9 8 7 6 5 4 3 2 1

ISBN 1-55583-806-5

the bent lens: a world guide to gay and lesbian film
[edited] by Lisa Daniel and Claire Jackson. – 2nd ed. p. cm.
Includes bibliographical references and indexes
1. Homosexuality in motion pictures. 2. Motion pictures–Catalogs. I. Daniel, Lisa. II. Jackson, Claire.
PN1995.9.H55 B45 2003

791.43'653–dc21

Credits

Main front cover image by Mush Emmon from *Her Urge* (Barry Gilbert, 2001)

Cover design by Redback Graphix

Contents

Acknowledgements

What began as a two-person squad putting *The Bent Lens* 2nd Edition together very quickly became a team effort. We'd like to thank the essay writers, Judith Halberstam, Daniel Mudie Cunningham, Helen Hok-Sze Leung and Barbara Hammer, for sharing their specialist knowledge with us, and our readers. To the kind and patient folk at Allen & Unwin who came on board to make sure this 2nd edition saw the light of day—particularly Elizabeth Weiss, Alexandra Nahlous and Emma Sorenson. Thank you to the talented crew at Redback Graphix who provided the fantastic cover concept, as well as the generous filmmakers and distributors who provided their stills both for the cover, and throughout the book—big thanks in particular to Barry Gilbert who kindly provided the main cover still of the smooching gals. A very big nod of appreciation goes to everyone who provided synopses over the past few years, including Richard Watts, Madeleine Swain, Joseph Alessi, Ben Zipper, Paul Andrew, Laura Deriu, as well as all of the festivals and distributors who allowed us to use synopses and information from their programs, catalogues and websites—particularly Maura King and Desi del Valle at Frameline, Gaye Naismith, Faye Shortal and Amree Hewitt from the Australian Centre for the Moving Image, Michael Lumpkin and the team at the San Francisco International Lesbian and Gay Film Festival, Jeff Crawford and Deidre Logue at Canadian Filmmakers' Distribution Centre. The book is chock full of fantastic stills, and we will forever be grateful to Marcus Hu from Strand Releasing who helped us out with literally hundreds of images. Thank you also to Chris Berry for sharing his expertise with us once again, and to Peter Tapp for supporting the project from its inception as a first edition, to kind support of the second. Thanks to our families and friends for giving us time out from any social life during the final months of putting the book together, as well as to the Melbourne Queer Film Festival for excusing us from the office for several weeks whilst we put this baby to bed. And last but not least, thank you to Sheila Drummond, who never wavered in her commitment to helping us see this project through to print.

Introduction

There's been an enormous amount of activity in the queer filmmaking world since the 1st Edition of *The Bent Lens* appeared in 1997. During that time there has been somewhat of a frenzy of films made with a queer bent. For short filmmakers in particular, the ever-increasing availability of cheaper and easier film technologies has made picking up a camera and capturing stories on film that much more accessible. Audiences and film financiers too, have seemed more willing to embrace the depiction of diverse lifestyles on the screen. The increased commercialisation of mainstream queer film is evident in the number of queer narratives produced by the larger production houses over the past five years. The box office success of films such as *Billy's Hollywood Screen Kiss* (1998), *Better than Chocolate* (1999), *Boy's Don't Cry* (1999), *Before Night Falls* (2000) and *Hedwig and the Angry Inch* (2001) have seen an increased confidence in the ability of narratives about non-mainstream characters to attract audiences. Depictions of queer lives on television have increased in number and popularity also, with *Queer as Folk* (1999 and 2000) and *Metrosexuality* (2001) attracting huge audiences.

Even more inspiring is the success, and critical acclaim of films such as *By Hook or By Crook* (2001), and *Walking on Water* (2002), whose narrative concerns are real world problems experienced by characters who just happen to be queer. While 'coming out' stories and stories about being queer will always be relevant as long as queer people exist, it is refreshing, and perhaps a sign of the maturing of modern Western popular culture, that we can also enjoy and embrace narratives that celebrate the telling of a good story by a collection of characters for whom sexuality is just one part of a much bigger picture.

There are over 1000 new titles featured in this edition of *The Bent Lens*. Since there have been so many films both in long and short form released over the past five years it has been impossible to include them all. We have tried as best we can to include queer films of ten minutes and over that have either had a cinema release, are formally distributed, or that have played at least two queer film festivals somewhere in the world.

In the same way as the first edition, the second offers readers a practical guide to gay and lesbian film. Wherever possible we have included and updated selected distribution information about the films, or in the age of internet shopping, where you might be able to purchase your favourite titles over the web. The information is by no means exhaustive, and there are many companies that now offer the facility to purchase over the internet that we did not have the space to list here.

The Bent Lens offers an A–Z listing of over 2600 films which are also indexed according to director, country, sexualities and genre. Direct representations of lesbians, gay men, bisexuals, as well as transgendered people are featured throughout, as well as mainstream films which contain strong queer sub-texts, or sub-plots such as *Velvet Goldmine* (1998), *Being John Malkovich* (1999), *Magnolia* (1999) and *American Beauty* (1999). For filmmakers and festival audiences, we have included a selected listing of some of the major queer film festivals around the world, as well as some great websites to visit.

The Bent Lens is the only guide of its kind to include queer cinema from all parts of the world while representing all genres and formats including features, documentaries, shorts and experimental works, as well as work from the Asian and Australian regions. Nowhere in print will you find such a comprehensive listing of lesbian and gay short films. We hope that the support shown to short filmmakers will provide the encouragement to keep making films, and maybe even get that feature script up and running.

In order to provide some context to the wealth of information that is contained within, we have included a series of essays which highlight some of the changes that have taken place in lesbian and gay cinema in recent times, as well as some speculation about future directions. Daniel Mudie Cunningham gives us his take on what has been happening in the world of queer cinema since 1997; Helen Hok-Sze Leung guides us through a recent history of queer Asian cinema; and Judith Halberstam tours through the fluid gender world of recent narratives with a transgender bent. Also featured is an interview with prolific and pioneering lesbian experimental filmmaker Barbara Hammer, who gives us an intimate insight into her significant body of film work, highlighting her most recent title *History Lessons* (2000).

We have endeavoured to make *The Bent Lens* 2nd Edition as inclusive, accurate and current as possible, and as it is an ongoing project, we encourage feedback, new information and suggestions, but above all we hope you enjoy the book.

Claire Jackson and Lisa Daniel
Email: bentlens@bigpond.net.au

How to use this book

All films are listed alphabetically and where possible we have included the following information in this order:

> Title
> Alternate Title (aka: first alternative; second alternative)
> Director (last name, first name)
> Year; Country; Running Time; Black & White; Genre

P: (producer); W: (scriptwriter, screenplay); C: (cinematographer, director of photography or camera); E: (editor); M: (music)

Cast:

Synopsis: (including foreign language films with subtitle information)

Awards: (selected listing from major festivals and organisations)

Prod Comp: (production company)

Dist/Sales: (distribution company, sales contact or print source)

Example:

Evening Dress

(aka: Tenue de Soirée; Menage)

Blier, Bertrand

1986; France; 84 min; Comedy

P: Philippe Dussart, René Cleitman; *W:* Bertrand Blier; *C:* Jean Penzer; *E:* Claudine Merlin; *M:* Serge Gainsbourg

Cast: Gérard Depardieu, Michel Blanc, Miou-Miou, Michel Creton, Jean-François Stevenin

> This black comedy is a clever gay variation on the traditional romantic triangle. Everything changes when a thief talks a financially struggling couple into burglary: the thief then falls, not for the sexy wife, but the boring, balding husband. French with English subtitles.

Awards: Cannes Film Festival, 1986: Best Actor (Michel Blanc)

Prod Comp: Ciné Valse, DD Productions, Hachette Première, Phillipe Dussart SARL

Dist/Sales: Roadshow, Cinecom, BFI

Distributor's details can be found beginning page 513, and are listed in alphabetical order by code. Not all distributors provide titles internationally—some may only service limited regions, or distribute to particular organisations.

For ease of use and to help with locating films we have included indexes of directors, country, genre, and films of bisexual, cross-dressing, transgender, transsexual, fringe, gay, lesbian and queer interest. Films denoted as fringe interest include titles with central queer characters, but with limited queer story content. Films listed as queer include titles with storylines which contain elements relevant to multiple sexualities, gay, lesbian, bisexual etc.

When synopses have been taken from other sources we have credited the source in brackets at the end of the synopsis. Abbreviations used when crediting synopses are MQFF: Melbourne Queer Film Festival, WMM: Women Make Movies, ACMI: Australian Centre for the Moving Image, CFMDC: Canadian Filmmaker's Distribution Centre.

Queer Cinema Since 1997

Daniel Mudie Cunningham

By 1997, the year *The Bent Lens* was first published, queer cinema found itself at somewhat of a crossroads, staring into an uncertain future. Queer cinema was fast being absorbed into the mainstream, something that was certainly troubling considering 'queer' was a term injected with a range of meanings that included just about anything except mainstream, or normative, logic. The six or seven years preceding 1997 were identified, especially in the United States, as a time when queer film was electric, pulsing with the discordant rhythms of a period that came to be known—first by critics, second by audiences and lastly (if ever) by its practitioners—as New Queer Cinema.

In brief, the moniker New Queer Cinema was coined by film critic B. Ruby Rich to identify and categorise the larger-than-usual number of independent queer films lap-dancing around the US film festival circuit during 1991–92. Rich was referring primarily to the 'flock of films that were doing something new, renegotiating subjectivities, annexing whole genres, revising histories in their image'.[1] The films to which Rich referred included, among others, *Poison* (Todd Haynes, 1991), *My Own Private Idaho* (Gus Van Sant, 1991), *Paris is Burning* (Jennie Livingston, 1990), *The Living End* (Gregg Araki, 1992) and *Swoon* (Tom Kalin, 1992): landmarks of the emergent queer cinema, but more importantly, prime cuts of a new generation of filmmakers who were utilising the discontents of queerness to reconsider the very language of narrative cinema.

One of the problems for some critics, audiences and filmmakers was the fact that this growing wave of films were located in the boy-zone, where the splintering subjectivities of gay men dominated. Lesbian content was ensured, however, by filmmakers like Sadie Benning, Barbara Hammer, Ana Kokkinos, Pratibha Parmar and Monika Treut. But it wasn't until Rose Troche's *Go Fish* made a splash in 1994, that audiences everywhere recognised lesbian content in queer film had been sadly lacking. The success of *Go Fish* and others like it allowed viewers to whet their appetites (and perhaps even wet their legs) on lesbian narrative film.

Like many groundbreaking cultural forms, New Queer Cinema eventually became commercially viable. In the latter part of the 1990s, numerous New Queer filmmakers had abandoned strict queer criteria or simply opted for a more mainstream market. In 2000, Rich published another essay on the topic, this time reminiscing on the way New Queer had grown up and in many cases traded its independent origins for the mainstream. Rich argues that 'the story is more complicated than that, its conclusions less clear-cut, the movement itself in question, if not in total meltdown'.[2] Reasons for the 'total meltdown' abound, but it must be said that the ideas of 'queer'—like all so-called cutting edge concepts—inevitably evolve into shrink-wrapped commodities, whose appeal depends on increased circulation within the mainstream.

For some, queer cinema may have sold out, become co-opted in the process of being pushed towards commercialisation. For others, it is this commercialisation that finally makes queer film digestible and less obsessed with avant-garde attempts to trash the rules of both identity and cinematic form. As an avid consumer of all things queer, I have found it difficult to decide a position to which I should subscribe. Surely if I elect the first, I am living in a fantasy world that expects Rose Troche to preside over the lesbian go-fishbowl, Todd Haynes to make *Poison 2* and Gregg Araki to get over his Larry Clark-like obsession with disaffected post-adolescent flesh. If I subscribe to the second position, I have to admit I enjoyed (and sometimes prefer) relatively mainstream fare like *Boys Don't Cry* (Kimberly Peirce, 1999), *The Broken Hearts Club* (Greg Berlanti, 2000), *The Opposite of Sex* (Don Roos, 1998), *Psycho Beach Party* (Robert Lee King, 2000), as well as those I'm not likely to admit in print.

I must note, however, that an increasing number of commercial queer films do try and have it both ways. A recurring joke in *All Over the Guy* (Julie Davis, 2001) is at the expense of *In & Out* (Frank Oz, 1997), seemingly because any self-respecting queer who enjoyed *In & Out* has failed to see it as nothing more than a Hollywood exercise in safe-guarding thinly veiled homophobic sentiments. *In & Out* was hardly a great film, but it wasn't *that bad*. At least the sight of Kevin Kline and Tom Selleck locked in an oral embrace was worth the price of a weekly video hire. In contrast, *All Over the Guy* could have been granted a scholarship to the Nora Ephron Academy of Het-Rom-Comedy had the queer couples been cast by the likes of Tom Hanks and Meg Ryan. But for something that better presents a brooding, contemplative idea of queer, I'd recommend we ditch the bitch fight sparked by *All Over the Guy* and rent instead the similarly titled *All Over Me* (Alex Sichel, 1997), a gritty teenage tale of sex, drugs and rock and roll set in Hells Kitchen, NYC, and starring Alison Folland.

This depiction of sex, drugs and rock and roll is not an isolated one. Such themes in queer cinema can be located when we connect some of the dots on Christine Vachon's résumé as producer. Though Vachon openly dismisses being concerned only with queer product, she has produced a healthy dose of the more interesting queer films to come out of the United States. Vachon's post-1997 projects include the glam rock odysseys *The Velvet Goldmine* (Todd Haynes, 1998) and *Hedwig and the Angry Inch* (John Cameron Mitchell, 2001): proof that queers and disco aren't always synonymous. Moreover, these two films to a large extent re-write popular histories and myths through a queer framework; the former through music icons like David Bowie and Iggy Pop; the latter through its queer eurotrash take on Plato's *Symposium*.

This is not to say that the distinct independent sensibility of queer film has been totally abandoned. Surely the two glam examples cited above are still distinctive in terms of narrative, style and content. They may have the ability to reach a rapidly growing, potentially mainstream audience, but many viewers would agree that these films still inhabit the confines of the arthouse. Even *Boys Don't Cry*, which was also produced by Vachon, is something of an arthouse film, despite its well-known cast of nineties/noughties brat-packers, its critical and commercial success, and the Oscar and Golden Globe accolades bestowed on Hilary Swank for her transgender turn. This is a major accomplishment for queer cinema, but had the film not been based around Brandon Teena's tragic life, you have to ask whether it would have resonated on so many levels.

Even though queer cinema has become a relatively commercial zone, much of it still derives from the context of independent filmmaking. It seems that indie films now have a decidedly commercial edge. Gems like *High Art* (Lisa Cholodenko, 1998) and *Head On* (Ana Kokkinos, 1998) demonstrate that independent films can happily exist outside of the Hollywood system, and still make an impact with audiences and in the market-place. *High Art* asks the powerful question: What do you find when investigating a leaky roof? Answers don't come easily, but when they do, you'll find Ally Sheedy, playing a has-been photographer who seduces 'the girl with the leak', while trying to stage a career comeback one minute and a drug run the next. Entertaining as the premise sounds, *High Art* is fiercely intelligent, darkly satirical, full of visual pleasure—clearly one of the best queer films of the last decade. The Australian film *Head On* finds raw poetry in its protagonist's fucked-up everyday. Identity, moreover, is not limited to queerness, because *Head On* is equally concerned with the attempt to locate one's sense of self within the nuclear family, and in relation to larger ethnic communities. *High Art* and *Head On* are successful examples of queer cinema primarily because their depictions of queer subjects and subjectivities is uncompromising. The simplistic demands for so-called 'positive' images of queer, lesbian and gay life has been replaced by beautifully flawed characters who resonate long after the final credits roll.

But the distinction between mainstream and independent (read Hollywood/non-Hollywood) has become increasingly blurred in recent times. *Being John Malkovich* (Spike Jonze, 1999) is a studio-financed, big budget piece that presents an unexpected and subversive lesbian happy ending for Catherine Keener and Cameron Diaz. On the one hand, this film is as commercial as it gets for queer. On the other, it goes beyond queer, and into territory that feels strangely new.

From *American Beauty* (Sam Mendes, 1999) to *American Psycho* (Mary Harron, 2000), much Hollywood cinema engages to varying degrees with queer themes, characters, subplots and subtexts. This doesn't mean such inclusiveness will always be embraced by queer audiences. Whether it be in Hollywood, the indie world or elsewhere, queerness only stands a chance of being interesting if it continues to revise and reinvent itself. The better films of New Queer Cinema or the more commercial recent past explode conventional modes of narrative and subject matter, all the while maintaining that the language of queer is always on the move, but also of the moment, from this moment on. By the time *The Bent Lens* is next revised, another moment will be upon us and up on the screen.

Daniel Mudie Cunningham is a writer specialising in screen cultures and art history. Based in Sydney, Australia, Daniel has worked as an independent visual art and film curator, having staged numerous exhibitions since 1994. Daniel is nearing completion of his doctoral thesis on 'white trash' film aesthetics titled *Trashing Whites: The 'Film' on Whiteness* (University of Western Sydney). Daniel can be contacted through his web site: www.showpony.com.au.

Footnotes

[1] B. Ruby Rich. 'Homo Pomo: The New Queer Cinema' [September, 1992]. Reprinted in Cook and Dodd, eds. *Women and Film: A Sight and Sound Reader*. Philadelphia: Temple University Press, 1993, p. 164.

[2] B. Ruby Rich. 'Queer and Present Danger' [2000] Reprinted in Hillier, ed. *American Independent Cinema: A Sight and Sound Reader*. London: British Film Institute, 2001, pp. 114–18.

Queer Asian Cinemas

Helen Hok-Sze Leung

In and Out of the Festivals

In recent years, Asian films have become a significant and influential presence in queer film festivals all over the world. In 2001–2002 alone, Asian cinemas had inspired special programming, lectures, and panel discussions at such high-profile venues as the Transgender Film Festival in Amsterdam, Inside Out in Toronto, Frameline in San Francisco, and Out On Screen in Vancouver. Closer to home, queer film festivals in Asian cities such as Hong Kong, Tokyo, Manila, and Seoul are moving away from the earlier tendency to program material primarily from Western cinemas and returning the spotlight to their own regional film industries. Contrary to opinions circulating in some of the more established festivals, queer Asian cinemas are not just latecomers on the global queer scene, mirroring an earlier phase of development found in the West. Rather, the diversity of Asian cultures and the complex histories of their negotiation with non-normative forms of gender practices and sexual desire have produced films that suggest alternative models of queer identity, politics, and aesthetics. Themes such as homophobia and colonialism (*Ke Kulana He Mahu*, Brent Anbe and Kathryn Xian, 2001), indigenous queer identities (*Friends in High Places*, Lindsey Merrison, 2000), local histories of queer desire (*The Intimates*, Jacob Cheung, 1997), and gender identities that do not neatly correspond to the categories of Lesbian, Gay, Bisexual and Transgender (LGBT) (*Shinjuku Boys*, Kim Longinotto and Jano Williams, 1995) are just a few examples of the ways in which Asian films are reconfiguring the parameters of queer cinema. Outside of the festival circuit, however, it becomes much more difficult to speak of the influence of these films as though they form a coherent body of work. The very notion of a 'Queer Asian Cinema' is in many ways a festival invention. It refers to films that differ immensely in local contexts of production and reception, in their relation to social and political movements for gender and sexual minorities, and in their status in mainstream culture. In the rest of the essay, I will briefly outline some of these differences to highlight the diversity of queer Asian films.

The Queer Mainstream

An interesting phenomenon in festival programming of queer Asian cinemas is the inclusion of 'unintentionally queer' films. These are mainstream films that implicitly or explicitly feature same-sex desire and/or gender transgressions without any commitment to queer politics or involvement of the queer community in their production. They tend to have high production value and an all-star cast. Because of the recent efforts amongst the film industries of east and southeast Asia to consolidate their film markets, many of these films also enjoy wide distribution amongst mainstream audiences throughout Asia. For instance, the majority of queer films from Hong Kong—from the 1991 martial arts epic *Swordsman II* to last year's period comedy *Wu Yen* (Johnnie To and Wai Kai-fai, 2001), both of which have recently been programmed in queer film festivals—are examples of this category. Although these films seldom provide a realistic glimpse into queer lives and do not usually offer the positive images or subversive politics that some queer audiences look for, they play an important role in the dissemination of queer representations and instigate a different kind of spectatorial pleasure.

Mainstream films that tackle queer themes often adhere to generic rules in order to ensure their general marketability. As a result, they end up revealing the repressed limits of the genre itself, exposing the queer undercurrent that has always been present. For instance, the Thai comedy *Iron Ladies* (Youngyooth Thongkonthun, 2000) derives many elements of its plot from a genre of Japanese TV drama that was immensely popular in Asia during the 1970s. In this genre, competitive sports create a homosocial space where same-sex players share an intense *esprit du corp*. *Iron Ladies* appropriates and transforms this space with a riveting story about a volleyball team made up of gay men, drag queens, and a trans woman. *Memento Mori* (Kim Tae-yong and Min Kyu-dong, 2000) from South Korea combines a girls' school love drama with a *Carrie*-like horror plot. The anxious repression of queer desire is a recurrent subtext in both adolescent drama and the horror genre. *Memento Mori* simply pushes this latent anxiety of the genres into the foreground of the film. In *Portland Street Blues* (Yip Raymond, 1998), a butch woman with a strong transgender identification is cast into the role of a typical hero in the gangster action genre. Her intense affection for another man in the film replicates *not* heterosexual romance but the intense homoerotic bond between men that is a staple in the genre since John Woo's *A Better Tomorrow*.

Aside from the queering of generic clichés, the casting of major stars in queer roles is another way in which mainstream films provide opportunities of queer appropriation. For example, the pairing of Tony Leung and Leslie Cheung in *Happy Together* (Kar-wai Wong, 1997) and the casting of Seiichi Tanabe as a gay man in *Hush!* (Ryosuke Hashiguchi, 2001) cast a much welcomed queer gaze over these heterosexualized idols. Conversely, the casting of queer icons in ostensibly straight roles—Akihiro Maruyama as the *femme fatale* in *Black Lizard* (Kinji Fukasaku, 1968) and Leslie Cheung as a homophobic straight man pondering his sexual identity in *He's a Woman She's a Man* (Peter Chan and Chi Lee, 1994) for instance—introduces an ironic queer subtext that only audiences 'in the know' could appreciate. Such irony can empower queer spectators and return them to a rare position of privilege in relation to mainstream cinema.

Because mainstream queer films reach such a wide audience and stay in the popular memory for a relatively long time, they provide a rich resource for innovative projects that reclaim queer spaces in everyday life. For instance, Stanley Kwan's documentary *Yin ± Yang: Gender in Chinese Cinema* (1996) uncovers undercurrents of homoeroticism and gender transgressions throughout the history of popular Chinese cinema. The clip show *Desi Dykes and Divas: Hindi Film Clips*, compiled by Gayatri Gopinath and Javid Syed for the San Francisco South Asian LGBT festival QFilmistan in 2001, recovers and highlights the rich queer subtexts that are everywhere in Bollywood films. These projects are brilliant examples of the ways in which a 'queer mainstream' may be appropriated from popular Asian cinemas.

Queer Indies and the Queer Underground

A smaller but equally important body of queer Asian films are made by independent filmmakers with a consciously queer politics. These films are usually produced with the active involvement of the local queer community, often working voluntarily on the film crew. As a result, even when these films are not explicitly telling stories about the queer community, they give a much more intimate flavour of contemporary queer lives in Asia. Compared to mainstream films, independent films are far more inclined to represent explicit queer sexuality, and they do so in creative, unrestrained and at times humorous ways. Queer indie films from Asia have also moved away from the melodramatic plots more typical of mainstream features, which often dwell on themes like the difficulty of coming out, the tension with family, the tragedy of unrequited love. Instead, indie films are more interested in more abstract and universal themes such as urban alienation, national identity and histories of injustice. By exploring these questions from the perspectives of queer characters and in a recognisably queer cinematic style, queer indie films have reclaimed some of the grand narratives of cinema for queer audiences. Recent features such as Yau Ching's *Let's Love Hong Kong* (*Hoa Yuk*, 2002) and Evans Chan's *Maps of Sex and Love* (2001) from Hong Kong and Desiree Lim's *Sugar Sweet* (2001) from Japan are fine examples of this exciting emergence of queer independent filmmaking from Asia. The problem faced by most independent films is that of distribution. Many of these films play far more often in film festivals abroad than to audiences at home. However, with the rise of digital media, indie films are widening their distribution through VCD and DVD releases. Many independent filmmakers also manage to show their work on television where they can reach a wider audience than film festival or arthouse theatre releases.

Similar in spirit but far more difficult in execution than the indie films is a flourishing body of work from the queer underground. These are works filmed in societies where queer content in the cinema is still outlawed. The underground character of these films results in a style that is typical of guerrilla cinemas, often with lots of handheld work, undercover location shoots, make-do sets, and active, passionate involvement of the crew in every aspect of the film's production. Some examples of such underground works are *In the Name of Allah*, a film about queer Muslims in the Middle East that is still in progress, the documentary *Just a Woman* (Mitra Farahani, 2001) which follows the everyday life of a transsexual woman in Iran, and recent dramatic features from Mainland China like *Man Man Woman Woman* (*NanNan NuNu*,

Liu Bingjian, 1999), *Fish & Elephant* (*Jin Nian Xia Tian,* Li Yu, 2001) and *Enter into Clowns*, (*Enter the Clowns*, Zi'en Cui, 2001) all of which cast a provocative look at queer lives in Beijing while starring some of the most prominent queer activists and artists from the community.

Queer Asian Diasporas

Finally, it is necessary to briefly mention the works of queer filmmakers in the Asian diaspora, which continue to be in active dialogue with the queer cinemas of Asia. Recent feature documentaries such as *Rewriting the Script* and *I Exist* (Peter Barbosa and Garrett Lenoir, 2002) explore being queer in, respectively, the South Asian and the Middle Eastern communities in North America. In their search for a culturally specific language, history and experience of queerness, filmmakers in the Asian diaspora draw from both their immigrant experience and the contemporary queer culture of Asia. Shorter works by directors such as Sheila James, Quentin Lee, Erin O'Brien, Winston Xin and Wayne Yung amongst many others, explore themes like racism and homophobia, inter-racial relationships, family negotiations, and the global movements and displacements of people and culture. Increasingly, these films are reaching audiences in the queer communities in Asia and opening new dialogues on intersecting concerns and experiences. They are an important part of a diverse queer Asian cinematic landscape that will continue to grow beyond and transform its borders.

Helen Hok-Sze Leung is Assistant Professor of Women's Studies at Simon Fraser University, Canada, where she teaches queer theory, gender theory, literature and film. Her current research focuses on Hong Kong's queer culture.

The Transgender Look

Judith Halberstam, UC San Diego

'We feel like we were thrown almost every curve in the game. And we managed to make this thing by hook or by crook.'[1] Harry Dodge and Silas Howard, directors, *By Hook or By Crook* (2000)

The potentiality of the body to morph, shift, change and become fluid is a powerful fantasy in post- or trans-modern cinema. Whether it is the image of surgically removable faces in John Woo's *Face Off*, the liquid mercury type of slinkiness of the Terminator in *T2*, the virtual bodies of *Matrix* or the living dead body in *Sixth Sense*, the body in transition indelibly marks late twentieth century and early 21st century cinematic fantasy. Nowhere has the fantasy of the shape-shifting and identity-morphing body been more powerfully realised, however, than in the transgender film. In films like *The Crying Game* (Neil Jordan, 1992) and *Boys Don't Cry* (Kimberly Peirce, 2000), the transgender character surprises audiences with his/her ability to remain attractive, appealing and gendered while simultaneously presenting a gender at odds with sex, a sense of gender identity not derived from the body and a sexual subjectivity which operates within the heterosexual matrix without conforming to it. But even as the transgender body becomes a symbol par excellence for flexibility, transgenderism also represents a form of rigidity, an insistence upon particular forms of gender recognition which are far from fluid. Those bodies, indeed, which fail to conform to the postmodern fantasy of flexibility that has been projected onto the transgender body may well be punished in popular representations even as they seem to be lauded. And so, Brandon in *Boys Don't Cry* and Dil in *The Crying Game* are represented as both heroic and fatally flawed. What would a transgender film look like that did not punish the transgender subject for his or her inflexibilities and for failing to deliver the fantasy of fluidity that cinematic audiences so desire? *By Hook or By Crook* (2000) by Harry Dodge and Silas Howard offers the spectator not one but two transgender characters and the two together represent transgender identity as less of a function of bodily flexibility and more a result of intimate bonds and queer, interactive modes of recognition.

By Hook or By Crook marks a real turning point for queer cinema. This no-budget, low-tech, high-concept feature, shot entirely on mini DV, tells the story of two gender bandits, Shy and Valentine. Described by its creators as 'utterly post-post-modern a little bit of country and a little bit of rock and roll', the film conjures up the twilight world of two loners living on the edge without trying to explain or rationalise their reality. The refusal to explain either the gender peculiarities of the heroes or the many other contradictions they embody allows Howard and Dodge instead to focus on developing eccentric and compelling characters. While most of the action turns on the bond between Shy and Valentine, their world is populated with a stunning array of memorable characters like Valentine's girlfriend Billie (Stanya Kahn) and Shy's love interest Isabelle (Carina Gia). The film also features fabulous guest appearances by queer celebrities like Joan Jett as a news interviewee, the late Kris Kovick typecast as a Crazy

Nut in the Park and Machiko Saito as the Gun Store Clerk. These cameos establish the world of *By Hook or By Crook* as a specifically queer universe and they clearly mark a studied indifference to mainstream acceptance by making subcultural renown rather than Hollywood glamour into the most desirable form of celebrity.

Both *The Crying Game* and *Boys Don't Cry* relied heavily upon the successful solicitation of affect—whether revulsion, sympathy, empathy—in order to give mainstream viewers access to a transgender gaze. And in both films, a relatively unknown actor (Jay Davidson and Hilary Swank) performs alongside a more well-known actor (Stephen Rea and Chloe Sevigny); the relative obscurity of the transgender actors allow them to pull off the feat of credibly performing a gender at odds with the sexed body even after the body has been brutally exposed. *By Hook or By Crook* resists the seduction of crying games and the lure of sentiment and works instead to associate butchness and gender innovation with wit, humour and style. The melancholia that tinges *The Crying Game* and saturates *Boys Don't Cry* is transformed in *By Hook or By Crook* into the wise delirium of Harry Dodge's character Valentine. Dodge and Howard knowingly avoid engaging their viewers at the level of sympathy, pity or even empathy and instead they 'hook' them with the basic tools of the cinematic apparatus: desire and identification.

In *By Hook or By Crook*, transgenderism is a complex dynamic between the two butch heroes: Shy and Valentine. The two collude and collaborate in their gendering and create a closed world of queerness which is locked in place by the circuit of a gaze which never references the male or the female gaze as such. The plot of *By Hook or By Crook* involves the random meeting of two trans-butches and the development of a fast friendship. Shy tries to help Valentine, who has been adopted, find his mother while Valentine introduces the lonely Shy, whose father has just died, to an alternative form of community. The dead or missing parents imply an absence of conventional family and afford our heroes with the opportunity to remake home, family, community and most importantly, friendship. As the story evolves into a shaggy dog tale of hide and seek, we leave family time far behind and enter the shadow world of queers, loners, street people and crazies. Transgenderism takes its place in this world as a quiet location outside the storm of law and order, mental health and financial stability. Unlike other trangender films which remain committed to seducing the straight gaze, this film remains thoroughly committed to the transgender look and it opens up, formally and thematically, a new mode of envisioning gender mobility.

Dodge and Howard pioneer some brilliant techniques of queer plotting in order to map the world of the wilfully perverse. As they say in interviews, neither director was interested in telling a story about 'being gay'. Nor did Dodge and Howard want to spend valuable screen time explaining the characters' sexualities and genders to unknowing audiences. In the press kit, Dodge and Howard explain their strategy in terms of representing sexuality and gender as follows: 'This is a movie about a budding friendship between two people. The fact that they happen to be queer is purposefully off the point. If you call them something, other than sad, rambling, spirited, gentle, sharp or funny—you might call them "*butches*".' Instead of a humanist story about gay heroes struggling to be accepted, Dodge and Howard tell a beautifully fragmented tale of queer encounter set almost entirely in a queer universe. In other words, the heroes are utterly unremarkable for their queerness in the cinematic world that the directors have created. In this way, Dodge and Howard offer a tribute to the San Francisco subcultural worlds that they inhabit. Howard explains: 'We've always hoped this project would reflect the creativity and actual valour of the community of people we came from. And I think it does. From the get-go, this movie had its roots in our extended family of weirdos in San Francisco.'

In the film, Shy and Valentine visit cafés, clubs, shops and hotels where no one reacts specifically to their butchness. This narrative strategy effectively *universalises queerness* within this specific cinematic space. Many gay and lesbian films represent their characters and their struggles as 'universal' as a way of suggesting that their film speaks to audiences beyond specific gay and lesbian audiences. But very few do more than submit to the regulation of narrative that transforms the specific into the universal: they tell stories of love, redemption, family and struggle which look exactly like every other Hollywood feature angling for a big audience. *By Hook or By Crook* actually manages to tell a queer story that is more than a queer story by refusing to acknowledge the existence of a straight world. Where the straight world is represented only through its institutions such as the law, the mental institution, commerce, the queer cinematic world comes to represent a truly localised place of opposition, an opposition moreover that is to be found in committed performances of perversity, madness and friendship. While some of Harry Dodge's comments in the press notes imply a humanist aim for the project ('We wanted to make a film about people with big ideas and big dreams who end up dealing with the shadowy subtleties of human life...' and 'I want to make work that touches people's hearts—I am interested in the human spirit...'), the film ultimately resists the trap of liberal humanism (making a film about gays who are, in the end, just like everybody else). So, *By Hook or By Crook* universalises queerness without allowing its characters to be absorbed back into the baggy and ultimately heterosexist concept of the 'human'.

Different key scenes from the film build, capture and sustain this method of universalising queerness. In one scene soon after they meet, Shy and Valentine go to a club together. The club scene, filmed in San Francisco's notorious Lexington Bar, is a riotous montage of queer excess. The camera lovingly pans a scene of punky, pierced, tattooed, perverted young queers. The montage lasts much longer than necessary signalling that the beauty and intrinsic worth of this world transcends its diegetic purpose. While Valentine dances, Shy sits apart from the crowd watching and then he steals Valentine's wallet before leaving. The theft of Valentine's wallet should create a gulf of distrust and suspicion between the two strangers but in this looking glass world, it actually bonds them more securely within their underground existence.

When Shy returns Valentine's wallet the next day, she is greeted like a long lost brother—this has the effect of inverting the morality of the world represented in this film by the police. Other scenes deepen this refusal of conventional law and order. The two wanna-be thieves try to hold up a drug store only to be chased off by an aggressive sales clerk, they try to scam a hardware store and, in a citation of De Niro's famous scene from *Taxi Driver*, they pose with guns in front of the mirror in Shy's run down motel room. All of these scenes show Shy and Valentine as eccentric but gentle outlaws who function as part of an alternative universe with its own ethics, sex/gender system and its own public space.

De Niro's taxi driver, muttering 'you looking at me' as he pointed a loaded gun at his own mirror image, is a vigilante loner, a man turned inward and lost to the city he skims across in his yellow cab. But while De Niro's character accidentally hits a vein of humour with his mohawked 'fuck you', Shy and Valentine deliberately ride butch humour rather than macho vengeance into the sunset. If the vigilante wants to remake the world in his image, the queer outlaws of *By Hook or By Crook* are content to imagine a world of their own making. When asked about the title of the film, Silas Howard responded: 'The title refers to what is involved in inventing your own world—when you don't see anything that represents you out there, how can you seize upon that absence as an opportunity to make something out of nothing, by hook or by crook. We take gender ambiguity, for example, and we don't explain it, dilute it or apologize for it—we represent it for what it is—something confusing and lovely!'

Judith Halberstam is Professor of Literary and Cultural Studies at UC San Diego. Halberstam teaches courses in queer studies, gender theory, art, literature and film. She is currently working on a book about queer subcultures called *What's That Smell?* and finishing a book about the Brandon Teena case titled *The Brandon Archive*.

Footnotes

[1] All quotes from Silas Howard and Harry Dodge are taken from the Press Kit for *By Hook or By Crook* available at www.steakhaus.com/bhobc/ unless otherwise attributed.

History Lessons

An interview with Barbara Hammer

Barbara Hammer is considered a pioneer of lesbian/feminist experimental cinema. She has made 80 films and videos and received the Frameline Award in 2000 for making a significant contribution to lesbian cinema. She chooses film/video as a visual art form to make the invisible visible. Her work reveals and celebrates marginalised peoples whose stories have not been told. Her cinema is multilevelled and engages an audience viscerally and intellectually with the goal of activating them to make social change. Her trilogy of documentary film essays (*Nitrate Kisses*, 1992, *Tender Fictions*, 1995, *History Lessons*, 2000) on lesbian and gay history has received numerous awards.

Hammer's most recent work has turned to global issues outside her community as she has investigated a revolutionary filmmaking 'collective' in Japan in the feature-length documentary, *Devotion, A Film About Ogawa Productions*, 2000, (Jurors' Merit Award at the Taiwan International Documentary Film Festival) and *My Babushka: Searching Ukrainian Identities*, 2001, funded by a grant from Soros Documentary Fund of the Open Society Institute.

Hammer is presently completing a 16 mm feature documentary film, *Resisting Paradise*, which compares the lives of Resistance Fighters with those of the painters Matisse and Bonnard during WWII in Provence, France.

In a film culture where lesbians have rarely been depicted, let alone acknowledged, Hammer's extraordinary body of film work has gone a long way to help redress the missing realities of lesbian lives on the screen. In particular, *History Lessons* has encapsulated and appropriated a lesbian screen history that in real terms has been lost forever, or in some ways, never really existed. In acknowledging the absence of lesbian screen and cultural history, Hammer has seen fit to commandeer and reclaim found and archival footage shot by men, and rework it into an irreverent celebration of an imagined account of lesbian life on celluloid.

You have an extensive history as a filmmaker and you have made some groundbreaking and extraordinary films. How does your latest film History Lessons *fit into the framework that you have created for yourself as a filmmaker?*

It all began when I was trying to find lesbian representation from the beginning of film, 1896 until Stonewall, 1969. The first film I made was *Nitrate Kisses* in 1992, followed by *Tender Fictions* in 1995. In *Nitrate Kisses* I searched in the US, Germany and France for aural and visual images from the 1930s to Stonewall. Mainly, I found emptiness, cracks, broken windows and burned letters. This 'unfinding' led me to use blank spaces, destroyed buildings, scratches and empty images in the film. I believe form and content cannot be separated, so the fragmentary nature of lesbian and gay history became snippets of montage images. At the end of *Nitrate Kisses* Joan Nestle, one of the founders of the Lesbian Herstory Archive in New York City, is speaking and asking the viewing audience to save every scrap of paper for a cultural archive of lesbians in the 20th and 21st century.

Tender Fictions grew directly out of this request as I realised I had boxes of archival materials of my own including 8mm and Super 8mm film. I needed to show my scraps to the world. After researching the fascinating questions revolving around 'truth' and 'fiction' in anthropology, sociology, literature and cinema studies, I incorporated these postmodern critiques of auto/bio/graphy into the film.

The final question I had to ask was about lesbian representation before Stonewall was left. Little did I know that this would be so much fun to research and find the images of lesbian pre-1969.

What kinds of images did you find in the archives?

Most of the images I found were made by men depicting what they thought were lesbians and the dominant mode of portrayal, was sexual. Are we surprised?

Why do you think these types of depictions were so prevalent?

Because we are so bad and mean and totally irreverent toward the heterosexual family unit! Our 'illicit' behaviour was *sexual* and, after all, this is America founded by puritanical men. It was really all about control and regulation.

What were the dominant approaches used in these films and how have you dealt with them?

The films utilised measurements, statistics, misuse of 'the scientific method', sadistic and overly asexualised image-making. That's why I focused on trying to overturn the existing 'history' and re-conceptualise the past through humour, irony and just plain naughtiness.

I really believe that history should not belong only to those who 'make it' but to those who unmake and remake it. History is not a dead and done activity of recorded novel events. History is alive and can be changed in a flash by a scrap of paper, an old photograph, a memory. Every cultural item, every personal memory, every dream and vision for a future can be considered history.

You have drawn on an extraordinary range of sources. How did you go about the actual research process? And how long did it take to finish?

I didn't have time to spend my life in archives searching out these images so I found lesbian archivists who had dedicated their lives to finding representations and misrepresentations of women who could be gay. The first archivist I found was Ann Maguire at the Prelinger Archive. For years she had been collecting images that she thought could be read as lesbian. These clips make up the majority of the images in *History Lessons*. Then I found Szu Burgess who scoured old bookstores for boxes of yellowing magazines and posters. She passed along a few of these images to me as well and assisted me in finding the 'scandal journalism' at the Lesbian Herstory Archive in Brooklyn. We had to burrow past the positive press and pull out old file drawers that I don't think have been looked at for years.

Jenni Olson, Planet Out entrepreneur and filmmaker, lent me a film from her collection of lesbian porn and told me how to find old 8mm and super 8mm porn films. I would order these films on titles alone and either edit the men out of the three-ways or find amazing baton footage!

In France, I met curator and collector Bertrand Grimault who came to trust me enough to loan me the amazing found collection of 100 glass stereoscopic negatives of a lesbian couple, Marie Jeanne and Mouchette, that he found in an abandoned house in Bordeaux. Here were what may be the first images of lesbians documenting their own lovemaking. (*Dyketactics* may have a mother after all!).

The music in the film is intriguing. How did you decide from what period to choose the music?

I can break down the music into four different sections. The first was the original 1950s lesbian renditions of popular songs by Lisa Ben. A friend introduced me to Lisa Ben who rewrote popular music with a lesbian cant and performed these transformed songs in lesbians' cabarets and bars in Los Angeles in the '50s. Lisa now lives with her 13 cats and when I located her she told me she had not heard her own music in over 30 years. She only had one tape, a large reel-to-reel, and no tape recorder to put it on. I was surprised and delighted when I listened to her music. It was perfect and I was also able to transfer the songs to a cassette for her so she could listen to them again. At 86, she attended the premiere in Los Angeles driven by one great young dyke over the hills from Burbank where she lives down to Hollywood where *History Lessons* premiered at The Director's Guild of America as part of LA OutFest (the annual lesbian and gay film festival).

The second is a contemporary creation by Eve Beglarian of *Twisted Tutus*. I had always wanted to work with Eve who is a wizard with electronic music and computer files. Watching *Twisted Tutus* in performance was a trip and to find that she was willing to compose an opening score for the film, the archive scenes and the doctor scene was fantastic. I felt the film needed all kinds of sound montage, not just historical period music, so Eve and I met in her studio a few times and the more she worked the more she realised the sense of sound I had for these scenes.

She brought her own creative innovations to the score as well which is what collaboration at its best promises.

The third section was done by Gretchen Phillips of *Two Nice Girls*, who was commissioned to create the sleazy music for the porn scenes. She had a lot of fun mixing sounds on a new drum machine she bought and tried to sync her voice in the pie-throwing scene.

The fourth section I can talk about is the music written and created by Mikael Karlsonn for the 'Meat Market scene'. Mikael is a young Swedish student studying composing for film at a local university and was a friend of the Assistant Director, Anna Viola Hahlberg. The 12 minute section of the film shot near my studio with non-professional actors (with the exception of Carmelita Tropicana) was his assignment. This section sometimes eludes viewers. It is a take-off on the work of the American 1940s photographer known as Weegee. Weegee followed police cars around Manhattan and filmed crime scenes, some of which were in lesbian bars or paddy wagons of lesbians after a police raid of a bar. I asked Mikael to create something a bit hokey that might sound like an old player piano.

Tell us about some of the written material you found.

I found some incredible written material, some of those that stick to memory are things like: 'Lesbians signal one another with rapid motions of tongue and lips'. 'The idea of lesbians holding open conventions—just as though they were Rotarians or Real Estate brokers is inconceivable'. 'Lesbians find a delicious thrill belonging to a forbidden world'. 'The most a psychiatrist can do for a confirmed lesbian is to convince her to live with her problem'. 'Ancient aristocratic ladies with leisure on their hands would spend hours pulling at the clitoris to elongate it'. 'Lesbians and nymphomaniacs can be found in any profession'. 'Heterosexuals quit clubs when they saw too many bulldikers'. 'Four hundred women transvestites fought in the civil war'.

Of course the lesbian convention idea worked perfectly with the Eleanor Roosevelt archival footage I had found. All I had to do was tweak the sound a bit and ask my lover who has a lovely voice if she wouldn't put on her most affected Eleanor voice and read the line: Welcome ladies to this first-ever Lesbian Convention!

I use text as image in both *Nitrate Kisses* and *Tender Fictions* and I think it works with the flow of the films. But in *History Lessons* there was so much radical montage and diverse textures that the text held the quasi-narrative back and kept the film from advancing.

How do you think lesbian filmmaking has changed during the time you've been making films?

It has changed radically. There has been tremendous growth in terms of numbers of lesbians making films. Digital video and nonlinear home editing systems have put the medium in many wonderful lesbian hands. The range of work is as wide and varied as the filmmakers. The only problem I see is that many young filmmakers might think that the narrative form is the queen of all forms and so forsake the impudent genre of experimental or the challenge of documentary essay film.

Do you see anything in current lesbian filmmaking that is inspiring, or has the potential to be groundbreaking?

No, but one never knows what is right around the corner. What I do see as groundbreaking is gay cinema from other countries and cultures, gay cinema that has not been allowed before. For example, I recently saw the narrative gay Chinese film *Lan Yu*. Here was a story that hadn't been told before. What if we had a Chinese lesbian film? That would be revolutionary. The specifics and details of other cultural lesbian representations is what I am looking for and has potential to be globally groundbreaking.

What would you say to aspiring lesbian filmmakers?

Make the work that intrigues you even if it is unpopular, others don't understand what you are doing, and maybe even you can't explain it. Trust your intuition and your critical skills. Read everywhere in all disciplines and develop to your full potential then give back—in film, in law, in medicine, in politics.

What can you tell us about your next project?

Oh, I thought you would never ask.

Resisting Paradise is a 90 minute documentary essay film set in France during WW II which asks what we would do during a time of war. Local villagers from Cassis tell stories of resistance during the Nazi occupation while the painters Pierre Bonnard and Henri Matisse exchange letters about their work. Walter Benjamin, the German philosopher/historian is smuggled out of France by Lisa Fittko and struggles over the Pyrenees Mountains with a heavy manuscript under his arm. His walk, like Sisyphus, is continual throughout the film and similarly to the myth, ends in suicidal despair as he is turned back by the Spanish border guards. So many different choices and circumstances during this difficult period as exemplified by the people in the film. The question asked is: What would you and I do given a similar situation?

Barbara Hammer
Radcliffe Fellow
Radcliffe Institute for Advanced Study
Cambridge, Massachusetts
February, 2002

A-Z listing of films

10 Attitudes

Gallant, Michael
2001; USA; 87 min; Comedy
P: Jason Stuart, Michael Gallant, Rob Bonet; *W:* Jason
Stuart, Michael Gallant; *E:* Alan Roberts; *M:* David
Benoit
Cast: Jason Stuart, Jim J. Bullock, Christopher Cowan,
David Faustino

The new millennium dawns in West Hollywood,
and with it comes upheaval in the life of Josh
Stevens. Josh is a semi-attractive, 30-something gay
caterer originally from Cleveland, who feels his life is
happy and complete. While Josh has retained his
Ohio roots, his long-time partner Lyle, who has
made the move with him, has gone all Hollywood.
After catching Lyle in a compromising situation with
a young West Hollywood gay boy, Josh decides to
move back to Ohio. His best friend Brandon
convinces him to stay by giving him a challenge:
find Mr Right in 10 dates. (10 Attitudes.com)

Dist/Sales: Gallant

10 Violent Women

Mikels, Ted V.
1982; USA; 97 min; Action
P: Ted V. Mikels; *W:* Ted V. Mikels; *C:* Yuval
Shousterman; *E:* James Jaeger; *M:* Nicholas Carras
Cast: Sally Gamble, Dixie Lauren, Sherri Vernon

A gang of women are thrown into a brutal prison
after they botch a million-dollar jewellery heist.
They are subjected to violent and degrading
treatment by sadistic lesbian guards.

Prod Comp: Cinema Features

100 Days Before the Command

(aka: Sto dnej do Prikaza)

Erkenov, Hussein
1990; Soviet Union; 67 min; Drama
W: Vladimir Kholodov, Yuri Polyakov; *C:* Vladislav
Menshikov; *E:* Galina Dmitriyeva, Vladimir Portnov
Cast: Vladimir Zamansky, Oleg Vasilkov

Five young Red Army recruits struggle for survival
against the merciless violence that surrounds them
on a daily basis. Their only means of saving their
dignity is by preserving the humanity and compassion they share for each other. Visually astonishing
and erotically charged, the film was banned by
Soviet censors upon its initial release. Amazingly, all
the roles are played by real-life soldiers except for
one professional actor. Russian with English
subtitles. (Water Bearer Films)

Prod Comp: Gorky Film Studios
Dist/Sales: WaterBearer, Salzgeber

101 Rent Boys

Bailey, Fenton / Barbato, Randy
2000; USA; 85 min; Documentary
P: Fenton Bailey, Randy Barbato; *C:* Sandra Chandler;
E: William Grayburn

This voyeuristic, feature-length documentary
explores the world of male prostitutes in Los
Angeles. The men interviewed for the film (who are
paid on camera for their time), talk candidly and
openly about love, sex, turn-ons, turn-offs, drugs
and kinky stuff, and while showing us their assets
and their vulnerability. Both arousing and unsettling, viewers will possibly question the ethics of the
filmmakers while simultaneously revelling in the
admissions the hustlers make. (MQFF)

Prod Comp: Cinemax, World of Wonder
Dist/Sales: WorldOfWonder, Strand, Wolfe

101 Rent Boys

101 Reykjavik

Kormákur, Baltasar
2001; Denmark, France, Iceland, Norway; 100 min;
Comedy
P: Baltasar Kormákur, Ingvar H. Thordarson,

Thorfinnur Omarsson; *W:* Baltasar Kormákur; *C:* Peter Steuger; *E:* Stule Eriksen, Sigvaldi Karason; *M:* Damon Albarn, Einar Orn Benediktsson
Cast: Hilmir Snær Gudnason, Victoria Abril, Hanna María Karlsdóttir, Baltasar Kormákur

Hlynur is about to hit 30 and stills lives the life of a slacker with his mother in their tiny cramped house, ravenously trawling the internet for porn and never bothering himself with employment issues. His appetite for sex takes an unexpected turn when he discovers that the woman he has just slept with happens to be his mother's lesbian lover, and may be carrying his child.

Prod Comp: Zentropa Entertainments
Dist/Sales: Sagittaire

17 Rooms

(aka: What do Lesbians do in Bed?)

Sheldon, Caroline
1985; UK; 10 min; Comedy

What do lesbians do in bed? With a star-studded soundtrack, we're shown everything from knitting to drinking tea and pillow fights. In these 17 rooms everything is shown...everything that is except 'doing it'. *17 Rooms* doesn't satisfy the curiosity of male voyeurs but it does make the viewer examine visual representations of women, sexual terminology, so-called erotic fiction and semiotics on the way. (Cinenova)

Dist/Sales: Cinenova, WMM

2 by 4

(aka: 2 x 4)

Smallhorne, Jimmy
1997; USA; 90 min; Drama
P: John Hall, Virginia Biddle; *W:* Jimmy Smallhorne, Terrence McGoff, Fergus Tighe; *C:* Declan Quinn; *E:* Laura Sullivan, Scott Balcerek; *M:* HuncaMunca Music
Cast: Jimmy Smallhorne, Chris O'Neill, Bradley Fitts, Joe Holyoake, Terrence McGoff

Johnny, an Irish immigrant, is working as a foreman for his unsavoury uncle on a New York building site. Tormented by his growing attraction for men, and by recurring nightmares, Johnny is torn between his love for girlfriend Maria, and the young hustler he has befriended on the streets. Rather than glorify or fetishise the labourers who populate its scenes, the film turns an unflinching eye upon them, and upon their gritty, claustrophobic environment. A difficult, dark, often brutal film announcing the arrival of an important new talent. (MQFF)

Prod Comp: Electric Head, Red Horse Films
Dist/Sales: Cowboy

2 or 3 Things But Nothing for Sure

DiFeliciantonio, Tina / Wagner Jane
1997; USA; 12 min; Documentary

Acclaimed author Dorothy Allison (*Bastard Out of Carolina*) is profiled in this moving, inspiring film. Combining poetic imagery with powerful readings, it evokes Allison's childhood in the poor white American South of the 1950s, her birth as a writer and feminist, and her coming to terms with a family legacy of incest and abuse. A beautifully realised portrait of an artist and survivor, this stirring film provides important insights into the roots of self-renewal and creativity. (WMM)

Prod Comp: Naked Eye Productions
Dist/Sales: WMM

2 Seconds

(aka: 2 Secondes; Deux Secondes)

Briand, Manon
1998; Canada; 100 min; Drama
P: Roger Frappier; *W:* Manon Briand; *C:* Louise Archambault, Pierre Crépô, James Gray; *E:* Richard Comeau; *M:* Sylvain-Charles Grand, Dominique Grand
Cast: Charlotte Laurier, Dino Tavarone, Jonathan Bolduc, Suzanne Clément

Laurie is a professional bicycle racer who becomes a courier when her team drops her after losing a race when she sacrificed the start by two seconds. While out on a job she meets the grumpy owner of an Italian bike shop, and despite her attraction to girls, begins a quirky relationship with him. In the meantime, she plots to win the employee's bike race. French with English subtitles.

Prod Comp: Max Films, Sodec, Téléfilm Canada
Dist/Sales: Cowboy, Wolfe, Millivres, ACMI

21st Century Nuns

Stephan, Tom
1993; UK; 15 min; Documentary

Since the establishment of the order of the Sisters of Perpetual Indulgence in the late 1970s, the good sisters have been a highly visible and important part of gay communities across Europe, America and Australia. This British documentary follows the activities of Sister Brigid over Troubled Water, Sister Frigidity of the Nocturnal Emission, and Sister Belladonna.

Dist/Sales: LIFS

24 Nights

Turner, Kieran
1998; USA; 97 min; Comedy
P: Kieran Turner; *W:* Kieran Turner; *C:* Scott Barnard;

E: Rachel Chancey
Cast: Kevin Isola, Aida Turturro, Stephen Mailer, Mary Louise Wilson, Mary Stout

Jonathan Parker is a chronically single 24-year-old pot-head and pill-popper who works in a gay bookstore, and who still believes in Santa Claus. When he writes to Santa and asks for a boyfriend for Christmas, no-one is more surprised than Jonathan when Toby walks through the door. There's just one problem. Toby has a boyfriend. A very modern gay black comedy for the cynical 1990s.

Prod Comp: Cynical Boy Productions
Dist/Sales: TLA, Wolfe, 10%

27 Pieces of Me

Donahoe, Gerald
1995; USA; 90 min; Drama
W: Gina Hicks; *C:* Gina Hicks
Cast: Ezra Buzzington, Tina Denning, Angelique von Halle

Two sisters, Tanya (a lesbian sculptor) and Ramona, haven't seen each other in 10 years when the younger sister, Ramona, arrives in Seattle for an unannounced visit that finds Tanya unprepared to suddenly deal with ancient family issues. Tanya's roommate Bold, a gay performance artist who dreams of being an Alaskan dogsledder, attempts to reconcile the two sisters, but when he inadvertently shocks Ramona with the news that Tanya is a lesbian, Ramona reveals the real reason behind her sudden arrival.

$30

Cooke, Gregory
2000; USA; 19 min; Drama
W: Christopher Landon

$30 is a coming of age film told through the eyes of Scott, a 16-year-old boy who finds his virginity on trial when his father arranges a sexual liaison with a prostitute named Emily. For one hour, at thirty bucks a pop in a cheap motel, an unlikely friendship is forged out of self-discovery, laughter and ultimately, the comfort of strangers. With Sara Gilbert, Erik MacArthur and Greg Itzin.

Dist/Sales: Strand

301 - 302

Park, Chul-soo
1995; Korea; 100 min; Thriller
P: Park Chul-soo; *W:* Lee Suh-goon
Cast: Bang Eun-jin, Hwang Sin-hye

Bang, who lives in apartment 301, is an amateur cook and spends her time making lavish meals.

Hwang, her neighbour in 302, is rather bookish and becomes ill at the mere sight of food. They share some common obsessions—problematic relationships and eating disorders. But when 302 goes missing we discover in retrospect the development of their relationship and the truth of her disappearance.

Dist/Sales: Arrow

45 Minutes of Bondage

Castro, Rick
1995; USA; 45 min; Erotica
Cast: Conan, Stu Blake, Velvet, Alex Austin

Explores what can happens when you hook-up willing street boys with various displays of bondage.

Prod Comp: Pyewackett Productions
Dist/Sales: Pyewackett

4pm

Bakhurst, Samantha / Morement, Lea
2000; UK; 13 min; Comedy

This award winning short is a sexy and humorous take on a one-night stand which takes a turn for the unexpected, including an unfortunate encounter with an aquarium, a closeted politician, and of course, two gorgeous women. (MQFF)

Dist/Sales: WiseWomen

$30

'68

Kovacs, Steven
1987; USA; 89 min; Drama
P: Steven Kovacs, Dale Djerassi, Isabel Maxwell;
W: Steven Kovacs; *C:* Daniel Lacambre; *E:* Cari Coughlin
Cast: Eric Larson, Robert Locke, Neil Young, Sandor Tesci, Terra Candergaw

A father who is an Hungarian immigrant and his two sons, one an activist, the other gay, collide head on when his old-world values conflict with the ideals and passions of the new generation of the late 1960s.

Prod Comp: New World, 68 Limited
Dist/Sales: Roadshow

7 Steps to Sticky Heaven

Nguyen, Hoang Tan
1995; USA; 24 min; Experimental

Gay Asian men talk about their lives and relationships with other gay Asian men in this short experimental piece.

90 Miles

Zaldivar, Juan Carlos
2001; USA; 79 min; Documentary
P: Juan Carlos Zaldivar, Nicole Betancourt; *E:* Zelda Greenstein

A personal account of how the tempestuous relationship between the US and Cuba impacts on a man's family. Shot over 5 years, director Zaldivar recounts his personal journey back to his Cuban homeland after 18 years in the US, with his homosexuality underscoring the film as an example of how family love and acceptance can conquer all in the end.

99% Woman

1999; USA; 50 min; Documentary

In October 1998, 45-year-old Benjy Nelson—former high school athlete and United States Air Force airman—had a sex-change operation. During his air force career, he began to dress as a woman—first at home, and then in public. For the last five years before his operation, Benjy dressed as a woman full-time. However, Benjy was a family man. His wife Debbie, appears to have been totally supportive of his decision to have a sex change operation and become Bridget. Their three sons, however, a 14-year-old and 12-year-old identical twins, did not take easily to having their father become a tall blonde with stiletto heels and an almost comic sense of the female. Confused and angry, they start getting into trouble. The film finds no easy answers as it sets the freedom of individual choice against family well-being. (Filmakers Library)

Prod Comp: Worldview Pictures, France2
Dist/Sales: FilmakersLibrary

99 Women

(aka: Isle of Lost Women; 99 Mujeres)

Franco, Jesus
1969; Germany, UK; 90 min; Drama
P: Erwin C. Dietrich, Luis L. Moreno; *W:* Milo G. Cuccia, Carlo Fadda, Jesus Franco; *C:* Manuel Merino, Xavier Pérez Grobet; *E:* Stanley Frazen; *M:* Bruno Nicolai
Cast: Mercedes McCambridge, Maria Schell, Luciana Paluzzi, Herbert Lom

A women-in-prison film with lots of scantily clad girls and lesbian sex. When women prisoners are brutally abused, a sympathetic warden investigates the conditions and treatment by the lesbian guards.

Prod Comp: Corona Filmproduktion, Towers of London Productions

A.K.A

Roy, Duncan
2001; UK; 120 min; Drama
P: Richard West; *W:* Duncan Roy; *E:* Lawrence Catford, John Cross, Jackie Ophir; *M:* Matt Rowe
Cast: Matthew Leitch, George Asprey, Lindsey Coulson, Diana Quick

Set in Thatcher's London of the 1980s, *A.K.A* follows Dean, a shy working-class lad from Romford, on his quest for retribution. Kicked out of home by his abusive father, Dean introduces himself to Lady Gryffoyn, who he believes to be a friend of his mother. Unbeknownst to him, his mother has only ever served Lady Gryffoyn as a waitress. Nevertheless Dean manages to wheedle his way into the posh London set of artists, aristocrats and Sloanes that are the very essence of Lady Gryffoyn's life. What unfolds is a mesmerising and engulfing adventure of duplicity and deception as Dean gets deeper into debt, and the credit card fraud team close in on him. Split over three screens, *A.K.A* has fleeting references to *Pygmalion* as Dean chases his fantasy of being someone else. As toffs and rent boys rub shoulders at parties, snorting cocaine, quaffing champagne and spending (other people's?) money, *A.K.A* is also a stark portrait of the British class system. (2002 London Lesbian & Gay Film Festival)

Dist/Sales: ThirdRock

Abandoned

(aka: Torzók)

Sopsits, Árpád
2002; Hungary; 98 min; Drama
P: László Kántor, Frerenc Kardos; *W:* Árpád Sopsits; *C:* Péter Szatmári
Cast: Tamás Mészáros, Szabolcs Csizmadia, Attila Zsilák, Péter Müller, Imre Thúri

Hungary in 1960—a few years after the revolution and during a time of social uncertainty and harsh living conditions. Young Aaron's father leaves him at an orphanage where rigid discipline dominates and where children are subjected to extreme cruelties. Bewildered at first, Aaron is punished by the other boys but is soon accepted as a fellow sufferer. The director of the home is a devoutly religious martinet and takes every opportunity to punish the boys. Even under these brutal conditions, however, the innate goodness and humanity of these young children cannot be extinguished and provide whatever redemption exists in their lives. *Abandoned* is a moving story of the survival of a young boy's spirit in the face of pervasive oppression by a society that ignores the human condition. Recreating part of his childhood, renowned Hungarian director Árpád Sopsits presents an evocative and moving autobiographical coming-of-age story about innocence, cruelty, and sexual awakening. (Cinequest 12: 2002 San Jose Film Festival)

Dist/Sales: PictureThis!

About Vivien

Sport, Kathy
2000; Australia; 14 min; B&W; Documentary

Wartime service and 1950s repression never looked so dazzling as in this remarkable documentary about a young gay man called up for active duty. The use of stills, re-enactments and stunning archival footage from the Australian War Memorial vividly brings this astonishing story to life. (MQFF)

Above the Sea

(aka: Au essus de la Mar)

Hattu, Jean-Pascal
1998; France; 11 min; Drama

A older man wanders on a sunny beach and meets a young man who strangely resembles a friend he just lost. French with English subtitles.

Dist/Sales: Kanpaï

Absolutely Positive

Adair, Peter
1990; USA; 88 min; Documentary
W: Peter Adair; *C:* Peter Adair, Janet Cole; *M:* Michael Becker
Cast: Marlon Riggs

A touching documentary about 11 people who speak openly about being HIV-positive and how they cope with the uncertainty and fear of developing AIDS. Includes interviews with outspoken gays, a black filmmaker and 'typical Americans'. Made for television.

Prod Comp: Adair & Armstrong Productions
Dist/Sales: Frameline

Absolution of Anthony, The

Slotar, Dean
1998; USA; 12 min; Drama

An Hispanic youth struggles with his sexuality, and especially his attraction towards the local priest.

Dist/Sales: Slotar

Abuse

Bressan Jnr, Arthur J.
1982; USA; 95 min; Drama
P: Steven McMillin; *W:* Arthur J. Bressan Jnr;
C: Douglas Dickinson; *M:* Shawn Philips
Cast: Richard Ryder, Raphael Sbarge

A young man, who was abused as a child, finds love with a homosexual filmmaker. A controversial and enthralling love story between a filmmaker and a 14-year-old child-abuse victim based on the filmmaker's own life.

Dist/Sales: TLA, Cinevista, VideoAmericain

Abysses, Les

Papatakis, Nico
1963; France; 90 min; Drama
P: Nico Papatakis; *W:* Jean Vauthier; *C:* Jean-Michel Boussaguet; *E:* Edwige Bernard, Denise de Casabianca, Pascale Laverrière; *M:* Pierre Barbaud
Cast: Colette Bergé, Paul Bonifas, Pascale de Boysson, Colette Régis

Drama about a family who decides to move to a smaller house from their large country mansion. The two maids working for the family become so concerned about losing their jobs that they kill the mother and daughter as the father helplessly looks on. Based on a real-life incident and the inspiration for Jean Genet's *The Maids*.

Prod Comp: Lenox

Achilles

Purves, Barry
1996; UK; 11 min; Animation
P: Glenn Holbertson; *W:* Barry Purves, Jo Cameron Brown; *C:* Paul Smith; *M:* Nigel Hess

A brilliant, hard-hitting and erotic tale using claymation to tell the story of the legendary love affair between the Greek hero Achilles and Patroculus, during the nine years of the Trojan War. Voices by Derek Jacobi, Simon Green and David Holt. (MQFF)

Awards: Turin Gay & Lesbian Film Festival, 1996: Audience Prize
Prod Comp: Bare Boards Productions, Channel 4
Dist/Sales: Flickerfest, Channel4

Acla

(aka: La Discesa di Aclà a Floristella)

Grimaldi, Aurelio
1992; Italy; 86 min; Drama
P: Camilla Nesbitt, Pietro Valsecchi; *W:* Aurelio Grimaldi; *C:* Maurizio Calvesi; *E:* Raimondo Crociani;
M: Dario Lucantoni

Cast: Francesco Cusimano, Tony Sperandeo, Luigi Maria Burruano

Set in the harsh and punishing sulphur mines of Italy, where a young 11-year-old boy, Acla, dreams of escape from his brutal surroundings. During breaks the men indulge in the sexual exploration of each other. The film is reminiscent of a *Caravaggio* painting with young beautiful men, dressed only in loincloths, displaying their sweaty bodies—a feast for the eyes. Italian with English subtitles.

Prod Comp: Cines Europa, Nova Films
Dist/Sales: SACIS

Acquiring a Taste for Raffaella

Lepore, Sandy
1996; Australia; 14 min; Drama

The onset of menstruation leads to a curious mix of events when Raffaella shares the news with her traditional Italian Aunt. Together they make some special Italian love biscuits, 'biscotti di amore', with a secret ingredient intimately linked with Raffaella's menarche. When the object of her affections tastes the love biscuits, surprisingly, he asks for the recipe. (ACMI)

Prod Comp: Australian Film TV & Radio School
Dist/Sales: ACMI, AFTRS, Atom

Across the Rubicon

Friedberg, Lionel
1987; South Africa; 54 min; Documentary

Pieter-Dirk Uys is a South African female impersonator/caricaturist whose finely-wrought satirical touring show elucidates apartheid while lampooning it. Uys walks a thin line between censorship and arrest as he occasionally steps out of characters that include P. W. Botha, Desmond Tutu, and Margaret Thatcher, to deliver pointed attacks on apartheid and the South African government. Uys's popularity with both white and black audiences insulates him somewhat from government interference, but he describes his balancing act as being 'like doing the tango in front of a firing squad'. *Across the Rubicon* brilliantly portrays the humour and grace with which Uys makes his contribution to the fight against apartheid. (www.tgwebbuilders.com)

Acting on Impulse

(aka: Eyes of a Stranger)

Irvin, Sam
1993; USA; 73 min; Comedy, Thriller
P: David Peters; *W:* Mark Pittman, Alan Moskowitz;
C: Dean Lent; *E:* Neil Grieve; *M:* Daniel Licht
Cast: C. Thomas Howell, Linda Fiorentino, Nancy Allen, Dick Sargent

A tongue-in-cheek comic thriller, made for television by an openly gay director, about a B-grade horror film goddess who is accused of murder when her producer is found dead.

Prod Comp: Spectacor Films
Dist/Sales: Showtime

Actions Speak Louder than Words

Kwietniowski, Richard
1992; UK; 23 min; Documentary

A diverse, colourful and overwhelming collage of interviews, discussion and performance by, and between, six performers who bring their experiences of being gay and deaf to bear on their art. British sign language with subtitles for the hearing.

Prod Comp: Alfalfa, Channel 4

Adam

Bugden, Paul
1975; Australia; 38 min; B&W; Drama
P: David Perry; *W:* Paul Bugden; *C:* David Perry;
E: Ronda MacGregor; *M:* Robert Hughes
Cast: Wayne van Heekeren, Robert Hughes, David Calcott, Luda Apinys, Noel Brady

A short drama that concerns a young man's inability to cope with his own sexuality when confronted with an unfulfilled relationship with an older man.

Prod Comp: Quest Films, Experimental Film & Television Fund
Dist/Sales: NFVLS

Adam's Rib

Cukor, George
1949; USA; 97 min; B&W; Comedy
P: Lawrence Weingarten; *W:* Ruth Gordon, Garson Kanin; *C:* George Folsey Snr; *E:* George Boemlar;
M: Miklós Rózsa
Cast: Katharine Hepburn, Spencer Tracy, Judy Holliday, David Wayne, Tom Ewell

Amanda Bonner is a defence attorney in the trial of Doris Attinger who is being tried for the attempted murder of her husband whom she discovers has a mistress. Amanda's husband, Adam is the prosecuting attorney in the same trial. As the trial progresses, Amanda and Adam find they cannot confine their battle to the courtroom, as the issues of sexual equality extend into their home. David Wayne plays Kip, a composer and closet gay, who is a confidant and friend to Hepburn, and who provides much witty and bitchy repartee.

Prod Comp: MGM
Dist/Sales: NFVLS, ACMI, Warner, MGM, Swank

Addicted to Love

(aka: Boku wa koi ni Muchu)

Yoshiyuki, Yumi
1999; Japan; 60 min; Comedy
W: Koichi Imaizumi
Cast: Tomoo Okada

A romantic comedy about four gay guys in Tokyo. Tadashi fantasises about his best school friend, Kota. Hiroki and Shiji are a young, gay couple living in Tokyo. The three meet and Hiroki and Shiji prove invaluable in Tadashi's coming out journey. Japanese with English subtitles.

Adieu Bonaparte

Chahine, Youssef
1985; Egypt; 110 min; Drama
P: Youssef Chahine; *W:* Youssef Chahine; *C:* Mohsen Nasr; *E:* Luc Barnier; *M:* Gabriel Yared
Cast: Michel Piccoli, Patrice Chereau, Mohsen Mohiedine, Mohsena Tewfik

Set during Bonaparte's assault through Egypt, *Adieu Bonaparte* tells the story of an Egyptian family living in Alexandria and how they survive on 1 July 1798 when Napoleon lands with his troops. One of the sons begins a rather uneasy friendship with one of Bonaparte's advisers who obviously is sexually attracted to the young man. Contains homoerotic elements. Egyptian with English subtitles.

Prod Comp: Lyric International, Misr International, Renn Productions, TF1 Films

Adiós Roberto

Dawi, Enrique
1984; Argentina; 90 min; Drama
P: Enrique Dawi, Jorge Dawi
Cast: Víctor Laplace, Carlos Calvo, Ana María Picchio, Héctor Alterio

Adios Roberto, is rumoured to be the first openly gay film from Argentina. Roberto leaves his wife and cannot afford to rent an apartment, so he goes to live with his cousin's friend, Marcelo, who lives openly as a gay man. They soon develop an intriguing relationship, which creates conflicts for Roberto. Spanish with English subtitles.

Awards: New York Gay Film Festival, 1987: Best Film
Dist/Sales: Altermedia

Adjuster, The

Egoyan, Atom
1991; Canada; 102 min; Drama
P: Atom Egoyan, Camilla Frieberg; *W:* Atom Egoyan; *C:* Paul Sarossy; *E:* Susan Shipton; *M:* Mychael Danna
Cast: Elias Koteas, Arsinée Khanjian, Maury Chaykin,

Gabrielle Rose, Jennifer Dale

Noah Render is an insurance adjuster who plays saviour to men and women whose lives have been uprooted by tragedy. His clients look to him for comfort, sexual and otherwise, and he obliges them all, losing his own identity in the process. Noah's wife, Hera, is a censor for the Canadian government, who spends her days watching pornographic films which she secretly videotapes for her sister—but not for the purpose of titillation. Noah enters into a troubled relationship with a homosexual client. Into their lives come Bubba and Mimi, a wealthy couple and spend their money staging erotic fantasies to sustain their relationship. Posing as a filmmaker, Bubba takes over Noah and Hera's home as the setting for their latest, and most dangerous, immersion in play-acting.

Prod Comp: Ego Film Arts, Alliance Entertainment, Téléfilm Canada
Dist/Sales: OrionClassics

Adventures in the Gender Trade

Marenco, Susan
1993; USA; 40 min; Documentary

In this fascinating documentary, transsexuals, feminists, drag queens and historians discuss the limitations of 1990s thinking on gender. Excerpts from Kate Bornstein's play (*Hidden: A Gender*), in which she investigates her own experiences of coming out as a transsexual lesbian, offer poignant testament to the struggles involved in gaining acceptance as a transsexual. As the title makes clear, this video explores gender not as a fixed category, but as a highly politicised and socially constructed division that binds all men and women into rigid and oppressive roles. (MQFF)

Dist/Sales: Cinenova, FilmakersLibrary

Adventures of Priscilla, Queen of the Desert, The

Elliott, Stephan
1994; Australia; 98 min; Comedy
P: Al Clark, Michael Hamlyn; *W:* Stephan Elliott; *C:* Brian J. Breheny; *E:* Sue Blainey; *M:* Guy Gross
Cast: Terence Stamp, Hugo Weaving, Guy Pearce, Bill Hunter

Two drag queens and a transsexual leave Sydney in a bus called Priscilla, and travel to Alice Springs to climb a rock and put on a show. Along the way they break down, get lost, paint the bus lavender, dress up when they can, perform where they shouldn't, and encounter hilarity, hostility, incomprehension and, occasionally, acceptance.

Prod Comp: Latent Image, New South Wales Film &

a

TV Office, PolyGram Filmed Entertainment
Dist/Sales: RoadshowEnt, ReelMovies, Swank, Wolfe, Sogepaq, NFVLS, ACMI, VideoAmericain

The Adventures of Priscilla, Queen of the Desert

Adventures of Sebastian Cole, The

Williams, Tod
1998; USA; 99 min; Drama
P: Karen Barber, Jasmine Kosovic; *W:* Tod Williams;
C: John Foster; *E:* Alfonso Gonçalves; *M:* Elizabeth Swados
Cast: Adrian Grenier, Clark Gregg, Aleksa Palladino, Margaret Colin

Sebastian's first adventure begins when his step-dad, Hank, suddenly announces that he is going to become a woman. While other family members run for cover, Sebastian decides to stay with Hank, who becomes Henrietta. The two of them form a unique and winning bond as Sebastian learns to cope with prejudice and the non-stop curve balls life keeps throwing him. (Wolfe)

Prod Comp: Culpan Productions
Dist/Sales: ParamountClassics, Wolfe

Advise and Consent

Preminger, Otto
1962; USA; 140 min; B&W; Drama
P: Otto Preminger; *W:* Wendell Mayes; *C:* Sam Leavitt;
E: Louis Loeffler; *M:* Jerry Fielding
Cast: Henry Fonda, Charles Laughton, Walter Pidgeon, Franchot Tone

An orderly and analytical vision of Washington politics. Superbly acted by a large cast. When a senator doesn't back a candidate, he is blackmailed for having an affair with a man when he was in the army. Based on the novel by Allen Drury.

Prod Comp: Columbia, Sigma
Dist/Sales: Ascanbee, Columbia

Affairs of Love, The

(aka: Las Cosas del Querer)

Chávarri, Jaime
1990; Spain; 100 min; Drama
W: Lázaro Irazábal, Antonio Larreta; *C:* Hans Burmann;
E: Pedro del Rey; *M:* Gregorio García Segura
Cast: Ángela Molina, Ángel de Andrés López, Manuel Bandera, María Barranco

Set in the 1940s in Madrid *The Affair of Love* follows three performers in a vaudeville troupe: Juan, his girlfriend Pepita and Mario a gay piano player. When Mario's advances are rejected by Juan he goes about seducing a variety of men. When Mario breaks up with a nobleman, his lover's mother decides to take revenge.

Prod Comp: Iberoamericana de Televisión SA, Lince Films SA
Dist/Sales: Iberoamerica

Affirmations

Riggs, Marlon
1990; USA; 10 min; Drama

From the maker of *Tongues United*, an exploration of black gay male desires and dreams. *Affirmations* starts with an affectionate, humorous confessional and moves on to a wish for empowerment and incorporation. (Frameline)

Dist/Sales: Frameline

Afflicted

Guttman, Amos
1982; Israel; 25 min; B&W; Drama

Afflicted tells the story of a young, closeted Israeli man who visits a drag bar one night in search of sexual expression. Hebrew with English subtitles. (Frameline)

Dist/Sales: Frameline

After Hours

Scorsese, Martin
1985; USA; 97 min; Comedy
P: Amy Robinson, Griffin Dunne, Robert F. Colesberry; *W:* Joseph Minion; *C:* Michael Ballhaus;
E: Thelma Schoonmaker; *M:* Howard Shore
Cast: Rosanna Arquette, Griffin Dunne, Tommy Chong, Verna Bloom

An ordinary man experiences the most bizarre happenings. Mild-mannered computer programmer Griffin Dunne starts out on a date and things just go downhill: his date suicides before he can see her home, he gets mixed-up with some goofy thieves, an S/M freak—and that's just the beginning. Along the way Dunne picks up a lonely homosexual, played by Robert Plunket.

Awards: Cannes Film Festival, 1986: Best Director
Prod Comp: Double Play
Dist/Sales: Roadshow, ReelMovies, Warner

After Stonewall

Scagliotti, John
1999; USA; 88 min; Documentary
P: John Scagliotti; *E:* Dan Hunt, Janet Baus
Cast: Sheila James Kuehl

Documentary that examines the enormous changes in the gay rights movement since the Stonewall Riots in 1969. Interviews include Larry Kramer, Rita Mae Brown and narration by Melissa Etheridge.

Dist/Sales: FirstRunFeatures, VideoAmericain

After the Bath

Greyson, John
1995; Canada; 45 min; Documentary

In London, Canada in 1993 a bag of porn films was dragged out of a river. The main subject of the films was teenage boys. The Police Chief Julian Fantino was accused of creating a homophobic witch-hunt as over 60 men were arrested. This documentary uses headlines and interviews with journalists, police, gay activists and social workers to describe how the media and police manipulated the truth and blew out of proportion the threat of a child pornography ring.

Dist/Sales: VTape

After the Break (1992)

Guzmán, Mary
1992; USA; 13 min; B&W; Documentary
P: Mary Guzmán; *W:* Mary Guzmán

Personality clashes occur when co-dependency and the ability to love are discussed in a lesbian therapy group.

Dist/Sales: Frameline

After the Break (1998)

Kennerley, Annette
1998; UK; 13 min; Comedy

This short poetic film looks at the gap between being in a relationship and being single again—how we sometimes cling onto feelings of pain rather than feel nothing at all. (Cinenova)

Dist/Sales: Cinenova

After the Game

Gray, Donna
1979; USA; 19 min; B&W; Drama

Nicole and Diana, both in their early twenties, have a very close and loving friendship. When one of the women jokes that if she were a man they would get married, the other divulges she has a sexual attraction for her. Suddenly both realise their relationship has reached a turning point.

Dist/Sales: Cinenova

After the War you have to Tell Everyone about the Dutch Gay Resistance Fighters

Muller, Klaus
1991; The Netherlands; 60 min; Documentary

Documentary detailing the contributions made in the Dutch Underground by gays and lesbians during World War II.

Afternoon Breezes

(aka: Kaze tachi No Gogo)

Yazaki, Hitoshi
1980; Japan; 105 min; B&W; Drama
P: Mitsuhiko Akita, Shunichi Nagasaki, Shiro Oiwake;
W: Shunichi Nagasaki, Hitoshi Yazaki

The rather bleak story of a young Tokyo woman, Natsuko, who becomes obsessed with her female roommate, Mitsu. Based on an actual newspaper report, the film shows great insight into how a suppressed lesbian crush becomes an obsession. Natsuko attempts to break up Mitsu's relationship with her boyfriend by sleeping with him. When Mitsu discovers this, she kicks Natsuko out of the apartment. As her obsession for Mitsu grows, Natsuko begins to follow her everywhere.

Age 12: Love with a Little L

Montgomery, Jennifer
1990; USA; 22 min; Experimental

Age 12 is a riveting amalgam of forbidden desire, transgression and piercing self-recognition. Raw adolescent memories of girl cliques in kilts, cruel games and a hidden stash of *Playboys* counterpoint staged scenes exploring mechanisms of power and submission.

Dist/Sales: WMM

Age of Dissent

Parry, William
1994; UK; 51 min; Documentary
P: Greta Schiller

A video diary that follows the filmmaker and his
boyfriend in their involvement in the efoorts to
lower the age of consent for homosexuals in Britain
from 21 to 16. We follow them for a year through
their encounters with the media, politicians and
queerbashers.

Agora

Kinney, Donald / Kinney, Robert
1992; USA; 75 min; Drama
Cast: Randy Rovans, Kerry Snyder, Tammy Hopkins

A complex melodrama in which an agoraphobic gay
man meets a gay couple and a lesbian couple in
Midwest hotel. Parallels are drawn between homophobia and repression.

Aide Mémoire

Brynntrup, Michael
1995; Germany; 16 min; Experimental

The filmmaker turns his camera on photographer
Jürgen Baldiga in a personal investigation of how to
deal with the complicated issues of life, death and
AIDS.

Dist/Sales: MBC

AIDS

Pugh, George
1985; Australia; 42 min; Documentary
P: George Pugh

Exames the history of the AIDS epidemic in the
United States and the spread to gay communities in
the Western World including Australia. Medical
authorities discuss their hopes to contain the spread
of AIDS, outlining symptoms and debunking myths
regarding transmission of the virus. A series of frank
interviews highlight the human cost of AIDS.

Prod Comp: ABC
Dist/Sales: ACMI

AIDS Show: Artists Involved with Death and Survival, The

Adair, Peter / Epstein, Robert
1986; USA; 58 min; Documentary
P: Peter Adair, Robert Epstein; *M:* John Lewis, Doug
McKechnie
Cast: Steve Abel, William Barksdale, Robert Coffman,
Donna Davis

Based on San Francisco's Theatre Rhinoceros stage
productions, this thoughtful and thought-provoking
documentary deals with the impact of the AIDS
epidemic on the community most affected by the
disease in America—gay men.

Awards: San Francisco International Lesbian & Gay
Film Festival, 1986: Audience Award for Best Docu-
mentary
Dist/Sales: DirectCinema, Telling

AIDS: Words from One to Another

Muxel, Paule / de Solliers, Bertrand
1993; France; 73 min; Documentary

This series of interviews provides an intelligent, in-
depth and wide-ranging discussion of the social and
political issues surrounding HIV/AIDS. The subjects
describe with candour and eloquence how they
found out they were infected, how they envisage the
future, and how their sex lives and daily relationships
have been affected. (MQFF)

Dist/Sales: Point-Du-Jour

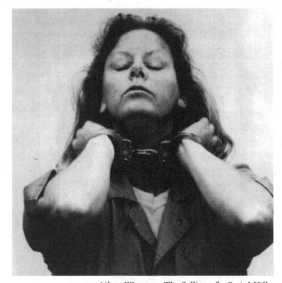

Aileen Wuornos: The Selling of a Serial Killer

Aileen Wuornos: The Selling of a Serial Killer

Broomfield, Nick
1992; UK; 85 min; Documentary
C: Barry Ackroyd
Cast: Nick Broomfield, Arlene Pralle, Aileen Wuornos

Aileen Carol Wuornos, a 35-year-old lesbian and
prostitute, was convicted of killing seven men in
Florida between 1990 and 1991 who were clients
she had picked up while hitchhiking. The FBI called
her America's first female serial killer. Nick

Broomfield digs through layers of hype to unearth an accurate portrait of Aileen Wuornos, her crimes and her fate. What becomes clear is the profiteering of the law enforcement agency and her friends, and the betrayal by her lover, Tyria.

Prod Comp: In Pictures, Channel 4
Dist/Sales: Ronin, 21stCentury, Strand, NFVLS

Aimée and Jaguar

Färberböck, Max
1998; Germany; 124 min; Drama
P: Hanno Huth, Günter Rohrbach;
W: Max Färberböck, Rona Munro; *C:* Tony Imi;
E: Barbara Hennings; *M:* Jan A. P. Kaczmarek
Cast: Maria Schrader, Juliane Köhler, Johanna Wokalek, Heike Makatsch

Set against snapshots of the glamorous illicit lesbian salons of wartime Berlin, *Aimée and Jaguar* tells the tragic true love affair between Lilly Wust (Aimée) and Felice Schragenheim (Jaguar). An intense and moody romance evolves when Lilly, the conventional blonde-blue-eyed epitome of Nazi motherhood, falls in love with Felice, a spirited Jewish lesbian who works for the underground and writes for a Nazi newspaper. German with English subtitles. (MQFF)

Prod Comp: Sentor Film
Dist/Sales: Senator, Zeitgeist, Mongrel, Wolfe, ACMI, VideoAmericain

Airport

Dunkhorst, Silke / Kay, Manuela
1994; Germany; 33 min; Comedy

A group of female flight attendants end up in a group sex session following a flight, and then finish off the night at a dyke leather party.

Alabaster Lions

Butera, Angelo
1990; Australia; 18 min; Drama

A florid and dramatic story of homosexual men and their lovers unfolds in this fast-moving and emotional tale.

Prod Comp: Australian Film TV & Radio School
Dist/Sales: AFTRS

Alexander: The Other Side of Dawn

Erman, John
1977; USA; 100 min; Drama
P: Wilford Lloyd Baumes
W: Walter Dallenbach, Dalene Young; *C:* Gayne Rescher; *E:* Neil Travis; *M:* Fred Karlin
Cast: Leigh McCloskey, Eve Plumb, Jean Hagen, Juliet Mills, Lonnie Chapman

Alexander moves to the big city but can't find a job, so takes up prostitution with both male and female clients. He finally moves in with an ex-football player, all the time denying his sexuality.

Prod Comp: Douglas S. Cramer Company
Dist/Sales: NBC

Alexandria... Why?

(aka: Iskanderija... lih?)

Chahine, Youssef
1978; Egypt; 132 min; Drama
P: Youssef Chahine; *W:* Youssef Chahine, Mohsen Zayed; *C:* Mohsen Nasr; *E:* Rashida Abdel Salam; *M:* Fouad El Zahiry
Cast: Farid Shawki, Naglaa Fathi, Ezzat El Alayli

Set in Alexandria in 1942, this film examines the illicit love affair of a Muslim man and a Jewish woman, and the relationship between an Egyptian teenager and a British soldier. Although not explicitly gay there is a very tender relationship between the two men, and the film is important for its Arabic treatment of the subject.

Awards: Berlin Film Festival, 1979: Best Director

Algie the Miner

Guy-Blaché, Alice
1912; USA; 13 min; Comedy

Rumoured to be one of the first queer comedies. Algie is a Nancy-boy Easterner who travels out West and finds a partner in a rough-around-the-edges miner.

Alias

Farrant, Kim
1998; Australia; 11 min; Documentary
P: Kate Riedl; *W:* Andrew Duvall, Kim Farrant

Alias takes us into the daily life of a male sex worker and introduces us to Jae, Todd, Toby and Craig—the four facets of his world. (MQFF)

Prod Comp: Australian Film TV & Radio School
Dist/Sales: AFTRS

Alicia was Fainting

Olivé-Bellés, Nuria
1994; USA; 37 min; Drama

The story of a 14-year-old girl who, after her mother's death, must deal with her own sexual awakening. Alicia, who doesn't like the idea of traditional women's roles, works in a butcher's shop, where she daydreams about her mother and writes letters to her best friend, a girl she's known all her life and with whom she must part upon their graduation from school.

Alien Prey

Warren, Norman J.
1983; USA; 85 min; Horror
P: Terence Marcel, David Wimbury; *W:* Max Cuff;
C: Derek V. Browne; *E:* Alan Jones; *M:* Ivor Slaney
Cast: Sally Faulkner, Glory Annan, Barry Stokes

An alien decides to satisfy its appetite by eating various people including two lesbian lovers. Graphic sex, violence and cannibalism abound in this film.

Prod Comp: Continent, Tymar Film Productions

Alive and Kicking

(aka: Indian Summer)

Meckler, Nancy
1996; UK; 100 min; Drama
P: Martin Pope; *W:* Martin Sherman; *C:* Chris Seager;
E: Rodney Holland; *M:* Peter Salem
Cast: Jason Flemyng, Antony Sher, Dorothy Tutin,
Anthony Higgins, Bill Nighy

Tonio's ambition as a young dancer at the peak of his career has allowed him to submerge his emotions under a carefree facade. The death of his best friend and mentor, Ramone, from an AIDS-related illness and the impending closure of his dance company, force Tonio to deal with his own HIV status. Added to this is the revival of *Indian Summer*, a pas de deux for two men, with Tonio in the lead role originally danced by Ramone. Escaping the pressure, Tonio meets Jack, an older, less flamboyant man, who works as a HIV counsellor. An unlikely couple, their relationship becomes a mirror to *Indian Summer*—a passionate expression of love, grief and an embrace of life.

Prod Comp: Channel 4, Martin Pope Productions
Dist/Sales: Channel4, FirstLook, Wolfe

Alkali, Iowa

Christopher, Mark
1995; USA; 17 min; Drama
P: Ann Ruark; *W:* Mark Christopher

Thoughtful and intelligent piece about the changing nature of the gay experience in the wide open spaces of America's heartland. J. D. Cerna plays a young man struggling with his sexuality, whose discovery of an old tin box in the ground leads him to think again about his family and the opportunities that were available to them in their lifetimes. With J. D. Cerna and Mary Beth Hurt. (MQFF)

Awards: Berlin International Film Festival, 1996: Teddy Award for Best Short Film
Dist/Sales: Forefront, Strand

All about Alice

Harrison, Ray
1974; USA; 80 min; Drama
Cast: Warren Fremming

A drag reworking of *All about Eve*, where Frieda plots to steal a Broadway star's career and muscle-bound boyfriend.

All about my Father

(aka: Alt om min Far)

Benestad, Even
2001; Norway; 75 min; Documentary
W: Even Benestad, August B. Hanssen; *E:* Erik
Andersson, Anders Refn; *M:* John Erik Kaada

All about my Father is a highly personal film about Esben Benestad, a well respected doctor—who also happens to be a transvestite—from a small, very close-minded Christian town in Norway. The film was directed by the one person most likely to convey the story with truth, warmth, humour and irony: Even Benestad, his son. 'Contrary to my father's idea that this film would promote him as a colourful character who uses all his time to combat conservative bureaucracy,' states the director, 'I wanted to make a portrait of him where his transvestism and strong self-realisation forms the basis of the film. I could not compromise—personal confrontation was paramount in making this a genuine film.' And genuine he is. Benestad's documentary is a candid, moving work exploring the two extremes of his dynamic dad's life as medico, author and politician juxtaposed with his identity as the exotic Esther Pirelli, sexual therapist and occasional actress. (2002 Melbourne International Film Festival) Norwegian with English subtitles.

Awards: Berlin Film Festival, 2002: Best Documentary
Prod Comp: Exposed Film Prods, Zentropa Real ApS
Dist/Sales: NorwegianFilm

All about my Mother

(aka: Todo sobre Mi madre)

Almodóvar, Pedro
1999; Spain; 100 min; Comedy
W: Pedro Almodóvar; *C:* Affonso Beato; *E:* José Salcedo;
M: Alberto Iglesias
Cast: Cecilia Roth, Penelope Cruz, Antonia San Juan,
Marisa Paredes, Candela Pena

Manuela is the perfect mother. A hardworking nurse, she's built a comfortable life for herself and her teenage son, an aspiring writer. But when tragedy strikes and her beloved only child is killed in a car accident, her world crumbles. The heartbroken woman learns her son's final wish was to know of his father—the man she abandoned when she was pregnant 18 years earlier. Returning to Barcelona in search of him, Manuela overcomes her grief and becomes caregiver to a colourful extended family: a pregnant nun, a transvestite prostitute, and two troubled actresses. (Wolfe)

Awards: Academy Awards, 1999: Best Foreign Language Film
Dist/Sales: Wolfe, SonyClassics, ACMI

All Fall Down

Foiles, Stacey
1993; USA; 30 min; Drama
P: Roberta Grossman

Dark memories erupt when a lesbian and her estranged sister travel to their mother's home on the anniversary of their brother's suicide. As they scatter his ashes in the spectacular Sierra Nevada mountains, Virginia and Amanda begin to confront their loss, their anger towards one another, and finally the incest suffered in their childhood and its profound impact on their lives.

Dist/Sales: WMM

All Girl Action: The History of Lesbian Erotica

Bright, Susie
1989; USA; 90 min; Documentary

Charts the recent history of lesbians making erotic film for lesbians.

All God's Children

Mosbacher, Dee / Reid, Frances / Rhue, Sylvia
1996; USA; 29 min; Documentary

Documentary made as a response to the increasing and deeply disturbing trend towards fundamentalist homophobia in the United States. The Traditional Values Coalition's notorious videotape, *Gay Rights/Special Rights: Inside the Homosexual Agenda*, was the spur that convinced the makers of *All God's Children* that a filmed response was definitely required. They have taken as their focus the African–American community in the US, highlighting what can often be a double dose of discrimination: racism and homophobia. The talking heads in the documentary include many religious figures such as the Reverend Jesse Jackson, while the political line-up features members of Congress, senators and the Mayor of Cambridge, Massachusetts. (MQFF)

Dist/Sales: WomanVision

All Men are Liars

(aka: Goodnight Irene)

Lee, Gerard
1994; Australia; 91 min; Comedy
P: John Maynard; W: Gerard Lee; C: Steve Arnold; E: Suresh Ayyar; M: Mark Moffatt, Wayne Goodwin
Cast: Toni Pearen, David Price, John Jarratt, Carmen Tanti, Jamie Peterson

A deadpan comedy of teenage love gone wrong. Mick, a 16-year-old boy, cross-dresses and joins an all-girl band in town for the local festival. He falls hopelessly in love with band member Angela who is flirting with lesbianism. She's hot for Mick, not just because he's cute and talented but, being a woman, he's honest.

Prod Comp: Arena Films
Dist/Sales: 21stCentury, 16MM, VSM

All of Me

Wilhelm, Bettina
1990; Germany; 76 min; Drama
W: Georgette Dee, Bettina Wilhelm; C: Frank Grunert; M: Terry Truck
Cast: Georgette Dee, Mechthild Grossmann, Miroslaw Baka

Orlanda is an androgynous performer who entertains with chansons and bawdy conversation in the old German 'Kleinkunst' tradition of the twenties. In a bewitching play on tradition and taboos Orlanda decides to marry the woman with the lowest voice in the world. On a concert tour to Warsaw, Orlanda and Elizabeth fall in love with a charming Polish man. The result is a complicated transcontinental love affair which resists the clichés that normally result from such entanglement. The film manages to succinctly question the limits of sexuality, gender and sexual attraction without sacrificing its entertainment appeal. (MQFF)

Dist/Sales: Wilhelm, VideoAmericain

All Out Comedy

Zachary, Bohdan
1993; USA; 78 min; Comedy

The first gay and lesbian stand-up comedy video, by the maker of *Loverville I & 2*. San Francisco comedians Scott Capurro, Marilyn Pittman, Tom Ammiano and Karen Ripley strut their stuff in live performances. (MQFF)

Dist/Sales: Zachary

a

All Over Me

Sichel, Alex
1997; USA; 89 min; Drama
P: Dolly Hall; *W:* Sylvia Sichel; *C:* Joe DeSalvo;
E: Sabine Hoffmann; *M:* Ani Difranco, Leisha Hailey,
Miki Navazio
Cast: Alison Folland, Tara Subkoff, Leisha Hailey,
Wilson Cruz, Cole Hauser

15-year-old Claude lives with her mom in New York City's Hell Kitchen, and is inseparable from her best friend Ellen. Claude's life revolves around the girl band she is trying to start with Ellen, working in the local pizza parlour with gay friend Jesse and the new musician in the building, Luke. Ellen's life increasingly revolves around drugs, and her new boyfriend, homophobic, macho Mark. But when Luke is murdered after a run-in with Mark, Claude's life is turned upside-down; her relationship with Ellen begins to disintegrate and she ventures out to a girl-punk club where she is attracted to Lucy.

Awards: Berlin International Film Festival, 1997: Teddy Award for Best Feature
Prod Comp: Baldini Pictures, Meducas Pictures, Slam Pictures
Dist/Sales: Palace, Alliance, FineLine, Wolfe, Millivres, ACMI, VideoAmericain

All Over the Guy

All Over the Guy

Davis, Julie
2001; USA; 95 min; Comedy
P: Susan Dietz, Donnie Land, Juan Mas, Dan
Bucatinsky; *W:* Dan Bucatinsky; *C:* Goran Pavicevic;
E: Glenn Garland, Mary Morrisey; *M:* Peter Stuart
Cast: Dan Bucatinsky, Richard Ruccolo, Christina
Ricci, Lisa Kudrow, Doris Roberts

Tom and Eli meet on a blind date set up by friends, but quickly find that they are complete opposites. Tom is a hunky, hard drinking, chain smoking school teacher who has a proclivity for one night stands and vintage stores. Eli is a cute and hopeless romantic who loves *The X Files*, and flies the flag for monogamy. They don't begin to hit it off until they start talking about movies, and even then it's obvious things will not happen over night. (MQFF)

Prod Comp: Niche Pictures
Dist/Sales: Wolfe, 10%

All the Queens Men

Ruzowitzky, Stefan
2001; Austria, Germany, Hungary, USA; 105 min;
Comedy
P: Marco Weber, Gabrielle Kelly, Zachary Feuer, Danny
Krausz; *W:* Daid Schneider, Jeff Stockwell; *C:* Wedigo
von Schultzendorff
Cast: Matt LeBlanc, Eddie Izzard, Nicolette Krebitz,
James Cosmo, David Birkin

A crew of Special Forces agents lead by cross-dressing Tony (a self-confessed 'bisexual lesbian trapped in a man's body') is sent to Germany, dressed as women, to infiltrate an Enigma factory and steal the much-coveted decoding device.

Prod Comp: Atlantic Streamline, Strand

All the Rage

Tec, Roland
1997; USA; 105 min; Comedy
P: Roland Tec; *W:* Roland Tec; *C:* Gretchen Widmer;
E: John Altschuler; *M:* Paul Outlaw, Roland Tec
Cast: John-Michael Lander, David Vincent, Jay
Corcoran, Paul Outlaw

Gorgeous, intelligent, with a great career and a hot gym sculpted body, Christopher is clearly a member of the gay urban 'A'-list. He is also an expert at one-night stands, and a master at brushing men off, once he's had them. But lately, Christopher is looking for a more meaningful relationship. Then he meets Stuart, an attractive, slightly chubby and down-to earth guy who spends as little time at the gym as he does selecting his wardrobe. Christopher is thrilled to finally be with a man who loves him for more than his looks, and the two begin a serious relationship... until temptation emerges in the form of Stuart's hunky and horny roommate. (Mongrel)

Prod Comp: Pinkplot Productions, Spade-a-Spade Pictures
Dist/Sales: JourDeFete, Mongrel, Pinkplot

All–American Story, An

Keitel, John
1991; USA; 28 min; Drama

A sharp, funny snapshot of the filmmaker as a young gay man, attending a Stanford reunion and shocking himself more than his straight pals. (www.cyborganic.com)

Alles Wird Gut

(aka: Everything will be Fine)

Maccarone, Angelina
1997; Germany; 88 min; Comedy
P: Claudia Schröder; *W:* Fatima El-Tayeb, Angelina Maccarone; *C:* Judith Kaufmann; *E:* Inge Bohmann; *M:* Jakob Hansonis
Cast: Kati Stüdemann, Chantal de Freitas, Pierre Sanoussi-Bliss, Isabella Parkinson

A warm and sexy comedy about two African women living in Berlin. Kim is a cool career woman on her way to the top, and is about to marry Dieter, her boss. Nabou is a younger, unemployed slacker who has just been dumped by her blue-haired girlfriend, and would do anything to win her back. Sparks fly when Kim and Nabou cross paths in the same apartment building. German with English subtitles.

Prod Comp: Multimedia, Norddeutscher Rundfunk
Dist/Sales: Multimedia

Alley of the Tranny Boys

Lee, Christopher / Zapata, J.
1998; USA; 50 min; Erotica

Gender outlaws reclaim their erotic and porno-graphic space in this celebration of transgender sexuality and fantasy.

Dist/Sales: LeeC

Almost the Cocktail Hour

Lin, Lana
1997; USA; 56 min; Drama

A personal meditation on the writer Jane Bowles.

Alone Together: Young Adults Living with HIV

Okazaki, Steven
1995; USA; 17 min; Documentary
P: Nobuo Isobe, Steven Okazaki; *C:* Tomas Tucker; *E:* Jay Hansell; *M:* Wade

Cast: Jennifer McGaugh, Justin Reed Early

Academy Award-winning filmmaker Steve Okazaki's powerful documentary shows the pain, frustration and extraordinary courage of nine young people living with HIV. Some live on the street, some in loving suburban families, while one is a professional figure skater. All speak with uncanny insight into their experiences. (MQFF)

Dist/Sales: Farallon

Alone Together: Young Adults Living with HIV

Alpsee

Mueller, Matthais
1994; Germany; 15 min; Experimental

An autobiographical essay on childhood, family and memory.

Dist/Sales: Canyon

Älskande par

(aka: Loving Couples)

Zetterling, Mai
1964; Sweden; 118 min; B&W; Drama
P: Göran Lindgren, Rune Waldekranz; *W:* Mai Zetterling, David Hughes;; *C:* Sven Nykvist; *E:* Paul Davies; *M:* Roger Wallis
Cast: Harriet Andersson, Gio Petre, Gunnel Lindblom, Anita Björk, Eva Dahlbeck

This drama, set at the beginning of the 20th century, is about three women in hospital all waiting to give birth. The three characters are Agda, a free spirit who has an arranged marriage with a gay man; Adele, stuck in a loveless marriage; and Angela, a lesbian living with her lover. The film uses a series of flashbacks to reveal the narrative.

Prod Comp: Sandrews

Alternative Conceptions

Sunley, Christina
1985; USA; 35 min; Documentary
P: Christina Sunley, Vicki Funari

An in-depth documentary, thoughtfully done, about lesbian parenting. Filmed in New York, it features interviews with several lesbian couples who talk about the problems associated with parenting, from the insemination, the sperm donor, the birth, legal aspects and the child's perception of growing up with same-sex parents.

Dist/Sales: WMM

Alternative, The

Eddey, Paul
1976; Australia; 75 min; Drama
P: Robert Bruning; *W:* Tony Morphett; *C:* Russell Boyd; *E:* Trevor Ellis; *M:* Bob Young
Cast: Wendy Hughes, Tony Bonner, Carla Hoogeveen, Peter Adams, Alwyn Kurts

Drama focussing on an unmarried mother and magazine-editor who has to make a choice between her new boyfriend and a former lover, after discovering she's pregnant. When she falls in love with a woman she questions the value of the traditional family unit.

Prod Comp: Grundy

Always Walter! An Inner View of Walter Larrabee

O'Driscoll Gray-Lee, Geoffrey
1999; USA; 117 min; Documentary

Walter Larrabee is a natural, intelligent, Salt Lake City boy trying to be a model human being. Believing his personal integrity to be truer than that of his family, young Walter cultivates himself as a multifaceted talent within the autocratic framework of The Church of Jesus Christ of Latter-day Saints. Following discord and coldness at Brigham Young University, Walter comes to terms with professional and personal maturity in this frank documentary.

Prod Comp: Balance Entertainment, World Class Educational Entertainment
Dist/Sales: Gray-Lee

Amazing Grace

(aka: Hessed Mufla)

Guttman, Amos
1992; Israel; 95 min; Drama
P: Doron Preiss; *W:* Amos Guttman; *C:* Yoav Kosh, Amnon Zlayet; *M:* Arkadi Duchin

Cast: Ada-Valery Tal, Sharon Alexander, Gal Hoyberger

This moving film is widely regarded as Israeli director Amos Gutman's masterpiece, and his swan song—he has since died of AIDS-related causes. Throughout his career Gutman was determined to make Israeli gays and lesbians visible to wider society and give them images of their own lives. In this feature, set in gay Tel Aviv, he adds AIDS to the picture. Sometimes humorous, sometimes melancholic, *Amazing Grace* follows spunky young Jonathan's move from carefree Miki to the older and HIV-positive Thomas, who has returned from New York to live with his mother. In the process, Jonathan learns about the serious side of his sexuality in a society where AIDS and homosexuality itself are hidden and young men like Miki have to do their stint in military service. Hebrew with English subtitles. (MQFF)

Prod Comp: Amazing Grace Productions
Dist/Sales: Mid-Bar, VideoAmericain

Ambiguous Feeling, An

Doundakov, Ilko
1997; Bulgaria; 57 min; Documentary

An in-depth look at homosexuality in Bulgaria. Bulgarian with English subtitles.

Dist/Sales: Bulgarian

Amelia Rose Towers

Farkas, Jackie
1992; Australia; 11 min; Experimental

A short film about perception, sexuality and maturity.

Prod Comp: AFTRS

American Beauty

Mendes, Sam
1999; USA; 121 min; Drama
P: Bruce Cohen, Dan Jinks; *W:* Alan Ball; *C:* Conrad L. Hall; *E:* Chris Greenbury, Tariq Anwar; *M:* Thomas Newman
Cast: Kevin Spacey, Annette Bening, Wes Bentley, Thora Birch

Winner of 5 Academy Awards including best picture, *American Beauty* tells the story of a seemingly perfect, but actually dysfunctional suburban family. Lester, is a self-described middle-aged loser, who is infatuated with a worldly teenage girl. His career-driven wife Carolyn drinks too much and is having an affair. Their daughter both loathes her parents, but falls for the new boy next door—whose hobby is documenting his life on videotape. The most well-adjusted characters of all are the gay couple next door who are happily ensconced in a long-term relationship. (Wolfe)

Awards: Academy Awards, 2000: Best Director, Best Picture, Best Actor (Kevin Spacey)
Prod Comp: DreamWorks SKG, Jinks/Cohen
Dist/Sales: Wolfe, UIP, Swank

American Fabulous

Dakota, Reno
1992; USA; 100 min; Comedy
P: Reno Dakota; *W:* Jeffrey Strouth; *C:* Travis Ruse;
E: Reno Dakota
Cast: Jeffrey Strouth

A one-man performance by Jeffrey Strouth who, from the back seat of a Cadillac, pontificates on any subject that enters his mind. Was released posthumously after Strouth's death from AIDS.

Prod Comp: Dead Jeffe Productions
Dist/Sales: FirstRunFeatures, VideoAmericain

American Gigolo

Schrader, Paul
1980; USA; 112 min; Drama
P: Jerry Bruckheimer; *W:* Paul Schrader; *C:* John Bailey;
E: Richard Halsey; *M:* Giorgio Moroder
Cast: Richard Gere, Lauren Hutton, Jessica Potter, William Dozier

A male escort for hire becomes a casualty of his profession when he is framed for murder. A rather homophobic film as all the gay characters are perceived as evil and/or murderous. There are scenes that include a gay killer, a gay wife-beater and a lesbian pimp.

Prod Comp: Paramount
Dist/Sales: Paramount

American Slices

Halwes, Shannon
2000; USA; 25 min; Comedy

Mitchell's life is turned upside down when his mother announces she's a lesbian. Normally this wouldn't faze Mitchell who is gay himself, but it's the fact that she's moving to a lesbian trailer park that's got him stunned.

Amerikanos

Dimas, Christos
1999; Greece, USA; 22 min; Drama

Tony, a Greek immigrant arrives in San Francisco hoping to start a new life, chasing his own kind of American dream.

Amic/Amat

(aka: Beloved/Friend)

Pons, Ventura
1998; Spain; 90 min; Drama
P: Ventura Pons; *W:* Josep Maria Benet i Jornet; *C:* Jesús Escosa; *E:* Pere Abadal; *M:* Carles Cases
Cast: José Maria Pou, Rosa Maria Sardà, Mario Gas

Jaume Clara, a brilliant and accomplished professor of medieval literature, should be enjoying the fruits of a life of hard work and achievement, but he is beset with failing health and is distraught over a passionate fixation on his beautiful, intelligent but withdrawn student, David. When a response to an anonymous call-boy's ad unexpectedly brings David to his door, Jaume foregoes the tempting opportunity for easy sex with his student and instead hatches an elaborate and dangerous plot to manifest his deep love, one which risks his career, his friendship with a beloved colleague, and the possibility of cruelty and violence at the hands of heartless David. The two men's mismatched passions and their well-matched intellects make for a feverish war of wills, one from which neither one will survive unharmed. (Strand) Catalan with English subtitles.

Prod Comp: Els Films de la Rambla, Generalitat de Catalunya
Dist/Sales: Lauren, Strand, VideoAmericain

Amigos

(aka: Friends)

del Valle, Claudio
1999; Chile; 21 min; Drama

A group of men who have been friends for many years meet in a bar to catch up. The dynamics change considerably when it is revealed that at least one of them is gay.

Dist/Sales: Insomnio

Among Good Christian Peoples

Gund Saalfield, Catherine / Woodson, Jacqueline
1991; USA; 30 min; Documentary

Demonstrates the pull between desire for religious community and personal freedom. Based on an autobiographical essay by Woodson where she looks at growing up, being one of the only black families on the block, the only writer in her family of Jehovah's Witnesses and being a lesbian. A powerful story that explores, for African–Americans, the relationship between their religious beliefs and their forbidden homosexuality. (Frameline)

Dist/Sales: Cinenova, Frameline, TWN

Among Men

Speck, Wieland
1980—1991; Germany; 80 min; Drama

A collection of five short films from German director Speck. David, spends an anxious afternoon spent with a man who struggles with his overwhelming desires in *Montgomery and I* (1980). *The Struggle of Fast Relief* (1983), tells of a night of feverish dreams and fantasies about an amorphous object of desire. *Chez Nous* (1981): the architecture of Berlin and its rooms figure prominently in this portrait of people 'loving life, living love'. *November* (1989), contrasts a sense of alienation with desire. Somewhere, people fight against state power, somewhere they celebrate afterwards. *Room 303* (1991), is a poignant view from a dying lover's bedside; the survivor sees a collage of scenes from the past: his lover, his lover's mother, his own mother and his father. (Frameline) German with English subtitles.

Dist/Sales: Frameline

Among Others

Vu, Trac
1998; USA; 17 min; Comedy

On a quiet evening charged with emotion, two men find themselves at intersecting crossroads. The life of a young male Asian hustler comes into focus through his chance meeting with a grieving stranger. (Big Film Shorts)

Dist/Sales: USC, BigFilm

Amor Maldito

Sampaio, Adélia
1983; Brazil; 90 min; Drama
W: José Louzeiro
Cast: Wilma Dias, Tony Ferreira, Monique Lafond, Mário Petráglia

Two women, who have been close friends, begin a lesbian affair. Unfortunately the affair ends in suicide, a murder charge and a trial. The lesbianism of the characters is described as an unnatural passion ending in murder. Supposedly the first Brazilian film to deal with lesbian sexuality. Portuguese with English subtitles.

Amorosa

Zetterling, Mai
1986; Sweden; 117 min; Drama
W: Mai Zetterling; *C:* Rune Ericson; *E:* Darek Hodor, Mai Zetterling; *M:* Roger Wallis
Cast: Stina Ekblad, Erland Josephson, Philip Zanden, Olof Thunberg

Based on the life of the Swedish author Agnes von Krusenstjerna who is famous for her treatment of lesbianism. The story is set during her last years in an insane asylum where she is sent to recuperate after suffering a nervous breakdown. During her time there she reflects on her tumultuous life, relationships and affairs.

Prod Comp: SVT Drama, Sandrews, Svenska Filminstitutet

Amos Gutman, Filmmaker

(aka: Amos Gutman, Bamay Kolnoa)

Kotzer, Ran
1997; Israel; 64 min; Documentary

From 1977 to his untimely death in 1993, Amos Gutman directed six films, all of them deeply personal reflections of his own life. Interviews with lovers, family and friends—including some of the most important people in Israeli cinema—tell the gripping story of a strikingly handsome, charismatic and deeply passionate gay man who has become a revered cult figure in Israeli cinema. (Frameline) Hebrew with English subtitles.

Dist/Sales: Frameline

Anatomy of a Hate Crime

Hunter, Tim
2000; USA; 93 min; Drama
P: Lawrence Bender, Bill Bannerman; *W:* Max Ember; *C:* Dan Nowak; *E:* Sunny Hodge; *M:* Dan Licht
Cast: Cy Carter, Brendan Fletcher, Ian Somerhalder, Amanda Fuller

This MTV produced drama recounts the story of the gay hate murder of Matthew Shepard in the USA.

Anatomy of Desire

Boullata, Peter Tyler / Monette, Jean-François
1995; Canada; 47 min; Documentary
P: Kenneth Hirsch, Jean-François Monette, Don Haig, David Wilson; *W:* David Wilson; *C:* Darren Biggs; *E:* Donna Reid, Jean-François Monette; *M:* Chris Crilly
Cast: Brad Fraser

Documentary which looks at how science is used to dissect and probe the causes of sexual orientation. Are lesbian and gay sexualities caused by socialisation? Or are they physiologically based? Or is it some complex interaction of the two? The film takes a provocative look at the growing debate on the origins of homosexuality and how it impacts on the issues surrounding lesbian and gay rights. Skilfully weaving together archival footage and interviews, the film traces the uneasy historical relationship between medicine and same-sex desire.

Prod Comp: National Film Board of Canada, Bare Bones Films
Dist/Sales: Heathcliff, CinemaGuild, NFVLS, NFBC

And the Band Played On

Spottiswoode, Roger
1993; USA; 140 min; Drama
P: Sarah Pillsbury, Midge Sanford; *W:* Arnold Schulman; *C:* Paul Elliott; *E:* Daniel Craven, Lois Freeman-Fox; *M:* Carter Burwell
Cast: Matthew Modine, Richard Gere, Lily Tomlin, Alan Alda, Anjelica Huston, Ian McKellen

> *And the Band Played On* attempts to expose the deadly role that inaction and infighting among government officials, blood banks, the scientific community and segments of the gay community played in the early spread of AIDS. Made for TV and based on the original story by Randy Shilts.

Prod Comp: HBO, Odyssey Entertainment
Dist/Sales: ReelMovies, Roadshow, Swank, Wolfe

And the Band Played On

And Then Came Summer

London, Jeff
2000; USA; 115 min; Drama
W: Jeff London; *M:* Greg Zocher
Cast: Jesse Petrick, Mathieu Smith

> Teenage boys discover their feelings for each other, only to be found out by their families. The exposed relationship leads to finding out one of the boys had been previously institutionalised for his homosexuality. (Wolfe)

Prod Comp: 10% Productions
Dist/Sales: Wolfe, 10%

And/Or=One

Kearney, Brian
1978; Australia; 45 min; Drama

> The true story of a Sydney prostitute and her lesbian relationships, and the unusual desire of one of her regular male customers.

Anders als die Anderen

(aka: Different from Others)

Oswald, Richard
1919; Germany; B&W; Drama
P: Magnus Hirschfeld; *W:* Magnus Hirschfeld, Richard Oswald; *C:* Max Fassbender
Cast: Conrad Veidt, Leo Connard, Fabers Vater, Ilse von Tasso-Lind

> A famous pianist falls in love with one of his students and the young man moves in with his teacher. Soon the pianist is blackmailed. Rather than paying off his blackmailer he goes to court and is found guilty and then imprisoned. Upon his release he suicides. His young lover makes a vow to change the law regarding homosexuality. One of the very first films to portray homosexuals in a positive light. The film was banned in the 1920s, and all prints were probably destroyed by the Nazis, but a short version was found in 1976 in the Ukraine.

Prod Comp: Richard-Oswald-Produktion

Anderson Tapes, The

Lumet, Sidney
1971; USA; 95 min; Thriller
P: Robert M. Weitman; *W:* Frank R. Pierson; *C:* Arthur Ornitz; *E:* Joanne Burke; *M:* Quincy Jones
Cast: Sean Connery, Dyan Cannon, Martin Balsam, Christopher Walken, Ralph Meeker

> This fast-paced caper is about an ex-con who schemes to rob a luxury apartment complex unaware that he is under surveillance. Martin Balsam plays a cowardly gay thief and antique dealer. Based on the novel by Lawrence Sanders.

Prod Comp: Columbia
Dist/Sales: Col-Tri, Columbia

Andy Warhol and his Work

Jokel, Lana
1973; UK; 51 min; Documentary

> This film is a fascinating insight into the man and his work as seen through his own eyes and those of his friends. As the sixties progressed, Warhol became more and more involved in filmmaking. A number of his films are classic examples of underground moviemaking and are valid reflections of the more extreme ends of life in late-sixties America.

Prod Comp: RM Productions
Dist/Sales: ACMI

Angel

O'Neil, Robert Vincent
1983; USA; 88 min; Thriller
P: Roy Watts, Donald P. Borchers; *W:* Robert Vincent

O'Neil, Joseph Michael Cala; *C:* Andrew Z. Davis;
E: Charles Bornstein; *M:* Craig Safan
Cast: Cliff Gorman, Susan Tyrell, Dick Shawn

A young high-school honours student in Hollywood
gets her kicks by spending nights working at the
world's oldest profession. When a madman goes on
the rampage she needs to use every trick in the book
just to survive. Among the characters are a lesbian
alcoholic and a very tacky drag queen.

Prod Comp: Adams Apple Film Company, Angel Venture
Dist/Sales: Roadshow, WaterBearer

Angelic Conversation, The

Jarman, Derek
1985; UK; 78 min; Experimental
P: James MacKay; *C:* Derek Jarman, James Mackay;
E: Peter Cartwright, Derek Jarman, Cerith Wyn Evans;
M: Coil
Cast: Paul Reynolds, Phillip Williamson, Judi Dench,
Dave Baby, Timothy Burke

As fourteen of Shakespeare's sonnets are being read,
we watch a young man isolated in a landscape of
fierce physical terror. It is his confrontation with
another man—at first antagonistic, then hesitant,
and finally sexual—which liberates the man and his
environment: rocks turn to water, physical struggle
turns to creativity. This beautifully shot experimental
film is a love poem dedicated to the artist's muse;
this time the love celebrated is between men and the
artist's liberation is defiantly homoerotic. The
sonnets are read by Judi Dench.

Prod Comp: BFI
Dist/Sales: BFI, Salzgeber, ACMI

Angelos

(aka: Angel)

Katakouzinos, George
1982; Greece; 126 min; Drama
W: George Katakouzinos; *C:* Tassos Alexakis;
M: Stamatis Spanoudakis
Cast: Michael Maniatis, Dionyssis Xanthos, Maria
Alkeou, Katerina Helmi

A downbeat film about a young man from a
dysfunctional family who meets and falls in love
with a macho sailor. Their relationship becomes
abusive and the young man is forced into prostitution on the streets of Athens. Based on a real-life
case, the film contains some brutally explicit love
scenes.

Prod Comp: Greek Film Centre
Dist/Sales: WaterBearer, VideoAmericain

Angels!

Martinez, Rico
2000; USA; 90 min; Comedy
P: T. J. Di Reda; *W:* Rico Martinez, John Stapleton;
C: Richard Avalon; *E:* Jim Makiej; *M:* Nazario Alonzo,
Craig Sherrad
Cast: John Stapleton, Ruben Zambrano, Raja, Monty
Freeman, Christian Campbell

Three 'female' private investigators from an elite Los
Angeles Detective agency are brought back to life
after 25 years of cryogenic sleep to fight crime in this
campy crime flick.

Prod Comp: Diet Angels

Anguished Love

Akarasainee, Pisan
1988; Thailand; 105 min; Drama

A gay-themed pseudo-documentary about gritty life
on the mean streets of Bangkok. A man now living
with an ex-lesbian goes to his ex-boyfriend's funeral.
The dead man's brother falls for him and the woman
has a relapse back into lesbianism and tracks down
her ex-lover. A gay aristocrat also emerges to borrow
money from his lesbian sister in order to open a new
club. Thai with English subtitles.

Dist/Sales: TMPPA

Animal Factory

Buscemi, Steve
2000; USA; 90 min; Drama
P: Julie Yorn, Steve Buscemi, Andrew Stevens, Eliie
Samaha; *W:* Edward Bunker, John Steppling; *C:* Phil
Parmet; *E:* Kate Williams; *M:* John Lurie
Cast: Edward Furlong, Tom Arnold, Seymour Cassel,
Mickey Rourke

Steve Buscemi's second film as a director, after the
impressive *Trees Lounge*, is a scintillating adaptation
of legendary crime scribe Edward Bunker's semi-
autobiographical novel. Set inside an American
penitentiary, *Animal Factory* follows the fortunes of
Ron Decker, a novice criminal who finds himself
plunged into the company of hardened cons. Luckily
for him, he is protected by the chief prison fixer and
gang leader, Earl Copen, who initiates him into the
ways of surviving prison life. Dark but not depressing, *Animal Factory* is a realistic and thoughtful
story, which shows how friendship and honour can
be maintained against all the odds. (BFI)

Prod Comp: Franchise Pictures
Dist/Sales: Col-Tri

Anita: Dances of Vice

(aka: Anita: Tanze des Lasters)

von Praunheim, Rosa
1987; Germany; 85 min; Drama
P: Rosa von Praunheim; *W:* Marianne Enzensberger,
Lotti Huber, Hannelene Limpach, Rosa von
Praunheim; *C:* Elfi Mikesch; *E:* Mike Shephard, Rosa
von Praunheim; *M:* Ed Lieber, Alan Marks, Rainer
Ruppert
Cast: Lotti Huber, Ina Blum, Mikael Honesseau

An old woman thinks she is the reincarnation of
Anita Berber, an infamous nude dancer in Berlin,
who was bisexual, a drug user and generally behaved
outrageously. Black and white dance segments are
intercut throughout the film.

Prod Comp: Exportfilm Bischoff & Company, Road
Movies Filmproduktion, ZDF
Dist/Sales: FirstRunFeatures

Anna und Edith

Neuhaus, Gerrit
1975; Germany; 77 min; Drama

Two female clerical workers fall in love while
fighting for better conditions at work. Made for
German television.

Anna und Elisabeth

Wysbar, Frank
1933; Germany; 74 min; B&W; Drama
W: Gina Fink, Frank Wysbar; *C:* Franz Weihmayr;
M: Paul Dessau
Cast: Dorothea Wieck, Hertha Thiele, Mathias Wieman

The paralysis suffered by the lady of the manor is
cured by the touch of a peasant girl. But the lady
soon discovers that she can't live without the girl.

Prod Comp: Kollektiv Film, Terra Film

Anne Trister

Pool, Léa
1986; Canada; 115 min; Drama
P: Claude Bonin; *W:* Marcel Beaulieu, Léa Pool;
C: Pierre Mignot; *E:* Michel Arcand; *M:* René Dupéré
Cast: Louise Marleau, Albane Guilhe, Lucie Laurier,
Guy Thauvette

A young Jewish painter named Anne, leaves Israel
for Montreal after the death of her father to stay
with her friend Alix, a psychologist. While she is
there she begins work on a huge mural. As the
painting develops, so does Anne's love for Alix,
causing confusion between the two women.

Prod Comp: Les Films Vision 4
Dist/Sales: BFI

Annie Sprinkle's Herstory of Porn: Reel to Real

Sprinkle, Annie / Harlot, Scarlot
1998; USA; 69 min; Documentary

An outrageous, irreverent and often hilarious review
of lesbian performer, filmmaker, porn star
extraordinaire Annie Sprinkle's 25 year career in film
porn as narrated by the 'Queen of Piss' herself.
Situated at bottom left of screen, Sprinkle talks us
through excerpts from dozens of her films as she
comments intelligently and humorously about
different porn genres and life in the risqué business.
Sprinkle's evolution through the sexual revolution
begins with rare vintage hippie porn, and then
progresses through to her 'kinky' period before
concluding with the era of women-made porn.
Despite the straight sex Sprinkle's sensibility is as
always inherently queer.

Dist/Sales: EroSpirit

Anniversary, The (1968)

Baker, Roy Ward
1968; UK; 95 min; Comedy
P: Jimmy Sangster; *W:* Jimmy Sangster; *C:* Harry
Waxman; *E:* Peter Weatherly; *M:* Philip Martell
Cast: Bette Davis, Sheila Hancock, Jack Hedley, James
Cossins

Bette Davis hams it up as a widow who uses her
wedding anniversary as an excuse for reuniting her
family. She gathers her sons together to celebrate the
death of her husband, whom she hated. She seems to
have an extraordinary hold over them, but when this
fails, she resorts to blackmail with her knowledge of
their various sexual activities, hetero, homo etc.
Based on the play by Bill McIlwraith.

Prod Comp: 20th Century-Fox, Hammer Film Productions, Seven Arts Productions
Dist/Sales: Ascanbee, 20thCenturyFox

Anniversary, The (1995)

Christensen, Garth
1995; USA; 14 min; Comedy

In this light-hearted comedy of errors from New
York, a misplaced anniversary note leads to confusion all round for two Manhattan couples and their
nosy neighbour. When the five finally get together,
the cat gets let out of the bag with the help of a very
special dessert. (MQFF)

Dist/Sales: Christensen

Another 45 Minutes of Bondage

Castro, Rick
1999; USA; 50 min; Erotica

More bondage hijinks from famed bondage

photographer Rick Castro. With Orlando, John Law, Kip Jaffey and Ralph Lower.

Prod Comp: Pyewackett Productions
Dist/Sales: Pyewackett

Another Country

Kanievska, Marek
1984; UK; 89 min; Drama
P: Alan Marshall; *W:* Julian Mitchell; *C:* Peter Biziou;
E: Gerry Hambling; *M:* Michael Storey
Cast: Rupert Everett, Colin Firth, Cary Elwes, Michael Jenn, Robert Addie

Guy Bennett is nearing the end of his last year at a leading English boarding school. His best friend, Tommy Judd, is a Marxist, committed to Lenin's brave new world. In a school permeated by homo-sexuality, affairs between the boys are accepted, provided discretion is practised. Bennett breaks this unwritten rule and the humiliating consequences establish within him a rejection of the system that excludes him. Scripted by Julian Mitchell from his own award winning play.

Prod Comp: Castlezone, Goldcrest, Eastern Counties Newspapers, NFFC, Virgin
Dist/Sales: ACMI, OrionClassics, VideoAmericain, Swank, BFI

Another Way

(aka: Egymásra Nézve)

Makk, Károly
1982; Hungary; 107 min; Drama
P: Andras Ozorai; *W:* Erzsébet Galgóczi, Károly Makk;
C: Tamás Andor; *E:* György Sívó; *M:* László Dés, Giorgio Moroder, János Másik
Cast: Hernadi Judit, Jadwiga Jankowska-Cieslak, Jozef Kroner, Andorai Peter

Eastern Europe's first film dealing with lesbian issues, this moving drama looks at the effects of political and social repression on the life of Eva, a journalist working for a weekly called Truth. She develops an obsessive passion for a fellow journalist, Livia, whose resistance is gradually broken down. Eva also finds that her investigative journalism is shackled by official censorship. These events are revealed in flashback as Eva is shot trying to cross the border. The love affair is treated lyrically while the scenes in the newspaper office are intense and realistic. Hungarian with English subtitles.

Awards: Cannes Film Festival, 1982: Best Actress (Jadwiga Jankowska-Cieslak)
Prod Comp: Mafilm Dialog Filmstudio, Meridian Films
Dist/Sales: NFVLS, ACMI, Sharmill

Antonia's Line

Gorris, Marleen
1995; The Netherlands; 93 min; Drama
P: Hans De Weers, Gerard Cornelisse, Antonino Lombardo; *W:* Marleen Gorris; *C:* Willy Stassen;
E: Marina Bodbijl, Wim Louwrier, Michiel Reichwein;
M: Ilona Sekacz
Cast: Willek van Ammelrooy, Els Dottermans, Dora van der Groen, Veerle van Overloop

The story of an independent-minded woman who comes to live in a small Dutch farming community at the end of World War II, and five generations of women who work, love and bond with each other. She looks back on her life and the lives of her daughter, granddaughter and great granddaughter, who is a lesbian. Continues the feminist allegorical themes in Gorris's work already established with films such as *Broken Mirrors* and *The Last Island*. Dutch with English subtitles.

Awards: Academy Awards, 1995: Best Foreign Language Film; Toronto International Film Festival, 1995: People's Choice Award
Prod Comp: Bard Entertainments, Bergen
Dist/Sales: NewVision, 21stCentury, FirstLook

Anxiety of Inexpression and the Otherness Machine, The

Lee, Quentin
1993; Hong Kong, USA; 53 min; Drama

Quentin Lee takes his video camera with him everywhere. Multilayered and covering everything from his appearance in a porn video to a family Christmas, sex with his bisexual lover, to doing drag and prostitution, to psychotherapy, this film is saturated with discourse and totally unabashed in its approach.

Dist/Sales: VTape

Any Wednesday

Miller, Robert Ellis
1966; USA; 109 min; Comedy
P: Julius J. Epstein; *W:* Julius J. Epstein, Muriel Resnik;
C: Harold Lipstein; *E:* Stefan Arnsten; *M:* George Duning
Cast: Jane Fonda, Jason Robards, Dean Jones, Rosemary Murphy, Jack Fletcher

A millionaire businessman spends every Wednesday with his mistress, but complications arise when his young associate is accidentally sent to use the company flat. When he finds out the truth he tells the businessman's wife and together they plot the husband's downfall. There is an effeminate interior designer, decorating the mistress's apartment, who receives a large amount of flack from the very macho Robards, who plays the businessman.

Prod Comp: Warner
Dist/Sales: Roadshow, Warner

Anything Once

Aeberhard, Dan
1998; USA; 23 min; Comedy
P: Antonio Manriquez, Joe Simon; *W:* Dan Aeberhard

Comedy which follows the friendship of roommates Joey, who happens to be openly gay, and Mike, who is straight. After a party one evening it becomes apparent that Joey has never slept with a woman, and Mike makes it his mission to try and persuade Joey to try it. As a result of Mike's efforts, Joey makes him a bet; if Joey is able to seduce a woman, Mike must pick up a guy.

Apariencias

Lecchi, Alberto
2000; Argentina; 94 min; Comedy
C: Marcelo Iaccarino; *E:* Alejandro Alem; *M:* Ivan Wyszogrod
Cast: Andrea Del Boca, Favio Posca, Diego Pérez, Fabian Mazzei

30-year-old Carmello has a crush on his co-worker Verónica, and is devastated when he finds out that she is about to get married. When he is spotted at a gay rally where he has accidentally become a spokesperson for the cause, Verónica naturally assumes that he's gay. Carmello goes along with the misunderstanding until his subterfuge brings about a most unexpected conclusion. Spanish with English subtitles.

Prod Comp: Patagonik Film Group, Pol-Ka Productions

Apart from Hugh

Fitzgerald, Jon
1994; USA; 87 min; B&W; Drama
P: Randy Allred, Jon FitzGerald; *W:* Jon FitzGerald;
C: Randy Allred; *E:* Randy Allred; *M:* James Clarke
Cast: David Merwin, Steve Arnold, Jennifer Reed

Elegantly shot in black and white, Jon Fitzgerald's thoughtful and intelligently written feature revolves around the first anniversary celebrations of Hugh and Collin. Unbeknownst to his lover, Collin is experiencing itchy feet and is already wondering whether leaving the relationship will make him stronger. His feelings are compounded by the arrival of the impulsive Frieda, an old friend from his wilder and more spontaneous days. Frieda has patently lost none of her attractive unpredictability and flagrant immorality. Who else would steal shoes from a goodwill store? Hugh throws an anniversary party for Collin, but will the man he loves still be there in the morning? (MQFF)

Prod Comp: Motion Media Company
Dist/Sales: TLA, WaterBearer, VideoAmericain

Apartment Zero

Donovan, Martin
1988; UK; 121 min; Thriller
P: Martin Donovan, David Koepp; *W:* Martin Donovan, David Koepp; *C:* Miguel Rodriguez; *E:* Conrad M. Gonzalez; *M:* Elia Cmiral
Cast: Dora Bryan, Liz Smith, Colin Firth, Hart Bochner, Cipe Lincovsky

A disturbing psychological thriller involving Adrian, a shy and sexually repressed young man who lives in an apartment in Buenos Aires and has a passion for old movie classics. He takes in a boarder, Jack, a charming and outgoing American. When gruesome murders begin to haunt the city, Adrian becomes suspicious that Jack may be the serial killer. Through the subtle use of suggestion, the film develops sexual tension between the two men.

Prod Comp: Summit Company, Producers Representative Organization
Dist/Sales: Col-Tri, Skouras, Wolfe, ACMI

Apartment Zero

Apartments

McMurchy, Megan
1977; Australia; 10 min; B&W; Drama
W: Megan McMurchy; *C:* Jeni Thornley, Wendy Freecloud; *E:* Megan McMurchy
Cast: Jeune Pritchard, Sandy Edwards, Michael Snelling

Two women living in the same apartment block are drawn to each other. Each is unaware of the other's desire, but a shared erotic fantasy develops between them. One woman's relationship with her lover disintegrates as the focus of her sexual desire shifts towards the other woman. The final meeting ensures a happy ending. (Cinenova)

Dist/Sales: Cinenova

Apostles of Civilised Vice

Achmat, Zackie
1999; South Africa; 104 min; Documentary
P: Jack Lewis; *W:* Zackie Achmat
Cast: Peter Krummeck, John Trengove, Denver
Vraagom, Ashley Brownlee

Apostles of Civilised Vice is a history of same-sex
desire which investigates lesbian and gay experience
and personalities from colonial times to the present.
Between 1910 and 1933 thousands of men were
convicted of sodomy and 'unnatural offences'. The
majority of those tried, convicted and imprisoned
were black. For over two centuries of South African
history, lesbian and gay stories have been silenced,
depriving contemporary queer life of a history.
Apostles of Civilised Vice gives voice to gays and
lesbians silenced by colonial rule and apartheid laws
that criminalised and marginalised same sex desire.
(Idol Pictures)

Dist/Sales: Idol

Apartments

Aqueles Dois

Amon, Sergio
1985; Brazil; 85 min; Drama
P: Gilberto Baum; *W:* Sergio Amon, Pablo Vierci;
C: César Charlone; *E:* Sergio Amon, Roberto Henkin;
M: Augusto Licks
Cast: Pedro Wayne, Beto Ruas

Raul is a lonely and sad man who has just left his
marriage. Saul is a shy and bitter man critical of the
world around him. The two lonely men meet at
their new workplace and become drawn to each
other. Although they are both clearly heterosexual,
their work colleagues believe differently and they
soon discover how far homophobia can go. A
thought-provoking study into male bonding and the
thin line between homosexuality and heterosexual
affection. Portuguese with English subtitles.

Prod Comp: Roda Filmes, Z Produtora

Arabian Nights

(aka: Il Fiore Delle Mille e una Notte)

Pasolini, Pier Paolo
1974; France, Italy; 130 min; Comedy
P: Alberto Grimaldi; *W:* Dacia Maraini, Pier Paolo
Pasolini; *C:* Giuseppe Ruzzolini; *E:* Nino Baragli,
Tatiana Casini Morigi; *M:* Ennio Morricone
Cast: Franco Citti, Margarethe Clementi, Tessa Boucha,
Ninetto Davoli

An erotic, dazzling and funny tale from *The Thousand
and One Nights*: featuring a series of stories within a
story about love and lovemaking, linked by the main
character Mur-El-Din as he searches for his kidnapped slave girl. The final instalment in the trilogy
of films preceded by *The Decameron* and *Canterbury
Tales*, it took Pasolini nearly two years to make.

Prod Comp: Les Productions Artistes Associés,
Produzioni Europee Associati
Dist/Sales: ReelMovies, UA

Arch Brown's Top Story

Brown, Arch
1993; USA; 118 min; Drama
Cast: John Finch, Jerry Ferracio

A gay soap opera from the 1990s about a group of
southern Californian men as they go about their
day-to-day life with all its traumas and problems.
The interlocking stories revolve around a group of
young men sharing a house together. An accurate
depiction of gay life through the lens of the director
of many adult, male porn flicks.

Are you Greedy?

Vuolo, Cristina / Tuzi, Federica
2000; Italy; 60 min; Documentary

Interviews with women both single and in couples
about relationships, sexual practices, roles and
negotiations. The filmmakers talk to women from
Europe, Africa, USA and South America.

Dist/Sales: Tuzi

Aren't you Lucky you Brought your Own Chair

Scott, Margaret
1999; Canada; 16 min; Experimental

Discussions about disability, access and sexuality.

Dist/Sales: VideoOut

Armistead Maupin is a Man I Dreamt Up

Clarke, Kristiene / Meynell, Kate
1992; UK; 60 min; Documentary
P: Kate Meynell, Kristiene Clarke

An entertaining portrait of one of America's most famous gay writers, the author of the *Tales of the City* series of books. The documentary includes interviews with colleagues, friends and with Maupin himself. There are also selected readings from his work, which are a nostalgic treat for those who love Maupin's writing.

Army of Lovers: or Revolt of the Perverts

von Praunheim, Rosa
1979; Germany; 97 min; Documentary
P: Rosa von Praunheim, Mike Shephard; *C:* Rosa von Praunheim; *E:* Rosa von Praunheim

A controversial documentary about the rise of gay militancy in America from 1950 to the late 1970s. It deals principally with the new gay consciousness that developed as a result of the Stonewall riots in 1970, the later schisms in the gay movement, anti-gay campaigns and official attitudes to the movement. The film is a deliberate attack on what von Praunheim categorises as a 'more straight, bourgeois, racist, sexist, middle-class gay audience'. As such, it is as much concerned with offending viewers as with informing them, raising issues about the role of the documentary filmmaker as agent provocateur.

Dist/Sales: Canyon, Exportfilm, NFVLS

Arrangement, An

Blasco, Didier
1998; France; 31 min; Drama

After closing his shoemaker shop in a high class neighbourhood, Alphonse Dutilleux goes to the Bois de Boulogne, a place where male prostitutes are solicited. His wife and his son are waiting for him... French with English subtitles.

Dist/Sales: Kanpaï

Art of Cruising Men, The

Litten, Peter McKenzie
1995; UK; 70 min; Documentary
P: Gary Fitzpatrick

Two cyber-hosts, the sexy and arrogant 'He-male' and the acid, sharp-tongued drag 'She-male', host a light-hearted inquiry into the cruising habits of gay men. From prehistoric man to the present day, they delve into the bars and toilets to find out exactly what the art of cruising men is all about.

Dist/Sales: WaterBearer, Salzgeber, TLA, VideoAmericain

As Far Away as Here

Carolfi, Jerome
1997; USA; 23 min; Experimental

Structured around footage shot on a road trip with a

former lover, *As Far Away as Here* is an extended visual metaphor exploring the nature of loss, employing a visual rather than vocal narrative.

As Good as it Gets

Brooks, James L.
1997; USA; 138 min; Comedy
P: James L. Brooks, Bridget Johnson, Kristi Zea;
W: Mark Andrus, James L. Brooks; *C:* John Bailey;
E: Richard Marks; *M:* Hans Zimmer
Cast: Jack Nicholson, Helen Hunt, Cuba Gooding Jnr, Greg Kinnear, Skeet Ulrich

Melvin Udall is the most dysfunctional of men, a romance novelist with a obsessive-compulsive disorder. He goes out of his way to offend and repulse people, But the only person who will stand up to him is Carol, a waitress and single mother. His neighbour across the hall is Simon, an art dealer and his gay lifestyle only further incites Melvin's malicious mouth. These three don't appear to have a hope in hell of finding happiness, but discover their fates intertwined with the fourth complicated character, an ugly, tiny dog named Verdell.

Awards: Academy Awards, 1997: Best Actress (Helen Hunt), Best Actor (Jack Nicholson)
Prod Comp: TriStar Pictures, Gracie Films
Dist/Sales: Col-Tri, 16MM, Wolfe

As Is

Lindsay-Hogg, Michael
1985; USA; 85 min; Drama
P: Iris Merlis; *W:* William M. Hoffman; *C:* René Ohashi; *E:* Ruth Foster; *M:* Peter Matz
Cast: Robert Carradine, Jonathan Hadary, Joanna Miles, Colleen Dewhurst

Based on the Broadway play by William Hoffman, this powerful made for television drama focuses on two ex-lovers who are drawn together through the AIDS crisis. Rich, a writer, leaves his long-time lover, Saul, for another man. But when Rich is tested positive for HIV, his new relationship ends and he is left alone. The only person who will stand by him is Saul. A humorous and revealing look at gay lifestyles.

Dist/Sales: TLA, ACMI

Asa Branca: A Brazilian Dream

Batista, Djalma Limongl / Pfahl, Berengar
1980; Brazil; 95 min; Drama
W: Djalma Limonge Batista
Cast: Edson Celulari, Walmor Chagas, Gianfrancesco Guarnieri

A story of homosexual repression and desire, set on the soccer field. A young man, Asa, finds he is becoming attracted to another man. This film provoked fury in Brazil when it was released as it suggested a homoerotic aspect to sport and its male fans. Portuguese with English subtitles.

Ashley 22

Nolan, Monica
1999; USA; 12 min; Comedy

Just when you think you've found the perfect date, you come to the stark realisation that everyone else is dating the same woman.

Astragale, L'

Casaril, Guy
1968; France; 102 min; Drama
P: Pierre Braunberger, Artur Brauner; W: Guy Casaril;
C: Edmond Richard; M: Joss Baselli
Cast: Marlene Jobert, Horst Buchholz, Magali Noel, Georges Géret

While escaping from prison to be with her lesbian friend, a 19-year-old girl breaks her ankle and is picked up by an ex-con, with whom she begins a passionate affair. She finally turns to prostitution and robbery to support herself.

Prod Comp: Film De La Plaeiade, CCC Filmkunst GmbH

At Home

Segal, Jonathan
1987; Israel; 29 min; Drama

Alex and his lover Gershon, both playwrights, have been living together for more than 10 years in Tel Aviv. Shadowed by artistic jealousy and questioning his relationship, Gershon spends his days at home, writing second-rate plays and sending articles out to local home-decorating magazines. Meanwhile, Alex is enjoying increased recognition as a playwright and brief liaisons with other men.

Dist/Sales: Frameline

Atomic Sake

Archambault, Louise
1999; Canada; 33 min; B&W; Comedy

Over dinner and sake, three women share secrets that will test the boundaries of their friendship and possibly have permanent ramifications for their relationship.

Attack of the Giant Moussaka, The

(aka: The Attack of the Giant Mousaka)

Koutras, Panos H.
1999; Greece; 103 min; Comedy

P: Panos H. Koutras; W: Panos H. Koutras;
C: Zafiris Epaminondas; E: Elissavet Chronopoulou;
M: Konstantinos Vita
Cast: Myriam Vourou, Yiannis Angelakis, Christos Mandakas, Grigoris Patrikareas

Around the year 2000, a terrible occurrence shocks the city of Athens. A huge piece of moussaka appears on the city streets spreading panic and death. Everyone keeps wondering: why, where, how, for what reason? but no one can give an answer. The ambitious Minister of Environment, his drug addicted wife, the director of the Observatory, his overweight girlfriend and a neurotic TV reporter, each for reasons of their own, meet with the frightening mass. All these people will became witness to a unique event, a new era will begin and a new family will be created. A camp comedy send up of 1950s American sci-fi classics. Greek with English subtitles.

Prod Comp: 100% Synthetic Film Production
Dist/Sales: GFC, AdVitam

Audit

To, Brian
2000; USA; 28 min; Drama

An unusual tax audit sets the stage for this biting satire of the Hollywood closet, featuring offbeat performances by Sally Kirkland and Alexis Arquette.

Avenge Tampa

Dyke TV
1993; USA; 10 min; Documentary

A shocking and disturbing film about homophobia in the United States. A woman's home is burned when shi is discovered to be HIV-positive. (Cinenova)

Prod Comp: Dyke TV
Dist/Sales: Cinenova

Away with Words

(aka: Kujaku)

Doyle, Christopher
1998; Hong Kong; 90 min; Drama
P: Hiro Tokimori; W: Christopher Doyle, Tony Rayns;
C: Christopher Doyle; E: Anne Goursaud, Sozo Morisaki; M: Fumio Itabashi
Cast: Tadanobu Asano, Christa Hughes, Kevin Sherlock, Mavis Xu

Asano has an amazing memory—the sort where words take on tangible shapes, tastes and colours. He is a world traveller who finds himself in Hong Kong and in the Dive Bar, which soon becomes a home away from home for him. The bar is run by Kevin, who has a terrible memory, and is an alcoholic. It seems that a relationship can develop between the two if only they didn't have to rely on words...

Prod Comp: Time Warp

B. D. Women

Blackman, Inge
1994; UK; 20 min; Documentary

This moving documentary investigates the experiences of black lesbians in Britain. Disparagingly referred to as 'bulldaggers', lesbians of colour occupy a precarious position that sees them confronting the homophobia of their ethnic communities, while at the same time having to challenge the racism of white-dominated queer spaces. A series of interviews with women of Caribbean, African and Asian descent is framed by a stylish fantasy set in the lesbian clubs of the Harlem Renaissance. (MQFF)

Dist/Sales: WMM

B.U.C.K.L.E.

Gund Saalfield, Catherine / Tolentino, Julie
1993; USA; 11 min; Comedy

A humorous fast-paced parody of women dancing, cruising and picking up other women at New York City's legendary Clit Club. (Cinenova)

Dist/Sales: Cinenova

B/side

Child, Abigail
1996; USA; 37 min; Experimental

B/side is an abstract portrait of a homeless woman at the edge of dystopia which implicates us all in her predicament.

Dist/Sales: Canyon

baba-It

(aka: At Home)

Sagall, Jonathan (aka: Segal, Jonathan)
1991; Israel; 29 min; Drama

Two gay playwrights try to keep their relationship afloat, but it proves difficult when one achieves success, and the other doesn't.

Baby

Elliot, Steven
2000; UK; 14 min; Experimental

A teenage boy revels in the pleasures of flesh and body collisions at a local swimming pool in this beautiful, surreal and most extraordinary coming of age film. (MQFF)

Dist/Sales: BFI

Baby Steps

Nauffts, Geoffrey
1999; USA; 26 min; Drama

Robert Kahn is a gay school teacher who wants to adopt a child. However, he encounters difficulties when he meets with Rose Melon (Kathy Bates), a Midwestern adoption agent who is resistant to the idea.

Dist/Sales: Rattled, Atom

Backroom

Morales, Guillem
1999; Spain; 13 min; Erotica

Chronicles the action in the back room of a gay male night club, providing an intimate look into the art of gay cruising.

Dist/Sales: PictureThis!

Bad Brownies

Mitchell, Allyson
1997; Canada; 20 min; Comedy

A mockumentary of memoires of childhood transgression. Former Brownies recall their lives in the organisation and two modern-day recruits—one a good Brownie and one a bad one are—demonstrate different reactions to the rules and rituals of the Brownie circle. (CFMDC)

Dist/Sales: CFMDC

Bad News Bachelors

Di Chiera, Franco
1990; Australia; 26 min; Drama

Set in gay Sydney, the film follows thirty-something Stuart as he roams the city's cafés, bars and cruising areas looking for a man to love but finding only sex with a series of likeable men—none of whom offer the likelihood of a relationship.

Prod Comp: Australian Film TV & Radio School
Dist/Sales: AFTRS

Badass Supermama

Inyang, Etang
1996; USA; 16 min; Comedy

This story of an African–American woman's search for identity mixes 1970s kitsch nostalgia with insightful observations about the adolescent lesbian experience. (Frameline)

Dist/Sales: Frameline

Baise-moi

(aka: Fuck Me; Rape Me)

Trinh Thi, Coralie
2000; France; 77 min; Erotica

P: Philippe Godeau; *W:* Coralie Trinh Thi, Virginie Despentes; *C:* Benoit Chamaillard, Julien Pamart; *E:* Ailo Auguste, Véronique Rosa, Francine Lemaitre; *M:* Varou Jan
Cast: Raffaela Anderson, Karen Lancaume, Delphine MacCarty, Lisa Marshall

Controversial film based on the novel by Virginie Despentes. Manu (a victim of rape) and Nadine (a witness of violence) embark on a revenge-inspired rampage of sex and murder. French with English subtitles.

Prod Comp: Le Studio Canal+
Dist/Sales: Remstar

Balcony, The

Strick, Joseph
1963; USA; 84 min; B&W; Drama
P: Ben Maddow, Joseph Strick; *W:* Ben Maddow; *C:* George Folsey; *E:* Chester W. Schaeffer; *M:* Igor Stravinsky
Cast: Shelley Winters, Peter Falk, Lee Grant, Ruby Dee

Interesting American adaptation of Jean Genet's symbolic play about life in a Parisian brothel. Winters plays the madam of the brothel who holds it together during the revolution, and Grant is her lesbian confidante.

Awards: Academy Awards, 1963: Best Cinematography
Dist/Sales: Ascanbee, Kino

Ballad of Little Jo, The

Greenwald, Maggie
1993; USA; 120 min; Western
P: Brenda Goodman, Fred Berner; *W:* Maggie Greenwald; *C:* Declan Quinn; *E:* Keith Reamer; *M:* David Mansfield
Cast: Suzy Amis, Bo Hopkins, Ian McKellen, David Chung

In the Wild West of the 1860s a woman had only two choices—she could be a wife or she could be a whore. Josephine Monaghan dared to be different—she realised that to survive in the West she needed to dress as a man. Inspired by a real-life legend.

Prod Comp: Joco, PolyGram Filmed Entertainment
Dist/Sales: REP, FirstRelease, FilmsInc, FineLine

Ballad of Reading Gaol

Kwietniowski, Richard
1988; UK; 12 min; Drama

An erotic, modern-day twist on Oscar Wilde's famous speech—delivered by Quentin Crisp—in defence of 'the love that dare not speak its name'. (Frameline)

Dist/Sales: Frameline, BFI, Salzgeber

Ballot Measure 9

MacDonald, Heather
1995; USA; 72 min; Documentary

Documentary about the 1992 ballot referred to as 'Measure 9 legislation' which was created by the Oregon Citizens' Alliance. The legislation set out to repeal and prohibit further state legislation that would protect homosexuals from discrimination.

Awards: Berlin Film Festival, 1995: Best Gay Film; Sundance Film Festival, 1995: Audience Award
Prod Comp: Oregon Tape Project
Dist/Sales: TLA, Zeitgeist

Bar Girls

Giovanni, Marita
1994; USA; 93 min; Comedy
P: Lauran Hoffman, Marita Giovanni; *W:* Lauran Hoffman; *C:* Michael Ferris; *E:* Carter De Haven; *M:* Lenny Meyers
Cast: Liza D'Agostino, Nancy Allison Wolfe, Camilla Griggs, Michael Harris

Bar Girls is a comedy about the amorous escapades of eight grown-up urban women who meet, retreat, and regroup in their home away from home, The Girl Bar. The plot revolves around the mysterious bittersweet and funny ways that lesbians can get their hearts and bodies tangled up with each other. (MQFF)

Prod Comp: Lavender Circle Mob, Orion
Dist/Sales: PictureThis!, Wolfe, Millivres, VideoAmericain, Swank

Barbarella

Vadim, Roger
1968; France, Italy; 98 min; Sci-Fi, Comedy
P: Dino de Laurentiis; *W:* Roger Vadim, Terry Southern, Claude Brule, Vittorio Bonicelli, Clement Biddle Wood, Brian Degas, Tudor Gates, Jean-Claude Forest; *C:* Claude Renoir; *E:* Victoria Mercanton; *M:* Michel Magne, Charles Fox, Bob Crewe
Cast: Jane Fonda, John Phillip Law, Anita Pallenberg, Milo O'Shea, Marcel Marceau

Set in the year 40,000 Barbarella is interrupted from her float amidst zero gravity by a call from the President of Earth. A young scientist named Duran-Duran is threatening the universal peace and Barbarella must find him and save the world. Anita Pallenberg plays the lesbian Black Queen and John Phillip Law plays the beautiful angel. A fabulous camp sci-fi classic from the 1960s.

Prod Comp: Marianne, Dino de Laurentiis Cinematografica, Paramount Pictures
Dist/Sales: Ascanbee, ReelMovies, Paramount

Bare

Strutt, Deborah
2000; Australia; 10 min; Comedy
P: Liz Baulch; *W:* Amanda Roberts

Tea Coffee? Scrambled eggs? Sex on toast? Erotic forces explode when two gay boys perve on their lesbian neighbours doing it for breakfast.

Prod Comp: Wild Iris Productions
Dist/Sales: CFMDC

Bare

Bargain Lingerie

Marcos, Teresa
1999; Spain; 15 min; Comedy

A young woman meets the big-breasted sales woman of her dreams while out shopping for lingerie. Spanish with English subtitles.

Dist/Sales: Deva

Barry Lyndon

Kubrick, Stanley
1975; UK; 178 min; Drama
P: Stanley Kubrick; *W:* Stanley Kubrick; *C:* John Alcott;
E: Tony Lawson; *M:* Leonard Rosenman
Cast: Ryan O'Neal, Marisa Berenson, Stephen Berkoff

An 18th century Irish rogue yearns for success among the English aristocracy, but in his quest for riches he loses his sense of perspective. There is a very homophobic scene depicting two gay men bathing in a river that is believed to have been conceived by Ryan O'Neal. Based on a novel by William Makepeace Thackeray.

Prod Comp: Warner, Hawk Films, Peregrine, Polaris
Dist/Sales: Warner

Basement Girl, The

Onodera, Midi
2000; Canada; 12 min; Experimental

Abandoned by her lover, a young woman finds comfort and safety in her basement apartment. Mundane routines, a diet of junk food and the warmth of the television insulate her from the pain and betrayal of her ill-fated relationship. Eventually, 'The Basement Girl' emerges—transformed and ready to 'make it on her own'. (WMM)

Dist/Sales: WMM, CFMDC

Basic Instinct

Verhoeven, Paul
1992; USA; 128 min; Thriller
P: Alan Marshall; *W:* Joe Eszterhas; *C:* Jan De Bont;
E: Frank J. Urioste; *M:* Jerry Goldsmith
Cast: Michael Douglas, Sharon Stone, George Dzundza, Jeanne Tripplehorn, Denis Arndt

Michael Douglas plays an ex-undercover cop, burnt out and recovering from drug and alcohol addiction who becomes involved with the investigation of a brutal murder. The prime suspect is a very rich, very beautiful bisexual woman whose calm and collected exterior belies a predatory and hedonistic soul. Sharon Stone has become a lesbian favourite on the strength of the role, and the film has become somewhat of a cult classic.

Prod Comp: Carolco, Canal Plus, TriStar Pictures
Dist/Sales: ReelMovies, Roadshow, ACMI, FilmsInc, Col-Tri, Wolfe

Basic Instinct

b

Basic Necessities

Miller, Tanya
1993; USA; 10 min; Drama

A hauntingly beautiful poetic text swoops and loops over home video imagery to explore the impact of sex work on a lesbian's life and especially on her relationship with her lover.

Basketball Diaries, The

Kalvert, Scott
1995; USA; 100 min; Drama
P: John Brad Manulis, Liz Heller; *W:* Bryan Goluboff; *C:* David Phillips; *E:* Dana Congdon; *M:* Graeme Revell
Cast: Leonardo DiCaprio, Bruno Kirby, Mark Wahlberg, Patrick McGaw, Lorraine Bracco

The story of a young basketball star at a Catholic high school who in a few short months becomes a strung-out heroin addict turning tricks for drugs. His coach is a closeted homosexual who makes passes at the young star. Jim's life gradually slips into the underworld of drug users, hookers and pimps. Meanwhile he records everything in his diary.

Prod Comp: Island Pictures, New Line Cinema
Dist/Sales: Roadshow, Lauren, NewLine

Battle of Tuntenhaus

Bashore, Juliet
1991; UK; 30 min; Documentary
P: Cheryl Farthing

Originally produced as part of Channel Four's *Out* series, this engaging documentary tells the story of thirty radical drag queens who claimed squatters' rights in a section of East Berlin after the fall of the Berlin Wall.

Prod Comp: Maya Vision, Channel 4
Dist/Sales: MayaVision

Be Careful what Kind of Skin you Pull Back, you Never know what Kind of Head will Appear

Brüning, Jürgen
1994; Germany; 26 min; Documentary
Ruminations on a gay skinhead lifestyle.

Beat

Walkow, Gary
2000; USA; 93 min; Drama
P: Andrew Pfeffer, Alain Silver, Donald Zuckerman; *W:* Gary Walkow; *C:* Ciro Cabello; *E:* Peter B. Ellis, Steve Vance, Gary Walkow; *M:* Ernest Troost

Cast: Courtney Love, Norman Reedus, Ron Livingston, Keifer Sutherland

The story of Beat author William Burroughs and his wife Joan Vollmer.

Dist/Sales: Nu-Image

Beau Travail
(aka: Good Work)

Denis, Claire
1998; France; 90 min; Drama
P: Jerome Minet
Cast: Gregoire Colin, Dennis Lavant, Michel Subor

Loosely based on Herman Melville's novella *Billy Budd, Beau Travail* is set in the North African camp of the French Foreign Legion. A new recruit, Sentain arrives and his physical beauty enraptures the whole platoon including the commandant. Only the Sergeant-Major, Galoup, remains resistant to Sentain's beauty, and his attempts to destroy the young recruit form the basis for the tragedy of this tale. But very much like an opera or a ballet, the narrative of this film is a thin pretext for a mesmerising spectacle that both celebrates the beauty of the male form while critically analysing the destructiveness of the rituals that attend masculinity; and just as these aggressive rituals assist in constricting men's freedom in the world, Denis draws a parallel with the colonisation of Africa which the Foreign Legion represents. The stunning cinematography recalls the transcendent beauty of early cinema, while the imaginative music score creates an eloquent aural equivalent to the ravishing strength of the images. We have for so long been used to the male gaze dominating the voyeuristic pleasures of film that Denis' firm, sympathetic but critical feminine gaze is experienced as a revolutionary moment in screen history: it is as if we are seeing men and women anew—there is none of the objectifying dismemberment of the misogynist gaze; and women are not made absent as so often happens in the aesthetics of homoeroticism. Almost wordlessly, we come to understand the enormity of the questions the film asks us about the connections between gender, sexuality and imperialism. (ACMI)
French with English subtitles.

Prod Comp: Pathe TV, SM Films, La Sept ARTE
Dist/Sales: ACMI

Beautiful Dreamers

Harrison, John Kent
1990; Canada; 110 min; Drama
P: Michael Maclear, Martin Walters, Sally Bochner; *W:* John Kent Harrison; *C:* François Protat; *E:* Ron Wisman; *M:* Laurence Shragge
Cast: Rip Torn, Colm Feore, Wendel Meldrum, Sheila

McCarthy, Colin Fox

Dr Maurice Bucke is the superintendent of a mental asylum in the 1880s. He is at odds with the medical establishment as he believes in treating patients with love and kindness. When he meets one of America's greatest writers, Walt Whitman, the two strike up a bond that sees them turn a place of horror into a place of beauty and joy. Whitman's homosexuality is only suggested when someone asks why he has never married. Based on a true story.

Prod Comp: Famous Players, Cinexus, National Film Board of Canada, Starway Films
Dist/Sales: Hemdale, ACMI

Beautiful Thing

MacDonald, Hettie
1996; UK; 87 min; Comedy
P: Tony Garnett, Bill Shapter; *W:* Jonathon Harvey;
C: Chris Seager; *E:* Don Fairservice; *M:* John Altman
Cast: Glen Berry, Scott Neal, Linda Henry, Ben Daniels

An hilarious comedy set in a working-class east London housing estate, which centres around two friends: Jamie, who hates sport and is constantly bullied at school, and Ste, who is good at sport but constantly bullied at home. When Ste has been battered once too often, Jamie's mother takes him in and he must share a bed with Jamie. Meanwhile Jamie is toying with the idea he might be gay and in love with Ste. Eventually Ste realises he's in love with Jamie also, and a love affair begins.

Prod Comp: World Productions, Channel 4
Dist/Sales: REP, Wolfe, SonyClassics, ACMI, VideoAmericain

Beatiful Thing

Beauty Before Age

Symons, Johnny
1997; USA; 22 min; Documentary
P: Johnny Symons

An exploration of the forces which divide gay men of different generations. Men ranging in age from 19 to 77 reflect on the process and prospects of growing older in a culture that objectifies young people and disdains its elders. Amidst gyms, bars, dance clubs and the streets, gay men discuss the cultural emphasis on appearance, the role of HIV, power dynamics between young and old, and mentorship and role modelling. Ultimately it reveals that glorifying youth and beauty has disturbing implications for gay men of all ages. (New Day Films)

Dist/Sales: NewDay

Because the Dawn

Goldstein, Amy
1988; USA; 40 min; Comedy, Musical
Cast: Sandy Gray

An alluring modern day lesbian vampire musical comedy, set in the shadowy metropolis of New York City, *Because the Dawn* combines the smoky feel of film noir with the dazzling beat of swing tunes. In this upbeat tale of obsession and transformation, the singing, sax-playing vampire Marie, seduces sports photographer Ariel from behind the camera. A contemporary fable of female desire.

Dist/Sales: WMM, Salzgeber

Because this is about Love

1992; USA; 28 min; Documentary
P: Shulee Ong

This is a touching profile of five lesbian and gay couples from multicultural backgrounds who have made a life-long commitment to each other by going through a marriage ceremony. Each couple tells their own story of how they met, why they decided to marry and how their family and friends responded. (Filmakers Library)

Dist/Sales: FilmakersLibrary

Becoming Colette

Huston, Danny
1992; Germany, USA; 100 min; Drama
P: Heinz J. Bibo, Peer J. Oppenheimer; *W:* Ruth Graham; *C:* Wolfgang Treu; *E:* Peter Taylor, Roberto Silvi; *M:* John Scott
Cast: Mathilda May, Klaus Maria Brandauer, Virginia Madsen, Paul Rhys

Based on the life of the famous writer. When the young Sidonie Colette is faced with the coldness of her philandering husband, she eventually enters into a ménage à trois with him and his mistress.

Prod Comp: Les Films Ariane
Dist/Sales: CastleHill

bed

Leder, Evie
1999; Canada; 14 min; B&W; Experimental

Black and white images of two women making love are juxtaposed with images of grainy images of city life, illuminating the contrast between public and private lives.

Dist/Sales: CFMDC

Bed of Lies

Graham, William A.
1992; USA; 90 min; Drama
P: Andrew Gottlieb; *W:* John Ireland; *C:* Isidore Mankofsky; *E:* Christopher Nelson; *M:* David Shire
Cast: Susan Dey, Chris Cooper, Tom Nolan, Fred Thompson, G. W. Bailey

Texas political golden boy Price Daniel Jnr, the son of one of the most popular Governors in Texan history, divorces his wealthy debutante wife to marry a waitress. This brash decision ends his political career and, ultimately, his life. He is murdered by the waitress in order to escape their abusive relationship. He is depicted as a latent homosexual, which appears to be the cause of his violence towards his wife. Made for television and based on a true story, and the novel *Deadly Blessing* by Steven Salerno.

Prod Comp: Elliot Friedgen & Company
Dist/Sales: Warner

Bedazzled

Donen, Stanley
1967; UK; 107 min; Comedy
P: Stanley Donen; *W:* Peter Cook, Dudley Moore; *C:* Austin Dempster; *E:* Richard Marden; *M:* Dudley Moore
Cast: Peter Cook, Dudley Moore, Eleanor Bron, Raquel Welch, Barry Humphries

This comedy cult film brings a new voice to the Faust legend. The laughs might seem a little tired to contemporary eyes, but Cook and Moore are hilarious. Moore plays a short order cook in a burger chain who is willing to give up his soul to have Margaret the waitress—and he does—but only once he sells his soul for seven wishes, along the way meeting the seven deadly sins. Two of the deadly sins, Vanity and Envy, are gay male stereotypes.

Prod Comp: 20th Century-Fox, Stanley Donen films
Dist/Sales: Ascanbee, ReelMovies, 20thCenturyFox

Bedrooms & Hallways

Troche, Rose
1998; UK; 95 min; Comedy
P: Ceci Dempsey, Dorothy Berwin; *W:* Robert Farra; *C:* Ashley Rowe; *E:* Chris Blunden
Cast: Kevin McKidd, Julie Graham, Simon Callow, Con O'Neill, Harriet Walter

Rose Troche's (*Go Fish*) second feature film is a gentle and amusing study into the nuances of sexual preference, dating and masculinity. Using Leo's 30th birthday bash as a basis, the film traces Leo's relationship to the guests; gay roommate Darren and his real estate agent boyfriend who have a penchant for using the bedrooms of the houses he's selling for their trysts; straight and single friend Angie; new Age guru and leader of Leo's men's group, Keith; Leo's previous boyfriend, Brendan and Brendan's current girlfriend, Sally, who also happens to be Leo's high school sweetheart. Central to the film are the gatherings of the men's group for masculine assertiveness, and when Leo admits his attraction to seemingly straight Irishman Brendan, it opens the floodgates for other members of the group with surprising results. (ACMI)

Prod Comp: ARP Selection, BBC, Pandora Cinema
Dist/Sales: Lauren, FirstRunFeatures, Wolfe, Mongrel, ACMI, VideoAmericain

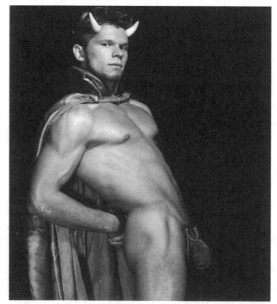
Beefcake

Beefcake

Fitzgerald, Thom
1999; Canada, France, UK; 93 min; Documentary
P: Thom Fitzgerald, Shandie Mitchell;

W: Thom Fitzgerald; C: Tom Harting; E: Susan Shanks, Michael Weir
Cast: Josh Peace, Daniel MacIvor, Carroll Godsman, Jack Griffin Mazeika

This engaging, amusing and classically camp homage to 1950s muscle magazines presents an alternate glisteningly buffed portrait of this era in which homoerotic images of musclemen were produced for an eager male subculture. In a seamless merging of fact and fiction, Thom Fitzgerald (*The Hanging Garden*) uses interviews, dramatic re-enactments and impressionistic fantasy sequences to trace male physique photography from its beginnings with Bob Mizer who controversially published *Physique Pictorial Magazine* and established the Athletic Model Guild.

Prod Comp: Channel 4, Alliance Independent
Dist/Sales: Cowboy, Millivres, Strand, Wolfe, ACMI, VideoAmericain

Beethoven's Nephew

(aka: Le Neveu de Beethoven)

Morrissey, Paul
1985; France; 99 min; Drama
W: Mathieu Carrière, Paul Morrissey; C: Hanus Polak; E: Claudine Bouché, Albert Jurgenson, Michèle Robert-Lauliac
Cast: Wolfgang Reichman, Keitmar Prinz, Jane Birkin, Nathalic Baye

This film explores the touching, maddening and humorous relationship between Beethoven and his sole heir, his nephew Karl. Beethoven's tragicomic obsession and the spiteful refusal by Karl of his uncle's affections are depicted in this drama. French with English subtitles.

Prod Comp: Orfilm
Dist/Sales: Roadshow

Before Night Falls

Schnabel, Julian
2000; USA; 130 min; Drama
P: Jon Kilik; W: Julian Schnabel, Cunningham O'Keefe, Lazaro Gomez Carriles; C: Xavier Pérez Grobet, Guillermo Rosas; E: Michael Berenbaum; M: Carter Burwell
Cast: Javier Bardem, Olivier Martinez, Andrea Di Stefano, Jonny Depp

An incredible journey through the personal life and work of the late, openly gay, Cuban poet Reinaldo Arenas, whose courageous fight for personal expression defied censorship and persecution. (Wolfe)

Prod Comp: El Mar Pictures, Grandview Pictures
Dist/Sales: 20thCenturyFox, FineLine, LolaFilms, Wolfe

Before Stonewall: The Making of a Gay and Lesbian Community

Rosenberg, Robert / Schiller, Greta
1984; USA; 84 min; Documentary
P: Robert Rosenberg, John Scagliotti, Greta Schiller

Stonewall is the name of a gay bar in New York where gay resistance to frequent police harassment came to a head over three days and nights in 1969. This marked the beginning of a large scale campaign to gain rights and respect for being different. Even as far back as the 1920s lesbians and gays had formed groups, produced newspapers, opened restaurants and discussed their problems. This film traces half a century of a parallel culture using film, photographs and accounts from participants.

Prod Comp: Before Stonewall Incorporated
Dist/Sales: CinemaGuild, FirstRunFeatures, Salzgeber, NFVLS, ACMI, VideoAmericain

Beguines, The

(aka: Le Rampart des Beguines)

Casaril, Guy
1972; France, Italy; 90 min; Drama
P: Raymond Hakim, Robert Hakim; W: Guy Casaril, Françoise Mallet-Joris; C: Andréas Winding; E: Louisette Hautecoeur; M: Roland Vincent, Michel Delpech
Cast: Nicole Courcel, Anicee Alvina, Venantino Venantini, Ginette Leclerc, Jean Martin

The lonely daughter of a widowed politician begins a passionate affair with her father's mistress. When the mistress finally marries her father, the girl realises it is only for material gain and decides to take the upper hand.

Behind Glass

Van Leperen, Ab
1981; The Netherlands; 69 min; Drama

Two men, one a middle-class reporter, the other a lower-class window cleaner, become lovers despite their obvious class difference. In the beginning things go smoothly, but after a while small battles begin to emerge and power games become predominant.

Dist/Sales: TLA

Behind Walls

Castro, Abel
1999; USA; 20 min; Drama

Josie is overcome with jealousy when her brother begins dating their cousin Papo.

Dist/Sales: Behind-Walls

Being at Home with Claude

Beaudin, Jean / Boisvert, Johanne
1992; Canada; 90 min; Thriller
P: Léon G. Arcand, Louise Gendron; W: Jean Beaudin;
C: Thomas Vámos; E: André Corriveau; M: Richard
Grégoire
Cast: Roy Dupuis, Jean-François Pichette, Jacques
Godin, Gaston Lepage, Hugo Dube

A murder-mystery thriller, set in Montréal, about a
young male prostitute who is accused of murdering
his gay lover. He turns himself in and is interrogated
by a cop who is determined to find the motive. An
absorbing drama dealing with gay passion and love.
Based on the play by René-Daniel Debois. French
with English subtitles.

Prod Comp: Les Productions du Cerf, National Film
Board of Canada
Dist/Sales: Cowboy, 21stCentury, Strand,
VideoAmericain

Being at Home with Claude

Being John Malkovich

Jonze, Spike
1999; USA; 112 min; Comedy
P: Steve Golin, Michael Stipe, Sandy Stern, Vincent
Landay; W: Charlie Kaufman; C: Lance Acord; E: Eric
Zumbrunnen; M: Carter Burwell
Cast: John Cusack, Cameron Diaz, Catherine Keener,
John Malkovich

Deliciously bizarre comedy about a puppeteer who
discovers a portal into the eponymous actor John
Malkovich's mind. Mainstream audiences may be
baffled, but this quirky, wildly imaginative oddity is
a must see for adventurous laugh-seekers. (Wolfe)

Prod Comp: Gramercy Pictures, Single Cell Pictures,
Propaganda Films
Dist/Sales: Wolfe, UIP, USAFilms, Swank

Bellas de Noche

Delgado, Miguel M.
1975; Spain; 110 min; Drama

P: Guillermo Calderón Stell; W: Francisco Cavazos;
C: Miguel Araña; E: José W. Bustos; M: Gustavo César
Carrión
Cast: Lalo El Mimo, Sasha Montenegro, Rafael Inclan,
Jorge Rivero

When a young Mexican pimp gets in too deep with
gangsters, he must repay them with sexual favours.

Prod Comp: Cinematográfica Calderón S.A.

Belle

Achten, Irma
1993; The Netherlands; 99 min; B&W; Drama
P: Kees Kasander, Denis Wigman; W: Irma Achten;
C: Néstor Sanz
Cast: Reinout Bussemaker, Do van Stek, Wivineke van
Groningen

The story is set in the early 1900s as a rebellious
young girl refuses to conform to the strict social and
sexual mores of the time. She develops a burning
passion for the housekeeper. As she grows older she
marries but, in her loveless marriage, she still
maintains her fascination with the housekeeper.
Considered by some to be the lesbian *Citizen Kane*.

Prod Comp: Allarts, Nos Television

Belle al Bar

(aka: Belles at the Bar)

Benvenuti, Alessandro
1994; Italy; 110 min; Comedy
P: Giorgio Leopardi; W: Alessandro Benvenuti, Ugo
Chiti, Nicola Zavagli; C: Blasco Giurato; E: Carla
Simoncelli; M: Patrizio Fariselli
Cast: Alessandro Benvenuti, Eva Robins, Andrea
Brambilla, Assumpta Serna, Anna Casalino

Leo's life has changed after meeting a mysterious
woman. He soon realises the beautiful lady was once
his male cousin, Giulio who has had gender
reassignment surgery. A whole new world opens up
to Leo where characters from every walk of life
surround themselves around his fabulous cousin. Leo
must face returning to his old life, or risking
everything to start afresh. Italian with English
subtitles.

Prod Comp: Union PN
Dist/Sales: UIP

Belle de Jour

Buñuel, Luis
1967; France, Italy; 100 min; Drama
P: Robert Hakim, Raymond Hakim, Henri Baum;
W: Luis Buñuel, Jean-Claude Carrière; C: Sacha Vierny;
E: Louisette Hautecoeur, Walter Spohr
Cast: Catherine Deneuve, Jean Sorel, Michel Piccoli,

Pierre Clémenti, Genevieve Page

Catherine Deneuve plays a beautiful young woman married to a rich young surgeon. Their life is a material success but the wife's frigidity is a strain on the marriage. Plagued by masochistic sexual fantasies, she takes a part-time job in a brothel, hoping that by playing the part of Belle de Jour, the high class prostitute, she can overcome her dislike for sex. This is a savagely funny, and often a very cruel film, as it pulls apart the consumerist psyche of a bourgeois woman to reveal her as soulless and empty of life. It is only as Belle de Jour that she can emotionally experience life. The brothel madam is a lesbian played by Genevieve Page. Based on the novel by Joseph Kessel. French with English subtitles.

Awards: Venice Film Festival, 1967: Best Film
Prod Comp: Paris Film, Five Film Roma
Dist/Sales: 21stCentury, NFVLS, AlliedArtists, Miramax, ACMI

Belle époque

Trueba, Fernando
1992; Spain; 108 min; Comedy
P: Fernando Trueba; *W:* Rafael Azcona; *C:* José Luis Alcaine; *E:* Carmen Frías; *M:* Antoine Duhamel
Cast: Penelope Cruz, Miriam Diaz-Aroca, Gabino Diego, Fernando Fernan Gomez

Spain, spring, 1931. Fernando, a young deserter fleeing through the Spanish countryside, meets Manolo, a wise and wizened elderly painter—now retired from both the art world and the world alike—who offers him assistance and protection. The day arrives, however, when Fernando must leave, making way for Manolo's four daughters who are coming from Madrid for a few days to see their father. When Fernando sees the four girls descend from the train, it isn't as though he consciously decides to return to Manolo's home, his feet decide for him. One of the sisters is a lesbian and is treated with dignity and respect by her family. Spanish with English subtitles.

Awards: Academy Awards, 1993: Best Foreign Language Film
Prod Comp: Animatógrafo, Producciones Cinematográficas SA, Lola Films
Dist/Sales: NewVision, 21stCentury, SonyClassics

Below the Belt

Colbert, Laurie / Cardona, Dominique
1998; Canada; 12 min; Comedy
P: Kate Gillen

Two 17-year-old girls fall in love and grapple with their feelings. Totally absorbed in each other, one makes the discovery that her mother, who she always

believed to be happily married to her father, is having an affair of her own.
Dist/Sales: CFMDC, Cinenova

Ben Hur

Wyler, William
1959; USA; 209 min; Action
P: Sam Zimbalist; *W:* Karl Tunberg; *C:* Robert L. Surtees; *E:* Ralph E. Winters, John D. Dunning; *M:* Miklós Rózsa
Cast: Charlton Heston, Jack Hawkins, Stephan Boyd, Hays Harareet, Ramon Novarro

Epic film about a Jewish prince who is betrayed and sent into slavery by a Roman friend. When he regains his freedom he returns for revenge. Highlights include the centrepiece chariot race, and a host of gladiators. Steeped in homoeroticism.

Awards: Academy Awards, 1959: Best Actor (Charlton Heston)
Prod Comp: MGM
Dist/Sales: Chapel, ACMI, MGM

Benjamin Smoke

Cohen, Jem / Sillen, Peter
2000; USA; 72 min; Documentary
W: Jem Cohen, Peter Sillen; *C:* Jem Cohen, Peter Sillen; *E:* Nancy Roach

Benjamin is a country boy with a sapphire-blue party dress singing for a punk-country-blues band called Smoke. This highly unorthodox documentary follows his crooked path in a hidden neighbourhood of Atlanta, Georgia called 'Cabbagetown'. Dragqueen, speed-freak, all-around renegade, Benjamin left the straight (in every sense of the word) world behind a long time ago. Introduced to Benjamin in 1989 by R.E.M.'s Michael Stipe, the filmmakers worked on and off for years, painting a complicated portrait of Benjamin and his environment. Both a window on a rarely documented underground music scene and an exploration of what it means to be queer, the film is as hilarious as it is harrowing. (Cowboy Pictures)

Prod Comp: Gravity Films
Dist/Sales: Cowboy

Bent

Mathias, Sean
1996; UK; 118 min; Drama
P: Dixie Linder, Michael Solinger; *W:* Martin Sherman; *C:* Yorgos Arvanitis; *E:* Isabelle Lorente; *M:* Philip Glass
Cast: Clive Owen, Lothaire Bluteau, Ian McKellan, Rupert Graves, Mick Jagger

Martin Sherman's famous play reminded the world that in the Nazi death camp a pink triangle could be more reviled than a yellow one. A success at Cannes, this screen adaptation features a rich cast including Mick Jagger in drag. The decadent lives of Max and Rudi are suddenly and irrevocably transformed when they are exposed as homosexuals and eventually made to experience the debasement and brutality of the concentration camp, where Max encounters Horst. There Max learns that love between two people can transcend and ultimately release from the assumed power of the tormentor.

Prod Comp: Channel 4
Dist/Sales: Goldwyn, OrionHV, Wolfe, ACMI, VideoAmericain, Swank, Salzgeber

The Berlin Affair

Berlin Affair, The

(aka: Interno Berlinese)

Cavani, Liliana
1985; Italy, West Germany; 121 min; Drama
P: Menahem Golan, Yoram Globus,; *W:* Liliana Cavani, Roberta Massoni; *C:* Dante Spinotti; *E:* Ruggero Mastroianni, Michael J. Duthie; *M:* Pino Donaggio
Cast: Gudrun Landgrube, Kevin McNally, Mio Takaki, Massimo Girotti, William Berger

Set in pre-war Germany, this film is an erotic and provocative tale of sexual obsession and power. Louise is the bored wife of a Nazi diplomat, Heinz. She becomes intrigued by a beautiful young Japanese woman, Mitsuko, whom she meets in her art class. The two begin a sensuous affair, but when Heinz begins to suspect something between the two women, he also becomes sexually involved with Mitsuko. Mitsuko then becomes dominating and manipulative through sex, drugs and blackmail. An interesting examination of sexual power, but the lesbian relationship is treated with tenderness.

Prod Comp: The Cannon Group
Dist/Sales: Col-Tri, MGM, VSM

Bertrand is Missing

(aka: Bertrand Disparu)

1986; France; 44 min; Drama

Bertrand is a young runaway who is saved from trouble by an older man who lets him stay at his house. A relationship soon develops.

Awards: San Francisco International Lesbian & Gay Film Festival, 1988: Audience Award Best Short Film

Best In Show

Guest, Christopher
2000; USA; 90 min; Comedy
P: Karen Murphy; *W:* Christopher Guest, Eugene Levy; *C:* Roberto Schaefer; *E:* Robert Leighton; *M:* Jeffrey C. J. Vanston
Cast: Jay Brazeau, Parker Poey, Christopher Guest

Prissy poodles, droopy-eyed bloodhounds, and neurotic Weimaraners compete for the gold in this largely improvised comedy that takes place at the Mayflower Kennel Club. A yuppie couple, a fly fisherman, and a pair of hairdressers are a few of the pet owners who primp, pamper, and prime their pooches for the big day in this hilarious 'dogumentary'. (Swank Motion Pictures)

Prod Comp: Castle Rock
Dist/Sales: Warner, Wolfe, Swank

Best Man, The

(aka: Gore Vidal's The Best Man)

Schaffner, Franklin
1964; USA; 102 min; B&W; Drama
P: Stuart Millar, Lawrence Turman; *W:* Gore Vidal; *C:* Haskell Wexler; *E:* Robert Swink; *M:* Mort Lindsey
Cast: Henry Fonda, Cliff Robertson, Margaret Leighton, Edie Adams

A political thriller about two presidential candidates in the same party who will stop at nothing to get the nomination. Both have a skeleton in the closet: Fonda had a mental illness and Robertson had a homosexual liaison.

Prod Comp: United Artists, Millar-Turman
Dist/Sales: ReelMovies, UA

Best of Out and Out on Tuesday, The

Ardill, Susan / Kwietniowski, Richard / Main, Stewart / Wells, Peter
1991; UK; 82 min; Documentary
P: Rebecca Dodds, Susan Ardill, Claire Beavan

UK television series hosted by Julian Clary, which was the first produced for a gay audience. Debuting in 1988 and running until 1994, the show was consistently stylish, informed and audacious. This collection brings together some of the best segments: 'Talking Hairs', 'Comic Cuts', 'Pride 91', 'Fasten Your Seatbelts', 'Postcard From New Zealand', 'Kush' and 'Girls in Boy Bars'.

Prod Comp: Channel 4
Dist/Sales: MayaVision

Best Way, The

(aka: La Meilleure façon de marcher)

Miller, Claude
1976; France; 85 min; Comedy
W: Luc Beraud, Claude Miller; *C:* Bruno Nuytten;
E: Jean-Bernard Bonis; *M:* Alain Jomy
Cast: Patrick Deware, Claude Pieplu, Patrick Bouchitey, Christine Pascal

A summer camp counsellor finds it difficult to face the fact that he has become attracted to another counsellor, after finding the young man dressed in women's clothes. Described by Vito Russo as '*Tea and Sympathy* with a French accent and guts'. French with English subtitles.

Dist/Sales: VideoAmericain

Bete Noire

Hunt, Victoria
1994; Australia; 15 min; B&W; Drama
P: Lesley Dyer

Lucinda Embers is cheating on her husband with a dazzling soprano. When she finds herself being blackmailed, she goes to the wrong side of town to hire Gil McNabe, a big, strong private eye who's handy with a gun and a quip.

Dist/Sales: Flickerfest

Betsy, The

Petrie, Daniel
1978; USA; 120 min; Drama
P: Harold Robbins, Robert Weston, Jack Grossberg;
W: William Bast, Walter Bernstein; *C:* Mario Tosi; *E:* Rita Roland; *M:* John Barry
Cast: Laurence Olivier, Robert Duvall, Katharine Ross, Tommy Lee Jones

The story of the sordid exploits, both sexual and financial, of a family of wealthy automobile manufacturers. The character of Loren Hardeman, played by Paul Rudd, is a homosexual who suicides. Based on the novel by Harold Robbins.

Prod Comp: Allied Artists, Harold Robbins International Company
Dist/Sales: ReelMovies, Warner, AlliedArtists

Better Dead than Gay

O'Hare, Christopher
1995; UK; 52 min; Documentary

'It hurts me to say goodbye. I wish ever so much that I could stay and live a healthy, normal life'. These words were written by 26-year-old Simon Harvey in a farewell letter to his parents. Simon wasn't ill. He decided to commit suicide, driving to the Sussex countryside where he killed himself with his car's exhaust fumes while the hymn *To God The Glory* played on the car radio. Simon was a Christian and gay and was tormented in his attempts to reconcile these two parts of his life. Treading carefully through sensitive areas, *Better Dead than Gay* reconstructs the background of the tragedy with the help of Harvey's diaries and the recollections of his parents and friends and clergymen at whose churches he worshipped. 'To discover my son was gay was as bad as losing him', says Simon's father. As a gay friend of Simon's says, 'Religion has a lot to answer for'. (20th San Francisco International Lesbian & Gay Film Festival)

Dist/Sales: Convergence

Better than Chocolate

Wheeler, Anne
1999; Canada; 98 min; Comedy
P: Sharon McGowan; *W:* Peggy Thompson; *C:* Gregory Middleton; *E:* Alison Grace; *M:* Graeme Coleman, Ani Difranco
Cast: Karyn Dwyer, Christina Cox, Ann-Marie MacDonald, Wendy Crewson

19-year-old Maggie is a law school drop out working in a lesbian bookshop when she meets and falls in love with Kim a travelling artist. Things are perfect until Maggie's parents break up and her mother and teenage brother arrive and move in to her apartment. Maggie madly juggles her new relationship and the problem of how to tell her mother about her sexuality. Meanwhile, Maggie's friends are involved in romantic dramas of their own. Her younger brother explores his burgeoning sexuality, her mother rediscovers her own long departed sexual self, while Maggie's boss is pursued by a transgendered nightclub performer coping with the rejection of her family. (MQFF)

Prod Comp: rave films inc.
Dist/Sales: Cowboy, Alliance, Wolfe, Millivres, ACMI, VideoAmericain

Betty Anderson

Kamitsuna, Mako
2000; USA; 40 min; Drama

A female detective must overcome her mysterious past before she can solve a homicide.

Dist/Sales: PictureRoom

Between the Lines

Constantinou, Sophie
1997; USA; 21 min; Experimental

A luminous study of self-mutilation, which focuses on sensual images and visual metaphors, as it explores the reasons behind the razor blade and the motivations of women who cut themselves.

Between Two Women

Woodcock, Steven
2000; UK; 92 min; Drama
P: Steven Woodcock; *W:* Steven Woodcock; *C:* Gordon Hickie
Cast: Barbara Marten, Andrina Carroll, Andrew Dunn

It is 1957 and Ellen Hardy, like many married women in the industrial, working-class North of England, where men are the 'providers' and women are 'housewives', feels vaguely dissatisfied. Ellen becomes friends with her 10-year-old son's teacher, the attractive Kathy Thompson. Kathy has taken a special interest in the son's artistic ability which causes conflicts with Ellen's husband, a factory worker, who cannot understand why people would pay money for his son's paintings. Ellen's and Kathy's friendship begins to develop further over the course of time, causing ripples in Ellen's marriage. Ellen's sense of isolation grows during a disastrous seaside holiday when she is torn between her duty as a wife and mother and her fear of admitting her growing affections for Kathy. Ellen searches for a way to come to terms with her love for Kathy and the prison of her prescribed role. Her search for the strength and courage to fly in the face of the social mores of her time makes *Between Two Women* a compelling drama. (12th Toronto Lesbian & Gay Film & Video Festival)

Prod Comp: North Country Pictures

Beware a Holy Whore

(aka: Warnung vor einer heiligen Nutte)

Fassbinder, Rainer Werner
1970; Germany; 100 min; Comedy
W: Rainer Werner Fassbinder; *C:* Michael Ballhaus;
E: Thea Eymèsz, Rainer Werner Fassbinder;
M: Peer Raben, Spooky Tooth
Cast: Eddie Constantine, Rainer Werner Fassbinder, Lou Castel, Hanna Schygulla

A film crew wait in an opulent Spanish hotel for the lead actor, director and production money, all the time arguing and getting drunk. One of the first Fassbinder films to depict homosexuality.

Prod Comp: Nova International Films

Beyond Gravity

Maxwell, Garth
1988; New Zealand; 50 min; Comedy
P: James H. Wallace
Cast: Robert Pollock, Iain Rea, Lucy Sheehan

Richard spends his time fantasising about outer space and the cosmos, an activity which antagonises friends and family. Then one day he meets Johnny, a handsome Italian man, with an enormous appetite for life, who offers him love and an escape from the monotony of work. This short New Zealand film is a joyous celebration of the love between two eccentrics.

Prod Comp: James Wallace Productions
Dist/Sales: ACMI

Beyond the Catwalk: The Search for Mr Gay Australia 2000

James, Grant
2001; Australia; 80 min; Documentary

A pecs-fest, abs epic. Guys from around Australia vie for the golden tanned adulation of Mr Gay Australia 2000.

Beyond the Valley of the Dolls

Meyer, Russ
1970; USA; 111 min; Comedy
P: Russ Meyer; *W:* Russ Meyer, Roger Ebert;
C: Fred J. Koenekamp; *E:* Dann Cahn, Dick Wormel;
M: Stu Phillips, William Loose
Cast: Dolly Read, Cynthia Myers, Marcia McBroom, John La Zar, Michael Blodgett

This is not a sequel to Susann's *Valley of the Dolls* but it follows a similar theme—the sexual adventures of three young women. In this case a rock trio out to make it big in show business. The three singers, along with their manager, go to Hollywood to break into the big time. Erica Gavin plays the obligatory lesbian. Classic vulgar exploitation from Meyer.

Prod Comp: 20th Century-Fox
Dist/Sales: ReelMovies, 20thCenturyFox

Beyond Therapy

Altman, Robert
1986; USA; 93 min; Comedy
P: Steven M. Hart; *W:* Robert Altman, Christopher Durang; *C:* Pierre Mignot; *E:* Jennifer Auge, Stephen P. Dunn; *M:* Gabriel Yared
Cast: Jeff Goldblum, Julie Hagerty, Tom Conti, Glenda

Jackson, Christopher Guest

Comic farce about two mixed-up Manhattanites who meet through the personal ads. Bruce, a bisexual in a relationship with Bob, goes on a date with a woman. When all fails he heads back to his therapist.

Prod Comp: New World Pictures, Sandcastle 5 Productions
Dist/Sales: Roadshow

Bezness

Bouzid, Nouri
1992; France; 100 min; Drama
W: Nouri Bouzid; *C:* Alain Levent; *E:* Kahéna Attia;
M: Anouar Braham
Cast: Abdel Kechiche, Jacques Penot, Ghalia Lacroix

When a French photographer is sent to Tunisia to do a story on the young male prostitutes there, he soon befriends Roufa, one of the boys. The photographer soon discovers the dichotomy of the boy's life, between the permissive ways of the West and the puritanical Arab life.

Prod Comp: Le Studio Canal+

Biches, Les

(aka: The Does)

Chabrol, Claude
1968; France, Italy; 94 min; Drama
P: André Génovès; *W:* Paul Gégauff, Claude Chabrol;
C: Jean Rabier; *E:* Jacques Gaillard; *M:* Pierre Jansen
Cast: Stephane Audran, Jean-Louis Trintignant, Jacqueline Sassard

A psychological thriller involving a triangle between a predatory older woman, Frederique, a young waif, 'Why', and Paul, an architect. Interest lies in the complexity of the human relationships with their changing combinations of homosexual and heterosexual attraction and the special sense of the unspoken shifts in these relationships. In this geometry of human relationships the triangle ultimately becomes a circle, as one personality consumes another. The milieu is rather more abstract than in the subsequent series of psychological dramas constituting Chabrol's mature phase, of which *Les Biches* was the first. French with English subtitles.

Prod Comp: Les Films la Boétie, Alexandra
Dist/Sales: NFVLS, ACMI, BFI

Big Business

Abrahams, Jim
1988; USA; 97 min; Comedy
P: Steve Tisch, Michael Peyser; *W:* Dori Pierson, Marc

Rubel; *C:* Dean Cundey; *E:* Harry Keramidas;
M: Lee Holdridge
Cast: Bette Midler, Lily Tomlin, Fred Ward, Edward Herrmann, Barry Primus

Big business complexities are further complicated by the fact that the main characters are discovered to have been exchanged at birth. Two of the corporate executives are homosexual lovers and have a great time camping it up.

Prod Comp: Silver Screen Partners III, Touchstone
Dist/Sales: Roadshow, ReelMovies, Touchstone, BuenaVista

Big Eden

Big Eden

Bezucha, Thomas
2000; USA; 117 min; Drama
P: Jennifer Chaiken; *W:* Thomas Bezucha; *C:* Rob Sweeney; *E:* Andrew London; *M:* Joseph Conlan
Cast: Arye Gross, Tim DeKay, Louise Fletcher, Eric Schweig

A multi-award winner, *Big Eden* is a celebration of the power of love, friends and family. Henry Hart is a successful New York artist with plenty of money, a cool New York loft and a non-existent love life. After hearing news that his beloved grandfather is seriously ill, he returns to sleepy home town Big Eden. Once there Henry rediscovers his unrequited love for high school friend Dean, while at the same time attracting the love of painfully shy, but handsome Pixie Dexter, a Native American who owns the general store and makes a mean Sunday roast. In a refreshing turn-around on the standard theme of small town bigotry, the folks of Big Eden embrace Henry and prove that love really does conquer all. A classic feel-good romantic story of family, love and redemption. (MQFF)

Prod Comp: Chaiken Films
Dist/Sales: JourDeFete, Mongrel, Wolfe, 10%, VideoAmericain

Big House, The

Ward, Rachel
2000; Australia; 24 min; Drama

The Big House tells of the relationship between an illiterate prisoner and his younger cellmate, who teaches the former to read. Together they discover the capacity to love.

Dist/Sales: NewTown

Big Sky, The

Hawks, Howard
1952; USA; 122 min; B&W; Western
P: Howard Hawks; *W:* Dudley Nichols; *C:* Russell Harlan; *E:* Christian Nyby; *M:* Dimitri Tiomkin
Cast: Kirk Douglas, Dewey Martin, Elizabeth Threatt, Arthur Hunnicutt

A trailblazing journey by an 1830 keelboat expedition of fur traders, and a handful of mountain men up the uncharted Missouri River through hostile Indian territory, provides the context for the realisation of personal interdependency and professional cooperation. This companion piece to *Red River* contains all the core elements of Hawks' 'male genre' films including male bonding (the Douglas-Martin relationship) with homosexual undertones closer to the surface than in most other Hawks films.

Prod Comp: RKO, Winchester Pictures
Dist/Sales: Ascanbee, NFVLS

Bigger Splash, A

Hazan, Jack
1974; USA; 105 min; Documentary
P: Jack Hazan; *W:* David Mingay, Jack Hazan; *C:* Jack Hazan; *E:* David Mingay; *M:* Patrick Gowers
Cast: David Hockney, Henry Geldzahler, Peter Schlesinger

A revealing documentary about the famous British gay artist and painter David Hockey. It is told through a series of witty interviews with the artist, his ex-lover, his friends and contemporaries.

Prod Comp: Buzzy Enterprises, Circle Associates
Dist/Sales: NewLine, BFI

Bike Boy

Morrissey, Paul / Warhol, Andy
1967; USA; 96 min; Drama
P: Andy Warhol; *W:* Andy Warhol; *C:* Paul Morrissey
Cast: Joe Spencer, Viva, Bridgit Polk, Ed Hood, Ingrid Superstar

Young working-class motorcyclist Joe Spencer, with a physique to die for, is the object of everyone's desire, but he's completely out of his element in the sophisticated world of Warhol's superstar friends—Viva, Ingrid Superstar, Bridgit Polk to name a few.

Prod Comp: Andy Warhol Films
Dist/Sales: NewVision, FilmmakersCoop

Bilitis

Hamilton, David
1977; UK; 100 min; Erotica
P: David Hamilton; *W:* Catherine Breillat; *C:* Bernard Daillencourt; *E:* Henri Colpi, Claire Painchault, Michel Valio; *M:* Francis Lai
Cast: Patti D'Arbanville, Mona Kristenson, Bernard Giraudeau, Mathieu Carriere

A rather slow-moving but beautifully shot film that tells of a 16-year-old girl's sexual and erotic awakening, particularly her relationship with an older woman. This was the first feature film by the well-known photographer of erotic art, made primarily for a straight male audience.

Prod Comp: Films 21

Bill Called William, A

Harvey, Alex
1997; UK; 51 min; Documentary

A Bill Called William concerns the controversial and historic campaign to legalise homosexuality in Britain which resulted in the Sexual Offences Act of 1967. This dramatised documentary supplements contemporary interviews and archive material with original Parliamentary speeches and convincing re-creations. In addition first hand accounts of pioneering gay rights campaigners are interwoven with specially shot footage and evocative 1960s music tracks to provide vivid glimpses of what gay life was like in London in the middle of the 'swinging sixties'.

Prod Comp: Channel 4

Billy Turner's Secret

Mayson, Michael
1990; USA; 26 min; Comedy
W: Michael Mayson

Billy and Rufus live together and share everything, except Billy's secret—he's gay. When the cousin of Rufus's girlfriend drops by unexpectedly, it looks like Billy's secret might be out of the bag.

Dist/Sales: Frameline, Forefront

Billy's Hollywood Screen Kiss

O'Haver, Tommy
1998; USA; 92 min; Comedy
P: David Moseley; *W:* Tommy O'Haver; *C:* Mark Mervis; *E:* Jeff Betancourt; *M:* Alan Ari Lazar

Cast: Sean Hayes, Brad Rowe, Richard Ganoung, Meredith Scott Lynn

Whimsical romantic comedy about Billy who becomes infatuated with handsome, but straight Gabriel. Billy is inspired to find a unique way to satisfy all three of his great obsessions—photography, old Hollywood movies and Gabriel.

Prod Comp: Revolutionary Eye
Dist/Sales: Trimark, Wolfe, VideoAmericain, 10%

Biloxi Blues

Nichols, Mike
1988; USA; 106 min; Comedy
P: Raymond Stark; *W:* Neil Simon; *C:* Bill Butler;
E: Sam O'Steen; *M:* Georges Delerue
Cast: Matthew Broderick, Christopher Walken, Corey Parker, Michael Dolan

A coming-of-age story set in a war-time boot camp which involves a group of young men: Jerome, a sensitive New York Jew who is harassed by a sadistic sergeant; Arnold, an intellectual who refuses to fit in; and Hennesy, a homosexual who is court-martialled and sent to Leavenworth Prison because his private sex life with another soldier is made public. It is essentially a story about trying to fit in to a brutal and insensitive system.

Prod Comp: Universal, Rastar
Dist/Sales: ReelMovies, ACMI, Universal

Bird in the Hand

Gund Saalfield, Catherine / Nelson, Melanie
1992; USA; 25 min; Drama

An ever so true-to-life dyke drama set in New York. Two women attempt to leave the city for a short vacation, but they are hampered by an endless who'll-look-after-the-cat type checklist and concern over an ex-lover's new conquest.

Dist/Sales: Frameline, Cinenova

Birdcage, The

Nichols, Mike
1996; USA; 120 min; Comedy
P: Mike Nichols; *W:* Elaine May; *C:* Emmanuel Lubezki; *E:* Arthur Schmidt; *M:* Jonathan Tunick, Mark Mothersbaugh
Cast: Robin Williams, Gene Hackman, Dianne Wiest, Nathan Lane, Dan Futterman

A Hollywood reworking of the classic camp French comedy *La Cage aux Folles* but this time without the subtitles. Armand and Albert have a home life many would envy. They share a long-time committed relationship encompassing their lives and careers and have, together, raised Armand's son Val to be a

caring, responsible and mature young man. So when Val arrives home and announces his engagement to the daughter of an ultraconservative US senator, what choice is there but to accept his decision of love? With the impending visit of his fiancee's rigid family, Val asks his father to straighten up the apartment, just a bit. All it entails is the removal of Armand's art collection, furnishings, clothes, job...and Albert. The arrival of the senator and his wife sets off a comedy of errors as Armand and Albert attempt to play out the roles of your typical American husband and wife.

Prod Comp: United Artists, MGM, Nichols
Dist/Sales: UIP, Wolfe, Warner, Swank, ACMI

b

The Birdcage

Birthday Time

Ferber, Lawrence
2000; USA; 19 min; Comedy

Christopher is three days away from his 18th birthday and desperate to get his first gay kiss.

Dist/Sales: Lilliput

Bisexual Kingdom, The

Schroder, Elizabeth G.
1987; Canada; 22 min; Comedy

An erotic and funny video about the adventures and misadventures of women and bisexuality. Entertaining, dramatic and serious, *The Bisexual Kingdom* challenges and explores our assumptions about bisexuality. (Groupe Intervention Video)

Dist/Sales: GroupeIntervention

Bishonen...Beauty

(aka: Meishaonian zhi lian)

Yonfan
1998; Hong Kong; 101 min; Drama
W: Yonfan; *C:* Henry Chung; *E:* Kam Ma; *M:* Chris Babida
Cast: Stephen Fung, Daniel Wu, Shu Qi, Jason Tsang

Everyone is in love with the arrogant and aloof Jet, a star gigolo in Hong Kong. That is until he meets and falls in love with Sam, a policeman on his local beat. Jet sets out to seduce Sam, but it seems Sam's past is as murky as Jet's present. Cantonese & Mandarin with English subtitles.

Prod Comp: Far Sun Film Company
Dist/Sales: Margin, GoldenHarvest, Salzgeber

Bishonen...Beauty

Bit of Scarlett, A

Weiss, Andrea
1996; UK; 70 min; B&W; Documentary
P: Rebecca Dobbs; *E:* Andrea Weiss

With the use of rare film footage, Weiss has put together a fascinating and personal look at the images of gays and lesbians in British cinema and culture. A queer post-modern 1990s soap opera—part musical, part comedy with heartbreak and a last-minute happy ending. Narrated by Sir Ian McKellen.

Prod Comp: Maya Vision
Dist/Sales: BFI, MayaVision

Bite Me Again

Jenkins, Scooter
1999; USA; 42 min; Documentary

Documentary about a hot and steamy erotic performance in San Francisco.

Dist/Sales: Valhalla

Bitter Harvest

Clark, Duane
1993; USA; 98 min; Thriller
P: Steven Paul, Gary Binkow, Eric M. Breiman;
W: Randall Fontana; *C:* Adam Kane; *E:* Paul Petschek;
M: Michael Tavera
Cast: Patsy Kensit, Stephen Baldwin, Jennifer Rubin, Adam Baldwin

Travis Graham is a restless young man whose dreams of world travel are grounded when he inherits the family ranch. He is soon joined by Kelly Ann Welsh, a young girl claiming to be lost, and Jolene Leder, a sophisticated beauty looking to purchase property. Jolene is used to getting what she wants—and she wants Travis. He finds himself involved with both women as he explores new emotional and sexual territories. But Travis soon realises the girls have a secret. It's a conspiracy that results in more adventure than he could ever have bargained for. Even though there is a lesbian element to the women's relationship, the film was made for a straight male audience.

Prod Comp: Prism Pictures
Dist/Sales: Rocvale

Bitter Moon

Polanski, Roman
1992; France, UK; 139 min; Drama
P: Roman Polanski; *W:* Roman Polanski, Gérard Brach, John Brownjohn, Jeff Gross; *C:* Tonino Delli Colli; *E:* Hervé de Luze; *M:* Vangelis
Cast: Peter Coyote, Emmanuelle Seigner, Hugh Grant, Kristin Scott-Thomas

A young English couple is spending their seventh wedding anniversary on a cruise liner in the Mediterranean. One evening they help a young cabaret star and become involved in her life and her relationship with her wheelchair-bound husband. A series of flashbacks reveals the tumultuous relationship between the cabaret star and her husband as they share their most intimate sexual experiences. There is a lesbian revelation at the end of the film where the two women end up in bed together, rather than the expected other man.

Prod Comp: Burrill Productions, Columbia, Le Studio Canal+
Dist/Sales: Roadshow, FineLine

Bitter Tears of Petra von Kant, The

(aka: Die Bitteren Tränen der Petra von Kant)

Fassbinder, Rainer Werner
1972; Germany; 125 min; Experimental
P: Rainer Werner Fassbinder, Michael Fengler;
W: Rainer Werner Fassbinder; *C:* Michael Ballhaus;
E: Thea Eymèsz; *M:* Giuseppe Verdi
Cast: Margit Carstensen, Irm Hermann, Hanna Schygulla, Eva Mattes, Katrin Schaake

This is the story of fashion designer, Petra, her young model lover, Karin, and their destructive and sadomasochistic relationship. Mind games become rampant when the maid gets involved. A controversial film and considered by some lesbians to be misogynistic.

Prod Comp: Filmverlag der Autoren
Dist/Sales: NFVLS, BFI

Bittersweet

Brave, Alice B.
1993; USA; 16 min; Drama

A steamy short film about a dominatrix who returns home from work to her submissive lover and continues her games of power and domination that she performs in her job. A violent and passionate film examining lesbian sex, piercing and S/M relationships. (Cinenova)

Dist/Sales: Cinenova

Black and White

(aka: Noir et Blanc)

Devers, Claire
1986; France; 80 min; B&W; Drama
W: Claire Devers; *C:* Daniel Desbois; *E:* Fabienne Alvarez, Yves Sarda
Cast: Francis Frappat, Jacques Martial, Josephine Fresson

A shy accountant takes a job in a health resort and gradually enters into a bizarre sadomasochistic relationship with a black masseur. As they both discover an attraction to pain, the massage sessions become more violent leading to an inevitable, horrifying conclusion.

Prod Comp: Les Films, Du Volcan
Dist/Sales: Greycat, ACMI

Black Glove, The

Beatty, Maria
1996; USA; 30 min; Drama

More stylish S/M erotica from underground filmmaker Maria Beatty who also made the short film *The Elegant Spanking*. *The Black Glove* has a decidedly darker edge, further exploring the mistress and slave scenario and playing with the boundaries of pleasure and pain.

Prod Comp: OutSpoken! Productions
Dist/Sales: VideoAmericain

Black Is... Black Ain't

Riggs, Marlon
1995; USA; 87 min; Documentary

A lively journey, hosted by award-winning director Marlon Riggs (*Tongues Untied*), exploring how African–Americans are defining their identities and asking what is 'black enough' and what isn't. (Cowboy Pictures)

Dist/Sales: CaliforniaNewsreel, Cowboy

Black Lizard

(aka: Kurotokage)

Fukasaku, Kinji
1968; Japan; 112 min; Comedy
P: Akira Oda; *W:* Masashige Narusawa; *C:* Hiroshi Dowaki; *E:* Keiichi Uraoka; *M:* Isao Tomita
Cast: Ko Kimura, Akihiro Maruyama, Yukio Mishima

A wild and campy detective-thriller starring Japan's celebrated female impersonator, Akihiro Maruyama, who plays a female crime boss and a mad scientist called the Black Lizard. Japanese with English subtitles.

Prod Comp: Shochiku Films
Dist/Sales: Cinevista

Black Mama, White Mama

Romero, Eddie
1972; USA; 82 min; Action
P: Eddie Romero, John Ashley; *W:* H. R. Christian; *C:* Justo Paulino; *E:* Asagni V. Pastor; *M:* Harry Betts
Cast: Pam Grier, Margaret Markov, Lynn Broden, Sid Haig

Deliciously campy exploitation version of *The Defiant Ones* where two women who are chained together escape from a Filipino prison camp. Lee (played by cult queen Pam Grier), and a revolutionary named Karen are brutalised by lesbian wardens and plan their escape, despite despising each other. The remainder of the film details the women's efforts to be rid of each other whilst keeping one step ahead of the authorities.

Prod Comp: American International Pictures, Four Associates
Dist/Sales: Orion

Black Nations/Queer Nations?

Frilot, Shari
1995; USA; 59 min; Documentary

This is an experimental documentary chronicling the March 1995 groundbreaking conference on lesbian and gay sexualities in the African diaspora. The conference brought together an array of dynamic scholars, activists and cultural workers including Essex Hemphill, Kobena Mercer, Barbara Smith, Urvashi Vaid and Jacqui Alexander to interrogate the economic, political and social situations of diasporic lesbians, gay men, bisexual and transgendered peoples. The film brings together the highlights of the conference and draws connections between popular culture and contemporary black gay media

b

production. The participants discuss various topics: Black and queer identity, the shortcomings of Black nationalism, and homophobia in Black communities. Drawing upon works such as Isaac Julien's *The Attendant*, this documentary illuminates the importance of this historic conference for Black lesbians and gays. (Third World Newsreel)

Dist/Sales: TWN

Black Sheep

Glover, Louise
1999; Australia; 27 min; Documentary
P: Penny McDonald; *W:* Louise Glover

Lou Glover grew up in Western Australia repeating the same homophobic and racist taunts she heard around her. Though she was raised in a white family, she was dark-haired and dark-eyed and was often asked if she was Aboriginal—a suggestion she vehemently denied. It wasn't until she came out as a lesbian and left the racist and homophobic environment in which she was raised that she began to explore her ancestry. And that's when she uncovered the secret that her father's family had been hiding for three generations. In this upbeat film from Australia, Lou Glover tells her own story as lesbian, one-time police officer, and recently-discovered Aboriginal woman. (WMM)

Prod Comp: Chili Films
Dist/Sales: Chili, WMM

Black Sheep Boy

Wallin, Michael
1995; 39 min; Drama

Black Sheep Boy explores the sexual thrill and emotional obstacles inherent in fantasies of fetishized youth.

Dist/Sales: WaterBearer, VideoAmericain

Black Sunday

(aka: La Maschera del Demonio)

Bava, Mario
1960; France, Italy; 83 min; B&W; Horror
P: Massimo de Rita; *W:* Mario Bava, Ennio de Concini, Mario Serandrei; *C:* Ubaldo Terzano, Mario Bava;
E: Mario Serandrei; *M:* Robert Nicolosi
Cast: Barbara Steele, John Richardson, Ivo Garrani

This is the story of Princess Asa who was burnt to death as a witch, her punishment for adultery. Two centuries later she returns, along with her lover, to kill and destroy her cursed family. It shocked audiences in the sixties due to its strong sexual (lesbian) suggestions and its explicit cruelty and was banned for many years. It is Bava's first solo feature and it also launched Steele's career as the ultimate

horror actress.

Prod Comp: Galatea Films, Jolly Films
Dist/Sales: NFVLS

Black Widow

Rafelson, Bob
1987; USA; 102 min; Thriller
P: Harold Schneider, Laurence Mark; *W:* Ronald Bass;
C: Conrad Hall; *E:* John Bloom; *M:* Michael Small
Cast: Debra Winger, Theresa Russell, Sami Frey, Dennis Hopper, Terry O'Quinn

A fascinating reworking of the film noir genre, with Teresa Russell as femme fatale Reni, who seduces then murders a string of unsuspecting men. Debra Winger takes on the role of the unsatisfied FBI agent Alex. Alex's investigation is complicated by her increasing obsession with Reni and the sexual tension between the two, which threatens to bring about the downfall of both. A gripping and intricate film that raises interesting questions about love, desire and death. Loaded with sexual tension and lesbian innuendo culminating with the two women in a slightly-longer-than-usual kiss.

Prod Comp: 20th Century-Fox, Amercent Films, American Entertainment Partners
Dist/Sales: ACMI, FilmsInc, 20thCenturyFox

Blair Princess Project, The

Goldberg, Paula
2000; USA; 20 min; Comedy
P: Joyce Marie Brusasco, Paula Goldberg, Christine Price

In August of 1999 three Jewish 'girls' set out to a synagogue in Malibu to document their friend Blair's wedding. A week later their footage was found.

Prod Comp: A Baby Tomata Production
Dist/Sales: PictureThis!

Blank Point: What is Transsexualism?, The

Wang, Xiao-Yen
1990; USA; 58 min; Documentary
P: Andy Martin; *W:* Xiao-Yen Wang, Andy Martin;
C: Xiao-Yen Wang; *E:* Xiao-Yen Wang, Andy Martin;
M: Jean-Pierre Tibi

A focus on two male-to-female transsexuals and one female-to-male transsexual who discuss their psychological and physical changes. We learn to understand transsexualism as a science that offers those who are tormented by a misaligned gender identity the opportunity to alter their physical sexual characteristics to correspond with their psychological gender identity.

Prod Comp: Beijing-San Francisco Film Group
Dist/Sales: EMA, CinemaGuild, NFVLS

Blazing Saddles

Brooks, Mel
1974; USA; 86 min; Comedy
P: Michael Hertzberg, Peter Wooley; *W:* Mel Brooks,
Alan Uger, Richard Pryor, Andrew Bergman, Norman
Steinberg; *C:* Joseph Biroc; *E:* Danford B. Greene, John
C. Howard; *M:* John Morris, Mel Brooks
Cast: Gene Wilder, Cleavon Little, Mel Brooks, Slim
Pickens, Don DeLuise

> Cleavon Little is a black railroad worker in the 19th
> century Midwest who with the assistance of an
> alcoholic gunfighter tries to foil the plans of a
> crooked attorney and his henchmen. In spite of the
> so-called plot, *Blazing Saddles* is an hilarious and
> camp parody of Hollywood westerns (and Holly-
> wood racism) featuring great comic performances.

Prod Comp: Warner, Crossbow Productions
Dist/Sales: ReelMovies, ACMI, Warner

Blessed are those who Thirst

(aka: Salige er de som Tørster)

Kiønig, Carl Jørgen
1997; Norway; 118 min; Thriller
P: Tomas Backström, Petter Borgli; *W:* Axel Hellstenius;
C: Kjell Vassdal; *E:* Inge-Lise Langfeldt; *M:* Aasmund
Feidje, Carl Jørgen Kiønig
Cast: Kjersti Elvik, Gjertrud Jynge, Lasse Kolsrud, Nils
Ole Oftebro

> Young medical student Kristine Håverstad is brutally
> raped in her apartment in Oslo. She is afraid, and
> her neighbour, the Iranian refugee Afase is not home
> that night. At the same time, police officer Hanne
> Wilhelmsen and police Inspector Håkon Sand are
> faced with a perplexing problem: the streets of Oslo
> are awash with terror from the mysterious 'Saturday
> Massacre'—but there are no corpses. Only blood.
> Attorney Karen Borg is working for refugees seeking
> asylum in Norway. She is attacked by a disturbed
> Bosnian refugee but rescued by Olaf Frydenberg
> from the immigration authorities. And then, the
> corpses surface and the scope of the brutalities
> become even more shocking. At the same time, the
> rape victim's father searches for the rapist. The
> police, the revenge-driven father and the rape victim
> herself all manage to pick up the tracks of the rapist.
> Set against the backdrop of racial tension in the
> immigrant community of Oslo, the manhunt
> becomes a question of life and death and the search
> for justice. The rape and the 'Saturday Massacre'
> converge to raise the question: Is it the perfect crime,
> or is it the perfect revenge? (Norwegian Film
> Institute)
> Norwegian with English subtitles.

Prod Comp: Nordic Screen Productions
Dist/Sales: NorwegianFilm

Blessed Art Thou

(aka: A Question of Faith)

Disney, Tim
2000; USA; 90 min; Drama
P: Bill Haney; *W:* Tim Disney; *C:* Claudio Rocha
Cast: Naveen Andrews, Bernard Hill, Paul Guilfoyle,
Daniel Von Bargen

> In this mystical parable about the inevitability of
> change, the monks in a monastery experience a test
> of faith when one of them undergoes a gender
> transition. Ancient traditions, modern technologies,
> and the non-traditional attitudes of the younger
> members of the order become a catalyst for dishar-
> mony. (2000 St Louis International Film Festival)

Prod Comp: Uncommon Productions
Dist/Sales: FirstLook, OFG

Blind Fairies

(aka: Le Fate Ignoranti; His Secret Life)

Ozpetek, Ferzan
2000; France, Italy; 105 min; Drama
P: Gianni Romoli, Tilde Corsi; *W:* Ferzan Ozpetek,
Gianni Romoli; *C:* Pasquale Mari; *E:* Patrizio Marone;
M: Andrea Guerra
Cast: Margherita Buy, Stefano Accorsi, Serra Yilmaz,
Andrea Renzi, Gabriel Garko

> A woman's encounter with her husband's gay lover
> changes their lives forever. Antonia is a wealthy
> Italian doctor who has been married to Massima for
> 15 years. Safe and secure in their relationship, she is
> shocked when he is suddenly killed. But nothing
> could have prepared her for the shock of then
> meeting her late husband's gay lover Michele, and
> discovering his secret life. The two are initially
> suspicious of one another, but eventually the
> realisation that they loved the same man, brings
> them together in ways they could never have
> expected. By the director of *Steam: The Turkish Bath*.
> Italian with English subtitles.

Dist/Sales: TF1, Strand

Blind Faith

Dickerson, Ernest
1998; USA; 118 min; Thriller
P: Nick Grillo; *W:* Frank Military; *C:* Rodney Charters;
E: Stephen Lovejoy; *M:* Ron Carter
Cast: Charles Dutton, Courtney B. Vance, Kadeem
hardison, Lonette McKee

> A police officer's son is arrested for the murder of a
> white boy in the Bronx in the repressive 1950s. His
> brother, John who is a lawyer, agrees to defend him,
> but soon realises that there is more to this story than
> meets the eye. The subsequent investigation leads
> John to uncover a conspiracy that goes beyond the

b

police, and causes him to reassess how he looks at himself and his country. An entertaining examination of bigotry and repression.

Prod Comp: Neufeld Rehme Productions Showtime
Dist/Sales: Showtime, Wolfe

Blind Moment, The

Peer, Ellie / Zinc, Felix
1991; UK; 16 min; Drama

The Blind Moment opens with a particularly twisted lesbian-bashing attack that leaves the victim comatose and totally helpless in her lover's hands. While the dream she experiences in this state is sensual and surreal, the film is still a disturbing encounter with illness and dependency. (MQFF)

Block Party

Block Party

Cronin, Laura Jean
2001; USA; 24 min; Comedy
P: Dillon Kreider; *W:* Laura Jean Cronin, Tara Morgan

Two lesbians work together to put on their very first street party, with a little love and friendship along the way.

Dist/Sales: BiProduct

Blond Man, The

Luketic, Robert
1994; Australia; 24 min; Drama
P: Robert Luketic; *W:* Robert Luketic

From his bedroom window Jason discovers the entrance to an exciting new world. The object of his love and jealous rage is unaware of the bleak consequences that arise from unrequited desire. With Alex Dimitriades.

Dist/Sales: VCA

Blonde Cobra

Jacobs, Ken
1963; USA; 25 min; Experimental
Cast: Ken Jacobs, Jack Smith

This very early gay avant-garde film, is a gritty and revealing investigation into homosexuals, transvestites and transsexuals. Very much made for a gay audience and designed to offend straights.

Blood and Concrete

Reiner, Jeffrey
1991; USA; 95 min; Drama
P: Richard LaBrie; *W:* Richard LaBrie, Jeffrey Reiner; *C:* Declan Quinn; *E:* Richard LaBrie, Jeffrey Reiner; *M:* Vinny Golia
Cast: Billy Zane, Jennifer Beals, Darren McGavin, James Le Gros

Joey Turks is a dim-witted car thief who has a knack for being in the wrong place at the wrong time. Joey is on the trail of a missing drug shipment, caught in the squeeze between a drug lord on a hell of a come down and a hard-boiled detective looking to make one final bust before he retires. Meanwhile the drug lord's gay psycho hoodlum, played by Le Gros, is hot on Joey's heals.

Dist/Sales: FirstRelease

Blood and Roses

Blood and Roses
(aka: Et Mourir de Plaisir)

Vadim, Roger
1960; France, Italy; 74 min; Horror
P: Raymond Eger; *W:* Claude Brulé, Claude Martin, Roger Vadim, Roger Vailland; *C:* Claude Renoir; *E:* Victoria Mercanton; *M:* Jean Prodromidès
Cast: Annette Vadim, Elsa Martinelli, Mel Ferrer

In the great tradition of the lesbian vampire genre,

Carmilla is seduced by her vampire ancestor who then takes over her body. Carmilla then goes about seducing and biting other beautiful young women, including her cousin. This adaption of Sheridan Le Fanu's *Carmilla*, is lots of fun and Vadim plays up the lesbian aspects of the story.

Prod Comp: Documento
Dist/Sales: TLA, FilmsInc, Paramount

Blood for Dracula

Morrissey, Paul / Margheriti, Antonio
1974; France, Italy; 103 min; Horror
W: Paul Morrissey
Cast: Joe Dallesandro, Udo Kier

Follow up to *Flesh for Frankenstein*. Morrissey at his campy, trashy best.

Blood Money

Brown, Rowland
1933; USA; 65 min; B&W; Drama
W: Rowland Brown, Hal Long; *C:* James Van Trees;
E: Lloyd Nosler; *M:* Alfred Newman
Cast: Sandra Shaw, Judith Anderson, George Bancroft, Frances Dee, Blossom Seeley

Sandra Shaw looks absolutely dashing in a tuxedo and has a passion for men's clothes. Even though she has a boyfriend, at one point she turns up dressed in a tweed suit with a woman on her arm.

Prod Comp: 20th Century Pictures, United Artists
Dist/Sales: NFVLS

Blood Splattered Bride, The

(aka: La Novia Ensangrentada)

Aranda, Vincente
1972; Spain; 95 min; Horror
P: Antonio Perez Olea, Jaime Fernández-Cid;
W: Vincente Aranda; *C:* Fernando Arribas; *E:* Pablo González del Amo; *M:* Antonio Pérez Olea
Cast: Simon Andreu, Alexandra Bastedo, Maribel Martin, Dean Selmier

Susan, a young bride, has difficulty enjoying sexual relations with her new husband at his Gothic mansion. When Carmilla, a mysterious woman who is a vampire, arrives Susan is immediately attracted to her. They become lovers and plot the murder of Susan's husband. Watch out for the very erotic blood-filled kiss.

Prod Comp: Morgana Films

Bloodbrothers

(aka: A Father's Love)

Mulligan, Robert
1978; USA; 120 min; Drama

P: Stephen Friedman; *W:* Walter Newman; *C:* Robert Surtees; *E:* Sheldon Kahn; *M:* Elmer Bernstein
Cast: Richard Gere, Paul Sorvino, Tony Lo Bianco, Lelia Goldoni

Gere portrays a young man who is caught between the construction life of his father and the desire to break away from family tradition. Paralleling the plot is the story of a gay jeweller played by Bruce French, who refuses to see his father. Based on the novel by Richard Price.

Prod Comp: Kings Road Entertainment, Warner
Dist/Sales: Warner

Bloodlust

Hewitt, Jon / Wolstencroft, Richard
1991; Australia; 84 min; Horror
P: Jon Hewitt, Richard Wolstencroft; *W:* Jon Hewitt, Richard Wolstencroft; *C:* Gary Ravencroft;
E: Jon Hewitt; *M:* Ross Hazeldine
Cast: Jane Stuart Wallace, Kelly Chapman, Robert James O'Neill, Max Crawdaddy, John Flaus

A stylish, macabre and ultra-violent action thriller exploitation flick laced with wicked humour that follows the plot line of *Fatal Attraction* as well as featuring an assortment of lesbian vampires. Lear, Frank and Tad are modern-day vampires who cruise the bizarre world of clubs and groovy hangouts. When their friend Dee is killed by a roving band of religious fanatics, they decide to embark on a heist they have been planning. The night before the heist they go on a drug-crazed orgy of sex and violence. The heist is held at a casino run by a ruthless syndicate boss Pastrioni and afterwards they find themselves on the run from the syndicate hit man Steig.

Prod Comp: Windhover Productions
Dist/Sales: ACMI

Bloodsisters: Leather Dykes and S/M

Handelman, Michelle
1995; USA; 70 min; Documentary

An examination of the political activities and sexual choices of women in the leather S/M community. The film focuses on nine central figures who represent a cross-section of the leather S/M community, and by following them, the film provides an in-depth look at the world of women into leather S/M.

Dist/Sales: WaterBearer

Bloody Mama

Corman, Roger
1970; USA; 89 min; Action
P: Roger Corman; *W:* Don Peters, Robert Thorn;

C: John A. Alonzo; *E:* Eve Newman; *M:* Don Randi
Cast: Shelley Winters, Don Stroud, Pat Hingle, Robert
De Niro, Bruce Dern

Sex crazy Ma Barker and her equally depraved gang hit town after town in a wild spree of robberies. Nothing seems to stop Bloody Mama. The ad promoting the film said 'The family that slays together, stays together'. It is basically a spoof of the gangster-family genre with gritty characters including Ma and four her sons—one's a junkie, another a homosexual. The family is held together by incest and murder. Look out for De Niro who's great as the glue-sniffing, model-plane making son.

Prod Comp: American International Pictures
Dist/Sales: Roadshow

Blow Job

Warhol, Andy
1963; USA; 35 min; Experimental

Warhol depicts a man's face as he receives the service referred to in the title.

Blue

Jarman, Derek
1993; UK; 75 min; Experimental
P: James MacKay, Takashi Asai; *W:* Derek Jarman;
M: Simon Fisher Turner
Cast: Nigel Terry, Tilda Swinton, Derek Jarman

Jarman's last film before he died of AIDS, is a startling experiment inspired by the works of the conceptual artist Yves Klein. A completely blue screen is used throughout the film as Jarman's journals are read by various actors, such as Tilda Swinton and Nigel Terry. At the time Jarman was working on the film his eyesight was severely impaired, in a way the film is taking us into his almost sightless world.

Prod Comp: Uplink Co, Channel 4, Arts Council of Great Britain
Dist/Sales: ArtificialEye, Zeitgeist, Salzgeber

Blue Boys

Marshall, Stuart
1992; UK; 25 min; Documentary
P: Rebecca Dobbs; *W:* Chris Woods

A riveting look at police powers and obscenity laws in Britain, which focuses on the infamous Operation Spanner case.

Dist/Sales: MayaVision

Blue Haven

Cautherley, Julian
2001; USA; 17 min; Comedy

Join Fakie and Henry as they chase the Blue Haven pool of their skater dreams. The Blue Haven isn't the only dream the boys are chasing, and pretty soon their harmless fun leads them into humorous times as they try to save the $40,000 they need for Fakie's gender reassignment surgery. (MQFF)

Blue Haven

Blue Hour, The

(aka: Die Blaue Stund)

Gisler, Marcel
1992; Germany; 87 min; Drama
W: Marcel Gisler, Andreas Herder, Rudolf Nadler;
C: Ciro Cappellari; *E:* Bettina Böhler; *M:* Paul Bley
Cast: Andreas Herder, Dina Leipzig, Cyrille Rey-Coquis, Christoph Krix

The Blue Hour deals with the ambiguous relationship between a gay hustler and a straight woman. On the surface, magnetically attractive Theo's life is calm and ordered. His apartment is the height of modernist decor, he dresses well and he even has two phones—one for work and one for his personal life. He works when he wants to and says he is most comfortable with sex when he gets paid at the end of it. However, still waters run deep and Theo is inexorably drawn into the messy world of emotional involvement: with a friend, a steady customer and an older female neighbour—at least until her boyfriend returns. This subtle psychological portrait moves far beyond the simple question of Theo's sexual orientation to confront the more difficult issues of how emotional needs relate to sex and whether it satisfies or blocks them. (MQFF)

Dist/Sales: WaterBearer, VideoAmericain

Blue Jeans

Burin des Roziers, Hughes
1981; France; 101 min; Drama
C: Jacques Assuérus; *E:* Gilles Amado; *M:* David MacNeil
Cast: Gilles Budin, Michel Gibet, Daniel Véry

A young French boy is sent to the English seaside to study English, where he falls in love with a young girl. She unfortunately rejects him and falls for an older boy. But the French boy soon becomes interested in the older boy himself.

Prod Comp: Chloé Productions

Blunt: The Fourth Man

Green, David
1985; UK; 85 min; Drama
P: Martin Thompson; *W:* Robin Chapman; *C:* John McGlashan; *E:* Jim Latham; *M:* Hector Berlioz
Cast: Anthony Hopkins, Ian Richardson, Michael Williams

This made for television film centres around the scandalous spy affair where Guy Burgess, Anthony Blunt, Kim Philby and Donald McLean, were all accused of spying for Russia. Blunt was a well-respected art historian for the Queen. He tries to cover up the network of fellow spies and especially the involvement of Guy Burgess, his ex-lover.

Prod Comp: BBC; *Dist/Sales:* TLA, BBC

Bob & Rose

Farino, Julian / Wright, Joe
2001; UK; 6 x 45 min; Drama
P: Ann Harrison-Baxter; *W:* Russell T. Davies
Cast: Alan Davies, Lesley Sharp, Jessica Stevenson

Set in Manchester, *Bob & Rose* expands the view of the city made famous by Davies' previous series *Queer as Folk*. We see Canal Street and the Babylon again, but we're also introduced to Deansgate, where 30-year-old Rose hangs out with her best mates. Rose is funny, sassy, down-to-earth, and, well, a bit bored with her life. Then she meets Bob...Bob is in his early thirties, a teacher, and a gay man with an overly-supportive mum. Having recently ended a relationship, he seems uneasy being single again. He certainly isn't expecting to meet someone like Rose. Meeting by chance, they are both surprised by how fast they click. They can't deny that something more than friendship is developing. Can they really be falling in love—a gay man and a straight woman? What will Holly, Bob's scarily off-kilter best friend, do about Bob choosing another woman over her? How do Bob & Rose themselves deal with the doubts and questions their relationship cause? (2002 New York Lesbian & Gay Film Festival)

Prod Comp: Red Production Co; *Dist/Sales:* RedProd

Bodies in Trouble

Bociurkiw, Marusia
1991; Canada; 15 min; Experimental

A video about the lesbian body under siege. Short vignettes describe a specific lesbian erotic language and a sense of the absurd. *Bodies in Trouble* is a call to action against the danger that the new Right poses to lesbian/feminist organising. By describing lesbian humour, eroticism and social space, it also evokes the funny, sexy and charming aspects of lesbian existence.

Dist/Sales: Frameline

Body of a Poet: A Tribute to Audre Lorde 1934–1992, The

Fernando, Sonali
1995; UK; 29 min; Drama
W: Sonali Fernando; *C:* Carolyn Chen; *E:* Nasser Aslam; *M:* Dominique Le Gendre
Cast: Rhetta Greene, Medusa, Nija Murphy

An imaginary biography of Audre Lorde—African–American, lesbian, feminist, professor, mother, visionary and 'warrior poet'—who died of breast cancer in 1992. (Cinenova)

Dist/Sales: Cinenova, WMM

Body without Soul

Grodecki, Wiktor
1996; Czech Republic; 90 min; Documentary

A deep and intimate look at the adult video industry in today's Czech Republic. Through interviews with the young models and by actually filming the production of an adult video, this film delves into the psyche of what it takes to sell your body to the camera for little reward. (Water Bearer Films) Czech with English subtitles.

Dist/Sales: WaterBearer

Bolo! Bolo!

Rashid, Ian Iqbal / Saxena, Gita
1991; Canada; 30 min; Documentary
Cast: Himani Bannerji, Sunil Gupta

More than one of the interviewees in this documentary about the South Asian community in Toronto remark that they often feel obliged to choose between being gay and being Asian. However, AIDS and AIDS education are making the need for visibility within the community more pressing, and this film is a powerful part of that process.

Dist/Sales: VTape

b

Bombay Boys

Gustad, Kaizad
1998; India; 105 min; Drama
P: Mahesh Naithani; *W:* Kaizad Gustad; *E:* Priya Krshnaswamy; *M:* Brad Steven Bergbom
Cast: Naseeruddin Shah, Rahul Bose, Naveen Andrews, Tara Deshpande

Nothing less than culture shocks and stunning self realisations tumble down on strangers of West Indian descent from three continents who come to share a flat and tumultuous life in the fast paced Megalopolis of Bombay. At times reminiscant of the heyday of Leslie Nielson, at others of key moments of *The Full Monty*, this partially gay coming out comedy keeps true to its hilarious Bollywood roots. (1999 Verzaubert Queer Film Festival)

Prod Comp: Kismet Talkies
Dist/Sales: Kismet

Bombay Eunuch

Bombay Eunuch

Gucovsky, Michelle / MacDonald, Sean / Shiva, Alexandra
2001; India, USA; 71 min; Documentary
P: Alexandra Shiva; *C:* Ajay Narohna, Bimal Biswas; *E:* Penelope Falk; *M:* John M. Davis

Rare are opportunities for Western eyes to explore the realm of the Third Sex of India—the subcontinent's answer to the Castrati: once revered in seats of government and religious rites alike, now forced into begging and prostitution to survive. The filmmakers were offered the privileged place of documenting the plight of Meena, a 37-year-old hijra and her adopted family of fellow eunuchs. Through their own voices, these 'girls' provide insights into why they volunteered a life under the sari—which includes full castration without anaesthetic, hostile families and near certain poverty. Whilst as much a story about

sex, gender and survival in the harsh slums of Bombay, the narration builds to a curiously optimistic ending—charged with almost heady irony through the manner in which a few eunuchs find themselves able to exploit their low status for financial gain. (MQFF)

Prod Comp: Gidalya Pictures
Dist/Sales: Gidalya

BOMgaY

Wadia, Riyad Vinci / Sethna, Jagu
1996; India; 11 min; Drama

Based around the poetry of R. Raj Rao, *BOMgaY* portrays the gay subculture in contemporary India, in what is said to be the first gay film to openly discuss the issue.

Dist/Sales: WadiaMovietone

Boots, Boobs and Bitches: The Art of G. B. Jones

Parker, Candy
1991; Canada; 15 min; Documentary

In addition to her roles as co-editor of JD's, co-founder of New Lavender Panthers and bad-girl filmmaker, G. B. Jones is a visual artist who has been described as 'the lesbian Tom of Finland'. This 'straight' documentary outlines the appeal of her controversial drawings. (MQFF)

Border Line...Family Pictures

Griffith, C. A.
1998; Mexico, USA; 29 min; Documentary

The life of African–American woman Linden Jordan, is evoked in this dramatised personal documentary recollection of her life, her lovers and her family.

Dist/Sales: DosEspiritus

Borderline

MacPherson, Kenneth
1930; UK; 61 min; B&W; Drama
W: Kenneth MacPherson
Cast: Paul Robeson, Eslanda Robeson, Helga Doorn, Gavin Arthur

Set in a small Swiss village, *Borderline* is the story of interracial love and, although not explicitly gay, there are a number of gay and lesbian undertones. Robeson holds the adoration of the inn's piano player and the owner of the inn is a cigar-smoking lesbian whose lover is the barmaid.

Prod Comp: Pool Group
Dist/Sales: NFVLS, BFI

b

Born in Flames

Borden, Lizzie
1983; USA; 79 min; Sci-Fi
P: Lizzie Borden; *W:* Lizzie Borden, Hisa Tayo;
C: Ed Bowes, Al Santana, Phil O'Reilly; *E:* Lizzie Borden
Cast: Honey, Adele Bertel, Jeanne Satterfield, Flo Kennedy, Pat Murphy

In New York 10 years after a peaceful social democratic revolution, the achievements of the revolution are celebrated by the official media but life in the streets remains the same—poverty, urban decay, unemployment and male harassment of women. A band of female anarchists, led by a black lesbian, battle an unresponsive government.

Prod Comp: Jerome Foundation
Dist/Sales: CinemaLibre, FirstRun/Icarus, FirstRunFeatures, NFVLS, VideoAmericain

Borstal Boy

Sheridan, Peter
2000; Ireland, UK; 93 min; Drama
P: Pat Moylan, Arthur Lappin; *W:* Nye Heron, Peter Sheridan; *C:* Ciaran Tanham; *E:* Stephen O'Connell;
M: Stephen McKeon
Cast: Shawn Hatosy, Danny Dyer, Lee Ingleby, Robin Laing, Michael York

Borstal Boy is an Irish film based on the memoirs of noted author and raconteur Brendan Behan. Behan, a 16-year-old Irish soldier, goes on a mission from Ireland to Liverpool during World War II. His mission is thwarted when he is apprehended, charged and imprisoned in Borstal, a reform institution for young offenders in East Anglia, England. At Borstal, Brendan is forced to live face-to-face with those he perceived as 'the enemy', a confrontation that reveals a deep inner conflict in the young Brendan, and forces a self-examination that is both traumatic and revealing. Events take an unexpected turn and Brendan is thrown into a complete spin. In the emotional vortex, he finally faces up to the truth. (Strand Releasing)

Dist/Sales: Strand, Clarence

Borstal Boy

Boston Strangler, The

Fleischer, Richard
1968; USA; 109 min; Thriller
P: Robert Fryer; *W:* Edward Anhalt; *C:* Richard Kline;
E: Marion Rothman; *M:* Lionel Newman
Cast: Tony Curtis, Henry Fonda, George Kennedy, Sally Kellerman, James Brolin

Based on the shocking true story of the murders that took place in Boston between 1962 and 1964. This unnerving thriller follows the tracks of schizophrenic Albert De Salvo and his strangulation rampage. A homosexual man, played by Hurd Hatfield, was originally accused of the crimes.

Prod Comp: 20th Century-Fox
Dist/Sales: 20thCenturyFox

Bound

Wachowski, Andy / Wachowski, Larry
1996; USA; 108 min; Thriller
P: Andrew Lazar, Stuart Boros; *W:* Larry Wachowski, Andy Wachowski; *C:* Bill Pope; *E:* Zach Staenberg;
M: Don Davis
Cast: Gina Gershon, Jennifer Tilly, Joe Pantoliano, John P. Ryan, Christopher Meloni

A very stylish lesbian film noir thriller with two very beautiful women looking for lust, love and loot. Violet and her Mafia boyfriend Caesar live next door to an apartment that Corky, a girl just released from prison is renovating. Through the walls Corky listens to the comings and going of Violet, Caesar and other mobsters. The two women meet, fall in love and decide to rip off the Mafia. A modern lesbian classic, and deservedly so.

Prod Comp: Dino De Laurentiis Productions, Spelling Films
Dist/Sales: Roadshow, Wolfe, ACMI

Bound and Gagged: A Love Story

Appleby, Daniel
1992; USA; 96 min; Comedy
P: Dennis J. Mahoney; *W:* Daniel Appleby; *C:* Dean Lent, Vincent Donohue, Roger Schmitz; *E:* Kaye Davis;
M: William Murphy
Cast: Elizabeth Saltarrelli, Ginger Lynn Allen, Karen Black, Chris Denton

Road movie featuring two bisexual women and a confused straight man. Cliff is depressed after the break up of his marriage, Elizabeth is a bisexual determined to cheer him up and Leslie, Elizabeth's lover, is in a marriage she would prefer to be out of. Comic and bizarre events happen as Leslie tries to escape back to her husband and Cliff tries to kill himself on numerous occasions.

Prod Comp: Cinescope Productions
Dist/Sales: NorthernArts

Bounty, The

Naczek, Jason
2001; USA; 18 min; Comedy

Two women that desperately want to have a baby steal a rare sperm sample. A cross-country chase ensues with a male chauvinist bounty hunter on their tail.

Box, The

Eddey, Paul
1975; Australia; 100 min; Comedy, Drama
P: Ian Jones; *W:* Tom Hegarty; *C:* Wayne Williams; *E:* Philip Reid; *M:* Gary Hardman
Cast: Barrie Barkla, Fred Betts, Belinda Giblin, Ken James, Paul Karo

A spin-off from the Australian television series of the same name set in a television station featuring the bawdy exploits of its staff, including bisexual reporter Vicki Stafford and high camp director Lee Whiteman. The film version expands on the television series by including high camp song and dance numbers, great 1970s clothes, and loads of gratuitous and explicit nudity.

Prod Comp: Crawford Productions
Dist/Sales: Roadshow

Boy Germs

Franko, Justine
1999; USA; 15 min; Comedy

Short comedy about a girl who suffers from blistering sores every time she kisses a boy. She is miraculously cured by her first kiss with a girl.

Prod Comp: All-Girl-Action Productions
Dist/Sales: All-Girl-Action

Boy Girl

Boschman, Lorna
1999; Canada; 14 min; Documentary

Three artists talk about their tomboy past, butch present and sexuality.

Dist/Sales: VideoOut

Boy like many Others, A

(aka: Un Ragazzo come Tanti)

Minello, Gianni
1983; Italy; 96 min; Drama
Cast: Stefano Mioni

The story of a fresh-faced young man who comes to the big city where he encounters poverty and exploitation. He becomes a prostitute and gets involved with drug dealing and crime as his depression mounts. He finally finds help and understanding with a male artist.

Boy Named Sue, A

Wyman, Julie
2000; USA; 57 min; Documentary

Filmed over several years, *A Boy Named Sue* plots Sue's transformation from butch dyke to Theo— 'self-confessed transman with pussy'. A unique insight into Theo's changing experiences as well as the difficulties encountered by his lesbian lover and friends. (MQFF)

Dist/Sales: WMM

Boy Next Door

Pfirman, Carl
1998; USA; 13 min; Comedy

A teenage brother and sister fight it out over their mutual love for the attractive new boy in the neighbourhood.

Awards: San Francisco International Lesbian & Gay Film Festival, 1999: Audience Award Best Gay Short
Dist/Sales: Atom

Boy Next Door? A Profile of Boy George

Kidel, Mark
1993; UK; 50 min; Documentary

Intimate portrait of famed gay pop singer Boy George.

Prod Comp: Channel 4

Boychick

Gaylord, Glenn
2001; USA; 12 min; Comedy

A Jewish teenager's crush on the handsome boy in school is helped along with a little assistance from an almost-imaginary friend. (MQFF)

Dist/Sales: NJB, FillingTheGap

Boyfriends (1995)

Hunsinger, Tom / Hunter, Neil
1995; UK; 82 min; Comedy
P: Tom Hunsinger, Neil Hunter; *W:* Tom Hunsinger, Neil Hunter; *C:* Richard Tisdall; *E:* John Trumper
Cast: James Dryfuss, Mark Sands, Michael Urwin, David Coffey

Boyfriends unfolds one Easter weekend as three gay friends and their partners spend the weekend together at a country cottage. Paul and Ben have been together for five years. It's beginning to seem a lot longer... Matt and Owen have going out for three months. Matt hears wedding bells but he's going to hear more than he bargained for by Sunday... Will picked Adam up the night before but it turns out that they already have a history. The question is whether or not they have a future. *Boyfriends* is a comedy about exploring the depths, and the shallows, of gay relationships in the 1990s. (Mongrel)

Prod Comp: Essex Features
Dist/Sales: FirstRunFeatures, Wolfe, Mongrel, VideoAmericain

Boyfriends (1999)

Horton, Simon
1999; UK; 11 min; Comedy

A classified ad, a coal shed, a threesome and a waiter. A novel way to find your dream man.

Dist/Sales: Absolute

Brad Bergman

Boychick

Boys Don't Cry

Peirce, Kimberly
1999; USA; 120 min; Drama
P: John Hart, Christine Vachon, Eva Kolodner, Jeffrey Sharp; *W:* Kimberly Peirce, Andy Bienen; *C:* Jim Denault; *E:* Tracy Granger; *M:* Nathan Larson
Cast: Hilary Swank, Chloe Sevigny, Peter Sarsgaard, Brendan Sexton II

Based on the life and death of Brandon Teena, *Boys Don't Cry* is a gripping and very moving account of difference and intolerance. Believing herself to be a male, Brandon constructs a masculine persona for herself and acts and lives as a man in a poverty stricken community in Nebraska. Within this 'white trash' locale she attempts to live her identity as best she can. She falls in love with Lana, and a tender romance ensues, which results in a group of local young men venting their homophobic violence on the lovers. One of a series of works in late 20th century American cinema which attempted to deal with the the increasing fracturing and alienation of working class life caused by unemployment and the rationalising of both economics and ethics, *Boys Don't Cry* resonates deeply as both a story of damaged lives as well being an inspiring challenge to conservative understandings of gender and sexuality. (ACMI)

Awards: Academy Awards, 1999: Best Actress (Hilary Swank)
Prod Comp: Killer Films, Hart-Sharp Entertainment
Dist/Sales: FoxSearchlight, 20thCenturyFox, Wolfe, ACMI

Boys from Brazil, The

Davidson, John-Paul
1993; Brazil, UK; 70 min; Documentary
P: Trudi Styler; *C:* Vittorio Dragonetti, Flávio Ferreira, Guy Gonçalves, Brian Sewell, Gigi Verga; *E:* Sara Bhaskaran, Ray Frawley

Documentary which explores the lives of transvestites, or 'travnesties' and 'she-males' as they are called in Brazil. It focuses on Samara, a once-famous male performer known as Bobby Fontal, and Luciana, a young 'tranvestie' who was befriended by Samara at the age of nine. We follow them for two years, confronting the horrible results of home silicon insertions for extra cleavage or fleshy hips. Their dream is to leave Brazil for Europe where they hope to find greater fortune. Readily acknowledging the European male attraction to dark-skinned Brazilians, Samara and Luciana believe their success is dependent on obeying the customs of 'Candomble', a voodoo religion that came to Brazil via the black slave ships from Africa. Sacrifices to spirits must be made to ensure that travel to Europe will be possible. A fascinating exploration of homosexuality, prostitution and gender identity in Brazil. (MQFF)
Some Portuguese with English subtitles.

Prod Comp: BBC, Xingu Films
Dist/Sales: Xingu

Boys in the Backyard

Kennerley, Annette
1997; UK; 22 min; Documentary

A slice of San Francisco life in the summer of 1993. Matt and Jo sit together in their back yard and talk about their daddy/boy relationship, transgender, life/love, tattoos and tomato plants. (Cinenova)

Dist/Sales: Cinenova

Boys in the Band, The

Friedkin, William
1970; USA; 120 min; Drama
P: Mart Crowley; *W:* Mart Crowley; *C:* Arthur Ornitz; *E:* Carl Lerner, Jerry Greenburg
Cast: Leonard Frey, Kenneth Nelson, Cliff Gorman, Frederick Combs, Robert La Tourneaux

This was the first Hollywood film in which all the principal characters were homosexual. As such, it was viewed at the time as a serious study of gay men

b

and mounted as a special project in which Crowley's off-Broadway play was adapted with great fidelity to the original text. To Vito Russo, *The Boys in the Band* is 'a perfunctory compendium of easily acceptable stereotypes who gather at a Manhattan birthday party and spend an evening savaging each other and their way of life'. Yet Russo also recognised it as a landmark film, 'part catharsis part catalyst', which opened the way for less stereotyped portrayals of homosexuality.

Prod Comp: Leo, Cinema Centre 100, National General Pictures
Dist/Sales: Ascanbee, 20thCenturyFox, Swank, BFI, NFVLS, ACMI, VideoAmericain

Boys Next Door, The

Spheeris, Penelope
1985; USA; 90 min; Drama
P: Sandy Howard, Keith Rubinstein; *W:* Glenn Morgan, James Wong; *C:* Arthur Albert; *E:* Andrew Horvitch; *M:* George S. Clinton
Cast: Maxwell Caulfield, Charlie Sheen, Patti D'Arbanville, Christopher McDonald

Explores the violence unleashed when a young man's suppressed homosexuality is finally released through anger and rage. Two teenage boys go on a killing spree just before their graduation. In the opening scene, the character played by Caulfield is shown as sexually repressed. He is contrasted with a high-school friend, Tom, who is openly gay.

Prod Comp: Republic Pictures Corporation, New World

Boys' Night Out

Caise, Yule
1996; USA; 34 min; Comedy

A homophobic man is coerced into running an AIDS charity race, where the only rule is the contestant must wear a minimum of 2-1/2" heels.

Boys of Cell Block Q

Daniels, Alan
1992; USA; 90 min; Comedy
P: Kevin M. Glover; *W:* Ralph Lucas; *C:* Ron Hamill; *M:* Shaun Guerin
Cast: Lewis Alante, Andrew Addams, Slade Burrus, Larry Maraviglia

A low-budget, humorous, tongue-in-cheek spoof of boys-in-prison films featuring sex, sadism and sin. They're all there from the pretty boys to sadistic priests. A very camp romp. Adapted from the play by John C. Will.

Prod Comp: Out & About Pictures
Dist/Sales: VideoAmericain

Boys of Manchester, The

Catania, John / Ignacio, Charles
2000; USA; 53 min; Documentary

Those randy Manchester lads are at it again in this US documentary that takes us deep behind the action on *Queer as Folk*, one of the most audacious gay TV programs ever made. Creator and writer, Russell T. Davies, and producer Nicola Shindler, chart the show's astonishing progression from small screen success to worldwide sensation. This candid 'behind-the-scenes' peek also features interviews with gay-for-pay actors Aiden Gillen, Craig Kelly and Charlie Hunnam. These men behaving badly happily expose all the dirty little secrets of the production. (MQFF)

Dist/Sales: In-The-Life

Boys on the Side

Ross, Herbert
1995; USA; 112 min; Drama
P: Arnon Milchan, Steven Reuther, Herbert Ross; *W:* Don Roos; *C:* Donald E. Thorin; *E:* Michael R. Miller; *M:* David Newman
Cast: Whoopi Goldberg, Mary-Louise Parker, Drew Barrymore, Matthew McConaughey

Three very different women share a car going west. During their road trip they go on a journey of self-discovery, but best of all they find they have each other. Parker plays a young uptight and conservative woman dying of AIDS, Barrymore is an impetuous, light-hearted white heterosexual and Goldberg is a black lesbian who has fallen in love with Parker. When Parker's illness worsens, they settle in a small town and make a life for themselves.

Prod Comp: Alcor Films, Hera Productions, Le Studio Canal+, Regency Enterprises
Dist/Sales: ReelMovies, ACMI, Warner, Swank

Brad

Noyce, Phillip
1977; Australia; 10 min; Drama
P: Tom Manefield; *C:* Mike Edols

Brad identifies as a homosexual. His mother expresses her feelings about Brad's sexuality. Brad is shown in his employment at a service station, and enjoying himself socially.

Prod Comp: Film Australia; *Dist/Sales:* NFVLS, ACMI

Bradfords Tour America, The

Morgan, U. B. / Nunn, Jan
1999; USA; 60 min; Documentary

This brave, sometimes frightening and blackly humorous mockumentary follows the adventures of

US queer filmmakers U. B. Morgan and Jann Nunn as they assume identities as a nice married Christian couple, Mr and Mrs Robert Bradford, and set off for a three week tour infiltrating America's religious right and obtaining video footage of outspoken homophobic rhetoric. Their video diary includes a visit to Jerry Falwell's church, The Jesse Helms Centre, the ghost town that was Jim and Tammy Faye Bakker's Heritage USA, and a private meeting with 'Reverend' Fred Phelps.

Brandon Teena Story, The

Muska, Susan / Olafsdottir, Greta
1997; USA; 90 min; Documentary
P: Susan Muska; *W:* Susan Muska, Greta Olafsdottir; *C:* Susan Muska; *E:* Susan Muska, Greta Olafsdottir

The documentary behind the Oscar winning feature film *Boys Don't Cry*. Based on a true story, *The Brandon Teena Story* traces the last few weeks in the life of the real-life Brandon Teena, who arrived in Falls City Nebraska in 1993. The revelation of Brandon's 'true' gender set off a chain of brutal events which culminated in Teena's horrific rape and murder at the hands of his girlfriend's brother. (MQFF)

Prod Comp: Bless Bless Productions
Dist/Sales: Zeitgeist, Wolfe, FilmsTransit, ACMI

Break of Day

Hannam, Ken
1977; Australia; 112 min; Drama
P: Patricia Lovell, Cliff Green; *W:* Cliff Green; *C:* Russell Boyd; *E:* Max Lemon; *M:* George Dreyfus
Cast: Sara Kestelman, Andrew McFarlane, Ingrid Mason, Tony Barry, John Bell

At the centre of this romantic drama set in a small Victorian rural community is the relationship between an older woman and a discontented returned soldier. She is a bisexual artist, escaping from city life, he is troubled by traumatic memories of combat at Gallipoli a few years earlier.

Prod Comp: Clare Beach Films
Dist/Sales: NFVLS, Roadshow, ACMI

Breaking the Code

Wise, Herbert
1997; UK; 90 min; Drama
P: Jack Emery; *W:* Hugh Whitemore; *C:* Robin Vidgeon; *E:* Laurence Mery-Clark
Cast: Derek Jacobi, Harold Pinter, Prunella Scales, Alun Armstrong

A biography of the English mathematician Alan Turing, who was one of the inventors of the digital computer and one of the key figures in the breaking of the Enigma code, used by the Germans to send secret orders to their U-boats in World War II. Turing was also a homosexual in Britain at a time when it was illegal. (Video Americain)

Prod Comp: BBC, The Drama House
Dist/Sales: BBC, VideoAmericain

Breaking the Silence

Chait, Melanie
1985; UK; 66 min; Documentary

This film gives voice to a variety of women of varying ages, races and class backgrounds who have had children. Some were lesbians when they decided to have children, others became lesbians after being involved in heterosexual relationships. As lesbian mothers they all have to learn to cope with living in a hostile society, with the ever-present possibility of losing their children (if they still have them), their lovers or their work.

Dist/Sales: Cinenova, BFI

Breaking the Surface

Stern, Steven Hilliard
1996; USA; 95 min; Drama
P: Mark Bacino; *W:* Alan Hines; *C:* Michael Slovis; *E:* Peter Svab; *M:* Richard Bellis
Cast: Mario Lopez, Michael Murphy, Rosemary Dunsmore, Jeffrey Meek

Seoul Olympics, 1988: Greg Louganis, while plunging towards the water, hits the diving board cutting his head open. Splashing into the water Greg begins to have flashbacks: Being ridiculed by the other neighbourhood children and his own unaccepting, overbearing father; winning an Olympic silver medal; the 1982 world champion-ship; two gold medals in Los Angeles; the struggles of an abusive relationship with Tom Barrett; his father's terminal cancer; Tom's losing battle with AIDS and Greg's own HIV-positive status. After doctors in Seoul stitch Greg's head wound, he returns to competition and picks up two more gold medals. After his dad's death and Tom's lost AIDS' battle, Greg courageously decides to go public with every aspect of his life. (Wolfe)

Prod Comp: Green/Epstein Productions
Dist/Sales: Wolfe, VideoAmericain

Breaking up Really Sucks

McGlone, Jennifer
2001; USA; 11 min; Comedy

From infatuation to the U-haul move-in to boredom and back again, this clever comedy sends up the foibles and follies of lesbian romance and one woman's search for true love. With *Baywatch*'s Alexandra Paul. (2002 Miami Gay & Lesbian Film Festival)

Brian Epstein Story, The

Wall, Anthony
1998; UK; 140 min; Documentary
P: Anthony Wall; *W:* Jon Savage; *C:* Luke Cardiff, Louise Caulfield; *E:* Guy Crossman, Roy Deverell

This BBC documentary about the notorious manager of The Beatles, a man whom Paul McCartney calls 'The Fifth Beatle', is a well-rounded look into the man behind the band which deals in part with his life as a gay man and Jew.

Prod Comp: BBC
Dist/Sales: BBC-Arena

Bright Eyes

Marshall, Stuart
1984; UK; 85 min; Documentary

Produced for Britain's Channel 4, this is one of the earliest films to deal with the AIDS crisis. It not only examines the historical facts but also deals with the emotional aspects. It shows how the media, partly due to its homophobia, ignored or badly handled early information about the disease.

Prod Comp: Channel 4
Dist/Sales: VDB

Bright Spell

(aka: L'Embellie)

Erreca, Jean-Baptiste
2000; France; 30 min; B&W; Drama
W: Jean-Baptiste Erreca

Saïd and Noria compete for the attention and affections of their adopted brother Karim when he returns from some time away from the family. Karim also has a secret he is anxious to keep to himself.

Dist/Sales: NoSacrifice

Brincando el Charco: Portrait of a Puerto Rican

Negrón-Muntaner, Frances
1994; USA; 55 min; Documentary

A film portrait of Claudia Marin, a Puerto Rican lesbian living in the United States, who attempts to construct a sense of community.

Dist/Sales: WMM

Britney Baby - One More Time

Boeken, Ludi
2001; USA; 82 min; Comedy

P: Gene Rosow, Richard Glandstein; *W:* Jonathan Bourne; *C:* David Carr-Brown; *E:* Sonja Schenck; *M:* Alexander Bubenheim
Cast: Mark Borchardt, Angel Benton, Mike Schank, Shannon Walker Williams

When an up-and-coming young filmmaker gets bounced off a shoot with teen-diva Britney Spears, he gloms on to the gay winner of a local Britney-lookalike contest. Hitting the road on the heels of the real pop-queen, Dude sends footage of his Britney-in-drag back to homebase—until the whole sorry masquerade inevitably starts to crumble. A loopy mockumentary spiked with spot-on observations about 'celebrity' docs. (2002 Seattle International Film Festival)

Prod Comp: Hungry Eye Lowland Pictures, Raphael Films
Dist/Sales: R&BFilms

Broadcast Tapes of Dr Peter, The

Paperny, David
1993; Canada; 45 min; Documentary
P: Arthur Ginsburg; *W:* Peter Jepson-Young; *E:* Arthur Ginsburg

Spanning a two-year period, Dr Peter Jepson-Young (a physician and educator living in Vancouver, British Columbia, who died of AIDS in November 1992), made a series of two-minute videos diaries about his illness and life that were aired weekly on Canadian television. They won widespread appeal and captured the imagination of the country.

Dist/Sales: DirectCinema

Broadway Damage

Mignatti, Victor
1997; USA; 110 min; Comedy
P: David Topel; *W:* Victor Mignatti; *C:* Michael Mayers; *E:* Victor Mignatti; *M:* Elliot Sokolov
Cast: Mara Hobel, Michael Lucas, Hugh Panaro, Aaron Williams

In an age when cynicism is considered cool, New York City is the perfect backdrop for three determined friends attempting to take the town by storm. Marc dreams of his big Broadway break, songwriter Robert dreams of Marc, and 'shop-a-holic' Cynthia dreams of landing her fantasy job at the top. When reality intervenes, the fun begins in this tale of unrequited love and relentless optimism. (Wolfe)

Prod Comp: Village Art
Dist/Sales: JourDeFete, Wolfe, Millivres

Broadway Melody, The

Beaumont, Harry
1929; USA; 105 min; B&W; Comedy, Musical

P: Irving Thalberg, Lawrence Weingarten; *W:* Norman Houston, Edmund Goulding, James Gleason; *C:* John Arnold; *E:* Sam S. Zimbalist; *M:* Herb Nacio Brown, Arthur Freed
Cast: Eddie Kline, Charles King, Bessie Love, Anita Page

An MGM musical about a romantic triangle involving two sisters and a song-and-dance man. A costume designer is the target of sexual innuendo as he flits around the set with his hands forever in mid-air.

Awards: Academy Awards, 1929: Best Film
Prod Comp: MGM
Dist/Sales: MGM

Broken Branches

(aka: Naeil Ui Hyahae Hurunun Kang)

Park, Jae-ho
1995; South Korea; 95 min; Drama
P: Sang-boem Kim; *W:* Jae-ho Park; *C:* Seung-ho Park; *E:* Kok-jee Park; *M:* Sang-hyon Cho
Cast: Ye-ryung Kim, Hong-sung Lee, Dae-yun Lee, In-chul Lee

A low-budget independent film that is said to be the first gay film from Korea. The story spans the years from 1955 to the present day and describes, in three chapters, the breakdown of traditional family structures, reflecting also the country's social and political change. The first chapter focuses on the feudal family in the sixties and the children rebelling against its patriarchal system. The second shows the decline of the father figure, and the third shows the narrator's attempts at a relationship with a married man.

Prod Comp: SamWoo Media Centre
Dist/Sales: KMPPC

Broken Goddess

Dallas, Peter
1969; USA; 29 min; B&W; Experimental
Cast: Holly Woodlawn

A rare underground short featuring Warhol superstar Holly Woodlawn. A beautiful black-and-white salute to both silent films and the Woodlawn image, the film is camp in the richest sense with Holly lounging besides fountains while Debussy plays in the background.

Broken Hearts Club: A Romantic Comedy, The

Berlanti, Greg
2000; USA; 95 min; Comedy
P: Mickey Liddell, Joseph Middleton; *W:* Greg Berlanti; *C:* Paul Elliott; *E:* Todd Busch; *M:* Christophe Beck

Cast: Timothy Olyphant, Dean Cain, Zach Braff, John Mahoney

A group of gay friends in West Hollywood have gathered together to celebrate the 28th birthday of Denis, a promising photographer. Among the boys are Denis's actor house mate, Cole, the cynical Patrick, drama-queen Taylor, and Jack, the surrogate mother to them all. Friendships are put to the test when tragedy strikes the group, resulting in unexpected changes for all of the characters. A 21st century *Boys in the Band*, the film explores and celebrates contemporary gay life in the West Hollywood ghetto. (MQFF)

Prod Comp: Banner Entertainment, Meanwhile Films
Dist/Sales: SonyClassics, Col-Tri, Wolfe, 10%

Bubbeh Lee and Me

Wilson, Andy Abrahams
1996; USA; 35 min; Comedy
W: Andy Abrahams Wilson

This Emmy-nominated documentary is an hilarious portrait of an extraordinary, ordinary Jewish grandmother and a touching account of her grandson's search for his place in the world. For her filmmaker grandson, a young gay man born to a Jewish mother and Protestant father, 87-year-old Bubbeh Lee is a vital link to self and cultural identity, and to unconditional love and acceptance. As the two of them relate feelings of love lost or hidden, kibbitz about strategies for shopping, and avoid meddling matchmakers, the strength of their bond emerges. (Open Eye)

Dist/Sales: OpenEye, NewDay

Bubbles Galore!

Roberts, Cynthia
1996; Canada; 93 min; Comedy
P: Greg Klymkiw; *W:* Cynthia Roberts, Greg Klymkiw; *C:* Harald Bachmann; *E:* Cynthia Roberts, Su Rynard, Sarah Peddie; *M:* Nicholas Stirling
Cast: Nina Hartley, Annie Sprinkle, Tracy Wright, Daniel MacIvor

A porn superstar falls for naive ingenue Dory Drawers and considers her for her next film—against the advice of her assistant Vivian, who argues that a virgin can't possibly be convincing in a porn film. Bubbles decides to give Dory a personal crash course in the sexual arts, upsetting Vivian, who harbours a secret crush on Bubbles. All hell breaks loose when rival porn kingpin Godfrey Montana hatches a plan to kill the women in order to make a snuff film. Some divine intervention is required from God, (played by Annie Sprinkle in a droll cameo) who has been overseeing proceedings all the while. More erotica than narrative, *Bubbles Galore!* successfully revamps the whole porn genre—moody montage sequences replace the moaning, groaning crotch close-ups, and the narrative, such as it is, focuses on women's love. (MQFF)

Dist/Sales: Showcase

Buck House

Cummins, Stephen / Hindmarsh, Gary / Wells, Brendon
1993; Australia; 18 x 20 min; Drama, Comedy
Cast: Jude Kuring, Anthony Hunt, Madeline Bridgett, Glen McKenzie, Elizabeth Tolley

A series of programs, in a soap-opera style, that centre on the comings and goings of a gay boarding house in Sydney. With all the drama, comedy and pathos expected from intertwining and complex relationships.

Prod Comp: Buck House, National Audio Visual Archives

Buckeye and Pinto

Pinder, Phil
1979; Australia; 29 min; B&W; Comedy
P: Tim Isaacson; *C:* Nino Martinetti
Cast: Mitchell Faircloth, Simon Thorpe

A spoof on American westerns that does not ignore the homosexual subtext. A film about men and their problems. A tale of two cowpokes who ride across the United States of Australia. Together they shoot everything that moves as they make their way from Syd Francisco to the Kingaroy badlands and Miss Kitty.

Prod Comp: Experimental Film & Television Fund
Dist/Sales: NFVLS

Buddies

Bressan Jnr, Arthur J.
1985; USA; 80 min; Drama
P: Arthur J. Bressan Jnr; *W:* Arthur J. Bressan Jnr;
C: Carl Teitelbaum; *E:* Arthur J. Bressan Jnr; *M:* Jeffery Olmstead
Cast: David Shachter, Geoff Edholm, Billy Lux, David Rose

A gay activist suffering from AIDS starts out hating the yuppie volunteer who comes to take care of him out of a sense of duty, but their brief relationship is both poignant and intense. One of the first narrative feature films to deal with the AIDS crisis in a very personal way.

Prod Comp: Film and Video Workshop
Dist/Sales: FilmsInc, Salzgeber, NewLine, BFI

Bugis Street

(aka: Yao jie huang hou)

Yonfan
1994; Singapore; 100 min; Drama
P: Katy Yew; *W:* Yonfan, Fruit Chan, Yuo Chan;
C: Jacky Tang; *E:* Ma Kam; *M:* Chris Babida
Cast: Hiep Thi Le, Michael Lam, Benedict Goh, Greg-O, Ernest, Gerald Chen

Set during the 1960s in Singapore, when Bugis Street was the centre for drag clubs and transvestite prostitution. The story centres on Lian, a young 16-year-old from Malacca, who gets a job as a receptionist at the Sin-Sin Hotel. It's the home of a gaggle of drag queens, all of whom have stories of broken hearts and drunken sailors. Lian learns more about life, lipstick and eyeliner than most—mainly from Drago, a Paris-based drag queen, back in town to look after her ailing mother.

Prod Comp: Jaytex Productions
Dist/Sales: Margin, VideoAmericain

Bugis Street

Bungee Jumping of their Own

(aka: Beonjijeonpeureul hada)

Kim, Dae-seung
2000; Korea; 99 min; Drama
P: Nak-kwon Choi; *W:* Eun-nim Ko; *C:* Hu-kon Lee;
E: Yu-kyeong Park
Cast: Byeong-heon Lee, Eun-ju Lee, Su-hyeon Hong, Hyun-soo Yea

When In-woo shares his umbrella with Tae-hee during a rainstorm in 1983, he falls hopelessly in love with her. So begins this unusual film, which was a box office hit in South Korea in 2001. In-woo is so dumbstruck that it takes him a while to figure out that Tae-hee has fallen in love, too. All he knows is he'll do anything for her—like pretending to be a smoker just because she gave him a lighter as a gift. On the night they finally go to a motel room to consummate their love, she promises to stay with him forever. But then she mysteriously disappears. Seventeen years later, In-woo is a married teacher riding herd on a classroom of boisterous boys. But this semester, something is different. There's something about one of his students, a boy named Hyun-bin... something that keeps taking In-woo back to the past. Soon In-woo is making odd late-night phone calls to the boy and fighting the urge to touch him in class. After a series of strange coincidences, In-woo begins to fear for his own sanity. And his students, co-workers and wife are starting to wonder as well. When Hyun-bin finally confronts his teacher and demands to know what is going on, things really begin to fall apart—only to fall back together again—in this tragic love story. In the end, student and teacher are united, if only in their conviction that true love can transcend anything, even death. (26th San Francisco International Lesbian & Gay Film Festival) Korean with English subtitles.

Prod Comp: Noon Entertainment
Dist/Sales: Cineclick

Burlesk King

Chionglo, Mel
1999; Philippines; 109 min; Drama
P: Robbie Tan; *W:* Ricardo Lee; *C:* George Tutanes;
E: Jess Navarro; *M:* Nonong Buencamino
Cast: Rodel Velayo, Nini Jacinto, Leonardo Litton, Raymond Bagatsing

At the rough end of male desire, *Burlesk King* does for South-East Asian cinema what films such as *Happiness* have done for middle America. Harry, a young Filipino–American, comes to Manila to look for his father and avenge his mother's death. Given his own troubled past—his father used to pimp him—Harry soon resettles into Manila's underbelly. He finds love in a friend, James, and Brenda, a superstitious teenage hooker. When James is killed by rival thugs, Harry starts pimping Brenda but realises he is mimicking his father's ways. Eventually he finds his father—dying of AIDS in a squatter's shack—who tells him the truth about his mother. *Burlesk King* is a powerhouse drama with wide-reaching currency. That films such as this are infrequently exported from the Philippines is testimony to its potency. (MQFF)
English & Tagalog with English subtitles.

Prod Comp: Seiko Films
Dist/Sales: Fortissimo, Strand, Wolfe

Burning Boy, The

Galvin, Kieran
2000; Australia; 12 min; Drama

Get Real meets *Head On* in this powerful and controversial drama of a teenage boy torn by his lust for a fellow classmate. A disturbing film for anyone who has been 16, in love and in the closet. (MQFF)

Burning Secret

Birkin, Andrew
1988; Germany, UK, USA; 106 min; Drama
P: Norma Heyman, Eberhard Junkersdorf; *W:* Andrew Birkin; *C:* Ernest Day; *E:* Paul Green; *M:* Hans Zimmer
Cast: Faye Dunaway, Klaus Maria Brandauer, David Eberts, Ian Richardson

While recuperating in a sanatorium in the mountains, a young boy becomes very close friends with an older baron. But the baron is only using the boy to get to know his mother, the wife of an older diplomat. When the boy realises the baron's intentions, he becomes jealous, moody and depressed. Queer audiences will spot the underlying homosexual subtext to the relationship between the boy and the baron.

Prod Comp: NFH, BA, CLG
Dist/Sales: Col-Tri

Burnt Money

Burnt Money
(aka: Plata Quemada; Burning Money)

Pineyro, Marcelo
2000; Argentina, France, Spain, Uruguay; 125 min; Drama
P: Oscar Kramer; *W:* Marcelo Pineyro, Marcelo Figueras; *C:* Alfredo F. Mayo; *E:* Juan Carlos Macías;
M: Osvaldo Montes
Cast: Leonardo Sbaraglia, Eduardo Noriega, Pablo Echarri, Letica Brédice

Set in Argentina in 1965, *Burnt Money* is based on the true story of the ruthless bank-robbing duo, Nene and Angel. Everyone calls them 'Los Mellizos'

b

(the twins), but they are actually lovers: lethal, thieving lovers. It's the story of a doomed relationship, confined to four rooms where intense passion and violence push the extremes. They flee from Argentina across the border to Uruguay after a large-scale hold-up turns bloody. With the cops closing in, the two lovers must confront their demons to survive. (Mongrel)
Spanish with English subtitles.

Dist/Sales: Strand, Mongrel, Wolfe

Bus Riley's Back in Town

Hart, Harvey
1965; USA; 93 min; Drama
P: Elliot Kastner; *W:* William Inge; *C:* Russell Metty; *E:* Folmar Blangsted; *M:* Richard Markowitz
Cast: Michael Parks, Ann-Margret, David Carradine, Janet Margolin, Brad Dexter

Bus Riley returns to his small town after time in the army. On his return, his ex-girlfriend wants to resume their relationship. The only problem is she has married in the mean time. Searching for fulfilment in his life, Bus decides to get a job with his gay friend who is a mortician. When the mortician makes a pass at him, Bus quickly gets out.

Prod Comp: Universal
Dist/Sales: Universal

Business of Fancydancing, The

Alexie, Sherman
2002; USA; 85 min; Drama
P: Larry Estes, Scott Rosenfelt; *W:* Sherman Alexie; *C:* Holly Taylor; *E:* Holly Taylor
Cast: Evan Adams, Michelle St John, Gene Tagaban, Swil Kanim

Famed author Sherman Alexie, whose stories were adapted in the 1998 arthouse hit *Smoke Signals*, makes his directorial debut with this complex and poetic drama focusing on the emotional reunion of former best friends. Seymour and Aristotle were best friends on the Spokane Indian Reservation growing up, but parted ways unhappily during college. Seymour embraced the advantages offered by white society, becoming a celebrated poet offering pre-packaged 'Native American wisdom' to a guilty white-liberal readership, and holding himself up as a spokesman for all Indians. Aristotle, meanwhile, floundered, returning to the reservation. Now, sixteen years later, the death of a childhood friend forces Seymour to leave his white lover, Steven, and head back to the reservation to confront his past and the choices that separated him from his friends and family. (2002 New York Lesbian & Gay Film Festival)

Prod Comp: FallsApart Productions
Dist/Sales: WelbFilm

Busting

Hyams, Peter
1974; USA; 89 min; Drama
P: Irwin Winkler, Robert Chartoff; *W:* Peter Hyams; *C:* Earl Rath; *E:* James Mitchell; *M:* Billy Goldenberg
Cast: Elliott Gould, Robert Blake, Allen Garfield, Antonio Fargas

Two Los Angeles vice squad officers find themselves up against their corrupt superiors when they try bringing a crime boss to justice. During the course of their investigation, the two cops disguise themselves as gays and raid a gay bar. When the gays refuse to go quietly, a riot ensues. One of the most homophobic and offensive films to come out of Hollywood in the 1970s.

Prod Comp: United Artists, Chartoff-Winkler Productions
Dist/Sales: ReelMovies, Warner, UA

But I was a Girl: The Story of Frieda Belinfante

Boumans, Toni
1998; The Netherlands; 69 min; Documentary
P: Bernard Neuhaus; *W:* Toni Boumans; *C:* Maarten Kramer

But I Was a Girl tells the story of Frieda Belinfante (1905–1995), a remarkable woman who was the first female conductor to have her own symphony orchestra, first in Holland and later in Orange County, California. Controversial, because of her sexuality, she showed a remarkably strong and positive will in everything she did. Born in a family of musicians in Amsterdam, she joined the resistance during World War II, then later fled to Switzerland. After the war she moved to the US where she resumed her musical career in the Hollywood studios, and formed her own symphony orchestra with Hollywood musicians. The story of Frieda's life is told by herself, her older sister Renee, old students and friends, and illustrated by the places she lived, archive materials of her orchestras and some of her most beautiful music. (First Run/Icarus)
Dutch with English subtitles.

Prod Comp: Frame Media Productions
Dist/Sales: Neter, FirstRun/Icarus

But, I'm a Cheerleader

Babbit, Jamie
1999; USA; 85 min; Comedy
P: Andrea Sperling, Leanna Creel; *W:* Brian Wayne Peterson; *C:* Jules Labarthe; *E:* Cecily Rhett; *M:* Pat Irwin
Cast: Natasha Lyonne, RuPaul Charles, Cathy Moriarty, Mink Stole, Clea Du Vall

There's a high belly laugh quota in this hilarious tale of a high school cheerleader whose suspect sexuality sees her sent off to a 'rehabilitation' camp run by Mike. Megan's parents are concerned by her attachment to Melissa Etheridge, Tofu and her lack of passion for her high school jock boyfriend. High camp hysterics and sorority house hi-jinks ensue once Megan arrives at 'True Directions' where she finds herself amongst a choice collection of up-and-coming queers. Will any of the group make it to hetero graduation? (MQFF)

Prod Comp: Ignite Entertainment, Kushner-Locke, HKM Films
Dist/Sales: Kushner-Locke, LionsGate, Wolfe, VideoAmericain, Swank, 10%

Butch Camp

De Gaetano, Alessandro
1997; USA; 101 min; Comedy
P: Steve Gellman, Timothy E. Sabo; *W:* Alessandro De Gaetano; *E:* Amy Harvey
Cast: Judy Tenuta, Paul Denniston, Jason Teresi, Jordan Roberts, Bill Ingraham

Matt Grabowski is a twenty-something sensitive gay man who has been put down one too many times. He's mad as hell and he's not going to take it anymore! Sam Rottweiller is an ageing sex God turned neo-fascist commandant who kicks butt at Butch Camp, a hysterical pseudo S/M style boot camp training centre for gay men to learn macho survival tactics. Matt and his fellow new recruits are guaranteed a masculine makeover of body, mind and soul. (Wolfe)

Dist/Sales: Wolfe, VideoAmericain

Butcher's Wife, The

Hughes, Terry
1991; USA; 101 min; Comedy
P: Wallis Nicita, Lauren Lloyd; *W:* Marjorie Schwartz, Ezra Litwak; *C:* Frank Tidy; *E:* Donn Cambern; *M:* Michael Gore, Steven Jae Johnson
Cast: Demi Moore, Jeff Daniels, George Dzundza, Frances McDormand

A country clairvoyant, played by Demi Moore, transfers a New York neighbourhood into a wondrous place of romantic awakenings and brings a sceptical psychiatrist under her spell. She begins dispensing advice to a lesbian boutique owner, a spinsterish choir director, a soap opera actress and others.

Prod Comp: Paramount
Dist/Sales: Paramount

Butley

Pinter, Harold
1974; Canada, UK, USA; 130 min; Drama
P: Ely A. Landau; *W:* Simon Gray; *C:* Gerry Fisher; *E:* Malcolm Cooke
Cast: Alan Bates, Richard O'Callaghan, Jessica Tandy, Susan Engel

Butley is set in Queen Mary's College, London and focuses on two English instructors, Ben Butley, a middle-aged former T. S. Eliot expert whose life is now in a shambles, and his protégé, Joey, a homosexual. With both Joey and his wife leaving, Butley faces a life alone, fighting back with wit, obscenity and booze.

Prod Comp: Landau, American Express

Butter & Pinches

Matthews, Mary C.
2000; USA; 15 min; Comedy

Meet Butter & Pinches—eccentric, oddball, lesbian detectives... without a clue.

Dist/Sales: Butter&Pinches

Butterflies on the Scaffold

(aka: Mariposas en el Andiamo)

Bernaza, Lius Felipe / Gilpin, Margaret
1996; Cuba; 70 min; Documentary
P: Margaret Gilpin; *W:* Luis Felipe Bernaza, Margaret Gilpin; *C:* Raúl Pérez Ureta; *E:* Luis Felipe Bernaza

A remarkable documentary about how the local citizens of a neighbourhood in Havana have befriended and accepted into their hearts, the drag queens and the drag subculture of the ghettos. Structured around interviews with the drag queens and locals, it tells how several powerful women on the new local government decided to support rather than suppress the drag culture, and asked them to perform at a café where the local workers eat. Spanish with English subtitles.

Prod Comp: Kangaroo Productions
Dist/Sales: WaterBearer, VideoAmericain

Butterfly Kiss

Winterbottom, Michael
1995; UK; 85 min; Thriller
P: Julie Baines, Sarah Daniel; *W:* Frank Cottrell Boyce; *C:* Seamus McGarvey; *E:* Trevor Waite; *M:* John Harle
Cast: Amanda Plummer, Saskia Reeves, Paul Brown, Kathy Jamieson, Des McAleer

Eunice is a dangerously unstable young woman who

b

is roaming the countryside looking for her girlfriend, Judith. While hitchhiking the motorways of northern England, passing through towns and cities scarred by decade-long recession and unemployment, she meets Miriam, a shy introverted woman who finds in Eunice the first person who has ever taken her seriously. Told in flashback by Miriam as she is interrogated by the police, *Butterfly Kiss*, is a powerful and disturbing examination of the psychologies of two people left discarded by the economic and social policies of Thatcherite Britain. A huge chasm emerges between the love shared by the two women for each other and the hatred and bitterness they share against a social order which ignores their existence and their desires. Though Eunice is obviously psychologically ill, Michael Winterbottom refuses any easy psychological or moral conclusions. For an audience torn between the intimate generosity shared between the two women, and the bloody results of their murderous rampage, the film proves both emotionally moving and intellectually confronting. (ACMI)

Prod Comp: British Screen, Dan Films, Lions Gate Films
Dist/Sales: Wolfe, Cowboy, FirstRunFeatures, ACMI

By Design

Jutra, Claude
1981; Canada, USA; 91 min; Comedy
P: Beryl Fox, Werner Aellen; *W:* David Eames, Claude Jutra, Joe Weisenfeld; *C:* Jean Boffety; *E:* Tony Trow, Ralph Rosenblum; *M:* Chico Hamilton
Cast: Patty Duke Astin, Sara Botsford, Saul Rubinek, Sonia Zimmer

Helen and Angela are fashion designers, business partners and lovers. They decide to have a child but are rejected by the adoption agency and have to make other plans. What follows are humorous attempts to find the right donor. They finally decide on Terry, a photographer, but things turn out differently than expected. Some very touching moments are handled well and with sensitivity.

Prod Comp: Atlantic, BDF Productions, Fox, Seven Arts Productions, Canadian Film Development Corporation

By Hook or by Crook

Dodge, Harry / Howard, Silas
2001; USA; 95 min; Drama
P: Steak House, Silas Howard, Harry Dodge; *W:* Silas Howard, Harry Dodge; *C:* Ann T. Rossetti; *E:* Silas Howard, Harry Dodge; *M:* Carla Bozulich
Cast: Silas Howard, Harry Dodge, Stanya Kahn, Carina Gia, Cash Askew, Joan Jett

By Hook or by Crook is a riveting and intimate portrayal of life in the queer mecca. Small-town Shy has big-town aspirations and hitches to San Francisco, determined to make a life out of petty crime. Along the way Shy stumbles into Valentine, the irrepressible and loveable eccentric who is on a quest to find her birth mother. The two join forces, and as they steal and grift their way through life they forge a friendship that is as unpredictable and unexpected as their characters. Shy, whose name says it all, struggles with a constant urge to fly, while the volatile and touchingly fragile Valentine unwittingly keeps Shy grounded. With wonderful performances and deft characterisation, San Francisco-based performance artists and directors Harry Dodge and Silas Howard have crafted this unique urban tale of friendship, trust and heroism with assurance and originality. Poignant and unforgettable, this is a story of misfits who subvert their stereotypes to confront their own truths like you've never seen before.

Prod Comp: Steakhaus Productions & NGB
Dist/Sales: Howard, Wolfe

By Hook or by Crook

By the Dawn's Early Light

Vesterskov, Knud
1993; Denmark; 77 min; Documentary

Road movie about the life of the writer, junkie, hustler, and artist David Wojnarowicz.

c-l-o-s-e-r

Mosvold, Frank
1997; Norway; 15 min; Drama

The spiky bud of love breaks through the fragments of a murky, muted colourless day in the life of a Police Captain father and his queer punk son.

Dist/Sales: NorwegianFilm

Cabaret

Fosse, Bob
1972; USA; 123 min; Drama, Musical
P: Cy Feuer; *W:* Hugh Wheeler, Jay Presson Allen;
C: Geoffrey Unsworth; *E:* David Bretherton;

M: Ralph Burns, John Kander
Cast: Liza Minnelli, Michael York, Helmut Griem, Joel Grey, Fritz Wepper

Stylish film based on the Fred Ebbjohn Kander Broadway musical, from John van Druten's play *I Am a Camera*. The story centres around nightclub singer Sally Bowles in pre-Second World War Berlin. The film also depicts the rise of the Nationalists and Fascism. York portrays Brian (the alter ego of openly gay writer Christopher Isherwood and based on his Berlin stories), a bisexual who is swept off his feet by the wealthy and debonair Maximillian.

Awards: Academy Awards, 1972: Best Actress (Liza Minnelli), Best Picture
Prod Comp: ABC Pictures, Allied Artists, American Broadcasting Company
Dist/Sales: ACMI, AlliedArtists, BFI, Warner, Wolfe

Cage aux Folles, La

Molinaro, Edouard
1978; France, Italy; 91 min; Comedy
P: Marcello Danon; *W:* Edouard Molinaro, Francis Veber, Marcello Danon, Jean Poiret; *C:* Armando Nannuzzi; *E:* Monique Isnardon, Robert Isnardon; *M:* Ennio Morricone
Cast: Ugo Tognazzi, Michel Serrault, Michel Galabru, Claire Maurier

The film's title refers to the name of a nightclub run by a pair of homosexual lovers, Renato and Albin. Albin is a renowed female impersonator. When Renato's son, from a heterosexual fling, decides to marry the daughter of a respectable official and a moral campaigner, her family wants to meets his. Some high camp comedy ensues when they decide to become 'respectable' themselves and Albin becomes 'Mother'. Based on the play by Jean Poiret. Very funny high camp romp but some subtle humour is lost due to the subtitling. French with English subtitles.

Prod Comp: United Artists France, Da Ma, Les Productions Artistes Associés
Dist/Sales: Warner, MGM, UA, ACMI, Swank

Cage aux Folles II, La

Molinaro, Edouard
1980; France; 100 min; Comedy
P: Marcello Danon; *W:* Francis Veber, Marcello Danon; *C:* Armando Nannuzzi, Luciano Tovoli; *E:* Robert Isnardon; *M:* Ennio Morricone
Cast: Ugo Tognazzi, Michel Serrault, Gianni Frisoni

The lives of Renato and Albin take an unusual turn when they become entangled in an international espionage ring and must deal with problems in their club. This high camp sequel to *La Cage aux Folles* is

often funny and with lots of twists. French with English subtitles.

Prod Comp: Da Ma Produzione, Les Productions Artistes Associés
Dist/Sales: ReelMovies, Warner, MGM, UA, Swank

Cage aux Folles III, La

Lautner, Georges
1985; France; 91 min; Comedy
P: Marcello Danon; *W:* Michel Audiard, Christine Carère, Marcello Danon, Gérard Lamballe, Georges Lautner, Philippe Nicaud; *C:* Luciano Tovoli; *E:* Michelle David; *M:* Ennio Morricone
Cast: Michel Serrault, Ugo Tognazzi, Antonella Interlenghi, Stephane Audran

In this third instalment of the *La Cage aux Folles* series, female impersonator Albin learns that he is to inherit £10,000,000 providing that he marries and fathers a child within 18 months. Unlike the earlier films, the gags have lost their freshness and the film lacks innovation. French with English subtitles.

Prod Comp: Columbia Films SA, Da Ma Produzione
Dist/Sales: 20thCenturyFox, 16MM

Caged

Cromwell, John
1950; USA; 95 min; B&W; Drama
P: Jerry Wald; *W:* Virginia Kellogg, Bernard Schoenfeld; *C:* Carl Guthrie; *E:* Owen Marks; *M:* Max Steiner
Cast: Eleanor Parker, Ellen Corby, Betty Garde, Agnes Moorehead, Hope Emerson

A naive young woman is sent to prison for helping her no-good husband in a robbery. On the inside she meets a sadistic and closeted prison matron, as well as Kitty, who tries to recruit her as an accomplice on her release. After several tragedies she becomes a hardened criminal. Much better than the usual women-in-prison films, in fact it was nominated for several Academy Awards including best actress.

Prod Comp: Warner
Dist/Sales: Swank, Warner

Caged Fury

Milling, Bill
1990; USA; 95 min; Action
P: Bob Gallagher; *C:* Kenneth Viatrak; *E:* Matthew Mallinson; *M:* Joe Delia
Cast: Erik Estrada, Blake Bahner, Richard Barathy, Roxanna Michaels

Yet another lesbian-behind-bars film. Two young women are en route to Hollywood to seek fame and fortune. But on their arrival in LA they are framed and found guilty of a sex crime they did not

C

commit. They are imprisoned in the Honeywell State Prison for Women where they are not only stripped of their dignity but their clothes as well.

Prod Comp: 21st Century-Fox
Dist/Sales: 21stCentury, Col-Tri

Calamity Jane

Butler, David
1953; USA; 101 min; Comedy, Musical, Western
P: William Jacobs; *W:* James O'Hanlon; *C:* Wilfred Cline; *E:* Irene Morra; *M:* Sammy Fain, Ray Heindorf
Cast: Doris Day, Howard Keel, Allyn McLerie, Phil Carey, Dick Wesson

Doris Day plays the tomboyish, cross-dressing Calamity Jane with great gusto. Her character maintains her sense of independence even while falling for Wild Bill Hickok. There's lots of fun and camp humour in this great musical, and lesbians will delight in creating their very own subtext.

Prod Comp: Warner
Dist/Sales: ACMI

California Suite

Ross, Herbert
1978; USA; 97 min; Comedy
P: Ray Stark; *W:* Neil Simon; *C:* David M. Walsh;
E: Michael A. Stevenson; *M:* Claude Bolling
Cast: Alan Alda, Michael Caine, Jane Fonda, Walter Matthau, Elaine May, Maggie Smith

This interesting drama delves into the personal dilemmas of five couples staying at the Beverly Hills Hotel. Michael Caine plays a bisexual antique dealer married to Maggie Smith, an actress who is in Hollywood for the Academy Awards ceremony. Based on the Broadway hit by Neil Simon.

Prod Comp: Columbia, Rastar
Dist/Sales: ACMI, Columbia

Caligula

Brass, Tinto
1979; Italy, USA; 146 min; Drama
P: Bob Guccione, Franco Rossellini; *W:* Gore Vidal, Bob Guccione; *C:* Silvano Ippoliti; *E:* Nino Baragli;
M: Paul Clemente
Cast: Malcolm McDowell, Teresa Ann Savoy, Peter O'Toole, Helen Mirren, John Steiner

Set in Rome between 37 and 41 AD, the plot follows the rise and fall of the crazed emperor Caligula Caesar. It primarily deals with the decadence and sexual freedom of the time rather than the actual facts. In one scene Caligula deflowers a virgin

and her fiancé just before their marriage. Both Tinto Brass and Gore Vidal took their names off the credits when *Penthouse* publisher Bob Guccione, had finished cutting the film, turning it into a sensationalist soft-porn flick.

Prod Comp: Penthouse, Felix
Dist/Sales: Roadshow

Call me your Girlfriend

Farthing, Cheryl
1992; UK; 20 min; Documentary
Cast: Rita Lynch

A no-holds-barred peek into the world, work and wardrobe of Rita Lynch, leading lesbian poet, singer and songwriter, as she embarks on a national tour of Britain.

Prod Comp: Alfalfa, Channel 4

Call to Witness

Walton, Pam
2000; USA; 60 min; Documentary
P: Pam Walton; *E:* Pam Walton

Every mainstream Protestant denomination in the USA is wrestling with same-sex marriage and the ordination of openly gay and lesbian pastors. *Call to Witness* documents that struggle within the Evangelical Lutheran Church in America. By focusing on the lives and trials of pastors who have taken a stand against their own church, this film explores the intersection of two communities of faith; those who support the ordination of openly gay and lesbian pastors and their committed relationships and those who don't. *Call to Witness* tells the stories of three Midwestern Lutheran pastors—Rev. Steve Sabin in Iowa, who has been outed by his bishop, supported by his congregation, and 'tried' by the national church because he refused to resign; Rev. Jane Ralph in Missouri, who was forced out of the ELCA with no process for recourse; and Pastoral Minister Anita C. Hill in Minnesota, who is working to be ordained as an openly lesbian pastor in the year 2000. (Filmakers Library)

Dist/Sales: FilmakersLibrary

Came out, it Rained, went back in Again

Evans Morris, Betsan
1991; UK; 10 min; Drama
Cast: Jane Horrocks

This short drama explores the perils of coming out as it follows a day in the life of one young lesbian.

Dist/Sales: WMM

Camp

Mead, Wrik
2000; Canada; 14 min; Experimental

Based on real-life experiences, *Camp* recounts the stories of homosexual survivors of World War II concentration camps. A series of short, expressionistic vignettes weave together these horrific experiences. Part documentary, part drama, *Camp* uses a variety of mediums to explore the emotional reality of those marked with the pink triangle. (CFMDC)

Dist/Sales: CFMDC

Camp Lavender Hill

Magnaye, Michael / Shepard, Tom
1997; USA; 28 min; Documentary

Documentary about the first summer camp for children who have gay, lesbian, and bisexual parents, which expresses the point of views of the campers who range in age from 6–15.

Campfire

(aka: Kampvuur)

Defurne, Bavo
1999; Belgium; 20 min; Drama
P: Yves Verbraeken

The temptation of nature takes over two young men when they spend a night alone in the bush. But after their bodies have met in a tangle of sexual exploration, their attitude over the experience is divided. Dutch with English subtitles. (MQFF)

Dist/Sales: Laika

Can I be your Bratwurst, Please?

von Praunheim, Rosa
1999; Germany, USA; 29 min; Comedy

Jeff Stryker (in his first non-porn role) plays a stranger from the Midwest who arrives in Hollywood, rents a motel room and becomes the fantasy of the owner, his mother and all the other guests. Young and old, male and female, black and white—everybody finds him delectable.

Prod Comp: Regina Ziegler Filmproduktion
Dist/Sales: Ziegler

Can't Stop Dancing

Falick, Steven / Zook, Ben
1999; USA; 97 min; Comedy
P: Joseph Merhi, Richard Pepin; *W:* Ben Zook, Steven Falick; *C:* Mac Ahlberg; *E:* Tony Lombardo; *M:* Nick Phoenix, Fred Rapoport
Cast: Ben Zook, Margaret Cho, Janeane Garofalo, Melanie Hutsell, Noah Wyle

When a very untalented group of six dancers and singers are sacked from a Kansas amusement park they decide to head off in a bus to Hollywood on a quest to find fortune and fame. They get one shot at it by performing at the Miss Orange County Beauty Pagent. Will they ever make it and do they have what it takes?

Prod Comp: PM Entertainment, Miramax

Can't Stop the Music

Walker, Nancy
1980; USA; 120 min; Comedy, Musical
P: Allan Carr, Jacques Morali, Henri Belolo;
W: Allan Carr, Bronte Woodward; *C:* Bill Butler;
E: John F. Burnett; *M:* Jacques Morali
Cast: The Village People, Valerie Perrine, Bruce Jenner, Steve Guttenberg

A group of singers played by The Village People join together to break into the music scene. The whole film abounds with gay subtext, with all manner of gay boy in-jokes and camp behaviour.

Prod Comp: AFD, EMI
Dist/Sales: TLA, Swank

Can't you Take a Joke?

Dun, Viki
1989; Australia; 28 min; B&W; Comedy
Cast: Kim Trengove, Melanie Bedde

This delightful, stylish comedy, in which boy meets girl and girl meets girl, uses the romantic music and visuals of Hollywood film noir to explore the ideal of love at first sight. (Cinenova)

Prod Comp: Victoria College of the Arts
Dist/Sales: Cinenova, WMM

Cancer in Two Voices

Phenix, Lucy Massie
1994; USA; 43 min; Documentary

A lesbian couple's eight-year relationship is put under strain when Barbara is diagnosed with breast cancer. Barbara is told she has three years to live, and so she and Sandy document their lives with courage and frankness. The two women talk about their identity as Jewish women and lesbians and speak openly about the difficult issues each is facing. A moving but balanced documentary on love and letting go.

Dist/Sales: WMM

Cap Tourmente

Langlois, Michel
1993; Canada; 112 min; Drama
P: Bernadette Payeur; *W:* Marcel Beaulieu, Michel

Langlois; C: Bernadette Payeur; E: Jean-Claude
Coulbois, Anne Whiteside
Cast: Andrée Lachapelle, Roy Dupuis, Elise Guilbault,
Gilbert Sicotte

A son's return home to his dysfunctional family
deeply affects both his mother and sister. The arrival
of an old lover causes chaos, as all members of this
tense and incestuous foursome struggle with their
inability to commit to each other or to their
individual futures. A first feature for screenwriter
Michel Langlois, this elegantly shot family drama is
austere, maddening and moving, weaving a tangled
web of suppressed passion. (MQFF)
French with English subtitles.

Prod Comp: Association Coopérative des Productions
Audio-Visuelles
Dist/Sales: Cinepix

Car Wash

Schultz, Michael
1976; USA; 97 min; Comedy
P: Gary Stromberg, Art Linson; W: Joel Schumacher;
C: Frank Stanley; E: Christopher Holmes; M: Norman
Whitfield
Cast: Richard Pryor, Franklin Ajaye, Sully Boyar,
George Carlin, Antonio Fargas

A boisterous offbeat farce, primarily staged in a Los
Angeles car wash to the pop music of Rose Royce
and the Pointer Sisters. Antonio Fargas plays the
transvestite, Lindy, who uses the fantastic line
'Honey, I'm more man than you'll ever be and more
woman than you'll ever get'.

Prod Comp: Universal
Dist/Sales: ReelMovies

Caravaggio

Jarman, Derek
1986; Italy, UK; 93 min; Drama
P: Sarah Radclyffe; W: Derek Jarman; C: Gabriel
Beristain; E: George Akers; M: Simon Fisher Turner
Cast: Nigel Terry, Sean Bean, Garry Cooper, Spencer
Leigh, Tilda Swinton

Not a conventional biopic, but the portrait of the
homosexual artist as a 'murderer imaged as a god'.
Caravaggio, according to Jarman, identified with the
murderer in St Matthew. The artist's extreme self
analysis becomes self destruction. In the film the
young painter lies dying, his mind drifting back over
his short life of intense passion, a triangle formed
with two of his models. One was the inspiration for
his repeated portrayal of the assassin in pictures of
martyrdom, the other the model for Mary
Magdalene and the dead virgin. The paintings are
the source of the film's characters as Jarman sought

to bridge the gap of centuries in recreating details of
his own life.

Prod Comp: BFI
Dist/Sales: Col-Tri, NFVLS, ACMI, Cinevista, BFI

Caretaker, The

(aka: The Guest)

Donner, Clive
1964; UK; 105 min; B&W; Drama
P: Michael Birkett; W: Harold Pinter; C: Nicolas Roeg;
E: Fergus McDonell; M: Ron Grainer
Cast: Alan Bates, Robert Shaw, Donald Pleasence

Bates plays the sadistic brother to Shaw, a mentally ill
man who lives in a house owned by Bates. When a
tramp, Pleasence, is invited to stay, he finds himself
moving in and out of favour between the two
brothers. Homosexual undertones abound as the
brothers compete for attention from the tramp,
particularly when the leather-clad Bates does his stuff.

Prod Comp: Caretaker Films
Dist/Sales: Ascanbee

Carmelita Tropicana: Your Kunst is your Waffen

Troyano, Ela
1993; USA; 28 min; Documentary

A Latina performance artist who supports herself as a
building superintendent on New York's Lower East
Side winds up in jail with some riot girls. Humorous
monologues, soapy melodramas, and campy
production numbers ensue. (First Run/Icarus)

Dist/Sales: FirstRun/Icarus, FirstRunFeatures

Carmilla

Beaumont, Gabrielle
1989; USA; 60 min; Horror
W: Sheridan Le Fanu
Cast: Meg Tilly, Roddy McDowall, Roy Dotrice, Ione
Skye

Set in a 19th century mansion, the story centres on
Marie, a lonely young woman. When legendary
vampire Carmilla arrives at the mansion the two
women soon form a bond and a friendship blossoms—before long Carmilla is seducing Marie and
sucking her blood. But all this comes to a swift end
when a famous vampirologist, played by McDowall,
arrives.

Carrington

Hampton, Christopher
1995; France, UK; 122 min; Drama
P: John C. McGrath, Ronald Shedlo; W: Christopher

Hampton; *C:* Denis Lenoir; *E:* George Akers;
M: Michael Nyman
Cast: Emma Thompson, Jonathan Pryce, Steven
Waddington, Samuel West, Rufus Sewell

Dora Carrington devoted her life to the gay writer
Lytton Strachey—a tall, thin, bearded bachelor and
member of London's famed Bloomsbury artistic set.
Even though their desire for each other was strong,
their relationship was based on friendship, a bond
that survived until the very end.

Prod Comp: Gramersy, PolyGram Filmed Entertainment, Le Studio Canal+
Dist/Sales: TLA, PolyGram, Sogepaq

Cass

Noonan, Chris
1978; Australia; 77 min; Drama
P: Don Harley; *W:* Laura Jones; *M:* Rory O'Donoghue
Cast: John Waters, Michele Fawdon, Max Cullen, Peter
Carroll

After making a documentary on tribal women, a
young female filmmaker finds it very difficult to
settle down to life with her husband on her return to
Australia. Her situation becomes even more
problematic when she finds herself attracted to
another woman. Made for television.

Prod Comp: Nine Network, Film Australia
Dist/Sales: NFVLS

Casta Diva

de Kuyper, Eric
1982; The Netherlands; 100 min; B&W; Experimental
W: Eric de Kuyper; *C:* Michel Houssiau; *E:* Ton De Graaf
Cast: Jack Post, Emile Poppe, Paul Verstraten

A celebration of the male form. A series of observations of men, filmed in beautiful black and white,
with an almost total absence of the spoken word.

Castro, The

Stein, Peter
1997; USA; 86 min; Documentary

Fascinating documentary which tells the story of
how a quiet, working-class neighbourhood of
European immigrants transmogrified into what is
now internationally recognised as the mecca of gay
liberation and lifestyle. Brilliant presentation of
archival material and interviews with noted San
Franciscans.

Cat and the Canary, The

Metzger, Radley
1979; UK; 98 min; Comedy
P: Richard Gordon; *W:* Radley Metzger;

C: Alex Thomson; *M:* Steven Cagan
Cast: Honor Blackman, Michael Callan, Edward Fox,
Olivia Hussey

Glencliff Manor, 1934...a dark and stormy night.
The family of a recently deceased, eccentric
millionaire has been summoned for the reading of
his final will and testament. Joining this group of
eight is an unexpected visitor: the chief psychologist
from the local mental hospital who is searching for a
dangerous criminal escapee from the psychiatric
ward! So turn off the lights, snuggle up to your loved
one, and get ready for a horrific night of suspense,
mystery and murder! (First Run Features)

Dist/Sales: FirstRunFeatures

Cat Nip

Taylor, Amanda
1994; USA; 14 min; B&W; Experimental
P: Amanda Taylor; *W:* Amanda Taylor; *C:* Amanda
Taylor

The age-old and often mythical relationships
between lesbians and their cats are whimsically
explored in this short film.

Prod Comp: Rocketgirl Productions

Cat on a Hot Tin Roof

Brooks, Richard
1958; USA; 104 min; Drama
P: Lawrence Weingarten; *W:* Richard Brooks, James
Poe; *C:* William Daniels; *E:* Ferris Webster
Cast: Elizabeth Taylor, Paul Newman, Burl Ives, Judith
Anderson, Jack Carson

In this original film version, the censors stepped in
and made the filmmakers remove all references to
homosexuality. The character played by Newman
becomes weak and insipid rather than a man dealing
with his sexual identity. The patriarch of the family
learns he is dying and his family visit him, some out
of greed, others to make their peace. Newman and
Taylor are a young married couple whose relationship is deeply troubled after the death of his closest
friend. Based on the play by Tennessee Williams.

Prod Comp: MGM, Avon
Dist/Sales: Chapel, ACMI, MGM

Cat People

Tourneur, Jacques
1942; USA; 73 min; B&W; Horror
P: Val Lewton; *W:* DeWitt Bodeen; *C:* Nicholas
Musuraca; *E:* Mark Robson; *M:* Roy Webb
Cast: Simone Simon, Kent Smith, Tom Conway, Jack
Holt, Jane Randolph

Irena, a New York fashion artist, believes she

C

descended from Serbian witches who could turn themselves into cats. She becomes obsessed with the fear that if she makes love to her husband she will undergo the same transformation. Ambiguity and restraint abound as it becomes unclear whether Irena is undergoing a supernatural metamorphosis, or whether she may be a lonely, neurotic, possibly lesbian woman driven to violence by her obsessive fears.

Prod Comp: RKO
Dist/Sales: NFVLS, ACMI

Cat Swallows Parakeet and Speaks!

Pietrobruno, Ileana
1996; Canada; 75 min; Experimental
P: Ileana Pietrobruno; *W:* Ileana Pietrobruno; *C:* John Houtman; *E:* Ileana Pietrobruno
Cast: Alex Ferguson, Rebecca Godin, Tara Frederick, Christine Taylor

Ambitious experimental drama that traces the troubled relationship between women and their bodies.

Dist/Sales: CFMDC

Cater Waiter

Lane, Eric
1996; USA; 14 min; Comedy

Follows the lives of two gay waiters over a four year period. Witty, moving and very human, it stars award winning actor David Drake.

Prod Comp: Orange Thought Productions
Dist/Sales: Forefront

Cats, The

(aka: Kattorna)

Carlsen, Henning
1964; Denmark; 93 min; B&W; Drama
P: Lorens Marmstedt; *W:* Valentin Chorell; *C:* Mac Ahlberg; *E:* Henning Carlsen
Cast: Eva Dahlbeck, Gio Petré, Monica Nielsen

The story of a group of women who work in a laundry, all of whom seem to be sexually starved. When Rike accuses Marta, the manager, of making sexual advances towards her, all hell breaks loose. When pressure is applied by the other women, Rike caves in and admits to lying about the sexual advance. In a turnaround Marta is attracted to Rike and Rike responds in a positive way.

Caught

Gotschall, Christopher
2000; USA; 21 min; Drama

Where does friendship end and romance begin, and what about the sex that comes between the two?

William and Jamie's illicit affair threatens to disrupt William's committed relationship with another man, in this handsome tale of love found and lost. (2002 Miami Gay & Lesbian Film Festival)

Caught in the Crossfire

Williams, Sandra R.
1997; USA; 26 min; Documentary

Black and Hispanic kids discuss their feelings about having queer parents.

Caught Looking

Giannaris, Constantine
1991; UK; 35 min; Comedy
P: Rebecca Dobbs; *W:* Paul Hallam; *C:* Denzil Armour-Brown, James Welland; *E:* William Diver, Deborah Field; *M:* John Eacott
Cast: Louis Selwyn, Bette Bourne

The ultimate gay computer game: pick your favourite sexual fantasy any time, any place and the boys of your choice. A voyeur selects four fantasy scenarios and, at the press of a virtual-reality button, takes part in them. Originally scheduled for the BBC's *Out* series, the film was dropped for being too explicit.

Awards: Berlin Film Festival, 1992: Teddy Award
Dist/Sales: Salzgeber, TLA, WaterBearer, MayaVision

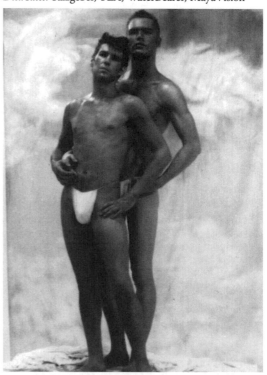

Caught Looking

Cavafy

(aka: Kavafis)

Smaragdis, Yannis
1996; France, Greece; 90 min; Drama
P: Helen Smaragdis; *W:* Yannis Smaragdis; *C:* Nikos
Smaragdis; *E:* Andreas Andreadakis; *M:* Vangelis
Cast: Manos Meletiou, Dimitris Katalifos, Vassilis
Diamantopoulos, Maya Lyberopoulou

The life of the famous Greek poet Constantine P.
Cavafy is told in flashback from his death bed.
While he is in hospital he receives a visit from a
young writer who reads passages from his biography
of Cavafy. It tells the story of his life as a young
wealthy man in Alexandria and his beautiful
widowed mother, and his partaking in the homosexual night life which he passionately wrote about.
Greek with English subtitles.

Prod Comp: Alexandros Film, Greek Films Centre,
Greek Television ET-1, Lumiére Services
Dist/Sales: Alexandros

Cecil B Demented

Waters, John
2000; France, USA; 88 min; Comedy, Action
P: Joseph M. Caracciolo Jnr, John Fielder, Mark Tarlov;
W: John Waters; *C:* Robert M. Stevens; *E:* Jeffrey Wolf;
M: Basil Poledouris, Zoe Poledouris
Cast: Melanie Griffith, Stephen Dorff, Rikki Lake,
Patricia Hearst, Alicia Witt, Mink Stole

Cecil B. DeMented is a quirky action-comedy about a
young underground filmmaker and his loyal cult of
film fanatics who declare war on bad cinema. As the
movie begins, Cecil and his 'Sprocket Holes' gang
kidnap Honey Whitlock, a long-time Hollywood
movie star visiting Baltimore for the premiere of her
latest blockbuster. They then force Honey to star in
their outlaw film, *Raving Beauty*. Though initially
she objects, Honey eventually converts to the group's
cause, and joins them as they wreak cinematic havoc
on the city of Baltimore. Eventually, even ordinary
citizens rally to DeMented's cause. (Wolfe)

Dist/Sales: Wolfe, ACMI

Celeste

Adlon, Percy
1981; Germany; 106 min; Drama
P: Eleonore Adlon; *W:* Percy Adlon; *C:* Jürgen Martin;
E: Clara Fabry; *M:* César Franck
Cast: Eva Mattes, Jürgen Arndt, Norbet Wartha, Wolf
Euba, Joseph Manoth

The moving drama of a young, uneducated peasant
girl who is hired as the housekeeper for the acclaimed writer and homosexual Marcel Proust. Their

relationship becomes one of caring companion and
friend. German with English subtitles.

Prod Comp: Artificial Eye Film, Bayerischer Rundfunk,
Pelemele Film
Dist/Sales: NFVLS, NewYorker

Celestial Clockwork

(aka: Mecaniques Celestes)

Torres, Fina
1994; Belgium, France, Spain; 86 min; Comedy
P: Gerard Costa; *W:* Fina Torres; *C:* Ricardo Aronovich;
M: Francois Farrugia, Michel Musseau
Cast: Ariadna Gil, Arielle Dombasle, Alma Rosa
Castellanos, Evelyne Didi, Frederic Longbois

Opera and song play a key role in the romantic
comedy *Celestial Clockwork* from award-winning
Venezuelan director Fina Torres. The Cinderella
story stars Ariadna Gil (one of the stars of the Oscar-
winning Spanish film *Belle Epoque*) as Ana, the
Venezuelan girl who leaves her fiancé at the altar and
hops a plane to Paris to fulfil her dream to become
an opera singer. What follows is a screwball comedy,
charting Ana's adventures with an apartment full of
crazy roommates and her seemingly improbable
destiny as the star of an impending production of
Rossini's *La Cenerentola*. The film's soundtrack
includes arias by Rossini and art songs by Schubert
and Schumann, as well as salsa numbers performed
by Venezuelan music star Alma Rosa, who also
appears in the film.
(www.womenandgender.buffalo.edu)
French & Spanish with English subtitles.

Prod Comp: Bastille Films, Paradise Films
Dist/Sales: October, Palace

Celine and Julie go Boating

(aka: Céline et Julie vont en Bateau)

Rivette, Jacques
1974; France; 185 min; Experimental
P: Barbet Schroeder; *W:* Juliet Berto, Eduardo de
Gregorio, Dominique Labourier, Bulle Ogier, Marie-
France Pisier, Jacques Rivette; *C:* Jacques Renard;
E: Nicole Lubtchansky; *M:* Jean-Marie Sénia
Cast: Juliet Berto, Dominique Labourier, Marie-France
Pisier, Bulle Ogier

A Librarian (Julie) begins a friendship with a
magician (Celine), who leads her to a haunted
house. The women eventually become involved with
the ghosts who live there. Although little happens
between the women, there is a subtle lesbian subtext,
and both women are physically affectionate towards
one another. French with English subtitles.

Prod Comp: Action Films, Les Films 7, Les Films du Losange
Dist/Sales: ACMI, NFVLS

C

Celluloid Closet, The

Epstein, Robert / Friedman, Jeffrey
1995; USA; 102 min; Documentary
P: Robert Epstein, Jeffrey Friedman; *W:* Robert Epstein,
Jeffrey Friedman, Sharon Wood, Armistead Maupin;
C: Nancy Schreiber; *E:* Jeffrey Friedman, Arnold
Glassman; *M:* Carter Burwell, k. d. lang
Cast: Lily Tomlin, Tom Hanks, Whoopi Goldberg,
Shirley MacLaine

The film version of the late Vito Russo's
groundbreaking book, *The Celluloid Closet*, explores
the history of the onscreen representations of gays
and lesbians with perception and wit. Lily Tomlin
delivers the narration written by Armistead Maupin,
which serves as a link between film clips and
interviews. Includes classic scenes from *Red River*,
with Montgomery Clift and John Ireland comparing
pistols, and Dietrich in a tuxedo giving mouth-to-
mouth to a female customer in *Morocco*. A highly
entertaining and, above all, important film.

Awards: Berlin International Film Festival, 1996: Teddy
Award for Best Documentary
Prod Comp: Telling Pictures, Channel 4, HBO, Sony
Pictures Classics
Dist/Sales: Palace, SonyClassics, Telling, Wolfe, Cowboy,
ACMI, VideoAmericain, FilmsTransit

The Celluloid Closet

Certain Grace, A

Nettlebeck, Sandra
1992; USA; 40 min; B&W; Comedy

Zelda meets Alice and together they begin working
on a photography project. The erotic tension builds
as Zelda's boyfriend gets jealous. Slowly feelings
develop between the two women.

Awards: San Francisco International Lesbian & Gay
Film Festival, 1992: Audience Award for Best Lesbian
Short
Dist/Sales: Frameline

Cha-Cha for the Fugitive, A

(aka: Gai Tao-wan-je de ChaCha)

Wang, Tsai-sheng
1996; Taiwan; 83 min; Drama
W: Wang Tsai-sheng; *C:* Wang Tsai-sheng; *E:* Christine
Huand; *M:* Tseng Shu-mei
Cast: Chieh-i Chen, Tsung-sien He, Hsien-yu Liu,
Julien Chen

Whatever else you may think about *A Cha-Cha for
the Fugitive*, it certainly doesn't look or sound like
any other Taiwanese movie you've ever seen. The
nameless bisexual protagonist, a young male dancer
with avant-garde leanings and dreams of escaping to
New York to his male lover, works nights in a sleazy
club and spends his days feeling trapped in his
studio in a grungy apartment block. His confused
thoughts about Taiwan, materialism, corrupt
politicians and murderous gangsters are splashed all
over the screen in shards of splintered imagery and
shades of blue and yellow. Tsai-sheng Wang, the
film's writer-director-designer-cinematographer,
pursues his protagonist's fantasies to the point that
they subside into memories of a more innocent
childhood. Along the way, he offers intriguing
glimpses of Taipei's neo-punk subculture and
explores the polymorphous hang-ups of Taiwan's
frustrated Generation-X kids. Taiwanese with
English subtitles. (1997 Berlin Film Festival)

Prod Comp: Fountain Films; *Dist/Sales:* Fountain

Chaero

Hayes, Matt
1989; Ireland; 15 min; Drama

Richie and his pal Chaero are two Dublin youths
who inhabit a world without rules. Cigarettes are big
currency and alcohol is the only escape. A nitty-
gritty short involving sex and blackmail with a trick
ending.

Dist/Sales: Frameline

Chain of Desire

López , Temistocles
1992; USA; 103 min; Drama
P: Brian Cox; *W:* Temistocles López; *C:* Nancy
Schreiber; *E:* Susanne Fenn; *M:* Nathan Birnbaum
Cast: Linda Fiorentino, Malcolm McDowell, Elias
Koteas, Angel Aviles, Patrick Bauchau

A witty observation about sexual yearning and
unrequited love in the time of AIDS. When Ann,
the owner of a nightclub, sleeps with Jesus, she starts
a chain reaction of erotic entanglements crossing
social and psychological boundaries.

Prod Comp: Distant Horizons
Dist/Sales: Warner, TLA

C

Chained Girls

Mawra, Joseph P.
1965; USA; 62 min; B&W; Comedy, Erotica
Cast: June Roberts

History lessons don't come much funnier than this. This 'exposé of Sapphic sexuality' apparently passed for serious documentary way back in the mid 1960s, but we doubt whether any of the practices depicted here will ring any bells of recognition. It may, however, prompt more than a few howls of derisive laughter. Check out this strange twilight world, where a gang of deviant dykes initiate a newcomer into their sinful fold by drawing straws to see who will get to do the (dis)honours. Funniest of all is the grave announcement during the opening credits, which tells us that the poor unfortunate creatures we are about to meet are each portrayed by a 'professional'.

Prod Comp: QC Film and Video
Dist/Sales: SomethingWeird, VideoAmericain

Chained Heat

Nicholas, Paul
1983; Germany, USA; 95 min; Drama
P: Billy Fine; *W:* Vincent Mongol, Paul Nicholas; *C:* Mac Ahlberg; *E:* Nino di Marco; *M:* Joseph Conlan
Cast: Linda Blair, Stella Stevens, John Vernon, Sybil Danning, Tamara Dobson

A shocking and explosive (exploitative?) look at the violence, cruelty and corruption which takes place in women's prisons. With the usual amount of shower scenes, along with cruel and sadistic lesbian guards. The sleaze classic of the women-in-prison genre. Definitely made for a straight male audience.

Prod Comp: Intercontinental, TAT, Heat GBR, Jensen Farley Pictures
Dist/Sales: Roadshow

Chained Heat II

Simandl, Lloyd
1993; USA; 99 min; Drama
P: Lloyd Simandl, John Curtis; *W:* Chris Hyde; *C:* Danny Nowak; *M:* Bruce Curtis
Cast: Brigitte Nielsen, Paul Koslo, Kimberley Kates

Deep inside the concrete jungle of an infamous communist-bloc prison, an innocent woman struggles to stay alive. Described as an exploitative lesbian *Midnight Express*, a young woman is wrongly imprisoned and now must contend with a warden into S/M, and a butch, knife-wielding henchwoman. Not for the politically correct, but you can still find a laugh or two at the ridiculous plot and ludicrous script.

Dist/Sales: NewLine

Chanel Solitaire

Kaczender, George
1981; France, UK; 118 min; Drama
P: Larry Spangler; *W:* Julian More; *C:* Ricardo Aronovich; *E:* Georges Klotz; *M:* Paul Jabara, Jean Musy
Cast: Marie-France Pisier, Karen Black, Rutger Hauser, Timothy Dalton

The story of Gabrielle Chanel, the woman who revolutionised the fashion industry and created the world famous perfume Chanel No. 5. Her torrid love affairs were once the talk of Europe. At one point she has a lesbian relationship but the film treats it only as an aberration.

Prod Comp: United Film Distribution, Fodrest, Gardenia Films

Change

Philpott, Ger
1995; Ireland; 12 min; Drama

A brilliant and involving monologue-driven drama that takes a look at a love affair cut short by AIDS. Both sad and sensual, this remarkable piece of gay Irish filmmaking leaves the heart aching. (MQFF)

Dist/Sales: Caspar

Change of Heart, A

Brown, Arvin
1998; USA; 96 min; Drama
P: Aaron Mendelsohn; *W:* Aaron Mendelsohn; *C:* John J. Campbell; *E:* Michael A. Hoey; *M:* Patrick Williams
Cast: Jean Smart, John Terry

This above average made-for-television movie tackles the subject of bisexuality and its effects on a seemingly happy, close-knit family. Jean Smart is quite memorable as a blindly contented mother of two teens who works as the efficient office manager at her medical doctor husband's offices. Her stability and her family's unity comes under a wrenching challenge when she discovers that her husband is having an affair with another man. Not only is she stunned, but their daughter and son are unable to deal with their father's homosexuality. The fascinating drama delves into how each member of the household must deal with the dramatic change in their lives. Smart is especially good as a Stepford Wife who is smacked with a dose of life-changing reality. (Wolfe)

Dist/Sales: Wolfe

Change the Frame

Rey, Cristina
1995; USA; 93 min; Drama
P: Cristina Rey; *W:* Cristina Rey; *C:* Ian Hardin;

C

E: Ian Hardin, Alex Kelly
Cast: Stephani Shope, Cristina Rey, Sarah Harmon, Cecila Saglio, Alex Kelly, Jan Hardin

Rey's film focuses on the relationship between Angela and Rachel, a couple who have been together for a while and are now having to re-evaluate their relationship. It seems they are both heading in different directions. The catalyst arrives in the form of another woman—a footloose and fancy-free singer from San Francisco who persuades Angela that there is something missing in her life. *Change the Frame* is often humorous, but strikes plenty of emotional chords. (MQFF)

Dist/Sales: FearlessProd

Changing Face

Roznowski, Robert / Tate, Robert
1993; USA; 103 min; Drama

An involving soap opera about a gay couple in the throes of a domestic mid-life crisis and their wacky group of friends.

Prod Comp: Rob Squared Films
Dist/Sales: TLA

Changing our Minds: The Story of Dr Evelyn Hooker

Changing our Minds: The Story of Dr Evelyn Hooker

Schmiechen, Richard
1991; USA; 75 min; Documentary
P: David Haugland; *W:* Richard Schmiechen, James Harrison

This fascinating documentary is a biography of Dr Evelyn Hooker, whose research into the psychological profiles of homosexual men was instrumental in the eventual declassification of homosexuality as a mental illness. This moving biography includes interviews with Hooker, and archival documentation of the 'underground' lesbian and homosexual communities in America during the 1950s and 1960s. Narrated by Patrick Stewart.

Awards: San Francisco International Lesbian & Gay Film Festival, 1992: Audience Award for Best Documentary
Prod Comp: Intrepid Productions
Dist/Sales: Ronin, Frameline, Salzgeber, NFVLS, ACMI

Chant d'Amour, Un

Genet, Jean
1950; France; 26 min; B&W; Drama
P: Jean Genet; *W:* Jean Genet; *C:* Jacques Natteau; *E:* Jean Genet
Cast: Lucien Sénémaud

Set in a men's prison wing housing convicted murderers in solitary confinement, the action shifts from individual cells to the minds of the prisoners and the guard-voyeur. The narrative depicts life in the prison and the prisoner's sexual misery and fantasies of homosexuality.

Dist/Sales: FilmmakersCoop, BFI, NFVLS

Charlie

Rosenzweig, Joshua
1999; USA; 49 min; Comedy

Camp, drag send up of 1970s US television show *Charlie's Angels*.

Dist/Sales: Tomorrow

Chasing Amy

Smith, Kevin
1997; USA; 111 min; Drama
P: Scott Mosier, Kevin Smith; *W:* Kevin Smith; *C:* David Klein; *E:* Scott Mosier, Kevin Smith; *M:* David Pirner
Cast: Ben Affleck, Joey Lauren Adams, Jason Lee, Dwight Ewell, Jason Mewes

The concluding chapter of Kevin Smith's New Jersey Trilogy, *Chasing Amy* is a drama/comedy about Holden, a successful comic-book creator, whose life takes a turn when he falls madly in love with Alyssa, a fellow artist. The first major shock awaiting Holden is Alyssa's apparent lesbian orientation. The second one comes after the two develop a strong friendship, and Alyssa decides not to limit her chances of love to women only. The two begin an affair, despite Holden's nagging doubts about her

promiscuous past. (ACMI)

Prod Comp: Viwe Askew Productions
Dist/Sales: Alliance, Lauren, Miramax, Wolfe, ACMI,
Swank

Chick in White Satin

Chastity

de Paola, Alessio
1969; USA; 83 min; Comedy
P: Sonny Bono; *W:* Sonny Bono; *C:* Ben Coleman;
E: Hugo Grimaldi; *M:* Sonny Bono
Cast: Cher, Barbara London, Stephen Whittaker, Tom
Nolan

Pop star Cher shares an intimate encounter with a
butch brothel madam in this trashy, hippy tale about
a mixed up teen. The film's title is steeped in irony
given that Cher named her daughter (lesbian activist
Chastity Bono) after her character's name, and
apparently became pregnant with her during
filming.

Prod Comp: American International Pictures, Progress
Motion Pictures

Chelsea Girls, The

Warhol, Andy
1966; USA; 210 min; Experimental
P: Andy Warhol; *W:* Ronald Tavel, Andy Warhol;
C: Andy Warhol; *M:* The Velvet Underground
Cast: Nico, Eric Emerson, Ingrid Superstar, Robert
Olivio, Ondine

Set in New York's famous Chelsea Hotel, this arthouse classic presents stories from different rooms
with the use of twin screens. The characters who live
in the hotel include an array of lesbians, homosexuals and drug users. One of the earliest underground
films, this is possibly Warhol's most famous.

Dist/Sales: MOMA

Chicks in White Satin

Holliman, Elaine
1993; USA; 25 min; Documentary
P: Jason Schneider

Nominated for an Academy Award for Best Short
Film in 1993, this film packs a feature-length's worth
of drama and comedy into a sparkling 20 minutes. It
documents the formal Jewish wedding of two San
Diego women, and the reverberations among each of
their families, at the same time incorporating a sly
critique of the traditional trappings of nuptials,
straight or gay. Tensions mount among the families
until the wedding day, when a miraculous transformation takes place and the previously alienated
mothers of the two brides waltz together on the
dance floor. (MQFF)

Awards: San Francisco International Lesbian & Gay
Film Festival, 1993: Audience Award for Best Short
Documentary
Dist/Sales: USC

Child-Play

Mohabeer, Michelle
1997; Canada; 15 min; Experimental

Ateesha Mansara, a woman in her late 60s has lived
her life haunted by the spirit of a child molester she
met as a young girl—50 years later in an attempt to
'claim her soul' he returns. (Third World Newsreel)

Dist/Sales: CFMDC, TWN

Children of Hannibal

(aka: Figli di Annibale)

Ferrario, Davide
1998; Italy; 93 min; Comedy
P: Maurizio Totti; *W:* Davide Ferrario, Diego
Abatantuono; *C:* Giovanni Cavallini; *E:* Claudio
Cormio, Luca Gasparini; *M:* Damiano Rota, Daniele
Sepe, Fabio Piazzalunga
Cast: Silivo Orlando, Diego Abatantuono, Valentina
Cervi, Flavio Insinna

Domenico is a chronically unemployed southerner
struggling to survive in Italy's unfriendly North.
Desperate to change his destiny once and for all, he
plans to rob a bank and head across the border to
Switzerland. Things go wrong, however, and
Domenico is forced to take a hostage: Tommaso, a
bankrupt businessman trapped in a loveless marriage. Tommaso is soon in command, and convinces
his captor to change direction and drive south. The
plan is to meet Tommaso's friend Orfeo in Puglia
and sail from there to Egypt. But once again things
don't go quite as planned. Domenico is shocked to

C

discover that Orfeo is not only a policeman—he's Tommaso's secret lover! (23rd San Francisco International Lesbian & Gay Film Festival) Italian with English subtitles.

Prod Comp: Mediaset, Colorado Film Production
Dist/Sales: Intra

Children of the Regime

Deocampo, Nick
1985; Philippines; Documentary
W: Nick Deocampo

> *Children of the Regime* is a graphic story about children forced by poverty into prostitution in the Philippines. Tagalog with English subtitles.

The Children's Hour

Children's Hour, The

Wyler, William
1961; USA; 107 min; B&W; Drama
P: William Wyler; *W:* John Michael Hayes; *C:* Franz Planer; *E:* Robert Swink; *M:* Alex North
Cast: Audrey Hepburn, Shirley MacLaine, James Garner, Miriam Hopkins, Fay Bainter

> This film version of Lillian Hellman's play *These Three* is more explicit in its depiction of lesbianism, than the original. The film lacks impact despite good performances by MacLaine and Hepburn as two teachers who operate a girls' boarding school. All is destroyed when a student accuses the two of having an affair and the unsubstantiated rumour runs wild in the self-righteous school community. In a turnaround at the end one of the women admits to having lesbian feelings and to being attracted to the other woman. An interesting film, full of suggestions of McCarthyism and one of the earliest films in Hollywood to openly mention lesbianism.

Prod Comp: Mirisch, United Artists
Dist/Sales: TLA, UA, NFVLS, ACMI, VideoAmericain, Swank

Chill Out

Struck, Andreas
2000; Germany; 90 min; Drama
P: Jost Hering; *W:* Andreas Struck; *C:* Andreas Doub; *E:* Philipp Stahl; *M:* Erlandas
Cast: Tatjana blacher, Sebastian Blomberg, Barnaby Metschurat

> Three dissimilar drifters find themselves intimately entwined in this cleverly constructed powerhouse of New Wave German cinema. At the heart is Anna, investigating family trees for a living and after work indulging in the occasional one-night stand. Anna crosses paths with Johann, always on the run with a stash of stolen credit cards from which he etches out a rough living. Johann moves in with Anna, and two becomes three when Max (one of Anna's fleeting lovers) arrives. Max sleeps with both Anna and Johann, but how long can lovers stay friends? Emerging German filmmaker Andreas Struck cut his teeth alongside Derek Jarman on *Edward II* and *Wittgenstein*. Like Jarman before him, Struck conveys a strong sense of interiority in this, his debut feature. His background in live theatre equally informs his ability to extract minutely refined performances from his actors, and convey character through minimal gestures and nuances. (MQFF) German with English subtitles.

Prod Comp: Jost Hering Filmproduktion, Studio Babelsberg
Dist/Sales: Fortissimo, Mongrel

Chill Out

China Dolls

Ayres, Tony
1997; Australia; 30 min; Documentary
P: Helen Bowden; *W:* Tony Ayres

> This stylish and moving portrayal of gays of Asian descent in Australia explores the relationship between race and sexuality. *China Dolls* probes the uncomfortable reality of racial stereotyping and discrimination in the gay world through interviews with Asian men who talk frankly, and often

humorously, of their experiences living within a double minority. The filmmaker himself tells a highly personal story of his journey from denial to self acceptance. *China Dolls* themes of diversity and acceptance make it a contemporary, universal story. (Filmakers Library)

Dist/Sales: FilmakersLibrary, ACMI

Chinese Characters

Fung, Richard
1986; Canada; 22 min; Documentary; *P:* Richard Fung

Asian men relate their histories and relationships to pornography.

Chocolate Babies

Winter, Stephen
1996; USA; 83 min; Comedy, Drama
P: Jason Kliot, Joana Vicente; *W:* Stephen Winter
Cast: Suzanne Gregg Ferguson, Dudley Findlay Jnr, Jon Lee, Michael Lynch

An underground band of HIV-positive, queer, urban, transvestite activists of colour is making headlines in New York. In an effort to expose political corruption surrounding the AIDS epidemic, these urban guerrillas stage a series of surprise attacks against conservative politicians whom they believe are collecting secret lists of HIV-positive individuals. Caught up in their extreme methods of activism and self-destructive drug and alcohol binges, the group becomes torn by infighting and begins to lose sight of their mission and loyalty to each other. Will they find the peace and justice they seek? Between fantasy, tragedy and comedy, *Chocolate Babies* is a roller-coaster ride that is sure to provoke laughter and dialogue. (Frameline)

Awards: New York Lesbian & Gay Film Festival, 1996: Best Feature
Prod Comp: Open City Films
Dist/Sales: Frameline, Wolfe, WaterBearer

Choirboys, The

Aldrich, Robert
1977; USA; 119 min; Drama
P: Lee Rich, Merv Adelson, William Aldrich, Lynn Guthrie; *W:* Christopher Knorf; *C:* Joseph Biroc; *E:* Maury Winetrobe, Irving Rosenblum, William Martin, Joseph Guresky; *M:* Frank de Vol
Cast: Charles Durning, Louis Gossett Jnr, Perry King, Clyde Kusatsu

Inside view of rank-and-file Los Angeles police life depicting both the fun and frustration of being a cop. One of the officers is chained naked to a tree in MacArthur Park and is confronted by a gay man walking his poodle. The gay subtext of the film is handled in a rather homophobic way as the cops clean up all the perverts in the city. Based on the novel by Joseph Wambaugh.

Prod Comp: Airone, Lorimar
Dist/Sales: 20thCenturyFox, Universal

Choosing Children

Chasnoff, Debra / Klausner, Kim
1984; USA; 45 min; Documentary

Documentary about the issues faced by women who become parents after coming out as lesbians. Six families share their experiences about donor insemination, non-biological motherhood, adoption, co-parenting with gay men and the impact on the children of growing up in a lesbian household. It challenges myths about gay people and children, and expands popular images of the family.

Awards: New York Lesbian & Gay Film Festival, 1985: Best Short Film
Dist/Sales: Cinenova, NFVLS, Frameline, WoMedia, Cambridge

Choosing Children

Chop Suey

Weber, Bruce
2000; USA; 98 min; Documentary
P: Leonard John Bruno; *W:* Bruce Weber, Maribeth Edwards; *C:* Lance Acord, Douglas Cooper, Jim Fealy; *E:* Angelo Corrao; *M:* John Leftwich

Bruce Weber's discovery of a gorgeous young hunk named Peter Johnson was the beginning of a marvellous collaboration that continued over four years. Plucking the young man from over a thousand boys in training as wrestlers, Weber turned Johnson into a highly-paid photographic model for Ralph Lauren, Versace, and Karl Lagerfeld. *Chop Suey* uses still photographs and live action footage to chart Johnson's transformation from a pretty young boy into a homoerotic icon. (Zeitgeist)

Prod Comp: Just Blue Films
Dist/Sales: Zeitgeist

Chopper Chicks in Zombie Town

Hoskins, Dan
1989; USA; 86 min; Comedy, Horror
P: Maria Snyder, Arthur Sarkissian, James Hardy;
W: Dan Hoskins; C: Tom Fraser; E: W. O. Garrett;
M: Dan May
Cast: Vicki Farrell, Kristina Loggia, Lycia Naff, Jamie Rose

This camp comedy contrasts the rampant hetero-sexuality of the Cycle Sluts with the outspoken lesbianism of their gang leader. An evil undertaker is resurrecting dead bodies to work as zombies in a radioactive mine. The Cycle Sluts ride into town and reluctantly save the day.

Prod Comp: Chelsea Partners
Dist/Sales: TLA, Troma

Chosen Family, The

Bradley, Maureen
2001; Canada; 13 min; Comedy

Families, whether chosen or biological, have a single aim—to drive us nuts, as this astute and comic film demonstrates.

Dist/Sales: CFMDC

Chrissy

North, Jacqui
1999; Australia; 52 min; Documentary
P: Jessica Douglas-Henry, Jacqui North

A far cry from the usual media depiction of women with HIV/AIDS as 'virgins, vamps or victims', Chrissy provides a revealing insight into the life of a young lesbian living with full-blown AIDS in inner-city Sydney. At 18, Chrissy Napier, the eldest in a family of four girls, was diagnosed with HIV. A teenage runaway and diabetic, she kept her positive status from her family for eight years. Filmmaker Jacqui North—Chrissy's best friend began recording Chrissy's life shortly after she reveals her illness to her family. The result is a film of great intimacy, compassion and sadness, as much about Chrissy's courage and resourcefulness as about her family's ultimate acceptance and unconditional support.

Prod Comp: North Productions
Dist/Sales: Frameline

Christine Jorgensen Story, The

Rapper, Irving
1970; USA; 98 min; Drama
P: Edward Small; W: Robert Kent, Ellis St Joseph;
C: Jacques Marquette; E: Grant Whytlock; M: Paul Sawtell, Bert Shefter
Cast: John Hansen, Joan Tompkins, Quinn K. Redeker

Based on the true story of George, a rather asexual man, who from a young age enjoyed dressing up in women's clothes. He believed he was trapped in the wrong body, and so finally decided to have a sex-change operation, turning him into Christine.

Prod Comp: Edprod
Dist/Sales: UA

Chuck and Buck

Arteta, Miguel
2000; USA; 96 min; Comedy
P: Matthew Greenfield; W: Mike White; C: Chuy Chavez; E: Jeff Betancourt
Cast: Mike White, Chris Weitz, Lupe Ontiveros, Beth Colt

Buck is an unemployed, infantile 27-year-old who becomes fixated on his childhood best friend, Chuck. Chuck, on the other hand, has moved on to living a successful adult life that includes a beautiful fiancée and a high-level job—and has no interest in rekindling this childhood friendship. Buck's obsession to re-friend Chuck motivates him to move to Los Angeles where he begins stalking Chuck and his fiancée. He calls continuously, hangs around in front of Chuck's office, appears at Chuck's home uninvited. With Chuck rejecting all these efforts, Buck takes dramatic measures and puts on a Children's Theatre play that he is certain will make Chuck become his best friend again. Finally, in great despair, Chuck finds a way to get Buck to leave him alone. (Wolfe)

Dist/Sales: Wolfe, ACMI

Chuck Solomon: Coming of Age

Dallas, Wendy / Huestis, Marc
1986; USA; 60 min; Documentary
P: Wendy Dallas, Marc Huestis

An intimate portrait of Chuck Solomon, a mainstay of the San Francisco theatrical community, who was diagnosed with AIDS in 1985. Includes interviews with many of Solomon's friends and colleagues, as well as with Chuck himself, in which he traces his growth as a gay man, his career as a committed gay artist and his courage in facing his illness.

Dist/Sales: CinemaGuild, Salzgeber

Chutney Popcorn

Ganatra, Nisha
1999; USA; 92 min; Comedy
P: Susan Carnival, Nisha Ganatra; W: Susan Carnival, Nisha Ganatra; C: Erin King; E: Jane Pia Abramowitz; M: Karsh Kale
Cast: Nisha Ganatra, Jill Hennessey, Madhur Jaffrey, Sakina Jaffrey

Reena is an aspiring photographer and beautician. As an Indian American lesbian she is happy living with her girlfriend Lisa, but struggles to find acceptance from her traditional mother, especially when she continually finds herself compared to her less radical sister, Sarita. Things become much more complicated when Sarita finds that she can't have children and Reena offers to become a surrogate mother. Sarita's hubby Mitch is all for the idea, but naturally nothing goes according to plan. *Chutney Popcorn* is a refreshing comedy about the ever-evolving tensions of modern life, individual desires, American queer lifestyles and Indian traditions. (MQFF)

Prod Comp: First Look Pictures, Mata Productions, Seneca Falls, Tribeca Productions
Dist/Sales: Mongrel, Wolfe, VideoAmericain

Cicely

Thompson, Rob
1992; USA; 52 min; Drama

Lesbian lovers arrive in Cicely, a small town on Alaska's Kenai Peninsula, at the turn of the century, determined to turn the little backwater mining town into a cultural mecca.

Cinema Fouad

Soueid, Mohammed
1994; Lebanon; 28 min; Documentary

A documentary on the life and ambitions of a young Lebanese cross-dresser. The filmmaker follows her journey from soldier to cabaret dancer in an effort to raise funds for her sex change operation. Shot in Beirut, *Cinema Fouad* weaves a complex and multilayered story of sexuality, identity and desire and paints a compelling portrait of its subject. (Third World Newsreel)

Prod Comp: Tele Liban
Dist/Sales: TWN

Circuit

Shafer, Dirk
2001; USA; 120 min; Drama
P: Gregory Hinton, Michael Roth, Steven J. Wolfe;
W: Dirk Shafer, Gregory Hinton; *C:* Joaquin Sedillo;
E: Glen Richardson; *M:* Tony Moran
Cast: Jonathan Wade-Drahos, Andre Khabbazi, Kiersten Warren, Brian Lane Green

From director Dirk Shafer (*Man of the Year* 1994) comes this controversial new film which puts the circuit party scene on the screen and under the microscope. John is an ex-cop who has left small-town life in search of an open new existence in West Hollywood. Here he is introduced to the beautiful people of the Circuit Party set, and their attendant lifestyle of sex, drugs, and gay abandon. Rapidly entrenched in a vicious cycle of hustling and deception, John must decide between his old and his new friends and his conflicting loyalties. (MQFF)

Prod Comp: Sneak Preview Entertainment
Dist/Sales: JourDeFete, TLA

Citizen Cohn

Pierson, Frank
1992; USA; 108 min; Drama
P: Doro Bachrach; *W:* David Franzoni; *C:* Paul Elliott;
M: Thomas Newman
Cast: James Woods, Joe Don Baker, Joseph Bologna, Ed Flanders

Based on the life of Roy Cohn, Senator Joseph McCarthy's right-hand man, who helped destroy some of the most powerful people in America during the McCarthy period of the 1950s. Told in a stream-of-consciousness style as he lies dying on his hospital bed. He was a closeted homosexual and died of AIDS in 1986. Made for TV and based on the novel by Nicholas Von Hoffman.

Dist/Sales: Warner, TLA, Swank

City of Lost Souls

(aka: Stadt der Verlorenen Seelen)

von Praunheim, Rosa
1983; Germany; 90 min; Comedy, Musical
W: Rosa von Praunheim; *C:* Stephan Köster; *E:* Rosa von Praunheim
Cast: Jayne County, Angie Stardust, Tara O'Hara, Lorraine Muthke

An hilarious low-budget musical satire about a group of expatriate Americans living in Berlin and working in a sleazy diner called the Burger Queen. The outrageous group include the transsexual Angie Stardust and transvestite Tara O'Hara. Described as a cross between Warhol, John Waters and *The Rocky Horror Picture Show*.

Dist/Sales: Exportfilm

Circuit

Claire

Thomas, Milford
2001; USA; 60 min; B&W; Drama
P: Milford Thomas; *W:* Milford Thomas; *C:* Jonathan
Mellinger; *M:* Anne Richardson
Cast: Toniet Gallego, Mish P. Delight, James Ferguson,
Allen Jeffrey Rein

Atlanta filmmaker Milford Thomas' *Claire* is a 60-minute black and white silent film shot on an antique hand-crank 35 mm camera. The film is designed to be accompanied by the 'Orchestra de Lune', a live 11-piece chamber orchestra performing an original score by Atlanta composer Anne Richardson. *Claire*'s story is loosely based on *Kaguyahime*, one of the oldest known Japanese fairy tales. Thomas' version tells the story of an elderly male couple on a farm in the rural 1920s South who find a girl from the moon and adopt her as their own. (www.clairefilm.com)

Prod Comp: Put Down the Plow Productions
Dist/Sales: Put-Down-the-Plow

Claire of the Moon

Conn, Nicole
1992; USA; 82 min; Drama
P: Pamela S. Kuri; *W:* Nicole Conn; *C:* Randolph
Sellars; *E:* Michael Solinger; *M:* Michael Allen Harrison
Cast: Trisha Todd, Karen Trumbo, Faith McDevitt,
Caron Graham

Two professional women meet at a writer's retreat and openly discuss their lesbianism and preconceptions of sexuality. An issue arises about Noel's decision about her sexuality and whether she could have a future with Claire who is so different from herself. The film sees a passionate affair slowly develop between the two women interspersed with much intellectualising about sexuality. Filled with simmering sexual desire, heavy breathing and hovering lips. The film is very slow moving as Noel painfully makes her decision. Finally when the deed is done, the film ends.

Prod Comp: Demi-Monde Productions
Dist/Sales: Wolfe, Strand, Potential, Millivres, ACMI

Clancy Street Boys

Beaudine, William
1943; USA; 66 min; B&W; Comedy
P: Sam Katzman, Jack Dietz; *W:* Harvey Gates; *C:* Mack
Stengler; *E:* Carl Pierson
Cast: Leo Gorcey, Huntz Hall, Bobby Jordan, Bennie Bartlett

Farcical eastside kids yarn, with Muggs enlisting the boys to be his siblings for the benefit of Uncle Beery. Hall in drag is a comic highlight.

Prod Comp: Monogram Pictures Corporation

Clancy's Kitchen

Roy, Duncan
1997; UK; 53 min; Comedy

Black comedy about Clancy who whilst a successful and handsome television chef, just can't seem to get his personal life in order. Trapped between his boyfriend and his girlfriend, he's terrified of the consequences of being outed, and so plots to dump the boyfriend and marry the girlfriend. But things don't go quite to plan.

Dist/Sales: ThirdRock

Claire of the Moon

Clay Farmers, The

Gonzalez, A. P.
1988; USA; 60 min; Drama
P: Michael Moore; *W:* Michael Moore; *C:* Meg
Partridge; *E:* A. P. Gonzalez; *M:* Robert Stine
Cast: Todd Fraser, Nicholas Rempel, Asbury Ward,
Liam McGrath

Set in a small farming community, two young men, Dan and Mike, take in a 10-year-old boy, Gary, who has been abused. Soon homophobic hatred is stirred up by the boy's father against the two men. When their friends and community turn against them they must confront their relationship.

Dist/Sales: VideoAmericain

Cleopatra Jones

Starrett, Jack
1973; USA; 89 min; Action
P: Max Julien, Bill Tennant; *W:* Sheldon Keller, Max Julien; *C:* David Walsh; *E:* Allan Jacobs; *M:* Carl Brandt, Brad Shapiro, J. J. Johnson
Cast: Tamara Dobson, Bernie Casey, Shelley Winters, Brenda Sykes, Antonio Fargas

A black, female former CIA martial-arts expert keeps the violence going until she has captured or killed all members of an international drug ring. Shelley Winters plays Mommy, the lesbian gang leader. Standard exploitation flick with a high mortality rate.

Prod Comp: Warner
Dist/Sales: Warner

Cleopatra's Second Husband

Reiss, John
2001; USA; 92 min; Drama
W: John Reiss; *C:* Matta Faw; *E:* Toby Yates; *M:* Cary Berger
Cast: Radha Mitchell, Boyd Kestner, Paul Hipp, Bitty Schram

Blackly comic, perversely erotic, and thoroughly unpredictable, this genre-bending story of sexual mind games stars indie favourite Radha Mitchell. (First Run Features)

Dist/Sales: FirstRunFeatures

Clinic E

Ward, Mark
1996; USA; 27 min; B&W; Drama
Cast: David Fenner

A summons to be tested for HIV sends Jack Everhart on a mission to track down the anonymous person who gave his name to the clinic. As he calls on the men and women he's had unprotected sex with, while keeping the whole thing secret from his current committed partner, he gradually comes to realise the destructive power of denial. By the time Jack gets the results of his test, he's learned a few lessons, but life still has a nasty trick or two in store. (Big Film Shorts)

Dist/Sales: BigFilm

Clinic, The

Stevens, David
1982; Australia; 92 min; Comedy
P: Robert Le Tet, Bob Weis; *W:* Greg Millin;

C: Ian Baker; *E:* Edward McQueen-Mason; *M:* Red Symons
Cast: Chris Haywood, Simon Burke, Gerda Nicolson, Rona McLeod

A hilarious send up of the day-in-the-life running of a STD clinic, with characters including a relaxed, experienced young doctor with a hangover, a young homophobic medical student, other doctors with various problems, a gay doctor and a bunch of patients. It reaches its highest point when the gay doctor, played by Haywood, has some anxious moments when he must meet his lover's parents.

Prod Comp: Film House, Generation Films
Dist/Sales: Roadshow, NFVLS

Clips

Kinney, Nan / Sundahl, Debi
1988; USA; 30 min; Experimental

An independent production that is a collection of three experimental vignettes which detail an erotic and safe-sex perspective to lesbianism. Areas covered include penetration, oral sex, dental dams, sex toys, power, and role playing.

Prod Comp: Blush Productions

Close to Home

Evans, Rodney
1998; USA; 24 min; Documentary

Documents the filmmaker's journey as he comes out to a conservative Jamaican family and negotiates a painful relationship with a 21-year-old heterosexual man. (TWN)

Dist/Sales: TWN

Closer

Gharavi, Tina
2000; UK; 24 min; Documentary

An experimental documentary which is a poignant character study of a 17-year-old lesbian living in Newcastle, England, *Closer* innovatively explores the process of documentary filmmaking and boldly challenges traditional forms of storytelling. From the streets of Newcastle—where we find Annelise speaking frankly to the camera about her experiences as a young lesbian—to the emotionally charged re-enactment of her coming out to her mother, this highly original film provides a rare auto-portrait where fiction and documentary collide. (WMM)

Dist/Sales: WMM

Closet Space

Farrelly, Colleen
2000; Australia; 38 min; Documentary
P: Karen Taylor

Honest and frank, this South Australian PFlag documentary delves into the minds of different mums and dads of gay, lesbian and bisexual children.

Prod Comp: PSPFlag, Cindigo Vision
Dist/Sales: ACMI

Closet, The

(aka: Le Placard)

Veber, Francis
2000; France; 85 min; Comedy
P: Patrice Ledoux; *W:* Francis Veber; *C:* Luciano Tovoli;
E: Georges Klotz; *M:* Vladimir Cosma
Cast: Gerard Depardieu, Daniel Auteuil, Thierry Lhermitte, Michele Laroque

Francois Pignon is a lonely, dull accountant at a condom factory. At home, he sits alone and pines for his ex-wife and his son, who find him too boring to visit. At work, he's the butt of many jokes, usually instigated by fellow worker Felix. To make things worse, it's all over the office that he's going to be fired. But all that changes one day when a rumour spreads that Francois is gay. Much to his surprise, his life takes an unexpected and hilarious turn for the better. French with English subtitles. (Wolfe)

Prod Comp: Le Studio Canal+, TF1 Films
Dist/Sales: Wolfe, Miramax, Sharmill, Swank, ACMI

Closets are for Clothes

Dezu
1995; Japan; 21 min; Comedy

A young Japanese lesbian is taken by surprise when her straight male friend starts to hit on her.

Dist/Sales: TokyoILGFF

Closets are Health Hazards

Mosbacher, Dee
1986; USA; 22 min; Documentary

Closets Are Health Hazards is a slideshow transferred to video in which sixteen lesbian and gay physicians discuss the medical profession and sexual orientation. (Woman Vision)

Dist/Sales: WomanVision

Closing Numbers

Whittaker, Stephen
1993; UK; 96 min; Drama
P: Jennifer Howarth; *W:* David Cook; *C:* Nic Knowland; *E:* Max Lemon; *M:* Moya Burns
Cast: Jane Asher, Tim Woodward, Nigel Chernock, Hazel Douglas, Jamie Glover

The life of a married couple is almost destroyed when the wife finds out her husband is having an affair—with another man. She, for some reason, meets and befriends the man, and thus becomes aware of the world of AIDS.

Dist/Sales: FilmFour

Club de Femmes

(aka: The Women's Club; Girl's Club)

Deval, Jacques
1936; France; 90 min; B&W; Comedy
W: Jacques Deval; *C:* Jules Kruger
Cast: Elize Argal, Danielle Darrieux, Josette Day, Valentine Tessier

This rarely seen comedy, *Club de Femmes*, is set in an all-women's hotel in Paris where the ideal is moral security and the motto is 'Men—keep out'. The main characters include Alice, an attractive lesbian, a young dancer who'll do anything to get her boyfriend inside, and a foreign student who becomes involved in a prostitution ring. With traces of the classic American screwball comedy, *Club de Femmes* expresses a variety of sexual attitudes. (MQFF) French with English subtitles.

Prod Comp: S.E.L.F.
Dist/Sales: BFI

Coal Miner's Granddaughter

Dougherty, Cecilia
1991; USA; 85 min; Drama
Cast: Leslie Singer, Kevin Killian

This humorous epic about a brutally realistic American family does for lesbians what John Waters did for Baltimore. Dougherty's sharp and skilfully original visual style recreates moments, like memories, which will resonate with an audience's own deeply felt emotions about family, illness and sexuality. Video artist Leslie Singer plays the protagonist Jane Dobson. Under the thumb of her sleazy, evil father, Jane is not the hero of her own life, she's simply there. But when Jane escapes from the structured life of her family back in Pennsylvania, *Coal Miner's Granddaughter* opens up into the impressionistic world of her sexuality. (MQFF)

Dist/Sales: VDB

Cockettes, The

Weber, Bill / Weissman, David
2002; USA; 100 min; Documentary
P: David Weisman; *C:* Marsha Kahm; *E:* Bill Weber; *M:* Richard Koldewyn

A feature length documentary that chronicles the flamboyant ensemble of hippies (women, gay men and babies) who decked themselves out in gender-bending drag and tons of glitter for a series of legendary midnight shows at the Palace Theatre in San Francisco during the 1960s and 1970s. It featured elaborate costumes, rebellious sexuality and exuberant chaos. (Strand Releasing)

Prod Comp: Blackfern, GranDelusion
Dist/Sales: Strand

The Cockettes

Coconut/Cane and Cutlass

Mohabeer, Michelle
1994; Canada; 30 min; Drama

A poetic rumination on exile, displacement and national identity from the perspective of a young Indo-Caribbean lesbian who migrated to Canada 20 years ago. Her autobiographical journey and the history of indenture and oppression of Indian people in the Caribbean are illuminated through beautifully layered imagery, location footage from Guyana, stylised dramatic sequences, personal narration, poetry and dance.

Dist/Sales: WMM, CFMDC

Coffee Date

Wade, Stewart
2000; USA; 17 min; Comedy

A straight guy is set up by his brother and accidentally meets the boy of dreams instead of the girl of his dreams on an email personals date.

Dist/Sales: CoffeeDate

Cold Footsies

Manzart, Richard
1991; Australia; 12 min; Comedy

Does Bradley love Cheryl and does Cheryl really love Bradley? Did Gerard love Bradley, and does Bradley love Gerard, or does Bradley love anyone at all?

Prod Comp: Australian Film TV & Radio School
Dist/Sales: AFTRS

Cold Lands, The

(aka: Les Terres Froides)

Lifshitz, Sébastien
1999; France; 62 min; Drama
W: Sébastien Lifshitz, Stéphane Bouquet; *C:* Pascal Poucet; *E:* Yann Dedet; *M:* Arvo Part
Cast: Yasmine Belmadi, Bernard Verley, Valérie Donzelli, Sébastien Charles

Djamel is a good looking young Arab who comes to Grenoble to meet a Frenchman he thinks may be his father. The 'father' gives him a poorly paid job at his factory, but rejects the notion that Djamel is his son. In the meantime, Djamel seems enamoured by his 'father's' gay and very handsome son, but it seems he has a hidden agenda that brings a conclusion he, nor we expected. French with English subtitles.

Prod Comp: Agat Films, La Sept-Arte
Dist/Sales: ArteFrance

Colegas

(aka: Pals)

de la Iglesia, Eloy
1980; Spain; 120 min; Drama
P: José Antonio Pérez Giner; *W:* Eloy de la Iglesia, Gonzalo Goicoachea; *C:* Hans Burmann, Antonio Cuevas; *M:* Miguel Botafogo
Cast: Antonio Gonzalez Flores, Rosario Gonzalez Flores, José Luis Manzano, José Manuel Cervino

The story of two young men who—in order to raise money so the girlfriend of one can have an abortion—prostitute themselves in a gay bathhouse. Unfortunately this doesn't work, and raising the money looks very difficult until they meet a gay drug-runner and get work smuggling drugs into Madrid. When they finally get the money, their friendship ends tragically.

Dist/Sales: VideoAmericain

Colonel Redl

(aka: Oberst Redl)

Szabó, István
1985; Hungary; 140 min; Drama
P: Manfred Durnick, József Marx; *W:* István Szabó, Péter Dobai; *C:* Lajos Koltai; *E:* Zsuzsa Csakany;

C

M: Zdenkó Tamássy
Cast: Klaus Maria Brandauer, Hans Christian Blech, Armin Mueller-Stahl, Gudrun Landrebe

Alfred Redl is one of the most infamous and ambitious figures of modern European history. The son of a poor railway worker, he invented the story of his life to gain acceptance to the ranks of the aristocracy, and to climb to the pinnacle of the Austro-Hungarian military regime. At his peak in the Austrian Intelligence, he was blackmailed by the Russians for being homosexual and a transvestite, and was forced to become a double agent. His case is often used as an example of how gays in the military are a security risk. German with English subtitles.

Awards: Cannes Film Festival, 1985: Jury Prize; BAFTA Award, 1986: Best Foreign Language Film
Prod Comp: MOKEP-Kerszi, Mafilm Studio Objektiv, Manfred Durniok Produktion, ZDF
Dist/Sales: NewVision, ACMI, OrionClassics

Color Purple, The

Spielberg, Steven
1985; USA; 152 min; Drama
P: Steven Spielberg, Kathleen Kennedy, Frank Marshall, Quincy Jones; *W:* Menno Meyjes; *C:* Allen Daviau; *E:* Michael Kahn; *M:* Quincy Jones
Cast: Whoopi Goldberg, Danny Glover, Oprah Winfrey, Margaret Avery

The Color Purple centres on a African American girl's struggle in America's deep south. Spanning a period of 40 years, the film tells of Celie who is mistreated by two men for 15 years until a blues singer enters her life and her real self begins to emerge. However, with one small scene deleted, the film dilutes the lesbian aspect that was present in the novel written by Alice Walker.

Prod Comp: Amblin, Warner, Guber-Peters Company
Dist/Sales: ReelMovies, Warner

Come and Go

Lau, Mishann
1998; Canada; 13 min; B&W; Drama

A single woman has a night out in a lesbian bar.
Dist/Sales: VTape

Come as you Are

Croghan, Emma-Kate / McGann, Brad
1996; Australia; 27 min; Documentary
P: Franziska Wagenfeld; *W:* Emma-Kate Croghan, Brad McGann; *C:* Susan Thwaites; *E:* Andrew Narozny; *M:* John Phillips
Cast: Miss Candy, Bridget Haire, Ron Walker

Three diverse individuals—a drag queen, a sexual

outlaw and a gay cowboy—find escape from life in the creation of colourful alter egos. This Melbourne-produced docudrama examines sexuality and identity and their place within the urban landscape.
Prod Comp: Film Fatale
Dist/Sales: ABC-International

Come Back to the Five and Dime, Jimmy Dean, Jimmy Dean

Altman, Robert
1982; USA; 110 min; Drama
P: Scott Bushnell; *W:* Ed Graczyk; *C:* Pierre Mignot; *E:* Joseph Rosenfield
Cast: Karen Black, Cher, Sandy Dennis, Sudie Bond, Kathy Bates

Set in a small town in Texas in 1975, five female members of the James Dean Fan Club hold their 20-year reunion at a five-and-dime store. The different directions their lives have taken, and the various degrees of success they have had, create numerous striking contrasts. The action works on two levels as incidents occurring at the reunion are paralleled with events 20 years earlier. One of the characters, exuberantly well-played by Karen Black, is a transsexual.

Prod Comp: Sandcastle 5, Viacom
Dist/Sales: Ascanbee, Cinecom

Comedy in Six Unnatural Acts, A

Oxenberg, Jan
1975; USA; 25 min; B&W; Comedy
P: Jan Oxenberg; *W:* Jan Oxenberg

A satire on the stereotyped images of lesbians, each scene is a takeoff of a different genre of Hollywood film—the source of so many of our stereotypes. (Cinenova)

Prod Comp: Good Taste Productions
Dist/Sales: Cinenova, Frameline, NFVLS

Comfort of Strangers, The

Schrader, Paul
1990; UK; 102 min; Drama
P: Angelo Rizzoli Jnr; *W:* Harold Pinter; *C:* Dante Spinotti; *E:* Bill Pankow; *M:* Angelo Badalamenti
Cast: Christopher Walken, Helen Mirren, Rupert Everett, Natasha Richardson

A chance encounter with a strangely seductive couple in Venice draws two young lovers into a forbidden zone of dark sexuality and hidden secrets, where pain equals pleasure and murder is the result. Based on the novel by Ian McEwan.

Prod Comp: Erre, Sovereign, Rank Organisation, Reteitalia
Dist/Sales: Col-Tri, FirstRelease, Skouras

Coming Home

Crary, Ashley
2000; USA; 57 min; Documentary

An intimate investigation of the coming out
processes of five gay and lesbians.

Dist/Sales: CinemaGuild

Coming of Age

Gorn, Phil
2001; USA; 81 min; Drama
P: Phil Gorn, Michael L. Pryfogle, Randi Acton;
W: Phil Gorn; *C:* Don Starnes; *E:* Phil Gorn
Cast: Ron Guinto, Marceia Fogg, Norman Gee, Kevin
Lasit

Stevie is apprehended for a gay bashing and
sentenced to serve community time in an AIDS
hospice. While there he realises that love can cross
many borders.

Dist/Sales: Wonderphil

Coming Out (1972)

Tarrant, Crea
1972; UK; 32 min; Documentary

The issues and problems associated with transvestism
and transsexualism are discussed in this film,
primarily using interviews.

Dist/Sales: NFVLS

The Comfort of Strangers

Coming Out (1989)

Carow, Heiner
1989; East Germany; 109 min; Drama
W: Wolfram Witt; *C:* Martin Schlesinger; *E:* Evelyn
Carow; *M:* Stefan Carow
Cast: Mathias Freihof, Dagmar Manzel, Dirk Kummer,
Walfriede Schnitt, Michael Gwisdek

An idealistic schoolteacher forms a relationship with
Tanya and they move in together. But when he has a
chance meeting with an old school friend to whom
he was sexually attracted, his relationship with Tanya
is put in jeopardy. He begins to delve into the gay
underground life of the city as he questions his
heterosexuality. German with English subtitles.

Prod Comp: DEFA-Studio für Spielfilme
Dist/Sales: Wolfe, FirstRunFeatures, NFVLS

Coming Out, Coming Home: Asian and Pacific Islander Family Stories

B., Hima
1996; USA; 44 min; Documentary

Five proud and very confident Asian Pacific Islander
families speak frankly, and emotionally about their
children's sexual orientation.

Dist/Sales: API-PFLAG

Coming Out of the Iron Closet

Peloso, Larry
1995; Canada; 40 min; Documentary

Of all the places in the world, the former USSR is
still one of the least secure for a gay man or lesbian
to live. The reason for this isn't so much due to the
traumas of living under an ongoing oppressive
regime, but rather those of living under such an
unstable one. Perestroika may have opened the closet
doors in some respects, but the political climate
since then has been so inconstant that what is
sanctioned one day may well be strictly taboo the
next. Shot during a fortnight's train trip through
Moscow, Riga and Tallinn, the video examines the
state of play for gay men and lesbians in the former
USSR, and includes an interview with the proud
editor of Russia's first gay magazine. (MQFF)

Awards: San Francisco International Lesbian & Gay
Film Festival, 1995: Audience Award for Best Video

Coming Out under Fire

Dong, Arthur
1994; USA; 71 min; Documentary
P: Arthur Dong; *W:* Allan Berube, Arthur Dong;
C: Stephen Lighthill; *E:* Veronica Selver; *M:* Mark Adler
Cast: Salome Jens

An extraordinary documentary about gays and
lesbians in the American military during the Second
World War. It goes beyond mere historical documentation to include riveting personal stories and
carefully chosen archival material. The film uncovers
the stories of men and women who found themselves fighting two wars: one for their country, and
the other against the armed forces who sought to

C

discharge them as undesirables.

Prod Comp: DeepFocus Productions
Dist/Sales: Wolfe, Zeitgeist, DeepFocus, VideoAmericain, ACMI

Coming to Terms

Postoff, Shawn
2000; Canada; 16 min; Drama

Damian sinks into desperation when he realises that both he and his family have an arduous journey ahead if they are to heal old wounds and come to terms with his dawning sexuality. (CFMDC)

Dist/Sales: CFMDC, Frameline

Common Flower, A

Bartoni, Doreen
1992; USA; 26 min; Drama

This moving short film concerns older couple Paula and Sylvia. They plan a trip to Sylvia's homeland, Russia, but when Sylvia dies Paula prepares to go anyway. This simple story gains poignancy and depth from its exploration of the difficulty of silent bereavement, when no-one knows the friend who has died is more than just a friend. (MQFF)

Common Ground

Deitch, Donna
2000; USA; 105 min; Drama
W: Paula Vogel, Terrence McNally, Harvey Fierstein; *C:* Jacek Laskus; *E:* Robin Katz; *M:* Frederic Talgorn
Cast: Beau Bridges, Ed Asner, Helen Shaver, Jonathan Taylor Thomas, Margot Kidder

Common Ground tells stories of three generations of gays in Homer, Connecticut. *Friends of Dorothy*, set in the 1950s, is about the rejection suffered by a local woman when she is discharged from the Navy under Section 8 (sexual deviancy). *Mr Roberts*, set in 1978, concerns a gay student/athlete who turns to his closeted French teacher for support after things get rough in the locker room. *2000* shows the pre-wedding jitters a gay man goes through, and explores his relationship with his military dad. (Wolfe)

Prod Comp: Winsome Entertainment
Dist/Sales: Wolfe, Showtime, ParamountHV

Common Threads: Stories from the Quilt

Epstein, Robert / Friedman, Jeffrey
1989; USA; 89 min; Documentary
P: Bill Couturie, Robert Epstein, Jeffrey Friedman;
W: Rob Epstein, Jeffrey Friedman, Cindy Ruskin;
C: Dyanna Taylor, Jean De Segonzac; *E:* Jeffrey Friedman, Rob Epstein; *M:* Bobby McFerrin

In the late 1970s, a mysterious new disease began infecting and killing gay men. *Common Threads* tells the powerful story of the first decade of the AIDS epidemic, as told through the lives of five very diverse individuals who shared a common fate. Using the monumental Names Project AIDS Memorial Quilt as its central metaphor, the film weaves together personal memories and television news stories to expose the US government's failure to respond to the growing epidemic, and the vibrant protest movement that was born as a result. From the Olympic athlete to the inner-city recovering drug addict, from the conservative naval commander to the New York gay activist, to the 11-year-old suburban boy with haemophilia, the film uses intimate details to tell an epic story of love, loss, anger and healing. (Telling Pictures)

Awards: Academy Awards, 1989: Best Documentary
Prod Comp: Mainstream, Telling Pictures
Dist/Sales: Ronin, BFI, Cowboy, Telling, FilmsTransit

Companions: Tales from the Closet

Bergström, Nina / Neant-Falk, Cecilia
1996; Sweden; 53 min; Documentary

In this documentary about lesbian love, five elderly Swedish women, ages 60 to 75, discuss their lives during a period when homosexuality was considered a perversion. In a poignant and often humorous manner, they talk about budding love and first relationships with women as well as the forced secrecy and loneliness, tracing their personal development from self loathing and forbidden love to a hard-won sense of emotional liberation and social openness. (Cinema Guild)
Swedish with English subtitles.

Dist/Sales: Wolfe, CinemaGuild

Company of Strangers, The

(aka: Strangers in Good Company)

Scott, Cynthia
1990; Canada; 97 min; Drama
P: David Wilson; *W:* Gloria Demers, Cynthia Scott, David Wilson, Sally Bochner; *C:* David De Volpi
E: David Wilson; *M:* Marie Bernard
Cast: Alice Diablo, Constance Garneau, Winifred Holden, Cissy Meddings

Seven old women are stranded at a deserted farmhouse, miles from civilisation after their bus breaks down. Through the ensuing days the group of strangers share their life stories, exchange once secret thoughts, and turn the crisis into a triumph of the human spirit. The group includes a shy Mohawk woman, a free thinker, a literary lesbian and an irrepressible woman from Dorset named Cissy.

Prod Comp: National Film Board of Canada, First Run Features
Dist/Sales: NewVision, CastleHill, Wolfe, ACMI, BFI

Complaints of a Dutiful Daughter

Hoffmann, Deborah
1994; USA; 44 min; Documentary

With profound insight and a healthy dose of levity, *Complaints of a Dutiful Daughter* chronicles the various stages of a mother's Alzheimer's Disease and the evolution of a daughter's response to the illness. The desire to cure the incurable, to set right her mother's confusion and forgetfulness, to temper her mother's obsessiveness, gives way to an acceptance which is finally liberating for both daughter and mother. Neither depressing nor medical, *Complaints of a Dutiful Daughter* is much more than a story about Alzheimer's and family caregiving. It is ultimately a life-affirming exploration of family relations, ageing and change, the meaning of memory, and love. (WMM)

Awards: San Francisco International Lesbian & Gay Film Festival, 1994: Best Documentary
Dist/Sales: WMM, Ronin, FilmsTransit, Cowboy

Compromised Immunity

Lipman, Andy
1985; UK; 47 min; Drama

A film version of one of the earliest stage dramas about AIDS, *The Normal Heart. Compromised Immunity* is the story of the developing friendship between Britain's first AIDS patient, a gay man, and a straight orderly in a typical London hospital.

Compulsion

Fleischer, Richard
1959; USA; 103 min; B&W; Thriller
P: Richard Zanuck; *W:* Richard Murphy; *C:* William C. Mellor; *E:* William Reynolds; *M:* Lionel Newman
Cast: Dean Stockwell, Bradford Dillman, Orson Welles, Diane Varsi

Recreation of the Leopold-Loeb murder case in 1920s Chicago, in which two young gay men, killed a boy for the thrill of it. The film contains well-dramatised courtroom scenes with Orson Welles playing the defence lawyer. See also Tom Kalin's film *Swoon* relating the same story.

Prod Comp: 20th Century-Fox
Dist/Sales: Ascanbee, 20thCenturyFox

Comrades in Arms

Marshall, Stuart
1990; UK; 50 min; Documentary
P: Rebecca Dobbs; *W:* Stuart Marshall

Six lesbians and gays recount their humorous and poignant memories of living, loving and serving in the armed forces during World War II. Their experiences range from the London Blitz to Japanese prisoner-of-war camps in Singapore, and from the drag show at the front line in Burma to Special Operations in Southeast Asia.

Prod Comp: Channel 4
Dist/Sales: FilmakersLibrary, Salzgeber, MayaVision

Conception

Sigal, David
1995; USA; 20 min; Comedy

An amusing and inventive look at the trials and tribulations of conceiving a child when one vital ingredient is missing. Sigal is, however, keen to stress that it's not just dykes who suffer the baby blues. *Conception* also includes a pregnant straight teen and a gay man with relationship problems. (MQFF)

Confession, The

Pfirman, Carl
2000; USA; 22 min; Drama

Nearing the end of his life, Joseph creates tension in his long-term relationship when he attempts to resurrect his Catholic faith.

Confessions of a Pretty Lady

Confessions of a Pretty Lady

Clarke, Kristiene / Mortimer, Sarah
1993; UK; 70 min; Documentary
W: Kristiene Clarke
Cast: Sandra Bernhard, Camille Paglia, Martin Scorsese

Engaging documentary by transsexual producer Kristiene Clarke, which follows Sandra Bernhard through the streets of tinsel town. Features snippets of Bernhard's own celluloid footage, live shows, home movies and interviews with family and friends like Martin Scorsese, LA's Dykes on Bikes and controversial enfant terrible academic, Camille Paglia.

Dist/Sales: BBC-Enterprises

Confessions of a Window Cleaner

Guest, Val
1974; UK; 90 min; Comedy
P: Greg Smith; W: Val Guest, Christopher Wood;
C: Norman Warwick; E: Bill Lenny; M: Sam Sklair
Cast: Robin Askwith, Anthony Booth, Linda Hayden,
Bill Maynard, Dandy Nichols

A bawdy British sex comedy about a window cleaner
who doesn't quite clean up his act. The first of the
UK 'Confessions' series of films. The window
cleaner is the voyeur who spends his time spying on
a nymphomaniac, a lesbian and a frustrated teacher.

Prod Comp: Columbia; Dist/Sales: 16MM, Col-Tri

Confessions of Felix Krull, The

(aka: Bekenntnisse des Hochstaplers Felix Krull)

Hoffmann, Kurt
1957; Germany; 116 min; B&W; Drama
P: Hans Abich, Eberhard Krause; W: Robert Thoeren,
Erika Mann; C: Friedl Behn-Grund; E: Caspar van den
Berg; M: Hans-Martin Majewski
Cast: Horst Buchholz, Liselotte Pulver, Ingrid Andree,
Susi Nicoletti

A rogue, in turn-of-the-century Germany, uses his
charm and good looks to acquire the finer things of
life without working. He indulges in a variety of
heterosexual and homosexual liaisons. His life takes a
strange twist when he falls in love with a trapeze
artist. Based on the original story by Thomas Mann.
German with English subtitles.

Prod Comp: Filmaufbau

Conformist, The

(aka: Il Conformista)

Bertolucci, Bernardo
1970; France, Germany, Italy; 108 min; Drama
P: Maurizio Lodi-Fe; W: Bernardo Bertolucci;
C: Vittorio Storaro; E: Franco Arcalli; M: Georges Delerue
Cast: Jean-Louis Trintignant, Stefania Sandrelli, Gastone
Moschin, Enzo Taroscio

In 1938 an inhibited and repressed homosexual
young man tries to conform to the prevailing mood
of Fascism, but after a series of events he gets out of
his depth when he turns informer and becomes an
unwilling murderer. Based on the original story by
Alberto Moravia. French with English subtitles.

Prod Comp: Mars, Marianne, Maran
Dist/Sales: Potential, Paramount

Confusion of Genders

(aka: La confusion des genres)

Cohen, Ilan Duran
2000; France; 94 min; Comedy

P: Didier Boujard; W: Ilan Duran Cohen, Philippe
Lasry; C: Jeanne Lapoirie; E: Fabrice Rouaud; M: Jay
Jay Johanson
Cast: Nathalie Richard, Pascal Greggory, Cyrille
Thouvenin, Vincent Martinez

Alain is a fortyish, bisexual attorney considering
settling down with his long-time law partner and
occasional lover Laurence. But suddenly the
beautiful young Christophe appears on the scene,
promising a taste of life on the wild side. And there's
also Babette, the enigmatic girlfriend of one of his
clients, Marc, who himself is rather cute.
(www.frenchculture.org)
French with English subtitles.

Prod Comp: Alta Loma Films, Fugitive Productions
Dist/Sales: PictureThis!, Haut-et-Court

Connections: Gay Aboriginal Men in Sydney

Dal, Reno
1997; Australia; 58 min; Documentary
P: Reno Dal

Connections is the first film to attempt an in-depth
understanding of gay Aboriginal men in Australia.
Filmed over two years, it sets out to understand what
it means to be gay and Aboriginal while living in the
urban environment of Sydney.

Prod Comp: Reno Dal Pty Ltd

Consenting Adult

Cates, Gilbert
1985; USA; 92 min; Drama
P: David Lavica, Ray Aghayan; W: Laura Z. Hobson,
John McGreevey; C: Frank Stanley; E: Melvin Shapiro;
M: Laurence Rosenthal
Cast: Martin Sheen, Marlo Thomas, Barry Tubb, Talia
Balsam

Drama about a family in turmoil when their 'perfect'
son discloses he's gay. A movie which explores the
ties that bind parent to child, wife to husband, lover
to stranger, body to soul. It's about becoming an
adult, a time when these ties often become tangled.
Based on the novel by Laura Z. Hobson, and
originally made for television.

Prod Comp: David Lawrence and Ray Aghayan
Productions, The Starger Company
Dist/Sales: ABC-US

Consequence, The

(aka: Die Konsequenz)

Petersen, Wolfgang
1977; Germany; 100 min; B&W; Drama
P: Peter Genée; W: Wolfgang Petersen, Alexander
Ziegler; C: Jörg Michael Baldenius; E: Hannes Nikel;
M: Nils Sustrate

Cast: Jürgen Prochnow, Ernst Hannawald, Werner Schwuchow, Hans-Michael Rehberg

The story of two men's illicit sexual relationship. One is an actor who is in prison for seducing a minor, the other is the teenage son of one of the guards. They attempt to make a life together, but with interference from the boy's family, tragedy ensues.

Prod Comp: Solaris Film

Conta Pra Mim

(aka: Trust Me)

Machado, Andre
2001; Brazil; 10 min; Drama

Anything can happen when a 17-year-old boy find himself in love with his best mate.

Dist/Sales: MixBrasil

Conversation Piece

(aka: Gruppo di famiglia in un interno)

Visconti, Luchino
1974; Italy; 117 min; Drama
P: Giovanni Bertolucci; *W:* Luchino Visconti, Suso Cecchi d'Amico, Ennric Medioli; *C:* Pasqualino de Santis; *E:* Ruggero Mastroianni; *M:* Franco Mannino
Cast: Burt Lancaster, Helmut Berger, Claudia Marsani, Silvana Mangano

When a reclusive professor is persuaded to let his top floor to a young couple he is brought face to face with his latent homosexuality and his approaching death.

Prod Comp: Rusconi, Gaumont
Dist/Sales: 20thCenturyFox, NewLine

Coonskin

(aka: Street Fight)

Bakshi, Ralph
1974; USA; 95 min; Comedy
P: Albert S. Ruddy; *W:* Ralph Bakshi; *E:* Donald W. Ernst; *M:* Chico Hamilton
Cast: Barry White, Charles Gordone, Philip M. Thomas, Scatman Crothers

This controversial animated feature from the man who made *Fritz the Cat* has superb design and a great voice track. The story attempts to trace the history of the African–American experience in America using rather misshapen animal characters. One of the characters is a black drag queen called Snowflake who spends most of his time having sex in the back of trucks or being beaten up, supporting the myth that homosexual behaviour is synonymous with sex and violence. A number of interest groups found the film offensive and it was taken out of circulation for nearly a decade and then later re-released under the less offensive title *Street Fight*.

Corpo, O

(aka: The Body)

García, José Antonio Fernández
1991; Brazil; 84 min; Drama
P: Adone Fragano, Anibal Massaini Neto; *W:* Alfredo Oroz; *C:* Antonio Meliande; *E:* Eder Mazzini, Danilo Tadeu; *M:* Paulo Barnabé
Cast: Antônio Fagundes, Marieta Severo, Cláudia Jimenez, Sérgio Mamberti

Story about a ménage à trois involving two women and a man. When the women find their man has been cheating on them with a prostitute, they become even closer. Their hatred for him begins to grow, they decide he must die and begin to plot his death.

Prod Comp: Cinearte, Olympus Filmes

Corps Imagé, Le

Cummins, Stephen
1986; Australia; 12 min; Experimental

Le Corps Imagé is a mood piece of photographs projected onto nude models. The images, ranging from classic nudes to a three-dimensional movie audience, are projected so that the distinction between the projected image and the model/screen is obscured. (Frameline)

Prod Comp: Australian Film TV & Radio School
Dist/Sales: AFTRS, Frameline

Corps Ouverts, Les

(aka: Open Bodies)

Lifshitz, Sébastien
1997; France; 44 min; Drama

18-year-old Rémi, studies commerce, works part-time in an Arab grocery, and, answering an ad for film actors, finds himself in a relationship with Marc, the director. His sexual identity, however, is an open book. French with English subtitles.

Dist/Sales: Kanpaï

Cosmic Demonstration of Sexuality, A

Frilot, Shari
1992; USA; 20 min; Experimental

A humorous comparison between female sexuality and cosmic structures, this video interviews five different women on topics such as menstruation, masturbation and ejaculation. The video proposes how sexuality may connect us with much more than just our partners. (Third World Newsreel)

Dist/Sales: TWN

C

Costa Brava

Balletbò-Coll, Marta
1994; Spain; 92 min; Comedy
P: Marta Balletbò-Coll; *W:* Marta Balletbò-Coll, Ana
Simon Cerezo; *C:* Teo López García; *E:* Olaguer
Cordoba; *M:* Miguel Amor, Emil Remolins Casas,
Xavier Martorell, Ikal Sena
Cast: Marta Balletbo-Coll, Desi Del Valle, Montserrat
Gausachs

Set in Barcelona, *Costa Brava* displays a clever,
simplistic style. A whimsical comedy, it weaves
through the day-to-day life of Anna, a tour guide
and struggling playwright. Anna's work brings her
into contact with Montserrat, a scientist who has
recently arrived in Barcelona from Israel. A friendship begins and the two women eventually fall in
love. Negotiating their way through the trials and
tribulations of a new relationship results in a few
comically confronting episodes. (MQFF)

Awards: San Francisco International Lesbian & Gay
Film Festival, 1995: Audience Award Best Film; Los
Angeles Gay & Lesbian Film Festival, 1995: Best Film
Prod Comp: Marta Balletbò-Coll
Dist/Sales: Forefront, Millivres, NorthernArts,
VideoAmericain

Could be Worse

Stratis, Zach
2000; USA; 84 min; Documentary
W: Zach Stratis, Vilma Gregoropoulous; *C:* Vilma
Gregoropoulous; *E:* Tom Ohanian, Jonathan Sahula,
Lynne Schwahn Parrella

Zach is making a film about his Greek–American
family in Boston for his parents' 50th wedding
anniversary party. Zach is the youngest in the family,
and wants to investigate what holds the family
together. He also wants to uncover how his family
feels about his homosexuality. But, he also doesn't
want to offend, so he decides to make a cheerful
musical comedy, rather than a straight documentary.
What follows is the Stratis family breaking into a
litany of lame songs, awful vocals, creeky choreography and completely over the top costumes. But it's
so utterly endearing that you can't help but fall in
love with them.

Prod Comp: Midburb Productions
Dist/Sales: Could-Be-Worse

Countess Dracula

Sasdy, Peter
1971; UK; 94 min; Horror
P: Alexander Paal; *W:* Jeremy Paul; *C:* Kenneth Talbot;
E: Henry Richardson; *M:* Harry Robertson
Cast: Ingrid Pitt, Nigel Green, Sandor Elès, Maurice

Denham, Lesley-Anne Down

Countess Elizabeth Bathory masquerades as her own
daughter, but she must bathe in the blood of virgins
to maintain her facade of youth. When her young
lover discovers the truth the countess reverts to an
old hag and tries to kill her own daughter to
rejuvenate herself. It is more a poignant study of
parents and the jealousy their children can inspire in
them rather than a vampire film.

Prod Comp: Hammer, Rank
Dist/Sales: Ascanbee, 20thCenturyFox, Carlton

Coup de Grace

(aka: Der Fangschuss)

Schlöndorff, Volker
1976; France, Germany; 95 min; B&W; Drama
P: Anatole Dauman; *W:* Genevieve Dormann, Jutta
Bruckner, Margarethe von Trotta; *C:* Igor Luther;
E: Jane Sperr; *M:* Stanley Myers
Cast: Margarethe von Trotta, Matthias Habich, Rüdiger
Kirschstein, Valeska Gert

Set in the 1918 civil war between German sympa-
thisers and Communist insurgents. Sophie, the
daughter of a once wealthy family, opens her house
to German soldiers and falls in love with Erich, the
commander of the unit. But her love for Erich is
unwelcomed as he is secretly in love with Sophie's
brother. Spurned by him and in desperation Sophie
finally turns to Communism, becoming a political
enemy. German with English subtitles.

Prod Comp: Argos, Bioskop Film
Dist/Sales: NFVLS

Crash and Burn

Graham, David
1999; USA; 25 min; Drama
P: David Graham, Brian Ash, Elizabeth Malcolm;
W: David Graham, Stephanie Urdang

Short film about a couple whose schedules keep
them apart at nights. One of the men's interest in
S/M bars almost gets him in to trouble one night.

Crazy Richard

Francis, Dean / Mathers, Katrina
2001; Australia; 64 min; Comedy
P: Dean Francis; *W:* Dean Francis, Katrina Mathers
Cast: Richard Viede, Dominic McDonald, Bonnie
Smith, Geoffrey Smith, Nick Farnell

From an early age Richard Viede led a charmed
life—a household-name starring in a top Australian
television soap opera. Then his life took a darker
turn when a drug overdose saw him vanish from the
nation's screens. *Crazy Richard* is a 'fly-on-the-wall'

C

mockumentary following Viede as he attempts to resurrect his illustrious career by taking a part in gay soap *I Can't Even Think Straight!*

Prod Comp: Long Shot Films

Creation of Adam, The

(aka: Sotvoreniye Adama)

Pavlov, Yuri
1993; Russia; 90 min; Drama
P: Dzhavanshir Kamandar, Anatolli Kasimov;
W: Vladimir Maslov, Vitaly Moskalenko; *C:* Sergei Machilsky; *E:* Raisa Lissova; *M:* Andrei Sigle
Cast: Irina Matlitskaya, Anzhelika Nevolina, Saulis Balandis, Sergei Vinogradov

Andrei's marriage is on the rocks because his wife thinks he's gay, and he gets himself into trouble when he helps a young gay man escape from some queer-bashers. But a work visit from a charismatic, wealthy businessman turns Andrei's life around. Russian with English subtitles.

Dist/Sales: WaterBearer, VideoAmericain

Creature

Creature

Patton, Parris
1998; USA; 77 min; Documentary
P: John Lepore; *C:* John Travers; *E:* Parris Patton;
M: Chad Smith
Cast: Stacey Hollywood Dean, Butch Dean, Dusty Dean, Filberto Barbarella Ascencio

Documentary which chronicles four years in the life of Stacey as she transforms her gender from male to female.

Prod Comp: Grapevine Films
Dist/Sales: 7thArt

Crimes of Passion

1991; UK; 17 min; Documentary

A short documentary about writers Ruth Rendell, Mary Wings and Katherine Forrest, who write books that represent contrasting lifestyles among lesbian detectives and share an interest in explicit eroticism.

Prod Comp: Channel 4

Criminal Lovers

Criminal Lovers

(aka: Les Amants Criminels)

Ozon, François
1999; France; 96 min; Comedy
P: Olivier Delbosc, Marc Missonnier; *W:* François Ozon; *C:* Pierre Stoeber; *E:* Dominique Petrot;
M: Philippe Rombi
Cast: Natacha Régnier, Jérémie Rénier, Miki Manojlovic, Salim Kechiouche

When Alice convinces her naive boyfriend Luc to prove his love for her by helping her murder a cocky classmate, the stage is set for a cross-country crime spree. While trying to dispose of the body the pair crosses paths with, and are ultimately trapped by, a terrifying hermit who brings their fling to a not-so-happy fairy tale ending. In *Criminal Lovers*, acclaimed director François Ozon weaves the story of a pair of lethal lovers-on-the-run with the fairy tale of *Hansel and Gretel*, twisting together a story of psychosexual tension that's guaranteed to titillate. French with English subtitles. (Strand)

Prod Comp: Fidélite Productions, La Sept Cinéma, Le Studio Canal+
Dist/Sales: Celluloid-Dreams, Strand, Millivres, VideoAmericain

Critical Mass: Gay Games Amsterdam

Manuel, William L.
1998; USA; 60 min; Documentary
P: William L. Manuel; *C:* Jose Lopez; *E:* Antonio Benetiz

A complete coverage of the Gay Games in Amsterdam in 1998.

Prod Comp: Manmade Multimedia
Dist/Sales: Manmade

Crocodile Tears

Coppel, Ann
1998; USA; 84 min; Horror
Cast: Dan Savage, Ted Sod, George Weiss Vando Wade Madsen

A remake of 'Faust' with a gay twist. An HIV-positive middle-school art teacher who has recently lost a drag-queen friend to suicide writes a letter to the devil asking for help. After a demon shows up at his door, he finds the price he has to pay to be very high, as he slowly transforms himself into a racist and homophobic heterosexual. (www.queerhorror.com)

Crocodiles in Amsterdam

(aka: Krokodillen in Amsterdam)

Apon, Annette
1989; The Netherlands; 88 min; Comedy
W: Annette Apon, Yolanda Entius, Henriëtte Remmers; *C:* Bernd Wouthuysen; *E:* Danniel Danniel; *M:* Henk van der Meulen, Michel Mulders
Cast: Joan Nederlof, Yolanda Entius, Hans Hoes, Marcel Musters

When a flighty blonde and a sulky activist meet up with Amsterdam as the backdrop, anything goes! And it sure does in this wacky girl-adventure movie. Gino and Nina meet under odd circumstances, and set about hatching a plan to blow up an arms factory. Apon creates a comedy that tests the limits of the female buddy film, without being overtly lesbian.

Dist/Sales: WMM, Netherlands, WaterBearer, VideoAmericain

Crossing, The

(aka: La Traversée)

Lifshitz, Sébastien
2001; France; 85 min; Documentary
W: Stáphane Bouquet; *C:* Pascal Poucet; *E:* Stéphanie Mahet

The Crossing is a film about trying to make sense of family and, to some extent, friendship. Stéphane's absent father has been banished to dreams. His mother, however, has become, in his eyes, the woman who has abandoned her own dreams to live her life through his. Somewhere, between those dreams is the reality of Stéphane's life. An exquisite selection of stilled frames and CinemaScope captures a poetic image of one young man's search for the father he has never met in a land where he has never been, America. Close-up, honest and self aware, each frame of the *The Crossing* documents the unfolding reality which it is artistically and respectfully observing. (16th London Lesbian & Gay Film Festival)

Prod Comp: Lancelot Films, CNC
Dist/Sales: AdVitam

Cruel

Del Valle, Desi
1994; USA; 20 min; Drama
P: Desi Del Valle; *W:* Desi Del Valle; *C:* Tracy Thompson; *E:* Amy E. Duddleston, Wendy Chien
Cast: Kristen Ochoa, Susan Papa

Isabel and Melanie are at the end of their relationship but, unwilling to let go, they remain together in the same household. Melanie avoids Isabel's pleas for reconciliation and begins dating another woman. Already wounded by the break-up, Isabel becomes outraged when she discovers that the woman Melanie is seeing is white. Isabel questions whether her being Latino, and not Anglo, is cause for Melanie to no longer love her. Melanie is unable to communicate her feelings and leaves Isabel alone to cope with the meaning of their break up. (Frameline)

Prod Comp: Chula Pictures
Dist/Sales: Frameline

Crueles, Las

(aka: The Cruel Ones)

Aranda, Vincente
1969; Spain; 100 min; Thriller
W: Vincente Aranda, Antonio Rabinad; *C:* Juan Amorós; *E:* Maricel Bautista, Bautista Treig; *M:* Marco Rossi
Cast: Haydée Politoff, Carlos Estrada, Raymond Lovelock, Capucine

After being jilted by her husband, Esther takes up with Parker who is a lesbian. Eventually, however, Esther takes her own life. To revenge her lover's death Parker entices the ex-husband to her house and shows him Esther's corpse which she keeps in the fridge. She begins to send him belongings of his ex-wife, such as dresses, but then begins to send severed pieces of the body.

Prod Comp: Films Montana

Cruising

Friedkin, William
1980; USA; 102 min; Drama, Thriller
P: Jerry Weintraub; *W:* William Friedkin; *C:* James Contner; *E:* Bud Smith; *M:* Jack Nitzsche

Cast: Al Pacino, Paul Sorvino, Karen Allen, Richard Cox, Don Scardino

One of the most controversial films of the 1980s, which tells the story of an undercover cop who enters the gay scene of Manhattan to search for a psychotic killer. Set in the leather bars of Greenwich Village, the straight cop not only begins his investigation into the murders but also his awakening sexuality. Based on the novel by Gerald Walker.

Prod Comp: Lorimar, United Artists
Dist/Sales: 20thCenturyFox, Warner, TLA, FilmsInc, UA, ACMI, Swank

Cruising

Cruising in the Channels

1991; UK; 21 min; Documentary

Short documentary which lokks at the depiction of lesbians and gays television.

Prod Comp: Channel 4

Crush (1992)

MacLean, Alison
1992; New Zealand; 97 min; Drama
P: Bridget Ikin; *W:* Alison MacLean, Anne Kennedy; *C:* Dion Beebe; *E:* John Gilbert; *M:* JPS Experience, Anthony Partos
Cast: Marcia Gay Harden, Caitlin Bossley, William Zappa, Donough Rees

Debut film from Alison MacLean about revenge and jealousy between two women and a 15-year-old girl after one of the women is crippled in a car accident. There is an unclear relationship between the two women. Were they lovers or ex-lovers, or just friends? A dark, modern fable about the teenage girl's developing awareness of her power and sexuality.

Prod Comp: Hibiscus Films, Movie Partners, New Zealand Film Commission
Dist/Sales: Wolfe, Strand, Cowboy, ACMI

Crush (2000)

Bartell, Phillip J.
2000; USA; 27 min; Drama

12-year-old Tina meets 16-year-old Robbie. They immediately strike up a friendship, which soon turns into a crush on Tina's part. But Robbie has a crush on a boy around town.

Dist/Sales: GoinBack

Crying Game, The

Jordan, Neil
1992; UK; 113 min; Thriller
P: Stephen Woolley; *W:* Neil Jordan; *C:* Ian Wilson; *E:* Kant Pan; *M:* Anne Dudley
Cast: Stephen Rea, Jaye Davidson, Forest Whitaker, Miranda Richardson, Adrian Dunbar

Full of surprises, this film has done more than win extraordinary critical acclaim throughout the world. It upstaged all competition by receiving six Academy Award nominations. Set in Ireland, this spellbinding thriller tells the story of a black British soldier, Jody, who befriends his reluctant IRA captor, Fergus. When Jody is killed in an ambush, Fergus fulfils his dying wish—to find his girlfriend Dil in England. When Fergus and Dil become romantically involved, the crying game begins. Electrifying and seductive, this groundbreaking movie had everyone talking.

Awards: Academy Awards, 1992: Best Screenplay
Prod Comp: Miramax, British Screen, Channel 4, Eurotrustees, Palace
Dist/Sales: Roadshow, TLA, FilmsInc, Wolfe, Miramax, ACMI, Swank

Crush (1992)

Curse of the Queerwolf

Pirro, Mark
1987; USA; 90 min; Comedy
P: Sergio Bandera, Mark Pirro; *W:* Mark Pirro;
M: Gregg Gross
Cast: Kent Butler, Michael Palazzolo, Taylor Whitney

When an all–American guy is bitten on the behind by a gay werewolf, he becomes a campy drag queen—a 'queerwolf'—when the moon is full.

Prod Comp: Pirromount Productions
Dist/Sales: TLA

Cuz it's Boy

Gund Saalfield, Catherine
1994; USA; 13 min; Experimental

Have you ever wanted to be a boy? Would that be different from being a lesbian or a passing woman? What does the story of Brandon Teena have to offer lesbians? (Kitchen)

Dist/Sales: Kitchen

Cynara: Poetry in Motion

Conn, Nicole
1996; USA; 40 min; Drama
Cast: Johanna Nemeth, Melissa Hellman

A sweeping romance set against the moody backdrop of the Northwest Coast of the USA in 1883. The story begins with the simple elegance of girl meets girl on a haunting shoreline. One is a sculptress in exile, the other is an expatriot—each woman is in search of herself—what they find is each other. Finally, lesbian romance and erotica meet on the silver screen in this resplendent romantic tale. *Cynara* is a high seas, Heathcliff on the Moors, larger than life romance. It is a lush, textured lesbian *Wuthering Heights* for our time. (Wolfe)

Dist/Sales: Wolfe, VideoAmericain

Daddy and the Muscle Academy

Pohjola, Ilppo
1992; Finland; 65 min; Documentary
P: Kair Paljakka, Alvaro Pardo
Cast: Isaac Julien

Tom of Finland's drawings have had an enormous impact on gay identity, not only for their intense physicality, but also for the permission they granted a whole generation to fantasise freely. This documentary centres on Tom's work and concentrates primarily on the impact that his drawings have had on focusing gay identity—particularly leather identity. With commentary provided by artist Nayland Blake and filmmaker Isaac Julien, among others, the phenomena of Madonna and Freddie

Mercury figure prominently in this tribute to one of the world's great gay artists. (MQFF)
Some Finnish with English subtitles.

Prod Comp: Filmtakemo, Yleisradio
Dist/Sales: Zeitgeist, Salzgeber, VideoAmericain

Daddy & Papa

Daddy & Papa

Symons, Johnny
2002; USA; 57 min; Documentary

Daddy & Papa explores the growing phenomenon of gay fatherhood and its impact on American culture. Through the stories of four different families, *Daddy & Papa* delves into some of the particular challenges facing gay men who decide to become dads. From surrogacy and interracial adoption, to the complexities of gay divorce, to the battle for full legal status as parents, *Daddy & Papa* presents a revealing look at some of the gay fathers who are breaking new ground in the ever-changing landscape of the American family. (www.daddyandpapa.com)

Dist/Sales: Daddy&Papa, NewDay, FilmsTransit

Dads

(aka: Papas)

Gypkens, Martin
2000; Germany; 35 min; Documentary

An in-depth and intimate look at the realities (good and bad) of gay parenting.

Dist/Sales: HFF

Dads Wanted

Pemberton, Justin
2001; New Zealand; 44 min; Documentary

Fascinating New Zealand documentary featuring three very different experiences of queer parenting. Theresa and Erin are a couple with twin baby boys who they are raising without any donor involvement. Leigh is a single lesbian looking for a gay father for her second child, and Glenn and Robert are a couple who share their two children with their lesbian mums. (queerDOC 2001)

Dadshuttle, The

Donoughy, Tom
1995; USA; 30 min; Drama
W: Tom Donoughy; *C:* Ellen Kuras
Cast: Peter Maloney, Matt McGrath

Based on the critically acclaimed play by Donoughy, this is the story of the change in the relationship between a father and son. A father drives his son to the station on Thanksgiving Night. Along the way the son tells his father that his lover is dying of AIDS.

Daisies

(aka: Sedmikrásky)

Chytilová, Vera
1966; Czechoslovakia; 78 min; Comedy
P: Bohumil Smida, Ladislav Fikar; *W:* Ester Krumbachová, Vera Chytilová; *C:* Jaroslav Kucera; *E:* Miroslav Hajek; *M:* Jiri Slitr, Jiri Sust
Cast: Jitka Cerhova, Ivana Karbonava, Julius Albert

This film is a study of the relationship between two bored young women, who decide to react to consumer-oriented society by performing a series of outrageous acts. These include destroying material goods owned by various people. It all ends with a banquet in a slapstick orgy of destruction. Although not obviously lesbian, the close relationship between the two women has helped this to become widely adopted as a lesbian film.

Prod Comp: Ceskoslovensk, Státní Film

Daisy Chain Project, The

D'Souza, Kevin / Noorani, Arif
1998; Canada; 15 min; Documentary

Documentary which brings together five South-Asian men from across Canada. Each of the men expresses in a short video-vignette a particular experience of their carnal body in relation to queer 'male' sexualities. (Video Pool)

Dist/Sales: VideoPool

Dakan

Camara, Mohamed
1997; Guinea, France; 87 min; Drama
P: René Féret; *W:* Mohamed Camara; *C:* Gilbero Azevedo; *E:* Dos Santos; *M:* Kouyate Sory Kandia
Cast: Mamady Mory Camara, Aboucar Touré, Cécile Bois, Koumba Diakite

Said to be the first West African film to deal with homosexuality. *Dakan* a coming out story which challenges the myth of a global gay culture, as well as traditional African attitudes towards homosexuality. French with English subtitles.

Prod Comp: Film Du 20ème Créations Cinématographiques
Dist/Sales: CaliforniaNewsreel

Dallas Doll

Turner, Ann
1993; Australia; 104 min; Comedy
P: Ross Matthews, Ann Turner, Tatiana Kennedy; *W:* Ann Turner; *C:* Paul Murphy; *E:* Mike Honey; *M:* David Hirschfelder
Cast: Sandra Bernhard, Victoria Longley, Frank Gallacher, Jake Blundell, Rose Byrne

A happy suburban family is thrown into chaos by the arrival of Dallas Adair—an American with no past but definite plans for the future. She manages to seduce all members of the family, bar one. A comic allegory of seduction, synchronicity ... and golf.

Prod Comp: Dallas Doll Productions
Dist/Sales: 21stCentury, ArtisticLicense, VSM

Damned if you Don't

Damned if you Don't

Friedrich, Su
1988; USA; 41 min; B&W; Experimental
P: Su Friedrich; *W:* Su Friedrich; *C:* Su Friedrich; *E:* Su Friedrich
Cast: Peggy Healey, Ela Troyano

Damned if you Don't is an experimental narrative about the seduction of a nun by another woman. Beginning with an amusing critique of the classic nun film, *Black Narcissus* (1947), the central narrative is interwoven with documentary footage of nuns in public places. In the audacious and beautifully choreographed final scene, Friedrich rejects the split between the spiritual and the sexual in Catholicism and, on another level, the denial of sensual pleasure in feminist filmmaking.

Awards: Athens Film Festival, 1988: Best Experimental Film
Dist/Sales: WMM, CFMDC, NFVLS

Damned, The

(aka: Gotterdammerung; La Caduta degli Dei)

Visconti, Luchino
1969; Germany, Italy; 164 min; Drama
P: Alfred Levy, Ever Haggiag; *W:* Nicola Badalucco,
Enrico Medioli, Luchino Visconti; *C:* Armando
Nannuzzi, Pasquale de Santis; *M:* Maurice Jarre
Cast: Dirk Bogarde, Ingrid Thulin, Helmut Berger,
Charlotte Rampling, Helmut Griem

Visconti's film probes the German soul on the eve of
Nazi power, meticulously dissecting the emotional
lives of members of a powerful munitions dynasty.
Dirk Bogarde portrays a modern Macbeth who
ruthlessly gains control of the steel empire during
Hitler's rise to power. Helmut Griem plays
Aschenbach, a leader in Hitler's SA troops whose
power grabbing schemes end when he is slaughtered
by the SS in a spectacular re-creation of the infamous 'Night of the Long Knives'. What develops is a
complex study in intrigue and obsessions, culminating in the weird power struggle involving Friedrich
and Martin. Visconti was forced to edit out much of
the homosexually-charged orgy that occurred just
before the slaughter. Look for Helmut Berger in drag
impersonating Dietrich.

Prod Comp: Pegaso, Praesidens
Dist/Sales: Warner

Dandy Dust

Scheirl, Hans
1998; Austria, UK; 94 min; Experimental, Sci-Fi
P: Hans Scheirl; *W:* Hans Scheirl; *C:* Jana Cipriani;
E: Hans Scheirl; *M:* Yossarian, Emma EJ Doubell, Bent
Cast: Suzie Krueger, Leonora Rogers-Wright, Tre
Temperilli, Hans Scheirl, Svar Simpson

This wild romp through a gender-fucked universe
was five years in the making, and what results is a
transgressive science-fiction splatter epic incorporating live action, miniature work, and computer and
film animation. The narrative follows a split-
personality cyborg of fluid gender, as s/he travels
through time while battling a genealogically-
obsessed family. A trippy and thought provoking
film, equal parts *Akira* and *Alice in Wonderland*, that
is everything reactionaries are afraid of. (MQFF)

Prod Comp: Dandy Dust Filmproduktion
Dist/Sales: Peccadillo, ACMI

Danger Girl, The

Badger, Clarence G.
1916; USA; 26 min; B&W; Comedy
P: Mack Sennett
Cast: Gloria Swanson, Mack Swain

Gloria Swanson dons up in male attire to seduce the
woman who is distracting the hero's attentions away
from her. Naturally it all ends heterosexually-ever-
after, but in the meantime there is plenty of
transgender fun and girl-girl tension.

Prod Comp: Keystone Film Company

Danny

Kybartas, Stashu
1987; USA; 20 min; Documentary

Danny is a moving personal documentary about
filmmaker Kybartas' friend Danny, who died of
AIDS in 1986. This powerful work explores the
reason for Danny's return home and his attempts to
reconcile his relationship with his family, who had
difficulty facing their son's homosexuality and his
imminent death.

Danza Macabra, La

(aka: Castle of Blood)

Margheriti, Antonio
1963; France, Italy; 87 min; B&W; Horror
P: Marco Vicario, Giovanni Addessi; *W:* Jean Grimaud,
Sergio Corbucci; *C:* Riccardo Pallottini; *E:* Otello
Colangeli; *M:* Riz Ortolani
Cast: Barbara Steele, George Rivière, Margaret Robsahn,
Henry Kruger

Our young hero is challenged by a friend to stay one
night in a very spooky castle. It turns out to be
inhabited by a pack of ghosts who act out the crimes
of passion for which they were killed. He realises
that they are after his blood and tries to flee the
castle only to be impaled on the gate. Steele returns
to her favourite genre and plays the central ghost
figure.

Prod Comp: Vulsinia Films, Jolly Films, Leo Lax, Ulysee
Dist/Sales: Sinister

Danzón

Novaro, María
1991; Mexico, Spain; 96 min; Drama
P: Jorge Sanchez; *W:* María Novaro, Beatriz Novaro;
C: Rodrigo García; *E:* María Novaro, Nelson Rodriguez;
M: Agustín Lara, Pepe Luis, Felipe Pérez, Consuelo
Velázquez
Cast: Tito Vasconcelos, María Rojo, Carmen Salinas

40-year-old Julia is a Mexican telephone operator.
When her long-time ballroom-dancing partner of 20
years suddenly goes missing, her search takes her to
the coastal town of Vera Cruz where she finds a new
friend, Susy, a transvestite nightclub entertainer. Susy
and her friends take on the task of lifting Julia's spirits.

Prod Comp: Instituto Mexicano de Cinematografía
Dist/Sales: SonyClassics

Dark and Lovely, Soft and Free

(aka: Nega Do Cabelo Duro)

Alberton, Paulo
2000; Brazil, South Africa; 52 min; Documentary

Based on research done by the Gay and Lesbian Archives of South Africa, this delightful documentary explores small town gay life in rural South Africa. Our host Zakhi Radebe introduces us to a variety of gay men—all of them hairdressers—and through them, their communities and their country.

Dist/Sales: Vidiola

Dark Habits

(aka: Entre Tinieblas)

Almodóvar, Pedro
1984; Spain; 116 min; Comedy
P: Luis Calvo; *W:* Pedro Almodóvar
Cast: Cristina Pascual, Carmen Maura

When nightclub singer Yolanda's boyfriend dies of an overdose, she seeks help from a group of over-the-top sexually ambiguous nuns in a local convent.

Dark Sun: Bright Shade

Kwoi
1993; Canada; 57 min; Drama

Focusing on themes of conflict between Eastern and Western values, feudalism and democracy, father and son, friend and lover, *Dark Sun: Bright Shade* follows the relationship of an exiled Tiananmen Square dissident and his lover as Confucian ethics collide with the temptations of Western complacency. (Frameline)

Dist/Sales: Frameline, CFMDC

Darker Side of Black, The

Julien, Isaac
1993; UK; 55 min; Documentary
P: Lina Gopaul, David Lawson; *W:* Isaac Julien;
C: Arthur Jafa, David Scott; *E:* Joy Chamberlain;
M: Trevor Mathison

The Darker Side of Black is a provocative investigation of the social and political influences of hip-hop and dance-hall music: its proponents, fans, detractors and critics. Allowing for a more complex response to his subject—which ritualises machismo, misogyny, homophobia and gun glorification—Julien never opts for easy judgements. Rather, the film explores issues of class, commercial marketing, the legacy of colonialism, fundamentalist faith and the fears governing accepted notions of masculinity.

Prod Comp: Arts Council of Great Britain, BBC
Dist/Sales: Drift, VTape, FilmakersLibrary

Darkness before Dawn

Wu, Feng
1996; China; 80 min; Documentary

Not so long ago the Chinese government declared that homosexuality did not exist in China. This brave and telling documentary shows the day-to-day lives of lesbians and gays in China in the 1990s. People from all areas of society, former stars of the Peking Opera, workers, intellectuals and one of the filmmakers, have been interviewed and allowed the camera into their very private worlds. Chinese with English subtitles.

Dist/Sales: Frameline

Darling

Schlesinger, John
1965; UK; 127 min; B&W; Drama
P: Joseph Janni; *W:* Frederic Raphael; *C:* Ken Higgins;
E: James Clark; *M:* John Dankworth
Cast: Julie Christie, Dirk Bogarde, Laurence Harvey, Roland Curran, Jose Villalonga

Julie Christie won an Academy Award for her performance as an ambitious young model who uses all her assets to achieve social success. Ultimately, she finds that the life to which she aspired is meaningless and empty. Her relationships with journalist Dirk Bogarde, company director Laurence Harvey, an effeminate photographer and an Italian Prince are never really satisfying. *Darling* was ground breaking in its time because it exposed the 'swinging sixties' with its more 'modern' attitudes towards sexuality, homosexuality and infidelity in a frank and adult manner.

Awards: Academy Awards, 1965: Best Actress (Julie Christie), Script
Prod Comp: Embassy, Anglo-Amalgamated Productions, Vic Films
Dist/Sales: ACMI

Darling International

Reeves, Jennifer Todd / Serra, M. M.
2000; USA; 22 min; Drama

A dark and sensual narrative that explores a metal worker's sexual fantasies during her nights as a femme on Manhattan's lower east side in this travelogue of desire.

Dist/Sales: FilmmakersCoop

Das Trio

(aka: The Trio)

Huntgeburth, Hermine
1997; Germany; 97 min; Comedy
P: Laurens Straub; *W:* Horst Sczerba, Volker Einrauch,

Hermine Huntgeburth; *C:* Martin Kukula; *E:* Renate Merck; *M:* Niki Reiser
Cast: Götz George, Christian Redl, Jeanette Hain, Felix Eitner

> When partners in crime become partners in bed, all hell breaks loose in this outrageous sex comedy that keeps it all in the family. (Wolfe)
> German with English subtitles.

Prod Comp: Next Film
Dist/Sales: MediaLuna, Attitude, TLA, Wolfe

Daughter of Dykes

Palmer, Amilca
1994; USA; 14 min; Documentary

> An upbeat approach is adopted as young teenage girls speak candidly about how they felt when they discovered their mothers were lesbians, their own coming-out process of being the daughter of a lesbian and feelings about their own sexual orientation.

Dist/Sales: WMM

Daughters of Darkness

(aka: Le Rouge aux Lévres)

Kümel, Harry
1971; Belgium, France, Germany, Italy; 96 min; Horror
P: Henry Lange, Paul Collet, Alain C. Guilleaume;
W: Pierre Drout, Jean Ferry, Harry Kumel; *C:* Edward van der Enden; *E:* Denise Bonan, August Verschueren, Hans Zeiler; *M:* François de Roubaix
Cast: John Karlen, Delphine Seyrig, Danielle Ouimet, Andrea Rau

> In an opulent Ostend hotel, eerily deserted in the off season, a young, but hardly innocent couple on their honeymoon encounter the apparently ageless, sunlight-fearing, lesbian Countess Bathory. Kümel imaginatively balances the erotic malaise and violence of vampire folklore and a European surrealistic tradition with 1930s Hollywood camp and comic strip tableaux. Perverse sexuality is located in a setting of decadent high life which seems to immobilise the victims.

Prod Comp: Showking Films, Maya Films
Dist/Sales: NFVLS, ACMI

Daughters of the Sun

Shahriar, Maryam
2000; Iran; 90 min; Drama
P: Jahangir Kosari; *W:* Maryam Shahriar; *C:* Homayun Payvar; *E:* Shahrzad Pouya; *M:* Hossein Alizadeh
Cast: Altinay Ghelich Taghani, Soghra Karimi, Zahra Mohammadi, Habib Haddad

> In her debut film about the bitter fate of Iranian women in the countryside, Shahriar takes a brave look at a controversial subject. Locks of Amagol's beautiful long black hair fall to the ground and are blown away by the wind, her father shaves her hair so that she looks like a boy. As the eldest of six daughters in a poor peasant family, Amagol is sent to a remote village, where she can work as a carpet weaver. Dressed in boy's clothes, she works, eats and sleeps in the small workshop. She remains a solitary figure since no one must find out that she is a girl. Her situation gets even more complicated and increasingly difficult when another girl from the workshop falls in love with her. (2001 Lesben Film Festival Berlin) Iranian with English subtitles.

Prod Comp: Farabi Cinema Foundation

David & Goliath

McHenry, Bryan
2001; USA; 28 min; Experimental

> A skinny 'David' falls for a 'Goliath', in this rewriting of the David and Goliath story. A witty rumination on the idea of body image in gay male culture.

David Searching

Smith, Leslie L.
1996; USA; 103 min; Comedy
P: John P. Scholz, Leslie L. Smith; *W:* Leslie L. Smith;
C: John P. Scholz; *E:* Toni Blye
Cast: Anthony Rapp, Camryn Manheim, Julie Halston, Joseph Fuqua

> *David Searching* is the story of an idealistic independent filmmaker's quest for romance. David is unable to pay his rent so he takes in a roommate, Gwen. The two become comrades-in-arms in the never ending search for a meaningful relationship. (Water Bearer Films)

Dist/Sales: WaterBearer, Millivres, VideoAmericain

Day for Night

(aka: La Nuit Américaine)

Truffaut, François
1973; France, Italy; 120 min; Drama
P: Marcel Berbert; *W:* François Truffaut, Jean-Louis Richard, Suzanne Schiffman; *C:* Pierre-William Glenn;
E: Martine Barraqué, Yann Dedet; *M:* Georges Delerue
Cast: Jacqueline Bisset, Valentina Cortese, Jean-Pierre Aumont, Alexandra Stewart

> Immensely enjoyable, richly detailed insider's view of the goings-on in a film studio. An ageing bisexual actor brings his new young lover onto the set but the actor is killed before shooting begins. Even though the relationship is presented in a positive light, it all ends in tragedy. Dubbed into English.

Awards: Academy Awards, 1973: Best Foreign Language Film
Prod Comp: Les Films du Carrosse, PECF, PIC
Dist/Sales: Ascanbee, ReelMovies, Warner

Day I Decided to be Nina, The

Jansen, Ingeborg
2000; The Netherlands; 15 min; Documentary

> 11-year-old Guido doesn't want to be a jet pilot or a policeman when he grows up. He'd rather be a girl. (queerDOC 2002)

Day in the Life of a Bull-Dyke, A

Dempsey, Shawna / Millan, Lorri
1995; Canada; 11 min; Experimental

> This experimental documentary tells the story of a big boned butcher looking for love. A unique chance to see the conventional world through unconventional eyes.

Dist/Sales: VideoPool

Day of the Jackal, The

Zinnemann, Fred
1973; France, UK; 114 min; Thriller
P: Julien Derode, John Woolf, David Deutsch;
W: Kenneth Ross; *C:* Jean Tournier; *E:* Ralph Kemplen;
M: Georges Delerue
Cast: Edward Fox, Alan Badel, Tony Britton, Cyril Cusack, Michel Auclair

> The complex story of an assassination attempt on French President General de Gaulle. Fox picks up a gay man in a bathhouse and uses his apartment as a hide out. When the man sees Fox's photograph on television, he is killed. The plot is revealed in great detail and can be hard work, but some great performances make it very engaging. Based on the novel by Fredrick Forsyth.

Prod Comp: Universal, Warwick Film Productions
Dist/Sales: ReelMovies, Universal

Day the Fish Came Out, The

(aka: Otan ta Psaria Vgikan sti Steria)

Cacoyannis, Michael
1967; Greece, UK; 109 min; Comedy
P: Michael Cacoyannis; *W:* Michael Cacoyannis; *C:* Walter Lassally; *E:* Vassilis Syropoulos; *M:* Mikis Theodorakis
Cast: Tom Courtenay, Candice Bergen, Colin Blakely, Sam Wanamaker, Ian Ogilvy

> A plane carrying dangerous weaponry goes down off the coast of Greece. To keep the locals calm the US officials arrive dressed as tourists to investigate. Only trouble is they are dressed so casually that the plane's pilots assume that they are all gay. The pilots must keep themselves hidden and can't contact the rescue team. The secrecy causes a comedy of errors that barely inspire a chuckle.

Prod Comp: 20th Century-Fox
Dist/Sales: Ascanbee

Days

(aka: Giorni)

Muscardin, Laura
2001; Italy; 90 min; Drama
P: Francesco Montini; *W:* Laura Muscardin, David Osorio, Monica Rametta; *C:* Sabrina Varani; *E:* Walter Fasano; *M:* Ivan Iusco
Cast: Thomas Trabacchi, Riccardo De Filippis, Monica Rametta, Davide Bechini

> Claudio is 35 years old, works as a bank manager and has been HIV-positive for ten years. One night, he meets Andrea and realises he has a particular attraction for him. There is a hidden aspect of Andrea's personality which induces Claudio to keep a distance from him. But Claudio soon abandons himself causing all the rules and restrictions which define his life to become superfluous. Italian with English subtitles. (Picture This! Entertainment)

Prod Comp: Movie Factory
Dist/Sales: PictureThis!

De Colores

Mosbacher, Dee
2001; USA; 28 min; Documentary

> *De Colores* is a bilingual documentary about how Latino families are replacing the deep roots of homophobia with the even deeper roots of love and tolerance. Through moving personal stories we learn about how families are breaking cultural barriers and how love always prevails. (Eye Bite Productions)

Prod Comp: EyeBite Productions, Woman Vision Productions
Dist/Sales: Eyebite, WomanVision

Dead Boys' Club, The

Christopher, Mark
1992; USA; 25 min; Drama
P: Mary Weisgerber Meyer; *W:* Mark Christopher;
C: Jamie Silverstein
Cast: Nat Dewolfe

> *The Dead Boys' Club* is the story of a young man in a world haunted by the absence of an entire generation of men: a generation that he should have known but, because of AIDS, that he can, for the most part, only imagine. Awkward and shy, Toby is visiting his New York cousin Packard, who gives him a pair of shoes previously owned by Packard's recently deceased

d

lover. When Toby dons the shoes, he's transported to 1970s the pre-AIDS world of promiscuity, hot guys and glitter balls. *The Dead Boys' Club* is an evocative, sexy and humorous exploration of a young man's coming out, and homage to the generation that paved the way (some with their lives) before him.

Awards: San Francisco International Lesbian & Gay Film Festival, 1992: Best Short
Dist/Sales: Frameline, Forefront, BFI

Dead Dreams of Monochrome Men

Hinton, David
1990; UK; 60 min; B&W; Musical

In this surprisingly homoerotic British film version of a dance/performance piece by the London-based DV8 Physical Theatre, anonymous sex is sweat-soaked, serious business with arousing, if sombre, consequences. The piece is based on the real-life murders of several gay men who were picked up in discos by a gay serial killer. Filmed in starkly-lit, muscle-enhancing black and white, *Dead Dreams* looks like a series of living George Platt Lynes photographs set in a fevered, prison-like bar world, pulsating with wordless sexual narratives, twitchy erotic appetites and well-shorn, hunky men. DV8's extreme choreography, while at times almost acrobatic, is appropriately rooted in urban sexual realism. (MQFF)

Deadfall

Forbes, Bryan
1968; UK; 120 min; Thriller
P: Paul Monash; *W:* Bryan Forbes; *C:* Gerry Turpin; *E:* John Jymson; *M:* John Barry
Cast: Michael Caine, Giovanna Ralli, Eric Portman, Nanette Newman

A jewel thief falls in love with a beautiful woman who is married to a homosexual man who turns out to be her father.

Prod Comp: Salamander, 20th Century-Fox
Dist/Sales: 20thCenturyFox

Deaf Heaven

Levitt, Steve
1993; USA; 25 min; Drama

A man must find the strength to battle his lover's parents who want to bring him home to die. An unexpected meeting with a Holocaust survivor at a sauna teaches him much about what it means to live through the pain of AIDS. (MQFF)

Awards: San Francisco International Lesbian & Gay Film Festival, 1993: Audience Award for Best Short
Dist/Sales: Frameline

Deal, The

Girolami, Lisa
1999; USA; 10 min; Comedy

Some Hollywood deals are more interesting than others. An aspiring actress is faced with a rather interesting deal proposed by a successful lesbian producer. (2000 Phoenix Lesbian & Gay Film Festival)

Dear Boys

(aka: Lieve Jongens)

De Lussanet, Paul
1980; The Netherlands; 90 min; Comedy
P: Matthijs van Heijningen; *W:* Paul de Lussanet, Chiem van Houweninge; *C:* Paul van den Bos; *E:* Hans van Dongen; *M:* Matthijs van Heijningen
Cast: Hans Dagelet, Bill Van Dijk, Albert Moll, Hugo Metsers

This film tells the story of Wolf, a middle-aged alcoholic writer who spends his time in self-absorbed sexual fantasies, and Tiger, a young man who is the centre of Wolf's obsession. Tiger befriends another young man, Muskrat, who is also in a relationship with an older man. Finally the two younger men leave their relationships with the desperate older men. Based on the novel by Gerald Reve.

Dist/Sales: Netherlands

Dear Jesse

Kirkman, Tim
1997; USA; 82 min; Documentary
P: Mary Beth Mann; *W:* Tim Kirkman; *C:* Norwood Cheek, Ashley McKinney; *E:* Joe Klotz

Filmmaker Tim Kirkman returns to his North Carolina hometown to come to grips with his own homosexuality while exposing the anti-gay sentiment led by Jesse Helms. A deeply moving and often hilarious meditation on controversial issues, *Dear Jesse* has universal appeal and timely political significance. (Cowboy Pictures)

Prod Comp: Bang Prods, North Caroline Film Foundation
Dist/Sales: Cowboy, Wolfe, NewYorker, VideoAmericain

Dear Mom

Bonder, Diane
1996; USA; 15 min; Experimental

The story about the formation of a girl's identity in relation to her powerful mother. When the young girl's fantasy of matricide comes true due to the ultimately death of her mother, she finds herself at a crossroads. She is left to reconstruct her own identity and finds out that her mother is more complex than she imagines.

Dear Rock

Walsh, Jack
1992; USA; 18 min; Documentary
W: Jack Walsh; *E:* Jack Walsh

Dear Rock is a powerful posthumous fan letter to Rock Hudson that uses Hudson as a springboard for an exploration of AIDS and homophobia.

Death in the Family, A

Main, Stewart / Wells, Peter
1987; New Zealand; 48 min; Drama
P: James H. Wallace; *W:* Peter Wells
Cast: John Bazier, Nancy Flyger, Bernadette Doolan, Ray Adkins

Although this is a dramatisation it is based on actual group experience of the process of dying. It covers the final 16 days of a man's life. Dying of AIDS he has returned to New Zealand to spend his last days with this friends. This film is perhaps unique in its portrayal of dying as both a practical process and a journey into 'a strange and foreign land', as one of the participants describes it. Despite the sadness, the group seems to be overcome by a kind of euphoria.

Prod Comp: New Zealand Film Commission, Television New Zealand
Dist/Sales: Ronin, Salzgeber, Heathcliff, ACMI

Death in Venice

(aka: Morte a Venezia)

Visconti, Luchino
1971; Italy; 128 min; Drama
P: Luchino Visconti; *W:* Luchino Visconti, Nicola Bandalucco; *C:* Pasquale de Santis; *E:* Ruggero Mastroianni; *M:* Gustav Mahler
Cast: Dirk Bogarde, Bjorn Andresen, Silvana Mangano, Marisa Berenson, Mark Burns

Gustav Aschenbach is a distinguished man, a world-famous conductor who embodies all the civilised virtues of the European culture he represents. Yet on a solitary holiday in Venice, he spies an innocent boy—and abandons himself to a secret passion that carries him to his doom. Lyrical, intelligent and heartbreakingly beautiful, *Death in Venice*, accompanied by the haunting music of Gustav Mahler, will leave its echo in your memory for years to come.

Awards: Cannes Film Festival, 1971: Grand Prix
Prod Comp: Warner, Alfa Cinematografica, PECF
Dist/Sales: ReelMovies, Warner, ACMI, NFVLS

Death in Venice, CA

Ebersole, P. David
1994; USA; 30 min; Drama
P: Maricel Pagulayan; *W:* P. David Ebersole; *C:* Amy Vincent; *E:* Poppy Das; *M:* Adam Fields
Cast: Robert Glen Keith, Nick Rafter, Shirley Knight

This update of Thomas Mann's novella sees handsome scholar Mason Carver's seaside convalescence interrupted by his landlady's vamping, hunky son. He is suddenly plunged into a passion he has studied but never known—with drop-dead gorgeous 18-year-old Sebastian Dickens.

Prod Comp: First Run Features
Dist/Sales: DesiFilms

Deathtrap

Lumet, Sidney
1982; USA; 116 min; Comedy
P: Burtt Harris; *W:* Jay Presson Allen; *C:* Andrzej Bartkowiak; *E:* John J. Fitzstephens; *M:* Johnny Mandel
Cast: Michael Caine, Christopher Reeve, Dyan Cannon, Irene Worth, Henry Jones

A no longer productive playwright conceives a complex plan to murder an upcoming rival and former student, and steal his script. But as it turns out, the two are gay lovers who actually concoct a plan to kill Caine's wife. The plot is so laden with twists and turns that not even the nosey psychic from next door can figure out the truth.

Prod Comp: LAH, Warner
Dist/Sales: ReelMovies, Warner, Swank

Deathwatch

Morrow, Vic
1966; USA; 88 min; B&W; Drama
P: Leonard Nimoy, Vic Morrow; *W:* Vic Morrow, Barbara Turner; *C:* Vilis Lapenieks; *E:* Verna Fields; *M:* Gerald Fried
Cast: Michael Forest, Paul Mazursky, Leonard Nimoy

Rarely seen film version of Jean Genet's play about a brutal prison love triangle. Three prisoners are thrown together—one a murderer, one a thief and the other a homosexual—as they fight for survival. See also *No Exit* which is based on a similar story.

Prod Comp: Castle Hill Productions, Beverly Productions

Debutantes, The

Oliver, Bill
1996; USA; 26 min; Drama

Crisis erupts over a dinner when an expatriated gay man returns to Savannah on the occasion of his sister's coming out—her debutante ball, that is. Every crisis presents an opportunity, and this one offers our hero and his sister a chance to come to terms with Southern tradition, family history, and their own truths. (Big Film Shorts)

Dist/Sales: BigFilm

Deccada

Sartain, Claudine
1999; Australia; 14 min; Experimental

Sweet, sexy, lyrical and visually gorgeous look at modern girls.

Dist/Sales: Queerscreen

Decodings

Wallin, Michael
1989; USA; 15 min; B&W; Experimental

A strongly affecting, allegorical compilation of found footage from the 1940s and 50s. Filmmaker Michael Wallin's unadorned narration describes the lonely social transition from boyhood to manhood, stapled to images of cliff-divers, stunt drivers and boys boxing blindfolded.

Dist/Sales: Canyon, WaterBearer

Deep End, The

McGehee, Scott / Siegel, David
2001; USA; 100 min; Thriller
P: Scott McGehee, David Siegel; *W:* Scott McGehee, David Siegel; *C:* Giles Nuttgens; *E:* Lauren Zuckerman; *M:* Peter Nashel
Cast: Tilda Swinton, Jonathan Tucker, Goran Visnjic, Peter Donat

With her navy officer husband away at sea, Margaret Hill has no one to turn to when the body of her gay son's older lover washes up on the beach, and she suspects Beau of murder. Her decision to hide the body propels her into an increasingly complicated and frightening situation—especially when blackmailers show up to threaten her with videotapes of her son. (Wolfe)

Prod Comp: i5 Films
Dist/Sales: 20thCenturyFox, FoxSearchlight, Wolfe

Deep Inside Clint Star

Alberta, Clint
1999; Canada; 89 min; Documentary
P: Louise Lore, Silva Basmajian; *C:* Marcos Arriaga;
E: Katharine Assals; *M:* James Cavalluzzo

The filmmaker, as title character 'Clint Star', interviews six friends about topics such as sex, identity, racism, suicide, and survival. The documentary careens up gritty city streets and down reservation roads into the hearts and minds of young Native men and women who are edgy, cool-and vulnerable. (Film & Video Centre: National Museum of the American Indian)

Prod Comp: National Film Board of Canada
Dist/Sales: NFBC

Deflatable Man, The

Bettell, Paul
1989; UK; 24 min; B&W; Experimental

Follows the mental wanderings of a loner in a quiet English suburb. Drawn towards the couples he sees, and the barber shop he has a fetish for, the pensive 'deflatable man' slips in and out of daydreams on the fears of loneliness and the absolution of the physical, and winds up sitting on the sidewalk. Bettell has long been seen as one of the leading filmmakers of Britain's gay avant-garde.

Dist/Sales: Frameline

Defying Gravity

Keitel, John
1997; USA; 92 min; Drama
P: Jack Koll, David Clayton Miller; *W:* John Keitel;
C: Tom Harting; *E:* Matthew Yagle
Cast: Daniel Chilson, Niklaus Lange, Don Handfield, Lianna Carter

Griff is the ultimate boy-next-door. Affable and cute, he's never had a problem fitting in. But Griff also has a secret—one that he has skilfully and diligently hidden from his fraternity brothers, his best friend Todd, and most of all, himself. Griff is in love with Pete, another member of his house. Rather than acknowledge his true feelings, though, Griff has conveniently convinced himself that it's only a phase. The tactic has worked, enabling him to operate, undetected, between two divergent worlds. But when Pete, no longer content with their surreptitious arrangement and string of one-night stands, moves out of the house and begins to explore his own sexuality more openly, Griff's two worlds stand ready to collide. (Jour de Fete)

Prod Comp: Boom Pictures
Dist/Sales: Wolfe, JourDeFete, Millivres, 10%

Deliverance

Boorman, John
1972; USA; 109 min; Drama
P: John Boorman; *W:* James Dickey; *C:* Vilmos Zsigmond; *E:* Tom Priestley; *M:* Eric Weissberg
Cast: Jon Voight, Burt Reynolds, Ned Beatty, Ronny Cox, James Dickey

The story of four ordinary men who embark on a canoe trip in the backwoods of America, determined to test themselves against a wilderness they only think they understand. Jon Voight, Burt Reynolds, Ned Beatty and Ronny Cox play the four friends whose three-dimensional roles heighten the film's impact and broader significance. Director John Boorman, renowned for his mastery of visual beauty and compelling mystery, maintains a narrative tension that never falters. This film is like a phantom; its images linger in our minds long after the river slows and returns us to real life. They meet up with some toothless hillbillies with buggery on their minds. Based on the original story by James Dickey.

Prod Comp: Warner, Elmer Productions
Dist/Sales: NFVLS, ReelMovies, Warner, ACMI

The Delta

Delta, The

Sachs, Ira
1996; USA; 85 min; Drama
P: Margot Bridger; *W:* Ira Sachs; *C:* Benjamin P. Seth; *E:* Alfonso Gonçalves; *M:* Michael Rohatyn
Cast: Shayne Gray, Thang Chan, Rachel Zan Huss, Colonious Davis

Lincoln is a nice Jewish boy with a car and a blonde girlfriend, a respectable family in the suburbs and nocturnal habits he'd rather they didn't know about. He is compulsively drawn to danger but not quite game for anything until he meets John, a troubled Vietnamese–African–American. They escape their lives by running away together on a boat down the Mississippi River. The film uses non-actors to give a real sense of, and insight into, the American South, teenagers, gay life, Jewish families and life as an Asian immigrant.

Awards: LA Outfest, 1997: Special Programming Committee Award Outstanding Emerging Talent (Ira Sachs)
Prod Comp: Charlie Guidance Productions
Dist/Sales: Wolfe, Strand, Cowboy, VideoAmericain

Demons

Kinney, Donald / Kinney, Robert
1994; USA; 70 min; Drama

This contemporary folk tale of survival is set in the rural Midwest in the early 1960s. Allie is a widow struggling to operate a small hog farm with the support of her teenage son, Dip, in spite of debts and vulturous corporate land prospectors. In the midst of these difficulties arrives her brother-in-law, Gray, who attempts to incorporate himself back on to the farm. Circumstances begin to knot when Grey pursues Dip, who reciprocates with the full passion of his burgeoning sexuality. Fearing that Dip will abandon both her and the farm, Allie devises a plan that will circumvent their desire.

Depart to Arrive

(aka: Weggehen um Anzukommen)

von Grote, Alexandra
1982; Germany; 89 min; Drama
Cast: Ute Cremer, Gabrielle Osburg

The debut film of Alexandra von Grote, who later went on to direct *November Moon*. Anna and Regina have been in a relationship for a year, but Regina slowly drifts away and begins an affair with another woman, Gaby. Anna, in trying to deal with the break-up, runs away to France to meditate. Even in this new location the wounds from the past keep surfacing. In order for Anna to move on to a new future she must look back and deal with the past, which holds a painful revelation.

Derrière, Le

(aka: From Behind)

Lemercier, Valérie
1999; France; 100 min; Comedy
P: Aissa Djabri, Manuel Munz, Farid Lahouassa; *W:* Valérie Lemercier, Aude Lemercier; *C:* Patrick Blossier; *E:* Maria Castro-Vasquez; *M:* Grégori Czerkinsky
Cast: Valérie Lemercier, Claude Rich, Dieudonné

After the death of her mother, Frédérique resolves to find her father, whom she has never met. She discovers the identity of her father on the back of an old photograph and sets out for Paris where he now lives. She is staying with some gay friends when she is persuaded to dress up as a gay man so that she can accompany them to a gay club. Frédérique later uses the same disguise when she discovers that her father is gay and is living with a younger, black man, hoping that her father will be more likely to accept a lost gay son than a lost straight daughter. To

d

complicate matters, Frédérique is simultaneously dating her boyfriend... French with English subtitles.

Prod Comp: TF1 Films, TPS Cinema, Vertigo
Dist/Sales: AMLF

Desert Hearts

Deitch, Donna
1985; USA; 91 min; Drama
P: Donna Deitch; *W:* Natalie Cooper; *C:* Robert Elswit;
E: Robert Estrin
Cast: Helen Shaver, Audra Lindley, Patricia Charbonneau, Andra Akers

Set in Nevada in 1959, Vivian Bell, a repressed college professor from New York, arrives at a ranch in Reno for a temporary stay to obtain a quickie divorce. Anticipating a quiet time reading and preparing for the academic year, she finds herself distracted and drawn to the ranch owner's fiery stepdaughter Cay Rivvers. As their friendship develops and Vivian's restrained and latent passion is unleashed, their lesbian relationship becomes an act of defiance against the accepted rules of society. Based on the novel *Desert of the Heart* by Jane Rule.

Prod Comp: Samuel Goldwyn Company, Desert Heart Productions
Dist/Sales: Roadshow, BFI, Wolfe, ACMI, TLA, SamuelGoldwyn, VideoAmericain

Deserter

(aka: Lipotaktis)

Korras, Giorgas / Voupouras, Christos
1988; Greece; 121 min; Drama
P: Greek Film Centre; *W:* Giorgos Korras, Christos Voupouras; *C:* Andreas Bellis; *E:* Giorgos Korras, Christos Voupouras; *M:* Eleni Karaindrou
Cast: Stelios Mainas, Leonidas Nomikos, Toula Stathopoulou, Stelios Pavlo

A fresco of life in a small provincial spa town. A comment on Greek society and the homosexual relationship between two young men, seen through the eyes of one of them. (www.hri.org)

Desi's Looking for a New Girl

Guzmán, Mary
2000; USA; 72 min; Drama
P: Fontana Butterfield, Mary Guzmán; *W:* Mary Guzmán; *C:* Sophia E. Constantinou; *E:* Lidia Szajko;
M: Alfred O. Guzman Jnr
Cast: Desi del Valle, Rosa Medina, Sandr Carola

From Cuban–American director Mary Guzmán comes a smart, sexy and exuberant trip through the world of Latina lesbian romance. A skateboarding baby-butch named J.T. narrates the tale of Desi, a cute young San Franciscan who's just dumped her two-timing girlfriend, and, the film's title notwithstanding, would rather curl up and die than look for a replacement. But cajoled by friends, soon enough Desi's on the prowl. From a New Age-type who's allergic to tea bags to a glamorous bombshell who likes to act straight, Desi's dating misadventures will make you laugh and cringe. Her family, amazingly supportive, nags her in Spanish that she needs a girlfriend. Her 'married' lesbian friends' precocious daughter won't stop bugging Desi about her ex. Meanwhile, J.T. has her own romantic fish to fry, positively obsessed with lesbian performer Marga Gomez. She's certain that, someday soon, she's destined to meet her idol. The entire ensemble delivers uniformly understated and down-to-earth performances, and in the title role, the irresistibly cute Desi del Valle plays miserably-single with winning charm. Punctuated by skateboard tricks and clever animated sequences, this groundbreaking diamond-in-the-rough first feature offers an irreverent and vibrant take on Latina lesbian life, and that universal and elusive quest for love. (2001 Miami Gay & Lesbian Film Festival) English & Spanish with English subtitles.

Dist/Sales: WaterBearer, Vagrant

Desire (1989)

Marshall, Stuart
1989; UK; 52 min; B&W; Documentary
P: Rebecca Dobbs; *W:* Frank Godwin
Cast: Peter Marc, Josie Bissett, Tamara Longley, Kay Parker, Dale Wyatt

An extraordinary documentary which looks at the history of homosexuality from the 1890s, with particular emphasis on the imprisonment of homosexuals by the Nazis during World War II.

Awards: Turin Gay & Lesbian Film Festival, 1991: Audience Prize
Dist/Sales: MayaVision, WaterBearer

Desire (1999)

Torregrossa, Jorge
1999; Spain, USA; 15 min; Drama

A married couple whose relationship is in trouble encounters a couple of handsome gay sailors in the woods, who offer a distraction.

Prod Comp: Reigen Films
Dist/Sales: OasisPC

Desperate Acquaintances

(aka: Desperate Bekjentskaper)

Wam, Svend
1998; Norway; 74 min; Drama
P: Svend Wam; *W:* Svend Wam, Dag Anders Rougseth;
C: Anders Leegaard; *E:* Frank Mosvold; *M:* Dag Anders

Rougseth
Cast: Anders Dale, Bjornar Teigen, Bjarte Hjelmeland, Kim Kolstad

> Three young men try to live up to masculine demands and myths When they can't find a sense of belonging or identity, they drift away from society—and protect themselves with bitter humour and drugs. Norwegian with English subtitles.

Dist/Sales: Mefistofilm

Desperate Living

Waters, John
1977; USA; 90 min; Comedy
P: John Waters; *W:* John Waters; *C:* Chris Lobingier, Allen Yarus; *E:* Charles Roggero; *M:* Chris Lobingier, Allen Yarus
Cast: Divine, Susan Lowe, Liz Renay, Mink Stole, Edith Massey

> Features a transvestite cop, leather-clad biker boys, tough-talking dykes and much more in this very queer and funny film from Waters. Peggy Gravel and her black maid kill her husband and escape to Mortville, a refuge for murderers, perverts and worse.

Prod Comp: Charm City Productions
Dist/Sales: NewLine, NFVLS, ACMI

Desperate Remedies

Desperate Remedies

Main, Stewart / Wells, Peter
1993; New Zealand; 93 min; Comedy
P: James Wallace; *W:* Peter Wells, Stewart Main; *C:* Leon Narbey; *E:* David Coulson; *M:* Peter Scholes
Cast: Jennifer Ward-Lealand, Kevin Smith, Lisa Chappell, Clifford Curtis

> Dorothea schemes to separate her opium-addled, sexpot sister from the lewd, addictively decadent Prince impersonator, Fraser. Dorothea engages the assistance of Lawrence, a penniless out-of-work hunk with a shady past and a fetching pout. A luscious, extravagant-looking film with fantastic art direction.

Very camp, humorous and highly stylised, with an overt lesbian relationship.

Prod Comp: James Wallace Productions, New Zealand Film Commission
Dist/Sales: NZFC, 21stCentury, NewVision, TLA, Swank, Miramax, ACMI

Destiny's Children

O'Keefe, Kevin
2001; Canada; 18 min; Documentary
The extraordinary story of David McInstry and his quest to be a father, against all odds. A moving and heart-warming story of someone who always believed his destiny was to raise children of his own. (queerDOC 2001)

Destroying Angel

Hoffman, Philip / Salazar, Wayne
1998; USA; 32 min; Documentary
P: Wayne Salazar

> *Destroying Angel* relates two stories of illness and weaves them into a tapestry of family history, memory and loss. The narrator, confronted with his own mortality, guides us through a landscape of recollections, dreams, close friendships and family ties. This is a moving portrait of the struggles involved in dealing with AIDS, cancer, memory and intimate relationships. (Frameline)

Prod Comp: Bar Nothin' Productions
Dist/Sales: Frameline, CFMDC

Detective, The

Douglas, Gordon
1968; USA; 114 min; Drama
P: Aaron Rosenberg; *W:* Abby Mann; *C:* Joseph Biroc; *E:* Robert Simpson; *M:* Jerry Goldsmith
Cast: Frank Sinatra, Lee Remick, Ralph Meeker, Jack Klugman

> A detective is assigned to find the killer of a wealthy gay man. He and his homophobic partner cruise the gay bars and areas in search of the murderer. Finally they coerce the murdered man's ex-lover to confess and he is sent to the electric chair. But it turns out he is innocent and the detective beings to uncover corruption in the police force.

Prod Comp: 20th Century-Fox
Dist/Sales: ReelMovies

Devil in the Holy Water, The

Balass, Joe
2001; Canada; 94 min; Documentary
P: Joe Balass; *W:* Joe Balass; *C:* Joe Balass, Andrei Khabad, Marjo Ferwerda, Giampaolo Marzi;

d

E: Joe Balass; *M:* Simon Carpentier

Two events collide in the Eternal City. As Catholics converge for the most important Church pilgrimage in modern times in Rome, thousands of gays and lesbians from around the planet gather for the first international Gay Pride Celebration. Joe Balass crafts a compelling portrait of the clash and controversy. The Vatican opposes the Pride March as an insult to Catholics. Parade organisers say the marchers will be 'an army of peace'. A Catholic activist calls the event 'an act of war against the Catholic Church', a fact he claims is proven by the march's support from 'radical' politicians, Masons and Jews—'always united... against the Catholic civilisation'. No wonder the church's allies in opposing the march are right-wing and neo-fascist parties. Organisers finally get permission from the waffling city officials to proceed with their rally just three days before it is set to begin. Ultimately, the march becomes a defining moment, not just for the Italian gay pride movement but for hundreds of thousands of proud queers from around the world. French & Italian with English subtitles. (2002 Vancouver Queer Film & Video Festival)

Prod Comp: Compass Productions
Dist/Sales: CinemaLibre

Devil's Playground, The

Schepisi, Fred
1976; Australia; 98 min; Drama
P: Fred Schepisi; *W:* Fred Schepisi; *C:* Ian Baker;
E: Brian Kavanagh; *M:* Bruce Smeaton
Cast: Arthur Dignam, Nick Tate, Simon Burke, Charles McCallum, John Frawley

A film told in a semi-autobiographical style about young boys at a Roman Catholic boarding school, reacting in different ways to puberty and their sexuality, and to their schoolmasters and priests. Schepisi's first feature is a powerful and insightful film.

Awards: Australian Film Institute Awards, 1976: Best Film, Director, Actor (Simon Burke, Nick Tate), Screenplay
Prod Comp: Film House
Dist/Sales: Sharmill

Devotion

Kaplan, Mindy
1994; USA; 120 min; Drama
P: Arlene Battishill; *W:* Mindy Kaplan, Arlene Battishill;
C: Mario Araya; *E:* Mindy Kaplan; *M:* Arlene Battishill
Cast: Jan Derbyshire, Kate Twa, Eileen Barrett, Cindy Girling

Sheila Caston is a stand-up lesbian comic whose life is going just fine. After a tour of the comedy circuits

Sheila is enjoying the company of her partner and friends and the familiarity of performing in her home town, Vancouver. Enter a childhood flame, throw in a theme of unrequited love and everything else in Sheila Caston's life begins to take a downward turn. Sheila gets a career break in the form of an offer of her own television show. Arriving at a preliminary meeting she is thrown off-balance when confronted with Lynn Webster—the object of her love 15 years ago. Both women are forced to confront the past, and tensions reach boiling point as respective partners realise something is awry. Interspersed with excerpts from Sheila's comedy routines, which poke fun at lesbian life and rituals, *Devotion* is sexy, funny, involving, and as satisfying as reading a good pot-boiler on a long flight. (MQFF)

Prod Comp: Auntie Em Productions, Dancing Arrow Productions
Dist/Sales: Forefront, NorthernArts, VideoAmericain, ACMI

Diabolique

Chechik, Jeremiah
1996; USA; 107 min; Thriller
P: Marvin Worth, James G. Robinson; *W:* Don Roos;
C: Peter James; *E:* Carol Littleton; *M:* Randy Edelman
Cast: Sharon Stone, Isabelle Adjani, Chazz Palminteri, Kathy Bates, Spalding Gray

This film is essentially a remake of *Les Diaboliques* (1955), which was directed by Henri-Georges Clouzot. For far too long, Nicole and Mia have suffered at the hands of Guy Baran, a cruel and heartless manipulator. As his mistress, Nicole has endured his lies and selfishness, while his wife, Mia, is nearly suicidal over his infidelities and callous humiliation of her. The two women form an intimate bond in their repression (although not obviously lesbian, the sexual nature of their relationship is very ambiguous) and devise a plan to murder him. With a seemingly foolproof scheme they kill him...or do they?

Prod Comp: Morgan Creek, Warner
Dist/Sales: Roadshow, ReelMovies, Warner

Diaboliques, Les

(aka: Diabolique)

Clouzot, Henri-Georges
1955; France; 106 min; B&W; Thriller
P: Henri-Georges Clouzot; *W:* Henri-Georges Clouzot, Jérôme Géronimi, René Masson, Frédéric Grendel;
C: Armand Thirard; *E:* Madeleine Gug;
M: Georges Van Parys
Cast: Simone Signoret, Vera Clouzot, Paul Meurisse, Charles Vanel, Michel Serrault, Pierre Larquey

A sadistic headmaster at a private boys school is

murdered by his long-suffering wife and his brutalised mistress. But when the two women return to the school and pretend no knowledge of the headmaster's disappearance they are unsettled by the schoolboys' sightings of his 'ghost'. Clouzot's famous horror film is imbued with a dark, malevolent atmosphere and perversity seems to lurk in every corner. The relationship between the two women is very ambiguous. Based on the book *Celle Qui N'Etait Plus* by Pierre Boileau and Thomas Narcejac (who also wrote *Vertigo*). French with English subtitles.

Prod Comp: Filmsonor, Vera Films
Dist/Sales: Ascanbee, SomethingWeird

Diane Linkletter Story, The

Waters, John
1969; USA; 15 min; Comedy
W: Divine, David Lochary, Mary Vivian Pearce, John Waters; *C:* John Waters; *E:* John Waters
Cast: Divine, David Lochary, Mary Vivian Pearce

Queer cult director Water tells the story of Diane Linkletter, which suggests that the daughter of famous television celebrity Art deliberately threw herself out of a window to get away from her stifling home life.

Prod Comp: Dreamland

Diary of a Male Whore

Wael, Tawfik Abu
2001; Palestine; 15 min; Drama

A haunting tale of a young man's sexual awakening and commodification, this short film by Palestinian filmmaker Tawfik Abu Wael depicts libidinal scenes and violent episodes without any sense of guilt. (www.arabfilm.com)

Dist/Sales: Trabelsi

Different Corner, A

Pham, Van M.
2001; UK, Wales; 12 min; Documentary

A Different Corner is a documentary about the positive relationships between lesbian parents and their children.

Different for Girls

Spence, Richard
1996; UK; 100 min; Comedy
P: John Chapman; *W:* Tony Marchant; *C:* Sean Van Hales; *E:* David Gamble; *M:* Stephen Warbeck
Cast: Rupert Graves, Steven Mackintosh, Miriam Marglyes, Saskia Reeves, Charlotte Coleman

Karl and Paul were best friends at school. Some 20 years later they met up again in London. But things are a little different now that Karl has become Kim, a transsexual. Amidst their problems they begin to fall in love, and after Kim seduces Paul he freaks out and the whole thing ends up in court. Now Kim has run away but will true love triumph?

Prod Comp: BBC
Dist/Sales: UIP, FirstLook, Wolfe, ACMI

Different Kind of Black Man, A

Wise, Sheila J.
2001; USA; 15 min; Documentary

A powerful look at the ideas and feelings of successful, black gay men on such issues as sexuality, masculinity and their perception of and their role within the black community. (Frameline)

Dist/Sales: Frameline

Different Kind of Love, A

Mills, Brian
1981; UK; 60 min; Drama
Cast: Nigel Havers, Joyce Redman, Rupert Frazer

A possessive mother, not long after her husband's death, pushes her son to get married by introducing him to a number of single women. She doesn't seem to understand that, at 30 and living with another man, he is not in the least bit interested.

Different Shades of Pink

Ku, Alexander
2001; Australia; 45 min; Documentary

Different Shades of Pink takes an intimate look at the lives of three Sydney multicultural gay couples as they relate their experiences of racism and Anglo angst.

Dist/Sales: Pinq

Different Story, A

Aaron, Paul
1978; USA; 108 min; Comedy
P: Alan Belkin; *W:* Henry Olek; *C:* Philip Lathrop; *E:* Lynn McCallon; *M:* David Frank
Cast: Perry King, Meg Foster, Peter Donat, Valerie Curtin, Richard Bull

A gay man and a lesbian marry to prevent his deportation from America, but somehow, despite initially hating each other, they fall in love. The film is terribly homophobic and they both come out of dysfunctional homosexual relationships and through their heterosexual tendencies maintain the status quo.

Prod Comp: Peterson Productions

Ding Dong

Hughes, Todd
1995; USA; 40 min; B&W; Comedy
P: David Carpender, David Colman, Todd Hughes;
W: Todd Hughes; C: David A. Carpender; E: Laurie
House; M: Cary Berger
Cast: Shawm Brydon, Marya Dosti, Mary Scheer,
Sandra Kinder

Reminiscent of early John Waters, *Ding Dong* is a very camp and decidedly warped account of two beauty product saleswomen turned serial killers. Working from the premise that if you can't beat 'em, join 'em, Hughes conjures up a witty riposte to the mainstream trend of lethal lesbians in such films as *Butterfly Kiss* and *Heavenly Creatures*. *Ding Dong* has an utterly queer sensibility, both in its outrageous narrative and skewed cinematography. *Ding Dong* also features celebrity cameos from the likes of Bob Hoskins and lesbian supermodel, Jenny Shimizu. (MQFF)

Prod Comp: Feminette Productions
Dist/Sales: KillerPix, DesiFilms

Dinner Guest, The

Wood, Andrew
1995; USA; 24 min; Drama

Soap opera style melodrama about a group of yuppie friends and their behind-the-scenes machinations. Coming together for a dinner party, a group of friends await one of their number with increasing trepidation. Wood's film shows how each of the characters reacts when they learn that their expected chum has tested HIV-positive. Although they have been asked to keep the information secret, one by one the story spreads and, once they realise they are all aware of the situation, they must decide how they will deal with this information when their friend arrives. In a short space of time they have to consider their relationships to him, his state of mind and, most difficult of all, the spectre of his death. (MQFF)

Diputado, El

(aka: The Deputy)

de la Iglesia, Eloy
1978; Spain; 111 min; Drama
W: Eloy de la Iglesia, Gonzalo Goicoachea; C: Antonio
Cuevas; E: Julio Peña; M: Julio Pena
Cast: José Sacristán, María Luisa San José, José Luis
Alonso, Enrique Vivó

When a prominent Spanish politician becomes involved in a love affair with a teenage boy, he becomes the target of blackmailers, putting his career in jeopardy.

Dirty Fingernails

Kennedy, Sarah
1996; USA; 21 min; Comedy

A love story about a girl and her motorbike.

Dist/Sales: Goodvibes

Dirty Laundry

Fung, Richard
1995; Canada; 31 min; Documentary

Dirty Laundry explores the hidden and lost histories of Asian–Canadian culture, while investigating issues of sexual and social behaviours that were misinterpreted by the dominant culture.

Dist/Sales: VDB

The Disco Years

Disco Years, The

King, Robert Lee
1991; USA; 30 min; Drama
P: Robert Lee King, John Peter James, Richard
Hoffman; W: Robert Lee King; C: Greg Gardiner;
E: Paul McCudden; M: Wendell Yuponce
Cast: Matt Nolan, Dennis Christopher, Gwen Welles

Filmmaker Robert King tells the story of Tom Peters, a gay teenager coming of age in the time of pet rocks, washing lines, and macramé. His proclivities become clear when Tom has his first sexual encounter with a male friend. While his mother is the epitome of the 'liberation' age, Tom finds that her permissiveness has some major limits and that he cannot seek the help he needs with her.

Prod Comp: RLK Productions
Dist/Sales: Strand, ACMI

Disgraceful Conduct

Weber, Eva
1995; UK; 17 min; Drama
Cast: Catherine White, Glynis Growe, Barry McCormick

Tells the story of Callum Morgan, a lesbian officer with the Royal Air Force, and the threats to her career that arise from the public knowledge that she is a lesbian.

Dist/Sales: Cinenova

Divine Trash

Yeager, Steve
1997; USA; 105 min; Documentary
P: Steve Yeager; *C:* Steve Yeager, Jeff Atkinson, Jim Harris; *E:* Terry Campbell, Tim Kahoe, Steve Yeager; *M:* Don Barto

An in-depth look at the early career of cult film-maker John Waters, from his childhood puppet shows in his native Baltimore to the successful release of what is widely regarded as the most important underground film ever made—*Pink Flamingos* (1972). *Divine Trash* features never-before-seen documentary footage shot behind the scenes during the rehearsal and filming of *Pink Flamingos* and 1972 interviews with a 25-year-old John Waters and many of the film's now-deceased cast members including Waters' discovery, the 300 pound drag superstar Glenn Milstead, aka Divine. (Wolfe)

Prod Comp: Stratosphere
Dist/Sales: Wolfe, Wellspring

Do you Think we can Talk about Anything but Love?

Ballyot, Sylvie / Kordon, Beatrice
2000; France; 40 min; Experimental

Three lesbians take us on a passionate excursion into melancholy, nomadism and ecstasy. An erotic, breathy French road movie with a difference. Together they traverse beautiful vistas and the psychobabble highways of a lesbian ménage à trois. True Gallic joie de vivre! (MQFF)

Dist/Sales: AMIP

Doctors' Wives

Schaefer, George
1971; USA; 100 min; Drama
P: Mike Frankovich; *W:* Daniel Taradash; *C:* Charles Lang; *E:* Carl Kress; *M:* Elmer Bernstein
Cast: Dyan Cannon, Richard Crenna, Gene Hackman, Carroll O'Connor, Rachel Roberts

A group of surgeons join forces when one of their sexually distraught wives is mysteriously murdered. One of the women, played by Rachel Roberts, confesses to having a lesbian affair.

Prod Comp: Frankovich Productions
Dist/Sales: Col-Tri

Disgraceful Conduct

Does your Mother Know?

Littleboy, Helen
1994; UK; 18 min; Comedy

Gay and lesbian teenagers discuss aspects of their lives to the tunes of 'Que Sera Sera' and Abba's 'Does Your Mother Know?'. They talk about everything from coming out at home and at school to first sexual experiences, age of consent, labelling and role models. (MQFF)

Prod Comp: Channel 4
Dist/Sales: Piranha

Dog Day Afternoon

Lumet, Sidney
1975; USA; 130 min; Drama
P: Martin Bergman, Martin Elfand; *W:* Frank Pierson;

C: Victor J. Kemper; E: Dede Allen
Cast: Al Pacino, John Cazale, Charles Durning, Sully Boyar, Penelope Allen

A New Yorker and his two accomplices are trapped in a bank with all the bank employees after his attempt to steal money to pay for his male lover's sex change operation goes horribly wrong. At times very humorous and tragic. Based on a ture story.

Awards: Academy Awards, 1975: Best Screenplay
Prod Comp: Warner, AEC
Dist/Sales: ReelMovies, Warner, ACMI, Swank

Dog's Dialogue

(aka: Colloque de chiens)

Ruiz, Raoul
1977; France; 22 min; Comedy
P: Hubert Niogret; W: Nicole Muchnik, Raoul Ruiz; C: Denis Lenoir; E: Valeria Sarmiento; M: Sergio Arriagada
Cast: Eva Simonet, Robert Darmel, Silke Humel

Footage of barking dogs, shots of streets and off-screen narration make up a hilariously tawdry melodrama of murder, prostitution, transsexuality and abandoned children.

Prod Comp: Filmoblic, L'Office de la Création Cinématographique

Doing Time on Maple Drive

Olin, Ken
1992; USA; 88 min; Drama
P: Paul Lussier; W: James Duff; C: Bing Sokolsky; E: Elba Sanchez-Short; M: Laura Karpman
Cast: James B. Sikking, Bibi Besch, William McNamara, Jayne Brook, Lori Loughlin, Jim Carrey

Made for TV movie about the Carter family who have gathered together to celebrate the impending marriage of their youngest son. As matters proceed, the gathering becomes confrontational as the secrets of each of the Carter's three children are unveiled—including the sensitively handled homosexuality of one of the sons. The mother and father are forced to take a closer look at reality and, at the same time, keep their family from falling apart.

Prod Comp: FNM Films
Dist/Sales: 20thCenturyFox, VSM

Domestic Bliss

Chamberlain, Joy
1984; UK; 52 min; Comedy

A situation comedy revolving around a lesbian couple Emma and Diana, who can't seem to find time to be alone. Emma has just left her husband and she and her daughter have moved in with Diana, who is a welfare doctor. Between Emma's unthinking husband, her daughter and Diana's demanding neighbour, how will they ever spend time together?

Dist/Sales: Cinenova

Don't Forget You're Going to Die

(aka: N'Oublie pas que tu vas Mourir)

Beauvois, Xavier
1995; France; 118 min; Drama
P: Christophe Lambert; W: Xavier Beauvois, Emmanuel Salinger, Anne-Marie Sauzeau, Zoubir Tligui;
C: Caroline Champetier; E: Agnés Guillemot;
M: John Cale
Cast: Xavier Beauvois, Chiara Mastroianni, Roschdy Zem, Bulle Ogier

Benoit is desperate to avoid military service and so fakes a suicide attempt. As a result he is shocked to find out that he is HIV-positive. He escapes to Italy and meets Claudia, and for a time things are good. However, he is still in denial about his condition and falls into prostitution and drug dealing. French with English subtitles.

Prod Comp: Why Not Productions
Dist/Sales: Leonor

Don't Tell Anyone

(aka: No Se Lo Digas a Nadie)

Lombardi, Francisco J.
1998; Peru; 114 min; Drama
P: Gustavo Sanchez; W: Giovanna Pollarolo
Cast: Santiago Magill, Lucia Jiménez, Christian Meier, Carmen Elias

Joaquin is a troubled youth from a well-to-do family in Peru who must overcome the domineering influences of his macho, racist father and obsessively religious mother to discover his true sexual nature. Spanish with English subtitles.

Prod Comp: Andres Vicente Gomez production
Dist/Sales: PictureThis!, Wolfe

Dona Herlinda and Her Son

(aka: Doña Herlinda y su hijo)

Hermosillo, Jaime Humberto
1985; Mexico; 90 min; Comedy
P: Manuel Barbachano Ponce; W: Jaime Humberto Hermosillo; C: Miguel Ehrenberg; E: Luis Kelly
Cast: Arturo Meza, Marco Antonio Trevino, Leticia Lupersio, Guadalupe del Toro

A cheerful yet subversive comedy about two gay men, one a surgeon and the other a student, who move in with the former's wilful mother. Liberating in its depiction of homosexual love.

Prod Comp: Clasa Films Mundiales
Dist/Sales: Cinevista, VideoAmericain

Doom Generation

Araki, Gregg
1995; France, USA; 84 min; Comedy
P: Gregg Araki, Andrea Sperling; *W:* Gregg Araki;
C: Jim Fealy; *E:* Gregg Araki, Kate McGowan;
M: Dan Gatto
Cast: James Duval, Rose McGowan, Johnathon
Schaech, Cress Williams

Add one hot chick, her loser boyfriend and a bleeding dude. Backdrop with a nightclub's techno music, race through fast food restaurants and rob a convenience store. In the end they are way more than friends and are being chased by crazy neo-Nazi jocks who want to kill them and end their Dorito-eating lives. Gregg Araki's homoerotic heterosexual movie. (Wolfe)

Dist/Sales: Wolfe, Trimark, Palace, Haut-et-Court

Doors Cut Down

Hens, Antonio
2000; Spain; 17 min; Drama
W: Antonio Hens

Amazingly self-assured, 16-year-old Guillermo cruises the bathroom of the local mall on a regular basis. Well versed in the art of the cruise, the boy has little trouble satisfying his desires with his daily partner of choice in any available stall. Problems arise, though, when the homophobic mall police cut down the bathroom stall doors to deter potential cruisers. Irritated, but undaunted, Guillermo has a few plans of his own to keep his sexual desires both fulfilled and defiantly public. (Picture This! Entertainment)

Dist/Sales: PictureThis!

Double Entente

Lawrence, Jacquie
1994; UK; 11 min; Comedy

It's been a hard day at the office, and Dulcie's not happy when her lover cancels their afterwork drink. Dulcie heads to the bar anyway, only to encounter a forward and mysterious stranger. Say hello to power dressing lipstick lesbians with attitude!

Double Face

Freda, Riccardo
1970; Italy, West Germany; 85 min; Thriller
P: Oreste Coltellacci, Horst Wendlandt; *W:* Robert
Hampton, Paul Hengge; *C:* Gábor Pogány; *E:* Anna
Amedei, Jutta Hering; *M:* Joan Christian
Cast: Klaus Kinski, Annabella Incontrera, Christiane
Krüger

Klaus Kinski plays a wealthy industrialist who kills his lesbian wife with a car bomb, only to find he is haunted by her image in pornographic films.

Prod Comp: Colt Produzioni Cinematografich, Mega
Film
Dist/Sales: Constantin

Double Strength

Hammer, Barbara
1978; USA; 20 min; Experimental

The study of four stages of a lesbian relationship.

Dist/Sales: WMM

Double the Trouble, Twice the Fun

Parmar, Pratibha
1992; UK; 25 min; Drama

Parmar profiles a man who is Indian, disabled and gay. As he searches for his community he has some revealing confrontations.

Dist/Sales: Cinenova

Double Trouble

Ayres, Tony
1991; Australia, UK; 24 min; Documentary

An insightful film with a sharp sense of humour that provides a response to the common white Australian refrain of, 'Lesbian and gay Aborigines? I didn't think there were any'.

Prod Comp: Big & Little Films, Channel 4
Dist/Sales: Big&Little

Dozens, The

Conrad, Randall / Dall, Christine
1981; USA; 80 min; Drama
P: Christine Dall, Randall Conrad; *W:* Randall Conrad,
Christine Dall, Marian Taylor; *C:* Joe Vitagliano;
E: Christine Dall, Randall Conrad
Cast: Deborah Margolis, Jessica Hergert, Edward
Mason, Michele Greene, Ethel Michelson

Based on a true story, *The Dozens* centres around Sally, a 21-year-old mother who has recently been released from prison. She is determined to create a normal life for herself and her daughter. Out in the wide world, she finds her only emotional support is from her lover who is still in prison.

Prod Comp: Calliope Films

Dr Jekyll and Ms Hyde

Price, David
1995; UK, USA; 90 min; Comedy
P: Frank K. Isaac, Jerry Leider, John Morrissey, Robert
Shapiro; *W:* Tim John, Oliver Butcher, William Davies,
William Osborne; *C:* Tom Priestley; *E:* Tony Lombardo;

d

M: Mark McKenzie
Cast: Sean Young, Timothy Daly, Lysette Anthony, Harvey Fierstein, Stephen Tobolowsky

> Based in New York, Dr Richard Jacks creates perfumes. But when he discovers that his great grandfather was Dr Jekyll, he tries to follow in his footsteps and creates a potion that turns him into a superwoman: Helen Hyde.

Prod Comp: Rank, Rastar/Leider-Shapiro, Savoy Pictures
Dist/Sales: 16MM, HBO, Rank

Dr Jekyll and Sister Hyde

Baker, Roy Ward
1971; UK; 93 min; Comedy, Sci-Fi
P: Albert Fennell, Brian Clemens, Samuel Z. Arkoff; *W:* Brian Clemens; *C:* Norman Warwick; *E:* James Needs; *M:* David Whitaker, Philip Martell
Cast: Ralph Bates, Martine Beswick, Gerald Sim, Dorothy Alison, Lewis Fiander, Susan Broderick

> Comic variation on the classic tale. Dr Jekyll experiments on himself with female hormones that he gets from prostitutes he has murdered. He turns into a big-breasted woman, who has an insatiable appetite for sex. In one scene Jekyll makes a pass at his girlfriend's brother, who is in fact Hyde's lover. The film attempts to examine sexual ambiguities but only just manages to scratch the surface of what could be a truly interesting idea.

Prod Comp: Hammer, EMI
Dist/Sales: Warner, OrionClassics, HBO, Republic

Dr T & the Women

Altman, Robert
2000; Germany, USA; 120 min; Comedy
P: Robert Altman, James McLindon; *W:* Anne Rapp; *C:* Jan Kiesser; *E:* Geraldine Peroni; *M:* Lyle Lovett
Cast: Richard Gere, Helen Hunt, Farrah Fawcett, Kate Hudson, Laura Dern

> Dr Sullivan Travis 'Dr T' is a Dallas gynaecologist whose clients are among the wealthiest women in Texas. Dr T is wealthy himself, but finds his cushy life taking a turn for the worse when his wife suffers a nervous breakdown, and is committed to an institution. Meanwhile his daughter Dee Dee's wedding is approaching, despite the fact that she is a lesbian and in a relationship with Marilyn, her maid of honour. His youngest daughter has an obsessive liking for conspiracy theories, while his secretary is attracted to him. The only sense he can make of the whole situation is through golf instructor Bree, who brings comfort and stability to him while everything else is falling down around him.

Prod Comp: Dr T Inc, Sandcastle 5 Productions, Splendid Medien AG
Dist/Sales: 20thCenturyFox, ACMI

Dracula's Daughter

Hillyer, Lambert
1936; USA; 70 min; B&W; Horror
P: E. M. Asher; *W:* Garrett Fort; *C:* George Robinson; *E:* Milton Carruth; *M:* Heinz Roemheld
Cast: Gloria Holden, Otto Kruger, Marguerite Churchill, Edward Van Sloan

> Made as the sequel to *Dracula* (1931), a young vampire, Dracula's daughter, tries to escape her nocturnal vampire life with the help of a sympathetic psychologist. But her lust for blood and young female flesh cannot be controlled. Considered to be one of the earliest films to depict a lesbian as a vampire, even though the lesbianism is subtle.

Prod Comp: Universal
Dist/Sales: Swank

Drag Attack

Kruger, Ken / Sodo, Mario
1994; Austria; 14 min; Comedy

> The humorous exploits of two very glamorous, globe-trotting drag queens. German with English subtitles.

Dragtime

Kaplan, Patti
1997; USA; 70 min; Documentary

> Get out your boas, your press-on nails, and your size thirteen pumps. *Dragtime*, a full-length documentary, attempts to answer three burning questions about drag performers: Why do they do it? How do they do it? And where did they get that cleavage? From a trendy lounge in Manhattan to a New Orleans Mardi Gras, from a popular revue in Atlanta, to a visit with Charles Busch in sunny California, *Dragtime* takes us on a tour of a cultural phenomenon, replete with poignant interviews, fabulous musical numbers, and plenty of chic, hip-hugging ensembles. (22nd San Francisco International Lesbian & Gay Film Festival)

Dist/Sales: PKProd

Drama in Blonde

Lambert, Lothar
1985; Germany; 90 min; Comedy
P: Lothar Lambert; *W:* Lothar Lambert; *C:* Helmut Röttgen; *E:* Lothar Lambert
Cast: Lothar Lambert, Dagmar Beiersdorff

If you've never seen this seldom screened, outrageous classic, you've probably heard of it. Lothar Lambert portrays a pudgy, middle-aged bank clerk who fulfils his secret desire to become a fabulous female impersonator. Dagmar Beiersdorff plays his sympathetic neighbour, who would like to have him as his beau but supports his endeavours selflessly.

Awards: New York Gay Film Festival, 1985: Audience Favourite

Drama Queen

Herd, Kelli
2001; USA; 45 min; Documentary

This comedy concert video showcases the talents of famed Canadian lesbian stand up comic Georgia Ragsdale.

Drawing Girls

McHenry, Bryan
1999; USA; 15 min; Drama

Autobiographical short about two Midwestern teen boys who draw comic books together. However, Bryan likes to draw his comic-book heroes with muscles while his best friend prefers drawing girls.

Dreaded Experimental Comedies, The

Topping, John
1992; USA; 16 min; Comedy

Three hysterical comic shorts (*How to Lessons*, *Body Rhythms* and *My New Lover*) in which the filmmaker uses another guy's backside as his drum, then tries to teach his soft-hearted lover how to be butch and sadistic and finally gives up altogether, becoming so desperate for the perfect lover that he creates his own. (MQFF)

Dream Girls

Longinotto, Kim / Williams, Jano
1993; UK; 50 min; Documentary

This fascinating documentary, produced for the BBC, opens a door into the spectacular world of the Takarazuka Revue, a highly successful musical theatre company in Japan. Each year, thousands of girls apply to enter the male-run Takarazuka Music School. The few who are accepted endure years of a highly disciplined and reclusive existence before they can join the Revue, choosing male or female roles. *Dream Girls* offers a compelling insight into gender and sexual identity and the contradictions experienced by Japanese women today. (WMM) Japanese with English subtitles.

Prod Comp: BBC
Dist/Sales: WMM, Cinenova, NFVLS

Dreamers of the Day

Spencer, Patricia / Wood, Philip
1990; Canada; 94 min; Drama
Cast: Lorna Harding, Julie Lemieux

The story revolves around Andra, an openly lesbian filmmaker dedicated to making lesbian films, and Claire, a married film producer. They begin to develop a friendship but Claire becomes increasingly uncomfortable with her own feelings and Andra's sexual attraction to her. They constantly deny any sexual relationship but in the end love and sex win out. A well-handled and tender film that deals with a very believable subject.

Dreck

(aka: Dirt)

Reding, Benjamin / Reding, Dominik
1995; Germany; 18 min; Experimental

A love story between a squatter, and the son of the policeman who is trying to evict him, and the consequences.

Dist/Sales: Schlammtaucher

Dream Girls

Dress Gray

Jordan, Glenn
1986; USA; 192 min; Drama
P: Glenn Jordan; *W:* Gore Vidal; *C:* Gayne Rescher; *E:* Paul Rubell, David A. Simmons; *M:* Billy Goldenberg

Cast: Alec Baldwin, Eddie Albert, Lloyd Bridges, Patrick Cassidy

Set in a military establishment, a classman is falsely accused of murdering a young gay cadet. In order to clear his name he decides to investigate the crime himself. A two-part series made for television.

Dist/Sales: NBC, Wolfe

Dressed to Kill

De Palma, Brian
1980; USA; 105 min; Thriller
P: George Litto; *W:* Brian De Palma; *C:* Ralf D. Bode; *E:* Jerry Greenberg; *M:* Pino Donaggio
Cast: Michael Caine, Nancy Allen, Angie Dickinson, Keith Gordon

Dr Elliot is a psychiatrist with a split personality: Robert, a man and very attracted to women, and Bobbi, a woman trapped in a man's body. When Bobbi is refused a sex-change operation, she takes her revenge by killing the women to whom Robert is attracted. The only witness to the murders is a prostitute, played by Nancy Allen, who becomes Bobbi's next victim.

Prod Comp: Filmways, Cinema 77, Warick Associates
Dist/Sales: MGM, Orion, Warner

Dresser, The

Yates, Peter
1983; UK; 118 min; Drama
P: Peter Yates, Ronald Harwood; *W:* Ronald Harwood, Peter Yates; *C:* Kelvin Pike; *E:* Ray Lovejoy; *M:* James Horner
Cast: Albert Finney, Tom Courtenay, Edward Fox, Eileen Atkins, Zena Walker

The compelling study of the intense relationship between the exhausted and ageing leader of a wartime Shakespearean company, 'Sir', and his homosexual dresser, Norman. Adapted by Ronald Harwood from his own play, *The Dresser* is based on the touring career of Donald Wolfit whose dresser the author was. A film rich in comedy, compassion and love for the theatre.

Prod Comp: World Film Service, Goldcrest
Dist/Sales: Col-Tri, TLA

Drift

Lee, Quentin
2000; USA; 85 min; Drama
W: Quentin Lee; *C:* Quentin Lee; *E:* Suan Toon Teo; *M:* Steven Pranoto
Cast: R. T. Lee, Greyson Dayne, Jonathon Roessler

Ryan, an Asian-Canadian writer has been with Joel for three years. Ryan loves Joel, but can't help questioning the intensity of their bond. At his agent's party, Ryan meets Leo, an aspiring novelist and college student. His confusion mounts when he imagines that Leo understands him like no one has ever before. He soon becomes infatuated with Leo and eventually decides to leave Joel. *Drift* then unfolds into a type of three pronged narrative structure where the audience gets to see how Ryan's life would have turned out had he made different decisions in life.

Prod Comp: De/Center Communications
Dist/Sales: Margin, Wolfe, VideoAmericain

Drift

Drifting

(aka: Nagu'a)

Guttman, Amos
1982; Israel; 104 min; Drama
P: Malka Assaf, Enrique Rottenberg; *W:* Amos Guttman, Edna Mazia; *C:* Yossi Wein; *E:* Anna Finkelstein; *M:* Erich Rudich
Cast: Ben Levine, Ami Traub, Jonathan Sagalle, Dita Arel, Amos Guttman

A gay Israeli filmmaker, while trying to finance his next project, runs into problems in homophobic Jerusalem, and with his family. They are ashamed of him and believe that if only he met the right woman he would be 'cured'. Considered to be a groundbreaking film for Israeli cinema as it is one of the first films from there to deal openly with homosexuality and its place in that society.

Prod Comp: Kislev Films
Dist/Sales: Nu-Image

Drop Dead Georgeous: The Power of HIV Positive Thinking

Bailey, Fenton / Barbato, Randy
1997; USA; 53 min; Documentary

HIV-positive comedian Steve Moore takes us on a tour of his life—from his Southern upbringing, to one nights stands both of the comedy and sexual kind.

Dist/Sales: WorldOfWonder, HBO

Drowning Lessons

Kennedy, Gregory
2001; USA; 20 min; Drama

Brother and sister, Jeremy and Barbara, share a flat and, even as adults, remain close. Both become attracted to a new neighbour and a battle ensues between them. Jeremy's fear of water is set up as a metaphor for him not being able to stand up to his sister and move forward with his life.

Drugs 'R' Us

Gregory, Tony
1994; Australia; 24 min; Documentary
P: Rebecca Dobbs

A provocative and anonymous comment that goes directly to the heart of the debate over drug use/abuse and queer lifestyles. This video charts the history of drug use in the gay scene from the 1890s to the present day.

Dist/Sales: MayaVision

Dry Cleaning

Dry Cleaning

(aka: Nettoyage à sec)

Fontaine, Anne
1997; France; 97 min; Drama
P: Alain Sarde, Philippe Carcassonne; *W:* Anne Fontaine, Gilles Taurand; *C:* Caroline Champetier;

E: Luc Barnier; *M:* Edouard Dubois
Cast: Miou-Miou, Charles Berling, Stanislas Merhar, Mathilde Seigner

This unusually compelling French psychosexual drama revolves around a staunchly 'normal' married couple and how their dormant sexuality is ignited when a young man—a bisexual drag queen performer—enters their lives. Nicole and Jean-Marie are a strait-laced married couple who operate a small-town dry cleaning shop. On a rare night out, they visit a club where they become enthralled by a brother-sister drag act. Through circumstances, the brother, Loic—an enigmatic but sexily androgynous young man—begins to work at the couple's shop. The story focuses on how both Marie and Jean-Marie are attracted to him (her, obviously for the sexual thrills, him either paternally, fraternally or homoerotically). (Wolfe)
French with English subtitles.

Prod Comp: Maestranza Films, Cinéa, Région Franche-Comté
Dist/Sales: Wolfe, Strand

Dry Kisses Only

Brooke, Kaucylia / Cottis, Jane
1990; USA; 75 min; Documentary

Dry Kisses Only is a transgressive look at the cultural icons of femininity and feminism through lesbian films. Clips of Hollywood films (which explicitly portray lesbians, or can be read as a narrative about the desire between women) are interwoven with tongue-in-cheek critical commentary, 'lesbians on the street' interviews, and gossip column revelations, among other media texts.

Dist/Sales: WMM

Duffer

Despins, Joseph
1971; UK; 75 min; B&W; Drama
Cast: Kit Gleave, Erna May, James Roberts, Marcelle McHardy

A musing of fantasy verses reality. Using voice-overs, the film tells its account of an attractive young man who spends most of his life submitting to a homosexual sadist and the rest of his time with a whore.

Dyke Blend

Weber, Eva
1996; UK; 11 min; Comedy
W: Eva Weber

A superior blend of film expertly created to capture the distinctive taste of sex, doubts and coffee. Eva Weber's humorous and passionate parody unfolds over nine mini-episodes. The story introduces the

Dyke Blend couple, Donna and Louise, and follows their evolving romance. (Cinenova)

Dist/Sales: Cinenova

Dykes and their Dogs

Godges, Mary Jo / Sotile, Renee
2000; USA; 17 min; Comedy

An uproarious musical/comedy 'dyke-umentary' about the popular Dykes and Their Dogs contest held annually in West Hollywood, California.

Dykes and Tykes

Devine, Christine
2000; Australia; 18 min; Documentary

Australian lesbians talk about their experiences of raising children.

Dist/Sales: Devine

e-male

Gibbs, Rolf
1998; UK; 23 min; Drama

A young woman intercepts the emails meant for her ex-boyfriend, and starts to write back. Her reply sets in motion a love affair on the net with surprising consequences.

Dist/Sales: SweetChild

Each Other

(aka: Rega'im)

Bat-Adam, Michal
1979; France, Israel; 90 min; Drama
P: Moshé Mizrahi; *W:* Michal Bat-Adam; *C:* Yves Lafaye; *E:* Sophie Coussein; *M:* Hubert Rostaing
Cast: Michal Bat-Adam, Brigitte Catillon, Assaf Dayan

With the use of flashback the film's narrative is structured around two women, Yola, an Israeli writer, and Anne, a French photographer on vacation. They meet on a Tel Aviv-Jerusalem train and become friends and, eventually lovers. The relationship between the two women endangers Yola's marriage to her husband, Avi.

Prod Comp: Mica Films, Rosa Productions

Eagle Shooting Heroes, The

(aka: Sediu yinghung tsun tsi dung sing sai tsau)

Lau, Jeffrey
1994; Hong Kong; 115 min; Comedy
P: Sung-lin Tsai; *W:* Louis Cha; *C:* Peter Pau; *E:* Kit-wai Kai; *M:* James Wong
Cast: Leslie Cheung, Brigitte Lin, Maggie Cheung, Tony Leung Chiu Wai

A wacky, gender-bender spoof from Hong Kong, produced and acted by some of the biggest names in Chinese cinema. The characters include two evil cousins who are fighting to take control of a kingdom, a young male priest played by a woman, and an emperor who in order to achieve nirvana must get a man to tell him he loves him. The plot is difficult to follow as the characters constantly swap genders but it is a huge amount of fun, and a great send-up of the martial arts films. Cantonese with English subtitles.

Prod Comp: Jet Tone Production Co.
Dist/Sales: RimFilm

Early Frost, An (1985)

Erman, John
1985; USA; 97 min; Drama
P: Perry Lafferty; *W:* Ron Cowen, Daniel Lipman; *C:* Woody Omens; *E:* Jerrold L. Ludwig; *M:* John Kander
Cast: Ben Gazzara, Aidan Quinn, Gena Rowlands, Sylvia Sidney

An emotional drama about a family who discover that their son is gay, and is also suffering from AIDS. A moving, powerful and sensitive drama, based on a story by Sherman Yellen. Made for television.

Prod Comp: NBC
Dist/Sales: NBC, Wolfe, ACMI

Early Frost, An (2000)

Pinaud, Pierre
1999; France; 17 min; Comedy
P: Laurent Lavolé, Isabelle Pragier; *W:* Pierre Pinaud

A 10-year-old girl learns that her pet rabbit is attracted to other boy rabbits. The news causes chaos with her parents and gay next door neighbours. With Amandine Sroussi. French with English subtitles.

Dist/Sales: Gloria, ACMI

East Palace West Palace

(aka: Dong Gong Xi Gong)

Zhang, Yuan
1996; China; 90 min; Drama
P: Yuan Zhang, Christophe Jung, Christophe Ménager; *W:* Yuan Zhang, Xiaobo Wang; *C:* Jian Zhang; *E:* Vincent Levy; *M:* Min Xiang
Cast: Han Si, Jun Hu

After a random raid one night in a local park, A Lan, a young gay writer is held for intensive interrogation. His questioning quickly transforms into an unexpected reminiscence of his tumultuous life: his childhood, parents, school, politically mandated peasant work in the country, and the slow drift into the quest for true love. These brief, intimate glances of A Lan's life blur the feelings Hu Jun, the interrogating officer, has for the prisoner. An awkward love-story unfolds. *East Palace West Palace* was shot without permission from Chinese authorities, and post-produced in France. Mandarin with English subtitles.

Prod Comp: Amazon Entertainment, Quelqu'un d'Autre Productions
Dist/Sales: Palace, Fortissimo, Wolfe, Strand

East Palace West Palace

Eat the Rich

Richardson, Peter
1987; UK; 89 min; Comedy
P: Tim Van Rellim; *W:* Peter Richardson, Pete Richens; *C:* Witold Stok; *E:* Chris Risdale
Cast: Lanah Pellay, Nosher Powell, Fiona Richmond, Ronald Allen, Koo Stark

The exploits of a transsexual waiter, who after losing his job at a restaurant called 'Bastards' gets his revenge by finally taking it over. He changes the name to 'Eat the Rich' and serves the management and rich customers for main course. Some rather wasted cameos that include Paul McCartney and Miranda Richardson.

Prod Comp: Iron Fist Motion Pictures, New Line Cinema
Dist/Sales: Palace, NewLine

Eban and Charley

Bolton, James
2000; UK, USA; 89 min; Drama
P: Chris Monlux; *W:* James Bolton; *C:* Judy Irola; *E:* Elizabeth Edwards; *M:* Stephin Merritt
Cast: Brent Fellows, Giovanni Andrade, Drew Zeller, Ellie Nicholson, Ron Upton

29-year-old Eban has returned to his hometown to live with his parents. He befriends a 15-year-old boy Charley, whose mother has just died. Gradually they

become romantically involved but when Charley's father finds out about their relationship, Eban must decide whether he is willing to risk imprisonment in order to be with Charley.

Prod Comp: Monqui Films, Harcamone Films
Dist/Sales: PictureThis!, Wolfe, 10%, VideoAmericain

Echte Kerle

(aka: Regular Guys)

Silber, Rolf
1996; Germany; 97 min; Comedy
P: Gerd Huber, Silvia Koller, Renate Seefeldt, Jochen Löscher; *W:* Rolf Silber, Rudi Bergmann; *C:* Jürgen Herrmann; *M:* Peter Schmitt
Cast: Christoph M. Ohrt, Carin C. Tietze, Oliver Stokowski, Tim Bergmann

Christoph, a cop and confirmed macho, wakes up after a night on the town in the bed of Edgar, a handsome gay car mechanic, who has fallen impetuously in love with him. Christoph's world seems to be coming apart at the seams when he loses both his girlfriend and his apartment shortly afterwards, and then gets a new and very self-confident colleague called Helen, who is clearly as interested in him as he is in her. What's more, he finds out that Edgar occasionally steals cars, and he is also no longer sure whether he likes guys or girls. A cop, an attractive detective, and a gay car thief cross paths in this turbulent romantic comedy. German with English subtitles.(www.goethe.de/uk)

Prod Comp: Cobra Film, Bayerischer Rundfunk
Dist/Sales: BuenaVista

Eclipse

Podeswa, Jeremy
1994; Canada; 95 min; Drama
P: Camelia Frieberg, Jeremy Podeswa; *W:* Jeremy Podeswa; *C:* Miroslav Baszak; *E:* Susan Maggi; *M:* Ernie Tollar
Cast: Von Flores, Jon Gilbert, Pascale Montpetit, Manual Aranguiz

Sex circulates like a good rumour as ten people unwittingly form a complex network of friends, lovers and casual encounters in an eerie game of carnal musical chairs—a business man picks up a rent boy, then goes home and sleeps with the family au pair, who in turn seduces a stranger. At the epicentre of all this feverish activity is an imminent solar eclipse set to plunge all into momentary darkness. English, French & Spanish with English subtitles.

Prod Comp: Fire Dog Films
Dist/Sales: Palace, Strand

Ed Wood

Burton, Tim
1994; USA; 124 min; B&W; Comedy
P: Denise De Novi, Tim Burton; W: Scott Alexander,
Larry Karaszewski; C: Stefan Czapsky; E: Chris
Lebenzon; M: Howard Shore
Cast: Johnny Depp, Martin Landau, Sarah Jessica
Parker, Patricia Arquette

A dramatised biography of Edward D. Wood Jnr, a
director who is generally considered to have made
some of the trashiest films ever committed to
celluloid. They include the cult greats *Glen or Glenda*
and *Plan 9 from Outer Space*. Wood was a well-
known transvestite, and often directed in a frock.
Martin Landau puts in a superb performance as Bela
Lugosi and Bill Murray is fantastic as a screaming
queen.

Prod Comp: Touchstone
Dist/Sales: Roadshow, ReelMovies, Touchstone,
BuenaVista, Swank

Edge of Seventeen

Edge of Seventeen
(aka: Edge of 17)

Moreton, David
1998; USA; 99 min; Comedy
P: David Moreton, Todd Stephens; W: Todd Stephens;
C: Gina DeGirolamo, Zak Othmer; E: Tal Ben-David;
M: Tom Bailey
Cast: Chris Stafford, Tina Holmes, Andersen Gabrych,
Stephanie McVay

1984. Boy George, Bronski Beat, Toni Basil, big
hair, skinny ties! Set in Ohio, in a decade where
make-up on boys was de rigeur and greed was good,
Edge of Seventeen traces the sexual turbulence and
insecurities of Eric, a sensitive high school boy. To
hide his lust for hunky gay co-worker Rod, Eric
begins a relationship with Maggie. His naive sexual
fumblings and hopeless romanticism make for
painfully honest yet upbeat viewing. Moreton's
recreation of the feather-haired era is picture perfect,

and is well-supported by a brilliant musical score by
Tom Bailey of the Thompson Twins. (MQFF)
Prod Comp: Blue Streak Films, Luna Pictures
Dist/Sales: Potential, PictureThis!, Strand, Wolfe,
Mongrel

Educate your Attitude

Berggold, Craig / Marshall, Teresa
1992; Canada; 30 min; Documentary

Young men and women, aged 15 to 27, share their
thought-provoking, humorous, and sometimes
painful reflections on growing up. They speak from a
wide range of experiences about love and fantasies,
gay identity, interracial relationships, masturbation,
peer pressure, media images, pornography, sexism,
sexual abuse, STDs, living with AIDS, condoms,
safer sex and more. (Frameline)

Dist/Sales: Frameline

Edward II

Jarman, Derek
1991; UK; 91 min; Drama
P: Steven Clark-Hall, Anthony Root; W: Ken Butler,
Steve Clark-Hall, Derek Jarman, Stephen McBride,
Antony Root; C: Ian Wilson; E: George Akers;
M: Simon Fisher Turner
Cast: Steven Waddington, Andrew Tiernan, Tilda
Swinton, Nigel Terry, Annie Lennox

Set in the 14th century and adapted from the 16th
century Christopher Marlowe play of the same
name, this is the story of King Edward's relationship
with a courtier, in what is believed to be the first
explicitly gay play written in English. The drama
revolves around Britain's only acknowledged gay
monarch, whose preference for his lover over his
queen sparked conflict with his barons and,
eventually, led to civil war.

Prod Comp: BBC, British Screen, Working Title Films
Dist/Sales: NewVision, NFVLS, BFI, FineLine

Eiger Sanction, The

Eastwood, Clint
1975; USA; 113 min; Thriller
P: Robert Daley; W: Hal Dresner, Rod Whitaker,
Warren B. Murphy; C: Frank Stanley; E: Ferris Webster;
M: John Williams
Cast: Clint Eastwood, George Kennedy, Vonetta
McGee, Jack Cassidy, Heidi Bruhl

A James Bond type film about a retired hit man and
mountain climber, who returns to his former
profession to assassinate a climber in an international
team attempting to climb the Eiger Mountain in
Switzerland. To prepare himself for the ordeal he
begins training in the magnificent cliffs of

Monument Valley. The climax includes some exciting action scenes in the Swiss Alps. Jack Cassidy plays a gay murderer with a dog named 'Faggot'.

Prod Comp: Universal, Jennings Lang, The Malpaso Company
Dist/Sales: ReelMovies, Universal

Eight Million

Child, Abigail
1991; USA; 24 min; Experimental

Eight Million is a video album combining documentary and narrative elements to rewrite women's drama. Short songs charting erotic tales in an urban environment profile the romantic myths of popular culture but with a twist, the genders are mixed, the social order is questioned and the narrative is fragmented.

Eika Katappa

Schroeter, Werner
1969; Germany; 144 min; Comedy, Musical
P: Werner Schroeter; *W:* Werner Schroeter; *C:* Werner Schroeter, Robert van Ackeren; *E:* Werner Schroeter; *M:* Georges Bizet
Cast: Magdalena Montezuma, Gisela Trowe, Rosa von Praunheim

A hysterical celebration of grand opera. It opens with previews of coming attractions and closes with a survey of past highlights. In between it shows scenes from some of the most loved and hated operas, which form the basis of the narrative, culminating in a tragic gay love story. Very high camp.

Eileen is a Spy

Frey, Sayer
1998; USA; 74 min; Documentary
P: Sayer Frey, John Kremer; *W:* Sayer Frey; *C:* Moe Flaherty; *E:* Sayer Frey; *M:* Barbara Cohen
Cast: Tami Hinz

Minneapolis based writer/director Sayer Frey draws inspiration for her debut feature from *Harriet the Spy*. This is the story of an eccentric and painfully shy loner who prefers to scrutinise the lives of others rather than pursue her own (sexual) desires. Like Harriet, the preteen heroine of Louise Fitzbugh's children's books, the thirty-something Eileen peers through binoculars and scribbles notes as if gathering information about a world she is not yet part of. Frey explores female friendships and same-sex attraction as Eileen meets Jayne, a hitchhiking free spirit who helps our anti-heroine overcome her disabling isolation. Frey combines the quirky details of Eileen's story with surrealistic digressions, snippets of home movies and audio taped interviews. The

result is an exquisite fusion of documentary, audio and dramatic fiction that flows gracefully from scene to scene. (Cinenova)
Dist/Sales: Cinenova

Ein Toter Hing im Netz
(aka: Girls of Spider Island)

Böttger, Fritz
1959; Austria, Germany; 80 min; B&W; Horror
P: Gaston Hakim, Wolfgang Hartwig; *W:* Fritz Böttger; *C:* Georg Krause; *M:* Karl Bette, Willy Mattes
Cast: Helga Frank, Barbara Valentin, Alex d'Arcy, Helga Neuner

A group of eight women are stranded on a deserted island after an air crash. Their manager is turned into a spider after being bitten by an insect. The whole film appears to be an excuse to show scantily dressed women doing their hair, taking showers and tugging at each other's breasts.

Prod Comp: International Film Management, Rapid-Intercontinetal
Dist/Sales: SomethingWeird

Eine Tunte zum Dessert
(aka: A Fairy for Dessert)

Beiersdorf, Dagmar
1992; Germany; 85 min; Comedy
P: Wolfgang Krenz; *W:* Dagmar Beiersdorf; *C:* Christoph Gies; *E:* Lothar Lambert
Cast: Suzanne Gautier, Lothar Lambert

Very funny, low-budget celebration of adopted families and colourful characters, featuring an overweight transvestite who takes parenting in his stride. German with English subtitles.

Einstein of Sex: The Life and Work of Dr Magnus Hirschfeld, The

von Praunheim, Rosa
1999; Germany; 100 min; Drama
P: Rosa von Praunheim; *W:* Chris Kraus, Valentin Passoni; *C:* Elfi Mikesch; *E:* Michael E. Shephard; *M:* Karl-Ernst Sasse
Cast: Friedel von Wangenheim, Ben Becker, Otto Sander, Wolfgang Volz

In 1897 Dr Magnus Hirschfeld (known as 'The Einstein of Sex' for his revolutionary work in sexual science) founded the first gay political group in history. In 1920 he opened his Institute of Sexual Science in Berlin. The film reveals Hirschfeld through the major figures in his life: from the unfulfilled love affair with Baron von Teschenberg to the happy years with young Karl Giese; from his struggle with his major gay opponent, right-wing

writer Adolf Brand, to the presence of his guardian angel, the transvestite Dorchen. Dr Hirschfeld died in 1935 only two years after the Nazis destroyed his Institute. Since this time, all attempts to organise an equivalent institute for sexual science have failed. Up to this day no one has surpassed the accomplishments of Dr Hirschfeld in the field of sexology. The Einstein of Sex tells the true story of the passion that drove his exceptional work and the destruction that lead to his exile and death. (Mongrel)
German with English subtitles.

Dist/Sales: TLA, Mongrel

Elegant Criminal, L'

(aka: Lacenaire)

Girod, Francis
1990; France; 120 min; Drama
P: Ariel Zeitoun; *W:* Georges Conchon, Francis Girod; *C:* Bruno de Keyzer; *E:* Geneviève Winding; *M:* Laurent Petitgirard ·
Cast: Daniel Auteuil, Jean Poiret, Jacques Weber, Francois Perier, Genevieve Casile

A period drama based on the life of the infamous gentleman criminal Pierre-Francois Lacenaire who scandalised (and entertained) 19th century France. Set in 1836, he is facing the gallows after committing a series of murders just for the thrill of it. He is a homosexual, very intelligent, and is able to charm both men and women. Based on the original story by Georges Conchon and Francis Girod.

Prod Comp: Centre National de la Cinématographie, Le Studio Canal+, UGC
Dist/Sales: 21stCentury

Elegant Spanking, The

Beatty, Maria / Delain, Rosemary
1994; USA; 30 min; B&W; Erotica
M: John Zorn
Cast: Rosemary Delain, Maria Beatty

A lesbian porn film featuring performance artist Rosemary Delain, who acts out the role of the Mistress and dominates and humiliates her lover Kitty. An exploration of S/M, power, dominance and submission.

Prod Comp: Bleu Productions
Dist/Sales: TLA

Elegy in the Streets

Hubbard, Jim
1990; USA; 30 min; Experimental

A political and personal perspective on the AIDS crisis in the USA.

Dist/Sales: Canyon

Elevation

Cummins, Stephen
1989; Australia; 11 min; Drama

An elegant and lyrical celebration of gay sexuality and flirtation. A story of love between two men set in an elevator. *Elevation* proves that passion can start in the strangest places.

Prod Comp: Australian Film TV & Radio School
Dist/Sales: AFTRS, Frameline, ACMI

Elevation

Ellen DeGeneres: The Beginning

Gallen, Joel
2000; USA; 65 min; Documentary
Cast: Ellen DeGeneres

Live from the Beacon Theatre in New York, after seven years on TV and the big screen, Ellen DeGeneres is back on stage, live, outspoken, outrageous and out. It's Ellen, back to stand-up at her most hilarious. From her secret for how to deal with forgetting people's names to the harsh realities of videotaping your sex life. (Wolfe)

Dist/Sales: Wolfe

Elton John: Tantrums and Tiaras

Furnish, David
1997; USA; 72 min; Documentary
P: Claudia Rosencrantz, Polly Steele; *C:* David Furnish; *E:* Martin Cooper

Cast: Elton John, David Furnish

Warts and all documentary by David Furnish about his partner—one of Britain's most successful modern pop musicians, Sir Elton John.

Prod Comp: Rocket Pictures
Dist/Sales: Cinemax

Emergence

Parmar, Pratibha
1986; UK; 18 min; Documentary

Common themes of identity, alienation and herstory in the context of the diasporan experience emerge in this powerful film. Four Black and Third World women artists, among them African–American feminist poet Audre Lorde and Palestinian performance artist Mona Hatoum, speak forcefully through their art and writing. (WMM)

Dist/Sales: WMM, GroupeIntervention

Emily and Gitta

Gold, Tami
1996; USA; 30 min; Drama

Emily, a painter, is the child of concentration camp survivors. Gitta, a photographer, grew up in Germany thinking of herself as innocent, removed from the actions of her parents and their generation under Hitler. The two meet and begin a dance of emotional and erotic intimacy. But almost as soon as it gets under way, their relationship threatens to be undone by the personal and historical legacies they do and do not share. (WMM)

Dist/Sales: WMM

Emmanuelle

Jaeckin, Just
1974; France; 94 min; Erotica
P: Yves Rousset-Rouard; *W:* Jean-Louis Richard;
C: Richard Suzuki, Marie Saunier; *E:* Claudine Bouché;
M: Pierre Bachelet, Francis Lai
Cast: Sylvia Kristel, Marika Green, Daniel Sarky

Emmanuelle is a naive young bride of an older and more knowledgeable man. While in Bangkok her husband introduces her to a world of sexual and sensual pleasures, both straight and lesbian. Although primarily made for a straight male audience, the lesbian love scenes are quite erotic.

Prod Comp: Trinacra, Orphee
Dist/Sales: Wolfe, Columbia, ACMI

Empire State

Peck, Ron
1987; UK; 102 min; Thriller
P: Norma Hayman; *W:* Ron Peck, Mark Ayres;

C: Tony Imi; *E:* Chris Kelly; *M:* Steve Parsons
Cast: Ray McAnally, Lee Drysdale, Cathryn Harrison, Martin Landau

A crime-thriller that involves a former male prostitute who attempts to take over a nightclub in the seedy East End of London. He gets caught between his old boss, Frank, and Chuck, an American businessman with whom he has tried to set up a deal. Features a strong gay sensibility, together with Jimmy Sommerville on the soundtrack, as well as a wide variety of rent boys.

Empty Bed, An

Gasper, Mark
1990; USA; 60 min; Drama
P: Mark Gasper, Victoria Larimore; *W:* Mark Gasper;
C: Oren Rudavsky; *E:* Gloria Whittemore; *M:* Glen Roven
Cast: Kevin Kelly, Thomas Hill, Harriet Bass, Conan McCarthy

Captures a day in the life of an elderly gay man living in Greenwich Village as he battles with a homophobic America. Using flashbacks, he spends the day recalling his youth. The only relationships he has had have all ended unhappily, leaving him full of regret and loneliness.

Dist/Sales: FirstRunFeatures

Enchantment, The

(aka: Yuwakusha)

Nagasaki, Shunichi
1989; Japan; 109 min; Thriller
Cast: Kumiko Akiyoshi, Masao Kusakari, Kiwako Harada, Takeshi Naito, Tsutomu Isobe

An involving and complicated drama about a Tokyo psychiatrist who becomes obsessed with a female patient when she reveals her bruises, given to her by her jealous girlfriend. Another patient turns up dead with a knife in his back and the film takes on a femme fatale twist.

Prod Comp: Fuji Television Network, Nippon Herald Films

Endangered

Hammer, Barbara
1988; USA; 19 min; Experimental

Examines the imminent disappearance of animals and life (and possibly the artist and her work), using split frames and featuring a prominent soundtrack. All forms of life are considered: spiders, seals, tigers, birds and microbes. The final cuts include a litany: 'extinct, done, gone, marginal, obliterated'. (Frameline)

Dist/Sales: NFVLS, Frameline

e

Enfants Terribles, Les

(aka: The Strange Ones)

Melville, Jean-Pierre
1949; France; 106 min; B&W; Drama
P: Jean-Pierre Melville; *W:* Jean-Pierre Melville, Jean Cocteau; *C:* Henri Decaë; *E:* Monique Bonnot; *M:* Paul Bonneau, Johann Sebastian Bach, Antonio Vivaldi
Cast: Edouard Dermithe, Nicole Stéphane, Renee Cosima, Jacques Bernard

With narration by the great gay poet, novelist and filmmaker, Jean Cocteau, Melville has created a film which exemplifies Cocteau's particular vision of childhood and fantasy, poetry and death. A brother and sister exist in a room together and rarely venture out. When they do, it leads to hilarious escapades as they wander about the world outside. Their confused narcissism and intense passion for each other, and the brother's sexual fluidity, finally leads to their destruction. French with English subtitles.

Prod Comp: Melville Productions
Dist/Sales: Ascanbee

Englishman Abroad, An

Schlesinger, John
1983; UK; 64 min; Comedy
P: Innes Lloyd; *W:* Alan Bennett; *C:* Nat Crosby;
M: George Fenton
Cast: Alan Bates, Coral Browne

This made for TV movie is a dramatisation of an actual unexpected meeting in Moscow, 1958, between actress Coral Browne and the former British spy Guy Burgess. Browne returns to Burgess's flat where she is introduced to his male lover. Browne approved the script based on her account of the incident and plays herself in the recreation of this humorous encounter.

Prod Comp: BBC

Enter into Clowns

(aka: Enter the Clowns; Choujue Dengchang)

Cui, Zi'en
2001; China; 82 min; Drama
P: Tongwei Zhang, Weifang Wu, Shujing Liu, Zi'en Cui; *W:* Zi'en Cui; *C:* Deqiang Yuan; *E:* Haixin Hu
Cast: Bing Chen, Na-ren-qi-mu-ge, Yu Bo, Xiaoyu Yu

Amazing narrative which explores sexual identity and gender orientation in modern Chinese society.

Dist/Sales: Cuizi Film Studio

Entertaining Mr Sloane

Hickox, Douglas
1970; UK; 90 min; Comedy
P: Douglas Kentish; *W:* Clive Exton;
C: Wolfgang Suschitzky; *E:* John Trumper;
M: Georgie Fame
Cast: Peter McEnery, Beryl Reid, Alan Webb

Joe Orton's plays eroticised the 'kitchen-sink' realist theatre of the 1960s. In *Entertaining Mr Sloane* a young man lodges with a safely bourgeois brother and sister only to find that they are both interested in sleeping with him, and they will let nothing get in the way of satisfying their sexual desires.

Prod Comp: Canterbury Film Productions
Dist/Sales: ACMI

Entre Nous

(aka: Coup de Foudre)

Kurys, Diane
1983; France; 110 min; Drama
P: Ariel Zeitoun; *W:* Diane Kurys, Alain le Henry; *C:* Bernard Lutic; *E:* Joële Van Effenterre; *M:* Luis Bacalov
Cast: Isabelle Huppert, Miou-Miou, Guy Marchand, Jean-Pierre Bacri

Lena, a housewife locked into the boring security of marriage and family, meets an artist. In contrast to Lena, Madeleine is vibrant and alive but like Lena she too is dissatisfied with her marriage. The two meet at the school that their children attend and become instant soul mates. They find in each other what is missing in their marriages and begin to drift together and away from their families. Through their complex but strong friendship Lena embarks on a journey of self-discovery. Diane Kurys based the story on her mother, and her mother's deep friendship with another woman.

Prod Comp: Partners Production, Alexandre Films, Films A2
Dist/Sales: UAClassics, Wolfe

Entwined

Harrington, Raquel Cecilia
1997; USA; 118 min; Drama
P: Raquel Cecilia Harrington, Jacqueline B. Frost; *W:* Raquel Cecilia Harrington
Cast: Verónica Sánchez, Koim Ostrenko, Iris Delgado, Marilyn Romero

The passion that has ignited between a film student and her lecturer causes drama as each is already committed to someone else.

Prod Comp: Corazón Films

Équilibristes, Les

(aka: Walking a Tightrope)

Papatakis, Nico
1991; France; 130 min; Drama
P: Humbert Balsan; *C:* William Lubtchansky
Cast: Michel Piccoli, Lilah Dadi, Polly Walker,

Doris Kunstmann, Patrick Mille

Based on an episode in the life of Jean Genet, Piccoli plays a great writer and poet who picks up a young man whose job is to sweep the floors. He falls in love with him and resolves to make him into a tightrope walker. But soon he tosses the boy aside when he falls for a woman who is an aspiring racing driver.

Dist/Sales: UGC

Equus

Lumet, Sidney
1977; USA; 137 min; Drama
P: Denis Holt, Elliott Kastner, Lester Persky; *W:* Peter Shaffer; *C:* Oswald Morris; *E:* John Victor Smith; *M:* Richard Rodnet Bennett
Cast: Richard Burton, Peter Firth, Joan Plowright, Eileen Atkins, Jenny Agutter

Peter Firth plays Alan Strang, a young man working as a stable boy at an upper-class riding school who one night brutally blinds the horses. Richard Burton is psychiatrist Dr Martin Dysart who is investigating the reasons for the young man's apparent senseless crime. Based on Peter Shaffer's acclaimed play, *Equus* is a film that explores and manages to traverse a rich field of themes and concerns: psychoanalysis and mythology; sexuality and repression; class and family; sex and power. The relationship between analyst and patient becomes increasingly complex as the mysteries of the boy's repressions become unravelled. The men's exchanges begin to be complicated by the echoes of homoeroticism and the psychological overtones of the Oedipal Complex. Initially dividing critics, *Equus* has become a cult favourite through the years and is acknowledged as one of Lumet's darker and innovative works. (ACMI)

Prod Comp: United Artists
Dist/Sales: ACMI

Erika's Passions

(aka: Erika's Leidenschaften)

Stöckl, Ula
1978; Germany; 67 min; Drama
C: Thomas Mauch
Cast: Karin Baal, Vera Tschechowa

A butch lesbian and her femme lover are accidentally locked in a room together after a long separation and are forced to confront each other's differences and complaints.

Ernesto

Samperi, Salvatore
1979; Italy; 98 min; Drama
P: José Frade; *W:* Amadeo Paganini, Salvatore Samperi,

Barbara Alberti; *C:* Camillo Bazzoni; *E:* Sergio Montanari; *M:* Carmelo Bernaola
Cast: Martin Halm, Virna Lisi, Michele Placido, Renato Salvatori, Turi Ferro

The story of a young Jewish boy's first sexual encounter with an older male worker at his uncle's factory. He discards the man and becomes attracted to twins—a brother and sister. He chooses heterosexuality and finally marries. But while he is truly loved by others, he is incapable of loving them. Based on the autobiographical novel by Umberto Saba.

Prod Comp: International Spectrafilm, Albatros Produktion
Dist/Sales: Facets

Erotica: A Journey into Female Sexuality

Gallus, Maya
1997; Canada; 75 min; Documentary
P: Julie Sereny; *C:* Zoe Dirse; *E:* Cathy Gulkin; *M:* Celina Carroll, Chip Yarwood

An evocative, sensuous, celebratory and, at times, dark journey through the female erotic imagination, *Erotica* travels behind-the-scenes with ten different women who reveal their inner fantasy lives and expose their most intimate secrets for the camera. Produced, directed and edited by women, and shot with an all-female crew, *Erotica* explores the range and variety of female eroticism, from the sadomasochistic rituals of a Parisian dominatrix, to the San Francisco lesbian nightclub scene. The film also features celebrity porn-star-turned filmmakers Annie Sprinkle and Candida Royale, renowned photographers Bettina Rheims and Phyllis Christopher, urban American rapper 'Lique', butch drag king 'Fairy Butch' and erotic novelist Alina Reyes. They openly discuss how their personal and professional lives merge. And they reveal the struggles and conflicts that they, like many women, have encountered, thereby illuminating the complex nature of female sexuality and its place in our ever-changing society. (Films Transit)

Prod Comp: Swept Away Productions
Dist/Sales: FilmsTransit

Erotique

Borden, Lizzie / Law, Clara / Treut, Monika
1993; Germany, USA; 90 min; Drama
P: Christopher Wood, Vicky Herman, Monika Treut, Michael Sombetzki, Teddy Robin Kwan, Eddie Ling-Ching Fong; *W:* Lizzie Borden, Susie Bright, Monika Treut, Eddie Ling-Ching Fong; *C:* Larry Banks, Elfi Mikesch, Arthur Wong; *E:* Jill Bilcock; *M:* Andrew Belling, Tats Lau
Cast: Kamela Lopez-Dawson, Liane Curtis, Bryan

Cranston, Priscilla Barnes, Marianne Sagebrecht

A compilation of three films by three female directors, each dealing with the erotic and sexual fantasies of women. *Let's Talk About Sex*: in Los Angeles, a young Latina works in a phone sex office to pay bills. She becomes obsessed with one of the male clients and finds him willing to participate in her fantasy. She enlists the aid of a policewoman friend to find out where he lives and a 'kidnap' is arranged where the resolution is a surprise to everyone. *Taboo Parlor*: in Hamburg, Claire and Julia are two stunning women in a lesbian relationship. The gentle, vulnerable and younger Julia receives Claire's approval for a heterosexual fling. Together, they search Hamburg's underbelly for the right young man. The ménage begins but jealousy flares and ends in the spectacular sequence where only two survive. *Wonton Soup*: An Australian-born Chinese boy travels out of Australia for the first time. In Hong Kong he reunites with his old girlfriend whom he met when she studied at his college in Melbourne. Though both are Chinese, they are products of totally different cultures. He is determined to prove that he can overcome all obstacles to restore the happy relationship they shared at school.

Dist/Sales: 21stCentury, Beyond

Escalier C

Tacchella, Jean-Charles
1985; France; 100 min; Comedy
P: Marie-Dominique Girodet; *W:* Jean-Charles Tacchella, Elvira Murail; *C:* Jacques Assuérus; *E:* Agnés Guillemot; *M:* Raymond Alessandrini
Cast: Robin Renucci, Jean-Pierre Bacri, Jacques Bonnaffé, Catherine Leprince, Jacques Weber

The tenants of Paris, 14 arrondissement, Stairs C, have one thing in common: their average age is 30. They include a widow, a novelist, an alcoholic and a very rude art critic. After a neighbour is murdered, the art critic has a moral turnaround and decides to move in with a caring gay man. He also goes on a pilgrimage to Jerusalem. An interesting character study which falls short of being a great film as it only superficially examines the issues raised. French with English subtitles.

Prod Comp: Films7, FR3 Films Cinéma
Dist/Sales: AMLF, NFVLS

Escape to Life: The Erika and Klaus Mann Story

Speck, Wieland / Weiss, Andrea
2000; Germany, UK; 84 min; Documentary
P: Thomas Kufus, Greta Schiller; *W:* Weiland Speck, Andrea Weiss; *C:* Nuala Campbell, Uli Fischer, Ann T. Rossetti; *E:* Prisca Swan, Andrea Weis; *M:* John Eacott

This compelling docudrama chronicles the lives of Klaus and Erika Mann, played out against the tumultuous history of the Roaring Twenties, the rise of Fascism and World War II. The openly gay children of German novelist Thomas Mann, Klaus and Erika were authors, cabaret performers, and committed antifascists. Their intense sibling relationship, which took root through the imaginative, make-believe world they shared as children, was strained by the demands of life in exile, by Klaus's drug addiction and Erika's gradual shift in loyalty from brother to father, with fatal consequences. Bringing together rare archival footage and period music, revealing anecdotes from colleagues and friends, TV interviews with Erika Mann, and re-created scenes based on Klaus Mann's writings, *Escape to Life* is a fascinating tribute to a extraordinary couple. (Cinema Guild)
English & German with English subtitles.

Prod Comp: Jezebel Productions, Zero Film
Dist/Sales: CinemaGuild

Escape to Life: The Erika and Klaus Mann Story

Escorte, L'

Langlois, Denis
1996; Canada; 92 min; Comedy
P: Bertrand Lachance, Denis Langlois; *W:* Bertrand Lachance, Denis Langlois; *C:* Yves Beaudoin; *E:* Meiyen Chan; *M:* Bertrand Chénier
Cast: Robin Aubert, Paul-Antoine Taillefer, Éric Cabana, Marie Lefebvre

In his first feature, a bittersweet comedy of manners, Langlois continues his study of love, hate, truth, lies, fidelity and promiscuity among a set of Montreal friends and lovers in the age of AIDS. The lives of Jean-Marc and Philippe, a gay couple struggling as their restaurant fails, are altered forever when the catalytic Steve, a young escort, enters their lives. He inspires the couple, and their friends, to act up and act out their desires. Long kept silences about HIV status are broken and confronted. French with English subtitles.

Prod Comp: Castor & Pollux
Dist/Sales: CinemaLibre

Et L'Amore

Kumiss, Mary / Seidler, Ellen
1993; USA; 23 min; Drama

This film is about a purely sensuous, erotic encounter between two women who meet and spend the rest of the film exploring each other's bodies in a realistic and passionate way.

Eve's Daughters

Ankele, John / Macksoud, Anne
1995; 27 min; Drama

'Beware of Eve the Temptress,' says St. Augustine, who was talking, apparently, about women who love other women. *Eve's Daughters* poignantly tells their story. (First Run Features)

Dist/Sales: FirstRunFeatures

Even Cowgirls get the Blues

Van Sant, Gus
1994; USA; 100 min; Comedy
P: Laurie Parker; *W:* Gus Van Sant; *C:* John Campbell, Eric Alan Edwards; *E:* Curtiss Clayton, Gus Van Sant; *M:* k. d. lang, Ben Mink
Cast: Uma Thurman, Lorraine Bracco, Rain Phoenix, Angie Dickinson, Pat Morita, Keanu Reeves

Cowgirls tracks the adventures of an unconventional heroine, a little girl born into the repressive 1950s with abnormally large thumbs. She transcends what would surely have been a huge handicap to most people by becoming the world's greatest hitchhiker. But though the lure of the wild and free open road is great, she comes to yearn for the security of a settled life and true love. She ends up at the Rubber Rose Ranch, falls in love with the head cowgirl, Bonanza Jellybean, and fights to save the whooping crane from extinction. Based on the cult novel by Tom Robbins.

Prod Comp: New Line Cinema, Fourth Vision
Dist/Sales: Roadshow, FilmsInc, FineLine, Lauren, ACMI

Evening Dress

(aka: Tenue de Soirée; Menage)

Blier, Bertrand
1986; France; 84 min; Comedy
P: Philippe Dussart, René Cleitman; *W:* Bertrand Blier; *C:* Jean Penzer; *E:* Claudine Merlin; *M:* Serge Gainsbourg
Cast: Gérard Depardieu, Michel Blanc, Miou-Miou, Michel Creton, Jean-François Stevenin

This black comedy is a clever gay variation on the traditional romantic triangle. Everything changes when a thief talks a financially struggling couple into burglary: the thief then falls, not for the sexy wife, but the boring, balding husband. French with English subtitles.

Awards: Cannes Film Festival, 1986: Best Actor (Michel Blanc)
Prod Comp: Ciné Valse, DD Productions, Hachette Première, Phillipe Dussart SARL
Dist/Sales: Roadshow, Cinecom, BFI

Evenings, The

(aka: De Avonden)

Van den Berg, Rudolf
1989; The Netherlands; 120 min; Drama
P: René Solleveld, Peter Weijdeveld; *W:* Jean Ummels; *C:* Willy Stassen; *E:* Maria Steenburgen; *M:* Bob Zimmerman
Cast: Thom Hoffman, Rijk de Gooyer, Viviane de Muynck, Pierre Bokma

The Evenings is based on Catholic gay author Gerald Reve's autobiography (Reve also wrote *The Fourth Man*) and follows Frits, a 20-year-old clerk, through six days leading to New Year's Eve of 1947. Frits is a Holden Caulfield figure, with a flatulent father and solicitous mother. He stumbles through parties, offices, school reunions and sexual encounters with Dutch boys. His sexually charged and anxiety-ridden daydreams are hilariously depicted as are his obsessions with time, thinning hair, the dark, sanity and bellybutton lint. Ardently inquisitive and an endearing bumbler, Frits attempts to assert his selfhood in a strange and hostile world. (MQFF)

Prod Comp: Concorde
Dist/Sales: Netherlands

Everlasting Secret Family, The

Thornhill, Michael
1988; Australia; 94 min; Drama
P: Michael Thornhill, Sue Carleton; *W:* Frank Moorhouse; *C:* Julian Penney; *E:* Pamela Barnetta; *M:* Tony Bremner
Cast: Arthur Dignam, Mark Lee, Dennis Miller, Heather Mitchell

A beautiful and ambitious youth becomes the lover of a powerful Senator who is a member of 'The Secret Family', a group of homosexual men who regularly meet to discuss politics. The young man (known as 'The Lover') soon realises that he can manipulate his position only as long as he retains his youth. With the help of an elderly judge, the young man hatches a plan to make a change in the world. To succeed, he must manipulate the Senator, his wife and the family chauffeur. Based on a book of short stories, *The Everlasting Secret Family and Other Secrets* by Frank Moorhouse.

Prod Comp: International Film Management, FGH

Everything in Between

Rony, Fatimah Tobing
2000; USA; 27 min; Drama

Rosa Wong Benitez, a struggling fashion designer of mixed Asian descent, protects herself from the vulnerability of falling in love by having a string of dead-end relationships. Abandoned by her mother when she was a baby, Rosa is obsessed with the old-style Hollywood movie star, Anna May Wong, who she fantasises to be her mother. Raised in downtown Los Angeles by her 'Uncle Otto', an older queen and former hairdresser, Rosa's deepest emotional relationships are with gay men, including her best friend Michael. Realising that she is in a rut, Rosa has decided to move to New York City. Before her departure, events force Rosa, Michael and Otto to end the masquerade that they play with each other and reveal their true feelings. (Frameline)

Dist/Sales: Frameline

Everything Relative

Pollack, Sharon
1996; USA; 110 min; Drama
P: Sharon Pollack; *W:* Sharon Pollack; *C:* Zakaela Rachel Othmer; *E:* Meredith Paige; *M:* Frank London
Cast: Stacey Nelkin, Monica Bell, Ellen McLaughlin, Harvey Fierstein

The story of a group of women, some lesbian and some straight, who went to school together and reunite after one of them has a baby. They come together for the weekend and travel to their old haunts, where they recount their old lives and discuss how they have changed since the 1970s.

Dist/Sales: Millivres, Wolfe

Excuse me Duckie, but Lucas Loved Me

(aka: Perdona Bonita, pero Lucas me queria a mi)

Sabroso, Félix / Ayaso, Dunia
1997; Spain; 92 min; Comedy
C: Arnaldo Catinari
Cast: Jordi Mollà, Repón Nieto, Roberto Correcher

Zany comic thriller in which three gay men fall for the same straight guy. Toni, Carlos, and Dani, best friends and roommates, need to find a fourth roommate to help pay the rent. Enter tall, sexy Lucas, who immediately sets each man's heart aflutter. Petty jealousies and fierce rivalries for handsome Lucas' attention come to a wickedly comic crescendo when Lucas' body is found, half-naked, with a complete set of kitchen knives buried in his chest. Only a repressed police inspector can solve this mystery as flashbacks reveal three very different versions of Lucas' life with the roommates. Each of the characters, instead of trying to prove his (or her) innocence, tells a story to try to prove that it

was he whom Lucas really loved. (Mongrel) Spanish with English subtitles.

Prod Comp: Cristal Producciones Cinematográficas
Dist/Sales: Sogepaq, Col-Tri, Mongrel

Execution of Justice

Ichaso, Leon
1999; USA; 103 min; Drama
P: Jeff Freilich; *W:* Michael Butler; *C:* Claudio Chea; *E:* Gary Karr; *M:* Daniel Licht
Cast: Peter Coyote, Tyne Daly, Stephen Young, Khalil Kain, Timothy Daly

The true story of the assassination of San Francisco Mayor George Moscone and openly gay City Supervisor Harvey Milk on 27 November 1978.

Prod Comp: Justice Productions, Paramount
Dist/Sales: Daly/Harris, Showtime, Wolfe, ParamountHV

Execution of Wanda Jean, The

Garbus, Liz
2001; USA; 88 min; Documentary
P: Rory Kennedy, Liz Garbus; *C:* Tony Hardmon; *E:* Mary Manhardt; *M:* Wendy Blackstone

Wanda Jean Allen was an attractive young woman with an appealing personality. In 1981 Allen served time for killing a friend, and in 1998, she shot and killed her lover, Gloria Leathers, after Leathers threatened to leave her. *The Execution of Wanda Jean* chronicles the last three months of her life, which culminated in her death by lethal injection on 11 January 2001. Using interviews with Allen, her clemency team and family members from both Allen's and the victim's families, Academy Award nominated director/producer Liz Garbus explores the many layers of her subject's complex personal history. (7th Art Releasing)

Prod Comp: HBO
Dist/Sales: Moxie

Exiles of Love

Kalitowski, Toby
1992; UK; 30 min; Documentary
P: Toby Kalitowski
Cast: Neil Bartlett, Derek Jarman, Constantine Giannaris, Robert Chevara

Inspired by the life and works of Jean Genet, this short video includes interviews with four contemporary gay filmmakers/writers—Derek Jarman, Neil Bartlett, Constantine Giannaris and Robert Chevara—to investigate the pleasure, the danger, the joy and fear involved in homosexual love and sex.

Prod Comp: 4BC, Greater London Arts
Dist/Sales: ACMI

Exploding Oedipus

Lafia, Marc
2001; USA; 84 min; Drama
P: Kenneth Peralta; *W:* Marc Lafia; *C:* Joplin Wu; *E:* Joe Bini; *M:* Petey Reniche, Juliana Hatfield
Cast: Bruce Ramsay, Juliana Hatfield, Charlotte Chatton, Tania Meneguzzi

When his father has a near-fatal heart attack, Hilbert descends into a surreal journey of self-discovery. Passionately experimenting with bisexuality, drugs, and art and testing his memories against home movies, he comes to realise that he can, in a sense, rewrite his past by confronting the future. (www.seattleweekly.com)

Dist/Sales: FDFilms

Extramuros

(aka: Beyond the Walls)

Picazo, Miguel
1985; Spain; 120 min; Drama
P: Antonio Martín; *W:* Jesús Fernández Santos, Miguel Picazo; *C:* Teodoro Escamilla; *M:* José Nieto
Cast: Carmen Maura, Mercedes Sampietro

A bleak tale about Sister Angela and her lover Sister Ana who conceive a plan to stop the demise of their convent. Sister Angela injures her hands and tells the people a miracle has happened—she has the mark of the stigmata. A bizarre and beautiful film using the ravages of the plague as a backdrop for the drama and isolation of the convent and the sensual relationship of the two nuns. Spanish with English subtitles.

Dist/Sales: Frameline, TLA, Wolfe

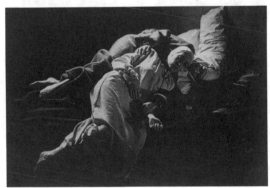

Extramuros

Eyes of Tammy Faye, The

Bailey, Fenton / Barbato, Randy
2000; UK, USA; 79 min; Documentary
P: Fenton Bailey, Randy Barbato; *C:* Sandra Chandler;

E: Paul Wiesepape; *M:* James Harry

Documentary wonderboys Fenton Bailey and Randy Barbato (*101 Rent Boys*, *The Real Ellen Story*) have done it again in this brilliant exploration of the life of one of the greatest living camp icons and Christian television poster girls of our time: Tammy Faye Bakker Messner. Narrated by RuPaul Charles this hilarious and at times moving documentary paints a fascinating and revealing portrait of a woman whose main crime was acceptance. Unlike her fundamental Christian contemporaries, Tammy Faye's brand of religion was always inclusive and celebratory. Her successes and failures, including her traumatic times with ex-husband Christian TV preacher Jim Bakker, are included, along with vital tips on make-up and hair, and the art of hand-puppetry. (MQFF)

Prod Comp: Cinemax, Channel 4, World of Wonder
Dist/Sales: LionsGate, Wolfe, Swank

F. is a Bastard

(aka: F. est un Salaud)

Gisler, Marcel
1998; France, Switzerland; 92 min; Drama
P: Pierre-Alain Schatzmann, Ruth Waldburger; *W:* Marcel Gisler, Rudolf Nadler; *C:* Sophie Maintigneux; *E:* Bettina Böhler; *M:* Rainer Lingk
Cast: Fréd´ric Andrau, Vincent Branchat, Urs Peter Halter, Jean-Pierre von Dach

Beni is a 16-year-old student who gets a job as a roadie for a rock band called 'The Minks'. He quickly develops a man size crush on the sexy and rebellious Fögi, the band's lead singer. Much to his surprise and delight the two become lovers. Fögi's career takes a turn for the worse and the singer's life spirals into a merry-go-round of drug use and insecurity, and he begins to take his failures out on Beni. But despite Beni's continuing devotion, the abuse careers out of control, and Beni has to decide between his lover and his own survival. French with English subtitles.

Prod Comp: Arena Films, Vega Film Productions
Dist/Sales: Vega

F2M

Latta, Cayte
1992; Australia; 15 min; Documentary

Jasper Laybutt is a well-known face on the Sydney queer scene, and through his involvement with the Ms Wicked events. Here he talks about his life as a pre-operative female-to-male transsexual and about his love of uniforms, women, and the arduous journey of recreating his identity as a man. (MQFF)

Fag Hag

Dietz, Damion
1998; USA; 75 min; Comedy
W: Damion Dietz; *E:* Vince Filippone
Cast: Stephanie Orff, Damion Dietz, Saadia Billman, Darryl Theirse

John Waters styled tongue in cheek story of how two hopeless no-talent losers find each other in a cruel world, and through the strength of their deep bond are empowered to become...two hopeless no-talent losers.

Prod Comp: Potemkin Productions
Dist/Sales: Potemkin, Troma

Faggots are for Burning

McKay, Barry
1997; Australia; 10 min; Experimental
P: Barry McKay

A young man is forced to seek a cure for his homosexuality when his tranquillity is unsettled by desire in this short film, which merges documentary and dramatised footage with a disturbing overlaid vocal collage.

Dist/Sales: Frameline

Fairy who didn't want to be a Fairy, The

Lynd, Laurie
1992; Canada; 17 min; Comedy
P: K. Lee Hall; *C:* Miroslaw Baszak; *E:* Miume Jan
Cast: Michael Kennard, John Turner

This black comedy is a musical fairy/morality tale for those who feel the grass is always greener on the other side of the fence. (MQFF)

Dist/Sales: BFI

Fall of Communism as Seen in Gay Pornography, The

Jones, William E.
1998; USA; 19 min; Documentary

An intriguing documentary made up entirely of images taken from gay pornography made in the Eastern bloc. It is constructed of images of young men being exploited.

Dist/Sales: NFVLS

Family Affair, A (1995)

Taylor, Amanda
1995; USA; 17 min; Experimental
P: Amanda Taylor; *W:* Amanda Taylor; *C:* Amanda Taylor

A Family Affair is an experimental documentary that chronicles a trip to Taylor's uncle's funeral. The video humorously examines the complexity of family dynamics, family histories and hereditary illness through Taylor's eyes as a lesbian.

Prod Comp: Rocketgirl Productions

Family Affair, A (2001)

Lesnick, Helen
2001; USA; 108 min; Drama
P: Valerie Pichney; *W:* Helen Lesnick; *C:* Jim Orr; *M:* Natasha's Ghost
Cast: Helen Lesnick, Arlene Golonka, Erica Shaffer, Barbara Stuart

Wayward New Yorker Rachel Rosen flees New York City and her capricious girlfriend for California in desperate pursuit of Ms Rightowitz. However, when she finds her, she's not so sure it's not Ms Wrongowitz she wants after all...

Prod Comp: Atta Girl Productions
Dist/Sales: AttaGirl, Wolfe

A Family Affair (2001)

Family Fundamentals

Dong, Arthur
2002; USA; 75 min; Documentary
P: Arthur Dong; *W:* Arthur Dong; *C:* Arthur Dong; *E:* Arthur Dong; *M:* Mark Adler

In this feature documentary, filmmaker Arthur Dong (*Licensed to Kill*, *Coming Out Under Fire*) continues his quest to understand American contempt for homosexuality and its effects on family, culture and the nation's political landscape. Armed with a digital camera, Dong takes viewers into the private, and sometimes very public lives, of three conservative Christian families with gay and lesbian children. (Deep Focus Productions)

Prod Comp: DeepFocus Productions
Dist/Sales: DeepFocus

Family Pack

Family Pack

(aka: Que Faisaient les Femmes Pendant que L'homme Marchait sur la Lune?)

Stappen, Chris Vander
2000; Canada, France; 105 min; Comedy
P: Catherine Burniaux, François Charlent, Jean-Luc Van Damme; W: Chris Vander Stappen; C: Michel Houssiau; E: France Duez; M: Frédéric Vercheval
Cast: Marie Bunel, Hélène Vincent, Tsilla Chelton, Masha Grenon

It's 1969, man is about to walk on the moon and Odile has an ultimatum for her girlfriend Sascha—come out to your mother or I'm leaving. And so Sascha travels from Montreal to her family home in Brussels with the intention of granting Odile's wish. However, first there is the small matter of admitting that she dropped out of medical school long ago. As Sascha hilariously tries to tell her family the truth, but is stifled at every turn, she begins to see that not all is as she had assumed. Her dwarf sister seems to enjoy the company of fish more than the family, and her father and grandmother both disappear mysteriously. What's more her mother's smelling salt addiction may be getting out of hand. (MQFF) French with English subtitles.

Prod Comp: Le Studio Canal+, Banana Films
Dist/Sales: M6

Family Values

Saks, Eva
2001; USA; 25 min; Documentary

Becky and Donna are a nice lesbian couple with a house in the suburbs, who run a family business cleaning up death scenes. They are an American family with traditional family values: two parents, two cars, one child, one day job, and a family business. But they're not exactly *The Donna Reed Show*. The two parents are women; their child Justin is Donna's son from a previous marriage; her day job is working as a Philadelphia police officer; the family cars are Donna's 'Homicide unit' van and Becky's 'Trauma Scene Restoration' van. (Big Short Films)

Dist/Sales: Reilly, BigFilm

Family Values: An American Tragedy

Walton, Pam
1996; USA; 57 min; Documentary

This intensely personal film documents lesbian videomaker Pam Walton's attempt to reconcile with her long estranged father. It is also her search for what family means to her. After her mother's death and her father's remarriage, her father Rus Walton broke off ties with his daughters. He evolved into a right wing fundamentalist and a 'family values' activist. In his writing he considered invoking the death penalty for practising homosexuals. Although Pam surrounded herself with a new lesbian family of nurturing and supportive friends, she yearned for her blood ties. Despite the emotional cost, she made repeated attempts to connect with him. This emotional saga is a journey through uncharted family terrain, evoking suspense, pain and wisdom. Told in the form of a video diary, *Family Values* shows how the longing for parental acceptance can never be extinguished. (Filmakers Library)

Dist/Sales: FilmakersLibrary

Fanci's Persuasion

Herman-Wurmfeld, Charles
1995; USA; 80 min; Comedy
C: David Rush Morrison; E: Michael A. Worrall
Cast: Jessica Patton, Justin Bond, Robert Coffman, Boa, Alyssa Wendt

The night before Fanci's wedding to her luscious girlfriend Loretta, a spell settles upon San Francisco. Fanci's friends and family are catapulted into a tantalising dream world where magic takes precedent over reality, and conventions crack. By the morning light, all of the players are transformed but one thing is certain: For Fanci and company, love is a many-gendered thing. (Water Bearer Films)

Dist/Sales: WaterBearer

Fantasm

Bruce, Richard (aka Richard Franklin)
1975; Australia; 90 min; Erotica
P: Antony I. Ginnane; W: Ross Dimsey; C: Vince Monton; E: Tony Paterson
Cast: Dee Dee Levitt, Maria Arnold, Bill Magold, Gretchen Gayle, Rene Bond

Ten sexual fantasies of women in the 1970s are presented episodically, and include sex in the beauty salon, fruit fetishism, and lesbianism in a sauna. Each episode is introduced by a German psychiatrist, Professor Jurgen Notafreud.

Prod Comp: TLN Film Productions, Australian International Films
Dist/Sales: VSM

f

Fantasm Comes Again

(aka: Fantasm 99)

Eggleston, Colin / Ram, Eric
1977; Australia; 94 min; Erotica
P: Antony I. Ginnane; *C:* Vince Monton; *E:* Tony
Paterson; *M:* John Mol
Cast: Angela Menzie-Willis, Clive Hearne, Uschi
Digart, Rick Cassidy, Liz Wolfe

> Libbie, a cadet newspaper reporter, is assigned to her
> paper's sexual advice column. She becomes privy to a
> number of colourful sexual experiences submitted by
> the readers.

Awards: Asian Film Festival, 1977: Special Award
Prod Comp: Australian International Film Corporation
Dist/Sales: VSM

Fantasy Dancer

Vista, Linda
1990; USA; 33 min; Drama

> An erotic fantasy dealing with voyeurism and the
> power of the gaze. A man takes his girlfriend, Nicole,
> to a strip club. She is shocked not at the club but at
> her own reaction to it. She becomes sexually drawn
> to an erotic black stripper, and is taken into the
> stripper's uninhibited world.

Farewell my Concubine

Farewell my Concubine

(aka: Ba wang bie ji)

Kaige, Chen
1993; China; 157 min; Drama
P: Feng Hsu; *W:* Lilian Lee, Wei Lu; *C:* Changwei Gu;
E: Xiaonan Pei; *M:* Jiping Zhao
Cast: Leslie Cheung, Fengyi Zhang, Li Gong, Qi Lu,
Da Ying

> *Farewell my Concubine* is based on Lilian Lee's
> popular novel and covers the changing fortunes and
> an intense relationship between two stars of the
> Peking Opera. One is a specialist in female roles,
> who has a lifelong attraction to his heterosexual

opera partner. It begins in the 1920s and describes
50 years of social and political turmoil in China. A
beautiful and lavish film and at times touching and
brutal. Chinese with English subtitles.

Awards: Cannes Film Festival, 1993: Best Film
Prod Comp: Mirimax, Maverick Picture, Tomson Films,
Beijing Film Studio
Dist/Sales: NFVLS, Swank, BuenaVista, Miramax,
ACMI, Swank

Farewell, The

(aka: Avskedet)

Niskanen, Tuija-Maija
1982; Finland, Sweden; 90 min; Drama
W: Eija-Elina Bergholm, Tuija-Maija Niskanen; *C:* Lasse
Karlsson, Esa Vuorinen
Cast: Carl-Axel Heikenrt, Sanna Hultman, Pirkko
Nurmi, Kerstin Tidelius, Gunnar Björnstrand

> Set between 1930s and 50s, *The Farewell* the story of
> Valerie, who lives in a household totally repressed by
> her stern father. When Valerie has a brief affair with
> another woman, her father is extremely angry and
> tries to end the affair with physical force. However
> Valerie's determination, independence and lesbian
> feelings cannot be crushed. Finnish with English
> subtitles.

Prod Comp: Swedish Film Institute
Dist/Sales: NewYorker

Farewell to Charms

Pontiac, Carla
1985; Australia; 13 min; Experimental
W: Carla Pontiac; *C:* Steve MacDonald, Alison Tilson,
Natalie Green; *E:* Carole Sklan, Chris Oliver
Cast: Radda Jordon, Helen Pankhurst

> An experimental feminist film that questions the
> goals of love and romance as a woman's ultimate
> fulfilment. Highlights the relationship between
> Emma and Cecily, two old school friends, and how
> that relationship changes when they meet a 'bionic
> bike dyke' called Stretch.

Prod Comp: Swinburne Film & TV School
Dist/Sales: NFVLS

Fascination

Rollin, Jean
1979; France; 78 min; Horror
P: Joe De Lara; *W:* Jean Rollin; *C:* Georges Fromentin,
Daniel Lacambre; *E:* Dominique Saint-Cyr;
M: Philippe d' Aram
Cast: Brigitte Lahaie, Franca Mai, Jean-Marie Lemaire,
Fanny Magier

> The visual delights of this film include sensual

lesbian lovemaking, the beautiful Lahaie as a scythe-wielding avenger and a group of blood-addicted women living in a castle, who must find a man to ritually slaughter. They capture a hoodlum but Mai, one of the women, falls in love with him and decides he must be saved. Eventually, her overwhelming hunger for blood drives her to kill him. French with English subtitles.

Prod Comp: Les Films, ABC, Comex
Dist/Sales: Siren

Fassbinder's Women

Fassbinder's Women

von Praunheim, Rosa
2000; Germany; 88 min; Documentary
P: Gerold Hofmann, Holger Prebe; *C:* Elfi Mikesch;
E: Mike Shephard; *M:* Peer Raben

Rosa von Praunheim's new documentary focuses on Rainer Werner Fassbinder through the people who knew him best—the women in his life and films. Hanna Schygulla, Jeanne Moreau, Irm Hermann, Juliane Lorenz, and many others relate their experiences working with the difficult auteur, and recount the influence he had on their personal and professional lives. Their memories and observations help illuminate the persistence of Fassbinder's legend, almost 20 years after his death. *Fassbinder's Women* is a fascinating and enlightening examination of one of the most influential filmmakers in German film history by one of the most renowned German directors working today. (2002 New York Lesbian & Gay Film Festival) German with English subtitles.

Prod Comp: ARTE, ZDF
Dist/Sales: ZDF

Fated to be Queer

Bautista, Pablo
1992; USA; 25 min; Documentary

Filipino men discuss the issues surrounding being queer and of colour in San Francisco.

Fear of Love

Vellenga, Frank
2000; The Netherlands; 24 min; Documentary

This insightful documentary reveals how Islamic gays in the Netherlands must reconcile their sexuality with the heavy burden of Islamic culture. (queerDOC 2002)

Fearless Vampire Killers, The

(aka: Dance of the Vampires)

Polanski, Roman
1967; UK, USA; 110 min; Comedy
P: Gene Gutowski; *W:* Gérard Brach, Roman Polanski;
C: Douglas Slocombe; *E:* Alistair McIntyre;
M: Christopher Komeda
Cast: Roman Polanski, Sharon Tate, Jack MacGowran, Alfie Bass, Jessie Robbins

Polanski plays the weird assistant to an even more weird professor from Transylvania who has come to obliterate the local vampires and rescue the sexy Sharon Tate from the bloodthirsty beasts. Filled with hilarious touches, including the Jewish vampire who is unfazed at the sight of a crucifix and the vampire's gay son who has a thing for Polanski.

Prod Comp: MGM, Filmways Pictures, Cadre
Dist/Sales: Ascanbee, MGM

Feed them to the Cannibals!

Cunningham Reid, Fiona
1992; Australia; 75 min; Documentary
P: Fiona Cunningham-Reid

In 1972 a small number of lesbians and gay men held the first Gay and Lesbian Mardi Gras in Sydney, a then militant solidarity march for gay rights. Since then the Sydney Gay and Lesbian Mardi Gras has become one of the biggest festivals in the world, attracting hundreds of thousands of international and domestic tourists every year. The film explores the history of the Sydney lesbian and gay community, and Mardi Gras. Many of the activists interviewed discuss the changes in Australian gay and lesbian politics over the last 20 years and the changes in the lived experiences of non-heterosexuality.

Prod Comp: Dangerous to Know, Baobab Productions
Dist/Sales: ACMI

Felicity

Lamond, John D.
1978; Australia; 60 min; Erotica
P: John D. Lamond, Russell Hurley; *W:* John D. Lamond; *C:* Gary Wapshott; *E:* Russell Hurley

Cast: Glory Annen, Christopher Milne, Joni Flynn, Jody Hansen, Marilyn Rodgers

The central character is Felicity, a student at a Catholic boarding school who tentatively explores her sexuality with other young female students. Which of course includes the obligatory nude shower scenes. She receives a letter from her father which invites her and a couple of friends to Hong Kong on a holiday where her sexual adventure continues. She meets Miles and begins an open and non-monogamous relationship with him.

Prod Comp: Krystal Motion Pictures
Dist/Sales: Roadshow

Female Closet, The

Hammer, Barbara
1998; USA; 60 min; Documentary
P: Barbara Hammer; *E:* Barbara Hammer;
M: Ikue More

Renowned filmmaker Barbara Hammer combines rare footage, interviews, and rich visual documentation to survey the lives of variously closeted women artists from different segments of the 20th century: Victorian photographer Alice Austen, Weimar collagist Hannah Höch, and present day painter Nicole Eisenman. In a compelling examination of the art world's treatment of lesbians, Hammer documents how the museum devoted to Austen ignores the implications of her crossdressing photos, how the Museum of Modern Art glossed over Höch's sexuality in a major exhibit, and how Eisenman's work based on patriarchal porn is described by critics as 'liberating, fun, and over the top'. Examining the museum as closet, and the negotiation of visibility and secrecy in lesbian history, this thoughtful video is a provocative look at the relationship between art, life, and sexuality. (WMM)

Dist/Sales: WMM, Cinenova, VTape

Female Misbehavior

Treut, Monika
1992; Germany, USA; 82 min; Comedy
P: Monika Treut, Raymond Wagner; *W:* Dennis Shryack, Jeff Levine, Michael Butler; *C:* Steven C. Brown, Elfi Mikesch; *E:* Renate Merck, James Mitchell; *M:* Peter Bernstein
Cast: Camille Paglia, Annie Sprinkle, Robert Springsteen

This fascinating work from cult lesbian director Monika Treut is actually several films in one. Two short films from the past, *Bondage* (1983) and *Annie* (1989) have been combined with two new documentaries, *Dr Paglia* and *Max*. The result is a series of portraits of 'misbehaving' women: a lesbian

sadomasochist who explains the appeal of breast torture, born again ex-porn star Annie Sprinkle; the enfant terrible of academia and infamous author of *Sexual Personae*, Camille Paglia; and a Native American lesbian who has crossed the gender barrier and now identifies as a heterosexual man. (MQFF)

Dist/Sales: Wolfe, FirstRunFeatures

Female Perversions

Streitfeld, Susan
1996; USA; 110 min; Drama
P: Mindy Affrime; *W:* Susan Steitfeld, Julie Hebert; *C:* Teresa Medina; *E:* Curtiss Clayton, Leo Trombetta; *M:* Debbie Wiseman
Cast: Tilda Swinton, Karen Sillas, Amy Madigan, Frances Fisher

Based on the book by Louise J. Kaplan, *Female Perversions* is the story of Eve Stephens who is on her way to a meeting with the Governor prior to proposing her for a judgeship. Even though she is self-confident, she goes through somewhat of an identity crisis, moving into wild sexual fantasies and winds up entering a relationship with a psychiatrist, Renee who shares a building with Eve.

Prod Comp: Trans Atlantic Entertainment
Dist/Sales: NewVision, 21stCentury, October, Wolfe

Female Trouble

Waters, John
1975; USA; 95 min; Comedy
P: John Waters; *W:* John Waters; *C:* John Waters; *E:* Charles Roggero
Cast: Divine, David Lochary, Mary Vivien Pearce, Mink Stole

The story of the outrageously insane life of Dawn Davenport (played by 300-pound transvestite—Divine) who ends up in the electric chair after her professions as waitress, go-go girl, hooker, mugger, acid-throwing victim, superstar and mass murderer. Classic cult camp.

Prod Comp: New Line Cinema, Dreamland
Dist/Sales: Wolfe, FineLine, NewLine

Fete des Peres, La

(aka: Dad's Day)

Fleury, Joy
1989; France; 80 min; Comedy
P: Jean-Claude Fleury; *W:* Pierre Grillet, Joy Fleury; *C:* Manuel Terán; *E:* Jacques Comets; *M:* Bob Telson
Cast: Thierry Lhermitte, Alain Souchon, Gunilla Karlzen

Stephane and Thomas are a gay couple who have

been living together for five years. They both work, share the same hobbies, and are very content, except for one thing: they want a child. They decide to adopt a baby, but while they are trying to set up the adoption, they are tricked out of their money. They then meet a girl who appears to be an ideal candidate to become a surrogate mother for them.

Prod Comp: TF1 Films

Fiction and Other Truths: A Film about Jane Rule

Fernie, Lynne / Weissman, Aerlyn
1995; Canada; 56 min; Documentary
P: Rina Fraticelli

An exceptional documentary about lesbian writer and activist Jane Rule, best known for her first novel, *The Desert of the Heart*, from which the classic lesbian film *Desert Hearts* was made. Beginning with that book's initial publication in 1964, the film presents a seamless exploration of Rule's writing, her ideas, and the political climate within which she worked. From the 1950s and 60s, when liberals generously pronounced that homosexuality was not an abomination but a treatable disease, and that homosexuals should be accorded compassion, up to the present, the film skilfully contextualises Rule's fiction within that history of prejudice and struggle. Central to the film's structure are the eloquent comments of Rule herself, intelligently balanced with sources as rich and diverse as news footage and reviews, the novels and film extracts, Rule's own correspondence, and interviews with friends and colleagues including Margaret Atwood, Donna Deitch and partner Helen Sonthoff. (MQFF)

Awards: San Francisco International Lesbian & Gay Film Festival, 1995: Best Documentary
Dist/Sales: FilmakersLibrary, NFBC

Fight to be Male, The

1979; UK; 50 min; Documentary
P: Edward Goldwyn; *W:* Edward Goldwyn

How do people become male or female? Scientific work in the past decade has revealed a remarkable battle within the womb in the fight to be male. In a Caribbean village, a few decades ago, forty young girls changed into muscular and active young men. Evidence is presented that says male and female brains are physically different and that homosexuals, through a lack of testosterone prior to birth, develop a female brain.

Prod Comp: BBC, Horizon
Dist/Sales: Roadshow, ACMI, NFVLS

Fighting Chance

Fung, Richard
1990; Canada; 30 min; Documentary

Fighting Chance is a combination of Fung's previous documentary, *Orientations* and newer footage, which tells of the personal struggles of Asian-Canadian gays and lesbians to express their sexual identities. When Fung produced *Orientations* in 1984, AIDS had not yet fully manifested itself, but by 1990 the epidemic had become widespread. Individuals and couples candidly discuss the various hurdles and challenges that AIDS has presented. Those affected must confront families, friends, the community and, most importantly, their inner selves.

Fighting in South-West Louisiana

Brunet, Jean-Francois / Friedman, Peter
1991; USA; 27 min; Documentary

Along his mail delivery route in his native Louisiana back country, Danny Cooper relates his experiences and struggles of being openly gay in his hometown.

Awards: LA Outfest, 1991: Best Short

Film for Two

Mignatti, Victor
1981; USA; 30 min; Drama

Two young men struggle to maintain their relationship.

Final Programme, The

(aka: The Last Days of Man on Earth)

Fuest, Robert
1973; UK; 85 min; Comedy
P: Sandy Lieberson, Jon Goldstone; *W:* Robert Fuest;
C: Norman Warwick; *E:* Barrie Vince; *M:* Paul Beaver, Bernard Krause
Cast: Jon Finch, Hugh Griffith, Patrick Magee, Jenny Runacre

Comedy about a man's quest to rescue his sister and the rest of the world from his brother's plot for world domination. Along the way he has to fight off the advances of a bisexual computer programmer.

Prod Comp: Goodtimes Enterprises, Gladiole

Finding North

Wexler, Tanya
1998; USA; 95 min; Comedy
P: Stephen Dyer, Steven A. Jones; *W:* Kim Powers;
C: Michael Barrett; *E:* Thom Zimny; *M:* Cafe Noir
Cast: Wendy Makkena, John Benjamin Hickey,

f

Jonathan Walker, Anne Bobby

Rhonda, a love-starved, big-haired girl, finally spots her ideal man, Travis. Unfortunately, Travis, suicidal and naked, is gay and on the verge of jumping off the Brooklyn Bridge. Thus, this modern day fairy tale begins with a multitude of misconceptions and mistaken identities to follow. A quirky chain of events finds them on the road together in Texas. This journey becomes a gift of life for both of them. (Wolfe)

Prod Comp: Redeemable Features, So No Productions
Dist/Sales: Cowboy, Millivres, Wolfe

Fingered!

Raymond, James
1992; USA; 12 min; Comedy

A sexually frustrated lesbian stalks a dextrous concert pianist, who will eventually become the answer to her chronically solo sexual peaks. (Frameline)

Dist/Sales: Frameline

Finished

Jones, William E.
1997; USA; 75 min; Documentary

An investigation into the life and death of porn star Alan Lambert.

Fire

Mehta, Deepa
1996; Canada, India; 104 min; Drama
P: Bobby Bedi, Deepa Mehta; *W:* Deepa Mehta; *C:* Giles Nuttgens; *E:* Barry Farrell; *M:* A. R. Rahman
Cast: Shabana Azmi, Nandita Das, Kulbushan Kharbanda, Jaaved Jaafri, Ranjiy Chowhry

Set in a household in contemporary New Delhi. Jetin's young prearranged bride Sita comes to live with the family. She becomes friends with Jetin's sister-in-law Radha. Sita's remarkably modern personality has a profound effect on Radha. Radha is at once surprised and fascinated. Eventually they develop a physical relationship that makes them both question every notion they ever had about their places in the world.

Prod Comp: Trial by Fire Films
Dist/Sales: Globe, Haut-et-Court, Zeitgeist, NFVLS

Fireworks

Anger, Kenneth
1947; USA; 14 min; B&W; Experimental
P: Kenneth Anger

This is a psychodrama (with Anger as the central character) cast in the form of a dream, remarkable for its intense self-analysis at a time when any direct allusion to homosexuality in the cinema was taboo.

Dist/Sales: NFVLS, BFI

First Base

Siler, Megan
1991; USA; 14 min; Drama

A coming of age comedy about two young girls masquerading as women. One tries for her first kiss from a boy but soon realises that it's better with her girlfriend. (Frameline)

Dist/Sales: Cinenova

First Breath

Georgiades, Jimmy
2002; USA; 19 min; Drama
W: Eric Lane

First Breath tells the story of a high school girl getting ready for her prom. Her life is touched by a gay garbage man who discovers a baby in the trash by her home. Their journey brings together two separate worlds and takes them to a place neither expected to travel. The film subtly explores the purpose we are born with—starting with an infant's first breath.

Prod Comp: Orange Thought Productions
Dist/Sales: Forefront

First Comes Love (1991)

Friedrich, Su
1991; USA; 22 min; B&W; Experimental

This contemplative short provokes a flow of ambivalent and intensely personal meditations on love and the ritualised institutions of marriage, and shows how incredibly evocative pop music can be when used on a well-chosen soundtrack. Controversial in some gay and lesbian film festivals—its images of heterosexual weddings alienating some—this work nonetheless provides a distinctly queer take on of society's most sacred institution.

Dist/Sales: WMM, CFMDC, Canyon

First Comes Love (1997)

O'Brien, Kelly
1997; Canada; 13 min; Comedy

Two best friends in their early 20s gaze into each other's eyes and recollect their sexcapades with a stupefying succession of boyfriends. The only true love here is their mutual adoration. (CFMDC)

Dist/Sales: CFMDC

First Love and Other Pains

Chung, Simon
2000; Hong Kong; 48 min; Comedy

A Hong Kong college student is smitten with his English instructor, an older, frustrated British playwright. Their common love of great literature leads both men into an erotic affair—the tenuous beginnings of a romance spanning two different worlds. (Wolfe)

Dist/Sales: FirstRunFeatures, Wolfe

Fish & Elephant

(aka: Jin Nian Xia Tian)

Li, Yu
2001; China; 96 min; Drama
P: Yong Cheng; *W:* Yu Li; *C:* Xiaoping Fei; *M:* Wei He
Cast: Pan Yi, Jilian Zhang, Tou Shi, Qiangian Zhang

Rumoured to be the first-ever lesbian film from mainland China, *Fish & Elephant* is an underground film with non-professional actors that honestly captures lesbian life in Beijing. Xiao Qun, an elephant keeper at a local zoo, has been meeting secretly with with Xiao Ling, a saleswoman in a clothing store, as the love between the two women grows. As if their secret love weren't enough to handle, Qun's life is further complicated by her mother's continuing obsession with marrying her off. Many humorous dates result, as Qun tries to placate her mother in order to prolong her time with Ling. As if all of this weren't enough to handle, Qun's ex-girlfriend suddenly appears back in her life, fleeing the police and asking for help. Qun decides to hide her ex in the zoo, while hiding even more truth from the ones she loves. (21st Chicago Lesbian & Gay International Film Festival)
Mandarin with English subtitles .

Dist/Sales: Yong

Fisher King, The

Gilliam, Terry
1991; USA; 137 min; Comedy
P: Debra Hill, Lynda Obst; *W:* Richard La Gravenese; *C:* Roger Pratt; *E:* Lesley Walker; *M:* George Fenton
Cast: Robin Williams, Jeff Bridges, Amanda Plummer, Mercedes Ruehl, Harry Shearer

After each falls from grace, Parry and Jack become friends and saviours to each other. Parry needs love but has an imperfect vision of the perfect woman and cannot approach the woman he secretly loves. Jack, the cynic, needs hope and is trying to redeem himself and erase the blight from his soul. Together these pure-hearted friends discover the true nature of love and life. Along the way they befriend a gay man who has lost most of his friends to AIDS.

Prod Comp: Columbia
Dist/Sales: Col-Tri, 16MM

Fixing Frank

Selditch, Michael
2001; USA; 103 min; Drama
P: Michael Selditch, Randi Snitz; *W:* Ken Hanes; *C:* Tamas Bojtor; *E:* Randi Snitz; *M:* Mark Strano
Cast: Dan Butler, Andrew Ellis Miller, Paul Provenza

Adapted by Ken Hanes from his stage play, and directed by Michael Selditch in his feature directorial debut, *Fixing Frank* is a powerful and unsettling drama exploring conversion therapy—the scientifically unproven method of turning homosexuals straight. Reporter Frank Johnston is sent undercover by his boyfriend, psychotherapist Jonathan Baldwin to write an exposé on Dr Arthur Apsey. Apsey claims to be able to successfully convert gays to straight, and Jonathan wants Frank to pose as a patient wanting to convert. But Jonathan and Frank underestimate Apsey's brilliance, leading Frank to doubt himself and his relationship with Jonathan. Caught in a psychological tug of war between the two therapists, Frank makes a series of life-changing decisions affecting all three men. (2002 New York Lesbian & Gay Film Festival)

Dist/Sales: Maximum-Vacuum

Flames of Passion

Kwietniowski, Richard
1989; UK; 18 min; B&W; Drama

A commuter steals an intriguing set of photographs from a train station photo booth, then comes face-to-face with the handsome doctor they depict. (Frameline)

Awards: Turin Lesbian & Gay Film Festival, 1990: Best Film; San Francisco Lesbian & Gay International Film Festival, 1990: Best Short Film
Dist/Sales: Frameline, ACMI, BFI, Salzgeber, NFVLS

Flaming Creatures

Smith, Jack
1961; USA; 43 min; B&W; Experimental
Cast: Joel Markman, Delores Flores

An underground film set in the 1920s depicting a world populated by drag queens and camp vampires and containing a rather innocent orgy. Interesting for its time as an examination of so-called perverse desire.

Dist/Sales: Canyon, NFVLS

Flaming Ears

(aka: Rote Ohren Fetzen Durch Asche)

Hans Schierl, Angela / Pürrer, Ursula / Schipek, Dietmar

1991; Austria; 83 min; Sci-Fi

P: Ursula Pürrer, A. Hans Schierl; *W:* Ursula Pürrer, Dietmar Schipek; *C:* Margarete Neumann, Manfred Neuwirth; *E:* A. Hans Schierl; *M:* Dietmar Schipek

Cast: Susanna Heilmayr, Angela Hans Schierl, Ursula Pürrer, Margarethe Neumann

Flaming Ears is a pop sci-fi lesbian fantasy feature set in the year 2700 in the burnt-out city of Asche. Following the tangled lives of three women, Volley, Nun and Spy, *Flaming Ears* becomes a story of love and revenge, and an anti-romantic plea for love in its many forms. An avowedly underground film, shot on super-8 and blown up to 16 mm, it is original in its playful disruption of narrative conventions, its witty approach to film genre and its visual splendour. German with English subtitles. (Cinenova)

Dist/Sales: WMM, Cinenova, WaterBearer

Flavor of Corn, The

(aka: Il Sapore del Grano)

de Campo, Gianni

1986; Italy; 90 min; Drama

P: Chantal Lenoble-Bergamo, Enzo Porcelli; *W:* Gianni Da Campo; *C:* Emilio Bestetti; *M:* Franco Piersanti

Cast: Lorenzo Lena, Marco Mestriner, Egidio Termine, Alba Mottura

A gentle and compassionate story of a handsome young high-school teacher, who, in spite of his best attempts at a heterosexual relationship, helplessly drifts into an intense and emotionally devastating relationship with a 12-year-old male student. Italian with English subtitles.

Flawless

Schumacher, Joel

1999; USA; 112 min; Comedy

P: Joel Schumacher, Jane Rosenthal; *W:* Joel Schumacher; *C:* Declan Quinn; *E:* Mark Stevens; *M:* Bruce Roberts

Cast: Robert De Nero, Philip Seymour Hoffman, Barry Miller, Chris Bauer, Skipp Sudduth

De Niro is Walt, a retired cop living in the same run-down building as Rusty, a flamboyant drag queen. When Walt suffers a stroke which partially paralyses his speech, he takes singing lessons from Rusty to strengthen his vocal cords. As expertly played by Hoffman, Rusty is a larger-than-life, cliché-quoting, all-out drag queen who doesn't seem to stop 'being on' for a minute. He's surrounded by an entourage of drags, though all of them stand up for themselves against anyone and everyone. Walt is a homophobe who slowly befriends Rusty and his friends. The only other gay characters are a group of gay Republicans with whom they come in conflict, and some butch lesbians who act as peacekeepers. (Wolfe)

Prod Comp: MGM, Tribeca
Dist/Sales: MGM, Wolfe, ACMI

Fleeing by Night

Fleeing by Night

(aka: Ye Ben)

Hsu, Li-kong / Yin, Chi

2000; Taiwan; 123 min; Drama

P: Li-kong Hsu , Shi-hao Chang; *W:* Hui-ling Wang, Ming-xia Wang; *C:* Cheng-hui Tsai; *E:* Po-wen Chen; *M:* Chris Babida

Cast: Rene Liu, Lei Huang, Chao-te Yin, Li-jen Tai, Ah-leh Gua

Set in China during the 1930s, *Fleeing by Night* recounts the unsettling relationship between three young characters. Ing'er, the daughter of a theatre owner is excited about the return of her cellist fiancee Shaodung, from a trip to America. Shaodung soon finds himself captivated by the opera *Fleeing by Night*, and its lead actor Lin Chung. Lin Chung is so immersed in his role, he has adopted the character's name and identity. The three begin to spend more time together, and eventually find themselves in an increasingly ambiguous relationship. While Shaodung attempts to blend eastern and western music without harmonious results, Ing'er is torn between her affection for both men, and an awareness of the growing intimacy between them. The makers of *Eat Drink Man Woman* have once again offered a sensuous visual feast and a complex story of forbidden emotions. (MQFF)
Mandarin with English subtitles.

Prod Comp: Zoom Hunt International, Central Motion Pictures, Broadband Films
Dist/Sales: Fortissimo, Strand

Flesh

(aka: Andy Warhol's Flesh)

Morrissey, Paul
1968; USA; 105 min; Comedy
P: Andy Warhol; *W:* Paul Morrissey; *C:* Paul Morrissey
Cast: Joe Dallesandro, Geraldine Smith, Patti d'Arbanville, Candy Darling

> A day-in-the-life look at a gay hustler, Joe, who sells his body so that his wife's lesbian lover can have an abortion. An independent classic from the 1960s sexual revolution that unfortunately lacks technical quality, particularly in the sound recording, making it difficult to decipher a lot of the dialogue.

Prod Comp: Warhol, Factory Films

Flesh and Paper

Parmar, Pratibha
1990; UK; 26 min; Documentary

> *Flesh and Paper* weaves a sensual tapestry of the life and writings of Indian lesbian poet and writer, Suniti Namjoshi. Born into an Indian royal family and now living in England, her poems and fables are characterised by her wry and satirical humour, informed by both lesbian consciousness and a deep Indian cultural framework. (WMM)

Prod Comp: Channel 4
Dist/Sales: WMM, VTape, Cinenova

Flesh for Frankenstein

Morrissey, Paul / Margheriti, Antonio
1974; France, Italy, USA; 95 min; Horror
W: Paul Morrissey, Tonino Guerra
Cast: Joe Dallesandro, Monique van Vooren, Udo Kier

> Baron Frankenstein attempts to create a new race of humans with leftover body parts.

Flesh Gordon

Benveniste, Michael / Ziehm, Howard
1972; USA; 84 min; Erotica
P: William Osco, Howard Ziehm; *W:* Michael Benveniste; *C:* Howard Ziehm; *E:* Abbas Amin; *M:* Ralph Ferraro
Cast: Jason Williams, Suzanne Fields, Joseph Hudgins, William Hunt, John Hoyt

> It's the 1930s and Flesh Gordon has to fight the mysterious sex ray that has plunged the Earth into chaos. A sex-orientated, but quite competent spoof on the Buster Crabbe serials of the 1940s. It features the queeny Prince Precious who saves the life of Flesh Gordon and is rewarded with 'blow job privileges'.

Prod Comp: Graffiti
Dist/Sales: ReelMovies, Ascanbee, TLA

Flesh on Glass

Turner, Ann
1981; Australia; 40 min; Experimental

> The graduation film from the director of *Dallas Doll*. Kate is a young woman who has fallen in love with her brother's wife, Aggie. In her frustration Kate enters a religious order and becomes a nun. A story of lesbian suppression.

Prod Comp: Swinburne Film & TV School
Dist/Sales: ACMI

Flight of Fancy

Sully, Andrew
1992; Australia; 15 min; Drama

> An adolescent who conjures up angels in his sexually charged dreams comes face-to-face with the living figments of his imagination. A vivid evocation of the confusion and games we play when we first discover we are gay. (MQFF)

Flirt

Hartley, Hal
1996; Germany, Japan, USA; 85 min; Drama
P: Ted Hope; *W:* Hal Hartley; *C:* Michael Spiller; *E:* Steve Hamilton; *M:* Ned Rifle, Jeffrey Taylor
Cast: Bill Sage, Dwight Ewell, Miho Nikaidoh, Parker Posey, Martin Donovan

> *Flirt* is the same story set in three different places and told in three different ways; an exploration of the universal themes of commitment, betrayal, indecision, catching a plane, losing a lover and getting shot in the face. New York: Bill's girlfriend Emily gives him an ultimatum to make a commitment before leaving for Paris, but Bill has another romantic interest, Margaret, a married woman. Berlin: Dwight, an American, lives on and off with Johan, an art dealer. As Johan leaves for a trip to New York he demands to know whether their relationship has a future. Dwight asks for 90 minutes to think about it and sets up a rendezvous with Werner, a married man he is fascinated with. Tokyo: Miho, a dance student, is kissed by her teacher, Mister Ozu. When Mister Ozu's wife finds out she gets a gun and threatens to shoot herself. At the same time Miho's boyfriend is packing to go to Los Angeles and wants to know if they have a future together. English, German & Japanese with English subtitles.

Prod Comp: Pandora Films; *Dist/Sales:* Dendy, Col-Tri

Flora's Garment Bursting Into Bloom

Baggott, Kevin
2002; USA; 92 min; Drama
P: Sarah Pirozek; *W:* Kevin Baggott; *M:* David Mansfield

Cast: Aldo Diaz, Marissa Manzanares, Claudina Del Guidice, Otto Sanchez, Jenette Sampson

Terry hits rock bottom after his girlfriend of nine years leaves him due to his sex addiction. This plunges him into the underbelly of New York City. He meets Flora in a chance encounter on the subway, a transsexual working in the peep shows, beaten but not broken, a survivor with an ascerbic wit. Despite Terry's reticence, Flora pushes him towards a relationship. The dramatic tension surrounding the mismatched couple leads them through a journey that becomes a powerful love story. (Damework)

Dist/Sales: DameWork

Florida Enchantment, A

Drew, Sidney
1914; USA; 63 min; B&W; Comedy
W: Marguerite Bertsch, Eugene Mullen;
C: Robert A. Stuart
Cast: Edith Storey, Sidney Drew, Charles Kent

While visiting her aunt in Florida, a young woman comes across an old chest containing seeds that can change a woman into a man and a man into a woman. She swallows the seeds and turns into a man. The next day, after shaving off her moustache, she pretends to still be a woman but her male instincts take over and she goes about seducing other women. Her maid and a male friend also partake of the seeds and go nightclubbing with hilarious results.

Prod Comp: Vitagraph Company of America
Dist/Sales: Frameline, Salzgeber

Flow

Lee, Quentin
1996; Canada, USA; 80 min; Experimental
P: Quentin Lee; *W:* Quentin Lee; *C:* Nathan Adolfson, Justin Lee, Christopher Smith; *E:* Quentin Lee;
M: Lee Yen, Scott Starrett
Cast: Tedd Szeto, Lela Lee, Ray Chang, B. P. Cheng

Experimental, episodic investigation of the personal lives of four young men, one of whom is gay.

Prod Comp: De/Center Communications
Dist/Sales: Margin

Flowing Hearts: Thailand Fighting AIDS

Goss, John
1992; Thailand, USA; 32 min; Documentary

This document of grassroots AIDS education in Thailand presents the unique approach of the White Line Dance Troupe, who combine traditional Thai dance, modern dance and Thai popular music in their educational performances. Also featured in the

film are scenes of safer-sex instruction from a gay bar owner and two handsome young men.

Dist/Sales: VideoOut

The Fluffer

Fluffer, The

Glatzer, Richard / West, Wash
2000; USA; 94 min; Comedy
P: Victoria Robinson, John Sylla; *W:* Wash West;
C: Mark Putnam; *E:* John Binninger; *M:* John Vaughn
Cast: Scott Gurney, Michael Cunio, Roxanne Day, Taylor Negron

Smear on the lip balm and grease up your bod for *The Fluffer*, one of the raunchiest and funniest feature films about the gay porn industry you'll see. This melodramatic romp zooms in on a world of sex, sleaze and sin. A 'fluffer', for those unfamiliar with hard-core porn, performs oral services to ready hunky actors for throbbing onset action. A dream job? Well Sean, the sexy and sweet lead character thinks so as he becomes the personal 'assistant' to Johnny Rebel, a gay-for-pay porno god. Obsessed with the well-endowed star, Sean has to contend with Johnny's girlfriend Babylon who similarly worships the self-involved stud. Loaded with sticky fumblings, the film also stars the legendary Deborah Harry and features drag porn director Chi Chi LaRue. (MQFF)

Prod Comp: Fluff and Fold LLC
Dist/Sales: MediaLuna, TLA, Wolfe, Mongrel, FirstRunFeatures

Flush

MacCubbin, Jeffrey
2001; USA; 68 min; Drama
P: Jeffrey MacCubbin; *W:* Jeffrey MacCubbin; *C:* Jeffrey MacCubbin; *E:* Jeffrey MacCubbin; *M:* John Stormrohn, Jeffrey MacCubbin
Cast: Tai Little, Brett Coy, Arlene Cooney, Shawn Quinlan

This feature-length film tells the story of Shannon, a

15-year-old student searching for a hobby, and her interesting relationship with two sexually ambiguous male classmates. One by one we meet the characters in Shannon's life, from her lonely mother to a indecisive pair of lovers. Seducing her two friends into encountering their growing love for each other, Shannon finds enough stimulus in this activity to keep her active mind satisfied. Through the film's experimental camera work and complex characters, the viewer is taken through an atmospheric, erotic tale of youthful curiosities. (21st Chicago Lesbian & Gay International Film Festival)

Dist/Sales: LittleBelly

Fly Away Homo

Hiller, Andrew
1998; USA; 15 min; Experimental

Revealed: the horrible consequence of being surrounded by straight men and never getting laid.

Dist/Sales: Fever

Fontvella's Box

Hayn, Stefan
1992; Germany; 17 min; Comedy

This surreal fairytale tells the love story of a 'queen' who lives in a Fontvella bottled water-plant and a bicycling farm boy in overalls.

Food of Love

Pons, Ventura
2001; Spain, USA; 105 min; Drama
P: Ventura Pons; *W:* Ventura Pons; *C:* Mario Montero; *E:* Pere Abadal; *M:* Carles Cases
Cast: Juliet Stevenson, Paul Rhys, Allan Corduner

Paul, a handsome and talented music student is employed as the page-turner at one of the world famous pianist Kennington's concerts in San Francisco. Not only is Paul diligent but also extremely attractive, a fact noticed by Kennington and his agent Mansourian, two men at the top of their chosen careers. Kennington and Paul meet again in Barcelona, where the boy is on holiday with his mother, Pamela, who is trying to get over her husband leaving her. Paul and Kennington fall in love but this has very different implications for both men. Kennington rushes back home escaping from commitment. Pamela, meanwhile, begins to recover her self-confidence but Paul is no longer a child. Back in the United States Paul learns that his musical career is not going to progress as desired; he simply is not talented enough. Paul and Pamela will learn through their living experience how to build a deeper relationship. *Food of Love* is the story of these two simple characters

awakening to the harsh reality of life. (TLA)

Prod Comp: Els Films de la Rambla
Dist/Sales: TLA

For a Lost Soldier

(aka: Voor een Verloren Soldaat)

Kerbosch, Roeland
1992; The Netherlands; 92 min; Drama
P: Matthijs van Heijningen; *W:* Roeland Kerbosch; *C:* Nils Post; *E:* August Verschueren; *M:* Joop Stokkermans
Cast: Maarten Smit, Jeroen Krabbe, Andrew Kelley, Elsje de Wijn, Feark Smith

During World War II a group of adolescents are evacuated from Amsterdam to a small fishing village. One of them, Jeroen, forms an intense attachment to Walt, a young soldier from the liberating Canadian army. Dutch & English with English subtitles.

Awards: Turin Gay & Lesbian Film Festival, 1993: Best Feature Film
Prod Comp: Sigma Films, AVRO
Dist/Sales: Potential, Strand, Fortissimo, Wolfe, ACMI

For a Lost Soldier

For Better or for Worse: A Celebration of Enduring Relationships

Collier, David
1993; 55 min; Documentary
P: David Collier; *C:* David Collier

Nominated for an Academy Award, this is a film that presents intimate portraits of five culturally diverse couples married for 50 years or longer, including a gay male couple (Mero and Harwood). We learn of Mero and Harwood's years of living secretly, of their becoming Grand Marshals for the Gay Pride parade, and finally the onslaught of Alzheimer's that left one of them institutionalised.

Dist/Sales: DirectCinema

For Straights Only

Gupta-Smith, Vismita
2001; USA; 22 min; Documentary

Explores the prejudices faced by the South Asian queer communities.

Forbidden Fruit

Bruce, Sue Maluwa / Kunath, Beate / Zuckmantel, Yvonne
2000; Germany, Zimbabwe; 30 min; Documentary

Zimbabwean filmmaker, Sue Maluwa Bruce, breaks long held taboos about sexual identity and lesbian love in African society in this groundbreaking film.

Dist/Sales: WMM

Forbidden Fruit: Unfinished Stories of our Lives

Wagner, Anton
1999; Canada; 27 min; Documentary

A moving and entertaining video documentary on the gay community in Toronto as seen through the life stories and performances of female impersonators/drag queens from the 1940s to the present. (CFMDC)

Dist/Sales: CFMDC

Forbidden Justice

(aka: Short Eyes)

Young, Robert M.
1977; USA; 92 min; Drama
P: Lewis Harris, Robert M. Young; *W:* Miguel Pinero; *C:* Peter Sova; *E:* Ed Beyer; *M:* Curtis Mayfield
Cast: Bruce Davison, Jose Perez, Nathan George, Donald Blakely, Shawn Elliott

Set in an American men's prison, this gritty, compelling film realistically tells of the lives of the prisoners as they endure violence, male rape and brutality in their fight for survival.

Forbidden Love of the Hero, The

Minerba, Giovanni
1995; Italy; 36 min; Drama

A deceased Israeli Medical Corps Colonel's surviving partner attempts to obtain widower rights from the State of Israel.

Dist/Sales: L'Altra

Forbidden Love: The Unashamed Stories of Lesbian Lives

Fernie, Lynne / Weissman, Aerlyn
1992; Canada; 85 min; Documentary
P: Margaret Pettigrew, Ginny Stikeman; *W:* Aerlyn Weissman, Lynne Fernie; *C:* Zoe Dirse; *E:* Cathy Gulkin, Denise Beaudoin

Ten women are interviewed about lesbian sexuality and survival in Canada during the 1950s and 1960s.

Against a backdrop of book covers from lesbian pulp novels, tabloid headlines referring to homosexuality, archival photographs and film clips, these women talk about love, beer parlours and bars for lesbians in Vancouver, Toronto and Montreal, male harassment and intolerance, and the butch/femme subculture. Their stories are interwoven with a fictional love story inspired by the then-popular lesbian paperback novels. Novelist Ann Bannon compares how lesbians were fictionalised with the reality of their lived experiences.

Prod Comp: National Film Board of Canada
Dist/Sales: REP, WMM, Salzgeber, EMA, NFVLS, ACMI, NFBC

Forbidden Passion: Oscar Wilde the Movie

Herbert, Henry
1986; UK; 120 min; Drama
Cast: Michael Gambon, Norman Rodway, Robin Lermitte, Emily Richard

A dramatisation of the last six years of the life of gay writer Oscar Wilde, including the dramatic court case where his sexuality and relationship with Lord Alfred Douglas became public knowledge, resulting in his imprisonment in Reading Gaol.

Forever (1991)

Black, Emma
1991; UK; 10 min; B&W; Drama

The point of departure in a relationship is a time when feelings and memories are heightened. A woman is leaving her lover. She is unable to tell her. Words no longer express anything. (Cinenova)

Dist/Sales: Cinenova

Forever (1994)

Graves, Chris / Wright, Douglas
1994; New Zealand; 54 min; Experimental

A striking and stylish performance piece, featuring the work of a Maori dance company, this atmospheric and energetic film covers numerous issues, including romance, death, AIDS, drag, gay-bashing, sex and show tunes. Meanwhile, homoerotic tension lingers throughout, and voyeurism is unambiguously invited. (MQFF)

Forever Mary

(aka: Mery per sempre)

Risi, Marco
1989; Italy; 100 min; Drama
P: Claudio Bonivento; *W:* Stefano Rulli, Sandro Petraglia, Aurelio Grimaldi; *C:* Mauro Marchetti; *E:* Claudio di Mauro; *M:* Giancarlo Bigazzi

Cast: Alessandro Di Sanzo, Michele Placido, Claudio Amedola, Francesco Benigno

An engaging and well-acted film about an idealistic teacher, Marco, who volunteers to work in a Sicilian reform school, home to some of the toughest delinquents in the area. He works hard to win the respect and affection of the boys, in part, by teaching them about poetry and love. Mario, a young transvestite (or Mary as he is called by the other boys) falls in love with Marco. But Marco rejects him and feels the need to punch him in the face to prove his manhood.

Prod Comp: Int Sel, Numero Uno International
Dist/Sales: Cinevista, BFI

Forgive & Forget

Walsh, Aisling
1999; UK; 96 min; Drama
P: Simon Passmore; *W:* Mark Burt; *C:* Kevin Rowley; *E:* Chris Buckland; *M:* Hal Lindes
Cast: Steve John Shepherd, John Simm, Laura Fraser, Maurice Roeves

Traces the tumultuous journey towards self-acceptance and coming out. David is a construction worker in London and unable to admit to himself or his best mate Theo that he is gay, and attracted to Theo. Sexual tensions arise and secrets are bared in this hard-hitting drama. (10%)

Prod Comp: Scottish Television
Dist/Sales: TLA, Wolfe, 10%

Forms and Motifs

Hetherman, Margaret
1994; USA; 40 min; Comedy

A young woman, CeCe, is not satisfied with the direction her life is taking when she discovers her grandfather's portfolio of designs. She decides that these exquisite patterns need to come to life and enlists the help of her surrogate family, three lively drag queens.

Forsaken

Mosvold, Frank
1994; USA; 11 min; Drama

An ageing priest recalls the struggle between sexuality and faith that led to his life-choice, as he remembers the man he left behind. The sensuality and melancholy of the flashbacks that describe the passion of his youth are contrasted with the restrained sadness of a meeting, decades later, with that same man. (MQFF)

Dist/Sales: Mosvold

Fortune and Men's Eyes

Hart, Harvey
1971; Canada, USA; 102 min; Drama
P: Lester Persky, Lewis M. Allen; *W:* John Herbert; *C:* Georges Dufaux; *E:* Douglas Robertson; *M:* Galt McDermot
Cast: Wendell Burton, Zooey Hall, Michael Greer, Danny Freedman, Larry Perkins

A shocking account of homosexuality in prison, directed with brilliant economy and force. Young Smithy, in prison for the first time, finds himself the prized sexual catch. Sexual domination, humiliation and abuse are to follow. Based on a play by John Herbert.

Prod Comp: MGM
Dist/Sales: ReelMovies, MGM, BFI, Swank

Forty Deuce

Morrissey, Paul
1982; USA; 90 min; Drama
P: Jean-Jacques Fourgeaud; *W:* Alan Bowne; *C:* Steven Fierberg, François Reichenbach, Stefan Zapasnik; *E:* Ken Eluto; *M:* Manu Dibango
Cast: Kevin Bacon, Orson Bean, Harris Laskaway, Mark Keyloun

A seedy look at the tough street life of New York as a male hustler tries to pin the murder of a 12-year-old boy on to a rich john he is blackmailing. Based on a play by Alan Browne.

Prod Comp: Island Pictures

Fostering

1991; UK; 18 min; Documentary

A look at the subject of fostering children with particular reference to lesbians and gay men.

Four Weddings and a Funeral

Newell, Mike
1994; UK; 117 min; Comedy
P: Duncan Kenworthy; *W:* Richard Curtis; *C:* Michael Coulter; *E:* Jon Gregory; *M:* Richard Rodney Bennett
Cast: Hugh Grant, Andie MacDowell, Simon Callow, Kristin Scott Thomas, James Fleet

This is the story of 8 friends, 5 priests, 11 wedding dresses, 16 parents-in-law, 2000 champagne glasses and 2 people who belong together—perhaps! Among the friends are a gay couple, one of whom dies suddenly during one of the weddings, hence the 'funeral' of the title. Nominated for a couple of Academy Awards including best film and screenplay.

f

Awards: Australian Film Institute Awards, 1994: Best Foreign Film
Prod Comp: Channel 4, Working Title, PFE
Dist/Sales: REP, Col-Tri, ACMI, MGM, PolyGram

Fourth Man, The

(aka: Di Vierde Man)

Verhoeven, Paul
1983; The Netherlands; 95 min; Thriller
P: Rob Houwer; *W:* Gerard Soetman; *C:* Jan De Bont;
E: Ine Schenkkan; *M:* Loek Dikker
Cast: Jeroen Krabbé, Renée Soutendijk, Thom Hoffman, Dolf de Vries, Geert de Jong

> Dutch black comedy-thriller with a winning combination of thematic preoccupations—sex, death and the occult. It is the story of Gerard Reve, a bisexual novelist with a very vivid imagination who becomes involved with a murderous and rich widow and her lover. He becomes obsessed with the young man and fantasises about him. Reve, using of his voyeuristic talents, discovers the woman's mysterious past and realises what his own fate will be—death. But he cannot leave the young man of his obsession. Dutch with English subtitles.

Prod Comp: De Verenigde Netherlandsche Filmcompagnie
Dist/Sales: NewVision, TLA, BFI

Fourth Sex, The

(aka: Le Quatrième sexe)

Wichard, Michel
1961; France; 82 min; B&W; Drama
P: José Bénazéraf
Cast: Nicole Burgot, Brigitte Juslin, Richard Winckler

> A wealthy Parisian woman who likes to paint her girlfriends in the nude is smitten by a beautiful, young newcomer in this cult classic of 1960s sexploitation. (First Run Features)

Dist/Sales: FirstRunFeatures

Fox and his Friends

(aka: Faustrecht der Freiheit)

Fassbinder, Rainer Werner
1975; Germany; 117 min; Drama
W: Rainer Werner Fassbinder, Christian Hohoff;
C: Michael Ballhaus; *E:* Thea Eymèsz; *M:* Peer Raben, Josef Niessen
Cast: Peter Chatel, Rainer Werner Fassbinder, Karl-Heinz Böhm, Adrian Hoven, Karl Boehm

> This tragicomedy of manners recounts the exploitation and ultimate destruction of Franz Fox at the hands of his lover Eugene. Fox (played by Fassbinder) is naive and good natured; he virtually gives away half a million marks won in a lottery. Fassbinder saw the homosexual theme as secondary to the theme of manipulation and exploitation that is possible within any sexual relationship. German with English subtitles.

Prod Comp: Tango Film Produktion, City-Film GmbH
Dist/Sales: NFVLS, BFI, Wolfe, ACMI, Wellspring

Fox, The

Rydell, Mark
1968; Canada, USA; 110 min; Drama
P: Raymond Stross; *W:* Lewis John Carlino, Howard Koch; *C:* William Fraker; *E:* Thomas G. Stanford;
M: Lalo Schifrin
Cast: Keir Dullea, Sandy Dennis, Anne Heywood, Glyn Morris

> Adapted from the D. H. Lawrence novella of the same name, the film centres on two lesbians, played by Dennis and Heywood, living on an isolated farm. Paul, a drifter, arrives at the farm and goes about seducing Heywood's character which causes great distress to Dennis. And, if that isn't enough, she ends up being crushed by a tree. A deceptively homophobic film where the truly lesbian character must die.

Prod Comp: Warner, Seven Arts, Motion Pictures International
Dist/Sales: ReelMovies, Warner, Swank, ACMI

Foxfire

Haywood-Carter, Annette
1996; USA; 100 min; Drama
P: Jeffrey Lurie, John Bard Manulis, John P. Marsh;
W: Elizabeth White; *C:* Newton Thomas Sigel;
E: Louise Innes; *M:* Michel Colombier
Cast: Hedy Burress, Angelina Jolie, Jenny Shimizu, Jenny Lewis

> It took them 17 years to learn the rules and one week to break them all. A breakthrough film about female friendship and rebellion. Based on the controversial novel by Joyce Carol Dates, *Foxfire* follows four suburban high school girls who are united when a mysterious stranger inspires them to take revenge on a sexually abusive teacher. But when the local jocks decide to teach the girls a lesson, their hard-won freedom becomes a violent trap. (Wolfe)

Framed Youth

(aka: Revolt of the Teenage Perverts)

1983; UK; 50 min; Documentary

> Young lesbians and gay men—including a youthful

Jimmy Sommerville—hit London's streets with cameras and microphones to confront heterosexuals with homosexuality, the results are humorous, musical and revealing. (Frameline)

Prod Comp: Lesbian & Gay Youth Project
Dist/Sales: Frameline

Framing Lesbian Fashion

Everett, Karen
1992; USA; 58 min; Documentary

This documentary explores how clothing has helped to shape and define the lesbian culture and image. It combines the personal story of the filmmaker with interviews with women including Sally Gearhart, JoAnn Loulan, Arlene Stein and Kitty Tsui. It chronicles the change in look from the butch/femme image to the more androgynous look of the 1990s.

Dist/Sales: Cinenova, Frameline, Wolfe, Everett

Franchesca Page

Sane, Kelley
1996; USA; 105 min; Comedy
P: Pietro Cuevas, D. J. Paul, Mark Downie; *W:* Kelley Sane; *C:* Chris Norr; *E:* Thomas Ostuni
Cast: Franchesca Leon, Rossy de Palma, Mark Dendy, Linda Smith, Varla Jean Merman

Franchesca has finally accomplished her dream role in a Broadway musical. Unfortunately she doesn't quite have the skill to pull it off in this campy trashy tale.

Prod Comp: Franchesca Page LLC, Ocelot Films

Francis Bacon

David Hinton
1985; UK; 54 min; Documentary

This seminal documentary, edited and narrated by Melvyn Bragg remains one of the 'stand out' documentaries that surveys the life, work and motivations of British painter, Francis Bacon, through a series of interviews. Bacon, an extraordinary man, laconically introduces the relationship between broad formalist concerns and attempts to connect with the subconscious. He articulates his response to images of a distressed humanity, revealing his deep fascination with the human body and its connection with much of Bacon's life philosophies. Gritty in content, Bacon's paintings reveal much of the 'violence of life and death' but seek to describe the normality of this with controlled sense of chaos, 'capturing the moment'. (ACMI)

Prod Comp: London Weekend Television, RM Arts
Dist/Sales: ACMI

Frankenstein Created Woman

Fisher, Terence
1967; UK; 92 min; Horror
P: Anthony Nelson Keys; *W:* John Elder; *C:* Arthur Grant; *E:* Spencer Reeve, James Needs; *M:* James Bernard
Cast: Peter Cushing, Susan Denberg, Thorley Walters, Robert Morris, Duncan Lamont

Baron Frankenstein covets the body of a young woman but bemoans her lack of life. He captures the soul of a young man who has been recently executed and installs it into the young woman. However, the memories from the young man are still within and the woman begins to kill the people whose false accusations led to the young man's execution.

Prod Comp: Seven Arts, Hammer
Dist/Sales: NFVLS, 20thCenturyFox

Frankie and Johnny

Marshall, Garry
1991; USA; 113 min; Comedy
P: Garry Marshall, Nick Abdo; *W:* Terence McNally; *C:* Dante Spinotti; *E:* Battle Davis, Jacqueline Cambas; *M:* Marvin Hamlisch
Cast: Al Pacino, Michelle Pfeiffer, Hector Elizondo, Kate Nelligan, Nathan Lane

This warm romantic comedy stars Michelle Pfeiffer as Frankie, a cynical waitress who is wooed by the gentle Johnny, a recently released petty criminal who takes a job as a chef in the restaurant in which Frankie works. Set around the working class neighbourhoods of New York City, the film is an engaging comedy about the fears and difficulties involved in learning to trust another person. Terrence McNally wrote the script which is based on his acclaimed play, Frankie and Johnny in the Clair de Lune. The cast includes Kate Nelligan as Frankie's fellow waitress; Nathan Lane as her generous spirited gay flatmate; and the underrated Hector Elizondo as Nick, the owner of the Greek restaurant where Frankie and Johnny work.

Prod Comp: Paramount
Dist/Sales: ReelMovies, ACMI, Paramount, UIP

Frantz Fanon: Black Skin, White Mask

Julien, Isaac
1996; UK; 52 min; Documentary
P: Mark Nash; *W:* Isaac Julien, Mark Nash

Frantz Fanon: Black Skin, White Mask explores for the first time on film the pre-eminent theorist of the anti-colonial movements of this century. Fanon's two

f

major works, *Black Skin, White Masks* and *The Wretched of the Earth*, were pioneering studies of the psychological impact of racism on both colonised and coloniser. Jean-Paul Sartre recognised Fanon as the figure 'through whose voice the Third World finds and speaks for itself'. This innovative film biography restores Fanon to his rightful place at the centre of contemporary discussions around postcolonial identity. (California Newsreel) English & French with English subtitles.

Prod Comp: Normal Films
Dist/Sales: CaliforniaNewsreel

Freddie Mercury: The Untold Story

Dolenzal, Rudi / Rosacher, Hannes
2000; UK; 68 min; Documentary

An intimate portrait of the personal and professional life of Freddie Mercury—flamboyant lead singer of the rock band Queen, who died from AIDS in 1991.

Dist/Sales: DoRo

Freebie and the Bean

Rush, Richard
1974; USA; 111 min; Comedy
P: Floyd Mutrux; *W:* Robert Kaufman; *C:* László Kovács; *E:* Michael McLean, Franz Steinkamp; *M:* Dominic Frontiere
Cast: James Caan, Alan Arkin, Loretta Swit, Christopher Morley, Paul Koslo

Two San Francisco cops nearly demolish the entire city while attempting to keep a known gangster alive. The cops are protecting him so he can testify against the mob who are involved in a numbers rackets. But the gangster is abducted by a transvestite and the chase is on. They almost meet their match, but unfortunately the transvestite is brutally killed by the cops.

Prod Comp: Warner
Dist/Sales: Warner

French Twist

Freebird

Silver, Suzie
1993; USA; 11 min; Comedy

What if there was an Academy Award for Having Loud Raucous Sex in a Women's Dressing Room at Bloomingdales? Nam June Paik meets Lynyrd Skynyrd with a glimpse of slippery sex and some dirty girl-talk. (MQFF)

Dist/Sales: VDB

French Dressing

(aka: Furenchi doressingu)

Hisashi, Saito
1997; Japan; 100 min; Drama
P: Tsutomu Tsuchikawa, Atsuyuki Shimoda; *W:* Hisashi Saito; *C:* Jun'Ichiro Hayashi
Cast: Munehisa Sakurada, Hiroshi Abe, Miako Tadano

Kishida thinks he is River Phoenix from *My Own Private Idaho*, complete with narcolepsy. Mercilessly teased and bullied by his schoolmates, Kishida reacts to stress and emotional turmoil by falling asleep. The film opens with the depressed schoolboy about to commit suicide. The person who pulls him back from the brink is his teacher, the enigmatic Mr Murai, who is supposed to have killed his own wife. Murai's brutal rape of Kishida jerks him back into life, and soon he is drawn into the vortex of a strange intense relationship with his teacher. His classmate Mari's curiosity gets the better of her and soon she is sucked into their relationship as well. Murai, with his glasses and tousled hair, becomes a rather unlikely 'papa' in their curious little family. Their ménage à trois makes *French Dressing* a disturbing and provocative film that looks at power, sexuality, family, the disaffection of youth, death, and in a perverse way, the reason to go on living. Deliberately understated, with an almost deadpan style, Saito Hisashi's moody debut feature is both disturbing and at the same time strangely compelling. (25th San Francisco International Lesbian & Gay Film Festival) Japanese with English subtitles.

Prod Comp: Daiei Studios
Dist/Sales: Tokuma

French Twist

(aka: Gazon Maudit)

Balasko, Josiane
1995; France; 100 min; Comedy
P: Pierre Grunstein; *W:* Patrick Aubrée, Josiane Balasko; *C:* Gérard de Battista; *E:* Claudine Merlin; *M:* Manual Malou
Cast: Alain Chabat, Victoria Abril, Josiane Balasko

A love triangle with a (French) twist. A madcap comedy that breaks the traditional formula of a love triangle, *French Twist* traces the hilarious adventures of Loli, a sexy yet scorned housewife and mother, who discovers a delicious way to avenge her two-timing husband. French with English subtitles.

Prod Comp: Le Studio Canal+
Dist/Sales: NewVision, 21stCentury, Swank, Wolfe, ACMI

Fresh Blood: A Consideration of Belonging

Yael, B. H.
1996; Canada; 55 min; Documentary

A hybrid documentary involving personal narrative and a video essay style. The piece engages issues of Jewish racialised identity; Arab/Jewish dichotomies and the ways these come together in Iraqi Jewish culture, and the personal implications of the politics of Palestine and of the Jewish holocaust. As a lesbian and Iraqi Jew, she examines issues of Jewish racialised identity and women's roles. (CFMDC)

Dist/Sales: CFMDC

Fresh Kill

Cheang, Shu Lea
1994; USA; 80 min; Drama
W: Jessica Hagedorn; *C:* Jane Castle; *E:* Lauren Zuckerman; *M:* Vernon Reid
Cast: Sarita Choudhury, Erin McMurty, José Zúñiga, Karen Finely

Tells the story of a lesbian couple in New York, their child, and the effects of living in a cloud of toxic waste. As a refuse barge full of nuclear waste circles the world in search of a port willing to accept it, strange things begin to happen. Pets start glowing in the dark, it begins to snow, not snow flakes but soap flakes, and people begin speaking in weird tongues. When the two women become involved, their child suddenly goes missing and it appears that the multinational corporation in charge of the waste is responsible.

Prod Comp: Independent Television Service, The Airwaves Project
Dist/Sales: Strand

Freunde: The Whiz Kids

Krüger, Jan H.
2001; Germany; 22 min; Drama

This intimate and luminous film explores the growing relationship between two young friends, and the challenges of a dangerous new identity.

Dist/Sales: AMAC

Fried Green Tomatoes

Avnet, Jon
1991; USA; 130 min; Drama
P: Jon Avnet, Jordan Kerner; *W:* Carol Sobieski, Fanny Flagg, Jon Avnet; *C:* Geoffrey Simpson; *E:* Debra Neil; *M:* Thomas Newman
Cast: Jessica Tandy, Kathy Bates, Mary-Louise Parker, Mary Stuart Masterson

Fried Green Tomatoes centres on the touching relationship between two pairs of women, one in the present day and the other in the 1930s. Evelyn meets the elderly Ninny who tells her of the relationship between Idgie and Ruth: their friendship, partnership in business and possible romantic involvement. A celebration of the verbal tradition of storytelling, it is also a tale of family, friendship, love, murder, and the compelling intimacies of life. Unfortunately most of the textual references to lesbianism found in the book are downgraded to subtextual readings in the film version.

Prod Comp: Universal, Act III
Dist/Sales: Roadshow, Swank, Wolfe, Carlton

Fried Green Tomatoes

Friend of Dorothy, A

O'Connell, Raoul
1994; USA; 12 min; Drama
P: Raoul O'Connell; *W:* Raoul O'Connell

Winston a young gay man follows his best friend
Anne to college in New York with a desperate yet
understated desire to fall in love and find himself a
boyfriend.

Awards: San Francisco International Lesbian & Gay
Film Festival, 1994: Audience Award Best Gay Short
Dist/Sales: Strand

Friends and Family

Coury, Kristen
2000; USA; 87 min; Comedy
P: Joseph Triebwasser, Linda Moran, Kristen Coury;
W: Joseph Triebwasser; *C:* John Leuba;
E: Tom Swartwout; *M:* Kurt Hoffman
Cast: Tony Lo Bianco, Greg Lauren, Christopher
Gartin, Tovah Feldshuh

Stephen and Danny are a gay male couple who are
enforcers for a New York Mafia family. Stephen's
parents, who know that their son is gay but not that
he works for the Mafia, decide to pay a surprise visit,
sending Stephen and Danny into a panic. Hilarious
complications ensue, as an ever expanding crazy-
quilt of characters adds to the fun.
(www.friendsandfamilythemovie.com)

Friends Forever

(aka: Venner for Altid)

Henszelman, Stefan
1986; Denmark; 95 min; Drama
P: Jens Ravn; *W:* Stefan Henszelman, Alexander
Korschen; *C:* Marcel Berga; *E:* Stefan Henszelman,
Camilla Skousen; *M:* Kim Sagild, Christian Skeed,
Morti Vizki
Cast: Claus Bender Mortensen, Thomas Sigsgaard,
Thomas Elholm, Lill Lindfors

A sensitive drama about a young boy, Kristian, who
is transferred to a new school and becomes friends
with two very different classmates. Henrik, independent and handsome, and Patrick, a troublemaker
who is dealing with his homosexuality. Kristian is
thrown into emotional turmoil when Patrick tells
him he's homosexual and introduces him to his
lover. He rejects Patrick but after realising his loss, he
re-establishes their friendship. Henszelman was an
openly gay filmmaker who died of AIDS in 1991.
Danish with English subtitles.

Awards: San Francisco International Lesbian & Gay
Film Festival, 1988: Audience Award for Best Feature
Prod Comp: Jens Ravn Film Produktion
Dist/Sales: DanishFilm

Friends in High Places

Merrison, Lindsey
2000; Germany, Switzerland; 86 min; Documentary
P: Lindsey Merrison; *W:* Lindsey Merrison; *C:* Lars
Barthel; *E:* Stewart Young

In Myanmar (formerly known as Burma), the cult of
nat spirit worship has survived both the triumph of a
devastating military dictatorship and the widespread
adoption of Buddhism. At the centre of the cult are
the spirit mediums, often homosexual men, who
communicate with the nats and take on their
flamboyant characteristics in ecstatic rituals. Guided
by two lively 70-year-olds, director Lindsey Merrison
explores the role of the spirit mediums in Burmese
society in this fascinating documentary. (2002 New
York Lesbian & Gay Film Festival) Burmese with
English subtitles .

Prod Comp: Arte/WDR, DRS, YLE, SBS
Dist/Sales: Merrison

Frisk

Frisk

Verow, Todd
1995; USA; 87 min; Drama
P: Marcus Hu, Jon Gerrans; *W:* James Dwyer, Todd
Verow; *C:* Greg Watkins; *E:* Todd Verow; *M:* Coil, Lee
Ranaldo, New E-Z Devils, Octarine
Cast: Michael Gunther, Alexis Arquette, Craig Chester,
Parker Posey

A first person narrative about the exploits of Dennis
a gay serial killer. Verow's cogent and dispassionate
cinematic study of Dennis Cooper's 1991 eponymous dark tale of the same name is inflected with
chilling and cheerless humour as it traces the
protagonist's slide into insanity through sex, sadism
and serial killing.

Dist/Sales: Cowboy, TLA, Strand, Wolfe

Frisson des Vampires, Le

(aka: Sex and the Vampire)

Rollin, Jean
1970; France; 90 min; Horror
P: Jean Rollin; *W:* Monique Natan, Jean Rollin;

C: Jean-Jacques Renon; *E:* Olivier Grégoire; *M:* Acanthus
Cast: Sandra Julien, Dominique, Michel Delahaye, Jacques Robiolles, Jean-Marie Durand

> Based on the conventional plot of a honeymoon couple who find themselves at a medieval castle inhabited by two ageing hippies and the mistress they share. At midnight a gorgeous vampire emerges from a grandfather clock and proceeds to make the bride one of her victims in a very sensuous scene in the cemetery. Mixing visually striking images, naked women and cryptic dialogue, this film conveys a bizarre, ritualistic sadism. Dubbed into English.

Prod Comp: Les Films, ABC, Films Modernes
Dist/Sales: Siren

From the Ashes

Cottam, Kevin
1997; Canada; 13 min; Drama

> Against a Chopinesque score and answering-machine messages narrative, Mark emerges from the paralysing 'survivor guilt' and grief over the death of his partner, David. A sensitively framed story told in tender images and colours.

Dist/Sales: BigFilm

From the Edge of the City

(aka: Apo tin akri tis polis)

Giannaris, Constantine
1998; Greece; 94 min; Drama
P: Dionyssis Samiotis, Anastasios Vasiliou;
W: Constantine Giannaris; *C:* Yorgos Argiroiliopoulos;
E: Ioanna Spillopoulou; *M:* Akis Daoutis
Cast: Stathis Papadopolous, Nicos Camondos, Panagiotis Chartomatsidis, Panayiotis Hartomatzidis

> Violent and energetic in its headlong rush into the abyss, *From the Edge of the City* takes an unsparing look at the lives of a gang of Pontian immigrants returning to Greece from the USSR. 17-year-old Sasha, sharp, streetwise and ambitious, is the leader of the gang. They roam Athens, hang out in clubs, hit brothels and cruise the streets. They make their money from petty crime and selling their bodies in Omonia Square. Adolescents hungry for adventure, they'll stop at nothing to get what they want. Kazakh with English subtitles. (Millivres)

Prod Comp: Hot Shot, Mythos, Rosebud
Dist/Sales: GFC, Millivres, PictureThis!, Wolfe, ACMI, 10%

Frostbite

Mead, Wrik
1996; Canada; 12 min; Experimental

> A lonely lighthouse keeper rescues his fantasy: a frost-bitten man on the rocks.

Dist/Sales: CFMDC

Fruit Machine, The

(aka: Wonderland)

Saville, Philip
1988; UK; 107 min; Drama
P: Steve Morrison; *W:* Frank Clarke; *C:* Dick Pope;
E: Richard Bedford; *M:* Hans Zimmer
Cast: Emile Charles, Tony Forsyth, Robert Stephens, Clare Higgins, Bruce Payne, Robbie Coltrane

> Set in Liverpool, against the backdrop of deprivation found in any modern city, *The Fruit Machine* follows the story of two 17-year-old gay boys, Eddie, innocent and on the run from home, and Michael, streetwise and a hustler who lives by his wits. They both desire to escape their less-than-perfect family lives, but end up on the run for different reasons when they witness the murder of a transvestite in their local gay bar. From the creator of *A Letter to Breshnev*.

Prod Comp: Granada Television, Ideal Communications
Dist/Sales: Col-Tri, Roadshow

Fucked in the Face

Durr, Shawn
2000; USA; 70 min; Comedy

> Henry Normal is a young gay man who is not having a good time of it lately. He's been kicked out of his apartment, he hasn't got a cent to his name, and he's being stalked by a rabid gang of lesbians out for blood. Henry gets so desperate he starts to believe that his only salvation is a hunky gay serial killer he's seen on FBI wanted posters in his neighbourhood. His search finds him in a hellish world of drugs, sex, lust and violence that he can't control.

Dist/Sales: Eccentric

Fuga, La

(aka: The Escape)

Spinola, Paolo
1966; Italy; 120 min; B&W; Drama
P: Alberto Casati, Mario Mariani, Vittorio Musy Glori;
W: Sergio Amedei, Piero Bellanova; *C:* Marcello Gatti, Armando Nunnuzzi; *E:* Nino Baragli; *M:* Piero Piccioni
Cast: Giovanna Ralli, Anouk Aimée, Paul Guers, Enric Maria Salerno

> A well-to-do wife who has everything finds fulfilment with an interior decorator who just happens to be a lesbian. Italian with English subtitles.

Prod Comp: Cine 3 SRL

Full Blast

Rodrigue, Jean
1999; Canada; 92 min; Drama
P: Ian Boyd, Jean Rodrigue; *W:* Jean Rodrigue, Nathalie

f

Loubeyre; *C:* Stefan Ivanov; *E:* Mathieu Bouchard-Malo; *M:* Robert Marcel LePage
Cast: David La Haye, Louise Portal, Patrice Godin, Martin Desgagné

Inspired by Martin Pître's Acadian novel L'ennemi que je connais, Full Blast tells the tale of four young adults—Steph, Piston, Charles and Marie-Lou—set against the backdrop of a strike at the local sawmill, which threatens the economic stability of the town. *Full Blast* touches upon the universal themes of human suffering, alienation and the never-ending search for love. Rodrigue Jean guides us on a realistic yet sensitive journey into a Canadian landscape rarely seen by outsiders. It is a story that draws us quickly into a web of social and personal upheavals. (Domino)

Prod Comp: Transmar Films, Les Films de I'sle Production
Dist/Sales: Domino

Full Monty, The

Cattaneo, Peter
1997; UK; 91 min; Comedy
P: Uberto Pasoloni; *W:* Simon Beaufoy;
C: John de Borman; *E:* David Freeman, Nick Moore;
M: Anne Dudley
Cast: Robert Carlyle, Mark Addy, William Snape, Steve Huison

You can't help pulling for these six unemployed guys in their attempt to make some real money. But will they have the guts to strip away all of their inhibitions and go the 'full monty'? This irresistible and heart-warming comedy reveals just about everything. (Wolfe)

Prod Comp: 20th Century-Fox, Channel 4, Fox Searchlight, Redwave Films
Dist/Sales: Wolfe, 20thCenturyFox, FoxSearchlight

Full Moon in New York

(aka: Ren zai Niu Yue)

Kwan, Stanley
1989; Hong Kong, USA; 88 min; Drama
P: Henry Fong; *W:* Acheng Zhong, Yau Tai On Ping;
C: Bill Wong; *E:* Steve Wang, Cheung-kan Chow;
M: Hung-yi Chang
Cast: Gaowa Siqin, Maggie Cheung, Sylvia Chang

Three women, representing three different Chinas, end up in New York: Chao Hong from China's mainland, Li Feng Jiao from Hong Kong and Wang Hsiung, a Taiwanese actress. Through the characters, we see the differences and similarities of their backgrounds, and the manner in which they try to deal with Western Culture. Chinese with English subtitles.

Prod Comp: Yu Raymond, Shio-bu Film, Golden Glory Productions
Dist/Sales: Kwan

Full Speed

(aka: À Toute Vitesse)

Morel, Gaël
1996; France; 85 min; Drama
P: Laurent Bénégui; *W:* Catherine Corsini, Gaël Morel;
C: Jeanne Lapoirie; *E:* Catherine Schwartz
Cast: Stéphane Rideau, Élodie Bouchez, Pascal Cervo, Mezziane Bardadi

Jimmy is the confident, sexy gang leader and best friend of Quentin, a young writer who betrays his background and his friends. Julie is the girlfriend of Quentin, but has designs on Jimmy. Samir is still healing from the loss of his first love, Rick, and falls for the sexually confused Quentin. When Samir is spurned, he starts to let go of his past and forms a close friendship with Julie and Jimmy—a bond so close, it will change his life permanently. (Millivres) French with English subtitles.

Prod Comp: Magouric Productions
Dist/Sales: Strand, Wolfe, Millivres

Full Speed

Fun

Zielinski, Rafal
1993; USA; 105; Drama
C: Jens Sturup; *E:* Monika Lightstone, Barry S. Silver;
M: Marc Tschanz
Cast: Renée Humphrey, Alicia Witt, William R. Moses, Leslie Hope

This controversial tale of a murder committed by two teenage girls interweaves fictional psychiatric interviews after the fact with events from their quickly-famed and very intense friendship before the event. (Cowboy)

Dist/Sales: Cowboy

Fun Down There

Stigliano, Roger
1989; USA; 110 min; Comedy
W: Roger Stigliano, Michael Waite; *C:* Peggy Ahwesh,
Eric Saks
Cast: Harold Waite, Michael Waite, Nickolas Nagurney,
Kevin Och

A young man from upstate New York decides to
move to New York City to explore his sexuality. He
finds what he is looking for in Greenwich Village. A
well-meaning coming-of-age film, but let down by
some poor performances.

Awards: Berlin Film Festival, 1989: Best Gay Feature
Dist/Sales: Frameline, Salzgeber, WaterBearer

Fun with a Sausage

(aka: L'Ingenue)

Wilhite, Ingrid
1985; USA; 30 min; Drama

This pair of shorts packaged together offers a now
dated look at lesbian life. In the first piece, a young
filmmaker from Idaho finds her sexual initiation in
San Francisco at the command of a leather woman.
The second film is a silent piece about the adventures of a young woman who decides to dress up as a
man—all the way down to the sausage she stuffs in
her jeans to obtain that proper 'bulging' silhouette.

Funeral Parade of Roses

(aka: Bara No Soretsu)

Matsumoto, Toshio
1969; Japan; 105 min; Drama
W: Toshio Matsumoto; *C:* Tatsuo Suzuki; *M:* Joji Yuasa
Cast: Emiko Azuma, Shinno Ikehata, Osamu
Ogasawaro

A modern parody of the Oedipus legend, except that
the Oedipus character, Eddie, must eliminate his
obstructive mother for the wild embrace of his
father. The first Japanese film to deal openly with
homosexuality. Japanese with English subtitles.

Funny Felix

(aka: Drôle de Félix; The Adventures of Felix)

Ducastel, Olivier / Martineau, Jacques
1999; France; 97 min; Comedy
P: Philippe Martin; *W:* Olivier Ducastel, Jacques
Martineau; *C:* Matthieu Poirot-Delpech; *E:* Sabine
Mamou
Cast: Sami Bouajila, Patachou, Ariane Ascaride, Pierre-
Loup Rajot

Cool and sexy Felix hits the road to Marseilles in
search of his father in this charming, light-hearted
road movie through the French countryside. At the
outset he becomes embroiled as a witness to a
bashing and ends up on-the-run from the perpetra-
tors. Through some kooky misadventures—
including spontaneous sex amongst the nettles—
Felix encounters a succession of chatty, quirky
individuals who impart their streetsmart wisdom and
become part of his 'family'. Will Felix find his father?
French with English subtitles. (MQFF)

Prod Comp: Le Studio Canal+, Pyramide Productions,
Les Films Pelléas
Dist/Sales: FPI, Mongrel, Wolfe, Wellspring, ACMI,
Salzgeber

Funny Lady

Ross, Herbert
1975; USA; 136 min; Musical
P: Ray Stark; *W:* Jay Presson Allen, Arnold Schulman;
C: James Wong Howe; *E:* Marion Rothman, Maury
Winetrobe; *M:* Peter Matz, John Kander
Cast: Barbra Streisand, James Caan, Ben Vereen, Omar
Sharif, Roddy McDowall

Barbra Streisand is the exuberant Fanny Brice,
Zeigfeld performer extraordinaire in this sequel to
the outstanding film *Funny Girl*. She is supported by
her close friend and confidant, a gay man, played by
Roddy McDowall. This lively, lavish musical opens a
new chapter in Fanny's career and love life. Now
divorced from the wealthy Nicky, she teams up with
songwriter Billy Rose, a brash and unkempt
showman who is bursting with enthusiasm and
theatrical ambitions. *Funny Lady* is a poignant story
of their show business magic, unbridled tempera-
ments and passionate romance.

Prod Comp: Columbia, Rastar, Vista
Dist/Sales: 20thCenturyFox, ACMI, 16MM, Columbia

Future is Woman, The

(aka: Il Futuro è Donna)

Ferreri, Marco
1984; Italy; 100 min; Drama
P: Achille Manzotti; *W:* Marco Ferreri, Piera Degli
Esposito, Dacia Maraini; *C:* Tonino Delli Colli;
E: Ruggero Mastroianni; *M:* Carlo Savina
Cast: Hanna Schygulla, Ornella Muti, Niels Arestrup,
Maurizio Donadoni

Gordon and Anna are a bored bourgeois couple who
have decided not to have children. When Anna
rescues Malvina, a young pregnant woman, in a
nightclub and brings her home to live with them,
her relationship with Gordon is put under stress as
both vie for Malvina's body and her child.

Prod Comp: Faso Films, Ascot Films, UGC
Dist/Sales: UGC

f

Gaea Girls

Longinotto, Kim / Williams, Jano
2000; Japan, UK; 106 min; Documentary
C: Kim Longinotto; *E:* Brian Tagg

This fascinating film follows the physically gruelling and mentally exhausting training regimen of several young wannabe 'Gaea Girls', a group of Japanese women wrestlers. The idea of them may seem like a total oxymoron in a country where women are usually regarded as docile and subservient. However, in training and in the arena, the female wrestlers depicted in this film are just as violent as any member of the World Wrestling Federation, and the blood that's drawn is very real indeed. (WMM) Japanese with English subtitles.

Dist/Sales: WMM

Gang Girls 2000

del Mar, Katrina
1999; USA; 25 min; Comedy
P: Katrina del Mar; *W:* Katrina del Mar

Forget *The Sopranos*, this gang of riot grrrls are ready rumble! Who will reign supreme—The Blades, The Glitter Girls, The Sluts or The Ponies?

Gang of Four, The

(aka: La Bande des Quatre)

Rivette, Jacques
1988; France; 150 min; Drama
P: Pierre Grise, Martine Marignac, Cyrus I. Yavneh; *W:* Pascal Bonitzer, Jacques Rivette, Christine Laurent; *C:* Caroline Champetier; *E:* Catherine Quesemand; *M:* Claudio Monteverdi
Cast: Bulle Ogier, Benoît Régent, Nathalie Richard, Laurence Côte, Fejria Deliba

Gang of Four, like many of Rivette's other films, focuses on the way women relate to each other. A renowned drama teacher, played by Bulle Ogier, hand picks four female actors to study for the performance of a play. They all share the same apartment and gradually the play begins to take over their real lives, which become disrupted when the lover of an ex-student of the drama teacher arrives.

Awards: Berlin Film Festival, 1989: Critic's Prize
Prod Comp: Limbo Films

Garbo Talks

Lumet, Sidney
1984; USA; 102 min; Comedy
P: Burtt Harris, Elliott Kastner; *W:* Larry Grusin;
C: Andrzej Bartkowiak; *E:* Andrew Mondshein;
M: Cy Coleman
Cast: Anne Bancroft, Ron Silver, Carrie Fisher,

Steven Hill, Harvey Fierstein

An eccentric dying woman has one final wish. She has worshipped Garbo for her entire life and now wants to meet her. Trying to fulfil her request, her divorced son begins an amusing search for the reclusive legend of the silver screen. There is a touching scene when the son befriends a gay man on the beach at Fire Island.

Prod Comp: United Artists, MGM
Dist/Sales: Warner, MGM

Garden, The

Jarman, Derek
1990; UK; 92 min; Drama
P: James MacKay; *W:* Derek Jarman; *C:* Derek Jarman;
E: Peter Cartwright; *M:* Simon Fisher Turner
Cast: Tilda Swinton, Derek Jarman, Spencer Lee,
Johnny Mills, Philip MacDonald

In this lush, innovative and complex film, Jarman leads the viewer on a magical journey through moods ranging from horror to humour, from melancholy to exhilaration, along the way contemplating the role of the Church in the persecution of homosexuals through the centuries. Considered an allegory for the AIDS epidemic.

Prod Comp: Channel 4, Screen Arts, Basilisk Productions, British Screen, Uplink Co, ZDF
Dist/Sales: NFVLS, TLA, Cowboy, BFI, ACMI

Gasp

Bernstein, Daniel
1995; USA; 20 min; Drama

This expansive and engaging short film follows an Ivy League college student's efforts to quell his anxieties about his attraction to other men. A sophisticated and mature coming out story, the young man's debates with friends and professors about gay stereotypes and lifestyles is expertly interwoven with fantastical images from his study of the classics and visual recollections of his casual sexual encounters with men in semi-public places on campus.

Dist/Sales: USC

Gaudi Afternoon

Seidelman, Susan
2001; Spain; 93 min; Comedy
W: James Myhre; *C:* Joseph M. Civit; *E:* Deidre Slevin;
M: Bernardo Bonezzi
Cast: Judy Davis, Marcia Gay Harden, Lili Taylor,
Juliette Lewis

Film noir takes a syringe of satire in this gender-inverting, genre-twisting comedic thriller that owes as much to *Bound* as it does *The Maltese Falcon*.

Femme fatale Frankie Stevens plays little-lost-American-sheep in Barcelona, lapping at the high heel of straight-and-narrow translator Cassandra Reilly. For a fee, Cassandra takes on the job of finding Frankie's husband who's mysteriously disappeared, but when hubbie Ben turns out to be less the man she expected, all eyes turn to Frankie who suddenly seems more fatale than femme. Kidnap, double-crossing and mistaken identities only go part way to dropping the penny on the endless twists of this punchy tale of queer family values. (MQFF)

Prod Comp: Lolafilms, Antena 3 Television, Via Digital
Dist/Sales: LolaFilms, Wolfe, ACMI

Gaudi Afternoon

Gay Agenda, The

1992; USA; 20 min; Documentary

Doctors, scholars, religious leaders, and 'recovering' gay men discuss the 'ills' of gay life.

Prod Comp: Christian Action Network

Gay Bombay

Khanna, Natthalie
1996; UK; 29 min; Documentary

Khanna investigates the structures of emerging gay life in India, and discusses the issues relevant to contemporary queers.

Gay Courage: 100 Years of the Gay Movement

von Praunheim, Rosa
1998; Germany; 90 min; Documentary

Rosa von Praunheim's documentary begins with 19th century gay personalities—including Oscar Wilde, sexologist Dr Magnus Hirschfeld, and lawyer Karl Heinrich Hossli—and ends in the queer mecca of San Francisco. Along the way, von Praunheim takes on the immense task of chronicling a mostly Western-European gay history. Using historical re-enactments as well as interviews with German historians and citizens, the film details some of the atrocities inflicted on gays through the ages for what

was formerly 'the love that dare not speak its name'. We've come a long way from the days of Nazi concentration camps and blackmailing. For von Praunheim there's no clearer picture of that change than present day San Francisco. He portrays the city over the rainbow as the nexus of a broader queer sensibility, a place where our identities have moved well beyond closed doors and into city hall. Von Praunheim captures bear love at the annual Folsom Street Fair, lesbian parents speaking out at a local PTA meeting, and drag queens campaigning for Presidential office. (www.queerculturalcenter.org)

Dist/Sales: Praunheim

Gay Cuba

de Vries, Sonja
1995; Cuba, USA; 57 min; Documentary
P: Sonja De Vries, Marlene Moleon; *C:* Ariel Fernández, Rafael Ruiz; *E:* Merle Mason, Catherine Ryan; *M:* Pablo Milanés, Silvio Rodríguez
Cast: Jennifer Maytorena Taylor

In Cuba the human rights of gays and lesbians are a controversial issue. This important work documents the lives and the history of gay and lesbian people in Cuba through the telling of their own stories—of harassment, coming out, expulsion from political organisations, and election to political leadership. De Vries has assembled a dynamic cast that demonstrates the diversity and changing reality of Cuban society. Her use of stunning archival footage provides the historical context central to an understanding of Cuba's sometimes contradictory contemporary political climate. In the words of a soldier interviewed by de Vries, 'there may be lesbians or homosexuals who are more revolutionary than anyone, not in theory, but in practice'. (MQFF) Spanish with English subtitles.

Prod Comp: Cuba's Felix Varela Centre
Dist/Sales: Frameline

Gay Deceivers, The

Kessler, Bruce
1969; USA; 90 min; Comedy
P: Joe Solomon; *W:* Jerome Wish; *C:* Richard C. Glouner; *E:* Renn Reynolds, Reg Browne; *M:* Stu Phillips
Cast: Kevin Coughlan, Brooke Bundy, Michael Greer

Two young men pretend that they are homosexual to escape being drafted into the army. They set up house in a gay neighbourhood, but realise that to complete the illusion, women are off limits. Basically homophobic and uses ridiculous stereotypes to represent gays.

Prod Comp: Fanfare Films Inc.
Dist/Sales: Wolfe, ACMI

g

Gay Games

Kotzer, Ran
1999; Israel; 55 min; Documentary

The story of the Israeli delegation to the Gay Games held in Amsterdam in 1998. Get a chance to meet some of the participants and a feel for the event and the night life during the games.

Dist/Sales: GilProd

Gay & Gray in New York City

Chesla, Nicholas / Creager, Cindi / Englander, Julie
1999; USA; 22 min; Documentary

Award winning documentary about the many silent pioneers whose 'long lives well lived' preceded the activism and reforms of the watershed 1968 Stonewall riots by several decades. An awe inspiring film that also ushers in the new millennium adage 'Life begins at 70'.

Dist/Sales: Fanlight

Gay Rock and Roll Years, The

Brown, Shauna
1991; UK; 50 min; Musical
P: Clare Beavan

In a stylish, witty and stunningly edited film, pop music clips starting from the 1950s encompass significant queer moments in recent British music history.

Prod Comp: Fulcrum, BBC

Gay Sera Sera

Ardill, Susan
1992; UK; 23 min; Documentary
P: Rebecca Dobbs

Are gay men and lesbians 'born that way' or is sexual orientation shaped later in life? It's the old nature/ nurture debate with a new twist in the form of Californian scientist Simon Levay's claim to have pinpointed the area of the brain that determines sexuality. Charting the changing attitudes through the decades to the nature of sexual identity up to the 'queer politics' of the nineties, the question 'What made you this way?' is asked once again.

Dist/Sales: MayaVision

Gay Tape: Butch and Femme

Dougherty, Cecilia
1985; USA; 29 min; Documentary

Examination of attitudes surrounding the butch/femme dichotomy in California, USA.

Gay USA

Bressan Jnr, Arthur J.
1977; USA; 78 min; Documentary

Bressan commissioned filmmakers throughout the USA to record all June 1977 Lesbian and Gay Pride parades and marches. He then cut on-the-street interviews (gay men and women talking about their lovers and how they came out) with the resulting footage, including lesbians marching against housework and drag queens protesting fascism.

Dist/Sales: Frameline

Gay Voices, Gay Legends

Various
1988; USA; 58 min; Documentary

Some famous and some not-so-famous gay men talk about their lives and their sexuality. Featuring Charles Pierce (female impersonator), Al Parker (porn star), Leonard Matlovich, Michael Murray, Norris Knight, Michael Hardwich and more.

Gay Voices, Gay Legends 2

Various
1989; USA; 58 min; Documentary

More famous and some not-so-famous gay men talk about their lives and their sexuality. Featuring Michael Kearns (gay actor), Rev. Troy Perry, Paul Monette (gay writer) and more.

Gay Youth

Walton, Pam
1992; USA; 40 min; Documentary

Young queer adolescents discuss the pressures of coming out within the school and home. Includes interviews the mother of Bobby Griffith who suicided in 1983 and whose diary is an eloquent testament to the painful oppression suffered by teenagers coming out in a conservative fundamental-ist environment. The Bobby Griffith Memorial Award is now awarded annually to teenage lesbians and gays who have contributed to fighting homopho-bia. Gina Gutierrez, a young Asian–American recipient of the award, describes her own painful coming out. In a brave move she performed a monologue about homophobia to a school audience and her friends and family discuss the consequences of her bravery. Although this documentary deals with often tragic material, the testimonies of the young people who are proud to forge ahead with queer lives and relationships are ultimately uplifting. (MQFF)

Dist/Sales: Cinenova, FilmakersLibrary, Wolfe

g

Gay'ze in Wonderland

Bocahut, Laurent / Brooks, Philip
1997; France; 52 min; Documentary

An irreverent look at the burgeoning contemporary gay lifestyle. Filmed during June 1997 when Paris hosted Europride, this documentary gives us an inside view of the European gay community.

Prod Comp: Dominant 7
Dist/Sales: Dominant7

Gaymes, The

Spiro, Ellen
1991; USA; 16 min; Documentary

Ellen Spiro provides a visual diary of an event, celebrating the collective lesbian/gay body while focusing a critical eye on the oppressive nature of ruthless competition. (MQFF)

Gemini Affair, The

Cimber, Matt
1974; USA; 88 min; Drama
Cast: Anne Seymour, Marta Kristen, Kathy Kersh

Jessica, a New York actress trying to break into the business, flies to Los Angeles to stay with her best friend, Julie, from high school. The two catch up and reminisce, finding they are close again and, despite Julie's house being rather large, they sleep in the same bed. Finally they make love, but afterwards Jessica is repulsed and runs away. Julie chases her and they discuss what's happened and, despite being attracted to each another, they know it is going to be difficult.

Prod Comp: Unicorn V
Dist/Sales: Moonstone

Gendernauts

Treut, Monika
1999; Germany; 86 min; Documentary
P: Monika Treut; *W:* Monika Treut; *C:* Elfi Mikesch; *E:* Eric Schefter; *M:* Georg Kajanus
Cast: Sandy Stone, Texas Tomboy, Susan Stryker, Jordy Jones, Stafford, Annie Sprinkle

A journey through shifting identities, *Gendernauts* explores gender fluidity at the end of the millennium in the Bay Area, California. It's a film about cyborgs, people who alter their bodies and minds with new technologies and chemistry, with particular focus on biological women who use the male sex hormone testosterone.

Prod Comp: Hyena Films
Dist/Sales: Millivres

Genesis Children, The

Aikman, Anthony
1972; Italy, USA; 85 min; Drama
P: Billy Byars; *W:* Anthony Aikman, Billy Byars; *C:* Bill Dewar; *E:* Jeremy Hoenack; *M:* Jerry Styner
Cast: Vincent Child, Peter Glawson, Greg Hill, Jack Good

A controversial film about a group of young American boys who go to a summer camp near Rome. They all answer a 'boys wanted' ad and are taken to an isolated beach by a mysterious man, for a reason that remains unknown. The boys decide that frolicking naked with each other is loads of fun and do it for the rest of the film.

Prod Comp: Lyric Films International

Gentlemen Prefer Blondes

Hawks, Howard
1953; USA; 91 min; Comedy, Musical
P: Sol C. Siegel; *W:* Charles Leaderer; *C:* Harry J. Wilde; *E:* Hugh S. Fowler; *M:* Jule Stynem, Leo Robin
Cast: Marilyn Monroe, Jane Russell, Charles Coburn, Tommy Noonan, Elliot Reid

Two American girls head for Paris to find love and money. Features Monroe's rendition of *Diamonds are a Girl's Best Friend*. Her best friend and fellow performer is played by Jane Russell. A classic favourite for gay and lesbian audiences who will enjoy the lesbian subtext.

Prod Comp: 20th Century-Fox
Dist/Sales: NFVLS, Fox, ACMI, 20thCenturyFox

Gently down the Stream

Friedrich, Su
1983; USA; 14 min; B&W; Experimental

A haunting succession of images and hand-scratched texts takes the viewer on a voyage down a stream of consciousness, suggesting that 'life is but a dream'. A film about conflict, rage and sexuality. (Cinenova)

Dist/Sales: NFVLS, Cinenova, WMM

Georgie Girl

Goldson, Annie / Wells, Peter
2001; New Zealand; 70 min; Documentary
P: Annie Goldson; *W:* Craig Wright

Born George Beyer, one-time prostitute turned politician Georgina Beyer was elected to New Zealand's Parliament in 1999, becoming the world's first transsexual to hold a national office. Amazingly a mostly white—and naturally conservative—rural constituency voted this former sex worker of Maori

g

heritage into office. Chronicling Georgina's transformations from farm boy to celebrated cabaret diva to grassroots community leader, the documentary couples interviews and sensual images of Beyer's nightclub and film performances with footage from a day in the life of the Minister of Parliament. The film presents a remarkable account of Beyer's precedent-setting accomplishment, revealing her intelligence, charisma, and humour. (Women Make Movies)

Dist/Sales: WMM

Gertrude Stein and a Companion

Cirker, Ira
1986; USA; 80 min; Drama
P: Nancy Walzog; *W:* Win Wells
Cast: Jan Miner, Marian Seldes

This film is a compelling exploration of the tempestuous 40 year relationship between the legendary American writer and lecturer, Gertrude Stein, and her beloved companion, Alice B. Toklas. Based entirely on historical materials and the personal letters of Toklas, it provides an intimate portrait of these two unique and unconventional women. Stein's thoughts on Alice, the arts, America's Hemingway and other characters are revealed. Scenes from their public and private lives are interwoven with Alice's recollections of their time together.

Dist/Sales: ACMI

Gertrude Stein: When you See this Remember Me

Miller Adato, Peter
1970; USA; 82 min; Documentary
P: Peter Miller Adato; *W:* Marianna Norris; *C:* Gardner Compton, Gerald Cotts, Jean Monsigny, Eliot Noyes, Ray Witlin; *E:* Alan Pesetsky

Documentary about the life of lesbian writer, famous personality and art collector Gertrude Stein and her relationship with Alice B. Toklas. With the use of newspaper articles and film clips, the film pays special attention to their days in Paris in the 1920s.

Dist/Sales: BFI

Geschlecht in Fesseln: dei Sexualnot der Gefangenen

(aka: Sex in Chains)

Dieterle, William
1928; Germany; 76 min; B&W; Drama
P: Leo Meyer; *W:* Herbert Juttke, Georg C. Klaren; *C:* Robert Lach; *M:* Pasquale Perris

Cast: William Dieterle, Mary Johnson, Carl Goetz, Paul Henckels, Gunnar Tolnaes

After accidentally killing a man in a fight Franz Sommer ends up in prison where he falls in love with one of the male convicts, who on departing prison promises to take care of Franz's wife. Franz is traumatised by the affair, and the effects it may have on his marriage. In the meantime his former prison lover has begun a relationship with Franz's wife. When he finally leaves prison he attempts to rekindle his relationship with his long-suffering wife, but his past catches up with him with tragic results. German with English subtitles.

Prod Comp: Essem Film

Get Bruce

Kuehn, Andrew J.
1999; USA; 75 min; Documentary
P: Andrew J. Kuehn; *C:* José Louise Mignone;
E: Maureen Nolan; *M:* Michael Feinstein

This touching and often funny documentary profiles one of the comedy industry's unsung heroes, Bruce Vilanch. Bruce writes for some of the biggest names in Hollywood including Bette Midler, Billy Crystal, Whoopie Goldberg, Robin Williams and Paul Reiser. An outspoken and lively person with enormous talent and a generous heart.

Prod Comp: AJK
Dist/Sales: Miramax, Wolfe

Get Out

Lewis, Pat
1999; USA; 20 min; Documentary

An investigation of the depictions of queer life in the US media.

Get Over It

Katsapetses, Nicholas
1995; USA; 90 min; B&W; Comedy
P: Marcus Hu; *W:* Nicholas Katsapetses
Cast: Nicholas Katsapetses, Tony Morgan, Deborah Cordell, Christian Canterbury, Dave McCrea

To help Steven get over his broken heart (having being dumped by his boyfriend Derek), his best friend Pam invites a group of people to stay. The guest-list comprises a rather mixed bag, including a lesbian couple, a straight man who believes he's fully in touch with his sexuality, and Robert with his new bratty young boyfriend. As it turns out, the boys keep swapping partners, the girls drive back to Los Angeles, and Steven is more miserable than ever.

Get Real

Shore, Simon
1998; UK; 110 min; Drama
P: Stephen Taylor; *W:* Patrick Wilde; *C:* Alan Almond;
E: Barrie Vince; *M:* John Lunn
Cast: Ben Silverstone, Charlotte Brittain, Brad Gorton,
Stacy Hart

What does growing up mean to an average, middle class adolescent who 'doesn't play football and has an IQ of over 20?' 16-year-old Steven Carter, with the help of his sassy best friend, Linda, is about to show us. *Get Real* is an engaging and entertaining journey through a crucible of suburban angst, which highlights the chasm some youth feel between social acceptance and individual freedom. The stage is set for melodrama when Steven's unrequited crush on the school's most eligible and popular student, John Dixon is acknowledged and returned. John, who is the material wet dreams are made of, is confused, scared and determined to keep his new relationship with Steven a secret. Steven on the other hand wants to openly acknowledge his lover and their sexual status. What unfolds is a warm and sensitive exploration of teenage sexuality that is at once gut-wrenchingly honest and incredibly humorous. Despite what he stands to lose, Steven finally 'comes out' to his parents, teachers and peers declaring, 'it's only love—what's everyone scared of?' His brave question reverberates in our minds, capturing the central premise of this award winning film, whilst highlighting the tensions associated with sexual rights of passage. (MQFF)

Prod Comp: Distant Horizons, Graphite Film Production
Dist/Sales: NewVision, Alliance, ParamountClassics, Wolfe, Cowboy, ACMI, Swank

Get the Bowheads

Hildebrand, David / Miller, Courtney
1997; USA; 22 min; Comedy
P: Mark Holden; *W:* Courtney Miller, David Hildebrand

Short horror/comedy spoof about a US sorority house which is infiltrated by lesbians.

Prod Comp: Revolution Entertainment
Dist/Sales: Miller/Hildebrand

Get Your Stuff

Mitchell, Max
2000; USA; 93 min; Comedy
P: Max Mitchell, Jasper Cole, Carl Peoples;
W: Max Mitchell; *C:* Jeff Orsa; *E:* Christopher Koefoed;
M: Barry Coffing

Cast: Cameron Watson, Anthony Paul Meindl, Elaine Hendrix, Kimberly Scott

Comedy about a young successful gay couple who find themselves hosting two foster kids from hell in their exquisite Beverly Hills home.

Prod Comp: Peoples Productions, Wey-Man Productions, reVision Films
Dist/Sales: reVision

Getting it On

Meyer, Armgard
1998; USA; 17 min; Drama

A young woman finds love where she least expects it.

Getting of Wisdom, The

Beresford, Bruce
1977; Australia; 100 min; Drama
P: Phillip Adams; *W:* Eleanor Witcombe; *C:* Donald McAlpine; *E:* William Anderson; *M:* Sigismund Thalberg
Cast: Susannah Fowle, Hilary Ryan, Terence Donovan, Sheila Helpmann, Candy Raymond

Laura Tweedle-Ramsbotham is about to enter another world. From her home in sleepy, rural Australia, she ascends to the spires of an exclusive college for young ladies, a very strict Victorian boarding school in Melbourne. Laura is strong willed and rebellious, which creates conflict with her peers and her teachers. In a desperate attempt to find acceptance with her peers, she weaves the most lurid stories imaginable. The only real soul mate she finds is one of the senior girls. This novel by Henry Handel Richardson was published in 1910, and was so shocking at the time that the author's name was stricken from the records of the school in which she set the thinly disguised autobiography.

Prod Comp: Southern Cross Film Productions, AFC, Nine Network
Dist/Sales: Roadshow, Sharmill, NFVLS, Ascanbee, ACMI

Ghost of Roger Casement, The

Gilsenan, Alan
2002; Ireland; 107 min; Documentary
P: John Murray; *W:* Alan Gilsenan

Filmed over two years in Ireland, England, the US, Europe and South America, this Irish television documentary brings back to life one of the great gay heroes of world history—whether the homophobes who still insist on denying the truth about his sexuality like it or not. Born in Dublin in 1864, Roger Casement gained fame and British knight-

g

hood for exposing the abuses inflicted by white colonial traders on the indigenous peoples of the Congo, Brazil and Peru. But after returning to Ireland, he realised that the Irish were as viciously oppressed by their British masters as any of the 'natives' he had worked so hard to save. So, Sir Roger went from loyal subject of the king to proud Irish nationalist. When he sought help for the rebellion from England's enemies in World War I, he was labelled a traitor, captured by the British and sentenced to death. At first it seemed that an international outcry would force his captors to spare his life. But when the British government produced Casement's 'black diaries,' which recorded in his own handwriting his extensive homosexual exploits with young men, his support vanished. He was executed without further protest. Ever since, the diaries' authenticity and meaning have been hotly contested by those who refuse to believe that a humanitarian and hero could also be a homosexual, or that a patriot could be a pederast. Now, this fascinating film takes us into the heart of that debate. (26th San Francisco International Lesbian & Gay Film Festival)

Prod Comp: Crossing the Line Films
Dist/Sales: Crossing-the-Line

Ghosts of the Civil Dead

Hillcoat, John
1989; Australia; 90 min; Drama
P: Evan English

Shattering experience set in an imaginary prison institution somewhere in the not too distant future. A crammed prison is the breeding ground for violence, drug trafficking and homosexual sadism. Authorities allow it all to breed in order to justify retaliatory crackdowns, in an escalating spiral of violence. The end product discharged from the institution is a new breed of social, disruptive misfits. (ACMI)

Dist/Sales: ACMI, Sharmill

Gia

Cristofer, Michael
1998; USA; 126 min; Drama
P: James D. Brubaker; *W:* Jay McInerney, Michael Cristofer; *C:* Rodrigo Garcia; *E:* Eric Sears; *M:* Terence Blanchard
Cast: Angelina Jolie, Mercedes Ruehl, Faye Dunaway, Elizabeth Mitchell

Gia dreams of sex, money, glamour and fame. Unfortunately her best laid plans don't come to fruition. Based on the tragic life and times of America's first supermodel Gia who enjoyed the high life in 1970s New York City—Studio 54, designer jeans, drugs and disco. She's living life in the fast lane, and has her pick of men and women alike. However, her life takes a tragic course. (Wolfe)

Prod Comp: Citadel Entertainment
Dist/Sales: HBO, Wolfe, Swank

Gilda

Vidor, Charles
1946; USA; 110 min; B&W; Drama
P: Virginia Van Upp; *W:* Marion Parsonnet; *C:* Rudolph Maté; *E:* Charles Nelson; *M:* Hugo W. Friedhofer
Cast: Rita Hayworth, Glenn Ford, George Macready, Joseph Calleia

Film Noir classic which tells the story of an emotional triangle between casino owner Macready, his assistant Ford and Macready's wife. It can also be read from a gay perspective, with insider references such as when Ford tells Macready, 'I was born the night I met you'.

Prod Comp: Columbia
Dist/Sales: Col-Tri, ACMI

Ginger Beer

Rea, Seamus
1999; UK; 17 min; Comedy, Musical

Short musical comedy about an ugly duckling who meets his prince during ballroom dancing lessons.

Dist/Sales: Cheek2Cheek

Girl in Every Port, A

Hawks, Howard
1928; USA; 64 min; B&W; Comedy
P: William Fox; *W:* Howard Hawks, Seton I. Miller, James K. McGuinness, Reginald Morris, Malcolm S. Boylan; *C:* William O'Connell, R. J. Berquist; *E:* Ralph Dixon
Cast: Victor McLaglen, Robert Armstrong, Louise Brooks, Natalie Joyce

A friendship or 'love story', as Hawks described it, between two womanising sailors is temporarily threatened by McLaglen's romance with a two-timing side show entertainer in this buoyant comedy which has a touch of romantic melodrama. The 'love story' anticipates male relationships in some later Hawks' films, particularly *The Big Sky*.

Prod Comp: Fox

Girl King

Pietrobruno, Ileana
2001; Canada; 80 min; Comedy
W: Ileana Pietrobruno; *C:* John Houtman; *E:* Ileana Pietrobruno

Playful and seductive, with a fistful of fetish in every frame, *Girl King* delivers an unabashedly original drag-king pirate adventure. The King has made off with the Queen's precious jewels, and without them there will be no more life on the island. Virgin Butch is pure and strong enough to recover her stolen treasure. In exchange for the return of her jewels, the Queen promises Butch the love of his life, the femme and beautiful Claudia. Lit by oversized moons and saturated by translucent waters, at times erotic and surreal and always camp, *Girl King* is, at heart, a sweetly perverse fable—a modern myth for our gender skewed times. (21st Chicago Lesbian & Gay International Film Festival)

Girl Power

Benning, Sadie
1992; USA; 15 min; B&W; Comedy

Shot on her usual Fischer-Price toy video camera, and set to music by Bikini Kill, an all-girl band from Washington DC, this is a raucous vision of what it means to be a radical girl in the 1990s. It is informed by the underground riot-girl movement, an attitude that is transforming the image politics of female youth today. (MQFF)

Dist/Sales: VDB, NFVLS

Girl Stroke Boy

Kellett, Bob
1971; UK; 88 min; Comedy
P: Ned Sherrin, Terry Glinwood; *W:* Caryl Brahms
Cast: Joan Greenwood, Michael Hordern, Patricia Routledge

Laurie's very straight parents are concerned when he arrives home with a West Indian 'girlfriend' of indeterminate gender.

Girl, The

Zeig, Sande
1999; France, USA; 84 min; Drama
P: Dolly Hall; *W:* Sande Zeig, Monique Wittig; *C:* George Lechapois; *E:* Keiko Deguchi, Geraldine Peroni; *M:* Richard Robbins
Cast: Claire Keim, Agathe de la Boulaye, Cyril Lecomte, Sandra N'kake

A beautiful painter who frequents a Paris nightclub has an affair with a singer. The Painter tells the story of her increasing obsession with the singer. She calls her The Girl. The Painter and The Girl continue to see each other but carry on relationships with other people. One night, a suspicious looking man, who seems to know The Girl, appears in the club. At first The Painter observes him from a distance, but

gradually she begins following him. She begins to understand that The Man is threatening The Girl. Suddenly, The Girl disappears. The Painter looks everywhere and eventually learns that The Girl and The Man have left Paris together. Then, all at once, The Girl is back, more elegant than ever. When The Painter finds The Girl in the arms of The Man, she is crushed. She attempts to lose herself in her work but she knows that she must return to The Girl's hotel room where she will find The Man and The Girl together. She also knows that it will be for the last time... (Mongrel)
English & French with English subtitles.

Prod Comp: Method Films, Dolly Hall Productions
Dist/Sales: ArtisticLicense, Mongrel, Wolfe

Girl Thing, A

Rose, Lee
2001; USA; 240 min; Drama
W: Lee Rose; *C:* Eric Van Haren Noman; *E:* Christopher Rouse; *M:* Terence Blanchard
Cast: Elle Macpherson, Kate Capshaw, Stockard Channing, Camryn Manheim, Mia Farrow

A Girl Thing tells four stories featuring women dealing with life's twists and turns. All are seeking advice from Psychiatrist Dr Beth Noonan. Facing her own personal struggles, Dr Noonan assists each of the women in making successful transitions in their lives. The first story features Lauren, an attorney who finds herself in an unexpected romance with Casey, an advertising executive. In the second story, three sisters learn how to deal with each other while coping with their controlling mother's death. The third story involves revenge, as a wronged wife and a private investigator collaborate with her husband's lover to give the cheater a taste of his own medicine. In the final story, an emotionally disturbed patient threatens Dr Noonan and her staff with a gun, with surprising results. (Wolfe)

Prod Comp: Hallmark, Showtime Networks
Dist/Sales: Wolfe, Showtime, 10%

Girl with the Golden Eyes, The

(aka: La Fille aux yeux d'or)

Albicocco, Jean-Gabriel
1961; France; 105 min; B&W; Drama
P: Gilbert de Goldschmidt; *W:* Jean-Gabriel Albicocco, Pierre Pelégri, Philippe Dumarçay; *C:* Quinto Albicocco; *E:* Georges Klotz; *M:* Narciso Yepes, Arcangelo Corelli
Cast: Marie Laforet, Paul Guers, Jacques Verlier, Françoise Prévost, Françoise Dorléac

A man working in the Paris fashion industry in the early 1960s falls for a woman he knows nothing

g

about. He soon discovers she is the lover of one of his female colleagues. He in turn becomes a threat to the women's relationship and it ends in a crime of passion with one of the women being stabbed to death.

Prod Comp: Madeleine Films

The Girl with the Golden Eyes

Girlfriends (1978)

Weill, Claudia
1978; USA; 86 min; Drama
P: Claudia Weill, Jan Sanders; *W:* Vicki Polon;
C: Fred Murphy; *E:* Suzanne Pettit; *M:* Michael Small
Cast: Melanie Mayron, Eli Wallach, Anita Skinner, Bob Balaban, Christopher Guest

This film explores the relationship between two women, Susan, a photographer and artist, and Ann, a writer, housewife and mother. In the past they have been best friends and roommates, but now that Ann is married, jealousy and tension enter into the friendship as they negotiate each other's lifestyles and characters. Susan picks up a hitchhiker who ends up staying with her. When the young hitchhiker tries to seduce Susan, she is asked to leave. The lesbianism is not handled well and there is the usual heterosexual triumph.

Prod Comp: Cyclops
Dist/Sales: Roadshow, Warner, Swank

Girlfriends (1993)

Bosko, Mark / Harold, Wayne
1993; USA; 90 min; Comedy
P: Mark Bosko; *W:* Wayne Harold; *C:* Alan Stevens;
E: Dick Myers; *M:* Sean Carlin, Matt Patterson
Cast: Lori Scarlet, Nina Angeloff

A rather strange and graphic film about two lesbian serial killers, Pearl and her lover Wanda, who pick up men, kill them and steal their wallets. During the course of all the killing, Pearl decides she wants to have a baby.

Prod Comp: Riot Pictures

Girls Can't Swim
(aka: Les filles ne savent par nager)

Birot, Anne-Sophie
2000; France; 101 min; Drama
P: Philippe Jacquier; *W:* Anne-Sophie Birot, Christophe Honore; *C:* Nathalie Durand; *E:* Pascale Chavance;
M: Ernest Chausson
Cast: Isild Le Besco, Karen Alyx, Pascale Bussieres, Pascal Elso

Gwen is a sunny, free-spirited 15-year-old who lives on the Brittany coast with her mother and fisherman father. Lise is her best friend, an intense city girl who comes every year with her mother and sisters to spend the summer. But this summer will be different: the death of her estranged father keeps Lise at home, the impassioned letters she exchanges with her cherished friend being the only thing that sustains her amidst the turmoil. Gwen, on the other hand, gets on with her life: hanging out with friends, sleeping on the beach, finding hideaways to have sex with local boys. Then, suddenly, Lise shows up at Gwen's house to stay for a couple of weeks. Their reunion is soon soured by Lise's resentment over the rapidly maturing Gwen's interest in the opposite sex. The following days are filled with awkwardness, tenderness and rage as the two girls revaluate their friendship, clinging to their fragile bond as the realities of ruthless, impending adulthood threaten to tear it apart. (www.frenchculture.org)
French with English subtitles.

Dist/Sales: Millivres, Wellspring

Girls in Boy's Bars

1991; UK; 16 min; Documentary

Looks at the role of straight women and drag in gay male bars.

Prod Comp: Channel 4

Girls Who Like Girls

Edwards, Pauline
2001; USA; 90 min; Documentary

A collection of favourite lesbian lovemaking scenes from the 1960s and 1970s including clips from landmark erotic films such as *Thérèse and Isabelle*, *Score*, *Olga's Girls* and many more.

Dist/Sales: FirstRunFeatures

Gladys, A Cuban Mother

Daniel, Xavier
2001; Spain; 11 min; B&W; Documentary

A mother tells her son that her greatest loves have been women. She recounts the story of raising two daughters left behind after the death of their mother, one of Gladys' former lovers. Shot clandestinely in Havana, *Gladys, A Cuban Mother* depicts the poignant experience of a lesbian mother living in a society driven by machismo. (Frameline) Spanish with English subtitles.

Dist/Sales: Frameline

Glasses Break

Buchanan, Justine
1991; UK; 18 min; B&W; Drama

A bittersweet recollection of a love affair. The lingering power of an ex-lover is explored and finally exorcised in this stylish black-and-white film. (MQFF)

Dist/Sales: WMM

Glen or Glenda

Wood, Edward D.
1953; USA; 61 min; B&W; Drama
P: George Wiess; *W:* Edward D. Wood; *C:* William C. Thompson; *E:* Bud Schelling
Cast: Bela Lugosi, Dolores Fuller, Daniel Davis, Lyn Talbot, Timothy Farrell

A turgid but sincere docudrama about transvestism and sex-change operations. An all-time great cult movie that is autobiographical in nature—Glen (played by Wood, under the name Daniel Davis) can't bring himself to tell his fiancée that he likes to wear frocks. By the director of that all-time turkey, *Plan 9 from Outer Space*.

Prod Comp: Screen Classics
Dist/Sales: Salzgeber, Englewood, Sinister, ACMI

Glider, The

(aka: Le Planeur)

Cantraine, Yves
1999; France; 17 min; Drama

Bruno is obsessed with a mysterious thief.

Dist/Sales: Need

Glitterbug

Jarman, Derek
1994; UK; 60 min; Experimental

Brian Eno provides the soundtrack for this atmospheric reminiscence of Jarman's life.

Go

Liman, Doug
1999; USA; 103 min; Comedy
P: Paul Rosenberg, Matt Freeman, Mickey Liddell; *W:* John August; *C:* Doug Liman; *E:* Stephen Mirrione
Cast: Sarah Polley, Katie Holmes, Desmond Askew, Taye Diggs

Told from three perspectives, *Go* is the story of a group of young Californians doing drugs, dealing drugs, experimenting with sex, and trying to make money in Las Vegas. Jay Mohr and Scott Wolf play two gay soap studs who agree to take part in an elaborate drug bust. After they successfully fulfil their duties, they accidentally run over a pedestrian while still wearing their police issue wires.

Prod Comp: Banner Entertainment, Saratoga Entertainment
Dist/Sales: Col-Tri, SonyPictures, Wolfe, ACMI, Swank

Go Fish

Go Fish

Troche, Rose
1994; USA; 85 min; B&W; Comedy
P: Rose Troche, Guinevere Turner; *W:* Guinevere Turner, Rose Troche; *C:* Ann T. Rossetti; *E:* Rose Troche; *M:* Brendan Dolan, Jennifer Sharpe, Scott Aldrich
Cast: Guinevere Turner, V. S. Brodie, T. Wendy McMillan, Anastasia Sharp

A fresh comedy about the contemporary lifestyles of lesbians living in San Francisco. Refreshing because it's not the usual coming-out story; these girls are out and about. The plot revolves around Max and her friend Kia. Kia decides to set up a date between Max and another woman, Ely, an ex-student of Kia's. Things don't run smoothly in the beginning. Ely must end a long-distance relationship with another woman first, but with help from their friends, things finally work out. A neatly performed, well-written comedy.

Prod Comp: Can I Watch, Islet, KPVI, Samuel Goldwyn Company
Dist/Sales: Dendy, Col-Tri, TLA, SamuelGoldwyn, Wolfe, ACMI

Goblin Market

Smith, Jo
1993; UK; 10 min; Drama

Based on the erotic lesbian poem by Christina Rossetti about two sisters who are tempted to eat the fruit given to them by a goblin. One of the sisters does and becomes ill. The only antidote is to eat more fruit.

Dist/Sales: Cinenova

g ▶ God, Gays and the Gospel

McEwen, Mary Anne
1991; USA; 58 min; Documentary

A profile of the Universal Fellowship of Metropolitan Community Churches that was founded by gays and lesbians under the premise that God loves everyone including homosexuals. After years of attacks, including fire bombings, it is one of the fastest-growing parishes in the world.

Dist/Sales: CinemaGuild

God, Sreenu & Me

Main, Stewart
2000; New Zealand; 52 min; Documentary

The celebration of male beauty as form of gay religion is called into question by Stuart Main as he and his young Indian assistant Sreenu travel the subcontinent to interview New Zealanders who have relocated in search of spiritual fulfilment.

Dist/Sales: MF-Films

Godass

Bell, Esther
2000; USA; 73 min; Drama
P: Rob Hall, Esther Bell, Lori Cheatle; *W:* Esther Bell;
C: Milton Kam; *E:* Rob Hall
Cast: Fred Schneider, Julianne Nicholson, Tina Holmes, Anna Grace

A young punk rock girl reconciles with her gay father.

Dist/Sales: HellsBells

Gods and Monsters

Condon, Bill
1998; UK, USA; 105 min; Drama
P: Paul Colichman, Gregg Fienberg, Mark R. Harris;
W: Bill Condon; *C:* Stephen M. Katz; *E:* Virginia Katz;
M: Carter Burwell, Steve Plunkett
Cast: Ian McKellen, Lynn Redgrave, Brendan Fraser, Lolita Davidovich

Biography of film director James Whale who created one of the screen's great mythic heroes in the classic version of Frankenstein. Beginning in the 1950s when Whale is largely forgotten or only remembered through camp nostalgia, the film traces Whale's increasing obsession with his gardener, Clayton. As Whale's health deteriorates, his memory increasingly draws him back to the pivotal moments of his life: his rejection of his harsh working-class youth; his service in World War I and his loving affair with a fellow soldier; and his years directing in the classic Hollywood era. Combining biography and a mature examination of the possible love between homosexual and heterosexual men, *Gods and Monsters* ends up being a loving tribute to both the classic Hollywood era and the possibility of transcendence for working-class people. (ACMI)

Awards: Academy Awards, 1998: Best Adapted Screenplay
Prod Comp: BBC, Lions Gate Films, Regent Entertainment, Showtime, Spike Productions
Dist/Sales: Globe, LionsGate, Wolfe, NFVLS, ACMI

Gohatto

(aka: Taboo)

Oshima, Nagisa
1999; Japan; 95 min; Drama
P: Nobuyoshi Otani, Jeremy Thomas, Jean Labadie;
W: Nagisa Oshima; *C:* Toyomichi Kurita; *E:* Tomoyo Oshima; *M:* Ryuichi Sakamoto
Cast: Ryuhei Matsuda, Shinji Takeda, Tadanobu Asano, Takeshi Kitano

Set in Kyoto in the Spring of 1865, *Gohatto* begins at the Temple Nishi-Honganji, where the Shinsengumi militia is choosing new recruits to become Samurai warriors. Commander Isami Kondo and lieutenant Toshizo Hijikata are supervising the recruiting process. Those hoping to be chosen must face off the best man in the militia, Soji Okita. Out of all the men present, only two are chosen: Hyozo Tashiro, a low-level samurai from the Kurume clan and Sozaburo Kano, a handsome young man whose good looks are bewitching. Tashiro is immediately attracted to Kano. Rigid rules and regulations keep order among this group of men and are the unifying force in the face of adversity... But suddenly the militia finds itself prey to rumours and jealousies... the fascination that the others hold for the young samurai Kano creates confusion all around. (New Yorker Films)

Prod Comp: Shochiku Films
Dist/Sales: Canal+, RimFilm, NewYorker

Going West

Mew, Michael
2001; Canada; 28 min; Comedy

Going West is an hilarious gay satire that follows small town boy Ben to the big city, where he gets caught up in a militant gay organisation, The Gay Liberation Army, determined to set the standard for a new generation. Their leader, Hared Banks, becomes obsessed with Ben, and goes to extraordinary lengths to get him. (www.goingwest.ca)

Gold Diggers, The

Potter, Sally
1983; UK; 90 min; Drama
P: Nita Amy, Donna Grey; *W:* Lindsay Cooper, Rose English, Sally Potter; *C:* Babette Mangolte; *E:* Sally Potter; *M:* Lindsay Cooper
Cast: David Gale, Julianne Christie, Colette Laffont

A feminist adventure tale about a beautiful blonde movie star who's saved from a life of being passed from man to man by a Black Frenchwoman on horseback.

Golden Threads

Winer, Lucy
1999; USA; 56 min; Documentary
P: Karen Eaton

Profiling the life of 93-year-old lesbian activist Christine Burton, founder of a global networking service for mid-life and elder lesbians, this documentary, exuberantly overturns our most deeply rooted stereotypes and fears of ageing. By adding the wry and introspective narrative of the director undergoing a mid-life crisis, the film generates a groundbreaking, intergenerational dialogue about sexuality, life choices, and ageing. (WMM)

Prod Comp: Independent Television Service
Dist/Sales: WMM

Gonin

(aka: The Five)

Ishii, Takashi
1995; Japan; 110 min; Thriller
P: Kazuyoshi Okuyama; *W:* Takashi Ishii; *C:* Yasushi Sasakibara; *M:* Goro Yasukawa
Cast: Takeshi Kitano, Koichi Sato, Masahiro Motoki, Jinpachi Nezu, Naoto Takenaka

Five down and out men, desperate to make some cash, get together and plot to perform a huge robbery. Unfortunately things don't go as planned, and the group are confronted by the local Yakuza. Lots of male bonding ensues in this drag infused,

action packed gay Japanese crime flick. Japanese with English subtitles.

Dist/Sales: Phaedra

Good Citizen: Betty Baker

Dempsey, Shawna / Millan, Lorri
1996; Canada; 27 min; Comedy

An hysterical, madcap adventure featuring Betty Baker—wife, mom and PTA member. Featuring cardboard cut-outs for sets and cut-out dolls clothes for costumes, this kitsch parody of 1950s suburbia is outrageous, camp fun. *Good Citizen* comprises five serial chapters, providing cliff-hangers and climaxes all the way through.

Prod Comp: Finger in the Dyke
Dist/Sales: CFMDC, VideoPool

Good Family, The

(aka: Thanksgiving Day)

Tanasescu, Gino
1990; USA; 90 min; Comedy
P: Marvin Miller; *W:* Steve Zacharias, Jeff Buhai; *C:* Fred Moore; *E:* Seth Flaum; *M:* Tom Hensley, Alan E. Lindgren
Cast: Mary Tyler Moore, Tony Curtis, Andy Hirsch, Jonathon Brandmeier, Kelly Curtis

Paula Schloss's family life is a whirl of people she can't seem to control...and when her husband dies unexpectedly—while carving the turkey—it sets off a chain of events that send the Schloss family on a wild and wacky roller-coaster ride. Eldest son Randy takes over the family business and it goes bankrupt within a year. Daughter Barbara announces she's going to live with another woman and no-one notices any change in young son Michael.

Prod Comp: NBC

Good Father, The

(aka: Fathers' Rites)

Newell, Mike
1986; UK; 86 min; Drama
P: Ann Scott; *W:* Christopher Hampton; *C:* Michael Coulter; *E:* Peter Hollywood; *M:* Richard Hartley
Cast: Anthony Hopkins, Jim Broadbent, Frances Viner, Harriet Walter, Simon Callow

Magazine designer, Bill Hooper, is distraught following the break-up of his marriage and the loss of contact with his six-year-old son. His wife has left him for another woman. Bill is a member of the 'forever young generation' who believed in open marriages and women's lib until he tried them and discovered the pain they can cause. Bill's friend,

g

Roger, is in a similar situation and when he learns that Roger's ex-wife plans to move to Australia, Bill is urged to fight a custody battle for his son in the courts.

Prod Comp: Channel 4, Greenpoint Films
Dist/Sales: NewVision, Skouras

Goodbye Emma Jo

Newbrough, Cheryl
1997; USA; 40 min; Drama

This is an unabashed story of erotic love and passion. Alex is mourning the loss of her beautiful Emma Jo on what would have been their anniversary. She has never felt more angry and alone—her day only gets worse when her car breaks down. Stranded, she is rescued by Haley, a gorgeous local, who offers her a place to spend the night. 'Come on, I'm not going to bite', promises Haley, yet Alex is wary. The two women turn a disastrous chain of events into a series of heightened sexual interludes, and it's more than a pleasure to watch them unfold. (Wolfe)

Dist/Sales: Wolfe

Goodbye Girl, The

Ross, Herbert
1977; USA; 110 min; Comedy
P: Ray Stark; *W:* Neil Simon; *C:* David M. Walsh;
E: John F. Burnett; *M:* Dave Grusin
Cast: Richard Dreyfuss, Marsha Mason, Quinn Cummings, Paul Benedict, Barbara Rhoades

An actor, played by Dreyfuss, and a divorcee, Mason, become unwilling co-tenants of an apartment. In spite of themselves they fall in love. One highlight of the film is a camp version of Richard III, put on by a gay stage director, where Dreyfuss camps it right up as the limp-wristed and lisping king.

Awards: Academy Awards, 1977: Best Actor (Richard Dreyfuss)
Prod Comp: MGM, Warner, Rastar Pictures
Dist/Sales: ReelMovies, Warner, MGM

Got 2B There

Torrealba, José M.
1998; Canada; 88 min; Documentary

Got 2B There offers guest-list access into the world of gay circuit dance parties—the hedonistic social epicentre of North America's 'A' list gay men. Born out of the AIDS epidemic of the 1980s, the circuit scene has become somewhat of a paradox. On one hand, the parties raise thousands of dollars for AIDS organisations. On the other, critics charge that the circuit itself contributes to the spread of the disease and encourages the widespread use of drugs such as crystal meth and GHB. This provocative film gives ample time to both sides. Shot at circuit events across North America, it combines throbbing footage of thousands of buffed, sweating torsos with a who's who line-up of commentators including party promoter Jeffrey Sanker, DJs David Knapp, Susan Morabito, Julian Mash and Buc and circuit critic Michelangelo Signorile. (CFMDC)

Dist/Sales: PictureThis!, CFMDC

Gotta Have Heart

(aka: Ba'al Ba'al Lev)

Fox, Eytan
1997; Israel; 36 min; Comedy

Gay fantasy film set in a small Israeli town. Guri is anxious to get to school in Tel Aviv before anyone learns that he's gay. Mitzi worries that she'll be left on the shelf. Nohav dreams of winning the local song contest.

Grace of God, The

L'Ecuyer, Gerald
1997; Canada; 75 min; Drama
P: Ann Medina; *W:* Gerald L'Ecuyer
Cast: David Bolt, David Cronenberg, Robbie Pennant, Michael Riley

A dark yet humorous psychological journey about the filmmaker's efforts to reconcile his socially awkward and sexually naive past with his mature present. Putting himself in front of and behind the camera, L'Ecuyer has forged a stunning hybrid of fiction and documentary. *The Grace of God* crackles and gleams with L'Ecuyer's aesthetic innovations and his impressive gifts for story telling and directing. *The Grace of God* is a labour of love, comprised of scenes gathered sporadically over a ten-year period. The resulting stream of consciousness film takes us on a metaphoric train ride home that slowly reveals the timeworn truth that moving is generally more important than arriving. (8th Inside Out Lesbian and Gay Film and Video Festival of Toronto)

Dist/Sales: CFMDC

Grapefruit

Dougherty, Cecilia
1989; USA; 40 min; Comedy
Cast: Suzie Bright

A mapping of lesbian content over the story of Yoko Ono, John Lennon, and the break-up of the Beatles.

Dist/Sales: VDB

Grass is Greener, The

Raine, Amanda
1999; UK; 17 min; Comedy

A butch lesbian and an affeminate gay man find themselves unexpectedly thrown together on a camping holiday in Wales.

Dist/Sales: PotentPussy

Green Plaid Shirt

Natale, Richard
1996; USA; 87 min; Drama
P: Lusa Norcen, Denis Chicola; *W:* Richard Natale;
C: Amit Bhattacharya; *E:* Hugo Rynders; *M:* Norman Noll
Cast: Gregory Phelan, Kevin Spirtas, Tony Campisi,
Richard Israel

It's the 1970s. Phil and Guy fall in love, have unrealistic expectations and an open relationship. Guy becomes ill, with 'the gay thing'. His departure is gradual. Flashback takes the viewer back to the ten years from gay liberation to the AIDS pandemic. A poignant, poetically crafted piece of cinema.

Prod Comp: A Vicious Circle
Dist/Sales: Wolfe, Millivres

Grief

Green Pubes

Arena, Tony (Anonymous Boy)
1995; USA; 25 min; Animation

A sexy, funny, queer punk love story, *Green Pubes* displays the punk movement's DIY ethics at its no-frills best. The simplistic animation makes up in sheer exuberance what it lacks in technique. You'll laugh, you'll cry, you'll mosh in your seats.

Greetings from Out Here

Spiro, Ellen
1993; USA; 60 min; Documentary

Ellen Spiro's video pilgrimage to Dixieland. Stopping to talk with some of the good old (queer) boys and girls along the way, this film captures the politics and

people of America's deep south, including the granny with a shotgun who runs the local pet cemetery and an out gay postman.

Dist/Sales: VDB

Greetings from Washington

Winer, Lucy
1981; USA; 27 min; Documentary
P: Robert Epstein, Frances Reid, Greta Schiller, Lucy Winer

A kaleidoscope of music, dance, stories and laughter shared at the first gay and lesbian rights march on Washington. (WMM)

Prod Comp: Greetings Films
Dist/Sales: WMM

Grief

Glatzer, Richard
1993; USA; 92 min; Comedy
P: Ruth Charny, Yoram Mandel; *W:* Richard Glatzer;
C: David Dechant; *E:* Robin Katz, Bill Williams;
M: Tom Judson
Cast: Alexis Arquette, Craig Chester, Jackie Beat, Illeana Douglas, Carlton Wilborn

A clever behind-the-scenes look at the lives of the scriptwriting department of a Z-grade television soap opera. This bittersweet comedy follows an eventful week in the life of the writer, Mark, a gay man who contemplates suicide on the anniversary of his lover's death from AIDS. When the executive producer decides to leave, the situation is set for some serious competition. Who will be Jo's successor?

Prod Comp: Grief Productions
Dist/Sales: Potential, Salzgeber, Strand, NFVLS, ACMI

Groove on a Stanley Knife

Krishnan, Tinge / Kotler, Beth
1997; UK; 42 min; Drama
P: Gary Holding; *W:* Tinge Krishnan

A frantic plunge into the dark history of two women fleeing violent crack dealers in the north of England. Holed up in a disused public toilet, the stress and claustrophobia of the long night forces the pair to confront the realities of their friendship.

Prod Comp: Disruptive Element Films
Dist/Sales: Cinenova

Group

de Marcken, Anne / Freeman, Marilyn
2001; USA; 106 min; Experimental
P: Anne de Marcken, Marilyn Freeman; *W:* Anne de Marcken; *C:* Anne de Marcken; *M:* Sleater-Kinney
Cast: Carrie Brownstein, Nomy Lamm, Kari Filipi,

g

Tracy Kirkpatrick, Tony Wilkerson

Marilyn Freeman has created a truly original film in *Group*, a startling experimental narrative following nine women for 21 weeks of 'queer friendly, sliding scale, downtown' group therapy. Utilising multiple frames to present the story from six simultaneous shifting angles, Freeman gets under the skin of the wildly different women—sex rocker, born-again Christian, bisexual punk amputee, hypochondriac, goody-two-shoes, tramp, bigot, binger, and lone therapist. The women challenge each other while they expose their own personal issues in an attempt to find a little happiness. Largely improvisational, the actors' performances are stunning, skirting the boundary of reality and drama. (2002 New York Lesbian & Gay Film Festival)

Prod Comp: Wovie
Dist/Sales: ArtisticLicense

Group, The

Lumet, Sidney
1966; USA; 150 min; Drama
P: Sidney Buchman; *W:* Sidney Buchman; *C:* Boris Kaufman; *E:* Ralph Rosenblum; *M:* Charles Gross
Cast: Candice Bergen, Joanna Pettet, Joan Hackett, Elizabeth Hartman, Shirley Knight

Based on the best-seller by Mary McCarthy, this film follows the interwoven stories of a group of women who graduated from school together in 1933. They meet again after a number of years, sharing and talking about their loves and the changes in their lives. Candice Bergen plays a lesbian who returns from Europe with the Baroness, a rather butch-looking woman who can certainly wear a suit. A frank look at lesbianism and considered quite shocking at the time of the film's release.

Prod Comp: United Artists, Famartists Productions
Dist/Sales: TLA

Guardian of the Frontier

(aka: Varuh Meje)

Weiss, Maja
2001; Slovenia; 100 min; Drama
P: Ida Weiss; *W:* Brock Norman Brock, Maja Weiss, Zoran Hocevar; *C:* Bojan Kastelic; *E:* Peter Braatz; *M:* Sewart Dunlop
Cast: Jonas Znidarsic, Iva Krajnc, Tanja Potocnik, Pia Zemljic

During their summer break, three girlfriends, Alja, Zana, and Simona, take a canoe trip down the Kolpa, the river separating Slovenia from Croatia. But what begins as a pleasure trip swiftly becomes a nightmarish voyage on the border between the permissible and the forbidden. Unknown to the young women, they are being watched by a self-appointed border guard, a conservative local politician bent on defending traditional values by eliminating anything transgressing his moral codes. When it becomes clear that Alja and Zana are more than just friends, they tempt the wrath of the *Guardian of the Frontier*. The first Slovenian feature directed by a woman, *Guardian of the Frontier* combines lush visuals and a powerful political message to create a feast for the eyes and the mind. (2002 New York Lesbian & Gay Film Festival) Slovenian with English subtitles .

Dist/Sales: SlovenianFF

Guess Who's Coming to Dinner?

Kwietniowski, Richard
1991; UK; 25 min; Documentary
P: Susan Ardill

Various hospitality workers (waiters, chefs, etc.), swap stories as they dine on a four course meal at a queer dinner party.

Dist/Sales: MayaVision

Gypsy 83

Stephens, Todd
2001; USA; 95 min; Comedy
P: Todd Stephens, Karen Jaroneski; *W:* Todd Stephens; *C:* Gina DeGirolamo; *E:* Annette Davey; *M:* Marty Beller
Cast: Sara Rue, Kett Turton, Karen Black, John Doe, Paulo Costanzo

Gypsy is a young woman in Stephens' hometown of Sandusky, Ohio, who is obsessed with Stevie Nicks. An aspiring musician herself, Gypsy heads for New York City with her best friend, Clive, an adorable misunderstood gay goth-boy, to compete in the legendary 'Night of a 1000 Stevies'. At the same time, Gypsy is searching for her mother, Velvet, who left her years ago. During the road trip, they run into a host of characters, including Bambi, a washed-up singer reduced to performing at a hick karaoke club; a hunky Amish boy looking for an escape from traditions; and a closeted college fraternity pledgemaster. (2002 New York Lesbian & Gay Film Festival)

Prod Comp: Velvet Productions
Dist/Sales: Gypsy83

Gypsy Boys

Shepp, Brian
1999; USA; 103 min; Comedy
P: Brian Shepp; *W:* Brian Shepp; *C:* Gay Rohan; *E:* Rick Lobo; *M:* Rich McCracken
Cast: Adam Gavzer, Robert Hampton, Tom McCann,

Jud Parker, Alberto Rosas

A wittily observed insider's journey through the swirl of alcohol, sex, heartbreak and hope that is the San Francisco gay nightlife. Featuring a number of hilarious fantasy scenes—from pornographic firemen to horny and accessible go-go boys—*Gypsy Boys* keenly captures the mix of heartbreak and hope that defines any community of singles wishing to become couples. (Wolfe)

Prod Comp: Another BS Production
Dist/Sales: Wolfe, 10%

Gypsy Boys

Habit

Bordowitz, Gregg
2001; USA; 52 min; Documentary

An autobiographical documentary that follows the current history of the AIDS epidemic along several personal and public trajectories. (VDB)

Dist/Sales: VDB

Hairspray

Waters, John
1988; USA; 88 min; Comedy
P: Rachel Talalay; *W:* John Waters; *C:* David Insley;

E: Janice Hampton; *M:* Kenny Vance
Cast: Ricki Lake, Divine, Deborah Harry, Sonny Bono, Ruth Brown

Tubby teenager Tracy Turnblad's dreams come true when she gets to appear on Baltimore's coolest pop show, 'The Corny Collins Show'. However, Tracy finds herself in bitter competition with the show's reigning teen queen, bitchy Amber Von Tussle. They battle not only for the crown but also for the true love of teen hunk, Link.

Prod Comp: New Line Cinema
Dist/Sales: Col-Tri, ACMI, NewLine, BFI

Half Mongrel

Chomicz, Alex
1999; Australia; 13 min; Drama

Fearful of impending fatherhood, a man is plagued by guilt-inspired dreams that send him into a tailspin of booze and sexual frustration.

Dist/Sales: Queerscreen

Hallelujah!

Gund Saalfield, Catherine
1997; USA; 90 min; Documentary
P: Catherine Gund Saalfield; *W:* Catherine Gund Saalfield

Raised by his grandmother to be a Pentecostal minister, Athey was speaking in tongues by the age of ten, a heroine addict by seventeen, and a performance artist by twenty-three. *Hallelujah!* is a compelling look into the life and work of a gay, HIV-positive performance artist, who practices sadomasochistic ritual as a personal religion. Through interviews with him and his troupe and featuring scenes from his touring show in Zagreb, Croatia and Mexico City, we are witness to a man who uses excessive means to test physical endurance. Pain and taboos are strikingly confronted in this meditative and autobiographical look at damnation, sacrifice and redemption. (Artistic License)

Dist/Sales: ArtisticLicense

Hamam: The Turkish Bath

(aka: Steam)

Ozpetek, Ferzan
1997; Italy, Turkey; 96 min; Drama
P: Marco Risi, Maurizio Tedesco, Cengiz Ergun, Aldo Sambrell; *W:* Ferzan Ozpetek, Stefano Tummolini; *C:* Pasquale Mari; *E:* Mauro Bonanni; *M:* Pivio, Aldo de Scalzi
Cast: Alessandro Gassman, Francesca d'Aloja, Halil Ergün, Serif Sezer

Francesco, a successful designer from Rome, arrives

in Turkey to oversee the disposition of an estate left to him by an estranged, recently deceased aunt. Once there, he discovers that the property is actually a hamam, a traditional Turkish steam bath, which had been run by his aunt until her death. From letters and friends' accounts, he discovers that his aunt was a remarkable and passionate woman, whose insights and meditations uncannily reflect his current experience. Enter Mehmet, the beautiful son of the hamam's custodian, who ushers Francesco into the sultry world of the Turkish baths, emblematic of men's erotic love and desire for one another. Enlightened and unbound, Francesco decides to remain in Istanbul and restore the hamam. (Strand) Italian & Turkish with English subtitles.

Prod Comp: Sorpasso Films, Promete Films, Asbrell Productions
Dist/Sales: Strand

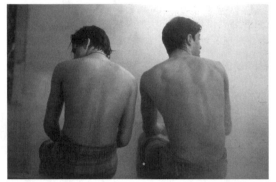

Hamam: The Turkish Bath

Hammer and Sickle
(aka: Serp i molot)

Livnev, Sergei
1994; Russia; 93 min; Drama
W: Sergei Livnev, Vladimir Valutsky; *C:* Sergei Machilsky; *E:* Alla Strelnikova; *M:* Leonid Desyatnikov
Cast: Aleksei Serebryakov, Yevdokiya Germanova, Marina Kajdalova

It is the mid 1930s. Stalin approves an experimental sex change operation. 'If Motherland needs soldiers, we'll make soldiers, if Motherland needs mothers, we'll make mothers'. So, in a Frankensteinian hospital above a forced labour camp, Yevdokia Kuznetsova is transformed. Yevdokim Kumetsov emerges, the model worker, a blond and bland 'new man'. He marries and adopts a child, steeps himself in Marxist philosophy and, as the pride of the Soviet state, becomes the real-life model for a monstrous statue at the World Exhibition in Paris. But while Stalin's regime presents this facade of human perfection to the outside world, Kumetsov harbours his grim secret. His ceaseless yearning for his non-Marxist lover is a romance that will eventually

disrupt the status quo. Whether the story is fact or fable, Livnev and cinematographer Sergei Matchilsky have created a sublime and tragic picture of the nightmare of Russia in the 1930s. (MQFF)

Dist/Sales: Intercinema

Hand on the Pulse

Warshow, Joyce P.
2002; USA; 52 min; Documentary

Using interviews, photos and archival footage, *Hand on the Pulse* is the poignant story of Joan Nestle, political and sexual 'bad girl'. Hand on the Pulse traces Joan's life; finding her community in Greenwich Village in the 1950s, celebrating the body in her writings and in her public readings in her black slip, having a lesbian archives in her home for 25 years, teaching students "from colonised backgrounds", participating in the Black civil rights movement as a freedom rider, becoming a feminist, and helping to forge a new lesbian and gay consciousness through grass roots organising. Now in her 60s, Joan continues to celebrate the body as an ageing woman and as a woman with cancer. Cofounder of the Lesbian Herstory Archives in New York City, Joan has made a significant contribution to our understanding of women's sexuality, gender issues, and the preservation of lesbian history and culture for the last half of the 20th century. (Frameline)

Dist/Sales: Frameline

Hanging Garden, The

Fitzgerald, Thom
1997; Canada, UK; 91 min; Drama
P: Thom Fitzgerald, Arnie Gelbert, Louise Garfield; *W:* Thom Fitzgerald; *C:* Daniel Jobin; *E:* Susan Shanks; *M:* John Roby
Cast: Ian Parsons, Peter MacNeill, Troy Veinotte, Kerry Fox

Director Thom Fitzgerald's remarkable debut follows the story of William and his dysfunctional family in Nova Scotia. The tormented, confused, and overweight teenager leaves only to return for his sister's wedding a changed man. In facing his family once again, William relives his painful life's journey. (Cowboy Pictures)

Prod Comp: Alliance Communications, Channel 4, Odean Films
Dist/Sales: Goldwyn, Palace, Wolfe

Happily Ever After
(aka: Além da Paixão)

Barreto, Bruno
1986; Brazil; 106 min; Drama

P: Lucy Barreto, Antônio Calmon; W: Antônio Calmon; C: Affonso Beato; E: Vera Freire
Cast: Regina Duarte, Paul Castelli, Patricio Bisso, Flavio Galvao

A housewife begins a passionate relationship with a bisexual transvestite. Unwittingly she is pulled into his dangerous and criminal world.

Dist/Sales: Facets, Wellspring

Happy Birthday Gemini

Benner, Richard
1980; USA; 108 min; Comedy, Drama
P: Bruce Calnan, Alan King, Richard Benner;
W: Richard Benner; C: James Kelly; E: Stephen Fanfara;
M: Rich Look, Cathy Chamberlain
Cast: Rita Moreno, Madelaine Kahn, Alan Rosenberg, Sarah Molcomb, David Marshall Grant

Francis, a student at Harvard, tries to figure out his sexuality amidst the strange characters and slums of South Philadelphia. His schoolmate, Judith, wants to continue their love affair but Francis finds himself attracted to her blond brother, Randy.

Prod Comp: King-Hitzig Productions
Dist/Sales: Warner, UA

Happy Gordons, The

Crickard, Paula
1994; Ireland; 26 min; Documentary
P: Marilyn Hyndman; C: Conor Hammond, David Hyndman; M: Zrazy

Once upon a time in Ireland a dance called the Gay Gordons had a name change to the Happy Gordons lest there be any confusion. This documentary looks at negotiating identity when being lesbian or gay and Irish. The St Patrick's Day Parade in New York City is a catalyst for identity exploration where Irish gays fight for inclusion to celebrate both their gay and Irish identities. Interviews with individuals who left Ireland because of their homosexuality feature, in particular a man who suffered sexual abuse at the hands of Christian Brothers and another who knew he would never work as a youth worker in Ireland if his sexuality was known. (MQFF)

Prod Comp: Lakme Productions
Dist/Sales: Cinenova

Happy Texas

Illsley, Mark
1999; USA; 104 min; Comedy
P: Mark Illsley, Rick Montgomery, Ed Stone; W: Mark Illsley, Phil Reeves, Ed Stone; C: Bruce Douglas Johnson; E: Norman Buckley; M: Peter Harris
Cast: Steve Zahn, Jeremy Northam, Ally Walker, William H. Macy

Escaped convicts Harry and Wayne flee to the small town of Happy, Texas, where they take on identities of gay, beauty pageant co-ordinators. From this masquerade blooms even stranger couplings and crushes and the possibility of bank robbery for the boys. (Wolfe)

Prod Comp: Marked Entertainment, Miramax
Dist/Sales: Wolfe, BuenaVista, Lauren, Miramax, Palace

Happy Together

(aka: Cheun gwong tsa sit)

Wong, Kar-wai
1997; Hong Kong; 96 min; Drama
P: Ye-cheng Chan, Chan Yecheng; W: Kar-wai Wong;
C: Christopher Doyle; E: William Chang, Ming Lam Wong; M: Danny Chung
Cast: Leslie Cheung, Tony Leung, Chang Chen

A mesmerising story of love lost and endured. Two gay lovers go to Buenos Aires to start over, but find themselves in a familiar vicious circle. Cantonese, Mandarin & Spanish with English subtitles.

Prod Comp: Block 2 Pictures, Jet Tone Production, Seowoo Film Company
Dist/Sales: Potential, Fortissimo, Siren, GoldenHarvest, Kino, Wolfe, NFVLS, ACMI

Happy Together

Hard

Huckert, John
1998; USA; 102 min; Thriller
P: John Huckert, John Matkowsky, Noel Palomaria;
W: John Huckert, John Matkowsky; E: John Huckert;
M: John Huckert, Phil Settle
Cast: Noel Palomaria, Malcolm Moorman, Charles Lanyer, Michael Waite, Steve Andrews

Raymond Vates is a closeted gay detective. Jack is a serial killer preying on young drifters and hustlers. Detective Vates has just been divorced; what the guys on the squad don't know is why, but that doesn't stop them celebrating. One night, Raymond meets Jack in a bar... *Hard* is a gruesome and suspenseful crime thriller that has caused controversy wherever it has screened; the film is the flip side of the campaign for 'positive representation', in cinema. (MQFF)

Prod Comp: MPH Entertainment
Dist/Sales: JourDeFete

Hard Fat

Moffet, Frederic
2002; Canada; 23 min; Documentary

Rick has his own unique way of addressing that time-honoured gay body-image worry. More is more! This fascinating and disturbing documentary takes us into the world of 'gainers', men who like to gain weight, and the men who like to encourage them. These are guys who actively reject the buffed ideals of gay male culture and find liberation in glorifying big bellies. (queerDOC 2002)

Hard God, A

Fitzwater, William
1981; Australia; 80 min; Drama
P: Alan Burke; *W:* Peter Kenna
Cast: Simon Burke, Dawn Lake, Martin Vaughan, Graham Rouse, Philippa Baker

Made for television movie about three brothers from a working-class Catholic family who go to the city home of their married brother after being driven off the family property by drought in the 1940s. In the middle of it all, the 16-year-old brother tries to cope with falling in love with his male friend.

Prod Comp: ABC

Hard Love & How to Fuck in High Heels

Rednour, Shar / Strano, Jackie
2000; USA; 96 min; Erotica
P: Jackie Strano, Shar Rednour
Cast: C. C. Belle, Jackie Strano

Porn made by lesbians for lesbians. Funky femmes, beautiful butches, hot tubs and high camp!

Prod Comp: SIRVideo Productions
Dist/Sales: SIRVideo

Harlequin Exterminator

Balletbò-Coll, Marta
1991; Spain, USA; 12 min; Comedy

A bittersweet comedy about obsessions, lies and cockroaches. Ana is from Barcelona but currently lives in New York City, writing 'roach-killer' commercials for a Hispanic advertising company. Before leaving Spain she had an affair with Mart, who was, and still is, involved with Eli. Difficulties arise when Eli comes to town.

Dist/Sales: Frameline

Harold and Hiroshi

Askinazi, Edward
1991; USA; 40 min; Drama

Harold, a New York Jew, finds himself falling in love with his Japanese college roommate, at the onset of the Second World War. As the two men grow closer, their countries head for conflict. A male-bonding film with sexual-political tensions and a cultural twist. (MQFF)

Dist/Sales: Forefront

Hate Crime

Hirsh, Arie
1992; Australia; 36 min; Drama
P: Arie Hirsh, Joady Weatherup; *W:* Joady Weatherup

Looking at 'gay-bashing', this film offers a complex context in which religion and ignorance about sexuality trigger an often fatal explosion of frustration and fear. Ultimately, the program proposes that unless this crime and its origins in confused sexuality are addressed through education and the media, it cannot be tackled effectively.

Dist/Sales: Marcom

Haunted Summer

Passer, Ivan
1988; USA; 102 min; Drama
P: Martin Poll; *W:* Lewis John Carlino; *C:* Giuseppe Rotunno; *E:* Cesare D'Amico, Richard Fields; *M:* Christopher Young
Cast: Eric Stoltz, Laura Dern, Philip Anglim, Alice Krige, Alex Winter

A beautifully filmed story of the fabled meetings between poets Lord Byron and Shelley in Switzerland in 1816. Among their visitors were novelist Mary Godwin, Shelley's lover, and her half-sister, Claire Clairmont, all of whom indulged themselves and experimented with drugs and sex.

Prod Comp: Cannon Group
Dist/Sales: Col-Tri, 16MM, FirstRelease

Haunted World of Edward D. Wood Jnr, The

Thompson, Brett
1995; USA; 110 min; Documentary
P: Crawford John Thomas, Brett Thompson; *W:* Brett Thompson; *E:* John Lafferty
Cast: Dolores Fuller, Paul Marco, Maila Nurmi, Reverend Lynn Lemon

A feature-length documentary on the controversial film director of the 1950s Edward D. Wood Jnr. He made only five films (some of the worst ever made), now considered cult classics., which include *Plan 9 from Outer Space*, *Glen or Glenda* and *Night of the Ghouls*. Among his many extraordinary traits was often appearing on the set dressed in a frock. Interviews with some of the people who worked with Wood help to build up a picture of this amazing person. A rather tragic figure and an alcoholic, he died at an early age. See the feature film *Ed Wood*.

Prod Comp: Wood-Thomas Pictures
Dist/Sales: Englewood

Haunting of Morella, The

Wynorski, Jim
1991; USA; 82 min; Horror
P: Roger Corman; *W:* R. J. Robertson; *C:* Zoran Hochstätter; *E:* Diane Fingado; *M:* Fredric Ensign Teetsel, Chuch Cirino
Cast: Nicole Eggert, David McCallum, Lana Clarkson, Chris Halstead

A witch places a curse on her daughter so that when the young girl turns 17, her body will be possessed by her own mother.

Prod Comp: New Horizon

Haunting, The

Wise, Robert
1963; UK, USA; 112 min; B&W; Horror
P: Robert Wise; *W:* Nelson Gidding; *C:* David Boulton; *E:* Ernest Walter; *M:* Humphrey Searle
Cast: Julie Harris, Claire Bloom, Richard Johnson, Russ Tamblyn

A 90-year-old New England house is the setting for a group of parapsychologists to study the effects of the supernatural phenomena that are occurring there. Included in the group are an unhappy spinster, a young girl with lesbian tendencies, an anthropologist and the young man who owns the house.

Prod Comp: Argyle Enterprises, MGM
Dist/Sales: Ascanbee, ReelMovies, MGM

He Bop!

Dannelly, Brian
1999; USA; 20 min; Comedy

Ryan is helped to find his gay boy soul by his eccentric (and dead!) grandmother.

Dist/Sales: Discodali

He's a Woman, She's a Man

(aka: Gum gee yuk yip)

Chan, Peter / Lee, Chi
1994; Hong Kong; 106 min; Comedy
P: Eric Tsang; *W:* James Yuen; *C:* Henry Chan; *E:* Kei-hop Chan; *M:* Yun Hui, Tsang-hei Tsui
Cast: Leslie Cheung, Carina Lau, Anita Yuen, Eric Tsang

Rose is a famous pop singer, and Weng idolises her

from afar, romanticising Rose's publicly perfect relationship with Sam, her agent. When Weng dresses as a boy and wins a talent contest organised by Sam, Weng realises her dream of meeting her idols. However to continue the deception Weng must live her new life as a man. Reminiscent of *Yentl*, a hilarious series of attractions, misunderstandings, and lessons in male deportment follow. The story works its way to a heart-warming conclusion, ultimately overcoming boundaries of gender and homophobia. (MQFF)

Prod Comp: United Filmmakers Organization

He's Bald and Racist, He's Gay and Fascist

Brüning, Jürgen
1994; Germany; 20 min; Documentary

This German film explores the fascination that many gay men have for skinheads, a fascination that is both erotic and repellent. Thought-provoking, sexy and challenging, this video tackles contentious material with intelligence and wit. (MQFF)

Dist/Sales: Brüning

He's Like

Goss, John
1986; USA; 26 min; Experimental

An engaging look at a never-seen man who is created by the contradictory descriptions and anecdotes of four men. Themes of masculinity and self-image are discussed.

Dist/Sales: VideoOut

He's My Girl

Beaumont, Gabrielle
1987; USA; 104 min; Comedy
P: Lawrence Mortorff, Angela Schapiro; *W:* Taylor Ames, Charles F. Bohl, Myrica Taylor; *C:* Peter Lyons Collister; *E:* Roy Watts; *M:* Kim Bullard, Roger Webb
Cast: David Hallyday, T. K. Carter, Jennifer Tilly, David Clennon, Monica Parker

The amusing moments are few and far between in this comedy about a man named Carter who dresses in drag so he can accompany his male friend on a free trip to Hollywood.

Prod Comp: International Video Entertainment
Dist/Sales: Roadshow

Head On

(aka: Loaded)

Kokkinos, Ana
1998; Australia; 104 min; Drama
P: Jane Scott; *W:* Ana Kokkinos, Andrew Bovell,

Mira Robertson; *C:* Jaems Grant; *E:* Jill Bilcock;
M: Ollie Olsen
Cast: Alex Dimitriades, Paul Capsis, William Zappa,
Julian Garner, Maria Mercedes

Ari is a young Greek man who is confronting both his traditional family and his sexuality. His journey of self-discovery takes him higher and wilder to the limits of desire and danger until he's on a collision course with reality. Based on the novel *Loaded* by Christos Tsiolkas. English & Greek with English subtitles.

Prod Comp: Great Scott Productions
Dist/Sales: Palace, Millivres, Strand, Wolfe

Head On

Headhunter

Schaeffer, Francis
1989; USA; 88 min; Horror
P: Jay Davidson, Barrie Saint Clair; *W:* Len Spinell;
M: Julian Laxton
Cast: Wayne Crawford, Kay Lenz, Steve Kanaly, June Chadwick, John Fatooh

A Miami cop discovers that his wife has a female lover, so he begins to have an affair with his female partner. Meanwhile, a voodoo demon from Africa arrives in Miami and begins beheading and possessing people—including the cop's wife.

Prod Comp: Gibraltar Entertainment
Dist/Sales: Palace

Health Status Survey

Randera, Safiya
2000; Canada; 12 min; Drama

The power dynamic shifts when one woman has an accident and her lover takes care of her.

Dist/Sales: CFMDC

Hearing Voices

Greytak, Sharon
1990; USA; 87 min; Drama
P: Sharon Greytak

Cast: Stephen Gatta, Michael Davenport, Erika Nagy,
Tim Ahearn

A model, after being physically scarred following reconstruction surgery, floats aimlessly through her empty life. She meets and begins a relationship with the gay lover of her doctor, and her life is turned around. A promising film about a romantic relationship between a straight woman and a gay man, which unfortunately misses the mark due to stilted acting and slow pacing.

Prod Comp: Leisure Time Features

Heart Exposed, The

(aka: La Coeur Découvert)

Laforce, Jean-Yves
1986; Canada; 100 min; Drama

A middle-aged teacher begins a relationship with an actor who is 15 years younger. Things become complicated when it is revealed that the young actor has a son. French with English subtitles.

Awards: San Francisco International Lesbian & Gay Film Festival, 1989: Audience Award for Best Feature
Dist/Sales: CanadianBroadcasting

Heart's Root, The

(aka: A Raiz Do Coração)

Rocha, Paulo
2000; Portugal; 120 min; Drama
P: Paulo Rocha, Gérard Vaugeois; *W:* Raquel Freire,
Paulo Rocha; *C:* Elso Roque; *E:* José Edgar Feldman;
M: José Mario Branco
Cast: Luis Miguel Cintra, Joana Bárcia, Melvil Poupaud,
Isabel Ruth

Sex, secrets, and politics are centre stage in this farcical tale of Cato, a right-wing mayoral candidate for the city of Lisbon, and the love that could ruin him. As the lavish preparations for the Feast of St Antony are underway, the election is heating up. Cato's reactionary supporters are out in force, with banners, songs, and slogans, but are rivalled in their parading and chanting by an outrageously costumed, flamboyant group of drag queens. Into this swirl of confusion and excitement comes word of a compromising videotape that could derail Cato's chance of victory. What no one knows is that the conservative, no-nonsense Cato is desperately in love with the lovely and proper Silvia. And that Silvia used to be Silvio. Just as success seems imminent, Cato's life and career are in danger of being consumed by the chaos all around. (21st Chicago Lesbian & Gay International Film Festival)
Portuguese with English subtitles.

Prod Comp: Suma Films, Boomerang Productions
Dist/Sales: Suma

Heat

Morrissey, Paul
1972; USA; 98 min; Comedy
W: Paul Morrissey, John Hollowell; *C:* Paul Morrissey;
E: Lara Jokel, Jed Johnson; *M:* John Cole
Cast: Joe Dallesandro, Sylvia Miles, Andrea Feldman

This is the story of an unemployed actor, hustler and
former child star, played by Dallesandro, who
returns to Hollywood to make a comeback. He
meets Sally Todd, a faded, ageing movie star. She
tells him she can help his career if he will help her in
the bedroom. But her lesbian daughter drops her
girlfriend and goes for the hustler instead.

Prod Comp: Andy Warhol Enterprises
Dist/Sales: Palace, ParamountHV

Heatwave

Stephens, Kathy
1994; UK; 15 min; Comedy
P: Erol Suleyman

Set in the summer of 1976, 15-year-old Sally has a
crush on her older and more sophisticated neighbour
Louise. But Sally is terrified to confide in Louise for
fear of rejection, so she spends her time in her tree-
house watching Louise sunbake.

Heaven, Earth and Hell

Harris, Thomas, Allen
1995; USA; 26 min; Experimental

Reflecting on the 'trickster' figure in African and
Native American culture recounting the story of his
first love, this beautiful work incorporates the critical
texts of Frantz Fanon, bell hooks and James Baldwin.
(Third World Newsreel)

Dist/Sales: TWN, EAI

Heaven-6-Box

(aka: Tengoku No Muttsu No Hako)

Oki, Hiroyuki
1995; Japan; 60 min; Documentary
P: Matsumoto Norihito; *C:* Hiroyuki Oki;
E: Hiroyuki Oki; *M:* Sato Atsushi, Tsunefuji Hiroki
Cast: Kiyooka Tasuhisa, Takasaki Gensho

Hiroyuki Oki has become something of a star in
Japan as their most famous avant-garde filmmaker.
The council of his local town, Kochi, asked him to
make a documentary on the opening of their new
Museum of Art. It is structured into six 10-minute
portraits of the people and their town. It includes
images of old people, schoolgirls, fishermen, priests
and lots of boys.

Prod Comp: Kochi Museum of Art
Dist/Sales: ImageForum

Heavenly Creatures

Jackson, Peter
1994; New Zealand; 95 min; Drama
P: Jim Booth; *W:* Frances Walsh, Peter Jackson;
C: Alun Bollinger; *E:* Jamie Selkirk; *M:* Peter Dasent
Cast: Melanie Lynsky, Kate Winslet, Sarah Peirse, Diana
Kent, Clive Merrison

Christchurch, New Zealand, 1952. Juliet Hulme
enrols in a new school and is immediately drawn to
Pauline Reiper, a creative genius and a bit of a social
outcast. Although the girls come from different
backgrounds, they both share an outrageous love of
fantasy. Their novel writing and dream world, at
least for a while, is balanced by their mutual
admiration for each other. The obsessive nature of
their relationship worries the girls' parents who
attempt to limit their contact. Both girls react to
their forced separation with violent temper tantrums
and coy manipulations. Juliet's parents decide to
divorce and her father's return to England is seen as
an ideal opportunity to split the girls up permanently. The girls respond by murdering Pauline's
mother. Based on true story.

Prod Comp: WingNut Films, Fontana, Miramax, New
Zealand Film Commission
Dist/Sales: Miramax, BuenaVista, Touchstone, Swank,
Wolfe, NFVLS, ACMI

Heavenly Creatures

Heavy Petting (1988)

Benz, Obie
1988; USA; 77 min; Documentary
P: Obie Benz; *W:* Pierce Rafferty; *C:* Sandi Sissel,
Dyanna Taylor; *E:* Judith Sobel, Joshua Waletzky
Cast: David Byrne, Laurie Anderson, Sandra Bernhard,
Spalding Gray, Alan Ginsberg

A memorable insight into the teenage sex lives of the
famous and not-so-famous during an era of
unprecedented change. A good amount of queer
representation.

Prod Comp: Fossil Films
Dist/Sales: Roadshow, Skouras

Heavy Petting (1991)

Haber, Rosalind
1991; UK; 10 min; Documentary

> Everything you always wanted to know about lesbians and gay men and their pets. Are they the secret ingredient of the 'pretend family'? Child substitutes? Lover substitutes?

Prod Comp: Maya Vision, Channel 4

Hedwig and the Angry Inch

Mitchell, John Cameron
2001; USA; 95 min; Musical
P: Christine Vachon, Katie Roumel, Pamela Koffler;
W: John Cameron Mitchell; *C:* Frank G. DeMarco;
E: Andrew Marcus; *M:* Stephen Trask
Cast: John Cameron Mitchell, Michael Pitt, Andrea Martin, Stephen Trask

> Wildly energetic Off-Broadway glam musical. An aspiring star undergoes a botched sex-change operation (thus the 'angry inch' that's left) and after one failed attempt at stardom, hits the road determined to do everything in her power to get the fame she rightly deserves. (10%)

Prod Comp: Killer Films, New Line Cinema
Dist/Sales: Wolfe, FineLine, NewLine, RoadshowEnt, 10%

Hell Bento!

Sully, Andrew / Broinowski, Anna
1997; Australia; 56 min; Documentary
P: Anna Broinowski; *W:* Anna Broinowski, Adam Broinowski

> An inclusive, uncompromising journey into Japanese subcultures including the Yakuza, the nationalists, the gay and lesbian community, the bikers and the homeless. The film also sets out to challenge assumptions about Japan's younger generation and what their rapidly westernising lifestyle might indicate for the future.

Prod Comp: Tetrapod
Dist/Sales: Ronin, ACMI

Hell For Leather

Scherrer, Dominik
1998; UK; 28 min; Comedy

> Satan falls from heaven—but this time it's London 1998.

Dist/Sales: Ulmann

Hell's Highway

Brown, Rowland
1932; USA; 62 min; B&W; Drama
W: Rowland Brown, Samuel Ornitz, Robert Tasker;
C: Edward Cronjager; *E:* William Hamilton
Cast: Richard Dix, Tom Brown, C. Henry Gordon, Rochelle Hudson, Oscar Apfel

> Frank 'Duke' Ellis, serving time on a chain gang, has to change his escape plans when his brother is brought in as a prisoner. It's tough and rough and covers everything from issues of race, to homosexuality.

Prod Comp: RKO

Hellion Heatwave

Castro, Rick
1999; USA; 86 min; Erotica
Cast: Tom Turbine, B. J. Bush, Bo Killer, Eddie T., Boo Johnson

> Filmed in Tucson, Arizona, photographer Rick Castro gets an assortment of non-porn men (musclemen, hunks, ex-cons) to recount sex stories and then gets them to strip for his camera. (Wolfe)

Prod Comp: Pyewackett Productions
Dist/Sales: Wolfe

Henry and June

Kaufman, Philip
1990; USA; 131 min; Drama
P: Peter Kaufman; *W:* Philip Kaufman, Rose Kaufman;
C: Philippe Rousselot; *E:* Vivien Hillgrove Gilliam, Dede Allen, William S. Scharf; *M:* Mark Adler
Cast: Fred Ward, Uma Thurman, Maria de Medeiros, Richard E. Grant, Kevin Spacey

> An intelligent and provocative drama about the passionate love triangle involving Anais Nin, writer Henry Miller and his wife, June. Set in Paris in the 1930s, it is beautifully photographed, producing a sensuous and atmospheric film. Based on the novel by Anais Nin.

Prod Comp: Universal, Walrus
Dist/Sales: UIP, Swank, Universal, Wolfe

Her Life as a Man

Miller, Robert Ellis
1984; USA; 96 min; Comedy
W: Joanna Crawford, Diane English;
C: Kees Van Oostrum
Cast: Joan Collins, Robert Culp, Marc Singer, Robyn Douglass, Laraine Newman

> An experienced female reporter disguises herself as a man to secure the sports-writing job she desires in this made for TV movie. She gets the job, and a lot of funny and embarrassing moments as well. Similar to the drag genre of *Victor/Victoria* and *Tootsie*.

Prod Comp: LS Entertainment

Her Urge

Gilbert, Barry
2001; USA; 15 min; Comedy

A cute girl with high academic ideals falls for an even cuter, yet ultra-cool chick, who at first doesn't even know she's alive.

Dist/Sales: Seduced

Her Urge

Heterosexual Agenda, The

Woods, Mark Kenneth
2001; Canada; 12 min; Comedy

A subversive take on anti-gay propaganda issues by religious types which looks at turning the tables on the consequences of choosing a heterosexual lifestyle. Presented with thought-provoking humour. (MQFF)

Dist/Sales: VTape

Heterosexuality

Beadle-Blair, Rikki
1998; UK; 25 min; Comedy

Kwame is a typical London teenager who lives for football and rap music, but his family life is different from other guys his age. His father is an outrageous, gay man who is devastated to find out that his son plans to lose his virginity—to a girl! An utterly queer twist on teen rebellion and generational conflict. How will Kwame' s father cope with his budding heterosexuality? Made in short form as a precursor to famed Channel 4 series *Metrosexuality*.

Prod Comp: Channel 4
Dist/Sales: Vicarious

Hey, Happy!

Gonick, Noam
2000; Canada; 75 min; Experimental
P: Laura Michalchyshyn; *W:* Noam Gonick, David McIntosh; *C:* Paul Suderman; *E:* Bruce Little; *M:* Chris Robinson
Cast: Jeremie Yuen, Craig Aftanas, Clayton Godson, Johnny Simone, Dita Vendetta

DJ Sabu spins Armageddon when his overactive libido leads him into teenage pregnancy. His mythic quest for two thousand boys ends with Happy, a paranoid UFO-ologist to whom aliens promise to appear (as his love child). Spanky is an evil hairdresser trying to foil Sabu's mission at every turn. He is the self-proclaimed 'biggest bitch in the world'. The action unfolds at a series of raves on old Garbage Hill in a strange place we call Winnipeg. *Hey, Happy!* depicts an optimistic vision of the apocalypse. Director Noam Gonick says that tens of millions of religious fundamentalists can't be wrong, 'There must be a connection between biblical 'end-times' and fags'. (Mongrel)

Prod Comp: Big Daddy Beer Guts, Mongrel Media
Dist/Sales: Mongrel

Hey, Happy!

Hey Sailor, Hey Sister

Spyke
1998; USA; 23 min; Erotica

Hey Sailor, Hey Sister is the story of a naval officer who, coming to port with just her duffel bag and leather chaps, goes looking for adventure—and finds it. Has the sailor resumed home for good or is she on weekend leave? Is the woman she meets on the docks a working girl or a kindred soul looking for fun? Do they fall in love, or do they just...? (Wolfe)

Dist/Sales: Wolfe

Hidden Assassin

(aka: The Shooter)

Kotcheff, Ted
1995; USA; 100 min; Action
P: Silvio Muraglia, Paul Pompian; *W:* Billy Ray, Meg Thyer, Yves André Martin; *C:* Fernando Argüelles; *E:* Ralph Brunjes; *M:* Stefano Mainetti
Cast: Dolph Lundgren, Maruschka Detmers, Asumpta Serna, John Ashton

After the assassination of the Cuban Ambassador in New York, Michael Dane, a CIA agent is sent to Prague to prevent any further terrorist attacks. Nikita, a lesbian nightclub owner, is one of the suspected killers. Things become more complicated and Dane finds he will have to fight to survive.

Prod Comp: PolyGram Filmed Entertainment, Le Studio Canal+, Arco Films SL
Dist/Sales: PolyGram, BuenaVista

Hidden Child

Whitley, Brian
1998; USA; 22 min; Drama

A young boy is haunted by memories of his late sister, and with family secrets that slowly present in a terrifying fashion. A queer perspective on love and loss.

Hidden Injuries

Finlayson, Kaya
Australia; 15 min; B&W; Drama
P: Kaya Finlayson, John Horniblow; *W:* Kaya Finlayson

A teenage boy is pushed by peer-group pressure to partake in a brutal gay bashing. A conflict between the leader of the gang and the boy leaves him behind after the bashing. The teenager then returns to the scene of the murder to appease his guilty conscience.

Hide and Seek

Friedrich, Su
1996; USA; 65 min; B&W; Documentary
P: Katie Roumel, Eve Kolodner; *W:* Su Friedrich, Cathy Nan Quinlan; *C:* Jim Denault; *E:* Su Friedrich
Cast: Chels Holland, Ariel Mara, Alicia Manta

Hide and Seek, mixes documentary and fiction to create a fascinating portrait of lesbian childhood. Revealing the imaginary universe of young lesbians, it's about being at an age when sexual feelings are still vague. The fictional narrative tells the story of Lou: a 12-year-old girl living in Brooklyn in the mid 1960s, coming to terms with her burgeoning sexuality. Her story is skilfully woven between interviews with 20 adult women who recount salient moments from their childhoods, including their first attractions, how they felt when they first heard the word lesbian and thoughts about the possible cause for their homosexuality. Mixing several genres, the film also includes more than 100 photographs of lesbians when they were young girls, and archival footage from educational films and home movies. (WMM)

Awards: LA Outfest, 1996: Best Documentary
Prod Comp: Downstream Productions, Independent Television Service
Dist/Sales: WMM

High Art

Cholodenko, Lisa
1998; Canada, USA; 101 min; Drama
P: Dolly Hart, Jeff Levy-Hinte, Susan A. Stover; *W:* Lisa Cholodenko; *C:* Tami Reiker; *E:* Amy E. Duddleston; *M:* Tracy McKnight
Cast: Ally Sheedy, Radha Micthell, Patricia Clarkson, Gabriel Mann

Syd is a young women with a perfectly nice boyfriend and a perfectly good job working for an upmarket photography magazine in New York City. But she is bored and keen for adventure, hoping to achieve more status and celebrity through work. A chance encounter with a legendary underground photographer, Lucy Berliner, enables Syd to move into the exotic fringes of the art world, as well as allowing her to explore her own sexuality and her own desires. But *High Art* is not a New Age film: we watch Syd's pursuit of Lucy and of fame, and we are asked to confront deeply disturbing questions about the amorality of contemporary relationships and culture. Art may be what all the characters in this film claim to care about, but their real pursuits are status and fame. Only Lucy Berliner, passionate about her photography, seems capable of committing herself to a notion of art that is not simply reducible to commerce. But Lucy's passion comes at a cost: life on the fringe, the dangers of drugs, and the continual question of where the rent money is going to come from. The final moments of this film, in which Syd faces what is really of value in the world of 'high art', are shattering. (ACMI)

Prod Comp: 391 Productions, October Films
Dist/Sales: October, Wolfe, ACMI

High Heels

(aka: Tacones lejanos)

Almodóvar, Pedro
1991; Spain; 115 min; Comedy
W: Pedro Almodóvar; *C:* Alfredo F. Mayo;
E: José Salcedo; *M:* Ryuichi Sakamoto
Cast: Victoria Abril, Marisa Paredes, Miguel Bosé

Becky has had almost as many husbands as gold records. She abandoned her daughter from her first marriage to focus on her career as a pop singer. Rebecca has been raised by her father since the age of 13, but remains obsessed by her absent mother to the point where she marries one of her mother's former lovers. A chance reunion between Becky and Rebecca's husband unleashes a chain of bizarre events. Spanish with English subtitles.

Prod Comp: Le Studio Canal+
Dist/Sales: Miramax, Warner

High Tech Rice

Cabatu, Joanne L. / Mirkin, Ekaterine
1996; Russia, USA; 25 min; Comedy

An exploration of how a Filipino–American lesbian must come to terms with living in two cultures at the same time, and her love-hate relationship with her answering machine.

Higher Learning

Singleton, John
1995; USA; 128 min; Drama
P: John Singleton, Paul Hall; *W:* John Singleton; *C:* Peter Lyons Collister; *E:* Bruce Cannon; *M:* Stanley Clarke
Cast: Omar Epps, Kristy Swanson, Michael Rapaport, Ice Cube, Jennifer Connelly

Higher Learning is the story of three new college students—track star Malik, who finds he must run faster and study harder than ever; innocent Kristen, who gets an abrupt initiation into this tough new world and has a lesbian affair with the head of the feminist group; and lonely Remy, an outsider who sparks a tragic chain of events that changes all of their lives.

Prod Comp: New Deal, Columbia
Dist/Sales: Col-Tri, 16MM, FirstRelease, Columbia

Hired to Kill

Mastorakis, Nico / Rader, Peter
1991; USA; 93 min; Action
P: Peter Rader; *W:* Nico Mastorakis, Kirk Ellis, Fred C. Perry; *C:* Andreas Bellis, Michael Stringer
Cast: Brian Thompson, Oliver Reed, George Kennedy, Jose Ferrer, Michelle Moffett

A mercenary poses as a gay photographer on a fashion shoot with six sexy models in order to break a rebel leader out of an impenetrable Latin American prison.

Dist/Sales: ParamountHV

History Lessons

Hammer, Barbara
2000; USA; 66 min; Documentary
P: Barbara Hammer, Anna Viola Hallberg; *C:* Barbara Hammer, Carolyn McCartney, Ann T. Rossetti
Cast: Carmolita Tropicana, Coco Fusco, Dred, Elvis Herselvis, Mo. B. Dick

History Lessons is an exploration of lesbian images shown in a compelling, humorous and empowering way. Focusing on pervading images prior to Stonewall the film exposes not only popular lesbian representations in culture and entertainment but also the controlling characterisations proliferated by medical, scientific and legal worlds.

Prod Comp: Barbara Hammer Productions
Dist/Sales: Hammer, Wolfe, FirstRunFeatures, FirstRun/Icarus, VideoAmericain

History of the World According to a Lesbian, The

Hammer, Barbara
1988; USA; 22 min; Experimental

Traces the invisible and visible reference to women who love women from prehistory to contemporary times with the sarcastic sounds of the 1950s lesbian quartet, The Sluts from Hell. (Frameline)

Dist/Sales: Frameline

Hit and Runway

Livingston, Christopher
1999; USA; 109 min; Comedy
P: Christopher Livingston, Andrew Charas, Chris D'Annibale; *W:* Christopher Livingston, Jaffe Cohen; *C:* David Timblety; *E:* Christopher Livingston, Rhonda l. Mitrani; *M:* Frank Piazza
Cast: Peter Jacobson, Michael Parducci, Kerr Smith, Judy Prescott

When Alex, a good Catholic heterosexual boy, teams up with Elliot a New York City Jewish gay boy to write a screen play it's hard enough to overcome their differences let alone finish the play. When Elliot scores a date with a gay waiter, Alex and Elliot's relationship and script takes a dramatic turn.

Prod Comp: Mirador Films
Dist/Sales: Lot47, Wolfe

hITCH

hITCH

Gray, Bradley Rust
1999; USA; 18 min; Drama

A journey of sexual self discovery for two sexy cowboys, in this brooding road movie.

HIV Rollercoaster

Lang, Paul
2001; USA; 27 min; Documentary

From cocktail therapy and community policing to gay male porn identity, life in prison, barebacking, and condom politics, this experimental documentary takes you on a rollercoaster ride through the ever-changing world of HIV. (2002 Mardi Gras Film Festival)

Dist/Sales: VTape

HIV Rollercoaster

Hold you Tight

(aka: Yue Kuai Le)

Kwan, Stanley
1998; Hong Kong; 95 min; Drama
P: Raymond Chow; *W:* Jimmy Ngai; *C:* Pung-leung Kwan; *E:* Maurice Li; *M:* Keith Leung, Yat-yiu Yu
Cast: Sunny Chan, Yue-lin Ko, Wing-kiu Lau, Eric Tsang

Four characters in search of an author (and love). Ah Moon is unhappily married; her husband, Fung Wai, only cares about his work; Tong is a deluded homosexual who divides his time between the bar and the bathhouse; and Jie is a young boy who is still sexually undecided. But above all, these are four portraits of the bitterness that comes from solitude and the incomprehension that derives from repressed emotions. This is the first film that Kwan directed after revealing he was gay and, as a result, it is the first time he no longer needs to use female alter egos in order to express his thoughts and experiences. (42nd Thessaloniki Film Festival)
Cantonese with English subtitles.

Prod Comp: Golden Harvest, Kwan's Creation Workshop
Dist/Sales: PonyCanyon

Holding

Beeson, Constance
1971; USA; 13 min; Drama
P: Constance Beeson

Romantic and impressionistic interpretation of a lesbian relationship exploring the fantasies of two women falling in love with each other.

Dist/Sales: NFVLS, Canyon

Hole

Cornell, Clare / Buxton, Rodney
2001; USA; 18 min; Experimental

A sultry, sweaty rumination on a man's trip to the local sauna.

Dist/Sales: DMC

Holi: Festival of Fire

Mehta, Ketan
1984; India; 114 min; Drama
P: Ketan Mehta, Pradeep Uppoor; *W:* Ketan Mehta, Mahesh Elkunchwar; *C:* Jehangir Choudhari; *E:* Subhash Sehgal; *M:* Rajat Dholakia
Cast: Rahul Ranade, Sanjeer Gandhi

When a holiday during the Holi spring festival is cancelled by the authorities of a hostel, the students riot in protest. A homosexual student is blackmailed into informing on the culprits and they retaliate. Hindi with English subtitles.

Dist/Sales: NFVLS

Hollow Reed

Pope, Angela
1995; UK; 100 min; Drama
P: Elizabeth Karlsen; *W:* Paula Milne;
C: Remi Adefarasin; *E:* Sue Wyatt; *M:* Anne Dudley
Cast: Martin Donovan, Joely Richardson, Ian Hart, Jason Flemyng, Sam Bould

Following the break-up of his marriage after revealing his homosexuality, GP Martin Wyatt loses custody of his son Oliver to his now ex-wife Hannah and her new partner Frank. Soon Oliver turns up at his father's house claiming to have been beaten up by thugs. After another incident, Martin puts two and two together and comes to the conclusion that Frank has been beating Oliver without Hannah's knowledge. Martin then begins a long courtroom custody battle to win back his son.

Prod Comp: Scala Productions, Senator Film, Channel 4
Dist/Sales: Wolfe, Col-Tri, LionsGate, FilmFour, Sogepaq

Home for the Holidays

Foster, Jodie
1995; USA; 99 min; Comedy
P: Jodie Foster, Peggy Rajski; *W:* W. D. Richter;
C: Lajos Koltai; *E:* Lynzee Klingman; *M:* Mark Isham
Cast: Holly Hunter, Robert Downey Jnr, Anne
Bancroft, Dylan McDermott, Steve Guttenburg

Often billed as Jodie Foster's first gay film, it stars
Holly Hunter as a woman at the end of her rope
who is forced to endure one of the greatest horrors
known... a family Christmas. Featuring an all-star
cast including Robert Downey Jnr as her gay sibling,
Anne Bancroft, Dylan McDermott and Steve
Guttenburg, this romantic comedy about one wildly
eccentric family will leave you not only smiling, but
also firm in the belief that the best family is your
queer family. (MQFF)

Prod Comp: PolyGram Filmed Entertainment, Paramount Pictures
Dist/Sales: 16MM, FilmsInc, Paramount, Sogepaq, Swank

Hollow Reed

Home Movie

Oxenberg, Jan
1973; USA; 12 min; Experimental

A warm and humorous semi-autobiographical look
at stereotypes and expectations of lesbianism. Using
home-movie footage of herself as a child and
cheerleader, Oxenberg talks about growing up as a
lesbian and the experience of coming out.

Dist/Sales: Cinenova, NFVLS

Home Sweet Home

Haber, Rosalind
1991; UK; 17 min; Documentary
P: Rebecca Dobbs

Lesbians and gays in various housing set-ups discuss
the different strategies that have been adopted by
them in order to integrate their housing needs with
their lifestyles.

Prod Comp: Maya Vision, Channel 4
Dist/Sales: MayaVision

Home You Go

Cullen, Colette
1993; UK; 11 min; Comedy

A tale of ordinary obsession about a dishevelled dyke
who discovers the keys to an older woman's art deco
flat. In an almost bewitched mood, she settles in to
raid the woman's life. (Cinenova)

Dist/Sales: Cinenova

Home-Made Melodrama

Duckworth, Jacqui
1982; UK; 51 min; Experimental
Cast: Lyndley Stanley, Cass Bream, Joy Chamberlain,
Madelaine McNamara

An autobiographical view, set in a domestic
landscape, of a lesbian-feminist ménage à trois
involving three women. The love triangle is seen as
difficult, even painful at times, while positive aspects
of the relationships, including sexual exploration, are
shown.

Dist/Sales: Cinenova

Homecoming Queen

Bracewell, Charles
1999; Australia; 45 min; Documentary

Documentary which chronicles the return of Miz
Ima Starr's/Charles Bracewell's return to his home
town to face an unhappy childhood, and to celebrate
his successful drag present.

Homicidal

Castle, William
1961; USA; 87 min; B&W; Horror
P: William Castle; *W:* Robb White; *C:* Burnett Guffey;
E: Edwin H. Bryant; *M:* Hugo W. Friedhofer

Cast: Glenn Corbett, Jean Arliss, Eugenie Leontovich, Patricia Breslin

The film opens with a young couple deciding to marry on impulse, and going to the registry office. After they have taken their vows the young bride stabs and murders the groom. She goes into hiding as the nurse of an elderly mute woman, but the old woman becomes suspicious and ends up dead too. The old woman's niece discovers that a male friend is actually the nurse in male drag. It turns out that the nurse has had a sex-change operation in order to cover up his/her crimes.

Prod Comp: William Castle Productions, Columbia
Dist/Sales: Columbia

Homme Blessé, L'

(aka: The Wounded Man)

Chéreau, Patrice
1984; France; 90 min; Drama
P: Ariel Zeitoun, Marie-Laure Reyre, Claude Berri;
W: Patrice Chéreau, Hervé Guibert; *C:* Renato Berta;
E: Denise de Casabianca; *M:* Albert Ayler, Fiorenzo Carpi
Cast: Jean-Hughes Anglade, Vittorio Mezzogiorno, Claude Berri, Roland Bertin

Henri is a shy, quiet man who comes right out of his shell and into obsession when he meets a street hustler. His lust for him finally explodes with horrible results.

Prod Comp: France 3 Cinéma, Gaumont

Homme Que J'aime, L'

(aka: The Man I Love)

Giusti, Stéphane
1997; France; 87 min; Drama
P: Alain Tortevoix, Michel Rivelin; *W:* Stéphane Giusti;
C: Jacques Bouquin; *E:* Catherine Schwartz;
M: Lazare Boghossian
Cast: Jean-Michel Portal, Marcial Di Fonzo Bo, Mathilde Seigner, Jacques Hansen

Gay pool boy Martin has made no secret of his crush on attractive, but straight lifeguard Lucas. Martin's attraction is so compelling that it's not long before Lucas is responding. However, when he learns that Martin has full-blown AIDS, he becomes confused by his feelings of fear and caring. Despite his feelings, he commits himself to Martin and takes on the role as Martin's main caregiver. French with English subtitles.

Prod Comp: Onya Production, La Sept-Arte, Ellipse Programme
Dist/Sales: ArteFrance

Homo Heights

(aka: Happy Heights)

Moore, Sara
1998; USA; 92 min; Comedy
P: Kate Lehmann; *W:* Sara Moore; *C:* David Doyle;
E: Vaughn Garland Smith; *M:* Evan Lurie
Cast: Quentin Crisp, Lea DeLaria, Stephen Sorrentino, David Fenley

Malcom, an ageing gay icon, is being held prisoner by Maria Callous, the all-powerful leader of the gay Mafia in Homo Heights. Planning his escape, Malcom seeks the help of Clementine, a tough-talking, soft-hearted driver for the Lavender Cab Company, who concocts an escape that is literally out of this world! (Wolfe)

Prod Comp: Lehmann-Moore Productions
Dist/Sales: Lehmann-Moore, Wolfe, 10%

Homo Promo

Homo Promo

Olson, Jenni
1991; USA; 75 min; Comedy
P: Jenni Olson

This fast-paced overview offers a crash course in gay and lesbian movie history from 1956–1976, and a colourful look at the best (and worst) Hollywood hard-sells of gay and lesbian subject matter. (Frameline)

Dist/Sales: Frameline, ArtisticLicense

Homophobia in Hollywood

Beavan, Clare
1991; UK; 24 min; Documentary
P: Shauna Brown

In 1992 the release of *Basic Instinct* and *The Silence of the Lambs* resulted in gay and lesbian activists organising nation-wide protests against Hollywood's portrayal of gay characters in films. Homophobia in Hollywood features interviews with director Paul Verhoeven (*Basic Instinct*), screenwriter Ted Tally (*Silence of the Lambs*) and producer Howard Rosenman (*Father of the Bride*) who discuss their reaction to gay and lesbian critics of their work. Gay director Tom Kalin (*Swoon*) discusses some of the difficulties he has with notions of 'positive' and 'negative' representation.

Prod Comp: Channel 4
Dist/Sales: ACMI

Homophobia: That Painful Problem

Bernard, Lionel
2000; France; 52 min; Documentary

Documentary which explores the realities of homophobia worldwide. Countries such as the US, China, Cuba, the UK, France and India report regular gay hate crimes that are endorsed by politicians, religious leaders, and the general public.

Dist/Sales: Dominant7

Homosexuality: A Film for Discussion

Creed, Barbara
1974; Australia; 43 min; B&W; Documentary

A group of lesbians and gay men discuss their lives, childhood, school years, growing up, prejudice, family and relationships. All describe the crucial importance of gay liberation and how it changed their lives. Also included are discussions with parents of the group and hilarious street interviews with an often hostile public.

Dist/Sales: ACMI

Homosexuality and Lesbianism

1976; USA; 26 min; Documentary

Psychologists, psychiatrists and queer people speak directly to high-school-age youngsters and respond to their questions, concerns and fears about homosexuality.

Prod Comp: Document Associates
Dist/Sales: CinemaGuild

Homoteens

Jubela, Joan
1993; USA; 60 min; Documentary

Five young gays and lesbians from New York talk about their very different lives and sexual identities. Vivid and candid autobiographical portraits that are worth seeing as they juxtapose cultural, racial and religious understandings of queerness. (MQFF)

Awards: San Francisco International Lesbian & Gay Film Festival, 1993: Audience Award for Best Video
Dist/Sales: Frameline

Hooking Up

Tec, Roland
1995; USA; 13 min; Comedy

Anyone who's ever done the casual-sex thing will smile/cringe with recognition as we follow the urban mating rituals of five pairs of gay men.

Dist/Sales: Pinkplot

Hope Along the Wind: The Life of Harry Hay

Slade, Eric
2001; USA; 57 min; Documentary

This much-anticipated documentary takes us through the fascinating and extraordinary life of Harry Hay; labour organiser, Marxist teacher, and founding member of the Mattachine Society, one of the first gay rights organisations in the US. Harry has been at centre stage of gay pride in the US for more than half a century. His story provides a chronicle of the gay rights movement, as well as a history of California in the 20th century. Harry Hay joined the Communist Party in the early 1930s and participated in the San Francisco General Strike of 1934. In the mid 1950s he was called before the House un-American Activities Committee, and around this time Harry started the Mattachine Society. This momentous film features poignant interviews with Harry and many of the surviving original members of this historic and brave group of gay men. In the last 40 years, Harry has immersed himself in the counterculture youth movement, the Radical Fairies, and Native American culture. (Frameline)

Dist/Sales: Frameline

Hope is a Thing With Feathers

Abrahams Wilson, Andy
1999; USA; 28 min; Experimental

A lush and lyrical film built around a poem which San Francisco poet and artist Beau Riley wrote as his lover of twelve years lay dying, the film shows one man plumbing the depths of his sorrow to find meaning through the strength of his mind, imagination, and devotion to his partner. (Open Eye Films)

Dist/Sales: OpenEye, NewDay

h

Horror Vacui: The Fear of Emptiness

(aka: Horror Vacui: Die Angst vor der Leere)

von Praunheim, Rosa
1984; Germany; 85 min; Drama
W: Cecil Brown, Marianne Enzensberger, Rosa von Praunheim; *C:* Elfi Mikesch; *E:* Mike Shephard, Rosa von Praunheim; *M:* Maran Gosov
Cast: Lotti Huber, Folkert Milster, Friedrich Steinhauer

Two young gay men, Hannes and Frankie, find their relationship crumbling as one of the men becomes obsessed with a religious cult called 'Optimal Optimism', run by Madame C, an old Nazi. When the members find out that Frankie is gay he is continually raped by both men and women of the cult. It is left up to Hannes to rescue him.

Prod Comp: Rosa von Praunheim Filmproduktion

Horse Dreams in BBQ Country

Baer, Daniel
1996; USA; 20 min; Documentary

This film charms gay and straight audiences alike with its funny, bittersweet portrayal of the long-time love between two gay ranchers in the patriotic, lottery-crazy land of South Texas. Though they struggle to make ends meet, Mario Borjas—Tejano to the core—and David Ewell, a Texas transplant, have somehow managed to fashion a rural life that has revolved around horses and each other for 14 years. (Frameline)

Dist/Sales: Frameline

Hotel New Hampshire, The

Richardson, Tony
1984; USA; 110 min; Comedy, Drama
P: Neil Hartley, Pieter Kroonenburg, David Patterson; *W:* Tony Richardson; *C:* David Watkin; *E:* Robert K. Lambert; *M:* Jacques Offenbach
Cast: Jodie Foster, Nastassia Kinski, Beau Bridges, Rob Lowe, Paul McCrane

In an attempt to unite his rather peculiar family, a man decides to buy an old girls' school and turn it into a family-run hotel. The result is a series of wild misadventures and sexual shenanigans, with a number a gay characters—Foster examines her sexuality with Kinski, dressed in a bear suit. Based on the novel by John Irving.

Prod Comp: Woodfall, Filmline Productions, Producers Circle, Yellowbill Productions
Dist/Sales: Palace, Orion

Hours and Times, The

Munch, Christopher
1991; USA; 58 min; B&W; Drama
P: Christopher Munch; *W:* Christopher Munch;
C: Christopher Munch; *E:* Christopher Munch
Cast: Ian Hart, David Angus

Munch ruminates on the possibilities that a relationship occurred between John Lennon and gay Beatles manager Brian Epstein during a trip to Barcelona in 1963.

Awards: Sundance Film Festival, 1992: Special Jury Recognition
Prod Comp: Antarctic Pictures
Dist/Sales: TLA, Strand, GoodMachine, NFVLS, ACMI

The Hours and Times

House of Pain

Hoolboom, Mike
1995; Canada; 80 min; B&W; Experimental
P: Mike Hoolboom; *W:* Mike Hoolboom; *C:* Mike Hoolboom; *E:* Mike Hoolboom; *M:* Earle Peach
Cast: Charles Costello, Paul Couillard, Janieta Eyre

Portrays different sexual acts in four chapters (*Precious*, *Scum*, *Kisses* and *Shiteater*) with industrial rock and soundscapes replacing dialogue.

Dist/Sales: CFMDC

How I Love You

(aka: Shou Bhebbak)

Zaatari, Akram
2001; Lebanon; 29 min; Documentary

Young, Lebanese gay men talk about identity, their sex lives, their relationships to their bodies and love. There identities remain secret due to the criminality of homosexuality in their home country.

Dist/Sales: Majnounak

How Old is the River?

(aka: Fuyu no Kappa)

Shiori, Kazama
1994; Japan; 115 min; Drama
P: Nishida Nobuyoshi, Nishimura Takashi;
W: Kazama Shiori, Ogawa Tomoko; *C:* Suzuki Akihiko;
E: Kazama Shiori
Cast: Ito Akiko, Cho Bang-Ho, Tanabe Seiichi, Wakuta Rijin

Three half-brothers share a house in the country near Tokyo. Ichitaro, the eldest, is a failed artist, turned piano teacher. Takeshi, the second, is a college dropout. The third, Tsuguo, who is not related by blood, is an art student and has a crush on Ichitaro. Their father decides to sell the farm and the film shows the last few weeks of their lives there. Problems begin when their female cousin Sakeko arrives and receives attention from Ichitaro.

Prod Comp: Fuyu no Kappa Unit Production, First Wood Entertainment
Dist/Sales: Uplink

How to Female Ejaculate

Kinney, Nan
1992; USA; 47 min; Documentary

Female ejaculation: what it is, what it is not, and how to achieve it. Beginning with a lecture that focuses on medical particulars and physical descriptions using charts and diagrams, Fanny Fatale uses her own vagina for a close-up look at feminine ejaculation. She explains that it is more than a simple orgasm, that particular vaginal exercises help bring it about and that there are two kinds of female ejaculation: clitoral and uterine (G-spot). The second half of the film finds Fatale joined by three women in discussion that concludes with group masturbation exercise that brings about several sexually graphic female eruptions.

How to Find your Goddess Spot

1993; USA; 36 min; Documentary

An exploration of women's G-spots (or better yet, Goddess spots) through the use of the Wondrous Vulva Puppet, drawings, a road map and, finally a personal, up-close demonstration. After just one viewing, no woman should ever get lost finding her own (and another's) pleasure zones.

Prod Comp: House O'Chicks

How to Have a Sex Party

Lane, Dorrie
1991; USA; 30 min; Erotica

How to Have a Sex Party is 30 minutes of provocative

and spontaneous lesbian sexual pleasure. The film begins with single and coupled women at a poetry reading. After a poem, the action begins.

How to Kill Her

Simo, Ana Maria
1990; USA; 15 min; B&W; Drama
P: Ela Troyano

A moody tale of romance and revenge by New York playwright Ana Maria Simo in a film noir style incorporating a jazz soundtrack. (WMM)

Dist/Sales: WMM

Howling II: Your Sister is a Werewolf

Mora, Philippe
1985; USA; 91 min; Horror
P: Steven Lane; *W:* Robert Sarno, Gary Brandner; *C:* Geoffrey Stephenson; *E:* Charles Bernstein;
M: Steve Parsons
Cast: Christopher Lee, Annie McEnroe, Sybil Danning, Reb Brown, Marsha A. Hunt

Widely lambasted sequel to *The Howling* sends up of the horror genre, with Christopher Lee as a werewolf and Sybil Danning playing Stirba, a bisexual queen witch from Transylvania. An investigator discovers a worldwide conspiracy of werewolves and with the help of a turncoat brother, Lee, puts an end to the coven.

Prod Comp: Granite, Hemdale, Cinema 86, Thorn EMI
Dist/Sales: Warner, Hemdale, HBO, Republic

Hu-Du-Men

(aka: Stage Door)

Shu, Kei
1996; Hong Kong; 100 min; Drama
P: Clifton Ko; *W:* Raymond To; *C:* Bill Wong;
E: Chi-leung Kwong, Kei Shu; *M:* Yoshihide Otomo
Cast: Josephine Siao, Anita Yuen, Daniel Chan, Waise Lee

More gender-bending confusion from Hong Kong in this powerful melodrama. Hu-Du-Men is the term for the imaginary line actors cross when taking to the stage and surrendering themselves to their roles, and no one crosses that line better than Lang Kim-sum, who is brilliant and believable playing the male roles in a successful Cantonese Opera troupe. But the gender confusion doesn't stop when she leaves the stage. People tend to see her only as her characters—one devoted female fan desperately wants to marry her—and when her teenage daughter Mimi falls in love with a girl, Lang begins to question her own femininity. Eventually Lang goes to the lesbian bar where Mimi's girlfriend Jojo works intending to straighten things out. Instead, Lang becomes convinced of Jojo's genuine feelings for Mimi and ends up supporting their relationship. Through it all, Lang must rely on the strengths and experiences of her on-stage characters to guide her through her often confusing real life in this award-winning film from director Kei Shu. Cantonese with English subtitles. (21st San Francisco International Lesbian & Gay Film Festival)

Prod Comp: Ko Chi-sum Productions
Dist/Sales: RimFilm

Hubo un Tiempo en que Los Suenos Dieron Paso a Largas Noches de Insomnio

Hernandez, Julian
1998; Mexico; 50 min; Drama

Bruno, a young man, works at putting up flyers around town. When he spies handsome Umberto working at a fairground, the two begin an on-again, off-again relationship—while Bruno himself is cruised by an elderly stranger, Paolo. The film's psychologically dense characterisations are capped by breathtaking black and white cinematography and austere direction that recalls Mexico's legendary Cinema D'Oro. (1998 LA Outfest)
Spanish with no subtitles.

Hunger, The

Scott, Tony
1983; UK; 94 min; Horror
P: Richard A. Shepherd; *W:* Ivan Davis, Thomas Davis Jnr, James Costigan; *C:* Stephen Galdblatt, Tom Mangravite; *E:* Pamela Power; *M:* Michael Rubin, Denny Jaeger
Cast: Catherine Deneuve, David Bowie, Susan Sarandon, Cliff De Young

A classic vampire story with Deneuve and Bowie as lovers. But as the fountain-of-youth wears out for Bowie, Deneuve is looking for a new mate, who turns up in the form of Sarandon, a doctor who is researching ageing. A very slick film, with Deneuve and Sarandon looking sumptuous, and making convincing lovers.

Prod Comp: MGM, United Artists, Peerford Ltd
Dist/Sales: Wolfe, MGM

Hungry Hearts

Kinney, Nan / Sundahl, Debi
1989; USA; 30 min; Drama

Set at an ocean resort where two real-life strippers, Pepper and Reva, engage in sensual and passionate lovemaking.

Prod Comp: Fatale Media

Hunting Season, The

Moreira, Rita
1989; Brazil; 22 min; Documentary

In Sao Paulo hunting is not tied to a season—not when it comes to the hunting down of homosexuals and transvestites. This disturbing documentary portrays the intolerant climate of the Brazilian metropolis where the police policy amounts to death to homos. Portuguese with English subtitles.

Hush!

Hush!

Hashiguchi, Ryosuke
2001; Japan; 135 min; Drama
P: Hiroo Tsukada, Tomiyasu Ishikawa; *W:* Ryosuke Hashiguchi; *C:* Shogo Ueno; *E:* Ryosuke Hashiguchi; *M:* Bobby McFerrin
Cast: Seiichi Tanabe, Kazuya Takahashi, Reiko Kataoka

Naoya is living a self-centred life as a gay man, but he has the sense that there is something missing in his life. By chance, he meets and falls in love with Katsuhiro, and they begin to see each other. Then a woman named Asako appears on the scene and proposes that they conceive a child together. Naoya opposes the idea, and he is irritated with Katsuhiro, who has hidden his homosexuality and is generally indecisive. While caught in these tangled emotions, the three are visited by Katsuhiro's brother and sister-in-law. The sister-in-law, obsessed with the division of the family's property, has learned about Asako and wants to end her relationship with Katsuhiro. As Naoya, Katsuhiro, and Asako struggle along, they reach a point where they must decide what family means and how they will choose to live their lives. (www.cine.co.jp)
Japanese with English subtitles.

Dist/Sales: Strand

Hustler White

Castro, Rick / La Bruce, Bruce
1995; Canada; 80 min; Erotica
P: Jürgen Brüning, Bruce La Bruce;

W: Rick Castro, Bruce La Bruce; C: Rick Castro, James Carman; E: Rider Siphron
Cast: Tony Ward, Bruce La Bruce, Alex Austin, Kevin Kramer

A wild tale about the street hustlers on the Santa Monica Boulevard in California, USA. It centres on Monti, a rather clumsy street stud, reminiscent of a Joe Dallesandro of the 1990s. We follow Monti on his daily routine of bizarre encounters, other hustlers and clients along the sleazy underground of Los Angeles.

Prod Comp: Dangerous to Know Swell Co., Hustler White Productions
Dist/Sales: Potential, Strand, Wolfe, Millivres, NFVLS, ACMI

Hustler White

I Almost Feel Like a Tourist

McKay, Barry
1999; Australia; 10 min; Experimental

A commentary on community and stereotypes from both sides of the Atlantic. Not all gays and lesbians feel like they belong.

I am a Camera

Cornelius, Henry
1955; UK; 98 min; B&W; Drama
P: Jack Clayton; W: John Collier; C: Guy Green;
E: Clive Donner; M: Malcolm Arnold
Cast: Julie Harris, Laurence Harvey, Shelley Winters, Ron Randell, Lea Seidl

In a story based on the same tale as *Cabaret*, Julie Harris portrays the half-courtesan Sally Bowles opposite Harvey's Isherwood with wit and intelligence, a role she had also played on the New York stage. By general consensus, *I am a Camera* is less successful in portraying the amoral, twilight world of Berlin during the last days of The Weimar Republic and the unconventional relationship between Bowles and Isherwood, repressing the latter's homosexuality. As it was, the film ran into censorship problems in the United States, and Isherwood harshly dismissed it as 'disgusting ... near pornographic trash'.

Prod Comp: Remus Films, Romulus
Dist/Sales: NFVLS, Carlton

I am a Man

Devakul, M. L. Bhandevanop
1988; Thailand; 115 min; Drama

A Thai film adaptation of *Boys in the Band*, a Matt Crowley play. A group of drag queens and a macho dancer celebrate the birthday of one of the 'girls'. Just as they are all dancing around, a straight friend unexpectedly walks in.

Dist/Sales: TMPPA

I am my Own Woman

(aka: Ich Bin Meine Eigene Frau)

von Praunheim, Rosa
1992; Germany; 90 min; Drama
W: Valentin Passoni; C: Lorenz Haarmann; E: Mike Shephard; M: Joachim Litty
Cast: Charlotte von Mahlsdorf, Jens Taschner, Ichgola Androgyn

True-life story of Charlotte von Mahlsdorf, the best-known transvestite in East Germany. Miss Charlotte survived the Nazi reign and the repression of the Communists as a transvestite and helped start the German gay liberation movement.

Dist/Sales: Cinevista

I am not What you Want

Hung, Kit
2001; Hong Kong; 49 min; Drama
W: Kit Hung

Having recently come out to his conservative family,

Ricky is now sleeping temporarily on the apartment floor of Mark, his best, straight friend. This meditative film explores the relationships which exist between lover, between friends, and the blurred boundaries between them. Cantonese with English subtitles.

Dist/Sales: Hung

I am the Camera Dying

Gilbert, Sky
1998; Canada; 30 min; Experimental
Cast: Tracy Wright

A gender-warped tale of Marvette, a recently deceased heroin addict, who returns to this world as a gorgeous gay sailor who just wants to cruise the boys. A who's who of local luminaries lend a hand in this funky, funny, experimental ode to mixing it up and making it work, no matter what the circumstances. (CFMDC)

Dist/Sales: CFMDC

I Became a Lesbian and so Can you

Donahue, Lizzie
1994; USA; 11 min; Comedy

Outlines a path to true happiness, an improved social life and magical powers in the form of an infomercial.

I Don't Just Want you to Love Me

(aka: Ich will nicht nur, daß ihr mich liebt)

Pflaum, Hans Günther
1992; Germany; 96 min; Documentary
P: Theo Hinz; *W:* Hans Günther Pflaum;
C: Manfred Burkle, Werner Kurz; *E:* Ingrid Wolff

Made to commemorate the tenth anniversary of Fassbinder's death, Pflaum negotiates the relationship between Fassbinder's life and his films by intercutting interviews with family and friends, such as Hanna Schygulla and Volker Schlondorff, with interviews of Fassbinder himself and excerpts from his 40-odd films.

I Don't Wanna be a Boy

Behrens, Alec / Muijser, Marijn
1994; The Netherlands; 30 min; Documentary

I Don't Wanna be a Boy goes right to the heart of the dangers of transsexual prostitution in the meat market district of New York City. Centring on six young black and Hispanic transsexuals from New York's poorest neighbourhoods, the ghettos in Brooklyn and the Bronx, this documentary follows them through the harsh reality of their daily lives. These 'girls' regularly face death by violence, AIDS, drug overdose or, when the options run out, suicide. Tragically, few transsexual prostitutes make it to their twenty-fourth birthday or to their dream of being a fully-fledged woman. Estranged from their families and from a society that refuses to accept that gender exists in the heart and the head as opposed to below the waist, they live day-by-day trading their bodies in one of the most dangerous markets around. (MQFF)

Dist/Sales: Wildshot

I, Eugenia

Finnane, Gabrielle
1998; Australia; 30 min; Drama
W: Gabrielle Finnane

The strange life of Eugenia Falleni, also known as Harry Crawford and Jean Ford: sailor, husband, convicted murderer, boarding house madam. Born in Italy, Eugenia came to Australia at the turn of the century.

Prod Comp: Curious Media

I Exist: Voices from the Lesbian and Gay Middle Eastern Community

Barbosa, Peter / Lenoir, Garrett
2002; USA; 56 min; Documentary
P: Peter Barbosa

An intimate look at how queers of Middle Eastern origin share a common experience despite the differences in their religious and cultural realities.

Prod Comp: EyeBite Productions
Dist/Sales: Eyebite

I Hate Faggy Fag Fag

MacCubbin, Jeffrey
2000; USA; 10 min; Drama

Three young gay men prepare for an evening of bitching, back stabbing and the destruction of other men's self esteem.

Dist/Sales: LittleBelly

I.K.U

Cheang, Shu Lea
2000; Japan; 74 min; Sci-Fi
P: Takashi Asai; *W:* Shu Lea Cheang;
C: Tetsusya Yamoto; *E:* Kazuhiro Shirao
Cast: Miho Ariga, Yumeko Sasaki, Ayumilas Tokito, Maria Yumeno

Early in the 21st century, the Genom Corporation advanced the sexual revolution to the GEN-XXX phase—creating a being virtually identical to a human—known as the GEN-XXX IKU Coder, superior in their hard-drive bodies, and at least equal in insatiability, to the programming engineers who created them. This is their story. Both live-action bisexual manga, and an erotic homage to Blade Runner, this sumptuously produced, visually startling film features breathtaking animation, gender fluidity, and lashings of hetero and homo action. Japanese with English subtitles. (MQFF)

Prod Comp: Uplink Co
Dist/Sales: Uplink

I Know a Place

Farrow, Jane / Mitchell, Roy
1999; Canada; 30 min; Documentary
W: Roy Mitchell

An intimate, funny and completely engaging family photo album of a thriving little queer community buried in the heart of a rugged and isolated Ontario steel town of Sault Ste. Marie. Bob Goddere is at the centre of this historic demimonde. Director/writer Roy Mitchell accesses this intriguing story through his personal relationship with Bob and the community as someone who grew up in the Sault, and like so many young queers, came out at Bob's parties in the 1970s and 80s. Mother Goddere, as he's known to most, hosted over two decades worth of queer dance parties in the basement of his small town house with his lover Jean-Guy. He was the central figure of Sault Ste Marie's gay underground, its organiser, therapist and archivist. *I Know a Place* is an important and refreshing contribution to queer history and geography. (CFMDC)

Dist/Sales: CFMDC

I Like You, I Like You Very Much

(aka: Anata-Ga Suki Desu, Dai Suki Desu)

Oki, Hiroyuki
1994; Japan; 60 min; Drama
P: Suzuki Akihiro; *W:* Hiroyuki Oki; *C:* Hiroyuki Oki;
E: Hiroyuki Oki
Cast: Shibuya Kazunori, Kitakaze Hisanori

Shin lives happily with his boyfriend Yu until one day he approaches a stranger with the proposition 'I like you...' Thus begins the ultimate voyeuristic trip, extremely candid in its sex scenes, as both boys embark on a series of sexual encounters. Japanese with English subtitles.

Prod Comp: Stance Company
Dist/Sales: WaterBearer, ACMI

I Love you Baby

Albacete, Alfonso / Menkes, David
2001; Spain; 110 min; Drama
P: Alfonso Albacete, David Menkes, Francisco Ramos;

W: Alfonso Albacete, David Menkes, Lucia Etxebarria;
C: Gonzalo F. Berridi; *E:* Miguel Santamaria;
M: Paco Ortga, M. A. Collado
Cast: Jorge Sanz, Santiago Magill, Boy George

An oddball exploration of the sacrifices we make to regain lost love, *I Love you Baby*, stars *Belle Epoque*'s Jorge Sanz as Marcos, a country boy who comes to Madrid to find his fortune. Instead he finds Daniel, a struggling actor with a penchant for Boy George and an idealistic approach to relationships. A sweet-natured romance blossoms between the two men, but fate intervenes when Marcos gets a blow to the head (mirroring Boy George's own real life stage accident some years back). In the resulting confusion, Marisol, a vivacious Dominican immigrant who has had an unrequited crush on Marcos, gets a chance to make her move (with the help of her gossipy circle of Latina girlfriends). How far is Daniel willing to go to get back the love of his life? Let's just say that, above the objections of his best gal-pal, he gets to put his acting skills to the ultimate test. Combining Hollywood-style high-concept comedy, a Caribbean bachata and merengue-flavored soundtrack featuring stars such as Chi Chi Peralta, and a post-modern sensibility, this film will entice even those it ultimately infuriates. (2002 Miami Gay & Lesbian Film Festival)
Spanish with English subtitles.

Prod Comp: 20th Century-Fox
Dist/Sales: Alquimia, 20thCenturyFox

I Love you, I'll Kill you

(aka: Ich Liebe Dich, Ich Töte Dich)

Brandner, Uwe
1971; Germany; 90 min; Drama
P: Uwe Brandner, Karin Thome; *W:* Uwe Brandner;
C: André Dubreuil; *E:* Heidi Genée; *M:* Uwe Brandner, Heinz Hetter, Kid Olanf
Cast: Rolf Becker, Hannes Fuchs, Helmut Brasch

A young schoolteacher moves to an apparently idyllic remote village. He meets a hunter and they begin a secret love affair. The teacher, for some reason, begins to lose his mind and starts poaching the village game. The hunter must now track down his escaped lover.

I Shall not be Removed: The Life of Marlon Riggs

Everett, Karen
1996; USA; 58 min; Documentary

Marlon Riggs was an African–American gay filmmaker, scholar, cultural commentator and activist. This documentary looks at his life, his special relationships with his family, his politics, his white lover and the frenetic pace of his work once he was diagnosed with AIDS.

Dist/Sales: CaliforniaNewsreel, Everett

I Shot Andy Warhol

Harron, Mary
1995; USA; 100 min; Drama
P: Tom Kalin, Christine Vachon; *W:* Mary Harron, Daniel Minahan; *C:* Ellen Kuras; *E:* Keith Reamer; *M:* John Cale
Cast: Lili Taylor, Jared Harris, Martha Plimpton, Stephen Dorff

Valerie Solanas is a self-described lesbian feminist who makes her living with a street hustle here and some prostitution there, but whose real drive in life is radical feminist writing. Through her friend Candy Darling she connects with Andy Warhol and his Factory gang, and comes to believe that he is going to produce one of her plays. He keeps stringing her along, and she keeps getting more desperate, and finally, in 1968, she goes over the edge.

Prod Comp: Valerie Pictures, Samuel Goldwyn Company
Dist/Sales: SamuelGoldwyn, Wolfe, Orion, Swank

I Shot Andy Warho

I, the Worst of All

(aka: Yo, la Peor de Todas)

Bemberg, María Luisa
1990; Argentina, France; 105 min; Drama
P: Lita Stantic; *W:* María Luisa Bemberg, Antonio Larreta; *C:* Félix Monti; *E:* Juan Carlos Macías; *M:* Luis María Serra
Cast: Dominique Sanda, Assumpta Serna, Hector Alterio, Alberto Segado

With the use of flashback the film reveals the story of 17th century Mexican poet and nun Sister Juana Inés de la Cruz, from her impoverished childhood to her exiled life in a convent. It shows her develop as a writer and her intimate relationship with a beautiful vicereine. At one point, she becomes involved in a plot to undermine the authority of the archbishop who has conspired to stop her work. A powerful and intense film with a superb performance by Assumpta Serna in the lead role. Spanish with English subtitles.

Prod Comp: Gea Cinematografica
Dist/Sales: FirstRunFeatures, TLA

I Think I Do

I Think I Do

Sloan, Brian
1997; USA; 90 min; Comedy
P: Marcus Hu, Lane Janger; *W:* Brian Sloan; *C:* Milton Kam; *E:* François Keraudren; *M:* Brahm Wenger
Cast: Alexis Arquette, Christian Maelen, Lauren Vélez, Jamie Harrold

Bob has a mad crush on college frat boy roommate Brendan. Brendan finds out, freaks out and sleeps with Sarah. Five years later they and college chums all reunite for a wedding. As everyone parties and consumes just enough booze, libidos are inflamed and inhibitions lowered. Is the bedroom-eyed Brendan really longing for Bob? Will Sarah bed Brendan, if only for old times' sake? Will Sterling marry Bob and get his hoped-for wedding? (Millivres)

Prod Comp: Danger Filmworks, Sauce Productions, House of Pain Productions
Dist/Sales: Millivres, Strand, Wolfe, 10%

I Vitelloni

(aka: The Young and the Passionate)

Fellini, Federico
1953; France, Italy; 104 min; B&W; Drama
P: Mario De Vecchi, Lorenzo Pegoraro; *W:* Federico Fellini, Ennio Flaiano, Tullio Pinelli; *C:* Carlo Carlini, Otello Martelli, Luciano Trasatti; *E:* Rolando Benedetti; *M:* Nino Rota
Cast: Alberto Sordi, Franco Interlenghi, Franco Fabrizi, Leopoldo Trieste, Riccardo Fellini

A study of five young men trapped in a small town

in the Adriatic who are restless middle-class layabouts unable to rise above the provincial wasteland they inhabit as they cope with their emerging adulthood. Italian with English subtitles.

Prod Comp: Peg Film, Cite Film, API Productions, Cité Films, Peg-Film
Dist/Sales: NFVLS, ACMI

I Want What I Want

Dexter, John
1972; UK; 90 min; Drama
P: Raymond Stross; *W:* Gillian Freeman;
C: Gerry Turpin; *E:* Peter Thornton; *M:* Johnny Harris
Cast: Anne Heywood, Michael Coles, Paul Rogers, Sheila Reid

A young man, played by Heywood, leaves his family in order to live his life fully as a woman called Wendy. Wendy is propositioned by a lesbian but turns her down and finally falls for a man. When he kisses and fondles Wendy he realises he's just kissed a man and beats her. In the end Wendy finally gets the sex-change operation she has always wanted.

Prod Comp: Marayan
Dist/Sales: OrionClassics, BFI

I Will not Think about Death Anymore

Buncel, Irene
1993; Canada; 19 min; Drama

A Jewish woman cannot sleep following the death of a friend from AIDS. She meets a handsome leather dyke called Death who takes her on a trip during which her fears of death are eloquently examined. (MQFF)

Dist/Sales: CFMDC

I'll Be your Mirror

Coulthard, Edmund / Goldin, Nan
1995; USA; 49 min; Documentary
P: Adam Barker; *W:* Edmund Coulthard, Nan Goldin;
C: Patrick Duval; *E:* Paul Binns;
M: Velvet Underground, Patti Smith, Eartha Kitt

An autobiographical account by Nan Goldin who photographed the drag scene of Boston in the 1970s and New York's gay heaven. She photographed it all, from the inside. AIDS changed her world as her friends both male and female died. A rare autobiography that manages to avoid being too egotistical or too coy.

Awards: Berlin International Film Festival, 1996: Teddy Award for Best Feature
Prod Comp: Blast Films
Dist/Sales: BBC-Enterprises

I'll Love you Forever - Tonight

Bravo, Michael Edgar
1992; USA; 80 min; B&W; Drama
E: Edgar Michael Bravo
Cast: Paul Marius, Jason Adams, Roger Shank, David Poynter

Billed as the first gay feature from a Latino, Bravo's debut film is shot in crisp black and white and boasts some fine performances from a cast of young unknowns. A sullen young photographer is coaxed by his sometime lover into spending the weekend with some friends at a Palm Springs hideaway. What is supposed to be a restful little vacation turns into a fairly joyless round of hard drinking and cold-blooded sexual games played by five gorgeous men who seem totally at a loose end with their lives in the urban fast lane. (MQFF)

Prod Comp: Cinema Bravo
Dist/Sales: TLA

I'm Starving

Yau, Ching
1998; USA; 12 min; Drama

An erotic love tale between a ghost and a woman who co-habit in a small apartment in New York's Chinatown. The ghost that eats Chinese takeout menus and paper money contrasts starkly with the human, a working class African–American woman, who eats only ramen. (Frameline)

Dist/Sales: Frameline

I'm the One that I Want

Coleman, Lionel
2000; USA; 96 min; Documentary

Famed bisexual US stand up comic Margaret Cho live in concert.

Dist/Sales: Wolfe

I've Heard the Mermaids Singing

Rozema, Patricia
1987; Canada; 83 min; Drama
P: Patricia Rozema, Alexandra Raffe; *W:* Patricia Rozema; *C:* Douglas Koch; *E:* Patricia Rozema;
M: Mark Korven
Cast: Sheila McCarthy, Paule Baillargeon, Ann-Marie MacDonald, John Evans

This is the delightful story of Polly, an awkward secretary for the curator of an art gallery. Polly is also an avid photographer and tries anonymously to get the curator to buy her photographs. She becomes infatuated with her lesbian boss, who is in a relationship with a beautiful young artist named

i

Mary. The film moves in and out of reality and fantasy with an interesting use of video and film technology which never becomes overpowering. A very warm and uplifting film that everyone can enjoy. It is the first feature film from Rozema who is also credited with *When Night is Falling*.

Awards: Cannes Film Festival, 1987: Young Cinema Award (Patricia Rozema)
Prod Comp: Vos, National Film Board of Canada, Téléfilm Canada
Dist/Sales: Palace, Miramax, BFI

Icarus

Balfour, Patricia
1998; Australia; 13 min; Drama

Icarus, a young Greek man, falls to his death on the shore of a rocky island. Was it just like the myth— 'Icarus getting too close to the sun'—or was something more sinister at hand? A tragic tale of a love triangle fuelled by jealousy and deception, set in the searing sun of the Greek islands.

Dist/Sales: BigFilm

Ice Palace, The

Blom, Per
1987; Norway; 80 min; Drama
W: Per Blom; *C:* Halvor Næss; *M:* Geir Bøhren, Bent Åserud
Cast: Hilde Martinsen, Line Storesund, Merete Moen, Sigrid Huun, Vidar Sandem

Two 11-year-old girls from a remote Norwegian town, Unn and Siss, form a deep friendship. One day while playing they remove each other's clothes, an act that awakens their sexual consciousness. They both become very disturbed by the feelings they discover. Unn, unable to face her friend the next day, runs away and finds herself lost in a frozen waterfall.

Prod Comp: Norsk Film

If

Anderson, Lindsay
1968; UK; 112 min; Drama
P: Michael Medwin, Lindsay Anderson; *W:* David Sherwin; *C:* Miroslav Ondricek; *E:* David Glodwell; *M:* Marc Wilkinson
Cast: Malcolm McDowell, David Wood, Richard Warwick, Robert Swann, Christine Noonan

Constructed in eight chapters *If* is an indictment on the British boy's school system. Through each chapter we follow Mick and his mostly younger friends through a series of indignities and abuse that makes any fond feelings toward these schools difficult. Mick and his friends eventually violently rebel.

Prod Comp: Memorial Enterprises, Paramount
Dist/Sales: Ascanbee, Paramount, VSM

If all Goes Well I'll Meet you on the Next Train

Rebehy, Mario Alves
1995; Brazil, Italy; 20 min; Drama

A thief manages to entangle an Italian officer in a scheme that will change the officer's life forever.

If She Grows Up Gay

Goodman, Karen Sloe
1983; USA; 23 min; Documentary

A blue collar African–American mother, talks about her pregnancy and raising her daughter with her lesbian lover. (Frameline)

Dist/Sales: Frameline

If She only Knew

Wynne, Stephanie
1999; USA; 30 min; Drama

Zaire develops a crush on Frankie, one of the delivery 'men' that come to her office. But it turns out Frankie isn't all that he seems.

Dist/Sales: GBF

If the Family Fits

Kearns, Patricia
1994; Canada; 51 min; Drama

The Delaneys are engaged in the process of reconfiguring their family—Mom leaves her role as happy housewife behind, Dad announces he is gay and the youngest daughter becomes a single mother.

Dist/Sales: CinemaLibre

If These Walls Could Talk 2

Anderson, Jane / Coolidge, Martha / Heche, Anne
2000; USA; 94 min; Drama
P: Mary Kane; *W:* Jane Anderson, Anne Heche, Alex Sichel, Sylvia Sichel; *C:* Paul Elliott, Peter Deming, Robbie Greenberg; *E:* Margaret Goodspeed; *M:* Basil Poledouris
Cast: Vanessa Redgrave, Chloe Sevigny, Michelle Williams, Ellen DeGeneres, Sharon Stone

One house—three generations of lesbians. This star-studded lesbian trilogy looks at three sets of lesbians from the 1960s to the present, creating an entertaining history of the modern lesbian experience. Edith mourns the loss of her long-term partner in the first segment, set in 1961, while her former partner's 'real family' take possession of the home she has lived in throughout their relationship. More than 10 years later, another lesbian moves into the house which is now the site of a politically correct obsessed feminist collective. Things get interesting when butch young Amy falls for femme Linda. The final third, written and directed by Anne Heche, sees a yuppy couple (played by Ellen Degeneres and Sharon Stone) happily ensconced in the home, but facing the pressures (and comedies) of searching for the perfect sperm donor. (MQFF)

Prod Comp: HBO, Team Todd
Dist/Sales: HBO, Wolfe, ACMI, Swank

Ifti

Majid, Hajira
1998; USA; 20 min; Documentary

A gay Pakistani poet makes waves in his adopted home of Chicago.

Dist/Sales: QueenFAD

Illegal Tender

Bettell, Paul
1988; UK; 14 min; Experimental

Shot in London's East End, Illegal Tender follows one punkish lad's pursuit of another—through a contemporary wasteland dripping with symbols. (Frameline)

Dist/Sales: Salzgeber

Image in the Snow

Maas, Willard
1945; USA; 30 min; B&W; Experimental
P: Willard Maas

A 'film poem' by a member of the early American film avant-grade, Willard Maas. This is a psychodrama expressing a young homosexual's isolation and alienation, accompanied by a lyrical abstract verse commentary.

Dist/Sales: NFVLS, Canyon

Images

Liss, Janet
1986; USA; 54 min; Drama

A lesbian couple, in a happy relationship, is tested by the arrival of another woman. A tender and erotic love story with good portrayals of the women.

Imagining October

Jarman, Derek
1984; UK; 27 min; Experimental

Influenced by the miners strikes of Thatcher's Britain, raids on gay culture and his questioning of the British film industry, *Imagining October* is a meditation on art and politics, the individual and the state.

Immacolata e Concetta - l'altra gelosia

Piscicelli, Salvatore
1979; Italy; 110 min; Drama
W: Carla Apuzzo, Salvatore Piscicelli; *C:* Emilio Bestetti;
M: Rudy Beytelman
Cast: Ida Benedetto, Tommaso Bianco, Marcella Michelangeli

Immacolata and Concetta meet and fall in love while both serving sentences in prison. When they are released, the two women move in together creating a scandal and pushing away their family, friends and Concetta's embittered husband. Probably the first Italian lesbian film too explicit at the time to find a distributor. Italian with English subtitles.

Prod Comp: Antea Films
Dist/Sales: AchabFilm

Immigration

1991; UK; 11 min; Documentary

A short documentary on the discrimination of immigration laws against lesbian and gay couples, showing different case histories.

Prod Comp: Channel 4

Impossible on Saturday

Joffé, Alex
1966; France, Israel, Italy; 115 min; Comedy
P: Jacques Steiner, Yitzhak Agadati, Joseph Carl;
W: Joseph Carl, Alex Joffé, John Perry, Jacques Steiner, Shabtai Tevet; *C:* Jean Bougoin; *E:* Eric Pluet; *M:* Sasha Argov
Cast: Robert Hirsch, Geula Noni

A conductor wills his vast holdings to the state of Jerusalem, but when his father's ghost tells him he must atone for his sins by getting his sons to marry before the Sabbath, his plan is in danger. One of his sons, a transvestite, refuses to marry.

Prod Comp: Athos Films, Meroz Films, Steno Film

Impromptu

Lapine, James
1991; France, UK; 106 min; Comedy
P: Stuart Oken, Daniel A. Sherkow; *W:* Sarah Kernochan; *C:* Bruno de Keyzer; *E:* Michael Ellis;
M: John Strauss
Cast: Julian Sands, Judy Davis, Hugh Grant, Mandy Patinkin, Bernadette Peters

A comic look at the love affair between the strong-willed novelist, George Sand, a cross-dressing, cigar-smoking woman and composer Frederic Chopin. It is set in an English mansion where Chopin, Liszt and artist Delacroix are on summer vacation. Sand, who has a crush on Chopin, arrives unexpectedly.

Prod Comp: Sovereign, CLG Films, Governor Productions, Les Films Ariane
Dist/Sales: Roadshow, ACMI, Col-Tri, Hemdale

Improper Conduct

(aka: Mauvaise Conduite)

Almendros, Néstor / Jiménez Leal, Orlando
1984; France; 115 min; Documentary
Cast: Susan Sontag, Lorenzo Monreal, Jorge Lago, Julio Medina

A powerful documentary revealing the persecution of intellectuals and homosexuals in Castro's Cuba. During that period thousands of homosexuals were rounded up, sent to labour camps and tortured—often having been betrayed by their families and friends, a situation reminiscent of Nazi Germany.

Awards: San Francisco International Lesbian & Gay Film Festival, 1984: Best Documentary
Prod Comp: Antenne-2, Les Films du Losange

In a Year of Thirteen Moons

(aka: In einem Jahr mit 13 Monden)

Fassbinder, Rainer Werner
1978; Germany; 123 min; Drama
W: Rainer Werner Fassbinder; *C:* Rainer Werner Fassbinder; *E:* Rainer Werner Fassbinder;
M: Peer Raben
Cast: Volker Spengler, Ingrid Caven, Gottfried John, Elisabeth Trissenaar, Eve Mattes

Tells the story of the doomed life of a transsexual who underwent a sex change operation to please another man. Now she must deal with rejection by friends and family alike. German with English subtitles.

Prod Comp: Filmverlag der Autoren, Pro-ject Filmproduktion, Tango Film
Dist/Sales: NFVLS, ACMI

In Bed with Madonna

(aka: Madonna: Truth or Dare)

Keshishian, Alek
1991; USA; 119 min; Documentary
P: Jay Roewe, Tim Clawson, Lisa Hollingshead;
C: Robert Leacock, Doug Nichol, Marc Reshovsky, Daniel Pearl, Christophe Lanzenberg, Toby Phillips;
E: Barry Alexander Brown, John Murray
Cast: Madonna, Sandra Bernhard, Pedro Almodóvar, Antonio Banderas, Warren Beatty

A frank look at the superstar during her 1990 world tour. For those with a queer interest, the most interesting parts of the documentary include a backstage visit from her old flame Sandra Bernhard, and some rather bitchy repartee as the only straight dancing boy gets a very hard time from the rest of the troupe.

Prod Comp: Propaganda, Boy Toy Productions, Miramax
Dist/Sales: Col-Tri, 16MM, Miramax

In My Father's House

Simmons, Aishah Shahidah
1996; USA; 15 min; Experimental

Award winning African–American director Simmons explores the coming out process, through introspection and interviews with her family and friends. Explores the issues of race, gender, homophobia, race and misogyny.

In on Earth as it is in Heaven

Crookshank, Ross
1996; UK; 36 min; Drama

Gabriel is a man obsessed with sex, yet unable to find the love he subconsciously craves. This gritty and often confronting tale explores one view of the adult life of gay men.

In & Out

Oz, Frank
1997; USA; 90 min; Comedy
P: Scott Rudin; *W:* Paul Rudnick; *C:* Rob Hahn;
E: Daniel P. Hanley, John Jympson; *M:* Marc Shaiman
Cast: Kevin Kline, Joan Cusack, Matt Dillon, Debbie Reynolds, Tom Selleck

Howard Brackett is a popular high school teacher whose life is thrown into chaos when, on the eve of his wedding, an ex-student (now a successful actor) mentions him in his Academy Award acceptance speech, and then inadvertently outs him as gay. The small town where he lives goes into turmoil with a media invasion desperate to cover the outing, and meet the 'gay' teacher. One of the reporters, (a gay man played by Tom Selleck), decides to do a large feature on the teacher for his TV show. Howard and the reporter notice a spark between them, and after a rather long kiss Howard must now face the truth.

Prod Comp: Paramount, Spelling Films
Dist/Sales: UIP, Wolfe, NFVLS, ParamountHV, Swank

In Pursuit of Prince/ess Charming

1991; UK; 20 min; Documentary

Magazine style documentary piece which looks at lesbian and gay relationships.

Prod Comp: Channel 4

In the Best Interests of the Children

Reid, Frances / Stevens, Elizabeth / Zheutlin, Cathy
1977; USA; 53 min; Documentary
Cast: Betty Knickerbocker, Lorraine Norman, Pat Norman

This groundbreaking documentary on lesbian mothering portrays the diversity of experience, race and class among eight lesbian mothers and their children. They describe the difficulties and prejudices they must overcome in order to live together, and their feelings about their family lives.

Prod Comp: Iris Films
Dist/Sales: NFVLS, WMM

In the Flesh (1997)

Taylor, Ben
1997; USA; 105 min; Drama
P: Julie R. Lee; *W:* Ben Taylor; *C:* Brian Gurley;
M: Eddie Horst
Cast: Dane Ritter, Ed Corbin, Roxzane T. Mims, Adrian Roberts

Oliver Beck is 21, good looking, clean-cut and a product of an upper class family. He's also leading a double life—student by day and street hustler by night. When he meets Philip Kirsch, undercover cop working Atlanta's drug enforcement branch, secrets collide. All too soon, their fragile trust is shaken when Oliver becomes the prime suspect in a murder case, and detective Kirsch reluctantly becomes his only alibi. (Wolfe)

Dist/Sales: Wolfe, 10%

In the Flesh (2000)

McLennan, Gordon
2000; USA; 45 min; Documentary

Introducing us to four very different people who identify themselves as transsexuals, *In the Flesh* explores traditional assumptions about gender and what happens when a person's inner sense of identity conflicts with society's expectations. Rose, Mirha, Peter and Chris speak frankly about sexuality, relationships, family and self. They also discuss the need for social support for transsexuals and for tolerance and equality. Most importantly, they talk about healing. This film is an inspiring look at how these individuals are trying to gain control of their lives in all aspects—in the mind, in the heart, and in the flesh. (Cinema Guild)

Dist/Sales: CinemaGuild, Heathcliff

In the Gloaming

Reeve, Christopher
1997; USA; 62 min; Drama
P: Nellie Nugiel; *W:* Will Scheffer; *C:* Frederick Elmes;

E: David Ray; *M:* Dave Grusin
Cast: Glen Close, Bridget Fonda, Whoopi Goldberg, Robert Sean Leonard, David Strathairn

Danny is dying of AIDS, and so decides to return home to his family for his last few months. He shares an incredible closeness with his mother, which causes problems with his father and sister.

Prod Comp: Frederick Zollo Productions
Dist/Sales: Wolfe, HBO, Swank

In the Shadow of the Sun

Jarman, Derek
1980; UK; 50 min; Experimental
P: James MacKay

Described as 'very personal' with a dreamlike repetitive quality, Jarman's film uses home movie footage to express a mythology and dabbles with ideas relating to magic alchemy and ritual, allowing dream-images to drift and collide at random.

Prod Comp: Dark Pictures
Dist/Sales: ACMI, BFI

In this House of Brede

Schaefer, George
1975; USA; 100 min; Drama
P: George Schaefer; *W:* James Costigan;
C: Chris Challis; *E:* Ronald J. Fagan; *M:* Peter Matz
Cast: Diana Rigg, Gwen Watford, Dennis Quilley, Pamela Brown

A sophisticated London businesswoman throws it all away to become a Benedictine nun. At the convent a young nun develops a crush on an older nun, but she finds it difficult to come to terms with her feelings and can't reciprocate. Based on the novel by Rumer Godden.

Prod Comp: Tomorrow Entertainment
Dist/Sales: CBS

Inauguration of the Pleasure Dome

Anger, Kenneth
1954; USA; 38 min; Experimental

Avant-garde film derived from an Aleister Crowley ritual where cult members take on the identity of gods or goddesses.

Dist/Sales: BFI

Incidental Journey

(aka: Haijiao Tianya)

Chen, Jofei
2001; Taiwan; 60 min; Drama
W: Jofei Chen; *C:* Liou Berg, Zh-van Zhang; *M:* Du-che Tu
Cast: Wan-jung Wang, Su-li Wu, Vicky Chiang

Incidental Journey is a road movie in which Ching is

forced to take another look at herself when she meets the mysteriously attractive Hsiang on her travels. (2002 Tokyo International Lesbian & Gay Film Festival) Mandarin with English subtitles.

Dist/Sales: ChenJ

Incredibly True Adventures of Two Girls in Love, The

Maggenti, Maria
1995; USA; 93 min; Comedy
P: Dolly Hall; *W:* Maria Maggenti; *C:* Tami Reiker;
E: Susan Graff; *M:* Terry Dame, Tom Judson
Cast: Nicole Parker, Laurel Holloman, Maggie Moore, Kate Stanfford, Sabrina Artel

This film is a teen romance with a twist. Evie, sheltered, rich and black, meets diesel dyke Randy. Their mixed marriage is spawned in the passing of locker-room love notes, and a shared appreciation of poetry. Their lifestyles are directly opposed. Evie lives a privileged uptown existence, and Randy lives in a happy home of wayward dykes with her lesbian aunt, her aunt's lover and a changing assortment of visitors. Together these dyklings struggle against school and home towards sharing the first kiss, the first touch and the first official display of affection in a public place. The film evokes memories of all those firsts, in what is a rich and tender portrayal of first-time love. Has become a lesbian classic. (MQFF)

Prod Comp: Fine Line Features, Smash Pictures
Dist/Sales: NewVision, 21stCentury, Wolfe, FilmsInc, FineLine, ACMI, Haut-et-Court

Indecent Acts

Parry, William
1994; UK; 54 min; Documentary

Just over one hundred years ago Oscar Wilde found himself at the Old Bailey charged with having committed an indecent act. The term 'gross indecency' was used to describe anything short of sodomy. Indecent Acts explores the circumstances of Wilde's trial and conviction and makes a contemporary link between the charge Wilde faced and the law as it stands today. A soldier shares his experience of being gay in the military while a clergyman reveals how he passed a note to a man in an adjoining toilet cubicle, only to find himself face to face with a detective and subsequently charged with 'soliciting'. This documentary also explores the 'transgressions' in Wilde's work that evidenced his homosexuality, his subsequent demise after his trial, and the political stakes involved in his conviction. (MQFF)

Prod Comp: Channel 4
Dist/Sales: Gimlet

Independently Blue

Neal, Sarah
1997; Australia; 11 min; Experimental
P: Sarah Neal, Julianne Lawson, Jo Erskine;
W: Sarah Neal

In a lesbian cabaret an older woman reminisces about a sultry jazz club, feather boas and exquisite looking women.

Dist/Sales: BigFilm

The Incredibly True Adventures of Two Girls in Love

Infidel

Gund Saalfield, Catherine
1989; USA; 45 min; Drama

An experimental film about a black lesbian designer, Arroe, dealing with such issues as racism in the fashion industry and the formulation of a positive self-image.

Inn Trouble

Rey, Cristina
1996; USA; 92 min; Comedy
P: Cristina Rey, Stephani Shope; *W:* Cristina Rey, Stephani Shope; *C:* Mark Petersen; *E:* Cristina Rey;
M: Celeste Carballo

Cast: Cristina Rey, Stephani Shope, Melissa Aronson, Alehandro Wooten

> Sofi attempts to pursue her dream of becoming a filmmaker in the face of society's efforts to crush her vision. But her plans get postponed for little bit when she kidnaps her best friend Chris, who is recovering from a broken heart, and takes her to the funeral of Maggie, the former proprietor of a lesbian inn. Sofi and Chris both worked at the inn and decide to take it over. With an assortment of colourful but difficult staff and a landlord who is trying to take the inn away from them and a wide assortment of lesbians looking for a room, will Sofi ever get her film made? A hilarious portrayal of growing up and falling in love—lesbian style.

Prod Comp: Fearless Productions
Dist/Sales: FearlessProd

Inside Monkey Zetterland

Levy, Jefery
1992; USA; 93 min; Comedy
P: Chuck Grieve, Tani Cohen, Jefery Levy; *W:* Steven Antin, John Boskovich; *C:* Christopher Taylor; *E:* Lauren Zuckerman; *M:* Jeff Elmassian, Rick Cox
Cast: Patricia Arquette, Sofia Coppola, Sandra Bernhard, Steven Antin, Tate Donovan

> A wacky family comedy mostly set during Thanksgiving. The characters include Monkey, a former teen star and screenwriter, his lesbian sister whose girlfriend is pregnant, and their soap-opera diva Jewish mother. Most of the cast is queer or queer friendly, helping to make it a charming and funny film.

Prod Comp: Coast Entertainment

Inside Out

Inside Out

Gould, Jason
1997; USA; 26 min; Comedy

> Jason Gould (real life son of Elliot Gould and Barbra Streisand) discusses the woes of being a celebrity kid, out gay man and actor, in this fictionalised satire.

Inspecteur Lavardin

Chabrol, Claude
1986; France; 100 min; Comedy
P: Marin Karmitz; *W:* Claude Chabrol, Dominique Roulet; *C:* Jean Rabier; *E:* Monique Fardoulis, Angela Braga-Mermet; *M:* Mathieu Chabrol
Cast: Jean Poiret, Bernadette Lafont, Jean-Claude Brialy, Jean-Luc Bideau

> Inspector Lavardin, a most unorthodox police detective, interrogates a family about the murder of a pious writer. The family members include, Helene an old flame of the detective, her teenage daughter and her gay brother, Claude, who paints glass eyes for a hobby.

Prod Comp: Films A2, MK2 Productions
Dist/Sales: MK2Diffusion

Internal Affairs

Figgis, Mike
1990; USA; 114 min; Thriller
P: Frank Mancuso Jnr; *W:* Henry Bean; *C:* John A. Alonzo; *E:* Robert Estrin; *M:* Mike Figgis, Anthony Marinelli, Brian Banks
Cast: Richard Gere, Andy Garcia, Laurie Metcalf, Nancy Travis, William Baldwin

> Raymond Avila is a detective who has been promoted to the Internal Affairs Division of the Los Angeles County Police. While researching a misconduct case, Avila becomes convinced that a respected street cop named Dennis Peck is involved in a complicated web of criminal activities. When Avila and his partner who is a lesbian, played by Laurie Metcalf of Roseanne fame, begin to investigate him, Peck retaliates by drawing Avila's wife, Kathleen, into what becomes an intense sexual and psychological struggle.

Prod Comp: Paramount, Out of the Town Films
Dist/Sales: UIP, ReelMovies, Paramount

Interview with the Vampire

Jordan, Neil
1994; USA; 122 min; Horror
P: Stephen Woolley, David Geffen; *W:* Anne Rice; *C:* Philippe Rousselot; *E:* Mick Audsley, Joke Van Wijk; *M:* Elliot Goldenthal
Cast: Brad Pitt, Christian Slater, Tom Cruise, Antonio Banderas, Stephen Rea, Kirsten Dunst

> Lestat is a vampire who when he so desires, awards his victims with immortality—whether they want it or not. Into Lestat's world, comes Louis de Pointe du Lac who is devastated by the loss of his beloved wife and infant daughter. Two hundred years later, in late 20th century San Francisco, Louis decides to tell his story to a young reporter—a vampire's story of

desire, love, yearning, grief, terror and ecstasy. A highly atmospheric, homoerotic story with a strong gay subtext, done in a very camp manner.

Prod Comp: Geffen, Warner
Dist/Sales: ReelMovies, Warner, Swank

Interviews with my Next Girlfriend

Nicolaou, Cassandra
2001; Canada; 13 min; Comedy

A lesbian conducts interviews to source her next girlfriend.

Dist/Sales: CFMDC, BuzzTaxi

Intimate Friendship, An

Hughey, Angela Evers
2000; USA; 82 min; Drama
P: Angela Evers Hughey, Sheri Owens;
C: Jessica Gallant; *E:* Shari Weinberg
Cast: Lsel M. Gorell, Stacy Marr, Rini Starkey, Tim McMillan

Kelly, Faygan and Danielle are close friends until Danielle muddies the water by coming out. Kelly goes through stages of disgust and anger before jumping on the support group bandwagon. Faygan, on the other hand, is supportive and understanding—a little too understanding perhaps? 'Coming to terms with how you feel is one thing. Telling your best friend you're in love with her is another...' For everyone who enjoys a little romantic illusion in their day. (MQFF)

Prod Comp: Filling The Gap Productions
Dist/Sales: FillingTheGap, Spectrum

Intimates, The

(aka: Ji Sor)

Cheung, Jacob
1997; Hong Kong; 117 min; Drama
P: Eric Tsang, Jacob Cheung; *W:* Man-ming Tong
Cast: Winston Chao, Kar Lok Chin, Teresa Lee, Charlie Yeung

The Intimates intercuts between past and present to tell the subtle and slow story of a lesbian relationship between a factory working girl and the factory owner. Cantonese & Mandarin with English subtitles.

Prod Comp: UFO
Dist/Sales: GoldenHarvest

Inverted Minstrel

Otalvaro-Hormillosa, Gigi
2000; USA; 25 min; Experimental

Experimental work which challenges racial binary systems of thought by questioning and

problematising the politics of hip hop in various 'cultures of resistance', including the queer community.

Dist/Sales: DevilBunny

Investigator, The

Oxley, Chris
1996; UK; 78 min; Drama
P: Sheryl Crown; *W:* Barbara Machin;
C: Neve Cunningham
Cast: Helen Blexendale, Ian Burfield, Anna Bolt, Laura Fraser

Recounts the true story of the persecution and expulsion of lesbians from the British army. In a witch hunt to rival *The Crucible* the confronting drama tells of Caroline Meagher, a staff sergeant who worked within the royal military police partaking in the investigations intent on exposing those with lesbian tendencies. Unable to cope with the brutality of the investigations she returns to a uniform post where she must come to terms with her own identity and realise love is worth taking risks for.

Prod Comp: September Films, Laurel Productions
Dist/Sales: Channel4

Invocation of my Demon Brother

Anger, Kenneth
1969; USA; 11 min; Experimental

A conjuration of pagan forces comes off the screen in a surge of spiritual and mystical power. (ACMI)

Prod Comp: Puck Film Productions
Dist/Sales: ACMI, BFI

Iris

Eyre, Richard
2001; UK, USA; 90 min; Drama
P: Robert Fox, Scott Rudin; *W:* Richard Eyre, Charles Wood; *C:* Roger Pratt; *E:* Martin Walsh;
M: James Horner
Cast: Judi Dench, Kate Winslet, Jim Broadbent, Hugh Bonneville

True story based on the life of bisexual novelist Iris Murdoch. Details the adventures of her student days, through her lifelong relationship with husband John Bayley through to her final struggle with Alzheimer's disease.

Prod Comp: BBC, Internedia Films, Mirage Enterprises
Dist/Sales: Miramax, Paramount, Swank

Irma Vep

Assayas, Olivier
1996; France; 98 min; Comedy
P: Georges Benayoun; *W:* Olivier Assayas;

C: Eric Gautier; *E:* Luc Barnier
Cast: Maggie Cheung, Jean-Pierre Léaud, Nathalie Richard, Bulle Ogier, Lou Castel

Action diva Maggie Cheung arrives in Paris to play the latex-clad cat-burglar Irma Vep in a latter day remake of Louis Feuillard's 1915 silent film *Les Vampires* to be directed by Rene Vidal. Rene is an ageing filmmaker who no longer connects with the audience and is on the verge of a nervous break-down. Shooting begins and Maggie attracts the attention of the lesbian costume designer and some malicious gossip ensues. One night before shooting is abandoned, Maggie merges with her role and burglarises rooms in the hotel she is staying in. Rene is taken off the picture and replaced. The new director doesn't want Maggie either and views a startling assemblage of scenes that Rene has edited himself. English & French with English subtitles.

Prod Comp: Dacia Films
Dist/Sales: Potential, Siren, Zeitgeist, NFVLS, Haut-et-Court

Iro Kaze

(aka: Colour Wind)

Oki, Hiroyuki
1991; Japan; 10 min; Experimental

An experimental film that uses a panorama of gay feelings and sentiments to make this a wonderful visual experience.

Dist/Sales: ImageForum

The Iron Ladies

Iron Ladies, The

(aka: Sa tree lex)

Thongkonthun, Youngyooth
2000; Thailand; 100 min; Comedy
Cast: Jesdaporn Pholdee, Sahaphap Tor, Ekachai Buranapanit

The Iron Ladies tells the true story of a Thai male volleyball team which won the national champion-

ships in 1996 with a team consisting mostly of gay men, drag queens, transsexuals and one straight guy. The film was a surprising success in Thailand, where it became the second-highest grossing film of all time. (Strand)

Awards: San Francisco International Lesbian & Gay Film Festival, 2000: Audience Award for Best Feature
Prod Comp: Tai Entertainment
Dist/Sales: Fortissimo, Strand

Is Mary Wings Coming?

Charman, Karen
1993; Australia; 15 min; Comedy

Wry, restrained but sharp, *Is Mary Wings Coming?* has its finger on the pulse of Melbourne's cafe society. Weaving among the tables, this humorous short picks up the conversations and thoughts of the student dyke community that congregates around inner suburban Melbourne, Australia. (MQFF)

Isle of Lesbos

Harmon, Jeff B.
1996; USA; 98 min; Musical
P: Jeff B. Harmon; *W:* Jeff B. Harmon; *C:* Clark Mathis; *E:* Duncan Burns; *M:* Jeff B. Harmon
Cast: Kirsten Holly Smith, Danica Sheridan, Sonya Hensley, Michael Dotson

The Rocky Horror Show meets *Oklahoma* in this outrageous musical comedy. Set in two towns, the god-fearing, one-horse small town and the Isle of Lesbos. It is in fact lesbian heaven, where all good dykes go when they die.

Dist/Sales: PictureThis!

It Dwells in Mirrors

Sbrizzi, Paul
1998; USA; 13 min; Experimental

A stylised look at a lonely man's journey through corridors of fetishised encounters and hungry looks. He feels like the eternal spectator, but then he hooks up with a guy he desires and things take a turn for the fantastical.

It is not the Homosexual who is the Pervert but the Society in which He Lives

(aka: Nicht der Homosexuelle ist pervers, sondern die Situation, in der er lebt)

von Praunheim, Rosa
1971; Germany; 65 min; Drama
W: Rosa von Praunheim; *C:* Robert van Ackeren;
E: Jean-Claude Piroué
Cast: Berryt Bohlen, Bernd Feuerhelm

A young homosexual man examines all the political, dogmatic, and anti-bourgeois aspects of his life in the process of coming out. This film assails media-created romantic illusions, capitalist principles, and sexist role playing.

It wasn't Love

Benning, Sadie
1992; USA; 20 min; B&W; Comedy

A sexy gender-fuck tale of lesbian love on the road.

Dist/Sales: VDB, NFVLS

It's a Boy! Journeys from Female to Male

Leech, Marla
2001; USA; 30 min; Documentary
P: Marla Leech

The stories of three people who have undergone the transition from female to male. Includes interviews with partners and friends.

It's a Queer World

Farthing, Cheryl
1993; UK; 40 min; Comedy

Using their pink satellite dish, Lily Savage and her lovely assistant Damian present an extremely entertaining visual sampling of gay television from around the world.

It's Elementary: Talking about Gay Issues in School

Chasnoff, Debra
1996; USA; 80 min; Documentary
P: Helen S. Cohen

Using interviews with teachers and children from kindergarten to high school this Academy Award-winning filmmaker presents a powerful case against the conservatives who attack the so-called gay agenda in schools. These brave teachers have put everything on the line to stop the hatred and prejudice that children learn from a very young age by addressing anti-gay issues in the classroom.

Awards: San Francisco International Lesbian & Gay Film Festival, 1996: Audience Award for Best Documentary
Prod Comp: Women's Educational Media
Dist/Sales: WoMedia, NewDay, Heathcliff

It's in the Water

Herd, Kelli
1996; USA; 100 min; Comedy
P: Dee Evans, Jonathan Ladd; *W:* Kelli Herd;
C: Michael Off; *E:* Rusty Martin
Cast: Keri Jo Chapman, Teresa Garrett, Derrick Sanders, Timothy Vahle

The charitably-minded society dames of Azalea Springs arm themselves with rubber gloves and buckets of prejudice when an AIDS hospice opens in their area. But their panic metres really go off the dial when a drunken gay resident announces that homosexuality can be caught from the town's water supply. Amidst the ensuing mayhem, Alex shocks her golfing hubby (and the rest of the town) by being caught in a passionate embrace with her old high school buddy, Grace; while Mark, the son of the local slander-mongering newspaper chief, deals with his own latent homosexuality when he meets the gorgeous Tomas.

Prod Comp: Kelli Herd Film Company
Dist/Sales: Wolfe, Millivres

It's my Life

Tilley, Brian
2001; South Africa; 74 min; Documentary
P: Phillip Brooks, Steven Markovitz; *C:* Giulio Biccari;
E: Ronelle Loots; *M:* Philip Miller

At the beginning of *It's my Life* we learn that there are 4.7 million South Africans currently infected with the HIV virus and, despite the fact that anti-retroviral medicines allow people with HIV to lead almost normal lives, the South African government has failed to provide them in public hospitals and clinics. More damning, the President of the country, Thabo Mbeki, has consistently questioned the link between HIV and AIDS. It is in this context that Zackie Achmat, the HIV-positive acting chairperson of the Treatment Action Campaign (TAC), has decided not to take anti-retroviral medicines until they are made available by the government in public hospitals and clinics. Filmed over five months, *It's my Life* follows Zackie as he leads a court battle against the multinational drug companies to allow the introduction of cheaper, generic drugs, and takes on the South African government for it's confusing policies around HIV/AIDS. As a leader in the campaign for affordable treatment, Zackie's provocative position is not one all his friends and colleagues support. When Zackie gets ill, everyone wants to know why he refuses to take the medicines that would let him lead a healthier life. *It's my Life* interweaves personal and public images to provide an intimate look at an internationally profiled defiance campaign and the complexities of its leading figure. (First Run/Icarus)

Prod Comp: Dominant 7, Big World Cinema
Dist/Sales: Dominant7, FirstRun/Icarus

It's my Party

Kleiser, Randal
1996; USA; 100 min; Drama
P: Joel Thurm, Randal Kleiser; *W:* Randal Kleiser;
C: Bernd Heinl; *E:* Ela Von Hasperg; *M:* Basil Poledouris
Cast: Eric Roberts, Gregory Harrison, Margaret Cho,
Bruce Davison, Lee Grant

A year after Nick and Brandon break up, Nick
learns he has just a few days to live due to a rare and
terminal AIDS-related condition. Rather than
succumb to the disease's debilitating effects, he
decides to end his life as he has lived it—with joy
and gusto. As a prelude to his death, Nick throws a
two-day farewell party to which dozens of friends
and family are invited. Uninvited, Brandon shows
up to a chorus of dissent from Nick's friends who
believe Brandon failed Nick when he most needed
him. What follows is a raft of camp one-liners and a
Hollywood roll-call of cameos: Marlee Matlin plays
Nick's sensitive sister Daphne, George Segal plays
the estranged father, and Olivia Newton-John (who
also sings on the soundtrack) plays a high-school
sweetheart. (MQFF)

Prod Comp: United Artists, MGM
Dist/Sales: UIP, TLA, Warner, Wolfe, Swank

It's not Unusual: A Lesbian and Gay History

Farthing, Cheryl / MacMillan, Ian
1996; UK; 3 x 50 min; Documentary

This three part documentary series, made for BBC
2, tells the hidden history of gay and lesbian lives in
the 20th century. Rare archival footage is intercut
with personal accounts from a wide ranging and
fascinating group of gay men and lesbians. Interviewees range from Evelyn Irons, 96-years old and
an ex-lover of Vita Sackville West to Welsh 16-year-
old Grace Hughes, who has been out to her family
and school since age 13.

Prod Comp: BBC 2, Piranha Productions

It's Personal

2000; 30 min; Documentary

It's Personal examines the development of sexual
behaviour in today's society, and how our ideals and
identities have changed. Follows two couples: a
lesbian couple who have been living together for
twenty years, and a heterosexual couple in the first
stages of their relationship. Evaluates the connection
between healthy sexuality and a person's self-worth,
as well as emotions, personality, and general health.
(EMA)

Dist/Sales: EMA

It's that Age

Kot, Hagar
1990; Israel; 40 min; Drama

A rare lesbian love story set in Tel Aviv.

J'embrasse pas

(aka: I Don't Kiss)

Téchiné, André
1991; France; 115 min; Drama
P: Maurice Bernart, Jacques-Eric Strauss, Jean Labadie;
W: Michel Grisolia, Jacques Nolot, André Téchiné;
C: Thierry Arbogast; *E:* Claudine Merlin, Edith Vassart;
M: Philippe Sarde
Cast: Philippe Noiret, Emmanuelle Béart, Manuel
Blanc, Hélène Vincent

Pierre decides to break away from the restrictive life
of his childhood in rural south-west France and
moves to Paris. He contacts the only person he
knows in the city, Evelyn, a middle-aged woman he
met at Lourdes. She manages to get Pierre a job as a
hospital orderly, but his childhood dream is to
become an actor. After losing his way, Pierre falls
into prostitution and finds it difficult to retain his
innocence. Based on an original story by Jacques
Nolot. French with English subtitles.

Prod Comp: Bac Films, Ciné Cinq, Gruppo Bema,
Président Films, Salomé
Dist/Sales: NewVision, 21stCentury, ACMI

Jackson: My Life your Fault

Roy, Duncan
1995; UK; 41 min; Drama

Trapped beneath the burdens of memories of a dead
father and a monstrously possessive mother, Jackson
seeks escape in the arms of policeman Hardy.
Believing his love can save Jackson from his tortured
existence, Hardy sets in action events that nearly
destroy all their lives in the process.

Dist/Sales: BFI, ThirdRock

Jake 'Today I Became a Man'

Foiles, Stacey
2000; USA; 14 min; Documentary

Jake is 12 years old and already firm about his
chosen career—professional drag queen!

Dist/Sales: ACMI

James Baldwin: The Price of the Ticket

Thorsen, Karen
1990; USA; 83 min; Documentary
P: Karen Thorsen, Douglas K. Dempsey, William Miles

Cast: Amiri Baraka, Dr Maya Angelou, David Baldwin, David Leeming, Lucien Happersberger

Profiles the life, works and beliefs of the late black American writer, civil-rights activist and homosexual, James Baldwin. Born in Harlem in 1924, to a religious family, he looked for equality and justice in his own country until he left what he saw as the suffocating society of the US in 1948 and moved to Paris. This engaging documentary uses a combination of interviews and actual footage of Baldwin to create a portrait of a passionate, angry and idealistic fighter.

Prod Comp: Maysles Films
Dist/Sales: Ronin, CaliforniaNewsreel, ACMI, BFI

James Baldwin: The Price of the Ticket

Janine

Dunye, Cheryl
1990; USA; 10 min; Experimental

Janine is a video about one black woman's resolution of a past relationship. The filmmaker candidly tells the story of her friendship with Janine, a white upper-middle-class girl whom she met in high school. The film documents Dunye's struggle for acceptance in Janine's world, despite their racial and cultural differences. (MQFF)

Dist/Sales: TWN

Jareena: Portrait of a Hijda

Kalliat, Prem
1990; USA; 24 min; Documentary

A bold and sensitive look at the lives of the Hijdas—

a society of eunuchs that has thrived in India for centuries. The film provides an assertion of the dignity of human individuality, a portrayal of the multiplicity of human dimensions and a story of a personal odyssey. (MQFF)

Jaundiced Eye, The

de la Pena, Nonny
1999; USA; 89 min; Documentary
P: Dan Gifford; *W:* Nonny de la Pena; *C:* Bestor Cram; *E:* Greg Byers; *M:* Michael Brook

This harrowing documentary chronicles the decade long trials and emotional traumas incurred by a gay Michigan man, Stephen Matthews, and his straight father, Melvin Matthews, who were wrongfully accused by Stephen's ex-girlfriend and her husband of molesting Stephen's son. Despite the fact that there was no physical evidence (although accusations included the torturous use of a machete), both Stephen and Melvin Matthews were sentenced to 35 years in jail. A chlamydia test which swayed the jury, was later revealed to give false positive results. Both the manufacturer, Abbott Laboratories, and The Centre for Disease Control say that it lacks forensic value for use in sexual abuse cases. Eventually released from incarceration on this fact, both men went into the world to find that the prosecution wanted to put them on trial again, despite a total lack of evidence. Stephen Matthew's story is a horrifying example of justice miscarried in a society of legal labyrinths where science is easily confused about fact, and sexual orientation can provoke prosecutorial vendettas based upon long-held biases. (www.thejaundicedeye.com)

Prod Comp: Fifth Estate Productions, Pyedog Productions
Dist/Sales: FifthEstate, Scrine

Je, tu, il, elle

Akerman, Chantal
1974; Belgium, France; 81 min; B&W; Drama
P: Chantal Akerman; *W:* Chantal Akerman;
C: Bénédicte Delesalle, Renelde Dupont, Charlotte Szlovak; *E:* Luc Fréché
Cast: Chantal Akerman, Niels Arestrup, Claire Wauthion

A film in three parts. In the first part a young woman living alone in a room writes a long letter over a period of several weeks. Becoming increasingly frustrated she suddenly leaves and is picked up by a truck driver who turns out to be rather self-absorbed. The third part involves the young woman's lesbian relationship with a taciturn lover (Elle), which seems to act out the sexual politics alluded to in the second part: the lover adopts the role of dutiful wife. Tu could also refer to the audience as Akerman is clearly concerned with achieving an awareness of the way the narrative is constructed, bringing together formalist and feminist concerns. French with English subtitles.

Prod Comp: Paradise Films
Dist/Sales: NFVLS

Jean Cocteau: Autobiography of an Unknown

Cozarinsky, Edgardo
1985; France; 58 min; Documentary

A biography of Jean Cocteau, the poet, painter and filmmaker. It looks at his life from his childhood to his death in 1963. It touches on areas like his cocaine addition, which he battled for many years, and his films such as *Orpheus*, *Blood of a Poet* and *Beauty and the Beast*. It also mentions his love for his friend Raymond Radiguey, who died quite young leaving Cocteau devastated. There are many interviews with people such as Jean Renoir, Pablo Picasso, Sergei Diaghilev, Henri Matisse and Charles Chaplin.

Jeffery's Hollywood Screen Trick

Downing, Todd
2001; USA; 11 min; Animation

An hilariously tongue-in-cheek spoof of feelgood gay flicks that is not for the faint of heart or weak of stomach.

Dist/Sales: BrokenHip

Jeffrey

Ashley, Christopher
1995; USA; 92 min; Comedy
P: Mark Balsam, Mitchell Maxwell, Victoria Maxwell;
W: Paul Rudnick; *C:* Jeffery J. Tufano;
E: Cara Silverman; *M:* Stephen Endelman
Cast: Steven Weber, Patrick Stewart, Sigourney Weaver, Michael T. Weiss, Bryan Batt

Jeffrey takes a look at one man's comic search for love and commitment in 1990s New York. Jeffrey decides to become celibate when the risk of AIDS takes some of the joy out of sex, but immediately after, finally meets Mr Right. Jeffrey has an all-star cast headed by Patrick Stewart as an over-the-top interior designer who is the only truly sane character in the film. Sigourney Weaver plays a silver-clad tele-evangelist, and a Mother Theresa look-alike who plays a mean piano solo. (MQFF)

Prod Comp: The Booking Office, Workin' Man Films
Dist/Sales: TLA, Col-Tri, Orion, Wolfe, ACMI, Swank

Jenny

Sharp, Jan
1977; Australia; 30 min; Documentary
P: Tom Manefield

A film focusing on a teenage girl in a lesbian relationship. Jenny discusses her perception of the 'gay' scene, her relationship and how she feels other people perceive her lifestyle. (ACMI)

Prod Comp: Film Australia
Dist/Sales: ACMI

Jerker

Harrison, Hugh
1992; USA; 90 min; Drama
P: Hugh Harrison, Smitty, Lou Toth;
W: Hugh Harrison; *C:* Ron Hamill; *M:* Michael Angelo
Cast: Joseph Stachura, Tom Wagner

Set in the early 1980s, *Jerker* is the story of two gay men who choose to have the safest sex possible, that is, over the phone. As the phone calls continue, the sexual content of their conversations begins to wane and it becomes more personal, and eventually the two men become friends. From the play by Robert Chesley.

Dist/Sales: TLA

Jewel's Darl

Wells, Peter
1985; New Zealand; 57 min; Drama
P: John Maynard, Bridget Ikin; *W:* Anne Kennedy, Peter Wells; *C:* Stuart Dryburgh
Cast: Richard Hanna, Georgina Beyer

From the seven-part television series *About Face*. In *Jewel's Darl*, Jewel, a transsexual, and Mandy, a transvestite, are in love and trapped on the fringes of a hostile, mocking society. Stars Georgina Beyer— the subject of the documentary *Georgie Girl*.

Prod Comp: Hibiscus Films, New Zealand Film Commission

Jim Loves Jack: The James Egan Story

Adkin, David
1995; Canada; 53 min; Documentary
C: Ali Kazimi; *E:* Ricardo Acosta
Cast: Jim Egan, Jack Nesbit

A powerful documentary about the lives and activism of James Egan and his lover Jack Nesbit. Egan was one of the first activists, operating before the term 'gay rights' was ever used. He wrote letters to the Canadian government and newspapers demanding changes to the political and social representation of gays and lesbians. In 1995 he fought a Supreme Court battle for constitutional changes involving same-sex spousal benefits. The film is structured around interviews with the two men at their home in Vancouver.

Dist/Sales: VTape, CinemaGuild

Jodie: An Icon

Parmar, Pratibha
1996; UK; 24 min; Documentary

Jodie is a fast paced, breezy look at the transatlantic phenomenon that has made Hollywood actress Jodie Foster an icon for lesbians who identify with, adore and celebrate the screen personas of her remarkable career. Fans and queer cultural critics share their favourite 'iconic' moments giving illuminating lesbian readings of Foster's key films which trace the charismatic actor's progression from early tomboy parts as a child star to mature performances depicting active, strong willed women with attitude. (WMM)

Dist/Sales: WMM, Cinenova

Jodie Promo, The

Olson, Jenni
1995; USA; 30 min; Comedy
Cast: Jodie Foster

From *Freaky Friday* to *Nell*, Jodie Foster has been one of the most versatile actresses of her generation. As a tomboy role model, as a budding adolescent, and as one of the strongest women in Hollywood, she is also one of our hottest heartthrobs. This compilation of trailers features some of the brightest highlights of Foster's distinguished career from 1969–1995.

Dist/Sales: PlanetOut

Joe-Joe

Dougherty, Cecilia / Singer, Leslie
1993; USA; 52 min; B&W; Comedy

Transposing swinging London into sunny San Francisco, Dougherty and Singer relive the legend of gay playwright Joe Orton in the privacy of their own apartment—with both of them playing Joe. Spaced out in Warhol-land, they argue over which one should answer when a call comes in for Joe, deal with their famous agent Peggy Ramsay and take time out for sex. There are cameos from queer hero(ine)s such as Sadie Benning and Angela Hans Schierl.

Dist/Sales: VDB

Joey Breaker

Hall, Dolly / Starr, Steven
1993; USA; 92 min; Comedy
P: Steven Starr, Amos Poe; *W:* Steven Starr;

C: Joe DeSalvo; *E:* Michael Schweitzer
Cast: Richard Edson, Fred Fondren, Cedella Marley, Erik King, Gina Gershon

A romantic tale about a New York talent agent, Joey, who lives a rather sheltered life in Manhattan. A co-worker asks him along to visit and deliver food to Alfred, a gay man who is dying of AIDS. Terrified and confronted, Joey leaves as quickly as possible, but eventually returns to Alfred's flat and they begin to form a friendship. He also meets a Jamaican nurse with whom he falls in love and a black gay comedian. His sheltered life will never be the same again.

Prod Comp: Poe Productions, Breakdown Productions
Dist/Sales: Skouras

Joey goes to Wigstock

Freed, Leonard
1992; USA; 10 min; Documentary

Joey Arias has entertained audiences around the world for 18 years. What makes Joey's performance a little off beat is that he is a drag queen. Freed follows Joey, publicly a very social butterfly, all over town—a wig contest at a New York restaurant, the infamous Pyramid Club, and the rather more upscale Tavern on the Green—with a cult of fans and fellow cross dressers. The piece culminates at the 'Wigstock' festival, an annual outdoor event attended by thousand of cross dressers. But Joey's private side is also revealed, as he reflects on homosexuality, AIDS, drugs, and what it means to live in the fast lane—and not fall off the edge. (First Run/Icarus)

Dist/Sales: FirstRun/Icarus

Joggernaught

Mobley, Doug
1994; USA; 50 min; Comedy

Joggernaught is a queer video-diary with a rousing soundtrack, following the ruminations of a confused twenty-nothing as he retreats from his urban woes to the pastoral jogging trails of his bucolic motherland. While pounding his body over 16 miles of dirt and pavement, the jogger ponders the shards of his troubled relationship, pathetic career and absurd erotic desires.

Johanna, D'Arc of Mongolia

(aka: Joan of Arc of Mongolia)

Ottinger, Ulrike
1989; Germany; 165 min; Action
W: Ulrike Ottinger; *C:* Ulrike Ottinger;
M: Wilhelm Dieter Siebert
Cast: Delphine Seyrig, Irm Hermann, Gillian Scalici, Xu Re Huor

Seven Western women travellers meet aboard the

Trans-Siberian Express, a rolling museum of European culture. Lady Windemere, an elegant ethnographer, regales a young companion with Mongol myths and folklore while other passengers revel in the dining-car cabernet. Suddenly ambushed by a band of Mongol horsemen, the company is abducted to the plains of Inner Mongolia and embark on a fantastic camel ride across the magnificent countryside. Has been described as a lesbian Lawrence of Arabia. (WMM)
German with English subtitles.

Prod Comp: La Sept Cinéma, ZDF
Dist/Sales: WMM

Johnny Eager

Le Roy, Mervyn
1941; USA; 107 min; B&W; Drama
P: John W. Considine Jnr; *W:* John Lee Mahin, James Edward Grant; *C:* Harold Rosson; *E:* Albert Akst; *M:* Bronislau Kaper
Cast: Robert Taylor, Lana Turner, Van Heflin, Robert Sterling, Patricia Dane

A gangster melodrama about a good-looking egotistical hood, played by Taylor, his homosexual whipping-boy, Heflin, and a young society woman. The hood seduces the young woman and convinces her she has killed a man. After some prodding by Heflin, the hood does the right thing.

Prod Comp: MGM
Dist/Sales: Ascanbee, ReelMovies, MGM

Johnny Greyeyes

Manzano, Jorge
2000; Canada; 75 min; Drama
P: Jorge Manzano, Timothy L. Hill; *W:* Jorge Manzano; *C:* Marcos Arriaga; *E:* Jacqueline Carmody; *M:* Reynaldo Valverde
Cast: Gail Maurice, Columpa C. Bobb, Jonathan Fisher, Georgina Lightning

Johnny Greyeyes is the powerful story of a Native American woman struggling to maintain strength, love and spirit within the walls of a women's prison. Since the shooting death of her father, Johnny has spent most of her life in prison. There, she forms a new family and falls in love with her cellmate Lana. But her responsibilities to the outside world weigh heavily as she attempts to pull together her fractured natural family. With her release date near, Johnny valiantly strives to keep her two worlds together. (Wolfe)

Prod Comp: Nepantla Films
Dist/Sales: Nepantla, Vagrant, Wolfe, VideoAmericain

Johnny Guitar

Ray, Nicholas
1954; USA; 110 min; Western
P: Herbert J. Yates; *W:* Philip Yordan; *C:* Harry Stradling; *E:* Richard Van Enger; *M:* Victor Young
Cast: Joan Crawford, Sterling Hayden, Mercedes McCambridge, Ernest Borgnine, Ward Bond

A reformed gunfighter returns to a woman he had abandoned years earlier. She is now the proprietor of a gambling saloon opened in anticipation of the arrival of the railroad and in the face of hostile opposition from the local townspeople. The film's bizarre, even baroque intensity derives in part from the central antagonism between two women (virtually unique in the western) and in Yordan and Ray's expressed intention of seeking an anti-McCarthy parable. A great confrontation between Crawford and McCambridge with rampant symbolism throughout. Crawford indulges in a bit of cross-dressing in her western outfit.

Prod Comp: Republic Pictures Corporation
Dist/Sales: ReelMovies, 20thCenturyFox, ACMI, Republic, NFVLS

Johns

Silver, Scott
1996; USA; 97 min; Drama
P: Beau Flynn, Stefan Simchowitz; *W:* Scott Silver; *C:* Tom Richmond; *E:* Dorian Harris; *M:* Danny Caron, Charles Brown
Cast: David Arquette, Lukas Haas, Tony Epper, John C. McGinley

Scott Silver's first feature *Johns* is a dark comic tragedy starring Lucas Haas and David Arquette as two young street hustlers working the hot grim landscape of Hollywood's Santa Monica Boulevard, the day before Christmas. It's a story about friendship and sacrifice—what we give of ourselves to help another human being. (Wolfe)

Prod Comp: bandeira Entertainment
Dist/Sales: Wolfe, FirstLook

Jollies

Benning, Sadie
1990; USA; 11 min; B&W; Experimental

A pixel-porn parallel between two enamoured Barbie dolls and Benning's own desire frame this frank dialogue on teenage sexual curiosity.

Dist/Sales: VDB, NFVLS

Journey Among Women

Cowan, Tom
1977; Australia; 89 min; Drama
P: John Weiley; *W:* Tom Cowan, John Weiley, Dorothy
Hewett; *C:* Tom Cowan; *E:* John Scott; *M:* Roy Ritchie
Cast: Jeune Pritchard, Nell Campbell, Diana Fuller, Lisa
Peers, Jude Kuring

During Australia's early colonial period a band of
escaped female convicts, freed by an upper-class
woman, learn to live off the land as they set up a
commune in the bush. They find ways of surviving
in a community of women free from sexual oppression. An adventure narrative competes with a more
poetic approach; the latter introducing a mythic
dimension which does not escape showing women as
mysterious and close to nature, more intuitive than
logical.

Prod Comp: Ko-An Film Productions
Dist/Sales: NFVLS

Journey Among Women

Journey of Jared Price, The

Black, Dustin Lance
2000; USA; 97 min; Drama
P: Bob Edgar, Robert Edgar, Greg Nimer;
W: Dustin Lance Black; *C:* Tony Croll; *E:* Tom Vater;
M: Damon Intrabartolo
Cast: Corey Spears, Josh Jacobson, Steve Tyler, Rocki
Craigg, Gillian Harris

Having moved to Los Angeles from the South, Jared
Price takes up temporary accommodation at a youth
hostel, where he meets the friendly and optimistic

Robert. Before long Jared finds work as the live-in
help for the elderly Mrs Haines, whose own son
Matthew is too busy to look after her. Jared falls for
Matthew, learning too late that the older man
already has a boyfriend. The natural pacing and
undeniable charm of the story will endear the film to
viewers, as well as the eroticism of its sex scenes.
(MQFF)

Prod Comp: 10% Productions, Sock Puppet Productions
Dist/Sales: 10%, Wolfe, SockPuppet

The Journey to Kafiristan

Journey to Kafiristan, The

(aka: Die Reise nach Kafiristan)

Dubini, Donatello / Dubini, Fosco
2001; Germany; 100 min; Documentary
P: Donatello Dubini, Fosco Dubini;
W: Donatello Dubini, Fosco Dubini, Barbara Marx; *C:*
Matthias Kaelin; *E:* Christel Maye; *M:* Jan Garbarek,
Wolfgang Hamm, Ustad Fateh Ali Khan, Madredeus
Cast: Jeanette Hain, Nina Petri

In 1939, the author Annemarie Schwarzenbach and the
ethnologist Ella Maillart travel together by car to
Kabul, but each is in pursuit of her own project.
Annemarie Schwarzenbach, who was among Erika and
Klaus Mann's circle of friends in the 1930s, is searching
for a place of refuge in the Near East to discover her
own self. Ella Maillart justifies her restlessness, her need
for movement and travel, with a scientific pretext: she
would like to explore the mysterious Kafiristan Valley
and make a name for herself with publications on the
archaic life of the nomads living there. Both women are
on the run, but political developments and their own
biographies catch up with them again and again. Their
mutual journey through the outside world, which runs
from Geneva via the Balkans and Turkey to Persia, is
compounded by the inner world of emotions with a
tender love story. As both women arrive in Kabul,
World War II breaks out and puts an end to their plans.
(www.german-cinema.de)
German with English Subtitles.

Prod Comp: Dubini Filmprodktion
Dist/Sales: MediaLuna

Joys of Smoking, The

Katsapetses, Nicholas
1999; USA; 86 min; Drama
P: Nick Katsapetses, Paul Miller, Eduardo Morell;
W: Nick Katsapetses; *C:* Nick Katsapetses, Eduardo
Morell; *E:* Nick Katsapetses; *M:* Andrea Terry, Errol
Stewart
Cast: Matthew Rozen, Steven Sorensen, Deborah
Cordell, Carrie Mogan

At the heart of the film are Gray and his lover
Daniel, just a week away from their commitment
ceremony. Daniel's ready to tie the knot, if only he
can give up his clandestine trysts at the local beat.
Also in focus is a lesbian couple going through a
horrendous, but blackly humorous break-up, with
one stalking the other. Dotted throughout this
emotionally charged frame lies the one thing all the
characters draw on for comfort: cigarettes.

Prod Comp: Verging Productions
Dist/Sales: Verging

Juggling Gender

Gold, Tami
1992; USA; 27 min; Documentary
P: Tami Gold; *C:* Tami Gold
Cast: Jennifer Miller, Circus Amok

A loving portrait of Jennifer Miller, a lesbian
performer who lives her life with a full beard. Miller
works as a performance artist, circus director, clown
and as the 'bearded lady' in one of the only remain-
ing side-shows in America. In public she is often
mistaken for a man, an experience she handles with
the wit and intelligence that characterise her stage
performances. Her lifestyle suggests the impossibility
of defining anyone as truly feminine or masculine.
Juggling Gender explores the fluidity of gender and
raises important questions about the construction of
sexual and gender identity. (WMM)

Prod Comp: Tamerik Productions
Dist/Sales: Ronin, WMM, NFVLS

Julia

Zinnemann, Fred
1977; USA; 115 min; Drama
P: Richard Roth; *W:* Alvin Sargent; *C:* Douglas
Slocombe; *E:* Walter Murch, Marcel Durham;
M: Georges Delerue
Cast: Jane Fonda, Vanessa Redgrave, Jason Robards,
Meryl Streep, Maximilian Schell

Based on her own novel, Lillian Hellman describes
her close relationship with her childhood friend,
Julia, and how she was drawn into the European
resistance movement in the 1930s by smuggling
money to Berlin. There are some strong lesbian

undertones to their friendship but 'it' is never really
mentioned. At the time Hellman was writing *The
Children's Hour* which has a strong lesbian theme.

Awards: Academy Awards, 1977: Best Adapted Screen-
play, Actress (Vanessa Redgrave)
Prod Comp: 20th Century-Fox
Dist/Sales: Ascanbee, ReelMovies, 20thCenturyFox,
ACMI

Julian Clary - The Mincing Machine Tour

1993; UK; 86 min; Comedy
Cast: Julian Clary

Filmed live in concert, Julian says 'climb aboard the
hem of my chiffon cape and fly to a land of eternal
double entendres and withering glances, a land
where sophisticated social comment gives way
graciously to sheer smut'.

Julie Johnson

Julie Johnson

Gosse, Bob
2000; USA; 94 min; Drama
P: Ray Angelic; *W:* Gosse, Wendy Hammond; *C:* David
M. Dunlap; *E:* David Leonard; *M:* Angelo Badalamenti,
Andrew Barrett
Cast: Lili Taylor, Courtney Love, Spaulding Gray, Bill
Golodner

Julie Johnson is a dutiful wife and caring mother in
working class Hoboken, New Jersey where everyone
knows everyone else's business. Her best friend
Claire has been her loyal companion since high
school. Away from their tight-knit circle of friends
Julie harbours a secret passion for theoretical physics,
and is terrified that if her friends found out they
would ridicule her. Although she never finished high
school, Julie convinces Claire to accompany her to
adult education computer classes behind her
disapproving husband's back. While there she meets
an inspirational professor, who immediately spots
her potential, and helps to nurture her talent.
Eventually Julie's husband discovers the subterfuge,
and the marriage falls apart. Julie and Claire move in
together, and Julie admits to her long-standing

feelings for Claire. A romance develops between the women—but will it survive the bigotry of their small community, and the changes in Julie's life? (MQFF)

Prod Comp: Shooting Gallery
Dist/Sales: Gosse

Jumping the Gun

Schneider, Jane
1993; Australia; 10 min; Drama

A woman takes a one night stand much further in her mind.

Jungle Boy, The

Greyson, John
1985; Canada; 15 min; Experimental

Greyson explores the aftermath of a raid on a men's bathroom in Canada.

Dist/Sales: VDB

Jupon Rouge, Le

(aka: Manuela's Loves)

Lefèbvre, Geneviève
1987; France; 90 min; Drama
W: Nicole Berckmans, Geneviève Lefèbvre; *M:* Joanna Bruzdowicz
Cast: Marie-Christine Barrault, Guillemette Grobon, Alida Valli

Three women of greatly differing ages and back-grounds engage in a complicated, and at times contradictory, ménage à trois. Bacha, the older, is a human rights activist and, Manuela, a fashion designer. When Manuela meets and starts an affair with the young and beautiful Claude, Bacha becomes intensely jealous. Manuela must now make a decision between the two women. French with English subtitles.

Dist/Sales: Wolfe

Just a Woman

Farahani, Mitra / B. Y.
2001; France, Iran; 29 min; Documentary

Moravid experiences life as a male-to-female transsexual in her homeland. How does she cope when that homeland is Tehran? This fascinating documentary challenges many of the Western clichés about Iranian society, and reveals a woman and a nation filled with surprising contradictions. (queerDOC 2002)

Just Because of who we Are

Norman, Abigail
1986; USA; 28 min; Documentary

A groundbreaking documentary that explores the issues of violence against lesbians. A neglected topic, the film uses interviews with a range of women to reveal stories of unprovoked violence, physical and psychological harassment and attempts at 'cures'.

Prod Comp: Heramedia Collective
Dist/Sales: Cinenova, WMM

Just call me Kade

Zolten, Sam
2001; USA; 26 min; Documentary

Kade Farlow Collins is a 16-year-old female to male transgendered teen residing in Tucson Arizona. Kade's parents maintain a supportive and nurturing relationship to Kade regarding the many challenges facing their teenage child. However, it hasn't always been easy. (MQFF)

Dist/Sales: Frameline, ACMI

Just Desserts

Pellizzari, Monica
1993; Australia; 13 min; Comedy
W: Monica Pellizzari

This delicious comedy about an Italian–Australian girl's sexual awakening and her love for her mama's cooking. Through the use of a split screen which separates the food from the experience, issues such as menstruation, masturbation, lesbianism and virginity are explored, against a backdrop of broth, venetian fritters, polenta, dumplings and pizza. (ACMI)

Prod Comp: NRG Films Australia
Dist/Sales: ACMI

Just for Fun

Olye, David
1994; USA; 30 min; Drama
P: Gordon Seaman

Olye confronts the sensitive issue of gay bashing and presents a dramatisation of a young man who, under the influence of his peers, sets out at night with his friends to deliberately assault a homosexual male 'just for fun'. The video raises issues of personal identity, peer pressure and prejudice.

Prod Comp: Whistle Productions
Dist/Sales: DirectCinema

Just like a Woman

Monger, Christopher
1992; UK; 105 min; Comedy
P: Nick Evans; *W:* Nick Evans; *C:* Alan Hume;
E: Nicolas Gaster; *M:* Michael Storey
Cast: Julie Walters, Adrian Pasdar, Paul Freeman, Susan Wooldridge

She stole his heart. He stole her clothes. A love

triangle with a real twist. When the wife of a financial adviser finds some ladies knickers in his drawer, she kicks her husband out. But the knickers weren't there for the usual reason. A funny and well-handled film about transvestism.

Prod Comp: Rank, LWT, Zenith, British Screen
Dist/Sales: REP, Col-Tri, SamuelGoldwyn

Just One of the Girls

(aka: Anything for Love)

Keusch, Michael
1993; USA; 100 min; Comedy
P: Robert Vince, Cal Shumiatcher; *W:* Raúl Fernández; *C:* Tobias A. Schliessler; *E:* Allan Lee; *M:* Amin Bhatia, Vincent Mai
Cast: Corey Haim, Cameron Bancroft, Nicole Eggert

Chris is a young high-school student who, in order to stop being harassed by the school bully, dresses up in drag. With the help of his sister, everything goes well until he falls in love with Marie. Marie convinces Chris to try for the cheer leaders' squad and he gets the job. Meanwhile the school bully has fallen in love with him. The gym teacher thinks Chris is a lesbian and his father thinks he's gay.

Prod Comp: Vidmark E, Jailhouse Productions

Just One of the Guys

Gottlieb, Lisa
1985; USA; 97 min; Comedy
P: Andrew Fogelson; *W:* Dennis Feldman, Jeff Franklin; *C:* John McPherson; *E:* Tony Lombardo; *M:* Tom Scott
Cast: Joyce Hyser, Clayton Rohner, Billy Jacoby, Toni Hudson, Sherilyn Fenn

Terry is convinced her high school teachers don't take her seriously just because she's a pretty girl. When she doesn't win a journalism contest, she decides to switch schools—and gender. She manages to fool everyone and is accepted as one of the guys until she meets and falls for Rick.

Prod Comp: Summa, Triton, Columbia
Dist/Sales: 20thCenturyFox, 16MM, Col-Tri

Just One Time

Janger, Lane
1999; USA; 93 min; Comedy
P: Jasmine Kosovic, Lane Janger, Exile Ramirez, Jeff Roth; *W:* Lane Janger, Jennifer Vandever; *C:* Michael St Hilaire; *E:* Mitch Stanley; *M:* Edward Bilous
Cast: Loelle Carter, Guillermo Diaz, Lane Janger

Lane Janger's first feature film follows the story of New York City couple Anthony and Amy as they prepare for their approaching wedding. Plans are thrown into chaos when just prior to the wedding, Anthony makes known his long-standing fantasy: that he and Amy indulge in a threesome with another woman. Amy eventually agrees on one condition: that Anthony return the favour with another man—and she has just the man in mind—their cute, gay, Latino neighbour Victor who harbours a man-sized crush on Anthony. Anthony enlists the help of his work mates from the New York City Fire Department to help see the plan through—with hilarious results—while Amy becomes enamoured with their sexy lesbian neighbour Michelle. Will the marriage eventuate, what will become of Victor, and what will those hunky firemen make of New York's gay clubs?

Prod Comp: Danger Filmworks
Dist/Sales: Cowboy, Wolfe, Atom

Just One Time

Just the Two of Us

Beerson, Jaque / Peeters, Barbara
1973; USA; 82 min; Drama
P: David Novik; *W:* David Novik, Barbara Peeters; *C:* Jaque Beerson; *E:* Richard Weber
Cast: Alicia Courtney, Elizabeth Plumb, John Aprea, Jamie Cooper, Elizabeth Knowles

Two lonely housewives living in suburban LA become close friends. While lunching at a restaurant one day, they spot two women at another table holding hands and later kissing. Both are transfixed—one excited and envious, the other perplexed but intrigued. An idyllic romance soon ensues between the two, but troubles brew when the bisexual woman thinks of their relationship more as a fling, soon becoming bored and eager to meet men, much to the other's frustration and jealousy.

Dist/Sales: SomethingWeird

Justine's Film

(aka: Le Film de Justine)

Crépeau, Jeanne
1989; Canada; 45 min; Comedy
Cast: Marie-Hélène Montpetit, Denis Ménard, Stéphanie Morgenstern, Danielle Trépanier

Left by the woman she still loves, Justine swears she will never love again and again and again. A tender and sympathetic film with moments of humour and, above all, intelligence. French with English subtitles.

Dist/Sales: CinemaLibre

Kali's Vibe

Carpenter, Shari
2001; USA; 92 min; Drama
P: Gingi Rochelle; *W:* Shari Carpenter; *E:* Brunilda Torres
Cast: Lizzy Davis, Phalana Tiller, Charles Malik Whitfield, Akanke McLean-Nur, Yvette Brooks

In her feature-film debut, Spike Lee protégé Shari Carpenter has created a slick and lively trip through bisexual confusion, with a young African American lesbian named Kali as our guide. Kali soon discovers her performance artist and completely self-absorbed girlfriend, Crystal, has been cheating on her. Kali kicks the girl out, but finds the singles game isn't any better. She gets a hickey from a sex-machine butch and smoke in her face from a pork chop-eating homegirl (Kali is a vegetarian). To Kali's surprise, she starts to develop feelings for her lady-killer co-worker Reese, Just as Kali starts to feel a hetero vibe herself, now ex-girlfriend Crystal shows up again, declaring her love. Confused and conflicted, Kali turns to her Tarot-priestess lesbian godmothers and receives some remarkably enlightened advice about the fluidity of desire. Watching the truly radiant Lizzy Davis as Kali rove from Crystal to Reese and back again, it's almost easy to accept director Carpenter's message of love being bigger than the narrow identities we inhabit. (2002 Vancouver Queer Film & Video Festival)

Dist/Sales: KalisVibe

Kalihgat Fetish

(aka: Kalighat Athikatha)

Avikunthak, Ashish
2000; India; 22 min; Documentary

A portrayal of ceremonial cross-dressing in Indian culture.

Kalin's Prayer

DeSales
1998; USA; 30 min; Documentary
P: DeSales, Melissa Hammel; *W:* DeSales

Part documentary, part re-enactment of the director's life, this stylishly shot, brutally honest portrayal of a woman dealing with the demons of her past is sure to

entertain. The director extracts superb performances from relatively inexperienced actors, and delivers a forceful story employing a unique visual style.

Dist/Sales: IN*SITE

Kamikaze Hearts

Bashore, Juliet
1986; USA; 80 min; Drama
P: Heinz Legler; *W:* Juliet Bashore, John Knoop, Tina 'Tigr' Mennett; *C:* David Golia; *E:* John Knoop;
M: Walt Fowler, Paul M. Young
Cast: Sharon Mitchell, Tina 'Tigr' Mennett, Jon Martin, Sparky Vasque, Robert McKenna

A gritty film that examines the lives of two women working in the porn industry. Sharon Mitchell is the porn star and Tigr Mennett plays her devoted lover and director. Problems begin to surface in the relationship as Tigr becomes increasingly jealous of the lesbian love scenes that Mitchell plays out in front of the camera.

Prod Comp: Legler/Bashore
Dist/Sales: Salzgeber

Kamikaze Summer

Collins, Chris
1996; USA; 60 min; Documentary

A lesbian and a gay man from San Francisco, in an effort to discover why the Religious Right perceives homosexuality as a threat to civilisation, embark on a road trip into the heartland of religious bigotry in America. Travelling through Oregon, Idaho and Colorado—three states which have sponsored antigay legislation—the filmmakers interview movement leaders, show clips from homophobic cable television programs, witness queer-hating demonstrations, and offer their own comments on these encounters. (Cinema Guild)

Dist/Sales: CinemaGuild

Kanada

Hoolboom, Mike
1993; Canada; 65 min; Sci-Fi
P: Mike Hoolboom; *W:* Mike Hoolboom; *C:* Steve Sanguedolce; *E:* Mike Hoolboom; *M:* Earle Peach
Cast: Babs Chula, Sky Gilbert, Mike Hoolboom, Andrew Scorer

Set in the future, during the Canadian-French civil war of separatism, a megalomaniac plans to end the world just after he kisses his boyfriend. A political prostitute and her lover take control in this futuristic patriarchal nightmare.

Dist/Sales: CinemaEsperanca

Kansas Anymore

Wilson, David
1996; USA; 30 min; Drama
P: David Wilson; *W:* David Wilson

A young band's bittersweet journey across the American heartland is complicated by encounters with rednecks, old friends and by the lead singer's growing attraction to the bass player.

Dist/Sales: Kinofist

Karen Black Like Me

Briggs, David
1997; USA; 15 min; Comedy

Hysterical campy homage to the 1970s cult classic *Trilogy of Terror*.

Dist/Sales: FirstRunFeatures

Karmarama

Galea, Lee
2001; Australia; 10 min; Drama

When the local homophobic thug finally sees the light and wants to 'experiment', he gets a rather rude awakening.

Dist/Sales: Queerscreen

Karmen Geï

Ramaka, Joseph Gaï
2001; Canada, France, Senegal; 82 min; Musical
P: Richard Sadler; *W:* Joseph Gaï Ramaka; *C:* Bertrand Chatry; *E:* Hélène Girard; *M:* Julien Jouga, David Murray, Doudou N'Diaye Rose
Cast: Djeïnaba Diop Gaï, Stéphanie Biddle, Magaye Niang, Thierno Ndiaye

This sensual, exciting version of the Carmen legend transports the action of Prosper Merimée's original story and Georges Bizet's celebrated opera to contemporary Dakar on the coast of West Africa. Djeïnaba Diop Gaï is Karmen, a statuesque goddess who is involved with smugglers while desired by both policeman Lamine Diop and female prison warden Angelique. Senegalese filmmaker Joseph Gaï Ramaka has created not only the first African Carmen, but arguably, in his words, the first African film 'musical.' However, instead of calling on Bizet's music, he has assembled some of Senegal's finest musicians and choreographers. Gaï Ramaka's characters and their destinies seem propelled by the frenetic rhythms of the music and dance, complemented by his striking imagery with its bursts of colour. His openly-bisexual Karmen proved a little too passionate for the censors, since the film was banned in Senegal. Lusty and exuberant, Karmen Geï is an imaginative reworking of a familiar tale. (Rafael Film Centre)
French & Wolof with English subtitles.

Dist/Sales: CaliforniaNewsreel

Kate's Addiction

DelaBarre, Eric
1999; USA; 97 min; Thriller
P: Robyn Norris, Laura Caulfield; *W:* Eric DelaBarre; *C:* Jeffrey Wilkins; *E:* Wendy Smith; *M:* Bill Conn
Cast: Kari Wurher, Farrah Forke, Matt Borlenghi, Joel Gretch, Matt Porretta, Natalie Radford

Kate arrives in Los Angeles to meet up with her old friend Sara, but when Sara gets a boyfriend, Kate's sociopathic tendencies come violently to the fore. Her obsession with Sara leads her to murder.

Prod Comp: Avalanche
Dist/Sales: Avalanche

Ke Kulana He Mahu: Remembering a Sense of Place

Ke Kulana He Mahu: Remembering a Sense of Place

Anbe, Brent / Xian, Kathryn
2001; USA; 67 min; Documentary
P: Kathryn Xian, Brent Anbe, Jaymee Carvajal, Connie M. Florez; *W:* Kathryn Xian; *E:* Kathryn Xian, Jaymee Carvajal

Ke Kulana He Mahu: Remembering a Sense of Place is

the story of a group of people, young and old, surviving stereotypes, indignation, homophobia, and marginalisation in a land where the ancient culture once accepted them as a part of society. Through the richness of their personal stories and the humour of their frequent jokes we witness the solidarity and soul of a 'minority' who uses humour and togetherness to redefine family in order to overcome the hate they encounter everyday. *Ke Kulana He Mahu* covers several aspects of the Honolulu gay scene; among them are Hawaiian culture and history, the drag scene, HIV, and religion. (Zang Pictures)

Prod Comp: Zang Pictures
Dist/Sales: Zang

Keep it Up, Jack!

(aka: Auntie)

Ford, Derek
1973; UK; 90 min; Comedy
W: Derek Ford, Alan Selwyn; *C:* Geoff Glover;
E: Pat Foster; *M:* Terry Warr
Cast: Mark Jones, Sue Longhurst, Maggi Burton, Steve Viedor, Linda Regan

When down-on-his-luck, Jack inherits his aunt's mansion and discovers she was actually a madam and ran a brothel from the house, Jack sees an opportunity to make money so he impersonates his aunt to continue running the business. All the girls turn out to be lesbians and the only way Jack can sleep with them is by staying in drag. The film sadly misses out on what could be a rather interesting and humorous exploration of gender.

Dist/Sales: Roadshow

Keep the River on your Right

Shapiro, David / Shapiro, Laurie Gwen
2000; USA; 94 min; Documentary
P: David Shapiro, Laurie Gwen Shapiro; *W:* David Shapiro, Laurie Gwen Shapiro; *C:* Jonathan Kovel;
E: Tula Goenka; *M:* Steve Bernstein

Documentary about the amazing life of Tobias Schneebaum, a gay ex-artist, who travelled to Peru in the 1950s. Deep into the Amazon River he encountered a native tribe that became his second family. Whilst there he witnessed cannibalism, and enjoyed a relationship with one of the tribesman.

Dist/Sales: FilmsTransit

Keep your Laws off my Body

Gund Saalfield, Catherine / Leonard, Zoe
1990; USA; 13 min; B&W; Documentary

A juxtaposition of intimate lesbian images with the monstrous footage of police who descended on an ACT UP (AIDS Coalition To Unleash Power)

demonstration in New York in 1989. The gloved and helmeted police break into the bedroom of two women. (Cinenova)

Dist/Sales: Cinenova, WMM

Kenneth Anger's Hollywood Babylon

(aka: Kenneth Anger)

Finch, Nigel
1991; UK; 60 min; Documentary
C: Tony Bragg

Part portrait of an artist as a young man, part deathstyles of the rich and famous. The film is supposedly even more irreverent than the best-selling books. See Lupe Velez's violent suicide, Fatty Arbuckle's disgrace, human-ashtray James Dean, Marianne Faithfull in person, and the man who embalmed Marilyn! Made by the director of *The Lost Language of Cranes*. (MQFF)

Prod Comp: BBC
Dist/Sales: Roadshow

Kesher Ir

(aka: Urban Feel)

Sagall, Jonathan
1998; Israel; 103 min; Drama
P: Jonathan Sagall, Eyal Shiray, David Mandil, Michael Tapuach; *W:* Jonathan Sagall; *C:* Dror Moreh;
E: Dalia Kastel; *M:* Joseph Bardanashvili
Cast: Dafna Rechter, Jonathan Sagall, Scharonn Alexander, Asi Levy

Eva and Robby are partners in a downward spiralling marriage. Robby has taken to answering 'lonely hearts' ads, while Eva, ripe with desire for a more passionate existence, waits for something to happen... until an unexpected visitor drops by to interrupt their empty domestic routine. He is Emanuel, Robbie's former best friend and Eva's charming and somewhat alcoholic ex-lover. Having cruelly abandoned Eva eight years ago, the couple is wary of his presence. But when the sex-charged Emanuel cons his way back into their lives, sparks fly and old passions long thought dead surface, providing the catalyst for Robbie and Eva's burning desire for change. (Mongrel Media)
Hebrew with English subtitles.

Dist/Sales: Mongrel

Kevin's Room

Zurek, Sharon
2001; USA; 60 min; Drama
P: Sharon Zurek; *W:* Sharon Zurek, Christina Timmins, Lora E. Branch, Martha Shaifer, Andrew Spieldenner;
C: Ines Sommer; *E:* Anna Nakajima
Cast: Keith Butler, Malik Middleton, Parry Cavitt,

Byron Stewart

Kevin's Room is the story of five African–American gay men, each of whom struggles with common issues related to our community, family and each other. Through participation in a support group, each of the men learn valuable lessons and change in ways that will forever impact their lives. Kevin, a young African–American social worker, receives a small grant to start a gay men's support group. Recruiting men to participate however has been difficult and his job is in jeopardy. One evening he is pleasantly surprised by the arrival of three group participants. Charles and Pharoah, motivated by a recent hate crime, and Teddy, a Christian student whose impending wedding to his childhood sweetheart is causing him apprehension and indecisiveness. (Black Cat Productions)

Prod Comp: Black Cat Productions
Dist/Sales: BlackCat

Khush

Parmar, Pratibha
1991; India, UK; 26 min; Drama

Khush is a sensual, visual discovery of the lives of South Asian lesbians and gays in Britain, North America and India. Real-life experiences are interspersed with dreamlike fantasies, Indian film clips and dance performances that evoke the sensibility of lesbian and gay desire.

Prod Comp: Hauer Rawlence Productions, Channel 4
Dist/Sales: Cinenova, WMM, VTape

Kicking On

Browne, Jaime
2000; Australia; 13 min; B&W; Comedy

Is the local thug at the Sunshine Footy Club a big poof? And did you hear he stuck it to some guy in Reserves who can't even drop-punt? A gay footy flick that scores. (MQFF)

Dist/Sales: Queerscreen

Kika

Almodóvar, Pedro
1993; Spain; 114 min; Comedy
P: Esther García; *W:* Pedro Almodóvar; *C:* Alfredo F. Mayo; *E:* José Salcedo; *M:* Enrique Granados, Enrique Granados
Cast: Veronica Forqué, Peter Coyote, Victoria Abril, Alex Casanovas

At this film's centre is the title character, Kika, a dizzy, good-hearted bombshell who works as a make-up artist and whose ingenuous sexiness affects everyone she meets. Even Ramon, a corpse whom

Kika has been hired to paint, responds to her effervescent chatter. It turns out that Ramon has only been in a cataleptic trance. Still Kika's friendliness is enough to wake the dead. Spanish with English subtitles.

Prod Comp: CiBy 2000, El Deseo SA
Dist/Sales: NewVision, 21stCentury, October

Killer Condom

(aka: Kondom des Grauens)

Walz, Martin
1996; Germany, Switzerland; 107 min; Comedy
P: Ralph S. Dietrich, Harald Reichebner;
W: Ralf König, Martin Walz; *C:* Alexander Honisch;
E: Simone Klier; *M:* Emil Viklicky
Cast: Udo Samel, Peter Lohmeyer, Marc Richter, Leonard Lansink

A living, squirming, and worst of all, biting condom, grips the city of New York in prophylactic panic. Especially hard hit is gay detective Luigi Mackeroni. As chomped corpses pile up, no one believes his carnivorous contraception theory. Then, when Mackeroni loses a testicle to the latex menace, his pursuit becomes personal. He blows the lid off a cult of supervillains bent on eliminating New York's sexual deviants. Their weapon: the Killer Condom. German with English subtitles. (Troma)

Prod Comp: ECCO Film, Ascot Film
Dist/Sales: Lauren, Troma

Killer in the Village

Nisbett, Alec
1983; UK; 55 min; Documentary

An update of the 1983 Horizon report on the spread of AIDS in the United States of America and those groups most affected by the disease. Documents medical research in relation to AIDS and follows AIDS patients through various treatments. Highlights the lifestyle changes initiated in the homosexual community. Some of the ideas expressed in this video have changed in light of recent research into AIDS. (ACMI)

Prod Comp: BBC
Dist/Sales: ACMI

Killer Nun

(aka: Suor Omicidi)

Berruti, Giulio
1978; Italy; 90 min; Horror
P: Enzo Gallo; *W:* Giulio Berruti, Alberto Tarallo;
C: Antonio Maccoppi; *E:* Mario Giacco;
M: Alessandro Alessandroni
Cast: Anita Ekberg, Joe Dallesandro, Lou Castel, Alida Valli, Massimo Serato

k

A cult horror film about a morphine addicted, crazed nun who is the head of a hospital where she rules over a regime of lesbianism and violence. She endangers the life of the staff and patients as she becomes more and more unhinged. Italian with English subtitles.

Prod Comp: Cinesud, Il Gruppo Di Lavoro Calliope
Dist/Sales: VSM

Killer, The

(aka: Die Xue Shuang Xiong)

Woo, John
1989; Hong Kong; 107 min; Action
P: Hark Tsui; *W:* John Woo; *C:* Wing-hang Wong, Peter Pao; *E:* Kung-ming Fan; *M:* Lowell Lo
Cast: Yun-fat Chow , Danny Lee, Sally Yeh, Kong Chu, Kenneth Tsang, Fui-on Shing

This is a highly kinetic male-bonding movie which is also something of a commentary on classic American and French gangster movies and even Sergio Leone's westerns. A maverick cop falls in love with the killer he has to apprehend. The killer in turn is fixated on a woman he has inadvertently blinded while carrying out a hit. The Killer is an outrageously high-camp mix of choreographed aggression fantasy combined with romantic fatalism and glossy melodrama. Dubbed into English.

Prod Comp: Golden Princess, Magnum, Film Workshop
Dist/Sales: NFVLS

Killing of Sister George, The

Aldrich, Robert
1968; UK; 138 min; Drama
P: Robert Aldrich; *W:* Lukas Heller; *C:* Joseph Biroc; *E:* Michael Luciano; *M:* Gerald Fried
Cast: Beryl Reid, Susannah York, Coral Browne, Ronald Fraser

Sometimes touching, but blackly comic story of an ageing lesbian actress, Beryl Reid, who is in the process of losing both her live-in lover, Susannah York, and her job on a popular television soap—her character (Sister George) is being killed off. Reid is superb as the embittered lesbian, as she goes from the dominant, in-control actor to the pathetic, lost woman. A breakthrough film in the sixties and possibly the first openly lesbian film for mainstream cinema, although it does have unfortunate lesbian stereotypes depicting the lesbian lifestyle as a sad and mostly traumatic existence.

Prod Comp: Palomar, American Broadcasting Company
Dist/Sales: Ascanbee, BFI, ACMI

Kim

Gajilan, Arlyn
1988; USA; 27 min; Documentary

Kim is a young Puerto Rican lesbian who describes her journey of coming out in New York City.
Dist/Sales: Frameline

Kind of Family, A

Koster, Andrew
1992; Canada; 54 min; Documentary

An inspiring docudrama about Glen, a gay city councillor, and his turbulent relationship with his adopted son, Michael. We follow Michael's perilous teenage years as he drifts towards drugs, alcohol and male prostitution. By the age of 18 he is HIV-positive. Although the street remains Michael's life, Glen remains constant in his unconditional love and commitment.
Dist/Sales: NFBC

Kindling Point, The

Rice, Teri
1993; USA; 45 min; Erotica

'Perhaps the most beautiful lesbian S/M film ever made ... intimately acted out rituals of domination and pleasure, by way of a crop, candles, and an exquisitely expressive camera'—Village Voice. Enter a vortex of voyeurism as this highly acclaimed experimental documentary unfolds. Warning: every scene may offend...or fixate.
Dist/Sales: Egocentric

King and Country

Losey, Joseph
1964; UK; 82 min; B&W; Drama
P: Norman Priggen, Joseph Losey; *W:* James Lansdale Hodson, Evan Jones, John Wilson; *C:* Denys Coop; *E:* Reginald Mills; *M:* Larry Adler
Cast: Dirk Bogarde, Tom Courtenay, Leo McKern, Barry Foster

Set during World War I, an officer is assigned to defend a young soldier who was the sole survivor of a battle and walked away. He now faces execution for desertion. The two men begin to develop a very close relationship with a subtle homosexual subtext.
Prod Comp: BHE, Landau/Unger
Dist/Sales: Col-Tri, NFVLS, ACMI, AlliedArtists

King Girl

Miller, Sam
1996; UK; 75 min; Drama
P: Hilary Salmon; *W:* Philomena McDonagh; *C:* Janet Tovey; *E:* Elen Pierce Lewis
Cast: Cathy Purcell, Louise Atkins, Maxine Campling, Angela Saville

The pain, fear and loneliness of a teenage girl's life

without love explode into anger and violence in the powerful film *King Girl*. Two Yorkshire teenagers give remarkable performances in the roles of a tough gang leader and her vulnerable victim. Sixteen-year-old Barnsley schoolgirl Louise Atkins—in her first-ever acting role—stars as Glenn, the fourteen-year old leader of an all-girl gang. Hard as nails on the outside Glenn strides, swears and bullies her way through life. On the inside she struggles with her adolescent fears, her sexual fantasies and her dreams while coping with an absent father and a mother who is virtually on the game. Glenn finds an outlet for her anger and frustration by victimising Gail, her timid classmate who is herself bewildered and vulnerable after the death of her beloved father. Out of all the fear and hatred that defines their relationship, a tense and highly ambivalent fascination arises between the two girls. (1998 Verzaubert International Queer Film Festival)

Prod Comp: BBC

King of the City

(aka: Club Life)

Vane, Norman Thaddeus
1985; USA; 90 min; Drama
P: Norman Thaddeus Vane; *W:* Norman Thaddeus Vane; *C:* Joe King; *E:* David Kern
Cast: Tom Parsekian, Michael Parks, Jamie Barrett, Tony Curtis, Pat Ast, Dee Wallace

A young man leaves Texas to find fame and fortune in Hollywood, but he soon discovers the seedier side of Tinsel Town when he becomes caught up in the world of drugs and crime. The film has a great rock soundtrack and Pat Ast appears as a lesbian bar owner named Butch.

Prod Comp: MPR, VTC
Dist/Sales: Troma

Kings

Ayoup, Colleen
2001; Canada; 25 min; Documentary

Short documentary about Montreal's Mambo Drag Kings—a group of sexy, suave and outrageous women who have taken the city's queer community by storm. (MQFF)

Dist/Sales: GroupeIntervention

Kings of the Road

(aka: Im Lauf der Zeit)

Wenders, Wim
1976; Germany; 168 min; B&W; Drama
P: Wim Wenders; *W:* Wim Wenders; *C:* Robby Müller, Martin Schäfer; *E:* Peter Przygodda; *M:* Axel Linstädt
Cast: Rüdiger Vogler, Hanns Zischler, Lisa Kreuzer,

Marquard Boehm, Rudolf Schündler

Bruno is a travelling cinema mechanic who picks up a hitchhiker, Robert, a psychologist who has problems with women. The road journey begins and signals the start of intimacy as the two share stories of their lives, dreams and hopes. Their intimacy gives rise to an underlying sexual tension between them. German with English subtitles.

Prod Comp: Filmverlag der Autoren, Argos, Westdeutscher Rundfunk
Dist/Sales: NFVLS, ACMI

Kinsey 3, The

Robinson, Angela
1998; USA; 13 min; Comedy

A crack team of sexual provocateurs attempts an unprecedented art heist.

Kipling Trilogy, The

Greyson, John
1986; Canada; 42 min; Documentary

This loosely related trilogy explores how the cultural legacy of British imperialism impacts on the taboos of homosexual desire. Using film versions of Kipling's oeuvre as a departure point, the films examine the veritable tug of war between the gay subculture and mainstream social values. The three films are *The Perils of Pedagogy*, *The Jungle Boy* and *Kipling Meets the Cowboys*.

Dist/Sales: VideoOut

Kings

Kiss in the Snow, A

Mosvold, Frank
1997; Norway; 22 min; Drama

A boy learns that his life needs some readjusting to accommodate his first love. A heart-warming short story about two boys with deep feelings for each other who can never find the right moment to express their love. Norwegian with English subtitles.

Dist/Sales: NorwegianFilm, Frameline

Kiss Me Guido

Vitale, Tony
1996; USA; 86 min; Comedy
P: Ira Deutchman, Christine Vachon; W: Tony Vitale;
C: Claudia Raschke; E: Alexander Hall; M: Randall
Poster
Cast: Nick Scotti, Anthony Barrile, Anthony DeSando,
Craig Chester, Dominick Lombardozzi

Frankie Zito, an Italian–American working in a
Bronx pizza parlour, yearns to be an actor. Catching
his girlfriend and his brother inflagrante delicto on
the kitchen table is the last straw for Frankie, and he
moves out. Assuming that the abbreviation GWM in
a classified ad means 'Guy With Money,' the naive
but hunky Frankie soon finds himself sharing a
Manhattan apartment with Warren, a gay actor and
choreographer. (MQFF)

Prod Comp: Capitol Films, Redeemable Features
Dist/Sales: ParamountHV, Wolfe, Swank

Kiss me Monster

(aka: Bésame Monstruo)

Franco, Jesus
1969; Germany; 75 min; Horror
P: Pier A. Caminnecci, Adrian Hoven, José López
Moreno; W: Jesus Franco, Luis Revenga; C: Jorge
Herrero, Franz Hofer; E: Francisco García Velázquez,
Maruja Soriano
Cast: Janine Reynaud, Rosanna Yanni, Adrian Hoven,
Michel Lemoine

A badly shot and routine horror film that is set in a
gothic castle. Gory experiments are carried out on
women who are mostly naked. Diana and Regina
suffer harassment from mutant body builders and
suspect lesbians. Sequel to *Sadisterotica* (1967).
Dubbed into English.

Prod Comp: Aquila Film Enterprises, Films Montana
Dist/Sales: Siren

Kiss of the Spider Woman, The

Babenco, Hector
1985; Brazil, USA; 114 min; Drama
P: David Weisman; W: Leonard Schrader; C: Rodolfo
Sánchez; E: Mauro Alice, Lee Percy; M: John Neschling,
Michael Jary
Cast: William Hurt, Raul Julia, Sonia Braga, Jose
Lewgoy

Set in a Latin American prison during a military
dictatorship, this film explores the relationship that
develops between two cellmates: a left wing
journalist and a homosexual window dresser. To
entertain his cellmate during the monotony and
horror of prison life, the latter recreates stories from
his favourite 1940s movies. Based on the novel by
Manuel Puig.

Awards: Academy Awards, 1985: Best Actor (William
Hurt)
Prod Comp: FilmDallas Pictures, HB Filmes, Sugarloaf
Films
Dist/Sales: Col-Tri, Ascanbee, BFI, Fox, ACMI

The Kiss of the Spider Woman

Kiss the Boys and Make Them Die

Stratton, Margaret
1994; USA; 30 min; Drama

This is an autobiographical film that explores how
memory, sexuality and the self are created and
enforced through the family story. It is a story of
childhood trauma and the adult need to exorcise the
past and create an independent self.

Dist/Sales: VDB

Kissing Jessica Stein

Herman-Wurmfeld, Charles
2001; USA; 94 min; Comedy
P: Brad Zions, Eden H. Wurmfeld; W: Heather
Juergensen, Jennifer Westfeldt; C: Lawrence Sher;
E: Kristy Jacobs Maslin, Gregory Tillman;
M: Marcelo Zarvos
Cast: Heather Juergensen, Jennifer Westfeldt, Tovah
Feldshuh, Esther Wurmfeld

Jessica is a sensitive but neurotic New York journalist
who's fed up with the dating life. One day, she
happens to read an intriguing personal ad, but it's in
the 'women seeking women' section. On a daring
whim, she answers the ad, and meets funky downtown hipster Helen for drinks. To Jessica's shock,
they click instantly, and a first kiss leads to an
earnest, hilarious, muddling courtship. (Wolfe)

Prod Comp: Cineric
Dist/Sales: 20thCenturyFox, FoxSearchlight, Wolfe

Kizuna Volume 1 & 2

Kodaka, Kazuma
1994; Japan; 60 min; Animation
W: Kazuma Kodaka; *M:* Fujio Takano

Sam's legendary champion fencing career is halted by a botched murder attempt. While his close friend, Enjoji, helps him recover, they recognise their intense love for one another. Enter Sagano, Enjoji's half brother who also has a crush on Sam. (Wolfe) Japanese with English subtitles.

Dist/Sales: Wolfe

Km. 0

Km. 0

(aka: Kilometro cero)

Iborra, Juan Luis / Serrano, Yolanda Garcia
2000; Spain; 102 min; Comedy
P: Gianni Ricci; *W:* Yolanda Garcia Serrano, Juan Luis Iborra; *C:* Angel Luis Fernandez; *E:* José Salcedo; *M:* Joan Bibiloni
Cast: Concha Velasco, Silke Hornillos Klein, Georges Corraface, Carlos Fuentes

It's the hottest day of the year in Spain and nobody at Madrid's Plaza del Sol wants to keep their clothes on! Kilometre Zero is the centre point from which distances are measured outward from the capital. But in this fast-paced and witty ensemble comedy, it becomes the meeting point for a host of colourful characters of various sexual orientations. Four sets of strangers independently arrange to meet at Km. 0 at the same time, which leads to most of them accidentally pairing off with the wrong person. This simple premise leads to a variety of entertaining situations, including the proverbial internet-inspired hook up between two horny guys and the male virgin who wants to connect with a hooker before his wedding but takes off with a man instead. (Mongrel)

Prod Comp: Media Park, Cuarteto Producciones Cinematografica
Dist/Sales: Sogepaq, Mongrel, UIP, TLA

Kore Cara Mia

Pendra
1999; Canada; 18 min; Erotica

Lesbian erotica at its most versatile in the age of AIDS.

Krámpack

(aka: Nico & Dani)

Gay, Cesc
2000; Spain; 90 min; Drama
P: Jordi Berenguer, Gerardo Herrero; *W:* Jordi Sànchez, Cesc Gay, Tomás Aragay; *C:* Andreu Rebés; *E:* Frank Gutierrez; *M:* Joan Diaz, Jordi Prats, Riqui Sabates
Cast: Fernando Ramolla, Jordi Vilches, Chisco Amado, Marieta Orozco

While his parents are away for the summer, 16-year-old Dani invites his best friend, the irrepressible Nico, to stay for the holidays. Jealously rears its head when Nico appears more interested in the local girls than in Dani. Hot summer nights and too many joints lead to experimentation which neither boy can talk about, a situation complicated by the appearance of the older and openly gay Julian, a published writer and old friend of Dani's father. A deftly handled film about adolescent discovery and exploration. Spanish with English subtitles. (MQFF)

Prod Comp: Messidor Films
Dist/Sales: Sogepaq, Mongrel, NewYorker, Wolfe, 10%

Krays, The

Medak, Peter
1990; UK; 114 min; Drama
P: Dominic Anciano, Ray Burdis; *W:* Philip Ridley; *C:* Alex Thomson; *E:* Martin Walsh; *M:* Michael Kamen, Chris Rea
Cast: Billie Whitelaw, Tom Bell, Gary Kemp, Martin Kemp, Susan Fleetwood

This fact based drama tells the story of evil twin brothers who grew up in London's tough East End during the years of the Second World War, their lives moulded and influenced by their mother. By the 1960s Reg and Ron Kray controlled London's gangster underworld through a reign of terror. Ron, a homosexual, began to show signs of mental instability and his savagery eventually brought them down.

Prod Comp: Parkfield, Fugitive
Dist/Sales: Palace, TLA, Miramax

L. I. E.

Cuesta, Michael
2001; USA; 97 min; Drama
P: René Bastian, Linda Moran, Michael Cuesta;
W: Stephen M. Ryder, Michael Cuesta; *C:* Romeo

Tirone; *E:* Eric Carlson, Kane Platt; *M:* Pierre Foldes
Cast: Brian Cox, Paul Franklin Dano, Billy Kay, Bruce Altman

Set in a world of contemporary suburban adolescence, *L.I.E.* (Long Island Expressway) begins as we join a group of boys who rob houses in the middle-class comfort of Long Island. While it seems that they break and enter strictly for kicks, they are good at it. Two of these boys, Howie and Gary, are the very best of friends. It is Gary's idea to rob the house belonging to an old guy named Big John, and when Big John quickly figures out exactly who to go to after the crime, Howie learns that his pal Gary has been leading a secret life. Gary and Big John have been engaged in a sex-for-pay relationship, and this secret life fascinates Howie. Perhaps for the first time he realises that he can truly live, like Gary, outside the bounds of school, of home, and that it may be OK that his feelings for Gary may run deeper than those for his other friends. Gary, in the meantime, has figured out how to run away from Long Island, and when he leaves it is Howie who suffers the greatest loss. (Lot 47)

Dist/Sales: Lot47, NewYorker, Wolfe

L Is for the Way you Look

Carlomusto, Jean
1991; USA; 23 min; Documentary

A fun-filled exploration of lesbian history, incorporating discussion of events, images, gossip and role models.

Dist/Sales: WMM

L-Shaped Room, The

Forbes, Bryan
1962; UK; 125 min; B&W; Drama
P: Richard Attenborough, James Woolf; *W:* Brian Forbes, Lynne Reid Banks; *C:* Douglas Slocombe; *E:* Anthony Harvey; *M:* John Barry
Cast: Leslie Caron, Tom Bell, Brock Peters, Cicely Courtneidge

Leslie Caron in one of her best roles as a pregnant girl left to face life in the gloomy surroundings of a London rooming house. Brock Peters plays a West Indian jazz musician in love with Tom Bell, who is also the object of Caron's desire. Cicely Courtneidge plays a lesbian tenant who also meets Caron's character.

Prod Comp: Romulus, British Lion
Dist/Sales: Ascanbee, FilmsInc, Columbia

Labor More than Once

Mersky, Liz
1983; USA; 52 min; Documentary
P: Liz Mersky

Marianne MacQueen is a lesbian mother who struggles against a homophobic judicial system to regain custody of her son. Her refusal to back down and abandon her fight led to a landmark court trial in 1981.

Labyrinth of Passion

(aka: Laberinto de pasiones)

Almodóvar, Pedro
1982; Spain; 100 min; Comedy
P: Pedro Almodóvar; *W:* Pedro Almodóvar, Terry Lennox; *C:* Ángel Luis Fernández; *E:* Jose Salcedo; *M:* Pedro Almodóvar, Bernardo Bonezzi, Fany McNamara
Cast: Cecilia Roth, Imanol Arias, Antonio Banderas

A film about several love stories. The main couple, around whom the film develops, are Sexilia, a young sex fiend who is in love with the heir to a fallen Arab empire, and Riza, who is more preoccupied with cosmetics and men than with internal politics. Spanish with English subtitles.

Prod Comp: Alphaville
Dist/Sales: Potential, Cinevista, NFVLS, ACMI

Ladies Please!

Saw, Andrew
1995; Australia; 55 min; Documentary
P: Phaedon Vass, Rebel Penfold-Russell; *W:* Andrew Saw; *C:* Brian J. Breheny
Cast: Adam Cahill, Ritchie Finger, Stuart Garskie

A rare and stimulating insight into the professional and personal lives of three of Australia's most innovative drag performers who inspired the hit film *The Adventures of Priscilla, Queen of the Desert.*

Dist/Sales: Minotaur

Lady

Sachs, Ira
1993; USA; 28 min; Comedy
Cast: Dominique Dibbell

Dominique Dibbell of New York's 'Five Lesbian Brothers' stars as a glamorous redhead in this understated but hilarious pastiche. Is she a femme playing a male-to-female trannie, or a butch playing a femme?

Prod Comp: Charlie Guidance Productions
Dist/Sales: Frameline

Lady in Cement

Douglas, Gordon
1968; USA; 93 min; Drama
P: Aaron Rosenberg; *W:* Marvin H. Albert, Jack Guss; *C:* Joseph Biroc; *E:* Robert Simpson; *M:* Hugo Montenegro

Cast: Frank Sinatra, Raquel Welch, Richard Conte, Martin Gabel, Lainie Kazan

In this sequel to *Tony Rome*, Sinatra is back as a Miami private eye. He is hired by a small-time hood to locate his missing girlfriend. His investigations lead him across the paths of many shady characters. A sharp twist in the plot sees Sinatra being accused of murder. Paul Henry appears as a vice-squad officer whose job involves working the street in drag.

Prod Comp: 20th Century-Fox, Arcola Pictures, Millfield
Dist/Sales: ReelMovies, 20thCenturyFox

Lakme Takes Flight

Lady in Waiting, The

Taylor, Christian
1992; USA; 30 min; Comedy
Cast: Virginia McKenna, Rodney Hudson

Nominated for an Academy Award, this short film spins a tale of what happens when a prim and proper Englishwoman is sent to New York to deliver a letter to her employer's mistress. However, a blackout sees her stuck in a highrise with only a black drag queen for company. (MQFF)

Ladyboys

Marre, Jeremy
1992; Thailand, UK; 53 min; Documentary

This film offers an intimate portrait of teenage boys who leave their impoverished homes in the north Thailand countryside to find fame and fortune as transvestite performers in the glamorous cabarets of the south. The film follows two boys, out of the thousands, who each year enter transvestite beauty contests and display themselves in extravagant costumes. We see the pain, prejudice, and humour that accompanies their transformation into women. (Water Bearer Films)

Dist/Sales: WaterBearer

Ladybugs

Furie, Sidney J.
1992; USA; 89 min; Comedy
P: Albert S. Ruddy, Andre E. Morgan; *W:* Curtis Burch; *C:* Dan Burstall; *E:* John W. Wheeler, Timothy N. Board; *M:* Richard Gibbs, D.A. Young
Cast: Rodney Dangerfield, Jackee Harry, Jonathan Brandis, Ilene Graff

Chester is an under-appreciated corporate employee who, hoping for a promotion, volunteers to coach the 'Ladybugs', a girls' soccer team sponsored by his boss. Previously a championship team, this year they are 13-year-old novices who know nothing about soccer. Out of desperation, Chester convinces his fiancée's jock son to join the team... as a girl.

Prod Comp: Paramount, Ruddy & Morgan, Ladybugs
Dist/Sales: Roadshow, Paramount

Lakme Takes Flight

James, Sheila / Young, Melina
2000; Canada; 10 min; Comedy

A parody of Bollywood musicals and a humorous love story between two women.

Dist/Sales: GroupeIntervention

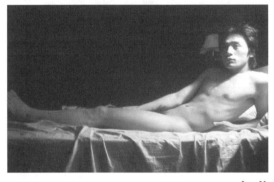

Lan Yu

Lan Yu

Kwan, Stanley
2001; Hong Kong; 86 min; Drama
P: Yongning Zhang; *W:* Jimmy Ngai; *C:* Tao Yang; *E:* William Chang; *M:* Yadong Zhang
Cast: Jun Hu, Ye Liu, Jin Su, Huatong Li, Fang Lu, Yongning Zhang

Beijing 1988. Middle-aged Chen Handong is the eldest son of a senior government bureaucrat, heads a fast-growing trading company and plays as hard as he works. Few know that Handong's tastes run to boys more than girls. Lan Yu is a country boy, newly arrived in Beijing to study architecture, who is short of money and willing to try anything to earn some.

He meets Handong in a pool hall and encounters a life changing sexual initiation. Handong and Lan Yu meet often, and the boy becomes very secure in his love for the man. But Handong insists that he merely wants a playmate, not a lifelong companion, and warns Lan Yu that he will eventually break up with him. They eventually move in together but, Handong continues to shy away from his feelings for the boy. But fate can play cruel tricks... Mandarin with English subtitles.

Dist/Sales: Celluloid-Dreams, Strand, Mongrel

Laramie Project, The

Kaufman, Moisés
2001; USA; 97 min; Drama
P: Declan Baldwin; *W:* Moisés Kaufman;
C: Terry Stacey; *E:* Brian A. Kates; *M:* Peter Golub
Cast: Steve Buscemi, Christina Ricci, Laura Linney, Camryn Manheim, Jeremy Davies, Janeane Garofalo

What happens to an American town when something unexpected, unconscionable and unforgivable rips it apart and thrusts it into the national media spotlight? That is the question that led a New York City theatre troupe to the town of Laramie, Wyoming, to seek out residents whose lives were changed after a gay college student named Matthew Shepard was brutally beaten, tied to a fence and left for dead off a rural road. This groundbreaking HBO Films drama recreates the efforts of the troupe who interviewed the residents of Laramie in an effort to uncover what such a heinous crime meant to the people, their town and their country. (Wolfe)

Prod Comp: Good Machine
Dist/Sales: HBO, Wolfe, Swank

Larry's Visit

Nero, Carlo Gabriel
1995; USA; 23 min; Drama

High-powered and over-stressed ad executive Frank Valentine gets a visit from an old private school friend. Over the course of his short visit, the truth about their boyhood relationship surfaces, much to the chagrin of Frank's wife. (Atom Films)

Dist/Sales: Atom

Last Bus Home, The

Gogan, Johnny
1997; Ireland; 93 min; Drama
P: Paul Donovan; *W:* Johnny Gogan; *C:* James Mather; *E:* Catherine Creed; *M:* Cathal Coughlan
Cast: Annie Ryan, Anthony Brophy, Brian F. O'Byrne, John Cronin

Two young punks, Reena and Jessop, meet on the day the Pope comes to Dublin in 1979. Their

unholy alliance leads to bed and the formation of The Dead Patriots. (Beyond International)

Prod Comp: Bandit Films

Last Call at Maud's

Poirier, Paris
1993; USA; 77 min; Documentary
P: Paris Poirier; *E:* Paris Poirier

A documentary which looks at the longest running lesbian bar in the United States—Maud's. It opened its doors in 1966 in San Francisco and continued doing business through the seventies and eighties. It finally closed in 1989. Included in the film are some wonderfully revealing personal accounts of lesbian life and culture from an earlier time.

Dist/Sales: Frameline, WaterBearer, ACMI

Last Coming Out, The

Anemogiannis, Con
1993; Australia; 90 min; Documentary
P: Con Anemogiannis; *W:* Con Anemogiannis

This film is Australia's first feature-length look at AIDS/HIV. It looks at the multicultural communities, both straight and gay, of Australia, showing how they've been affected by the disease. The film looks at how in Australia, more than any other country in the world, AIDS is a gay disease with 93% of all cases being homosexual men. It examines issues such as homosexuality, homophobia and racism, suggesting that AIDS and these issues have been inextricably linked.

Last Emperor, The

Bertolucci, Bernardo
1987; China, Italy, UK, USA; 162 min; Drama
P: Jeremy Thomas; *W:* Bernardo Bertolucci, Mark Peploe, Enzo Ungar; *C:* Vittorio Storaro; *E:* Gabriella Cristiani; *M:* Ryuichi Sakamoto, David Byrne, Cong Su
Cast: John Lone, Joan Chen, Peter O'Toole, Ying Ruocheng, Victor Wong

An amazing and remarkable film inspired by the true story of Pu Yi, the last emperor of China, who, in 1908, was crowned at the age of three and lived a cloistered life in the Forbidden City until he was deposed. He was made puppet emperor of Manchuria by the Japanese but after the Second World War was arrested by the communists and imprisoned. Later he was released to live as an ordinary citizen. Based on a book written by Pu Yi's English tutor, which chronicles his life from the absolute extravagance and excesses as emperor to his existence of poverty in modern day China.

Awards: Academy Awards, 1987: Best Film, Director, Adapted Screenplay, Cinematography

Prod Comp: Thomas, Columbia, AAA, Hemdale, Recorded Pictures
Dist/Sales: 20thCenturyFox, Ascanbee, 16MM, ReelMovies, Col-Tri

Last Empress, The

(aka: Wei dai huang hou)

Chen, Jialin / Sun, Qingguo
1985; China; 105 min; Drama
Cast: Hong Pan

The story of the fate of three women, including the wife and cousin of who have a lesbian relationship. The deposed Chinese Emperor Pu Yi's life is shown in detail in Bernardo Bertolucci's *The Last Emperor*. Chinese with English subtitles.

Prod Comp: Changchun Film Studio

Last Exit to Brooklyn

Edel, Ulrich
1989; Germany, USA; 102 min; Drama
P: Bernd Eichinger, Herman Weigel; *W:* Desmond Nakano; *C:* Stefan Czapsky; *E:* Peter Przygodda; *M:* Mark Knofler
Cast: Stephen Lang, Jennifer Jason Leigh, Alexis Arquette, Burt Young, Steve Baldwin

A down-to-earth and bleak look at life on the mean streets of Brooklyn, USA, 1952. It centres around a strike against a local factory. Lang plays a married shop steward from the union who is caught stealing from the till to pay for his homosexual affair. Leigh is a prostitute who, when she has had a few too many drinks, gets gang raped in the local bar. Based on the controversial novel by Hubert Selby Jnr.

Prod Comp: Allied, Neue Constantin, Bavaria
Dist/Sales: 16MM, Col-Tri, Cinecom, ACMI

Last Island, The

Gorris, Marleen
1990; The Netherlands; 101 min; Drama
P: Laurens Geels, Dick Maas; *W:* Marleen Gorris; *C:* Marc Felperlaan; *E:* Hans van Dongen; *M:* Boudewijn Tarenskeen
Cast: Kenneth Colley, Paul Freeman, Patricia Hayes, Shelagh McLeod

In a brilliant, modern version of the classic ship-wreck tale, director Marleen Gorris manages to capture both a gay male's and feminist perspective. After a large airliner crashes on a deserted island killing most of the passengers, two women, five men and a dog survive: an Eastern European, a Canadian lawyer, a French biologist, a prosperous Scottish financier, a young American, an extrovert Australian and a major in the British army. Hopes of rescue

fade as the survivors come to realise that the world may have suffered a major disaster. They have to rely on their own resources and at first manage to live harmoniously. But gradually tensions rise after a failed attempt to escape. Intolerance threatens their very existence as one of the men begins to put himself forward as the leader of the group. (MQFF)

Prod Comp: First Floor Features
Dist/Sales: FirstFloor

Last Married Couple in America, The

Cates, Gilbert
1980; USA; 103 min; Comedy
P: Ed Feldman, John Herman Shaner; *W:* John Herman Shaner; *C:* Ralph A. Woolsey; *E:* Peter E. Berger; *M:* Charles Fox
Cast: George Segal, Natalie Wood, Dom DeLuise, Valerie Harper, Richard Benjamin

A happily married couple are so upset at the break-up of all their friends' marriages that they begin to question their own relationship. The only happy couple in neighbourhood just happens to be gay.

Prod Comp: Universal
Dist/Sales: ReelMovies, Universal

Last Metro, The

(aka: Le Dernier métro)

Truffaut, François
1980; France; 133 min; Drama
P: Jean-José Richer, François Truffaut; *W:* François Truffaut, Suzanne Schiffman, Jean-Claude Grumberg; *C:* Néstor Almendros; *E:* Marie-Aimee Debril, Martine Barraqué-Curie; *M:* Georges Delerue
Cast: Catherine Deneuve, Gerard Depardieu, Jean Poiret, Heinz Bennent

Set during the German occupation of France in World War II, a theatre company owner is forced to hide out in his cellar, while his actress wife struggles to keep his business running. She is supported in her efforts by the rest of the company which includes a gay director and a lesbian actress. French with English subtitles.

Prod Comp: Films du Carrosse, Société Française de Production, TF1 Films
Dist/Sales: Ascanbee, Palace, MK2Diffusion, UAClassics, Wellspring

Last of England, The

Jarman, Derek
1987; UK; 87 min; Drama
P: James MacKay, Don Boyd; *W:* Derek Jarman; *C:* Derek Jarman, Christopher Hughes, Cerith Wyn Evans, Richard Heslop; *E:* Peter Cartwright, Angus Cook, John

Maybury, Sally Yeadon; *M:* Simon Fisher Turner
Cast: Tilda Swinton, Spencer Leigh, Gay Gaynor, Matthew Hawkins, Gerard McArthur

This is both a lament for what Jarman sees as the terminal state of the nation and what has been described as 'a defiant fist waved in the face of Thatcher's Britain'. Jarman calls it 'a dream allegory [in which] the present dreams the past future'. Several strands of video and super-8 imagery—urban decay, home movies from the twenties to the fifties, angry stylised homoerotic images, reflexive scenes of Jarman at work—are complemented by music and voice-over.

Prod Comp: Anglo International, British Screen, Channel 4, Tartan Productions
Dist/Sales: Cowboy

The Last of England

Last of Sheila, The

Ross, Herbert
1973; USA; 119 min; Thriller
P: Herbert Ross; *W:* Anthony Perkins, Stephen Sondheim; *C:* Gerry Turpin; *E:* Edward Warschilka; *M:* Billy Goldenberg
Cast: James Coburn, Dyan Cannon, James Mason, Raquel Welch, Joan Hackett

A murder-mystery thriller set on a yacht in the south of France. A film producer invites a group of friends to stay for a week on the yacht; the purpose, it seems, is to discover his wife's murderer. As it happens he gets an ice pick in the neck—while he's in drag. With lots of twists and turns towards the end, we find out it is the homosexual who did it.

Prod Comp: Warner
Dist/Sales: Warner

Last Song, The

Akarasainee, Pisan
1986; Thailand; 90 min; Drama
Cast: Somying Daorai

Boontherm (whose name means 'long stem') is a young boy from the Thai countryside. He moves to the city to make a life for himself, where he meets a drag queen who falls in love with him and begins to support him. Boon, however, leaves the drag queen, and meets and falls in love with Orn, but Orn turns out to be a lesbian.

Dist/Sales: TMPPA

Late Bloomers

Dyer, Julia
1996; USA; 107 min; Comedy
P: Gretchen Dyer, Julia Dyer, Stephen Dyer; *W:* Gretchen Dyer; *C:* Bill Schwarz; *E:* Gretchen Dyer, Julia Dyer; *M:* Ted Pine, Suzanne Ciani
Cast: Connie Nelson, Dee Hennigan, Gary Carter, Jonah Marsh

A high school secretary wrongly suspects a geometry teacher of having an affair with her husband, then ends up having a passionate romance with her. Once the affair becomes public, their lives are turned upside down by a suburban community not willing to accept them. (Cowboy Pictures)

Dist/Sales: Strand, Wolfe, Cowboy, Millivres

Latin Boys go to Hell

Troyano, Ela
1997; USA; 70 min; Comedy, Drama
P: Jürgen Brüning; *W:* Ander Salas, Ela Troyano; *C:* James Carman; *E:* Brian A. Kates; *M:* John Zorn
Cast: Irwin Ossa, John Bryant Davila, Jenifer Lee Simard, Alexis Artiles

A comedy drama set in New York's Latino community. The lives of a group of young gay and straight friends gets complicated by desire and jealousy and starts to resemble the Spanish soap opera they are all dedicated to.

Dist/Sales: Potential, Strand, Siren, Mongrel, Wolfe, Millivres

Latin Queens: Unfinished Stories of our Lives

Wagner, Anton
1999; 55 min; Documentary

Latino drag queens fleeing persecution in South America struggle for survival in the gay community in Toronto. There is little legal protection for homosexuals in many Latin American countries. Several gays, transgendered persons and drag queens featured in this documentary were subject to police brutality in their countries and have been granted refugee status in Canada on the basis of their sexual orientation. (CFMDC)

Dist/Sales: CFMDC

Laughing Policeman, The

Rosenberg, Stuart
1973; USA; 112 min; Drama
P: Stuart Rosenberg; *W:* Thomas Rickman; *C:* David
M. Walsh; *E:* Robert Wyman; *M:* Charles Fox
Cast: Walter Matthau, Bruce Dern, Louis Gossett Jnr,
Anthony Zerbe, Albert Paulsen

> Two San Francisco policemen hunt down a deranged
> killer who has randomly murdered a number of
> innocent people on a city bus. Once again the mad
> mass-murderer turns out to be homosexual. Based
> on a novel by Per Wahloo and Maj Sjowall.

Prod Comp: 20th Century-Fox
Dist/Sales: 20thCenturyFox

Late Bloomers

Laura

Luketic, Robert
1996; Australia; 14 min; Comedy
W: Robert Luketic

> Laura is a *Twin Peaks* meets *Natural Born Killers*
> meets *Priscilla* kind of girl. A glamorous transsexual
> with a bizarre and deadly secret. Starring Pax (first
> name Sarah) in the title role, this psycho-sexual
> thriller follows Detective Steve Ransard, the man
> assigned to catch a serial killer with a disturbing
> modus operandi—a penchant for men with blue
> eyes. His boyfriend, Mark, gets more than he
> bargained for during the couple's holiday at a coastal
> caravan park. (MQFF)

Dist/Sales: VCA

Lavender Limelight: Lesbians in Films

Mauceri, Marc
1997; USA; 45 min; Documentary

> From *Go Fish* to *Paris is Burning* to *The Watermelon
> Woman*, *Lavender Limelight: Lesbians in Films* goes
> behind the scenes to reveal America's most successful
> lesbian directors. These talented moviemakers
> enlighten and entertain as they explore their sexual
> identity, growing up gay, inspirations and tech-
> niques, Hollywood vs. Indie, and of course, love and
> sex, onscreen and off. (First Run Features)

Dist/Sales: FirstRunFeatures, Wolfe

Lavender Tortoise

Woodward, Ken
1991; USA; 14 min; Comedy
Cast: Greg Taylor

> Join Greg Taylor and his merry band of fags and
> dykes as they make their way to America's ultimate
> fantasy world—Disneyland.

Law of Desire

(aka: La Ley del Deseo)

Almodóvar, Pedro
1986; Spain; 102 min; Drama, Comedy
P: Esther García; *W:* Pedro Almodóvar; *C:* Angel Luis
Fernandez; *E:* José Salcedo
Cast: Eusebio Poncela, Carmen Maura, Antonio
Banderas, Miguel Molina

> The plot centres on Pablo's love for Juan, frustrated
> and unrequited as it is at times. Adding to the brew
> is Pablo's sister, Tina, a transsexual who is in love
> with a model. The antics of these four, plus several
> others, reach a fevered crescendo where they must all
> challenge the very real laws of desire. (MQFF)
> Spanish with English subtitles.

Prod Comp: El Deseo SA, Lauren Film
Dist/Sales: NewVision, Cinevista, Lauren, ACMI

Lawless Heart, The

Hunsinger, Tom / Hunter, Neil
2001; UK; 100 min; Drama
P: Martin Pope; *W:* Tom Hunsinger, Neil Hunter;
C: Sean Bobbitt; *E:* Scott Thomas; *M:* Adrian Johnston
Cast: Tom Hollander, Ellie Haddington, Douglas
Henshall, Sukie Smith

> *The Lawless Heart* is a sharp, modern love story
> where lust, love and loyalty are stretched to their
> limits. Shocked by the death of a friend, Dan, Nick
> and Tim, decide to take their lives in hand but

reckon without the three beguiling women they're about to meet. Dan is a faithful if frustrated husband and father—until he meets the gorgeous and glamorous Corinne who awakens a sense of belated adventure in him. Nick is struggling to come to terms with the loss of his boyfriend Stuart, but the effervescent Charlie is determined to bring him out of his shell. Tim has spent eight years searching the globe for something meaningful, little realising that the girl of his dreams lives in his own home town—surely nothing could be easier than winning her heart? Told from three different perspectives, *The Lawless Heart* reveals the comic and subtle realities of modern relationships. (www.lawlessheart.co.uk)

Dist/Sales: FirstLook

Leather

Haberman, Hardy
1995; USA; 10 min; B&W; Documentary

A subjective documentary about the world of leathermen in the form of a film poem. Interviews and sound bites combine with a lyric narrative and crisp graphic images of sadomasochistic activity.

Dist/Sales: Frameline

Leather Boys, The

Furie, Sidney J.
1963; UK; 108 min; B&W; Drama
P: Raymond Stross; *W:* Gillian Freeman; *C:* Gerald Gibbs; *E:* Reginald Beck; *M:* Bill McGuffie
Cast: Colin Campbell, Rita Tushingham, Dudley Sutton, Gladys Henson, Avice Landon

The disillusion of a disappointing marriage leads a young mechanic into a relationship with a fellow motorcyclist in this often perceptive study of masculinity, shot on a small budget in a London working-class environment. The homosexuality at the heart of the relationship is sympathetically (for the time) brought into the open, negating the myth of the buddy relationship as a neutral escape route from the role-playing in male-female relationships.

Prod Comp: British Lion, Garrick, Raymond Stross Productions
Dist/Sales: Col-Tri, AlliedArtists, VSM, NFVLS, ACMI

Leather Jacket Love Story

DeCoteau, David
1997; USA; 85 min; B&W; Drama
P: Jerry Goldberg; *W:* Rondo Mieczkowski; *C:* Howard Wexler; *E:* Jeffrey Schwarz; *M:* Jeremy Jordan
Cast: Christopher Bradley, Sean Tataryn, Geoffrey Moody, Hector Mercado, Mink Stole

In this sexually explicit film, Kyle, a serious film poet takes post in nonconformist Silverlake, California

and befriends a cast of locals who, in varying degrees, become agents in his sentimental education: a trinity of transvestites, a senior bard with muse in tow and hunky bikie, Mikey. Counterpoised to his adventure is the experience of his best friend, who leads the predictable 'lifestyle' of the 'professionally' gay man, specialising in serial partnering and physique fetishism and cultivating that requisite, oh-so-cool, morning-after, ennui. But our intrepid protagonist wants to love... monogamously, thereby prompting Mike to reconsider the priorities in his own life.

Prod Comp: Leather Jacket Productions
Dist/Sales: Wolfe

Leave It!

Cronin, Laura Jean
2002; USA; 27 min

A cute girl changes everything at dog obedience school.

Leave It!

Legacies

Wekland, Sean
1995; USA; 30 min; Documentary

In depth documentary about how the Mormon Church has dealt with homosexuality. Features the traumatic experiences of four gay ex-Mormons who were subject to all manner of psychological ill-treatment.

Legal Memory

Steele, Lisa / Tomczak, Kim
1992; Canada; 80 min; Drama
P: Lisa Steele, Kim Tomczak; *W:* Lisa Steele, Kim Tomczak; *C:* Julie Warren; *E:* Dennis Day
Cast: Lisa Steele, Kim Tomczak

A docudrama about Leo Mantha, the last man

hanged in British Columbia who, in 1958 murdered his male lover on a Victoria naval base. The film explores the crime within the context of mainstream society and the gay subculture in 1950s Canada.

Prod Comp: Legal Memory Inc
Dist/Sales: VTape

Legend of Fong Sai-Yuk, The

Yuen, Corey
1993; Hong Kong; 105 min; Action
P: Jet Li; *W:* Kung-yung Chai, Kin Chung Chan, Jay On; *C:* Jingle Ma; *E:* Peter Cheung; *M:* Romeo Díaz, Mark Lui, James Wong
Cast: Jet Li, Josephine Siao, Sung Young Chen

The mother of a young man dresses up as a man to defend the family's honour in this drag meets Kung Fu action adventure comedy flick. She goes into battle with the mother of another family but, as it turns out, the two women fall in love. Cantonese with English subtitles.

Prod Comp: Eastern Production
Dist/Sales: RimFilm, BuenaVista

Legend of Lylah Clare, The

Aldrich, Robert
1968; USA; 130 min; Drama
P: Robert Aldrich; *W:* Hugo Butler, Edward DeBlasio, Jean Rouverol, Robert Thom; *C:* Joseph Biroc; *E:* Michael Luciano; *M:* Frank de Vol
Cast: Peter Finch, Kim Novak, Milton Selzer, Rossella Falk, Ernest Borgnine

A film director's wife dies only a few hours after they are married. He attempts to recreate his wife's image as the great star, Lylah Clare, by using other young women for a screen biography. A rather heavy-handed approach to the subject. Rossella Falk plays a rather predatory lesbian.

Prod Comp: MGM
Dist/Sales: MGM

Lesbian Avengers Eat Fire Too

Baus, Janet / Friedrich, Su
1993; USA; 55 min; Documentary

Looks at the accomplishments of a group of lesbian activists in their first year together.

Lesbian Bed Death: Myth or Epidemic

Foiles, Stacey
1995; USA; 15 min; Comedy

This wild spoof of TV magazine journalism takes a mock-serious look at a phenomenon which is reportedly sweeping through the lesbian community. The satirical interviews with members of the afflicted group are a hoot. The Camille Paglia stand-in is flawless, and the lines are hilarious. (Cinenova)

Dist/Sales: Cinenova

Lesbian Health Matters

1995; UK; 46 min; Documentary

Devised by London Lesbians in Health Care, a diverse multidisciplinary group of healthcare workers, this film is intended to raise the awareness of lesbians as service users. It seeks to alert healthcare workers to the needs of lesbians and to demonstrate how assumptions of heterosexuality may inadvertently lead to a damaging consultation. (Cinenova)

Prod Comp: Ukulele Productions; *Dist/Sales:* Cinenova

Lesbian Physicians on Practice, Patients & Power

Mosbacher, Dee
1991; USA; 30 min; Documentary

Lesbian Physicians on Practice, Patients & Power introduces you to a fascinating group of lesbians, from surgeons to psychiatrists. It provides a rare opportunity to hear them candidly assess the impact of being out on their professional and personal lives. The video uses the unique vantage point of these physicians to consider specific concerns of lesbians and gay men as patients within the medical system. (Woman Vision)

Dist/Sales: WomanVision

Lesbian Teenagers in High School

Salmon, Norah
1998; USA; 23 min; Documentary

Discusses the experiences of young lesbians in high school.

Lesbian Tongues

1989; USA; 90 min; Documentary
Cast: Peggy Shaw, Lois Weaver, Donna J. McBride, Barbara Greir

Using interviews with a number of lesbians, this educational documentary details how they live and work openly, their relationships and lovers. Among the eclectic group of interviewees are comedians, performance artists, dairy owners and publishers.

Lesbians Behaving Badly

McKibben, Kerry
2001; UK; 46 min; Documentary

Find out what London's lesbians get up to in their natural habitat.

Dist/Sales: WorldOfWonder

Lesbians Go Mad in Lesbos

Kent, Gabi
2000; UK; 50 min; Documentary

A group of debauched dykes from London's candy Bar plan their first ever package holiday to Lesbos. And they've got the lot laid on for them: wet T-shirt competitions, prizes for the hussy of the week and to cap it all off, the 'wet pussy pool party'. However, it's the flyers for the last event that particularly rile the local Mayor, who comes down hard and fast on the proposed water sports. Will he have his wicked way, or will the fun-hungry females get to make a splash? (MQFF)

Dist/Sales: WorldOfWonder

Lesbians in the Pulpit

1991; USA; 28 min; Documentary

Sally Boyle, an ordained minister has been living openly with her lesbian lover for four years. Her courageous stand has provoked controversy. (Filmakers Library)

Dist/Sales: FilmakersLibrary

Lesbians Olé

Gorham, Caz
2002; UK; 50 min; Documentary

Fifty lesbians arrive in Sitges in Spain, Europe's most popular gay destination for a week of hard partying. It's a holiday the organisers won't forget easily, and one the locals probably want to forget as soon as possible. Pool parties, strip shows and an invasion of the local theme park aside, this World of Wonder Production is a fast-paced and funny fly-on-the-wall documentary. (2002 London Lesbian & Gay Film Festival)

Dist/Sales: WorldOfWonder

Lesson 9

Taylor, Mark
1999; USA; 16 min; Experimental

A shifting montage of abstract imagery, animation, and archival footage is combined with a haunting soundtrack and original footage to illustrate the brooding poetic journal entries of a lover gone mad. Taylor uses text scrawled on the screen, to draw us into the writer's troubled mind. (Frameline)

Dist/Sales: Frameline

Let Me Die, Again

Knight, Leone
1994; Australia; 15 min; Comedy
P: Megan McMurchy; *W:* Viki Dun

Cast: Nicholas Hope, Paul Capsis, Jenny Vuletic

A musical melodrama about the queerness of opera, and the operatic in everyday life. It's opera night at an Australian corner pub, and a series of impossible love scenarios are being played out by couples caught in the ordinary tragedy of human relationships.

Awards: Turin International Gay & Lesbian Film Festival, 1996: Best Short Film
Prod Comp: Suitcase Films

Let Me Die, Again

Let's Love Hong Kong

(aka: Ho Yuk)

Yau, Ching
2002; Hong Kong; 87 min; Drama
P: Ching Yau; *W:* Ching Yau; *C:* Kam Cam, Hung-yut Chen; *E:* Po-wen Chen; *M:* Chi Shing Kung
Cast: Wong Chung-ching, Erica Lam, Colette Koo, Maria Cordero

Zero, who, like many Hong Kong youngsters, has a handful of unsteady jobs. She takes a fancy to Chan Kwok Chan, whom she begins stalking. Chan in turn, has a job donning exotic costumes as a cyber papel doll for a porn website, and a sex-worker lover who has a son and a separate husband on the mainland. Then there's Nicole, who gets her orgasmic intimacy watching Chan every night. All these games of chasing, rejecting and seducing are played out in an economically and spiritually depressed Hong kong. (2002 Hong Kong International Film Festival)
Cantonese with English subtitles.

Let's Play Prisoners

Zando, Julie
1988; USA; 22 min; B&W; Drama

A haunting look at the hidden issues of erotic power relationships between women told through the reconstructed story of two girlhood friends. The origins of desire and domination are traced to the childhood relationship between mother and daughter as revealed in the often fearful and cruel framework of childhood play.

Dist/Sales: VDB

Letters from Home

Hoolboom, Mike
1996; Canada; 15 min; Experimental

A filmic reflection on AIDS, life, love and death.

Lez B Friends: A Biker Bitch Hate Story

House, Uncle Steak / Lovanne, Auntie Lou
1998; USA; 20 min; Comedy
P: Uncle Steak House, Auntie Lou Lovanne

In a spoof of John Waters films, a girl biker gang cruises the city looking for recruits.

Prod Comp: Uncle Steak Auntie Lou Productions
Dist/Sales: Steakhaus

Lez Be Friends

Hayes, Lisa
2000; Canada; 13 min; Comedy

After making a short film about her best friend Abbey's struggle to accept her sexual orientation, Lily is assumed to be the true subject of the film. While Abbey, the film's star, becomes a legend in the lesbian community, Lily is trapped in a netherworld between heterosexuality and homosexuality, continually trying to set the record straight. (CFMDC)

Dist/Sales: CFMDC

Lianna

Lianna

Sayles, John
1983; USA; 110 min; Drama
P: Jeffrey Nelson, Maggie Renzi; *W:* John Sayles;
C: Austin De Besche; *E:* John Sayles; *M:* Mason Daring

Cast: Linda Griffiths, Jane Hallaren, Jon de Vries, Jo Henderson

Lianna drops out of university to become a wife and mother. She decides to go back to night class where she meets and falls in love with Ruth, her psychology teacher. They begin an affair, but when Lianna tells her husband, he kicks her out of their house and separates her from her children. Even her close friend Sandy suddenly avoids her. Now Lianna must make her own way in life, find a job, somewhere to live and new friends. She tries to win back her children and friends while dealing with her relationship with Ruth. The film is not just another coming-out story, it looks at the consequences of Lianna's actions in the real world. An interesting and complex film for the era in which it was made.

Prod Comp: Winwood
Dist/Sales: Swank, BFI, UAClassics

Liberace

Hale, William
1988; USA; 100 min; Drama
P: Jeanne Van Cott; *W:* Anthony Lawrence, Nancy Lawrence; *M:* Gary William Friedman
Cast: Andrew Robinson, John Rubinstein, Maris Valainis, Louis Giambalvo

The life of the extremely flamboyant pianist, Liberace, who must be the most famous closet homosexual in entertainment history. Even up to his death of AIDS in 1987, he refused to acknowledge his homosexuality. In this very sanitised made for television version of his life, homosexuality and AIDS are never mentioned.

Dist/Sales: Roadshow

Liberace: Behind the Music

Greene, David
1988; USA; 100 min; Drama
W: Gavin Lambert
Cast: Victor Garber, Saul Rubinek, Maureen Stapleton, Michael Dolan

Another man-behind-the-music film of Liberace, this time from the view of his long-time personal manager Seymour Heller. A more honest account of his life, Liberace's life story is approached more directly than in the other version released in 1988, particularly with respect to his death from AIDS.

Dist/Sales: Roadshow, TLA

Licensed to Kill

Dong, Arthur
1997; USA; 80 min; Documentary
P: Arthur Dong; *W:* Arthur Dong; *C:* Robert Shepard;
E: Arthur Dong

Cast: Donald Aldrich, Corey Burley, Raymond Childs, William Cross

Licensed to Kill goes behind the media headlines of high-profile anti-gay murders to investigate their causes. Attacked by gay bashers in 1977, filmmaker Arthur Dong probes the hearts and minds of murderers convicted of killing gay men—he faces them in one-on-one cell block interviews and asks them directly: "Why did you do it?" (Deep Focus Films)

Prod Comp: DeepFocus Productions
Dist/Sales: DeepFocus

Lickerish Quartet, The

(aka: The Erotic Quartet)

Metzger, Radley
1970; USA; 88 min; Erotica
P: Radley Metzger; *W:* Michael DeForrest, Radley Metzger; *C:* Hans Jura; *M:* Stelvio Cipriani
Cast: Frank Wolff, Silvana Venturelli, Erika Remberg, Paolo Turco

Set in an opulent Italian castle, a family invites a young female performer from a touring circus to stay with them. She seduces the whole family, including the mother, father and teenage boy, who in turn act out their sexual fantasies, which include watching pornographic films. This is a badly made film with poor acting, cinematography and editing. The so-called erotic fantasies are not so erotic and the lesbianism will seem fairly tame for today's audiences.

Dist/Sales: Col-Tri, FirstRunFeatures

Lie Down with Dogs

White, Wally
1995; USA; 85 min; Comedy
P: Wally White, Anthony Bennett; *W:* Wally White; *C:* George Mitas; *E:* Hart F. Faber; *M:* Douglas J. Cuomo
Cast: Bash Halow, Darren Dryden, James Sexton, Wally White

A coming-of-age sexual odyssey which takes place one summer in Provincetown—dubbed the 'Ultimate gay resort'. Tommie leaves Manhattan with his friend Eddie with the promise of lots of available men at the resort—and he's not disappointed.

Prod Comp: Miramax
Dist/Sales: Dendy, Swank, Miramax

Life

(aka: Containment; Out of the Blue)

Johnston, Lawrence
1995; Australia; 85 min; Drama
P: Elisa Argenzio; *W:* John Brumpton, Lawrence Johnston; *C:* Mandy Walker; *E:* Bill Murphy; *M:* John Clifford White
Cast: John Brumpton, David Tredinnick, Robert Morgan, Ian Scott, Noel Jordan

A film adaptation of John Brumpton's play *Containment*, this powerfully acted drama is set in a prison where Des, a tough criminal, is placed in T2 division after he tests positive to HIV. His cellmate is the sensitive Ralph. The characters share their stories and both carry a lot of emotional baggage. Flashbacks are used to develop the interactions between the two men, the other inmates and wardens.

Prod Comp: Rough Trade Pictures
Dist/Sales: Dendy, Intra, Col-Tri

Life

Life and Death

Wam, Svend / Vennerod, Peter
1980; Norway; 90 min; Drama
P: Mephisto Films

Jacob is married, but falls in love with John. Whilst initially shocked, Jacob's wife Jennifer slowly warms to the idea, and finds herself drawn into a romantic triangle.

Life and Death on the A-List

Corcoran, Jay
1996; USA; 45 min; Documentary

Many Americans will remember Tom McBride as the devilishly handsome actor from the well known laundry detergent ads with Dana Delany and as the dancing Dr Pepper man. As the subject of Jay Corcoran's gripping documentary, Tom grapples with the very real-life complications of living with AIDS while coming to terms with his inevitable fall from (gay) grace. (Water Bearer Films)

Dist/Sales: WaterBearer

Life and Times of Allen Ginsberg, The

Aronson, Jerry
1990; USA; 82 min; Documentary

A candid and intimate look at the life of the visionary poet Allen Ginsberg. Aronson spent ten years compiling the footage for this documentary. In the process he developed a warm friendship with Ginsberg. Through black and white stills, home movies, television news footage, various interviews and poetry readings; we watch Ginsberg grow from a pained boy into an unpretentious literary giant. Included are interviews with Timothy Leary, Ken Kesey, Herbert Hunke, Amiri Baraka (LeRoi Jones) and Abbie Hoffman; as well as two partial reading of *Howl* and a full reading of *Kaddish*. (www.kerouac.com)

Life History of a Star

Gentile, Jennifer M.
1999; 13 min; Drama

Angie takes us on a magical journey as she recounts the events leading up to the destruction of her relationship with Dave and into her strange encounter with Claire. (Big Film Shorts)

Dist/Sales: Infected, BigFilm

Life is a Woman

(aka: Zhizn-Zhenshchina)

Serikbayeva, Zhanna
1991; Kazakhstan; 80 min; Drama

Women in prison saga with a 1970s flavour. Madina is imprisoned for murdering her boyfriend's enemy. When she learns that he has married another woman, it sparks a series of betrayals and depression. As with any film of this genre there are the lesbian love affairs, the jealous, vicious fights, steamy shower scenes and sadistic, cruel guards. Russian with English subtitles.

Dist/Sales: FeminaleEV

Life is Like a Cucumber

(aka: Affengeil)

von Praunheim, Rosa
1990; Germany; 87 min; Documentary
W: Rosa von Praunheim; *C:* Klaus Janschewsky, Mike Kuchar; *E:* Mike Shephard; *M:* Maran Gosov, Thomas Marquard
Cast: Lotti Huber, Rosa von Praunheim, Helga Stoop

A documentary that examines the filmmaker's friendship with German actress Lotti Huber, who survived a Nazi concentration camp during the Second World War and then went to Israel. She later became a television personality and an outspoken supporter of the gay community.

Life that we Dreamt, The

(aka: Het Leven dat we Droomden)

De Hert, Robbe
1981; Belgium; Drama
W: Fernand Auwera, Robbe De Hert
Cast: Arlette Weygers, Karen van Parijs, Herman Gilis

Two women fall in love with the same man, but soon discover that they are actually in love with each other.

Prod Comp: Belgische Radio en Televisie

Life's a Butch!

Rosser Goodman, A.
2000; USA; 14 min; Comedy

A true femme realises she must pose as a butch to win the femme of her dreams.

Dist/Sales: KGB

Life's Evening Hour

Life's Evening Hour

Murray, Karen
2000; Canada; 48 min; Documentary

When fine arts photographer John Dugdale lost most of his sight to an AIDS-related stroke, it not only made him re-evaluate his life, but also made his career become both therapy and salvation. This inspirational and moving documentary portrays the courage and personal faith of a talented man, who not only overcame his obstacles but used them to challenge standard methodologies of photography. Using a video diary format, the film chronicles the accolades for and celebrity interest in Dugdale's work (Sir Elton John being just one collector) as well as the passion that fuels it. A beautiful depiction of the human spirit and its power to overcome. (2002 Mardi Gras Film Festival)

Lifetime Commitment: A Portrait of Karen Thomson

Zeldes, Kiki
1987; USA; 30 min; Documentary

Tells story of Karen Thomson who struggled through the courts for legal access to her hospitalised lover, Sharon, who was severely injured in a car accident 1980s. Sharon's family denied she was a lesbian, although the two women had exchanged rings and made a lifetime commitment to each other, and had blocked Karen from rights usually given to family members. This version was updated in 1993 when Karen won the right to care for her lover.

Dist/Sales: WMM

Lifetime Guarantee: Phranc's Adventures in Plastic

Udelson, Lisa
2001; USA; 58 min; Documentary

Phranc has gone through some Madonna-sized transformations in her life. She began her singing career as a member of the Los Angeles punk scene in the 1970s. In the 1980s she came out as a lesbian folk singer who looked and dressed like a man, and sang cheery acoustic ditties about surfing and her love for Martina Navratilova. And now she's embraced the most American of middle-American products: Phranc's selling Tupperware. This funny and suprisingly moving documentary follows Phranc as she arranges Tupperware parties, sings her original Tupperware song, fills Tupperware orders, and finally attends a national convention for crackerjack Tupperware salesladies. But the film's not a satire or a critique. Sporting a flattop haircut, her retro jeans, and her polka-dot tie, Phranc is definitely the freakiest Tupperware lady ever. And yet, she genuinely believes in what she sells and approaches her encounters with middle-American housewives without a trace of irony or condescension. The resulting clash of cultures and backgrounds reveals

both painful homophobia and also inspiring acceptance. *Lifetime Guarantee* is a very funny film as well as a powerfully emotional examination of an outsider struggling for recognition. (2002 Mardi Gras Film Festival)

Dist/Sales: Roadside

Lightship, The

Skolimowski, Jerzy
1985; USA; 88 min; Thriller
P: Bill Benenson, Moritz Borman; *W:* William Mai, David Taylor, Siegfried Lenz; *C:* Charly Steinberger; *E:* Barrie Vince, Scott Hancock; *M:* Stanley Myers
Cast: Robert Duvall, Klaus Maria Brandauer, Tom Bower, Robert Costanzo, Badja Djola

A psycho-suspense thriller set on a lightship anchored off the coast of Norfolk. which picks up a drifting boat with three psychopathic crooks on board who are on the run. They take over the lightship and the suspense builds as the crew of the lightship becomes hostile and begins to fall apart under the pressure of the increasingly bizarre acts of the leader, played by Duvall. Duvall is almost unrecognisable as a slimy homosexual thug.

Prod Comp: CBS Television
Dist/Sales: Col-Tri, 20thCenturyFox, CastleHill

Like Grains of Sand

Like Grains of Sand
(aka: Nagisa no Shindobaddo)

Hashiguchi, Ryosuke
1995; Japan; 130 min; Drama
P: Kiyomi Kanazawa, Yuuka Nakazawa; *W:* Ryosuke Hashiguchi; *C:* Shogo Ueno; *M:* Kaziya Takahashi
Cast: Yoshinori Okada, Kota Kusano, Ayumi Hamazaki, Koji Yamaguchi

When Kasane moves to a new school she soon realises that Shuji, the most interesting boy in the class, is hopelessly in love with a fellow male student, Hiroyuki. But Hiroyuki isn't interested in Shuji. Shuji and Kasane become close friends and are mistaken for a couple. When Hiroyuki begins to show interest in Kasane, Shuji's reaction is rather immature. A moving film about passionate yet thwarted first love. Japanese with English subtitles.

Prod Comp: Toho Co, PIA Corporation

Like it is

Oremland, Paul
1997; UK; 90 min; Drama
P: Tracey Gardiner; *W:* Robert Gray;
C: Alistair Cameron; *M:* Don McGlashan
Cast: Steve Bell, Ian Rose, Dani Behr, Roger Daltrey

An unlikely romance between a working class youth and a up-and-coming record producer forms the basis of this candid and endearing British feature. Craig is a bare-knuckles boxer from working-class Blackpool. Matt is a record producer who has the golden touch—at least as far as boy bands are concerned. This cross-class love story—arousing, endearing, and romantic—features a superbly bitchy cameo by The Who's Roger Daltrey as Matt's cynical and sleazy boss. Daltrey threatens to steal the film...and Craig.

Prod Comp: Channel 4
Dist/Sales: Potential, FirstRunFeatures, Salzgeber, Wolfe, Mongrel, ACMI

Lilies

(aka: Lilies - les Feluettes)

Greyson, John
1996; Canada; 96 min; Drama
P: Anna Stratton, Arnie Gelbart, Ronib Cass; *W:* Michel Marc Bouchard; *C:* Daniel Jobin; *E:* André Corriveau, Jane Tattersall; *M:* Mychael Danna
Cast: Brent Carver, Marcel Sabourne, Aubert Pallascio, Jason Cadieux

Death, sexuality and religion are intertwined in this moving adaptation of Michel Marc Bouchard's hit play. An ageing bishop is held hostage in a Quebec prison by inmates who perform a play recounting his role in a teenage boy's murder. (Cowboy)

Awards: Genie Awards, 1996: Best Film; Montreal World Film Festival, 1996: Best Film
Prod Comp: Triptych Media, Gaga Film
Dist/Sales: TurbulentArts, Wolfe, Alliance, Cowboy, Millivres, VideoAmericain

Lilith

Rossen, Robert
1964; USA; 114 min; B&W; Drama
P: Robert Rossen; *W:* Robert Rossen; *C:* Eugen Schüfftan; *E:* Aram Avakian; *M:* Kenyon Hopkins
Cast: Warren Beatty, Jean Seberg, Peter Fonda, Kim Hunter

This story of the shifting involvement of a trainee therapist, Vincent, with a schizophrenic young woman is a reworking of the legend of Lilith, a female devil who, according to ancient Jewish mythology, is simultaneously the embodiment of madness and beauty. In the film Lilith fascinates and humiliates Vincent and uses him as an accomplice in a lesbian affair. Lilith has moments of lucidity which place her between two worlds. Vincent becomes obsessed with the fear of losing her when she finally crosses over.

Prod Comp: Columbia, Centaur
Dist/Sales: ReelMovies, NFVLS

Limites

Torrealba, José M.
1997; Canada; 50 min; Documentary

In *Limites* Peruvian photographer Carlos Quiroz unveils the artistic process behind capturing the male nude. This documentary visits Quiroz' private photo sessions, permitting us to witness the intimate relationship between camera and subject. (CFMDC)

Dist/Sales: CFMDC

Lip Gloss

Siegel, Lois
1995; Canada; 68 min; Comedy
P: Lois Siegel; *W:* Lois Siegel
Cast: Armand Monroe

Armand Monroe guides the audience through a who's who of Montreal's drag queens. Meet Gilda, Black Emmanuelle, Stella Spotlight and more...shopping for lingerie and high heels, on stage and backstage, and engaging in extracurricular activities.

Dist/Sales: TLA, WaterBearer

Liquid Sky

Tsukerman, Slava
1982; USA; 107 min; Sci-Fi
P: Slava Tsukerman; *W:* Slava Tsukerman, Anne Carlisle, Nina V. Kerova; *C:* Yuri Neyman; *E:* Sharyn L. Ross; *M:* Brenda I. Hutchinson, Slava Tsukerman
Cast: Anne Carlisle, Paula E. Sheppard, Bob Brady, Susan Doukas, Otto Von Wernherr

This darkly comic fairytale is populated by mythical characters in a New York underworld: a lesbian performance artist, a German astrophysicist, drug addicts and 'posturing artists'. Aliens from a miniature flying saucer find a chemical compound produced in the brain at the moment of orgasm which is a suitable substitute for heroin (liquid sky). Russian émigré Tsukerman keeps this afloat with a satirical wit, a psychedelic eye belying the low budget and intriguingly interwoven thematic threads.

Prod Comp: Z Films; *Dist/Sales:* NFVLS, ACMI

Listen

Wilding, Gavin
1996; USA; 101 min; Thriller
P: Diane Patrick-O'Connor; *W:* Jonas Quastel, Michael Bafaro; *C:* Brian Pearson; *E:* Melinda Seabrook; *M:* David Davidson
Cast: Brooke Langton, Gordon Currie, Sarah Buxton, Joel Wyner, Andy Romano

When Sarah discovers her phone line can tap into other people's conversation, particularly when they're having phone sex, her life is under threat as she begins to uncover the identity of a serial killer. Her life is already complicated, as she is torn between her new relationship with a man and her obsessive ex-lover Krista. A stylish film about manipulation and seduction with a reasonable amount of suspense, and despite some homophobic aspects, the girls do end up happily together.

Prod Comp: Devin Entertainment, Rampage Entertainment
Dist/Sales: 16MM

Listening for Something

Brand, Dionne
1996; Canada; 56 min; Documentary

This intriguing exchange between eminent American poet Adrienne Rich and Trinidadian-Canadian poet/filmmaker Dionne Brand, who share strong feminist and lesbian identities but are different in generation, race and class, invites viewers into the conversation and art of two remarkable women. Their open-ended dialogue, intercut with their interpretive readings of their poems, embrace subjects as diverse as citizenship, racism, political activism, ethnicity, sexuality, love, and the poetic process. (WMM)

Dist/Sales: WMM, Heathcliff

Little Bit of Lippy, A

Bernard, Chris
1992; UK; 75 min; Comedy
P: George Faber; *W:* Martyn Hesford; *C:* Rex Maidment; *E:* Sue Wyatt; *M:* Richard Blackford
Cast: Alison Swann, Danny Cunningham, Rachel Davies, Kenneth Cranham

Legendary English soap opera *Coronation Street* meets *Oranges Are Not the Only Fruit* by way of Danny La Rue in this cross-dressing comedy set in the north of England. Marian and Rick are caught in the tedium of working-class heterosexuality. When

Marian decides to re-ignite the spark in their marriage, she finds Rick has found solace in her make-up collection. Beyond all the laughs, *A Little Bit of Lippy* attempts to dispel some of the myths that still surround transgenderism by drawing attention to the finer distinctions between homosexuality and transvestism, and transvestism and female illusionism. (MQFF)

Dist/Sales: Roadshow, BBCTV

Liu Awaiting Spring

Soo, Andrew
1998; Australia; 11 min; Drama

An award-winning visual poem about a young Chinese boy's remembrances of his gay uncle's death, and his developing awareness of his own sexuality. Beautifully shot and constructed, the absence of dialogue just heightens this evocative and moving tale.

Prod Comp: Over Exposed Productions
Dist/Sales: Frameline, ACMI

Live Flesh

(aka: Carne Trémula)

Almodóvar, Pedro
1997; France, Spain; 103 min; Comedy
P: Austin Almodovar; *W:* Pedro Almodovar, Jorge Guerricaechevarria, Ray Loriga; *C:* Affonso Beato; *E:* José Salcedo; *M:* Alberto Iglesias
Cast: Liberto Rabal, Francesca Neri, Javier Bardem, Angela Molina

Victor is caught up in a violent encounter that sees him entangled in the lives of two cops, a philandering wife and a diplomat's daughter in this tale of life, love and lust. Spanish with English subtitles.

Prod Comp: CiBy 2000, France 3 Cinema, El Deseo SA
Dist/Sales: Siren, 20thCenturyFox, Goldwyn

Live Nude Girls

Lavin, Julianna
1995; USA; 89 min; Comedy
P: Cara Tapper, Steve White, Barry Bernardi; *W:* Julianna Lavin; *C:* Christopher Taylor; *E:* Adam Bernardi, Kathryn Himoff; *M:* Anton Sanko
Cast: Dana Delany, Kim Cattrall, Laila Robins, Cynthia Stevenson

Jamie, a woman in her thirties, is about to get married for the third time. Her childhood friends throw her a slumber party. It's been years since they have all been together for the whole night. As the night moves on, they reveal more and more about themselves. One of the women admits to being bisexual. The drama reaches a crisis about 3.30 in the morning due to fatigue...and that's when the trashy fun really begins.

Prod Comp: Republic Pictures Corporation, Spelling Entertainment
Dist/Sales: Republic, ACMI

Live Nude Girls UNITE!

Query, Julia / Funari, Vicky
2000; USA; 70 min; Documentary
P: John Montoya, Julia Query; *W:* Vicky Funari, Julia Query; *C:* Vicky Funari, Julia Query, John Montoya, Sarah Kennedy; *E:* Vicky Funari, Heidi Rahlmann Plumb; *M:* Allison Hennessy
Cast: Stephanie Batey, Julia Query, Dr Joyce Wallace

Live Nude Girls UNITE! is a record of the time stand up comedian Julia Query and her erotic-dancing colleagues at the Lusty Ladies strip joint in San Francisco started a campaign to unionise and provide better working conditions for strippers. And the dramatic tension isn't confined to the stand-off between the working girls and their money-grubbing bosses. Query's mother is Dr Joyce Wallace, a woman famous in her field for her pioneering activist work with prostitutes in the US. But, as the film makes abundantly clear, there is always a big difference between having liberal beliefs and how you feel when your own flesh and blood is involved. (MQFF)

Dist/Sales: FirstRunFeatures

Live to Tell: The First Gay and Lesbian Prom in America

Lang, Charley
1995; USA; 27 min; Documentary

This award-winning film documents the first gay and lesbian prom in America, organised by the students of the EAGLES centre, a gay and lesbian high school in Los Angeles. The film celebrates these students and their reclaiming of a teenage rite of passage previously denied them. *Live to Tell* also provides an insight into the lives of gay teens, as they deal with relationships, social prejudice and what to wear on prom night! (MQFF)

Awards: LA Outfest, 1995: Best Documentary Short
Dist/Sales: CinemaGuild

Living and Dying

(aka: Ich Lebe Gern, Ich Sterbe Gern)

Acklin, Claudia
1990; Switzerland; 72 min; Documentary

'My name is Andre Ratti, I am 50 years old, I am a homosexual and I've got AIDS.' When Andre Ratti, a Swiss television interviewer, dropped this bomb shell on 2 July 1984 at the press conference organ-

ised for the founding of AIDS-Help Switzerland, it prompted a tremendous reaction. *Living and Dying* provocatively examines the life of a complex and salty character—a man who refused to make things easy for the people around him by bowing to their perceptions of illness and sexuality. (Frameline)

Dist/Sales: Frameline

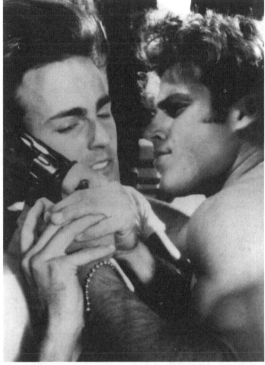

The Living End

Living End, The

Araki, Gregg
1992; USA; 92 min; Drama, Comedy
P: Marcus Hu, Jon Gerrans; *W:* Gregg Araki;
C: Gregg Araki; *E:* Gregg Araki; *M:* Cole Coonce
Cast: Craig Gilmore, Mike Dytri, Mark Finch, Mary Woronov

A post-modern love story and black comedy inspired by the AIDS crisis and propelled by a hard core-industrial soundtrack. Also a road movie that focuses on the relationship between two HIV-positive outcasts, Jon and Luke, who ditch their life in Los Angeles filled with lesbian serial killers, dangerous homophobes, murderers and lunatics, and hit the road for San Francisco.

Prod Comp: Desperate Pictures
Dist/Sales: NewVision, 21stCentury, October, Wolfe, Strand, Swank, ACMI

Living Out Loud

LaGravenese, Richard
1997; USA; 102 min; Drama
P: Danny DeVito, Michael Shamberg, Stacey Sher;
W: Richard LaGravenese; C: John Bailey; E: Jon
Gregory, Lynzee Klingman; M: George Fenton
Cast: Holly Hunter, Danny DeVito, Queen Latifah,
Martin Donovan

Newly divorced Judith Nelson is consumed by
vindictive fantasies of her ex-husband and his young
bride. Her life is empty until she finds unexpected
companionship in a bold and sassy jazz singer at a
local club and the down-on-his-luck elevator
operator in her fashionable Fifth Avenue building.
Although no longer alone, her life still seems
unfulfilled until a passionate kiss from a stranger
opens her eyes to all that she's been missing. (Wolfe)

Prod Comp: New Line Cinema, Jersey Films
Dist/Sales: Wolfe, NewLine

Living Proof: HIV and the Pursuit of Happiness

Cole, Kermit
1993; USA; 73 min; Documentary
P: Kermit Cole

A group of people are brought together by a
photographer documenting the lives of people living
with AIDS. They are a diverse group, ranging from a
swimmer and policeman to a 19-year-old scout
leader. Many of those interviewed have had the HIV
virus for several years, all are, however, active in
either athletic or artistic pursuits. The photographs
that emerge at the end of the shoot vividly capture
each subject's life, energy and individualism.
(MQFF)

Prod Comp: Jane Balfour Films
Dist/Sales: Ronin, FirstRunFeatures

Living with AIDS

Mooney, Shayne
1989; Australia; 57 min; Documentary
P: Shayne Mooney

Interviews with four men with who have two things
in common—they are all gay and HIV positive. Two
of the men, Colin, a photographer, and Ian, were
filmed in the final stages of their lives. Peter
Charlton and Chris Carter were HIV-positive but
had not then developed AIDS. The four men discuss
how the illness has affected their lives, the discrimination they have experienced and how they have
come to terms with the prospect of death with the
help of AIDS support workers.

Prod Comp: SBS
Dist/Sales: Marcom, ACMI

Living with Pride: Ruth Ellis @ 100

Welborn, Yvonne
1999; USA; 60 min; Documentary
P: Yvonne Welborn; C: Catherine Crouch, Ines
Sommer; E: Amanda Ault
Cast: Ruth C. Ellis

A must-see inspirational biopic about America's
oldest lesbian icon Ruth Ellis. Ruth's recollections of
dancing, a musical family, aeroplanes, two world
wars, Illinois riots, racial lynchings, Martin Luther
King, The Black Panther Party and the Stonewall
riots are compelling touchstones from an extraordinary life devoted to social justice, human rights and
bowling championships. (MQFF)

Prod Comp: Our Film Works
Dist/Sales: PictureThis!, Wolfe

Loads

McDowell, Curt
1980; USA; 22 min; Experimental

Explicit meditations on male masturbation.

Dist/Sales: Canyon

Lola and Billy the Kid

(aka: Lola and Bilidikid)

Ataman, E. Kutlug
1998; Germany; 93 min; Drama
P: Martin Hagemann, Martin Wiebel, Zeynep Özbatur;
W: E. Kutlug Ataman; C: Chris Squires; E: Ewa J. Lind;
M: Arpad Bondy
Cast: Inge Keller, Murat Yilmaz, Michael Gerber, Erdel
Yildiz, Gandi Mukli

Murat, a gay Turkish teenager is trying to come out
in a traditional immigrant neighbourhood in Berlin.
Murat's life becomes even more complicated when
he must choose whether or not to avenge the murder
of his newly-found brother Lola, the reigning queen
of the gay Turkish community. (Cowboy)
German & Turkish with English subtitles.

Prod Comp: Zero Films, Boje Buck Produktion,
Westdeutscher Rundfunk
Dist/Sales: Cowboy, PictureThis!, Millivres,
GoodMachine, Wolfe

Lone Star Hate

Yule, Paul
1997; UK; 76 min; Documentary
P: Jonathan Stack

The banality of evil is one of the subjects in this
Channel 4 documentary on the gruesome 1993 gay-
bashing murder of Nicholas West in conservative
Tyler, Texas. The story unfolds in graphic detail,
through forensic photographs, visits to the crime

scene, courtroom and police interrogation transcripts, death row interviews with the killers, and conversations with West's friends in the gay community. (Frameline)

Prod Comp: Gabriel Films
Dist/Sales: Frameline

Lonely Lady, The

Sasdy, Peter
1983; USA; 92 min; Drama
P: Robert R. Weston; *W:* John Kershaw, Shawn Randall; *C:* Brian West; *E:* Keith Palmer; *M:* Charlie Calello
Cast: Pia Zadora, Lloyd Bochner, Bibi Besch, Joseph Cali, Anthony Holland

After being raped, a young writer decides to sleep her way to the top. This includes sleeping with anyone and everyone, men and women. But she finds when she gets there, that it's a lonely place to be. Described as tasteless and tacky, based on the original story by Harold Robbins.

Prod Comp: Harold Robbins International Company, KGA, Universal Pictures
Dist/Sales: Roadshow

Lonely without You

De Bisschop, Sarah
1999; Belgium; 16 min; Comedy

Lena Stromans is 27, handsome, intelligent, and single, but not for long. Lena has a plan that is so secret that it will not be made public before the year 2031. Thanks to the website of love, he will be able to realise her near perfect utopia. A film about new families, new love and old fashioned passion.

Dist/Sales: Incident

Lonesome Cowboys

Warhol, Andy
1968; USA; 110 min; Comedy
P: Andy Warhol, Paul Morrissey; *C:* Paul Morrissey; *E:* Paul Morrissey
Cast: Joe Dallesandro, Viva, Louis Waldon, Taylor Mead

A band of gay cowboys arrive in a small and lonely desert town where they are greeted by two frustrated women, a transvestite sheriff and a seductive young man. All manner of sexual mayhem ensues.

Prod Comp: The Factory, Andy Warhol Films

Long Awaited Pleasure

Manana, Giovanna
1989; USA; 90 min; Comedy
Cast: Peggy Shaw, Lois Weaver

A New York dentist moves to a small town where she meets Sue, an undertaker and, after a very tentative beginning, they start a relationship.

Long Day Closes, The

Davies, Terence
1992; UK; 85 min; Drama
P: Olivia Stewart, Angela Topping; *W:* Terence Davies; *C:* Michael Coulter; *E:* William Diver; *M:* Bob Last, Robert Lockhart
Cast: Marjorie Yates, Leigh McCormack, Patricia Morrison, Nicholas Lamont, Anthony Watson

In the style of *Distant Voices, Still Lives*, Terence Davies continues his portrayal of childhood memories and recollections from Liverpool in the 1950s. A series of lyrical vignettes takes us into the childhood world of home, school, cinema and church, and reveals an altogether warmer and more sympathetic view of the struggle of growing up and coming to terms with his sexuality.

Prod Comp: BFI, Film Four International
Dist/Sales: Dendy, Col-Tri, TLA, SonyClassics

Long Time Comin'

Brand, Dionne
1993; Canada; 52 min; Documentary
Cast: Grace Channer, Faith Nolen

Long Time Comin' profiles two African-Canadian lesbian artists who bring political commitment and passion to their work and to their communities. Grace Channer's large evocative canvases relay her world views, her sexuality and the recovery of her African heritage. Singer, songwriter and community activist, Faith Nolan, speaks in her music of black people's daily struggles and of a lesbian feminist vision. *Long Time Comin'* connects the creative process to political and sexual being. (WMM)

Dist/Sales: WMM, NFBC

Long Voyage Home, The

Ford, John
1940; USA; 109 min; B&W; Drama
P: Walter Wanger; *W:* Dudley Nichols; *C:* Gregg Toland; *E:* Sherman Todd; *M:* Richard Hageman
Cast: John Wayne, Thomas Mitchell, Ian Hunter, Barry Fitzgerald

Set on a freighter loaded with ammunition making a dangerous journey to England during the early days of World War II, this is a mood piece with an episodic narrative based on Eugene O'Neill's work, who apparently approved of the film adaptation of three of his one-act plays. The sensuality of the dark, moody images is linked with death. There are frequent references to 'going home'. The men are propelled by fate causing them to constantly ship out. Ole is the innocent who must be saved by making 'the long journey home'. There is an undercurrent of homosexuality, and, with one exception, the emotional ties between the men are stronger than with any of the women.

Prod Comp: Argosy Films, Walter Wanger Productions
Dist/Sales: Ascanbee, UA

Long Weekend, The

(aka: The Long Weekend (O'Despair))

Araki, Gregg
1989; USA; 93 min; Drama
Cast: Bretton Vail, Maureen Dondanville, Andrea Beane

Three college friends get together for a long weekend. They share their angst about living in the late eighties and the politics of sexuality. An exploration of gay, lesbian and straight relationships.

Longtime Companion

Longtime Companion

René, Norman
1990; USA; 96 min; Drama
P: Stan Wlodkowski; *W:* Craig Lucas; *C:* Tony Jannelli; *E:* Katherine Wenning; *M:* Greg De Belles
Cast: Campbell Scott, Stephen Caffrey, Patrick Cassidy, John Dossett, Mary-Louise Parker

A powerful and wonderful fictional film dealing with the AIDS crisis in the USA. The story revolves around a group of mainly gay friends and depicts how the disease affects them all. It starts with the sexually liberated early 1980s and progresses to the fear of the late 1980s as death and disease take their toll. Director Norman Rene describes the film as 'a human drama above all, one that focuses not just on the heroics of a single character but rather on the interrelated struggles of an entire community'.

Prod Comp: American Playhouse Theatre, Samuel Goldwyn Company
Dist/Sales: Wolfe, BFI, TLA, SamuelGoldwyn, Swank, ACMI

Looking for a Space

1994; USA; 38 min; Documentary
P: Kelly Anderson

One of the ironies of the Cuban Revolution was

that, from the beginning, it persecuted many of its loyal supporters because of their sexual orientation. *Looking for a Space* examines the cultural, political and historical reasons behind the persecution of lesbians and gay men during the early years of the Revolution, and takes a fresh look at this issue from the perspectives of Cubans who are living on the island today. We meet a diverse group of people, from a wide range of age groups and occupations, who express differences of opinion. Older people recall the repression of the late sixties when gay people were sent to 'UMAP' camps for 're-education'. During the Mariel boat lift of 1980, many gay people were seen as 'counterrevolutionary' for fleeing the country. Many younger Cubans feel there is more tolerance today, as an emerging gay subculture demonstrates. Given the uncertain political and economic climate of today's Cuba, the future remains unclear. The documentary raises critical questions about political ideology and sexual identity. (Filmakers Library)

Dist/Sales: FilmakersLibrary

Looking for Angel

(aka: Tenshi No Rakuen)

Suzuki, Akihiro
1999; Japan; 61 min; Drama
P: Akihiro Suzuki, Toshiko Takashi; *W:* Akihiro Suzuki, Akihiro Suzuki, Jun Kurasawa; *C:* Jun Kurosawa, Akihiro Suzuki; *E:* Akihiro Suzuki; *M:* Hiroyuki Oki
Cast: Koich Imaizumi, Hataru Hazuki, Akira Kuroiwa, Akira Suehiro

Shinpei, a country boy alone in Tokyo with ambiguous sexual preference, is invited to a party by a girl he hasn't seen in a while. It turns out to be a wake for Takachi, a gay guy who appeared in straight porn, and who was apparently murdered in a casual pickup. During the night Shinpei pieces together fragments of Takachi's story: his friendship with a beautiful rent boy, his move to Kochi where 'the boys are like angels', his return to Tokyo... and his heart breaking plea for gentleness in the last night of his life. Japanese with English subtitles. (2001 Hong Kong Lesbian & Gay Film Festival)

Looking for Common Ground

Akeret, Julie
1999; USA; 30 min; Documentary

When Massachusetts enacted an anti-discrimination law establishing the rights of gay and lesbian high school students, the citizens of Westhampton were embroiled in controversy. Parents, students, school committee members and local citizens were polarised. Those opposed to the new law questioned the morality of the issue and feared the consequences of introducing a 'gay curriculum' in school. Supporters of this law worried about escalating dropout and suicide rates if gay and lesbian students were not more fully accepted. The film gives voice to the gay and lesbian students who talk about their struggle for acceptance. It also allows us to hear articulate and passionate testimony from all sides of the controversy, both in interviews and community meetings. Surprisingly, in this small town environment, the diversity of opinion rivals that of any metropolis. Among the issues raised are parents versus governments in determining the education of minors; community values versus the rights of the individual; nature versus nurture in determining sexual orientation. (Filmakers Library)

Prod Comp: Akeret Films
Dist/Sales: FilmakersLibrary

Looking for Langston

Julien, Isaac
1988; UK; 40 min; B&W; Experimental
Cast: Ben Ellison, Matthew Baidoo, John Wilson, Akim Magaji

A 'poetic meditation' on the black poet Langston Hughes. This haunting, lyrical film examines the relationship of gay sexuality to the 1920s American artistic movement known as the Harlem Renaissance. Beautifully filmed and edited, it could have become too arty but remains fresh, strong and interesting.

Prod Comp: Channel 4
Dist/Sales: Facets, ACMI, WaterBearer, NFVLS, BFI

Looking for Mr Goodbar

Brooks, Richard
1977; USA; 136 min; Drama
P: Freddie Fields; *W:* Richard Brooks; *C:* William Fraker; *E:* George Grenville; *M:* Artie Kane
Cast: Diane Keaton, Tuesday Weld, Richard Gere, Tom Berenger, William Atherton, Richard Kiley

A film about a woman's self-destructive lifestyle based on the novel by Judith Rossner. By day the female protagonist is a model citizen, a teacher, but by night she cruises the singles bars in search of men. The men she finds, either emotionally or physically, abuse her then dump her. Tom Berenger plays a repressed homosexual who goes to a bar and is picked up by Keaton. When he can't perform sexually and she asks him to leave, he flies into a rage. Another homophobic portrait from Hollywood, where sexual difference is met with violence and death.

Prod Comp: Paramount
Dist/Sales: ReelMovies, Paramount

Loose Connections

Eyre, Richard
1983; UK; 80 min; Comedy
P: Simon Perry; *W:* Maggie Brooks; *C:* Clive Tickner; *E:* David Martin; *M:* Dominic Muldowney, Andy Roberts
Cast: Lindsay Duncan, Stephen Rea, Robbie Coltraine, Gary Olsen, Ken Jones

A humorous battle-of-the-sexes and road movie combined. When Sally is left to drive on her own from London to Munich to attend a feminist convention, she places an ad in a newspaper for a companion. The only person to answer it is Harry who, although not a woman, is gay, or so he says. The trip begins and they stumble from one disaster to another.

Prod Comp: Umbrella, Greenpoint Films, NFFC, Virgin
Dist/Sales: 20thCenturyFox, OrionClassics

Loose Ends

Nettlebeck, Sandra
1996; Germany; 90 min; Drama
Cast: Jasmin Tabatabai, Regula Grauwiller, Natascha Bub

The story of three women and their search for happiness. Sarah begins a passionate affair while making arrangements for her wedding day; Katherine, re-establishes her relationship with her ex-boyfriend; and Nina meets her match, waking up with the same girl more than once.

Dist/Sales: Frameline

Loot

Narizzano, Silvio
1970; UK; 96 min; Comedy
P: Arthur Lewis; *W:* Ray Galton, Alan Simpson; *C:* Austin Dempster; *E:* Martin Charles; *M:* Keith Mansfield, Richard Willing-Denton
Cast: Richard Attenborough, Lee Remick, Hywel Bennett, Milo O'Shea, Dick Emery

A gruesome, fast-paced comedy with Richard Attenborough as a caricature of the law and Lee Remick as a nymphomaniac Jean Harlow look-alike. It's basically the story of two mates who decide to get rich quick by robbing a bank. They hide the money in a coffin that is supposed to house one of the crook's mothers, but there isn't enough room for both, so mum gets put in the lavatory. All hell breaks loose when they try to retrieve the loot before anyone one else gets to it. See *Entertaining Mr Sloane*, another film of a Joe Orton play, and *Prick Up your Ears*, which tells part of his life story.

Prod Comp: British Lion, Performing Arts

Lorenza

Stahlberg, Michael
1992; Chile, Germany; 20 min; B&W; Documentary

This brutally honest portrait of a Chilean-German gay artist with no arms could all too easily have descended into freak-show sensationalism. However, Lorenza forestalls the intrusions of voyeurism by declaring himself an exhibitionist and deliberately engaging public interest by performing and painting with his feet.

Dist/Sales: Hocschule

Losing Lois

Hill, Julie / Richter, Kathy / Rosenthal, Barbara
2001; USA; 18 min; Documentary

Relates the events of the death of Tampa Police-woman Lois Marrero, and her lesbian partner's fight for her pension rights.

Loss of Heat

Deville, Noski
1994; UK; 20 min; Drama
W: Noski Deville; *M:* Derek Richards, Tanya Syed
Cast: Anjum Mouj, Susan Paul, Valantina Gomez-Martinez, Carol Coombes

Loss of Heat weaves the stories of two lesbians—one in London, the other in Spain. They don't know each other but are connected by their experiences of epilepsy. The film examines the nature of lesbian relationships when dealing with the illness of one partner.

Prod Comp: Heartbreak Productions
Dist/Sales: WMM, Cinenova

Loss of Innocence

(aka: The Greengage Summer)

Gilbert, Lewis
1961; UK; 100 min; Drama
P: Edward Small, Victor Saville; *W:* Howard Koch;
C: Freddie Young; *E:* Peter Hunt; *M:* Richard Addinsell
Cast: Susannah York, Kenneth Moore, Danielle Darrieux, Claude Nollier

A young, innocent English girl, along with her mother and three younger children, go on summer holidays to a pension in France. Her mother unexpectedly becomes ill and is hospitalised leaving the girl to her own devices. She soon grows to be a woman after a relationship with one of the other boarders. The film takes for granted the lesbian relationship between the mistress of the house and another French woman. Based on the novel *The Greengage Summer* by Rumer Godden.

Prod Comp: Columbia

Lost and Delirious

Pool, Léa
2000; Canada; 100 min; Drama
P: Lorraine Richard, Louis-Philippe Rochon, Greg Dummett; *W:* Judith Thompson; *C:* Pierre Gill;
E: Gaetan Huot; *M:* Yves Chamberland
Cast: Piper Perabo, Jessica Pare, Mischa Barton, Jackie Burroughs

Mouse Bradford has just arrived at boarding school. Her two senior roommates, the striking, sharp-witted Paula and the charming and beautiful Tori, quickly adopt the homesick girl. When Paula and Tori are found to be lovers, Mouse, caught in the role of accomplice and confessor, is left torn between her two friends. (10%)

Prod Comp: Cité-Amérique, Dummett Films
Dist/Sales: LionsGate, Wolfe, Swank, 10%

Lost in the Pershing Point Hotel

Pierrepont III, Julie Jay
2000; USA; 106 min; Comedy
P: Julie Jay Pierrepont III, Erin Chandler;
W: Leslie Jordan; *C:* Sacha Sarchielli; *E:* Ila von Hasperg; *M:* Dan Gilboy
Cast: John Ritter, Marilu Henner, Michelle Phillips, Sheryl Lee Ralph

A gay, Southern writer, in search of spiritual meaning, is entertainingly lead astray by a beautiful, runaway debutante (who is an expert in 'self medication') and tempted by a seductive, heroin-addicted street hustler. Together, this trio of misfits embark on a wild, dark journey of self-discovery through the underground drug scene of the mid 1970s. (www.perishingpointhotel.com)

Lost Language of Cranes, The

Finch, Nigel
1991; UK; 88 min; Drama
P: Ruth Caleb; *W:* Sean Mathias; *C:* Remi Adefarasin;
E: Sue Wyatt; *M:* Julian Wastall
Cast: Corey Parker, Angus MacFadyen, John Schlesinger, Brian Cox, Eileen Atkins

Based on the best-selling novel by David Leavitt, *The Lost Language of Cranes* is a faithful made-for-television translation of the book's themes and meanings, despite its relocation to England. Rose and Owen are a married couple, content in their routine. They live in a rented apartment in a fashionable suburb. Their son, Philip, now in his twenties, is fairly close to the family but keeps his distance because he is gay. When Philip finally comes out to his family he stirs up a hornet's nest of secrets and hidden feelings within his parents marriage, culminating in his father coming to terms with his own homosexuality.

Prod Comp: BBC TV
Dist/Sales: BBCTV, Wolfe

Lot in Sodom

Watson Jnr, James Sibley / Webber, Melville
1933; USA; 28 min; B&W; Drama
Cast: Friedrich Haak, Hildegarde Watson, Dorthea
House, Lewis Whitbeck

Said to be one of the first American sound experimental films, *Lot in Sodom* represents the Biblical story in a blend of semi-erotic imagery and the manipulation of light and shadow, featuring semi-maked men amidst filmed body fragments and faces.

Love and Human Remains

Love and Death on Long Island

(aka: Amour et mort à Long Island)

Kwietniowski, Richard
1997; Canada, UK; 93 min; Drama
P: Steve Clark-Hall, Christopher Zimmer; *W:* Gilbert
Adair, Richard Kwietniowski; *C:* Oliver Curtis; *E:* Susan
Shipton; *M:* Richard Grassby-Lewis
Cast: John Hurt, Jason Priestley, Fiona Loewi, Sheila
Hancock, Harvey Atkin

Giles D'Ath is an old fashioned widower whose trips

to the movies see him fall in love with screen idol Ronnie Bostock. He becomes obsessed with Ronnie and his movie and eventually travels to Long Island to meet him, dramatically confronting the young actor's reality.

Prod Comp: BBC, Arts Council of England, British
Screen
Dist/Sales: Siren, Alliance, Cinepix, LionsGate,
Universal, Wolfe

Love and Human Remains

Arcand, Denys
1993; Canada; 100 min; Drama, Comedy
P: Roger Frappier; *W:* Denys Arcand, Brad Fraser;
C: Paul Sarossy; *E:* Alain Baril; *M:* John McCarthy
Cast: Thomas Gibson, Ruth Marshall, Mia Kirshner,
Cameron Bancroft

The story focuses on the lifestyles of two friends—David, a gay, sardonic, witty actor turned waiter, and his flatmate, Candy, an optimistic book reviewer—and their search for meaningful relationships. This leads them both into a number of hilarious and sometimes heartbreaking encounters, which take on a dangerous twist when someone they know reveals a darker side. An astute look at what it means to fall in love in the era of AIDS.

Prod Comp: Max Films, Atlantis Films, First Choice,
Super Ecran, Téléfilm Canada
Dist/Sales: NewVision, 21stCentury, Wolfe,
SonyClassics, ACMI

Love and Marriage

Ardill, Susan
1991; UK; 40 min; Documentary
P: Rebecca Dobbs

Produced for Britain's *OUT* series, *Love and Marriage* is a discussion of the issues raised by the push for domestic partnership laws in Britain, the US and Denmark.

Dist/Sales: MayaVision

Love and Other Catastrophes

Croghan, Emma-Kate
1996; Australia; 76 min; Comedy
P: Stavros Andonis Efthymiou; *W:* Yael Bergman,
Emma-Kate Croghan, Helen Bandis; *C:* Justin Brickle;
E: Ken Sallows; *M:* Oleh Witer
Cast: Frances O'Connor, Alice Garner, Radha Mitchell,
Matthew Dyktynski

An original comedy-romance very much set in the 1990s. It's essentially a day-in-the-life story of five university students as they move across town and across campus, in and out of relationships. With the use of diverse characters, including two lesbians, all in their twenties, the film captures the youth experience with spirit and energy.

Prod Comp: Screwball Five, Newvision Films, Beyond Films
Dist/Sales: NewVision, Beyond, 21stCentury, ReelMovies, ACMI, FoxSearchlight

Love in a Women's Prison

(aka: Diario Segreto da un Carcere Femminile)

di Silvestro, Rino
1972; Italy; 100 min; Action
P: Giuliano Anellucci; *W:* Rino di Silvestro;
C: Fausto Rossi; *E:* Angelo Curi; *M:* Franco Bixio
Cast: Anita Strindberg, Eva Czemerys, Jenny Tamburi, Olga Bisera

Exploitation film about women behind bars. Includes lesbianism, women fighting, bondage and spanking. The loose plot involves the mafia, drug smuggling and gangs. Dubbed into English.

Prod Comp: Aquarius Film, Overseas Film Company

Love in Progress

(aka: Amori in corso)

Bertolucci, Giuseppe
1989; Italy; 82 min; Comedy
P: Ferninando O, Flavia Villevielle; *W:* Giuseppe Bertolucci, Mimmo Rafele, Lidia Ravera;
C: Fabio Cianchetti; *E:* Fiorella Giovanelli
Cast: Francesca Prandi, Amanda Sandrelli, Stella Vordemann

A young woman plans a weekend rendezvous with a man at a beautiful villa in the Italian countryside. To legitimise the weekend to her parents, she invites along a female friend she doesn't know well, as the excuse for the getaway. Through a variety of circumstances, the man arrives late, giving the two young women time to get to know each other, which leads to the beginnings of an attraction.

Prod Comp: Rai Due, Mito Film
Dist/Sales: Academy

Love is the Devil

Maybury, John
1998; France, Japan, UK; 102 min; Drama
P: Chiara Menage; *W:* John Maybury; *C:* John Mathieson; *E:* Daniel Goddard; *M:* Ryuichi Sakamoto
Cast: Derek Jacobi, Daniel Craig, Tilda Swinton, Anne Lambton

A filmic portrait in the style of controversial British painter Francis Bacon. Like Bacon's confronting yet compelling portraits, John Maybury's film intensely focuses on its subject—revelling in distortion and pain. The film follows the turbulent, sadomasochistic relationship Bacon had with George Dwyer, who he meets when he accidentally stumbles upon Dwyer attempting to burgle Bacon's meagre apartment. Francis simply says to George: 'Take off your clothes. Come to bed and you can have whatever you want'. The relationship has a destructive effect on the passive George who feels uncomfortable with Bacon's eccentric friends, and who is continually tortured by Bacon's sadistic enjoyment of pain and suffering. (ACMI)

Prod Comp: BBC
Dist/Sales: BFI, Strand, Wolfe, ACMI, Sharmill, Haut-et-Court, Salzgeber

Love is the Devil

Love Letter, The

Chan, Peter
1999; USA; 88 min; Comedy
P: Kate Capshaw, Sarah Pillsbury, Midge Sanford;
W: Maria Maggenti; *C:* Tami Reiker; *E:* Jacqueline Cambas; *M:* Luis Bacalov
Cast: Kate Capshaw, Ellen DeGeneres, Gloria Stuart, Tom Selleck, Blythe Danner

A charming, low-keyed romantic comedy with Capshaw as a bookstore owner who finds an unsigned love letter and thinks it's meant for her. But who sent it? Complications arise when the letter finds its way into the hands of others in her small New England coastal town, each thinking it's meant for them as well. DeGeneres is a natural sidekick as the store's manager, and Selleck is quite appealing as the local fire chief in love with Capshaw. (Wolfe)

Prod Comp: DreamWorks
Dist/Sales: Wolfe, UIP

Love Like Any Other, A

(aka: Eine Liebe wie andere auch)

Stempel, Hans / Ripkens, Martin
1983; Germany; 102 min; Drama

W: Martin Ripkens, Hans Stempel

Weiland and Wolf are a young gay couple living in Berlin. Their relationship is threatened by differing political and personal needs.

Love Ltd.

Phang, Jennifer
1999; USA; 24 min; Comedy

Quirky and very funny take on a young woman's attempt to come out to her dysfunctional Asian–American family over a tension filled dinner party. Can she spill the beans before the rest of the family?

Dist/Sales: Frameline

Love Machine, The

Snee, Patrick
1994; USA; 20 min; Comedy

It's 1968 in Greenwich Village and a psychiatrist is becoming aware of a host of young homosexual men falling victim to the dangerous charm of 'The Love Machine'. This hilarious send-up of conventional Hollywood treatment of queers is a well-aimed kick in the face to all straight movies and romance novels that have sensationalised homosexuality in the guise of tolerance.

Love Makes a Family: Gay Parents in the '90s

Kobufs, Remco / Leech, Marla / Veltri, Danl
1991; USA; 16 min; Documentary

This touching documentary interviews queer people who are raising children of their own. We meet a lesbian single mother, a lesbian couple raising a son, and two gay men who have two adopted children. Non-sensational and thoughtful, this video makes clear the important role queer parents have in broadening our understanding of love and families. (MQFF)

Dist/Sales: Fanlight

Love=ME3

Fernandez, Agustin
2000; USA; 92 min; Comedy
P: Agustin Fernandez, Greg Huge; *W:* Agustin Fernandez; *C:* M. A. Morels; *E:* Sandro Philips
Cast: Angelica Ordoñes, Evly Pacheco, Agustin Fernandez

Love=ME3 is a romantic comedy, based on a true story, about one man and two women who fall deeply in love with each other and try to lead a normal life, despite the doubts and judgements of those around them.

Dist/Sales: Babylegs

Love of a Man, The

(aka: Amor de Hombre)

Iborra, Juan Luis / Serrano, Yolanda Garcia
1997; Spain; 96 min; Drama
W: Yolanda Garcia Serrano, Juan Luis Iborra;
C: Paco Femenia
Cast: Loles Léon, Andrea Occhipinti, Pedro Mari Sanchez, Armando del Rio

It's Esperanza's 40th birthday party and she can't help noticing the irony of her life. Here she is without a boyfriend, yet all the guests at her party are intelligent, witty and handsome men. Of course, these guys are gay, and Esperanza loves them all. Her favourite of the bunch is Ramon, a sexy lawyer who is also searching in vain for Mr Right. Together they commiserate and laugh at the foibles of their love lives and try (unsuccessfully) to fix each other up. When Ramon is temporarily confined to bed after an accident, Esperanza makes the mistake of introducing him to Robert, an attractive masseur who she hopes can help Ramon's rehabilitation. Ramon quickly becomes obsessed and will do anything to satisfy the very sexy Robert, including sacrificing his close friendship with Esperanza. (Mongrel Media) Spanish with English subtitles.

Dist/Sales: Mongrel

Love Story: Berlin 1942, A

Clay, Catrine
1997; UK; 60 min; Documentary
P: Catrine Clay; *C:* John Goodyer; *E:* Edward Roberts

In 1942 Berlin, Lilly Wurst was a model Aryan hausfrau with a picture of the Führer on the wall, a husband in the army, and a German motherhood medal for bearing four sons. With this distinction came mother's helper Ulla Schaaf, who unbeknownst to Lilly was deeply involved with the Jewish underground. When Lilly boasted that she could 'smell a Jew', Ulla tested her by introducing her to Felice Schraderheim, aka Felice Schrader, a 20-year-old Jewish woman living in hiding. The result of that meeting is an unusual love story whose arc is followed through recollections, documents, and archival footage in this beautifully made documentary. (WMM)

Prod Comp: BBC, Timewatch
Dist/Sales: WMM

Love! Valour! Compassion!

Mantello, Joe
1997; USA; 115 min; Comedy
P: Doug Chapin, Barry Krost; *W:* Terence McNally;
C: Alik Sakharov; *E:* Colleen Sharp; *M:* Harold Wheeler
Cast: Jason Alexander, John Glover, Stephen Spinella,

Stephen Bogardus

Eight friends leave the city behind for three simple weekends of rest and relaxation in the country. What they find is an outrageous mix of *The Big Chill* meets *The Birdcage* in this film version of Terrance McNally's Tony Award-winning play. (Wolfe)

Prod Comp: Krost/Chapin
Dist/Sales: Wolfe, FineLine

Love/Juice

Kaze, Shindo
2001; Japan; 78 min; Drama
P: Chikako Nakabayashi, Tsuyoshi Sugino, Kazutoshi Wadakura; *W:* Shindo Kaze; *C:* Koji Kanaya;
E: Ikio Watanabe; *M:* Kenichiro Isoda
Cast: Chika Fujimura, Mika Okuno, Toshiya Nagasawa

Love/Juice explores a familiar but oh so painful situation: what can happen when a young girl falls for her straight best friend. Chinatsu and Kyoko live together, but when Kyoko's curiosity and provocative behaviour lead Chinatsu to reveal how she really feels, their cosy world is changed forever. (MQFF) Japanese with English subtitles.

Prod Comp: Cine Baxar

Love/Juice

Loved One, The

Richardson, Tony
1965; USA; 116 min; B&W; Comedy
P: John Calley, Haskell Wexler; *W:* Terry Southern, Christopher Isherwood; *C:* Haskell Wexler; *E:* Antony Gibbs, Hal Ashby, Brian Smedley-Aston;
M: John Addison
Cast: Robert Morse, Rod Steiger, John Gielgud, Dana Andrews, Liberace, Jonathan Winters, Milton Berle

Morse plays a British poet who must help organise his uncle's burial in California. As he encounters some bizarre and humorous aspects of the funeral business, he falls in love with the funeral parlour's cosmetician. Along with a great cast, Liberace camps

it up as a casket salesman. Based on Evelyn Waugh's classic novella.

Prod Comp: MGM, Filmways Pictures
Dist/Sales: Chapel, Ascanbee

Loverfilm

Brynntrup, Michael
1996; Germany; 21 min; Experimental
W: Michael Brynntrup

A video-diary and collage of the director's many lovers over the past twenty years. This film passes through self-indulgence into the realms of the starkly personal, and involves the viewer to an intimate degree. German with English subtitles.

Prod Comp: MBC- Filmproduktion
Dist/Sales: MBC, CFMDC

Loverville 2: The Honeymoon

Zachary, Bohdan
1993; USA; 10 min; Comedy

The sequel to the popular hit Loverville. An annoying waiter comes between 2 male protagonists on a long awaited trip to gay Paris. (MQFF)

Dist/Sales: Zachary

Low-Fat Elephants

Marzella, Phillip
2000; Australia; 90 min; Comedy
P: Phillip Marzella; *W:* Phillip Marzella; *C:* Peter Falk
Cast: Christopher Gabardi, Tessa Wells, Karen Pang, Phillip Marzella

Low-Fat Elephants is a comedy that revolves around Greta—a neurotic-poetry-loving-chef—and Yuri—a bad actor, as they fight for the love of the same woman. The film draws together romance, wedding cakes, poetry and African music.

Prod Comp: Acrobat Films
Dist/Sales: Acrobat

Low-Fat Elephants

Lucifer Rising

Anger, Kenneth
1969; USA; 28 min; Experimental

A film about the love generation—the birthday party of the Aquarian age showing actual ceremonies to make Lucifer rise. Lucifer is the light god, not the devil—the rebel angel behind what's happening in the world today. His message is that the key of joy is disobedience. Isis wakes. Osiris answers. Lilith climbs to the place of Sacrifice. The Magus activates the circle and Lucifer, bringer of light, breaks through.

Prod Comp: Puck Film Productions
Dist/Sales: BFI

Ludwig

Visconti, Luchino
1972; France, Germany, Italy; 245 min; Drama
P: Ugo Santalucia, Dieter Geissler; *W:* Luchino Visconti, Enrico Medioli, Suso Cecchi D'Amico;
C: Armando Nannuzzi; *E:* Ruggero Mastroianni;
M: Robert Schumann, Franco Mannino
Cast: Helmut Berger, Trevor Howard, Silvana Mangano, Helmut Griem, Gert Frobe

A lavish film about the attractive but obsessive homosexual Mad King of Bavaria—from his patronage of Richard Wagner to his extravagant and extensive castle building. The main character is so cold that it is hard to identify with him or feel any sympathy for him. Italian with English subtitles.

Prod Comp: Divina, Cinete, Mega, Dieter Geissler Filmproduktion
Dist/Sales: BFI, Ascanbee, Salzgeber, MGM

Ludwig: Requiem for a Virgin King

(aka: Ludwig: Requiem für einen Jungfräulichen König)

Syberberg, Hans Jürgen
1972; Germany; 140 min; Drama
W: Hans Jürgen Syberberg; *C:* Dietrich Lohmann;
M: Richard Wagner, Franz Lehar, Kurt Weill
Cast: Harry Baer, Balthasar Thomas, Oskar von Schab, Ingrid Caven

The film relates the story of Ludwig II, the mad, virgin homosexual king, a visionary and builder of impossible castles. It is part of a trilogy of films that examines the chaos of German history from the rise of Bismarck to the rise of Hitler in the 1930s.

Prod Comp: TMS Films
Dist/Sales: BFI

Lulu

Thiele, Rolf
1962; Austria; 100 min; Drama
P: Otto Dürer; *W:* Rolf Thiele; *C:* Michel Kelber;
M: Carl de Groof
Cast: Nadja Tiller, Mario Adorf, O. E. Hasse, Hildegarde Neff

A remake of Pabst's 1929 film *Pandora's Box*, which was based on the play by Franz Wedekind. Tells the story of a young woman who is taken off the streets by a doctor and turned into a sophisticated woman. She marries the doctor but he dies, she then goes through a succession of relationships and ends up in prison. She is released by one of her ex-husband's sons and his lesbian friend. She later becomes a victim of Jack the Ripper.

Prod Comp: Gloria-Film GmbH, Vienna Film

Luminous Procuress

Arnol, Steven
1971; USA; 81 min; Experimental

Avant-garde film from the early 1970s featuring the legendary drag group The Cockettes. (See also *The Cockettes*)

Lunch with Eddie

Preece, David John
2001; USA; 13 min; Drama

Lunch with Eddie is about friends you thought you knew and the lover you never forget.

Dist/Sales: MollyBeGood

Lune

Eltringham, Billie
1992; UK; 28 min; Drama

A gentle story from the United Kingdom about the sexual awakening of a fisherman's daughter in a remote coastal village. When a storm-damaged sailing boat brings an older woman to the harbour, the daughter becomes fascinated with her and invites her into their home. (MQFF)

Lust and Liberation

1991; UK; Documentary

Two generations talk about sex and politics.

Prod Comp: Channel 4

Lust for a Vampire

(aka: To Love a Vampire)

Sangster, Jimmy
1971; UK; 95 min; Horror
P: Harry Fine, Michael Style; *W:* Tudor Gates;
C: David Muir; *E:* Spencer Reeve; *M:* Harry Robertson
Cast: Yutte Stensgaard, Suzanna Leigh, Ralph Bates, Barbara Jefford, Michael Johnson

Set in 1870, this is the story of Mircalla, who ravages

the girls of a finishing school close to her castle. Included in her victims are two male teachers. Finally the outraged villagers burn down the school and Mircalla is accidentally staked and killed by a falling beam. Unfortunately this film does not quite meet the standard set by Jean Rollin's sensuous and erotic lesbian vampire films.

Prod Comp: Hammer
Dist/Sales: Warner

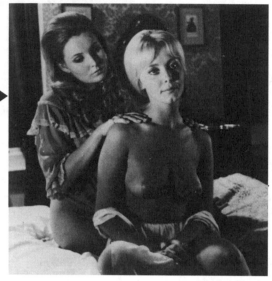

Lust for a Vampire

Lust in the Dust

Bartel, Paul
1985; USA; 85 min; Comedy
P: Tab Hunter, Alan Glaser; *W:* Philip John Taylor;
C: Paul Lohman; *E:* Alan Toomayan; *M:* Peter Matz
Cast: Tab Hunter, Divine

Trashy camp western spoof starring drag legend Divine.

Luster

Lewis, Everett
2001; USA; 90 min; Drama
P: Robert Shulevitz; *W:* Everett Lewis;
C: Humberto De Luna; *M:* Michael Leon
Cast: Justin Herwick, Pamela Gidley, Shane Powers, Jonah Blechman

Luster is a refreshingly funny and sexy look at unrequited love. Jackson, a cute, lanky, blue-haired poet who works in a record store, is at the center of Everett Lewis' twisted black LA comedy. He's got a crush on the sexy young blonde, Billy, who he met at an orgy the other night. But Billy's not into him—

he's in love with Sonny, a musician into SM. And although Billy doesn't want Jackson, two other guys do: Derek, a clean-cut record store customer, and Sam, the straight record store owner. Into this mix is thrown Jed, Jackson's hunky cousin, which leads Jackson to seriously contemplate the technicalities of incest. Before he can do anything about it, though, Jed is seduced by Jackson's lesbian artist friend. What's a boy to do? (2002 New York Lesbian & Gay Film Festival)

Dist/Sales: Luster

Luv Tale, A

Smith, Sidra
1999; USA; 45 min; Drama

Candice is the editor of Meridian Magazine where she's being overworked and overlooked by her boss/ boyfriend. Then she meets Taylor, a photojournalist who's tiring of the industry. Their two worlds come together in a seductive and memorable tale. (Wolfe)

Dist/Sales: Bizarre, Wolfe

Lycanthrophobia

Victor, Harry
1998; USA; 15 min; Comedy

A full moon. A smoky bar. All Ted wanted was a drink. What he gets instead might change his life forever. This tight, well made film is a frightening drama of werewolves and mistaken identity. (Big Film Shorts)

Dist/Sales: Rednavel, BigFilm

Luster

Lysis

Markopoulos, Gregory
1948; USA; 24 min; Experimental

A study in stream-of-consciousness poetry of a lost, wandering, homosexual soul.

M Butterfly

Cronenberg, David
1993; USA; 97 min; Drama
P: Gabriella Martinelli; *W:* David Henry Hwang;
C: Peter Suschitzky; *E:* Ronald Sanders; *M:* Howard Shore
Cast: Jeremy Irons, John Lone, Barbara Sukowa, Ian Richardson

> A French diplomat serving in Beijing in 1964 develops an obsession with a beautiful Chinese opera singer. But this fevered fantasy cannot last when he discovers that he has been the object of a deadly game of international political manipulation and the woman he desires turns out to be a man.

Prod Comp: Warner, Geffen, Miranda Productions
Dist/Sales: Warner, Swank

M! Mom, Madonna and Me

Siddiqi, Atif
2001; Canada; 54 min; Experimental

> In this very personal exploration of identity, the narrator-filmmaker looks for reflections of himself and finds them in the images of his mother, a Pakistani homemaker and Madonna, the international pop icon. On his journey toward self-love and maturity, he sees how his gender identity and professional life have been framed by his admiration of these two women. Dramatisations of intense personal events from the past 15 years demonstrate how the dreams and ambitions of Mom became the filmmaker's own. From a schoolboy in Pakistan, to a fashion designer in Los Angeles, to a performance artist and filmmaker in Montreal, M! traces the filmmaker's personal journey as he lets go of judgement, both about himself and others and grows to self-acceptance and self-love. With this new sense of acceptance he develops the ability to love others as he never has before. (V Tape)

Dist/Sales: VTape

M.U.F.F. Match

Jenkins, Julie
1995; UK; 50 min; Comedy

> This is a wacky British muffdiving sex romp in the Benny Hill tradition. Chaos erupts when the Comps hockey team takes on the M.U.F.F.s for a bit of rough and tumble. These girls just can't seem to keep themselves out of trouble, both on the field and in the locker room. Harriet gets caught in the toilet with her hands full, while the school nurse treats one of the injured players with the unusual set of implements from the first aid cabinet. (20th San Francisco International Lesbian & Gay Film Festival)

Dist/Sales: WaterBearer, VideoAmericain

Ma Vie

(aka: My Life)

Langlois, Denis
1992; Canada; 21 min; Comedy
Cast: Denis Langlois, Claudine Paquette, Mario Thibeault

> Seeking a way out of his writer's block, Jeannot turns to his past for inspiration and produces a fictional biography in several parts. The resulting film is split into chapters, including chapter five, 'The appeal of stripped pine and casual sex'. An amusing romp through time and space, made poignant as characters disappear from chapter to chapter due to the toll of AIDS. French with English subtitles.

Dist/Sales: CinemaLibre

Ma Vie en Rose

(aka: My Life in Pink)

Berliner, Alain
1997; Belgium, France, UK; 89 min; Drama
P: Carole Scotta; *W:* Chris Vander Stappen, Alain Berliner; *C:* Yves Cape; *E:* Sandrine Deegen;
M: Dominique Dalcan
Cast: Michéle Laroque, Jean-Philippe Écoffey, Hélène Vincent, Georges Du Fresne

> Ludovic is a seven-year-old boy who lives with his family in an affluent French neighbourhood. He also likes dressing up in girls clothing and chooses to make his grand entrance as a girl at his parents' housewarming party. His obsession with femininity increases with time and the family are coldly rejected by their local community. The family, in turn, reject their own son. French with English subtitles.

Dist/Sales: SonyClassics, Haut-et-Court, Wolfe, ACMI

Macho Dancer

Macho Dancer

Brocka, Lino
1988; Philippines; 125 min; Drama
W: Ricardo Lee, Amado Lacuesta; *C:* Joe Tutanes;
E: Ruben Natividad

Cast: Allan Paole, Jacklyn Jose, Daniel Fernando, Charlie Catalla, William Lorenzo

Paolo, a young country boy, moves to Manila and, to earn money, is quickly drawn into the gay bars and nightclubs, and a world of prostitution and sexually explicit dancing. A realistic low-budget, independent film that became one of the favourites of the queer film festival circuit. Tagalog with English subtitles.

Dist/Sales: Strand, Wolfe

Macumba

Mikesch, Elfi
1982; Germany; 88 min; Experimental

Isabel has given herself over to her musings in her lounge chair on the roof, and to her mysterious yearning, which she has named Macumba, the embodiment of what is lacking in her life. One day a stranger stumbles into her half-demolished apartment building. She refuses to let him intrude so she decides to co-opt him into a fictional character. What follows is a detective story and the impetus for Isabel, her girlfriend and Max to break out into the unknown world outside. (Frameline)

Dist/Sales: Frameline

Mad, Bad and Barking

Chambers, Sara / Zalcock, Bev
1996; UK; 30 min; Comedy

A film that uses the female buddy movie to explore the relationship between a woman and her dog. In the face of constant harassment, they undergo a crucial transformation and this gentle comedy turns into a female revenge movie. (Cinenova)

Dist/Sales: Cinenova

Madagascar Skin

Newby, Christopher
1995; UK; 95 min; Comedy
P: Julie Baines; *W:* Christopher Newby;
C: Oliver Curtis; *E:* Christopher Newby, Annabel Ware
Cast: Bernard Hill, John Hannah

Harry is a lonely man, who loses himself in a London disco with a threesome in the back room. But when the lights come on he's rejected. You see, he has a birth mark on his cheek that is the same shape as Madagascar. In his depression he goes to the seaside. There he comes across a burly tattooed man, Flint, who has been beaten up on the beach. Although they have nothing in common they slowly begin to fall in love and live a rather domestic life in a cottage by the seaside.

Prod Comp: BFI, Channel 4
Dist/Sales: BFI, Wellspring

Madam Wang's

Morrissey, Paul
1981; USA; 95 min; Comedy
Cast: Virginia Bruce, Patrick Schoene, Paul Ambrose

A Communist agent infiltrates America only to be influenced by its popular culture. He finds himself in a world of transvestites, lesbians, prostitutes and more, at Madam Wang's Chinese Restaurant.

Madame Sousatzka

Schlesinger, John
1988; UK, USA; 122 min; Drama
P: Robin Dalton; *W:* Ruth Prawer Jhabvala, John Schlesinger; *C:* Nat Crosby; *E:* Peter Honess; *M:* Gerald Gouriet
Cast: Shirley MacLaine, Peggy Ashcroft, Twiggy, Leigh Lawson, Shabana Azmi

Madame Sousatzka is set in a very particular kind of London household. The shabby rooming house is on a once-distinguished street that has now been targeted by realtors for gentrification. The house is owned by Lady Emily, a sweet-tempered old lady who lives in the basement and peacefully coexists with her tenants, who include Madame, the model, and Cordle, a decayed civil-servant type who has occasional, furtive homosexual adventures. Based on the novel by Bernice Rubens.

Prod Comp: Cineplex Odeon
Dist/Sales: ReelMovies, Roadshow, Universal

Madame X: An Absolute Ruler

(aka: Madame X: Eine Absolute Herrscherin)

Ottinger, Ulrike
1977; Germany; 140 min; Experimental
C: Ulrike Ottinger
Cast: Tabea Blumenschein, Irena von Lichtenstein, Yvonne Rainer, Ulrike Ottinger

A rarely screened film that has become something of a lesbian cult classic. Women cannot resist the pirate Madame X, and board her ship in the quest for gold, love and adventure. A light-hearted lesbian portrayal.

Prod Comp: Autoren Film
Dist/Sales: Exportfilm

Mädchen in Uniform (1931)

(aka: Girls in Uniform)

Sagan, Leontine
1931; Germany; 84 min; B&W; Drama
P: Carl Froelich; *W:* F. D. Andam, Christa Winsloe;
C: Reimar Kuntze, Franz Weihmayr; *E:* Oswald Hafenrichter; *M:* Hansen Milde-Meissner
Cast: Dorothea Wieck, Ellen Schwannecke, Hertha

Thiele, Emilia Unda, Hedwig Schlichter

Central to the film, set in a boarding school for the daughters of German officers prior to World War I, is the relationship between a young student and her teacher. Interwoven emotional and institutional pressures result in near tragedy. The atmosphere of Prussian authoritarianism in the school is expertly evoked and the film has long been seen as an attack on German militarism. More recently, however, attention has been given to its delicate yet forceful treatment of lesbianism. Remade in 1957 under the same title. Dubbed into English.

Prod Comp: Deutsche Film-Gemeinschaft
Dist/Sales: BFI, NFVLS, ACMI

Mädchen in Uniform (1957)
(aka: Girls in Uniform)

von Radványi, Géza
1957; Germany; 91 min; Drama
P: Artur Brauner, Joseph Spigler; *W:* Franz Hollering, F. D. Andam; *C:* Werner Krien; *E:* Ira Oberberg
Cast: Romy Schneider, Lilli Palmer, Therese Giehse, Christine Kaufmann

This classic story of the infatuation of a schoolgirl for her tender teacher was first filmed in 1931. The 1957 version is much more lavish and was influenced as much by Hollywood as by pre-war Germany. The setting is still a turn-of-the-century girls' boarding school in Germany and the theme is outlawed love in an authoritarian system. (MQFF)

Prod Comp: CCC Filmkunst GmbH, Les Films Modernes
Dist/Sales: Altermedia, SevenArts

Made in Heaven

Rudolph, Alan
1987; USA; 103 min; Comedy
P: Raynold Gideon, Bruce A. Evans, David Blocker; *W:* Bruce A. Evans, Raynold Gideon; *C:* Jan Kiesser; *E:* Tom Walls; *M:* Mark Isham, Neil Young
Cast: Kelly McGillis, Timothy Hutton, Maureen Stapleton, Ann Wedgeworth, James Gammon

Romantic fantasy in the style of *Heaven Can Wait* and *Here Comes Mr Jordan*. A young man dies and goes to heaven where he meets and falls in love with a yet-to-be-born woman. The big question is how long will it take them to meet in their new identities on earth. Debra Winger is almost unrecognisable when she cross-dresses to play Hutton's guardian angel.

Prod Comp: Lorimar
Dist/Sales: Roadshow, Warner

Madras Eyes

Freccia, Ilaria
1998; Italy; 80 min; Drama
P: Eve Silvester; *W:* Ilaria Freccia; *C:* Gianenrico Bianchi; *E:* Giula Ciniselli; *M:* Sergio Gribanovski

An intoxicating blend of fiction and documentary fleshes out the story of a young Eunuch living in India. Tamil with English subtitles.

Dist/Sales: RaiTrade

Mafu Cage, The
(aka: My Sister, My Love)

Arthur, Karen
1978; USA; 100 min; Thriller
P: Diana Young; *W:* Don Chastain; *C:* John Bailey; *E:* Carol Littleton; *M:* Roger Kellaway
Cast: Lee Grant, Carol Kane, Natalie Delon, Will Geer, James Olsen

An exploration of incest and madness. Cissy, the younger and creative sister, is in love with her dead father and her older sister, Ellen. They were bought up in Africa and have turned their living room into a replica of the jungle which includes an orang-utan. When Ellen begins a relationship with a male co-worker, their special world is threatened. Visually beautiful, the film is saved from falling into an exploitative piece by the tender and loving relationship between the two sisters.

Magic Christian, The

McGrath, Joseph
1969; UK; 92 min; Comedy
P: Denis O'Dell; *W:* Peter Sellers, John Cleese, Graham Chapman, Joseph McGrath, Terry Southern; *C:* Geoffrey Unsworth; *E:* Kevin Connor; *M:* Ken Thorne
Cast: Peter Sellers, Ringo Starr, Isabel Jeans, Caroline Blakiston, Leonard Frey

The Magic Christian tells the unlikely story of an eccentric multimillionaire who spends his days working out ways to demonstrate that people will do anything for money. There are some comic moments throughout the film, most notably Yul Brynner dressed in drag, singing 'Mad About the Boy', while picking up Roman Polanski in a bar; and a boxing match that turns to romance when the two fighters fall in love. The film is loaded with double entendres and gay sight gags, and some great cameos.

Prod Comp: Grand Commonwealth
Dist/Sales: Roadshow, Republic

m

Magnolia

Anderson, Paul Thomas
1999; USA; 190 min; Drama
P: Joanne Sellar, Paul Thomas Anderson;
W: Paul Thomas Anderson; *C:* Robert Elswit;
E: Dylan Tichenor; *M:* Jon Brion
Cast: Tom Cruise, Julianne Moore, William H. Macy, Jason Robards

A magnificent ensemble cast fleshes out the stories of nine people over one day in California. Each of the protagonists is connected in some way, and their lives span tragic and triumphant in the most unexpected ways. William H. Macy plays Donnie Smith, child quiz show has-been who has moved from childhood success to abject failure in his adult years, and has a hopeless obsession with a totally out of reach hunky barman at his local gay hang out.

Prod Comp: Ghoulardi Film Company, New Line Cinema
Dist/Sales: NewLine, Alliance

Mahogany

Gordy, Berry
1975; USA; 110 min; Drama
P: Rob Cohen, Jack Ballard; *W:* John Byrum, Bob Merrill; *C:* David Watkins; *E:* Peter Zinner;
M: Michael Masser
Cast: Diana Ross, Billy Dee Williams, Anthony Perkins, Jean-Pierre Aumont

A photographer discovers a young Chicago model who dreams of becoming a fashion designer. When the photographer takes her to France to become famous, she must leave her roots and her boyfriend behind. When her dreams are finally realised she finds life in the fashion world empty and loveless and decides to go back to the arms of the man who loves her. Perkins plays the photographer who is gay but tries in vain to bed the beautiful Mahogany to prove his manhood.

Prod Comp: Paramount, Motown
Dist/Sales: Paramount

Mai's America

Poras, Marlo
2002; USA; 72 min; Documentary
P: Marlo Poras; *W:* Marlo Poras; *C:* Marlo Poras;
E: Michelle Gisser

A spunky Vietnamese teenager named Mai gets the chance of a lifetime—to study in the United States. Expecting Hollywood, she instead lands in rural Mississippi, a crazy quilt of self-proclaimed rednecks, cliquish teenagers, South Vietnamese exiles and transvestite soul mates. As she tries to fit in and to make ends meet, Mai discovers that 'America' is both less and far more than she bargained for. From cosmopolitan Hanoi to the heart of the Deep South, Mai's unforgettable journey offers an outsider's glimpse inside America. (WMM)

Prod Comp: Independent Television Service
Dist/Sales: WMM

Maid of Honor

Arnold, Jennifer
1999; USA; 25 min; Drama
P: Steven Friedland, Jennifer Arnold; *W:* Jennifer Arnold

Two young lesbians are forced to re-examine their level of commitment when they attend a close 'straight' friend's wedding.

Prod Comp: Bean Productions
Dist/Sales: PictureThis!

Maiden Work

Wang, Guangli
1998; China; 67 min; Drama
P: Rong Ye, Da-yu Li; *W:* Guangli Wang, Lui Man;
C: Xiaoming Ma; *M:* Guang-tian Zhang

The romance of Xue and her lover Yu shatters over a portrait of Yu painted by the artist, Jinian. When Jinian injures his eye in a bar fight, his mind (and the film) becomes a swirl of fragments—the women's relationship, old Chinese war movies, Maoist discos—as a haunting past clash and meld. Jinian feels compelled to make a movie about the women and himself, and we take part in his attempt to get the film made, despite plenty of obstacles, real and imagined. *Maiden Work* is an independent underground film shot outside the official Chinese film system, and yet to be screened in China. (23rd San Francisco International Lesbian & Gay Film festival)

Maids, The

Kinney, Donald / Kinney, Robert
1990; USA; 53 min; Drama

Jean Genet's The Maids provides the text for this film by the Kinney brothers that explores their relationship as twins and their gay sexuality. Robert and Donald play the title roles of sisters, Claire and Solange, domestic servants in service to a wealthy mistress. While the mistress is away the sisters play out the fantasy and horror of their own lives.

Making Love

Hiller, Arthur
1982; USA; 111 min; Drama
P: Allen Adler, Danny Melnick; *W:* Barry Sandler;
C: David M. Walsh; *E:* William Reynolds;

M: Leonard Rosenman
Cast: Michael Ontkean, Kate Jackson, Harry Hamlin, Wendy Hiller

A successful doctor married to a television executive, leaves his wife after he meets a gay writer and they begin a relationship. One of the first mainstream films made in Hollywood to deal openly with homosexuality and show two men kissing.

Prod Comp: 20th Century-Fox, IndieProd
Dist/Sales: ReelMovies, 20thCenturyFox

Making of Monsters

Greyson, John
1990; Canada; 35 min; Comedy, Musical
P: Laurie Lynd; *W:* John Greyson; *E:* Miume Jan;
M: Glenn Schellenberg
Cast: Christopher Anderson

Drawing from Kurt Weill, Bertolt Brecht, Queer Nation and a gay-bashing incident in Toronto in 1985, this wild and crazy all-singing, all-dancing musical satire is one of the most compelling and entertaining films to hit the lesbian and gay film festival circuit.

Awards: Berlin International Film Festival, 1991: Teddy Award for Best Short Film

Mala Noche

(aka: Bad Night)

Van Sant, Gus
1985; USA; 78 min; B&W; Drama
P: Gus Van Sant; *W:* Gus Van Sant; *C:* John Campbell;
E: Gus Van Sant; *M:* Peter Daamaan, Karen Kitchen, Creighton Lindsay
Cast: Tim Streeter, Doug Cooeyate, Ray Monge, Sam Downey

Walt, a cynical young man who spends most of his time selling liquor to vagrants, becomes infatuated with 16-year-old Johnny, an illegal Mexican immigrant. He pursues him but ends up with his gun-toting friend Pepper. Van Sant's first feature film is a refreshing, if somewhat off-the-wall, low budget film.

Dist/Sales: Salzgeber

Mama, I Have Something to Tell You

Salvo, Calogero
1996; USA; 41 min; Documentary

This autobiographical video, in which the filmmaker reveals his homosexuality to his mother, explores the awkward situation of being 'out' to friends but closeted to family. Prompted by the deaths of his father and best friend, Salvo returns to his native Venezuela to 'come out' to his mother. In this intimate dialogue she discusses her preconceptions, fears and love, and he reveals childhood memories, adolescent thoughts and fears, and affirms his present loving relationship. Supplementing this story are interviews with other Latino lesbian and gay friends who offer further insights into family responsibilities, death and continuity, and the importance of honesty. (Cinema Guild)

Dist/Sales: CinemaGuild

Man in Her Life, The

(aka: Ang lalaki sa buhay ni Selya)

Siguion-Reyna, Carlos
1997; Philippines; 96 min; Drama
P: Malou N. Santos, Charo Santos-Concio;
W: Bibeth Orteza; *C:* Daniel Delinna, Yam Laranas;
E: Manet A. Dayrit; *M:* Ryan Cayabyab
Cast: Ricky Davao, Gardo Versoza, Rosanna Roces, Alan Paule

A steamy melodrama from the Philippines which explores the sexual and emotional experiences of the film's four main characters—Seyla, Bobby, Ramon and Carding—and how their lives become intertwined. A passionate film that challenges conventional family values. (Millivres)

Prod Comp: Star Cinema
Dist/Sales: Millivres

Man in the Irony Mask, The

Andrew, Paul
1998; Australia; 28 min; Documentary
P: Kath Shelper; *W:* Paul Andrew

A visually beautiful film that captures a sense of the life and personality of the late Sydney artist and AIDS activist Brenton Heath-Kerr, as well as the essence of his work.

Prod Comp: Scarlett Pictures
Dist/Sales: ACMI

Man is a Woman

(aka: L'Homme est une Femme Comme les Autres)

Zilbermann, Jean-Jacques
1998; France; 96 min; Drama
P: Régine Konckier, Jean-Luc Ormières; *W:* Jean-Jacques Zilbermann, Gilles Taurand; *C:* Pierre Aïm;
E: Monica Coleman
Cast: Antoine de Caunes, Elsa Zylberstein, Gad Elmaleh, Michael Aumont

Simon is a talented clarinettist who has turned his back on family, duty and his Jewish tradition to pursue his main interest: men. Rosalie comes from a New York Hasidic Jewish family and secretly keeps herself pure while she waits for the man of her dreams. Together, they make an unlikely match. Rosalie, a singer of secular Yiddish songs falls in love with Simon when she sees him playing Klezmer clarinet at a wedding reception. When Simon's family blackmails him into marriage (in order to preserve the family name), Rosalie seems the most obvious choice for a wife. The marriage ought to be a disaster. After all, Simon lives for guys, Rosalie lives for God. And yet, together they provide each other with an opportunity to explore life in a new way. French with English subtitles. (Mongrel)

Prod Comp: Les Films Balenciaga, M^ Films
Dist/Sales: UGC, Millivres, Mongrel, PolyGram

Man like Eva, A

(aka: Ein, Mann wie Eva)

Gabrea, Radu
1983; Germany; 90 min; Drama
P: Horst Schier, Laurens Straub; *W:* Radu Gabrea, Laurens Straub; *C:* Horst Schier; *M:* Verdi
Cast: Eva Mattes, Lisa Kreuzer, Charles Regnier, Werner Stocker

During the shooting of a version of *The Lady of the Camellias*, there is more drama off the screen than on. The transsexual star Eva leaves her lover, marries the leading lady, and seduces the leading man. A rather bleak film ending in tragedy. Although Rainer Werner Fassbinder is not mentioned directly, the film can be read as an apocryphal portrait of the famous filmmaker.

Prod Comp: Blue Dolphin, Cinevista
Dist/Sales: BFI

Man Man Woman Woman

(aka: Nannan Nünü; Men and Women; Men Men Women Women)

Liu, Bingjian
1999; China; 90 min; Drama
P: Jinliang Li; *W:* Zi'en Cui, Bingjian Liu; *C:* Jiang Liu, Jun Xu; *E:* Ah Yi
Cast: Yang Qing, Yu Bao, Kang Zhang

Independent filmmaking is alive and well in China if Liu Bingjian's offering is anything to go by. Clothes shop owner Qing and her husband take in country boy Xiao Bo when he arrives in Beijing to find himself. Slowly Qing begins to suspect that Xiao Bo is gay, and shares her concerns with her husband. Xiao Bo runs away when Qing's husband makes a clumsy attempt to rape him. Liu frames his story with fantasy scenes which imagine what Beijing might be like in a more enlightened world and give the film an entertaining blend of realism and idealistic daydream. (MQFF)
Mandarin with English subtitles.

Dist/Sales: Asparas

Man of no Importance, A

Krishnamma, Suri
1994; UK; 99 min; Drama
P: Jonathan Cavendish; *W:* Barry Devlin; *C:* Ashley Rowe; *E:* David Freeman; *M:* Julian Nott
Cast: Albert Finney, Brenda Fricker, Michael Gambon, Tara Fitzgerland

The story of a Dublin bus conductor and loveable old gay man, Alfie Byrne, who amuses his passengers with monologues and poetry by Oscar Wilde, particularly *Salome*, which has been branded immoral by the local church. Alfie decides to stage the play, casting a young unmarried mother in the lead role.

Prod Comp: Majestic, BBC, Little Bird, Newcomm
Dist/Sales: Wolfe, TLA, NewYorker

Man of the Year

Shafer, Dirk
1994; USA; 85 min; Comedy
P: Matt Keener; *W:* Dirk Shafer; *C:* Stephen Timberlake; *E:* Barry Silver, Ken Solomon; *M:* Peitor Angell
Cast: Dirk Shafer, Vivian Paton, Claudette Sutherland

In 1992 Dirk Shafer was *Playgirl*'s 'Man of the Year'. *Man of the Year* is Shafer's mockumentary about his experiences. Will the Playgirl editors take his title away if they find out he's gay.

Prod Comp: Artisan Productions, Foundation Films, Seven Arts Productions
Dist/Sales: UIP, Wolfe, 7thArt

Man who Drove with Mandela, The

Schiller, Greta
1998; The Netherlands, South Africa, UK; 82 min; Documentary
P: Greta Schiller, Mark Gevisser; *W:* Mark Gevisser; *C:* Michelle Crenshaw, Tania Hoser
Cast: Corin Redgrave

A creative mix of documentary and fiction, this remarkable film examines the life of little know gay activist Cecil Williams, a white South African who fought against both Apartheid and homophobia in his native country. Williams is a successful and open Johannesburg theatre producer/director whose home became a centre of gay and politically leftist life in the 1940s through the 1960s. This was at a time when homosexuality was both criminal and hidden and the separation of blacks and whites the law of the land. Schiller adds interviews with his gay and communist friends, gays and lesbians today and amazing home movie footage in her effort to learn about William's tumultuous life. (Wolfe)

Prod Comp: Jezebel Productions, Channel 4, BFI
Dist/Sales: CinemaGuild, Wolfe

Mandragora

Grodecki, Wiktor
1997; Czech Republic; 130 min; Documentary
C: Vladimir Holomek; E: Wiktor Grodecki;
M: Wolfgang Hammerschmid
Cast: Mirek Caslavka, David Svec, Miroslav Breu, Pavel Skripal

16-year-old Marek leaves his dreary small-town life for the beautiful but treacherous streets of Prague, a city where everything can be had for a price. He is quickly lured by a greasy pimp into selling his body to the many tourists who flock to the city for its cathedrals, castles and tender male flesh. Emboldened by his clear marketability (he's gorgeous), Marek and his handsome streetwise buddy David decide to enter the teen flesh trade on their own. But kinky johns, all-too-available drugs and their own self-destructive natures propel them instead into a hellish world in which the instinct to survive is their only hope. Czech with English subtitles. (Water Bearer Films)

Dist/Sales: WaterBearer, Millivres, ACMI, Salzgeber

Manhattan

Allen, Woody
1979; USA; 96 min; B&W; Comedy
P: Charles H. Joffe; W: Woody Allen, Marshall Brickman; C: Gordon Willis; E: Susan E. Morse; M: Tom Pierson, George Gershwin
Cast: Woody Allen, Diane Keaton, Michael Murphy, Meryl Streep, Mariel Hemingway

Bittersweet slice-of-life about a New York comedy writer, Isaac Davis, who has an obsession with Manhattan. After his wife leaves him for another woman, he tries to find fulfilment in a relationship with a 17-year-old girl, but the age difference is too much. Throughout the film this pathetic character attempts to rebuild his waning manhood, even resorting to trying to kill his ex-wife by driving his car through her front window.

Prod Comp: United Artists, Jack Rollins & Charles H. Joffe Productions
Dist/Sales: Ascanbee, ReelMovies, Warner, UA

Manila: In the Claws of Darkness

(aka: Maynila: Sa mga kuko ng liwanag)

Brocka, Lino
1975; Philippines; 125 min; Drama
W: Clodualdo del Mundo Jnr; C: Miguel De Leon
Cast: Rafael Roco Jnr, Hilda Koronel, Lou Salvador Jnr, Juling Bagaboldo

A young fisherman, Julio, leaves his small village to find his girlfriend who has disappeared in Manila.

He wanders the dirty streets, shanty towns, street markets and brothels of the city in his search for her. When his money runs out, he reluctantly turns to male prostitution to survive.

Manji

(aka: All Mixed Up)

Yasuzo, Masumura
1964; Japan; 91 min; Drama
P: Yonejiro Saito; W: Kaneto Shindo; C: Setsuo Kobayashi; E: Tatsuji Nakashizu; M: Tadashi Yamauchi
Cast: Ayako Wakao, Kyoko Kishida, Yusuke Kawazu, Eiji Funakoshi

Married housewife Sonoko falls madly in love with fellow art student Mitsuko who is the daughter of a wealthy industrialist. A relationship between them begins. Sonoko's policeman husband soon becomes suspicious. In the meantime, it is revealed that Mitsuko also has a male lover Eijiro. What follows is a mess of infidelity, blackmailing and seduction. Japanese with English subtitles.

Dist/Sales: Daiei

Mannequin

Gottlieb, Michael
1987; USA; 90 min; Comedy
P: Art Levinson; W: Michael Gottlieb, Edward N. Rugoff; C: Tim Suhrstedt; E: Richard Halsey; M: Albert Hammond, Sylvester Levay, Diane Warren
Cast: Andrew McCarthy, Kim Cattrall, Meshach Taylor, Estelle Getty, James Spader

A romantic comedy about a stockroom clerk, Jonathan, who falls in love with his work and a department store mannequin. She comes to life, when only he is around, and anything can happen! Taylor plays the flamboyant window dresser, Hollywood Montrose, a true gay stereotype, but he manages to steal the show anyway.

Prod Comp: Gladden Entertainment
Dist/Sales: Col-Tri, Warner, 20thCenturyFox

Manodestra

Ubelemann, Cleo
1986; Switzerland; 53 min; Experimental

Considered highly controversial wherever it is screened, this film explores our fascination with sexual cruelty in the dungeon of the dominatrix. Manodestra is an art film extravaganza of flesh and fetish, which takes an experimental approach to sadomasochistic lesbianism. S/M culture is presented as subtle and complex and much more than the mere enjoyment of pain.

m

Map of Sex and Love, The

(aka: Qingse ditu)

Chan, Evans
2001; Hong Kong; 131 min; Drama
P: Willy Tsao; *W:* Evans Chan; *C:* O. Sing-pui
Cast: Bernardo Chow, Victor Ma, Cheri Ho

Through three interrelated stories—*Rubber Band*, *Belgrade*, and *Nazi Gold*—Evans Chan explores history past and present, and love gay and straight in *The Map of Sex and Love*. In *Rubber Band*, a gay dancer recalls how in high school, a counsellor advised him to wear a rubber band in order to heal his perversity; in *Belgrade*, a girl tries to hide from herself and the world, a traumatic revelation that occurred during her Eastern European travels; and in *Nazi Gold*, a filmmaker encounters a lingering mystery from the Third Reich in the unlikely setting of his childhood home. (www.amamedia.org/movies) Mandarin with English subtitles.

Marble Ass

(aka: Dupe od Mramora)

Zilnik, Zelimir
1995; Serbia; 80 min; Drama
W: Zelimir Zilnik; *C:* Miodrag Milosevic;
E: Vladimir Milenkovic; *M:* Dejan Kijevcanin
Cast: Aleksandar Brujic, Luna Lu, Vjeran Miladinovic, Nenad Milenkovic

Set in Belgrade, the story centres around Merlyn, a transvestite prostitute, and her roommate, Sanela. Their life and routine is thrown into turmoil when Johnny, an ex-lover, is thrown out of the army and arrives on their doorstep. He is quite crazed and filled with suppressed rage, putting their lives at greater risk than they already are in the dangerous world of gay prostitution. Serbian with English subtitles.

Awards: Berlin International Film Festival, 1995: Teddy Award for Best Feature Film
Prod Comp: Radio B92 Beograd

March in April

Kinsella, Stephen
1993; USA; 60 min; Drama
Cast: Keith Meinhold, Barney Frank, Pat Schroeder

Family, friends and lovers gather for an historic March on Washington as Mark, the main character, confronts having never come out to his ailing mother. (First Run Features)

Dist/Sales: Wolfe, FirstRunFeatures

March on Washington, The

Scagliotti, John
1993; USA; 30 min; Documentary
P: John Scagliotti

This film chronicles the April 1993 March on Washington for Lesbian, Gay and Bisexual Equal Rights and Liberation, one of the largest civil rights rallies in American history, with an estimated one million people marching on the nation's capital. The film features highlights from speeches and comedy and musical performances, as well as interviews with politicians and celebrities in attendance, and a brief history of gay rights activism in the USA.

Dist/Sales: CinemaGuild

Marching into Darkness

Spano, Massimo
1995; Italy; 110 min; Drama

20-year-old Saro Franzese is assigned to an elite helicopter unit for his national service. He takes to it like a fish to water. But everything disintegrates when his sergeant, Gianni Tricario, reveals to Saro that he is gay. Saro runs away, but is found and viciously raped by Captain Roatta, a brilliant soldier who is the leader of a secret military faction. Now Saro begins a difficult fight for justice. He must face the military and civil institutions, some of which are willing to help him, while others are prepared to support Roatta. Italian with English subtitles.

Dist/Sales: Intra

Mare, Il

(aka: The Sea)

Griffi, Giuseppe Patroni
1962; Italy; 110 min; B&W; Drama
P: Gianni Buffardi; *W:* Giuseppe Patroni Griffi, Alfio Valdarini; *C:* Ennio Guarnieri; *E:* Ruggero Mastroianni; *M:* Giovanni Fusco
Cast: Umberto Orsini, Francoise Prévost, Dino Mele

While on holiday in Capri, an actor meets a moody young man in the midst of a self-destructive drinking binge. The young man is obviously interested in the older actor but before anything can happen they befriend a woman who has come to sell her house and her presence begins to cause complications. Beautifully shot with great performances, *Il Mare* creates a feeling of sexual tension laced with violence and unrequited love.

Prod Comp: Buffardi SpA

Mark of Lilith, The

Fionda, Bruna / Gladwin, Polly / Mack-Nataf, Isiling
1986; UK; 32 min; Horror

Zena is a black filmmaker and her latest project is on the goddesses of the past who slowly declined and became demons. Her research leads her to watch horror films. Lillia is one of the characters in the films, a white vampire. Zena and Lillia meet and begin an affair. As Zena makes the analogy between the creation of female monsters and the way society views blacks and lesbians, this helps Lillia overcome her role as a male fantasy.

Prod Comp: Revamp Productions
Dist/Sales: BFI, Cinenova

Markova: Comfort Gay

Portes, Gil M.
2000; Philippines; 97 min; Documentary
W: Clodualdo del Mindo Jnr; *C:* Johnny Araojo;
E: George Jarlego; *M:* Joy Marfil
Cast: Eric Quizon, Loren Legarda, Jeffrey Quizon

Markova: Comfort Gay tells the unconventional true story of Walter Dempster Jnr, otherwise known as Markova. After watching a documentary about the suffering of women forced into prostitution during the Japanese occupation of the Philippines, Markova decides to tell his own painful story to reporter Loren Legarda. Escaping the torment of growing up with an abusive older brother, he and his friends find further suffering at the hands of Japanese soldiers, forced into sex work to survive. But even after the war, Markova's struggle continued. Starring beloved Filipino comic actor Dolphy in the lead, and two of his sons, Eric and Jeffrey Quizon, as younger versions Markova at different points in his story, *Markova: Comfort Gay* is a moving, intense, and, ultimately, life-affirming story. (2002 New York Lesbian & Gay Film Festival)
Tagalog with English subtitles.

Prod Comp: RVQ Productions
Dist/Sales: RVQ

Marlene

Vilsmaier, Joseph
2000; Germany; 125 min; Drama
P: Jutta Lieck-Klenke, Katharina M. Trebitsch, Joseph Vilsmaier; *W:* Christian Pfannenschmidt; *C:* Joseph Vilsmaier; *E:* Barbara Hennings; *M:* Harald Kloser
Cast: Monica Bleibtreu, Heino Ferch, Katja Flint, Cosma Shiva Hagen, Herbert Knaup

Detailed biopic on German film star Marlene Dietrich.

Prod Comp: Perathon Film
Dist/Sales: Senator

Martin Four

Hackworth, Ben
2000; Australia; 21 min; Drama

Caught up in the claustrophobic world of his mother, who lives in a drunken haze of romantic memories of exotic places, an aimless young gay man tries to make a connection with love and life in the present. (ACMI)

Prod Comp: Victorian College of the Arts
Dist/Sales: ACMI

Martirio

(aka: Sufferance)

Escanilla, Claudia Morgado
2000; Canada; 19 min; Drama

Elissa, a famous trapeze artist, is being forced by her father to marry an up and coming trapeze impresario that she doesn't love. Her disabled identical twin sister witnesses her pain and makes an incredible sacrifice for love.

Dist/Sales: BuzzTaxi

Mary's Place

Lee, Melissa
1998; Australia; 50 min; Documentary

This powerful documentary combines vox pop commentary with the story of a lesbian assault survivor to explore issues surrounding homophobic violence and the community's response to this problem. Walking home from a club one night, Mary is assaulted in Floods Lane, Sydney, Australia. The film charts her brave journey from victim to outspoken survivor, and demonstrates the activism and support she found in the community through the act of renaming the lane where she was attacked as Mary's Place.

Mascara

Conrad, Patrick
1987; Belgium, France, USA; 100 min; Thriller
P: Pierre Drouot, Henry Lange, René Solleveld
W: Hugo Claus, Patrick Conrad, Pierre Drouot, Susana Rossberg; *C:* Gilbert Azavedo; *E:* Susanna Rossberg; *M:* Egisto Macchi
Cast: Michael Sarrazin, Charlotte Rampling, Derek de Lint, Jappe Claes

A sexually repressed police inspector is brought to the brink of murderous insanity, triggered by a dress he fancies. He and his sister, the object of his incestuous desires, meet a fashion designer and the sister falls for the designer.

Prod Comp: Dédalus, Iblis Films, Praxino Pictures
Dist/Sales: Warner

Mask of Desire

(aka: Shades of Black)

Haverstick, Mary
1993; USA; 115 min; Drama
P: Mary Haverstick
Cast: Jennifer MacDonald, Trisha McCormick

Described as *Personal Best* meets *Psycho*, the story centres around Kate, a 23-year-old photographer and athlete, who is hired to photograph a contemporary dance piece and is instantly attracted to Lilly, one of the dancers. Lilly, an older woman, sweeps Kate off her feet and makes her the focus of a series of masks she is designing for an exhibition. Kate begins to feel that she is losing power in the relationship. She suspects Lilly is having an affair as Lilly's manipulative powers become evident.

Prod Comp: Haverstick Films
Dist/Sales: PictureThis!, WaterBearer

Mass Appeal

Jordan, Glenn
1984; USA; 96 min; Drama
P: David Foster, Lawrence Turman; *W:* Bill C. Davis;
C: Donald Peterman; *E:* John Wright; *M:* Bill Conti
Cast: Jack Lemmon, Zeljiko Ivanek, Charles Durning, Louise Latham, Talia Balsam

A newly appointed deacon takes up the challenge to defend two suspected gay seminarians and in their defence he admits to his own homosexual affairs. The homophobic Monsignor is determined to expel him from the church and when the young deacon asks for help from one of his colleagues, he refuses as he doesn't want to be presumed gay if he sides with him.

Prod Comp: Jalem Productions, Operation Cork, Turman-Foster Company
Dist/Sales: ReelMovies, Universal

Massillon

Jones, William E.
1991; USA; 70 min; Experimental

William E. Jones returns to his hometown to construct an unconventional and moving autobiography. Challenging some of the most firmly entrenched notions of filmmaking, *Massillon* tells its story without a single human actor, by combining beautiful images with a seductive voice-over narration. (Canyon Cinema)

Dist/Sales: Canyon

Match that Started My Fire, The

Cook, Cathy
1991; USA; 19 min; Comedy

This unconventional comedy explores women's sexuality through candid stories of sexual discoveries, fantasies and pleasures; a montage of found and original footage, the phone rings, girl-talk starts and secrets emerge.

Dist/Sales: Cinenova, WMM

Matt

Kennerley, Annette
1998; UK; 20 min; Documentary

Video conversation with well-known San Francisco transgender identity Matt, where he recounts the changes in his life over the last few years as he has progressed from female to male.

Dist/Sales: Cinenova

Matter of Taste, A

(aka: A Question of Taste; Une Affaire de Goût)

Rapp, Bernard
1999; France; 90 min; Thriller
P: Chantal Perrin, Catherine Dussart; *W:* Bernard Rapp, Gilles Taurand; *C:* Gérard de Battista; *E:* Juliette Welfling; *M:* Jean-Philippe Goude
Cast: Bernard Giraudeau, Jean-Pierre Lorit, Florence Thomassin, Charles Berling

Nicholas, a handsome young waiter, is befriended by Frederic Delamont, a wealthy middle-aged businessman. Delamont, a man of power, influence, and strictly refined tastes, is immediately smitten by Nicholas' charms. Lonely and phobic, Frederic offers Nicholas a lucrative job as his personal food taster. In spite of their differences, a close friendship begins to emerge between the two men. However, their bond of trust and admirations soon spirals downward into a dangerous game of deceit and obsession for which neither is prepared. (Attitude Films) French with English subtitles.

Prod Comp: Le Studio Canal+, France 3 Cinéma
Dist/Sales: TLA, Attitude

Maurice

Ivory, James
1987; UK; 138 min; Drama
P: Ismail Merchant; *W:* Kit Hesketh-Harvey, James Ivory; *C:* Pierre Lhomme; *E:* Katherine Wenning; *M:* Richard Robbins
Cast: James Wilby, Hugh Grant, Rupert Graves, Denholm Elliott, Simon Callow

Based on the novel by E. M. Foster, *Maurice* is set in pre-World War I England and examines the social repression of a college student dealing with his homosexuality. Maurice studied at Cambridge where he meets and falls in love with Clive Durham. Under pressure from his family Durham marries, but Maurice finally consummates his inclinations with Durham's gamekeeper. A gay love story that transcends wealth and class.

Prod Comp: Merchant-Ivory, Channel 4
Dist/Sales: Wolfe, October, BFI, Cinecom, ACMI

Maybe I can Give you Sex?

Brüning, Jürgen / Layumas, Rune
1992; Germany; 75 min; Drama

Rune Layumas in Manila and Jürgen Brüning in Berlin collaborated to make this two part docudrama film that confronts Western audiences with issues of racism, sexism and neo-colonialism as it compares and contrasts the construction of male gender roles between East and West. Macho dancers of the Philippines, bar boys and their customers are portrayed to highlight the import of Western sexual structures. (MQFF)

Dist/Sales: Brüning

Maybe we're Talking about a Different God

Ankele, John / Macksoud, Anne
1995; USA; 28 min; Documentary

In Rochester, New York, a woman with 90% support from her congregation is barred from serving as a pastor of her Presbyterian church because she is a lesbian. Her protesters argue that lesbianism is contrary to God's order. This film presents interviews and footage of the Rochester religious court hearings. One parishioner who once described himself as homophobic asks, 'If this woman is thoroughly decent, how is that inconsistent with basic Christianity?' (First Run Features)

Dist/Sales: FirstRunFeatures

Mayhem

Child, Abigail
1987; USA; 20 min; Documentary
Cast: Diane Torr, Ela Troyano

Through a catalogue of looks, movements, and gestures, *Mayhem* presents a social order run amok in a libidinous retracing of film noir conventions. Sexuality flows in an atmosphere of sexual tension, danger, violence, and glamour; antagonism between the sexes is symbolised in the costuming of women in polka dots and men in stripes. Censored in Tokyo for its use of Japanese lesbian erotica, *Mayhem* creates an image bank of what signifies the sexual and the seductive in the history of image-making, pointing to the way we learn about our bodies, and how to use them from images. (VDB)

Dist/Sales: NFVLS, VDB

Me and the Girls

Shallcross, Alan
1985; UK; 54 min; Drama
P: Alan Shallcross
Cast: Tom Courtenay

George Banks is dying, and from his hospital bed he reflects on his colourful, unconventional and at times poignant years as the leader of a travelling troupe of dancing girls. He remembers the good and bad times, his friends and loved ones, especially his one great love, Harry. Set in Switzerland in 1938, this drama is based on the play by Noel Coward. (ACMI)

Dist/Sales: ACMI

Meeting Magdalene

Freeman, Marilyn
1995; USA; 34 min; B&W; Drama

This moody black-and-white film brings together the unlikely coupling of the 'all work and no play' city-chick Sarah, with Magdalene, part manipulator, part earth mother. It is Magdalene's psychic powers that give her seduction of Sarah an alarming level of assurance. Through the rituals of New Age healing, herbal tea drinking, and a series of farcical visits from friends, their high-energy flirting leaves them both breathless. (MQFF)

Meeting of Two Queens

Barriga, Cecilia
1991; Spain; 14 min; Comedy

This charming and witty film reconstructs the films of Greta Garbo and Marlene Dietrich to create an entirely new movie where a hot romance between the two can't help but erupt. Dyke dreams do come true. (MQFF)

Dist/Sales: WMM

Melody for Buddy Matsumae

(aka: Matsumae-Kun No Senritsu)

Oki, Hiroyuki
1989; Japan; 50 min; Experimental

The last in Oki's *Matsumae* trilogy, this film focuses on 10 days that Oki spent at a seaside town, the first half is spent with his lover, the next five days depict the time after his lover has left.

Dist/Sales: ImageForum

Memento Mori

(aka: Yeogo Guidam II)

Kim, Tae-yong / Min, Kyu-dong
2000; South Korea; 97 min; Drama

P: Chun-yeon Lee; W: Tae-yong Kim, Kyo-dong Min; C: Yoon-soo Kim; E: Sung-woo Cho; M: Sung-woo Cho
Cast: Min-hee Kim, Yeh-jin Park, Young-jin Lee, Min-sun Kim

Min-ah finds a strange diary, capable of arousing hallucinations, kept by two of her senior fellow-students, Hyo-shin and Shi-eun, who seem to have an unusually close bond. But Hyo-shin suddenly kills herself for no obvious reason and the entire school is shocked and depressed. Min-ah, however, starts to feel different. It's almost as if she's somehow possessed by the dead girl.... 'Memento Mori' is the incantation left in a dead student's diary. The death of the girl who was neither child nor adult is recalled through this spiritual dialogue that sadly ordains the diary. (2001 Slamdance Film Festival)
Korean with English subtitles.

Dist/Sales: Mirovision

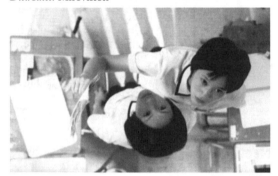

Momento Mori

Memory Pictures

Parmar, Pratibha
1989; UK; 24 min; Documentary

A beautifully composed profile of gay Indian photographer, Sunil Gupta, and the way his work portrays issues of sexual and racial identity in relation to personal and familial history. (WMM)

Dist/Sales: WMM, GroupeIntervention

Memsahib Rita

Parmar, Pratibha
1994; UK; 20 min; Experimental

Using magic realism, Memsahib Rita looks at the physical and emotional violence of racism. Shanti is haunted by both the racist taunts of nationalist white youths and the memory of her white mother. (WMM)

Dist/Sales: WMM

Men in Love

Huestis, Marc
1990; USA; 93 min; Drama
P: Scott Catamas; W: Emerald Starr, Scott Catamas;

C: Fawn Yacker, Marsha Kahm; E: Frank Christopher;
M: Donald James Regal
Cast: Emerald Starr, James A. Taylor, Joe Tolbe, Doug Self

A young gay man takes the cremated remains of his lover, who has died of AIDS, to Hawaii. Along the way a lot of soul searching is done, and with the support of his friends he manages to put his life back together again.

Prod Comp: Crystal Clear Comms, Tantric Films
Dist/Sales: WaterBearer, Salzgeber

Men Like Me

Long, Susan
1994; Australia; 25 min; Documentary
P: Sylvie Shaw; W: Susan Long

Explores the physical and social transformation of Dale Michaels, a female-to-male transsexual. This film broke new ground in video computer technology at the time. If this is Dale's story, it is also an account of the filmmaker's journey.

Dist/Sales: VTape

Men Like Me

Men Men Men

(aka: Uomini Uomini Uomini)

de Sica, Christian
1996; Italy; 90 min; Comedy
P: Aurelio De Laurentiis; W: Christian de Sica, Enrico Vanzina, Giovanni Veronesi; C: Gianlorenzo Battaglia; E: Raimondo Crociani; M: Manuel de Sica
Cast: Christian de Sica, Massimo Ghini, Leo Gullotta

A comedy about four best friends: Vittorio, an architect who is obsessed with his ex-lover; Dado, a doctor who seduces straight football players; Vittorio, a fashion designer who finds sex by picking up hustlers; and Sando, an independent filmmaker who has just come out and is having problems with his son. They play sexual games, exploiting everyone including straights, gays, men and women. But their sex games turn sour when they betray Simonetta, a wardrobe mistress. Italian with English subtitles.

Dist/Sales: SACIS, Lauren

Menmaniacs: The Legacy of Leather

Hick, Jochen
1995; Germany; 86 min; Documentary
P: Jochen Hick; W: Jochen Hick; C: Jochen Hick;
E: Micheline Maske; M: Charly Schoppner

This fascinating documentary takes a look at the S/M leather scene one summer in Chicago, New York and San Francisco, particularly the Mr Leather competition in Chicago, which attracts over 2000 men and women who identify with leather. The film focuses on the erotic and sexual side of the leather lifestyle as well as the community's commitment to raising funds for HIV. This is an intimate look at a movement in which membership is not just a hobby, but more a way of life. Features footage from the New York Gay Games and the International Mr Drummer competition, wherein participants enact their sexual fantasies. A must see even for non-leather lovers, this documentary sheds light on a scene that has long mystified many. (MQFF)

Prod Comp: Galeria Alaska Productions
Dist/Sales: TurbulentArts

Mercy (1989)

Child, Abigail
1989; USA; 10 min; B&W; Experimental

Child masterfully composes a rhythmic collage of symmetries and asymmetries in a fluid essay that forefronts the treatment of the body as a mechanised instrument—placing the body in relation to the man-made landscape of factories, amusement parks and urban office complexes. (VDB)

Dist/Sales: VDB

Mercy (1999)

Harris, Damian
1999; USA; 94 min; Thriller
P: Andrew Stevens, Amedeo Ursini, Elie Samaha;
W: Damian Harris; C: Manuel Terán; M: B. C. Smith
Cast: Ellen Barkin, Julian Sands, Wendy Crewson, Peta Wilson

A gritty female detective enters a sordid world of sexual deviance to catch a serial killer. (Wolfe)

Prod Comp: Jazz Pictures, Franchise Pictures, Phoenician Entertainment
Dist/Sales: Wolfe, Col-Tri, HBO

Merry Christmas, Mr Lawrence

Oshima, Nagisa
1983; Japan, New Zealand, UK; 122 min; Drama
P: Jeremy Thomas; W: Nagisa Oshima, Paul Mayersberg; C: Toichiro Narushima; E: Tomoyo Oshima; M: Ryuichi Sakamoto

Cast: David Bowie, Ryuichi Sakamoto, Tom Conti, Jack Thompson, Takeshi

A battle of wills begins during the Second World War in a Japanese prisoner-of-war camp between the camp commander, and a British major. There seems to be a homosexual attraction between the two men that is finally played out at the end by a rather awkward kiss, just before the major is executed. A visually beautiful film, it was Oshima's first English-speaking venture and a triumphant psychological drama about survival. English & Japanese with English subtitles.

Prod Comp: Asahi National Broadcasting Company, Cineventure Productions, Oshima Productions
Dist/Sales: ReelMovies, Universal, BFI

Metalguru

Colker, Flavio
1999; Brazil; 30 min; Drama

A precocious preteen girl befriends two travelling motorcycle babes and gets a taste for adventure.

Metamorphosis: Man into Woman

Leeman, Lisa
1990; USA; 58 min; Documentary
P: Claudia Hoover

Gary, a 39-year-old transsexual, has been convinced since childhood that he is a woman trapped in a male body. At age 36, Gary decided to begin the extraordinary process of changing his gender. Shot over three years, this compassionate yet unsentimental film follows Gary's transformation into Gabi. Before he can be accepted for sex-reassignment surgery, Gary must prove that he can successfully live and work as a woman, 24 hours a day, for at least one year. We see Gary sorting out his masculine and feminine traits, undergoing facial plastic surgery, electrolysis, hormone therapy, and psychological counselling. A lively discussion among Gabi's co-workers raises questions about the very nature of masculinity and femininity. Gabi attends a trans-sexual support group, and wrestles throughout the film with religious conflicts. By the end of the film she reconciles with her mother, and attends her high school reunion. (Filmakers Library)

Dist/Sales: FilmakersLibrary, NFVLS

Metamorphosis: The Remarkable Journey of Granny Lee

Debarros, Luiz
2001; South Africa; 52 min; Documentary

When Leonard Christian Du Plooy was born on the 18 March 1919 to a mixed race, working class family, he embodied all the contradictions of a country ruled by racism and hypocrisy. The first part of his life was spent in his hometown of Kimberley and then Durban as a teacher. Then he changed his mind (and his skin colour). In his fifties, he moved to Johannesburg and proceeded to become the city's most famous club-goer and drag queen. Due to a skin condition he was now able to pass himself off as white, which held many advantages in Apartheid South Africa. By outfitting himself with outrageous costumes, feather boas, heavy makeup and a retinue of young admirers, the pensioner transformed himself and became Granny Lee, Queen of the Discos. In death Lee continued to flaunt the rules, mistakenly being the first non-white buried in a whites only Johannesburg cemetery. (www.grannylee.co.za)

Meteor and Shadow

(aka: Meteoro kai Skia)

Spetsiotis, Takis
1985; Greece; 101 min; Drama
P: Takis Spetsiotis; *W:* Takis Spetsiotis; *C:* Philipos Koutsaftis; *E:* Despina Danae Maroulakou
Cast: Michael Marmarinos, G. Palamiotis, E. Franco, Takis Moschos

A poignant and harrowing account of the rise and fall of Napoleon Lapathiotis (1888–1944), Greece's most esteemed poet. Acclaimed director Takis Spetsiotis conveys, with sensitive daring and finesse, the poet's life as a romantic charmer, literary genius, communist sympathiser, depraved drug addict and, most importantly, as a national icon whose openly gay lifestyle created a scandal in conservative Athenian society. (Water Bearer Films)

Prod Comp: Greek Film Centre
Dist/Sales: WaterBearer

Metrosexuality

Beadle-Blair, Rikki
2001; UK; 6 x 24 min; Drama
P: Carol Harding; *W:* Rikki Beadle Blair
Cast: Rikki Beadle Blair, Noel Clarke, Rebecca Varney, Paul Keating

The story of two gay dads, their straight teenage son and his two gay best mates, *Metrosexuality* is a fresh new take on contemporary queer life in London. 17-year-old Kwame is terminally straight, but his best friend is in love with Kwame's dad Max, who has just dumped his husband and jumped back into single life. Meanwhile, Kwame's lesbian aunt has discovered that her ex-boyfriend from high school is in love with Max too! Sound complicated? It is—as well as fast, funny and fever-pitched. (MQFF)

Prod Comp: Channel 4
Dist/Sales: Wolfe, TLA

Mi Novia El

Salaberry, Enrique Cahen
1975; Spain; 90 min; Comedy
W: Oscar Viale
Cast: Alberto Olmedo, Susana Giménez

Laucha accepts a dare to pick up a famous transvestite called Moninique. But later, on closer inspection he is not sure whether Moninique is a man dressed as a woman or a woman dressed as a man dressed as a woman.

Prod Comp: Aries Cinematográfica Argentina

Michael, a Gay Son

Glawson, Bruce
1980; Canada; 27 min; Documentary

This sympathetic portrayal will help professional and general audiences gain insight into the dilemmas facing the homosexual. It reveals the feelings and needs of Michael, his parents, and his brother and sister on learning that he is gay. Michael's decision to 'come out' was difficult, but he was supported by a peer group of homosexuals. Unprepared for his parents' total inability to discuss the matter with him, he suggests a group session with a social worker.

Prod Comp: Bruce Glawson Productions
Dist/Sales: NFVLS, FilmakersLibrary

Metrosexuality

Midnight Cowboy

Schlesinger, John
1969; USA; 113 min; Drama
P: Jerome Hellman; *W:* Waldo Salt; *C:* Adam Holender; *E:* Hugh A. Robertson; *M:* John Barry
Cast: Dustin Hoffman, Jon Voight, Brenda Vaccaro, Sylvia Miles, John McGiver

A slightly dim-witted Texan hustler goes to New York to offer his services as a stud for rich ladies, but finds the real market is homosexual men. He spends a hard winter trying to help a tubercular con man played by Dustin Hoffman. Desperate for money they travel to the warmer climate of Florida. The two men form a tender, caring, homo-emotional friendship. Based on James Leo Herlihy's novel.

Awards: Academy Awards, 1969: Best Film, Director
Prod Comp: United Artists, Florin Productions
Dist/Sales: ReelMovies, ACMI, Warner, UA, Swank

Midnight Dancers

Midnight Dancers

(aka: Sibak)

Chionglo, Mel
1994; Philippines; 128 min; Drama
P: Richard Tang; *W:* Ricardo Lee; *C:* George Tutanes;
E: Jess Navarro; *M:* Nonong Buencamino, Ramon Reyes
Cast: Alex del Rosario, Lawrence David, Gandong Cervantes, Luis Cortez

The director of this gut-wrenching film has drawn on his own experiences to create a powerful document about the lives of young prostitutes in Manila's sex industry. Combining documentary-like realism with melodramatic flourishes, *Midnight Dancers* follows three brothers who are all macho dancers in one of the city's gay bars. At 23, Joel, the eldest brother, is considered a has-been and is torn between the demands of his wife and his gay lover. The second brother, Dennis, prefers to descend fully into the nightmare world of drugs, sex and gang warfare that dominate the street life of the prostitutes. It is only Sonny, the youngest brother, who is able to experience joy in his sexuality, and it is through Sonny's eyes we witness the drama between the brothers unfold. (MQFF)
Filipino with English subtitles.

Prod Comp: Tangent Films International
Dist/Sales: TLA, Salzgeber, FirstRunFeatures, Wolfe, Fortissimo, Cowboy, ACMI

Midnight Express

Parker, Alan
1978; UK, USA; 120 min; Drama
P: Alan Marshall, David Puttnam; *W:* Oliver Stone;
C: Michael Seresin; *E:* Gerry Hambling; *M:* Giorgio Moroder
Cast: Brad Davis, Randy Quaid, John Hurt, Irene Miracle, Bo Hopkins

Based on the autobiography of Billy Hayes, *Midnight Express* is about the traumatic years Hayes spent in a Turkish prison for drug running. The relationship Hayes had with another prisoner during his time in detention is only hinted at. Alan Parker is quoted as saying, 'it is acceptable for drug runners to be heroes but you can't remain one if you love another man'.

Prod Comp: Casablanca Filmworks
Dist/Sales: 20thCenturyFox, Col-Tri, TLA, ACMI

Midnight in the Garden of Good and Evil

Eastwood, Clint
1998; USA; 155 min; Drama
P: Clint Eastwood, Arnold Stiefel; *W:* John Lee Hancock; *C:* Jack N. Green; *E:* Joel Cox; *M:* Johnny Mercer, lennie Niehaus
Cast: Kevin Spacey, John Cusack, Jack Thompson, Jude Law

Focuses on the life and crime of Jim Williams, art collector, antiques dealer, man about town and homosexual. Reporter John Kelso finds himself in Savannah to write a story about Williams' notorious Christmas parties, and ends up completely fascinated by him when he meets his young lover Billy. When Billy turns up dead, Kelso naturally stays around to report on the murder trial, along the way meeting a wide variety of eccentric characters that manage to make his Savannah visit even more intriguing.

Prod Comp: Silver Pictures, Malpaso Productions, Warner
Dist/Sales: Warner, Wolfe

Midwife's Tale, The

Siler, Megan
1995; USA; 75 min; Drama
P: Michael Lowe; *C:* Adam Teichman
Cast: Gayle Cohen, Stacey Havener

Told as a fantasy fairy tale bedtime story, the film is set in medieval times and is the story of Lady Eleanor, a noblewoman who marries against her will and is expected to bear children. She seeks the help of the town's midwife, in the hope that she will have a potion to stop Eleanor conceiving. But the midwife is gaoled and charged with being a witch. The midwife's apprentice, Gwenyth, steps in to help Eleanor, but only if she promises to help Gwenyth release the midwife. Through the course of their adventure, the two become attracted to each other and end up in Eleanor's bed chamber.

Dist/Sales: NorthernArts

Miguel/Michelle

Portes, Gil M.
1998; Philippines; 110 min; Drama
W: Ricardo Lee, Gil M. Portes
Cast: Ronnick Sarmienta, Gloria Diaz, Future Ray, Cris Villanueva

Miguel's Filipino family eagerly awaits his return from a 5 year stay in the US, where they hope he has made lots of money and married an American. They are in for a shock when they find that Miguel has had major surgery whilst in the US, and has returned as Michelle. Tagalog with English subtitles.

Mikaël

(aka: Chained)

Dreyer, Carl
1924; Germany; 75 min; B&W; Drama
P: Erich Pommer; *W:* Carl Dreyer, Thea von Harbou;
C: Karl Freund, Rudolph Maté; *M:* Hans Joseph Vieth
Cast: Walter Slezak, Benjamin Christensen, Nora Gregor

Zoret, an ageing artist is driven to despair and grieves over the loss of his young male model and student to Princess Zamikoff. Sigmund Freud makes a brief appearance. Based on the book by Hermann Bang, which was reportedly based on the life of Auguste Rodin, the famous French artist.

Prod Comp: Universum Film AG

Mike's Murder

Bridges, James
1984; USA; 110 min; Drama
P: Jack Larson; *W:* James Bridges; *C:* Reynaldo Villalobos; *E:* Dede Allen, Jeff Gourson;
M: Joe Jackson, John Barry
Cast: Debra Winger, Mark Keyloun, Paul Winfield, William Ostrander, Darrell Larson

A young woman investigates the murder of a man she has been seeing. Mike, a tennis pro, is killed when he and his friend get involved in cocaine dealing. During the course of her investigation Winger soon discovers an underworld of sex and drugs, and a male record executive who was in love with Mike.

Prod Comp: Skyewiay
Dist/Sales: Warner

Militia Battlefield

Bokova, Jana
1975; UK; 61 min; Documentary

An unusual documentary that looks at the gay clubs and expatriate entertainers in London.

Milou in May

(aka: Milou en Mai; May Fools)

Malle, Louis
1989; France; 108 min; Drama
P: Louis Malle; *W:* Louis Malle, Jean-Claude Carriere;
C: Renato Berta; *E:* Emmanuelle Castro; *M:* Stéphane Grappelli
Cast: Michel Piccoli, Miou-Miou, Michel Duchassoy, Harriet Walter, Bruno Carette, François Berleand

Set in a large villa in the Southwest of France, Milou, a 60-year-old man, invites the members of his family to the funeral of his mother. He has been living with her and taking care of the property. It is 1968 and student demonstrations have just started in Paris. The family spend their time either dividing up and fighting over the matriarch's belongings or playing sexual games. Included in the guest list is her granddaughter who is a lesbian. French with English subtitles.

Prod Comp: TF1 Films, Ellepi Films, Nouvelles Éditions de Films
Dist/Sales: NewVision, ACMI, OrionClassics

Minor Disturbances

Ashley, Carol
1992; USA; 17 min; Drama

A disenchanted housewife, her lesbian lover and her jealous husband form a triangle in this almost wordless household melodrama played out against a background collage of 1950s educational films. (Frameline)

Dist/Sales: Frameline

Minoru and Me

Nakata, Toichi
1992; UK; 45 min; Documentary

A brutally honest drama of a man with cerebral palsy trying to come out to the filmmaker, his friend. As the filmmaker becomes increasing obsessed with portraying the physically challenged man as disabled and dependent, the man with cerebral palsy becomes increasingly disgusted and unable to state what he's travelled all the way from Japan to say. English & Japanese with English subtitles.

Dist/Sales: Frameline

Miracle Alley

(aka: El Callejon de los Milagros)

Fons, Jorge
1994; Mexico; 144 min; Drama
P: Alfredo Ripstein Jnr, Gerardo Barrera; *W:* Vicente Leñero; *C:* Carlos Marcovich; *E:* Carlos Savage;
M: Lucía Álvarez

Cast: Ernesto Gómez Cruz, María Rojo, Salma Hayek

This film deals with the conflict between the desires and the expectations of people in a small Mexican community. Rutilio, a gruff macho tavern owner, develops a taste for handsome young men; Chava, his son, longs for a better life in America; Alma, a strong-willed beauty, is tempted to marry a wealthy, elderly shop owner; Abel is an earnest but penniless young barber who loves Alma; and Susanita is a spinsterish apartment-house owner who looks for love in all the wrong places. Does anyone get what he or she wants? Based on the Nobel prize winning novel by Naguib Mahfouz.

Prod Comp: Alameda Films, MCINE
Dist/Sales: Roadshow, UIP

Mirror Images II

Hippolyte, Gregory
1993; USA; 90 min; Erotica
M: Ashley Irwin
Cast: Shannon Whirry, Luca Bercovici, Tom Reilly, Eva Larue

One identical bisexual twin, thought to be dead, enjoys pretending to be her sister and sleeps with her sister's husband, work mates and friends. Meanwhile, the sister starts an affair with her therapist.

Prod Comp: Axis Films International
Dist/Sales: 20thCenturyFox

Mirror, Mirror

(aka: Lille Spejl)

Fleming, Edward
1978; Denmark; 107 min; Comedy
P: Nina Crone; *W:* Edward Fleming; *C:* Claus Loof;
E: Edward Fleming, Gert Fredholm, Grete Møldrup;
M: Ole Høyer
Cast: Frits Helmuth, Bodil Kjer, Preben Kaas

A rather bitchy comedy that centres around a group of middle-class drag queens. At the centre of the group is Bent, an out-of-work shoplifter. The film focuses on his relationship with his mother, who lives in an imaginary past. Danish with English subtitles.

Prod Comp: Crone Film, Edward Fleming Produktion
Dist/Sales: DanishFilm

Mob Queen

Carnoy, Jon
1999; USA; 87 min; Drama

Brooklyn, 1957. In the world of dockworkers, mobsters and streetwalkers, two small time hoods set up their boss with the new prostitute on the docks, only to discover that she has an unbelievable secret.

Dist/Sales: FirstRunFeatures

Modesty Blaise

Losey, Joseph
1966; UK; 119 min; Comedy
P: Joseph Janni; *W:* Evan Jones; *C:* Jack Hildyard;
E: Reginald Beck; *M:* Johnny Dankworth
Cast: Monica Vitti, Dirk Bogarde, Terence Stamp, Harry Andrews, Michael Craig

Monica Vitti is the comic-strip character of the title in this spoof of spy thrillers, with stylish pop art set design and a great mix of gay and lesbian characters—it's great camp fun.

Prod Comp: Janni, 20th Century-Fox
Dist/Sales: Ascanbee, ReelMovies, 20thCenturyFox, VSM

Moffie Called Simon, A

Greyson, John
1986; Canada; 14 min; B&W; Documentary

A collage of photographs, letters, TV footage and dramatic sequences present the case of Simon Nkodi, a black gay activist and student leader in South Africa, who has been in jail for nearly two years. The film also explores connections between antiapartheid struggles and gay liberation. (CFMDC)

Dist/Sales: CFMDC

Moments: The Making of Claire of the Moon

Conn, Nicole
1992; USA; 70 min; Documentary

Behind-the-scenes look at the making of the 1992 lesbian classic *Claire of the Moon*. Includes funny moments like Karen and Trisha's first kiss, rehearsals, bloopers and out-takes never seen, and stars the cast and crew of the film.

Dist/Sales: Wolfe, Millivres

Mona Lisa

Jordan, Neil
1986; UK; 105 min; Thriller
P: Stephen Woolley, Patrick Cassavetti; *W:* Neil Jordan, David Leland; *C:* Roger Pratt; *E:* Lesley Walker;
M: Michael Kamen
Cast: Bob Hoskins, Cathy Tyson, Michael Caine, Robbie Coltrane, Sammi Davis

George, short in stature as well as intellect, is just out of prison and trying to pick up the pieces of his life. Simone is a tall, slender black whore who plies the poshest London hotels for her upmarket trade. George gets a job driving Simone to her various appointments and, though he's not very good at it, and feels awkward and ill at ease, he finds himself falling in love with her. But Simone's desires lie elsewhere. The object of her desire, Cathy, has

m

disappeared—Simone and George find themselves in the dangerous and nightmare world of the sordid underworld of London—in search of her.

Prod Comp: Handmade Films
Dist/Sales: Col-Tri, BFI, ACMI, TLA

The Monkey's Mask

Monkey's Mask, The

Lang, Samantha
2000; Australia; 93 min; Thriller
P: Robert Connolly, John Maynard; *W:* Anne Kennedy;
C: Garry Phillips; *E:* Dany Cooper
Cast: Kelly McGillis, Susie Porter, Marton Csokas, Abbie Cornish

Dorothy Porter's prose novel, *The Monkey's Mask* was a tantalising blend of the noir aesthetic, nocturnal sexual desire and the back stabbing Sydney literary scene. Given that, director Samantha Lang's task to translate it into a coherent cinematic whole proves a challenging task. Lesbian private detective Jill Fitzpatrick is called in to investigate the mysterious disappearance of literature student and grunge poet, Mickey Norris. Jill's investigation leads her to Mickey's lecturer, the sensuous Diana, who although married and a potential suspect, is soon embarking on a passionate affair with Mickey. (ACMI)

Prod Comp: Arenafilm, New South Wales Film & TV Office, TVA, Le Studio Canal+
Dist/Sales: Canal+, Strand, Wolfe, ACMI

Monsieur Hawarden

Kümel, Harry
1968; Belgium; 106 min; B&W; Thriller
W: Jan Blokker, Harry Kümel; *C:* Eduard van der Enden; *M:* Pierre Bartholomée
Cast: Ellen Vogel, Hilde Uitterlinden, Dora Van Der AGroen, Johan Remmelts

A lesbian cross-dressing murder-mystery about a young maid who is found dead, and whose employer becomes the suspect. Set at the turn of the century and based on a true story, the film is at times slow moving but this adds to the unfolding mystery.

Prod Comp: Sofidoc, Parkfilm

Montgomery Clift: The Prince

Masenza, Claudio
1988; Italy; 59 min; Documentary
P: Donatella Baglivo; *C:* Giancarlo Formichi;
E: Maurizio Baglivo

A documentary incorporating footage of Montgomery Clift's most memorable films; interviews with family and friends, and rare archival material stretching back to his childhood. What develops is the story of an intense young boy who yearned for stardom, achieved notable success in such classic films as *From Here to Eternity* and *I Confess*, only to be ruined by alcohol addiction and his inability to face his own fears and homosexual desires. Montgomery Clift, as this video portrays him, may not have been a happy man but he never compromised his acting talents for Hollywood.

Prod Comp: Ciak Studio

Montreal Main

Vitale, Frank
1974; Canada; 90 min; B&W; Drama
P: Frank Vitale, Allan Moyle; *W:* Stephen Lack, Allan Moyle, Frank Vitale; *C:* Eric Bloch; *E:* Frank Vitale;
M: Beverly Glenn-Copelann
Cast: Frank Vitale, Stephen Lack, Allan Moyle

An open and honest autobiographical account of male sexuality centred on Frank, an unemployed photographer, and his circle of mainly gay friends. He and his best friend, Bozo, attempt to have sex, although they consider themselves straight. But things begin to fall apart when Frank meets and falls in love with Johnny, a 13-year-old boy.

Prod Comp: Canadian Film Development Corporation, Videograph of Montreal

More Love

Shimada, Koshi
1984; Japan; 60 min; Drama
P: Ken Togoh

A coming-out story about a Japanese man in a culture that is built on male bonding but is extremely threatened by homosexuality. A beautifully filmed melodrama that is perhaps the first gay-focused film to come out of Japan.

More than Friends: The Coming Out of Heidi Leiter

1994; USA; 29 min; Drama
W: Bruce Harmon

Two teenage girls fall in love after a friendly game of basketball, and decide to come out by going to their class prom together. With Claire Danes

Prod Comp: Itel, HBO; *Dist/Sales:* Marcom, Swank

Morocco

von Sternberg, Josef
1930; USA; 92 min; B&W; Drama
P: Hector Turnbull; *W:* Jules Furthman; *C:* Lee Garmes,
Lucien Ballard; *E:* S. K. Winston; *M:* Karl Hajos
Cast: Marlene Dietrich, Gary Cooper, Adolphe Menjou,
Francis McDonald

> In her first film in the USA, and one that consoli-
> dated her legend, Dietrich's sexually suggestive
> cabaret act still raises eyebrows today. Cooper plays
> the legionnaire lover she follows across the desert.
> Described as the 'mannish lesbian' of the 1920s and
> 30s, her androgynous qualities and cross-dressing
> make her a true lesbian icon.

Prod Comp: Paramount
Dist/Sales: Wolfe

Morocco

Morris Loves Jack

Hofmann, Sonia
1978; Australia; 27 min; Comedy
W: David Marsh, Sonia Hofmann
Cast: Kris McQuade, John Hargreaves, Bill Hunter,
David Boyd

> The sweet story of Morris, an out-of-work, would-be
> actor with homosexual tendencies, and his girlfriend.

Prod Comp: Australian Film TV & Radio School
Dist/Sales: NFVLS, ACMI

Moscow Does not Believe in Queers

Greyson, John
1986; Canada; 27 min; Documentary

> Based on John Greyson's experience of attending the
> 1985 Moscow youth festival as an out gay delegate,
> this film is an eccentric, ten day diary of that trip.

Dist/Sales: VideoOut

Moscow Fags

Poselski, Iakov
1995; Russia; 25 min; Documentary

> Young gay men living their lives openly in Russia are
> working to change the country's legal stance on
> homosexuality. The film not only looks at the
> workers involved in change but at prisoners and the
> prison system.

Most Unknowable Thing, The

Patierno, Mary
1999; USA; 57 min; Documentary
P: Mary Patierno

> Mary Patiernio set out to make a documentary
> about what she thought might be the last few years
> of her brother's life when she found out about his
> HIV-positive status. However, as the title suggests,
> things didn't quite pan out as she expected. Begin-
> ning with the video footage from her brother's
> surprise marriage to his female chiropractor,
> following his break up with boyfriend Carlo, the
> documentary (which was five years in the making),
> cleverly unwinds to tell one of those stories you
> simply wouldn't believe in a fictional film. You know
> those people to whom extraordinary things just seem
> to happen? David was one of those. And then some.

Awards: LA Outfest, 1999: Grand Jury Award for Most
Outstanding Documentary

Mountain King, The

Tucker, Duncan
2000; USA; 20 min; Drama

> A persuasive young street hustler disrupts a young
> man's quiet day at the beach, and teaches him to
> appreciate life's element of surprise.

Dist/Sales: JourDeFete

Mountains of the Moon

Rafelson, Bob
1990; USA; 135 min; Drama
P: Daniel Melnick; *W:* Bob Rafelson, William Harrison;
C: Roger Deakins; *E:* Thom Noble; *M:* Michael Small
Cast: Iain Glen, Patrick Bergin, Fiona Shaw, Richard E.
Grant, Peter Vaughan

> A compelling drama based on William Harrison's

m

biographical novel, Burton and Speke, about Richard Burton and John Hanning Speke, two adventurers who attempted to find the source of the Nile. In 1854 they set out on two expeditions through the African jungle finally culminating in the discovery of Lake Victoria. Speke was homosexual and quite taken with Burton. Their male bonding is handled well by Rafelson.

Prod Comp: Carolco, Indieprod
Dist/Sales: 16MM, ACMI, Col-Tri

Mr Christie

Peehl, Scott
2000; USA; 24 min; Comedy

A young man find Jesus watching televison soap operas on his couch.

Dist/Sales: FilmIngk

Mrs Doubtfire

Columbus, Chris
1993; USA; 122 min; Comedy
P: Marsha Garces Williams, Robin Williams, Mark Radcliffe; *W:* Leslie Dixon, Randi Mayem Singer; *C:* Donald McAlpine; *E:* Raja Gosnell; *M:* Howard Shore
Cast: Robin Williams, Sally Field, Pierce Brosnan, Harvey Fierstein

Mrs Doubtfire is a comedy about Daniel and Miranda Hillard, a couple with three children, who go through a divorce—at her instigation. Because Daniel is an out-of-work voice-over artist, Miranda gets temporary custody of the kids, leaving Daniel distraught over the minuscule amount of time he gets to spend with his family. Needing the child care, Miranda advertises for a housekeeper, which prompts the clever but desperate Daniel to disguise himself as an elderly British woman—and he gets the job. Daniel enlists the help his brother (Harvey Fierstein), a gay make-up artist, and his lover, who offer advice, make-up and frocks.

Prod Comp: 20th Century-Fox, Blue Wolf
Dist/Sales: ReelMovies, 20thCenturyFox

Mujeria

Hidalgo de la Riva, Teresa
1992; USA; 20 min; Animation

Mujeria combines two animations that focus on the influence of the Olmeca culture on the filmmaker, who has attempted to go beyond the stereotypical use of Aztec iconography to represent Chicano and Mexican cultural identity by choosing a lesser-known but equally important culture in Mexico. In doing so her animations both celebrate the beauty and strength of this culture—particularly as it relates to women and lesbians—as well as providing an understanding of the history and identity of Third World women.

Dist/Sales: WMM

Mulholland Drive

Lynch, David
2001; France, USA; 146 min; Thriller
P: Neal Edelstein, Mary Sweeney, Alain Sarde, Tony Krantz, Michael Polaire; *W:* David Lynch; *C:* Peter Deming; *E:* Mary Sweeney; *M:* Angelo Badalamenti
Cast: Naomi Watts, Laura Harring, Justin Theroux, Ann Miller

The king of surreal, David Lynch is back with a tale beginning with a car crash on Mulholland Drive. When Rita is dragged from her car at gunpoint by two men, they are almost immediately struck and killed by an oncoming car. Rita has amnesia and staggers her way back to an apartment building where she runs into an aspiring actress who helps her attempt to put the pieces of her life back together, and with whom she forms a relationships of sorts. Lynch uses this as his spring board to take us into the interlocking lives of several interesting characters including a man who's dreams keep coming true, a difficult film director, two gangsters and a pair of deadpan LAPD detectives. A sense of evil binds this ever-tightening group of strangers in this gripping thriller. (Swank)

Prod Comp: Asymmetrical Productions, Le Studio Canal+, Touchstone Television
Dist/Sales: Canal+, Universal, Wolfe, RoadshowEnt, Swank

Mull

(aka: Mullaway)

McLennan, Don
1988; Australia; 90 min; Drama
P: Howard D. Grigsby; *W:* Jon Stephens; *C:* Zbigniew Friedrich; *E:* Zbigniew Friedrich; *M:* Michael Atkinson
Cast: Nadine Garner, Sue Jones, Bill Hunter, Craig Morrison, Brad Kilpatrick

This is a witty and compassionate story of a teenage girl coming to terms with her family and herself when her mother falls critically ill. She decides to leave school to look after her family, which turns out to be an enormous challenge, as she has to deal with her father's fanatical religion, her brother's experimentation with drugs and homosexuality, her desire for the wrong boy, and her younger brother and sister's inability to cope with the family's instability. This is a well-handled rites-of-passage film in a modern setting. Based on the original story, *Mullaway* by Bron Nicholls.

Prod Comp: International Film Management, Ukiyo Films
Dist/Sales: Roadshow, ACMI

Multiple Maniacs

Waters, John
1971; USA; 94 min; Comedy
W: John Waters
Cast: Divine, Mink Stole

The film director Waters claimed 'flushed religion out of my system' is about a travelling carnival called 'Lady Divine's Cavalcade of Perversions,' which lands in Baltimore and disrupts the lives of the creeps living there. We're treated to a junkie shooting up on a church altar, bearded transvestites, the sight of Divine being raped by a 15-foot lobster, Mink Stole's rosary beads, cannibalism, Kate Smith's rendition of 'God Bless America' and, perhaps most disturbing of all, shots of downtown Baltimore. (www.queertheory.com)

Mum's the Word

Carriere, Paul
1996; France; 53 min; Documentary

Offers a candid portrait of four French Canadian women who adopt surprising new roles as they approach their 50s. Leaving behind, husbands and children these women discuss the courage it took to embark on their quests for lesbian lifestyles.

Dist/Sales: Mediatique

MURDER and murder

Rainer, Yvonne
1996; USA; 113 min; Documentary
W: Yvonne Rainer; *C:* Stephen Kazmierski; *E:* Yvonne Rainer

Mildred is a professor who has lived as a lesbian for as long as she can remember. Doris, a mother of grown children, is taking classes and is falling in love with a woman for the first time. From different backgrounds and circumstances, Mildred and Doris try to carve out a life together. Mainly from Doris' perspective, the film investigates the pleasures, uncertainties and ambiguities of late-life emotional attachment and lesbian identity within the confines of a culture that glorifies youth and heterosexual romance. That is the narrative backbone of *MURDER and murder*, but Yvonne Rainer is one of the mothers of feminist, experimental narrative and this film is much more than that. The story is haunted by the ghosts of Doris' mother Jenny and an 18-year-old Mildred. Running parallel is a commentary by Rainer, disturbing the narrative with the

asymmetries of her mastectomised chest. *MURDER and murder* deals with 'deviant' sexuality, female ageing and breast cancer, reflecting upon cultural and scientifically determined perceptions of disease. (CFMDC)

Prod Comp: MURDER and murder Productions
Dist/Sales: Zeitgeist, CFMDC

Muriel's Parents have had it up to Here
(aka: Muriel fait le désespoir de ses Parents)

Faucon, Philippe
1995; France; 74 min; Drama
P: Ognon

Muriel tells her mother that she 'prefers girls to boys'. Mother is aghast and father remains aloof. Thankfully, there's much more to this story than the despair, or lack thereof, of Muriel's parents. In fact, this is a story about a shy young woman coming to terms with her identity. Muriel has left the nest to study in Paris where she falls under the spell of Nora—a sexy and saucy young girl who revels in her seductive powers. Sensing Muriel's burgeoning crush, Nora flirts shamelessly, all the while reminding shy and cautious Muriel that her romantic gestures are 'just for fun'. Nora's idea of fun takes an interesting twist during a vacation to the seaside where she engages in heavy petting and skinny dipping with mutual friend Fred as Muriel stands by, but Muriel doesn't give up. (24th San Francisco International Lesbian & Gay Film Festival)

Dist/Sales: Ognon

Murmur of Youth
(aka: Mei li zai chang ge)

Lin, Cheng-sheng
1997; Taiwan; 106 min; Drama
P: Shun-ching Chiu, Li-kong Hsu; *W:* Su-ching Ko, Cheng-sheng Lin; *C:* Cheng-hui Tsai
Cast: Rene Liu, Jing Tseng, Chin-hsin Tsai

Both Lin's protagonists are called Mei-li and both are young, but come from two different worlds. One comes from a middle-class family living in a Taipei tower block. She silently watches her siblings pursue a materialistic lifestyle as their parents endure their long, hard marriage. The other Mei-li lives in a rickety old house at the edge of the city. Her parents are construction workers—people who have had to endure hardship and are trying desperately to steer their children onto an easier path. Fate brings the two girls together when they find themselves trapped inside the boxoffice of a cinema, and a bond develops as they share their fantasies and frustrations. Spending so much time together in very close

m

proximity brings them to a level of intimacy that allows the exploration of many taboo subjects, such as boys, sex and menstruation, and eventually leads to an explosion of young passion. Mandarin with English subtitles.

Prod Comp: Central Motion Pictures
Dist/Sales: CentralMotion

Muscle

Sato, Hisayasu
1993; Japan; 60 min; Drama
P: Syuji Kataoka; *W:* Shirô Yumemoto; *C:* Kouichi Saitô; *E:* Seiji Sakai; *M:* So Hayakawa
Cast: Takeshi Ito, Simonn Kumai, Koyoma Hageki

Set in Tokyo, a journalist working for a bodybuilding magazine falls into a sadomasochistic and obsessive relationship with a dangerously charismatic bodybuilder. Their affair becomes dominated by S/M games. Japanese with English subtitles.

Prod Comp: ENK Promotion
Dist/Sales: TLA, Strand

Music Lovers, The

Russell, Ken
1971; UK; 119 min; Drama
P: Roy Baird, Ken Russell; *W:* Melvyn Bragg, Catherine Drinker Bowen; *C:* Douglas Slocombe; *E:* Michael Bradsell; *M:* André Previn
Cast: Glenda Jackson, Richard Chamberlain, Christopher Gable, Max Adrian, Isabelle Telezynska

Russell's controversial biography of Tchaikovsky is a flamboyant and visually kinetic attempt to match the romanticism of the composer's music. Though talented, charismatic and handsome, Tchaikovsky's life was compromised by confusion over his homosexuality. The film traces his disastrous marriage to Nina and the platonic love he shared with his wealthy patron, Countess von Meck, a woman whom he never met.

Prod Comp: United Artists, Russfilms
Dist/Sales: Warner, TLA, Swank

Must be the Music

Perry, Nickolas
1996; USA; 20 min; Drama

Four gay boys do the rounds of the gay nightclub scene in Los Angeles.

Dist/Sales: Strand

My Addiction

Gilbert, Sky
1993; Canada; 60 min; Comedy
P: Dennis Mohr; *W:* Sky Gilbert; *C:* Gregg Bennett

E: Sky Gilbert; *M:* Dennis Mohr
Cast: Caroline Gillis, Ellen-Ray Hennessey, Tracy Wright

Matt, although married, is completely in love with a hustler called Dick. One night Matt leaves his wife and goes to Dick's apartment where he waits for his loved one. But Dick's roommate tells Matt that if Dick catches him there he will kill him.

Dist/Sales: CFMDC

My Babushka

Hammer, Barbara
2001; USA; 53 min; Documentary

Hammer brings her vital search for her own ethnic roots and identity to the screen. *My Babushka* not only explores personal history but is a journey to a nation just beginning to open to the West. Questions of human rights, anti-Semitism, homophobia, feminism, and cultural difference are encountered as the artist meets diverse Ukrainians including a long-lost relative, a controversial feminist sex-researcher, a lesbian activist, and a fellow artist who travels with her to the killing fields of Babi Yar. (25th San Francisco International Lesbian & Gay Film Festival)

Dist/Sales: Hammer

My Beautiful Laundrette

Frears, Stephen
1985; UK; 91 min; Drama
P: Sarah Radclyffe, Tim Bevan; *W:* Hanif Kureishi; *C:* Oliver Stapleton; *E:* Mick Audsley; *M:* Stanley Myers, Ludus Tonalis
Cast: Saeed Jaffrey, Roshan Seth, Daniel Day-Lewis, Gordon Warnecke

A young south London Indian and his white, working-class, racist boyfriend take over his uncle's laundrette. They turn it from a dump into a salubrious palace. A thoughtful and intelligent examination of race relations and the economic state of Britain.

Prod Comp: Channel 4, SAF, Working Title Films
Dist/Sales: Dendy, ACMI, OrionClassics, BFI

My Best Friend's Wedding

Hogan, P. J.
1997; USA; 105 min; Comedy
P: Jerry Zucker, Ronald Bass; *W:* Ronald Bass; *C:* László Kovács; *E:* Garth Craven, Lisa Fruchtman; *M:* James Newton Howard
Cast: Julia Roberts, Dermot Mulroney, Cameron Diaz, Rupert Everett, Philip Bosco

A blood-oath that Julianne Porter has with ex-college

beau Michael, promising to marry if both are still single at age 28, is just about due. When Julianne receives an invitation to Michael's forthcoming wedding to a billionaire heiress, the occasion could only call for deceit, sabotage and, perhaps forgiveness with the aid of her closest confidante, a stylish gay man named George.

Prod Comp: TriStar Pictures, Predawn Productions, Zucker Brothers
Dist/Sales: Col-Tri, FirstRelease, 16MM, Wolfe

My Body

Moffett, Joel
1997; USA; 30 min; Comedy

A laugh-out-loud tale about a neurotic but cute young man in denial about his sexual orientation. (First Run Features)

Dist/Sales: AmericanFilm, FirstRunFeatures

My Brother's Keeper

Jordan, Glenn
1995; USA; 120 min; Drama
P: Gregory Goodell; *W:* Gregory Goodell; *C:* Tom Del Ruth; *E:* David Simmons; *M:* David Shire
Cast: John Lithgow, Annette O'Toole, Veronica Cartwright, Ellen Burstyn

A moving made-for-television drama, based on a true story, about twin brothers Bob and Tom, who are well-loved schoolteachers from Long Island. Tom, who is HIV-positive, has the unique opportunity to receive a bone-marrow transplant from his brother to slow the progression of the disease. Just before they are about to go ahead with the procedure, Tom's insurance company refuses to cover it and a court battle begins. John Lithgow puts in a great performance as both twins.

Prod Comp: RHI Entertainment
Dist/Sales: 21stCentury

My Cousin Mike

Hannon, Gerald
1999; Canada; 10 min; Comedy

An older man, a younger man, a masturbation fantasy and an intrusive cat.

Dist/Sales: VTape

My Father is Coming

Treut, Monika
1991; Germany, USA; 80 min; Comedy
P: Monika Treut; *W:* Monika Treut, Bruce Benderson; *C:* Elfi Mikesch; *E:* Stev Brown; *M:* David Van Tieghen
Cast: Annie Sprinkle, Shelley Kastner, Michael Massee, Alfred Edel

Vicky, an out-of-work actress, struggling waitress and lesbian has her whole life thrown into turmoil when her father comes from Germany to visit. The main problem is that Vicky has told him she is a successful actress and happily married. She enlists the help of a gay friend to play her husband. Using a large range of characters—gay, lesbian, straight, transsexuals—the film creates a funny and touching view of family dynamics and sexuality.

Prod Comp: Hyane
Dist/Sales: FirstRunFeatures, Millivres, Wolfe

My Feminism

Cardona, Dominique / Colbert, Laurie
1997; Canada; 55 min; Documentary

In an era of antifeminist backlash, this articulate documentary by the makers of *Thank God I'm a Lesbian* forcefully reminds us that the revolution continues. Powerful interviews with feminist leaders including bell hooks, Gloria Steinem, and Urvsahi Vaid are intercut with documentary sequences to engagingly explore the past and present status of the women's movement. Discussing the unique contributions of second wave feminism, they explore their racial, economic and ideological differences and shared vision of achieving equality for women. An essential component of women's studies curricula, *My Feminism* introduces feminism's key themes while exposing the cultural fears underlying lesbian baiting, backlash, and political extremism. (WMM)

Dist/Sales: WMM

My Femme Divine

Everett, Karen
1999; USA; 52 min; Documentary
P: Karen Everett

Skilfully combining personal memoir with performances and lively group discussion, Everett reveals the complex dynamics at play in contemporary relationships between butch and femme lesbians. Drawing on her encounters with religion and psychology she poignantly recounts the spiritual reawakening she experienced while weathering the storms of an explosive love affair with a beautiful femme—an affair which precariously straddles the boundaries between obsession and passion, and yet is told with a disarming humour. Woven into this narrative are the insights of lesbian women talking butch-to-butch and femme-to-femme about yin/yang chemistry and a love that borders on worship.

Dist/Sales: Everett, Wolfe

My First Suit

Main, Stewart
1985; New Zealand; 57 min; Comedy
P: John Maynard, Bridget Ikin; *W:* Peter Wells;

m

C: Alan Locke; *E:* Peter Evans; *M:* Keith Ballantyne
Cast: Conrad Crawte, Martyn Sanderson

From the seven-part television series *About Face. My First Suit* is a comedy about a gay adolescent's struggle to find his place in the world. He is confronted by the conflict between how he is required to dress and how he wants to dress to express his identity.

Prod Comp: Hibiscus Films, New Zealand Film Commission
Dist/Sales: NFVLS, VideoAmericain

My Friend Su

Bhasin, Neeraj
2001; India; 55 min; Documentary

My Friend Su is an insightful examination of one man's feelings and struggles with being a 'man' on the outside but feeling distinctly feminine otherwise. His acceptance of what he is from within, a real 'woman', and his dreams to be with a man who can love him as a woman become the core issues that unravel in the film. (15th Singapore International Film Festival)

Dist/Sales: Ihsan

My Girlfriend did It

West, Dawn
1995; USA; 40 min; Documentary

Domestic violence in lesbian relationships is something most people don't want to talk about, and we have managed to keep it safely in the closet for too long. Dawn West tackles this important issue head-on in her powerful documentary *My Girlfriend Did It*. The stories of a wide range of women who have been in abusive relationships and have managed to survive are juxtaposed with the examination of one relationship that ended in tragedy. Through interviews with survivors, therapists, attorneys, advocates and researchers, this film provides firsthand accounts, defines the cycle of violence in relationships and presents issues of 'coming out' as a battered lesbian. (20th San Francisco International Lesbian & Gay Film Festival)

My Hustler

Warhol, Andy / Wein, Chuck
1965; USA; 67 min; B&W; Comedy
P: Andy Warhol; *W:* Chuck Wein, Andy Warhol;
C: Andy Warhol
Cast: Paul America, Ed Hood, Genevieve Charbon, Joseph Campbell

My Hustler marks a further stage in the development of the Factory's films from their beginnings focusing on the process of filming per se through the tentative emergence of spectacle and performance towards the coherent and planned narratives of Paul Morrissey. Wein came up with the original idea about an ageing homosexual who rents a boy from Dial-a-Hustler, who then feels he has to protect his 'property'. The negotiated gestures of grooming and seduction between men in a bathroom become a voyeuristic documentation of the intimacies of private ritual.

Prod Comp: Factory Films
Dist/Sales: NFVLS, MOMA

My Left Breast

Rogers, Gerry
2000; Canada; 57 min; Documentary

Incorporating a unique blend of wit, wisdom and resilience, filmmaker Gerry Rogers bravely recounts her story of breast cancer survival to share with the world that life, indeed, can continue with full force and vigour. Shortly after being diagnosed at age 42, Rogers and her female partner began to document their ordeal on camera in an attempt to confront Rogers' questions and fears about breast cancer. Rather than present a sombre and morose meditation on this difficult experience, she decides to invoke humour to frankly reflect on the meaning of this disease on her life, as well as on the lives of her friends and family. The result is a one-of-kind approach to positively coping with a potentially fatal disease. (WMM)

Dist/Sales: WMM, FilmsTransit

My Mother is an Alien

Evans, Bronwen
1995; UK; 34 min; Documentary

The British documentary *My Mother is an Alien* gives voice to the adult children of 'out' lesbians. What did they think of their childhood? Their mothers' politics? Their mothers being out? The value system they grew up in? These questions and more are addressed in funny and moving interviews with the lesbian moms and their grown-up kids. (20th San Francisco International Lesbian & Gay Film Festival)

My Own Private Idaho

Van Sant, Gus
1991; USA; 102 min; Drama
P: Laurie Parker, Allan Mindel; *W:* Gus Van Sant;
C: John Campbell, Eric Alan Edwards;
E: Curtiss Clayton; *M:* Bill Stafford
Cast: River Phoenix, Keanu Reeves, William Richert, James Russo, Rodney Harvey

A poetic journey that focuses on the life of Mike, a young burnt-out male prostitute, and the object of his love, Scott, as they travel the back roads of the US and Europe searching for Scott's mother. A dreamlike quality pervades this tender and insightful film which explores the place where the need to survive and the need to be loved and belong meet personal choices in the transition to adulthood.

Prod Comp: New Line Cinema
Dist/Sales: Wolfe, ACMI, FilmsInc, BFI, FineLine

My Own Private Idaho

My Pal Rachid

Barassat, Philippe
1999; France; 19 min; Comedy
W: Philippe Barassat

Short comedy about a boy who has an obsession with his friend's penis and continually asks to see it. The friend will only oblige if he receives money and sweets in return. French with English subtitles.

Dist/Sales: LaVieEstBelle, UniFrance

My Summer Vacation

Gilbert, Sky
1995; Canada; 90 min; Comedy
W: Sky Gilbert; *E:* Karen Saunders
Cast: Sky Gilbert, Caroline Gillis, Ellen-Ray Hennessy, Daniel MacIvor

Joe is determined to find his perfect man and fill his soul with love and romance. Along the way he plans to document his adventures with his new video camera. In Joe's hands, the camera becomes a tool of seduction. *My Summer Vacation* takes a wry look at Generation-X gay life. Featuring scenes of city life, wacky lesbians on dope and ad-libbed dialogue, this is nineties cinéma-vérité with a wickedly comic edge! (MQFF)

Dist/Sales: CFMDC, WaterBearer

My Survival as a Deviant

Zoates, Toby
1980; Australia; 60 min; Documentary

The myths of deviancy are explored and the realities of survival are experienced in the city of Sydney between 1979 and 1980 from the point of view of a broke and homeless gay male cartoonist and the many fellow travellers he meets on the streets.

Dist/Sales: ACMI

My Two Loves

Black, Noel
1986; USA; 100 min; Drama
W: Reginald Rose, Rita Mae Brown; *M:* Gary William Friedman
Cast: Mariette Hartley, Lynn Redgrave, Barry Newman, Sada Thompson

The story of a recently widowed woman and mother, Gail, who is torn between her new boyfriend and another woman, Marjorie, a co-worker at her new job. When the two women become lovers, Gail must deal with her teenage daughter's reaction to the relationship. Made for television.

Prod Comp: ABC-TV
Dist/Sales: ABC-US

Myra Breckinridge

Sarne, Michael
1970; USA; 93 min; Comedy
P: Robert Fryer; *W:* Michael Sarne, David Giler; *C:* Richard Moore; *E:* Danford B. Greene; *M:* John Philips
Cast: Mae West, John Huston, Raquel Welch, Rex Reed, John Carradine, Farrah Fawcett

A film that created quite a stir in the 1970s, it tells the story of a film critic who has a sex-change operation and then sets out to destroy the male movie-star stereotype. Features early screen appearances by Farrah Fawcett and Tom Selleck and a large number of archival cameos, among them Carmen Miranda and Marlene Dietrich. Full of in-jokes about the movie industry, and based on the novel by Gore Vidal.

Prod Comp: 20th Century-Fox
Dist/Sales: 20thCenturyFox, CBS

Mystère Alexina, Le
(aka: The Mystery of Alexina)

Féret, René
1985; France; 90 min; Drama
P: René Féret; *W:* René Féret, Jean Gruault; *C:* Bernard Zitzermann; *E:* Ariane Boeglin; *M:* Anne-Marie Deschamps
Cast: Valérie Stroh, Phillippe Vuillemin, Véronique Silver, Bernard Freyd, Pierre Vial

Dramatisation of a true 19th century case history, based on the diaries of the hermaphrodite 'Alexina', who was raised as a girl from birth. It is not until she

m

falls in love with another girl, Sara, that she finds out she is actually a boy. Sara is uncomfortable about the idea of a lesbian relationship, and when the two become sexually intimate she is delighted to find that Alexina is a man. But Alexina suffers a severe identity crisis. When Alexina reveals to the bigoted French provincial society that she is actually a man, she/he is persecuted and finally suicides at the age of 22.

Prod Comp: Cinéaste Animaliers Associés, Les Cinéastes Associés, TF1 Films

Myth of Father

Hill, Paul
2001; USA; 60 min; Documentary
P: Laura Dahlinger, Paul Hill; *C:* Steve Carter; *E:* Paul Hill, Steve Carter; *M:* Marc Purslow

An intimate documentary about Paul and his family's journey towards understanding his trans-sexual father, Jodie.

Dist/Sales: AstroBaby

Nadja

Almereyda, Michael
1994; USA; 90 min; B&W; Horror
P: Mary Sweeney, Amy Hobby; *W:* Michael Almereyda; *C:* Jim Denault; *E:* David Leonard; *M:* Simon Fisher Turner
Cast: Elina Löwensohn, Nic Ratner, Karl Geary, Peter Fonda

Nadja, born by the Black Sea, has moved to present-day Manhattan. With her short, dark hair and pale skin, Nadja fits right into downtown New York life. When Van Helsing drives a stake through the heart of her father, he entangles his own nephew, Jim, in his efforts to kill Nadja and her accursed twin brother. But Jim's wife has already fallen under Nadja' spell, as the story shuttles to the darker regions of Brooklyn, then to Transylvania for the final confrontation.

Prod Comp: Globe Film Co, Kino Link Company
Dist/Sales: UIP, 21stCentury, October

Naked Civil Servant, The

Gold, Jack
1975; UK; 78 min; Drama
P: Barry Hanson, Verity Lambert; *W:* Quentin Crisp, Philip Mackie; *C:* Mike Fash; *E:* Mike Taylor; *M:* Carl Davis
Cast: John Hurt, Patricia Hodge, Liz Gebhardt, Stanley Lebor

This biographical film, based on the life of Quentin Crisp, is briefly introduced by Crisp himself. Crisp is an effeminate homosexual, a flamboyant and witty exhibitionist whose conversation is as glittering as the lipstick and mascara he used to effect. The film, drawn from his own book, tells the story of his life: his youth in the 1930s, his volatile relationship with his father, his ill-fated friendships, his encounters with authority in an extremely homophobic and intolerant society, and his rare moments of true happiness. Above all, it tells the story of a good and honest man, determined to confront the world with the truth about himself, in order that they can learn that he, too, is a human being with dreams and feelings just like everybody else.

Prod Comp: Thames Television
Dist/Sales: TLA

Naked Highway

West, Wash
1997; USA; 75 min; Erotica
W: Wash West
Cast: Jim Buck, Joey Violence

Sultry Southern sexuality sets the pace for Wash West's award winning gay erotic tale of the search for love on the American road. Seeking renewal of a tortured love affair, Colorado abandons his southern roots in search of his former lover, Billy Jo. While Colorado has been pining away, Billy Jo is doing for money what he wouldn't do for love. On the way to tinseltown's gay sex industry, Colorado crosses paths with Dude, a street hustler with a problem—he looks for lust in all the wrong places. Before travelling the naked highway, Dude engages a trick in one of the most erotically mesmerising underwater sexual 'dances' ever filmed. Colorado and Dude's journey runs from suspenseful to sexual with plenty of action on all fronts. (Wolfe)

Dist/Sales: Wolfe

Naked in New York

Algrant, Dan
1994; USA; 93 min; Comedy
P: Frederick Zollo; *W:* Dan Algrant, John Warren; *C:* Joey Forsyte; *E:* Bill Pankow; *M:* Angelo Badalamenti
Cast: Eric Stoltz, Ralph Macchio, Tony Curtis, Mary-Louise Parker, Jill Clayburgh

Joanne and Jake's romance begins to unravel as Jake moves to New York to produce his first off-Broadway play, and Joanne encounters the guiding hand of a dashing gallery entrepreneur. Jake is exposed to a series of life's little surprises never encountered by him before. He finds out his best friend is gay, he is seduced by the leading lady who's not right for the part, and he believes his girlfriend is cheating on him. When his play is a failure, he discovers the down side of success, which he believes reflects on his own life. Through this comical haze of love and life, Jake comes to find his own destiny and self understanding.

Prod Comp: Some Film
Dist/Sales: Ronin, 16MM, FineLine

Naked Killer

(aka: Chiklo gouyeung)

Yiu-leung, Clarence Fok
1992; Hong Kong; 110 min; Action
P: Jing Wong; *W:* Jing Wong; *C:* Peter Pau, William Yim; *M:* Lowell Lo
Cast: Chingmy Yau, Simon Yam, Carrie Ng, Madoka Sugawara

The sparks fly as the genres collide: lesbian crime fiction meets Hong Kong martial-arts action movie. Watch out for cops, private detectives, lurid costumes, outrageous sets, poisonous lipstick, wild martial arts scenes, Sister Cindy, dykes who jump out of first-floor windows onto motorbikes and loads of lesbian lust. (MQFF)

Prod Comp: Golden Harvest, Wong Jing's Workshop
Dist/Sales: RimFilm, ACMI

Naked Lunch

Cronenberg, David
1991; Canada, UK; 115 min; Sci-Fi, Experimental
P: Jeremy Thomas; *W:* David Cronenberg; *C:* Peter Suschitzky; *E:* Ronald Sanders; *M:* Howard Shore, Ornette Coleman
Cast: Peter Weller, Roy Scheider, Judy Davis, Ian Holm, Julian Sands

Loosely based on the classic book by famous gay author, William S. Burroughs, the main character, William Lee, (also an author), faces his demons when roach powder (read drugs) takes over his life. He enters the nightmarish Interzone: a fictitious place populated by spies, junkies, witches and shape-changing monsters. Davis has a very interesting scene with another woman in uniform. A bizarre film that gives you the feeling of being in a drug haze, with an emphasis on surrealism as typewriters turn into mechanical insects.

Prod Comp: Thomas
Dist/Sales: Col-Tri, ACMI, 20thCenturyFox

Nana, George and Me

Balass, Joe
1998; Canada; 48 min; Documentary

What do you get when you ask your 92-year-old Nana and a 72-year-old man you've just met questions you've only dared to dream of about identity and sexuality? *Nana, George and Me* is a funny, intimate, sometimes shocking and always heart-warming look at two Iraqi Jewish lives—one a traditionally raised woman and the other a completely unconventional gay man. (Cinema Libre)

Prod Comp: Compass Productions
Dist/Sales: CinemaLibre

Naomi's Legacy

Levy, Wendy
1994; USA; 26 min; Drama

Naomi's Legacy records three generations of women in a Jewish family. The story is told by the daughter, Naomi, as she reinterprets home movies and audio cassettes. Coming to terms with her past, she develops a new understanding about her mother, her grandmother and her own identity as a Jewish lesbian. (WMM)

Dist/Sales: WMM

Naughty Little Peeptoe

Maxwell, Garth / Wells, Peter
2000; New Zealand; 28 min; Documentary

Charismatic Doug George talks about his lifelong obsession with women's shoes.

Dist/Sales: MF-Films

Naya Zamana

Rupa, Mandrika
1996; New Zealand; 11 min; Comedy

The traditional expectations of an Indian family in modern day New Zealand are confronted in this short drama with a twist. A young Indian woman living in a West Auckland housing estate seems caught between two irreconcilable sets of expectations. While Shobhanam's aunt discusses a suitable match for her niece, Shobhanam has other ideas but her intended is not what her aunt might expect. (Cinenova)

Dist/Sales: Cinenova

Nea: The Young Emmanuelle

(aka: Nea)

Kaplan, Nelly
1976; France; 140 min; Drama
P: Yvon Guézel, André Génovès; *W:* Jean Chapot, Nelly Kaplan; *C:* Andréas Winding; *E:* Hélène Plemiannikov; *M:* Michel Magne
Cast: Ann Zacharias, Sami Frey, Francoise Brion, Heinz Bennent, Micheline Presle

A spoilt, rich, 16-year-old girl (Nea) is an accomplished writer of erotic literature. She writes a novel and publishes it secretly under an assumed name.

She then encourages her lesbian mother to leave her marriage to be with her lover. Nea also takes a lover to experience eroticism for herself. An ingenious film that is a deft examination of sexual politics.

Prod Comp: Les Films la Boétie

Need and Want

Poklar, Micki / Crocetti, Daniela
2000; USA; 35 min; Documentary

A group of lusty lesbians talk frankly about sex—what they like to do, and how they like to do it; in raunchiest reality and in their wildest, wettest dreams. (queerDOC 2001)

Neptune's Rocking Horse

Roznowski, Robert / Tate, Robert
1996; USA; 104 min; Drama
P: Robert Roznowski, Robert Tate; *W:* Robert Roznowski, Robert Tate; *C:* Renato Falcao;
E: Robert Tate
Cast: David Beach, Joe Capozzi, Tony Fair, Helen Gallagher, Laura Kenyon

A poignant and thought provoking film about how 'the fucking system screws the little guy, the little guy in the dress'. Set in the Upper West side of New York City, the film explores the reaction of five witnesses to the violent arrest of a black transvestite. An impassioned civil libertarian, a gay handyman, a frustrated office worker, a black doorman and a invalid care giver weave in and out of a story exploring prejudices, conscious or otherwise.

Prod Comp: Rob Squared Films

Nervos de Aco

(aka: Nerves Made of Steel)

Andrade, Ed
2001; Brazil; 20 min; Drama

Peixoto, a private eye, is hired by the beautiful and mysterious Ana Claudia. He has been assigned to find her ex-boyfriend Sebastian. In the middle of the investigation, the detective's sexuality becomes suspicious.

Dist/Sales: MixBrasil

Nervous Energy

Stewart, Jean
1995; UK; 110 min; Drama
P: Ann Scott; *W:* Howard Schuman; *C:* Nicholas D. Knowland; *E:* Ardan Fisher; *M:* Stephen Warbeck
Cast: Alfred Molina, Cal Macaninch, John McGlynn, Siobhan Redmond

Tom and Ira are two gay men living in London. Tom, from Scotland, has AIDS and is living his life to the fullest, indulging in music, art and shopping. He decides to return to Scotland to see his family and friends in the hope of finding love and acceptance. It all goes well in the beginning, but when Tom's health deteriorates and dementia sets in, Ira arrives to take Tom back to London for treatment. When Tom finally returns he finds that his true family is not his relations in Scotland but his adopted family of friends in London.

Prod Comp: BBC
Dist/Sales: BBC-Scotland

Neurosia: 50 Years of Perversity

von Praunheim, Rosa
1995; Germany; 90 min; Comedy
Cast: Rosa von Praunheim, Desiree Nick, Lotti Huber, Evelyn Kunneke

A very camp and satirical autobiographical comedy from one of the most prolific guerrilla filmmakers and gay activists, Rosa von Praunheim. A filmmaker is murdered while hosting a tribute to himself. A tabloid journalist decides to investigate the murder and learn more about the German underground filmmaker. She turns up a whole array of interesting and colourful characters including ex-lovers, actors, porn stars and his loving mother, all of whom admit to wanting to kill him. German with English subtitles.

Dist/Sales: FirstRunFeatures, Wolfe

Never Look Back

Kinsella, Stephen
1996; USA; 85 min; Drama
W: Stephen Kinsella; *M:* Jaime Mendoza-Nava
Cast: Girlina, Candis Cayne, Nicole Freeman, Chris Sery

Jill is a bright beautiful young woman whose life in a small Florida town is made unbearable by her unhappy parents and her mood swinging, steroid using, physically abusive fiancé. She ditches them all and moves to South Beach where she meets and is immediately embraced by gender illusionists Mona and her lover Billee, who operate a cabaret. They teach her about self confidence, the world of modelling and how to survive on her own. She falls in love with the glamour, stardom, money and all that goes with it. Trouble starts to brew when Jill's former fiancé shows up determined to 'take her back where she belongs'. (Wolfe)

Dist/Sales: Wolfe

Never Met Picasso

Kijak, Stephen
1995; USA; 100 min; Comedy
P: Patrick Cunningham, Stephen Kijak;

W: Stephen Kijak; *C:* David Tames; *E:* Angelica Brisk;
M: Kristin Hersh, Bill Lee
Cast: Alexis Arquette, Margot Kidder, Georgia Ragsdale,
Don McKellar

A humorous film depicting the day-to-day concerns of queers and their drive for creativity. While a young gay artist is struggling to find new direction with his work, he is also having problems with his rather unstable new boyfriend. Meanwhile his mother is writing a performance for an experimental theatre and she, in turn, is being pursued by a lesbian artist who channels famous dead female artists through her soul and into her work.

Prod Comp: Mighty Reel Productions
Dist/Sales: TurbulentArts, WaterBearer

New Women, The

Hughes, Todd
2001; USA; 89 min; Sci-Fi, Comedy
P: Edward Nachtrieb, John Schliesser; *W:* Tood Hughes,
P. David Ebersole; *C:* Larra Anderson; *E:* Daniel Gabbe;
M: Cary Berger
Cast: Mary Woronov, Jamie Tolbert, Sandra Kinder,
Jane Ray

The New Women is a post-apocalyptic, wacky, science-fiction farce about a mysterious rainstorm that puts all males into a coma, where their only function is to get erections every 45 minutes. The women must band together to rebuild their world and save the human race.

Prod Comp: Interzone
Dist/Sales: KillerPix

Next Best Thing, The

Schlesinger, John
1999; USA; 108 min; Comedy
P: Linne Radmin, Tom Rosenberg, Leslie Dixon;
W: Thomas Ropelewski; *C:* Elliot Davis; *E:* Peter Honess
Cast: Madonna, Rupert Everrtt, Benjamin Bratt, Illeana
Douglas, Lynn Redgrave

An unexpected night of passion between two best friends—a straight woman and a gay man—leads to an unconventional family situation.

Prod Comp: Lakeshore Entertainment, Paramount
Dist/Sales: Wolfe, Paramount, ACMI

Next Stop, Greenwich Village

Mazursky, Paul
1976; USA; 111 min; Comedy
P: Paul Mazursky, Tony Ray; *W:* Paul Mazursky;
C: Arthur Ornitz; *E:* Richard Halsey; *M:* Bill Conti
Cast: Lenny Baker, Shelley Winters, Lois Smith,
Christopher Walken, Ellen Greene

Set in 1953 in Greenwich Village, *Next Stop* depicts an aspiring young actor and his life and relationships with a group of people he befriends. Shelley Winters puts in a warm performance as a Jewish momma and Antonio Fargus plays a misunderstood black gay man with pathos.

Prod Comp: 20th Century-Fox
Dist/Sales: ReelMovies

Nice Girls Don't

Kerridge, Nicola
1994; UK; 10 min; Comedy

A cautionary tale for young dykes planning on taking their girlfriend home to meet the folks. Things go from bad to worse when Anna brings her freshly-shorn scalp and her lover Lisa home for Dad's birthday dinner at the middle-class family abode. (MQFF)

Dist/Sales: RoyalCollege

Nice Girls Don't Do It

Daymond, Kathy
1990; USA; 13 min; B&W; Documentary

A daring, graphic exposé on the pleasures of female ejaculation. Dismissed by the medical profession as urinary incontinence, this film, with the use of several genres, deconstructs the conventional meanings attached to male and female sexuality and destabilises notions around specific visual representations of the female body.

Dist/Sales: Cinenova, CFMDC

Nietta's Diary

Romano, Gabriella
1996; Italy, UK; 30 min; Drama

Nietta's Diary is a film about the lesbian relationship of Nietta Apra and Linda (Flafi) Mazzuccato in pre and post war Italy. The film centres upon the passionate love story as recounted through Nietta's unpublished diary. (Cinenova)

Dist/Sales: Cinenova

Night Larry Kramer Kissed Me, The

Kirkman, Tim
2000; USA; 85 min; Comedy
C: James Carman; *E:* Caitlin Dixon; *M:* Steve Sandberg
Cast: David Drake

Originally a monster hit off-Broadway, *The Night Larry Kramer Kissed Me* brings to film David Drake's one-man show exploring the highs and lows of urban gay male life. Based loosely on his own life, Drake gives a powerful performance that sparks uproarious laughter and heartfelt tears. The stories he tells include the indelible impression Larry Kramer's play *The Normal Heart* made on him, the emotion of his first kiss, his take on the gay club and gym scenes and more. (Wolfe)

Prod Comp: Montrose Pictures
Dist/Sales: Wolfe, TLA

Night of Varennes, The

(aka: La Nuit de Varennes)

Scola, Ettore
1982; France; 133 min; Drama
P: Renzo Rossellini; *W:* Sergio Amedei, Ettore Scola; *C:* Armando Nannuzzi; *E:* Raimondo Crociani; *M:* Armando Trovajoli
Cast: Marcello Mastroianni, Hanna Schygulla, Harvey Keitel, Jean-Claude Brialy

In 1791 Louis XVI and Marie-Antoinette (the King and Queen of France) tried to escape from Revolutionary Paris to join monarchist allies outside France, only to be arrested in Varennes. The incident engendered distrust and suspicion of the monarchy. Using this historical event as a reference point, the film imagines a group of travellers on the same road, including the American patriot Thomas Paine, the noted seducer Casanova, the French novelist Restif de La Bretonne, and one of the queen's ladies-in-waiting. The group illustrate various attitudes toward the changes taking place in their troubled society. French with English subtitles.

Prod Comp: Gaumont, Opera Film, France 3
Dist/Sales: NewVision

Night Out

Night Out

Johnston, Lawrence
1989; Australia; 48 min; B&W; Drama
P: Lisa Doherty, Lawrence Johnston; *W:* Lawrence Johnston
Cast: Colin Batrouney, John Brumpton, Luke Elliott, Andrew Larkins

A homosexual is bashed in a toilet block and taken for a nightmare car ride while his lover is interstate. While this serves as a harsh introduction to the film,

within the narrative it becomes a divisive incident in the lovers' relationship as they begin to question each other's commitment. The second half of the film is a quiet and often poignant contrast to the first, which covers not only the bashing but also a gay party. Thus it becomes not only a film about homosexual assaults and homophobia but also promiscuity and relationships in the era of AIDS.

Prod Comp: Swinburne Film & TV School
Dist/Sales: NFVLS, ACMI

Night Porter, The

(aka: Il Portiere di notte)

Cavani, Liliana
1974; Italy; 115 min; Drama
P: Robert Gordon Edwards, Esa De Simone; *W:* Barbara Alberti, Liliana Cavani, Italo Moscati; *C:* Alfio Contini; *E:* Franco Arcalli; *M:* Danièle Paris
Cast: Dirk Bogarde, Charlotte Rampling, Philippe Leroy, Gabriele Ferzetti

It is a dozen years after World War II and a group of ex-Nazis and Gestapo meet regularly in an exclusive hotel in Vienna. The porter at the hotel is an ex-SS concentration camp officer who one day recognises one of the hotel's guests as a former prisoner whom he raped when she was fourteen and then proceeded to use as his sex-slave till the end of the war. In meeting again they continue their sadomasochistic relationship which inevitably, and horrifically, leads to tragedy. This controversial film has been praised as profound, denounced as morally corrupt and ridiculed as high camp. Italian with English subtitles.

Prod Comp: Ital Noleggio Cinematografico, Lotar Films
Dist/Sales: ReelMovies, Ascanbee, Col-Tri

Night Rhythms

Hippolyte, Gregory
1992; USA; 99 min; Thriller
P: Andrew W. Garroni; *W:* Alan Grifs, Robyn Sullivent; *C:* Wally Pfister; *E:* Kent Smith; *M:* Ashley Irwin
Cast: Delia Sheppard, Martin Hewitt, Tracy Tweed, David Carradine

Burt hosts a late-night talk show on radio where he gives advice on love, sex and relationships. One night he gets a call from Honey, a lesbian, who has decided to end her relationship with her lover. She goes to Burt's studio and, as it turns out, he is accused of her murder, but all is not what it appears.

Dist/Sales: Palace

Night Trade

Karpinski, Barbara
2001; Australia; 10 min; Drama

Reality bites hard in this beautiful, dark, and moody

piece about love, war, and the resilience of the human spirit. Using authentic voice-over and filmed re-enactments, *Night Trade* travels from the war zones and strip clubs of post-Communist Eastern Europe to the gritty streets of Kings Cross. (queerDOC 2001)

Night Visions

Bociurkiw, Marusia
1989; Canada; 60 min; Drama

Racism and homophobia are explored in two overlapping stories, one about a Native–American single mother fighting social welfare authorities and her white ex-husband for custody of her daughter, the other about a lesbian photographer whose erotic photographs have been seized by the police.

Dist/Sales: CFMDC, Salzgeber

Night Warning

Asher, William
1982; USA; 96 min; Thriller
P: Stephen Breimer, Eugene Mazzola; *W:* Stephen Breimer, Boon Collins, Alan Jay Glueckman; *C:* Robbie Greenberg; *E:* Ted Nicolaou; *M:* Bruce Langhorne
Cast: Jimmy McNichol, Bo Svenson, Susan Tyrrell

A good psychological thriller about a young college basketball player, Billy, and his overprotective aunt, Cheryl. When Cheryl kills a television repairman who refuses her advances, a cop with a closed mind investigating the case links it to a homosexual basketball coach, leaving Billy as the prime suspect.

Prod Comp: Royal American, S2D Associates

Night with Derek, A

Kwietniowski, Richard
1995; UK; 23 min; Documentary

An engaging biopic about the late avant-garde filmmaker Derek Jarman, subverting traditional documentary style. This evocative, dreamlike film features interviews with Jarman's friends and lovers, and excerpts from several of his films.

Nighthawks

Peck, Ron
1978; UK; 110 min; Drama
P: Paul Hallam, Ron Peck; *W:* Paul Hallam, Ron Peck; *C:* Joanna Davis; *E:* Mary Pat Leece; *M:* David Graham Ellis
Cast: Ken Robertson, Tony Westrope, Rachel Nicholas James, Maureen Dolan

A gritty, realistic story about the dual life of a homosexual schoolteacher who by day is a model upstanding citizen, but by night cruises discos and nightclubs looking for male partners. In the end he is finally outed by his own students.

Dist/Sales: BFI, WaterBearer, ACMI

Nightwork

Schneider, Jane
1994; Australia; 12 min; Comedy
P: Nicki Roller; *W:* Marele Day
Cast: Gosia Dobrowolska, Shayne Foote, Deborah Kennedy, Tatea Riley, Raj Sidhu

Rachel believes her girlfriend is doing more than just playing her saxophone at the nightclub where she works. When she hires a detective to investigate her lover's 'affairs' the results are not what she expected. Great comedy about the dangers of jealousy and a vivid imagination. (MQFF)

Prod Comp: Australian Film TV & Radio School
Dist/Sales: ACMI, AFTRS

Nijinsky

Ross, Herbert
1980; UK; 125 min; Drama
P: Nora Kaye, Stanley O'Toole; *W:* Hugh Wheeler, Romola Nijinsky; *C:* Douglas Slocombe; *E:* William Reynolds; *M:* John Lanchberry
Cast: Alan Bates, George De La Pena, Leslie Browne, Alan Badel

A beautiful looking film that chronicles the early career of the legendary Russian ballet dancer Vaslav Nijinsky and his passionate love affair with the impresario Sergei Diaghilev. His other relationships included the Hungarian aristocrat Romola de Pulsky (while on the rebound from Diaghilev) and a wealthy homosexual patron.

Prod Comp: Hera
Dist/Sales: TLA, Paramount

Nijinsky

(aka: The Diaries of Vaslav Nijinsky)

Cox, Paul
2002; Australia; 95 min; Documentary
P: Paul Cox, Aanya Whitehead; *W:* Paul Cox; *C:* Paul Cox, Hans Sonneveld; *E:* Paul Cox; *M:* Paul Grabowsky
Cast: Derek Jacobi, Delia Silvan, Chris Haywood, Hans Sonneveld

A dramatised documentary about Vaslav Nijinsky, which details his struggle with mental illness as well as his relationship with ballet impresario Sergei Diaghilev, and marriage to his Italian wife.

Prod Comp: Illumination Films, SBS Independent
Dist/Sales: Sharmill, Wellspring

n

Nine Days

Magrina, Gala
2001; USA; 13 min; Drama

An overprotective mother tries to find the right husband for her lesbian daughter. Her daughter has other plans.

Dist/Sales: MCrown

Nitrate Kisses

Hammer, Barbara
1992; USA; 62 min; Documentary
P: Barbara Hammer; *W:* Barbara Hammer; *C:* Barbara Hammer; *E:* Barbara Hammer

A collage of different elements—found footage, interviews, optical reprinting and filmed footage of lesbian and gay lovemaking—is used to relate a lesbian and gay history that has been repressed or distorted. The film's main strategy is densely associative, operating on different levels: allegorical, historical and erotic. The found footage includes one of the earliest gay films, Watson and Weber's *Lot in Sodom* (1933), and German narrative feature films of the 1930s.

Prod Comp: B. Grummels
Dist/Sales: Frameline, NFVLS, ACMI

No Backup

Tal, Efrat
2000; USA; 13 min; Documentary

A gay Los Angeles Police Department officer discusses the hypocrisies and difficulties of serving as part of one of America's most infamous police force. (2001 Imageout Film Festival)

No Dumb Questions

Regan, Melissa
2001; USA; 25 min; Documentary
These three sisters absolutely adore their Uncle Bill. But will they feel the same way when he becomes their Aunt Barbara? This funny and touching doco follows the 6, 9, and 11-year-old sisters as they struggle with, and ultimately accept, this new concept in their lives. (queerDOC 2001)

No Exit

Danielewski, Tad
1962; Argentina, USA; 85 min; Drama
P: Hector Olivera, Fernando Ayala; *W:* George Tabori; *C:* Ricardo Younis; *E:* Jacques Bart, Carl Lerner, Atilio Rinaldi; *M:* Vladimir Ussachevsky
Cast: Carlos Brown, Rita Gamm, Elsa Dorian, Mario Horna

Another version of Sartre's famous drama about three strangers who find they are to spend eternity locked in a seedy hotel room. One is a widely acclaimed journalist, one a social-climbing housewife and the third is a lesbian. Through their isolation they begin to relate stories about themselves and the truth becomes apparent.

No Exit

(aka: Huis Clos)

Audry, Jacqueline
1955; France; 100 min; B&W; Drama
W: Pierre Laroche; *C:* Robert Juillard; *M:* Joseph Kosma
Cast: Arletty, Frank Villard, Gaby Sylvia, Yves Deniaud

A weak man, a sexy woman and an embittered lesbian share the confines of a hotel room for eternity, where they act out their dislikes and rivalry. The film is based on the famous play by Jean-Paul Sartre, where hell is not a place, but other people.

Prod Comp: Les Films Marceau

No One Sleeps

Hick, Jochen
2000; Germany; 108 min; Drama
P: Jochen Hick; *W:* Jochen Hick; *C:* Michael Maley, Tom Harting; *E:* Helga Scharf; *M:* James Hardway
Cast: Tom Wlaschiha, Irit Levi, Jim Thalman, Richard Conti

Stephan arrives in San Francisco to prove that the AIDS Virus was deliberately introduced into the general population. Before his death, Stephan's father, a medical researcher, identified some of the experimenters and survivors involved. Armed with this evidence, Stephan attempts to track them down—only to discover that they are being systematically murdered. (Wolfe)

Prod Comp: Galeria Alaska Productions
Dist/Sales: MediaLuna, Wolfe, 10%

No Ordinary Love

Witkins, Doug
1994; USA; 104 min; Drama
P: Eli Kabillio; *W:* Doug Witkins; *C:* Armando Basulto; *E:* John Orland; *M:* Bob Christianson
Cast: Tymme Reitz, Koing Kuoch

Kevin struggles with his grandchild-obsessed mother. Wendy is a rock singer looking for love in all the wrong places. Andy is a butch bisexual. Vince is a gorgeous young Asian drag-queen. Ben is the new housemate from Hell. No desire is forbidden in this twisted suspense-comedy about a group of 20-something, sexually ambivalent, promiscuous housemates living in the Hollywood Hills.

Prod Comp: No Ordinary Limited Partnership
Dist/Sales: PictureThis!, Wolfe

No Rewind

Mozen, Paula
1992; USA; 23 min; Documentary

Fast-paced documentary that educates teenagers about HIV/AIDS awareness in the 1990s. Teens speak for themselves through interviews and peer-group discussions that promote abstinence and safe-sex education.

No Sad Songs

Sheehan, Nick
1985; Canada; 60 min; Documentary
P: Nick Sheehan; *C:* Paul Mitchnick; *M:* Allen Booth, David Woodhead
Cast: Kate Reid

Jim Black and Catherine Hunt talk about their experiences of living with AIDS. Jim talks about his life, his affection for his best friend, his family's rejection of him and the death he is facing. Catherine talks about her brother who is dying of AIDS.

Prod Comp: AIDS Committee of Toronto, Cell Productions
Dist/Sales: Salzgeber, CFMDC

No Skin Off My Ass

No Skin Off My Ass

La Bruce, Bruce
1990; Canada, Germany; 75 min; B&W; Erotica
W: Bruce La Bruce; *E:* Bruce La Bruce
Cast: Klaus von Brucker, G. B. Jones, Caroline Azar, Bruce La Bruce

Bruce La Bruce, Toronto's underground gay filmmaker extraordinaire, plays a punk hairdresser who picks up a young, baby-faced skinhead in the park and locks him up in his apartment. In this raw and dirty, sweet and charming, and unabashedly erotic movie, Klaus von Brucker suggests a skinhead Joe Dallesandro for the 1990s. Bruce La Bruce's

deadpan style, shot in gritty black and white, belies a keen artistic awareness as he walks a fine line between a home-movie aesthetic and mainstream narrative technique. (MQFF)

Dist/Sales: TLA, Strand, Millivres, ACMI

No Way Out

Donaldson, Roger
1987; USA; 120 min; Thriller
P: Laura Ziskin, Robert Garland, Mace Neufeld; *W:* Robert Garland; *C:* John Alcott; *E:* Neil Travis, William Hoy; *M:* Maurice Jarre
Cast: Kevin Costner, Gene Hackman, Sean Young, Howard Duff, Will Patton

This political sex thriller reworks the plot of the 1947 thriller, *The Big Clock*. Costner plays a Lieutenant-Commander who has an affair with the lover of his boss. The beautiful woman ends up dead and it looks like Costner's the villain. Great suspense drama with a particularly good twist at the end. Will Patton plays Hackman's gay assistant who would do anything for his boss.

Prod Comp: Orion Pictures
Dist/Sales: Roadshow, ReelMovies, MGM, Orion

Noche de Walpurgis, La

Klimovsky, León
1970; Germany, Spain; 85 min; Horror
P: Salvadore Romero; *W:* James Molin, Hank Munkel; *C:* Leopoldo Villasenor; *E:* Tony Grimm; *M:* Antón García Abril
Cast: Paul Naschy, Paty Shepard, Gaby Fuchs, Barbara Capell

This rather incoherent narrative follows the life of the Count Waldemar, a werewolf who is resurrected after doctors remove a silver bullet from his chest. He goes in search of the Countess Waldessa, a vampire who was staked and killed by a cross. With the help of two young female students he revives her. There is a particularly erotic scene when one of the women cuts herself and drips blood into the mouth of the Countess. When she awakens she bites one of the women and abducts the other.

Prod Comp: Plata Films
Dist/Sales: SomethingWeird, Universal

Nocturne (1989)

Harris, Mark T.
1989; USA; 100 min; Drama
P: Mark T. Harris; *W:* Mark T. Harris; *C:* Ed Talavera
Cast: Gabriel Amor, T. Ryder Smith

A contemplative coming-of-age story about Martin, a shy pianist newly arrived in New York, who meets the handsome Gino. Martin thinks he's found his

n

match, but Gino only wants a casual sexual liaison. As Martin slides into obsession he is forced to deal with a terrible secret from his past.

Nocturne (1990)

Chamberlain, Joy
1990; UK; 60 min; Drama
P: Rebecca Dobbs; W: Tash Fairbanks
Cast: Lisa Eichhorn, Maureen O'Brian, Caroline Paterson

This is the story of Marguerite, a 45-year-old woman who returns to her childhood home after an absence of many years to attend her mother's funeral. Discovering that the house itself has the power to repress her in the same way that her mother did, she is determined to find the key to that power and rid herself of its control. The chance intervention of two lesbian runaways with a penchant for role-playing serves as catalyst to release the passions and possibilities that have lain dormant within our heroine.

Prod Comp: Maya Vision, Channel 4
Dist/Sales: MayaVision

Nocturne (1990)

Non, Je Ne Regrette Rien

(aka: No Regret)

Riggs, Marlon
1992; USA; 42 min; Documentary
P: Jonathan Lee

Through music, poetry and quiet—at times chilling—self-disclosure, five sero-positive black gay men speak of their individual confrontations with AIDS, illuminating the difficult journey African–American men make in coping with the personal and social devastation of the epidemic. This is the third film in the series *Fear of Disclosure*. (Frameline)

Dist/Sales: VDB, Frameline

None of the Above

Fowler-Smith, Penny
1993; Australia; 13 min; Drama
P: Sally Regan; W: Penny Fowler-Smith, Linda Murdoch

Is this a hard-nosed investigation of the world of bondage and discipline? A light-hearted musical tribute to dominance and submission? A dark journey through the steamy underbelly of adult perversion? Or is it none of the above?

Prod Comp: Australian Film TV & Radio School
Dist/Sales: AFTRS

None of the Above

Norang Mori 2

(aka: Running Blue; Yellow Hair 2)

Kim, Yoo-min
2001; Korea; 102 min; Drama
W: Yoo-min Kim; C: Kang-min Lee, Dong-eun Kim
Cast: Ri-soo Ha, Yi Shin, Hong-jin Mo, Chan Yoon

Three lonely outcasts unexpectedly meet at a convenient store and find themselves caught in a murder. One is an aspiring actress, named Y, who is used by a deceitful agent that promises to make her into a star. Another is an aspiring student filmmaker, named R, who searches for the truth with his camera and videotapes anything he finds interesting. Finally, there's a motorcycle delivery girl, named J, who dreams to fall in love again, but must cope with her transsexual identity in a society that finds it hard to tolerate. These three hide the body in storage and bolt out of the store. Three strangers, having to hide in the dark corners of the streets, experience a fast-paced journey they'll never forget. (Cinema Service) Korean with English subtitles.

Prod Comp: Fiction Bank
Dist/Sales: CinemaService

Norman, is that You?

Schlatter, George
1976; USA; 90 min; Comedy
P: George Schlatter; *W:* George Schlatter; *C:* Gayne Rescher; *E:* George Folsey Jnr; *M:* William Goldstein
Cast: Dennis Dugan, Michael Warren, Tamara Dobson, Redd Foxx, Pearl Bailey

Norman, a 23-year-old black man, and his lover, Garson, who is white, find themselves in some tricky and humorous situations when Norman's parents, who don't know he's gay, come to visit.

Prod Comp: MGM
Dist/Sales: ReelMovies, NFVLS, Swank

North of Vortex

Giannaris, Constantine
1991; UK; 60 min; B&W; Drama
P: Rebecca Dobbs; *W:* Paul Hallam; *C:* James Welland; *E:* Deborah Field; *M:* John Eacott
Cast: Stavros Zalmas, Howard Napper, Valda Drabla

This rapturously beautiful black-and-white road movie follows a trio of characters—a poet, a sailor and a girl named Jackie—through a sensual, but ultimately tragic love triangle.

Dist/Sales: WaterBearer, Salzgeber, MayaVision, ACMI

Not all Parents are Straight

1986; USA; 60 min; Documentary
P: Kevin White, Annamarie Faro

This film examines the dynamic of the parent-child relationship within several different households where children are being raised by gay and lesbian parents. Through open and honest interviews with the children and their parents, the film explores emotional conflicts within the family, legal custody problems and the social discrimination that these families face.

Dist/Sales: CinemaGuild

Not Alone: A Hallowe'en Romance

Hasick, Paul
1995; Canada; 26 min; Comedy

Mushroom soup, an anti-gay bashing march, and a surprise dinner guest are the background for this story about one young gay man, his semi-dream lover, and his mischievous dyke roommate. A comedic portrait of one man's failed attempts to avoid a relationship before it even develops. (CFMDC)

Dist/Sales: CFMDC

Not Angels, But Angels

Grodecki, Wiktor
1994; Czechoslovakia; 80 min; Documentary
P: Frank Beauvais, Peter Lencses, Miro Vostiar;
W: Wiktor Grodecki; *C:* Vladimír Holomek;
E: Wiktor Grodecki; *M:* Jan Cenek

Set in Prague, this moving documentary about teenage boy prostitutes, whose best customers are tourists, is astonishingly frank and unsentimental. The story is told through a series of interviews with 19 young men.

Dist/Sales: WaterBearer, Salzgeber

Not Just Passing Through

Carlomusto, Jean / Gund Saalfield, Catherine / Perez, Dolores / Thistlethwaite, Polly
1994; USA; 54 min; Documentary

This film is a celebration of the richness of lesbian life. Photographs and oral history pay tribute to African–American Mabel Hampton (1902–89), who helped inspire the founding of the Lesbian Herstory Archives. The rescue of Marge McDonald's collection of diaries, books and artefacts documenting her life in the Midwest in the 1950s is recorded in two parts. Part Three focuses on Asian Lesbians of the East Coast, an organisation that is a source of support and pride for its members. Part Four takes us backstage to the New York's WOW Cafe where theatre and comedy explode oppressive images. (WMM)

Dist/Sales: WMM

Not Love, Just Frenzy

(aka: Mas Que Amor, Frenesi)

Albacete, Alfonso / Bardem, Miquel / Menkes, David
1996; Spain; 104 min; Drama
P: Fernando Colomo, Beatriz de la Gándara; *W:* Alfonso Albacete, Miquel Bardem, David Menkes; *C:* Néstor Calvo; *E:* Miguel Angel Santamaria; *M:* Juan Bardem
Cast: Nancho Novo, Cayetana Guillen Cuervo, Ingrid Rubio, Beatriz Santiago

The story of a sexual crime, of young people who play with fire, who disguise the truth and try to make it what they would like it to be. It is a film of emotions in which love is confused with desire and the fear of being alone. Secrets, confession, crazy happenings, dreams, outbursts, disappointments and escape. Characters who look for friendship, love their own identity or just money... in sex. They all

n

have three things in common: their youth, music and the furious delirium that is 'Not Love, Just Frenzy.' (Jour de Fete)
Spanish with English subtitles.

Prod Comp: Canal+ España, Television Española
Dist/Sales: TLA, Wolfe

Notorious C.H.O.

Machado, Lorene
2002; USA; 95 min; Comedy
P: Lorene Machado; *W:* Margaret Cho; *C:* Kirk Miller;
E: Lorene Machado

Filmed live in Seattle, bisexual comedienne Margaret Cho's hilarious follow-up to her hit comedy *I'm the One That I Want* captures Cho's boisterously entertaining one-woman show, which successfully toured thirty-seven cities throughout North America in 2001–2. (Wolfe)

Prod Comp: Cho Taussig Productions
Dist/Sales: Vagrant, Wellspring, Wolfe

November Moon

(aka: Novembermond)

von Grote, Alexandra
1985; Germany; 107 min; Drama
W: Alexandra von Grote; *C:* Bernard Zitzermann; *E:*
Susanne Lahaye; *M:* Egisto Macchi
Cast: Gabriela Osburg, Christine Millet, Daniele Delorme, Bruno Pradal

Set in 1939, a Jewish girl called November flees Germany for Paris, where she meets and falls in love with another woman Ferial. The film charts the development of their relationship and parallels the emergent events of the Second World War. When the Nazis occupy France their relationship is jeopardised, they have to separate, and with the help of the French underground, November is hidden. Ferial works for the Nazi information department in the hope of shielding her lover from detection. When the Allies liberate France, the women should be safe from persecution. The violence of the Nazis is, however, replaced by that of the Resistance who take unrestrained vengeance on those they perceive as collaborators—such as Ferial.

Dist/Sales: Cinenova, Wolfe, BFI

Nowhere

Araki, Gregg
1997; USA; 82 min; Drama
P: Gregg Araki, Andrea Sperling; *W:* Gregg Araki;
C: Arturo Smith; *E:* Gregg Araki
Cast: James Duval, Rachel True, Nathan Bexton, Debi Mazar

A darkly funny film which tackles teen angst with a

vengeance. An overtly sexual and achingly real look at an 18-year-old searching for love. (Wolfe)

Prod Comp: Why Not Productions
Dist/Sales: FineLine, Wolfe, Haut-et-Court

Nuestra Salud: Violencia Domestica

Cuadra, Teresa / Newman, Suzanne
1999; USA; 17 min; Documentary

Is there domestic violence between women? What are the signs of an abusive relationship? Lesbian Latinas in the US share their stories and insight to create a moving portrait of a hidden problem.

Dist/Sales: Salud, Fanlight

Number 96

Number 96

Bernardos, Peter
1974; Australia; 113 min; Drama
P: Bill Harmon; *W:* David Sale, Johnny Whyte;
C: John McLean; *E:* Alan Lake, Ron Williams;
M: Tommy Tycho
Cast: Johnny Lockwood, Philippa Baker, Gordon McDougall, Sheila Kennedy, Pat McDonald

A movie length spin-off of the Australian television series, this high camp, high drama theatrical release was filmed with the same cast and the same episodic formula, with pack-rape, attempted murders, suicide, homosexuality, alcoholism and marriage.

Prod Comp: Cash-Harmon

Nun, The

(aka: La Religieuse)

Rivette, Jacques
1966; France; 130 min; Drama
P: Georges de Beauregard; *W:* Jacques Rivette, Jean Gruault; *C:* Alain Levent; *E:* Denise de Casabianca;
M: Jean-Claude Eloy
Cast: Anna Karina, Liselotte Pulver, Micheline Presle, Christine Lenier

Based on Diderot's novel of 18th century convent life, this film is one of the towering achievements of French cinema in the 1960s. A young woman is forced to join a convent where, half-starved and beaten, she fails to take her annual vows. She is sent to another convent where the Mother Superior makes lesbian advances towards her. She escapes with the help of a priest but is almost raped by him. Banned in France because of its anticlericalism. French with English subtitles.

Prod Comp: Films Rome-Paris, SDC
Dist/Sales: Ascanbee

Nunzio's Second Cousin

DeCerchio, Tom
1994; USA; 18 min; Drama

A gay detective gets revenge on a young gay basher. An early role for Hollywood actor Vincent D'Onofrio.

Dist/Sales: Strand

O Boys: Parties, Porn & Politics, The

Gassman, Allan
1999; USA; 66 min; Documentary
M: Michael Callen

The O Boys is Allan Gassman's award winning and provocative behind-the-scenes look at LA's notorious O Boy private orgies. The O Boys organisation began in the early 1990s with LA's hottest hunks combining safe sex education with group sex theme parties. Their strategy was to reclaim sex and desire from an era of dread and self-hatred by establishing an unadulterated group sex practice. Underlying the numerous hard-core sequences featured in the film is the emphasis on safe sex in all its multifunctional possibilities, with strict rules and procedures applying to all participants. This sexually charged documentary is efficiently paced for maximum pleasure, as all decorum and modesty is left on the cutting room floor. (MQFF)

Dist/Sales: Gassman

Object of My Affection, The

Hytner, Nicholas
1998; USA; 112 min; Drama
P: Laurence Mark; *W:* Wendy Wasserstein;
C: Oliver Stapleton; *E:* Tariq Anwar; *M:* George Fenton
Cast: Paul Rudd, Jennifer Aniston, Alan Alda, Allison Janney, John Pankow

When George Hanson is dumped by his boyfriend, Nina Borowski is sympathetic and offers him a spare room in her Brooklyn apartment. In a few months Nina and George become the best of friends, which is fairly unsettling to Nina's boyfriend Vince. But

things get even more disturbing for Vince when Nina announces she is pregnant and wants to bring the child up with George instead.

Prod Comp: 20th Century-Fox
Dist/Sales: 20thCenturyFox, Wolfe

Odd Girl Out

Carland, Tammy Rae
1994; USA; 17 min; Experimental

Video diary relating the filmmaker's crush on a school friend.

Ode

Reichardt, Kelly
1999; USA; 50 min; Drama

Scorning the demands of her overbearing family, Bobbie Lee Hartley and Billy Joe McAllister meet at their usual Choctaw Ridge trysting place and attempt to consummate their forbidden love. Using the storied love of Bobbie Lee and Billy Joe as its crucial metaphor, *Ode* attempts to reconcile modern moralities with a tradition-bound faith, and asks whether it's possible to commit a sin against a religion that won't even have you as a member.

Ode to Billy Joe

Baer, Max
1976; USA; 100 min; Drama
P: Max Baer, Roger Camras; *W:* Herman Raucher;
C: Michel Hugo; *E:* Frank E. Morris; *M:* Michel Legrand
Cast: Robby Benson, Glynnis O'Connor, Joan Hotchkis, Sandy McPeak

Bobbie Gentry's song gets turned into a movie and you get to find out what Billy Joe was doing up there on Tallahatchee Bridge. Billie's desperate to lose his virginity but his girlfriend won't come forth. He winds up in bed with another boy. The next day, feeling ashamed and disgraced and unable to prove his manhood to his girl, he plunges to his death.

Prod Comp: Warner
Dist/Sales: Warner

Off the Straight and Narrow: Lesbians, Gays, Bisexuals and Television

Sender, Katherine
1998; USA; 63 min; Documentary
P: Katherine Sender; *W:* Katherine Sender; *E:* Katherine Sender

Off the Straight and Narrow has been acclaimed as the first in-depth documentary to cast a critical eye over the growth of gay, lesbian and queer images on TV. It does for television what *The Silver Screen: Color Me Lavender* did for the big screen. Media scholars from diverse perspectives deconstruct three decades of news coverage, sitcoms, TV dramas, talk shows, sports and commercials. A fine scalpel is used to make incisions into the coverage of Rock Hudson's death in 1985, Andrew Cunanan's murder of Gianni Versace, and Ellen's coming out. Through a panoramic lens, *Off the Straight and Narrow* navigates the TV landscape from virtual invisibility before 1970 to 'gay chic' of the 1990s.

Prod Comp: Media Education Foundation
Dist/Sales: MediaEdFound

Offering, The

Lee, Paul
1999; Canada; 10 min; Drama
W: Paul Lee

A meditation on the passing of life, through the story of love and friendship between a Japanese monk and his novice. In rejecting his own faith and drowning in self-doubts, the novice leaves his life of unfulfilled potentials. (CFMDC)

Prod Comp: Ganymedia Inc
Dist/Sales: CFMDC

Oh Baby, a Baby!

(aka: Zwei Frauen, ein Mann und ein Baby)

Murnberger, Wolfgang
1999; Austria; 91 min; Comedy
P: Danny Krausz, Kurt Stocker; *W:* Sabine Reichel;
C: Helmut Wimmer; *E:* Uschi Efber;
M: Stefan Bernheimer
Cast: Nicloe Ansari, Eva Herzig, Ralf Bauer, Peter Matic, Viktoria Schubert

Sandra and Iris' eight year relationship has stalled. Sandra is a very sexy and successful architect, and Iris is a florist who's addicted to romance and yearns for a baby—only trouble is, Sandra is not too keen. While Sandra ruminates, Iris begins her search for the perfect donor, quickly seizing upon good-looking Antonio when he finds himself in her florist shop. After a drunken night at a bar with Iris, Antonio agrees to be the couple's donor. Meanwhile Sandra has begun lusting after the gorgeous new architect at work, and soon begins an affair with him. Convinced that Sandra would make the perfect mother, Iris surprises Sandra with the sperm and she is inseminated. Soon after Sandra finds she's pregnant, and in true screwball tradition, things begins to get really complicated. What ensues is a riotous comedy of misunderstandings, raunchy sex scenes and surprises—and a wedding that could have any number of brides turning up! German dubbed into English.

Prod Comp: ORF, RLT
Dist/Sales: ORF

Oi Queer

Reding, Benjamin / Reding, Dominik
1996; UK; 13 min; Drama
P: Dominik Reding, Benjamin Reding

A skinhead must decide between his gang and his boyfriend.

Oi! Warning

Reding, Benjamin / Reding, Dominik
1999; Germany; 90 min; B&W; Drama
W: Benjamin Reding, Dominik Reding;
C: Axel Henschel; *E:* Margot Neubert-Maric;
M: Tom Ammermann
Cast: Sascha Backhaus, Simon Goerts, Sandra Borgmann, Jens Veith

A disconcerting and intense first film by the twins Dominik and Benjamin Reding, following the trajectory of a boy in a crisis of identity. He is in search of his masculinity in a world where all of the male standards have been lost. Janosch is tired of his life with the family, impatient to prove that he is now a man, and he seeks out his former school friend Koma. He must base himself on a model, and Koma—now a skinhead, although with no clear vision of what this might, in fact, represent—is happy to have an admirer, someone who will follow him. Koma transforms Janosch into a replica of himself. When Janosch, however, meets Zottel, a stranger, proud of being leftist, he romantically changes position and arouses Koma's wrath. The consequences are tragic. Lyrical, but frightening, the film provides evidence of homophobic violence. It is also a technical tour-de-force with a fine sound track and black and white photography that evokes the beauty and balance that Janosch seeks, and the cruelty he will encounter. (www.mostra.org) German with English subtitles.

Prod Comp: Schlammtaucher Filmproduktion
Dist/Sales: Schlammtaucher

Okoge

Nakajima, Takehiro
1992; Japan; 120 min; Comedy
P: Yoshinori Takazawa, Masashi Moromizato;
W: Takehiro Nakajima; *C:* Yoshimasa Hakata; *E:* Kenji Goto; *M:* Hiroshi Ariyoshi
Cast: Misa Shimizu, Takehiro Murata, Takeo Nakahara

A clever satire of Japanese morés focusing on a young woman, Sayoko, who becomes friends with Goh, a leather craftsman, and his lover, Tochi. The only problem is that Tochi is married and his wife threatens to reveal his homosexuality if he does not break up with Goh. So Sayoko offers them her apartment for their secret rendezvous. But Goh's happiness disintegrates when Tochi finally returns to his wife. Japanese with English subtitles.

Prod Comp: Nakajima Productions, Into Group

Olga's Girls

Mawra, Joseph P.
1964; USA; 72 min; Erotica, Comedy
P: George Weiss; *C:* Warner Rose; *M:* Clyde Otis
Cast: Gil Adams, Rita Barrie, Rickey Bell, Audrey Campbell, Ava Denning

Headquartered in New York's Chinatown, where Communists provide a steady stream of dangerous drugs from the Orient, sadist Olga Saglo deals in narcotics and white slavery. Her drug-addicted slaves, brutally tortured for the slightest offense, some of them locked into chastity belts, have only one another for comfort. When Olga suspects there is an informant among them, she stops at nothing in trying to ferret out the snitch. But some of her girls have another plan in mind, a plan of revenge... A classic of early sexploitation films, *Olga's Girls* deserves its place in the pantheon of classic cult films. (First Run Features)

Dist/Sales: SomethingWeird, FirstRunFeatures

Olive Tree, The

Camarda, George
1999; USA; 26 min; Drama

Eddie is devastated when he finds his best friend has decided to get someone else to father her child.

Oliver

Deocampo, Nick
1983; Philippines; Documentary
W: Nick Deocampo

Oliver, although married with a child, refers to himself as gay. He supports his family by working in a Manila bar with his drag act. A graphic look at poverty and prostitution in the Philippines. Tagalog with English subtitles.

Olivia

(aka: The Pit of Loneliness)

Audry, Jacqueline
1950; France; 88 min; B&W; Drama
W: Colette Audry, Pierre Laroche; *C:* Christian Matras;
M: Pierre Sancan
Cast: Edwige Feuillère, Simone Simon, Claire Olivia, Suzanne Dehelly

A lesbian cult classic, rarely screened. This film comes with great credentials—a screenplay by Colette, based on Dorothy Busey Strachey's superbly written autobiographical novella of the same name. *Olivia* has often been described as the French version of the German classic *Mädchen in Uniform*. But where *Mädchen* inhabits a harshly disciplined and militaristic world, the school in *Olivia* provides a luxurious and sensuously Gallic backdrop for the action. Here the schoolgirls have single rooms with lacy bedspreads. The school is run by two headmistresses and any newcomers are swiftly divided into one of the two camps/fan clubs. New girl Olivia is immediately attracted to Mademoiselle Julie. It seems the passion is mutual as the simpering Mademoiselle Cara is soon fiercely jealous. One of the film's highlights is Feuillère's inspiring performance as Mademoiselle Julie. Her late night offer of a sweet to the adoring Olivia is one that none could refuse. (MQFF)

Prod Comp: Memnon Films; *Dist/Sales:* Cinenova

Olivier, Olivier

Holland, Agnieszka
1992; France; 110 min; Drama
P: Marie-Laure Reyre; *W:* Agnieszka Holland;
C: Bernard Zitzermann; *E:* Isabelle Lorente;
M: Zbigniew Preisner
Cast: Grégoire Colin, Marina Golovine, Frédéric Quiring, François Cluzet, Faye Gatteau

A family's life is destroyed when their youngest child, Olivier, goes missing. Six years later he returns and re-establishes his relationship with his sister and parents after years on the streets as a homosexual prostitute. But the question soon arises, is he really Olivier? Some very fine performances make this true story a powerful and absorbing film. French with English subtitles.

Prod Comp: Oliane Productions, Canal, Sofica Investimage 3, CNC
Dist/Sales: NewVision, 21stCentury, SonyClassics

On Becoming

Rizzo, Teresa
1993; Australia; 26 min; Documentary

Documentary which looks at the concept of gender and gender fluidity. A visual affirmation and exploration of the concept that gender is a performance that needs to be thought outside dualisms and binaries.

Dist/Sales: NFVLS

On Being Gay: A Conversation with Brian McNaughton

1986; Ireland; 80 min; Documentary

An entertaining documentary by the lecturer, counsellor, activist and Irish Catholic, Brian McNaughton, about being gay in the straight world.

O

On Guard

On Guard

Lambert, Susan
1984; Australia; 52 min; Drama
P: Digby Duncan; *W:* Sarah Gibson, Susan Lambert; *C:* Laurie McInnes; *E:* Catherine Murphy
Cast: Liddy Clark, Jan Cornall, Kerry Dwyer, Mystery Carnage

Four women plan to sabotage a firm involved in reproductive engineering. Within the form of an adventure film, the women's sexuality and emotional lives are explored together with the complexity of their domestic responsibilities. Tensions increase between the women as the day of the heist draws near. One of the characters is a lesbian and in a relationship with another woman who has children. Conflicts arise as her care for her children interrupts their affair.

Prod Comp: Women's Film Fund, Australian Film Commission, Red Heart Pictures
Dist/Sales: NFVLS, ACMI

ON_LINE

Weintroub, Jed
2001; USA; 86 min; Drama
P: Tanya Selvar, Adam Brightman, Tavin Marin Titus;
W: Andrew Osborne, Jed Weintroub; *C:* Toshiaki Ozawa; *E:* Stephanie Sterner; *M:* Roger Neill
Cast: Josh Hamilton, Harold Perrineau, Isabel Gillies, John Fleck

Set deep in the world of cyberspace, this favourite from the Sundance and Berlin film festivals, is a humorous and engaging inquiry into the quest for sexual fulfilment, human contact and love. John and Moe are old college buddies who start a cyberporn site called Intercon-X that links visitors to live erotic chat sessions. John spends most of his time managing the site (i.e., watching the sessions), while Moe indulges in real-life sexual fantasies with his new girlfriend Moira, another web junky. Among Intercon's most popular hosts is gay 'daddy' Al, who's in a cyber-relationship with Ed, a hungry gay college student from Ohio. Director Jed Weintrob employs groundbreaking new digital technology, including expert use of split-screen images, to create a very believable online world where six characters learn about what it is they really want. (2002 LA Outfest)

Prod Comp: Internet Stories Productions
Dist/Sales: Indican

On the Bus

Black, Dustin Lance
2001; USA; 100 min; Documentary
Cast: Dustin Lance Black, Billy Kaufman, Charles Kinsley, Jason Webb

On the Bus is a self-aware documentary covering the stories of five young men (including the producer and director) who have all just become a part of a 'Real World-esque' television show. Together, they are travelling to the wild Burning Man pagan festival. Included in this trip is Damon, a bitingly witty music composer; JMY, a Swedish Olympic diver; Billy, the intellectual; Jason, a young porn star; Charles, the beautiful guy everyone lusts after; and Lance, the narrator. As they get to love—and hate—each other, the erotic tension builds, spilling over when they reach the festival with its 'anything goes' party atmosphere. (Wolfe)

Dist/Sales: SockPuppet, Wolfe, 10%

Once is not Enough

(aka: Jacqueline Susann's Once is not Enough)

Green, Guy
1975; USA; 121 min; Drama
P: Howard W. Koch Jnr; *W:* Julius J. Epstein;
C: John A. Alonzo; *E:* Rita Roland; *M:* Henry Mancini
Cast: Kirk Douglas, Alexis Smith, David Janssen, George Hamilton, Brenda Vaccaro

A film based on Jacqueline Susann's trashy novel of the scandalous goings-on among celebrities and a young woman, who is fixated on her father.

Prod Comp: Paramount, Aries Productions, Sujac Productions
Dist/Sales: ReelMovies, Paramount

Once upon a Time in the East

(aka: Il était une fois dans l'est)

Brassard, André
1974; Canada; 100 min; Drama
P: Pierre Lamy; *W:* Michel Tremblay, André Brassard; *C:* Paul van der Linden; *E:* André Corriveau; *M:* Jacques Perron
Cast: Denise Filiatrault, Michelle Rossignol, Frédérique Collin

> The first feature film by stage director André Brassard centres on the lives of a number of people who frequent a transvestite nightclub. They range from a young man preparing to do the drag performance of his life as Cleopatra, to a young girl thinking about having an abortion, and an old woman who wins one million trading stamps. The lives of people who are living on the edges of conventional society are dealt with empathy and humour. French with English subtitles.

Prod Comp: Les Productions Carle-Lamy

On the Bus

One Nation Under God

Maniaci, Teodoro / Rzeznick, Francine
1993; USA; 83 min; Documentary

> *One Nation Under God* is a comprehensive historical document of homosexuality in America over the past 30 years. It focuses on the discursive construction of homosexuality as an undesirable and reversible condition, an 'illness' that both religion and science have tried to eradicate through a variety of techniques, including aversion therapy, exorcisms and 'orgasmic reorientation'. The film documents the work of Exodus International (the male founders of which left and fell in love with each other) and its efforts to assist recovery from 'sexual brokenness'. Through interviews with psychologists, activists, conservatives and case studies of former 'ex-gays', *One Nation Under God* presents a powerful picture of the historical, political, social and religious fight for and against gay rights. (MQFF)

Awards: San Francisco International Lesbian & Gay Film Festival, 1993: Audience Award for Best Documentary
Dist/Sales: FirstRunFeatures, FilmsTransit, Wolfe

One of Them

Main, Stewart
1997; New Zealand; 46 min; Drama
P: Michele Fantl; *W:* Peter Wells

> Two teenage boys come to grips with their homosexuality in the bleak and punitive environment of post-war 1960s New Zealand. Lemmy and Jamie are in denial about their attraction for men, and one another. A film that deals with growing up gay and youth suicide.

Prod Comp: Zee Films
Dist/Sales: NZFC, FirstRunFeatures, Wolfe, ACMI, NFBC

One + One

Chiang, S. Leo
2001; USA; 27 min; Documentary

> John and Noel are in a panic. The condom broke during sex, and John happens to have AIDS. Joanne breaks down when the counsellor asks about her HIV-positive husband Robert. In their six-year marriage, Joanne has been tested twice a year, each time more stressful than the last. *One + One* takes an unflinching look at the lives of two couples—one straight, one gay—as they navigate the sexual and emotional minefield inherent in every sero-discordant (mixed HIV status) relationship. This poignant film gives insights to how sero-discordant couples cope with the difficult task of negotiating death and love on a daily basis, and the deep bond they share because of it. (New Day Films)

Dist/Sales: WalkingIris, NewDay

One Shadowless Hour

Sasagawa, Narusa
1995; Japan; 30 min; Documentary

> A documentary on the second Tokyo Lesbian and Gay Parade with interviews with some of the women involved, depicting the diverse lifestyles and backgrounds of lesbians living in Japan.

One Small Step

Crouch, Catherine
1999; USA; 30 min; Comedy, Drama

Set in South Carolina on the event of the 1969 Apollo 11 moon walk, this film is a dramatic comedy about a rambunctious 8-year-old tomboy whose parents teach her that she can do anything she wants. She learns there is one exception when she announces that she wants to marry the girl next door.

Dist/Sales: CFMDC

Only the Brave

Only the Brave

Kokkinos, Ana
1994; Australia; 61 min; Drama
P: Fiona Eagger; *W:* Ana Kokkinos, Mira Robertson; *C:* Jaems Grant; *E:* Mark Atkin; *M:* Philip Brophy
Cast: Elena Mandalis, Dora Kaskanis, Maude Davey, Helen Athanasiadis, Bob Bright

Alex and Vicki are wild girls living life on the edge. They share a dream: to leave school and go north. But the tension between them grows when Alex begins to acknowledge her attraction to Vicki. Their lives move out of control toward a harrowing climax. A powerful and touching film about two Australian-Greek girls growing up on Melbourne's outer western edge, marked by great performances and brilliant direction from Kokkinos.

Awards: Australian Film Institute Awards, 1994: Best Short Film, Screenplay; San Francisco International Lesbian & Gay Film Festival, 1994 Audience Award for Best Feature
Prod Comp: Pickpocket Films
Dist/Sales: NFVLS, NewVision, 21stCentury, FirstRunFeatures, ACMI

Only When I Laugh

Jordan, Glenn
1981; USA; 120 min; Comedy, Drama
P: Roger M. Rothstein, Neil Simon; *W:* Neil Simon;
C: David M. Walsh; *E:* John Wright; *M:* David Shire
Cast: Marsha Mason, Kristy McNichol, James Coco, Joan Hackett

A 17-year-old girl moves back in with her mother, who gave up custody of her six years previously. As they get to know one another again, their relationship evolves from that of strangers to mother and daughter. James Coco plays the mother's best friend, a struggling gay actor.

Prod Comp: Columbia, Rastar
Dist/Sales: Col-Tri, 16MM, Columbia

Opening Closet X: A Voice for Queer Youth

Kelly, Max / Polish, Diana
1998; USA; 17 min; Documentary

A diverse, short documentary, that deals with gay, lesbian and transgender youth. Raw and thought provoking.

Opposite of Sex, The

Roos, Don
1998; USA; 105 min; Drama
P: Michael Besman, David Kirkpatrick; *W:* Don Roos;
C: Hubert Taczanowski; *E:* David Codron;
M: Mason Daring
Cast: Christina Ricci, Lisa Kudrow, Martin Donovan, Ivan Sergei, Lyle Lovett

Dedee Truitt is 16 and runs away to live with her half brother Bill, managing to turn his life upside down in the process. Bill is a dedicated and caring teacher who happens to be gay. After his long-time partner has died, he tries to resurrect his life with his new boyfriend Matt. Lucia, a friend of Bill's distrusts the newcomer and tries to protect Bill. Her suspicions are confirmed when Dedee seduces Matt and gets him to steal $10,000.

Prod Comp: Rysher Entertainment
Dist/Sales: Col-Tri, 16MM, SonyClassics, Wolfe, ACMI

Oranges are not the Only Fruit

Kidron, Beeban
1989; UK; 205 min; Drama
P: Phillippa Giles; *W:* Jeanette Winterson;
C: Ian Punter; *E:* John Strickland; *M:* Rachel Portman
Cast: Geraldine McEwan, Charlotte Coleman, Margery Withers, Cathryn Bradshaw

A humorous and sometimes sad and touching look at the coming-of-age of a young lesbian, Jess. Jess' mother is a fiercely Charismatic Evangelist who fights to dominate and suppress Jess who was adopted from birth. She wants her to become a missionary but Jess has other ideas and interests, particularly the bewitching Melanie, an older

O

woman. Based on the novel by Jeanette Winterson *Oranges Are Not the Only Fruit* was a landmark lesbian made-for-television movie.

Awards: San Francisco International Lesbian & Gay Film Festival, 1990: Audience Award for Best Feature
Prod Comp: BBC
Dist/Sales: BBC-Enterprises, NFVLS

Order to Kill

(aka: El Clan de los Immorales)

Gutiérrez Maesso, José
1973; Italy; 90 min; Thriller
W: Massimo De Rita, José Gutiérrez Maesso, Eugenio Martín, Santiago Moncada; *C:* Aiace Parolin;
E: Ángel Serrano; *M:* Adolfo Waitzman
Cast: Helmut Berger, Sydne Rome, José Ferrer, Kevin McCarthy, Elena Berrido

An action drama about an assassin who is ordered to kill an old friend, and the repercussions when he refuses. At the same time, although it has nothing to do with the plot, there seems to be a relentless undercurrent of sadism and masochism with a homosexual aura.

Prod Comp: BRC Produzione Film, Excisa SA, FRAL, Televisión y Cine SA
Dist/Sales: Roadshow, VSM

Ordinary Sinner

Ordinary Sinner

Davis, John Henry
2001; USA; 93 min; Drama
P: J. B. White, John Henry Davis, Chris Bongirne;
W: William Mahone; *C:* Mathieu Roberts;
E: Paul Zehrer; *M:* Brian Adler
Cast: Brendan P. Hines, Kris Park, Elizabeth Banks, Joshua Harto

A compelling tale of three college students on the brink of adulthood, struggling to find their place in a violent and profane world. It is a story of friendship, love and betrayal, as well as a look at the way religion in America both supports and condemns

violence against gays. Shot on location in the beautiful Vermont countryside, this coming of age drama delivers a moral tale that rocks the lives of its complex characters. (2002 Stonybrook Film Festival)

Prod Comp: Magic Lantern, Shorelands Productions
Dist/Sales: Shorelands

Orientations

Fung, Richard
1984; Canada; 56 min; Documentary

Men and women of different Asian backgrounds speak frankly, humorously and often poignantly about their lives as members of a minority within a minority. They speak about coming out, homophobia, racism, cultural identity, sex, and the ways that being gay and Asian have shaped who they are.

Dist/Sales: TWN

Original Schtick

Wszelaki, Maciej
1999; Australia; 55 min; Documentary
P: Bronwyne Smith, Peter George; *C:* Maciej Wszelaki;
E: Jane Usher; *M:* Stephen Joyce

In 1997, a flamboyant American artist, Bob Fischer, came to Melbourne from California to work with local artists and stage exhibitions of his work. He wanted stellar fame and recognition, and was willing to do anything for his 15 minutes in the limelight. By ruthlessly manipulating the media and Melbourne's art world, Bob created a chain reaction of ill-fated events that veer wildly from the hilarious and peculiar to the disastrous. (www.sbs.com)

Prod Comp: Windy City Warhol Productions

Orlando

Orlando

Potter, Sally
1992; UK; 92 min; Drama
P: Christopher Sheppard; *W:* Sally Potter;
C: Alexei Rodionov; *E:* Hervé Schneid; *M:* David Bedford, Fred Frith, David Motion, Sally Potter

Cast: Tilda Swinton, Billy Zane, Charlotte Valandrey, Quentin Crisp, Dudley Sutton

An exciting and witty adaptation of Virginia Woolf's 1928 novel structured around the intriguing notion of a character who lived for 400 years, changing sex during time. Some fantastic casting with Quentin Crisp as the ageing Queen Elizabeth I; and delightful scenes of Swinton, playing a man, seducing beautiful women. Directing her first feature Sally Potter has made a ravishing film translation of one of the 20th century's most controversial novels.

Prod Comp: Adventure Pictures, Lenfilm, Mikado Film, Rio Sigma Film
Dist/Sales: Ronin, ACMI, NewYorker, Wolfe, Cowboy

O▶ Osaka Story

Nakata, Toichi
1994; UK; 75 min; Documentary
P: Ichiro Matsumoto, Toichi Nakata; *W:* Toichi Nakata;
C: Simon Atkins; *E:* Toichi Nakata

The Nakatas are a family of conflicting Korean and Japanese cultures. Toichi's father, a Korean immigrant, cannot reconcile his Korean and his wife's Japanese families. Toichi's mother is preoccupied with her present and future position, his brother is torn between the family business empire and a cult religious sect, and his sister has opted out of the scenario altogether to go her own way. Tolstoy may have been correct in his assessment that every family is unhappy in its own way, but the problems of the Nakata family seem universal. The filmmaker himself is not exempt. Should he return to Japan and fulfil the traditional role of an eldest son? Or should he come out to his family with his homosexuality and choose his own way forward? (First Run/Icarus) Japanese & Korean with English subtitles.

Dist/Sales: FirstRun/Icarus, Uplink

Other Mothers

Shallat, Lee
1993; USA; 54 min; Drama
Cast: Meredeth Baxter Birney, Joanna Cassidy, Justin Whalin

Made for television drama about a teenage boy who is shunned by his homophobic school friends because his mother is in a relationship with another woman. They think that he might be gay and feel they'll be guilty by association.

Other Side, The

(aka: Del Otro Lado)

Griffith, C. A.
1999; Mexico, USA; 79 min; Drama
P: Mario Callitzin, Gustavo Cravioto, C. A. Griffith;

C: Juan Carlos Martin Torres
Cast: Eduardo Lopez Rojas, Patricia Reyes Spindola, Maria Ybarra, Gustavo Cravioto

The Other Side is a tale about love, trust, AIDS and Immigration as well as an intimate portrait of a gay couple living in Mexico. Alejandro and Beto live an almost idyllic life except that Alejandro must live with the challenge of having AIDS. Lifesaving medication is unavailable in Mexico and he must travel to the US for treatment but unfortunately his visa is rejected. He must decide whether to wait for treatment in Mexico, or cross the border illegally. Spanish with English subtitles.

Prod Comp: Dos Espiritus
Dist/Sales: DosEspiritus

Other Voices, Other Rooms

Rocksavage, David
1997; UK, USA; 95 min; Drama
P: Peter Wentworth; *W:* David Rocksavage, Sara Flanigan; *C:* Paul Ryan; *E:* Cynthia Scheider;
M: Chris Hajian
Cast: Lothaire Bluteau, Anna Thomson, David Speck, April Turner, Frank Taylor

Based on Truman Capote's highly acclaimed first novel, the film follows a young boy's odyssey of self-discovery as he seeks to solve the puzzle surrounding his father's infirmity. Joel Sansom, a young by of 13, is summoned to a sprawling decaying plantation house in the deep South to meet the father he has not seen for nine years. On his arrival, he meets Amy Skully, the mistress of the house, and Randolph, her debauched and eccentric cousin. His father is nowhere in sight. Joel later discovers the man lying paralysed in the attic of the crumbling mansion, whereupon he begins to unravel the mysterious secrets that lie within the house. (Artistic License Films)

Prod Comp: Golden Eye Films
Dist/Sales: ArtisticLicense

Otra Historia de Amour

(aka: Another Love Story)

de Zárate, Américo Ortiz
1986; Argentina; 80 min; Drama
W: Américo Ortiz de Zárate; *C:* Hector Morini
Cast: Arturo Bonín, Mario Passik, Carlos Muñoz, María José Demare

Set in contemporary Argentina, the film centres on Jorge, a brash and attractive clerk who knows what he wants from life and is determined to get it. These desires include Raul, his extremely straight and conservative boss. Before long, it's Raul who learns that there is more to life than the virtues of a middle-class family and climbing the corporate ladder. A refreshing tale of man meets man, and man and man fall in love. But not, of course, without Raul and Jorge bearing the brunt of a social milieu which would prefer its leading men to be straight. (MQFF)

Our Brothers, Our Sons

Arnold, Jim
2001; USA; 25 min; Documentary

In the early 1980s, a new disease called AIDS began to ravage a generation of gay men in the US. The gay community watched in horror as tens of thousands of its contemporaries suffered and died with few or no treatment options. At the same time, a new generation was being born into a world forever changed. While young gay boys of this new generation were learning on the playgrounds of America that they were different from other boys, their older brothers were in the trenches, laying the groundwork to save a community from extinction. Due in large part to unrelenting pressure from gay activists of the Baby Boomer generation, attitudes were changed, safer-sex guidelines were adopted and potent new drugs were developed for the treatment of this devastating disease. A diminished community thrived. *Our Brothers, Our Sons* explores a surprising generation gap around AIDS in the gay community by examining personal stories of representatives of both Generation X and the Baby Boomer generation. The gay men interviewed include HIV-positive and negative activists, writers, sex workers and others who tell of their experiences with this issue. (Eureka)

Dist/Sales: Eureka

Our House: A Very Real Documentary

Spadola, Meema
1999; USA; 57 min; Documentary

This US documentary profiles children in five diverse families as they face the challenges and joys of growing up in gay and lesbian households. (ACMI)

Prod Comp: Sugar Pictures
Dist/Sales: CinemaGuild, ACMI

Our Lady of the Assassins

(aka: La Virgen de los sicarios)

Schroeder, Barbet
2000; Colombia, France, Spain; 100 min; Drama
P: Barbet Schroeder, Margaret Menegoz, Jaime Osorio Gomez; *W:* Fernando Vallejo; *C:* Rodrigo Lalinde; *E:* Elsa Vasquez; *M:* Jorge Arriagada
Cast: German Jaramillo, Anderson Ballesteros, Juan David Restrepo, Manuel Busquets

From Barbet Schroeder—the director of *Barfly* and *Reversal of Fortune*—comes this powerful, critically acclaimed story about the search for love and redemption in a society gone mad. World-weary author Fernando has returned to his native Columbia to live out his days in peace. But Fernando's once-quiet hometown has become a hotbed of violence, drugs and corruption. On the brink of despair, Fernando meets Alexis, a beautiful but hardened street kid who lives by the rule of the gun. Together, they forge an unlikely relationship.(Wolfe) Spanish with English subtitles.

Prod Comp: Le Studio Canal+
Dist/Sales: Wolfe, ParamountClassics

Our Mom's a Dyke

1995; USA; 23 min; Documentary
P: Juliette Olavarria

This is a charming documentary about adolescent girls who have to deal with an unexpected complication in their suburban life. Their mother suddenly dissolves her marriage and then tells the girls in strictest confidence that she is a lesbian. This secret makes them feel isolated from their friends and especially from their father who was not privy to this information. The oldest sister, Juliette, made this funny and poignant video which reveals their coming to terms with their mother's new sexual identity. It captures their initial shock, embarrassment and anger. They try to make sense out of their parents' former life together. 'Did you ever love daddy?', they want to know. But as time goes on, the sisters relaxed about their mother's new lifestyle. They understand that now she is being true to herself and is happier. When the secrecy was lifted their friends were accepting, and even thought their mom was 'cool.' They came to realise that their own heterosexuality was not threatened. These days they are activists for gay rights and march proudly with their mother. (Filmakers Library)

Dist/Sales: FilmakersLibrary

Our Private Idaho

Gallagher, Daniel / Muller, Clare
1998; UK; 32 min; Documentary

Documentary about the battle over an Idaho gay rights amendment.

Dist/Sales: DevilsAdvocate

Our Sons

(aka: Too Little, Too Late)

Erman, John
1991; USA; 100 min; Drama
P: Philip Kleinbart; *W:* William Hanley; *C:* Tony Imi; *E:* Robert Florio; *M:* John Morris
Cast: Julie Andrews, Ann-Margret, Hugh Grant, Zelijko

Ivanek, Tony Roberts

Made for television story of two mothers, one who accepts her son's relationship with another man, and the other who can't. But things change when one of the men is diagnosed with AIDS. Compassionate and compelling viewing.

Prod Comp: Greenwald Films
Dist/Sales: Roadshow

Out At Work: America Undercover

Anderson, Kelly / Gold, Tami
1996; USA; 58 min; Documentary

This disturbing documentary addresses the startling reality that in forty American states, at the time of filming, it is legal to fire an employee for being homosexual. It reveals the ongoing perils that gays and lesbians face in companies in many states across the US, through moving case studies of two gay men and one lesbian worker, who are exposed to job discrimination and finally take action to fight for their rights. Cheryl Summerville, a cook at a Cracker Barrel restaurant in Bremen, Georgia, for more than three years, was fired when a corporate policy was instituted announcing that the 'family' restaurant could no longer employ individuals 'whose sexual preference failed to demonstrate normal heterosexual values.' Mark Anderson, a trainee at the Los Angeles branch of Cantor Fitzgerald, a prestigious securities trading firm, was also fired when rumours started spreading through the office that he was gay. He became the target of degrading slurs and vandalism initiated by both co-workers and, surprisingly, the branch's top partners. Ron Woods, a third generation auto worker in Detroit, was physically attacked by co-workers and management after they learned he was gay. He initiated a lawsuit alleging that Chrysler had failed to provide a safe work environment. (Filmakers Library)

Dist/Sales: FilmakersLibrary, Frameline

Out for a Change: Homophobia in Women's Sports

Mosbacher, Dee
1995; 27 min; Documentary

A documentary which addresses the issues of homophobia in women's sports. In particular, homophobia is seen as a political tool which is used to control the lucrative sports industry. Interviews with aspiring young women athletes, coaches, administrators and professional athletes such as Zina Garrison-Jackson and Martina Navratilova offer a rare insight into the insidious nature of homophobia and how athletes can confront and deal with the problem. (ACMI)

Dist/Sales: WomanVision, ACMI

Out in Africa

Symons, Johnny
1994; USA; 17 min; Documentary

In a collection of interviews, five gay black African men speak of their personal and political struggles, their work as activists, hairdressers and prostitutes, their future within the global gay community, and their struggle to remain true to both their cultures and their sexuality. (MQFF)

Out in Nature: Homosexual Behaviour in the Animal Kingdom

Alexandresco, Stéphane / Loyer, Bertrand / Menéndez, Jessica
2001; UK; 52 min; Documentary
P: Bertrand Loyer; *W:* Jessica Menéndez, Jo Stewart Smith, Jacqueline Farmer

The wild kingdom takes on a whole new meaning in this truly groundbreaking documentary about homosexuality in the animal kingdom. With never-before-seen footage of dyke monkeys hunting for some butch/femme bumping, and sissy elephants sizing up local studs, this meticulously researched film is slicker than any BBC documentary. Scientific in its approach, yet completely hilarious, this worldwide hit is a belated Pride March for queer animals. (MQFF)

Prod Comp: Le Studio Canal+, Saint Thomas Productions
Dist/Sales: Explore

Out in South Africa

Hammer, Barbara
1994; USA; 51 min; Documentary
P: Barbara Hammer

Out in South Africa documents Barbara Hammer's experiences as an official guest of the first gay and lesbian film festival on the African continent in June 1994, shortly after the introduction of South Africa's new interim constitution, one of the few constitutions in the world which explicitly proscribes discrimination on the grounds of sexual orientation. Much of the film's material is taken from video workshops Hammer held in the townships. At a time of monumental change in South African society, a diverse group of Black, Afrikaner and English-speaking gays and lesbians speak frankly about their personal histories, their desires, and their hopes for the future. (MQFF)

Dist/Sales: Hammer, VTape, WMM

Out in Suburbia

Walton, Pam
1988; USA; 29 min; Documentary
P: Pam Walton; *W:* Pam Walton

Eleven lesbians who represent a variety of ages, occupations and ethnic backgrounds share their experiences of their chosen lifestyle. Filmed in homes and in work settings, they discuss family relationships, religion, motherhood, marriage and dealing with discrimination.

Awards: San Francisco International Lesbian & Gay Film Festival, 1989: Audience Award for Best Documentary

Dist/Sales: FilmakersLibrary, Wolfe, NFVLS, GroupeIntervention

Out in Suburbia

Out in the Open

Barbosa, Peter
2001; USA; 54 min; Documentary

Out in the Open takes us on an intimate excursion through gay sex in public places.

Dist/Sales: Eyebite

Out Loud

Gaulke, Cheri
1995; USA; 19 min; Documentary

A by-the-people, for-the-people approach to queer youth video, *Out Loud* provides a forum for an age group which often receives short shrift. What is it like to be gay bashed? Can a gay boy grow up to be president? Does being gay really matter? In nine installments, gay and lesbian teens discuss their hopes, fears, challenges, and achievements in their words, and with their own vision. (Frameline)

Dist/Sales: Frameline

Out of Our Time

Pacilio, Casi
1989; USA; 70 min; Drama

Valeri and Marilyn are a lesbian couple living in contemporary times. The film contrasts their lives and choices with the life lead by Valeri's grandmother in the 1930s.

Prod Comp: Back Porch Productions

Out of Season

Buck, Jeanette L.
1998; USA; 98 min; Drama
P: Kim McNabb, Jeanette L. Buck; *W:* Kim McNabb; *C:* Ed Talavera; *E:* Sharon Teo; *M:* Miki Navazio
Cast: Carol Monda, Joy Kelly, Dennis Fecteau, Nancy Daly, Rusty Clauss

Micki is a leather-clad, love 'em and leave 'em lesbian who finds herself in a small seaside resort long after the last tourist has gone, caring for her dying Uncle Charlie. Touchy, hip, and alone, Micki has spent her whole life fleeing from commitment, until she meets Roberta, a friend of her uncle's, a small town lesbian, and an older woman. Seemingly comfortable with her simple life, Roberta is uneasy with Micki's brazen advances. But a shared concern and love for Charlie—and a growing attraction neither woman can deny—begin to create a complex and enduring bond.

Prod Comp: imj Productions
Dist/Sales: PictureThis!, JourDeFete, Wolfe

Out of the Closet, Off the Screen: The Life & Times of William Haines

Bailey, Fenton / Barbato, Randy
2001; USA; 45 min; Documentary

In 1930, Joan Crawford and William Haines were the top box office stars in Hollywood. Although Ms Crawford is remembered around the world, many readers might ask, 'William WHO?' Alas, Haines sacrificed his celluloid career for the love of not the woman, but the MAN in his life. 70 years later, Billy Haines remains Hollywood's only 'out' gay male screen idol. Haines, a gay teen runaway, was discovered by a talent agent and shipped to Tinseltown, where he appeared in a long list of films. In the Roaring Twenties, Hollywood was a haven for free lovers, and since the studios controlled the press, Billy and other actors lived openly gay lives without repercussion. That is until the depression changed American morality and in 1933, Louis B. Mayer ordered Billy to leave his long-time lover, Jimmie Shields, and publicly marry a woman. When Billy refused, his shining career ended for good. Shortly after, friends Joan Crawford and Carole Lombard helped Billy kick off a new, lucrative career decorating mansions for the stars, and he lived to share a 50-year love with Jimmie. 25 years after his death, Billy Haines' furniture pieces are prized at auction, and though his films may not be familiar to modern moviegoers, his most important legacy is his story of authenticity and it's place in the early history of Hollywood. (World of Wonder)

Dist/Sales: WorldOfWonder

O

Out of the Past

Dupre, Jeff
1997; USA; 67 min; Documentary
P: Jeff Dupre; W: Michelle Ferrari; C: Buddy Squires; E: Toby Shimin, George O'Donnell; M: Matthias Gohl
Cast: Gwyneth Paltrow, Stephen Spinella

The incredible stories of gay civil rights activists are profiled in this powerful film. Told through the eyes of a high school student in Salt Lake City, Out of the Past explores her history-making experience of forming a Gay Straight Alliance in her public school. (Wolfe)

Dist/Sales: Wolfe, PBS

Out: Stories of Lesbian and Gay Youth

Adkin, David
1993; Canada; 78 min; Documentary
P: Silva Basmajian; C: Joan Hutton, John Walker; E: Steve Weslak; M: Aaron Davis, John Lang

According to Scott Thompson, 'You're going into a world that is changing—drastically. And in ten years, it's going to be as uncool to hate homosexuals as it is to be a racist. So you better get ready for that world'. Out offers positive images of gay youth from a variety of racial and cultural heritages while examining the emotional, societal and familial conflicts they face in their everyday lives. (MQFF)

Prod Comp: National Film Board of Canada
Dist/Sales: FilmakersLibrary, Salzgeber, NFVLS, ACMI, Heathcliff, NFBC

Out: The Making of a Revolutionary

Collins, Rhonda / de Vries, Sonja
2000; USA; 60 min; Documentary

Convicted of the 1983 US Capitol building bombing and 'conspiring to influence, change and protest policies and practices of the US government through violent and illegal means', Laura Whitehorn, an out lesbian and one of six defendants in the Resistance Conspiracy Case, spent 14 years in prison. Out is the story of her life and our times: five tumultuous decades of struggle for freedom and justice. Whether you agree or disagree with radical left politics, this is a documentary that will challenge you to think about what you might be willing to risk for your own beliefs.

Prod Comp: Film Arts Foundation
Dist/Sales: CollinsR

Outcasts, The

(aka: Niezi; The Outsiders)
Yu, Kan-ping
1986; Taiwan; 102 min; Drama
W: Yeong Shiang

Cast: Ming-ming Su, Hsin Shao, Sun Yuek Tai Ling

A groundbreaking film from Taiwan, which centres on a photographer who decides to help gay teenage boys who have been abandoned by their families because of their sexuality, and are struggling to survive on the streets. He takes them in and with the help of his landlady, the boys open Taipei's first gay nightclub, the Blue Angel. Chinese with English subtitles.

Dist/Sales: Facets

Outlaw

Lebow, Alisa
1994; USA; 26 min; Documentary

Leslie Feinberg, a self-identified 'gender outlaw' who has spent much of her life passing as a man, speaks with passion and intelligence about her experiences in this video manifesto. Raw and confrontational, this videotape asks its audience to examine their assumptions about the 'nature' of gender and calls for more sensitivity and awareness of the human rights and the dignity of transgendered people. (WMM)

Dist/Sales: WMM

Outrageous!

Benner, Richard
1977; Canada; 100 min; Comedy
P: William Marshall, Henk van der Kolk; W: Richard Benner; C: James B. Kelly; E: George Appleby;
M: Paul Hoffert
Cast: Craig Russell, Hollis McLaren, Richert Easley, Allan Moyle, Helen Shaver

A gay female impersonator and hairdresser start an unlikely but touching friendship with an escaped schizophrenic woman who is pregnant.

Prod Comp: Film Consortium of Canada
Dist/Sales: Ascanbee

Outtakes

Brooks, Katherine / Klopfenstein, Karen
1998; USA; 72 min; Drama
P: Katherine Brooks, Karen Klopfenstein; W: Katherine Brooks, Karen Klopfenstein; C: Jennifer Lane
Cast: Katherine Brooks, Samantha, Flate, Sean Carlos Larkin, Karen Klopfenstein

The sexual tension is high when Cassy, (an upcoming indie film director with ego and libido to match) hires Lauren as her assistant director. Their filmmaking skills match perfectly, and soon the romantic side of things follows suit.

Prod Comp: Fearless Pictures
Dist/Sales: FearlessPictures

Over Our Dead Bodies

Marshall, Stuart
1991; UK; 75 min; Documentary
P: Rebecca Dobbs

This film powerfully documents the origins of the AIDS activist movement in the United States. It also chronicles the genesis of Queer Nation, springing from a newly politicised sense of pride and community fuelled by AIDS activism. *Over Our Dead Bodies* celebrates the real success of these movements, which were born from the gay community's anger and frustration with the inadequate response of the US political and medical establishments. It also sheds light on the debates surrounding the relationship between homophobia, racism and sexism and the need for the community to integrate its grief with its political activism.

Awards: LA Outfest, 1991: Best Documentary
Dist/Sales: MayaVision

Over the Rainbow: Parts 1–4

USA; 2 x 60 min; Documentary

Combining rare archival footage with revealing firsthand accounts, *Over the Rainbow* traces the struggles and gains of the gay rights movement in the United States by going behind the headlines to the experiences of the people who were there. From the Stonewall riot in Greenwich Village in 1969 to the discussions of the possible future of the gay and lesbian rights movement.

Override

Ginsburg, Lisa
2000; USA; 10 min; Comedy

A femme office meets a butch bike courier in this rock narrative.

Dist/Sales: Riveter

Oy Gay

Haber, Rosalind
1992; UK; 31 min; Documentary

Lesbian and gay Jews straddle two communities that have much in common in terms of history and experience but who rarely recognise the similarities of their situations and often view each other with a great deal of suspicion. An affectionate examination and celebration of being lesbian or gay and Jewish.

Dist/Sales: MayaVision

P(l)ain Truth

Pohjola, Ilppo
1993; Finland; 15 min; Documentary
W: Ilppo Pohjola; *C:* Arto Kaivanto; *E:* Heikki Salo;

M: Gionn Branoa

Documentary based on the experiences of Rudi, a female-to-male transsexual. This compelling and cathartic piece from the director of *Daddy and the Muscle Academy*, has played at film festivals around the world.

Awards: Berlin International Film Festival, 1993: Teddy Award for Best Short Film
Prod Comp: Crystal Eye Ltd
Dist/Sales: Zeitgeist

P. S. Your Cat is Dead

Guttenberg, Steve
2001; USA; 90 min; Comedy
P: Kule A. Clark, Christopher Vogler; *W:* Jeff Korn;
C: David Armstrong; *E:* Derek Vaughn
Cast: Steve Guttenberg, Lomardo Boyar, Cynthia Watros, Shirley Knight

Two desperate men, thrown together one New Year's Eve when their lives have crumbled, are willing to kill each other, until they discover that each is the other's only salvation. Actor-cum-fledgling writer Jimmy Zoole has lost it all this New Year's Eve. His girlfriend is seeing someone else. His groundbreaking yet ill-conceived one-man show has closed after one day. His best friend died a few short months ago. His soon-to-be-demolished apartment has been robbed twice. And now his beloved cat is dead. But Jimmy's downward spiral is just beginning. The aforementioned burglar has returned, and Jimmy's caught him. This New Year's will be like no other, as Jimmy holds Eddie the burglar hostage for an emotionally charged, soul-searching, and often hilarious night.

Dist/Sales: TLA

Pandora's Box

(aka: Die Büchse der Pandora)

Pabst, G. W.
1928; Germany; 110 min; B&W; Drama
P: George C. Horsetzky, Seymour Nebenzal;
W: G. W. Pabst, Laszlo Wajda, Joseph Fleisler;
C: Günther Krampf; *M:* Timothy Brock
Cast: Louise Brooks, Fritz Kortner, Franz Lederer, Alice Roberts, Carl Gotz

Brooks and Pabst's collaboration did not win favour in Hollywood or Germany and this film was not only censored, it received limited release in Europe and the USA, as well as a cool reception from critics. It took decades before *Pandora's Box* was recognised as the classic it is seen as today. Brooks plays Lulu, an insatiable woman who uses men for erotic pleasure and then seduces or kills them. She finally reaps what she sows at the hand of Jack the Ripper. An important film for lesbians as it has a well-developed lesbian character, the Countess, who falls in love with Lulu.

Prod Comp: Nero Films
Dist/Sales: NFVLS, ACMI, BFI

Panic Bodies

Hoolboom, Mike
1998; Canada; 70 min; Experimental
W: Mike Hoolboom
Cast: Tom Chomont, Ed Johnson

> Filmed in the shadow of AIDS, *Panic Bodies* is a testament to the permanent impermanence of the flesh. The film's six parts show the range of Hoolboom's engagement with mortality, from rage to reverie.

Dist/Sales: CFMDC

Pansexual Public Porn

(aka: The Adventures of Hans and Del)

Volcano, Del LaGrace
1998; UK; 11 min; Documentary

> Female to male transsexuals Del and Hans, armed with camcorders, cruise public parks to get it on with other boys on film.

Dist/Sales: Volcano

Paper Cranes

Reed, Peter
1991; USA; 18 min; Drama

> Set during three different periods (1950, 1970 and 1990), *Paper Cranes* investigates aspects of male bonding while simultaneously examining the cultural notions of an honourable death.

Paradise Bent

(aka: Fa'afafines in Paradise)

Croall, Heather / Wunderman, Eva
1999; Australia; 51 min; Documentary
P: Heather Croall, Alison Elder

> This is one of the first explorations of the Samoan fa'afafines, boys who are raised as girls, fulfilling a traditional role in Samoan culture. The film shows how in the large Samoan family there may be one or two fa'afafines who are not only accepted but appreciated. They cheerfully share the women's traditional work of cooking, cleaning and caring for children and the elderly. Today's fa'afafines are becoming more westernised and look more like drag queens. Dance has always been an important part of Samoan culture. From an early age, the fa'afafines dance the female role, and many continue to dance

as entertainers in nightclubs. We meet Cindy, a popular dancer, who has fallen in love with a representative of the Australian High Commission. They live together in the Australian compound, which lands him in trouble. He is transferred to Australia, but gives up his job and returns to be with Cindy. Several anthropologists, including Derek Freeman and Tom Pollard comment on the phenomenon. *Paradise Bent* brings up issues of culture and gender and the complexities of sexual identity. (Filmakers Library)

Prod Comp: Re Angle Productions
Dist/Sales: FilmakersLibrary

Paragraph 175

Epstein, Robert / Friedman, Jeffrey
1999; Germany, UK, USA; 81 min; Documentary
P: Janet Cole, Michael Ehrenzweig, Rob Epstein, Jeffrey Friedman; *C:* Bernd Meiners; *E:* Dawn Logsdon; *M:* Tibor Szemzö

> An estimated 10,000–15,000 men were imprisoned in Nazi concentration camps in the 1930s and 40s for the crime of having same-sex relationships. Only 10 of those men survive today, and until now, they have not spoken openly about their histories. In this riveting documentary firsthand accounts of queer life in Nazi Germany are delicately and compassionately drawn out of gay and lesbian Holocaust survivors and interwoven with astonishing archival footage. Made by the team responsible for *The Celluloid Closet* and narrated by Rupert Everett. (MQFF)

Prod Comp: Channel 4, Cinemax, HBO, Telling Pictures, Zero Film GmbH
Dist/Sales: Cowboy, NewYorker, Wolfe, NFVLS, ACMI, VideoAmericain

Parallel Sons

Young, John G.
1995; USA; 93 min; Drama
P: Nancy Larsen, James Spione; *W:* John G. Young; *C:* Matthew M. Howe; *E:* James Spione, John G. Young; *M:* Ed Menasche
Cast: Gabriel Mick, Lawrence Mason

> Seth is an aspiring artist who lives a boring life in a quiet upstate New York town. But all that changes when he meets Knowledge, a black escapee from a detention centre. A deep connection forms between the two men as they embark on a journey of freedom and escape.

Awards: San Francisco International Lesbian & Gay Film Festival, 1995: Audience Award for Best Feature
Prod Comp: Black Brook Films, Eureka Productions
Dist/Sales: Forefront, Greycat, Strand

Parents of Gays

Lacey, Margaret
1983; Australia; 20 min; Documentary

Six parents talk about their experiences of coming to terms with the homosexuality of their children. The video stresses the value of sharing difficult experiences with others.

Dist/Sales: ACMI

Paris is Burning

Livingston, Jennie
1990; USA; 102 min; Documentary
P: Nigel Finch, Davis Lacy, Jennie Livingston;
C: Paul Gibson; *E:* Jonathan Oppenheim
Cast: Anji Xtravaganza, André Christian, Dorian Corey

Paris is Burning is the result of the five years that filmmaker Jennie Livingston spent amongst New York City's black and Hispanic transvestite community. Often poor and homeless the young gay men and drag queens form 'houses' which conduct dances and balls dedicated to vogueing: the celebration of fashion, style and beauty. This is a fascinating documentary which confronts the viewer with a blurring of traditional notions of gender and sexuality, it also celebrates sexual, ethnic and racial diversity and difference. Features a great soundtrack of house and funk music.

Awards: San Francisco International Lesbian & Gay Film Festival, 1990: Audience Award for Best Documentary; Sundance Film Festival, 1991: Best Documentary
Prod Comp: Off-White Productions
Dist/Sales: 21stCentury, ACMI, Swank, NFVLS

Paris was a Woman

Schiller, Greta
1996; USA; 75 min; Documentary
P: Frances Berrigan, Greta Schiller, Andrea Weiss;
W: Andrea Weiss; *C:* Nurith Aviv, Greta Schiller, Renato Tonelli, Fawn Yacker; *E:* Greta Schiller
Cast: Gisele Freund, Berthe Cheyrergue, Catherine R. Stimpson

A fascinating film portrait of the women writers, artists and photographers who flocked to the left bank in the early decades of this century, *Paris was a Woman*, recreates the mood and flavour of this female artistic community in Paris during its most magical era. Among the community of women on the Left Bank, many were lesbian or bisexual, and all felt a primary emotional if not sexual attachment to other women. (Wolfe)

Dist/Sales: Zeitgeist, Wolfe, ACMI

Parting Glances

Sherwood, Bill
1986; USA; 90 min; Drama
P: Yoram Mandel, Arthur Silverman; *W:* Bill Sherwood;
C: Jacek Laskus; *E:* Bill Sherwood
Cast: John Bolger, Richard Ganoung, Steve Buscemi, Patrick Tull, Adam Nathan

Two men, Robert and Michael, attempt to keep their relationship strong and meaningful when Robert is transferred overseas to a job in Kenya. Other pressures come into play, including the fact that Michael's ex-lover is dying of AIDS. The transfer could mean the end of Robert and Michael's six-year relationship.

Prod Comp: Rondo Productions
Dist/Sales: Wolfe, TLA, October, BFI, FirstRunFeatures, Palace, ACMI

Partners

Burrows, James
1982; USA; 98 min; Drama
P: Aaron Russo; *W:* Francis Veber; *C:* Victor J. Kemper;
E: Danford B. Greene, Stephen Lovejoy;
M: Georges Delerue
Cast: Ryan O'Neal, John Hurt, Kenneth McMillan, Robyn Douglas, Darrell Larson

Two Los Angeles cops, one straight, the other gay, investigate the murder of a homosexual. In order to lure the murderer out they take an apartment together and pose as a gay couple. All the homosexual characters that appear are absolute clichés, limp-wristed and lisping. It is supposed to be a parody of *Cruising* but turns out to be even more offensive.

Prod Comp: Paramount, Titan Productions
Dist/Sales: Ascanbee, Paramount

Party Favor, The

Udelson, Lisa
1994; USA; 21 min; Comedy

What happens when lesbian couple, Debbie and Susie attend Debbie's future sister-in-law's bridal shower? It's not what you might expect in Lisa Udelson's very funny, bright comedy about untraditional people caught up in the preparations for the age-old tradition of marriage. Also starring David Schwimmer (*Friends*), *The Party Favor*, whose title has more than one meaning, is a sharply etched, cleverly written and good natured film. Wedding showers were never so entertaining! (1997 Toronto Jewish Film Festival)

p

Party Monster

Bailey, Fenton / Barbato, Randy
1997; UK, USA; 60 min; Documentary
P: Fenton Bailey, Randy Barbato; *E:* Scott Gamzon,
Tim Atzinger

The astonishing, true story of what really happened
behind the scenes at the Limelight nightclub in New
York City. From Fenton Bailey and Randy Barbato,
comes the shockumentary that reveals the NYC
Club-Kid turned cold-blooded murderer. (Picture
This!)

Prod Comp: Cinemax, Channel 4, World of Wonder
Dist/Sales: PictureThis!, Wolfe

Party Safe with DiAna and Bambi

Spiro, Ellen
1992; USA; 25 min; Documentary

Sequel to *DiAna's Hair Ego. Party Safe* takes viewers
on a relentlessly sexy journey to safer sex game show-
style parties across America. Explores a method of
promoting safe sex in a very explicit fashion.

Pasajes

(aka: Passages)

Calparsoro, Daniel
1996; Spain; 86 min; Drama
P: Agustin Almodovar; *W:* Daniel Calparsoro;
C: Kiko de la Rica; *E:* José Torrecilla; *M:* Alberto Iglesias
Cast: Najwa Nimri, Alfredo Villa, Charo Lopez, Ion
Gabella

Gabi is a young petty thief with little direction in life
who is part of a gang who are constantly being
hounded by the police. She manages to convince her
friends that they can help her escape her bleak life.
Carmina, an alcoholic cleaning woman becomes
Gabi's key to escape, and they begin a relationship
along the way. Spanish with English subtitles.

Prod Comp: El Deseo SA
Dist/Sales: Goldwyn

Passed Away

Peters, Charlie
1992; USA; 96 min; Comedy
P: Larry Brezner, Timothy Marx; *W:* Charlie Peters;
C: Arthur Albert; *E:* Harry Keramidas, Garth Craven;
M: Richard Gibbs
Cast: Bob Hoskins, Jack Warden, William L. Petersen,
Diana Bellamy

When his father suddenly drops dead, a man is
forced to organise the funeral. In the meantime we
are introduced to his colourful and quirky family
which includes his mother and his very pregnant, yet
unmarried, sister. He has another sister, rebellious in

nature, who ran away to marry a dancer not
knowing he iwas gay. We also meet a mysterious
young woman who steals Hoskins' heart but turns
out to his father's mistress.

Prod Comp: Hollywood Pictures, Touchwood Pacific
Partners
Dist/Sales: BuenaVista

Passengers

Fleck, Paula / Zuckerman, Francine
2000; Canada; 15 min; Drama

Evocative, passionate and poetic, this film is a
compelling and moving exploration of the relationship between a daughter and her father as she
matures from childhood to adulthood. On the day
of his funeral, she draws on the legacy of his love,
understanding and compassion and comes to term
with her sexual identity.

Dist/Sales: CFMDC

Passengers

Passing Resemblance

Wascou, Daniel
2000; USA; 16 min; Drama

This beautiful film adds a twist to the coming out
story, as well as lashings of sexual tension and
realistically inarticulate teenage dialogue.

Passion of Remembrance, The

Blackwood, Maureen / Julien, Isaac
1986; UK; 82 min; Drama
Cast: Anni Domingo, Joseph Charles, Antonia Thomas,
Jim Findley

Produced by Sankofa, a collective of gay filmmakers
and black feminists, *The Passion of Remembrance* is
structured around the confrontation between a black
radical woman and a young gay black man. Using
montages of documentary and dramatised footage,

they act as devices to examine the complexities and disputes of the black experience in Britain from the 1950s to the present day.

Prod Comp: Sankofa Film
Dist/Sales: TWN, WMM

Past Caring

Eyre, Richard
1985; UK; 80 min; Drama
P: Kenith Trodd; *W:* Tom Clarke;
C: Kenneth MacMillan; *M:* Stanley Myers
Cast: Denholm Elliott, Emlyn Williams, Coonie Booth, Joan Greenwood

A rather roguish man approaching old age finds himself incarcerated in a home for senile senior citizens. Williams plays an elderly homosexual who is determined to relive his youth.

Paul Cadmus: Enfant Terrible at 80

Sutherland, David
1987; USA; 57 min; Documentary
P: David Sutherland; *C:* Joe Seamans;
E: Michael Colonna
Cast: Jon Andersson, Paul Cadmus

A documentary on the life and work of the artist Paul Cadmus, who stylised the homoerotic painting. His first painting, called *The Fleet's In*, was considered outrageous and scandalous by the Navy. He claims that he was never trying to be controversial, but that the Navy did great things for his career by causing such a furore.

Paul Monette: The Brink of Summer's End

Bramer, Monte
1997; USA; 90 min; Documentary
P: Lesli Klainberg; *W:* Monte Bramer; *E:* Joshua Butler, Chris Reiss; *M:* Jon Ehrlich

A provocative and deeply personal film biography of the late gay writer and activist Paul Monette. Shot over the course of three and a half years, Monette's life and work is explored from his seemingly idyllic New England boyhood and his closeted adolescence, to his development into a successful writer, committed lover and activist, until his death from AIDS in February 1995. (First Run/Icarus)

Dist/Sales: FirstRunFeatures, Cinemax, FirstRun/Icarus

Peach

Parker, Christine
1993; New Zealand; 16 min; Drama
P: Caterina de Nave; *W:* Christine Parker;
C: Stuart Dryburgh; *M:* David Bridgman
Cast: Tania Simon, Joel Tobeck, Lucy Lawless

Lucy Lawless (*Xena*) appears in this seductive and sexy tale about a young Maori woman who meets another woman with an even more impressive tow truck than her boyfriend. It's a hot and oppressive afternoon when Sal discovers unexpected desire and crosses the invisible line between merely seeing beauty and experiencing it.

Prod Comp: Oceanic Parker Films
Dist/Sales: NZFC, FirstRunFeatures, BFI

Peccatum Mutum

(aka: The Silent Sin)

Silver, Suzie / Steger, Lawrence
1988; USA; 35 min; Comedy

This film explores relationships among cloistered nuns. Using gothic expressionistic sets, humour, serious kissing and melodrama, this work expresses the contradictions and ironic similarities between physical desire and spiritual fervour. A rare glimpse at the other side of catholic guilt.

Pedagogue

Marshall, Stuart
1988; UK; 10 min; Comedy
Cast: Neil Bartlett

Performing artist Neil Bartlett plays a gay lecturer whose attempt to go back into the closet is betrayed by the contents of his briefcase.

Peixe-Lua

(aka: Moon-Fish)

Morais, Jose Alvaro
1999; France, Portugal, Spain; 124 min; Drama
P: Paulo Branco; *W:* Jose Alvaro Morais, Jeanne Waltz;
C: Edgar Moura; *E:* Jackie Bastide; *M:* Riccardo Del Fra
Cast: Beatriz Batarda, Marcello Urgeghe, Ricardo Aibeo, Afonso Melo

A young Portuguese woman (Maria) who is about to be married decides it's not what she wants to do after all. In a rather confusing narrative, it turns out that Maria's father's bisexual Godson Gabriel has had sex with both Maria, and her two siblings—Ze Maria, and married bisexual Alfonso. Portuguese with English subtitles.

Prod Comp: Madragoa Films, Gemini Films
Dist/Sales: Gemini

Pencas de Bicuda

Pinheiro, Dacio
2001; Brazil; 10 min; Documentary

Bianca's exotic video diary, complete with interviews and performances.

Penitentiary

Fanaka, Jamaa
1979; USA; 99 min; Drama
P: Jamaa Fanaka; W: Jamaa Fanaka; C: Marty Ollstein;
E: Betsy Blankett; M: Frankie Gaye
Cast: Leon Isaac Kennedy, Hazel Spear, Thommy
Pollard, Badja Djola

This Blaxploitation flick finds Too Sweet Gordon
behind bars, after spending one hot night with Linda
and ending up being unfairly convicted of a murder
that Linda actually committed. To survive in prison
he begins training for the fight of his life, the
welterweight crown and his manhood. A hard-
hitting look at violence, corruption and homosexuality in prison life.

Prod Comp: Jerry Gross Productions

Pensao Globo

Mueller, Matthais
1997; Germany, Portugal; 15 min; Experimental

A man facing his approaching death takes what is
perhaps his last journey and ends up in 'Pensao
Globo' in Lisbon, where he sets out on aimless
excursions throughout the city. With over-saturated
colours, both sanguine and succulent, vision swims
and slips away in echoing super-impositions. These
overlapping exposures convey a sense of the
permeable boundaries between life and death.
(CFMDC)

Dist/Sales: CFMDC

Peony Pavilion

(aka: Youyuan jingmeng)

Yonfan
2001; Hong Kong; 122 min; Drama
P: Kunhou Chen, Ann Hui; W: Yonfan; C: Henry
Chung; E: Chileung Kong; M: Antony Lun, Yun-ging Ye
Cast: Joey Wong, Daniel Wu, Rie Miyazawa

Set in Suzhou amongst the decaying nobility of
1930s China, Peony Pavilion is the final instalment
in director Yonfan's trilogy about 'alternative' love.
The story centres on Jade, a beautiful courtesan, and
her decidedly modern, cross-dressing cousin Lan.
Lan is smitten, yet the women initially only express
their longing for each other through the songs of
traditional Chinese Opera, as several men come and
go from the courtesan's life. Only the surprise of
seeing Lan with a male lover jolts Jade into realising
the adoration she's been taking for granted. While
Yonfan may be a little coy for some in depicting the
women in love, this is a sumptuous and bold
melodrama about two women who are passionately

committed to one another, and the most extravagant
'women in love' story ever made in China. (2002
London Lesbian & Gay Film Festival)
Mandarin with English subtitles.

Peony Pavilion

Peony Pavilion, The

Chen, Kuo-fu
1995; Taiwan; 95 min; Drama
W: Kuo-fu Chen, Shih-chieh Chen;
C: Christopher Doyle; M: Wei-ji Lin
Cast: Rene Liu, Ben-yu Chang, Shin Tien

Adapted from the traditional Chinese Opera and
updated to contemporary Taipei, The Peony Pavilion
mixes sexual ambiguities with supernatural melodrama in a campy yet sensitive style. Lily is troubled
by a recurring dream in which she falls in love with a
handsome young scholar from ancient times. One
day upon seeing the face of the man from her
dreams on a commercial billboard, she accidentally
falls from a flat and dies. The person who is featured
in the billboard is in fact an up and coming female
singer Yuk-mei. Some years later, Yuk-mei moves
into the flat where Lily once lived. She starts to have
the same dream as Lily. (2001 Hong Kong Lesbian
& Gay Film Festival)

Peoria Babylon

Diller, Steven
1994; USA; 90 min; Comedy
W: Steven Diller
Cast: David Drake, Ann Cusack, Matthew Pestorius

Worlds collide in this screwball comedy when Candy
Dineen and gay fashion victim Jon Ashe, owners of a
flat broke Peoria II art gallery, team up with a con
artist to come up with a harebrained publicity
scheme that happens to trigger a screwball series of
events that lead to the destruction of the museum
after an explosive shoot-out. At the end, nothing is
left standing except Candy and Jon's friendship and
unfortunately the rest of Peoria. (Wolfe)

Dist/Sales: Wolfe

p

Pepi, Luci and Bom

Almodóvar, Pedro
1980; Spain; 80 min; Comedy
P: Pepon Corominas, Pastora Delgado, Ester Rambal;
W: Pedro Almodóvar; C: Paco Femenia; E: Pepe Salcedo
Cast: Carmen Maura, Felix Rotaeta, Olvido 'Alaska'
Gara, Eva Siva

After she is raped by a policeman, Pepi seeks revenge
and enlists the help of her friend, Bom, her lesbian
lover and members of Bom's band. When she
discovers her friends have mistakenly beaten up the
rapist's twin brother, Pepi embarks on another
revenge plot by taking knitting lessons from the
policeman's drab wife, Luci. After Luci is introduced
to the world of Pepi and Bom she leaves her
husband. Spanish with English subtitles.

Prod Comp: Figaro Films
Dist/Sales: Cinevista, ACMI

Peppermills

Hegner, Isabel
1998; Switzerland, USA; 14 min; Comedy

An obsessive thief wines and dines her dates in order
to get to her booty—peppermills.

The Prefect Son

Perfect Son, The

Farlinger, Leonard
2000; Canada; 93 min; Drama
P: Jennifer Jonas; W: Leonard Farlinger; C: Barry Stone;
E: Glenn Berman; M: Ron Sures
Cast: Colm Feore, David Cubitt, Chandra West, John
Boylan

Secrets exert powerful forces in every family. When
two brothers finally come clean, which one is the
perfect son? Both brothers' lives seem headed in
different directions. Theo has spent his life in and
out of drug rehab centres, while Ryan has enjoyed
success as a conservative lawyer. Neither particularly
likes the other. Reunited at their father's funeral,
Ryan surprises Theo by revealing that he is gay. As
Theo is drawn into Ryan's private world, the two
brothers develop a complex, loving bond neither
ever thought possible. (Wolfe)

Prod Comp: New Real Films, Téléfilm Canada
Dist/Sales: Wolfe

Performance

Cammell, Donald / Roeg, Nicolas
1970; UK; 105 min; Drama
P: Sandford Lieberson; W: Donald Cammell;
C: Nicolas Roeg; E: Antony Gibbs, Brian Smedley-
Aston; M: Randy Newman, Jack Nitzsche
Cast: James Fox, Mick Jagger, Anita Pallenberg, Michele
Breton, John Burdon

James Fox is Chas, a working-class London hit man,
who is violent, cunning and ruthless. His growing
arrogance results in a murder which sets his gangster
boss against him. On the run, and fearing for his
life, Chas holes up in the basement apartment of an
ex-rock star who lives with his two bisexual girlfriends. The two men experience an initial repulsion
then increasing fascination with each other, and
under the influence of hallucinogenic drugs, they
begin slowly to merge personas. This startling,
original film uses the techniques and experiments of
underground cinema to investigate the dislocation
suffered by both bourgeois and working-class
sexualities when confronted by the permissiveness of
the hippie subculture. Fox, hard and masculine, and
Jagger, soft and androgynous, both give two superb
homoerotic performances.

Prod Comp: Goodtimes Enterprises
Dist/Sales: Roadshow ReelMovies, Warner

Persona

Bergman, Ingmar
1966; Sweden; 81 min; B&W; Drama
P: Lars-Owe Carlberg; W: Ingmar Bergman;
C: Sven Nykvist; E: Ulla Ryghe; M: Lars Johan Werle
Cast: Liv Ullman, Bibi Andersson, Gunnar Björnstrand,
Margaretha Krook

A nurse begins to identify with her mentally ill
patient, and then has a mental breakdown. The
patient, an actress, decides not to speak again and is
placed in the care of the nurse. A struggle for
identity begins as the intimacy between the women
increases. An absorbing and compelling drama,
possibly Bergman's best film. Swedish with English
subtitles.

Prod Comp: Svensk Filmindustri
Dist/Sales: Ascanbee, MGM, UA

p

Personal Best (1982)

Towne, Robert
1982; USA; 124 min; Drama
P: Robert Towne; W: Robert Towne;
C: Michael Chapman; E: Bud Smith, Jere Huggins, Ned Humphreys, Jacqueline Cambas, Walt Mulconery;
M: Jack Nitzsche, Jill Fraser
Cast: Mariel Hemingway, Patrice Donnelly, Scott Glenn, Kenny Moore

Two elite woman athletes have a close relationship that eventually turns to love. Their relationship collapses as one of them accuses the other of deliberately setting her up to be injured, and the younger one eventually finds 'true love' with a man. Could be considered a lesbian exploitation film as there are a lot of scenes in the sauna and shots of the women's athletic bodies, but has long been a lesbian favourite.

Prod Comp: Warner, Geffen
Dist/Sales: Warner, Swank, Wolfe, ACMI

Personal Best (1982)

Personal Best (1991)

Kwietniowski, Richard
1991; UK; 20 min; Documentary

A celebration of lesbian and gay involvement in sport and fitness training that asks: What are the appeals of sport and exercise for participants and spectators? How do sport and sexuality interact? Are we the only ones honest enough to acknowledge it? Gay London swimmers break a major taboo by swimming naked, and lesbian footballers fondle on and off the field. (MQFF)

Prod Comp: Alfalfa, Channel 4

Personals

Shadbolt, Jane / Vivienne, Sonja
1996; Australia; 10 min; Documentary
W: Jane Shadbolt, Sonja Vivienne

'Seeking stories. Sleazy, sexy or sordid tales sought for short documentary on the experience that is women's personals'. Three women talk about their various expectations and experiences with lesbian personal columns.

Prod Comp: Australian Film TV & Radio School
Dist/Sales: AFTRS

Perverted Justice

Clark, Donna
1996; UK; 51 min; Documentary
P: Valentine Schmidt

Producer Valentine Schmidt asks, 'Do lesbians kill more than other women or are they being targeted for capital punishment?' Of 20,000 convicted murderers in the US, 1% receive the death penalty; and of all the women on death row, 40% are lesbian. They are also predominantly poor and/or women of colour. Hot on the heels of *Butterfly Kiss* and *Basic Instinct*, *Perverted Justice* fiercely examines how pre-existing prejudice influences prosecution. Through news footage, commentary from lawyers, scholars, and activists, and an interview with Andrea Jackson (sentenced to death for killing a police officer), *Perverted Justice* uses the power of media to give faces to those dehumanised by the American trial process. (21st San Francisco International Lesbian & Gay Film Festival)

Dist/Sales: Channel4

Petals

Natarajan, Suresh
2001; India; 16 min; Drama

Two years ago the newspapers in Kerala South India broke a shocking tale of two young lesbian girls who ended their lives beneath a train. A note they carried stated that they were ending their lives as they had failed in their long struggle to live together in the harsh and hypocritical society of Kerala. This film picks up on the agony of those innocent girls and many others who still struggle for their emotional rights.

Dist/Sales: CFMDC

Peter Allen: The Boy from Oz

MacLean, Stephen
1995; Australia; 55 min; Documentary
P: Ben Gannon, Fran Moore
Cast: Peter Allen, Jack Thompson

The story of Peter Allen, Australia's beloved variety entertainer and songwriter. As one of the first openly gay entertainers, Allen won a unique stardom with a mainstream public who loved him for his honesty.

Prod Comp: ABC
Dist/Sales: Minotaur, ACMI

p

Peter's Friends

Branagh, Kenneth
1992; UK; 101 min; Comedy, Drama
P: Kenneth Branagh, Martin Bergman; W: Rita Rudner,
Martin Bergman; C: Roger Lanser; E: Andrew Marcus;
M: Gavin Greenaway
Cast: Kenneth Branagh, Alphonsia Emmanuel, Stephen
Fry, Rita Rudner, Emma Thompson

Ten years after a close-knit group of six university
friends celebrated New Year's Eve with the farewell
performance of their musical-comedy revue, they
meet again on New Year's Eve. Amid the seasonal
trappings and stirring music from their youth, the
friends slip easily back into their relationships. It's a
weekend of high comedy and drama, quarrels and
reconciliations, as old friendships are tested and
renewed while the dawn of a new year approaches.
The host, Peter, reveals his homosexuality and HIV-
positive status.

Prod Comp: Channel 4, Goldwyn, Renaissance, BBC
Dist/Sales: BuenaVista, ReelMovies, TLA,
SamuelGoldwyn, Swank

Phantom

Phantom

(aka: O Fantasma)

Rodrigues, Joao Pedro
2000; Portugal; 90 min; Drama
P: Amandio Coroado; W: Paulo Rebelo, Joao Pedro
Rodrigues, Jose Neves, Alexandre Melo; C: Rui Poças
Cast: Ricardo Meneses, Bertriz Torcato, Eurico Vieira,
Andre Barbosa

Handsome young garbage collector Sergio spends his
nights working on the streets of Lisbon, and his
spare time engaged in the pursuit of passionate but
anonymous sex with strangers under unusual
circumstances, such as a cop he finds handcuffed in
the back of his own car. Although his co-worker
Fatima offers him romance, he can only respond to
her with violence. When Sergio meets the man of his
dreams, his interest quickly takes a dark turn towards
obsession. He breaks into the young man's house to
mark his territory like a dog; sorts through his

garbage; and makes fetishes of the man's cast off
motorcycle gloves and speedos. When he is rejected,
Sergio realises that he is totally alone. The intensity
of its sex scenes and the charisma of its sultry star are
sure to grab you right from the opening scene.(MQFF)
Portuguese with English subtitles .

Prod Comp: ICAM, RTP, Rosa Filmes
Dist/Sales: Fortissimo, PictureThis!

Phantom Pain

Matsumoto, Neil
1996; USA; 83 min; B&W; Drama
P: Tina Alexis; W: Neil Matsumoto; C: Jeff Wilkins;
E: Jeffrey Schwarts
Cast: Tina Alexis, Holly Woodlawn, Scott Ramirez,
Sean Cory

A mesmerising slice-of-life study of a transsexual
looking for love in all the wrong places. The film's
central character Christy Nichols meets with her
share of hard to watch tragic events (her confused
Johns inevitably turn on her whether she begs them
to love her or leave her alone), but it is the searing
and gentle emotion engendered through the startling
superstar-like debut of lead actor Tina Alexis that
shines through the loudest. (2000 Silverlake Film
Festival)

Prod Comp: White Streak Productions

Philadelphia

Demme, Jonathan
1993; USA; 115 min; Drama
P: Edward Saxon, Jonathan Demme; W: Ron Nyswaner;
C: Tak Fujimoto; E: Craig McKay; M: Howard Shore,
Bruce Springsteen, Neil Young
Cast: Tom Hanks, Jason Robards, Mary Steenburgen,
Antonio Banderas, Denzel Washington

Up-and-coming young lawyer Andrew Becket has
been fired from his prestigious law firm. His former
colleagues claim he's just not good enough; Andrew
says he's been fired because he's got AIDS. Andrew
then defends his reputation with a brilliant attorney
and battles against prejudice and fear of homosexuals. Critically acclaimed, well-acted tear-jerker.

Awards: Academy Awards, 1993: Best Actor (Tom
Hanks)
Prod Comp: TriStar Pictures, Clinica Estetico
Dist/Sales: Wolfe, Col-Tri, FilmsInc, ACMI, Swank

Pianese Nunzio

(aka: Fourteen in May; Sacred Silence)

Capuano, Antonio
1996; Italy; 115 min; Drama
P: Gianni Minervini; W: Antonio Capuano; C: Antonio

p

Baldoni; *E:* Gregiò Franchini; *M:* Umberto Guarino
Cast: Fabrizio Bentivoglio, Emanuele Gargiulo, Manuela Martinelli, Tonini Taiuti, Rosario de Cicco

The sounds, smells, sights of Naples flesh out the sensuality, carnality, and humanity of a story wherein the pressures of love, crime and survival are pitted one against the other with inexorable force. Within this tableau vivant, Nunzio, a choir boy from a broken family, has, for the first time in his thirteen and a half years, found the affection and guidance he has always craved in his teacher, mentor and lover, the local priest, Lorenzo. The priest, locked into a personal and social struggle against the cammorristi who control the city's dilapidated neighbourhoods, inspires his flock to resist the lure of organised crime's easy money. Eventually, Nunzio and Lorenzo's liaison becomes the target of both criminals and the police who aim to destroy the one rare thing that is life affirming in this harsh social order. Italian with English subtitles. (MQFF)

Prod Comp: AMA Films, Instituto Luce, GMF, Mediaset
Dist/Sales: PictureThis!, Wolfe

Piccadilly Pickups

Peart, Amory
1999; UK; 88 min; Drama
Cast: Alexis Arquette, B. J. Wallace, Chris Green, Spike St John

A quirky, satirical seduction into the glorious world of prostitution and pornography from Piccadilly, Manchester to Piccadilly, London. Teenager Jake sets off for London with the promise of making easy money as a rent boy. But difficulties arise as he breaches another boy's patch, is pimped by a pro and is tempted into the sleazy world of gender-bending pornography by the worldly Henri De La Plus Oooh Arrgh. (Millivres)

Dist/Sales: Millivres

Pierre et Gilles, Love Stories

Aho, Michael
1997; France; 57 min; Documentary

With over 20 years of collaboration behind them, Pierre and Gilles, a photographer and a painter, have become perhaps the most important pop artists of their generation. They are truly promiscuous cultural borrowers, blending religious imagery from East and West, glamour photography, kitsch art, and erotica, to create images of paradoxical naiveté and sophistication. *Pierre et Gilles, Love Stories* follows a year in the life of this glam couple, revealing not only the precision of their working methods, but also the intimacy and

affection of their close circle of friends, which includes Catherine Deneuve, Rupert Everett, Jean-Paul Gaultier, Nina Hagen and Marc Almond, who all share their love and admiration for these grand doyens of Parisian gay life in this illuminating documentary. (1998 New York Lesbian & Gay Film Festival)

Dist/Sales: WaterBearer

Pillow Book, The

Greenaway, Peter
1996; France, UK; 126 min; Drama
P: Kees Kasander; *W:* Peter Greenaway;
C: Sacha Vierny; *E:* Peter Greenaway, Chris Wyatt
Cast: Ewan McGregor, Vivian Wu, Yoshi Oida, Ken Ogata

Jerome is a bisexual Englishman who is involved with Nagiko, an obsessed young woman, and an older man who is one of the object's of Nagiko's obsession.

Dist/Sales: Wolfe, Cinepix

Pillow Talk

Gordon, Michael
1959; USA; 102 min; Comedy
P: Ross Hunter, Martin Melcher; *W:* Maurice Richlin, Clarence Greene; *C:* Arthur E. Arling;
E: Milton Carruth; *M:* Frank De Vol
Cast: Doris Day, Rock Hudson, Tony Randall, Thelma Ritter, Nick Adams

Jan Morrow, a single interior designer has to share a telephone party-line with Brad Allen, a playboy musician. His best-friend, a millionaire, is in love with Jan. Brad thinks it would be fun to pretend to be someone else and see if he can woo Jan away from his friend. Things turn a little crazy, however, when he finds himself falling in love for the first time. The problem: Jan hates Brad. This crazy, funny love story is one of Hollywood's camp classics, a delicious comedy about sex, virginity, and the games girls and boys play with each other. Though initially criticised as 'superficial' by contemporary critics, in hindsight, the Hudson/Day romantic comedies still seem fresh in comparison to the 'serious' Hollywood fare of its day. In part this comes from the playfulness with which Hudson and Day approach their roles, immersing themselves in their characters (she's pure and virginal, he's manly and a womaniser) at the same time investing enough subversive 'queerness' in their roles to amuse those amongst us who may or may not be heterosexual. (ACMI)

Awards: Academy Awards, 1959: Best Screenplay
Prod Comp: Universal, Arwin Production
Dist/Sales: ACMI

Pink Angels, The

Brown, Larry G.
1971; USA; 90 min; Comedy
P: Patrick J. Murphy, Gary Radzat; *W:* Larry G. Brown, Margaret McPherson; *E:* Grant Hoag; *M:* Mike Settles
Cast: Tom Basham, Don Haggerty, John Alderman

A gang of transvestite bikers heads out for Los Angeles. A queer cult film classic, a camp version of those bikie genre films like *Easy Rider*.

Prod Comp: Plateau Productions

Pink Flamingos

Waters, John
1973; USA; 95 min; Comedy
P: John Waters; *W:* John Waters; *C:* John Waters; *E:* John Waters
Cast: Divine, Edith Massey, David Lochary, Cookie Mueller, Mink Stoll

Sleaze queen Divine lives in a caravan with her loony hippie son Crackers and her 250-pound mother Mama Edie, living up to the tag of 'the filthiest people alive'. But nearby competition is looming in the form of Connie and Raymond Marble, who sell heroin to schoolchildren and kidnap and impregnate female hitchhikers, selling the babies to lesbian couples. Finally, they challenge Divine directly, and battle begins. Madcap John Waters at his politically incorrect best.

Prod Comp: Dreamland
Dist/Sales: Wolfe, FineLine, NewLine

Pink Narcissus

Pink Narcissus

Bidgood, Jim
1971; USA; 70 min; Erotica
E: Martin Jay Sadoff; *M:* Gary Goch, Martin Jay Sadoff
Cast: Bobby Kendall

The legendary gay underground classic. A young

male hustler escapes the reality of his street life through a series of highly exotic costumed and sadomasochistic fantasies. Still astonishingly explicit after all those years.

Dist/Sales: Potential, Strand, NFVLS, ACMI

Pink Pimpernel, The

Greyson, John
1989; Canada; 32 min; Experimental

Deals with an underground AIDS treatment drug-smuggling network, highlighted by classics of gay cinema reworked as public service announcements.

Pink Triangle: A Study of Prejudice Against Gays & Lesbians

1982; USA; 35 min; Documentary

Documentary which takes a look at the nature of discrimination against lesbians and gay men and challenges some of society's attitudes towards homosexuality. It also examines historical and contemporary patterns of racial, religious, political and sexual persecution.

Prod Comp: Cambridge Documentary Films
Dist/Sales: NFVLS, Cambridge, ACMI

Pink Ulysses

de Kuyper, Eric
1989; The Netherlands; 100 min; Experimental
P: Suzanne van Voorst; *W:* Eric de Kuyper; *C:* Stef Tijdink; *E:* Ton De Graaf
Cast: Eric De Bruyn, Jos Ijland, Jose Teunissen

A sex-drenched oddity from the director of *Naughty Boys*, this is a nostalgic tribute to those thinly disguised homoerotic bodybuilding magazines of the 1950s. The story is loosely based on Ulysses' return from Troy after 20 years in exile, which is a great excuse to show lots of muscular boys in loin clothes.

Dist/Sales: TLA, Strand

Pink Ulysses

P

x

Pink Video: Out-Rageously Pink, The

1995; UK; 70 min; Comedy
Cast: Scott Capurro, Steve Best, Ian Keable

Welcome to the outrageous world of gay and gay-friendly entertainment. Viewers will be treated to a sensational menu of music, comedy and speciality acts, including the BBC's Bret Tyler Moore's hilarious true tales of coming out!

Dist/Sales: Warner

Pixel Pose

Graves, Lisa
1996; Canada; 11 min; Experimental

A lesbian's life is depicted in three stages: the single lesbian, the lesbian couple and lesbian family. This movement based video uses queer text and carnal poses to explore issues of lesbian intimacy and representation. (Video Pool)

Dist/Sales: VideoPool

Pixote: A Lei do Mais Fraco

Babenco, Hector
1981; Brazil; 127 min; Drama
P: Sylvia B. Naves, Paulo Francini, Jose Pinto;
W: Hector Babenco, Jorge Duran; *C:* Rodolfo Sánchez;
E: Luiz Elias; *M:* John Neschling
Cast: Fernando Ramos de Silva, Marilia Pera, Jorge Juliao, Gilberto Moura, Edilson Lino

A chilling drama about a 10-year-old street criminal named Pixote and two other youths who escape a detention centre and get involved with a homosexual drug dealer. The film tries to deal with the shocking results of street life for young boys in Brazil. The actors are actual street kids and the child in the lead role returned to the streets only to be shot and killed by police in 1987. Portuguese with English subtitles.

Prod Comp: Embrafilme, HB Filmes
Dist/Sales: Ascanbee, Palace, Facets

Place Between our Bodies, The

Wallin, Michael
1975; USA; 33 min; Experimental

The Place Between Our Bodies seems to come from another planet, another epoch, in its frank and tender extrapolation of gay sexual hunger and the kindling of a first relationship. The film is stridently pre-AIDS—much more so than any mid 1970s porno. This is partly because it is a personal film that discusses sexual hunger and love in a context that endows them with transcendent powers .... Sexual love overcomes the light of gay alienation and sexual hunger. And that is what begins to turn the film around, so that its most beautiful moments become its most painful. Wallin's indescribable expression during orgasm, and the enveloping tenderness with which he (unsafely) fucks his boyfriend, left me chilled with sadness barely discernible beneath the usual tough-skinned attempt—on my part, on everyone's—to endure. (Todd Haynes, Afterimage, 1988 - Canyon Cinema)

Dist/Sales: Canyon

Place Called Lovely, A

Benning, Sadie
1992; USA; 20 min; B&W; Experimental

Benning's film forcefully questions the motives of a violent world through some difficult childhood memories.

Dist/Sales: VDB, NFVLS

Place in the Sun, A

Giannaris, Constantine
1994; UK; 44 min; Drama
P: Christopher Collins; *W:* Constantine Giannaris
Cast: Stavros Zalmas, Panagiotis Tsetsos

18-year-old Panagiotis, an Albanian economic refugee, arrives in Athens and meets Ilias, a 35-year-old man looking for someone to distract him from his empty life. A lyrical exploration of homosexual desire and cultural difference with cinematic references to Genet and Godard. Greek with English subtitles.

Dist/Sales: MayaVision

Place of Rage, A

Parmar, Pratibha
1991; UK; 52 min; Documentary
Cast: Angela Davis, June Jordan, Alice Walker, Trinh T. Minh-ha

This compelling documentary examines the achievements of African–American women in the civil rights, black power, feminist, and lesbian and gay movements. Interviews with Angela Davis, June Jordan, Alice Walker and filmmaker Trinh T. Minh-ha, and archival footage, are interwoven with contemporary images to form a polemic that links homophobia, racism, US imperialism and liberation struggles. Period protest anthems and contemporary music by Prince and Janet Jackson provide a fitting soundtrack to complement this reclamation of black women's fundamental contributions to black feminism. (WMM)

Dist/Sales: VTape, WMM

Play Dead

Jenkins, Jeff
2001; USA; 80 min; Comedy
P: Jeff Jenkins, Tino Sage, Gary Kohn; *W:* Jeff Jenkins;
C: Mark Putnam; *E:* Curtiss Clayton, David R.
Finkelstein; *M:* Peter Golub
Cast: Diva Zappa, Nathan Bexton, Jessica Stone, Sherrie
Rose, Jason Hall

Just when you thought black comedy couldn't get
any darker, how about a wacky romance between a
young man and... a corpse? While baby-sitting after
school for white trash sex pot Darlene Murphy,
bumbling high school drama geek Dale Splitler
dreams of romancing the hunky yet unreachable
Raymond Haver, captain of the wrestling team. But
when Dale's best friend Violet Wertzema causes a
hit-and-run accident resulting in the freak explosion
of a pickup truck, Dale discovers that his unrequited
fantasy is about to come true in a most unexpected
way. Dale, Violet, and Darlene's morbid, wisecracking, seven-year-old daughter Dustine return to the
scene of the crime to discover that the driver of the
truck is none other than Raymond, lying gorgeous
but very dead on the road. Stuffing the body in the
trunk of Violet's beat up old car, the culprits embark
on a wild journey which pushes our imagination to
the limit. In a delightfully bizarre way, this marvellous cast of kooky characters show us just how far
the human species will go for love. (12th Reel
Affirmations Film Festival)

Prod Comp: Headstrong Entertainment, Managing
Artists Concepts

Play it as it Lays

Perry, Frank
1972; USA; 94 min; Drama
P: Frank Perry, Dominick Dunne; *W:* Joan Didion,
John Gregory Dunne; *C:* Jordan Cronenweth;
E: Sidney Katz; *M:* Spring McKendree
Cast: Tuesday Weld, Anthony Perkins, Tammy Grimes,
Adam Roarke

An intense drama about a young actress's attempts to
deal with a nervous breakdown. She is supported
and helped by a close friend, a gay film producer
played by Perkins, who also has his problems.

Prod Comp: Universal
Dist/Sales: Universal

Playing Gay

1991; UK; 21 min; Documentary

Hollywood actors discuss their lesbian and gay
performances.

Prod Comp: Channel 4

Playing the Part

McCabe, Mitch
1994; USA; 40 min; Comedy

A very humorous short film made in a
mockumentary style about a lesbian coming out to
her mother. Mitch (or Michelle as her family know
her) is studying at Harvard and has a girlfriend
called Katya. When she returns to the family home
in Michigan for the holidays she tries to decide
whether to tell her unknowing parents of her
lesbianism.

Dist/Sales: FirstRunFeatures

Please Don't Stop: Lesbian Tips for Givin' and Gettin' it

Bolden, Oriana
2001; USA; 74 min; Documentary
P: Sarah Kennedy; *W:* Oriana Bolden
Cast: Simone de la Getto, Hella Getto, Moyocoyotzin,
Toni Sparrow, Trick Ready

An instructional video by and for lesbians of colour.
It features information on sexual activities and toys
illustrated with erotic scenes.

Prod Comp: Sexpositive Productions
Dist/Sales: Goodvibes

Pleasure Beach

Bressan Jnr, Arthur J.
1982; USA; 78 min; Erotica

The sexual escapades of two lifesavers in California.

Pleasure Principle, The

Cohen, David
1991; UK; 100 min; Drama
P: David Cohen, Stephen Woolley; *W:* David Cohen;
C: Andrew Spellar; *E:* Joe McAllister; *M:* Sonny Southon
Cast: Peter Firth, Lynsey Baxter, Lysette Anthony,
Haydn Gwynne, Sara Mair-Thomas

A journalist can't resist women, who in turn, seem
unable to resist him. He has entanglements with a
young divorcee, who is waiting for him to sexually
liberate her; his ex-wife who has become a radical
lesbian; a female brain surgeon; and a lawyer.

Plushies & Furries

Castro, Rick
2001; USA; 19 min; Documentary

Famed underground filmmaker Rick Castro brings
to the surface a sexual subculture of people suiting
up in animal costumes to express the beast within.

Dist/Sales: WorldOfWonder

P

Poetry for an Englishman

Daley, Martin
1987; Australia; 25 min; Drama
P: AFTRS

Janie reminisces about the summer her brother had a secret that she was desperate to uncover.

Dist/Sales: AFTRS

Point of Departure, A

McLennan, Don
1974; Australia; 31 min; B&W; Drama
P: Don McLennan, Hilton Bonner
Cast: Hilton Bonner, Karen Corbett, Neil Henson, Marcia Scales, Sharon Jackson

A young man's seeming incapability to form a relationship with a girl appears to be caused by past homosexual encounters.

Prod Comp: Experimental Film & Television Fund
Dist/Sales: NFVLS

Poison

Haynes, Todd
1991; USA; 85 min; Drama
P: Christine Vachon; *W:* Todd Haynes; *C:* Maryse Alberti, Barry Ellsworth; *E:* Todd Haynes, James Lyons; *M:* James Bennett
Cast: Edith Meeks, Millie White, Buck Smith, Larry Maxwell, Susan Norman

An ambitious and daring first feature film, *Poison* features three separate but interwoven stories inspired by the work of Jean Genet. *Hero* is a mother's account of her son's disappearance; in *Horror* a scientist's experiments lead to contagion and decay; and in *Homo* a prisoner falls in love with a beautiful but cruel fellow inmate and becomes drowned in obsession, a fantasy and, ultimately, violence.

Awards: Sundance Film Festival, 1991: Grand Jury Prize
Prod Comp: Bronze Eye, Poison L.P.
Dist/Sales: 21stCentury, NFVLS, ACMI, Zeitgeist

Poisoned Blood

Fleras, Jomar
1991; Philippines; 32 min; Documentary

Video documentary which discusses various issues related to life in the Philippines, including homosexuality, prostitution and AIDS-prevention efforts.

Dist/Sales: Brüning

Politics of Fur, The

Nix, Laura
2002; USA; 70 min; Comedy
P: Laura Nix; *W:* Laura Nix; *C:* Winnie Heun;

E: Jeffrey Schwarz
Cast: Katy Selverstone, Tim Young, Brynn Horrocks

Una, a health-obsessed music producer with a baby tiger for a pet and a full-time personal assistant falls for a punk rock dyke named Bea. Soon Bea, the antithesis of the healthy living movement, moves in and what ensues is a relationship made in hell. (www.dykediva.com)

Awards: Outfest, 2002: Best Narrative Feature
Dist/Sales: Automat

Polskiseks

Kwietniowski, Richard
1991; UK; 20 min; Documentary
P: Ardill Susan, Clare Beavan

In the UK, the combination of Solidarity government and traditional Polish Catholicism has brought into question the future of homosexuality in a country that has had, until the 1990s, very liberal legislation.

Prod Comp: Channel 4
Dist/Sales: Channel4

Polyester

Waters, John
1981; USA; 89 min; Comedy
P: John Waters; *W:* John Waters; *C:* David Insley; *E:* Charles Roggero; *M:* Debbie Harry, Michael Kamen, Chris Stein
Cast: Divine, Tab Hunter, Edith Massey, David Samson, Stiv Baton, Mary Garlington

Exploitation flick about the tragic life of Francine Fishpaw, an obese housewife whose mere existence burdens her so-called loved ones. Unjustly mistreated by her chauvinistic husband Elmer who runs the local porn theatre and money hungry mother, La Rue, she turns to the bottle for love and support. Life is on the downslide for the Fishpaw household with son Dexter, the reputed neighbourhood phantom foot stomper, daughter Lulu, a crazed pregnant disco groupie and the family dog resorting to suicide. Then, in a Cinderella fantasy, Francine meets her Polyester Prince, Todd Tomorrow and blissfully, they fall in love. Originally released in 'Odorama'.

Prod Comp: New Line Cinema
Dist/Sales: ACMI, NewLine

Pony Glass

Klahr, Lewis
1997; USA; 15 min; Animation

The story of comic book character Jimmy Olsen's secret life. Superman's pal embarks on his most adult adventure ever as he navigates the treacherous shoals of early 1960s romance trying to resolve a sexual identity crisis of epic proportions. (Canyon Cinema)

Dist/Sales: Canyon

Pool Days

Sloan, Brian
1993; USA; 45 min; Drama
P: Brian Sloan; *W:* Brian Sloan; *C:* Jonathan Schell; *E:* Brian Sloan, Andy Hafitz; *M:* Hundred pound Head
Cast: Josh Weistein, Nick Poleti, Kimberly Flynn

Handsome 17-year-old Justin gets a summer job as a lifeguard/attendant in a gym. Still confused about his sexuality, the gay world comes to him as steam room sex, naked male bodies and in the form of one particularly enticing swimmer.

Prod Comp: House of Pain Productions
Dist/Sales: Strand

Pool Days

Portion of a Lady

Chiandetti, Marco
2000; UK; 75 min; Documentary
Cast: Juana La Cubana

Fly-on-the-wall documentary about three London drag performers.

Dist/Sales: Skarda

Portland Street Blues

Yip, Raymond
1998; Hong Kong; 114 min; Action
P: Raymond Chow, Jing Wong; *W:* Manfred Wong;
C: Yiu-fai Lai; *M:* Ji-chi To
Cast: Sandra Ng, Kristy Yeung, Alex Fong, Vincent Wang

Set in the ultra-violent world of Hong Kong triads, *Portland Street Blues* takes you on an exhilarating journey into the life and memories of Sister Thirteen, a powerful female member of one of the most important gangs in the city. After a particularly vicious war, two battling gangs enter into a brief cease-fire. During negotiations between the gangs, Thirteen is caught in an intense battery of betrayals, battles and unlucky twists of fate, resulting in the death of her father as he tries to defend her life. His violent end triggers a flashback to her formative teenage years, and memories of others she has loved and lost—most notably her girlfriend Yun and the ways in which they shared their love of a local boxer, and their love for each other. But when Thirteen returns to the present, the people from her memories start to come back into her life in a flurry of unexpected and shocking situations. Finally, events climax in a gang showdown which is both breathtakingly brutal and heart-rending. (23rd San Francisco International Lesbian & Gay Film Festival) Cantonese & Mandarin with English subtitles.

Dist/Sales: Splendid

Portrait of a Marriage

Whittaker, Stephen
1990; UK; 220 min; Drama
P: Colin Tucker; *W:* Penelope Mortimer; *C:* David Feig;
E: Dick Allen; *M:* Barrington Pheloung
Cast: Janet McTeer, David Haig, Cathryn Harrison, Peter Birch

Portrait of a Marriage is the story of the tempestuous relationship between Vita Sackville West and Violet Trefusis-Keppel. After five years of marriage Vita's husband, Harold Nicholson, confesses his homosexuality. Ironically, at the same time, Vita's childhood friend, Violet, tells her that she has always loved her. This is the beginning of the women's passionate and moody relationship.

Prod Comp: BBC
Dist/Sales: BBC-Enterprises

Portrait of a Young Girl at the End of the '60s in Brussels

(aka: Portrait d'une jeune fille de la fin des années 60 à Bruxelles)

Akerman, Chantal
1993; France; 60 min; Drama
P: Georges Benayoun, Marilyn Watelet, Yannick Casanova, Elisabeth Devoisse, Francoise Guglielmi, Paul Rozenberg; *W:* Chantal Akerman; *C:* Raymond Fromont; *E:* Martine Lebon; *M:* Yarol Poupaud
Cast: Circé, Julien Rassam, Joelle Marlier, Cynthia Rodberg

Fifteen year-old Michelle, having decided to quit school, sits at a train station idly forging absentee notes, with excuses ranging from an illness in the family to her own death. She goes to the movies and succumbs with no qualms, but with no particular enthusiasm, to the amorous advances of a Parisian army deserter, Paul. They wander the streets while the camera ambles along with them, mimicking their pleasurably unhurried gait. Then follows a scene in an empty apartment where they dance and then slip between the sheets. But the film's real emotional thrust comes when Michelle keeps a prearranged appointment with Danielle: clearly the true object of her affections and maybe her secret lover. French with English subtitles.

Prod Comp: IMA Productions, La Sept-Arte
Dist/Sales: IMA

Portrait of Jason

Clarke, Shirley
1967; USA; 100 min; B&W; Documentary
P: Shirley Clarke; *C:* Jeri Sapanen; *E:* Shirley Clarke
Cast: Jason Holliday

A documentary in which Jason, a black homosexual hustler and entertainer, talks directly to the camera about his life.

Dist/Sales: MOMA

Positiv

von Praunheim, Rosa
1990; Germany; 80 min; Documentary

Praunheim investigates the realities and impacts of AIDS in New York City. Features AIDS activist Phil Zwickler.

Positive Story

(aka: Sipur Hiyuvi)

Kotzer, Ran
1996; Israel; 42 min; Documentary

Avinof was born in Giva'ataim with the given name Avi. His childhood resembled that of many gay men like him: loneliness, social isolation, secrecy, fear and mockery. As a child Avi used to sit for hours on one of the hills overlooking Tel-Aviv, dreaming of the day he would be free to live his life openly in the big metropolitan city. At the age of 17, Avi added the word 'nof' (Hebrew for view) to his first name and began discovering the gay world of Tel-Aviv: secret gardens, night clubs, cafes. At the age of 19, in a routine examination for HIV, Avinof tested positive. Positive Story is a first-time glance into the world of people living with HIV/AIDS in Israel. It is a rare instance in which an Israeli person carrying the HIV virus is willing to tell his story honestly and openly. (Frameline)

Dist/Sales: Frameline

Possible Loves

(aka: Amores Possiveis)

Werneck, Sandra
2000; Brazil; 93 min; Drama
P: Sandra Werneck; *W:* Paulo Halm; *C:* Walter Carvalho; *E:* Isabelle Rathery; *M:* João Nabuco
Cast: Murilo Benício, Carolina Ferraz, Emílio de Mello, Beth Goulart, Irene Ravache

Love-struck student, Carlos, arranges to meet the object of his passions at a cinema. The girl doesn't show up and Carlos is left cooling his heels in the foyer. But as he waits, something happens that will change his life forever. Fifteen years later, we see three possible versions of his life. In the first, he finds himself torn between the consolations of a secure if, dull, married life, and the desire to have a passionate affair; in the second, he is a gay man whose life revolves around sex; and in the third, he has never known true love and stumbles from relationship to relationship, in search of the ideal woman. One of these versions is his real life; one a possible alternative; and one, the life he would really like to live. The question is: which is which? Portuguese with English subtitles. (www.braziliancinema.com)

Prod Comp: Petrobrás Distribuidora, Cineluz
Dist/Sales: GNCTV

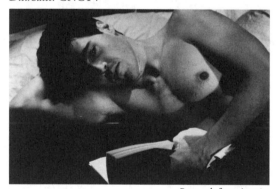

Postcards from America

Postcards from America

McLean, Steve
1994; UK, USA; 93 min; Drama
P: Craig Paull, Christine Vachon; *W:* Steve McLean;
C: Ellen Kuras; *E:* Elizabeth Gazzara; *M:* Stephen Endelman
Cast: James Lyons, Michael Tighe, Olmo Tighe, Michael Imperioli

Postcards from America is a visual feast as it moves back and forth through three stages in the life of its central character. Based on the autobiographical writings of the late David Wojnorowicz (one of the most influential queer writers/artists of our time), it traces the transition of America from the 1960s to the 1990s. We are treated to snippets of the experiences of the preadolescent boy, the sexy teenage hustler and the hunky adult, as he journeys through his dysfunctional and violent family relationships, his sexual and emotional encounters, and the wild and breathtaking American landscape. This confronting movie looks behind the façade of traditional family and values systems, exploding their myths through its stylised cinematography, often harrowing narrative, and sizzling sexual imagery. (MQFF)

Prod Comp: Channel Four Films, Islet, Normal
Dist/Sales: Potential, Strand, Cowboy, Wolfe

Postman

(aka: Youchai)

He, Jianjun
1994; China; 101 min; Drama
P: Kei Shu; *W:* Jianjun He, Ni You; *C:* Di Wu;
E: Xiaojing Liu; *M:* Yoshihide Otomo
Cast: Yuanzheng Feng, Danni Liang, Quanxin Pu, Xin Huang

Adultery, prostitution and drugs are just the appetisers in a banquet of temptations laid out before Xiao Dou. A slow-witted young man overprotected by his older sister, he is unprepared for Beijing's shadow world, and titillation rapidly turns to moral confusion and tragedy. Chinese with English subtitles.

Prod Comp: United Frontline
Dist/Sales: Fortissimo

Potluck and the Passion, The

Dunye, Cheryl
1993; USA; 30 min; Drama

A film exploring racial, sexual and social politics at a lesbian potluck. *The Potluck and the Passion* challenges tradition narrative presentation through the use of direct address talking heads, pseudo-documentary, and humour. Dunye's video is a commentary on interracial lesbian relationships and the historical relationship of African–American women to issues of race, sexuality and gender.

Dist/Sales: Frameline, TWN, EAI

Pourquoi Pas Moi?

(aka: Why Not Me?)

Giusti, Stéphane
1999; France, Spain, Switzerland; 94 min; Comedy
P: Marie Masmonteil, Caroline Adrian; *W:* Stéphane Giusti; *C:* Antoine Roch; *E:* Catherine Schwartz

Cast: Johnny Hallyday, Marie-France Pisier, Amira Casar, Julie Gayet, Bruno Putzulu

Camille is the only one in her close-knit group of friends who is out to her family. Out? Her mother is flying a rainbow flag in the garden! Agreeing that there is strength in numbers Eva, Ariane and Nico agree to bring their parents to a coming out dinner, hosted by Camille's perpetually optimistic parent. Hysteria ensues as family secrets spill out, and partnerships are redefined and formed. French with English subtitles.

Prod Comp: Elzevir Films
Dist/Sales: UGC, Millivres, Mongrel

Pouvoir Intime

Simoneau, Yves
1986; Canada; 87 min; Thriller
P: Claude Bonin; *W:* Pierre Curzi, Yves Simoneau;
C: Guy Dufaux; *E:* André Corriveau; *M:* Richard Grégoire
Cast: Jacques Lussier, Robert Gravel

Martial, a security guard, is in a relationship with Janvier, a waiter. Through an unexpected twist of fate, Martial ends up in the back of a truck that is used for a robbery and, unbeknownst to the thieves, is taken back to their warehouse. When they discover Martial they try in vain to persuade him to leave, but Martial is convinced that his only hope of survival is to stay. French with English subtitles.

Prod Comp: Téléfilm Canada, National Film Board of Canada

Prefaces

Child, Abigail
1981; USA; 10 min; Experimental

Prefaces is composed of wild sounds constructed along entropic lines, placed tensely beside bebop rhythms, and a resurfacing narrative cut from a dialogue with poet Hannah Weiner. (VDB)

Dist/Sales: VDB, Canyon

Presque Rien

(aka: Come Undone; Almost Nothing)

Lifshitz, Sébastien
2000; Belgium, France; 98 min; Drama
P: Jean-Christophe Colson, Cécile Amillat, Christian Tison; *W:* Sébastien Lifshitz, Stéphane Bouquet;
C: Pascal Poucet; *E:* Yann Dedet; *M:* Peery Blake
Cast: Jérémie Elkaim, Stéphane Rideau, Dominique Reymond, Marie Matheron

Mathieu is a quiet 18-year-old boy spending the holidays with his depressed mother. His life changes when he gets involved with the more experienced Cédric. Their relationship sets off an emotional firestorm in Mathieu as he moves towards adulthood and independence. (Wolfe) French with English subtitles.

Prod Comp: Lancelot Films, RTBF, arte France Cinema
Dist/Sales: PictureThis!, Wolfe, VideoAmericain, 10%, Salzgeber

Pretty Baby

(aka: Maybe...Maybe Not; Der Bewegte Mann; The Most Desired Man)

Wortmann, Sönke
1994; Germany; 95 min; Comedy
P: Bernd Eichinger; *W:* Sönke Wortmann, Ralf König;
C: Gernot Roll; *E:* Ueli Christen; *M:* Torsten Breuer
Cast: Til Schweiger, Katja Riemann, Joachim Krol, Rufus Beck

Axel has been kicked out of his apartment by his girlfriend Doro after she discovers he has been cheating. He finds himself sharing an apartment with Norbert, a homosexual, and Axel is introduced to the gay scene of contemporary Germany. When Norbert's queenie friend Waltraud attends a 'Straight Men's Support Group' as the gay man who can teach them about gayness, hilarious dialogue highlights a film rich with insightful sexual characterisations. As the narrative unfolds, Axel finds spending time with Norbert and his drag-queen friends both fun and liberating, so liberating that Doro suspects that Axel is actually gay. German with English subtitles.

Awards: German Film Awards, 1995: Most Outstanding Feature Film
Prod Comp: Neue Constantin Film GmbH, Olga Film
Dist/Sales: Globe, OrionClassics, Lauren

Pretty Boy

(aka: Smukke Dreng)

Sønder, Carsten
1993; Denmark; 82 min; Drama
P: Peter Aalbæk Jensen, Ib Tardini; *W:* Carsten Sønder;
C: Jacob Banke Olesen; *E:* Henrik Fleischer;
M: Joachim Holbek
Cast: Christian Tafdrup, Benedicte W. Madsen, Rami Nathan Sverdlin, Sune Otterstrøm

Pretty Boy is a seedy tale of lost innocence and betrayal. Nick is a 13-year-old runaway who, through a series of misadventures, is caught up in a gang of rent boys living a life of sordid sex and violence. This is a realistic street drama which moves rapidly towards a shocking conclusion. (MQFF)

Prod Comp: Zentropa Entertainments
Dist/Sales: Nordisk

Prick up Your Ears

Frears, Stephen
1987; UK; 99 min; Drama
P: Andrew Brown; *W:* Alan Bennett;
C: Oliver Stapleton; *E:* Mick Audsley; *M:* Stanley Myers
Cast: Gary Oldman, Alfred Molina, Vanessa Redgrave, Julie Walters

The biographical account of the cult British figure Joe Orton, a playwright and homosexual, and his lover, Kenneth Halliwell. Their turbulent and complex relationship culminated in Orton's violent murder by Halliwell, who then killed himself. Halliwell killed Orton because of his fear that Joe would leave the relationship. Oldman puts in a powerful and insightful performance as Orton and Stephen Frears again shows his great talent for directing queer-friendly films.

Prod Comp: Zenith, Civilhand-Zenith Productions
Dist/Sales: Wolfe, SamuelGoldwyn, BFI, NFVLS, ACMI, Carlton

Prick up Your Ears

Pride Divide

Poirier, Paris
1997; USA; 56 min; Documentary
P: Karen Kiss

A ground breaking exploration of the gender gap between gays and lesbians. Politically united against global homophobia, they are poles apart on many life issues. Oddly enough, their struggle of male versus female mirrors many traditional conflicts inherent to straight relationships. The gay and lesbian community is not immune to gender conditioning. Here is the classic battle of the sexes from a totally new perspective, leavened with humour. *Pride Divide* looks at the issues around male domination versus female submission;

p

promiscuousness versus commitment; exaltation of the body versus the spirit; AIDS versus breast cancer support. We hear about the subtle chauvinism by gay activists who excluded lesbians from their political and social life, especially in the conformist 1950s. Now, however, both sides seem willing to discuss these differences openly. Individuals involved in this dialogue include Martin Duberman, Barney Frank, Barbara Gittings, Simon LeVay, Camille Paglia and others. (Filmakers Library)

Dist/Sales: FilmakersLibrary

Pride in Puerto Rico

Oliver, Jorge
1999; Puerto Rico, USA; 17 min; Documentary

In 1991 Puerto Ricans held the first-ever Gay, Lesbian, Bisexual, Transgender and Transexual Pride March. Eight years later, director Jorge Oliver documented the 1999 Pride March, now an annual event on the island. Together with footage from the festivities are interviews with prominent Puerto Rican activists—including the first openly gay Puerto Rican candidate for the House of Representatives—working for social change. As much a document of the struggle against discrimination and ignorance, *Pride in Puerto Rico* is a story of community and dignity. (Frameline)

Dist/Sales: Frameline

Pride, Politics and Pissheads

Belliveau, Lulu
1998; UK; 16 min; Documentary
P: Linda Riley

We follow a gang of loose and lascivious lesbians as they embark on their last throes of political activism to the Anti-Poll Tax march and riots of 1990, and on a trip to Manchester with a busload of dykes for the Anti-Clause 28 demonstration.

Priest

Bird, Antonia
1994; UK; 103 min; Drama
P: George Faber, Josephine Ward; *W:* Jimmy McGovern; *C:* Fred Tammes; *E:* Susan Spivey; *M:* Andy Roberts
Cast: Linus Roache, Tom Wilkinson, Cathy Tyson, Robert Carlyle

Father Greg Pilkington is a *Times*-reading Catholic priest, who comes to his new Liverpool parish preaching a doctrine of self-reliance and self-help to his congregation. Eventually his homosexuality comes to the fore through an unexpected relationship, and he struggles to deal with a young girl's disclosure in the confessional that she is being abused by her father. Resolution is found, but while uplifting, it does not gloss over the central conflict between what the priest as a man can do, and what those in Rome demand of him.

Awards: Berlin Film Festival, 1995: Best Film, International Critic's Jury
Prod Comp: BBC, Electric Pictures, Miramax, PolyGram Filmed Entertainment
Dist/Sales: Wolfe, Miramax, ACMI, Swank

Priest

Prince in Hell

(aka: Prinz in Holleland)

Stock, Michael
1993; Germany; 94 min; Drama
C: Lorenz Haarmann
Cast: Harry Baer, Stefan Laarmann, Michael Stock

A street performer's tale about the *Prince in Hell* parallels the street lives of Stefan and Jockel, one a heroin addict and the other hopelessly politically correct. Graphic and sexually explicit, ex-Rosa von Praunheim assistant Michael Stock's debut feature drops any romantic delusions about the freedom of street life for a more aggressive depiction of both its ecstasies (in all senses) and its agonies. A powerful film about the price paid for nonconformity in the nineties. (MQFF)

Dist/Sales: Stock

p

Prince of Tides, The

Streisand, Barbra
1991; USA; 132 min; Drama
P: Barbra Streisand, Cis Corman, Andrew S. Karsch,
James T. Roe; *W:* Pat Conroy, Becky Johnston, Jay
Presson Allen; *C:* Stephen Goldblatt;
E: Don Zimmerman; *M:* James Newton Howard
Cast: Barbra Streisand, Nick Nolte, Melinda Dillon,
Blythe Danner, Brad Sullivan

After years of torment, and with the help of a
psychiatrist, a man and his sister unravel their past
and the brutal rape that he endured as a 13-year-old.
Though painful, he rebuilds his life and supports his
sister in her own endeavours. A neighbour to
Streisand is gay and is portrayed as a sympathetic
and warm character, still unusual for Hollywood.

Prod Comp: Barwood Films, Columbia, Longfellow
Pictures
Dist/Sales: 16MM, Col-Tri

Princesa

Princesa

Goldman, Henrique
2000; Brazil, Germany, Italy; 96 min; Drama
P: Rebecca O'Brien; *W:* Henrique Goldman, Ellis
Freeman; *C:* Guillermo Escalon; *E:* Kerry Kohler;
M: Giovanni Venosta
Cast: Ingrid de Souza, Cesare Bocci, Lulu Pecorari,
Johnny Guimares, Sonia Morgan

This bittersweet drama tells of Fernanda, a stunning
nineteen-year-old Brazilian transvestite who arrives
in Italy with two dreams: become a woman and find
a respectable husband. With her above-the-rails
looks, prostituting herself to raise money for the
operation at first comes easy. As streetwalking
'Princesa', Fernanda meets Gianni, a client who takes
to her and promises to leave his wife and pay for her
operation. But more urgently than whether Gianni
can accept Fernanda as she is, Fernanda must decide
if she's ready to change for herself. Starring mostly

non-professional actors in lead roles, *Princesa* is a
powerhouse of cinematic realism and a rare gem that
quickly transcends its core story line of the transsexual experience. (MQFF) Italian with English
subtitles.

Dist/Sales: Strand

Prisonnières

Silvera, Charlotte
1988; France; 100 min; Drama
P: Roger Andrieux; *W:* Charlotte Silvera;
C: Bernard Lutic; *E:* Danielle Fillios; *M:* Michel Portal
Cast: Marie-Christine Barrault, Agnès Soral, Annie
Girardot, Bernadette Lafont

Set in a women's prison, *Prisonnières* is the story of
cruelty, violence and rebellion of life behind bars.
This film attempts not to sensationalise the subject
matter and avoids many of the clichés, unlike other
films of the genre. Tensions arise when Sabine falls in
love with Lucie who has given up on life and never
wants to be released.

Prod Comp: Capital Cinéma

Private Benjamin

Zieff, Howard
1980; USA; 110 min; Comedy
P: Nancy Meyers, Charles Shyer, Harvey Miller;
W: Nancy Meyers, Charles Shyer, Harvey Miller;
C: David M. Walsh; *E:* Sheldon Kahn; *M:* Bill Conti
Cast: Goldie Hawn, Eileen Brennan, Armand Assente,
Sam Wanamaker, Robert Webber

After the death of her husband, a rich young Jewish
woman decides to join the army. Immediately she
goes into battle with the hard-nosed lesbian sergeant
of her platoon. A slightly humorous film but the
characterisation of the lesbian is very clichéd.

Prod Comp: Warner
Dist/Sales: ReelMovies, Warner

Private Wars

Deocampo, Nick
1996; Philippines; 60 min; Documentary

Deocampo takes us on a deeply personal journey on a
search for his father. Along the way he must confront
his sexuality, and his relationship with his family.

Privates on Parade

Blakemore, Michael
1982; UK; 107 min; Comedy
P: George Harrison, Denis O'Brien, Simon Relph;
W: Peter Nichols; *C:* Ian Wilson; *E:* Jim Clark;
M: Denis King

Cast: John Cleese, Nicola Pagett, Patrick Pearson, Michael Elphick, Joe Melia

A wacky comedy about a British Army unit, whose members dress in drag, and are assigned the thankless task of entertaining the troops stationed in the Malayan Jungle during the Second World War. There are some humorous moments as the boys impersonate great stars of the 1940s such as the Andrews Sisters and Carmen Miranda.

Prod Comp: Handmade Films
Dist/Sales: OrionClassics, BFI

Privilege

Rainer, Yvonne
1990; USA; 103 min; Comedy, Drama
P: Yvonne Rainer; *W:* Yvonne Rainer; *C:* Mark Daniels; *E:* Yvonne Rainer
Cast: Alice Spivak, Novella Nelson, Yvonne Rainer, Blaire Baron

This pseudo-documentary style films sees a filmmaker interviewing a group of middle-aged women about menopause. The footage is paralleled with hilarious educational archival film from the fifties with ridiculous male doctors. The film focuses on one woman, Jenny, as she reveals a lesbian encounter and recalls a rape she experienced and has kept hidden for 25 years.

Dist/Sales: Zeitgeist

Protagonist, The

(aka: Shujinko)

Oki, Hiroyuki
1991; Japan; 26 min; Experimental
W: Hiroyuki Oki; *C:* Hiroyuki Oki
Cast: Hiroyuki Oki

Video diary format, which chronicles 13 days in the life of a young man in his rented room. It asks the question 'Who is the actual protagonist?' It ends quite literally with an orgasmic climax with Oki himself in front of the camera.

Dist/Sales: ImageForum

Psycho Beach Party

King, Robert Lee
2000; Canada; 94 min; Comedy
P: Virginia Biddle, Jon Gerrans, Marcus Hu, Victor Syrmis; *W:* Charles Busch; *C:* Arturo Smith; *E:* Suzanne Hines; *M:* David Tobocman, Ben Vaughn
Cast: Charles Busch, Lauren Ambrose, Thomas Gibson, Nicholas Brendon, Kimberley Davies

Wax the washboard and slip into bikini mode! It's beach party time—with a capital M for Murder. New York playwright-cum-drag performer Charles

Busch screenwrites and 'acts' in this hammed-up tribute to 1950s B-movie scream queens, 1960s surf movies and 1970s slasher flicks. Perky Florence 'Chicklet' Forest cruises Malibu beach, curiously monitoring the gaggle of beefy-tight-togs-beach-boys, including the Great Kanaka. Just one problem: Chicklet is constantly at the scene when bloodied bodies wash ashore. Quick to the scene is Sheriff's Captain Monika Stark, who tags Chicklet as her number 1 suspect. Soon the suspects and bodies pile up, amidst a cast of hilarious film stereotypes from surf bums to beach bunnies. A bucket of film references, top-notch performances and a shovel in the side of Hollywood's whitewashed beach daze all make for one riotous whodunit. (MQFF)

Prod Comp: New Oz Productions, Red Horse Films, Strand Releasing
Dist/Sales: Sagittaire, Strand, Wolfe

Psycho Beach Party

Public Opinion

Dvoracek, Ted
1993; USA; 24 min; Drama

Stylised short involving an actor, a priest and a sauna.

Pump

Severance, Abigail
1999; USA; 17 min; Comedy

Sleek production values underpin this award winning short of a young woman's unremitting determination to be rid of her broken heart.

Dist/Sales: bellecote

Punks

Polk, Patrik-Ian
2000; USA; 104 min; Comedy
P: Patrik-Ian Polk, Tracey E. Edmonds, Michael McQuarn; *W:* Patrik-Ian Polk; *C:* Rory King; *E:* Anne Misawa; *M:* Mervyn Warren
Cast: Seth Gilliam, Dwight Ewell, Jazzmun, Renoly

p

Santiago, Rockmond Dunbar

Hopelessly romantic Marcus, a successful photographer, struggles with his inability to acclimate to the mores of contemporary urban gay life. His neighbour and love interest, Darby, tries to balance his own happiness with that of his girlfriend. HIV-positive Hill, copes with his romantic travails after catching his European boyfriend Gilbert locking lips with someone else. Dante, a Latino boy-toy from Beverly Hills, revels in youth while trying to deny his privileged upbringing. And Cris, an imperious transgender diva, is blithely ignorant of how her lead singer affectations are disrupting the harmony of her singing ensemble. Throw in a trio of veritable hunks put to good use as eye-candy and supporting roles and cameos by Loretta Devine, Thea Vidale, and Devon O'Dessa, and you've got a very entertaining stew of black gay experience. (24th San Francisco International Lesbian & Gay Film Festival)

Prod Comp: A Tall Skinny Black Boy, e2 Filmworks
Dist/Sales: e2Filmworks

Quai des Orfèvres

(aka: Jenny Lamour)

Clouzot, Henri-Georges
1947; France; 105 min; B&W; Drama
P: Roger De Venloo; *W:* Henri-Georges Clouzot, Jean Ferry; *C:* Armand Thirard; *E:* Charles Bretoneiche; *M:* Francis Lopez
Cast: Louis Jouvet, Bernard Blier, Suzy Delair, Simone Renant

An entertaining detective thriller using sleazy music halls as the backdrop. Jouvet gives a human face to the role of the police inspector. Delair plays a voluptuous singer and her husband becomes the prime suspects in a murder case. Simone Renant, who plays a lesbian photographer, was said, at the time, to be the most beautiful actress in Paris. Based on the novel by S. A. Steeman.

Awards: Venice Film Festival, 1947: Best Director
Prod Comp: Majestic Films

Queen Christina

Mamoulian, Rouben
1933; USA; 101 min; B&W; Drama
P: Walter Wanger; *W:* H. M. Harwood, Salka Viertel, S. N. Behrman; *C:* William H. Daniels; *E:* Blanche Sewell; *M:* Herbert Stothart
Cast: Greta Garbo, John Gilbert, Lewis Stone, Elizabeth Young, Ian Keith

The androgynous 17th century Swedish queen who gives up the throne for her lover, is arguably Garbo's finest role. Garbo's character was brought up as a boy to succeed the throne form her father. But her career

disintegrates when she falls in love with a Spanish envoy and must decide where to leave the throne. At one point she is attracted to the Countess Ebba, whom she kisses on the lips and promises to go with on a trip to the country. But the Countess betrays Christina by falling in love with a man.

Prod Comp: MGM, United Artists
Dist/Sales: Chapel, NFVLS, Swank

Queen: Marianne Hoppe, The

(aka: Die Königin: Marianne Hoppe)

Schroeter, Werner
2000; France, Germany; 101 min; Documentary
P: Elke Peters; *W:* Werner Schroeter, Monica Keppler; *C:* Alexandra Kordes, Thomas Plenert; *E:* Flo Köhler; *M:* Peer Raben

An intimate documentary portrait of Marianne Hoppe, one of the most fascinating German actresses of her time. Includes in-depth interviews with Hoppe herself, who discusses her sometimes heartbreaking personal life, and amazing career in German cinema. German with English subtitles.

Prod Comp: Mira Filmproduktion, Sender Freies Berlin
Dist/Sales: Transit

Queen of the Night

(aka: La Reina de la Noche)

Ripstein, Arturo
1994; Mexico; 177 min; Drama
P: Jean-Michel Lacor; *W:* Paz Alicia Garciadiego; *C:* Bruno de Keyzer; *E:* Rafael Castanedo; *M:* Lucía Álvarez
Cast: Patricia Rayes Spindola, Blanca Guerra, Alberto Estrella, Ana Ofelia Murguia

The fictionalised account of the famed torch singer of the 1930s and 40s, Lucha Reyes, and her troubled lesbianism. She began as a child performer and, on a tour of the US, married at 15. Lucha had an abortion a year later that left her sterile. She settled down and adopted a daughter but her inner torment continued to surface. Amidst alcohol, drugs and sexual excess she slid into despair.

Prod Comp: Instituto Mexicano de Cinematografía

Queen of the Whole Wide World

Hyde, Roger
2001; USA; 82 min; Documentary
P: Roger Hyde; *E:* Roger Hyde

The Miss USA beauty pageant never looked like this! This pageant of drag queens started in 1989 in LA to raise money for sufferers of HIV/AIDS; 11 years later, this pageant has grown into a gala event attracting crowds of over 2000 and raising more then $225,000. This film tells an outrageous story of the 2000 pageant complete with swimsuit, evening gown and talent competitions. You will meet seven contestants: Misses Mexico, France, Ireland, Antarctica, Norway, Russia, and Saudi Arabia as they work to get their hairstyles, glitzy sets, and insane costume designs ready in time for pageant night. While we become familiar with these very different men, we learn of their personal triumphs and failures in love and life. Of course, as the big day approaches, behind-the-scenes footage shows all the competitiveness and egos that emerge as each vie for the coveted title of Queen of the Whole Wide World. (12th Reel Affirmations Film Festival)

Queen, The

Simon, Frank
1968; USA; 68 min; Documentary
P: Lewis M. Allen
Cast: Andy Warhol, Jack Doroshow, Terry Southern

An hour-long documentary about a Miss All-America Beauty contest held in New York in 1967. It's not your usual beauty contest however, as all the entrants are male transsexuals. Considered at the time to be cutting edge.

Prod Comp: MDH, Vineyard
Dist/Sales: TLA, FirstRunFeatures, BFI

Queen's Cantonese Conversational Course, The

Yung, Wayne
1998; Canada; 33 min; Comedy

In three easy lessons, you'll pick up many phrases that are useful in a gay bar, a cruising park, and a bathhouse.

Queens Don't Lie

(aka: Tunten Lügen Nicht)

von Praunheim, Rosa
2001; Germany; 90 min; Documentary
C: Lorenz Haarmann; E: Mike Shephard

Documentary about four famed Berlin drag queens. German with English subtitles .

Prod Comp: Rosa von Praunheim Filmproduktion
Dist/Sales: Praunheim

Queens Logic

Rash, Steve
1991; USA; 112 min; Comedy
P: Russell Smith, Stuart Oken; W: Tony Spiridakis;
C: Amir Mokri; E: Patrick Kennedy; M: Joe Jackson
Cast: Kevin Bacon, John Malkovich, Linda Fiorentino, Joe Mantegna, Jamie Lee Curtis

Queens Logic begins with a group of people gathering in the New York borough of Queens for a bachelor party and a wedding. Over the next few days these events will be the occasion for various moments of truth and self-revelation, discovery and disappointment. Like reunion films such as Return of the Secaucus 7 and The Big Chill, the plot gives the characters, who are now mostly in their thirties, an opportunity for a mid-life evaluation. Malkovich plays a homosexual who acts on his sexuality but prefers a life of celibacy.

Prod Comp: New Visions Pictures
Dist/Sales: Roadshow, SevenArts

Queer as Folk (1998)

Harding, Sarah / McDougall, Charles
1998; UK; 280 min; Drama
P: Nicola Shindler; W: Russell T. Davies;
C: Nigel Walters; E: Tony Cranstoun; M: Murray Gold
Cast: Aidan Gillen, Craig Kelly, Charlie Hunnam, Denise Black

Queer as Folk is an important story based around the lives of three young gay men that explores the intoxicating extremes of modern-day life and love. It's refreshingly non-judgmental and atypical in its avoidance of stereotype. With a delightful comic script drawing fine performances from the young cast, Queer as Folk is a vibrant, vital and honest reflection of how gay life can be. There's never a dull moment in this lively drama following the lives of three men living large in Manchester's gay village. Stuart Jones has got it all. He's rich, drop-dead gorgeous and always the centre of attention. He can be forgiven the arrogance because he's pretty close to perfection. His best mate Vince Tyler is funny, adorable and definitely a babe but, unlike his friend, has zero confidence in himself. Since time began, Vince has carried a torch for Stuart but his love remains firmly unrequited. They're both 29, hitting Canal Street every night, stalwarts of the scene but just starting to wonder where else their lives may be going. Then along comes Nathan Maloney. Young, wild and coming out with a vengeance, he crowbars his way into their world and once he arrives, nothing is ever the same again. (Wolfe)

Prod Comp: Red Production Company
Dist/Sales: Wolfe, RedProd, ACMI

Queer as Folk 2

Huda, Menhaj
2000; UK; 111 min; Drama
P: Nicola Shindler; W: Russell T. Davies; M: Murray Gold
Cast: Aidan Gillen, Craig Kelly, Charlie Hunnam, Denise Black

Follow up to the controversial first series which

follows the trials and sexual exploits of a group of gay men in London. This second series was created as a one off finale and re-teams the three main protagonists from the first season. The hedonistic Stuart, his long suffering best friend Vince, and the recently 'out' teenager Nathan. *Queer as Folk 2* still focuses on the same milieu of Canal street, the gay district of the first series, but this time around centres on the relationship between Vince and Stuart. Will the two best friends finally consummate their relationship? Will Stuart come out to his parents? Will the impressionistic Nathan finally get over Stuart or follow in his footsteps? (ACMI)

Prod Comp: Red Production Company
Dist/Sales: Wolfe, RedProd, ACMI

Queer as Folk (2000)

Various
2000; USA; 60 min; Drama
P: Sheila Hockin; *W:* Various; *C:* Thom Best;
E: Bill Goddard, Lisa Grootenboer, Wendy Hallam Martin; *M:* Mitch Magonet, Tom Third
Cast: Michelle Clunie, Robert Gant, Thea Gill, Gale Harold, Randy Harrison

Queer as Folk is the outrageous story of a group of gay men and lesbians living in Pittsburgh. Focusing on their relationships, careers, loves and ambitions, this made for television series (based on the British version) is a brave, realistic, funny and sometimes graphic portrayal of modern gay life. (Wolfe)

Prod Comp: Cowlip Productions, Temple Street Productions
Dist/Sales: Showcase, Showtime, Wolfe

Queer Geography: Mapping our Identities

Bolden-Kramer, Rachel / Hernandez, Theresa
2001; USA; 12 min; Documentary

Queer Geography is a short documentary which explores the lives of four queer youth, ages 16-20. It examines sexual orientation, coming out, family life and dealing with being 'out' in school. (Frameline)

Dist/Sales: Frameline

Queer Son

Seitchik, Vickie
1993; USA; 49 min; Documentary

Queer Son is a compelling portrait of parents coping with their children's lesbian or gay sexual orientation. The parents and children Seitchik interviews each come from different social and ethnic backgrounds. Some accepted their children's orientation easily; others had grief to compound their ordeal from the start. (Frameline)

Dist/Sales: Frameline

Queer Story, A

(aka: Jilao Sishi)

Shu, Kei
1997; Hong Kong; 100 min; Drama
Cast: Jordan Chan, George Lam, Fredric Mao

Director Shu Kei's latest film, *A Queer Story*, is a slick, highly entertaining melodrama that deals head-on with themes of gay sexuality and homophobia in Hong Kong—and is refreshingly optimistic in its belief that prejudice can be overcome. Law Kar-sing is a gay 46-year-old marriage counsellor whose trepidation is mounting about his own wedding to his childhood sweetheart Chuen. While puzzling over what to do, Law discovers that his cocky young hairdresser boyfriend has been having an affair. Subplots proliferate as Law recovers from the ordeal by running straight into the arms of a hustler. Watch what happens when Chuen makes a surprise visit and finds Law and his boyfriend caked in green mud-masks! Shu Kei's deft handling of confrontational scenes provides many enjoyable and often extremely funny moments in what is definitely one of the gayest films ever to come out of Hong Kong. (21st International Lesbian & Gay Film Festival) Cantonese & Mandarin with English subtitles.

Queercore: A Punk-u-mentary

Treleaven, Scott
1996; Canada; 20 min; Documentary

This dynamic documentary explores the queer punk underground from its beginnings in the mid 1980s. Features interviews with Bruce La Bruce, G. B. Jones, band members of Pansy Division, and others, plus music by dyke legends Team Dresch and Tribe 8.

Dist/Sales: VTape

Querelle

Fassbinder, Rainer Werner
1982; Germany; 120 min; Drama
P: Dieter Schidor; *W:* Rainer Werner Fassbinder, Burkhard Driest; *C:* Xaver Schwarzenberger, Josef Vavra; *E:* Jiliane Lorenz, Rainer Werner Fassbinder
Cast: Brad Davis, Franco Nero, Jeanne Moreau, Laurent Malet

Based on the novel by Jean Genet, Querelle, a drug smuggling sailor, murders a fellow sailor and takes refuge in a brothel, where he discovers his homosexuality. The film, whose themes echo of sexual submission, violence and passion, was Fassbinder's last. Brad Davis, who plays Querelle, died of AIDS in 1992.

Prod Comp: Gaumont, Planet, Albatros Filmproduktion
Dist/Sales: ACMI, 21stCentury, TLA, FilmsInc, BFI, Wolfe, ACMI

Quest for Love

Noguerira, Helena
1988; South Africa; 95 min; Drama
P: Shan Moodley; *W:* Helena Nogueira;
C: Roy MacGregor; *M:* Tony Rudner
Cast: Jana Cilliers, Sandra Prinsloo, Joanna Weinberg,
Wayne Bowman

Alexandra is a bisexual writer and activist who goes on a cruise with Dorothy, the woman she deeply loves, and Mabel, who in turn loves Dorothy. More complications arise when Alexandra's boyfriend joins the cruise. Set against the political turmoil of South Africa, it is a powerful and un-stereotypical view of lesbian love. This was the first commercial feature film to be produced by a South African woman.

Question of Attribution, A

Schlesinger, John
1992; UK; 70 min; Drama
P: Innes Lloyd; *W:* Alan Bennett; *C:* John Hooper;
E: Mark Day; *M:* Gerald Gouriet
Cast: James Fox, David Calder, Geoffrey Palmer

An intense drama that focuses on the 'Fourth Man' of the Cambridge spy ring. Thirty years after the discovery of the ring the fourth man, Anthony Blunt, a well-known homosexual and art dealer to the Queen, was exposed after his identity was covered up by the British government.

Prod Comp: BBC

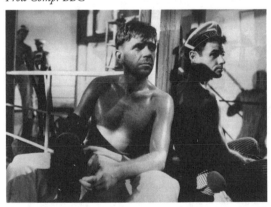

Querelle

Question of Love, A

Thorpe, Jerry
1978; USA; 100 min; Drama
P: William Blinn, Jerry Thorpe; *W:* William Blinn;
C: Charles G. Arnold; *E:* Byron Chudnow;
M: Billy Goldenberg
Cast: Gena Rowlands, Jane Alexander, Ned Beatty,
Bonnie Bedelia

Based on the true story of a nurse and her two sons, who moves in with her lesbian lover. When the oldest boy decides to go back to his father, a hard-fought court battle begins. Well scripted and sensitively handled with a great cast, originally made for television.

Prod Comp: Blinn/Thorpe Productions, Viacom Productions
Dist/Sales: NBC

Questioning Faith

Alston, Macky
2002; USA; 85 min; Documentary
P: Macky Alston; *C:* Tom Hurwitz; *E:* Chris White;
M: Camara Kambon

Macky Alston wants to be a minister. But in this age of AIDS and terrorism how does one preach about God's mercy when everyone around you is suffering from some kind of intimate tragedy. In this personal essay documentary, Alston spends his two years in seminary interviewing friends and learning how their different faiths reconcile them with a theology that stands up to even the most cruel loss. A thoughtful and inspiring film that handles tough questions without losing trust in an ultimate goodness. (2002 Double Take Documentary Festival)

Prod Comp: Cinemax Reel Life
Dist/Sales: Riverfilms

Rachel, Rachel

Newman, Paul
1968; UK; 100 min; Drama
P: Paul Newman; *W:* Stewart Stern; *C:* Gayne Rescher;
E: Dede Allen; *M:* Jerome Moross
Cast: Joanne Woodward, Estelle Parsons, James Olson,
Kate Harrington

Charts the events in the life of a middle-aged schoolteacher in a small New England town. Her close friend is a lonely and repressed lesbian schoolteacher, who in one passionate moment kisses Woodward. Vito Russo describes it as a touching and pathetic moment as Parson's character has been in the closet for years.

Prod Comp: Warner, Kayos
Dist/Sales: Warner

Rachel Williams Documentary

Cunliffe, Mike
1996; UK; 20 min; Documentary

Supermodel Rachel Williams talks straight about her uncompromising view of her sexuality. She talks openly about her relationship with rock singer Alice Temple, what it is like to come out when you're famous, the media's reaction and the not-so-glamorous world of the supermodel.

Prod Comp: Channel 4
Dist/Sales: Channel4

Radical Harmonies

Mosbacher, Dee
2002; USA; 90 min; Documentary
P: Dee Mosbacher

Radical Harmonies chronicles the Women's Music Cultural Movement and its evolution from a 'girl with guitar' to a revolution in the roles of women in music and culture. The movement gave birth to an alternative industry that changed women and music forever. Through festival and performance footage, interviews, and archival material, the film delves into the rich and beautiful history of women creating a cultural life based in a commitment to diversity, personal integrity, feminism and women loving women. In its heyday, during the 1970s and 80s, women's music offered a different message than mainstream musical culture. It opened doors for women musicians, producers, sound and light technicians and for new women-owned recording companies and women-oriented shows. Pioneers like Cris Williamson, Bernice Johnson Reagon, Margie Adam and Linda Tillery recall the frustrations and the triumphs of finding women sound engineers and other professionals in a completely male-dominated industry. (Woman Vision)

Dist/Sales: WomanVision

Rainbow Serpent, The

(aka: Haltéroflic)

Vallois, Philippe
1983; France; 90 min; Thriller
P: Daniel Vassaire; *W:* Philippe Vallois;
C: François About
Cast: Serge Avedikian, Ged Marlon

A suspense thriller about a rookie cop who is investigating a murder and the prime suspect who is a body builder. The cop soon becomes enraptured by the erotic world of gyms and male bodies, and the two men begin to develop an S/M, homoerotic relationship even though they are both straight. French with English subtitles.

Dist/Sales: Frameline

Rainbow, The

Russell, Ken
1989; UK; 107 min; Drama
P: Ken Russell; *W:* Ken Russell, Vivian Russell;
C: Billy Williams; *E:* Peter Davies; *M:* Carl Davis
Cast: Sammi Davis, Glenda Jackson, Amanda Donohue,

Christopher Gable, David Hemmings

A striking drama about sensuality, sexuality and independence. Amanda Donohue plays a lesbian gym instructor who seduces the young main character, Ursula, a wilful, intelligent and independent woman. Their relationship is uninhibited and exploratory, until Ursula falls for a man. Based on the novel by D. H. Lawrence.

Prod Comp: Vestron
Dist/Sales: Col-Tri, Roadshow

Rainmakers - Zimbabwe

Hart, Robbie
1999; Canada; 26 min; Documentary

The spectre of President Mugabe's oppressive and homophobic regime is the backdrop for this gripping account of the fight for human rights and native justice in Zimbabwe.

Dist/Sales: Adobe

Raising Heroes

Langway, Douglas
1995; USA; 90 min; Action
P: Douglas Langway, Rose M. Langway, Henry White;
W: Douglas Langway, Edmond Sorel, Henry White;
C: Stephen Schlueter; *E:* Douglas Langway;
M: Fractured Cylinder
Cast: Troy Sostillio, Henry White, Edmond Sorel

A low budget action/adventure gay film. Paul and Josh are a happy couple and about to embark on the most important event in their lives—adopting a child. But just as they are about to attend the final court hearing for the adoption approval, Josh witnesses a mob killing and becomes the next target. As they are stalked by professional killers they turn to guns, killing and violence to protect their dream of having an alternative family.

Prod Comp: Doppelganger Films
Dist/Sales: WaterBearer, Millivres

Rape of Ganymede, The

Whitman, Tom / Woehmann, Dustin
2000; USA; 10 min; Comedy

The Greek mythological story surrounding Ganymede is retold from Ganymede's point of view. Through his eyes, we tour an Olympus populated by leather daddies (Zeus), circuit queens (Apollo), bull dykes (Athene) and lipstick lesbians (Aphrodite). Skewering both the euphemising of the myth as well as current gay stereotypes and icons, *The Rape of Ganymede* is a sarcastic romp through ancient and contemporary gay culture. (Prometheus)

Dist/Sales: Prometheus

Ray's Male Heterosexual Dance Hall

Gordon, Bryan
1988; USA; 23 min; Comedy

Sam Logan is looking for a job—and not just any job. And it may all depend on who he chooses as his next dance partner at Ray's Male Heterosexual Dance Hall!

Awards: San Francisco International Lesbian & Gay Film Festival, 1989: Audience Award Best Short Film; Academy Awards, 1988: Best Short Film Live Action

Razor Blade Smile

West, Jake
1998; UK; 101 min; Horror
P: Robert Mercer, Jake West; *W:* Jake West;
C: James Slolan; *M:* Richard Wells
Cast: Eileen Daly, Grahame Wood, Christopher Adamson, Isabel Brook

Razor Blade Smile is an over-the-top camp vampire flick that manages to send up the whole Lilith myth in very stylish and fun manner.

Reaching for the Moon

Goulding, Edmund
1930; USA; 91 min; B&W; Comedy
W: Edmund Goulding; *C:* Ray June, Robert Planck;
E: Hal C. Kern, Lloyd Nosler; *M:* Irving Berlin
Cast: Douglas Fairbanks Sr, Bebe Daniels, Edward Everett Horton, Claud Allister, Jack Muhall

A girl-shy Wall Street millionaire, played by Fairbanks, takes lessons in love from his valet (in a hilarious scene of homosexual innuendo). He plucks up his courage and follows an aviatrix to Europe on a luxury liner. In mid-voyage he hears that he has lost all his money in the 1929 stock market crash.

Prod Comp: United Artists, Feature Productions
Dist/Sales: NFVLS, UA

Reaching Out to Lesbian, Gay and Bisexual Youth

Rokab, Sylvie
1996; USA; 21 min; Documentary

This film, sponsored by the Gay, Lesbian and Straight Teachers Network, features interviews with young gay men and lesbians who discuss how homophobic attitudes of not only fellow students but also their adult teachers negatively affects their school work. These articulate young people also comment on their own feelings about their sexual orientation, their 'coming out' experiences, the importance of being 'out' to friends and family, and the need for a gay and lesbian community. Their

commentary is supplemented by interviews with doctors and psychologists who underline the need for sensitivity training of teachers and other adults who work with gay and lesbian youth. (Cinema Guild)

Dist/Sales: CinemaGuild

Real Ellen Story, The

Bailey, Fenton / Barbato, Randy
1998; USA; 42 min; Documentary

This documentary traces the 'coming out' episode of *The Ellen Show* from its earliest beginnings, when a TV executive first suggested to Ellen that she needed a love interest, and would she consider a puppy, as a lesbian was deemed too threatening? An important and entertaining look at a pivotal moment in mainstream US television history. (MQFF)

Dist/Sales: WorldOfWonder, PictureThis!, Wolfe

Rebel Rebel

Burke, Betsy
2001; USA; 21 min; Drama

Dolores' life has become depressing and aimless, until she takes temporary custody of her wayward teenage second cousin. Both of their lives are transformed by the surprise relationship that develops between them.

Red Dirt

Purvis, Tag
1999; USA; 110 min; Drama
P: Cyril Bijaoui, Sean Gibbons; *W:* Tag Purvis;
C: Theodore Cohen; *E:* Nikko Tsiotsias; *M:* Nathan Barr
Cast: Karen Black, Dan Montgomery Jnr, Aleksa Palladino, Walton Goggins

Set in a small town in rural Mississippi, *Red Dirt* is an intimate, character-driven drama focusing on the dreams and desires of small-town boy Griffith Burns, as he struggles to escape the stifling confines of his home. Encouraging him to stay are his sensual cousin Emily and his agoraphobic Aunt Summer. Snared by the women he loves, Griffith threatens to tear free when an attractive stranger, Lee Todd drifts into town. *Red Dirt* is lushly shot, and is sure to appeal to fans of Tennessee Williams. (MQFF)

Prod Comp: Sweet Tea Productions
Dist/Sales: Wolfe, VideoAmericain, 10%

Red Heat

Collector, Robert
1985; Germany, USA; 104 min; Thriller
P: Mario Kassar, Andrew G. Vajna, Ernst R. von Theumer; *W:* Robert Collector, Gary Drucker;

r

C: Wolfgang Dickman; *E:* Anthony Redman;
M: Tangerine Dream
Cast: Sylvia Kristel, Linda Blair, Sue Kiel, William Ostrander

A women-behind-bars film set behind the iron curtain. An innocent American woman is captured and must endure all sorts of traumas. Kristel plays a lesbian warden who terrorises the woman. A particularly anti-gay film, all the lesbians are torturing, murderous heathens, but good for a laugh if you are interested in hair-pulling, underwear-clad lesbians.

Dist/Sales: Palace

Red Label

Dun, Viki
1987; Australia; Comedy

A send up of the gangster genre with our detective, Laura Hunt, a Red Label whiskey swilling, lesbian. She is hired by a woman to find a stolen leather jacket and finds herself in the world of lesbian leather bars.

Red Rain

Plotkin, Laura
1998; USA; 60 min; Documentary
P: Laura Plotkin; *C:* Catlin Manning;
E: Gabriel Rhodes; *M:* E. J. Sharpe, Jon Birdsong
Cast: Gina 'Boom Boom' Guidi

'I was a lesbian way before I was a fighter' says Gina 'Boom Boom' Guidi in this outstanding behind-the-scenes account of the life of a professional female boxer. The film follows the charismatic Guidi's compelling story from working-class roots to struggles with addiction and domestic violence, through a gruelling daily training regime to the biggest fight of her career the women's IBFA junior middleweight world title. Tenderly cradling a rabbit in her massive arms, pounding an opponent and then suggesting they keep in touch, weeping in frustration and rage after a cruel homophobic act, Guidi emerges as an outrageous, compelling, and humane representative of a sometimes inhuman sport.

Prod Comp: Lolafilms
Dist/Sales: Lola, Wolfe

Red Ribbon Blues

Winkler, Charles
1995; USA; 100 min; Comedy
P: Brad Wyman, Dale Rosenbloom; *W:* Charles Winkler; *C:* Larry Blanford; *E:* Clayton Halsey;
M: John Frizzell
Cast: Paul Mercurio, Ru Paul, John Epperson, Debi Mazar

Troy is 29-years-old and is HIV-positive. He has been to 23 funerals for friends who have died of AIDS. His one hope is a miracle AIDS drug called D-64 but it is far too expensive to buy and the chance of getting on the drug trial is very low. Darcy and Duke are from Troy's HIV support group and decide that if they can't buy the drug why not steal it. Troy reluctantly goes along with their plan. They rob a number of drug stores and steal more than they need and decide to distribute it to the rest of the community. Now they have a great mission in life and finds their biggest target—the drug company's warehouse.

Prod Comp: Red Ribbon Productions
Dist/Sales: Kushner-Locke, Col-Tri

Red River

Hawks, Howard / Rosson, Arthur
1948; USA; 133 min; B&W; Western
P: Howard Hawks; *W:* Charles Schnee, Borden Chase;
C: Russell Harlan; *E:* Christian Nyby; *M:* Dimitri Tiomkin
Cast: John Wayne, Montgomery Clift, Joanne Dru, Walter Brennan, Colleen Gray

This classic western stars the legendary John Wayne at the peak of his career and Montgomery Clift in his screen debut. The film is an account of the first cattle drive over the Chisolm Trail, from deep Texas to Abilene, Kansas. Authentic detail and stunning cinematography bring to life the trials and tribulations of this extraordinary challenge for the men who battled the dust, rain, heat and frustration of the long, hard drive. The demands of this rigorous journey further strain the edgy relationship between the film's key characters. An epic western in every sense and loaded with repressed sexuality.

Prod Comp: Monterey Productions, Charles K. Feldman Group
Dist/Sales: ACMI, Warner, NFVLS, UA

Red Shoe Diaries 3: Another Woman's Lipstick, The

Eisenman, Rafael / King, Zalman / Kotcheff, Ted
1993; USA; 90 min; Drama
P: Rafael Eisenman, Avram 'Butch' Kaplan, Zalman King, David Saunders, Jeff Alan Young; *W:* Chloe King, Zalman King, Ed Silverstein; *C:* Larry Fong, Daniel Mindel, Ronn Schmidt; *E:* James Gavin Bedford, Curtis Edge, Marc Grossman; *M:* George S. Clinton
Cast: David Duchovny, Nina Siemaszko, Lydie Denier, Christina Fulton

A classy soft porn erotic film series for the straight man, it tells the story of a woman who discovers lipstick on her husband's collar and decides to follow him. He goes to a restaurant to meet his lover, the wife sees the beautiful woman and becomes obsessed with her. Finally she dresses as a man and picks up the other woman in a nightclub and they begin a sexual relationship.

Prod Comp: Red Shoes Inc., The Zalman King Company
Dist/Sales: Col-Tri

Reflecting Skin, The

Ridley, Philip
1990; UK; 93 min; Horror
P: Roy Burdis, Dominic Anciano; *W:* Philip Ridley;
C: Dick Pope; *E:* Scott Thomas; *M:* Nick Bicât
Cast: Viggo Mortensen, Lindsay Duncan, Jeremy Cooper, Duncan Fraser, Sheila Moore

An almost non-narrative, poetic horror film set in the Midwest in the 1950s. Seth is an eight-year-old boy who is virtually ignored by his neurotic mother and father. He creates an imaginary world of his own and when he finds a dead foetus in the barn he believes it to be a dead friend who has been turned into an angel. But his world begins to collapse and reality takes hold when his father is accused of killing and sexually abusing young boys in the local area. Seth's brother returns in a rather disturbed state from the Pacific during World War II to his lover, a widow with a necrophilic fetish. No one and nothing is conventional in this macabre film.

Prod Comp: Fugitive, BBC, British Screen, Zenith
Dist/Sales: Col-Tri, BBC, Miramax, Cowboy

Reflections

Ellsworth, Robert
1993; USA; 18 min; Drama

A disturbing short concerning a woman's descent into madness. A couple move into a flat unaware that the previous tenant, a gay man, was murdered there. (MQFF)

Reflections in a Golden Eye

Huston, John
1967; USA; 110 min; Drama
P: Raymond Stark, John Huston; *W:* Gladys Hill, Chapman Mortimer; *C:* Aldo Tonti; *E:* Russell Lloyd; *M:* Toshiro Mayuzumi
Cast: Marlon Brando, Elizabeth Taylor, Julie Harris, Brian Keith

A US Army soldier's repressed homosexuality is about to threaten his life and career. A landmark exploration of a taboo theme, it is also rich with humour. Based on the novel by Carson McCullers.

Prod Comp: Warner, Seven Arts
Dist/Sales: Warner, SevenArts, Swank

Reform School Girls

De Simone, Tom
1986; USA; 90 min; Drama
P: Jack Cummins; *W:* Tom De Simone;
C: Howard Wexler; *E:* Michael Spence
Cast: Sybil Danning, Wendy O. Williams, Pat Ast, Linda Carol, Charlotte McGinnis

A young first-time offender learns hard and fast that the rules of the outside world do not apply in reform school. She is determined to stop corruption at the school but runs headlong into the iron-fisted, leather-clad lesbian played by Williams.

Prod Comp: New World, Balcor Film Investors, International Cinevision Productions
Dist/Sales: Roadshow

Reframing AIDS

Parmar, Pratibha
1987; UK; 35 min; Documentary

The film investigates how AIDS has been used to increase state harassment of gay men, lesbians, black people and women in Britain. Framing the problem in terms of a left politic, it reveals how homophobia and puritanism have caused the slow government response to AIDS.

Dist/Sales: GroupeIntervention

Reframing AIDS

Relationships

1997; 50 min; Documentary

This film focuses on married, cohabiting, gay and lesbian couples and establishes the similarities and differences between these couples in how they handle conflict, their views on work and the role played by their support network of family and friends. The program also considers the role play by gender and society in influencing personal relationships. (EMA)

Dist/Sales: EMA

Relax

Newby, Christopher
1990; UK; 30 min; B&W; Drama
P: Mehdi Norowzian
Cast: Philip Rosch

London, 1990. Steve scrubs himself neurotically prior to going to the doctor for an HIV test. Once there the doctor tells him, 'Relax'. The examination is intercut with scenes of Steve and his pal Ned watching porn films and sunbathing on the roof. Later, Steve picks up Keith, a cyclist, but the encounter is tense because Steve is too frightened of the disease. Keith urges him on, 'Relax'. A well-shot film, in beautiful black and white, which encapsulates the fears and hopes of living in the time of AIDS. (Frameline)

Awards: Melbourne International Film Festival, 1991: Best Experimental Film; Berlin Film Festival, 1991: Best Gay Film
Prod Comp: BFI
Dist/Sales: Frameline, Ronin, BFI

Relax... It's Just Sex

Castellaneta, P. J.
1998; USA; 108 min; Comedy
P: Steven J. Wolfe, Megan O'Neill, Harold Warren;
W: P. J. Castellaneta; *C:* Lon Magdich; *E:* Tom Seid;
M: Lori Eschler Frystak
Cast: Jennifer Tilly, Lori Petty, Mitchell Anderson, Cynda Williams, Timothy Paul Perez

Relax...It's Just Sex revolves around a close-knit group of thirty-something friends—heterosexual, homosexual and bisexual. Lovelorn gay playwright Vincy desperately wants a lover. Vincy's friend Tara desperately wants to get pregnant with her boyfriend Gus, who desperately wants to find himself. Gus' brother Javi announces he's HIV-positive and falls in love with loudmouth artist Buzz. Long time lesbian couple Sarina and Megan fall out of love, and in love with Robin and Jered respectively, while their clean-cut Christian friends, the sickeningly perfect couple Dwight and Diego, pray for them all. Confused? Sprinkled with plenty of smart banter and eye-popping sex, *Relax...It's Just Sex* portrays the trials and tribulations of sex and love in the 1990s in a playful, humorous and poignant way. (MQFF)

Prod Comp: Forefront Films, Sneak Preview Entertainment
Dist/Sales: Millivres, JourDeFete, Haut-et-Court, Wolfe, Mongrel, ACMI

Rendez-vous d'Anna, Les

Akerman, Chantal
1978; Belgium; 121 min; Drama
P: Alain Dahan; *W:* Chantal Akerman; *C:* Jean Penzer;
E: Francine Sandberg
Cast: Aurore Clement, Helmut Griem, Lea Massari, Jean-Pierre Cassel

Anna, a film director, goes on a train journey across Europe in order to publicise her latest film. Along the way she meets an assortment of characters. During the course of the journey, she describes to her mother a sexual experience with another woman. An austere, affecting portrait of a woman lost. French with English subtitles.

Prod Comp: Paradise Films, Hélène Films, Unité Trois, ZDF
Dist/Sales: NFVLS

Reno Finds Her Mom

Dean-Pilcher, Lydia
1997; USA; 90 min; Documentary
P: Lydia Dean-Pilcher, Reno, Tina Di Feliciantonia;
W: Reno; *C:* Trish Govoni; *E:* Jane Wagner
Cast: Reno, Mary Tyler Moore, Lily Tomlin

In this made-for-HBO docudramedy, lesbian stand-up comic Karen Reno, adopted at birth by lily-white suburbanites, goes in search of her biological mother and her ethnic roots. Hilarious at times, poignant at others, Reno's film gives Madonna's *Truth or Dare* a run for the money in the Media Personality Allows Camera To Capture Unflattering Moments Of Real Emotion department. Reno jokes, screams, rants, rails, mugs, curses, cries and connives her way through a Kafkaesque adoption bureaucracy, exhibiting all the bravado and vulnerability that so endears Reno to her fans. When a clandestine source in the adopted underground scores the vital information as to Reno's mother's name and present whereabouts, Reno must face a moment she has dreaded and longed for her whole life. Brief fantasy-scene cameos by Lily Tomlin and Mary Tyler Moore add deft, comic touches to lighten the tone whenever the material threatens to get too heavy. The film is ultimately uplifting because, corny as it sounds, not only does Reno find her Mom—she finds herself in the process of searching. (1998 Austin Gay and Lesbian International Film Festival)

Prod Comp: HBO
Dist/Sales: Reno

Replay
(aka: La Répétition)

Corsini, Catherine
2000; France; 96 min; Drama
P: Philippe Martin; *W:* Catherine Corsini, Pascale Breton, Pierre Erwan Guillaume, Marc Syrigas;
C: Agnés Godard; *E:* Sabine Mamou; *M:* Pierre Bondu, Fabrice Dumont
Cast: Emmanuelle Béart, Pascale Bussières, Dani Levy,

Jean-Pierre Kalfon

Imagine *Mina Tannenbaum* morphing into *Single White Female*! or *Beaches* becoming *All About Eve* and you'll get some idea of what to expect in Catherine Corsini's engrossing drama about two best friends who fall out and then meet up again several years later to resume their push-me-pull-you relationship. What makes the film so interesting, however, is Corsini's refusal to fall back on stereotypes. Just when you've pegged one character as a prime example of that old and not-so-lamented Hollywood favourite—the psycho dyke—you realise neither woman is the villain here. Unlike Diane Kurys' similarly themed *Six Days and Six Nights*, they are both flawed women for whom love burns so furiously it can't help but be destructive as well as positive. These are in-depth brilliantly drawn characters, played with tremendous skill and intelligence by Emmanuelle Béart and Pascale Bussiéres. French with English subtitles. (MQFF)

Prod Comp: Le Studio Canal+
Dist/Sales: FPI

Replay

Requiem pour un Vampire

(aka: Vierges et Vampires)

Rollin, Jean
1971; France; 95 min; Horror
P: Jean Rollin, Sam Selsky; *W:* Jean Rollin;
C: Renan Polles; *M:* Pierre Raph
Cast: Marie-Pierre Castel, Mireille D'Argent, Philippe Gasté, Dominique

A classic of the sexual supernatural, when shown in its original version. It's the story of two young women on the run who shelter in an old castle inhabited by a vampire and his cohorts. They become captive and must lose their virginity to be initiated into the group. What follows is a sado-erotic blend of vampirism and sex. Rollin's fourth film in his examination of vampire sex.
French with English subtitles.

Prod Comp: Les Films, ABC

Rescuing Desire

Rogers, Adam
1995; USA; 115 min; Comedy
P: Patrick Sisam; *M:* Wendy Blackstone
Cast: Melinda Mullins, Caitlin Dulanyt, Tamara Tunie, Ellen Cleghorne, Lea Delaria

Toni Wilson is a respected nurse who works in a small private hospital. At 46 years old she is engaged to Ralph, a doctor, but instead of experiencing the joy and expectation usually associated with this event, she is becoming more and more anxious. Suddenly she has become attracted to women. Ralph thinks it's all hormonal but Toni knows better. She begins expeditions to gay bookstores and lesbian bars where she meets a co-worker, Van, and her friend Evonne. Toni is instantly attracted to the beautiful and mysterious Evonne and the two begin an affair. A humorous look at coming out for older women.

Dist/Sales: Pilgrims4

Residencia, La

(aka: The House that Screamed)

Ibáñez-Serrador, Narcisco
1969; Spain; 94 min; Thriller
P: Arturo Gonzalez; *W:* Luis Verner Penafiel, Narcisco Ibáñez-Serrador; *C:* Manuel Berenguer;
E: Reginald Mills; *M:* Waldo de los Rios
Cast: Lilli Palmer, Cristina Galbó, John Moulder-Brown, Mary Maude

La Residencia is set in a school for runaway girls run by a ruthless teacher who believes in absolute discipline. Of course the girls get up to all sorts of mischief, including rampant sex, lesbian affairs and torture. Meanwhile girls are being murdered, one by one. Spanish with English subtitles.

Prod Comp: Anabel Films
Dist/Sales: Ascanbee

Resident Alien

Nossiter, Jonathan
1992; USA; 85 min; Documentary
P: Chantal Bernheim, Jonathan Nossiter; *W:* Jonathan Nossiter; *C:* John Foster; *E:* Jonathan Nossiter
Cast: Quentin Crisp, John Hurt, Holly Woodlawn, Paul Morrissey

Documentary on the life of famous queer Quentin Crisp, (author of *The Naked Civil Servant*). Includes his views of homosexual pop culture.

Dist/Sales: Greycat

Resonance

Cummins, Stephen / Hunt, Simon
1991; Australia; 12 min; B&W; Drama
P: Paul Fogo; *W:* Stephen Cummins, Simon Hunt;

C: Brendan Young; *E:* Annette Davey; *M:* Simon Hunt
Cast: Mathew Bergan, Chad Courtney, Annette Evans

Beginning with a gay-bashing in the back streets of Sydney, the film uses gesture and dance as an interior monologue to explore acts of violence.

Prod Comp: Resonance Productions
Dist/Sales: Ronin, Frameline, NFVLS

Resonance

Return of Sarah's Daughters, The

Jarmel, Marcia
1997; USA; 56 min; Documentary

The Return of Sarah's Daughters is a compelling personal documentary about secular women drawn to Jewish Orthodoxy. Rus, a no-nonsense social worker, discovers fulfilment in the Hasidic community. Myriam, a spiritually-oriented lesbian, struggles to fit in, but ultimately leaves to become a rabbi. Their stories challenge the filmmaker to give more than a feminist tour of this closed world. She must confront her own lack of ethnic identity. What does tradition have to offer? At what price? Ultimately, her journey illuminates the modern conflict between assimilation and tradition, community and individualism. (WMM)

Dist/Sales: WMM

Return to Go!

(aka: Zürück Auf Los!)

Sanoussi-Bliss, Pierre
1999; Germany; 92 min; Drama
P: Frank Löprich, Katrin Schlösser; *W:* Pierre Sanoussi-Bliss; *C:* Thomas Plenert; *E:* Christian Cloos
Cast: Pierre Sanoussi-Bliss, Bart Klein, Doris Dörrie, Dieter Bach

Best friends Sam and Sebastian are searching for Mr Right and the meaning of life. When Sam's relationship with Manne begins to sour, he seeks comfort with Sebastian, a Barbra Streisand impersonator and TV commercial dancing tomato. When Manne is admitted to hospital, Sam goes to his side, and Sebastian moves in to care for Sam. Along the way, each takes a lover (a male nurse/model and a British painter) and the four end up sharing the two bedroom flat where they survive casual flings, cigarettes and booze, lack of money, and the odd tragedy. An inspiring film about alternative family, the value of home, and the importance of learning to love ourselves. (MQFF)
German with English subtitles.

Dist/Sales: O-Filmproduktion

Revoir Julie

(aka: Julie and Me)

Crépeau, Jeanne
1998; Canada; 92 min; Drama
P: Jeanne Crépeau; *W:* Jeanne Crépeau;
C: Michel Lamothe, Stephan Ivanov; *E:* Myriam Poirier;
M: Karen Young
Cast: Dominique Leduc, Stephanie Morgenstern, Marcel Sabourin, Muriel Dutil

Sweet, sunny and fresh, *Revoir Julie* tells the story of two friends who reconcile after having lost touch for 15 years. Juliet is recovering from another traumatic break up when she begins to think about her school friend Juliet. The women meet up and over the course of a couple of days are confronted with unresolved feelings that having been lying dormant since their school days. French with English subtitles.

Prod Comp: Box Films
Dist/Sales: Crepeau

Revolutionary Girl Utena: The Movie

(aka: Shôjo kakumei Utena: Adolescence mokushiroku)

Ikuhara, Kunihiko
1999; Japan; 87 min; Animation
P: Toshimichi Otsuki; *W:* Yoji Enokido;
C: Toyomitsu Nanajo; *E:* Shigeru Nishiyama

A new student comes to a strange school and is

caught up in a battle for the affection of a beautiful and mysterious girl. Sounds like a familiar plot, doesn't it. But *Revolutionary Girl Utena: The Movie* is not your typical high school drama. For one thing, the new student isn't all he seems to be—and neither is the school. Duels, mystery, conspiracy, hate, love and millions of roses fill this award-winning animated movie. In 1997, director Kunihiko Ikuhara and popular female comic artist Chiho Saito created the TV series *Revolutionary Girl Utena*, which broke new ground in portraying an intense emotional relationship between two girls, gender-bending Utena and femme Anthy. In the TV series, Ikuhara and Saito created a world in which the beautiful and powerful students of exclusive Oohtori Academy each suffer for their secrets, even as they try to win the mysterious 'power to revolutionise the world.' With the movie, Ikuhara takes the relationship between Utena and Anthy to the next level. (26th San Francisco International Lesbian & Gay Film Festival) Japanese with English subtitles.

Prod Comp: Shojo Kakumei Utena Production
Dist/Sales: ProductionIG

Revolutions Happen like Refrains in a Song

Deocampo, Nick
1987; Philippines; 85 min; Documentary
Cast: Reynaldo Villarma

The third film in a trilogy that focuses on the links between poverty and prostitution in the Philippines. It follows the lives of the people in the first two films, *Oliver* (1983) and *Children of the Regime* (1985). It is an uncompromising look at street life and we find Oliver is still supporting his family by working in a gay bar in Manila and children are still selling their bodies in order to survive.

Rewriting the Script: Love Letter to Our Families

2001; Canada; 46 min; Documentary
P: Leela Acharya, Amina Ally, Farzana Doctor, Anjula Gogia, Zeenat Janmohamed, Nasreen Khan, Deena Ladd, Anuja Mendiratta, Arif Noorani

Rewriting the Script features frank discussions with parents, siblings and extended family members of South Asian gays, lesbians, bisexuals and transgendered people. Poignant testimonies are shared not only about the coming out experience but how these families transformed themselves to include their queer children, changing the larger South Asian community in the process. The documentary speaks not only to experiences of South Asians (which includes people originating from the Indian subcontinent), but to other

diasporic communities as well. (V Tape)

Prod Comp: Friday Night Productions
Dist/Sales: VTape

Rhythm & Blues

Lennhoff, Stephen
2000; UK; 90 min; Comedy
P: Hugh Bygott-Webb, Dominic Denny;
W: Michael Jones; *C:* Fiona Cunningham-Reid;
E: Patrick McDonnell; *M:* Michael Conn
Cast: Angus MacInnes, Paul Blackthorne, Ian Henderson, Phillipe Sartori, Richard Ritchie

Rhythm & Blues follows the adventures of a Scottish skinhead Byron and his enigmatic Adonis protégé John. A gay comedy about rent boys and sugar daddies set in fantasy Great Britain circa 1980.

Prod Comp: Life on Mars
Dist/Sales: Equator

Rice and Potatoes

Biasatti, John / Wilson, Todd
1998; USA; 58 min; Documentary

Rice: Slang for gay Asians. Potatoes: Slang for gay Caucasians. Filmed in San Francisco, *Rice and Potatoes* presents a candid look at the issues and stereotypes surrounding interracial gay relationships. Often funny, always thought provoking commentary by a diverse cast of 17 gay men, both Asian and Caucasian.

Dist/Sales: TLA

Richard's Things

Harvey, Anthony
1980; UK; 104 min; Drama
P: Mark Shivers; *W:* Frederic Raphael;
C: Freddie Young; *E:* Lesley Walker; *M:* Georges Delerue
Cast: Liv Ullmann, Mark Eden, Gwen Taylor, Amanda Redman, Amanda Walker

Slow-moving drama of marital infidelity. A woman and her late husband's girlfriend come together for companionship and to mourn their loss. But they soon become attracted to one another and fall in love.

Prod Comp: Southern Pictures

Right to be Different, The

Cipelletti, Claudio
1998; Italy; 61 min; Documentary
W: Claudio Cipelletti

Gay and straight students from three Italian high schools discuss the difficulties encountered when growing up in a homophobic society.

Right Wing, Right Off, Right Hons, Right?

Kwietniowski, Richard
1991; UK; 100 min; Documentary
P: Susan Ardill, Clare Beavan

From devout conservatives to the merely politically incorrect, homosexuals on the Right have tended to escape the limelight. This film redresses the balance, probing those who join the Tories, become yuppies, go to the opera and feature in upmarket glossies.

Prod Comp: Channel 4
Dist/Sales: Channel4

Righteous Babes, The

Parmar, Pratibha
1998; UK; 50 min; Documentary

Inspired by the likes of Chrissie Hynde, only to be dumbed-down again by The Spice Girls, women are stripping both the pop and the cock from rock. To steal a phrase from Skunk Anansie's Skin, it's all about 'Clit Rock'. British lesbian filmmaker Pratibha Parmar delivers an urgent dose of male ego deflation in this uncompromising rockumentary that re-evaluates feminism in an era when even some of its most vocal vocalists are hesitant to wave the flag. Splashes of funky vid clips are tucked between head grabs from Sinead O'Connor, Tori Amos, Chrissie Hynde, Skin and Ani DiFranco, as well as academics Gloria Steinem and Camille Paglia.

Dist/Sales: Cinenova

Rights and Reactions

Lippman, Jane / Zwickler, Phil
1987; USA; 56 min; Documentary
P: Paul Zwickler

Documentary about the struggle for civil rights for gay and lesbian people, centred on the 1986 public hearings in New York City Council Chambers on a proposed local bill to outlaw discrimination on the basis of sexual preference; a Bill which was finally passed.

Dist/Sales: ACMI, Salzgeber

Rites of Passage

Salva, Victor
1999; USA; 95 min; Thriller
P: J. Todd Harris; *W:* Victor Salva;
C: Don E. Fauntleroy; *E:* Ed Marx; *M:* Bennett Salvay
Cast: Dean Stockwell, Jason Behr, James Remar, Robert Keith

The Farraday men are men with secrets. And when all of them end up at the family's mountain get-a-way unexpectedly—one secret turns deadly in this unique and chilling thriller from writer/director

Victor Salva. Old wounds and resentments between father and son arise as Dell realises that his homophobia may be pushing his youngest boy, Jason Behr, into the arms of a much darker and deadlier father. (Wolfe)

Dist/Sales: Daly/Harris, Wolfe

Ritual

Bennett Clay, Stanley
1998; USA; 78 min; Drama
P: Beth Hubbard, Michael Hubbard;
W: Stanley Bennett Clay; *C:* David Mullen;
E: Nicholas Eliopoulos, Eric Kahn, Michael Schulz;
M: Lumelle Humes
Cast: Clarence Williams III, Denise Nicholas, Shawn Michael Howard, Angelle Brooks

Through the shimmering glass of their beautiful Malibu home, the Beckers appear to be the ideal family. Their father is a successful attorney; their mother, a former Broadway actress. Their two children, Mason and Teresa, are everything parents could hope for. But beneath their supposedly perfect home and perfect lives, lie secrets that threaten to destroy them. When handsome gay Mason drops out of college, and suddenly returns home, the precarious balance of power within the family shifts, threatening to destroy their carefully constructed façade. (2000 Tampa International Gay & Lesbian Film Festival)

Prod Comp: Gotham Entertainment Group

Ritual Nation

Kaminsky, Sean
2000; USA; 29 min; Documentary

Over the course of two years, New York filmmaker Sean Kaminsky travelled alone for two years with a digital video camera filming his visits to three unique alternative communities: the Rainbow Family in Oregon, the Radical Faeries in Tennessee and the Burning Man Festival in Nevada.

Dist/Sales: Spectrum, CFMDC

Ritz, The

Lester, Richard
1976; UK; 88 min; Comedy
P: Denis O'Dell; *W:* Terence McNally; *C:* Paul Wilson;
E: John Bloom; *M:* Ken Thorne
Cast: Jack Weston, Jerry Stiller, Rita Moreno, Treat Williams, Kaye Ballard, F. Murray Abraham

In an attempt to get away from his hit-man brother-in-law, a Cleveland sanitation worker hides out in a gay bathhouse where he is certain that he won't be found but his brother-in-law's business dealings are spread far and wide. A riotous farce (some may call it tasteless and tacky) with some fabulous musical numbers to boot.

Prod Comp: Warner, Courtyard Films
Dist/Sales: ReelMovies, Warner

Rock Hudson

Nicolella, John
1990; USA; 89 min; Drama
P: Diana Kerew, Renee Palyo; *W:* Dennis Turner;
C: Newton Thomas Sigel; *E:* Peter Parasheles;
M: Paul Chihara
Cast: Thomas Ian Griffith, Daphne Ashbrook, William R. Moses, Andrew Robinson

Made for TV biopic about the life and career of Rock Hudson. It begins with his truck-driving days, his acting career and rise to fame, and finally his death from AIDS. Based on the book by his ex-wife, Phyllis Gates, and on the court records from the civil suit brought by his former lover, Marc Christian.

Prod Comp: Konigsberg International, The Sanitsky Company
Dist/Sales: Warner

Rock Hudson's Home Movies

Rappaport, Mark
1992; USA; 63 min; Documentary
W: Mark Rappaport
Cast: Eric Farr

Documentary about the career and eventual death from AIDS of movie star Rock Hudson. Film clips from over 30 of his films illustrate ways in which his sexuality was played out on the screen.

Prod Comp: Couch Potato Productions
Dist/Sales: ArtisticLicense, WaterBearer, NFVLS, ACMI

Rock the Boat

Houston, Robert
1998; USA; 88 min; Documentary

Filmmaker Robert Houston joins the crew of the sloop 'Survivor' to capture the experiences of 11 HIV-positive men during competition in the 2000 mile Trans-Pacific Yacht Race from Los Angeles to Hawaii in 1997.

Rockwell

Less, Vadan
1999; USA; 22 min; Drama

In the small town of Rockwell, football is the only thing that matters, but with the arrival of city boy Cody, star player Jake soon has other things on his mind. (MQFF)

Dist/Sales: FloridaUni

Rocky Horror Picture Show, The

Sharman, Jim
1975; UK, USA; 95 min; Comedy
P: Michael White, John Goldstone; *W:* Richard O'Brien, Jim Sharman; *C:* Peter Suschitzky; *E:* Graeme Clifford; *M:* Richard Hartley, Richard O'Brien
Cast: Tim Curry, Susan Sarandon, Barry Bostwick, Richard O'Brien, Little Nell, Patricia Quinn

When Brad and Janet, the clean-cut all-American couple, can't get their car to start, they end up at the castle of Dr Frank N. Furter, a transvestite, bisexual alien scientist. A very enjoyable sci-fi hi-camp spoof with memorable songs which has become a cult favourite.

Prod Comp: 20th Century-Fox
Dist/Sales: Wolfe, 20thCenturyFox

Roi Danse, Le
(aka: The King is Dancing)

Corbiau, Gérard
2000; France; 114 min; Drama
P: Dominique Janne; *C:* Gérard Simon; *E:* Philippe Ravoet, Ludo Troch; *M:* Jean-Bastiste Lully
Cast: Benoit Magimel, Tchéky Karyo, Boris Terral, Colette Emmanuelle

Historians didn't call Louis XVI of France 'the Sun King' for nothing. The first modern monarch to declare himself the centre of his country's governmental universe, he was also the prototypical media darling. After seizing power from his mother and her advisors, he gained public fame—and popularised the relatively new art of ballet—by becoming a dancer himself. He simultaneously used music and theatre to help glorify and streamline his own image. *Le Roi Danse* revolves around Louis' partnership with his choreographer and court musician, Jean-Baptiste Lully. Corbiau liberally blends historical fact with juicy, soap-opera fiction, creating a vibrant portrait of an unstable, passionate world where music can heal and harm with equal facility. (Gemma Files, Toronto Eye Weekly) French with English subtitles.

Prod Comp: Le Studio Canal+

Room of Words, The
(aka: La Stanza della parole)

Molé, Franco
1990; Italy, USA; 115 min; Drama
W: Francesco Molè; *E:* Kathleen Stratton; *M:* Gianni Silano
Cast: Martine Brochard, David Brandon, Linda Carol

Another version of the steamy relationship between artist and writer Anais Nin, writer Henry Miller, and his wife, June, the woman they both loved.

Prod Comp: Wind Film

r

Roommates

Metzger, Alan
1994; USA; 100 min; Drama
W: Robert W. Lenski; C: Geoffrey Erb;
M: Lee Holdridge
Cast: Eric Stolz, Randy Quaid, Elizabeth Peña, Charles Durning

Two men, one gay and the other straight, both have an AIDS-related illness. They become unwilling roommates in an apartment building run for AIDS patients. Quaid's character is a homophobic ex-con who contracted the virus through a blood transfusion, Stolz is an educated and wealthy man. The two clash aggressively at the beginning but start to soften as their disease progresses.

Prod Comp: Hollywood Pictures, PolyGram Filmed Entertainment

Rope

Hitchcock, Alfred
1948; USA; 81 min; Thriller
P: Sidney Bernstein, Alfred Hitchcock; W: Arthur Laurents; C: Joseph Valentine, William V. Skall;
E: William Ziegler; M: David Buttolph
Cast: James Stewart, Farley Granger, John Dall, Joan Chandler, Cedric Hardwicke

A great psychological thriller about power, ego and murder. Two young gay students murder a friend in their luxury apartment and throw a cocktail party serving drinks to the victim's father and girlfriend from the trunk in which the corpse is concealed. There is no apparent reason for the murder except that they believe they are too intelligent to be caught. Loosely based on the real-life Loeb and Leopold case. (See also: Swoon)

Prod Comp: Transatlantic Pictures, Warner
Dist/Sales: UIP, Ascanbee, Universal, Warner, NFVLS, ACMI

Rose, The

Rydell, Mark
1979; USA; 134 min; Drama
P: Marvin Worth, Aaron Russo; W: Michael Cimino, Bo Goldman, Bill Kerby; C: Vilmos Zsigmond;
E: Robert Wolfe, Carroll Timothy O'Meara;
M: Paul A. Rothchild
Cast: Bette Midler, Alan Bates, Frederic Forrest, Harry Dean Stanton, Barry Primus

Very loosely based on the life of Janis Joplin, *The Rose* tells of a bisexual rock singer as she struggles with booze, drug addition, success and her inability to find a fulfilling relationship, straight or lesbian. This was Bette Midler's debut film; her performance is strong and believable, and she was nominated for an Academy Award for Best Actress.

Prod Comp: 20th Century-Fox
Dist/Sales: ReelMovies, 20thCenturyFox

Rosebud

Farthing, Cheryl
1992; UK; 14 min; Drama
P: Leontine Ruette; W: Cheryl Farthing;
C: Cinders Forshaw; E: Peter Webber
Cast: Doreene Blackstock, Julie Graham

When Kay moves into a new flat, she finds herself unexpectedly intrigued by the open sexuality of the lesbian couple who live next door. Surprised by the intensity of her feelings, Kay embraces her own repressed desires and sets out to turn fantasy into reality. (Cinenova)

Prod Comp: BFI, Channel 4
Dist/Sales: Cinenova, WMM, BFI

Rough Sketch of a Spiral

(aka: Rasen No Sobyo)

Yasufumi, Kojima
1990; Japan; 103 min; Documentary
P: Takeshige Kunio; C: Dobashi Hedeyuki; E: Kojima Toshihiko, Nakaba Yumiko, Okayasu Hajime

A very personal documentary that looks at the lives of gay men living in Osaka. One of the men, Yoshhiichi, is a playwright who hopes his play will change the status of gays in contemporary Japan, where deep-rooted homophobia and prejudice is still rife. With humour, the film examines the day-to-day life of the play's production, the actors and friends that make it possible. It also deals with Yoshhiichi's relationship with his lover Takashi. Japanese with English subtitles.

Dist/Sales: HeraldAce

Roy Cohn/Jack Smith

Godmilow, Jill
1993; USA; 90 min; Comedy
P: Ted Hope, James Schamus, Marianne Weems;
W: Gary Indiana, Jack Smith; C: Ellen Kuras;
E: Merrill Stern; M: Michael Sahl
Cast: Ron Vawter, Coco McPherson

These two legendary and equally infamous contemporaries could not have been more different, except for the fact that they were gay white men living through oppressive times. Both political in their respective ways, closeted Cohn used his back room conservative politics as 'drag' (a guise to conceal his sexuality), while out and outrageous Smith went from back room to centre stage turning drag into sexual politics through his *Arabian Nights*/B-movie kitsch-inspired performances.

Prod Comp: Good Machine, Pomodori Foundation
Dist/Sales: GoodMachine

Roy Cohn/Jack Smith

RSVP

Lynd, Laurie
1991; Canada; 23 min; Experimental
M: John McCarthy
Cast: Daniel MacIvor, Ross Manson

A lyrical piece that explores the emotions felt by a group of people when Andrew dies. There is almost no dialogue, but rather a central piece of music—*La Spectre de la Rose by Berlioz*, which forms a link between various family members and friends listening to it; through their images, reactions and memories we learn about Andrew's life and his death from AIDS.

Dist/Sales: Frameline, CFMDC, BFI

Rules of the Game

Fockele, Jorge
1998; Germany, USA; 50 min; Documentary

In *Rules of the Game*, members of New York's Hetrick-Martin Institute for queer youth have an opportunity to stage a fantasy scene complete with professional make-up and costume design, in which they reveal usually unseen parts of themselves. Results? A suave drag-king crooner, a sexy femme drag dance number, an encounter with a vampire, and a death metal music video. (22nd San Francisco International Lesbian & Gay Film Festival)

Rules of the Road

Friedrich, Su
1993; USA; 31 min; Drama
P: Su Friedrich; *W:* Su Friedrich; *C:* Su Friedrich;
E: Su Friedrich

Footage of a 1983 Oldsmobile Cutlass Cruiser shared by a lesbian couple is combined with a voice-over account of the history of their relationship.

Friedrich seeks to subvert male car culture by questioning the culture's social space defined by dominant heterosexual values.

Dist/Sales: WMM, NFVLS, Cinenova, CFMDC

Running Gay: Lesbian and Gay Participation in Sport

Chowdhry, Maya
1991; UK; 20 min; Documentary

Examines the participation of lesbians and gay men in sports, focusing on the homophobia they confront in mainstream sporting events and their efforts to organise gay teams, organisations and events. (Cinema Guild)

Prod Comp: Sheffield Film Co-op, Channel 4
Dist/Sales: CinemaGuild

Ruthie & Connie: Every Room in the House

Dickson, Deborah
2002; USA; 55 min; Documentary
P: Sandra Butler, Deborah Dickson, Donald Goldmaker

Ruthie and Connie are Jewish grandmothers who are lesbians and national heroines. They spend much of their lives 'doing the right thing'—until they discover it isn't right for them. By taking risks and challenging values they add a powerful chapter to the dialogue on the meaning of family in America today. Set against the backdrop of working-class Jewish Brooklyn and framed by the emergence of feminism and gay liberation, this powerful film reveals that revolutions are often made up of small, daily decisions. In committing to each other, Ruthie and Connie jettison their previous heterosexual marriages, wound their children, and establish a whole new social life. As activists, they embrace the struggle for dignity and respect, and as lovers they change the course of their lives, paving the way for a significant domestic-partners battle that they eventually win! (2002 San Francisco Jewish Film Festival)

Dist/Sales: Berkeley

S.

Henderickx, Guido
1998; Belgium; 94 min; Drama
P: Luc Reynaerts; *W:* Guido Henderickx;
C: Jan Vancaillie; *M:* Patrick Riguelle
Cast: Natalie Broods, Katelijne Damen, Josse De Pauw, Jan Decleir

A woman kills her boyfriend and his mistress after she's recorded them having sex. Dutch & French with English subtitles.

Dist/Sales: Leonor, Strand

Sabor a Mi

(aka: Savour Me)

Escanilla, Claudia Morgado
1997; Canada; 22 min; Experimental
P: Seanna McPherson, Claudia Morgado Escanilla;
W: Claudia Morgado Escanilla, Seanna McPherson,
Lori Hagan

An erotic short film about sensual yearnings, the guilty pleasures of watching, and the secret complicity of desire. Two women secretly watch the most intimate moments of each other's lives. Chance meetings between the two soon become deliberate encounters and the women discover their mutual longing for each other. (WMM) Spanish with English subtitles.

Dist/Sales: WMM, CFMDC

Sacred Lies, Civil Truths

Gund Saalfield, Catherine / Phipps, Cyrille / Williams, Rachael / Wright, Suzanne
1993; USA; 58 min; Documentary

Documents the dangerous, hateful lies of the US Far Right whose anti-lesbian and gay campaigns have led to homophobic violence. The film reveals the real agenda of the Christian Right to gain power and impose a 'Biblical rule'. (Cinenova)

Dist/Sales: Cinenova

Sad Disco Fantasia

Reinke, Steve
2001; USA; 24 min; Experimental

An episodic tour through the void of Los Angeles, slips of pop culture and Reinke's own astringent self-regard. Despite the blasts of dry wit and the hopeful embrace of gay porn, this is a lament. (VDB)

Dist/Sales: VDB

Sadness

Ayres, Tony
1993; Australia; 52 min; Documentary

Based on photographer William Yang's acclaimed stage performance of the same name, Sadness is a mesmerising and poetic montage of storytelling, photography and stylised re-enactment, Yang explores his Chinese–Australian identity and family history and his experience of losing friends to AIDS. (Film Australia)

Dist/Sales: FilmAust

Safe is Desire

Sundahl, Debi
1993; USA; 60 min; Comedy

Allie and Dianne, a lesbian couple, can't agree on whether to have safe sex or not. So Dianne takes Allie to a safe-sex club where they both discover the pleasures of latex and other assorted rubber goods. A very hot and sexy look at the safe-sex proposition for lesbians that is humorous and informative.

Prod Comp: Blush Entertainment

Safe Journey

Chiang, S. Leo
2001; USA; 15 min; Drama

Two strangers meet by chance on a windy autumn night. The boy is homeless; the man has just lost the one he loves. Will their differences unite them, or drive them apart?

Dist/Sales: WalkingIris

Safe Place, A

Guttman, Amos
1977; Israel; 29 min; Drama

Guttman's first short film explores a high school boy's struggle with his emerging gay identity. Danny fakes a stomach ache so that he can avoid playing football, and go to the cinema instead. His perspective is that of a young man on the verge of discovering his sexuality; the world is filled with straight couples and the longing stares of gay men. In a dream sequence reminiscent of Sleeping Beauty, his tentative touch wakes a naked man and signifies his own awakening. After avoiding a gay sexual encounter in the cinema, he returns there to find whatever the promise of the dark theatre holds. This short is a wonderful story of sexuality, individuality and adulthood. (Frameline) Hebrew with English subtitles.

Dist/Sales: Frameline

Sagitario

Foix, Vincent Molina
2001; Spain; 105 min; Drama
Cast: Eusebio Poncela , Angela Molina, Enrique Alcides

A compelling character study of two middle-age friends (who both happen to be Saggitarians) trying to come to terms with their relationships involving younger men. Spanish with English subtitles.

Dist/Sales: Lauren

Sailor

(aka: Matroos)

Defurne, Bavo
1998; Belgium; 16 min; Experimental

Dreaming about exotic countries, marvellous starry skies and the inevitable homesickness that would bring his sailor friend back, a teenager faces the fragility of his colorful illusions.

Dist/Sales: ACMI, Laika

Saint

Defurne, Bavo
1996; Belgium; 11 min; Drama

An indirect tribute to Genet's homoerotic classic, *Un Chant d'Amore*, and a meditation on the violent death of Saint Sebastian.

Dist/Sales: BFI, ACMI, Laika

Salivation Army

Treleaven, Scott
2001; Canada; 22 min; Experimental

A tale of blood, sex, spit, spunk & cult recruitment: for three years the Salivation Army operated a counterculture 'zine aimed at restless queer punk youth. But during their brief existence what began as a small, local gang transformed into an increasingly dangerous cult network. Part confessional, part recruitment drive. A vicious, erotic and instructional cut'n paste portrait of the underground. (www.salivationarmy.org)

Salmonberries

Adlon, Percy
1991; Germany; 94 min; Drama
P: Eleonore Adlon; *W:* Percy Adlon, Felix O. Adlon;
C: Newton Thomas Sigel; *E:* Conrad M. Gonzalez;
M: Bob Telson
Cast: k. d. lang, Rosel Zech, Jane Lind, Eugene Omiak, Oscar Kawagley

Set in an isolated village in Alaska, an orphaned female Eskimo becomes infatuated with the town librarian, an exiled German woman. They are both from very different backgrounds but manage to develop a deep emotional bond. On a trip to Berlin their relationship is nearly consummated but Zech's insecurity gets in the way. k. d. lang looks perfect as the androgynous Eskimo but her acting leaves something to be desired. She sings the title song Barefoot, and her music brings a haunting quality to the film.

Prod Comp: Pelemele Film
Dist/Sales: Col-Tri, Wolfe

Salo

(aka: The 120 Days of Sodom)

Pasolini, Pier Paolo
1975; Italy; 117 min; Erotica
P: Alberto De Stefanis, Antonio Girasante, Alberto Grimaldi; *W:* Sergio Citti, Pier Paolo Pasolini;
C: Tonino Delli Colli; *E:* Nino Baragli, Tatiana Casini Morigi; *M:* Ennio Morricone
Cast: Paolo Bonacelli, Giorgio Cataldi, Umberto Paolo Quintavalle, Caterina Boratto

Set in the Nazi-controlled, northern Italian state of Salo in 1944, a group of four Fascist rulers kidnap six teenage boys and girls and systematically force them into sexually degrading and repugnant acts and eventually, murder. Pasolini's last film before he was murdered, it is a descent into the evil of the human spirit. A revamp of the Marquis de Sade's novel *The 120 Days of Sodom*, it is bound to shock, and has been banned in several countries.

Prod Comp: Les Productions Artistes Associés, Produzioni Europee Associati
Dist/Sales: 21stCentur, BFI

Salome's Last Dance

Russell, Ken
1988; UK; 90 min; Comedy
P: Penny Corke; *W:* Ken Russell; *C:* Harvey Harrison;
E: Timothy Gee
Cast: Stratford Johns, Glenda Jackson, Nickolas Grace, Douglas Hodge

In a brothel in Victorian London, Oscar Wilde, luxuriating on cushions with his lover, watches a private production of his banned play, *Salome*, acted by friends, clients and prostitutes. A very stylised film, it treads tenuously between fantasy and reality with much overacting.

Prod Comp: Jolly Russell Productions
Dist/Sales: Col-Tri, Roadshow

Salon Kitty

(aka: Madam Kitty)

Brass, Tinto
1976; France, Germany, Italy; 120 min; Drama
P: Ermanno Donati, Giulio Sbarigia; *W:* Tinto Brass, Ennio De Concini, Maria Pia Fusco;
C: Silvano Ippoliti; *E:* Tinto Brass; *M:* Fiorenzo Carpi
Cast: Helmut Berger, Ingrid Thulin, Bekim Fehmiu, Teresa Ann Savoy, John Steiner

An SS officer will do anything to get gossip on his fellow officers and their wives. An erotic and disturbing look at a man's slide into madness. Similar in theme to films such as *Salo* and *The Night Porter*, which deal with Nazi sexual degeneracy.

Prod Comp: Cinema Seven Film, Coralto Cinematografica, Les Productions Fox Europa
Dist/Sales: 20thCenturyFox, VSM

Salt Mines, The

Aikin, Susan / Aparicio, Carlos
1990; USA; 47 min; Documentary

The Salt Mines observes the lives of young Latino transvestites who, finding themselves homeless in New York City, make a shelter in a row of abandoned garbage trucks.

Dist/Sales: Frameline

Salut Victor!

Poirier, Anne Claire
1989; Canada; 80 min; Drama
P: Anne Claire Poirier; W: Anne Claire Poirier;
C: Michel Brault; M: Joël Bienvenue
Cast: Jean-Louis Roux, Jacques Godin, Julie Vincent

Two elderly gay men meet in a home for the aged. Philippe is a quiet and distinguished gentleman, while Victor has a strong spirit even though his flesh is weak. They are complete opposites, but through loneliness they slowly become friends. A touching story about ageing and relationships. French with English subtitles.

Dist/Sales: Frameline, FilmsTransit, Strand

S

Sambal Belacan in San Francisco

Lim, Madeleine
1997; USA; 25 min; Documentary

Fragrant chilli and shrimp paste, 'sambal belacan', is a staple of Singaporean cooking. Representing the cultural mingling of many ethnic groups, it serves as a central metaphor for the experiences of expatriate Singaporean lesbians in this creative examination of identity and belonging. In intimate interviews, three women who emigrated to live openly as lesbians share their feelings of exclusion both from their families and culture of origin and the United States. (WMM)

Dist/Sales: WMM

Sammy and Rosie Get Laid

Frears, Stephen
1987; UK; 104 min; Drama
P: Sarah Radclyffe, Tim Bevan; W: Hanif Kureishi;
C: Oliver Stapleton; E: Mick Audsley; M: Stanley Myers
Cast: Shashi Kapoor, Frances Barber, Claire Bloom, Roland Gift, Ayub Khan Din

Tells the story of Sammy, the hedonistic, thoroughly English son of a prominent Pakistani politician (Rafi), who abandoned Sammy and his mother in London years before to seek wealth and power in his homeland. Sammy, who scrapes out a living as an accountant, lives in a dangerous and decaying black neighbourhood with his wife Rosie, a sexually adventurous 'modern woman' supportive of fashionable radical issues. Rafi re-enters Sammy's life when he is forced to flee his political enemies in Pakistan. Struggling to maintain his self-dignity and his sanity in the terrifying environment of the city he no longer knows, Rafi rapidly becomes disenchanted by Sammy and Rosie's unanchored world and tolerance of sexual liberty, drugs and revolutionary violence. An affectionate lesbian couple are among some of the characters that preside in this harsh and brutal environment.

Prod Comp: Working Title, Channel 4
Dist/Sales: ACMI, Cinecom

Sand and Blood

(aka: De Sable et de Sang)

Labrune, Jeanne
1987; France; 100 min; Drama
P: Jean Nainchrik; W: Jeanne Labrune;
C: Dominique Delguste, André Neau;
E: Nadine Fischer; M: Nina Corti, Anne-Marie Fijal
Cast: André Dussollier, Clémentine Célarié, Sami Frey

A romantic triangle underlies this erotically charged thriller. The trio consist of a young matador, a wealthy doctor who is opposed to bullfighting, and a beautiful young woman.

Prod Comp: Centre National de la Cinématographie, Septembre Productions

Sando to Samantha: The Art of Dikvel

Lewis, Jack / Phungula, Thulanie
1998; South Africa; 52 min; Documentary

The true story of Sando Willemse, aka Samantha Fox, a drag queen from Bonteheuwel in Cape Town, who became a soldier for the South African Defence Forces in 1991. Sando perfected the art of dikvel—a real thick-skinned queen who never let life's challenges get the better of him. Having survived, thrived and found a place in the army, Sando was tested for HIV without his permission. His HIV-positive status was disclosed to his entire squad by the army command and he was summarily dis-charged. He turned to the road to survive, finding a new home and support from other drag queens working Cape Town's streets. He died of HIV related causes in 1996 aged 22. This docudrama is narrated by Sando and blends interview material (shot three weeks before his death) and drama to provide testimony to his courage and daring. (Idol Pictures)

Dist/Sales: Idol

Sari Red

Parmar, Pratibha
1988; UK; 12 min; Documentary

Eloquently examines the effect of the ever-present threat of violence on the lives of Asian women in both private and public spheres. In this moving visual poem, the title refers to red, the colour of blood spilt and the red of the sari, symbolising sensuality and intimacy between Asian women. (WMM)

Dist/Sales: WMM

Satan's Princess

(aka: Malediction)

Gordon, Bert I.
1989; USA; 90 min; Horror
P: Bert I. Gordon; *W:* Stephen Katz; *C:* Thomas F.
Denove; *E:* Barbara Boguski; *M:* Norman Mamey
Cast: Lydie Denier, Robert Forster, Caren Kaye, Phillip
Glasser

A crippled ex-cop is hired to investigate a missing
daughter but winds up in the occult world of a
wealthy woman who claims to have lived for 500
years and killed 1000 men. An offbeat film with a
confused plot and some interesting characterisations.
Fairly tame lesbian vampire flick.

Prod Comp: Sun Heat Pictures
Dist/Sales: ParamountHV

Satdee Nite

Armstrong, Gillian
1973; Australia; 15 min; Drama
C: Fred Richardson, Bill Constable, David Gribble;
E: Kit Gyatt

A downbeat slice of gay life in the early 1970s in
which a young man's expectations of a Saturday
night give way to loneliness and disappear in an
alcoholic haze.

Prod Comp: Australian Film TV & Radio School
Dist/Sales: AFTRS, NFVLS

Saturday Night at the Baths

Buckley, David
1974; USA; 90 min; Drama
P: David Buckley, Steve Ostrow; *W:* David Buckley,
Franklin Khedouri; *C:* Ralf D. Bode; *E:* Suzanne Fenn,
Jackie Raynal
Cast: Robert Aberdeen, Ellen Sheppard, Don Scotti,
Janie Olivor, Steve Ostrow

Approached in an almost semi-documentary style,
the film follows the story of a musician as he goes
from a heterosexual relationship to a homosexual
one. Set against the Continental Baths of New York.

Prod Comp: Mammoth Films

Saturn's Return

Byrne, Wenona
2000; Australia; 26 min; Drama

Written by Christos Tsiolkas (*Loaded*), this road
movies charts a journey of reconciliation and grief
navigated by a young gay couple. An intimate and
sexually candid drama.

Dist/Sales: Flickerfest, Frameline, ACMI

Satyricon

Fellini, Federico
1969; Italy; 129 min; Drama
P: Alberto Grimaldi; *W:* Federico Fellini, Bernardino
Zapponi, Brunello Rondi; *C:* Giuseppe Rotunno;
E: Ruggero Mastroianni; *M:* Tod Dockstader, Ilhan
Mimaroglu, Nino Rota, Andrew Rudin
Cast: Martin Potter, Hiram Keller, Salvo Randone, Max
Born

Based on Petronius' classic about the moral decay of
ancient Rome, it is the adventure of two young
students, who become obsessed and infatuated with
the same young man. A dreamlike and visually
stunning film, *Satyricon* is filled with
homoeroticism.
Italian with English subtitles.

Prod Comp: Artistes Associes, Produzioni Europee
Associati
Dist/Sales: Ascanbee, 21stCentury, NFVLS, Warner,
ACMI

S

Saturn's Return

Sauve Qui Peut

(aka: Slow Motion)

Godard, Jean-Luc
1979; France; 84 min; Drama
P: Alain Sarde, Jean-Luc Godard; *W:* Jean-Claude
Carriere, Anne-Marie Mieville, Jean-Luc Godard;
C: William Lubtchansky, Renato Berta; *E:* Anne-Marie
Miéville, Jean-Luc Godard; *M:* Gabriel Yared
Cast: Isabelle Huppert, Jacques Dutronc, Nathalie Baye

Godard's film marked his return to cinema after a decade of video experimentation. The themes are not new—prostitution as a metaphor for alienation, the impossibility of durable relationships—although the connection between misogyny and repressed homosexuality is given a new emphasis. While basic oppositions—country v. city, commerce v. independence, sex v. work—are set out very simply, the narrative is developed with ambiguities and unexplained events contained in a dense stylistic weave. French with English subtitles.

Prod Comp: Sara Films
Dist/Sales: NFVLS

Savage Nights

(aka: Les Nuits Fauves)

Collard, Cyril
1992; France; 126 min; Drama
P: Nella Banfi; *W:* Cyril Collard; *C:* Manuel Terán; *E:* Lisa Beaulieu; *M:* René-Marc Bini, Cyril Collard
Cast: Cyril Collard, Romane Bohringer, Carlos Lopez, Corine Blue

This film is a defiant shout in the face of AIDS, the disease that killed this gifted 35-year-old filmmaker shortly before his film swept France's national awards. A bisexual, Jean who is HIV-positive, is involved with Samy, an angry young immigrant from Spain, and with Laura, an aspiring actress whom Jean meets at an audition. Confronting and compelling. French with English subtitles.

Prod Comp: PolyGram Filmed Entertainment, Procirep, SNC, Sofinergie 2
Dist/Sales: NewVision, 21stCentury, Swank

Scarecrow in a Garden of Cucumbers

Kaplan, Robert J.
1972; USA; 82 min; Comedy
P: Robert J. Kaplan, Henry J. Alpert; *W:* Sandra Scoppettone; *C:* Paul Glickman; *E:* Dick Cohen; *M:* Jerry Blatt
Cast: Holly Woodlawn, Tally Brown, Suzanne Skillen

A very funny spoof of the star-is-born genre. It stars Holly Woodlawn, of Warhol fame, as Eve Harrington, who goes to New York in order to find fame and fortune. Along the way she must deal with creeps and slimeballs and men who will break her heart, as well as the music of Bette Midler.

Prod Comp: Sliding Pond Productions

Scenes from a Queer Planet

1992; Argentina, India, Peru, Russia; 90 min; Documentary

This documentary focuses on four countries: Peru, India, Argentina and Russia; and through the use of video footage it shows the shocking human rights abuses against gays, lesbians and transvestites. Presented by Julie Dorf, the Executive Director of the International Gay and Lesbian Human Rights Commission.

Prod Comp: International Gay & Lesbian Human Rights Commission

Scenes from the Class Struggle in Beverly Hills

Bartel, Paul
1989; USA; 102 min; Comedy
P: Jim C. Katz; *W:* Bruce Wagner, Paul Bartel; *C:* Steven Fierberg; *E:* Alan Toomayan; *M:* Stanley Myers
Cast: Jacqueline Bisset, Ed Begley Jnr, Ray Sharkey, Mary Woronow, Robert Beltran

Two comically complicated Beverly Hills families are forced to share one measly mansion for an entire weekend. A sitcom queen and a socialis t undergo temptations as a result of a bet between their house boys. A sex romp ensues.

Prod Comp: North Street Films
Dist/Sales: Roadshow, ACMI

Scent Uva Butch

Rosenfeld, Shoshana
1998; USA; 35 min; Documentary

A sexy, personal, gender-bending documentary that bends stereotypical notions of butchness beyond recognition. Butch women offer an entertaining insight into their identification, their friendships, their sexual attractions and, most importantly, how to 'pack' successfully.

Dist/Sales: BlowUp

School Fag

Fung, Richard / McCaskell, Tim
1998; Canada; 17 min; Documentary

Documentary about 19-year-old Shawn who recounts his life as a young queer growing up in a conservative small town Canadian suburb. Shawn is a natural stand up comic and his stories are alternatively hilarious, biting and poignant.

Dist/Sales: VTape, VDB

School's Out: Lesbian and Gay Youth

Spalding, Ron
1993; USA; 30 min; Documentary

Examines the difficulties facing gay and lesbian teenagers and the emergence of new special educational programs designed for them.

Dist/Sales: CinemaGuild

Score

Metzger, Radley
1972; USA, Yugoslavia; 90 min; Drama
W: Jerry Douglas; *C:* Frano Vodopivec;
E: Doris Toumarkine
Cast: Casey Donovan, Claire Wilbur, Gerald Grant,
Calvin Culver

> Radley Metzger's erotic masterpiece, starring gay-porn icon Casey Donovan, is about two swinging couples who mix it up one weekend. (First Run Features)

Prod Comp: Jadran Film
Dist/Sales: FirstRunFeatures

Scorpio Rising

Anger, Kenneth
1963; USA; 37 min; Experimental

> *Anger Magick Lantern Cycle Series* featuring several short films, including: *Kustom Kar Kommandos*: A young man strokes his customised car with a powder puff. *Scorpio Rising*: A death mirror held up to American culture—Brando, bikes and black leather; Christ, chains and cocaine. A high view of the myth of the American motor cyclist. The machine as totem from toy to terror. (ACMI)

Prod Comp: Puck Film Productions
Dist/Sales: ACMI, BFI

Scout's Honor

Shepard, Tom
2001; USA; 57 min; Documentary
P: Tom Shepard; *W:* Meg Moritz

> *Scout's Honor* traces the conflict between the anti-gay policies of the Boy Scouts of America and the broad-based movement by many of its members to overturn them. The story is told predominantly through the experiences of a 13-year-old boy and a 70-year-old man – both heterosexual, both dedicated to the Scouts, and both determined to change the course of Scouting history. Their challenge is being waged in their hometown of Petaluma, California – a place more familiar with agriculture than activism. Yet it is here where they began an international petition drive and media campaign to overturn the BSA's anti-gay policy. (New Day Films)

Dist/Sales: ScoutsHonor, NewDay

Scream, Teen, Scream

Rosenzweig, Joshua
1996; USA; 38 min; Comedy

> A wacky piss-take on teen horror films that's full of campy pop culture references and even features a visit by the ghost of Karen Carpenter.

Scrubbers

Zetterling, Mai
1982; UK; 93 min; Drama
P: Don Boyd; *W:* Susannah Buxton, Roy Minton, Jeremy Watt, Mai Zetterling
C: Ernest Vincze; *E:* Rodney Holland;
M: Michael Hurd
Cast: Amanda York, Chrissie Cotterill, Kate Ingram, Elizabeth Edmonds

> An intense drama about women in prison without any of the sensation, exploitation or clichés that usually accompany this genre. Among the characters is a young lesbian who breaks the law so she can go back inside to prison to rejoin her lover. A large cross-section of inmates, from black lesbians to young white innocents is portrayed. A violent and disturbing study.

Prod Comp: Handmade Films
Dist/Sales: ACMI, OrionClassics

Scream, Teen, Scream

Sea in the Blood

Fung, Richard
2000; USA; 26 min; Experimental

> A personal documentary about living with illness, tracing the relationship of the artist to thalassemia in his sister Nan, and AIDS in his partner Tim.

Dist/Sales: VDB

Seamen

Boreham, Craig
1999; Australia; 12 min; Experimental

A tragicomic short from the underbelly of middle Australia. Urban myths as told by a not-quite-straight cab driver, a wannabe model and a sensitive goth-fag create a twisted triumvirate of tales and takes on gritty city living. (MQFF)

Dist/Sales: Pineapple

Search for Intimacy, The

Kennedy, Michael
1989; Canada; 24 min; Documentary
W: Michael Kennedy

This film takes an in-depth look at relationships and sexuality in the mature years. The need for companionship, stability, vitality and enrichment is examined through visits with a variety of married, single, widowed, divorced and homosexual seniors who talk frankly and openly about their experiences.

Prod Comp: SC Communications
Dist/Sales: NFVLS

Seashell and the Clergyman, The

(aka: La Coquille et le Clergyman)

Dulac, Germaine
1928; France; 44 min; B&W; Drama
W: Antonin Artaud; *C:* Paul Guichard
Cast: Alex Allin, Genica Athanasiou, Lucien Bataille

Considered to be the first surrealist film, this avant-garde classic is a story of sexual repression and crazed fantasies. A celibate clergyman's dreams become full of lust and bizarre fantasies.

Sebastian

Wam, Svend
1995; Norway; 90 min; Drama
W: Svend Wam; *C:* Per Källberg
Cast: Hampus Björch, Nicolai Cleve Broch, Ewa Fröling, Helge Jordal

A gay teenage romance from Norway. Five young teenage friends must deal with all the angst that only teenage years can offer: their parents, friends, trying to fit in and, at the same time, the need to rebel against the social structures of their society. It is a difficult time for all, but it is perhaps more difficult for Sebastian, who is sexually attracted to his best friend, Ulf, and suddenly must question everything and everyone around him. Norwegian with English subtitles.

Prod Comp: Mefistofilm A/S, Nordisk Film & Television
Dist/Sales: NorwegianFilm

Sebastiane

Humfress, Paul / Jarman, Derek
1976; UK; 81 min; Drama
P: James Whaley, Howard Malin; *W:* Derek Jarman, Paul Humfress; *C:* Peter Middleton; *E:* Paul Humfress; *M:* Brian Eno
Cast: Leonardo Treviglio, Barney James, Neil Kennedy, Richard Warwick

This film is a profane version of the martyrdom of Sebastian who, in AD 303, was banished by the Emperor Diocletian for his Christian sympathies. The legend of Catholic mythology is here transformed into a psychological exploration of male sexuality with Sebastian as a homosexual icon. Jarman's film was an innovative independent production for British cinema, its most unusual feature being the fact that its dialogue is in Latin, thus avoiding the anachronisms and banalities of the dialogue in most historical films and the problems of deploying a multinational cast. Latin with English subtitles.

Prod Comp: Cinegate Ltd
Dist/Sales: NFVLS, ACMI, BFI

Second Awakening of Christa Klages, The

(aka: Das Zweite Erwachen der Christa Klages)

von Trotta, Margarethe
1977; Germany; 93 min; Drama
W: Margarethe von Trotta, Luise Francia; *C:* Franz Rath; *E:* Annette Dorn; *M:* Klaus Doldinger
Cast: Tina Engel, Sylvia Reize, Katharina Thalbach, Peter Schneider

A young mother and her boyfriend rob a bank and with the money hope to stop the closure of a childcare centre. While on the run they are pursued not only by the police but also by a mysterious woman whom they kept hostage briefly during the robbery. The first feature film by the renowned filmmaker Margarethe von Trotta, whose films examine and define the relationships between women.

Prod Comp: Westdeutscher Rundfunk
Dist/Sales: NewLine, NFVLS

Second Coming, The

Walsh, Jack
1995; USA; 53 min; Experimental

A deft combination of narrative and experimental filmmaking, Jack Walsh's *The Second Coming* is the coming of age story of Carlos, a bi-racial gay teen who becomes a politically aware activist. Set in the near future during a Fundamentalist group's attempted coup d'état in the United States, this conspiracy-theory-wrought film examines overriding social crises such as homophobia and racism. Carlos, alienated from most of his peers and family, finds love and companionship with a classmate, Ben. Together the two join forces with a group of teens who are making and broadcasting videotapes that question the crisis created by the Fundamentalist threat. Through a series of betrayals and a death squad-like kidnapping, Carlos is murdered. However, in the face of these devastating circumstances, a new voice of resistance appears that gives hope to those whom Carlos has left behind. *The Second Coming* shows how individuals swept up in a chain of historical events can resist and have an impact on a seemingly hopeless situation. (20th San Francisco International Lesbian & Gay Film Festival)

Dist/Sales: WaterBearer

Second Serve

Page, Anthony
1986; USA; 100 min; Drama
W: Gavin Lambert, Stephanie Liss; *C:* Robbie Greenberg; *E:* John C. Horger; *M:* Brad Fiedel
Cast: Vanessa Redgrave, Martin Balsam, Louise Fletcher, Jeff Corey, William Russ

The moving story of transsexual Rene Richards, the male surgeon turned female tennis champion. It is a story of deep pain, long struggle and great bravery leading to a real victory of the human spirit. Redgrave's riveting performance is unforgettable—ageing from 22 to 54 and changing from man to woman. She imbues every gesture with dignity and truth as a transsexual who did what she knew was right. Based on the book of the same title by Rene Richards with John Ames.

Prod Comp: Lorimar
Dist/Sales: ACMI, Roadshow, CBS

Second Skin

(aka: Segunda Piel)

Vera, Gerardo
1999; Spain; 100 min; Drama
P: Andres Vicente Gomez; *W:* Angeles Gonzalez Sinde; *C:* Julio Madurga; *E:* Nicholas Wentworth; *M:* Roque Banos
Cast: Jordi Molla, Javier Bardem, Ariadna Gil, Cecilia Roth

Alberto is a closeted aerospace engineer, whose can't decide to stay with his wife and young son, or be with his lover Diego, an orthopaedic surgeon. Eventually his wife finds out about his affair, his lover becomes more demanding of his time, and his two worlds begin to collide. Spanish with English subtitles.

Prod Comp: Lolafilms, Via Digital
Dist/Sales: LolaFilms

Secret Ceremony

Losey, Joseph
1968; UK; 107 min; Drama
P: Norman Priggen, John Heyman; *W:* George Tabori; *C:* Gerry Fisher; *E:* Reginald Beck; *M:* Richard Rodney Bennett
Cast: Elizabeth Taylor, Mia Farrow, Robert Mitchum, Peggy Ashcroft, Pamela Brown

An ageing prostitute, is adopted by a rather strange and mysterious wealthy young woman. The surrogate mother-daughter relationship works for both of them as the young woman's need for a mother is fulfilled and the prostitute is financially rewarded. When the girl's stepfather returns, it is revealed that Farrow is a sexual psychotic and that her seduction of Mitchum helped ruin his marriage to her mother. There are lesbian undertones as the close and erotically charged relationship develops between the two women.

Prod Comp: Universal, WFS
Dist/Sales: NFVLS, Universal

Secret Policeman's Private Parts, The

Temple, Julien / Graef, Roger
1981; UK; 80 min; Comedy
M: Alan Brewer, Pete Townshend
Cast: John Cleese, Dame Edna Everage, Peter Cook, Graham Chapman, Terry Gilliam

This sequel to *The Secret Policeman's Ball* features a bent cop, a transvestite lumberjack, and more, in this irreverent outing from the Monty Python team.

Dist/Sales: 21stCentury, Miramax

Secrets

Ralph, Sheryl Lee
1997; USA; 13 min; Comedy

A woman seeks out the advice of friends at a wedding when she discovers her husband is gay.

Dist/Sales: IslandGirl

Seducers, The

(aka: Death Game)

Traynor, Peter S.
1977; USA; 90 min; Thriller
P: Larry Spiegel, Peter S. Traynor; *W:* Anthony Overman, Michael Ronald Ross; *C:* David Worth; *M:* Jimmie Haskell
Cast: Sondra Locke, Seymour Cassel, Colleen Camp

When a man allows two women into his house to make a phone call on a stormy evening, he ends up enduring a night of physical and mental torture at their hands.

Prod Comp: First American Films; *Dist/Sales:* Liberty

S

Seduction of Innocence

Bijan, Ali
1995; USA; 101 min; Drama
P: Ali Bijan; *W:* Ali Bijan; *C:* David Blood; *E:* Sandy
Schwartz; *M:* Amin Emam, Dave Innis
Cast: Kathleen Blake, Lisa Cawthron, Fran Gonzalez,
Patrick Otero

> When a small-town girl travels to the big city to see
> her sister, she faces some new challenges in her life.
> It turns out her is a stripper and is involved with a
> drug ring and living with a lesbian. The young sister
> decides to take up stripping herself. Fairly exploita-
> tive film with lots of nudity but there is a mainly
> positive portrayal of the lesbian character.

Prod Comp: Artist View Entertainment, Intermedia
Film Corporations, New City Releasing
Dist/Sales: ArtistView

Seduction: The Cruel Woman

(aka: Verführung: Die Grausame Frau)

Mikesch, Elfi / Treut, Monika
1985; Germany; 85 min; Erotica
P: Michael McHernan; *W:* Elfi Mikesch, Monika Treut;
C: Elfi Mikesch; *E:* Renate Merck; *M:* Maran Gosov
Cast: Mechthild Grossmann, Sheila McLaughlin,
Georgtte Dee, Carola Regnier

> This film is based on two classic sadomasochistic
> novels; *Venus in Furs*, and *The Story of O. Venus in
> Furs* (Leopold von Sacher-Masoch) portrays the
> insatiable desire of one man to submit to one very
> cruel woman—indeed his love-ridden slavishness is
> so demanding that it takes a considerable toll on her.
> Wanda is the cruel woman, and through the course
> of the film, all Wanda's primary relationships change:
> and yet the show and performance art of sadomaso-
> chism, goes on. German with English subtitles.

Prod Comp: Hyena Films
Dist/Sales: Palace, FirstRunFeatures, Salzgeber, Millivres,
ACMI

See how they Run

Morse, Emily
2001; USA; 54 min; Documentary

> *See how they Run* is a humorous portrait of American
> politics played out in San Francisco. With behind
> the scenes access, this film follows Mayor Willie
> Brown in his fight for re-election. The story takes a
> remarkable turn when an openly gay city supervisor
> and stand-up comedian, Tom Ammiano, stages a
> historic write-in campaign to create a David and
> Goliath showdown. This verite film chronicles an
> election in which power, race and sexual orientation
> ended up on the back-burner for locals more
> concerned about the expansion of Starbucks and the

'dot-coms' in their backyards. *See how they Run*
captures the humour and scandals from inside
personal and political battles.
(www.seehowtheyrun.org)

See the Sea

(aka: Regarde la Mer)

Ozon, François
1997; France; 52 min; Thriller
W: François Ozon

> On the beautiful holiday island of Yeu, the solitude
> of Sasha, a young mother awaiting her husband's
> return, is broken by the appearance of Tatiana, a
> brooding backpacker who asks to camp outside her
> cottage. Sasha grows increasingly fascinated with her
> mysterious visitor whose demeanour gradually
> becomes more ominous as she insinuates herself into
> Sasha's home. With its stunning cinematography, See
> the Sea provocatively uncovers the dark and sinister
> undercurrents swirling beneath curiosity and
> attraction, ultimately challenging our assumptions
> about desire, identity and motherhood. (Zeitgeist)
> French with English subtitles.

Dist/Sales: Zeitgeist

Self-Destruction of Gia, The

Martin, J. J.
2002; USA; 72 min; Documentary

> Supermodel Gia Carangi was a leading symbol of the
> extravagant 1980s, and, in a way, that decade's
> greatest sacrificial lamb. Catapulted to fame in a
> field she ironically viewed with contempt, her career
> and life were cut short when she died of AIDS in
> 1986 after a long struggle with drug addiction. This
> moving and provocative documentary traces her
> meteoric rise and fall. A voracious lover of women,
> Gia today occupies a troubling place as a symbol of
> female power whose very image masked her
> vulnerability and pain. Intimate home movies and
> archival interview footage of the icon bring her eerily
> close to the viewer. These combine with interviews
> with Gia's psychiatrist, her family members and
> fashion world luminaries (including designers Vera
> Wang and Diane von Furstenberg, photographer
> Francesco Scavullo and Gia's former lover, make-up
> artist Sandy Linter), to shed light on the enigmatic
> life of a pivotal female persona of the late 20th
> century. (2002 LA Outfest)

Dist/Sales: CineL'Mod

Separate Peace, A

Peerce, Larry
1972; USA; 104 min; Drama
P: Robert Godston, Otto Plaschkes; *W:* Fred Segal;

C: Frank Stanley; *E:* John C. Howard; *M:* Charles Fox
Cast: Parker Stevenson, John Heyl, William Roerick, Victor Bevine, Peter Brush

Two young men, who are roommates in a 1940s prep school, become friends and develop an unspoken love, and face the transition to manhood in the last years of World War II. Although not overtly homosexual, there are lusty scenes of half-naked boys.

Prod Comp: Paramount
Dist/Sales: Ascanbee

Sergeant Matlovich vs. the U.S. Air Force

Leaf, Paul
1978; USA; 100 min; Drama
P: Paul Leaf; *W:* John McGreevey; *C:* Mario Tosi;
E: Thomas Stanford; *M:* Teo Macero
Cast: Brad Dourif, Marc Singer, Frank Converse, William Daniels, Stephen Elliott

The story of Sergeant Matlovich, a Vietnam veteran who declared to his commander that he was gay, causing him to be dishonourably discharged. He fought the case in the courts and was still discharged—this time honourably.

Prod Comp: Tomorrow Entertainment
Dist/Sales: Roadshow, NBC

Sergeant, The

Flynn, John
1968; USA; 110 min; Drama
P: Richard Goldstone; *W:* Dennis Murphy;
C: Henri Persin; *E:* Françoise Diot, Charles Nelson;
M: Michel Magne
Cast: Rod Steiger, John Phillip Law, Ludmila Mikaël, Frank Latimore

Set in France in 1952, this is the story of a repressed homosexual army sergeant who desires one of the handsome privates. Finally the sergeant loses control and kisses the private who pushes him away and refuses his advances. Humiliated, the sergeant takes his own life.

Prod Comp: Warner, Seven Arts
Dist/Sales: Warner, Swank

Servant, The

Losey, Joseph
1963; UK; 115 min; B&W; Drama
P: Joseph Losey, Norman Priggen; *W:* Harold Pinter;
C: Douglas Slocombe; *E:* Reginald Mills;
M: John Dankworth
Cast: Dirk Bogarde, Sarah Miles, Wendy Craig, James Fox

A socio-psychological drama in which a servant, Barratt, is hired by an upper-class, self-centred young man. He has moved into a new house in Chelsea where he plans to live with his fiancee after their marriage. Gradually the relationship between the servant and master, with its suggestion of homosexuality, changes as the latter finds himself falling slowly under Barratt's control.

Prod Comp: Springbok Films, Elstree

Serving in Silence: The Marguerite Cammermeyer Story

Bleckner, Jeff
1995; USA; 88 min; Drama
P: Richard Heus, Cis Corman; *W:* Alison Cross;
C: Glen MacPherson; *E:* Geoffrey Rowland;
M: David Shire
Cast: Glenn Close, Judy Davis, Jan Rubes, Wendy Makkena

After 25 years of exemplary military service and a Bronze Star in Vietnam, Colonel Cammarmeyer's career is in jeopardy as she finds herself entangled in a hostile human rights battle after she admits to being a lesbian. At risk is not only her career, but also the love of her sons, the respect of her friends and her own sense of integrity. Although this made for TV story is generally well handled, the lesbianism is treated in a rather coy manner. The only physical touch is a very short and discreet kiss on the lips.

Prod Comp: Barwood Films, Storyline Productions, Trillium Productions
Dist/Sales: Col-Tri, ACMI

Set it Off

Gray, F. Gary
1996; USA; 122 min; Action
P: Oren Koules, Dale Pollock; *W:* Takashi Bufford, Kate Lanier; *C:* Marc Reshovsky; *E:* John Carter;
M: Busta Rhymes, Christopher Young
Cast: Jada Pinkett Smith, Queen Latifah, Viveca A. Fox, Kimberly Elise, Blair Underwood

Four childhood friends have endured tough lives growing up in the mean streets of LA. Eventually when they've had enough of being ripped off, taken advantage of, abused by crooked cops, the four girls, one a lesbian, become determined to get their own back. A tragic chain of events brings them even closer than they could have imagined. Virtually overnight, the women become enmeshed in a world of crime, and it looks like prison could be the only future for them.

Prod Comp: New Line Cinema, Peak Films
Dist/Sales: Constantin, NewLine, RoadshowEnt, Wolfe

S

Set Me Free

(aka: Emporte-moi)

Pool, Léa
1998; Canada, France, Switzerland; 95 min; Drama
W: Léa Pool, Nancy Huston, Isabelle Raynault;
C: Jeanne Lapoirie; E: Michael Arcand;
M: Robyn Schulkowsky
Cast: Karine Vanasse, Nancy Huston, Pascale Bussières, Charlotte Christeler

13-year-old Hanna's sexual awakening includes an infatuation with her best friend and a teacher. She's also taken with Nana, a character in the Jean-Luc Godard New Wave film Vivre Sa Vie, which Hanna watches again and again. Meanwhile, Hanna's home life is complicated by conflicts between her frustrated father and her overworked mother. (Wolfe) French with English subtitles.

Prod Comp: Merchant Ivory Films, Haut et Court
Dist/Sales: TF1, ArtisticLicense, Wolfe, Haut-et-Court

Seven Women

Ford, John
1966; USA; 87 min; Drama
P: John Ford, Bernard Smith; W: Janet Green, John McCormick; C: Joseph La Shelle; E: Otho S. Lovering; M: Elmer Bernstein
Cast: Anne Bancroft, Flora Robson, Sue Lyon, Margaret Leighton

John Ford's last film is the story of seven women who are isolated on a mission for women in China in 1935. The establishment becomes overrun by a Mongolian barbarian and his troop of bandits, and the women are subjected to gross indignities. Bancroft memorably plays a newly arrived doctor, a cross-dressing, cigar-smoking, hard-talker, who comes into conflict not only with the bandits but also with the self-righteous leader of the mission. Lots of latent lesbianism.

Prod Comp: MGM
Dist/Sales: MGM, Swank

Sex 121 and the Gulag

Kwietniowski, Richard
1991; UK; 100 min; Documentary
P: Susan Ardill, Clare Beavan

Investigates sexual politics in the glasnost era, the supposedly impending decriminalisation of homosexuality in the former USSR, the rise of erotica and Western-style pornography, and the effects of AIDS on that society.

Prod Comp: Channel 4
Dist/Sales: Channel4

Sex and Balls

Jansen, Doerthe
1994; Australia; 53 min; Documentary
Cast: Nina Hartley

Ten ordinary Australians bare their sexual souls in this film about sex in the 1990s: a man into threesomes, an S/M lesbian couple and a male stripper who disrobes nightly for crowds of lusty women. This film challenges sexual stereotypes and examines whether traditional concepts of family and monogamy are dominant cultural customs or a convenient myth.

Dist/Sales: Scrine

Sex and the Sandinistas

Broadbent, Lucinda
1991; UK; 25 min; Documentary

Nicaragua is known for the Sandinista Revolution, an inspiring struggle for national liberation. What has never been told before is the story of how homosexuals battled for their own space within the revolution. This unique story is related through the drama of personal experience. Without assuming any prior knowledge of Nicaraguan history, the film brings to life the extraordinary and valuable experience of lesbians and gays coming out in the whirlwind of a Latin American revolution. (WMM)

Dist/Sales: WMM

Sex and the Single Gene?

1997; 29 min; Documentary

Focuses on the science behind a controversial piece of genetic research, the so-called gay gene. The film considers the findings of this research—that homosexuality may indeed be genetically determined. (EMA)

Dist/Sales: EMA

Sex Becomes Her: The True Life Story of Chi Chi LaRue

Aho, Michael
2000; UK; 65 min; Documentary
M: Christian Henson
Cast: Chi Chi LaRue, Cole Tucker, Steve Rambo

This documentary traces the career of the man behind the camera and under the make-up—famed drag porn director Chi Chi LaRue. Always a bit player in other porn docos, Chi Chi finally takes centre stage in this titillating romp through the sex industry. Nothing in this film is left to the imagination. From sleazy action on set, to the Gay Porn Awards, and entry into private sex parties, this shrewd industry player hilariously exposes it all. (MQFF)

Prod Comp: Planet Rapido
Dist/Sales: Rapido

Sex Bytes

Jammeh, Kasi
2001; USA; 15 min; Drama

Two roommates discover that surfing the net provides the hottest action in town.

Dist/Sales: MyAss

Sex Change: Shock! Horror! Probe!

Jackson, Jane
1989; UK; 50 min; Documentary

Male and female transsexuals speak about their trials and tribulations, politics, gender-identity formation, and other issues in this intriguing documentary.

Sex, Drugs and Democracy

Blank, Jonathan
1995; USA; 87 min; Documentary
P: Jonathan Blank, Barclay Powers

A documentary looking at the rather relaxed laws in Holland covering things such as abortion, euthanasia, use of soft drugs, gay marriages, nude beaches, universal health care and the banning of personal handguns. Holland has the lowest AIDS infection rate, one of the lowest murder rates, the lowest imprisonment rate in Western world and one of the highest life expectancies. The filmmaker talks to judges, police, doctors and legislators, as well as drug users and prostitutes, to record their views on the country's legal system—if it works and how.

Prod Comp: Barclay Powers

Sex Flesh in Blood

Lee, Christopher
1999; USA; 57 min; Erotica

Gender anarchy rules in this tribute to the punk porn scene with a transgender twist.

Dist/Sales: LeeC

Sex Is...

Huestis, Marc
1993; USA; 80 min; Documentary
P: Marc Huestis; *C:* Fawn Yacker; *E:* Hrafnhildor Gunnarsdottir, Marc Huestis, Lara Mac; *M:* MJ Lallo
Cast: Larry Brinkin, Danny Castellow, Alex Chee, Wayne Corbitt

This celebration of gay male sexuality was a smash hit in the US, breaking box-office records set by such films as *Edward II* and *Without You I'm Nothing*, and winning multiple exclamation-mark headlines in *Variety*. A must-see film interspersed with flashes of hot erotic activity and laced with interesting archival footage, it comprises interviews with men from ex-priests to drag queens, of differing races, classes and generations who tell all: from back room antics, to beats, to safe-sex invention to lifetime companionships. (MQFF)

Awards: Berlin Film Festival, 1993: Best Gay Film
Prod Comp: Outsider Productions
Dist/Sales: Salzgeber, WaterBearer

Sex is Sex: Conversations with Male Prostitutes

Bergen, Brian / Milici, Jennifer
1995; USA; 50 min; Documentary

A candid video documentary which looks at the lives of a selection of male prostitutes in New York City. This involving portrait of sex workers in the nineties targets such topics as power, AIDS, sexual identity, relationships and the dangers and rewards of hustling.

Dist/Sales: WaterBearer

Sex Monster, The

Binder, Mike
1999; USA; 96 min; Comedy
P: Jack Binder, Scott Stephens; *W:* Mike Binder;
C: Keith L. Smith; *E:* Lee Grubin
Cast: Mariel Hemmingway, Mike Binder, Renée Humphrey, Taylor Nichols

In an hilarious look at marriage and sexuality in the late 1990s, a happily married man persuades his loving wife to help him live out the ultimate male fantasy—another woman and not just for himself, but for his wife, too. Unfortunately, she gets more out of it than he bargained for. (Wolfe)

Prod Comp: Sun-Lite Pictures
Dist/Sales: Trimark, Wolfe

Sex Warriors and the Samurai

Deocampo, Nick
1995; Philippines, UK; 25 min; Drama

An unusual story of a transgender sex-worker in the Philippines who, due the closure of United States military bases in the region and the crackdown on prostitution by the government, must move to Japan to work so he can support his large family.

S

Sex Wars

Farthing, Cheryl
1992; UK; 39 min; Documentary

A look at the conflicts between gay men and lesbians, how tension is already being felt within the queer coalition and how 'lesbian boys' are turning radical drag on its head. (MQFF)

Sex Warriors and the Samurai

Sex/Life in LA

Hick, Jochen
1997; Germany, USA; 90 min; Documentary
P: Jochen Hick; *W:* Jochen Hick; *C:* Jochen Hick;
E: Ingrid Molnar; *M:* James Hardway
Cast: Tony Ward, Kevin Kramer, Ron Athey, Matt Bradshaw

Glossy magazines, porn stars, washboard stomachs, and street hustlers: Hollywood faithfully provides the public with a seemingly inexhaustible flood of male erotica. *Sex/Life in LA* brings together nine young men who earn their livings with their bodies. There are porn stars: Matt Bradshaw, porn actor and hairdresser; Kevin Kramer, who's planning his transformation from porn legend to legitimate actor; and Cole Tucker, porn star and successful entrepreneur. And there is Ron Athey, a performance artist. Finally, there are unemployed hustlers and models like Patrick and David, and ex-porn stars like John Garwood. To each of the men interviewed, the body is both the object of desire and the subject of art, and they all show their bodies freely. The scene of Tony Ward in the bathtub is worth the price of admission. For some it's been their ticket to success, and for others it's been their downfall. In the end, *Sex/Life in LA* entertainingly depicts the survival strategies of some of the male image industry's major players. (22nd San Francisco International Lesbian and Gay Film Festival)

Prod Comp: Galeria Alaska Productions
Dist/Sales: Strand, Wolfe, MediaLuna, Millivres

Sexe des étoiles, Le

(aka: Sex of the Stars)

Baillargeon, Paule
1993; Canada; 100 min; Drama

P: Pierre Gendron, Jean-Roch Marcotte;
W: Monique Proulx; *C:* Eric Cayla; *E:* Hélène Girard;
M: Yves Laferrière
Cast: Denis Mercier, Marianne Mercier, Tobie Pelletier

A sensitive, detailed look at how a young girl copes with the return of her estranged father, who is now a transsexual woman. However the film side-steps the issues in the end as the father, in order to reconcile with the daughter, begins to dress as a man again. French with English subtitles.

Prod Comp: National Film Board of Canada, Téléfilm Canada
Dist/Sales: Facets

Sexing the Label: Love and Gender in a Queer World

Broinowski, Anna
1996; Australia; 58 min; Documentary
P: Anna Broinowski, Lisa Duff; *W:* Anna Broinowski

The sexual label—gay, lesbian, bisexual, transsexual, straight etc.—has become a political tool which can either empower or dispossess its user. This film examines the complex tensions associated with these issues. It sets out to map the valid principles of empowerment underlying the use of sexual labels both past and present and charts the shifting relationship between the mainstream and non-straight communities.

Prod Comp: Froxoff Films
Dist/Sales: ACMI

Sexual Identity

1982; UK; 27 min; Documentary
P: Frances J. Berrigan

In considering the questions of sexual identity and its importance in our lives today, the work of Havelock Ellis is examined in this documentary. It looks at the meaning of sexual identity for individuals in their lives, the way this identity is related to their sense of gender, and also shows how society sets up sexual categories within which we can form a sense of sexual identity.

Prod Comp: BBC
Dist/Sales: NFVLS

Sexual Orientation: Reading Between the Labels

1992; USA; 28 min; Documentary

This film focuses on issues facing gay and lesbian youth and is designed to help build respect between individuals of divergent sexual orientation. Ignorance about homosexuality has contributed to a climate of fear, isolation, discrimination and violence toward those perceived as homosexual. Rather than relying solely on testimony from professionals, *Sexual Orientation: Reading Between the Labels* provides a forum for gay and lesbian teens to speak of their concerns.

Prod Comp: Newist
Dist/Sales: EMA

Shades

Ajalon, Jamika
1994; USA; 12 min; Drama

Explores the issues around dark and light skin in the African–American community. Drawing on erotic imagery and the relation between a light skinned woman and a darker skinned lesbian, this video questions what exactly is meant by 'black enough'. (TWN)

Dist/Sales: TWN

Shades of Gray

DePaepe, Tim
1999; USA; 73 min; Documentary
P: Edward P. Stencel, David Michael Allen;
C: Edward P. Stencel, Tim De Paepe, Bill Pryor;
E: Tim De Paepe, Bill Pryor
Cast: Michael Lovegrove, Bill Mullin, Ben Zimmer, Lea Hopkins

Shades of Gray is a documentary that focuses on the lives of five ordinary people leading normal lives in Lawrence, Kansas who happen to be gay and lesbian. When the Lawrence City Council is approached with a proposal to add the words 'sexual orientation' to its discrimination policies, a struggle ensues between the citizens of Lawrence, outside anti-gay influences, religious organisations and activists. *Shades of Gray* illustrates how homosexual women and men are very much a part of the moral fibre that comprises American society. (7th Art Releasing)

Dist/Sales: ShadesOfGray, 7thArt

Shadey

Saville, Philip
1985; UK; 116 min; Comedy
P: Otto Plaschkes; *W:* Snoo Wilson; *C:* Roger Deakins;
E: Chris Kelly; *M:* Colin Towns
Cast: Anthony Sher, Patrick Macnee, Billie Whitelaw, Leslie Ash, Bernard Hepton

On the face of it, there is nothing odd about Oliver Shadey, who owns a car repair business in London. You would not be wrong to consider him ordinary, unless you knew a few more facts. Shadey has the bizarre ability to transmit pictures from his mind onto film, and is desperate for a sex-change.

Prod Comp: Larkspur Films, Channel 4
Dist/Sales: NewVision, Skouras

Shall We Dance

Sloan, Brian
1992; USA; 15 min; B&W; Drama

It's Graduation Night at the Fort Stephens Military College and Ed's date has collapsed drunk at their table. He is called over by another cadet who discreetly seduces him. By the end of the night Ed's conviction about his own sexuality has been well and truly shaken.

Shame No More

Krokidas, John
1999; USA; 12 min; B&W; Comedy

Inspired by the US Public Service Announcements of the 1950s, *Shame No More* is a satire of conformist mentality. Set in idyllic suburb of Cherry Creek, the film warns of the disease infecting the town's men and women, the disease known as heterosexuality.

Dist/Sales: NewVague

Shampoo Horns

(aka: Cuernos de Espuma)

Toledano, Manuel
1996; Spain; 89 min; Drama
P: Elias Querejeta; *W:* Manuel Toledano; *C:* Alfredo F. Mayo; *E:* Nacho Ruiz Capollas; *M:* Angel Illarramendi
Cast: Jason Reeves, Cheyenne Besch, Jonathan Lawrence

Set primarily in that New York institution of the nightclub scene, Club 2000, in this 'one night in the life of' we get to experience close-up exactly what transpires behind the velvet rope that doesn't get lifted for everybody. This Spanish production was written and directed by Manuel Toledano who says about his first club visit, "I became a 'member' of a family determined to live life to its fullest without being affected by rules or conventions". Using the club kids' never-ending search for drugs and thrills, Toledano has interwoven three parallel stories. Punk Jonathan is a hard-core club-goer who in reality is a hopeless romantic searching for his prince. Tony is a novice on his first visit who loses his date; and Dennis is an ageing drag queen whose discovery of his HIV-positive status causes him to abandon the scene and take matters into his own hands. Sometimes funny, sometimes sad, *Shampoo Horns* ultimately documents an era and a place that may one day be recalled with fond nostalgia. (1997 Berlin Film Festival) Spanish with English subtitles.

Prod Comp: Esicma Productions

Shanghai Panic

(aka: Wo men hai pa)

Cheng, Andrew
2001; Australia, China; 87 min; Drama

W: Andrew Cheng; *C:* Andrew Cheng;
E: Andrew Cheng; *M:* Ke Zhao
Cast: Mian Mian, Zhinan Li, Yuting Yang, Zijie Zhou

Adapted from the novel *We Are Panic* by Mian Mian, in a hilarious performance as divorced writer Kika, *Shanghai Panic* is *Slackers* with Chinese characteristics in glittering Shanghai. Pretty face Bei is the source of the panic. "I think I have AIDS", he mutters. It turns out to be false alarm but soon other panics, older and more enduring, surface. Shot in a quasi-documentary style with bold camera movements and energised editing, the video sums up the madness of a city hell-bent on revitalising its past glories. The slow motion sequence on the Bund delivers a mesmerising, drugged and alienating effect, as if to remind us that 'all that glitters is not gold'. (26th Hong Kong International Film Festival) Mandarin with English subtitles .

Prod Comp: Western Dragon
Dist/Sales: WesternDragon

Shantay

Bailey, Fenton / Barbato, Randy
1995; USA; 15 min; Comedy

RuPaul plays a supermodel/secret agent who ends ending a hostage stand-off and clashes with fashion villain Toyota Carter.

Dist/Sales: WorldOfWonder

Shatzi is Dying

Shatzi is Dying

Carlomusto, Jean
2000; USA; 55 min; Documentary

Jane and Jean's beloved 16-year-old Doberman Shatzi is dying. Carlomusto's documentary casts an intimate, but light-hearted look at queers and their pets, and how we deal with death in Western society.

Dist/Sales: RockingHorse

She Don't Fade

Dunye, Cheryl
1991; USA; 23 min; Comedy
Cast: Cheryl Dunye

She Don't Fade chronicles the experiences of one woman's search for love. Dunye plays Shae, a black lesbian who is trying out her 'new approach' to women. Her use of narrative and humour are effective not only in showing the intimacies of lesbian relationships but also in portraying, a black lesbian sexuality in the context of a broader lesbian community.

Dist/Sales: TWN, EAI

She Even Chewed Tobacco

Freedman, Estelle / Stevens, Elizabeth
1983; USA; 40 min; B&W; Documentary

Meet Babe Bean, the 'trouser puzzle' who escaped the hot glare of tabloid headlines by disguising herself as Jack Garland and serving in the Spanish American War. Or Jeanne Bonnet who scored a record of 22 plus arrests for wearing male attire, went to prison for her indiscretions and later organised a group of prostitutes into a shoplifting ring! (WMM)

Dist/Sales: WMM

She Must be Seeing Things

McLaughlin, Sheila
1987; USA; 95 min; Drama
P: Sheila McLaughlin; *C:* Mark Daniels; *M:* John Zorn
Cast: Sheila Dabney, Lois Weaver, John Erdman, Kyle De Camp

Agatha is an international lawyer, Jo a filmmaker. The two women are lovers. While Jo is on the road showing her film, Agatha discovers and reads her diaries. Problems ensue as Agatha's transgression leads to jealousy and a spiralling cycle of sexual obsession. Throughout the film, Jo's and Agatha's professional lives pose a contrast to the intimacy of their life together. The tensions of their sexual attraction and the details of that intimacy become a framework for the film's more explicit narrative. (MQFF)

Dist/Sales: FirstRunFeatures

She Wears Cufflinks

Brodie, Diana J.
2002; USA; 18 min; Documentary
Poet K. Anne Richardson provides a guide to proper butch attire. (queerDOC 2002)

S

She's Real Worse than Queer

Thane, Lucy
1996; USA; 50 min; Documentary

A video-film-music documentary by and about dykes who are beginning to find culture they can stand through Punk Rock. Featuring Tribe 8, Fifth Column, Cunts With Attitude, Riot Girl NYC, Team Dresch, Sister George, Phranc, Free to Fight. (Cinenova)

Dist/Sales: Cinenova

Sherlock, Louise and Mina

Brown, Emma
1996; UK; 13 min; Drama

Set in the 1920s, Louise and Mina are two 17-year-old girls sharing a room in an English boarding school. Louise is obsessed with Sherlock Holmes and Mina is in love with Louise and desperately tries to find out if her love is reciprocated.

Shifting Positions

High, Kathy
1999; USA; 28 min; Drama
P: Kathy High

A semi-autobiographical/fictional trilogy exploring becoming queer later in life, High's father's dementia, and of mid and end-of-life crises. (VDB)

Dist/Sales: VDB

Shinjuku Boys

Longinotto, Kim / Williams, Jano
1995; UK; 53 min; Documentary
P: Kim Longinotto; *C:* Kim Longinotto;
E: John Mister; *M:* Nigel Hawks
Cast: Gaish, Tatsu, Kazuki

Shinjuku Boys takes us into the heart of the queer underbelly of Tokyo, to the aptly named Marilyn Club, where roles have been completely reversed and straight women spend their time and money with female cross-dressers called 'Annabe'. Giving incredibly frank interviews and insights into their lives, the film centres on three 'Annabe' employees of the Marilyn Club. Although they live as men and have girlfriends they do not identify as lesbians. Japanese with English subtitles.

Prod Comp: 20th Century Vixen
Dist/Sales: WMM, Cinenova, NFVLS

Shinjuku Triad Society

(aka: Shijuku Kuro Shakai)

Takashi, Miike
1995; Japan; 102 min; Drama
W: Ichiro Fujita; *C:* Naosuke Imaizumi;
E: Taiji Shimamura; *M:* Atorie Shira
Cast: Shiina Kippei, Taguchi Tomoro, Sabu

Miike Takashi's appallingly depraved debut inaugurated a trilogy of features about turf wars and struggles for supremacy between Japanese yakuza and Chinese triads. The Dragon's Claw gang from Taiwan is muscling in on various rackets in Shinjuku, including dope, extortion and gay prostitution. A lone-wolf cop tries to stem the tide, but his younger brother becomes the gang-leader's gay lover... Gleefully violent, perversely funny and dazzlingly stylish. (BFI)
Japanese with English subtitles.

Dist/Sales: Daiei

Shooting Porn

Larsen, Ronnie
1997; USA; 75 min; Documentary
P: Caryn Horwitz, Doug Lindeman; *W:* Ronnie Larsen;
C: Bruce McCarthy; *E:* James Lyons

Go backstage with Blue Blake, BJ, Hunter, Rip and a cast of dildos in this chatty factory floor tour of everyday life in the gay porn industry in Los Angeles. Go on the set of cum shots and douche scenes. Meet stunt cocks and gay-for-pay straight porn stars. Includes a loving homily to the late Joey Stefano. Candid and explicit. (MQFF)

Dist/Sales: Horwitz

Shinjuku Boys

Shoplifting Chanel

Cohn, Marya
2001; USA; 61 min; Comedy

As Oona Stone, poetry's once-promising young talent, crosses into her thirties without a word printed in years, she tries to Zelda-and-Scott her days away with gay pal Jack in vapid style—with plenty of drink, of course, and glamorous threads lifted from the costume museum at which she works. But her sister Madison's breast cancer rears its ugly head again, and Oona reluctantly agrees to take the reins of the tiring feminist literary magazine Madison edits. In a bold move to breathe some life into its pages (and sales), Oona publishes the stalwart mag's first male-authored piece in its long history. In the process, she changes the course of her relationships with Madison and Jack forever, while conversely re-igniting a passion for words she thought had gone. Not merely a sly satire on the lesbian and gay literary scene, *Shoplifting Chanel* also takes a sharp stab at the medical community's reluctance to attend to women's health issues. (25th San Francisco International Lesbian & Gay Film Festival)

Show Me Love

Show me Love
(aka: Fucking Åmål)

Moodysson, Lukas
1998; Denmark, Sweden; 89 min; Drama
P: Lars Jönsson; *W:* Lukas Moodysson; *C:* Ulf Brantås; *E:* Michal Leszczylowski, Bernhard Winkler
Cast: Alexandra Dahlström, Rebecka Liljeberg, Erica Carlson, Mathias Rust

> This insightful and realistic film about teenage sexuality is set in a small Swedish town. Elin is beautiful and popular but the limitations of a small town lead her to increasing experimentation with alcohol, sex and drugs. Agnes is finding that after nearly two years in her new high school she is still largely friendless and alone. Elin and Agnes inhabit two very different social worlds but when they do finally meet they discover a disturbing and exciting sexual attraction for each other. Elin deals with this knowledge by throwing herself into a relationship with a shy diffident boy, while Agnes increasingly comes to accept her lesbianism. Refusing easy moralism or neat conclusions, Lukas Moodysson crafts an intelligent examination of contemporary youth culture. This is a gritty love story tenderly and convincingly performed by its young cast. (ACMI) Swedish with English subtitles.

Awards: Berlin International Film Festival, 1999: Teddy Award
Prod Comp: Memfis Films
Dist/Sales: Strand, Wolfe, Potential, ACMI

Show me your Pic

Baldwin, Robbie
2001; Australia; 26 min; Documentary

> Traces the lives of five gay men as they search for love on line. An hilarious and sometimes moving look at Sydney's gay cyber-scene.

Dist/Sales: Queerscreen

Siberia

Suenke, Orlow
1995; The Netherlands; 50 min; Drama

> Frans is a music teacher who takes a new job at a secondary school on a small island off the coast of Holland. There he meets and begins a passionate affair with Duits, the German teacher. Duits becomes concerned that the small conservative island community will discover their relationship so he plans to marry, keeping his affair with Frans in the closet. Frans is not happy with this choice and he leaves the island and Duits. Thirty years later he returns to celebrate Duits's retirement as headmaster of the school. They find their love for each other is still as passionate as ever. But will Duits follow his heart?

Siege
(aka: Self Defense)

Donovan, Paul / O'Connell, Maura
1983; Canada; 81 min; Action
P: Michael Donovan, John Walsch, Maura O'Connell; *W:* Paul Donovan; *C:* Les Krizsan; *E:* Ian McBride; *M:* Drew King, Peter Jermyn
Cast: Tom Nardini, Brenda Bazinet, Daryl Haney, Doug Lennox

> A group of thugs, known as 'the New Order', bring nothing but disorder to the town when they decide to clean up the homosexuals who inhabit a gay nightclub where the clubbing never seems to stop. Based on a true story, and highly controversial at the time of its release.

Prod Comp: Salter Productions
Dist/Sales: ReelMovies, NewLine, VSM

Siegfried

Domalik, Andrzej
1986; Poland; 90 min; Drama
W: Andrzej Domalik; *C:* Grzegorz Kedzierski; *M:* Jerzy Satanowski
Cast: Adam Ferency, Gustaw Holoubek, Tomasz Hudziec

> Set in 1934, an art collector, who is feeling his age and impending death, becomes invigorated when he meets a circus acrobat named Siegfried and embarks on a homosexual relationship.

Prod Comp: Zespol Filmowy-Tor

S

Sign of the Cross, The

De Mille, Cecil B.
1932; USA; 120 min; B&W; Drama
P: Cecil B. De Mille; *W:* Sidney Buchman, Waldemar Young; *C:* Karl Struss; *E:* Anne Bauchens;
M: Rudolph G. Kopp
Cast: Fredric March, Elissa Landi, Charles Laughton, Claudette Colbert

> The decline and fall of Western civilisation according to De Mille. The moral tale of the Christian victory over paganism. Perverse, enjoyable film with fine performances, especially Laughton's definitive and queer Nero.

Prod Comp: Paramount
Dist/Sales: Ascanbee, Paramount

Signed: Lino Brocka

Blackwood, Christian
1987; USA; 80 min; Documentary
P: Christian Blackwood; *W:* Christian Blackwood;
C: Christian Blackwood; *E:* Monika Abspacher

> A documentary on the Philippine film director, Lino Brocka, who talks openly about filmmaking, politics and his sexuality.

Awards: Berlin International Film Festival, 1988: Peace Award Christian Blackwood

Silence=Death

(aka: Die AIDS-Trilogie: Schweigen=Tod)

von Praunheim, Rosa / Zwickler, Phil
1990; USA; 60 min; Documentary
C: Mike Kuchar; *M:* Diamanda Galas
Cast: Alan Ginsberg, Keith Haring, Rafeal Gambas, David Wojnorowicz

> A documentary which looks at the way AIDS has devastated the gay arts community, particularly in New York. Various artists are interviewed, revealing their shock, anger and frustration, not only with the disease, but with society as well.

Awards: Berlin International Film Festival, 1990: Teddy Award for Best Feature
Dist/Sales: FirstRunFeatures

Silence of the Lambs, The

Demme, Jonathan
1991; USA; 118 min; Thriller
P: Edward Saxon, Kenneth Utt, Ron Bozman;
W: Ted Tally; *C:* Tak Fujimoto; *E:* Craig McKay;
M: Howard Shore
Cast: Anthony Hopkins, Jodie Foster, Scott Glenn, Ted Levine

> A young FBI agent, Clarice Starling, is enlisted to get information from a serial killer-psychiatrist who may have knowledge of a killer committing horrible murders against young women. The tension and suspense build as the psychiatrist slowly releases clues to the killer's identity. A horribly homophobic film with the revelation that the killer is a homosexual-transvestite who wants to be transformed into a woman. He thinks he can achieve this by killing and skinning young women, and making a suit of their flesh. Based on the best-selling book by Thomas Harris.

Awards: Academy Awards, 1991: Best Film, Actor (Anthony Hopkins), Actress (Jodie Foster), Direction, Adapted Screenplay
Prod Comp: Orion, Strong Heart
Dist/Sales: ReelMovies, Col-Tri, Lauren, OrionHV, ACMI

Silence that Silences, The

Kinney, Donald / Kinney, Robert
1990; USA; 25 min; Experimental

> A video that offers an initially hypercorrect but eventually invigorating, funny and painful critique of the media's portrayal of AIDS.

Silence, The

(aka: Tystnaden)

Bergman, Ingmar
1963; Sweden; 88 min; B&W; Drama
P: Allan Ekelund; *W:* Ingmar Bergman;
C: Sven Nykvist; *E:* Ulla Ryghe; *M:* Ivan Renliden
Cast: Ingrid Thulin, Gunnel Lindblom, Hakan Jahnberg, Birger Malmsten

> Thought provoking narrative about two sisters who stop at a hotel in a northern European city. One sister is a frustrated lesbian, the other is a free-spirited mother of a 10-year-old boy. Thulin suppresses her sexual desire for her sister, Lindblom picks up a waiter and brings him back to the hotel. The film deals with the need for human tenderness and emotional warmth. Swedish with English subtitles.

Prod Comp: Svensk Filmindustri
Dist/Sales: Ascanbee, NFVLS, BFI

Silences

Cullen, Colette
1995; Ireland; 21 min; Drama
W: Colette Cullen
Cast: Adrienne Rich

> Niamh is home in Ireland with her producer, Helen, looking at locations in which to film her prize-winning short story. They're staying with her parents, which is causing underlying tensions to surface as Helen falls for Niamh's sister. (Cinenova)

Dist/Sales: Cinenova

Silencis

(aka: Silent Moments)

Xavier, Daniel
1983; Spain; 14 min; Drama

A Spanish army officer struggles with his attraction to his gay son. His repressed feelings instill a voyeurism in him that he can't control.

Silent Pioneers

Winer, Lucy
1984; USA; 45 min; Documentary
P: Pat Snyder, Lucy Winer, Harvey Marks, Paula DeKoenigsberg

Silent Pioneers creates a portrait of strong and active women and men who face not only issues of ageing, but also concerns related to sexual orientation. Nominated for an Emmy Award in 1986.

Prod Comp: Silent Pioneers
Dist/Sales: ACMI, FilmakersLibrary, Salzgeber, WaterBearer, BFI

Silent Thrush, The

(aka: Shisheng Huamei)

Cheng, Sheng-fu
1991; Taiwan; 100 min; Drama
Cast: Yu-shan Li, Yi-ch'An Lu, Chia-p'ei Yuan, Ying-chen Chang

Amidst the shouting and turmoil of a present-day Taiwanese opera group, a young girl, Yuh, joins the company and its star, Chia-feng, falls in love with her. Unfortunately this provokes jealousy from her long-time lover Ai-ching. A fascinating mixture of eroticism and exoticism among the colour and music of the opera.

Silkwood

Nichols, Mike
1983; USA; 130 min; Thriller
P: Mike Nichols, Michael Hausman; W: Nora Ephron, Alice Arlen; C: Miroslav Ondricek; E: Sam O'Steen; M: Georges Delerue
Cast: Meryl Streep, Cher, Kurt Russell, Diana Scarwid

Based on the true story of Karen Silkwood, a worker in a nuclear plant, who, after finding problems with safety within the plant, goes headlong into battle with a lazy and uncaring management. Against this background she has to deal with a troubled love affair, a custody battle for her child, and unwanted lesbian affection from her close friend, played by Cher. The plant management almost wins when they try to cover up Karen's mysterious death in a car

accident.

Prod Comp: ABC, 20th Century-Fox
Dist/Sales: Roadshow, ACMI, 20thCenturyFox

Silver Screen: Color me Lavender, The

Rappaport, Mark
1997; USA; 103 min; Documentary
W: Mark Rappaport; C: Mark Rappaport

The Silver Screen: Color Me Lavender studies the way Hollywood treated or ignored the issue of homosexuality during its Golden Age. Sometimes shocking, often funny and sarcastic, this investigation describes the subterfuges that directors used to allude to homosexuality without naming it, let alone identifying it—that is, by avoiding the subject. At the same time, Rappaport offers us a fascinating essay on the genders, showing how they were perceived and perpetuated by the 'dream factory' for almost thirty years, from the 1930s to the 60s. (1998 Tampa International Gay & Lesbian Film Festival)

Prod Comp: Couch Potato Productions
Dist/Sales: WaterBearer

Silverlake Life: The View From Here

Joslin, Tom / Friedman, Peter
1993; USA; 99 min; Documentary

Silverlake Life: The View From Here is a landmark documentary since it was the first time a film both documented and intimately exposed viewers to the ravages of AIDS. When filmmaker Tom Joslin and his long time lover Mark Massi were both diagnosed with AIDS, Joslin decided to shoot a video diary. This film combines the intimacy and urgency of a dying man's diary with his striking visual style. As Joslin's strength began to fail, filmmaker Peter Friedman took over the project and finished the film. Silverlake Life is a unique, gay couple's harrowing record of the disease told from the time they were diagnosed to their deaths. The unflinching camera and the probing honesty with which the pair talk make a unique firsthand journal and a deeply moving experience. (Films Transit)

Dist/Sales: FilmsTransit, Cowboy

Simon and I: Steps for the Future

Ditsie, Beverley Palesa / Newman, Nicky
2001; South Africa; 52 min; Documentary

Sultry lesbian activist and singer Ditsie recounts the amazing life and heritage of Simon Nkodi. Ditsie's honey voice and languid reminiscences tell the story of an extraordinary friendship with Simon and their shared struggles, joys and songs for same sex social justice in South Africa. (MQFF)

S

Simone

Ehm, Christine
1984; France; 103 min; Drama

> Stylised drama of a love affair between the beautiful
> and mysterious Simone and the gamine Francoise,
> first seen in hospital recovering from a suicide
> attempt. The two meet on the metro, when
> Francoise is arguing with her well-meaning but
> patronising brother. Simone intercedes, the three
> laugh it off and part as abruptly as they met. But
> Simone reappears and she and Francoise begin to
> establish a sensual relationship. French with English
> subtitles.

Dist/Sales: Altermedia

Sincerely Yours

Douglas, Gordon
1955; USA; 115 min; Drama
P: Henry Blanke; *W:* Irving Wallace; *C:* William H.
Clothier; *E:* Owen Marks; *M:* Liberace
Cast: Liberace, Joanne Dru, Dorothy Malone, William
Demarest

> Liberace's portrayal of a concert pianist seemed too
> close to the bone for most people. The pianist's life
> changes abruptly when he loses his sight. A camp
> classic written by Irving Wallace, it was an absolute
> bomb when it was released, but has curiosity value
> now.

Prod Comp: International Artists, Warner
Dist/Sales: Ascanbee, Warner

Sink or Swim

Friedrich, Su
1990; USA; 48 min; B&W; Drama
Cast: Jessica Meyerson

> An autobiographical film about the relationship
> between a father and daughter. A young girl narrates
> 26 short stories that recount memories of a father
> she both fears and admires.

Dist/Sales: NFVLS, WMM, CFMDC, ACMI

Sir: Just a Normal Guy

La Rosa, Melanie
2001; USA; 57 min; Documentary

> A candid look at the life of Jay Snider, who started
> life as Jennifer. Through in-depth interviews, we
> learn about the process of his transition, charting the
> physical and emotional changes he went through,
> and the sense of normality he felt when he finally
> began to live as a man. (2002 Mardi Gras Film
> Festival)

Siren

Swords, Sara
1996; USA; 45 min; Erotica

> Ella is captivated by Jodie, a writer of erotic fiction.
> Sent to her majestic country estate, Ella is titillated
> by what she sees there. *Siren* is an erotic lesbian
> fantasy drama made by women for women, featuring
> exquisite imagery combined with a powerful
> soundtrack. (Wolfe)

Dist/Sales: Wolfe

SIS: The Perry Watkins Story

Cartagena, Chiqui
1994; USA; 52 min; Documentary
P: Chiqui Cartagena, Suzanne Newman

> This groundbreaking documentary explores the
> explosive issue of gays in the military. It examines the
> case of Perry J. Watkins, the first openly gay man to
> defeat the ban against gays in the military. The case
> established a powerful legal precedent that acted as an
> inspiration to the gay and black communities. His
> story is funny and compelling and sheds light on the
> social, political and historical context of the lesbian
> and gay movement. Drafted in 1968, Perry Watkins
> served 15 years in the US Army as an openly gay man
> who even did female impersonations on base, to
> entertain the troops. In 1982, he was discharged
> under the provisions that ban homosexuals from
> serving in the Armed Forces. With the help of the
> American Civil Liberties Union, Sgt. Watkins fought
> for reinstatement for nine years. In the end, the
> United States Supreme Court ruled in his favour and
> refused to hear the Army's appeal. (Filmakers Library)

Dist/Sales: FilmakersLibrary

Sir: Just a Normal Guy

Sissy

Gittens, Debbie
2000; Australia; 27 min; Documentary

Koori queens proudly get out and about in this high-spirited and affirming documentary. Battling homophobia within their community, and the ongoing violence of racism, these queers of colour demand visibility, space and one hell of a fabulous time. (MQFF)

Dist/Sales: ArtemisInt

Sister Louise's Discovery

Heatherman, Margaret
1994; USA; 10 min; B&W; Comedy

Sister Louise is torn between her marriage to God, and her real-life sister's lesbian lifestyle. She discovers the delights of lesbianism, and the sins of the flesh aren't all bad when she ends up in a dyke bar. Can she be distracted from her own moral path by the promise of cheap thrills in darkened wine-bar corner?

Sister My Sister

Sister My Sister

Meckler, Nancy
1994; UK; 102 min; Drama
P: Norma Heyman; *W:* Wendy Kesselman; *C:* Ashley Rowe; *E:* David Stiven; *M:* Stephen Warbeck

Cast: Julie Walters, Joely Richardson, Jodhi May, Sophie Thursfield

Les Mans, France, 1933. Two sisters, maids in the bourgeois household of Madam and Isabelle Danzard, savagely murder their employers after leading a harrowing existence since early childhood. Left by their poverty stricken mother in an abusive convent as children, separated and sent into service as adolescents, they spend their adult days in the oppressive home of Madame and Isabelle Danzard. Only in their cold, cramped attic room, isolated from the unfeeling world around them, can they create a secret world of their own and give each other the tenderness and love they so crave.

Prod Comp: NFH Productions, British Screen, Channel 4
Dist/Sales: Wolfe, 7thArt, ACMI

Sister Smile

(aka: Suor Sorriso)

Deutsch, Roger
2001; Italy; 95 min; Documentary
P: Kass Thomas; *W:* Roger Deutsch, Francesca Terrenato; *C:* Guilio Pietromarchi; *E:* Andrea Pica; *M:* Andreas Salvatori
Cast: Ginevra Colonna, Antonio Salines, Simona Caparrini, Francesca Bianco

Jeanine Deckers (aka 'Sister Smile') was a young nun in a Belgian convent in the 1960s who wrote the song Dominique. It became an international smash hit and sold more than 1.5 million copies, even bumping the Beatles off the top spot. Hollywood eventually cast Debbie Reynolds in the cheesy 1966 'inspired by' musical, *The Singing Nun*. Jeanine leaves the convent to become a missionary and a musician. Searching for a replacement for the lack of love she received from her cold father, she falls in and out of love with a woman named Clara. All the while, even though Jeanine donated all of her royalties from Dominique to her convent, the government hounds her for tens of thousands of dollars in back taxes. Over 20 years after her brush with fame, Jeanine eventually falls in love with the doomed Annie Pecher and descends into mental illness and addiction. With eloquent performances and delicate cinematography, *Sister Smile* travels from innocence to tragedy without a false note. (2002 Chicago Lesbian & Gay International Film Festival) Italian with English subtitles.

Prod Comp: Neo Film
Dist/Sales: Neofilm

Sisters Lumiere, The

(aka: Sisters of Light)

Vanderborght, Karen
2000; Belgium; 28 min; Experimental

Two friends—Stella, an astronomer, and Lucia, a salesgirl in a lamp store—who know each other only through correspondence, are separated by death. Lucia, the surviving friend, drives off at night, heading for the Belgium of twinkling motorways, searching for Stella's angel which should have become Lucia's guardian angel. With an empty heart, she drives, accompanied by strange light phenomena around her (UFOs? angels?) to find enlightenment around her loss. (Frameline)

Dist/Sales: Frameline

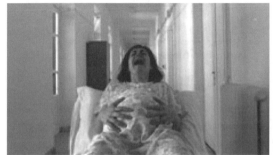

Sister Smile

Sitcom

Ozon, François
1998; France; 85 min; Comedy
P: Olivier Delbosc, Marc Missonnier;
W: François Ozon; *C:* Yorick Le Saux;
E: Dominique Petrot; *M:* Éric Neveux
Cast: François Marthouret, Evelyne Dandry, Adrien de Van, Marina de Van, Lucia Sanchez

Director François Ozon's own words give the best description of his first feature film. He calls it 'essentially a sitcom, but loaded with other cinematic genres—the family film, horror, gore, melodrama and farce'. The combination creates an outrageously comical, yet surprisingly poignant, black farce in the best Buñuelian tradition, with no taboo left unbroken. Things begin to get weird when Jean brings home a pet rat for his family which unleashes all manner of chaos revolving around the themes of homosexuality, incest, bisexuality, violence, suicide and S/M. The whole family including mother Helene, son Nicholas and daughter Sophie start acting strangely. Nicholas announces he is gay and proceeds to conduct orgies in his bedroom. Sophie turns suicidal. Maria, the maid, stops doing her duties and starts messing with Sophie's boyfriend David, who shows off a fully erect penis in one scene. And Helene takes motherly love to extremes in an attempt to 'cure' her son's homosexuality. (MQFF)
French with English subtitles.

Prod Comp: Fidélité Productions
Dist/Sales: Celluloid-Dreams, NewYorker, ACMI

Six Degrees of Separation

Schepisi, Fred
1993; USA; 112 min; Drama
P: Fred Schepisi, Arnon Milchan; *W:* John Guare;
C: Ian Baker; *E:* Peter Honess; *M:* Jerry Goldsmith
Cast: Donald Sutherland, Stockard Channing, Ian McKellen, Will Smith

When wealthy Manhattan art dealers Ousia and Flan Kittredge open their door to a young man, Paul, who has been stabbed and mugged in Central Park, their world is changed forever. He poses as Sidney Poitier's son and says he went to Harvard with their daughter. The next morning, Ousia finds Paul in bed with another man and her illusions of him are shattered.

Prod Comp: MGM, New Regency
Dist/Sales: Warner, TLA, MGM, UIP, Swank

Sixth Happiness, The

Hussein, Waris
1997; India, UK; 97 min; Drama
P: Tatiana Kennedy; *W:* Firdaus Kanga;
C: James Welland; *E:* Laurence Mery-Clark
Cast: Firdaus Kanga, Souad Faress, Khodus Wadia

Brit is born with a disease that makes his bones brittle, and affects his growth so that he will never be more than four feet tall. Despite his physical challenges, Brit has his own spirited way of dealing with the world, and the cast of characters that surrounds him helps ensure that life is never dull: an eccentric mom, a dad with movie star looks, a doting sister, and numerous other mentors. Although he is committed to a future arranged marriage to a deaf girl, he falls in love, and has a relationship, with the very handsome Cyrus. Adapted from the autobiography of Firdaus Kanga.

Dist/Sales: BFI

Size 'Em Up

Size 'Em Up

Russo, Christine
2001; USA; 15 min; Comedy

Buying a bra becomes a major trauma for sporty

dyke Samantha—especially when she's surrounded by lusty sales ladies, and an especially cute girl.

Dist/Sales: BustinOut

Skin and Bone

Lewis, Everett
1995; USA; 110 min; Comedy
P: Claudia Hoover, Gardner Monks; *W:* Everett Lewis;
C: Fernando Argüelles; *E:* Everett Lewis;
M: Geoff Haba, Mark Jan Wlodarkiewicz
Cast: B. Wyatt, Alan Boyce, Garrett Scullin

The story of three hustlers who are all working the streets for different reasons, or so they think. Together they must deal with the gritty realities of street life and face up to their fading dreams.

Dist/Sales: Strand, Alliance, JourDeFete, Wolfe

Skin Complex

Lennhoff, Stephen
1992; UK; 20 min; Documentary
P: Rebecca Dobbs

For those of you who loved *No Skin off My Ass*, here's a look at the increasingly widespread adoption of skinhead fashions by gay men. Since the 1970s gay men have been drawing inspiration for their own looks from heterosexual macho images. But can this particular style of dress be separated from the fascist homophobic politics it represents? Stephen Lennhoff opens up a controversial and enlightening debate by confronting skinheads of differing persuasions, race and sexuality. (MQFF)

Dist/Sales: MayaVision

Skin Deep

Onodera, Midi
1994; Canada; 85 min; Drama
P: Midi Onodera, Lentin Mehernaz; *W:* Midi Onodera;
C: Robert MacDonald; *E:* Sarah Peddie;
M: Kathryn Moses
Cast: Melanie Nicholls-King, Natsuko Ohama, Keram Malicki-Sánchez

Alex is a filmmaker who is obsessed with tattooing. She places an ad in a tattooing magazine and it is answered by young androgynous Chris. Chris describes to Alex the sexual pleasure gained from tattooing and, as they share their obsession, Chris finds that he is falling madly in love with Alex. But Alex's girlfriend, Montana, is put off-side when it becomes obvious that Alex enjoys the new attention and infatuation. When Alex rejects Chris, he tries desperately to gain Alex's attention.

Prod Comp: Daruma Pictures
Dist/Sales: FilmsTransit, WaterBearer, Domino

Skin Flick

(aka: Skin Gang)

La Bruce, Bruce
1999; Canada, Germany; 70 min; Erotica
P: Jürgen Brüning; *W:* Bruce La Bruce; *C:* James Carman
Cast: Steve Masters, Eden Miller, Tom International, Ralph Steel

Bruce La Bruce is increasingly queer cinema's most maverick filmmaker, not only producing films that defy the conventions of mainstream Hollywood but also creating queer and bisexual characters who are heretical to the homosexual mainstream itself. *Skin Flick* is a pornographic film that allows itself to experiment with both representation and the techniques of film and video. Continuing La Bruce's fetishising of skinheads, *Skin Flick* is about a group of fascist youths who spend their time having sex with one another when they are not bashing homosexuals and people of colour. The film contrasts the aggression and violence of the skinheads with the bourgeois emptiness of a mixed-race gay couple. After being raped and tortured by the skins, the couple turn the table and extract their revenge. However, they find that the pleasure of violence is addictive. (ACMI)

Prod Comp: CAZZO Film
Dist/Sales: Brüning, Millivres, ACMI

Skindeep

Cox, Paul
1970; Australia; 37 min; Drama
P: Paul Cox; *C:* Edward Keogh; *M:* Ian Wallace
Cast: Jan Hurrell, Anthony Ward, Pat Allen

A mood piece involving two lesbian lovers and a disturbed young man contemplating suicide.

Dist/Sales: NFVLS, ACMI

Skud

Swan, Donna
1996; Australia; 26 min; Comedy
P: Donna Swan; *W:* Donna Swan

Scud takes us to the edge of the lives of Tash and Matt—two young people in search of themselves and a release from their existence. Tash at fifteen is stubbornly independent and fights against the external forces that sweep her to the 'edge'. Matt recklessly lives on the borderline of life and death as he pushes the limits with train surfing. Tash in seeking time out from a well meaning but 'out of control' mother meets Matt at a youth refuge. They connect through their individual struggles and share their outlets of trainsurfing and boxing, eventually confronting 'the edge' within themselves—with devastating consequences.

Slaves to the Underground

Peterson, Kristine
1996; USA; 92 min; Comedy
P: Kristine Peterson, Bill Cody, Raquel Caballes
Maxwell; *W:* Bill Cody; *C:* Zoran Hochstätter;
E: Eric Vizents; *M:* Mike Martt
Cast: Molly Gross, Marisa Ryan, Jason Bortz, Bob
Neuwirth, Natacha La Ferriere

This funny and hip portrait of life on the margins of
the Seattle music scene is an upbeat, fresh and
honest look at bisexual love. Girl-positive and sex-
positive, it also features a killer soundtrack. Shelley
dumps Jimmy, joins an all-girl band and starts a
relationship with the singer Suzy who is wild and
outrageous both on and off stage. Soon the pair are
cruising around Seattle, making no apology for their
sexuality and stealing pornography from hapless
convenience store clerks. But when Shelley runs into
Jimmy again she realises that she is still attracted to
him. Jimmy also discovers something she has
managed to hide from him...

Prod Comp: NEO Motion Pictures
Dist/Sales: FirstLook, Wolfe

Sleep Come Free Me

Schmidt, Laurie
1998; USA; 19 min; Comedy

Natalie, a disenchanted office worker, lives in the
space between dreams and reality. When her dream
life overlaps with reality, her dull 9 to 5 existence is
flooded with overwhelming and unexpected desire,
and Natalie is forced to sink or swim. *Sleep Come
Free Me*—comedic and intelligent—brims with
discord, lust and symbolic imagery. (Frameline)

Dist/Sales: Frameline

Sleep in a Nest of Flames

Dowell, James / Kolomvakis, John
2000; USA; 117 min; Documentary
P: James Dowell, John Kolomvakis; *W:* James Dowell;
C: Scott Barnard; *E:* David Lindblom
Cast: Rich Bernatovech, Eric Cole

Filmmakers James Dowell and John Kolomvakis had
never heard of Charles Henri Ford when they found
one of his books during a holiday in Greece. But
they soon became fascinated by this little-known,
though influential poet, novelist, filmmaker, and
publisher. An outspoken gay man throughout his
life, Ford began his arts career in the 1930s, when he
co-wrote what is believed to be the first gay novel
with a happy ending, *The Young and the Evil*. That
same decade, Ford read poetry in Gertrude Stein's
salon, and he organised The Paper Ball at the

Hartford Athenaeum, a fabulously queer costume
party, shown here with amazing footage. Throughout the next 30 years, Ford played a part in the
major art movements of the time, including
Surrealism, the Beat movement, and Pop Art: as a
member of Andy Warhol's factory, Ford made an
explicitly homoerotic underground film evocatively
titled Johnny Minotaur. *Sleep in a Nest of Flames* is
chock-full of powerful homoerotic dramatisations,
music by Paul Bowles and Ned Rorem, and lively
interviews with William S. Burroughs, Paul
Morrissey, Edmund White, Allen Ginsberg, and
Ford himself, who's still alive: an impish, creative,
modest man with a twinkle in his octogenarian eyes.
(2002 Mardi Gras Film Festival)

Dist/Sales: Symbiosis

Sleep in a Nest of Flames

Sleepy Haven

Mueller, Matthais
1993; Germany; 15 min; Experimental

A mesmerising blend of original and found footage,
including floating naked sailors, and solar system
images. A powerful meditation on desire.

Dist/Sales: Canyon

Slight Fever of a 20-Year-Old

(aka: Hatachi No Binetsu)

Hashiguchi, Ryosuke
1993; Japan; 115 min; Drama
W: Ryosuke Hashiguchi; *C:* Junichi Tozawa;
E: Hiroshi Matsuo; *M:* Akira Isono, Ryuji Murayama,
Kôhei Shinozaki
Cast: Yoshihiko Hakamada, Reiko Kataoka, Masashi
Endô, Sumiyo Yamada

The film centres around two young hustlers, Tatsuro
and Shin, and their two female best friends. Tatsuro,
the better hustler, spends his days skipping school
and entertaining clients, but when Shin declares his
love for him, Tatsuro has to enter the real world.
Japanese with English subtitles.

Prod Comp: Akira Ishigaki, Pony Canyon

Sluts and Goddesses Video Workshop

Beatty, Maria / Sprinkle, Annie
1993; USA; 52 min; Documentary
P: Annie Sprinkle, Maria Beatty; *M:* Pauline Oliveros
Cast: Annie Sprinkle, Barbara Carrellas

A very humorous and absurd look at sex with that
wonderful sexpert Annie Sprinkle. It features many
exotic ways to simulate sexual and sensual pleasures.
These encounters include tattooing, striptease,
Chinese-sword dancing, piercing and shaving. You
will also be witness to female ejaculation and a five
minute orgasm! A controversial but thought-
provoking examination of female sexuality.
(Cinenova)

Dist/Sales: Cinenova

Smear

Zalutsky, Sam
1998; USA; 10 min; Drama

It's tough being a teenager in love—especially when
you're in love with your (straight) best friend.

Dist/Sales: PictureThis!

Smoke

D'Auria, Mark
1993; USA; 90 min; Drama

Michael, a loner who works as a bathroom attendant
in a fancy Manhattan hotel, has a penchant for older
men. Lost in his search for a father figure he pursues
a married detective, and is, in turn, pursued by his
ex-boyfriend who bullies and intimidates him
throughout the film.

Dist/Sales: WaterBearer

Smokers Only

(aka: Vagón Fumador)

Chen, Verónica
2002; Argentina; 87 min; Drama
P: Donald Ranvaud; *W:* Verónica Chen, Alejandro
Sapogniikoff; *C:* Nicolás Theodossiou;
E: Verónica Chen; *M:* Pablo Siriani
Cast: Cecelia Bengolea, Leonardo Breznicki, Adrian
Fondari, Pablo Razuk

Andrés is a 20-year-old 'taxiboy' who flies through
the Buenos Aires night on rollerblades. Under the
unerring eye of a surveillance camera, Andrés turns
tricks with men he meets in an enclosed ATM at a
bank in the centre of the city. Reni is also twenty, a
singer in a struggling band, already living on the
edge. Spying Andrés connecting with a john, she is
fascinated with what she sees. She enters the ATM
and Andrés' world, initiating a dangerous game, and
is drawn into the dark side of Buenos Aires and its
rent-boy circuit. Reni believes in the redemptive
power of love, but Andrés' world threatens to
destroy her. Scanning the crowded sidewalks, Andrés
is both innocent urchin and savvy hustler, scoping
out his next score. As Reni walks, and then works,
the streets with Andrés, the two become trapped in a
dance of mutual discovery and inevitable loss. First-
time feature film director Veronica Chen's Vagón
fumador captures the mesmerizing erotic dreamscape
of Buenos Aires at night with a fractured narrative
that mirrors the urban rhythms that infuse the film.
Edgy, hip and romantic all at once, it is a haunting,
sexy meditation on the thrill, but also the ephemeral
and precarious nature, of connection in the big city.
(2002 Miami Gay & Lesbian Film Festival)

Dist/Sales: Strand

Snake Boy, The

Chen, Michelle / Li, Xiao
2001; China; 61 min; Documentary
P: Michelle Chen, Ethan Hou; *W:* Arthur Jones,
Michelle Chen; *C:* Xiao Li; *E:* Jinglei Kong;
M: Coco Zhao
Cast: Coco Zhao

An engaging look at the life of Coco Zhan, a
homosexual jazz singer in Shanghai. Mandarin with
English subtitles.

Dist/Sales: ChenM

Snatch it

Stafrace, Inka
2000; USA; 14 min; Comedy

Light-hearted social commentary, shadowed with
black humour, exposing the fickleness of friendship

when matched with the primal power of sexual desire.

Dist/Sales: PollyTickle

Sodom

Price, Luther
1989; UK; 25 min; Drama

A reworking of gay porn that evokes Genet's *Un Chant d'Amour* and Kenneth Anger's *Fireworks*, while bouncing off texts by Sade and Bataille. Like his precursors Genet and Anger, Luther Price challenges traditional notions of sexual portrayal and, as with their work, his film is certain to be controversial.

Soft Hearts

(aka: Pusong Mamon)

Lamangan, Joel / Quizon, Enrico
1998; Philippines; 112 min; Comedy
W: Ricardo Lee, Mel Mendoza-Del Rosario;
C: Romeo Vitug; *E:* Jess Navarro; *M:* Dennis Garcia
Cast: Lorna Tolentino, Albert Martinez, Eric Quizon

Annie is a hopeless romantic who has her sights set on gorgeous, but distant co-worker Ron. She aims to make him her husband, and successfully lures him into bed after a drunken night at the office. According to plan she becomes pregnant and demands Ron marry her. She is shocked to learn that he's gay and in a long term relationship with Nick. What transpires is a comedy of errors that highlights the possibility of constructing alternative families, and the enduring power of love.

Dist/Sales: Viva

Soliloquy of Dale Cunningham, The

MacGeorge, Samuel
1994; Australia; 21 min; B&W; Drama
P: Samuel MacGeorge

A film about a teenage boy exploring his sexuality. It is the story of a boy, his dog and a toilet block.

Solos Y Soledades

Berrios, Javier Antonio
1992; Cuba; 22 min; Drama

Two men meet at a bus stop, but find it hard to find a suitable place to consummate their meeting. Spanish.

Some Aspect of a Shared Lifestyle

Bordowitz, Gregg
1986; USA; 22 min; Documentary

Focusing on early media reporting of the AIDS

epidemic and the struggle for gay rights, Bordowitz successfully portrays the complexity of issues surrounding the AIDS epidemic as it emerged in the early 1980s in the USA, forcefully arguing for the need to confront AIDS as an equal-opportunity threat to all members of society.

Some Ground to Stand On

Warshow, Joyce P.
1998; USA; 35 min; Documentary
P: Janet Baus, Joyce P. Warshow

This compelling documentary tells the life story of Blue Lunden, a working class lesbian activist whose odyssey of personal transformation parallels lesbians' changing roles over the past 40 years. Starting with Blue's experience of being run out of the 1950s New Orleans gay bar scene for wearing men's clothing, *Some Ground to Stand On* combines interviews, rare photos, and archival footage to trace her experiences: giving up her child for adoption and getting her back; getting sober; and coming into her own as a lesbian rights, feminist, and antinuclear activist. Now 61 and living in Sugarloaf Women's Village, Blue reflects on ageing, activism, and a life spent 'doing what she wanted' in this touching, inspiring look at a generation's struggle for a lesbian identity and consciousness. (WMM)

Dist/Sales: WMM, Cinenova

Some Like it Hot

Some Like it Hot

Wilder, Billy
1959; USA; 119 min; B&W; Comedy
P: Billy Wilder; *W:* Billy Wilder, I. A. L. Diamond;
C: Charles Lang; *E:* Arthur Schmidt; *M:* Adolph Deutsch
Cast: Marilyn Monroe, Tony Curtis, Jack Lemmon, Joe E. Brown, George Raft

A legendary comedy about two musicians who, after witnessing the St Valentine's Day Massacre in Chicago, flee from gangsters by taking refuge in an all-girl band. Of course this leads to complications when the boys start to fall for the girls, and a millionaire falls for Jack Lemmon. With lots of slapstick humour and verbal innuendo, this gender-bender makes a great drag classic.

Prod Comp: United Artists, Ashton Productions, Mirisch Company
Dist/Sales: NFVLS, ReelMovies, ACMI, Warner, MGM, UA, Swank

Some of my Best Friends Are

Nelson, Mervyn
1971; USA; 110 min; Drama
P: John Lauricella, Martin Richards;
W: Mervyn Nelson; *E:* Richard Cadenas, Angelo Ross;
M: Phil Moore, Gordon Rose
Cast: Candy Darling, Rue McClanahan, Sylvia Sima, Fannie Flagg

Set on Christmas Eve, this is one night in the life of a pre-Stonewall bar in Greenwich Village, the centre of gay life in New York. This collection of lonely and unhappy people includes gays, drag queens and fag hags who seem to have nowhere else to go—the bar is their only refuge.

Some of These Days

Miller-Monzon, John
1994; USA; 33 min; B&W; Drama
W: John Miller-Monzon

The final film in New York writer/director John Miller-Monzon's trilogy. Hal is devastated by the sudden end of a long-term relationship, but before he has even begun his emotional recovery he takes the plunge with a handsome new acquaintance.

Dist/Sales: Forefront

Some Prefer Cake

Arnesen, Heidi
1997; USA; 96 min; Comedy
P: Matthew J. Siegel, Jeannie Kahaney; *W:* Jeannie Kahaney; *C:* Matthew J. Siegel; *E:* Heidi Arnesen
Cast: Kathleen Fontaine, Tara Howley, Tirza Naramore

A tale of sex, chocolate and lesbian desire, set in San Francisco's comedy circuit scene. With a winning mix of engaging characters, including the angsty comedienne who can't get a laugh, her oriental stalker and the straight best mate who prefers chocolate cake to sex. (Millivres)

Prod Comp: Up All Nite productions
Dist/Sales: Wolfe, Millivres

Something Close to Heaven

Black, Dustin Lance
2000; USA; 28 min; Drama

The story of a boy's struggle with sexual awakening

in a household with no father. His only support can be found in a half-present mother consumed in a promiscuous search for her own self worth, and a Winged Woman he's caged up in the backyard of his dreams. (Sock Puppet)

Dist/Sales: SockPuppet

Something for Everyone
(aka: Black Flowers for the Bride)

Prince, Harold
1970; USA; 112 min; Comedy
P: John Flaxman; *W:* Hugh Wheeler; *C:* Walter Lassally; *E:* Ralph Rosenblum; *M:* John Kander
Cast: Angela Lansbury, Michael York, Anthony Corlan, Heidellinde Weis

A black comedy about a bisexual young man who takes advantage of the staff and family of an impoverished countess.

Prod Comp: Cinema Center 100 Productions, Media Productions Incorporated
Dist/Sales: Ascanbee

Somewhere in the City

Niami, Ramin
1997; USA; 93 min; Comedy
P: Ramin Niami, Karen Robson; *W:* Ramin Niami, Patrick Dillon; *C:* Igir Sunara; *E:* Ramin Niami, Elizabeth Gazzara; *M:* John Cale
Cast: Sandra Bernhard, Peter Stormare, Bai Ling, Robert John Burke, Ornella Muti

This hilarious underground comedy deftly threads the overlapping stories of six eccentric but lovable residents of a New York City tenement apartment building, include a self-obsessed therapist, a Chinese exchange student, an incompetent crook, and a brilliant, gay Shakespearean actor. All have hopes and dreams, and most are looking for love-but settling for sex. (First Run Features)

Prod Comp: Sideshow Inc
Dist/Sales: FirstRunFeatures, ArtisticLicense

Song of the Loon

Herbert, Andrew
1970; USA; 90 min; Drama
W: Richard Amory
Cast: John Iverson, Lancer Ward, Morgan Royce

Campy early independent period piece about a gay man searching for love, set on the late 1800s.

Dist/Sales: SomethingWeird

Sonny Boy

Carroll, Robert Martin
1987; USA; 99 min; Drama, Comedy
P: Ovidio G. Assonitis; *W:* Graham Whiffler;

C: Roberto D'Ettore Piazzoli; *E:* Claudio M. Cutry;
M: David Carradine, Carlo Maria Cordio
Cast: Michael Griffin, David Carradine, Paul L. Smith,
Brad Dourif

Wacky black comedy drama about a baby boy who is
accidentally kidnapped by a transvestite and a
psychopathic criminal and brought up in a steel
cage. Treated like an animal, they teach him to kill,
and then release him as a fully grown teenager.

Prod Comp: Trans World Entertainment
Dist/Sales: Col-Tri

Sordid Lives

Shores, Del
2000; USA; 111 min; Comedy
W: Del Shores; *C:* Max Civon; *E:* Ed Marx;
M: George S. Clinton
Cast: Bonnie Bedelia, Beth Grant, Ann Walker, Delta
Burke

A family in a small Texan town are preparing for the
funeral of their mother. The family includes an
eccentric cast of characters: a son who has spent the
past 23 years dressed as Tammy Wynette, a gay
grandson trying to make his mark in West Hollywood, and two sisters fighting over whether their
dead mother should be wearing a mink stole during
the funeral. Despite the hilarious problems, the
eccentric cast of characters band together in the end
to send their mother on her way.

Prod Comp: Haly-Harris Productions
Dist/Sales: Vagrant

Sospiro d'amore nell'attesa

Governi, Valeria
Italy; 13 min; Drama

This film deals with the theme of desire for the
unattainable. Blurring the boundaries between
fantasy and reality, we are led into Antonio's home
and his consuming passion...for an angel! There is
teasing and foreplay but no union in the very real
world of Antonio's home, so he attempts to solve this
problem as the film moves towards its fiery climax.
(MQFF)

Sotto Sotto

(aka: Softly, Softly; Sotto... sotto... Strapazzato da Anomala Passione)

Wertmüller, Lina
1984; Italy; 104 min; Comedy
P: Mario Cecchi Gori, Vittorio Cecchi Gori; *W:* Enrico
Oldoini, Lina Wertmüller; *C:* Dante Spinotti; *E:* Luigi
Zitta; *M:* Paolo Conti
Cast: Enrico Montesano, Veronica Lario, Luisa de
Santis, Massimo Wertmüller

A wild sex comedy set in Naples, about two married
women, Adele and Ester, friends who fall in love
while on holiday. They return to their husbands but
both fret for each other. Ester's husband, thinking
she is in love with another man, goes into a jealous
rage. However he becomes even more violent when
he discovers her love interest is another woman. A
disappointing end from a lesbian perspective.

Prod Comp: Intercapital; *Dist/Sales:* TLA

Soufflé

Sharp, Andrew
1986; Australia; 20 min; Documentary

A film dealing with the issues of homosexuality and
AIDS.

Prod Comp: Australian Film TV & Radio School
Dist/Sales: AFTRS

Southern Comfort

Davis, Kate
2001; USA; 90 min; Documentary
P: Kate Davis; *C:* Kate Davis; *E:* Kate Davis;
M: Joel Harrison

Peter Fonda look alike Robert travels life's highways
in America's Deep South. This is a must-see biopic
from the transgender conduits of a different Middle
America, that owes more to David Lynch than
Norman Rockwell. Robert meets serene southern
belle Lola, who looks like a woman but walks like a
man and whose life's philosophy is 'nature loves
diversity why can't people'. This poignant documentary portrays their profound love story from the
gender divide surrounded by friends at the annual
Southern Comfort 'retreat'. Life deals Robert a cruel
hand. His odyssey into masculinity is not all he and
Lola hope for and he falls prey to terminal ovarian
cancer. (MQFF)

Prod Comp: HBO, Next Wave Films
Dist/Sales: Cowboy, FilmsTransit

Souvenir

Cholodenko, Lisa
1994; USA; 13 min; Drama

Two dykes arguing within the close confines of their
car are on a road trip from hell. Escapees from a
family visit, Thelma and Louise have nothing on
these two. Early film from Cholodenko who has
since directed *High Art*. (MQFF)

Spacked Out

(aka: Mo yan ka sai)

Ah Mon, Lawrence
2000; Hong Kong; 91 min; Drama

P: Johnny To; *C:* Yiu-fai Lai; *E:* Chi Wai Chan
Cast: Debbie Tam, Christy Cheung, Angela Au Man-si, Maggie Poon

> *Spacked Out* follows four schoolgirls—Cookie, Banana, Bean Curd and Sissy—through a few days in their lives as they hang out in tacky shopping malls. They get high, go to parties and cut other girls, and themselves, with box cutters all under the watchful eyes of the Sanrio pantheon—Hello Kitty, Bad Batz Maru, all the lovable cartoon characters that bring joy and cuteness to every young girl's life. But Hello Kitty's never seen kids like this. Banana makes phone sex calls on her cell phone during class, Bean Curd and Sissy are lovers engaged in a tumultuous relationship that swings like a manic depressive. Cookie's best friend is being sent to reform school and, desperate for human contact, she calls late night radio shows, drowning in the misery and boredom of her own life. This film reeks of lives on hold, wasted hours turning into wasted lives, hit-and-run sex, and all the self-mutilation, self-loathing, and self-importance of adolescence. (www.subwaycinema.com)
> Cantonese with English subtitles.

Prod Comp: Mei Ah Films, Milkyway Image
Dist/Sales: Seng

Sparky's Shoes

Caims, Glen
1994; Canada; 16 min; Experimental

> A beautifully shot, meditative, and deeply spiritual short that explores the boundaries of love, loss and denied eroticism in a gay relationship overshadowed by AIDS. (MQFF)

Spartacus

Kubrick, Stanley
1960; USA; 161 min; Drama
P: Edward Lewis; *W:* Dalton Trumbo; *C:* Russell Metty, Clifford Stine; *E:* Robert Lawrence; *M:* Alex North
Cast: Kirk Douglas, Laurence Olivier, Jean Simmons, Peter Ustinov

> One of the most intelligent historical 'epics' of the period, with Kirk Douglas as the slave leading the revolt against Republican Rome. Laurence Olivier plays Crassus, the bisexual emperor, and Tony Curtis is his young slave who escapes to join Douglas. Spectacular, literate and exciting, a true masterpiece of cinema which can be enjoyed on many levels.

Awards: Academy Awards, 1960: Best Supporting Actor (Peter Ustinov), Cinematography
Prod Comp: Bryna, Universal
Dist/Sales: ACMI, Universal

Speaking for Ourselves

Coppel, Ann / Mifsud, John
1994; USA; 27 min; Documentary

> Five diverse young people provide personal stories about coming-out, and the issues and emotions confronting gay and lesbian youth and their parents.

Dist/Sales: Diversity

Special Day, A

(aka: Una Giornata particolare)

Scola, Ettore
1977; Canada, Italy; 115 min; Drama
P: Carlo Ponti; *W:* Maurizio Costanzo, Ruggero Maccari, Ettore Scola; *C:* Pasqualino de Santis; *E:* Raimondo Crociani; *M:* Armando Trovaioli
Cast: Sophia Loren, Marcello Mastroianni, Alessandra Mussolini, John Vernon

> Set in Fascist Italy, on the same day that Hitler is due to visit, *A Special Day* is the story of a lonely housewife and her friendship with a homosexual radio announcer. They are drawn together as it becomes evident that he is about to be arrested.

Prod Comp: Champion, Canafox

Special Guest Star

Hitchins, Geoff
1999; Australia; 11 min; Comedy
W: Geoff Hitchins

> One Sunday morning tensions come to a head in a share house, when one of the housemates claims to have brought rock star Nick Cave home.

Speedway Junky

Speedway Junky

Perry, Nickolas
1998; Israel, USA; 104 min; Drama
P: Randall emmett, Rafi Stephan, Rodney Omanoff, George Furla, Jeff Rice; *W:* Nickolas Perry;

S

C: Steve Adcock; *M:* Stan Ridgway
Cast: Jesse Bradford, Jordan Brower, Daryl Hannah, Jonathan Taylor Thomas, Patsy Kensit

> Johnny has run away from home to pursue his fantasy to race cars—but he runs into trouble and out of money in Las Vegas. Gay street hustler Eric befriends Johnny and introduces him to his gang, including brash Steven and charming Wilma. Johnny also meets Eric's surrogate mom Veronica. As the two boys become close, they are confronted with a life-threatening situation involving drugs, money and betrayal, and Johnny must decide if he has what it takes to follow his dream. (Wolfe)

Prod Comp: Magic Entertainment
Dist/Sales: Wolfe, 10%

Speedy Boys

Herbert, James
1999; USA; 80 min; Experimental
P: James Herbert; *C:* James Herbert; *E:* Mark Jordan
Cast: Andy Piedilato, Carter Davis, Kari Malievich, Aline Nari

> *Speedy Boys* continues James Herbert's ambitious motion picture study of the human body, as two frequently naked Americans spend a summer in Italy lying about the apartment, chasing women and cycling through the countryside.

Prod Comp: Cargo Cult Productions
Dist/Sales: CargoCult

Spent

Romilly, Jason
1998; Canada; 27 min; Experimental

> Eric is a secret agent who's double identity and dangerous missions are completely hidden from the people closest to him. As his lies and betrayal come to the forefront due to reckless behaviour, his relationships crumble and his secret life becomes all-consuming. (CFMDC)

Dist/Sales: CFMDC

Spikes and Heels

Ataman, E. Kutlug
1994; USA; 53 min; Documentary
P: Phillippe Brooks

> A breathless highlights package of the Unity Gay Games of 1994, stuffed with interviews, beautiful rippling bodies, excerpts from the opening and closing ceremonies, and an engaging look at the lesbian and gay rights movement in the 1990s.

Dist/Sales: FilmakersLibrary

Spin the Bottle

Yerkes, Jamie
1997; USA; 82 min; Drama
P: Kevin Chinoy, Kris Homsher, Jamie Yerkes; *W:* Amy Sohn; *C:* Harlan Bosmajian; *E:* Jamie Yerkes, Josh Apter; *M:* Ed Tomney
Cast: Michelle Riggs, Kim Winter, Jessica Faller

> A sweet tale of sexual revenge. Five smart, attractive twenty-somethings reunite at the old lake house where they spent their summers. As kids, they played truth or dare by spinning a bottle, but one friend still nurses wounds from the old game. Late one night, the opportunity for revenge comes when they spin the bottle one more time. (Wolfe)

Prod Comp: Cineblast productions
Dist/Sales: Wolfe, TLA, 10%

Split: Portrait of a Drag Queen

(aka: Split: William to Chrysis)

Fisher Turk, Ellen / Weeks, Andrew
1992; USA; 58 min; Documentary
P: Ellen Fisher Turk; *W:* Dan Chayefsky

> Chrysis, the victim of her own creation, lived 39 years and died of cancer caused by seepage from wax and silicone breast implants. A New York 'show girl' and drag queen, one of Salvador Dali's inner circle, a woman from the waist up and a man from the waist down, Chrysis lived in a hidden world of transsexuals and drag queens, hormones, drugs and prostitution and illuminated it with her humour, wit and glamour.

Dist/Sales: WaterBearer

Split World, The

Cipelletti, Claudio
1994; Italy; 12 min; Drama

> A film about a young man's refusal to continue to divide his world between his straight university friends and family and his homosexuality.

Spokes

Fockele, Jorge
1996; Germany; 19 min; Drama

> A chance meeting in a park leads Tamas and Malik on a journey of desire and self discovery that must end with the arrival of the dawn.

Spot the Lesbian

East, Kippy
1985; Australia; 46 min; Documentary
C: Deborah Howlett, Heather Williams; *E:* Kippy East,

Gill Sellar

This documentary attempts to dispel many myths and misconceptions about lesbianism. A number of lesbian women speak candidly about a range of issues including their coming out experiences with family, friends and in the workplace, and lesbian motherhood.

Prod Comp: Women's Film Fund, Australian Film Commission
Dist/Sales: NFVLS

Sprinter, The

Böll, Christoph
1984; Germany; 90 min; Comedy
W: Christoph Böll, Wieland Samolak, Nicole Schürmann; *C:* Peter Gauhe
Cast: Dieter Eppler, Jürgen Mikol, Renate Muri

A young man, having problems coming to terms with his homosexuality, decides to become a professional track-and-field athlete, with the idea that it may turn his life around.

Dist/Sales: Verlag

Spy Who Came, The

Wertheim, Ron
1970; USA; 70 min; Drama

A detective goes into a bar in Greenwich Village and picks up a young girl. Soon he is involved in the darker side of life including white slavery. The woman in charge of the girls is a lesbian and likes to try her wares.

Dist/Sales: SomethingWeird

Squeeze

Turner, Richard
1980; New Zealand; 80 min; Drama
P: Richard Turner; *W:* Richard Turner; *C:* Ian Paul; *E:* Jamie Selkirk; *M:* Andy Hagan, Morton Young
Cast: Robert Shannon, Paul Eady, Donna Akersten, Peter Heperi, David Herkt

Made under the difficulties of a very small budget and harassment from some quarters, this film is a drama set in the gay subculture of Auckland. It centres on the double life of Grant, whose career prospects are strengthened by his adoption of a heterosexual role, including his engagement to Joy, but endangered by his involvement in the gay scene and his affair with a younger man.

Prod Comp: Trilogic Films
Dist/Sales: 20thCenturyFox, NFVLS

Staceyann Chin - A Poetry Slammer

Schepelern, Mette-Ann / Wivel, Ullrik
2001; USA; 27 min; Documentary

Staceyann Chin, 29 years old, is one of the major American slam poets. This film is a portrait of her and the world of poetry slam. Slam is like a boxing match in which poets compete against other with each poet having a time limit of three minutes. Judges are chosen from the audience to rate the poems. Staceyann is a talented, fascinating, creative artist. Her poems are very personal reflecting her turbulent childhood, her mixed race background, and her realisation that she is a lesbian. (Filmakers Library)

Prod Comp: Barok Film
Dist/Sales: FilmakersLibrary

Staircase

Donen, Stanley
1969; France, UK, USA; 110 min; Comedy
P: Stanely Donen; *W:* Charles Dyer;
C: Christopher G. Challis, Philipe Brun;
E: Richard Marden; *M:* Dudley Moore
Cast: Richard Burton, Rex Harrison, Cathleen Nesbitt

The story of two middle-aged homosexuals who live above their barber shop in London and have been in a relationship for over 30 years. Both men are enveloped by self-hatred and regret. They hate the world and each other. Gay audiences at the time found it insulting and it's easy to see why.

Prod Comp: 20th Century-Fox
Dist/Sales: FilmsInc

Stand on your Man

Ardill, Susan
1991; UK; 20 min; Musical
P: Rebecca Dobbs

The world of lesbian country music is put under the microscope in this slick and entertaining tribute to its stars and fans. Footage includes k. d. lang, Patsy Cline, The Well Oiled Sisters and the Stetson Sisters.

Dist/Sales: MayaVision

Stand Together

Nicol, Nancy
2002; Canada; 120 min; Documentary
P: Nancy Nicol; *C:* Carolyn Wong, Robin Bain, Kim Derko; *E:* Ed Sinclair

Documents the history of the lesbian and gay rights movement in Ontario, from 1967–87.

Star is Porn, A

Austin, Todd
1997; UK; 50 min; Documentary

A documentary commissioned by UK Channel Four about the making of the porn film *Butt Buddies* which won an Erotic Oscar.

Star Maps

Arteta, Miguel
1997; USA; 86 min; Comedy
W: Miguel Artera
Cast: Douglas Spain, Efrain Figueroa, Martha Velez, Kandeyce Jorden

Carlos has ideas about becoming an actor, but his father has ideas about him joining the family business—in male prostitution. Carlos reluctantly agrees—hoping it might help him meet someone to make his acting dream a reality. Eventually one of his wealthy clients helps him begin his path to Hollywood stardom.

Prod Comp: 20th Century Fox

Stargaze

McBride, Jason
1998; Canada; 12 min; Drama

Toronto, 1952. 18-year-old Derek undergoes painful aversion therapy designed to 'cure' his homosexuality.

Dist/Sales: CFMDC

Steers and Queers

Gauthier, Paula
2000; USA; 30 min; Documentary

This short documentary features an engaging and eclectic group of competitors, including a woman who fooled the judges to compete at one of the most unique and exciting events in queer culture, the gay rodeo! (queerDOC 2001)

Dist/Sales: BigFilm

Stephen

Kinney, Donald / Kinney, Robert
1990; USA; 28 min; Drama

Stephen is the final instalment in a series of three productions by Robert and Donald Kinney. The work is broadly based on a chapter from Thorton Wilder's *The Bridge of San Luis Rey*. It focuses on the story of siblings (in this case twins) locked in an emotional and sexual relationship.

Stepping Out

Hofmeyr, Nicolaas
1994; South Africa; 26 min; Documentary

Denzel, a teenager from the 'coloured' township of Ennerdale, takes part in the Miss Gay Transvaal competition—a drag show. The cameras are on Denzel, as well as his mother, and a local gay rights activist in attendance. A film about a mother and son coming to terms with each other and themselves, and an incisive look at gay life in South Africa. (First Run/Icarus)

Prod Comp: Mail & Guardian Television Production
Dist/Sales: FirstRun/Icarus

The Sticky Fingers of Time

Sticky Fingers of Time, The

Brougher, Hilary
1997; USA; 81 min; Sci-Fi, Thriller
P: Sysan A. Stover, Isen Robbins, Jean Castelli;
W: Hilary Brougher; *C:* Ethan Mass;
E: Sabine Hoffmann; *M:* Miki Navazio
Cast: Belinda Becker, Leo Marks, Terumi Matthews, James Urbaniak

A sci-fi thriller extraordinary for its female predominance. A 1950s fiction writer steps out of her New York City apartment to buy coffee and finds herself transported into the future, where she discovers a kindred connection to a modern woman. The pair join together in a time-travel journey of self-exploration and survival. (Cowboy Pictures)

Prod Comp: Good Machine, Crystal Pictures
Dist/Sales: Strand, Wolfe, Cowboy

Stiff Sheets

Goss, John
1989; USA; 19 min; Documentary

An anonymous collection of gay artists presents an agitprop/drag fashion show to protest the lethal lack of AIDS care and facilities in Los Angeles.

Dist/Sales: VideoOut

S

Still Sane

Ingratta, Brenda / Patuasz, Lidia
1990; Canada; 58 min; Documentary

A moving testament to Sheila Gilhooly's strength of character in succeeding in getting herself out of enforced psychiatric care. *Still Sane*'s overriding theme is one of defiance and survival: we can maintain our choices, even in the face of mind-numbing oppression.

Stolen Diary, The

(aka: Le Cahier Volé)

Lipinska, Christine
1992; France, Italy; 110 min; Drama
P: Tves Gasser; *W:* Christine Lipinska, Paul Fournel;
C: Romain Winding; *E:* Marie-Claude Lacambre;
M: Arié Dzierlatka
Cast: Élodie Bouchez, Edwige Navarro, Benoit Magimel, Malcolm Conrath

Set in France at the end of World War II, this gem of a film is the story of Virginie and Anne, 17-year-olds who have just come back to their village from boarding school. Their friends Jean-Claude and Alain come back from the war injured and disillusioned. There is no longer any innocence in their vision of the world. War, suffering and horror have changed them all. Jean-Claude desperately wants to marry Virginie, but she is in love with Anne, and writes profusely of her love in her diary. In an effort to repel Jean-Claude's advances, Anne tries to convince him that Virginie is in love with another boy. She erases her own name from Virginie's diary entries and fills in the name Paul. But when Alain gets a hold of the diary, he's not just put off—he threatens to read it to the whole village. (21st San Francisco International Lesbian & Gay Film Festival) French with English subtitles.

Prod Comp: Providence Films, Scena Group SFPGSA
Dist/Sales: Cinexport

Stolen Moments

Wescott, Margaret
1997; Canada; 91 min; Documentary
P: Silva Basmajian; *W:* Joan Nestle, Leslie Feinberg, Audrey Lorde; *C:* Zoe Dirse

A comprehensive and contemporary exploration of lesbian lives *Stolen Moments* offers an engaging glimpse into a diverse community that will entertain and educate viewers, regardless of the sexual orientation. Narrated by Kate Nelligan, the film takes us on an odyssey across North America and Europe to capture the stolen moments of lesbian history: lesbian culture in pre-war Paris, Berlin and Amsterdam; the experience of women in Nazi concentration camps; and the butch/femme scene in New York in the 1950s, are just a few of the aspects of lesbian history and identity explored in this provocative film.

Prod Comp: National Film Board of Canada
Dist/Sales: NFBC, Wolfe, FirstRunFeatures, FirstRun/Icarus, ACMI, Heathcliff, NFBC

Stonewall

Stonewall

Finch, Nigel
1995; UK, USA; 99 min; Drama
P: Christine Vachon, Ruth Caleb; *W:* Rikki Beadle Blair; *C:* Chris Seager; *M:* Michael Kamen
Cast: Guillermo Diaz, Frederick Weller, Brandan Corbalis, Duane Boutte, Bruce MacVittie

Grab your wig and eyeliner sweetie. It's 1969, New York. Matty is young, gay, full of dreams and new to the city where the Stonewall Inn, haunt of fabulous diva drag queens, has just been raided. The Vietnam War is on, man is walking on the moon and Matty winds up in a relationship that stretches the heartstrings to breaking point. Stonewall gets busted again and the girls hit back—a riot of high-kicking, power-fisted drag queens, fighting for gay pride. Based on the original story by Martin Duberman.

Awards: San Francisco International Lesbian & Gay Film Festival, 1996: Audience Award for Best Feature
Prod Comp: BBC, Arena NY
Dist/Sales: Wolfe, Col-Tri, Strand, ACMI

Stonewall 25: Voices of Pride and Protest

Nasile, Vic
1994; USA; 90 min; Documentary

Documentary about the advances made in the gay rights movement since the Stonewall riots of 1969. Includes archival material featuring Quentin Crisp, Sir Ian McKellen, Joan Rivers, Stockard Channing, Petula Clark and more.

Storm in a Teacup

Hindley, Emma
1992; UK; 60 min; Documentary

A documentary about London's lesbian and gay history, celebrating the scene from the 1940s to the 1970s.

Storme: The Lady of the Jewel Box

Parkerson, Michelle
1987; USA; 21 min; Documentary

An intimate portrait of Storme DeLarverie, a black woman and former MC, and male impersonator with the legendary Jewel Box Revue—America's first integrated female impersonation show. A forerunner to *La Cage aux Folles*, the multiracial revue was a favourite act of the black theatre circuit and attracted mixed mainstream audiences from the 1940s through to the 1960s, a time marked by the violence of segregation. (WMM)

Dist/Sales: WMM

Story of a Bad Boy, The

Donaghy, Tom
1998; USA; 93 min; Drama
P: Jean Doumanian; *W:* Tom Donaghy;
C: Garrett Fisher; *E:* Barbara Tulliver;
M: Angelo Badalamenti, Chris Hajian
Cast: Jeremy Hollingworth, Christina Camargo, Giampiero Judica, Stephen Lang

Pauly falls in love with his high school drama teacher (Noel) in New Jersey 1982. He tries out for the upcoming musical, and then falls into an uneasy relationship with Noel.

Story of PuPu, The

(aka: PuPu No Monogatari)

Watanabe, Kensaku
1998; Japan; 73 min; Action
P: Miyoshi Kikuchi; *W:* Kensaku Watanabe;
C: Naoto Muraishi; *M:* June Miyake
Cast: Sakura Uehara, Rei Yamanaka, Jun Kunimura, Reiko Matsuo

Two girls, Fu and Suzu, are on the road to visit the grave of a baby pig named PuPu. Along the way, Suzu decides to pay a visit to Kijima, a man with whom she once had a relationship. It becomes clear that she is planning to blackmail him. On the road, the two encounter a gay couple and a golfer in a blue convertible. Thanks to Suzu's unbridled personality, they get into trouble from time to time. But whenever they do, a mysterious hero called the

TrunkMan always appears and rescues them. With the TrunkMan's emergence, the relationship between Fu and Suzu becomes strained. This is because Suzu has fallen in love with him. Eventually, Fu decides to leave her. Japanese with English subtitles.

Dist/Sales: LittleMore

Story so Far, The

Deville, Noski / Sharif, Rif
1994; UK; 39 min; Drama

A forgotten classic about a robbery, a taxi and a stolen bus with a mighty cast of local black and white dyke stars. Dyke noir at its best with great location shots across London as a group of sparky and bright lesbians plot a night-time robbery that could change their lives. (Cinenova)

Dist/Sales: Cinenova

Straight Agenda, The

Binninger, John / Turnure, Jackie
1994; USA; 19 min; Comedy
Cast: Jackie Beat, Craig Chester, Suzie Berger

The first blatantly anti-straight propaganda film, this hilarious parody exposes the moral corruption inherent in heterosexual relations. Made in response to the right-wing anti-gay film, *The Gay Agenda*.

Straight Down the Aisle: Confessions of Lesbian Bridesmaids

Hankin, Kelly / Russo, Christine
2000; Canada, USA; 23 min; Documentary
P: Christine J. Russo

'Always the bridesmaid, never the bride'. What does it mean for lesbians to publicly support an institution they are denied? And what does it mean that heterosexuals ask them to? This entertaining documentary explores the contradictions and ambiguities of this role for lesbians through revealing interviews with a diverse group of lesbian bridesmaids. Their candid responses range from frustration, at being asked to 'de-dyke' for the big day or having their girlfriends ignored, to humour and confusion about past and present relationships with the bride.

Straight for the Money: Interviews with Queer Sex Workers

B., Hima
1994; USA; 58 min; Documentary
Cast: Annie Sprinkle, Joan Nestle, Carol Queen

Hima B. interviews eight lesbian and bisexual

women—lap-dancers, peepshow dancers and prostitutes—who talk about their identities as queer women whose jobs make them 'straight for the money'. This sex-positive documentary also incorporates fascinating archival footage and interviews with sexperts and social commentators Annie Sprinkle, Joan Nestle and Carol Queen. (MQFF)

Dist/Sales: Himaphiliac

Straight from the Heart: Gay and Lesbian Children

Mosbacher, Dee / Reid, Frances
1994; USA; 24 min; Documentary

Internationally acclaimed film and Academy Award nominee, Straight from the Heart examines the issues parents face in coming to terms with a gay or lesbian child. It presents interviews with parents and children and tackles issues in a positive and thought provoking manner including the diagnosis of a child with HIV/AIDS. (ACMI)

Dist/Sales: CinemaGuild, Wolfe, ACMI

Straight from the Suburbs

Ducharme, Carole
1998; Canada; 24 min; Comedy
P: Nathalie Ducharme, Carole Ducharme;
W: Carole Ducharme

A comedy spoof about a family who is struck by the curse of heterosexuality.

Dist/Sales: CinemaLibre

Straight in the Face

Demas, Peter
2002; Canada; 12 min; Comedy

Two gay dads, in the midst of an open relationship, are sceptical about the fashionable and cultured boy their daughter has brought home.

Dist/Sales: BuzzTaxi

Straight to the Heart

(aka: À Corps Perdu)

Pool, Léa
1988; Canada; 92 min; B&W; Drama
P: Denise Robert, Robin Spry; *W:* Marcel Beaulieu, Léa Pool; *C:* Pierre Mignot; *E:* Michel Arcand;
M: Osvaldo Montes
Cast: Matthias Habich, Johanne-Marie Tremblay, Michel Voïta, Jean-François Pichette

When a photojournalist arrives home in Montreal from an assignment in Nicaragua, he is devastated to find both his lovers, Sarah and David have left him

after ten years. After some frustrating encounters with his ex-lovers he embarks on a relationship with Quentin, a deaf-mute. A haunting and affecting film from the director of the lesbian classic *Anne Trister*. French with English subtitles.

Prod Comp: Les Films Telescene, Xanadu Productions
Dist/Sales: Alliance

Straightman

Berkowitz, Ben
1999; USA; 101 min; B&W; Drama
P: Ben Berkowitz, Ben Redgrave; *W:* Ben Berkowitz, Ben Redgrave; *C:* Jerome Biron; *E:* Michael Palmerio
Cast: Ben Berkowitz, Ben Redgrave, Joaquin De La Puenta, Butch Jerinic

Witty, authentic and powerful, Straightman is the story of best friends David Leibowitz and Jack Webster. David, overweight, sleazy, and in denial about his Jewish heritage, manages a Chicago comedy club and sleeps with any woman he can lay his hands on, while simultaneously idolising the apparently perfect relationship Jack, a construction worker, has with his partner Maxine. Both men are stunned when Maxine walks out on Jack, leaving him for a job on the west coast. After the two men move in together, Jack begins the difficult task of addressing his increasing attraction towards other men, forcing both men to reassess their relationship with one another. *Straightman* is a film about identity, and the difficulties of navigating friendships between men. The film's complex and completely believable characters and situations are sure to provoke discussion and debate among audiences. (MQFF)

Prod Comp: Benzfilm Group
Dist/Sales: Vagrant

Strange Fits of Passion

McCredie, Elise
1999; Australia; 84 min; Drama
P: Lucy McLaren; *W:* Elise McCredie; *C:* Jaems Grant;
E: Chris Branagan, Ken Sallows;
M: Cezary Skubiszewski
Cast: Michela Noonan, Mitchell Butel, Steve Adams, Samuel Johnson

Meet 'She', a twenty-something Australian who embarks on a crusade to lose her virginity. Meet Francis, the enigmatic and elusive poet who frequents the second-hand bookshop where She works. The conundrum: despite her obsession with romantic poetry, She is intellectually convinced that romance is a patriarchal plot to enslave women. Like a modern day Alice, She falls down a rabbit hole full of the most unlikely characters who all, initially, seem to offer the solution to her quest. A bittersweet fable with an unpredictable ending, *Strange Fits of Passion* is a young woman's discovery of the meaning of love, sex and desire in a post-everything world. (Mongrel)

Prod Comp: ABC, Arena, Film Victoria, Meridian Films
Dist/Sales: Beyond, Mongrel

Strange Life and Death of Dr Turing, The

Sykes, Christopher
1992; USA; 50 min; Documentary

When Dr Alan Turing died of cyanide poisoning in 1954, he left a legacy of ideas—scientific theories on the nature of life and the mind. Turing was the originator of modern computing science and the concept of artificial intelligence, without which the modern computer would not have been possible. He also had a secret life as a wartime code-breaker and a homosexual. This film investigates the life story of an unsung hero.

Dist/Sales: Roadshow

Strange Love Affair, A

de Kuyper, Eric / Verstaaten, Paul
1985; The Netherlands; 92 min; Drama

An American gay man teaching film in Holland begins a relationship with one of his students. Dutch with English subtitles.

Dist/Sales: Howard Hensel, Karel Scheydt, Leike Leo

Strange One, The

(aka: End as a Man)

Garfein, Jack
1957; USA; 100 min; B&W; Drama
P: Sam Spiegel; *W:* Calder Willingham; *C:* Burnett Guffey; *E:* Sidney Katz; *M:* Kenyon Hopkins
Cast: Ben Gazzara, Mark Richman, George Peppard, Pat Hingle, James Olson

Ben Gazzara in a dazzling debut role as a sadistic upper-class and closeted homosexual in a Southern military school. When his schemes threaten the other freshmen, they rebel against the bullying menace who turns into a cowardly wimp. From Calder Willingham's play *End as a Man*. George Peppard also had his debut role in this film.

Prod Comp: Columbia, Horizon Films
Dist/Sales: Ascanbee, Columbia

Stranger Inside

Dunye, Cheryl
2000; USA; 96 min; Drama
P: Michael Stipe, Jim McKay, Effie Brown; *W:* Cheryl Dunye, Catherine Crouch; *C:* Nancy Schreiber

Cast: Yolanda Ross, Medusa, Alma Dixon, Davenia McFadden, Rain Phoenix

Treasure Lee, a young African American, has just been transferred to the Women's State Prison. There, she schemes to meet the incarcerated mother who gave her up years ago. But when she connects with Brownie, a seasoned convict and 'lifer', Treasure finds the path to reconciliation both twisted and dangerous. (Wolfe)

Dist/Sales: HBO, Wolfe

Strawberry and Chocolate

(aka: Fresa y Chocolate)

Alea, Tomás Gutiérrez / Tabío, Juan Carlos
1993; Cuba; 70 min; Drama
P: Miguel Mendoza; *W:* Tomás Gutiérrez Alea, Senel Paz; *C:* Mario García Joya; *E:* Osvaldo Donatién, Miriam Talavera; *M:* José María Vitier
Cast: Jorge Perugorría, Vladimir Cruz, Mirta Ibarra, Francisco Gattorno

Entertaining story from Cuba about the unlikely friendship between two very different men. Cultured Diego, a gay artist, invites David, a naive, macho, heterosexual communist, who knows nothing about art, to his apartment one afternoon. The experience changes the naive young college student forever. A similar theme to *Kiss of the Spider Woman*—the gay subverts the communist—but this time the smart one is the homosexual. A sharp and acid social commentary, loaded with swipes against the Castro regime. This is the first Cuban film to be nominated for an Academy Award (Best Foreign Film). Spanish with English subtitles.

Prod Comp: Franca Pelster Films
Dist/Sales: Palace, 21stCentury, Swank, Miramax, ACMI

Stray Dogs

Crouch, Catherine
2001; USA; 97 min; Drama
P: Yvonne Welborn; *W:* Julie Jensen; *C:* Marie-Joëlle Rizk; *E:* Sharon Zurek; *M:* Ray Nardelli, Josh Horvath
Cast: Guinevere Turner, Bill Sage, Dot Jones, Ryan Kelly

Set in 1958, and adapted from the award-winning stage play by Julie Jensen, *Stray Dogs* is a Southern Gothic film in which a young mother must choose between her troubled marriage and her children. Darla feels like a prisoner—she married Myers Carter on a whim, but is now bound to him and subject to his alcohol-induced mood swings and violence. She is protected by her butch sister-in-law, Jolene, who has her own, decidedly non-sisterly dreams about providing for Darla. One horrible

S

night, a turning point is reached as Darla and Jolene risk everything to stand up against Myers. (2002 New York Lesbian & Gay Film Festival)

Prod Comp: Stray Dogs LLC
Dist/Sales: CottonLover

Streamers

Altman, Robert
1983; USA; 118 min; Drama
P: Nick Mileti, Robert Altman; *W:* David Rabe;
C: Pierre Mignot; *E:* Norman Smith; *M:* Stephen Foster
Cast: Matthew Modine, Michael Wright, Mitchell Lichtenstein, David Alan Grier

Set in an Army barracks in 1965, about a group of young soldiers awaiting assignment to Vietnam. The draftees come from diverse backgrounds: two are African–Americans, one a country boy and the other a Yale-educated homosexual. They are confronted by two brutal ex-Korean War veteran sergeants. Sexual and racial tensions build as the men wait in their claustrophobic barracks and, eventually, shocking violence erupts. The barracks are a microcosm of the explosive emotions and issues that surfaced in America at the time.

Prod Comp: Rank, Streamers International
Dist/Sales: ACMI, TLA, UAClassics

Strip Jack Naked: Nighthawks II

Peck, Ron
1991; UK; 91 min; Documentary
P: Ron Peck, Paul Hallam; *W:* Ron Peck, Paul Hallam;
C: Ron Peck, Christopher Hughes; *M:* Adrian James Carbutt
Cast: John Brown, John Daimon, Nick Bolton, Derek Jarman, Ken Robertson

Strip Jack Naked is a low-budget exploration of the London gay club scene. Using a combination of new scenes shot on video and out-takes, loops and production notes from the original film, Peck has created a sequel which examines not only the personal struggles of a filmmaker to come to an understanding of his sexuality, but also documents the struggles of young filmmakers to gain funding and encouragement to create their visions on screen. Part autobiography, part film-making journal, part a history of the contemporary gay movement, *Strip Jack Naked* celebrates an aesthetic and a personal sexual expression which are not represented in mainstream cinema: this film is an encouragement to any artist working from the margins.

Prod Comp: BFI, Channel 4
Dist/Sales: TLA, BFI, WaterBearer, NFVLS, ACMI

Strippers

Ameer, Jorge
2000; USA; 71 min; Drama
P: Jorge Ameer, John Greenlaw; *W:* Jorge Ameer;
C: Aaron Kirsch, Gary Tachell; *E:* Rollin Olson;
M: Paul McCarty
Cast: Tony Tucci, John Greenlaw, Jorge Ameer, Kerrie Clark

Roundly lambasted film about men and women in power suits who'll stop at nothing to get ahead in the world.

Prod Comp: AJ Productions
Dist/Sales: Hollywood

Strung Up

Johnstone, Cathy
1996; Australia; 10 min; Drama

Intense, symbolic portrait of a relationship between a circus performer and photographer that meets a sizzling end.

Such a Crime

Newbrough, Cheryl
1998; USA; 48 min; Comedy
Cast: Heather King, Michelle Maloy

Skip, the top agent of a band of lesbians, puts her organisation in jeopardy with her indiscreet sexual behaviour. Wounded and at risk, she must hide out at a safe house where she is tended to by the beautiful Jenn. Jenn wants a normal life and one other thing—Skip. (Wolfe)

'Sucker

Murton, Iain
2001; Australia; 13 min; Horror

Where will the night take you? To heaven, or to hell? A boy's gotta get off—but what should you know about your one night stand? A sexy boy vampire short.

Dist/Sales: IMM

Suddenly, Last Summer (1959)

Mankiewicz, Joseph L.
1959; USA; 114 min; B&W; Drama
P: Sam Spiegel; *W:* Gore Vidal, Tennessee Williams;
C: Jack Hildyard; *E:* William Hornbeck, Thomas Stanford; *M:* Buxton Orr, Malcolm Arnold
Cast: Elizabeth Taylor, Montgomery Clift, Katharine Hepburn, Albert Dekker

Another brilliant Tennessee Williams adaptation. After a mental breakdown a young woman and her mother with the help of her doctor, try to unravel the reason why she had a breakdown while on vacation with her homosexual brother, Sebastian. It turns out he's been attacked and killed by street urchins whom he preyed on to fulfil his sexual desires.

Prod Comp: Columbia, Horizon Films
Dist/Sales: Ascanbee, Col-Tri

Suddenly Last Summer (1991)

Beavan, Clare
1991; UK; 18 min; Comedy
P: Shauna Brown
Cast: Martina Navratilova

Together with women from all over Britain and abroad, Tyneside comedienne 'Hufty' travels to the Mecca of lesbian fandom, the Pilkington Glass Ladies of Tennis Championships in Eastbourne. For many of the women any sacrifice is worth the opportunity to see their idol, Martina Navratilova, in the flesh.

Prod Comp: Channel 4
Dist/Sales: ACMI

'Sucker

Sugar and Spice

Trepanier, Tania
1997; Canada; 10 min; Drama

Radha and Anna are expecting a visitor from India. In anticipation of her aunt's arrival, Radha uncharacteristically covers up evidence of her relationship with Anna, while Anna is determined to impress Durga Aunty with her Indian chai. Unexpected outcomes follow Durga's arrival, leaving the audience to determine for themselves what Durga Aunty makes of the two women's relationship. (Video Pool)

Dist/Sales: VideoPool

Sugar Cookies

Gershuny, Theodore
1973; USA; 90 min; Horror
P: Ami Artzi, Jeffrey Kapelman, Oliver Stone;
W: Theodore Gershuny, Lloyd Kaufman;
C: Hasse Wallin; *E:* Dov Hoenig; *M:* Gershon Kingsley
Cast: George Shannon, Mary Woronov, Lynn Lowry, Monique van Vooren

Two lesbian lovers are set up to be murdered by a filmmaker who makes pornographic films.

Prod Comp: Armor Films
Dist/Sales: Troma

Photo: Phyllis Christopher

Sugar High, Glitter City

Sugar High, Glitter City

Rednour, Shar / Strano, Jackie
2001; USA; 83 min; Erotica
Cast: Aimee Pearl, Charlie Skye

Urban encrusted glam... Gutter glitter lust... Join us in a sticky belly crawl through the underworld of 'Glitter City'. It's the future. Sugar is outlawed and cane-addicted dykes will stop at nothing to get it— even selling their own bodies. A fabulously diverse cast and multiple dyke sexualities take sticky centre stage in this fast-paced, futuristic farce. *Sugar High* will satisfy your hunger for screen-melting chemistry, mind-blowing dirty talk fantasy-play and real-life, full-force, glam-sleazy dyke sex. Lesbian porn made by lesbians for lesbians. (SIRVideo)

Prod Comp: SIRVideo Productions
Dist/Sales: SIRVideo

Sugar Sweet

Lim, Desiree
2001; Japan; 67 min; Drama
P: Toshiyuki Fuse, Kouichi Kobayashi; *W:* Desiree Lim,

S

Carole Hisasue; *C:* Natsuyo Nakamura;
E: Takao Yamanaka
Cast: Saori Kitagawa, C. Snatch Z., Mao Nakagawa

Desiree Lim, the first out queer filmmaker in Japan to direct a lesbian feature, turns in a delightfully sassy, saucy and sexy feature debut. Naomi is an aspiring TV director who pays the bills by directing lesbian porn. Her callous male bosses deride her work for its unsuitability for male viewers, and her lesbian friends see her as a sell-out. Her only confidante is 'Sugar', a secret chat-room friend on the Internet. When Naomi gets a chance to direct an episode of a popular 'matchmaking' TV show, she casts her friend Azusa, who's experiencing lesbian bed death with her long-term girlfriend and looking to spice up her life. Romantic sparks fly on the set—scorching even Naomi! Can she keep her job, her dreams and Sugar—especially Sugar—online? (2002 LA Outfest) Japanese with English subtitles .

The Sum of us

Sum of us, The

Burton, Geoff / Dowling, Kevin
1994; Australia; 97 min; Comedy
W: David Stevens; *C:* Geoff Burton;
E: Frans Vandenburg; *M:* Dave Faulkner
Cast: Jack Thompson, Russell Crowe, John Polson, Deborah Kennedy

Jeff and his dad are an odd couple of lonely hearts. One an open-hearted widower, the other a young single gay guy. Both men need some romance in their otherwise boring lives and decide to look for new ways to find it. Dad enrols in a computer dating service to find his lady love. Son Jeff, sick of one-night stands and noisy gay bars, wants a real commitment. But when he finds his Mr Right, what will dad have to say?

Prod Comp: Southern Star International, Great Sum Film, Samuel Goldwyn Company
Dist/Sales: UIP, TLA, ACMI, SamuelGoldwyn

Summer Dress, A

(aka: Une Robe d'été)

Ozon, François
1997; France; 15 min; Drama

On summer holiday with his boyfriend, Frederic's encounter with a stranger on the beach further complicates his already ambivalent teenage sexuality. (Zeitgeist) French with English subtitles.

Dist/Sales: Fidelite, Zeitgeist

Summer in my Veins (Director's Cut)

Saran, Nish
1999; India, USA; 40 min; Documentary

A gay Indian filmmaker travels across America with his family visiting from India, as he struggles to come out to them. He was tested for HIV before he left for the trip and will not receive his results until they return. Under the threat of terminal illness, made very real by an unsafe encounter with an HIV-positive man, the filmmaker explores the dynamics of secrecy and love that mark this very close family. Pushing the limits of personal documentary every moment, every achingly intimate moment—including coming out to his mother—is caught on film. (Frameline)

Dist/Sales: Frameline

Summer of Miss Forbes, The

(aka: El Verano de la señora Forbes)

Hermosillo, Jaime Humberto
1988; Spain; 86 min; Drama
P: Evelio Delgado, Max Marambio; *W:* Jaime Humberto Hermosillo; *C:* Rodrigo García;
E: Nelson Rodríguez; *M:* Sergio Vitier
Cast: Hanna Schygulla, Francisco Gattorno, Alexis Castanares

The story of a frustrated and slightly unhinged governess with a passion for Greek tragedies and alcohol who is hired to mind two children at a holiday house for six weeks. She becomes obsessed with a beach boy, called Achilles, who is adopted by the family. The governess goes mad when she eventually discovers that he is gay.

Prod Comp: Televisión Española

Summer Vacation 1999

(aka: 1999 Nen No Natsu Yasumi)

Kaneko, Shusuke
1988; Japan; 90 min; Drama
P: Yutaka Okada, Eiji Kishi; *W:* Michiyo Kishida;

C: Kenji Takama; *E:* Isao Temita; *M:* Yuriko Nakamura
Cast: Eri Miyagima, Tomoko Otakra, Miyuki Nakano, Rie Mizuhara, Eri Fukatsu

Four teenagers are left at a boarding school for the summer vacation of 1999. They are caught up in an adolescent love triangle. One of them suicides but a new boy appears who is the image of the dead boy and the circle continues. This muted, romantic fusing of love and death, in which the roles of the boys are played by girls, has roots in Japanese popular culture: cross-dressing from certain theatrical spectacles and male homosexuality in comics for teenage girls. Although Kaneko sees the film as a re-examination of his own childhood, he chose to abstract the story by setting it in the future. He wanted to deal with 'love' in a pure and abstract sense, not primarily with homosexual love. Japanese with English subtitles.

Prod Comp: CBS Sony Group, New Century, Shibata Organisation
Dist/Sales: NFVLS

Sun and Rain

(aka: Taiyang Yu)

Zeming, Zhang
1988; China; 90 min; Drama
Cast: Chun Sun, Xiaopin Yan, Xinxin Yi

Set in the modern city of Shenzhen, an introverted young woman slowly moves away from her brash boyfriend and, despite her inhibitions, develops a crush on another young teenage woman. An eye-opening view of modern China.

Sunday, Bloody Sunday

Schlesinger, John
1971; UK; 100 min; Drama
P: Joseph Janni; *W:* Penelope Gilliatt; *C:* Billy Williams; *E:* Richard Marden; *M:* Ron Geesin
Cast: Glenda Jackson, Peter Finch, Murray Head, Peggy Ashcroft

Glenda Jackson, a career woman separated from her husband, and Peter Finch, a Jewish doctor, are caught in a love triangle with a young bisexual designer. Although the arrangement appears perfect, the trio must deal with jealousy, fear and self-doubt. This absorbing character study, originally shocking, is regarded as a forerunner of cinema's increasingly mature treatment of homosexuality. Includes fantastic performances by Jackson and Finch, both of whom were nominated for Academy Awards.

Prod Comp: United Artists, Vectia
Dist/Sales: ReelMovies, TLA, UA, ACMI

Sunflowers

Hainsworth, Shawn
1996; USA; 50 min; Documentary

Exploring traditional cultural perceptions of homosexuality and sexual identity, *Sunflowers* is a moving portrait of a spirited group of gay men living in a rural Filipino town, who perform, in drag, a traditional festival known as the Santa Cruzan. Accepted by the local townspeople in this small farming community, the sunflowers were organised in 1975 to promote the visibility and talents of its members. As they prepare for the Santa Cruzan, these outspoken men share childhood memories, coming out stories, and their thoughts about the Catholic church. Interviews with townspeople are combined with the honest, often funny stories of the Sunflowers, revealing an evolving culturally rich community.

S

Super 8 1/2

Super 8 1/2

La Bruce, Bruce
1994; Canada; 85 min; Erotica
P: Jürgen Brüning; *W:* Bruce La Bruce; *C:* Donna Mobbs; *E:* Manse James, Robert Kennedy
Cast: Bruce La Bruce, Liza La Monica, Chris Teen

A surprisingly hard-core film-within-a-film, an autobiographical drama about a washed-up porn star whose life changes when a lesbian filmmaker begins to make a film about him. From the director of *No Skin off my Ass*.

Prod Comp: Jürgen Brüning Filmproduktion, Strand
Dist/Sales: TLA, Strand, Millivres, ACMI

Superdyke

Hammer, Barbara
1975; USA; 20 min; Comedy

A comedy about a troop of shield-bearing Amazons who take over city institutions before relaxing in the country. (www.barbarahammer.com)

Superstar: The Life and Times of Andy Warhol

Workman, Chuck
1990; USA; 90 min; Documentary
P: Marilyn Lewis, Peter English Nelson, Chuck Workman; *W:* Chuck Workman; *C:* Burleigh Wartes; *E:* Stephen Stept

Through the works and views of people such as David Hockney, Tom Wolfe, Dennis Hopper, Sylvia Miles, Grace Jones and the Campbell's soup spokesman, we gather an insight into one of the world's most famous contemporary artists and a master of publicity. Also included are interviews with the man himself.

Prod Comp: Marilyn Lewis Entertainment
Dist/Sales: PictureThis!, Wellspring, ACMI

Surrender Dorothy

DiNovis, Kevin
1998; USA; 87 min; B&W; Comedy
P: Richard Goldberg; *W:* Kevin DiNovis; *C:* Jonathan Kovel; *E:* Kevin DiNovis; *M:* Christopher Matarazzo
Cast: Peter Pryor, Kevin DiNovis, Jason Centeno, Elizaeth Casey

A dark comedy of gender manipulation. When slacker Lahn gets into trouble, lonely Trevor agrees to hide him—but only if he disguises himself as Dorothy, Trevor's ideal woman. But Lahn isn't happy as a gal, and Trevor's not gay. The solution? Trevor can make Dorothy into a real woman, and Lahn need never know! (Wolfe)

Prod Comp: Rich Entertainment
Dist/Sales: Wolfe, TLA

Surviving Friendly Fire

Nelson, Todd
1997; USA; 60 min; Documentary
P: Todd Nelson, Michael Hofacre; *C:* Todd Nelson; *E:* Michael Hofacre; *M:* Rich Meyers

Narrated by Sir Ian McKellen, this moving documentary allows gay and lesbian street kids to tell their stories through a theatre workshop and performance. Together they create a play about abuse in the home, growing up gay, and lesbian and surviving on the streets.

Prod Comp: Surviving Films/TW Nelson Production
Dist/Sales: Frameline

Surviving Sabu

Rashid, Ian Iqbal
1997; UK; 14 min; Drama

A complex story of generational conflict in a Muslim Asian family. The Indian film actor Sabu is the focal point for the troubled relationship between Amin and his father Sadru. (MQFF)

Dist/Sales: Frameline

Susana

Munoz, Susana
1980; Argentina, USA; 25 min; Documentary

An autobiographical film about the lesbian filmmaker leaving her native Argentina to live her life outside the strictures of her Latin American culture and family.

Dist/Sales: WMM

Swann in Love

(aka: Un Amour de Swann)

Schlöndorff, Volker
1983; France; 110 min; Drama
P: Eberhard Junkersdorf, Margaret Ménégoz; *W:* Peter Brook, Jean-Claude Carrière, Marie-Hélène Estienne, Volker Schlöndorff; *C:* Sven Nykvist; *E:* Françoise Bonnot; *M:* David Graham, Hans Werner Henze, Gerd Kuhr, Marcel Wengler
Cast: Jeremy Irons, Alain Delon, Ornella Muti, Fanny Ardant, Marie-Christine Barrault

An elegant and educated bachelor, Charles Swann, moves in the powerful and fashionable circles of Paris in the 1890s. He falls in love with a courtesan, but his friends warn him not to get too close to her. His friends cast him aside when he doesn't listen to their warnings. Features Alain Delon as the homosexual Baron.

Prod Comp: Gaumont, Bioskop Film, Films du Losange
Dist/Sales: ACMI, Palace, OrionClassics

Sweet Boy

Everett, Karen
2001; USA; 29 min; Documentary

Sweet Boy reveals an imaginative lesbian world where erotic fantasies bring sexual healing. Filmmaker Karen Everett's thoughtful, stylised and highly personal memoir documents the passionate complications a lesbian couple experience as they play out a relational mother/boy dynamic.

Dist/Sales: Everett

Sweet Thing

Robinson, Mark
2001; Australia; 14 min; Drama

When a trailer park mum abandons her kids, the resident drag queen steps into her rather unglamorous shoes with a hairpiece and Pyrex dish at the ready. Guess who turns up to parent teacher interviews? (MQFF)

Dist/Sales: Queerscreen

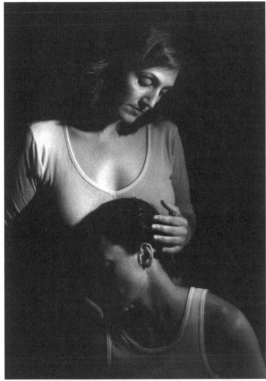

Sweet Boy

Swimming

Siegel, Robert J.
2000; USA; 98 min; Drama
P: Robert J. Siegel, Linda Moran; *W:* Lisa Bazadona, Grace Woodard, Robert J. Siegel; *C:* John Leuba; *E:* Frank Reynolds; *M:* Mark Wike
Cast: Lauren Ambrose, Jennifer Dundas Lowe, Joelle Carter, Jamie Harrold

It's the start of another Carolina summer, and it's becoming increasingly clear to Frankie Wheeler, a young local, that she wants more out of life than Myrtle Beach can offer her. She spends her days working in her family's restaurant and wastes her nights hanging out on the boardwalk with her best friend, Nicola, proprietor of a piercing shop and self-proclaimed trouble seeker. Frankie has always played sidekick to Nicola, so neither is prepared when two new arrivals, a young siren hired as a waitress, and a drifter selling tie-dyes out of the back of his van, court only Frankie. Nicola's ensuing jealousy sets in motion a series of betrayals driving a wedge into their friendship and forces Frankie to take a stand for herself. *Swimming* is an intimate look at friendship, love and breaking away, set amidst the backdrop of a bustling beach town. (Swimmingthemovie.com)

Dist/Sales: Oceanside

Swimming Prohibited

(aka: Yuei Kinshi)

Oki, Hiroyuki
1989; Japan; 89 min; Experimental
W: Hiroyuki Oki; *C:* Hiroyuki Oki
Cast: Hiroyuki Oki

Oki documents three weeks in his life. The film is not edited and is shown as it would have run through the camera. It is open and frank, and deals with his routines, pleasures, affairs, regrets and encounters; his diary becomes a small masterpiece of queer subjective cinema.

Dist/Sales: ImageForum

Swimming Upstream: A Year in the Life of Karen and Jenny

Freedman, Jennifer
2001; USA; 73 min; Documentary
P: Jennifer Freedman; *W:* Jennifer Freedman

Swimming Upstream chronicles a year in the life of a lesbian couple planning their first child together. The film opens with Karen discovering that she is indeed pregnant through artificial insemination. Throughout the next year, as Karen's belly grows, the couple must deal with a variety of complex emotional issues. Both Karen and Jenny candidly discuss being lesbian, and worry about how their unborn child will be treated in the world. While dealing with lesbian issues, the film is also about relationships as Karen and Jenny are forced to deal with their roles and perceptions of one another throughout the year as their lives change. The ensuing stress of their upcoming family reveals itself through the couple's financial strains and sexual issues. When their baby is born with health problems, their world is dramatically turned upside down once again. (MQFF)

Prod Comp: Pie Town Productions
Dist/Sales: PieTown

S

Switch (1991)

Edwards, Blake
1991; USA; 99 min; Comedy
P: Tony Adams; W: Blake Edwards; C: Dick Bush;
E: Robert Pergament; M: Don Grady, Henry Mancini
Cast: Ellen Barkin, Jimmy Smits, Jobeth Williams,
Lorraine Bracco, Tony Roberts

Steve and Walter used to have a preference for
blondes. Then Steve was murdered ... and came back
as one. Will being a woman make him a better man?
A ploy used many times, usually to extract laughs,
it's Hollywood's way of innocently examining
homoeroticism without getting its hands dirty. A
rather lame comedy but there is one interesting
scene when Steve has an encounter with a lesbian
who tries to come on to him/her.

Prod Comp: Cinema Plus, HBO, Beco Films
Dist/Sales: 16MM, Col-Tri, Lauren, Warner, Swank

Switch (1999)

Thompson, Hope
1999; Canada; 22 min; Drama
P: Sharon Brooks; W: Hope Thompson

It's 1949. Isabelle, a telephone operator is leading a
double life. She is having a clandestine affair with
another operator, Alice, while her boyfriend Ricky is
secretly making plans to elope with her to Niagara
Falls. (CFMDC)

Prod Comp: Red Bandit Productions
Dist/Sales: CFMDC

Switchblade Sisters

Hill, Jack
1975; USA; 91 min; Action
W: Jack Hill

Dominic is president of the Silver Daggers, a gang of
young thugs that controls the drug and prostitution
rackets in the local high school. Lace is Dominic's
girl—until Maggie on the scene and turns his head.
When a rival gang led by Crabs tries to muscle in on
the Daggers' territory and shoots Dominic's brother
Guido, the result is a gang shootout at a roller
skating rink in which Crabs kills Dominic. Maggie
then rallies the girls of the gang to kick out the
surviving boys as ineffectual cowards and makes an
alliance with a revolutionary black, girls' gang led by
Muff to eliminate Crabs and his organisation by
force of arms. This is accomplished by a devastating
gun battle in the street that features a home-made
armoured car. Lace's best friend Patch, convinces
Lace that Maggie has to be eliminated as a threat to
Lace's leadership. Maggie and Lace then face off in a
bloody knife duel that leaves Lace dead. Cult lesbian
trash at its best. (Picture This! Entertainment)

Dist/Sales: PictureThis!

Swollen Stigma

Pucill, Sarah
1998; UK; 21 min; B&W; Experimental

A visual, surrealist narrative of a woman travelling
both literally and psychically through an interior
space of several rooms. Memories, or fantasies, of
another woman fill her imaginary space. Femininity,
as a construction, is explored within a lesbian
context where the assertion of lesbian symbolic
imagery is created. (Cinenova)

Dist/Sales: Cinenova

Swoon

Kalin, Tom
1992; USA; 92 min; B&W; Drama
P: Christine Vachon; W: Tom Kalin, Hilton Als;
C: Ellen Kuras; E: Tom Kalin; M: James Bennett
Cast: Daniel Schlachet, Craig Chester, Robert Read,
Ron Vawter, Michael Kirby

Tells the true story of Richard Loeb and Nathan
Leopold—rich, young gay lovers and intellectuals
with an interest in Nietzsche, who murder a boy as a
thrill-killing in Chicago in the 1920s. Their only
motive was to prove that they could get away with it.
They later escaped the death penalty because of an
impassioned defence case conducted by Clarence
Darrow. Darrow argued that they were insane and
used their homosexuality as proof. Inspired by other
films on the same subject, Rope (Alfred Hitchcock)
and Compulsion (Richard Fleischer).

Awards: Berlin Film Festival, 1992: Gay Teddy Award
Prod Comp: Intolerance, American Playhouse
Dist/Sales: ACMI, FilmsInc, FineLine, NFVLS

Swordsman II

(aka: Xiao ao Jiang hu zhi Dong Fang bu bai)

Ching, Siu-tung / Tong, Stanley
1991; Hong Kong; 110 min; Action
P: Hark Tsui; W: Hanson Chan, Pik-yin Tang, Hark
Tsui; C: Moon-tong Lau; E: Chi-sin Mak;
M: Richard Yuen
Cast: Jet Li, Brigitte Lin, Michelle Reis, Waise Lee,
Rosamund Kwan, Kar Lok Chin

A continuation of the story began in Swordsman
(1990). Before retiring his martial arts school to an
isolated mountain, Blademaster visits Princess Yin-
Yin, who is his love interest, and the leader of a tribe
of snake-wielding female warriors. He finds that they
have been attacked, and the Princess abducted. The
attacker is revealed to be the Princess's evil uncle
Fong, who years before overthrew and imprisoned
Yin-Yin's father and took over their sect. Fong has
also stolen a sacred scroll which reveals the secrets of
achieving unbeatable martial arts power. Blademaster
attempts to help free Yin-Yin and her father.

However, his romantic attachments become more complicated when his childhood friend and Yin-Yin are joined by a new rival, who at first Blademaster believes to be an innocent village girl he has saved. He is shocked when she turns out to be Fong! It is then revealed that to gain ultimate martial arts power one must perform self-castration and become female. Cantonese & Mandarin with English subtitles.

Prod Comp: Film Workshop Ltd.
Dist/Sales: MeiAh

Swordsman III: The East is Red

(aka: Dung Fong bat Baai 2: Fung wan joi hei)

Lee, Raymond / Ching, Siu-tung
1992; Hong Kong; 90 min; Action
P: Hark Tsui; *W:* Hanson Chan, Pik-yin Tang, Hark Tsui; *C:* Moon-tong Lau; *E:* Chi-sin Mak; *M:* William Wu, Richard Yuen
Cast: Brigitte Lin, Shun Lau, Joey Wong

A spectacular action fantasy film that follows our transsexual hero, Asia, as she goes on an incredible fighting and killing spree to win back the love of her beautiful Snow. Like any good kung-fu film there are some amazing special effects and gymnastic live action. This gender-bender is a must-see, particularly the lesbian love scene. Cantonese with English subtitles.

Prod Comp: Film Workshop, Golden Harvest Company
Dist/Sales: RimFilm

Sydney - Living with Difference

1999; Australia; 30 min; Documentary

In just over 20 years, Sydney (Australia) has transformed itself from an outpost of the British Empire to one of the most cosmopolitan cities in the world. Using Sydney's Gay and Lesbian Mardi Gras as a starting point, this film opens up questions about Sydney's reputation for openness and tolerance towards social diversity and alternative lifestyle choices. Featuring interviews with members of an Aboriginal dance group, new migrants from the Cook Islands and people from gay and lesbian communities, the program considers the social interactions between disparate groups that go to make up Sydney's distinctive cultural life. (EMA)

Dist/Sales: EMA

Sylvia Scarlett

Cukor, George
1935; USA; 97 min; B&W; Comedy
P: Pandro S. Berman; *W:* Gladys Unger, John Collier, Mortimer Offner; *C:* Joseph August; *E:* Jane Loring; *M:* Roy Webb, Alberto Colombo

Cast: Katharine Hepburn, Cary Grant, Brian Aherne, Edmund Gwenn

Directed by legendary filmmaker George Cukor, the dazzling talents of Katharine Hepburn and Cary Grant light up the screen in this engaging lovingly filmed comedy adventure. When her father runs afoul of the law in pre-war Paris, a plucky young girl disguises herself as a boy to aid in their escape. But when they team up with a lowbrow con-man, Kate's scheming soon precipitates a disastrous series of uproarious romantic misunderstandings. She/he becomes the love interest of a beautiful young woman.

Prod Comp: RKO
Dist/Sales: NFVLS, ACMI, FilmsInc, BFI

Symposium: Ladder of Love

Sheehan, Nick
1996; Canada; 72 min; Documentary
P: Greg Klymkiw; *C:* Harald Bachmann; *E:* Caroline Christie; *M:* Nicholas Stirling

A documentary about the meaning of love from a queer perspective.

Sync Touch

Hammer, Barbara
1981; USA; 10 min; Experimental

In Sync Touch, lesbian images are juxtaposed with common clichés, providing an ironic and humorous inquiry into the nature of the lesbian aesthetic. (WMM)

Dist/Sales: WMM

TABU V (About Which one Cannot Speak)

Brynntrup, Michael
1997; Germany; 13 min; Experimental

Death is not an event in life. One does not experience death. If one understands eternity to mean timelessness rather than eternal time, then he who lives in the present will live forever. Our life is as endless as our field of vision is boundless. (Brisbane International Film Festival)

Dist/Sales: CFMDC

Take Out

Monette, Jean-François
2000; Canada; 38 min; Drama

In this coming of age tale, Rory is a typical high school student—he runs track, smokes, and has a lousy after-school job. His career so far consists of delivering chicken to customers. Excitement at work is limited to exchanges between his teasing co-worker and hungry grunting suburbanites. But on a delivery like any other, Rory meets Pete, a middle aged man in the midst of a breakdown. Fascinated by Pete's material trappings of success and intrigued by the source of his breakdown, Rory is drawn into a friendship with him. Their platonic friendship proves to be a catalyst: Rory's sexuality forces him to reconsider his small world as his curiosity propels him to take a risk. (CFMDC)

Dist/Sales: CFMDC, PictureThis!

Tales of the City

Tales of the City

Reid, Alastair
1993; UK, USA; 3 x 100 min; Drama
P: Alan Poul; *W:* Richard Kramer; *C:* Walt Lloyd;
E: David Gamble; *M:* John E. Keane
Cast: Olympia Dukakis, Donald Moffat, Laura Linney, Chloe Webb

Armistead Maupin's cult queer novel series *Tales of the City* makes it to the screen. This modern gay classic takes an original and thoroughly entertaining look at life in San Francisco in the 1970s.

Prod Comp: American Playhouse, Channel 4

Tales of the City 2

(aka: More Tales of the City)

Gang, Pierre
1998; Canada, UK, USA; 330 min; Drama
P: Kevin Tierney; *W:* Armistead Maupin, Nicolas Wright; *C:* Serge Ladouceur; *E:* Philippe Ralet
Cast: Olympia Dukakis, Laura Linney, Colin Ferguson, Bill Campbell, Barbara Garrick

Sequel to the hugely successful *Tales of the City*—the film version of Armistead Maupin's series of much-loved books about life in the queer mecca of San Francisco.

Prod Comp: Showtime
Dist/Sales: Showtime

Tales of the City 3

(aka: Further Tales of the City)

Gang, Pierre
2001; Canada, USA; 180 min; Drama
P: Alan Poul; *W:* Armistead Maupin, James Lecesne;
C: Serge Ladouceur
Cast: Olympia Dukakis, Paul, Hopkins, Laura Linney, Barbara Garrick, Jackie Burroughs

More of Armistead Maupin's series of much-loved books about life in the queer mecca of San Francisco.

Prod Comp: Showtime
Dist/Sales: Showtime

Talk of the Town

(aka: Stadtgespräch)

Kaufmann, Rainer
1995; Germany; 89 min; Comedy
P: Henrik Meyer; *W:* Ben Taylor; *C:* Klaus Eichhammer;
E: Ursula Mai; *M:* Stefan Traub
Cast: Katja Reimann, August Zirner, Martina Gedeck, Kai Weisinger

A multilayered sexual comedy centred around Monika, a single open-minded woman who hosts a morning radio program for those in need of advice on romance and relationships. The love pentagon that ensues involves Monika, her married lover Erik, her best friend Sabine, her brother Rene and his male lover. Needless to say each cast member uses Monika's radio program for their own essential absolution. German with English subtitles.

Prod Comp: Studio Hamburg Produktion, ZDF
Dist/Sales: ZDF

Talk to me like the Rain

Kinney, Donald / Kinney, Robert
1989; USA; 17 min; Drama

Part of the trilogy of films from brothers Robert and Donald Kinney, *Talk to me like the Rain* is a languid, subtle tale of love gone wrong. Based on a poem by Tennessee Williams, the film is a tribute to the writer. (MQFF)

Tampon Thieves

(aka: Ladronas de tampones)

Lozano, Jorge
1996; Colombia; 22 min; Drama

Zena and Tita are due in court for stealing tampons; they refuse to pay for the privilege of menstruating. They live in an abandoned warehouse on the edge of Toronto and pay for college by selling phone sex. Reflective and insightful, *Tampon Thieves* gently weaves reflections on family with love between friends to tell a rich story of how women and gay men of colour are treated in a racist, homophobic culture. (Frameline)

Dist/Sales: Frameline

Tanaka

Jacobson, Clayton
2001; Australia; 23 min; Drama
W: Clayton Jacobson
Cast: Kim Dryden, Kathy Smith, Katsuhiko Suzuki Sai

Mori comes to Australia from Japan to arrange his uncle's funeral. But Mori's life is changed when he discovers his uncle's secret.

Tangible Fathers

Poirier, Bob
1999; USA; 57 min; Documentary

A documentary which tells the story of a Catholic Priest as he discovers his homosexuality and struggles with family relationships, his vows to the church and his self acceptance.

Dist/Sales: BobbyRoger

Tank Girl

Talalay, Rachel
1995; USA; 93 min; Sci-Fi
P: Richard Lewis, Pen Densham, John Watson;
W: Tedi Sarafian; *C:* Gale Tattersall; *E:* James R. Symons; *M:* Graeme Revell
Cast: Lori Petty, Naomi Watts, Malcolm McDowell, Ice T, Don Harvey, Iggy Pop

Futuristic, cutting-edge action adventure based on the cult British comic strip. Set in the year 2033, when an ecological cataclysm has devastated the land and left water the most rare and precious resource. Out of this brutal landscape emerges Tank Girl, a new kind of hard-edged heroine who heads the revolt against the evil Department of Water. A great camp romp, with Petty as a tough-talking, gunslinging modern girl pretending to be lovers with another woman in order to protect her.

Prod Comp: United Artists, Trilogy, MGM
Dist/Sales: UIP, ReelMovies, Warner, Swank

Tarch Trip

Oki, Hiroyuki
1994; Japan; 65 min; B&W; Experimental
P: Jürgen Brüning; *W:* Hiroyuki Oki; *C:* Hiroyuki Oki;
E: Hiroyuki Oki
Cast: Masashi Mori, Takashi Furukawa, Tadayuki Kataoka, Seiji Otsuta

Shot in black and white with no dialogue in the home of the filmmaker. This is an avant-garde film with a personal view that includes a series of images, creating feeling and mood, which focus on three gay friends, one of whom is HIV-positive.

Taste

Dombroski, Lisa
2000; Australia; 22 min; Comedy

Meet Suz—her relationship with Pete is going sour. Meet Danny—a chef who offers her something sweet and a little spicy. It's all a matter of taste in this sexy gender-bending comedy. (MQFF)

Dist/Sales: NFVLS

Taste of Honey, A

Richardson, Tony
1961; UK; 100 min; B&W; Drama
P: Tony Richardson; *W:* Shelagh Delaney, Tony Richardson; *C:* Walter Lassally; *E:* Antony Gibbs;
M: John Addison
Cast: Rita Tushingham, Murray Melvin, Dora Bryan

Film version of Shelagh Delaney's play about a young girl who becomes pregnant to a black sailor. She leaves an unsympathetic home and finds care and tenderness with a homosexual. A poignant, moving and remarkable film, although somewhat dated, with sensitive performances.

Prod Comp: Bryanston
Dist/Sales: Ascanbee

Taste the Sweat

Reding, Benjamin / Reding, Dominik
1997; Germany; 13 min; B&W; Experimental

A young skinhead enquires about getting his first tattoo, dreams about how he will be treated by his peers once he is inked, and fantasises about the punk he meets in the tattoo studio. German with English subtitles.

Dist/Sales: Schlammtaucher

Taxi to Cairo

(aka: Taxi nach Kairo)

Ripploh, Frank
1987; Germany; 90 min; Comedy
W: Tamara Kafka, Frank Ripploh; *C:* Dodo Simoncic;
E: Peter R. Adam; *M:* Peter Breiner
Cast: Frank Ripploh, Udo Schenk, Christine Neubauer

Frank must marry a woman in order to remain in his

t

mother's will. The only problem is that he and his wife have fallen in love with the same man. See also Frank Ripploh's film *Taxi to the Toilet* (aka: *Taxi zum Klo*).

Taxi to the Toilet

(aka: Taxi zum Klo)

Ripploh, Frank
1981; Germany; 100 min; Comedy
W: Frank Ripploh; *C:* Horst Schier; *M:* Hans Wittstadt
Cast: Frank Ripploh, Bernd Broaderup, Tabea Blumenschein, Magdalena Montezuma, Gitte Lederer

An autobiographical account of how filmmaker Frank Ripploh, a gay teacher who is having problems with his relationship, spends his nights picking up men in public toilets. He immerses himself in the gay culture of Berlin while still holding on to his lover and job.

Dist/Sales: Cinevista, ACMI

Tea and Sympathy

Minnelli, Vincente
1956; USA; 120 min; Drama
P: Pandro S. Berman; *W:* Robert Anderson;
C: John Alton; *E:* Ferris Webster; *M:* Adolph Deutsch
Cast: John Kerr, Deborah Kerr, Leif Erickson, Edward Andrews

A sensitive youth is in conflict about his sexuality and is teased by the other boys and called 'Sister-Boy'. He doesn't fit in with their view of life and refuses to adopt their cruel and callous behaviour. Finally he comes to terms with his sexual identity when he has an affair with his teacher's wife, proving his 'manhood'. The homosexual nature of the story was well and truly watered down by censorship in the mid 1950s.

Prod Comp: MGM
Dist/Sales: MGM

Tea Leaf

Novaczek, Ruth
1986; UK; 10 min; Drama

The story of a Jewish woman growing up in London in the 1960s. Denying her culture and sexuality for years she awakens in the 1980s, fighting the system and poverty by stealing food from supermarkets and learning to love women.

Dist/Sales: Cinenova

Teenage Tupelo

McCarthy, John Michael
1995; USA; 83 min; Drama
P: John Michael McCarthy; *W:* John Michael

McCarthy; *C:* Darin Ipema; *E:* Darin Ipema, John Michael McCarthy, Dave Thompson, Brian Churchill; *M:* Impala
Cast: D'Lana Tunnell, Sherri Ann Bandham, Sophie Couch, Kris Kremmers

Set in Tupelo, Mississippi, in 1962, a young woman becomes pregnant to a womanising man who leaves town. She must face life as a single mother at the same time that her own mother is trying to force her to have her pregnancy terminated. Things look grim until a gang of lesbians and a film star come to her assistance.

Prod Comp: Big Broad Guerrilla Monster
Dist/Sales: SomethingWeird

Tell me no Lies

Hunter, Neil
1993; UK; 30 min; Comedy

Set among college students in London, this coming-out comedy revolves around three best friends, all of whom are gay but are unable to come out to the others.

Tell me that you Love me, Junie Moon

Preminger, Otto
1969; USA; 112 min; Drama
P: Otto Preminger; *W:* Marjorie Kellogg; *C:* Boris Kaufman; *E:* Henry Berman, Dean Ball; *M:* Pete Seeger, Philip Springer
Cast: Liza Minnelli, Ken Howard, Robert Moore, Kay Thompson, James Coco

The moving story of three misfits who, after meeting in hospital, decide to share an apartment together. They are a young woman with bad facial scars, an epileptic, and a wheelchair-bound homosexual. A rather dated effort that never achieves any real depth, based on a novel by Marjorie Kellogg who also adapted the script.

Prod Comp: Paramount, Sigma Productions
Dist/Sales: Ascanbee, Paramount

Tell me the Truth about Love

White, Susanna
2000; UK; 60 min; Documentary

This hauntingly beautiful BBC documentary examines the words and wisdom of Pulitzer Prize-winning poet W. H. Auden. When he died in 1973, Auden left behind some of the greatest love poems of the 20th century. He also left two short journals containing diagrams and notes about the nature of love, journals which reveal that Auden's poetry came not just from inspiration but also from a scientific analysis of love itself. Auden fuelled his analysis through his real-life relationships with Christopher

Isherwood, Don Bachardy, Humphrey Spender, and other major literary and social figures of the 20th century, many of whom are interviewed in the film. *Tell Me the Truth About Love* is full of gorgeous poetry, fascinating archival footage, and colourful characters – a wonderful and illuminating film. (2002 Mardi Gras Film Festival)

Tell me the Truth about Love

Tell me Why: The Epistemology of Disco

Di Stefano, John
1991; USA; 25 min; Comedy

An often humorous, and poignant look at the role that disco music has played in the formation of gay male identity. The film challenges the notion of disco as merely a 'leisure activity' by positing disco as an important cultural expression of gay sexuality.

Tender

Dimas, Christos
1995; Greece; 13 min; Documentary

An intimate portrait of a transsexual sex worker in Athens. Greek with English subtitles.

Tender Fictions

Hammer, Barbara
1995; USA; 60 min; Experimental

Innovative, funny, and historic, *Tender Fictions* is an autobiographical exploration of the search for and meaning of gay community. From a childhood spent being groomed as the next Shirley Temple to her current work as an activist and maker of over 70

films and videos, groundbreaking filmmaker Barbara Hammer casts a wry eye on her life and changing world. In a rich montage of home movies, experimental films, news footage, and personal photographs, Hammer charts her growth from 1950s child star 'wannabe' to 1960s straight earth mother to 1990s lesbian artist and activist. (WMM)

Dist/Sales: Hammer, WMM

Tenebrae Lessons
(aka: Leçons de Ténèbres)

Dieutre, Vincent
2000; France; 77 min; Experimental
P: Emmanuel Giraud; *W:* Vincent Dieutre; *C:* Jean-Marie Boulet, Benoît Chamaillard, Gilles Marchand; *E:* Ariane Doublet
Cast: Andrzej Burzynski, Hubert Geiger, Vincent Dieutre, Leo Bersani

Shot in alternating film and video, *Tenebrae Lessons* ia a very densely constructed documentary narrative with flashes of beauty. The film cuts between Renaissance paintings and monologues about fisting, along with French existentialism and a man talking in second person about his lover.

Prod Comp: Carrré Noir, Les Films de la Croisade
Dist/Sales: Grisé

Teorema
(aka: Theorem)

Pasolini, Pier Paolo
1968; Italy; 104 min; Drama
P: Franco Rossellini, Manolo Bolognini; *W:* Pier Paolo Pasolini; *C:* Giuseppe Ruzzolini; *E:* Nino Baragli; *M:* Ennio Morricone
Cast: Terence Stamp, Silvana Mangano, Massimo Girotti, Anne Wiazemsky

A mysterious stranger enters the lives of a bored bourgeois family. He seduces all the members one by one and then leaves as mysteriously as he arrived, leaving their life in tatters as they all slowly lose their sanity. Pasolini's obsessions with eroticism, homosexuality, religion and social position are all examined in this politically allegoric, controversial and often erotic film. Italian with English subtitles.

Prod Comp: Aetos
Dist/Sales: Ascanbee, TLA, ACMI, BFI

Terence Davies Trilogy, The

Davies, Terence
1976–1983; UK; 97 min; Drama
W: Terence Davies; *C:* William Diver; *E:* Digby Rumsey
Cast: Phillip Maudsely, Robin Hooper, Val Lilley, Terry O'Sullivan, Sheila Raynor

In this partly autobiographical trilogy, Davies

t

outlines Liverpudlian Robert Tucker's develop-ment—from victimised schoolboy, in *Children* (1976), through a Catholic repressed gay middle age, *Madonna and Child* (1980), to senility and death in hospital, *Death and Transfiguration* (1983)—'into a rich, resonant tapestry of impressionistic detail'. The bleakness is relieved by a wry wit, imaginative use of music and flashes of surrealism foreshadowing Davies' subsequent autobiographies, *Distant Voices, Still Lives* and *The Long Day Closes*.

Prod Comp: BFI
Dist/Sales: Frameline, Strand

Terms of Conception

Taylor, Amanda
1994; USA; 30 min; Documentary
P: Amanda Taylor; *W:* Amanda Taylor; *C:* Amanda Taylor

Terms of Conception is a documentary about a lesbian couple and their decision to have a child through artificial insemination with a known donor. Through candid interviews with a nurse practitioner, family and marriage counsellor, lawyer, friends, relatives and the parents-to-be, this complex and increasingly common issue is examined.

Prod Comp: Fish Tayl Productions

Terror in the Crypt

(aka: La Cripta e L'Incubo)

Miller, Thomas
1964; Italy, Spain; 80 min; B&W; Horror
P: William Mulligan; *W:* Julian Berry, Robert Bohr, Maria del Carmen, Martinez Ramón, José L. Monter; *C:* Julio Ortas, Giuseppe Acquari; *E:* Herbert Mark; *M:* Herbert Buchman, Carlo Savina
Cast: Adriana Ambessi, Christopher Lee, Ursula Davis, José Campos

Another reworking of the Sheridan Le Fanu's *Carmilla*, which has been made many times and often more successfully than in this particular version. A Count believes there is a curse on his family and one of his descendants will be reincarnated as the evil witch Sheena. Although it appears it is his daughter, Laura, her friend Lyuba is the one reincarnated as the witch.

Prod Comp: MEC Cinematographica, Hispaner Films

Terry and Julian (Vol. 1 and 2)

Oldroyd, Liddy
1992; UK; 90 min; Comedy
P: Toni Yardley; *W:* Julian Clary, John Henderson, Paul Merton; *M:* Russell Churney, Barb Jungr, Michael Parker
Cast: Julian Clary, Lee Simpson, Kate Lonergan

Julian is a homeless Channel 4 celebrity. He answers an ad for a flatmate, arriving on the doorstep of Terry, a rough and ready South London lad. Julian soon turns the dowdy flat into a glittering, bejewelled objet d'art, more in keeping with Julian's aesthetic requirements. Thus with a cheery wave, the occasional song and one or two sordid innuendoes, this incongruous couple settle down to domestic bliss together ... Or do they?

Prod Comp: Wonderdog Productions
Dist/Sales: ReelMovies, Channel4

Thank God I'm a Lesbian

Colbert, Laurie / Cardona, Dominique
1992; Canada; 55 min; Documentary
Cast: Sarah Schulman, Dionne Brand, Nicole Brossard

An uplifting and entertaining documentary about the diversity of lesbian identity. The women speak frankly and articulately about issues ranging from coming out, racism, bisexuality and S/M, to the evolution of the feminist and lesbian movements, outing and compulsory heterosexuality. (WMM)

Dist/Sales: WMM, CFMDC

That Certain Summer

Johnson, Lamont
1972; USA; 75 min; Drama
P: Richard Levinson, William Link; *W:* Richard Levinson, William Link; *C:* Vilis Lapenieks; *E:* Edward M. Abroms; *M:* Gil Melle
Cast: Hal Holbrook, Joe Don Baker, Martin Sheen, Marilyn Mason

A son has trouble understanding why his middle-aged parents are separating in this made for television movie. When he visits his father during the summer break, he meets his father's 'close friend'. Soon it is revealed that the young man is his father's lover. Considered to be groundbreaking at the time it went to air in 1972.

Awards: Golden Globe Awards, 1973: Best Film Made for TV
Prod Comp: Universal
Dist/Sales: ABC-US

That Tender Touch

Vincent, Russell
1969; USA; 88 min; Drama
P: Russel Vincent; *W:* Russel Vincent; *C:* Robert Caramico; *E:* Maurice E. Wright
Cast: Sue Bernard, Bee Tompkins, Rick Cooper, Margaret Read

A rarely screened camp lesbian thriller starring Sue Bernard (*Playboy*'s Miss December 1966), whose lesbian relationship with an ageing woman eventually catches up with her. When the older woman attempts to rekindle their relationship tragedy ensues.

Dist/Sales: Frameline

That's a Family

Chasnoff, Debra
2000; USA; 35 min; Documentary

Children from a wide variety of families share their experiences of having lifestyles deemed different from the 'norm'—gay and lesbian families, adoptive families, single parent families to name a few. From Academy Award winning director Debra Chasnoff (*It's Elementary*). (MQFF)

Dist/Sales: WoMedia, NewDay

Thelma

Meier, Pierre-Alain
2001; France, Greece, Switzerland; 95 min; Drama
P: Robert Boner, Pierre-Alain Meier, Fenia Cossovitsa, Xavier Grin; *W:* Jacques Akchoti, Lou Inglebert, Pierre-Alain Meier, Barbara Sobeck; *C:* Thomas Hardmeier; *E:* Loredana Cristelli; *M:* Yiorgos Mandas
Cast: Laurent Schilling, Pascale Ourbih, Nathalia Capo d'Istria, François Germond

Vincent Fleury, a taxi driver in Lausanne, lives apart from his wife and son. One night he meets Thelma, a young woman who offers him a large amount of money to take her to Crete and help her get revenge on an ex-lover. Vincent and Thelma become close during the trip, but Thelma remains a bit evasive. Vincent has trouble understanding her game, until one night, when their flirting gets slightly more serious and he finds out... that she is also a man. He is shocked and pushes her away. However, when he discovers Thelma's 'other' secret, he begins to see her differently... (www.thelma.ch) French with English subtitles.

Prod Comp: Thelma Films
Dist/Sales: Vagrant

Thelma and Louise

Scott, Ridley
1991; USA; 128 min; Drama, Action
P: Ridley Scott, Mimi Polk Gitlin; *W:* Callie Khouri; *C:* Adrian Bibble; *E:* Thom Noble; *M:* Hans Zimmer
Cast: Susan Sarandon, Geena Davis, Harvey Keitel, Brad Pitt, Michael Madsen

When unhappy housewife Thelma and her wise-cracking friend Louise decide to take a break from their lives, they embark on a trip that leads to a tragic incident at a roadside honky tonk. In an instant, their weekend 'getaway' becomes just that as they flee across the American Southwest with the police one step behind. A stylish and witty action film, with a rather long kiss between the two women at the end. Although not on the surface a lesbian narrative, *Thelma and Louise* has become one of the great lesbian favourites of cinema.

Awards: Academy Awards, 1991: Best Screenplay
Prod Comp: MGM, Pathé Entertainment, United International Pictures
Dist/Sales: UIP, Warner, ACMI, MGM

Theme: Murder

Swetzoff, Martha
1998; USA; 54 min; Documentary

A real life story of murder, secrets and sexuality, set in the art world of the 1950s and 60s, *Theme: Murder* takes the viewer on an immersive journey into the struggles and frustrations of living with an unsolved homicide. The filmmaker was nine years old in 1968 when her father, the Boston art dealer Hyman Swetzoff, was beaten and left to die in his home. Martha's search to make sense of her father's unsolved murder uncovers the price of homophobia and also reveals many of the subtle attitudes that accompany murder. Probing and disquieting, using lush visual and aural textures in contrast with the brutality of its subject, this film presents the experience of homicide from the inside out. (New Day Films)

Dist/Sales: NewDay

There is no Pain in Paradise
(aka: En el Paraiso no Existe el Dolor)

Saca, Victor
1994; Mexico; 90 min; Drama
P: Victor Saca, Georgina Teja; *W:* Victor Saca;
C: Jorge Medina; *E:* Menahem Peña
Cast: Miguel Angel Ferriz, Evangelina Elizondo

After the death (from AIDS) of his lover and business partner, Manuel heads to the Mexican city of Monterey where he finds a disturbing world of violence, lust and lies. He must find his way out of this nether world, so he can begin life afresh. Spanish with English subtitles.

Prod Comp: Instituto Mexicano de Cinematografía
Dist/Sales: IMCINE

Thérèse and Isabelle

Metzger, Radley
1968; France; 102 min; B&W; Drama
P: Radley Metzger; *W:* Jesse Vogel; *C:* Hans Jura;
E: Humphrey Wood; *M:* Georges Auric
Cast: Essy Persson, Anna Gaël, Simone Paris, Barbara Laage

Based on the autobiographical novel by Violette

Leducet, *Thérèse and Isabelle* is the sensitive drama of buddy female sexuality set in an all-girl Catholic boarding school. It delves into the emotions and passion of two young women who meet and fall in love. Even with some fairly explicit sex scenes for its time it manages to remain non-exploitative.

Prod Comp: Amsterdam Films
Dist/Sales: TLA, Wolfe Video, FirstRunFeatures

They are Lost to Vision Altogether

Kalin, Tom
1989; USA; 13 min; Documentary

They are Lost to Vision Altogether acts as an erotic retaliation to the Helms Amendment, the United States government's refusal to fund explicit AIDS prevention information for gay men, lesbians and intravenous drug users. The film addresses the contradictions of sexuality and romance in the face of a monolithic and culturally compulsory hetero-sexuality.

Dist/Sales: VDB, Drift, EAI

Thin Ice: Passion on the Pink Rink

Cunningham Reid, Fiona
1994; UK; 88 min; Drama
P: Fiona Cunningham-Reid; *W:* Fiona Cunningham-Reid, Geraldine Sherman; *C:* Belinda Parsons; *E:* Rodney Sims; *M:* Diana McLoughlin
Cast: Sabra Williams, Charlotte Avery, Ian McLellen

Thin Ice is the story of Steffi, an ambitious photographer, and her journalist partner, nice gay boy Greg, who concoct a scheme to make big bucks by writing a story about love and lesbians on ice at the Gay Games in New York in the mainstream press. The particular lesbians in question are none other than Steffi and her lover, Lisa. That is, until Lisa dumps Steffi within weeks of the competition. Not to be thwarted, Steffi tracks down a new skating partner: the innocent, naive and straight Natalie. Through bribery, flirtation, a few white lies and a little seduction, Steffi convinces Natalie to sign on for New York. Unfortunately it doesn't all go to plan. (MQFF)

Prod Comp: Thin Ice Productions

Things we Said Today

Miller-Monzon, John
1992; USA; 34 min; Drama
P: John Miller-Monzon; *W:* John Miller-Monzon

The story of a few days in the life of a young lesbian in New York—a pillow fight, a near affair, a major battle with her lover, trouble paying the rent—and not a cliché in the whole 34 minutes.

Dist/Sales: Frameline

Things you can Tell Just by Looking at Her

Garcia, Rodrigo
2000; USA; 109 min; Drama
P: Jon Avnet, Lisa Lindstrom, Marsha Oglesby; *W:* Rodrigo Garcia; *C:* Emmanuel Lubezki; *E:* Amy E. Duddleston; *M:* Edward Shearmur
Cast: Glen Close, Calista Flockhart, Kathy Baker, Cameron Diaz, Holly Hunter, Valeria Golina

Comprised of five interwoven vignettes, the film binds the lifelines of several seemingly disconnected San Fernando Valley residents. Detective Kathy Farber arrives at a crime scene to discover the body of Carmen, an old acquaintance. In the days preceding Carmen's death, we see her skirt unnoticed around the periphery of our protagonists' lives: Dr Elaine Keener, who tends to her infirm mother and waits anxiously for a male colleague to call; self-reliant Rebecca Weyman, who, on discovering she is pregnant, confronts a difficult, desolate choice; single mother Rose, who develops a fanciful, comedic obsession with her new neighbour; Christine, who wrestles with the imminent death of her ailing lesbian lover Lilly; and investigator Kathy's acerbic, blind sister, Carol, who speculates on what might have driven Carmen to suicide. (www.nhk.or.jp)

Prod Comp: Franchise Pictures
Dist/Sales: Wolfe, MGM, Showtime, UA, RoadshowEnt

Third Sex, The
(aka: Anders als du und ich)

Harlan, Veit
1957; Germany; 75 min; Drama
W: Felix Lützkendorf; *C:* Kurt Grigoleit; *E:* Walter Wischniewsky; *M:* Erwin Halletz
Cast: Christian Wolff, Paul Dahlke, Paula Wesley

Klaus's father confesses to a family friend early in the film that Klaus shows no interest in girls. Klaus's friend Manfred then comes under suspicion as the focus and cause of Klaus's 'sickness'. The family takes desperate measures to curtail Klaus's friendship with Manfred. Klaus is forced to attend a heterosexual gathering in the hope that closer proximity to the opposite sex will encourage 'normality'. Manfred is jealous and Klaus leaves suddenly, seeking protection with the mysterious music teacher who lives in a secluded mansion on the outskirts of town (and who has among his students an array of nubile young lads). Klaus is then pursued across the city by his father—a search which leads us through the gay nightclubs of 1950s Berlin. (MQFF)

Prod Comp: Arca-Filmproduktion GmbH
Dist/Sales: 21stCentury, Constantin

Thirst

(aka: Törst; Three Strange Loves)

Bergman, Ingmar
1949; Sweden; 90 min; B&W; Drama
P: Helge Hagerman; *W:* Herbert Grevenius; *C:* Gunnar Fischer; *E:* Oscar Rosander; *M:* Erik Nordgren
Cast: Eva Henning, Birger Malsten, Mimi Nelson, Birgit Tengroth, Hasse Ekman

A couple, going through the disintegration of their childless marriage go on a train trip to Stockholm, stuck in a claustrophobic compartment. Intercut with their story is the tale of the husband's ex-wife, Viola, who has a sympathetic relationship with a female ballet dancer who becomes a lesbian. Based on a collection of three stories by Birgit Tengroth.

Prod Comp: Svensk Filmindustri
Dist/Sales: Kino

This I Wish and Nothing More

(aka: Nincsen Nekem Vagyam Semmi)

Mundruczo, Kornel
2000; Hungary; 80 min; Drama
P: Viktoria Petranyi, Zsofia Kende, Nota Petak, Gyorgy Durst; *W:* Farkas Hegyi, Kornel Mundruczo, Viktoria Petranyi; *C:* Szilard Makkos; *E:* Bela Barsi; *M:* Gabor Ruzsa, Csaba Faltay, Zsofia Taller
Cast: Ervin Nagy, Roland Rába, Imre Csuja, Martina Kovacs

Idyllic fantasy collides with brutal reality in Kornél Mundruczó's energetic feature debut. Handsome Bruno and his pretty gymnast wife Mari live in the country and dream of escaping their humdrum existence. But without Mari knowing, Bruno travels to the city each week to pull petty thefts and turn bizarre tricks along with Mari's drag queen skinhead brother Ringo, who wants Bruno. Bruno is also involved in a complex love/hate relationship with an older married man. Able to juggle his lies for only so long, Bruno is forced to determine which he truly is—dreamer or hustler. (2002 New York Lesbian & Gay Film Festival) Hungarian with English subtitles.

Dist/Sales: MagyarFilmunio

This is Dedicated: Grieving When a Partner Dies

Mathew, Jan
1991; UK; 25 min; Documentary

The death of a loved one is difficult enough to deal with, hemmed in as it is with taboos and the fear of strong emotions. For lesbians and gay men the pain of loss is frequently sharpened by the insensitivity and, at times, the quite astounding emotional cruelty of a straight world that denies the legiti-

macy—and sometimes even the very existence—of lesbian and gay relationships.

Prod Comp: Alleycat Productions, Channel 4
Dist/Sales: FilmakersLibrary

This is not a Very Blank Tape Dear

Cottis, Jane
1989; USA; 22 min; Comedy

A woman sends her mother a questionnaire about her sexuality and her life.

This Marching Girl Thing

This Marching Girl Thing

Simpson, Kelli
1994; Australia; 20 min; Comedy
P: Ann Turner; *W:* Kelli Simpson
Cast: Toni Collette, Matt Day, Jenny Apostolou, Toni Rickards

Cindy is a baton twirler with The Southern Twirlettes. She looks like she fits in. She's just beginning to feel like she doesn't.

Prod Comp: Victoria College of the Arts
Dist/Sales: ACMI, VCA

This Special Friendship

(aka: Les Amitiés Particulières)

Delannoy, Jean
1964; France; 100 min; B&W; Drama
P: Christine Gouze-Rénal; *W:* Jean Aurenche, Pierre Bost; *C:* Christian Matras; *E:* Louisette Hautecoeur
Cast: Francis Lacombrade, Didier Haudepin, Michel Bouquet, François Leccia

A moving film set in a strict Catholic school in France, where a young boy falls in love with one of his younger classmates. After repeated attempts to stop the boys meeting, a priest lies to one of the boys to get him to leave the school and end the relationship but tragically the boy kills himself. Based on the novel by Roger Peyrefitte. French with English subtitles.

Dist/Sales: Facets

Those who Love me can Take the Train

Chéreau, Patrice
1998; France; 122 min; Drama
P: Charles Gassot; W: Patrice Chéreau, Pierre Trividic, Daniele Thompson; C: Eric Gautier; E: François Gédigier; M: Éric Neveux
Cast: Vincent Perez, Pascal Greggory, Valeria Bruni-Tedeschi, Charles Berling

> Those who Love me can Take the Train is a beautifully moving celebration of new life blossoming from tragic loss. The film follows the journey of a group of family, friends and lovers of painter Jean-Baptiste from Paris to Limoges to attend his funeral. Featuring a talented cast of France's best contemporary actors, luminous cinemascope photography and an eclectic rock soundtrack, Those who Love me is an important film which handles an intricate story line with finesse. Even more significantly, it presents a group of well-defined characters, of varying gender and sexual orientation, with a degree of sensitivity and compassion rarely seen in movies today. (Kino International)
> French with English subtitles.

Prod Comp: Le Studio Canal+
Dist/Sales: Kino, ArtificialEye

Thousand Miles, A

Feranti, Sharon
2000; USA; 23 min; Drama

> Jesse is a lesbian who hasn't spoken to her mother for eight years. Her younger brother Clay convinces her to return home for a visit, and so Jesse goes home hoping for a reconciliation, and to face her demons.

Dist/Sales: 2XTexan

Three

(aka: Tatlo... magkasalo)

Siguion-Reyna, Carlos
1998; Philippines; 86 min; Drama
P: Armida Siguion-Reyna; W: Bibeth Orteza;
C: Romulo Araojo; E: Manet A. Dayrit; M: Ryan Cayabyab
Cast: Rita Avila, Gina Alajar, Ara Mina, Tonton Gutierrez

> Elsie, a young Filipino housewife, is unhappily married to macho Tito. When she finds that her former secret lover has cancer, Elsie leaves her husband for Alice. No sooner does Elsie come out than she discovers she is pregnant, and she, Alice and Tito must learn to get along for the sake of the baby.

Eventually, tensions explode. (Wolfe)
Filipino with English subtitles.

Prod Comp: Reynafilms
Dist/Sales: Wolfe

Three Bewildered People

(aka: Three Bewildered People in the Night)

Araki, Gregg
1987; USA; 92 min; Drama
P: Gregg Araki; W: Gregg Araki; C: Gregg Araki; E: Gregg Araki
Cast: Mark Howell, John Lacques, Darcy Marta

> Araki's first feature film follows three young people in a café in Los Angeles, USA, as they work out their feelings and sexuality, amidst the despair and angst of the modern world.

Three Drags and a Wedding

Sugarman, Andrew
Australia; 44 min; Documentary
P: Andrew Sugarman

> A light-hearted look at the success, both popular and critical, of the two films Muriel's Wedding and The Adventures of Priscilla, Queens of the Desert. Sugarman looks at their success locally and internationally—themes covered in the film include sexuality, tolerance, acceptance and Australian humour.

Dist/Sales: Roadshow

Three of Hearts

Bogayevicz, Yurek
1993; USA; 101 min; Comedy
P: Matthew Irmas, Joel B. Michaels; W: Mitch Glazer, Adam Greenman; C: Andrzej Sekula; E: Dennis M. Hill, Suzanne Hines; M: Joe Jackson
Cast: Kelly Lynch, William Baldwin, Sherilyn Fenn, Joe Pantoliano, Gail Strickland

> A woman employs a male prostitute to pursue and break the heart of her lesbian ex-lover, believing that if she is hurt badly enough, and put off men, she will come back. Unfortunately her ex-lover falls for the boy. Thought to be a groundbreaking lesbian film for Hollywood, but sadly misses out, even in 1992 the boy must get the girl. The film has one good point in that Kelly Lynch's character retains her strength and dedication to lesbianism throughout.

Prod Comp: New Line Cinema
Dist/Sales: Roadshow, NewLine

Three on a Match

Robbins, Fred A.
1999; USA; 87 min; Comedy
P: Fred Cobar
Cast: Erica Shaffer, Janet Lark, Ingrid Sthare, Te-See Bender, Gregg Hoffman

> This light-hearted sexy comedy begins at Annie's annual birthday bash, a special time for a group of old friends to reminisce about their good old days and to catch up on each other's lives. This year's hot topic is Beth and Claire. Last year they moved in together and this year Beth's maternal instinct has hit overdrive—much to Claire's dismay. Since artificial insemination is too cold and adoption takes forever, Beth, the confirmed lesbian, goes on a manhunt. Her search leads her to David, a nightschool teacher, who happens to be secretly in love with Claire. While Beth wants to dip into David's gene pool, David wants to dip into Claire. (Wolfe)

Dist/Sales: Wolfe

Three to Tango

Santostefano, Damon
1999; USA; 98 min; Comedy
P: Bobby Newmyer, Jeffrey Silver, Bettina Sofia Viviano; *W:* Rodney Vaccaro, Aline Brosh McKenna; *C:* Walt Lloyd; *E:* Stephen Semel; *M:* Graeme Revell
Cast: Matthew Perry, Neve Campbell, Dylan McDermott, Oliver Platt

> A business tycoon thinks it's safe to ask his gay client Oscar to spy on his mistress. Oscar isn't 'gay', but to keep the tycoon happy, he agrees—and falls madly in love. (Wolfe)

Prod Comp: Outlaw Productions
Dist/Sales: Wolfe, Warner

Threesome

Fleming, Andrew
1994; USA; 93 min; Comedy
P: Brad Krevoy, Steve Stabler; *W:* Andrew Fleming; *C:* Alexander Gruszynski; *E:* William C. Carruth *M:* Thomas Newman
Cast: Josh Charles, Stephen Baldwin, Lara Flynn Boyle, Alexis Arquette

> When they said the dorms were co-ed, they didn't mean guys and girls would be assigned to the same rooms. But Alex has a name that puts her in the male column as far as the university computer is concerned, so she finds herself squeezed into the most intimate of living arrangements! Alex has her eye on Eddy who has his eye on Stuart!

Prod Comp: Motion Picture Corporation of America, TriStar Pictures; *Dist/Sales:* 16MM, Col-Tri

Throwback

(aka: Spike of Bensonhurst)

Morrissey, Paul
1988; USA; 97 min; Comedy
P: David Weisman; *W:* Alan Bowne; *C:* Herbert Kirkpatrick, Allen G. Thompson; *E:* Bernard Loftus; *M:* Coati Mundi
Cast: Sasha Mitchell, Maria Patillo, Ernest Borgnine, Geraldine Smith

> An ambitious boxer tries to climb his way to the top. He falls in love with the local don's daughter and is banished from the area, so he sets up shop with a hilarious Puerto Rican family. His mother is a lesbian.

Prod Comp: FilmDallas Pictures, Sugarloaf Films
Dist/Sales: Roadshow

Thug

Economopoulis, Spiro / Tsiolkas, Christos
1998; Australia; 12 min; Experimental

> Explores issues surrounding pornography, masculinity and memory.

Thunderbolt and Lightfoot

Cimino, Michael
1974; USA; 115 min; Comedy, Action, Drama
P: Robert Daley; *W:* Michael Cimino; *C:* Frank Stanley; *E:* Ferris Webster; *M:* Dee Barton
Cast: Clint Eastwood, Jeff Bridges, Geoffrey Lewis, Catherine Bach, Gary Busey

> Four men conspire to rob an armoured car, in this rather vulgar comedy-drama. Bridges gives a first-rate performance as a young drifter after quick riches and spends most of the film in drag. A fairly homophobic film with no openly gay characters but most of the males spend an inordinate amount of time trying to hide their fear of homosexuality.

Prod Comp: United Artists, The Malpaso Company
Dist/Sales: ReelMovies, Warner, UA

Thundercrack!

McDowell, Curt
1975; USA; 150 min; Comedy, Horror
P: Charles Thomas, John Thomas; *W:* George Kuchar; *C:* Curt McDowell; *E:* Curt McDowell; *M:* Mark Ellinger
Cast: Marion Eaton, George Kuchar, Mookie Blodgett, Melinda McDowell

> A bizarre black comedy that's become a cult classic. This spoof is difficult to categorise as either comedy or horror. During a storm, a group of travellers, including a gorilla, find themselves at cackling

Gertie's Old Dark Masturbatorium. They are terrorised by a bunch of perverts who sexually assault them. A sexually graphic hoot that is rarely seen in its original uncut version.

Tidy Endings

Millar, Gavin
1988; USA; 60 min; Drama
P: Patrick Whitley, Rick McCallum; *W:* Harvey Fierstein; *C:* John Michaels; *E:* Ruth Foster; *M:* Stanley Myers
Cast: Stockard Channing, Harvey Fierstein, Nathaniel Moreau, Jean De Baer

A made-for-television drama, this is a touching story about an unusual friendship. When a man dies of AIDS, his male lover, and his ex-wife develop a bond where they find support in their grief. A strong and powerful drama that explores its emotional subject with depth and understanding.

Prod Comp: Sandollar

Ties that Bind, The

Friedrich, Su
1984; USA; 55 min; B&W; Documentary

Lesbian filmmaker, Su Friedrich examines her mother's life during the Nazi rule of Germany. Far different from the usual documentary and more than a daughter interviewing a mother.

Dist/Sales: WMM, Cinenova, CFMDC

Tillsammans

(aka: Together)

Moodysson, Lukas
2000; Denmark; 106 min; Comedy
P: Lars Jönsson; *C:* Ulf Brantås; *E:* Fredrik Abrahamsen, Michal Leszczylowski
Cast: Lisa Lindgren, Emma Samuelsson, Michael Nyqvist, Sam Kessel

A group of twenty-somethings in a hippie share house in mid 1970s Sweden start to question their social, moral and sexual beliefs. Elisabeth has fled her alcoholic husband in the hope of starting a new life for herself and her two children. The house leader and his wife have an open marriage, although it's clear the wife enjoys her sexual freedom more than her husband. Anna and Lasse are recently separated, and Anna thinks she may be a lesbian, whilst Lasse is confused and angry—even more so when he is propositioned by one of the household's few single males. Swedish with English subtitles.

Prod Comp: Zentropa Entertainments

Tim Miller: Loud and Queer

Harrison, Richard
1992; USA; 29 min; Documentary

Widely acclaimed performance artist Tim Miller conducts a workshop for gay men, performs excerpts from *My Queer Body* and discusses the importance of autobiographical storytelling to lesbians, gay men and other marginalised communities. Interviews, performance footage and images spanning his 15-year career are interwoven as Miller confronts fear and loss, violence, censorship, homophobia and the politics of AIDS in America.

Dist/Sales: VDB

Time Being, The

Sherman, Kenneth
1997; Canada; 52 min; Drama

A visually stunning, powerful meditation on one man's struggle for survival and forgiveness after assisting with his lover's euthanasia. The film begins with Michael and Sebastian moving into their new home. They are in love; embraced by friends and Sebastian's unconditionally loving mother. Still, they are not immune to social problems or human weaknesses: Michael has AIDS and he betrays Sebastian by sleeping with someone else, though it is not clear which precedes the other. After Michael's death, Sebastian is filled with doubt about helping him die and a consuming need to forgive not only Michael, but himself. (Frameline)

Dist/Sales: Frameline, CFMDC

Time Off

Fox, Eytan
1990; Israel; 45 min; Drama

Brave first film from Fox which is a drama about homosexuality in the Israeli Army. Hebrew with English subtitles.

Time Piece

Petraska, Brian / Sprenkel, Kenn
1994; USA; 96 min; Drama
Cast: Eric Brizee, Markas O'Donnell, Brian Petraska

From discussions of group sex, to monogamy, to coming out, a surprise 30th birthday party is the catalyst for this story based on the experiences of seven San Francisco gay men in the early 1990s. A fictional story shot in documentary style, the film explores issues that touch the personal and intimate lives of most gay men. (Water Bearer Films)

Dist/Sales: WaterBearer

Time Regained

(aka: Le Temps retrouvé)

Ruiz, Raoul
1999; France; 158 min; Drama
W: Raoul Ruiz, Gilles Taurand; *C:* Ricardo Aronovich;
E: Denise de Casabianca; *M:* Jorge Arriagada
Cast: Catherine Deneuve, Emmanuelle Béart, John
Malkovich, Vincent Perez, Pascal Greggory

Marcel Proust (1871–1922) is on his deathbed.
Looking at photographs brings memories of his
childhood, his youth, his lovers, and the way the
Great War put an end to a stratum of society. His
memories are in no particular order, they move back
and forth in time. Marcel at various ages interacts
with Odette, with the beautiful Gilberte and her
doomed husband, with the pleasure-seeking Baron
de Charlus, with Marcel's lover Albertine, and with
others; present also in memory are Marcel's beloved
mother and grandmother. It seems as if to live is to
remember and to capture memories is to create a
work of great art. The memories parallel the final
volume of Proust's novel. (Mongrel Media) French
with English subtitles.

Prod Comp: Le Studio Canal+
Dist/Sales: Kino, Mongrel, ArtificialEye, NFVLS

Time Zones

Jarman, Derek
1976; UK; 32 min; Documentary
P: James MacKay

Three short films featuring personal video diary
work: a portrait of William Burroughs, and clips
produced for the band Throbbing Gristle.

Prod Comp: Dark Pictures
Dist/Sales: ACMI

Times of Harvey Milk, The

Epstein, Robert
1984; USA; 90 min; Documentary
P: Richard Schmiechen; *W:* Judith Coburn, Carter
Wilson; *C:* Frances Reid; *E:* Robert Epstein, Deborah
Hoffmann; *M:* Mark Isham
Cast: Harvey Fierstein, Harvey Milk, Anne Kronenberg,
Tory Hartmann

An exceptionally moving documentary about
Harvey Milk, the first openly gay candidate elected
to San Francisco's Board of Supervisors. A courageous activist, Milk worked hard to express the
political concerns of not only gays and lesbians, but
also of African–Americans, Hispanics and other so-
called American minorities. After 11 months in
office Milk and the Mayor of San Francisco were
assassinated by Dan White, a conservative member
of the Board of Supervisors. The subsequent trial, in
which White received a lenient sentence, resulted in
massive rioting in San Francisco by gay and lesbian
activists. But amidst the tragedy the film builds a
convincing and impassioned picture of a man
committed to human rights and human dignity.

Awards: Academy Awards, 1984: Best Documentary;
San Francisco International Lesbian & Gay Film
Festival, 1985: Audience Award for Best Documentary
Prod Comp: Black Sand Productions
Dist/Sales: ACMI, October, Telling, BFI, Wolfe,
NewYorker, Cowboy

Times Square

Moyle, Allan
1980; USA; 111 min; Drama
P: Robert Stigwood, Jacob Brackman; *W:* Jacob
Blackman; *C:* James A. Contner; *E:* Tom Priestley;
M: Blue Weaver, Robin Gibb
Cast: Trini Alvarado, Robin Johnson, Tim Curry, Peter
Coffield

A teenage rock 'n' roll rebel story about two young
women involved in a psychiatric experiment who
become close friends and decide to escape. They
begin living on the streets and put together an all-
girl rock band and fall in love. Music supplied by the
Patti Smith Group, Lou Reed and Suzi Quatro,
amongst many others. Has become a cult favourite,
particularly since revelations about more overt
lesbian scenes that were dropped from the final cut.

Prod Comp: Robert Stigwood Organisation
Dist/Sales: BFI, Swank

Tiny and Ruby: Hell Drivin' Women

Tiny and Ruby: Hell Drivin' Women

Schiller, Greta / Weiss, Andrea
1988; USA; 30 min; Documentary

This sequel to The International Sweethearts of
Rhythm profiles one of the band's star performers,
the legendary jazz trumpeter Ernestine 'Tiny' Davis,
and her partner for 40 years, drummer Ruby Lucas.
The film includes colourful interviews with Tiny and
Ruby in their Chicago home, compelling archival

material, lively musical performances, imaginative computer animation, and an evocative narration by Cheryl Clarke.

Awards: San Francisco International Lesbian & Gay Film Festival, 1988: Best Documentary
Prod Comp: Jezebel Productions
Dist/Sales: CinemaGuild, BFI, Salzgeber

Titanic 2000

Fedele, John Paul
1999; USA; 85 min; Comedy
P: Michael L. Raso; *W:* Clancy Fitz Simmons;
C: Timothy Healy
Cast: Tammy Parks, Michael R, Thomas, Jacob Bogert, Suzanne Lenore

> Vampire Vladamina is a passenger on the maiden voyage of the ocean liner Titanic 2000. She's there for the ride, but also to find a woman she can turn into a vampire queen. Shari, a rock groupie looks to be the perfect conquest, and she eventually must choose between an eternal life as Vladamina's sex slave, or death.

Dist/Sales: Seduction

To an Unknown God

(aka: A un Dios Desconocido)

Chávarri, Jaime
1977; Spain; 95 min; Drama
W: Elías Querejeta; *C:* Teodoro Escamilla;
M: Luis de Pablo
Cast: Héctor Alterio, Ángela Molina, María Rosa Salgado

> This enigmatic story centres around Jose, a gay magician, now living with his younger lover. He goes into what could be called a mid-life crisis and decides to review his life. He travels to his childhood home in Granada and is flooded with the memory of witnessing the assassination of the gay poet and activist Federico Jose Lorca. An oblique meditation on ageing, homoeroticism and childhood.

To Die for

(aka: Heaven's a Drag)

Litten, Peter McKenzie
1994; UK; 97 min; Drama
P: Gary Fitzpatrick; *W:* Johnny Byrne; *C:* John Ward;
E: Jeffrey Arsenault; *M:* Roger Bolton
Cast: Thomas Arklie, Ian Williams, Dilly Keane, Tony Slattery, Ian McKellen

> The story of the relationship between Simon, a hunky television repairman, and Mark, a HIV-positive drag queen. The expressive, sensitive, witty and very camp Mark does not let a small event such

as death separate him from his laconic boyfriend, who attempts to escape from the serious issues of life via a hedonistic lifestyle. Simon's troubles have only just begun when his attempts to date other men are met by haunting obstruction and harassment from the 'other side'. This well-shot British production combines wit, seriousness, meaty portrayals of gay life, comic situations, and a great soundtrack in a manner that will bring both laughter and tears to any audience. (MQFF)

Prod Comp: Victor, British Screen
Dist/Sales: TLA, FirstRunFeatures

To Forget Venice

(aka: Dimenticare Venezia)

Brusati, Franco
1979; Italy; 90 min; Drama
P: Franco Brusati, Claudio Grassetti; *W:* Franco Brusati, Jaj Fiastri; *C:* Romano Albani; *E:* Ruggero Mastroianni;
M: Benedetto Ghiglia, Saverio Mercadante
Cast: Erland Josephson, Mariangela Melato, David Pontremoli, Eleanora Giorgi

> A comedy/drama about a middle-aged gay man, Nicky and his young lover, who stay with Nicky's sister, Marta, at her country estate. Marta is an opera star, now dying, who lives with her adopted niece, Anna. The visit of her brother brings back a series of childhood memories, both painful and pleasant. Italian with English subtitles.

Prod Comp: Rizzoli, Action
Dist/Sales: ACMI

To my Women Friends

Sharandak, Natasha
1993; Germany, Russia; 64 min; Documentary

> A series of revealing interviews with six Russian lesbians which depicts the subjects' joys and hardships, touching on issues like women's prisons, coming out, homophobia, transsexuality and gay and lesbian community groups.

Dist/Sales: Frameline

To Play or to Die

(aka: Spelen of Sterven)

Krom, Frank
1990; The Netherlands; 50 min; B&W; Drama
P: Maria Peters, Hans Pos, Dave Schram, Jose Steen;
W: Frank Krom, Anne van de Putte; *C:* Nils Post;
M: Ferdinand Bakker, Kim Hayworth
Cast: Tjebbo Gerritsma, Geert Hunaerts

> Kees, a 15-year-old boy, has developed a crush on Charel, a classmate. When Kees's parents go away he embarks on a plan of seduction and invites Charel to

his house. But his plan is ultimately for revenge against the bullying and cruel Charel. A psycho-sexual drama dealing with insanity, which is unfortunately equated with homosexual desire.

Dist/Sales: WaterBearer

To Ride a Cow

Deeya, Loran / Lee, Quentin
1992; Hong Kong, USA; 24 min; Drama

A sumptuously moody film about a young Asian man who is finding commitment a problem—both to his girlfriend and the man he is seeing when he just wants to have sex.

To Wong Foo, Thanks for Everything, Julie Newmar

Kidron, Beeban
1995; USA; 108 min; Comedy
P: G. Mac Brown; *W:* Douglas Carter Beane; *C:* Steve Mason; *E:* Andrew Mondshein; *M:* Rachel Portman
Cast: Wesley Snipes, Patrick Swayze, John Leguizamo, Stockard Channing

Vida and Noxeema are two sophisticated New York drag queens who let hard-luck 'drag princess' Chi-Chi tag along with them as they drive to Hollywood in a pink Cadillac for a major drag competition. On the way, they run afoul of a sexist, homophobic cop, get stuck in a small Nebraskan town, and change the lives of everyone they encounter there. Made for a straight audience.

Prod Comp: Amblin, Universal
Dist/Sales: UIP, Wolfe, TLA, Swank

Toc Storee

Ma, Ming-yuen S.
1992; Hong Kong, USA; 21 min; Drama

A film addressing the issues of sexuality, tradition and identity in Asian gay contexts. Stories from Chinese and Japanese history are juxtaposed with contemporary accounts and texts by authors such as James Baldwin and Trinh T. Minh-ha, to create a sense of continuity from past to present in self-identification as gay Asians. (MQFF)

Todd Killings, The

Shear, Barry
1970; USA; 90 min; Drama
P: Barry Shear; *W:* Dennis Murphy, Joel Oliansky; *C:* Harold E. Stine; *E:* Walter Thompson; *M:* Leonard Rosenman
Cast: Robert F. Lyons, Richard Thomas, Belinda Montgomery, Barbara Bel Geddes

Skipper is a good-looking dropout who hates old people, women and his teachers. Bored with his drug use, he begins to live more dangerously. He falls in love with another tough boy who has just been released from a remand home. They begin a rampage of thrill-killings of young women.

Prod Comp: National General Pictures
Dist/Sales: Warner

Together Alone

Castellaneta, P. J.
1991; USA; 84 min; B&W; Drama
P: P. J. Castellaneta; *W:* P. J. Castellaneta; *C:* David Dechant; *E:* P. J. Castellaneta, Maria Lee; *M:* Wayne Alabardo
Cast: Todd Stites, Terry Curry

Two gay men casually meet in a bar, go home together and have sex. Together Alone peels away the veneer of faked intimacy dredged up by a typical one night stand. The two men humorously and antagonistically discuss the many levels of mistrust evident in this sort of relationship, and their sexuality. Beautifully filmed it is Castellaneta's first feature film and has won many awards. Described as the gay *My Dinner with Andre*.

Awards: Berlin Film Festival, 1992: Best Gay Film; San Francisco Gay & Lesbian Film Festival, 1995: Audience Award for Best Feature
Dist/Sales: Wolfe, Forefront, BFI

Together and Apart

Lynd, Laurie
1986; USA; 26 min; B&W; Drama

A delightful musical drama about sexual and professional choices, *Together and Apart* is a tale of reunited lovers and has the cast singing part of the narrative in bed, across dinner tables, and on the road. (CFMDC)

Awards: Berlin Film Festival, 1992: Best Gay Film
Dist/Sales: CinemaGuild, CFMDC

Toilers and the Wayfarers, The

Froelich, Keith
1995; USA; 80 min; B&W; Drama
P: Keith Froelich; *W:* Keith Froelich; *C:* James D. Tittle
Cast: Matt Klemp, Andrew Woodhouse, Ralf Schirg

Lush tale of two gay teenage boys growing up in the conservative Midwest of America. The pressure of hiding their sexuality from their family and the local community reaches boiling point when they meet a mysterious stranger and the three decide to escape to find a new life in the big city. German with English subtitles.

Prod Comp: KJF Productions
Dist/Sales: PictureThis!, Wolfe

Token of Love

Motyl, H. D.
1993; USA; 31 min; Drama

Twisted tales of gay break-ups. Was banned in Japan due to brief full frontal nudity.

Tokyo Cowboy

Garneau, Kathy
1994; Canada; 94 min; Drama
P: Richard Davis; *W:* Caroline Adderson; *C:* Kenneth Hewlett; *M:* Ari Wise
Cast: Hiromoto Ida, Christianne Hirt

No Ogawa, who works in a Tokyo burger palace, dreams of going West to become a cowboy. His childhood pen-pal Kate lives in the wilds of Canada and No decides to visit her. Kate has returned to her small town with her lover Shelley and No falls for Shelley.

Dist/Sales: WaterBearer

Tokyo Fist

(aka: Tokyo-ken)

Tsukamoto, Shinya
1995; Japan; 87 min; Drama
P: Shinya Tsukamoto; *W:* Shinya Tsukamoto; *C:* Shinya Tsukamoto; *E:* Shinya Tsukamoto; *M:* Chu Ishikawa
Cast: Fujii Kaori, Kôji Tsukamoto, Shinya Tsukomoto, Takenaka Naoto

Tsuda, an insurance agent, encounters Takuji, an old school chum, now a professional boxer. During a subsequent visit and scuffle, a jealous Tsuda is KO'd by Takuji who has attempted to seduce his fiancée, Hizuru. This violent episode is the catalyst for change with Tsuda who is now consumed by the desire for revenge. He attends boxing training just as Hizuru moves in with Takuji after piercing every available appendage and getting heavily tattooed. Has all the usual Tsukamoto homoerotic undercurrents. Japanese with English subtitles.

Prod Comp: Kajiyu Theater
Dist/Sales: Manga

Tom

Hoolboom, Mike
2002; Canada; 80 min; Documentary
P: Mike Hoolboom; *W:* Mike Hoolboom; *C:* Caspar Stracke; *E:* Mike Hoolboom

Tom is an 'experimental' feature-length documentary made almost entirely of found footage. This is cinema as déjà vu, or déjà voodoo; many moments will feel all too familiar, though they've been projected now onto the surface of a life to make up this most unusual of biographies. The history of a city, New York City, the most photographed city in the world, operates as a backdrop for the life of Tom Chomont, a key member of the New York underground, a notorious video artist, AIDS sufferer, raconteur. His fantastical stories punctuate the weave of pictures, recounting infanticide, a mobster's love, incest, and a rare white light, which he imagines as both the beginning and end of all life. As the decades roll past, excerpts from hundreds of films, some archival documents, some well-known Hollywood moments, stream past in a hypnotic rush offering a subject whose skin is cinema, whose flesh and blood has been remade into the picture plane. This is a biography about biographies. Tom travels the length of his own life without arriving. Perhaps the most important parts of his own life are never witnessed, experienced or understood by him. The unconscious. The stolen footage is a way to reflect on a new kind of identity (socially formed, as an image). This biography is made possible even, by the society of the spectacle. (Mike Hoolboom)

Dist/Sales: CFMDC

Tongues Untied

Tom Clay Jesus

Duong, Hoang A.
2001; USA; 17 min; Drama

A multilayered examination of one man's experience of a one night stand.

Dist/Sales: HeavyBlow

Tomboychik

DuBowski, Sandi Simcha
1993; USA; 15 min; Documentary

A series of intimate Video-8 vignettes depicting the fierce love between Malverna, who is 88 years old, and her grandson, Sandi, 22 years old. The two playmates dress up drag-esque. It is a moving portrait of a woman's life and struggle with gender and sexuality across three generations.

Dist/Sales: VDB

Tongues Untied

Riggs, Marlon
1989; USA; 55 min; Documentary
Cast: Kerrigan Black, Bernard Brannier, Gerald Davis, Blackberri

This is the acclaimed account of black gay life by Emmy Award-winning director Marlon Riggs. Using poetry, personal testimony, rap and performance, *Tongues Untied* describes the homophobia and racism that confront black gay men.

Awards: Berlin International Film Festival, 1990: Teddy; San Francisco International Lesbian & Gay Film Festival, 1990: Audience Award
Dist/Sales: Frameline, BFI, Wolfe, NFVLS, ACMI, Strand

Too Much Sun

Downey Snr, Robert
1991; USA; 91 min; Comedy
P: Lisa M. Hansen; *W:* Robert Downey Jnr, Laura Ernst, Al Schwartz; *C:* Robert Yeoman;
E: Joe D'Augustine; *M:* David Robbins
Cast: Robert Downey Jnr, Eric Idle, Ralph Macchio, Andrea Martin, Leo Rossi, Jennifer Rubin

Two eccentric children of a Beverly Hills millionaire learn that they will lose $200 million in inheritance unless one of them produces an heir within one year. The only problem is that the son is gay and the daughter is a lesbian. The characters are only there for laughs and the film basically falls short of anything more interesting.

Prod Comp: Cinetel Films
Dist/Sales: Col-Tri, NewLine

Too Outrageous!

Benner, Richard
1987; Canada; 110 min; Comedy
P: Roy Krost; *W:* Richard, Benner; *C:* Fred Guthe;
E: George Appleby
Cast: Craig Russell, Hollis McLaren, Rusty Ryan, Norman Weiler

A sequel to the film *Outrageous!* Living in New York, a wisecracking hairdresser and female impersonator's life is hampered by his schizophrenic roommate. Some great impersonations of Tina Turner, Eartha Kitt and Mae West. Both Benner and Russell died of AIDS in 1990.

Prod Comp: Téléfilm Canada

Too Young

(aka: Ye Maque)
Huang, Min-chen
1997; Taiwan; 40 min; Drama

An introverted teenager with an obsession for self-help tapes, develops a crush on a classmate with a mysterious past.

Tootsie

Pollack, Sydney
1982; USA; 112 min; Comedy
P: Sydney Pollack, Dick Richards; *W:* Larry Gelbart, Murray Shisgal; *C:* Owen Roizman; *E:* Frederick Steinkamp, William Steinkamp; *M:* Dave Grusin, Stephen Bishop
Cast: Dustin Hoffman, Jessica Lange, Teri Garr, Dabney Coleman, Charles Durning, Bill Murray

Comedy about a struggling New York actor who is having problems getting work because he is considered difficult. To find work he dons drag and becomes a superstar on a soap opera. Things get a little tricky when he falls for his co-lead, Jessica Lange and, in a moment of intimacy, makes a move on Lange who, of course, reads it as a lesbian advance.

Prod Comp: Columbia, Delphi, Mirage, Punch Productions
Dist/Sales: 20thCenturyFox, 16MM, ReelMovies, Col-Tri, Swank

Torch Song Trilogy

Torch Song Trilogy

Bogart, Paul
1988; USA; 118 min; Comedy, Drama
P: Howard Gottfried; *W:* Harvey Fierstein; *C:* Mikael Salomon; *E:* Nicholas C. Smith; *M:* Peter Matz
Cast: Harvey Fierstein, Anne Bancroft, Matthew Broderick, Brian Kerwin, Karen Young

Set around three incidents in the life of a drag artist: in 1971 there is a one-off affair with a schoolteacher firmly in the closet; in 1973 he falls deeply in love with a young man who comes to live with him; in 1980 his mother discovers his homosexuality as an old lover moves back in. Moving and thoughtful reworking of the Broadway success written by one of the few openly gay actors and writers, Harvey Fierstein.

Prod Comp: New Line Cinema
Dist/Sales: Col-Tri, Wolfe, BFI

Total Eclipse

Holland, Agnieszka
1995; Belgium, France, UK; 110 min; Drama
P: Jean-Pierre Ramsay-Levi; *W:* Christopher Hampton; *C:* Yorgos Arvanitis; *E:* Isabelle Lorente; *M:* Jan A. P. Kaczmarek
Cast: Leonardo DiCaprio, David Thewlis, Romane Bohringer, Dominique Blanc

The sensational story of Arthur Rimbaud, the 19th century French poet, and his affair with fellow poet Paul Verlaine, an older and not so successful poet. The film follows their messy relationship up until it turns violent and destructive.

Prod Comp: Capital Films, FIT Productions, Fine Line Features, K2 Film
Dist/Sales: FilmsInc, FineLine, Wolfe, UIP

Total Loss

Nechustan, Dana
2000; The Netherlands; 84 min; Drama

Opening and ending with a spectacular and harrowing tunnel car crash, *Total Loss* moves backwards to tell us (*Memento*-like) the twisted narrative arc. Duco, a rich arrogant doctor, and his house guest/lover Reinier take in a man, Jeroen, after his failed suicide attempt. Duco plans to arrive at his parents' New Year's Eve party with a surprise: both men. His parents and fiancee don't know he's gay and living with a shady drug dealer, one who holds secrets to both of their pasts. A dark, stylish thriller that drops pieces of the puzzle in the viewer's lap every so often, while simultaneously offering up questions about escape, manipulation and those last few minutes of life. (2002 Chicago Lesbian & Gay International Film Festival) Dutch with English subtitles.

Totally Confused

Pritikin, Greg / Rosen, Gary
1998; USA; 88 min; Comedy
P: Bob Fagan; *W:* Greg Pritikin, Gary Rosen; *C:* Alan Thatcher
Cast: Greg Pritikin, Gary Rosen, Heather Donaldson

Rock star wannabe Johnny is continually being led on by Murray, his pathologically-lying manager, who claims that he's already made it big in the overseas market. Johnny's best friend Wiley, a porn-addicted bookstore clerk, is desperately trying to figure out if he's attracted to women or men. The already complex friendship heads up, when Wiley puts the moves on Johnny. But what will happen when Johnny's live-in girlfriend finds out?
(1998 Verzaubert Queer Film Festival)

Totally F***ed Up

Araki, Gregg
1993; USA; 85 min; Drama
P: Andrea Sperling, Gregg Araki; *W:* Gregg Araki; *C:* Gregg Araki; *E:* Gregg Araki
Cast: James Duval, Roko Belic, Susan Behshid, Jenee Gill

An open-structured and angst filled look into the lives of six gay and lesbian teenagers living in Los Angeles. They share their views on sex, their parents and relationships, and show their anger and frustration at living in the homophobic 1990s.

Prod Comp: Desperate Pictures, Muscle + Hate Studios
Dist/Sales: Potential, Strand, Fortissimo, Wolfe, NFVLS, ACMI

Touch Me (1994)

Cox, Paul
1994; Australia; 30 min; Drama
W: Paul Cox, Barry Dickins, Margot Wilburd
Cast: Gosia Dobrowolska, Claudia Karvan

Two women escape their frustrating relationships and spend a weekend alone together in the country.

Touch Me (1997)

Boos, H. Gordon
1997; USA; 107 min; Drama
P: David Rubin, Michael Sourapas; *W:* H. Gordon Boos, Greg H. Sims; *C:* Giles Dunning; *E:* Steve Nevius; *M:* Claude Foisy
Cast: Amanda Peet, Michael Vartan, Greg Louganis, Peter Facinelli, Kari Wuhrer

Life is pretty good for Amanda as she has a new job and a new relationship. But a telephone call changes everything when she is told her former lover in dying of AIDS.

Prod Comp: Devin Entertainment

Touch of Evil

Welles, Orson
1958; USA; 105 min; B&W; Thriller
P: Albert Zugsmith; *W:* Orson Welles; *C:* Russell Metty; *E:* Edward Curtiss, Aaron Stell, Virgil W. Vogel; *M:* Henry Mancini

Cast: Charlton Heston, Janet Leigh, Orson Welles, Joseph Calleia, Marlene Deitrich

Charlton Heston plays Hank Quinlan, a police captain in a corrupt city on the Mexican–American border who pursues his own notion of justice. It's a wonderful thriller that delves into the murky depths of corruption, justice, worship and betrayal. There's a scene where Janet Leigh is roughed up by a gang of thugs and raped, one of the gang members, Mercedes McCambridge, is a dyke in male drag who just wants to watch. From the novel by Whit Masterson.

Prod Comp: Universal
Dist/Sales: Potential, ReelMovies, NFVLS, Universal, ACMI

Touch of Love, A

(aka: Thank you all very Much; The Millstone)

Hussein, Waris
1969; UK; 105 min; Drama
P: Max Rosenberg, Milton Subotsky; *W:* Margaret Drabble; *C:* Peter Suschitzky; *E:* Bill Blunden; *M:* Michael Dress
Cast: Sandy Dennis, Ian McKellen, Eleanor Bron, John Standing

Realistic, unsentimental British drama. Ph.D. Student Sandy Dennis decides to keep her baby despite being unmarried. The father of the child is a bisexual news reader.

Prod Comp: Columbia, Palomar-Amicus
Dist/Sales: Columbia

Touchables, The

Freeman, Robert
1968; UK; 97 min; Comedy
P: John Bryan; *W:* Ian La Frenais; *C:* Alan Pudney; *M:* Ken Thorne
Cast: Rick Starr, Ester Anderson, Judy Huxtable, Harry Baird

Set in the fabulous swinging sixties in London, *The Touchables* is the story of four gorgeous female models who kidnap a rather pretty-boy pop star and take him to a huge inflatable dome in the country. Meanwhile gangsters pursue the group and a very muscle-bound black wrestler has the hots for the young pop star. Lots of fun, very camp and psychedelic.

Prod Comp: Film Designs Ltd
Dist/Sales: ReelMovies, 20thCenturyFox, VSM

Tour Abroad

(aka: Auslandstournee)

Polat, Ayse
1999; Germany; 91 min; Drama
P: Elke Peters; *W:* Ayse Polat, Basri Polat; *C:* Martin Gressmann; *E:* Margot Neubert-Maric
Cast: Oezlem Blume, Siir Eloglu, Oezay Fecht, Martin Glade, Hilmi Soezer

Tour Abroad is a tender road movie that follows the adventures of a gay Turkish folk singer and the 11-year-old daughter of his recently deceased friend. German & Turkish with English subtitles.

Prod Comp: Mira Filmproduktion, ZDF
Dist/Sales: MiraFilm

Toward Intimacy

McGee, Debbie
1992; Canada; 61 min; Documentary
P: Nicole Hubert

A woman with a disability retains both her sexuality and her right to seek, develop and sustain a relationship with the partner of her choice. In this documentary, four disabled women from across Canada share their personal experiences and raise important issues including sexuality, self-esteem, stereotyping and parenting.

Prod Comp: National Film Board of Canada
Dist/Sales: ACMI, FilmakersLibrary

Toxic Queen

Cunningham Reid, Fiona
1997; Australia; 25 min; Documentary

In 1994 film maker Fiona Cunningham Reid recorded several hours of interviews with her friend David McDiarmid. In these intimate conversation David reflects on his life as an artist, and a sick queen 'who refuses to be bitter' in the bewildering age of AIDS.

Prod Comp: Starfish Films
Dist/Sales: Starfish

Traditional Family Vampires

Poirier, Bob
2000; USA; 17 min; Comedy

Wacky comedy about a right wing vampire family claiming victims door to door until they meet one particularly unsavoury character.

Dist/Sales: BobbyRoger

Tragedy of Samantha Biggle and the Twins, The

Himmel, Lauren
1998; USA; 32 min; Comedy

Tells the story of the friendship between Sam, a high school girl and her two new friends, twin sisters Darcie and Charlotte. The film explores several themes as it traces the relationship between the trio: ebbing sexuality, sister jealousy, socio-economic class dynamics, and the psychological setting of the nuclear family.

Dist/Sales: TunnelVision

Tragic but True

Burt, Malcolm
1996; Australia; 18 min; Comedy
P: Lori-Jay Ellis, Robyn Evans; *W:* Malcolm Burt

Take one bored raver, his dizzy sister, a macho cop and a jilted queen and what do you get? Lloyd's Heaven!

Dist/Sales: Attitude

Transanimals

Antell, Rachel / Hill, Amy / Weiner, Rebecca
2001; USA; 15 min; Comedy

Ever wondered why Kitty has been scratching and clawing more than usual? Did you happen to catch Fido sniffing around your make-up? Take an hilarious sneak-peak inside the world of transitioning pets. (MQFF)

Transeltown

Paci, Myra
1992; USA; 23 min; Drama

A morbid and tender love story that begins when a lonely girl drags home the naked body of a coma-tose, genital-less blonde woman. (Cinenova)

Transexual Menace

von Praunheim, Rosa
1995; Germany, USA; 60 min; Documentary

From one of Germany's most prolific gay filmmak-ers, a factual yet captivating documentary about the biology of the transgender process. Transgendered queers discuss the technical aspects and the com-plexities of male-to-female and female-to-male transition.

Dist/Sales: Praunheim, VDB

Transformation, The

Aparicio, Carlos / Aikin, Susan
1995; USA; 58 min; Documentary

The Transformation is a documentary that explores the changes that Ricardo, a former homeless prostitute transvestite, undergoes after discovering that he is HIV-positive and deciding that he is not going to die on the streets. In order to move out of his street life he accepts help from a group of Born Again Christians who in exchange demand his

complete transformation: that of homosexual to heterosexual. Ricardo is taken to Dallas where he tries very hard to transform himself: inside and out. During this process he becomes a Christian and ends up marrying Betty, a woman he meets through the church. Together they try to start a new life away from his past. Meanwhile the church organises a trip to New York to 'rescue' other transvestite street walkers and invites Ricardo to go along with them and preach his example. Ricardo travels to New York and meets up with his old friends Gigi and Giovanna, both of whom refuse the offer to come back with him to Dallas to be redeemed from their sexuality. They also refuse to believe in the truth of his transformation, and regard it openly as a desperate exercise in survival. Ricardo and the church committee return to Dallas empty handed. As time goes by and Ricardo is affected by the onset of AIDS-related illness, he looks back on his life and reflects that if he could choose all over again he would still want to be a woman. (Frameline)

Dist/Sales: Frameline

Transformers/AIDS

Kinney, Robert
1988; USA; 28 min; Documentary

Transformers/AIDS takes a speech by President Reagan to the American Foundation for AIDS Research in 1987 as the point of departure for a critique of conservative policies regarding the epidemic. The tape uses an assortment of lively visual juxtapositions to explore the language and representations that have been produced to shape public perceptions of the disease.

Transit: Adventures of a Boy in the Big City

Cameron, Heather
1999; Canada, Germany; 20 min; Documentary

A young Berliner reflects on how the radical changes to Berlin's architecture and flow influences the emergence of his transgenderism. Ati walks through the city and shows the locations and spaces which help shape his daily life: cruising in the Tiergarten, going shopping for suits or hardware, getting ready to dance fox-trot in Cafe Fatale, Berlin's 'queer carousel', on a Sunday night. A portrait of a thoughtful boy confronting the unfinished state of both his body and his city. (CFMDC)

Dist/Sales: CFMDC

Transsexual Journey, A

Sedghi, Behzad
1995; USA; 44 min; Documentary

Profiles Katherine Cohen (formerly Bruce Cohen)

and her decision to undergo male-to-female sex reassignment surgery. In interviews before the surgery, Cohen discusses her prior life, including a marriage and two children, relations with her family and her lifelong conflicted feelings about her sexuality. In separate interviews conducted a few weeks and a full year after the operation—illustrated in a computer animated sequence—she discusses her decision, her new life, and her hopes for the future. (Cinema Guild)

Dist/Sales: CinemaGuild

Trappings of Transhood

Hurwitz, Elise / Lee, Christopher
1997; USA; 27 min; Documentary

Fascinating and revealing documentary about the experiences of female to male transsexuals.

Dist/Sales: LeeC

Trash

Morrisey, Paul
1970; USA; 93 min; Drama
P: Andy Warhol; *W:* Paul Morrissey; *C:* Paul Morrissey;
E: Jed Johnson, Paul Morrissey
Cast: Joe Dallesandro, Holly Woodlawn, Bruce Pecheur, Geri Miller

Joe Dallessandro plays a character driven by his need for drugs which also render him sexually impotent. He has a series of encounters with characters: a young 'swinging' married couple each with a homosexual yen; a welfare worker with a shoe fetish and so on. Through this apparent episodic randomness the relationship between Joe and his girlfriend emerges as the film's central focus.

Prod Comp: Paul Morrisey, Filmfactory
Dist/Sales: NFVLS, JourDeFete

Treading Water

Himmel, Lauren
2001; USA; 95 min; Drama
P: Lauren Himmel; *W:* Julia Hollinger; *C:* Gary Henoch; *E:* Hilary Schroeder; *M:* Kristopher Carter
Cast: Angie Redman, Nina Landey

Treading Water is a touching, sincere look at the relationship between two women as they struggle to lead quiet, normal lives in a staid, conservative New England town. Living directly across the bay, Casey's family maintains a desperate unwillingness to accept her lesbian identity. It doesn't help that Casey never introduces them to Alexandra who, at one point, waits in the car during a Christmas party. Familial tensions mount as Casey's mother struggles to maintain control and keep up appearances at any cost. Himmel uses great care in avoiding stereotypes

and clichés to fashion a tender, subtle, tense and sometimes funny look at repression and the idea of family. (2002 Santa Cruz Film Festival)

Prod Comp: Tunnel Vision Productions
Dist/Sales: TunnelVision, Wolfe

Treading Water

Treasure Island

King, Scott
1999; USA; 86 min; B&W; Comedy
P: Adrienne Gruben; *W:* Scott King; *C:* Phillip Glau;
E: Dody Dorn; *M:* Chris Anderson
Cast: Lance Baker, Nick Offerman, Jonah Blechman, Pat Healy

Two World War II US Navy cryptographers write letters for a corpse in an attempt to fool the Japanese Army. But as the letters they write reveal the secrets of their lives, the body comes alive and invades their memories, their fantasies and their world. (Redeemable Features)

Prod Comp: King Pictures, Redeemable Features
Dist/Sales: KingPix

Treaty of Chance, The

(aka: Le Traité du Hasard)

Mimouni, Patrick
1998; France; 95 min; Comedy
W: Patrick Mimouni; *C:* Vicent Buron, Florent Montcouquiol, Yann Carcedo; *E:* Patrick Mimouni;
M: Ika
Cast: Eliane Pine Carringhton, Nini Crépon, Laurent Chemda, Bruni Anthony de Trigance

Blurring the gap between biography and fiction, *The Treaty of Chance* inhabits an entirely queer world, focusing on a group of friends approaching middle-age, the nature of their survival in the face of AIDS, and the complex fluidity of their relationships. Director Patrick Mimouni stars as a filmmaker (also called Patrick) who, like his oldest friend and sometime lover, Bruno, has avoided the virus. 'Dykess' Lou Rockerfeller III and the sexy young

t

Julien are not so lucky, though in metaphor that is typical of the film's humour, Julien continually mistakes AZT for Ecstasy! Littered with Firbankian bon mots ('now that everyone's dead, living has become so vulgar') and juggling a range of references—*La Maman et la Putain, La Ronde, The Boys in the Band, Carmen*—Mimouni has created a film that nevertheless avoids archness and is remarkable for its tenderness and authenticity. (1998 London Lesbian & Gay Film Festival)

French with English subtitles.

Prod Comp: CNC, Les Films du Labyrinthe, National Film Cetre
Dist/Sales: Grisé

Trembling BeforeG-d

Trembling Before G-d

DuBowski, Sandi Simcha
2000; Israel, USA; 84 min; Documentary
P: Sandi Simcha DuBowski, Marc Smolowitz; *C:* David W. Leitner; *E:* Susan Korda; *M:* John Zorn

In the midst of Western media dishing out flimsy and stereotyped portraits of religious fundamentalism in action, *Trembling Before G-d* offers an urgently needed context to the collision between monotheistic religion and western sexual mores. This award-winning documentary offers remarkably detailed insights into the experiences of Orthodox Jews who come out as lesbians and gays. Unlike in other major religions, the subject matter is seldom discussed, largely because Judaism tends to keep publicly quiet on the matter. As such Jewish lesbians and gays tend not to be vocal on their religious experiences, which makes this documentary—shot over five years in Brooklyn, Jerusalem, Los Angeles, San Francisco, Miami and London—a vital addition to any dinner party conversation. Orthodox gays and lesbians offer frank insights into their personal reconciliations with themselves, hostile families, intolerant rabbis and fringe communities. (MQFF)

Prod Comp: Simcha Leib Productions, Turbulent Arts
Dist/Sales: Cowboy, Mongrel, NewYorker

Trevor

Rajski, Peggy
1994; USA; 18 min; Comedy
P: Peggy Rajski, Randy Stone; *W:* James Lecesne; *C:* Marc Reshovsky; *E:* John Tintori; *M:* Danny Troob
Cast: Brett Barsky, Judy Kain, John Lizzi

Academy-award winning short film about a 13-year-old boy who can't decide whether to kill himself or become Diana Ross. An excellent piece, very funny and touching at the same time, which was funded in part by Jodie Foster. (MQFF)

Awards: Academy Awards, 1994: Best Live Action Short; Berlin International Film Festival, 1995: Best Short Film; San Francisco International Lesbian & Gay Film Festival, 1995: Audience Award
Dist/Sales: WaterBearer, Atom

Trey Billings Show, The

Briggs, David
1999; USA; 35 min; Comedy

David Drake stars in this celebrity talk show pastiche.

Dist/Sales: Wolfe

Treyf

Lebow, Alisa / Madansky, Cynthia
1998; USA; 54 min; Documentary
P: Alisa Lebow, Cynthia Madansky; *W:* Alisa Lebow, Cynthia Madansky

An unorthodox documentary about two Jewish lesbians who meet and fall in love at a Passover Seder. If something is 'treyf,' it's not kosher. Like, pork, say, or pickles... lesbians. With its compelling visual style and moving narrative, *Treyf* follows Alisa and Cynthia, an enlightened, socially involved, secular Jewish couple as they engage with the world they inhabit—be that Israel or New York. Let them take you to their local supermarket, and then to the Holy City; let them tell you about their lives; and let them introduce you to their 'treyf' friends.

Dist/Sales: WMM

Trials of Oscar Wilde, The

Hughes, Ken
1960; UK; 120 min; Drama
P: Harold Huth, Irving Allen, Albert R. Broccoli; *W:* Ken Hughes; *C:* Ted Moore; *E:* Geoffrey Foot; *M:* Ron Goodwin
Cast: Peter Finch, James Mason, Yvonne Mitchell, Nigel Patrick

Based on the court transcripts of the trial of the celebrated author Oscar Wilde. Produced after the 1957 Wolfenden Report that shifted homosexuality from the unmentionable to a subject of enthusiastic debate. Finch puts in a moving performance as the ill-fated writer who sued the marquess of Queensberry, his lover's father, for libel. He lost the case and was later charged with sodomy and imprisoned.

Awards: Golden Globe Awards, 1961: Best English Language Foreign Film
Prod Comp: Warwick
Dist/Sales: TLA, UA

Trevor

Triche, La

(aka: The Cheat)

Bellon, Yannick
1984; France; 101 min; Thriller
P: Denise Petitdidier; *W:* Yannick Bellon, Rémi Waterhouse; *C:* Houshang Baharlou, Dominique Le Rigoleur; *E:* Kenout Peltier; *M:* Catherine Lara
Cast: Victor Lanoux, Valérie Mairesse, Anny Duperey, Xavier Deluc, Michel Galabru

Michel is a modern police inspector: cultured, lucid, disillusioned, but has an understanding view of the world. Although he is married and has a son, he is bisexual. His whole life is on the edge of ruin when he becomes involved with Bernard, the prime suspect in a murder case. Does he protect or arrest him? French with English subtitles.

Prod Comp: Les Films de l'Equinoxe, Les Productions du Daunou
Dist/Sales: NFVLS

Trick

Fall, Jim
1999; USA; 90 min; Comedy
P: Jim Fall, Ross Katz, Eric d'Arbeloff; *W:* Jason Schafer; *C:* Terry Stacey; *E:* Brian A. Kates
Cast: Christian Campbell, John Paul Pitoc, Tori Spelling, Brad Beyer

Romantic comedy about an aspiring Broadway

composer who desires a go-go dancer from his local club. Thinking her doesn't have a chance, he is shocked to find the dancer shares his attraction. The only problem is they can't find a venue to fulfil their attraction.

Prod Comp: Good Machine, Roadside Attractions
Dist/Sales: GoodMachine, FineLine, Wolfe, 10%, Roadside

Trip, The

Swain, Miles
2001; USA; 93 min; Comedy
P: Houston King; *W:* Miles Swain; *C:* Charles Barbee, Scott Kevan; *E:* Carlo Gustaff; *M:* Steven Chesne
Cast: Larry Sullivan, Steve Braun, Alexis Arquette, Sirena Irwin, Jill St John

This romantic comedy-drama chronicles the highs and lows of an 11-year romance that began in 1973 between Alan, a straight writer and young Republican, and queer activist Tommy. The two meet through an older, closeted lawyer, Peter, while Alan is researching and writing an anti-gay book entitled *The Straight Truth*. The attraction between Alan and Tommy is immediate, although Alan convinces himself it is nothing more than friendship. Tommy pries Alan out of his closet in a whirlwind of romance, politics and polyester (it is the seventies after all). Four years later, it is Peter who has his eye on Alan and, in a bid to get his man, he orchestrates the publication of Alan's long-forgotten book. Tommy, feeling deceived and betrayed, leaves Alan and runs away to Mexico. Fast-forward to 1984: Tommy is ill and longs to see Alan again. Meanwhile, Alan is persuaded by his mother, ex-girlfriend and best friend to leave the scheming Peter and sets off to see Tommy. (2002 Toronto Lesbian & Gay Film & Video Festival)

Dist/Sales: FalconLair

Triple Echo

Apted, Michael
1973; UK; 93 min; Drama
P: Graham Cottle; *W:* Robin Chapman; *C:* John Coquillon; *E:* Barrie Vince; *M:* Marc Wilkinson
Cast: Glenda Jackson, Oliver Reed, Jenny Lee Wright, Brian Deacon, Anthony May

A young man is AWOL from the army during World War II. He runs away to the country and persuades a lonely woman to put him up. He disguises himself as a woman and pretends to be her sister. He finds that he has attracted the attention of a visiting army sergeant, who invites him to a dance. The sergeant gets a rather large shock after a bit of fondling in the back room. Based on the novel by H. E. Bates.

Prod Comp: Senta, Hemdale
Dist/Sales: Equator

t

Troika

Montgomery, Jennifer
1998; USA; 96 min; Drama
P: Jennifer Montgomery; *W:* Jennifer Montgomery;
C: Mark Serman, Horacio Marquinez, Matthew
Buckingham; *E:* Jennifer Montgomery, Lana Lin
Cast: Jenny Bass, Lev Shektman, Marina Shterenberg,
Valery Manenti

Jennifer is doubly challenged. As a professional
journalist, she's trapped on a pleasure boat with
Russian ultra-nationalist and macho pig Vladimir
Zhirinovsky, conducting an interview that turns into
a battle of wills. At home, her lesbian lover teases
and insults her relentlessly. Weaving together scenes
that present encounters with both characters,
Montgomery reveals their unlikely similarity by
employing a dispassionate style that renders each
power play all the more insidious. As a result, the
politics of personal beliefs become impossible to
imagine separately. (1998 New York Lesbian & Gay
Film Festival)

Prod Comp: Guardiez-bien

Trois

Hardy, Rob
1999; USA; 90 min; Drama
P: William Packer; *W:* Rob Hardy, Valencia Walker,
William Packer; *C:* Charles Mills; *E:* Griff Thomas;
M: Steven Gutheinz
Cast: Gretchen Palmer, Gary Dourdan, Kenya Moore

A marriage turns sour when the husband talk his
wife into a threesome with another man.

Prod Comp: Rainforest Productions, TRF Productions
Dist/Sales: Rainforest, Col-Tri

True Blue Camper

Cannon, Cairo
1996; UK; 12 min; Comedy

The filmmaker returns to the American girls' camp
of her childhood to relive old memories of togetherness in the wild. Was it all that living in tents with
natural girls and strong women leaders every
summer that made her a lesbian? Did they know?
Do they know now? Maybe they, too, are lesbians. A
hilarious journey into healthy living that produces a
few surprises. (Cinenova)

Dist/Sales: Cinenova

True Faith

Johnston, Lawrence
1988; Australia; 25 min; Drama
P: Swinburne Film and Television School

True Faith is a dramatic examination of fidelity and

relationships in the era of AIDS. At a nightclub,
Alan bumps into Stewart, a past lover who has just
recently returned to Melbourne. Stewart has been
tested as HIV-positive and his lover has recently died
as a result of AIDS. Allan decides to get tested for
AIDS. This is a delicately handled drama about a
young man coming to terms with an HIV-positive
result, and how to break the news to his partner.
(ACMI)

Dist/Sales: ACMI

True Inversions

Boschman, Lorna
1992; Canada; 24 min; Documentary

A documentary that looks at the limits and censorship of erotic images. The two actresses who are real-
life lovers discuss how much of their performance
together is real or acting. (Cinenova)

Dist/Sales: Cinenova, GroupeIntervention

True Inversions

Truth about Gay Sex, The

Clarke, Kristiene
2001; UK; 60 min; Documentary

We hear so much about gay rights, but the idea of
what gay men actually do with one another remains
something of a taboo. In this documentary, the
secrets of gay sex are unpacked and we find that
there's plenty to learn for straight girls and boys.
(World of Wonder)

Prod Comp: Channel 4
Dist/Sales: WorldOfWonder

Truth about Jane, The

Rose, Lee
2000; USA; 91 min; Drama
W: Lee Rose; *C:* Eric Van Haren Noman; *E:* Peter V.
White; *M:* Terence Blanchard
Cast: Ellen Muth, Stockard Channing, RuPaul Charles,
Kelly Rowan

Jane's mom assumes her popular daughter is just like
every other fifteen-year old girl. Then Jane meets
Taylor and falls madly in love with her. Suddenly,

everyone is trying to figure out how to cope with the realisation that Jane is a lesbian. Her classmates are having trouble treating her like a human being, and her mom refuses to have anything to do with Jane's 'experiment'. The trouble is, this is not just a phase. Jane knows she is gay. If her mom can't or won't accept that fact, their relationship could be broken forever. Based on a true story, and made for television. (Wolfe)

Prod Comp: Hearst Entertainment
Dist/Sales: Wolfe

Truth Game, The

Cole, Jeff
1990; UK; 16 min; Drama

Paul, 18, is gay and wants to tell his father the truth. They go on holiday together and with the aid of a video camera, they play the Truth Game. Back home, they have to live with the results.

Turnabout

Roach, Hal
1940; USA; 80 min; Comedy
P: Hal Roach; *W:* Mickell Novak, Berne Giler, John McLain; *C:* Norbert Brodine; *E:* Bert Jordan; *M:* Arthur Morton
Cast: Carole Landis, John Hubbard, Adolphe Menjou

A squabbling husband and wife, constantly complain about their marital roles. Through the magical powers of an Indian sculpture they change bodies. She must now cope as an advertising executive and he is left with the household chores. The leads aren't convincing, Hubbard's camped-up posturings are painful, but the supporting cast actually do bring the film to life.

Prod Comp: Hal Roach Studios Inc., United Artists
Dist/Sales: UA, Strand

Twice a Man

Markopoulos, Gregory
1963; USA; 47 min; Experimental
P: Gregory Markopoulos

This film poem by Gregory Markopoulos adopts the Greek legend of Hippolytus. Film phrases are used in clusters to mix the memories and prophecies of a young man, his mother and his male lover. Dialogue and music are used as heightening elements.

Dist/Sales: NFVLS

Twice a Woman

(aka: Twee vrouwen)

Sluizer, George
1979; The Netherlands; 90 min; Drama

P: Anne Lordon, George Sluizer; *W:* George Sluizer, Jurriën Rood; *C:* Mat van Hensbergen; *E:* Leo De Boer; *M:* Willem Breuker
Cast: Bibi Andersson, Sandra Dumas, Anthony Perkins

A middle-aged woman, Laura, picks up a younger woman, Sylvia, and they begin an affair. After Sylvia moves in, their relationship begins to deteriorate, mainly due to the difference in their age and social status. Then Sylvia meets Laura's ex-husband and they begin an affair resulting in a web of passion and deceit. A fairly awful film, but may yet fall into the realm of cult status.

Prod Comp: MGS Film
Dist/Sales: Netherlands

Twilight Girls, The

Hunebelle, Andre
1961; 83 min; B&W; Drama

Seeking to escape a family scandal, a young woman enters an exclusive boarding school for girls, and is immediately absorbed into a clique of attractive and wealthy young vixens. (First Run Features)

Dist/Sales: FirstRunFeatures

Twilight of the Gods

Main, Stewart
1995; New Zealand; 15 min; Drama
P: Michele Fantl; *W:* Stewart Main; *C:* Simon Raby; *M:* David Coulson
Cast: Greg Mayaor, Marton Csokas, Joel Lund, Adam Cohen, Craig Jenkins

An explosive clash of two cultures occurs when two men meet. One is a Maori warrior, the other, a European soldier. Set in the lush rainforest of New Zealand the Maori nurses the wounded soldier back to health, and the two become lovers. But their idyllic and innocent existence is devastated by the invasion of the outside world. Maori with English subtitles.

Prod Comp: Zee Films
Dist/Sales: NZFC, FirstRunFeatures

Twilight of the Golds, The

Marks, Ross
1997; USA; 92 min; Drama
P: Paul Colichman, John Davimos, Mark R. Harris; *W:* Jonathan Tolins, Seth Bass; *C:* Tom Richmond; *E:* Dana Congdon; *M:* Lee Holdridge
Cast: Brendan Fraser, Jennifer Beals, Garry Marshall, Faye Dunaway, Jon Tenney

Following a genetic analysis, pregnant Suzanne Stein discovers that her unborn child will more than likely be born gay, like her brother David. A family crisis

t

ensues while she decides whether to keep the baby, or have an abortion.

Prod Comp: Regent Entertainment
Dist/Sales: Wolfe, Showtime

Twin Bracelets

(aka: Shuang Cho)

Huang Yu, Shan
1992; Hong Kong, Taiwan; 100 min; Drama
Cast: Chen Te Jung, Liu Hsiao Hui

> The story of one young woman's fight against oppression and patriarchy in a small Chinese fishing village, and her efforts to capture the heart of the woman she loves. Hui-hua is desperately in love with Hsiu, her childhood friend, and jealous of her arranged marriage which Hsiu finally manages to leave. Hui-hua begs her to fulfil their childhood vow to live and die together. Mandarin with English subtitles.

Awards: San Francisco International Lesbian & Gay Film Festival, 1992: Audience Award for Best Feature
Dist/Sales: RimFilm

Twin Cheeks: Who Killed the Homecoming King?

Wild, Osker
1995; USA; 60 min; Comedy

> Queer spoof of the US television series *Twin Peaks*.

Twinkle

(aka: Kira Kira Hikaru)

Matusoka, Joji
1992; Japan; 103 min; Drama, Comedy
Cast: Hioko Yakushimaru, Etsushi Toyokawa, Michitaka Tsutsui

> Comedy drama about Matsuki, a handsome gay doctor, and Shoko, a translator with a drinking problem. When their parents arrange their marriage, Matsuki's boyfriend Kon becomes jealous and tensions rise. The sparks fly as both families find out the secrets kept by their in-laws, while meanwhile Shoko experiences a sense of failure at not being able to keep her husband happy. This film is a brave look at the difficulties of gay life in Japan. (MQFF) Japanese with English subtitles.

Dist/Sales: HeraldAce

Twinkle Toes

Milton, Keith
1999; USA; 15 min; Comedy
P: Keith Milton; *W:* Keith Milton

> Black comedy about a suicidal man who's recently

been rejected at yet another dance audition and can't take it any more. Just in time, he meets a cop, with a similar interest in dance—and a secret.

Twins of Evil

(aka: The Gemini Twins)

Hough, John
1971; UK; 87 min; Horror
P: Harry Fine, Michael Style; *W:* Tudor Gates;
C: Dick Bush; *E:* Spencer Reeve; *M:* Harry Robinson
Cast: Madeleine Collinson, Mary Collinson, Peter Cushing, Dennis Price, Kathleen Byron

> Identical Austrian twins, played by real-life twins and *Playboy* playmates Madeleine and Mary Collinson, become devotees of a vampire cult. With some mild lesbianism, they feed from their women prey by not only biting on the neck but on the breast as well. Made as a follow-up to *Vampire Lovers*, but doesn't quite keep up the tradition.

Prod Comp: Hammer, Rank Organisation
Dist/Sales: Rank, Universal

Twisted

Donsky, Seth Michael
1996; USA; 86 min; Comedy
P: Adrian Agramonte, Seth Michael Donsky; *W:* Seth Michael Donsky; *C:* Hernan Toro; *E:* Seth Michael Donsky, Tom McArdle
Cast: Ray Aranha, Elise Ballard, Keivyn McNeill Graves, Billy Porter, William Hickey

> Based on Charles Dickens' *Oliver Twist*, this dark near-millennium fable set in New York City follows the travails of Lee, a 10-year-old African American runaway. Unwittingly taken in by Andre, a lecherous brothel owner played with devious delight by William Hickey, Lee quickly becomes immersed in a dangerous underworld of prostitution and drugs. Angel befriends Lee and rescues him from the evil lords of this apocalyptic subculture. (Water Bearer Films)

Prod Comp: Miravista Films; *Dist/Sales:* WaterBearer

Twisted Sheets

Deacon, Chris
1996; Canada; 14 min; Experimental

> When Sue dashes to the store in her nightgown, she doesn't count on running into her ex-boyfriend and his decidedly beautiful new girlfriend. On a whim, disillusioned Sue accompanies gal pal Shelley to a lesbian bar and runs into.... Worlds collide and retribution is sweet in this 1990s take on the classic love triangle. (CFMDC)

Dist/Sales: CFMDC

Two Brides and a Scalpel: Diary of a Lesbian Marriage

Achbar, Mark
1999; Canada; 60 min; Documentary
P: Mark Achbar, Jennifer Abbott; C: Georgina Scott, Linda Fraser; E: Mark Achbar, Jennifer Abbott; M: Doug Blackley

Video diary documentary by Mark Achbar (*Manufacturing Consent*) which follows two years in the lives of transsexual Georgie, and Linda, the woman Georgie falls in love with, and eventually marries. Follows their battles at work and with their own families.

Two Brothers

Bell, Richard
2000; Canada; 60 min; Drama
P: Richard Bell; W: Richard Bell; C: Richard Bell; E: Dennis Tal; M: Paul Moniz de Sa
Cast: Norbet Orlewicz, Cody Campbell, Karen Rae, Kevin MacDonald

After the death of his mother Riley, a gay man, moves back to the West End to live with his older brother Chad. Chad is unemployed and only concerned with how much money is left in his mother's estate. Chad's girlfriend Tobie befriends Riley and introduces him to Gavin. Riley and Gavin soon fall for each other but their happiness is only short lived. Chad's tormented internal world explodes as he's left trying to make sense of his abusive upbringing and the patterns he is doomed to repeat.

Prod Comp: BellMovies
Dist/Sales: BellMovies, TLA

Two Girls and a Baby

Simpson, Kelli
1997; Australia; 27 min; Comedy
P: Penny Robins; W: Kelli Simpson

Catherine and Liz want to have a baby. Well, Catherine does, but Liz is not sure. A baby will change everything. Doesn't Catherine realise that? No, she's too busy on the phone to the sperm bank.

Prod Comp: Annamax Films
Dist/Sales: NFVLS, PictureThis!, ACMI, Atom

Two in Twenty

Chiten, Laurel / McCollum, Rachel / Qamar, Cheryl
1988; USA; 160 min; Drama

Consists of five humorous and dramatic episodes of the amusing and entertaining lesbian soap opera, which was called Two in Twenty because it sounds more fun than 'one in ten'. It has all the elements of any good soap (including poor production quality and some hilarious ads for fictional products)—the only difference is they're all dykes. Now a cult classic on the home video market.

Dist/Sales: Wolfe

Two in Twenty

Two Men

Cole, Jeff
1989; UK; 13 min; Drama

An English lad on holiday in Portugal finds good company with a hot-bodied Portuguese gent, who is seen lying naked on the beach. A spirited holiday romance ensues. Back in London distance and language difficulties show the inadequacy of a postcard relationship.

Two Moon Junction

King, Zalman
1988; USA; 104 min; Drama
P: Donald P. Borchers; W: Zalman King; C: Mark Plummer; E: Marc Grossman; M: Jonathan Elias
Cast: Sherilyn Fenn, Richard Tyson, Louise Fletcher, Kristy McNichol, Burl Ives

Despite her approaching marriage, a rich Southern belle, April, begins an affair with a handsome carnival worker, Perry. Her grandmother and the local sheriff get together to stop the union. April has the choice between privilege and passion. McNichol has a cameo as a likeable and perky bisexual cowgirl.

Prod Comp: Lorimar, DDM Film Corporation
Dist/Sales: Roadshow, ReelMovies

Two of Us
(aka: Mates)

Tonge, Roger
1987; UK; 75 min; Drama
P: Roger Tonge; W: Leslie Stewart; C: Andrew Dunn; E: Peter Barber, Caius Julyan; M: David Chilton, Nicholas Russell-Pavier

Cast: Jason Rush, Lee Whitlock, Judy Gridley, John Judd, Jenny Jay

The dramatic coming out story of two young working class teenage boys Phil and Matthew, who fall in love but runaway to the seaside because of pressure from their families and friends. A scene in the locker room of a swimming pool where the two boys kiss was cut from the original release. Made for television.

Prod Comp: BBC TV
Dist/Sales: TLA

Two or Three Things I Know about Them

Mak, Anson
1991; Hong Kong; 39 min; Experimental
Cast: Kim-fai Yum

A four-part experimental film looking at the issues that concern the newly emerging lesbian community in Hong Kong. It also profiles the lesbian opera star Yum Kim-fai who performs in male drag. Cantonese with English subtitles.

Two Point Five

Sirota, Greg
1999; USA; 12 min; Comedy

David is planning to conceive a child with a female friend. Only problem is he hasn't told his lover Carl yet.

Dist/Sales: FallingDoor

Two Roads

Gebhardt, Amy
1998; Australia; 11 min; Comedy

Two Roads follows the path of friendship, love and growing up in a small country town. Over just one night the relationship between three school friends can change forever.

Uh-Oh!

Zando, Julie
1993; USA; 38 min; Experimental
P: Josephine Anstey; *W:* Julie Zando
Cast: Emanuela Villorini, Eileen Myles

Zando retells The Story of O within and against a contemporary love story, employing an all-female cast of 'cowboys' in romantically-staged S/M rituals in the basement of a diner.

Dist/Sales: Drift, VDB, EAI

Unconditional Love

Hogan, P. J.
2002; USA; 121 min; Drama
W: P. J. Hogan, Jocelyn Moorhouse

Cast: Kathy Bates, Rupert Everett, Jonathan Pryce, Dan Ackroyd

A middle-aged housewife and a gay British valet are thrown together after the death of his long-time lover, who happens to be her favourite singer.

Prod Comp: New Line Cinema

Uncut

Greyson, John
1997; Canada; 90 min; Drama
P: John Greyson; *W:* John Greyson; *C:* Kim Derko; *E:* Dennis Day; *M:* Andrew Zealley
Cast: Michael Achtman, Matthew Ferguson, Damon D'Oliveira, Maria Reidstra

A typist, Peter, is obsessed with Pierre Trudeau. A student, Peter, is perplexed by circumcision. A Jackson Five fan, Peter, wants to break into broadcast. They meet, make love and make art in this Kafkaesque fable by John Greyson. (Millivres)

Prod Comp: Grey Zone
Dist/Sales: TurbulentArts, Millivres, Domino, ACMI

Under Heat

Reed, Peter
1994; USA; 92 min; Drama
P: Denise Kasell, Frances M. Mordock, Peter Reed; *W:* Peter Reed, Michael David Brown; *C:* Manfred Reiff; *E:* Irene Kassow; *M:* Elizabeth Swados
Cast: Lee Grant, Eric Swanson, Robert Knepper, David Conrad

A stylish contemporary feature set on a leafy upstate ranch. Hunky Eric Swanson plays Dean, who returns home to break the news that he's gay and has AIDS. Events intervene and family problems emerge from every handy closet. The coming-out scene is up there with the funniest of family outings. Eric and Simon, the stable-hand, do a great roll in the hay. Dean, his older brother and his mother are a vulnerable trio, seemingly bent on self-destruction. Dean's mellow journey to despair to a commitment to the here and now is both believable and gratifying. (MQFF)

Prod Comp: Furious Films
Dist/Sales: PictureThis!, 21stCentury, Wolfe

Undercover

Stevens, David
1983; Australia; 88 min; Drama
P: David Elfick; *W:* Miranda Downes; *C:* Dean Semler; *E:* Tim Wellburn; *M:* Bruce Smeaton
Cast: Genevieve Picot, John Walton, Michael Pare

Set in the 1920s, the story of a girl's rise within the international Berlei underwear company, founded by Australian Fred Berlei. The film deals sensitively with historical material, without stooping to glamorise an industry that has dominated women's perceptions of their bodies for over one hundred years. The secretary at Berlei is a gay man, and lead designer is a lesbian.

Prod Comp: Palm Beach Pictures, Filmco
Dist/Sales: Roadshow, ACMI

Union in Wait, A

Butler, Ryan
2001; USA; 28 min; Documentary

Susan Parker and Wendy Scott were members of the Wake Forest Baptist Church in North Carolina. In 1997 the couple decided to have a union ceremony in Wake Forest University's Chapel, but the university prevented this from happening. *A Union in Wait* recounts the struggle of Parker and Scott to have their union recognised and the controversy that divided a community. (Frameline)

Dist/Sales: Frameline

Unknown Friend

Unknown Cyclist, The

Salzman, Bernard
1997; USA; 96 min; Drama
P: Matthew Carlisle, Betsy Pool; *W:* Matthew Carlisle, Howie Skora, Betsy Pool; *C:* Bernard Salzmann;
E: Irit Raz; *M:* Sydney Forest
Cast: Vincent Spano, Stephen Spinella, Danny Nucci, Lea Thompson

Christopher Cavetelli's dying wish was for the four

most important people in his life to join together for the 450 mile West Coast Cycle for AIDS. When his homophobic identical twin brother Frank, a New York cop, arrives in Hollywood for Chris's funeral, he finds that he must make the ride with Chris's lover Doug, ex-wife Melissa, and slacker best friend Gaetano. The gruelling five-day bike ride down the spectacular California coast tests the foursome to their limits. Untrained for the physical exertion and unprepared for the emotional journey, the four riders must navigate the geography of the land and of their own fears and desires. As humour gives way to anger and phobia to understanding, the four come to terms not only with their differences, but also with their loss. Ultimately, each of them realises that personal transformation was the final destination Chris intended for them, and that his spirit will bind them all together for the rest of their lives. (22nd San Francisco International Lesbian & Gay Film Festival)

Prod Comp: Watermark Films
Dist/Sales: Trident

Unknown Friend

(aka: Fremde Freundin)

Krohn, Anne Høegh
1999; Germany; 83 min; Drama
P: Sigrid Hoerner, Anne Leppin, Martin Walz; *W:* Anne Høegh Krohn; *C:* Sebastian Edschmid; *M:* Bernd Jestram, Ronald Lippok
Cast: Inga Busch, Karoline Eichhorn, Birol Uenel

Unknown Friend is an intensely atmospheric thriller set in Berlin in which Ellen, newly released from five years in prison, tries to find out the truth about what happened the night she was arrested. To do that she seeks out her best friend, the beautiful Katrin, who was present on the night of the crime. Katrin initially wants nothing to do with her old friend, but is soon won over by Ellen's persistence. Flashbacks fill in their shared past, including Katrin's relation-ship with her husband, and makes evident Ellen's love for her friend. But what exactly did happen that night? Anne Høegh Krohn's feature debut is a sexy and taut psychological drama guaranteed to keep audiences on the edge of their seat up through the last minute. (2002 New York Lesbian & Gay Film Festival)

Prod Comp: Moneypenny Films, ZDF
Dist/Sales: Moneypenny

Up!

Meyer, Russ
1976; USA; 72 min; Comedy
P: Russ Meyer; *W:* Reinhold Timme, Russ Meyer, Jim Ryan; *C:* Russ Meyer; *E:* Russ Meyer; *M:* Paul Ruhland,

William Loose

Cast: Robert McLane, Edward Schaaf, Elaine Collins, Su Ling

Piranhas in the bath, multiple rapes, lesbians, homosexuals, voluptuous barmaids and martial arts action can all be found in this Redwood Country whodunit. Lots of fun and as with all Russ Meyer films, never to be taken seriously.

Prod Comp: RHM
Dist/Sales: Ascanbee

Up the Academy

Downey Snr, Robert
1980; USA; 84 min; Comedy
P: Marvin Worth, Danton Rissner; *W:* Jay Tarses, Tom Patchett; *C:* Harry Stradling; *E:* Bud Molin, Ron Spang
Cast: Ralph Macchio, Wendall Brown, Tommy Citera, J. Hutchison

Four freshmen attending a military academy wreak havoc with an endless series of wild pranks. Look out for the gay dance teacher. The soundtrack features the music of Pat Benatar, The Kinks, Blondie and Cheap Trick.

Prod Comp: Warner; *Dist/Sales:* Warner

Urbania

Urbania

Shear, Jon
1999; USA; 103 min; Drama
W: Daniel Reitz, Jon Shear; *C:* Shane F. Kelly; *M:* Marc Anthony Thompson
Cast: Dan Futterman, Alan Cumming, Matt Keeslar, Josh Hamilton

Charlie is a lonely gay man who yearns for his lost boyfriend Chris. He stumbles through New York City looking for a mysterious stranger who he believes holds the key to his existence. He seems to be living out a series of creepy urban legends—or is Charlie making up this whole story? (Wolfe)

Dist/Sales: Blackwatch, Wolfe, 10%

Urinal

(aka: Pissoir)

Greyson, John
1988; Canada; 100 min; Comedy
P: John Greyson; *W:* John Greyson; *C:* Adam Swica; *M:* Glenn Schellenberg
Cast: Lance Eng, Pauline Carey, Paul Bettis, Keltie Creed

A group of famous dead gay and lesbian artists, including Langston Hughes, Frida Kahlo and Mishima, have been transported to modern-day Toronto to the garden of two dead sculptors. They talk about the attraction of public-toilet sex. Their purpose is to research the policing of toilet sex in Ontario and propose solutions to this serious crisis for the gay community. An irreverent and hilarious film, made in a surrealist style.

Awards: Berlin Film Festival, 1989: Best Feature Film
Prod Comp: Greyson Productions
Dist/Sales: Frameline, CinemaLibre, WaterBearer

Valentine's Day

Hoolboom, Mike
1994; Canada; 80 min; B&W; Sci-Fi
P: Mike Hoolboom; *W:* Mike Hoolboom; *C:* Steven Sanguedolce; *E:* Mike Hoolboom; *M:* Earle Peach
Cast: Babs Chula, Gabrielle Rose

In the near future, Canada is at war with Quebec, battles are determined by television ratings, and weapons are sponsored by McDonalds and IBM. In the midst of social chaos, a lesbian couple, Barb and Alex, dress themselves in protective masks, gowns and rubber boots to spend a quiet afternoon at the zoo. Barb is gang-raped by soldiers while taking a short cut through a restrictive zone. Fearful of infection, Alex begs her to take an AIDS test. With a world imploding around them, Barb decides to announce her result as the punch line of a comic routine. At first, Alex can't see the joke, but she eventually joins in and engineers an attempt to make love without touching.

Valentine's Day

Valentino

Russell, Ken
1977; UK; 132 min; Drama
P: Irwin Winkler, Robert Chartoff; *W:* John Byrum;
C: Peter Suschitzky; *E:* Stuart Baird; *M:* Stanley Black,
Ferdinand Grofe
Cast: Rudolf Nureyev, Leslie Caron, David De Keyser,
Seymour Cassel

Beginning with his death and using flashbacks to his
early days in the US, Valentino tells the story of one
of the screen's greatest legends. Selective facts and
historical settings are used in an attempt to isolate
the real nature of the adulation of Valentino. The
film works well in the first half but becomes
disjointed towards the end. A film that views the
legend with humour and pathos. Rudolf Nureyev's
debut film role.

Prod Comp: United Artists, Aperture Films, Chartoff-
Winkler Productions
Dist/Sales: Ascanbee, ReelMovies, UA

Vampire Lovers, The

Baker, Roy Ward
1970; UK; 88 min; Horror
P: Harry Fine, Michael Style; *W:* Tudor Gates, Harry
Fine, Michael Style; *C:* Moray Grant; *E:* James Needs;
M: Harry Robinson
Cast: Ingrid Pitt, Pippa Steele, Peter Cushing, George
Cole, Douglas Wilmer

Hammer's chiller about lesbian vampires adapted
from Sheridan Le Fanu's *Carmilla*. Our luscious
vampire enjoys sinking her teeth into the bosoms of
beautiful young women. An enjoyable film,
sprinkled with humour, made Ingrid Pitt a major
horror cult figure.

Prod Comp: Hammer, American International Pictures
Dist/Sales: Ascanbee, MGM, OrionHV, ACMI

Vampire Nue, La

(aka: The Naked Vampire)

Rollin, Jean
1969; France; 82 min; Horror
P: Jean Rollin, Jean Lavie; *W:* Jean Rollin, S. H. Mosti;
C: Jean-Jacques Renon; *M:* Yvon Serault
Cast: Oliver Martin, Maurice Lemaitre, Caroline
Cartier, Bernard Musson

With a convoluted story-line mixing elements of
horror and science fiction, this film chronicles the
obsession of a guilty Catholic voyeur, wallowing in
perversion and sin. Our hero gets involved with a
young woman and soon finds himself mixed up with
a suicide cult, an old castle infested with vampires
and women wearing spikes on their nipples. It is the
second vampire offering from Rollin. Dubbed into
English.

Prod Comp: Les Films, ABC; *Dist/Sales:* Siren

Vampyres, Daughters of Dracula

Vampyres, Daughters of Dracula

(aka: Blood Hunger)

Larraz, José Ramón (aka: Larraz, Joseph)
1974; UK; 86 min; Horror
P: Brian Smedley-Aston; *W:* Diana Daubeney; *C:* Harry
Waxman; *E:* Geoff R. Brown; *M:* James Clarke
Cast: Marianne Morris, Anulka Dziubinska, Murray
Brown, Brian Deacon

An explicit male fantasy film where women are seen
both as objects of terror and desirable. Two beautiful
lesbian vampires living in a decaying mansion lure
men there for lust and blood. One of the women,
however, falls madly in love with her victim. He
decides to stay and gradually gets weaker and weaker,
but finally is saved by the dawn.

Prod Comp: Essay Films, Lurco Films

Vampyros Lesbos

(aka: Lesbian Vampires; Die Erbin des Dracula)

Manera, Franco (Franco, Jesus)
1970; Germany, Spain; 90 min; Horror
P: Arturo Marcos; *W:* Franco Manera, Jaime Chávarri;
C: Manuel Marino; *E:* Clarissa Ambach; *M:* David
Khune, Manfred Hubler, Siegfried Schwab
Cast: Susan Korda, Dennis Price, Ewa Stroemberg,
Andrés Monales, Paul Mueller

Nadina is the beautiful descendant of Count
Dracula. She lives on an isolated island to which she
entices young women, where she does what she
wants to them in order to maintain her youth. There
were two versions released, the Spanish one was a

little more tame than the German, which included salacious scenes of lesbianism and bloodsucking.

Prod Comp: Fenix Films, CCC Telecine

Vanished

Kulik, Buzz
1971; USA; 240 min; Drama
W: Dean Riesner; *C:* Lionel Lindon; *E:* Robert Watts;
M: Leonard Rosenman
Cast: Richard Widmark, Tom Bosley, Skye Aubrey,
Larry Hagman, James Farentino

A presidential adviser disappears in mysterious circumstances. The FBI has information that says he was a homosexual; why won't the President make a statement? Made for television and based on Fletcher Knebel's best-selling novel.

Prod Comp: Universal TV
Dist/Sales: NBC

Vaudeville

Sachs, Ira
1990; USA; 55 min; Drama

The events of one relatively typical performance night document the complex interrelationships of a group of wandering entertainers. Events unfold around Charlie Guidance, the mischievous and provocative cast member who seduces the manager's boyfriend. He infuriates the neurotic star singer, and plays off just about everyone else.

Vegas in Space

Ford, Phillip R.
1991; USA; 85 min; Comedy
P: Phillip R. Ford; *W:* Doris Fish, Miss X, Phillip R.
Ford; *C:* Robin Clarke; *E:* Ed Jones;
M: Joshua Raoul Brody
Cast: Doris Fish, Miss X, Ginger Quest, Romona
Fischer

The four-man crew of the USS Intercourse races on a secret mission to the planet Clitoris, a twenty-third century all-female pleasure planet where men are forbidden to touch down. Ordered by the Empress of Earth to swallow gender-reversal pills, the spacemen swap their sex to go undercover as 20th century showgirls and are propelled into a dizzying caper to capture the perpetrator of a heinous crime that has hurled the orbiting resort on its path to doom.

Prod Comp: Troma Films
Dist/Sales: Troma

Velocity of Gary, The

Ireland, Dan
1998; USA; 102 min; Drama
P: Dan Lupovitz; *W:* James Still; *C:* Claudio Rocha;
E: Luis Colina, Debra Goldfield; *M:* Peitor Angell
Cast: Vincent D'Onofrio, Salma Hayek, Thomas Jane,
Ethan Hawke

A hard-edged love fable set among the hustlers, trannies and homeless of New York City. It tells the tale of the strained love triangle between a charismatic bisexual, a male prostitute and a tempestuous Latina. The sultry but annoyingly whinny Hayek stars as Mary Carmen, a hot-tempered beauty desperately in love with Valentino, a small-time porn actor with big-time attitude. Things change when Gary, a sensitive rookie male prostitute, also falls in love with the magnetic, longhaired Valentino. Mary Carmen and Gary take a jealous dislike for each other as they battle for Valentino's affections. But when Valentino becomes ill with AIDS, the two, in a fight to be his caretaker, are forced to look at themselves less as rivals and more as family. (Wolfe)

Prod Comp: Cineville Inc, Columbia TriStar
Dist/Sales: Col-Tri, Wolfe

Velvet Goldmine

Haynes, Todd
1998; UK, USA; 125 min; Comedy
P: Christine Vachon; *W:* Todd Haynes; *C:* Maryse
Alberti; *E:* James Lyons; *M:* Carter Burwell
Cast: Jonathan Rhys-Meyers, Ewan McGregor, Christian Bale, Toni Collette

It's 1971. Bisexual rockstar Brian Slade has grown to hate the glamrock role model status he has created for himself, and so plots to have himself murdered. When his fans discover that the murder was faked, his career takes a dive. The action fast forwards to 1984 when a journalist for a New York newspaper begins to investigate what has become of the faded rock star.

Prod Comp: Channel 4, Miramax, Goldwyn Films
Dist/Sales: Miramax, Lauren, ACMI

Velvet Vampire, The

(aka: The Waking Hour)

Rothman, Stephanie
1971; USA; 80 min; Horror
P: Charles S. Swartz; *W:* Stephanie Rothman, Charles S.
Swartz, Maurice Jules; *C:* Daniel Lacambre; *E:* Stephen
Judson, Barry Simon; *M:* Roger Dollarhide, Clancy B.
Grass III

Cast: Sherry Miles, Michael Blodgett, Celeste Yarnall, Gene Shane

> Another female vampire film, in which a vampire invites a young married couple to stay at her home in the Californian desert. She attempts to vampirise the young man but, in the meantime, Miles is bitten by a snake and the vampire sucks out the venom saving her life. Yarnall finally kills the man and, after finding his body, the young woman flees to Los Angeles hotly pursued by the vampire. There is a definite attraction between the two women and the film has been described as having a strong feminist slant. It is an interesting film from one of the very few female directors of horror.

Prod Comp: New World Pictures

Vendetta

Logan, Bruce
1985; USA; 86 min; Drama, Action
P: Jeff Begun, Ken Dalton, Ken Solomon, Sidney D. Balkin; *W:* Laura Cavestani, Emil Farkas, Simon Maskell, John K. Adams; *C:* Robert New; *E:* Glenn Morgan; *M:* David Newman
Cast: Karen Chase, Sandy Martin, Roberta Collins

> A young woman kills a man who attempts to rape her, and ends up in prison for manslaughter, only to be brutally murdered by a lesbian prison gang leader. The authorities return a verdict of suicide and the case is quickly forgotten, except by Laurie, the dead girl's sister who commits a crime to get herself in to the prison to exact revenge on her sister's murderer.

Prod Comp: Chroma III, International Cinevision Productions

Venus Boyz

Baur, Gabriel
2001; Germany, Switzerland, USA; 104 min; Documentary
W: Gabriel Baur; *C:* Sophie Maintigneux; *E:* Jean Vites, Daniela Roderer, Salome Pitschen; *M:* David Shiller

> Documentary which focuses on drag kings, female masculinity, and gender performance in New York City and London, featuring a star-studded cast of local celebrities including Dréd Gerestant, Storme Webber, Diane Torr, and Mo Fischer, among others. Director Gabriel Bauer follows a wide range of subjects, finding out about their personalities, the male characters they've created, and their perceptions of gender and performance. Why do these women perform as men? How does it feel taking on a male persona? Bauer also expands the scope of the documentary by talking to FTMs like Hans Scheirl and Svar Simpson, and intersexed persons like Del

LaGrace Volcano, and explores their transformations through male hormones. (2002 New York Lesbian & Gay Film Festival)
English & German with English subtitles.

Prod Comp: ONIX Filmproduktion GmbH

Vera

Toledo, Sergio
1986; Brazil; 87 min; Drama
W: Sergio Toledo
Cast: Ana Beatriz Nogueria

> A young woman leaves a boarding school for girls. She finds she is attracted to women but cannot see that she may be a lesbian, so she begins to adopt a male persona. Portuguese with English subtitles.

Prod Comp: Embrafilme, Grange
Dist/Sales: Kino

Veronica 4 Rose

Chait, Melanie
1983; UK; 48 min; Documentary

> This warm and engaging film explores the ups and downs of being a lesbian in a predominantly heterosexual and homophobic society. Young women between the ages of 16 and 23 speak openly about their experiences of coming out, many of them recall how they were told by their friends and family that it was 'only a phase'. (Cinenova)

Dist/Sales: Cinenova

Very Funny

Zachary, Bohdan
1994; USA; 16 min; Comedy

> This San Francisco 'comedy competition' takes a bleak and bitter look at homophobia in America as six stand-up acts satirise and leave us speechless.

Dist/Sales: Zachary

Very Natural Thing, A

Larkin, Christopher
1973; USA; 80 min; Drama
P: Christopher Larkin; *W:* Joseph Coencas, Christopher Larkin; *C:* C. H. Douglass; *E:* Terry Manning; *M:* Gordon Gottlieb, Bert Lucarelli
Cast: Curt Gareth, Robert Joel, Bo White

> A young man leaves the priesthood and moves to New York City in the hope of finding a meaningful gay relationship, and very quickly falls in love with a young advertising executive. Considered an important film in gay culture as it was the first feature film made by an openly gay man about gay

issues to get a commercial release in America.

Prod Comp: Montage Creations
Dist/Sales: NewLine, WaterBearer

Via Appia

Via Appia

Hick, Jochen
1993; Germany; 90 min; Drama
P: Norbert Friedlander; *W:* Jochen Hick; *C:* Peter
Christian Neumann; *E:* Claudia Vogeler; *M:* Charly
Schoppner
Cast: Peter Senner, Guilherme de Pádua, Margaret
Schmidt, Yves Jansen

A young German flight attendant in Rio has a one
night stand with a street hustler. The next morning
he finds a message on the bathroom mirror,
'Welcome to the AIDS club'. When the disease
becomes evident he returns to Brazil with a film
crew in order to find the young hustler. Along the
way he interviews male prostitutes and lowlifes.
German with English subtitles.

Prod Comp: Friedlander Filmproduction
Dist/Sales: TLA, Strand, Wolfe

Vicious

B., Hima
1999; USA; 20 min; Documentary

Queer women discuss their experiences of violence
in relationships. The documentary footage is
blended with nonfictional testimonies.

Dist/Sales: Himaphiliac

Victim

Dearden, Basil
1961; UK; 100 min; B&W; Drama
P: Michael Relph; *W:* Janet Green, John McCormick;
C: Otto Heller; *E:* John D. Guthridge; *M:* Philip Green
Cast: Dirk Bogarde, Sylvia Sims, Dennis Price, Norman
Bird, Anthony Nicholls

A restrained dramatisation of the problems created
by the criminalisation of homosexual acts between
consenting adults. Bogarde gives one of his finest
performances as a successful barrister who places his
career on the line by coming out in order to expose a
blackmail racket. This was the first British film to
centre its narrative on male homosexuality and was
made with the specific intention of supporting the
new recommendations of the 1957 Wolfenden
Committee for the partial decriminalisation of male
homosexual acts.

Prod Comp: Allied Filmmakers, Parkway, Rank
Organisation
Dist/Sales: NFVLS, Carlton

Victor/Victoria

Edwards, Blake
1982; UK; 129 min; Comedy
P: Tony Adams, Blake Edwards; *W:* Blake Edwards,
Hans Hoemburg; *C:* Dick Bush; *E:* Ralph E. Winters;
M: Henry Mancini, Leslie Bricusse
Cast: Julie Andrews, James Garner, Robert Preston,
Lesley Anne Warren, Alex Karras

Comic farce about gender confusions, in which a
female singer in 1934 Paris becomes successful when
she poses as a female impersonator. Robert Preston
plays her gay friend and confidante and is great in
the role, but again the gay character is just the
harmless friend of a woman.

Prod Comp: MGM, United Artists
Dist/Sales: UIP, Ascanbee, Warner, MGM, Swank

Video 28

1988; UK; 20 min; Documentary

A celebration and record of the fight against Section
28 of the Local Government Act. A focus for
campaigning and inspiration to action. (Cinenova)

Prod Comp: Vera Productions
Dist/Sales: Cinenova

Viktor/Viktoria

Schünzel, Reinhold
1933; Germany; 101 min; B&W; Comedy
W: Reinhold Schünzel; *C:* Konstantin Irmen-Tschet;
M: Franz Doelle
Cast: Hermann Thimig, Renate Müeller, Hilde
Hildebrand, Fritz Odemar

Viktor is a drag queen who persuades a young singer,
Susanne, to perform as a male female impersonator.
She becomes an instant success and they begin a tour
of Europe with a series of sexual escapades. The
inspiration for Blake Edwards's *Victor/Victoria*.

Village Affair, A

Armstrong, Moira
1994; UK; 108 min; Drama
P: Jane Wellesley; *W:* Alma Cullen
Cast: Sophie Ward, Kerry Fox, Nathaniel Parker, Claire Bloom, Michael Gough

In this beautifully crafted and sexy melodrama, Alice is a lovely young wife and mother of three who moves with her lawyer husband Martin to a dream house in an English country village. Martin's roving eye is quickly captured by Clodagh, the wild daughter of the wealthy neighbours, but Clodagh is interested only in Alice. The two women develop a close friendship that deepens into a passionate affair. Shy, unhappy Alice gradually learns to put her own needs on par with those of her family and to stand up to her domineering mother-in-law. But Martin's jealous older brother Anthony spitefully exposes the two women's affair, throwing their families—and the entire village—into an uproar. The love scenes, in which the emotionally reserved Alice's sense of propriety is swept away in a torrent of self-revelation and pent-up longings, are exciting and sensuous. *A Village Affair* offers more than a simple romance. Its combination of high production values and remarkably nuanced performances and writing offers a powerful portrait of a community struggling to come to terms with homosexuality in its midst. (22nd San Francisco International Lesbian & Gay Film Festival)

Prod Comp: Warner Sisters, Carlton

Village Voices

Clarke, Kristiene
1997; UK; 52 min; Documentary

Chronicles the development of a queer enclave in Manchester UK.

Villain

Tuchner, Michael
1971; UK; 98 min; Thriller
P: Alan Ladd Jnr, Jay Kanter; *W:* Dick Clement, Ian La Frenais; *C:* Christopher Challis; *E:* Ralph Sheldon; *M:* Jonathan Hodge
Cast: Richard Burton, Ian McShane, Nigel Davenport, Donald Sinden, Fiona Lewis

A violent crime thriller set in London's East End, with Burton playing an evil and brutal homosexual crime boss who has a thing about a petty criminal. He moves from beating him up to bedding him. His only barrier is the dedicated police inspector who is determined to pin a crime on him.

Prod Comp: Anglo-EMI, Kastner/Ladd/Kanter
Dist/Sales: Warner, MGM, VSM

Vintage: Families of Value

Allen Harris, Thomas
1995; USA; 72 min; Documentary
W: Thomas Allen Harris

Vintage is a meditative and reflexive look at black families through the eyes of black lesbian and gay siblings. In contrast to traditional documentaries, *Vintage* places the camera in the hands of family members to construct a collective autobiographical presentation of family. Interweaving conversations among family members, verite documentary footage, dramatic portrayals, experimental recreations, visual abstractions, music television strategies and archival photographs, *Vintage* is a mosaic of extended black families. (EAI)

Dist/Sales: EAI

Viol du Vampire, Le

Rollin, Jean
1967; France; 100 min; B&W; Horror
P: Jean Rollin, Sam Selsky; *W:* Jean Rollin;
C: Guy Leblond, Antoine Harispé
Cast: Bernard Letrou, Ursule Pauly, Solange Pradel, Nicole Romian

Made on a shoestring budget, this is the first feature and lesbian/sex vampire film from the noted French horror director, Jean Rollin. The narrative is fragmented, making the film almost incomprehensible, but it centres on two young women who think they are vampires. The film was released under many titles, including *Les Femmes Vampires, Le Reine des Vampires, The Rape of the Vampire, Queen of the Vampires* and *Vampire Women*. French with English subtitles.

Prod Comp: Les Films, ABC

Violet's Visit

Turner, Richard
1995; Australia; 90 min; Comedy
P: Andrew Steuart; *W:* Barry Lowe, Andrew Creagh;
C: Edmund Milts; *E:* Kathryn Fenton;
M: Paul Anthony Smith
Cast: David Franklin, Rebecca Smart, May Lloyd, Caleb Packham, Graham Harvey

15-year-old Violet runs away from her small home town to pay a surprise visit to her Dad whom she's never met. The surprise is more of a shock to Dad's long-standing boyfriend, Pete, whom she meets first. To her dad she is an unwelcome reminder of a past he'd put well and truly behind him. Can two gay men whose sole previous experience of parenting is a pair of love birds cope with a teenage daughter and can the daughter cope with them?

Prod Comp: Spandau Productions; *Dist/Sales:* Wolfe

V

Virgin Larry, The

Dietz, Damion
2001; USA; 80 min; Comedy
P: Vince Filippone, Damion Dietz, Lisa Dennis
Kennedy; *W:* Damion Dietz; *C:* Vince Filippone; *E:*
Vince Filippone
Cast: Saadia Billman, Damion DietzMichael McMullen,
Stephanie Block

Larry Gantry is a gay, self-proclaimed 'artist' with a
penchant for the absurd and outrageous, who is
hired by the unsuspecting arts council of Sunnymead
to put together a local artist showcase. In humorously workmanlike fashion, Larry assembles his cast
and starts rehearsals, but the show's controversial
combination of sexual and religious themes is
definitely not what the local government and
churches had in mind. When Larry's right to
freedom of expression is put to the test, he responds
with an ultimate act of artistic defiance that is both
hilarious and ironically satisfying.
(Potemkin Productions)

Prod Comp: New Media Entertainment
Dist/Sales: Potemkin

Virgin Machine

(aka: Die Jungfrauenmaschine)

Treut, Monika
1988; Germany; 85 min; B&W; Drama
P: Monika Treut; *W:* Monika Treut; *C:* Elfi Mikesch;
M: Mona Mur, Laibach, Blazing Redheads, Pearl Harbour
Cast: Ina Blum, Marcelo Uriona, Dominique Gaspar,
Susie Sexpert, Shelly Mars, Glad Klein

The Virgin Machine follows a young West German
woman's exploration of her own sexuality. Dorothy is
bored with her life in Hamburg and so goes to San
Francisco in search of her mother. But the fun and
sexual discoveries begin on her arrival as she
encounters a series of characters that bring alive her
lesbianism. German with English subtitles.

Prod Comp: Hyena Film Production, Norddeutscher
Rundfunk
Dist/Sales: 21stCentury, FirstRunFeatures, Millivres,
NFVLS, ACMI

Virus knows no Morals, A

(aka: Ein Virus kennt keine Moral)

von Praunheim, Rosa
1985; Germany; 82 min; Comedy
P: Rosa von Praunheim; *W:* Rosa von Praunheim;
C: Elfi Mikesch; *E:* Rosa von Praunheim, Michael
Schaeffer; *M:* Maran Gosov
Cast: Rosa von Praunheim, Dieter Dicken, Maria
Hasenaecker

A gay bathhouse owner is worried that AIDS will
put him out of business. Things become quite
surreal when the owner and his lover both contract
the disease, in this blackly comic, campy satire on
society's attitudes towards homosexuality and AIDS.

Dist/Sales: FirstRunFeatures

A virus knows No Morals

Visitors

Angguish, Dallas
1997; Australia; 13 min; Comedy

A bevy of gorgeous, dangerous and kitsch lesbian
vampires from another world visit earth to sample
local cuisine.

Viva Eu!

Cypriano, Tania
1989; Brazil; 18 min; Documentary
Cast: Wilton Braga

Documentary which follows the life of Brazilian
artist Wilton Braga for eight years, while he lived in
Barcelona, New York and Sao Paulo. During this
time he was suffering from AIDS. Portuguese with
English subtitles.

Dist/Sales: TWN

Vive l'Amour

(aka: Aiqing Wansui)

Tsai, Ming-liang
1994; Taiwan; 118 min; Drama
P: Hu-ping Chung, Wei-hua Tzon; *W:* Ming-liang Tsai,
Yi-chun Tsai, Pi-ying Yang; *C:* Peng-jung Liao, Ming-
kuo Lin; *E:* Fan-chen Sung
Cast: Kuei-mei Yang, Lee Kang Sheng, Chen Chao Jung

Despite the romantic title, this film is about lack of
love and fulfilment in the overworked 1980s. A real
estate agent uses her empty apartments for quick sex.
Spare keys fall into the hands of a lover and another
young man unsure of his sexuality, and all three end up
using the one space. Taiwanese with English subtitles.

Awards: Venice Film Festival, 1994: Golden Lion
Prod Comp: Central Motion Pictures
Dist/Sales: Strand, Mongrel

Vive l'Amour

Voices from the Front

Elgear, Sandra / Hutt, Robyn / Meieran, David
1991; USA; 90 min; Documentary

A powerful distillation of words and pictures from events organised across America to try to alter public consciousness about AIDS, to expose profiteering by pharmaceutical companies, and to challenge government inaction and neglect concerning AIDS and those who suffer from it.

Awards: Berlin Film Festival, 1992: Teddy
Dist/Sales: Frameline, Salzgeber, Strand

Voicing the Legacy

Savage, Eleanor
1996; USA; 35 min; Documentary

Documentary examining the experiences of middle-aged and senior lesbians.

Dist/Sales: Savage

Voleurs, Les

(aka: Thieves)

Téchiné, André
1996; France; 90 min; Drama
P: Alain Sarde; *W:* André Téchiné, Gilles Taurand, Michel Alexandre; *C:* Jeanne Lapoirie;
E: Martine Giordano; *M:* Philippe Sarde
Cast: Daniel Auteuil, Benoît Magimel, Catherine Deneuve, Laurence Côte

Lustful tale which revolves around a streetwise cop, his gangster brother and their families as they seek out money and sex. Côte plays Deneuve's tomboy lover Juliette. From the director of *Wild Reeds*. French with English subtitles.

Prod Comp: Le Studio Canal+, TF1 Films
Dist/Sales: SonyClassics, ACMI

Waiting

Hasson, Patrick
2000; USA; 80 min; Comedy
P: John Stefanic; *W:* Patrick Hasson;
C: Michael Perlman; *E:* Patrick Hasson
Cast: Will Keenan, Kerri Kenney, Hannah Dalton, Bill Robertson

Sean McNutt is losing his mind. Customer complaints, fifty cent tips, raw chicken parmigiana and Mafioso management are gnawing away at what sanity he has left. Welcome to the world of *Waiting*, a comedy about the seamy underbelly of the restaurant industry as told through the eyes of Sean McNutt, a waiter trying to muster the ambition to move on in life. Recently dumped and still living at home, Sean drinks himself into oblivion each night until an impulsive visit to a fetish club to see an old flame results in an ejection from the club and a taste of leather clad justice. This is the last straw, and Sean soon embarks on a campaign of romantic retaliation. (2000 Brooklyn International Film Festival)

Prod Comp: Manayunk Pictures
Dist/Sales: TLA

Waiting for the Moon

Godmilow, Jill
1987; USA; 87 min; Drama
P: Sandra Schulberg; *W:* Mark Magill; *C:* Andre Neau;
E: Georges Klotz; *M:* Michael Sahl
Cast: Linda Hunt, Linda Bassett, Bruce McGill, Bernadette Lafont, Jacques Boudet

A fictional look at the life of writer Gertrude Stein, and her complex relationship with her long-time companion and lover, Alice B. Toklas. A slow-moving portrait in a production that was made for television.

Prod Comp: New Front Films, AB Films, American Playhouse, Channel 4, Skouras Pictures
Dist/Sales: Facets, Skouras

Waiting 'round Wynyard

Di Chiera, Franco
1983; Australia; 13 min; Drama

A young man, gay and unemployed, waits on the street, open to a sexual encounter. A film about suspicion, desire and ambivalence towards a first pickup with another man. A sensitive observation of men, straight and gay, on the prowl on city streets.

Prod Comp: Australian Film TV & Radio School
Dist/Sales: ACMI

Walk on the Wild Side

Dmytryk, Edward
1962; USA; 112 min; B&W; Drama

W

P: Charles K. Feldman; *W:* John Fante, Edmund Morris; *C:* Joseph MacDonald; *E:* Harry Girstad; *M:* Elmer Bernstein

Cast: Capucine, Jane Fonda, Laurence Harvey, Barbara Stanwyck, Anne Baxter

In the 1930s, a penniless farmer finds the woman he once loved working in a New Orleans brothel. He believes he can save her from, among other things, her 'special' relationship with the brothel madam. And so begins a battle of heterosexual power and dominance. A watered-down version of the original story that aimed not to offend the audience with too much lesbianism or prostitution.

Prod Comp: Columbia, Famartists Productions, Famous Artists Productions

Dist/Sales: Columbia

Walking on Water

Walking on Water

Ayres, Tony
2002; Australia; 90 min; Drama
P: Liz Watts; *W:* Roger Monk; *C:* Robert Humphreys; *E:* Reva Childs; *M:* Antony Partos
Cast: Vince Colosimo, Maria Theodorakis, Nathaniel Dean , Judi Farr, Anna Lise Phillips

Charlie and Anna are Gavin's two best friends. They made a pact to assist the terminally ill Gavin to die when the time came. However, despite a massive overdose of morphine, Gavin stays alive. Charlie ends up slipping a plastic bag over Gavin's head and suffocating him. This is hardly the dignified death that they had all planned. But it's the beginning of an emotional roller coaster ride, which takes Charlie and Anna through the highs and lows of the grief experience—from illicit affairs and left over morphine—to devastating accusations and unwitting betrayals. At the end of the day, Charlie and Anna are forced to face the true meaning of friendship, loyalty and love. (www.walkingonwater.net.au)

Awards: Berlin Film Festival, 2002: Teddy Award for

Best Gay Feature
Prod Comp: Porchlight Films
Dist/Sales: Fortissimo, Globe, Dendy

Wallowitch & Ross: This Moment

Morris, Richard
1998; USA; 77 min; Documentary
P: Robert Morris-Purdee; *C:* Don Lenzer; *E:* Marsha Moore, Richard Morris

A documentary celebration of the 30-year relationship and professional partnership of cabaret duo Bertram Ross and John Wallowitch.

Prod Comp: Karmic Productions

War on Lesbians

Cottis, Jane
1992; USA; 35 min; Drama

How do you know if you really are a lesbian? Drawing on various pop-culture conventions and references (film, television news and traditional talking-head documentaries), Cottis poses a gallery of characters and throws lesbianism into every imaginable arena.

War Widow, The

Bogart, Paul
1978; USA; 83 min; Drama
W: Harvey Perr
Cast: Frances Lee McCain, Pamela Bellwood

Amy, the lonely wife of a World War I soldier, meets and becomes friends with the free-spirited Jenny; soon their relationship turns to a passionate love affair, scorned by her family and society at that time. As Amy's husband is about to return from the war, she must make a decision between her family and the woman she loves. Made for television.

Awards: San Francisco International Lesbian & Gay Film Festival, 1988: Best Video

Was Sie nie Über Frauen Wissen Wollten

(aka: All you Never Wanted to know about Women)

Lambert, Lothar
1991; Germany; 80 min; B&W; Comedy
P: Lothar Lambert; *W:* Lothar Lambert;
C: Lothar Lambert, Albert Kitti
ler; *E:* Lothar Lambert
Cast: Lothar Lambert, Nilgün Taifun, Dennis Buczma, Doreen Heins, Renate Soleymany

A feast of strange women, undertaking all manner of sexual adventures with other women, and men, in this hysterically camp underground classic.

W

Watching Lesbian Porn

McLeod, Dayna
2001; Canada; 10 min; Comedy

A pornographic parody, that advocates the use of feminism as lesbian foreplay. This film is directed specifically at a lesbian audience attending a screening at a gay and lesbian film festival. (V Tape)

Dist/Sales: VTape, GroupeIntervention

Watching Lesbian Porn

Watching You

Abramovich, Stephanie
2000; Israel; 32 min; Drama

Sharon is a single mother hemmed in by a possessive girlfriend and a controlling boss. She escapes her reality by watching and taking photos of her attractive, but obviously troubled neighbour.

Water Drops on Burning Rocks

(aka: Gouttes d'Eau sur Pierres Brûlantes)

Ozon, François
1999; France; 90 min; Comedy
P: Olivier Delbosc, Christine Gozlan, Kenzô Horikoshi, Marc Missonnier, Alain Sarde; *W:* François Ozon;
C: Jeanne Lapoirie; *E:* Laurence Bawedin, Claudine Bouché
Cast: Bernard Giraudeau, Malik Zidi, Ludivine Sagnier, Anna Levine

Based on Rainer Werner Fassbinder's play *Tropfen auf hiesse Steine* this richly perverse and very funny sex comedy stars Bernard Giraudeau as Leopold, an ultra successful and ultra conservative businessman who seduces the young Franz. But when Franz moves in, all expectations are overturned when it is Leopold who refuses to compromise to Franz's old fashioned sense of morality and domesticity. Franz turns to his ex-girlfriend for comfort but she too ends up falling for Leopold's cold seductive charms. Their bizarre ménage à trois is then interrupted when Leopold's ex, Vera, a male to female transsexual, comes for a visit. (ACMI)

French with English subtitles.
Prod Comp: Euro Space, Fidélite Productions, Studio Images 6
Dist/Sales: Celluloid-Dreams, ArtificialEye, Zeitgeist, Haut-et-Court, ACMI

Watermelon Woman, The

Dunye, Cheryl
1996; USA; 90 min; Drama
P: Alexandra Juhasz, Barry Swimar; *W:* Cheryl Dunye;
C: Michelle Crenshaw; *E:* Cheryl Dunye
Cast: Guinevere Turner, Cheryl Dunye, Valerie Walker, Cheryl Clarke

Cheryl is an aspiring black filmmaker who works in a video store. She becomes obsessed with a mammie character actress of the 1930s, known only as the Watermelon Woman, and decides to make a documentary about her. As she works on the documentary her own life undergoes a sudden change when she falls for a rich white girl, Diana. The ensuing turmoil causes Cheryl to question her own identity, her relationship with Diana, her community, her life and actions. One of the first feature films made by an out black lesbian, it opened the San Francisco Lesbian and Gay Film Festival in 1996.

Awards: Berlin Film Festival, 1996: Teddy Award; LA Outfest, 1996: Audience Award
Prod Comp: Dancing Girl Productions
Dist/Sales: FirstRunFeatures, Salzgeber, Wolfe, ACMI

Wavelengths

Parmar, Pratibha
1997; UK; 15 min; Comedy
P: Janine Marmot; *W:* Jaden Clark

After breaking up with her girlfriend, a young lesbian on the lookout for someone new is convinced by a friend to try cybersex. Her virtual lover turns out to have more substance than she anticipated. (MQFF)

Dist/Sales: Cinenova, WMM

Waves

(aka: Bølgene)

Mosvold, Frank
1998; Norway; 11 min; Drama
P: Frank Mosvold, Ivan Gasparini; *W:* Frank Mosvold, Øyvind Ellenes

Waves looks at the friendship between 18-year-olds Tim and Morten as they stand at the cusp of adulthood, and employs only natural lighting and handheld photography to tell its story. (MQFF)

Dist/Sales: NorwegianFilm

W

Wax Me

Simpson, Kelli
1993; Australia; 10 min; Comedy

The story of Camille, a beauty worker caught between the disapproval of her colleagues and her desire for a beautiful client. Who says dykes and drags don't mix? (MQFF)

We Always Danced

Marquez, Nettie
1996; USA; 10 min; Drama

Anna is trying to come to terms with the loss of her best friend to AIDS. The contradictions between her traditional Latin upbringing and her identity as a lesbian leave her conflicted on how to handle her grief. (TWN)

Dist/Sales: TWN

We are Family

Sands, Aimee
1987; USA; 58 min; Documentary

A moving profile of life in three gay families, full of funny moments and everyday wisdom. Children and parents have their say about a situation that is too often regarded with hysteria.

Awards: San Francisco Film Festival, 1988: Golden Gate Award
Dist/Sales: FilmakersLibrary

We are Transgenders

Ogawa, Lulu
1998; Japan; 78 min; Documentary

An intimate look at the thriving transgender movement in contemporary Japan. A diverse range of activists and personalities are interviewed, and issues of gender discussed. Japanese with English subtitles.

Dist/Sales: TokyoILGFF

We Think the World of You

Gregg, Colin
1988; UK; 90 min; Comedy
P: Tommaso Jandelli; *W:* Hugh Stoddart; *C:* Mike Garfath; *E:* Peter Delfgou; *M:* Julian Iacobson
Cast: Alan Bates, Gary Oldman, Frances Barber, Max Wall, Liz Smith

Frank is very, very confused. His best friend and former lover, Johnny, has been sent to prison. Suddenly Frank has fallen in love with Evie, the girl Johnny left behind. And Evie's a real dog (we are talking four legs and a wet nose)!

Prod Comp: British Screen, Film Four International, Gold Screen
Dist/Sales: Cinecom, BFI

We Think the World of You

We were Marked with a Big A

Weishaupt, Joseph / Jeanron, Elke
1991; Germany; 44 min; Documentary

Powerful and thorough documentary featuring gay man and women who share their experiences of surviving Nazi Germany.

We were One Man

(aka: Nous étions un Seul Homme)

Vallois, Philippe
1979; France; 90 min; Drama
W: Philippe Vallois; *C:* François About; *E:* Philippe Vallois; *M:* Jean Jacques Ruhlmann
Cast: Serge Avédikian, Piotr Stanislas, Catherine Albin

Set during World War II, Guy, an escapee from a mental hospital, hides in an isolated cottage. He finds a wounded German soldier, Rolf, and takes him back to the cottage where he can recuperate. Soon they become friends, and their friendship develops into a homosexual affair. Guy tries to stop Rolf leaving, but the outside world intrudes when Rolf is captured. French with English subtitles.

Prod Comp: Philippe Vallois
Dist/Sales: Frameline

We're Funny that Way

Adkin, David
1998; Canada; 86 min; Documentary
P: Harry Sutherland, David Adkin; *C:* Ali Kazimi;
E: Steve Weslak; *M:* Aaron Davis, John Lang

Eleven of North America's funniest gay and lesbian comedians star in this documentary showcasing the wit and wisdom of an unusual group of performers who have, for years, taken the professional risk of coming out onstage. Included in the line-up are: Scott Capurro, Lea DeLaria, Kate Clinton, Jaffe Cohen. Live performance clips are combined with behind-the-scenes footage and interviews in which the performers candidly share their life experiences, offer insights into the art of comedy, and discuss the obstacles facing gays and other minorities within the entertainment industry.

Prod Comp: Fabulous Pictures
Dist/Sales: Fabulous

We've Been Framed

Farthing, Cheryl
1991; UK; 25 min; Documentary

Another film made for the British Channel 4 *Out* series. Women of different ages, races and class backgrounds talk about the best, the worst and the first lesbian films they've seen.

Webcam Boys

RADD
2001; USA; 57 min; Documentary

Webcam Boys follows ten men over four months and films them 24 hours a day. Candid interviews dig deep into their personal lives. Video verite at its most voyeuristic.

The Wedding Banquet

Wedding Banquet, The

(aka: Hsi yen)

Lee, Ang
1993; China, Taiwan, USA; 111 min; Comedy
P: Ted Hope, James Schamus, Ang Lee; *W:* Ang Lee, James Schamus, Neil Feng; *C:* Jong Lin; *E:* Tim

Squyres; *M:* Mader
Cast: Winston Chao, May Chin, Mitchell Lichtenstein, Ah-Leh Gua, Sihung Lung

Wai-tung is happily settled in Manhattan in a gay relationship with Simon, but is pestered by his parents in Taiwan to marry and maintain the family tradition. One of his tenants, an illegal immigrant from Shanghai needs a green card, so a marriage of convenience is arranged. But no-one has reckoned on the possibility of a Chinese wedding. Nominated for an Academy Award for Best Foreign Language Film, 1993. Some Taiwanese with English subtitles.

Prod Comp: Central Motion Pictures, Good Machine
Dist/Sales: Palace, SamuelGoldwyn, GoodMachine, Wolfe, Swank

Wedding Video, The

Cowen, Clint / Korpi, Norman
2001; USA; 84 min; Comedy
Cast: Norman Korpi, Heather B. Gardner, Cory Murphy, Julie Oliver, Rachel Campos

Norm and his muscular boyfriend, Sky, are about to tie the knot. Norm wants to remember it forever, so he hires a videographer to make a wedding video. Fortunately for us, the unseen videographer and relentless interviewer leaves the camera running when it probably should be turned off. For example, things don't go over quite so well when the wedding planners find out there are two grooms. Via pre-wedding interviews, we get introduced to Norm's eclectic and diverse circle of friends. When the whole, messy group assembles at Norm's Beverly Hills castle to prepare for the big day, the ride really gets bumpy. A hayride, a red dildo, and an out of control bachelor party may end up on the cutting room floor, but we get to see it all first. And did someone forget to tell Norm that his new spouse is a porn star? (2002 Austin Gay & Lesbian International Film Festival)

Prod Comp: Fruit Films, Rewind Services
Dist/Sales: FruitFilms

Weekend, The

Skeet, Brian
1999; UK, USA; 97 min; Drama
P: Ian Benson; *W:* Brian Skeet; *C:* Ron Fortunato; *E:* Chris Wyatt; *M:* Sarah Class, Dan Jones
Cast: Gena Rowlands, Brooke Shields, Deborah Kara Unger, Jared Harris, David Conrad

Marian and John Kerr are expecting an old friend, Lyle for a weekend visit to their beautiful upstate New York home. Emotions run high since it is the one-year anniversary of the death of John's brother, the handsome and charismatic Tony, who had also been Lyle's lover. Marian, who is still inconsolable after losing Tony to AIDS, is upset when Lyle brings his new boyfriend, a young artist, Robert. Meanwhile, the situation is just as tense at the Kerr's neighbours house, where oft-widowed, free spirit Laura Ponti gets a surprise visit from her resentful, angry daughter, Nina, and her married lover, Thierry. Matters worsen when the battling mother-daughter duo joins the Kerr household for a dinner party, where the pain-riddled diners engage in a messy emotional showdown. (Strand Releasing)

Prod Comp: Granada Films, Lunatics and Lovers
Dist/Sales: Strand, Wolfe

The Weekend

Weeki Wachee Girls

Cummings, Kim
1999; USA; 22 min; Comedy

Best friends forever, Katie and Maura have dreamed of being part of the live mermaid show at the Wekki Wachee Spring. It's the summer of 1979, they're 15 and everything is changing, especially when Katie discovers Maura kissing another girl.

Dist/Sales: Atom, CFMDC

Weiner Brut

Fädler, Hans
1985; Austria; 98 min; Comedy

Set among the ousted aristocracy of Austria, this outrageous parody tells the story of a group of punks who help the aristocrats maintain their drug supply. In return, however, the punks want the crown jewels and to turn the opera house into a rock venue.

Weininger's Nacht

Manker, Paulus
1989; Austria; 104 min; Drama
C: Walter Kindler; *E:* Marie Homolkova, Ingrid Koller; *M:* Hans Georg Koch
Cast: Andrea Eckert, Paulus Manker, Sieghardt Rupp

Weininger's Nacht is a fascinating, disturbing glimpse

into the psyche of a man whose repressed homosexuality and cultural identity produces madness. Otto Weininger was a contemporary of Freud; his contribution to the world of psychoanalysis was *Sex and Character* a misogynist rant that elevated the male to godlike status and cited the female as the root of all evil. His denial of his own homosexual nature was expressed through the revulsion he felt toward women; the guilt he experienced being a Jew in turn-of-the-century Vienna resulted in a vicious anti-Semitism and a conversion to Christianity. Based on the Volkstheater Wien's production of Joshua Sobol's stage play, *Weininger's Nacht* describes the uneasy relationship between oppression and self-hatred, and between homophobia and anti-Semitism. (MQFF)

Welcome to Africville

Inkster, Dana
1999; 15 min; Documentary

Tells the stories of three black women (two of them lesbians) as they recount their lives in Africville on the eve of its destruction.

Dist/Sales: VideoOut, GroupeIntervention

Well Lit Shadows

Collins, Paul
1994; Australia; 15 min; Drama

He is repressed and middle-class. His escape? The personal columns of *Truth* newspaper, and a sexual adventure with a young transvestite. Fantasy and reality blur, but will he ever come out of the shadows? (MQFF)

Well Sexy Women

Believeau, Lulu / Hickson, Michele / Moorcock, Sophie / North, Liz
1993; UK; 55 min; Documentary

Featuring six lesbians captured during a group discussion that involves suggestions on how lesbians can reduce their risk to STDs and generally lead safer sex lives.

Dist/Sales: Wolfe

Well, The

Lang, Samantha
1997; Australia; 100 min; Thriller
P: Sandra Levy; *W:* Laura Jones; *C:* Mandy Walker; *E:* Dany Cooper; *M:* Stephen Rae
Cast: Pamela Rabe, Miranda Otto, Paul Chubb, Frank Wilson, Steve Jacobs

The sun can't seem to shine in this eerie thriller that

suffuses the otherwise sun-baked Australian outback with a sickly pallid light. Ageing spinster Hester brings home the spirited Katherine to assist with the chores around her decrepit ranch home. In contrast to the burdens of her ailing father, Katherine's youthfulness offers Hester a ray of golden sunshine in her dismal gloom, and their developing relationship helps her overcome her frustrations and giddily inspires her beyond the everyday. When the old man dies, Hester supplements the inheritance with the sale of the old ranch house, and the two women find an ideal fantasy world in a new cottage home. Then one night everything changes—Katherine runs over a man out on their deserted road. Fantasy turns into feverish nightmare, as distrust, paranoia, and horror begin to run rampant. (24th San Francisco International Lesbian & Gay Film Festival)

Prod Comp: New South Wales Film & TV Office, Southern Star Xanadu
Dist/Sales: Globe

Wellness

1996; Canada; 29 min; Documentary

A community health centre gives priority to marginalised women whose needs are not met by the medical system, a group of women with multiple sclerosis share common concerns about health care, and a researcher studies the health care needs of lesbian and bisexual women in Nova Scotia. (EMA)

Dist/Sales: EMA

West Coast Crones

Muir, Madeline
1991; USA; 28 min; Documentary

An articulate group of nine white, mostly middle-class women meet to discuss issues as diverse as their initial sexual experiences, coming out, their decision to have or not have children, their self-perception, friendships and relationships with other women as well as the expectancy and mental preparation for approaching infirmary and death.

Dist/Sales: Wolfe, Frameline

West Fickt Ost

(aka: West Fucks East)

Brüning, Jürgen
2001; Germany; 60 min; Experimental

West Fickt Ost follows three attractive men: Erik, who works at the stock market; Cyrus, who spends his days as a waiter; and Tim, who manages a sex store. The three are good friends, and, it quickly becomes apparent, are involved in a seemingly uncomplicated sexual relationship. In a series of

loosely-structured, documentary-like scenes, Brüning presents their lives as refreshingly free of angst or conflict—they spend their time having fun, dancing, cruising, modelling for photos, hustling for money, and having sex. *West Fickt Ost* emerges as an experimental portrait of unashamedly sensual gay male sexuality. (2002 New York Lesbian & Gay Film Festival) German with English subtitles.

Prod Comp: Jürgen Brüning Filmproduktion
Dist/Sales: Brüning

Westler: East of the Wall

Speck, Wieland
1985; Germany; 90 min; Drama
W: Egbert Hörmann, Wieland Speck; *C:* Klemens Becker; *E:* Gabriele Bartels, Wieland Speck; *M:* Engelbert Rehm
Cast: Sigurd Rachman, Rainer Strecker, Sala Kogo, Andy Lucas

This low-budget feature from Germany tells the story of Felix, a young man from West Berlin, who on a day trip, meets and falls in love with Thomas, a waiter from East Berlin. The boys decide on an escape plan for Thomas but they are thwarted by suspicious border guards. Even though made on a low budget, this first feature from Speck is refreshing, uplifting and fascinating—it includes illegal video footage shot in the East. German with English subtitles.

Awards: San Francisco International Lesbian & Gay Film Festival, 1986: Audience Award for Best Feature
Dist/Sales: Frameline, Salzgeber, Strand

What a Pretty Sister

Thomas, Yvette
1991; New Zealand; 25 min; Documentary

A sensitive exploration of a transsexual's journey from boyhood to her present-day life as a woman.

Dist/Sales: AucklandUni

What have I Done to Deserve This?

(aka: Qué he hecho yo para Merecer esto?!!)

Almodóvar, Pedro
1984; Spain; 100 min; Comedy
P: Tadeo Villalba, Hervé Hachuel; *W:* Pedro Almodóvar; *C:* Ángel Luis Fernández; *E:* José Salcedo; *M:* Bernardo Bonezzi
Cast: Carmen Maura, Juan Martinez, Luis Hostalot, Angel de Andres-Lopez

Gloria is a typical Spanish housewife—or is she? She has an indifferent taxi driver husband, two sons who have discovered the fringe benefits of drug-dealing, and a self-reliant mother-in-law with a pet lizard. When the family run out of money, one of the sons is sold to a gay dentist. Gloria craves a better life or, at least for starters, sex with a potent man.

Prod Comp: Tesauro SA, Kaktus Producciones Cinematográficas SA
Dist/Sales: ACMI, Potential, Cinevista

What is the Relationship between Rosa von Praunheim and the Male Strippers of San Francisco?

Brüning, Jürgen / Goldstein, Mark
1990; USA; 15 min; Documentary

Interviews with the legendary filmmaker Rosa von Praunheim are interspersed with explicit porn movie scenes, stripping scenes and interviews with male strippers.

What Kind of Music!

(aka: Ma Che Musica!)

Cecchi, Antonio / Gatti, Gianni
1999; Italy; 13 min; Drama

A young boy longs to be in a marching band.

What Makes a Family

Greenwald, Maggie
2001; USA; 91 min; Drama
P: Wendy Grean; *W:* Robert L. Freedman; *C:* Rhett Morita; *E:* Keith Reamer; *M:* David Mansfield
Cast: Brooke Shields, Cherry Jones, Anne Meara

After a brief but passionate courtship, two young women, Janine Nielssen and Sandy Cataldi, seal their commitment to each other with a beautifully moving lesbian wedding. As they settle into domestic life together, Sandy realises she wants to start a family. Shortly after giving birth to a daughter, Sandy falls ill and Janine has to fight for the custody of her daughter. (2001 Verzaubert International Queer Film Festival)

Prod Comp: Lifetime Television

What you Take for Granted

Citron, Michelle
1983; USA; 75 min; Documentary
P: Michelle Citron

The tentative friendship of Anna, a feisty truck driver, and Diana, an upper middle-class doctor, provides the core for an unusual, intimate and moving look at women's experiences in jobs traditionally held by men. *What You Take for Granted* creatively confronts issues of race and class and examines the cultural contradictions and stereotypes

these women cannot 'take for granted'.

Prod Comp: Iris Feminist Collective
Dist/Sales: WMM

What's Cooking?

Chadha, Gurinder
2000; UK, USA; 110 min; Comedy
P: Jeffrey Taylor; *W:* Gurinder Chadha, Paul Mayeda Berges; *C:* Jong Lin; *E:* Janice Hamton; *M:* Craig Pruess
Cast: Joan Chen, Julianna Margulies, Mercedes Ruehl, Kyra Sedgwick

What's Cooking? celebrates the quintessential American holiday Thanksgiving through the stories of four diverse families: African–American, Jewish, Latino and Vietnamese. But there's more than turkey being served, and the side dishes include family secrets, affection, tension and more. All-star cast includes Kyra Sedgewick and Julianna Margulies as lesbian lovers. (Wolfe)
English, Spanish & Vietnamese with English subtitles.

Prod Comp: Flashpoint, Stagescreen, Because Entertainment
Dist/Sales: Trimark, LionsGate, Wolfe

When Boys Fly

When Boys Fly

Halpern, Stewart / Rolov, Lenid
2001; USA; 62 min; Documentary
P: Stewart Halpern, Lenid Rolov, Kevin Weiler;
C: Clay Westervelt; *E:* Stewart Halpern, Lenid Rolov;
M: Robert Johnson

This erotically charged documentary focuses on four men as they soar through the fast-paced world of the USA's biggest circuit party, a weekend of debauchery where rules don't apply, boundaries are non-existent and physical perfection is demanded. Brandon, 23, is a shy circuit virgin whose straight-laced life collides head-on with Tone, 21, an extroverted party boy trying to keep himself out of the emergency room. Todd, a handsome 35-year-old businessman, recklessly plays the field while trying to maintain a

W

relationship with Jon, his 19-year-old 'soul mate'. Circuit parties allow professional gay men to travel to 'Wonderland' to play Peter Pan, hoping to forge the kind of relationships we're all looking for...love, friendship and self-worth. *When Boys Fly* is a provocative, startling, no-holds-barred peek into the lives of a new generation. (2002 LA Outfest)

Prod Comp: New Voices Production
Dist/Sales: NewVoices, TLA

When Love Comes

Maxwell, Garth
1998; New Zealand; 94 min; Drama
P: Michele Fantl, Jonathan Dowling; *W:* Garth Maxwell, Rex Pilgrim, Peter Wells; *C:* Darryl Ward; *E:* Cushla Dillon; *M:* Angus McNaughton, Chris Anderton, Dave Goodison, Darryl Ward
Cast: Dean O'Gorman, Rena Owen, Sophia Hawthorne, Nancy Brunning, Simon Westaway

Stephen is old friends with Katie (a has-been singer from 1970s) but is in love with Mark. Lesbian punk rockers Fig and Sally are excited about their band and the lyrics Mark is writing for their songs. Eddie loves Katie but does she still want him? All the characters come together in a round of revelations and recriminations which are handled with pathos and humour by Maxwell. (MQFF)

Prod Comp: MF Films
Dist/Sales: NZFC, Millivres, JourDeFete, Wolfe, ACMI

When Night is Falling

Rozema, Patricia
1995; Canada; 82 min; Drama
P: Barbara Tranter; *W:* Patricia Rozema; *C:* Douglas Koch; *E:* Susan Shipton; *M:* Leslie Barber
Cast: Pascale Bussières, Rachael Crawford, Henry Czerny, David Fox

Camille is a Christian academic, engaged to be married to a fellow theologian. Then she meets Petra, a flamboyant performer in an avant-garde circus. Much to her surprise, Camille finds herself falling deeply, almost magically, in love. Forced to choose between the woman she wants and the man who loves her, Camille discovers that the true duty of the soul is desire. A beautiful, sensitive and often funny film from the director of *I've Heard the Mermaids Singing*.

Awards: Melbourne International Film Festival, 1994: Best Film; Berlin Film Festival, 1994: Audience Award
Prod Comp: Crucial Pictures
Dist/Sales: UIP, Wolfe, TLA, October, Cowboy, ACMI, Swank, Haut-et-Court

When Shirley Met Florence

Bezalel, Ronit
1994; Canada; 27 min; Documentary

'When I first saw Shirley, I fell in love with her', exclaims Florence in describing a rich relationship that she believes 'was made in heaven'. Now, after a lifetime together in Montreal, the two Jewish women continue to cherish the ties that have bound them together for 55 years and to celebrate their passion for music which first drew them to each other.

Prod Comp: National Film Board of Canada
Dist/Sales: Heathcliff, NFBC

When Night is Falling

When the Cat's Away
(aka: Chacun Cherche Son Chat)

Klapisch, Cédric
1995; France; 95 min; Comedy
P: Farid Lahouassa, Aissa Djabri, Manuel Munz;
W: Cédric Klapisch; *C:* Benoit Delhomme;
E: Francine Sandberg; *M:* Frédéric Chopin
Cast: Garance Clavel, Renee Le Calm, Olivier Py, Zinedine Soualem

When make-up artist Chloe decides to take a week's holiday at the sea side, the only person that she can get to mind her beloved cat, Gris Gris, is Madame Renee', an eccentric old biddy with an apartment full of the fur balls. Finding that on her return to Paris Madame Renee has misplaced her cat, her grief has Madame organising a posse of elderly matrons and local folk to help Chloe and her gay flatmate Michel hunt down the cat. As the neighbourhood gets involved in the search, with a local lad developing a crush on Chloe, and Chloe, a crush on the drummer who keeps everyone up at night. French with English subtitles.

Prod Comp: Vertigo, Le Studio Canal+, France 2 Cinéma
Dist/Sales: Palace, ArtificialEye

W

When the Party's Over

Irmas, Mathew
1992; USA; 115 min; Drama
P: James A. Holt, Matthew Irmas, Ann Wycoff; *W:* Ann Wycoff, Matthew Irmas; *C:* Alicia Weber; *E:* Dean Goodhill, Jerry Bixman; *M:* Joe Romano
Cast: Rae Dawn Chong, Sandra Bullock, Elizabeth Berridge, Kris Kamm

The film focuses on three very different young women and a homosexual man sharing a house in contemporary Los Angeles, as they negotiate the difficult transition into adulthood. All the characters find love at some stage except for the gay man.

Prod Comp: Emby Eye

When the Penny Drops

Clifford, Barbara
1993; Australia; 20 min; Documentary

In this film several Australians talk about how they have been targeted for violence, loss of employment, denial of immigration because of their sexuality.

Where is My Love?

(aka: Qiangpo Puguang)

Chen, Jofei
1995; Taiwan; 56 min; Drama
P: Jojo Wu; *W:* Jofei Chen; *C:* Jiping Liu; *E:* Xiaodong Chen
Cast: Jixing Wen, Anchen Qui, Shuqing Ke, David Wang

The debut feature from Jofei Chen, centres on two very different men. Ko is a writer and gay, but terrified of intimacy with another man and even more terrified of coming out. Ko has a one-night stand with Pierre, who is openly gay. Pierre wants more from Ko and begins to wear down the writer's inhibitions. Chinese with English subtitles.

Dist/Sales: ChenJ

Where Lies the Homo?

Monette, Jean-François
1998; Canada; 34 min; Experimental
W: Jean-Françios Monette

A film diary that explores the construction of gay identities through an analysis of media clips and coming out tales. The narrative's focus is on demystifying stereotypical representations of queerness in film while offering a personal view of growing up queer in a heterosexist culture. (CFMDC)

Dist/Sales: CFMDC

Where the Sun Beats Down

(aka: Onde Bate o Sol)

Pinto, Joaquim
1989; Portugal; Drama
P: João Pedro Bénard; *W:* Joaquim Pinto; *C:* Joaquim Pinto; *E:* Claudio Martínez
Cast: Antonio Pedro Figueiredo, Marcello Urgeghe, Manuel Lobão

Set in modern-day Portugal, Nuno returns from the city to his sister's farm where he develops a relationship with a young farm worker, Alberto. The relationship threatens the stability of Nuno's snobbish family, but he is a young man determined to break the sexual and class taboos of his culture.

Prod Comp: Grupo de Estudos e Realizações

Whether you Like it or Not: The Story of Hedwig

Nix, Laura
2001; USA; 85 min; Documentary
P: Laura Nix; *E:* Jeff Groth; *M:* Stephen Trask

A fascinating documentary on the making of the film *Hedwig and the Angry Inch* from its conception in the New York underground club scene to its reception at the Sundance Film Festival. In addition to rare archival footage you won't see anywhere (including Hedwig's first appearance), you'll find intimate interviews with leading players John Cameron Mitchell and Stephen Trask. (2002 Chicago Lesbian & Gay International Film Festival)

Prod Comp: Automat Pictures
Dist/Sales: Automat, NewLine

White People's Business

Dacic, Diana / Seelenmeyer, Melissa
2001; Australia; 26 min; Documentary

An urban perspective on non-indigenous involvement in the reconciliation movement in Australia. Features interviews with Rob Lake from Black, White and Pink—a Sydney-based group of queers who work towards providing information and action plans for the queer community about reconciliation.

Dist/Sales: WhitePeople

White to be Angry, The

Davis, Vaginal
1999; USA; 15 min; Experimental

Davis makes a definitive statement about American race, gender and class relations in *The White to be Angry*.

Who Happen to be Gay

Beldin, Dale / Krenzien, Mark
1979; USA; 23 min; Documentary

A highly-acclaimed American Broadcasting Corporation television documentary which profiles six professionals, three men and three women (an engineer, a college professor, a psychologist, a registered nurse, a real estate agent and a doctor) who have decided to lead openly gay lives.

Dist/Sales: DirectCinema

Who Killed Pasolini?

(aka: Pasolini, an Italian Crime; Pasolini, un delitto Italiano)

Giordana, Marco Tullio
1995; Italy; 100 min; Drama
P: Claudio Bonivento, Rita Cecchi Gori, Vittorio Cecchi Gori, Jean-François Lepetit; *W:* Marco Tullio Giordana, Sandro Petraglia, Stefano Rulli; *C:* Franco Lecca; *E:* Cecilia Zanuso; *M:* Ennio Morricone
Cast: Carlo DeFilippi, Nicoletta Braschi, Toni Bertorelli

When the famous Italian film director, poet and social critic Pier Paolo Pasolini was murdered in a Rome slum in 1975, the official view was that he was murdered by an enraged teenage boy he had picked up for a sexual encounter. This film, made in the form of a docudrama, looks at the murder first in a straightforward manner, but then raises several provocative questions: was the boy acting alone or with a gang, was it an impulse killing or was the killer (or killers) hired to murder Pasolini?

Prod Comp: Flach Film
Dist/Sales: Alliance

Who's Afraid of Project 10?

Greene, Scott
1990; USA; 24 min; Documentary

The special needs of gay and lesbian teenagers are seldom dealt with by conventional high-school guidance counsellors. Project 10 is a program in southern Californian high schools that meets the counselling needs of gay teens. This videotape moves between the program's director discussing how it works, the gay and lesbian teenagers who have benefited from the program, and fundamentalist protesters who consider this important social program immoral and anti-family. (MQFF)

Who's the Woman, Who's the Man

Chan, Peter
1996; Hong Kong; 107 min; Comedy
C: Henry Chan
Cast: Anita Yuen, Anita Mui, Jordan Chan, Leslie Cheung

Wing is obsessed with pop idol Rose and her partner and producer Sam. When she hears that Sam is on the lookout for fresh male talent, Wing dresses up as a man to win a talent competition and ends up entangled in a love triangle with them. Rose becomes attached to Wing, so Wing tells 'he' is gay to rebut her advances, only to be overheard by Sam who decides he is attracted to 'him'. Cantonese & Mandarin with English & Chinese subtitles.

Prod Comp: Golden Harvest, United Filmmakers Organisation, Second Studio
Dist/Sales: RimFilm

Why am I Gay?

1995; UK; 57 min; Documentary

An accessible and timely look at homosexuality which tackles it from the angle of development of sexual orientation. Is it just a social problem? Are homosexuals 'made' by their social world or are homosexuals born as they are?

Prod Comp: Itel
Dist/Sales: Marcom

Why Not!

(aka: Pourquoi Pas!)

Serreau, Coline
1979; France; 93 min; Comedy
P: Michèle Dimitri; *W:* Coline Serreau; *C:* Jean-François Robin; *E:* Sophie Tatischeff; *M:* Jean Pierre Mas
Cast: Mário González, Sami Frey, Nicole Jamet, Christine Murillo

A threesome involving two men and a woman is going along happily until another woman enters the scene and it becomes a foursome.

Prod Comp: Dimage, SND
Dist/Sales: NewLine

Wigstock: The Movie (1987)

Rubnitz, Tom
1987; USA; 20 min; Documentary

A documentary about the annual New York 'storywig-in' organised by The Lady Bunny, featuring Lypsinka, John Sex, John Kelly, Baby Gregor, Hapi Phace, Taboo, among many others. (The Kitchen)

Dist/Sales: Kitchen

Wigstock: The Movie (1995)

Shils, Barry
1995; USA; 85 min; Documentary
P: Dean Silvers, Marlen Hecht; *E:* Marlen Hecht, Tod Scott Brody, Barry Shils; *M:* Gerry Gershman
Cast: Alexis Arquette, Candis Cayne, Crystal Waters, Coco Peru, RuPaul Charles

Part concert, part frockumentary this engaging and fun film journeys beneath the glamour and make-up of the annual Wigstock Festival in New York. Features great performances from drag queen luminaries such as RuPaul and Deee-lite along with some cute drag kings as well.

Dist/Sales: 21stCentury, Wolfe

Wild Life

Goss, John
1985; USA; 40 min; Drama

A portrait of two 15-year-old gay Latinos, combining documentary-style interviews with fictional segments in which they act out their typical Los Angeles day. It explores the life of Carlos and Caesar, two school friends, and how they deal with being gay and coming out.

Dist/Sales: VideoOut

Wild Party, The

Arzner, Dorothy
1929; USA; 76 min; B&W; Drama
W: E. Lloyd Sheldon, John V. A. Weaver, George Marion Jnr; *C:* Victor Milner; *E:* Otho Lovering; *M:* John Leipold
Cast: Clara Bow, Fredric March, Marceline Day, Shirley O'Hara

Set in an all-girls school, *The Wild Party* is the story of a young student in love with one of the professors. The relationships between the girls is depicted in a very sensual manner, although there is no overt lesbianism. Dorothy Arzner was the most prominent female director in Hollywood from the late 1920s to the 1940s; she was also an overt lesbian and was tolerated by Hollywood because she was considered 'one of the boys'.

Prod Comp: Paramount Famous Lasky Corporation
Dist/Sales: Paramount

Wild Reeds, The

(aka: Les Roseaux Sauvages)

Téchiné, André
1994; France; 110 min; Drama
P: Georges Benayoun, Alain Sarde; *W:* André Téchiné, Olivier Massart, Giles Taurand; *C:* Jeanne Lapoirie; *E:* Martine Giordano
Cast: Élodie Bouchez, Gaël Morel, Stéphane Rideau, Frédéric Gorny

The Wild Reeds is set in 1962, the year in which the independence of Algeria was confirmed by the Evian Treaty. An intricate web of sexual and political tensions unexpectedly unites four young people as they each struggle for independence and maturity. Among the four is the sensitive, bourgeois, François, who is coming to terms with his sexuality and finds he is attracted to the rather butch, working-class Serge. French with English subtitles.

Awards: Cesar Awards, 1994: Best Film, Direction, Screenplay, New Actress
Prod Comp: IMA Productions, Les Films Alain Sarde, Strand
Dist/Sales: Strand, Ronin, 21stCentury, Wolfe

The Wild Reeds

Wild Side

Brauner, Franklin (aka Cammell, Donald)
1996; USA; 96 min; Thriller
P: Elie Cohn, John Langley, Nick Jones, Hamish McAlpine; *W:* China Kong, Donald Cammell; *C:* Sead Mutarevic; *E:* Frank Mazzola; *M:* Jaimie Muhoberac, Ryuichi Sakamoto, Jon Hassell
Cast: Christopher Walken, Joan Chen, Anne Heche, Steven Bauer

The story centres on Alex, a loan officer in a bank, who moonlights as a high class prostitute when there is the threat of losing her house. She meets up with a new client, Bruno a money launderer, his driver, who rapes Alex and turns out to be an undercover cop, and his lesbian wife. Alex somehow gets involved in a money-laundering deal and falls in love with the wife. There are some erotic lesbian sex scenes, but the best part is that the women get away with the loot. There is also a Director's Cut of the film (*Donald Cammell's Wild Side* released in 1999) which was pieced together by the editor after Cammell apparently suicided when the studio cut was not to his liking. The Director's Cut is said to be an outstanding piece of cinema and far superior to the studio release. Cammell had his name removed from the 1996 version.

Prod Comp: Nu Image, Channel 4, Mondofin BV, Wild Side Productions
Dist/Sales: 20thCenturyFox, Wolfe

Wild Things

McNaughton, John
1998; USA; 108 min; Thriller
P: Rodney M. Liber, Steven A. Jones; *W:* Stephen Peters;
C: Jeffrey L. Kimball; *E:* Elena Maganini;
M: George S. Clinton
Cast: Matt Dillon, Neve Campbell, Denise Richards,
Kevin Bacon, Bill Murray

A respectable Florida high school guidance counsellor's life is upended when he is accused of rape by
two rebellious students. Detective Ray Duquette is
brought in to investigate, but it seems that not
everything is as it appears, and more than one person
is being deceived.

Prod Comp: Mandalay Entertainment
Dist/Sales: Col-Tri, RoadshowEnt, SonyClassics

Wilde

(aka: Oscar Wilde)

Gilbert, Brian
1997; UK; 118 min; Drama
P: Marc Samuelson, Peter Samuelson; *W:* Julian
Mitchell; *C:* Martin Fuhrer; *E:* Michael Bradsell;
M: Debbie Wiseman
Cast: Stephen Fry, Jude Law, Vanessa Redgrave

In 1883, Irish-born Oscar Wilde returned to
London bursting with exuberance from a year long
lecture tour of the United States and Canada. Full of
talent, passion and, most of all, full of himself, he
courted and married the beautiful Constance Lloyd.
A few years later, Oscar Wilde's wit, flamboyance
and creative genius were widely renowned. His
literary career had achieved notoriety with the
publication of *The Picture of Dorian Gray* and he and
Constance had two sons. One evening Robert Ross,
a young Canadian house guest, tempted Oscar and
forced him to finally confront his homosexual
feelings that had gripped him since his school days.
Oscar's work thrived on the realisation that he was
gay, but his private life flew increasingly in the face
of decidedly anti-homosexual conventions of late
Victorian society. As his literary career flourished,
risk of a huge scandal grew ever larger. By 1892, on
the opening night of his acclaimed play *Lady
Windermere's Fan*, Oscar was reintroduced to
handsome young Oxford undergraduate, Lord
Alfred Douglas, who was nicknamed 'Bosie'.
Instantly mesmerised by the confident, dashing and
intelligent young man, Oscar began the passionate
and stormy relationship which consumed him and
ultimately destroyed him.

Dist/Sales: Wolfe, SonyClassics

Wildflowers

Smith, Robert
1989; UK; 65 min; Drama
P: Chris Harvey; *W:* Sharman Macdonald;
E: John Davies
Cast: Colette O'Neil, Beatie Edney, Stevan Rimkus

Sadie, a young woman, goes to visit her boyfriend's
family in a small seaside town in Scotland. She meets
his mother and becomes increasingly fascinated by
her, even more so when she discovers the mother is
bisexual. Made for television.

Prod Comp: Channel 4, Frontroom Films
Dist/Sales: Frameline

William Burroughs: Commissioner of the Sewers

Maeck, Klaus
1986; USA; 60 min; Documentary

Documentary portrait on the life of author and Beat
personality William Burroughs.

Willie Dynamite

Moses, Gilbert
1974; USA; 100 min; Action
P: Richard D. Zanuck, David Brown; *W:* Ron Cutler;
C: Frank Stanley; *E:* Aaron Stell; *M:* J. J. Johnson
Cast: Roscoe Orman, Diana Sands, Thalmus Rasulala,
Roger Robinson

An action film set in New York City that includes
some very colourful characters. A pimp sets out to
topple big-shot Roger Robinson, who camps it up as
an outrageous homosexual.

Prod Comp: Universal
Dist/Sales: Universal

Willkommen im Dom

(aka: Welcome to the Dome)

Hick, Jochen
1992; Germany; 15 min; Documentary
P: Elke Peters; *C:* P. C. Neumann; *E:* Jochen Hick

A visual record of the spectacular ACT UP (AIDS
Coalition To Unleash Power) action that took place
during the final service of the German Bishop's
Conference on 26 August 1991. The footage was
shot during the making of a television film about
this conference and the first Atheists' Congress in the
Federal Republic of Germany.

Prod Comp: Galeria Alaska Productions

W

Willy/Milly

(aka: Something Special)

Schneider, Paul
1986; USA; 90 min; Comedy
P: David Chilewich; *W:* Walter Carbone, Carla Reuben;
C: Dominique Chapuis; *E:* Michael R. Miller;
M: David McHugh
Cast: Pamela Segall, Patty Duke, John Glover, Eric
Gurry

Milly Niceman's dream comes true when she wishes
to be a boy and grows 'a guy thing down there'. Now
all the girls are taking a different interest in Milly,
now Willy, and with the right equipment Willy is
determined to have a good time as well. Not sighted
since it's release, Willy Milly is a rare example of a
Hollywood transgender comedy where the girl gets
to be a boy.

Dist/Sales: 20thCenturyFox

Wilma's Sacrifice

Lanteigne, Kat
1999; Canada; 15 min; Drama

This film tells the tale of young Wilma's romantic
escapades with Christine a woman from the 'outside'
world. Surrealistically set in the 1950s, the town of
Eden is a place where the air is haunted with silence.
Wilma has to choose whether to redeem herself in
the eyes of her religiously obsessed brother James,
her neurotic chain-smoking Mother, and her
opprobrious Father; or escape Eden, a place where
one can never feel quite clean enough. (CFMDC)

Dist/Sales: CFMDC

Windows

Willis, Gordon
1980; USA; 88 min; Thriller
P: Mike Lobell; *W:* Barry Siegel; *C:* Gordon Willis;
E: Barry Malkin; *M:* Ennio Morricone
Cast: Elizabeth Ashley, Talia Shire, Joseph Cortese, Kay
Medford

Thriller set in New York involving a homicidal
lesbian, who develops a fatal passion for a straight
young woman who is her neighbour. Ashley stalks
Shire, turning peeping Tom, and taking dire actions
to secure her affections. Very lesbophobic.

Prod Comp: Mike Lobell Productions, United Artists
Dist/Sales: ReelMovies, Warner, UA, VSM, ACMI

Witches, Faggots, Dykes and Poofters

One in Seven Collective
1979; Australia; 45 min; Documentary
P: Digby Duncan; *C:* Wendy Freecloud, Jan Kenny, Jeni

Thornley, David Perry; *E:* Melanie Read; *M:* Hens
Teeth

This film examines the individual and collective
oppression of homosexuals in Australia against the
background of such oppression throughout history.
It grew out of a gay liberation protest march in
Sydney where police clashed with homosexuals.
Believed to be the first Australian documentary
made on gay rights and the gay liberation movement.

Prod Comp: One in Seven Collective
Dist/Sales: NFVLS

Withnail and I

Withnail and I

Robinson, Bruce
1987; UK; 108 min; Comedy
P: Paul M. Heller; *W:* Bruce Robinson; *C:* Peter
Hannan; *E:* Alan Strachan; *M:* David Dundas, Rick
Wentworth
Cast: Paul McGann, Richard E. Grant, Richard
Griffiths, Ralph Brown

Set at the end of the swinging 1960s, the film
documents the tale of two down-and-out actors who
flee their London flat for a weekend country idyll
that turns into a vine-covered hell. The cottage,
offered to them by Withnail's gay uncle, has no
power, lights or running water, and their nightmare
begins. An intelligent and funny film with a witty
script and entertaining gay subtext.

Prod Comp: Handmade Films
Dist/Sales: Col-Tri, Equator

Without you I'm Nothing

Boskovich, John
1990; USA; 90 min; Comedy, Musical
P: Jonathan D. Krane; *W:* Sandra Bernhard, John
Boskovich; *C:* Joseph Yacoe; *E:* Pamela Malouf-Cundy;
M: Patrice Rushen
Cast: Sandra Bernhard, John Doe, Steven Antin, Lu
Leonard

W

Based on Sandra Bernhard's one-woman show, *Without You I'm Nothing* is an ecstatic celebration of deviancy and sexual difference. Bernhard is a sardonic and biting comedian who, in a series of inspired personas, exposes the hypocrisy and shallowness that dominate contemporary American culture. Whether sending up her suburban Jewish upbringing or the excesses of Hollywood stardom, Bernhard's stand-up routines reclaim the transgressive bitchiness of camp.

Prod Comp: MCEG Productions
Dist/Sales: Wolfe, ACMI

Wittgenstein

Wittgenstein

Jarman, Derek
1993; UK; 75 min; Drama
P: Tariq Ali; *W:* Derek Jarman, Terry Eagleton, Ken Butler; *C:* James Welland; *E:* Budge Tremlett; *M:* Jan Latham-Koenig
Cast: Tilda Swinton, Karl Johnson, Michael Gough, Clancy Chassay, Jill Balcon

The film traces Ludwig Wittgenstein's life and thoughts on the philosophy of language and meaning through the First World War; his career as a schoolteacher and eventually as an academic at Cambridge University; to his final abandonment of classical philosophy and the development of a challenging deconstruction of language which was to bring him into conflict with more positivist philosophies. Scripted by renowned English academic, Professor Terry Eagleton, the film revolves around a series of arguments and discussions between Wittgenstein, Bertrand Russell and their university peers. In the long run, Wittgenstein's break with the hierarchy at Cambridge is not only a product of intellectual speculation but is also rooted in his problematic and alienated homosexuality which could not find direct expression in the highly austere and conventional environment of 'high academia'.

Prod Comp: BFI, Channel 4, Uplink Co., Bandung
Dist/Sales: ACMI, Zeitgeist, BFI

Wolves of Kromer, The

Gould, Will
2000; UK; 80 min; Horror
P: Charles Lambert; *W:* Charles Lambert, Matthew Read; *C:* Laua Remacha; *E:* Carol Salter; *M:* Basil Moore-Asfouri
Cast: Angharad Rees, Kevin Moore, Rita Davies, Margaret Towner, Rosemary Dunham

Two young wolves fall in love, while two old maids plot to murder their mistress and frame the wolves for the crime.

Prod Comp: Discodog Productions
Dist/Sales: FirstRunFeatures, Wolfe

The Wolves of Kromer

Woman Accused, A

(aka: In the Glitter Palace)

Butler, Robert
1977; USA; 90 min; Drama
P: Jay Daniel, Jerrold L. Ludwig; *W:* Jerrold L. Ludwig;
C: Gerald Perry Finnerman; *E:* Richard Bracken,
Herbert H. Dow; *M:* John Carl Parker
Cast: Barbara Hershey, Chad Everett, Howard Duff,
Salome Jens, Carole Cook

A lesbian is accused of murder when the man blackmailing her is found dead. Everett plays her defence lawyer determined to discover the truth. At the time of its release it was a groundbreaking film in its treatment of lesbianism. Made for television.

Prod Comp: Columbia Pictures TV, The Writers' Company
Dist/Sales: Columbia, NBC

Woman Hunt

Romero, Eddie
1972; Philippines, USA; 80 min; Action
P: John Ashley, Eddie Romero; *W:* David Hoover;
C: Justo Paulino; *E:* Ben Barcelon, Joseph Zucchero
Cast: John Ashley, Sid Haig, Lisa Todd, Pat Woodell

An action adventure where kidnapped women are used as prey. Todd's dull performance as a black-leather-clad lesbian sadist wouldn't even amuse her fans.

Prod Comp: New World Pictures

Woman in Flames, A

(aka: Flaming Desire; Die Flambierte Frau)

van Ackeren, Robert
1982; Germany; 105 min; Drama
P: Robert Van Ackeren; *W:* Catherine Zwerenz, Robert van Ackeren; *C:* Jürgen Jürges; *E:* Tanja Schmidbauer;
M: Peer Raben
Cast: Mathieu Carrière, Gudrun Landgrebe, Gabriele Lafari, Hanna Zischler

A woman leaves her boring marriage and husband to become a high-class hooker. She teams up with a bisexual gigolo whom she falls in love with. A study of obsessive sex and passion, and sex without passion. A very slick and glossy portrayal of the complex psychology of sexual politics, but not always from an optimistic view. German with English subtitles.

Prod Comp: Dieter Geissler Filmproduktion

Woman Inside, The

Van Winkle, Joseph
1981; Canada; 95 min; Drama
P: Sidney H. Levine; *W:* Joseph Van Winkle; *C:* Ron Johanson; *E:* John Duffy; *M:* Eddy Manson
Cast: Gloria Manon, Michael Champion, Dane Clark, Joan Blondell

Gloria Manon plays the role of a male Vietnam veteran who decides to have a sex-change operation.

Prod Comp: 20th Century-Fox
Dist/Sales: 20thCenturyFox

Woman Like Eve, A

(aka: Een Vrouw als Eva)

van Brakel, Nouchka
1979; The Netherlands; 100 min; Drama
P: Matthijs van Heijningen; *W:* Judith Herzberg, Nouchka van Brakel; *C:* Nurith Aviv; *E:* Ine Schenkkan;
M: Laurens van Rooyen
Cast: Maria Schneider, Monique van de Ven, Marijke Merckens

This early positive portrayal of lesbians tells the sensitive story of Eve, a bored housewife, who leaves her marriage, finds feminism and falls in love with Liliane, a free-spirited lesbian folk singer.

Prod Comp: Sigma Films

Woman on Top

Torres, Fina
2000; USA; 92 min; Comedy
P: Alan Poul; *W:* Vera Blasi; *C:* Thierry Arbogast;
E: Leslie Jones; *M:* Luis Bacalov
Cast: Penelope Cruz, Murilo Benicio, Harold Perrineau Jnr, Mark Feuerstein

Isabella is a great cook, which is largely why her husband's restaurant in Brazil has been a success. She also has severe motion sickness, and to control it, she has to insist on doing the driving, and she must be on top during sex. Her misogynist husband, Toninho, uses this as an excuse to stray. Eventually Isabella can't take anymore, and moves to San Francisco to be with her childhood friend, Monica, a cross-dresser. Toninho eventually arrives in San Francisco with the intention of winning her back. However, he finds her hosting a popular food show on TV, whilst accepting the advances of her producer.

Prod Comp: Fox Searchlight
Dist/Sales: FoxSearchlight, 20thCenturyFox

Woman to Woman

Sheedy, Laura
1994; Australia; 23 min; Documentary

Interviews with young Melbourne lesbians, who talk about life, work and getting married... (MQFF)

W

Women I Love

Hammer, Barbara
1976; USA; 25 min; Experimental

Portraits of Hammer's friends and lovers.

Dist/Sales: Canyon, WMM

Women in Cages

(aka: Women's Penitentiary III)

de Leon, Gerardo
1971; USA; 73 min; Action
P: Ben Balatrat, Roger Corman, Cirio H. Santiago;
W: Jim Osterhout, James Watkins; *C:* Felipe Sacdalan;
E: Ben Barcelon
Cast: Judy Brown, Roberta Collins, Pam Grier, Jennifer Gan

Women-behind-bars melodrama, with lots of sadism and scantily dressed women. Pam Grier plays a lesbian prison guard who tortures her prisoners in a chamber called the Play-pen.

Prod Comp: New World Pictures, Premiere Productions

Women in Love

Russell, Ken
1969; UK; 128 min; Drama
P: Larry Kramer; *W:* Larry Kramer; *C:* Billy Williams;
E: Michael Bradsell; *M:* Georges Delerue
Cast: Glenda Jackson, Oliver Reed, Jennie Linden, Alan Bates

A powerful adaptation of D. H. Lawrence's novel about two sisters who have relationships with two men. Bates's character seems unable to be fulfilled by a woman and craves the companionship of men. This craving culminates in a very homoerotic nude wrestling scene by the fireside between his character and Reed's. The film ends with Reed killing himself because he can't return Bates's affection and Bates crying 'He should have loved me. I offered it'.

Awards: Academy Awards, 1970: Best Actress (Glenda Jackson), Best Adapted Screenplay (Larry Kramer)
Prod Comp: United Artists, Brandywine Productions
Dist/Sales: ReelMovies, ACMI, UA

Women in Revolt

Morrissey, Paul
1971; USA; 89 min; Comedy
P: Andy Warhol; *W:* Paul Morrissey; *C:* Jed Johnson, Andy Warhol; *E:* Paul Morrissey
Cast: Holly Woodlawn, Candy Darling, Jackie Curtis, Penny Arcade, Betty Blue

Three drag queens, Jackie Curtis, Candy Darling, and Holly Woodlawn are members of feminist group PIGs (Politically Involved Girls). Covers their boredom with the workforce, along with the trials and tribulations of relationships with men (and women), their feminist attacks on men. A politically incorrect farce not to be taken seriously.

Dist/Sales: NewVision

Women Like us/Women Like that

Neild, Suzanne / Pearson, Rosalind
1990; UK; 49 min; Documentary

Two part series featuring sixteen older lesbians from diverse backgrounds, ranging in age from 50 to 80+, as they tell about their lives from the 1920s to the present. Moving and intimate portraits explore the experiences of women during the World War II, butch/femme roles, the emergence of modern feminism and coming out later in life to husbands and children. *Women Like That* is a poignant sequel to *Women Like Us* in which eight participants discuss their changed lives since the film's popular broadcast in England. (WMM)

Dist/Sales: WMM

Women of Brewster Place, The

Deitch, Donna
1989; USA; 189 min; Drama
P: Reuben Cannon, Patricia K. Meyer; *W:* Karen Hall;
C: Alexander Gruszynski; *E:* Jerrold L. Ludwig;
M: David Shire
Cast: Oprah Winfrey, Robin Givens, Paula Kelly, Mary Alice, Olivia Cole, Moses Gunn

A portrait of seven black women living in an apartment building whose crumbling walls have turned the address of Brewster Place into both a real and symbolic dead end. The cast of characters ranges from welfare mothers to a sophisticated lesbian couple. Based on the novel by Gloria Naylor and made for TV by the director of *Desert Hearts*.

Prod Comp: Harpo Productions, King Phoenix Entertainment
Dist/Sales: 21stCentury

Women of Gold

Abbink, Marilyn / Lee, Eileen
1990; USA; 30 min; Documentary

'Being athletic is not something that we, as Asian women, were encouraged to be' says body builder Kitty Tsui in this engaging record of the experiences of Asian-Pacific athletes who participated in the 1990 Gay Games. (MQFF)

Dist/Sales: WMM

Women on the Roof

(aka: Kvinnorna på taket)

Nykvist, Carl-Gustaf
1989; Sweden; 90 min; Drama
P: Katinka Faragó; *W:* Carl-Gustaf Nykvist, Lasse
Summanen; *C:* Jörgen Persson, Ulf Brantas; *E:* Lasse
Summanen; *M:* Håkan Möller
Cast: Helena Bergstrom, Amanda Ooms, Stellan
Skarsgård, Percy Brandt

Set in 1914, this slow-moving film is the story of a
timid young woman, Linnea, who befriends a
sophisticated photographer, Anna. They soon
develop a romantic interest in each other but things
change when the young girl's ex-boyfriend arrives in
town. Carl-Gustaf Nykvist is the son of the great
Swedish cinematographer, Sven Nykvist, who has
worked with, among others, Ingmar Bergman.
Swedish with English subtitles.

Prod Comp: Swedish Film Institute, Filmhuest, Svensk
Filmindustri
Dist/Sales: SwedishFilminstitute

Wonder Boys, The

Hanson, Curtis
2000; Germany, Japan, UK, USA; 112 min; Drama,
Comedy
P: Curtis Hanson, Scott Rudin; *W:* Steve Kloves;
C: Dante Spinotti; *E:* Dede Allen; *M:* Leonard Cohen,
Christopher Young
Cast: Michael Douglas, Tobey Maguire, Frances
McDormand, Robert Downey Jnr

In this touching comedy drama, Michael Douglas
stars as Grady Tripp, a university professor struggling
to write a second novel after the wild success of his
first book seven years ago. The action takes place on
the Pittsburgh campus where Tripp teaches, during a
weekend literary festival. Tripp, stoned and depressed
by the departure of his third wife, drifts from mishap
to mishap clad in a fuzzy pink bathrobe. In one
humorous subplot, Robert Downey Jnr, playing
Tripp's gay editor, shows up at the festival with a
transvestite he's picked up, then dumps him to
pursue one of Tripp's students. (Wolfe)

Prod Comp: BBC, Paramount
Dist/Sales: Wolfe, Paramount, Warner, Swank

Word is Out

Adair, Peter
1977; USA; 124 min; Documentary
P: Nancy Adair, Peter Adair, Andrew Brown, Robert
Epstein, Lucy Massie Phenix, Veronica Selver

A documentary that focuses on the conversations of
26 American gays and lesbians from a variety of
backgrounds (class and ethnic groups) who talk
about their experiences, how they deal with their
sexuality and society's attitudes towards them. The
film is neither militant nor analytical, and is an
important document of gay and lesbian culture.

Prod Comp: Mariposa Film Group

Work

Reichman, Rachel
1996; USA; 90 min; Drama
P: Susan A. Stover; *W:* Rachel Reichman
Cast: Cynthia Kaplan, Sonja Sohn

The story of two women trapped in an economically
ravaged small town. Jenny is out of work and stuck
in a loveless marriage with a boring man. She spends
her days in the depressing search for work. The only
light in her life is an affair with her next-door
neighbour, June. June is a 20-year-old student and
plans to leave the town she hates. Conflict arises
when Jenny doesn't seem to mind her situation and
is happy to stay.

Dist/Sales: District, ACMI

Working Class Dykes from Hell

Lawrence, Jacquie
1992; UK; 20 min; Documentary

Similar experiences have shaped a working-class gay
lifestyle, but even the lesbian who purges class from
personal or political agendas lives a life generated by
class-based experience. Class, though not the only
factor, can become an important one in the choice of
a lover.

Working Girls

Working Girls

Borden, Lizzie
1986; USA; 90 min; Drama
P: Lizzie Borden, Andi Gladstone; *W:* Lizzie Borden,
Sandra Kay; *C:* Judy Irola; *E:* Lizzie Borden; *M:* David
Van Tieghen

W

Cast: Louise Smith, Deborah Banks, Liz Caldwell, Marusia Zach, Amanda Goodwin

A comical and non-judgmental look at prostitution, where it is viewed as an economic alternative and a business transaction. Set in Manhattan, it is the story of Molly, an aspiring photographer, who lives with her black lesbian lover and child.

Prod Comp: Alternative Current
Dist/Sales: Col-Tri, ACMI, Miramax, NFVLS, BFI

World According to Garp, The

Hill, George Roy
1982; USA; 131 min; Comedy
P: George Roy Hill, Robert L. Crawford; *W:* Steve Tesich; *C:* Miroslav Ondrícek; *E:* Ronald Roose, Stephen A. Rotter; *M:* David Shire
Cast: Glenn Close, Robin Williams, Mary Beth Hurt, John Lithgow, Jessica Tandy

A complex, unpredictable man takes an eccentric journey through life. He's the bastard son of a nurse and as an adult marries and pursues a career as a writer. Some great performances, including those by Close and Lithgow (who plays a transsexual), make this a most intelligent, well-crafted and enjoyable film. Lithgow was nominated for an Academy Award. Based on the novel by John Irving.

Prod Comp: Pan Arts Productions, Warner
Dist/Sales: Roadshow, Warner

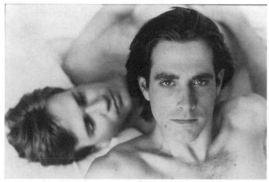

World and Time Enough

World and Time Enough

Mueller, Eric
1994; USA; 90 min; Drama
P: Andrew Peterson, Julie Hartley; *W:* Eric Mueller; *C:* Kyle Bergersen; *E:* Laura Stokes; *M:* Eugene Huddleston
Cast: Gregory G. Giles, Matt Guidry, Kraig Swartz, Peter Macon

Mark is a sculptor who is HIV-positive and mounts politically based environmental installations, and Joey is his teddy-bear boyfriend, a highway garbage collector. When Mark's father dies, Mark starts to make a cathedral with his own hands—he wants to build 'something that's going to last forever'.

Awards: San Francisco International Lesbian & Gay Film Festival, 1995: Audience Award for Best Feature
Prod Comp: 1 in 10 Films
Dist/Sales: Strand, Wolfe, 10%

World is Sick (sic), The

Greyson, John
1989; Canada; 38 min; Documentary

A humorous account of activism and journalism at the Fifth International Conference on AIDS in Montreal in June 1989.

Worthy Mothers

Bega, Jessica Anna
1996; USA; 63 min; Documentary

Worthy Mothers is a powerful and touching video documentary which looks into the everyday lives of two lesbian couples who chose to raise children. Through candid interviews, the members of the two multiracial, multicultural families portrayed share the personal, social and legal experience in becoming mothers.

Woubi Chéri

Bocahut, Laurent / Brooks, Philip
1998; France, Ivory Coast; 62 min; Documentary
P: Philip Brooks, Laurent Bocahut

Woubi Chéri is the first film to give African homosexuals a chance to describe their world in their own words. Often funny, sometimes ribald, but always real, this documentary introduces us to gender pioneers demanding their right to construct a distinct African homosexuality.
(California Newsreel)
French with English subtitles.

Dist/Sales: CaliforniaNewsreel

Wrecked for Life: The Trip & Magic of Trocadero Transfer

Goss, John
1993; USA; 60 min; Documentary

Goss interviews the past employees of San Francisco's famed gay nightclub Trocadero Transfer.

Wrestlers, The

(aka: Uttara)

Dasgupta, Buddhadeb
2000; India; 98 min; Drama
P: Buddhadeb Dasgupta; *W:* Buddhadeb Dasgupta,

Samaresh Bose; *C:* Asim Bose; *E:* Rabi Ranjan Maitra;
M: Biswadep Dasgupta
Cast: Jaya Seal, Tapas Pal, Shankar Chakraborty, Tapas
Adhikari, R. I. Asad

Dasgupta's visually rich feature focuses on the lives of
Balram and Nemai, two station masters who while
away their days on remote railway station, working
together and sharing their passion for wrestling.
Exploring the boundaries of Dosti—the Indian
concept of close relationships between men—
Dasgupta reveals an undercurrent of homoeroticism
that resonates throughout the film. But this rural
idyll is threatened when Balram unexpectedly arrives
back from a visit home with a new wife and the local
priest becomes the target of an anti-Christian gang.
Dasgupta has created a unique and mysterious world
populated with Hindu folk dancers and a community of small people, and his influences appear to run
from Fellini to photographer Diane Arbus. This is a
standout example of contemporary Indian arthouse
cinema, both ravishing and provocative to watch.
(BFI)
Bengali with English subtitles.

Dist/Sales: LesGrands

Wrong Son, The

Oliver, Bill
1993; USA; 15 min; Comedy

Poaching material from an old television game show
in which the contestants have to guess who is telling
the truth and who is lying, this clever film neatly
captures the ridiculous dilemmas facing gays in the
military. (MQFF)

Wu Yen

Wai, Kai-fai / To, Johnnie
2001; Hong Kong; 120 min; Drama
P: Johnnie To, Kai-fai Wai; *W:* Kai-fai Wai, Nai-hoi Yau,
Ben King-fai Wong; *C:* Siu-keung Cheng; *E:* Wing-
cheong Lau, Wing-ming Wong; *M:* Raymond Wong
Cast: Anita Mui, Sammi Cheng, Cecilia Cheng,
Raymond Wong

Wu Yen is a collaboration by director/producers
Johnnie To and Ka-fai Wai, who set the standard for
quality in the post-1997 Hong Kong film industry
with their Milkyway Image film company productions. *Wu Yen* is their first Chinese New Year film.
The plot is based on an old Chinese folk legend that
has been depicted in several earlier Hong Kong films
and featured in Cantonese opera. As portrayed in the
current film, the story concerns a complicated love
triangle set in the distant past. A female outlaw
warrior Zheng Wuyan (aka Chung Mo-yim, aka Wu

Yen) and a Fairy Enchantress who moves between
male and female personas vie for the affections of the
Emperor Qi. (Shelly Kracier with Sebastian Tse,
Chinese Cinema)
Cantonese with English subtitles.

Dist/Sales: Seng

X Y and Zee

(aka: Zee and Co.)

Hutton, Brian G.
1971; UK; 105 min; Drama
P: Jay Kanter, Alan Ladd Jnr; *W:* Edna O'Brian; *C:* Billy
Williams; *E:* Jim Clark; *M:* Stanley Myers
Cast: Elizabeth Taylor, Michael Caine, Susanna York,
Margaret Leighton

A well-to-do architect has an affair with a young
designer but events change when his wife discovers
the young woman's bisexuality and exacts her revenge.
She fights tooth and nail to get her husband back,
and winds up in the young woman's bed herself.

Prod Comp: Columbia, Zee Company
Dist/Sales: Col-Tri

XXXY

Gale, Porter / Soomekh, Laleh
2000; USA; 13 min; Documentary

Moving portrait of two intersex individuals born
with ambiguous genitalia, and their struggle with the
medical establishment and society's rigid gender
system. (MQFF)

Y tu Mamá También

Y tu Mamá También

(aka: And your Mother Too)

Cuaron, Alfonso
2001; Mexico, USA; 105 min; Drama
P: Jorge Vergara; *W:* Alfonso Cuaron, Carlos Cuaron;
C: Emmanuel Lubezki

Cast: Diego Luna, Gael Garcia Bernal, Maribel Verdu,

Y tu Mamá También is a dynamic coming-of-age road movie. Like most teen males, Tenoch and Julio are on a crotch-first rush into adulthood. With their girlfriends away in Europe, they collect beautiful 'older woman' Luisa on the road and head for an imaginary beach paradise. Competing for her affections, unspoken jealousies throw open matters of friendship and the heart. (2002 Melbourne International Film Festival)
Spanish with English subtitles.

Dist/Sales: GoodMachine, Dendy, Globe

Yang±Yin: Gender in Chinese Cinema

Kwan, Stanley
1996; Hong Kong, UK; 77 min; B&W; Documentary
W: Elmond Yeung; *C:* Christopher Doyle; *E:* Maurice Li

Uncovers depictions of homosexuality, cross-dressing, and gender fluidity across 100 years of Chinese cinema.

Prod Comp: BFI
Dist/Sales: BFI, NFVLS

Yearning for Sodom

Baethe, Hanno
1988; Germany; 44 min; Drama
E: Michael F. Huse
Cast: Hans Hirschmüller, Kurt Raab

During the 1970s, actor Kurt Raab collaborated with director Rainer Werner Fassbinder on over 30 films. In 1982, he wrote about this intense creative period in *Die Sensuchtdes Rainer Werner Fassbinder*. When he was later asked to write about himself and the New German Cinema, Raab decided to present the subject in the form of 33 video scenes entitled *Sensucht Nach Sodom* (*Yearning for Sodom*). Only six scenes had been completed when Raab was diagnosed with AIDS. With the assistance of his friends, actor Hans Hirschmuller and director Hanno Baethe, Raab continued to work on this, his last film, a moving mixture of diary and performance that shows Kurt for the fierce fighter and gifted artist that he was. (MQFF)

Prod Comp: Hanno Baethe Film und Videoproduktion

Yellow Fever

Yeung, Raymond
1998; UK; 26 min; Comedy
P: Johann Insanally

A love story set in 1990s London, following the life of Monty, a gay Chinese Anglophile, desperately seeking his 'white knight'. A modern comedy of manners, a sizzling stir-fry with more than a hint of oriental spice, a dash of camp and a trace of glamour. (Frameline)

Prod Comp: Sankofa Film
Dist/Sales: Frameline

Yentl

Streisand, Barbra
1983; USA; 130 min; Drama
P: Barbra Streisand, Rusty Lemorande; *W:* Jack Rosenthal, Barbra Streisand; *C:* David Watkins; *E:* Terry Rawlings; *M:* Michel Legrand, Alan Bergman, Marilyn Bergman
Cast: Barbra Streisand, Mandy Patinkin, Amy Irving, Steven Hill, Nehemiah Persoff

Set around the turn of the century in Eastern Europe, and tells the story of Yentl a young woman who, in order to study the scriptures, disguises herself as a boy. The disguise is perfect, almost too good, as Yentl, ends up marrying Hadass.

Awards: Golden Globe Awards, 1984: Best Director, Motion Picture
Prod Comp: United Artists
Dist/Sales: ACMI, Warner, MGM, Swank

Yes

(aka: To Ingrid my Love Lisa; Kvinnolek)

Sarno, Joseph W.
1968; Sweden; 90 min; Drama
W: Joseph W. Sarno; *C:* Åke Dahlqvist
Cast: Gun Falck, Heinz Hopf, Lars Lind, Mimi Nelson

Lisa is a fashion designer who falls in lust with her neighbour's daughter, Ingrid. After a lot of hard work, food and drink, Lisa finally succeeds in getting Ingrid into bed, but it's a long and painful time before she submits. An over-the-top lesbian obsession film that still manages to be enjoyable.

Prod Comp: Omega Film

Yo Yo Gang

Jones, G. B.
1992; Canada; 20 min; Action

An exuberant girl-gang action-adventure film involving intrigue, yo-yos, skateboards, romance, go-go boy slaves and sparkling dialogue.

You are not Alone

(aka: Du er ikke Alene)

Johansen, Ernst / Nielsen, Lasse
1978; Denmark; 90 min; Comedy
P: Steen Herdel; *W:* Lasse Nielsen, Bent Petersen;

C: Henry Herbert; *E:* Hanne Hass; *M:* Sebastian
Cast: Peter Bjerg, Anders Agensø

A funny and charming account of two boys who fall in love at a Danish boarding school. One of the boy's fathers, who happens to be the principal, finds out and threatens to destroy the relationship. Fortunately, love conquers all.

Prod Comp: Steen Herdel Filmproduktion

You don't know Dick: Courageous Hearts of Transsexual Men

Cram, Bestor / Schermerhorn, Candace
1996; USA; 75 min; Documentary
P: Candace Schermerhorn, Bestor Cram; *C:* Bestor Cram, Mike Majoros, Michael A. Gorenberg, Bruce Johnson; *E:* Mike Majoros

"I kept waiting for that facial hair to come ... instead l got breasts." *You don't know Dick* presents a series of honest and self-effacing insights into the lives and minds of female-to-male transsexuals. Ted, Michael, James, Max, Stephan and Loren discuss their experiences of 'living a lie', bilateral mastectomies, genital reconstruction, testosterone injections, intimate relationships, 'doing it' and 'fitting in'.

Prod Comp: Northern Light Productions
Dist/Sales: FilmsTransit

You Taste American

Greyson, John
1986; Canada; 24 min; Experimental

Michel Focault and Tennessee Williams have an affair in Orillia, Ontario, and get caught up in the Canadian washroom arrests of 1983.

You've had Worse Things in Your Mouth

Liddi, Allison
1994; USA; 50 min; Comedy
Cast: Billi Gordon

Food takes a back seat to the 400-pound transsexual Billi Gordon's one-liners as she tries to host the cooking show from hell.

Dist/Sales: TLA

Young Soul Rebels

Julien, Isaac
1991; UK; 103 min; Drama
P: Nadine Marsh-Edwards; *W:* Paul Hallam, Isaac Julien, Derrick McClintock Saldaan; *C:* Nina Kellgren;

E: John Wilson; *M:* Simon Boswell
Cast: Valentine Nonyela, Mo Sesay, Dorian Healy, Frances Barber, Sophie Okonedo

Set during the Queen's Silver Jubilee in 1977, Young Soul Rebels depicts the youth, music and passion of the era in the UK through the eyes of two black men, one gay, the other straight, who both operate a pirate radio station.

Awards: Cannes Film Festival, 1990: Critic's Award
Prod Comp: BFI, Film Four International
Dist/Sales: Dendy, Col-Tri, Swank, BFI

Young Soul Rebels

Your Brother, my Tidda

Martin, Kelrick
2002; Australia; 20 min; Documentary

Coming out to family and living with HIV are some of the life-changing situations faced by two Aboriginal gay men, Sam and Aaron. (queerDOC 2002)

Your Heart is all Mine

Gotz, Elke
1992; Germany; 50 min; Comedy

The story centres around two women who not only have to contend with who is the butchest but a clinging, semi-incestuous mother as well.

Your Mother Wears Combat Boots

Swenson, Laurel
1996; USA; 16 min; Documentary

A defiant montage of testimony, home video footage, interviews and rants. Young, angry and in-your-face, these women talk about poverty, classism, and the day-to-day trials, absurdities and joys of being a young, low-income lesbian mother.

Dist/Sales: VideoOut

Youth Outloud!

Burklee, Becky / Hines, Kathy
2000; USA; 50 min; Documentary

The complexities of coming out and the injustice of homophobia are the true essence of this documentary.

Dist/Sales: Sun&Moon

Zanjeer

(aka: The Chain)

Mehra, Prakash
1973; India; 146 min; Drama
P: Prakash Mehra; *W:* Javed Akhtar, Salim Khan;
C: N. Satyen; *E:* R. D. Mahadik; *M:* Kalyanyi Anandji
Cast: Amitabh Bachchan, Jaya Bhaduri, Pran, Om Prakash

This adaptation of the Hollywood crime melodrama to the Hindi entertainment film was a major success for superstar Amitabh Bachchan, who plays a man consumed by the desire for revenge. As a child, Vijay saw his parents murdered by a gunman following his father's release from prison. In adulthood Vijay becomes a police officer who treats criminals as personal enemies: he breaks the law while ostensibly upholding it. He threatens the criminal activities of a highly respectable businessman who trades in illicit liquor. Vijay forms what amounts to a homoerotic relationship with an honest Pathan, Sher Khan, but according to codes of Indian destana (male friendship) the relationship cannot be acknowledged as homosexual. Vijay's masculinity is affirmed in action scenes and through his relationship with Mala, a knife grinder. Hindi with English subtitles.

Dist/Sales: NFVLS

Zazie dans le Métro

Malle, Louis
1959; France; 88 min; Comedy
P: Louis Malle; *W:* Jean-Paul Rappeneau, Louis Malle;
C: Henri Raichi; *E:* Kenout Peltier; *M:* Fiorenzo Carpi, André Pontin
Cast: Vittorio Caprioli, Yvonne Clech, Hubert Deschamps, Annie Fratellini, Jacques Dufilho

Scandalous and maniacal surrealist comedy by the director of *Pretty Baby* and *Atlantic City*. A precocious 11-year-old with too much time on her hands is sent to spend the weekend with her uncle in Paris. She is greeted at the door by her uncle who is wearing a dress. French with English subtitles.

Prod Comp: Nouvelles Éditions de Films
Dist/Sales: Ascanbee

Zero Budget

Hindley, Emma
1996; UK; 25 min; Documentary

An inspirational documentary looking at independent film productions from the US. It deals in particular with lesbian feature filmmakers and shows clips from films such as *Go Fish*. There are also stories from, and interviews with, filmmakers like Christine Vachon.

Prod Comp: Channel 4
Dist/Sales: Frameline, Channel4

Zero de Conduite

(aka: Zero for Conduct)

Vigo, Jean
1933; France; 47 min; B&W; Drama
Cast: Jean Daste, Robert le Lon, Louis Lefebvre

A marvellously subversive film about the rebellion of four boys at a French provincial school. Banned for many years, it was re-released in 1945 although it was considered to contain anti-French sentiment. Included is a young homosexual boy who develops a tender friendship with a classmate. French with English subtitles.

Dist/Sales: NFVLS, ACMI

Zero Patience

Greyson, John
1993; Canada; 95 min; Comedy, Musical
P: Louise Garfield, Anna Stratton; *W:* John Greyson;
C: Miroslaw Baszak; *E:* Miume Jan; *M:* Glenn Schellenberg
Cast: John Robinson, Norman Fauteux, Dianne Heatherington, Richard Keens-Douglas

Z

This AIDS musical tells the story of 70-year-old sexologist, Sir Richard Burton, who is preparing a sensationalist museum display about Patient Zero, Gaetan Dugas, the airline steward accused of bringing AIDS to America. Zero's ghost is on hand to set the record straight. It includes a number of Busby Berkeley-style musical numbers such as *The Butthole Duet*.

Prod Comp: Zero Patience Productions
Dist/Sales: Potential, Fortissimo, Cinevista, Cowboy, NFVLS, ACMI

Zindagi Zindabad

(aka: Long Live Life)

Bhave, Sumitri / Sukthankar, Sunil
2000; India; 130 min; Drama
P: Sumitri Bhave, Sunil Sukthankar; *W:* Sumitri Bhave; *C:* Charudatta Dukhande; *E:* Sumitri Bhave, Sunil Sukthankar; *M:* Anand Modak
Cast: Mita Vasisht, Milind Gunaji, Uttara Baokar, Abhiram Bhadkamkar

Three stories merge to illustrate the realities of HIV/AIDS in modern urban India. A rare Indian perspective on a worldwide problem. Hindi with English subtitles.

Zippers & Tits

(aka: Fasuna to Chibusa)

Shirakawa, Koji
2001; Japan; 60 min; Drama
W: Koji Shirakawa; *E:* Koji Shirakawa; *M:* Kiyohito Komatsu
Cast: Kentaro Takayama, Sachiko Ejiri, Manami Ogawa, Yoshifumi Tsubota

Shirakawa Koji's film gets inside the heads of two prostitutes, a young rent boy and a 30-year-old woman. The boy in *Zipper* works the city streets, servicing his johns in back-alleys, and goes home to a boyfriend who takes him completely for granted. Thanks to the hypocrisy/hostility of many of the johns, the boy's self-esteem is so low it barely registers on the scale. The woman in *Tits* works in the small apartment she shares with a boyfriend who cooks for her and serves as her banker. The episode centres on the day she receives her first female client, a brittle, unsympathetic woman who turns out to have an ulterior motive for coming. Not long after, the boyfriend moves out. (2001 Vancouver International Film Festival)
Japanese with English subtitles.

Zorro, the Gay Blade

Medak, Peter
1981; USA; 93 min; Comedy
P: George Hamilton, E. O. Erickson; *W:* Greg Alt, Hal Dresner, Don Moriarty, Bob Randall; *C:* John A. Alonzo; *E:* Hillary Jane Kranze; *M:* Ian Fraser
Cast: George Hamilton, Lauren Hutton, Brenda Vaccaro, Ron Leibman

A very likeable and funny spoof of the original story with George Hamilton playing the two Zorros. When the real Zorro hurts his foot, he calls on his effeminate gay brother to temporarily assume his heroic role with some humorous results.

Prod Comp: 20th Century-Fox, Melvin Simon Productions
Dist/Sales: 20thCenturyFox

Films of Particular Interest

Bisexual

2 Seconds
  (aka: 2 secondes; Deux secondes)
Adjuster, The
Anita: Dances of Vice
  (aka: Anita: Tanze des Lasters)
Audit
Becoming Colette
Berlin Affair, The (aka: Interno Berlinese)
Beyond Therapy
Bisexual Kingdom, The
Bob & Rose
Bound and Gagged: A Love Story
Break of Day
Cabaret
California Suite
Cha-Cha for the Fugitive, A
  (aka: Gai Tao-wan-je de ChaCha)
Change of Heart, A
Chasing Amy
Clancy's Kitchen
Cleopatra's Second Husband
Confessions of Felix Krull, The
  (aka: Bekenntnisse des
  Hochstaplers Felix Krull)
Confusion of Genders
  (aka: La confusion des genres)
Day for Night
  (aka: La Nuit Américaine)
Desire (1999)
Don't Forget You're Going to Die
  (aka: N'Oublie pas que tu vas Mourir)
Dry Cleaning (aka: Nettoyage à sec)
Équilibristes, Les
  (aka: Walking a Tightrope)
Exploding Oedipus
Final Programme, The (aka: The
  Last Days of Man on Earth)
Geschlecht in Fesseln: dei Sexualnot
  der Gefangenen (aka: Sex in Chains)
Happily Ever After
  (aka: Além da Paixão)
Henry and June
Iris
Kali's Vibe
Karmen Geï
Kesher Ir (aka: Urban Feel)

Kinsey 3, The
Kissing Jessica Stein
Larry's Visit
Life History of a Star
Life that We Dreamt, The
  (aka: Het Leven dat we Droomden)
Lonely Lady, The
Love=ME3
Marlene
Mirror Images II
North of Vortex
Notorious C.H.O.
Peixe-Lua (aka: Moon-Fish)
Pillow Book, The
Reflections in a Golden Eye
Roi Danse, Le
  (aka: The King is Dancing)
Room of Words, The
  (aka: La Stanza della parole)
Rose, The
Sand and Blood (aka: De sable et de sang)
Score
Second Skin (aka: Segunda Piel)
Seduction: The Cruel Woman
  (aka: Verführung: Die grausame Frau)
Slaves to the Underground
Smokers Only
  (aka: Vagón Fumador)
Something for Everyone
  (aka: Black Flowers for the Bride)
Straight to the Heart
  (aka: À Corps Perdu)
Sunday, Bloody Sunday
To Ride a Cow
Totally Confused
Touch of Love, A (aka: Thank You
  All Very Much; The Millstone)
Trois
Velocity of Gary, The
Why Not! (aka: Pourquoi Pas!)
Woman in Flames, A
  (aka: Flaming Desire; Die
  Flambierte Frau)
X Y and Zee (aka: Zee and Co.)
Y tu Mamá También
  (aka: And Your Mother Too)

Cross-dressing, Transgender & Transsexual

99% Woman
About Vivien
Across the Rubicon
Adventures in the Gender Trade
All about My Father
  (aka: Alt om min far)
All Men are Liars
  (aka: Goodnight Irene)
Alley of the Tranny Boys
Always Walter! An Inner View of
  Walter Larrabee
Angels!
Ballad of Little Jo, The
Battle of Tuntenhaus
Belle al Bar (aka: Belles at the Bar)
Black Lizard (aka: Kurotokage)
Blank Point: What is Transsexualism?, The
Blessed Art Thou
  (aka: A Question of Faith)
Blue Haven
Bombay Eunuch
Boy Named Sue, A
Boys Don't Cry
Boys from Brazil, The
Boys in the Backyard
Brandon Teena Story, The
Bugis Street
  (aka: Yao jie huang hou)
Butterflies on the Scaffold
  (aka: Mariposas en el andiamo)
By Hook or by Crook
Cage aux Folles, La
Cage aux Folles II, La
Cage aux Folles III, La
Calamity Jane
Christine Jorgensen Story, The
Cinema Fouad
Come Back to the Five and Dime,
  Jimmy Dean, Jimmy Dean
Coming Out (1972)
Creature
Crying Game, The
Curse of the Queerwolf
Danger Girl, The

Danzón
Day I Decided to be Nina, The
Derrière, Le (aka: From Behind)
Different for Girls
Dog Day Afternoon
Dr Jekyll and Ms Hyde
Drag Attack
Dragtime
Dream Girls
Dressed to Kill
Eat the Rich
Ed Wood
Eine Tunte zum Dessert
   (aka: A Fairy for Dessert)
F2M
Fanci's Persuasion
Fight to Be Male, The
Flawless
Flora's Garment Bursting into Bloom
Florida Enchantment, A
Fontvella's Box
Forever Mary (aka: Mery per sempre)
Forms and Motifs
Gendernauts
Georgie Girl
Girl Stroke Boy
Glen or Glenda
Haunted World of Edward D.
   Wood Jnr, The
He's My Girl
Heart's Root, The
   (aka: A Raiz Do Coração)
Her Life as a Man
Homecoming Queen
Homicidal
Hu-Du-Men (aka: Stage Door)
I Am My Own Woman
   (aka: Ich Bin Meine Eigene Frau)
I Don't Wanna Be a Boy
I Want What I Want
If She Only Knew
Impossible on Saturday
In a Year of Thirteen Moons
   (aka: In einem Jahr mit 13 Monden)
In the Flesh (2000)
Iron Ladies, The (aka: Sa tree lex)
It's a Boy! Journeys from Female to Male
Jake 'Today I Became a Man'
Jareena: Portrait of a Hijda
Jewel's Darl
Joey Goes to Wigstock
Juggling Gender
Just a Woman

Just Call Me Kade
Just like a Woman
Just One of the Girls
   (aka: Anything for Love)
Kalihgat Fetish
   (aka: Kalighat Athikatha)
Ladies Please!
Lady
Lady in Waiting, The
Ladyboys
Lip Gloss
Liquid Sky
Little Bit of Lippy, A
Luminous Procuress
Ma Vie en Rose (aka: My Life in Pink)
Made in Heaven
Mascara
Matt
Men Like Me
Metamorphosis: Man into Woman
Metamorphosis: The Remarkable
   Journey of Granny Lee
Mi Novia El
Miguel/Michelle
Mirror, Mirror (aka: Lille spejl)
Monsieur Hawarden
Mrs Doubtfire
My Friend Su
Mystère Alexina, Le
   (aka: The Mystery of Alexina)
Myth of Father
Never Look Back
No Dumb Questions
Norang Mori 2
   (aka: Running Blue; Yellow Hair 2)
On Becoming
Orlando
Outlaw
Outrageous!
P(l)ain Truth
Pansexual Public Porn (aka: The
   Adventures of Hans and Del)
Paradise Bent
   (aka: Fa'afafines in Paradise)
Paris is Burning
Pencas de Bicuda
Phantom Pain
Pink Angels, The
Portion of a Lady
Princesa
Queen of the Whole Wide World
Queen, The

Queens Don't Lie
   (aka: Tunten Lügen Nicht)
Salt Mines, The
Sando to Samantha: The Art of Dikvel
Second Serve
Sex Change: Shock! Horror! Probe!
Sex Flesh in Blood
Sex Warriors and the Samurai
Sexe des étoiles, Le
   (aka: Sex of the Stars)
Shadey
Shantay
Shinjuku Boys
Sir: Just a Normal Guy
Some Like It Hot
Southern Comfort
Speaking for Ourselves
Split: Portrait of a Drag Queen
   (aka: Split: William to Chrysis)
Stepping Out
Storme: The Lady of the Jewel Box
Surrender Dorothy
Sweet Thing
Switch (1991)
Swordsman II (aka: Xiao ao jiang
   hu zhi dong fang bu bai)
Swordsman III: The East is Red
   (aka: Dung fong bat baai 2: fung
   wan joi hei)
Sylvia Scarlett
Taste
Tender
Thelma
To Wong Foo, Thanks for Every-
   thing, Julie Newmar
Tootsie
Transanimals
Transexual Menace
Transformation, The
Transit: Adventures of a Boy in the
   Big City
Transsexual Journey, A
Trappings of Transhood
Trevor
Triple Echo
Turnabout
Two Brides and a Scalpel: Diary of
   a Lesbian Marriage
Vegas in Space
Venus Boyz
Vera
Victor/Victoria
Viktor/Viktoria

Wax Me
We Are Transgenders
What a Pretty Sister
Whether You Like It or Not: The Story of Hedwig
Who's the Woman, Who's the Man
Wigstock: The Movie (1995)
Willy/Milly (aka: Something Special)
Woman Inside, The
Woman on Top
XXXY
You Don't Know Dick: Courageous Hearts of Transsexual Men
Zazie dans le Métro

Fringe

Abysses, Les
Acting on Impulse
   (aka: Eyes of a Stranger)
Adam's Rib
Adieu Bonaparte
After Hours
Alexandria...Why? (aka: Iskanderija...lih?)
Alien Prey
All the Queens Men
American Beauty
Anderson Tapes, The
Angel (1983)
Anniversary, The (1968)
Any Wednesday
Aqueles Dois
Astragale, L'
Barry Lyndon
Basketball Diaries, The
Beat
Beau Travail (aka: Good Work)
Beautiful Dreamers
Bed of Lies
Bedazzled
Beethoven's Nephew
   (aka: Le Neveu de Beethoven)
Belle de Jour
Belle époque
Ben Hur
Best Man, The
   (aka: Gore Vidal's The Best Man)
Betsy, The
Beware a Holy Whore (aka:
   Warnung vor einer heiligen Nutte)
Big Business
Big Sky, The

Bitter Harvest (1993)
Black and White
   (aka: Noir et Blanc)
Black Mama, White Mama
Blazing Saddles
Blood and Concrete
Blood Money
Bloodlust
Blunt: The Fourth Man
Borderline
Boston Strangler, The
Boys Next Door, The
Breaking the Code
Broadway Melody, The
Burning Secret
Bus Riley's Back in Town
Butcher's Wife, The
Calamity Jane
Cat and the Canary, The
Cat on a Hot Tin Roof
Cat People
Cecil B Demented
Celeste
Celestial Clockwork
   (aka: Mecaniques Celestes)
Chain of Desire
Chained Heat
Chanel Solitaire
Choirboys, The
Chuck and Buck
Clancy Street Boys
Cleopatra Jones
Comfort of Strangers, The
Company of Strangers, The
   (aka: Strangers in Good Company)
Confessions of a Window Cleaner
Coonskin (aka: Street Fight)
Coup de Grace
   (aka: Der Fangschuss)
Crush (1992)
Daisies (aka: Sedmikrásky)
Darling
Day of the Jackal, The
Deadfall
Deliverance
Devil's Playground, The
Diabolique
Diaboliques, Les (aka: Diabolique)
Doctors' Wives
Doom Generation
Double Face
Eiger Sanction, The

Ein Toter Hing im Netz
   (aka: Girls of Spider Island)
Enfants Terribles, Les
   (aka: The Strange Ones)
Equus
Escalier C
Fearless Vampire Killers, The
   (aka: Dance of the Vampires)
Fisher King, The
Flirt
Four Weddings and a Funeral
Foxfire
Frankie and Johnny
Freebie and the Bean
Full Monty, The
Full Moon in New York
   (aka: Ren zai Niu Yue)
Funny Lady
Garbo Talks
Genesis Children, The
Gentlemen Prefer Blondes
Getting of Wisdom, The
Gilda
Girl in Every Port, A
Girl Thing, A
Girlfriends (1978)
Go
Gold Diggers, The
Good Family, The
   (aka: Thanksgiving Day)
Good Father, The (aka: Fathers' Rites)
Goodbye Girl, The
Haunted Summer
Haunting, The
Headhunter
Hearing Voices
Hell's Highway
Hidden Assassin (aka: The Shooter)
Higher Learning
Hired to Kill
I Am a Camera
I Vitelloni (aka: The Young and the Passionate)
In Bed with Madonna
   (aka: Madonna: Truth or Dare)
In This House of Brede
Inspecteur Lavardin
Internal Affairs
Johnny Guitar
Journey Among Women
Julia
Just One of the Guys

Killer, The
   (aka: Die Xue Shuang Xiong)
King and Country
King Girl
King of the City (aka: Club Life)
Kings of the Road
   (aka: Im Lauf der Zeit)
L-Shaped Room, The
Lady in Cement
Ladybugs
Last Emperor, The
Last Married Couple in America, The
Last Metro, The
   (aka: Le Dernier métro)
Last of Sheila, The
Laughing Policeman, The
Legend of Lylah Clare, The
Lightship, The
Live Nude Girls
Living Out Loud
Long Voyage Home, The
Loose Connections
Loot
Loss of Innocence
   (aka: The Greengage Summer)
Love in a Women's Prison
   (aka: Diario Segreto da un
   Carcere Femminile)
Love Letter, The
Loved One, The
Lulu
Madame Sousatzka
Magic Christian, The
Magnolia
Mahogany
Manhattan
Mannequin
Merry Christmas, Mr Lawrence
Mike's Murder
Milou in May
   (aka: Milou en Mai; May Fools)
Miracle Alley
   (aka: El Callejon de los Milagros)
Mona Lisa
Morocco
Mountains of the Moon
Mull (aka: Mullaway)
My Best Friend's Wedding
Naked in New York
Nea: The Young Emmanuelle (aka: Nea)
Next Stop, Greenwich Village

Night of Varennes, The
   (aka: La Nuit de Varennes)
Night Rhythms
No Way Out
Ode to Billy Joe
Only When I Laugh
Order to Kill
   (aka: El Clan de los Immorales)
Other Voices, Other Rooms
Passed Away
Peter's Friends
Pillow Talk
Play It as It Lays
Pleasure Principle, The
Postman (aka: Youchai)
Prince of Tides, The
Private Benjamin
Quai des Orfèvres
   (aka: Jenny Lamour)
Question of Attribution, A
Rachel, Rachel
Reaching for the Moon
Red River
Reflecting Skin, The
Reform School Girls
Sammy and Rosie Get Laid
Scenes from the Class Struggle in
   Beverly Hills
Second Awakening of Christa
   Klages, The (aka: Das Zweite
   Erwachen der Christa Klages)
Secret Ceremony
Secret Policeman's Private Parts, The
Seducers, The (aka: Death Game)
Separate Peace, A
Set It Off
Seven Women
Sex, Drugs and Democracy
Shanghai Panic (aka: Wo men hai pa)
Sign of the Cross, The
Silence of the Lambs, The
Silence, The (aka: Tystnaden)
Silkwood
Sincerely Yours
Spy Who Came, The
Streamers
Strippers
Summer of Miss Forbes, The (aka:
   El Verano de la señora Forbes)
Swann in Love
   (aka: Un Amour de Swann)

Tell Me That You Love Me, Junie Moon
Thelma and Louise
Things You Can Tell Just by
   Looking at Her
Thirst (aka: Törst; Three Strange Loves)
Three to Tango
Throwback
   (aka: Spike of Bensonhurst)
Thunderbolt and Lightfoot
Todd Killings, The
Tokyo Fist (aka: Tokyo-ken)
Touch of Evil
Two Moon Junction
Undercover
Up the Academy
Velvet Goldmine
Well, The
When the Cat's Away
   (aka: Chacun Cherche Son Chat)
Wild Party, The
Wild Things
William Burroughs: Commissioner
   of the Sewers
Willie Dynamite
Withnail and I
Woman Hunt
Women of Brewster Place, The
Wonder Boys, The
World According to Garp, The
Wrestlers, The (aka: Uttara)
Yentl
Zanjeer (aka: The Chain)

Gay

10 Attitudes
100 Days Before the Command
   (aka: Sto dnej do prikaza)
101 Rent Boys
2 by 4 (aka: 2 x 4)
24 Nights
$30
45 Minutes of Bondage
'68
7 Steps to Sticky Heaven
90 Miles
A.K.A
Abandoned (aka: Torzók)
Above the Sea (aka: Au essus de la Mar)
Absolution of Anthony, The
Abuse

Achilles

Acla
  (aka: La Discesa di Aclà a Floristella)

Actions Speak Louder than Words

Adam

Addicted to Love
  (aka: Boku wa koi ni muchu)

Adiós Roberto

Adventures of Priscilla, Queen of
  the Desert, The

Adventures of Sebastian Cole, The

Advise and Consent

Affairs of Love, The
  (aka: Las Cosas del Querer)

Affirmations

Afflicted

Aide Mémoire

Alabaster Lions

Alexander: The Other Side of Dawn

Algie the Miner

Alias

Alive and Kicking (aka: Indian Summer)

Alkali, Iowa

All about Alice

All Over the Guy

All the Rage

All-American Story, An

Alpsee

Alternative, The

Amazing Grace (aka: Hessed Mufla)

American Fabulous

American Gigolo

Amerikanos

Amic/Amat (aka: Beloved/Friend)

Amigos (aka: Friends)

Among Men

Among Others

Amos Gutman, Filmmaker
  (aka: Amos Gutman, Bamay Kolnoa)

Anatomy of a Hate Crime

And the Band Played On

And Then Came Summer

Anders als die Anderen
  (aka: Different from Others)

Angelic Conversation, The

Angelos (aka: Angel)

Animal Factory

Anniversary, The (1995)

Another 45 Minutes of Bondage

Another Country

Anxiety of Inexpression and the
  Otherness Machine, The

Anything Once

Apariencias

Apart From Hugh

Apartment Zero

Arabian Nights (aka: Il Fiore delle
  mille e una notte)

Arch Brown's Top Story

Armistead Maupin is a Man I
  Dreamt Up

Arrangement, An

Art of Cruising Men, The

As Far Away as Here

As Good As It Gets

As Is

Asa Branca: A Brazilian Dream

At Home

Away with Words (aka: Kujaku)

baba-It (aka: At Home)

Baby

Baby Steps

Backroom

Bad News Bachelors

Ballad of Reading Gaol

Be Careful What Kind of Skin You
  Pull Back, You Never Know
  What Kind of Head Will Appear

Beautiful Thing

Beauty Before Age

Bedrooms & Hallways

Beefcake

Before Night Falls

Behind Glass

Behind Walls

Being at Home with Claude

Bellas de Noche

Benjamin Smoke

Bent

Bertrand is Missing
  (aka: Bertrand Disparu)

Best In Show

Best Way, The
  (aka: La Meilleure façon de marcher)

Better Dead than Gay

Beyond Gravity

Beyond the Catwalk: The Search
  for Mr Gay Australia 2000

Bezness

Big Eden

Big House, The

Bigger Splash, A

Bike Boy

Billy Turner's Secret

Billy's Hollywood Screen Kiss

Biloxi Blues

Birdcage, The

Birthday Time

Bishonen...Beauty
  (aka: Meishaonian zhi lian)

Black Sheep Boy

Blind Fairies
  (aka: Le Fate Ignoranti)

Blind Faith

Block Party

Blond Man, The

Blonde Cobra

Bloodbrothers (aka: A Father's Love)

Blue

Blue Hour, The (aka: Die Blaue Stund)

Blue Jeans

Body without Soul

Bombay Boys

BOMgaY

Borstal Boy

Boy like Many Others, A
  (aka: Un Ragazzo come Tanti)

Boy Next Door

Boychick

Boyfriends (1995)

Boyfriends (1999)

Boys in the Band, The

Boys' Night Out

Boys of Cell Block Q

Boys of Manchester, The

Brad

Breaking the Surface

Brian Epstein Story, The

Bright Spell (aka: L'Embellie)

Britney Baby - One More Time

Broadway Damage

Broken Branches (aka: Naeil Ui
  Hyahae Hurunun Kang)

Broken Hearts Club: A Romantic
  Comedy, The

Bubbeh Lee and Me

Buck House

Buckeye and Pinto

Buddies

Bungee Jumping of Their Own
  (aka: Beonjijeonpeureul hada)

Burlesk King
Burning Boy, The
Burnt Money (aka: Plata quemada;
    Burning Money)
Business of Fancydancing, The
Busting
Butch Camp
Butley
c-l-o-s-e-r
Cage aux Folles, La
Cage aux Folles II, La
Cage aux Folles III, La
Camp
Campfire (aka: Kampvuur)
Cap Tourmente
Caravaggio
Caretaker, The (aka: The Guest)
Carrington
Casta Diva
Cater Waiter
Caught
Caught Looking
Cavafy (aka: Kavafis)
Chaero
Change
Changing Face
Chant d'Amour, Un
Children of Hannibal
    (aka: Figli di Annibale)
Children of the Regime
Chill Out
Chinese Characters
Chop Suey
Chuck Solomon: Coming of Age
Circuit
Citizen Cohn
Claire
Clay Farmers, The
Clinic E
Clinic, The
Close To Home
Closet, The (aka: Le Placard)
Closets Are Health Hazards
Closing Numbers
Coffee Date
Cold Footsies
Cold Lands, The (aka: Les Terres Froides)
Colegas (aka: Pals)
Colonel Redl (aka: Oberst Redl)
Coming of Age
Coming Out (1989)
Coming to Terms

Compromised Immunity
Compulsion
Confession, The
Conformist, The
    (aka: Il Conformista)
Connections: Gay Aboriginal Men
    in Sydney
Consenting Adult
Consequence, The (aka: Die Konsequenz)
Conta Pra Mim (aka: Trust Me)
Conversation Piece (aka: Gruppo di
    famiglia in un interno)
Corps Imagé, Le
Corps Ouverts, Les (aka: Open Bodies)
Could Be Worse
Crash and Burn
Crazy Richard
Creation of Adam, The
    (aka: Sotvoreniye Adama)
Crocodile Tears
Crossing, The (aka: La Traversée)
Cruising
Crush (2000)
Daddy and the Muscle Academy
Daddy & Papa
Dads (aka: Papas)
Dadshuttle, The
Daisy Chain Project, The
Dakan
Damned, The (aka: Gotterdammer-
    ung; La Caduta degli Dei)
Dark and Lovely, Soft and Free
    (aka: Nega Do Cabelo Duro)
Dark Sun: Bright Shade
Darker Side of Black, The
Das Trio (aka: The Trio)
David & Goliath
David Searching
Day the Fish Came Out, The
    (aka: Otan ta psaria vgikan sti steria)
Days (aka: Giorni)
Dead Boys' Club, The
Dead Dreams of Monochrome Men
Deaf Heaven
Dear Boys (aka: Lieve Jongens)
Dear Rock
Death in the Family, A
Death in Venice (aka: Morte a Venezia)
Death in Venice, CA
Deathtrap
Deathwatch
Decodings

Deep End, The
Deep Inside Clint Star
Deflatable Man, The
Defying Gravity
Delta, The
Demons
Deserter (aka: Lipotaktis)
Desperate Acquaintances
    (aka: Desperate Bekjentskaper)
Detective, The
Diary of a Male Whore
Different Kind of Black Man, A
Different Kind of Love, A
Different Shades of Pink
Dinner Guest, The
Diputado, El (aka: The Deputy)
Disco Years, The
Doing Time on Maple Drive
Don't Tell Anyone
    (aka: No Se Lo Digas a Nadie)
Dona Herlinda and Her Son
    (aka: Doña Herlinda y su hijo)
Doors Cut Down
Double the Trouble, Twice the Fun
Drama in Blonde
Drawing Girls
Dreaded Experimental Comedies:
    How to Lessons, Body Rhythms,
    My New Lover, The
Dreck (aka: Dirt)
Dress Gray
Dresser, The
Drift
Drifting (aka: Nagu'a)
Drowning Lessons
Duffer
Dyke Blend
Early Frost, An (1985)
Early Frost, An (2000)
East Palace West Palace
    (aka: Dong Gong Xi Gong)
Eban and Charley
Echte Kerle
    (aka: Regular Guys)
Eclipse
Edge of Seventeen (aka: Edge of 17)
Edward II
Eika Katappa
Einstein of Sex: The Life and Work
    of Dr Magnus Hirschfeld, The
Elegant Criminal, L' (aka: Lacenaire)
Elegy in the Streets

Elevation

Elton John: Tantrums and Tiaras

Empire State

Empty Bed, An

Englishman Abroad, An

Entertaining Mr Sloane

Ernesto

Escorte, L'

Evening Dress
   (aka: Tenue de Soirée; Menage)

Evenings, The (aka: De Avonden)

Everlasting Secret Family, The

Execution of Justice

Exiles of Love

F. is a Bastard (aka: F. est un salaud)

Faggots are for Burning

Fairy Who Didn't Want to Be a
   Fairy, The

Fall of Communism as Seen in Gay
   Pornography, The

Fated to be Queer

Fear of Love

Fete des Peres, La (aka: Dad's Day)

Fighting in South-West Louisiana

Film for Two

Finding North

Finished

Fireworks

First Breath

First Love and Other Pains

Fixing Frank

Flames of Passion

Flaming Creatures

Flavor of Corn, The
   (aka: Il Sapore del Grano)

Fleeing By Night (aka: Ye Ben)

Flight of Fancy

Flow

Fluffer, The

Flush

Fly Away Homo

Food of Love

For a Lost Soldier
   (aka: Voor een verloren soldaat)

For Better or for Worse: A Celebration of Enduring Relationships

Forbidden Justice (aka: Short Eyes)

Forbidden Love of the Hero, The

Forbidden Passion: Oscar Wilde the Movie

Forgive & Forget

Forsaken

Fortune and Men's Eyes

Forty Deuce

Fox and His Friends
   (aka: Faustrecht der Freiheit)

Francis Bacon

Freddie Mercury: The Untold Story

French Dressing
   (aka: Furenchi doressingu)

Freunde: The Whiz Kids

Friend of Dorothy, A

Friends and Family

Friends Forever (aka: Venner for Altid)

Friends in High Places

Frisk

From the Ashes

From the Edge of the City
   (aka: Apo tin akri tis polis)

Frostbite

Fruit Machine, The (aka: Wonderland)

Full Speed (aka: À Toute Vitesse)

Fun Down There

Funeral Parade of Roses
   (aka: Bara No Soretsu)

Funny Felix (aka: Dróle de Félix;
   The Adventures of Felix)

Garden, The

Gasp

Gay Agenda, The

Gay Bombay

Gay Deceivers, The

Gay Voices, Gay Legends

Gay Voices, Gay Legends 2

Get Real

Get Your Stuff

Ghosts of the Civil Dead

Ginger Beer

Girls in Boy's Bars

Glider, The (aka: Le Planeur)

Glitterbug

God, Sreenu & Me

Godass

Gods and Monsters

Gohatto (aka: Taboo)

Going West

Gonin (aka: The Five)

Got 2 B There

Gotta Have Heart (aka: Ba'al Ba'al Lev)

Grace of God, The

Green Plaid Shirt

Green Pubes

Grief

Guardian of the Frontier
   (aka: Varuh Meje)

Gypsy Boys

Habit

Half Mongrel

Hallelujah!

Hamam: The Turkish Bath
   (aka: Steam)

Hanging Garden, The

Happy Birthday Gemini

Happy Texas

Happy Together
   (aka: Cheun gwong tsa sit)

Hard

Hard Fat

Hard God, A

Harold and Hiroshi

Hate Crime

He Bop!

He's Bald and Racist, He's Gay and Fascist

He's Like

Head On (aka: Loaded)

Heart Exposed, The
   (aka: La Coeur Découvert)

Heaven, Earth and Hell

Heaven-6-Box
   (aka: Tengoku No Muttsu No Hako)

Hellion Heatwave

Hidden Injuries

Hit and Runway

hITCH

HIV Rollercoaster

Hold You Tight (aka: Yue Kuai Le)

Hole

Holi: Festival of Fire

Hollow Reed

Home for the Holidays

Homme Blessé, L'
   (aka: The Wounded Man)

Homme Que J'aime, L'
   (aka: The Man I Love)

Hooking Up

Hope Along the Wind: The Life of
   Harry Hay

Hope is a Thing With Feathers

Horror Vacui: The Fear of Emptiness
   (aka: Horror Vacui: Die Angst
   vor der Leere)

Horse Dreams in BBQ Country

Hours and Times, The

House of Pain

How I Love You (aka: Shou Bhebbak)

How Old is the River?
   (aka: Fuyu no Kappa)

Hubo un Tiempo en que Los
  Suenos Dieron Paso a Largas
  Noches de Insomnio
Hush!
Hustler White
I Am a Man
I Am Not What You Want
I Don't Just Want You to Love Me
  (aka: Ich will nicht nur, daß ihr
  mich liebt)
I Hate Faggy Fag Fag
I Know a Place
I Like You, I Like You Very Much
  (aka: Anata-Ga Suki Desu, Dai
  Suki Desu)
I Love You Baby
I Love You, I'll Kill You
  (aka: Ich Liebe Dich, Ich Töte Dich)
I Shall Not Be Removed: The Life
  of Marlon Riggs
I Think I Do
I'll Love You Forever - Tonight
Icarus
If
If All Goes Well I'll Meet You on
  the Next Train
If the Family Fits
Ifti
Illegal Tender
Image in the Snow
In on Earth as It Is in Heaven
In & Out
In the Flesh (1997)
In the Gloaming
In the Shadow of the Sun
Inauguration of the Pleasure Dome
Inside Out
Interview with the Vampire
Invocation of My Demon Brother
Iro Kaze (aka: Colour Wind)
It Dwells in Mirrors
It is Not the Homosexual Who is
  the Pervert but the Society in
  Which He Lives
  (aka: Nicht der Homosexuelle ist
  pervers, sondern die Situation, in
  der er lebt)
It's My Party
J'embrasse pas
  (aka: I Don't Kiss)
Jackson: My Life Your Fault

James Baldwin: The Price of the
  Ticket
Jean Cocteau: Autobiography of an
  Unknown
Jeffery's Hollywood Screen Trick
Jeffrey
Jerker
Jim Loves Jack: The James Egan Story
Joey Breaker
Joggernaught
Johnny Eager
Johns
Journey of Jared Price, The
Jungle Boy, The
Just for Fun
Karmarama
Keep the River on Your Right
Kevin's Room
Kicking On
Killer in the Village
Kind of Family, A
Kipling Trilogy, The
Kiss in the Snow, A
Kiss Me Guido
Kiss of the Spider Woman, The
Kizuna Volume 1 & 2
Km. 0 (aka: Kilometro cero)
Krámpack (aka: Nico & Dani)
Krays, The
L. I. E.
Lan Yu
Last Bus Home, The
Last Exit to Brooklyn
Last of England, The
Latin Boys Go To Hell
Laura
Lawless Heart, The
Leather
Leather Boys, The
Leather Jacket Love Story
Legacies
Legal Memory
Lesson 9
Letters from Home
Liberace
Liberace: Behind the Music
Lie Down with Dogs
Life
  (aka: Containment; Out of the Blue)
Life and Death
Life and Death on the A-List

Life and Times of Allen Ginsberg, The
Like Grains of Sand
  (aka: Nagisa no Shindobaddo)
Like It Is
Lilies (aka: Lilies - les Feluettes)
Limites
Liu Awaiting Spring
Living End, The
Living with AIDS
Loads
Lola and Billy the Kid
  (aka: Lola and Bilidikid)
Lone Star Hate
Lonely without You
Long Day Closes, The
Longtime Companion
Looking for Angel
  (aka: Tenshi No Rakuen)
Looking for Langston
Looking for Mr Goodbar
Lorenza
Lost in the Pershing Point Hotel
Lost Language of Cranes, The
Lot in Sodom
Love and Death on Long Island
  (aka: Amour et mort à Long Island)
Love and Human Remains
Love is the Devil
Love Like Any Other, A
  (aka: Eine Liebe wie andere auch)
Love Machine, The
Love of a Man, The
  (aka: Amor de hombre)
Love! Valour! Compassion!
Loverfilm
Loverville 2: The Honeymoon
Lucifer Rising
Ludwig
Ludwig: Requiem for a Virgin King
  (aka: Ludwig: Requiem für einen
  jungfräulichen König)
Lunch with Eddie
Luster
Lycanthrophobia
Lysis
M! Mom, Madonna and Me
Ma Vie (aka: My Life)
Macho Dancer
Madagascar Skin
Madras Eyes
Maids, The

Making Love
Mala Noche (aka: Bad Night)
Mama, I Have Something to Tell You
Man in Her Life, The
    (aka: Ang lalaki sa buhay ni Selya)
Man is a Woman (aka: L'Homme
    est une femme comme les autres)
Man Man Woman Woman
    (aka: NanNan NuNu; Men and Women)
Man of No Importance, A
Man of the Year
Man Who Drove with Mandela, The
Mandragora
Manila: In the Claws of Darkness
    (aka: Maynila: Sa mga kuko ng liwanag)
Map of Sex and Love, The
    (aka: Qingse ditu)
Marble Ass (aka: Dupe od Mramora)
March in April
Marching into Darkness
Mare, Il (aka: The Sea)
Markova: Comfort Gay
Martin Four
Mass Appeal
Massillon
Matter of Taste, A (aka: A Question
    of Taste; Une affaire de goût)
Maurice
Maybe I Can Give You Sex?
Me and the Girls
Melody for Buddy Matsumae
    (aka: Matsumae-Kun No Senritsu)
Memory Pictures
Men in Love
Men Men Men
    (aka: Uomini uomini uomini)
Menmaniacs: The Legacy of Leather
Meteor and Shadow
    (aka: Meteoro kai Skia)
Michael, a Gay Son
Midnight Cowboy
Midnight Dancers (aka: Sibak)
Midnight Express
Midnight in the Garden of Good and Evil
Mikaël (aka: Chained)
Minoru and Me
Moffie Called Simon, A
Montgomery Clift: The Prince
Montreal Main
More Love
Morris Loves Jack

Moscow Fags
Mountain King, The
Mr Christie
Muscle
Music Lovers, The
Must be the Music
My Addiction
My Beautiful Laundrette
My Body
My Brother's Keeper
My Cousin Mike
My First Suit
My Hustler
My Own Private Idaho
My Pal Rachid
My Summer Vacation
My Survival as a Deviant
Naked Civil Servant, The
Naked Highway
Nana, George and Me
Naughty Little Peeptoe
Nervos de Aco
    (aka: Nerves Made of Steel)
Nervous Energy
Next Best Thing, The
Night Larry Kramer Kissed Me, The
Night Out
Night Trade
Night Warning
Nighthawks
Nijinsky
Nijinsky
    (aka: The Diaries of Vaslav Nijinsky)
No Backup
No One Sleeps
No Ordinary Love
No Skin Off My Ass
Nocturne (1989)
Norman, is that You?
Not Angels, But Angels
Not Love, Just Frenzy
    (aka: Mas Que Amor, Frenesi)
Number 96
Nunzio's Second Cousin
O Boys: Parties, Porn & Politics, The
Object of My Affection, The
Offering, The
Oi Queer
Oi! Warning
Okoge
Oliver

Olivier, Olivier
On Being Gay: A Conversation
    with Brian McNaughton
ON_LINE
On the Bus
Once upon a Time in the East
    (aka: Il était une fois dans l'est)
One of Them
One + One
Opposite of Sex, The
Ordinary Sinner
Original Schtick
Other Side, The
    (aka: Del Otro Lado)
Otra Historia de Amour
    (aka: Another Love Story)
Our Brothers, Our Sons
Our Lady of the Assassins
    (aka: La Virgen de los sicarios)
Our Sons (aka: Too Little, Too Late)
Out in the Open
Out of the Closet, Off the Screen:
    The Life & Times of William Haines
Outcasts, The
    (aka: Niezi; The Outsiders)
Outrageous!
P. S. Your Cat is Dead
Panic Bodies
Paper Cranes
Paragraph 175
Parallel Sons
Parting Glances
Partners
Passing Resemblance
Past Caring
Paul Cadmus: Enfant Terrible at 80
Paul Monette: The Brink of
    Summer's End
Pedagogue
Penitentiary
Pensao Globo
Peoria Babylon
Perfect Son, The
Peter Allen: The Boy from Oz
Phantom (aka: O Fantasma)
Philadelphia
Pianese Nunzio
    (aka: Fourteen in May; Sacred Silence)
Pierre et Gilles, Love Stories
Pink Narcissus

Pink Ulysses
Pixote: A Lei do Mais Fraco
Place Between Our Bodies, The
Place in the Sun, A
Play Dead
Pleasure Beach
Poetry for an Englishman
Point of Departure, A
Poison
Pony Glass
Pool Days
Portrait of Jason
Positiv
Positive Story (aka: Sipur Hiyuvi)
Possible Loves (aka: Amores Possiveis)
Postcards from America
Pouvoir Intime
Presque Rien
   (aka: Come Undone; Almost Nothing)
Pretty Baby (aka: Maybe...Maybe
   Not; Der Bewegte Mann; The
   Most Desired Man)
Pretty Boy (aka: Smukke Dreng)
Prick Up Your Ears
Priest
Prince in Hell
   (aka: Prinz in Holleland)
Private Wars
Protagonist, The (aka: Shujinko)
Public Opinion
Punks
Queen's Cantonese Conversational
   Course, The
Queens Logic
Queer Story, A (aka: Jilao Sishi)
Querelle
Questioning Faith
Rainbow Serpent, The
   (aka: Haltéroflic)
Raising Heroes
Ray's Male Heterosexual Dance Hall
Red Dirt
Red Ribbon Blues
Reflections
Relax
Resident Alien
Resonance
Return to Go! (aka: Züruck Auf Los!)
Revolutions Happen like Refrains
   in a Song
Rhythm & Blues
Rice and Potatoes

Rites of Passage
Ritual
Ritz, The
Rock Hudson
Rock Hudson's Home Movies
Rock the Boat
Rockwell
Roommates
Rope
Rough Sketch of a Spiral
   (aka: Rasen No Sobyo)
Roy Cohn / Jack Smith
RSVP
Sad Disco Fantasia
Safe Journey
Safe Place, A
Sagitario
Sailor (aka: Matroos)
Saint
Salome's Last Dance
Salut Victor!
Satdee Nite
Saturday Night at the Baths
Saturn's Return
Satyricon
Sauve Qui Peut (aka: Slow Motion)
Savage Nights (aka: Les Nuits fauves)
School Fag
Scorpio Rising
Scout's Honor
Sea in the Blood
Seamen
Sebastian
Sebastiane
Second Coming, The
Secrets
Sergeant Matlovich vs. the U.S. Air Force
Sergeant, The
Servant, The
Sex Becomes Her: The True Life
   Story of Chi Chi LaRue
Sex Is...
Sex is Sex: Conversations with Male
   Prostitutes
Sex/Life in LA
Shall We Dance
Shampoo Horns
   (aka: Cuernos de espuma)
Shinjuku Triad Society
   (aka: Shijuku Kuro Shakai)
Shooting Porn
Show Me Your Pic

Siberia
Siege (aka: Self Defense)
Siegfried
Silencis (aka: Silent Moments)
Silverlake Life: The View From Here
Sissy
Six Degrees of Separation
Sixth Happiness, The
Skin and Bone
Skin Complex
Skin Flick (aka; Skin Gang)
Sleep in a Nest of Flames
Sleepy Haven
Slight Fever of a 20-Year-Old
   (aka: Hatachi No Binetsu)
Smear
Smoke
Snake Boy, The
Sodom
Soft Hearts (aka: Pusong Mamon)
Soliloquy of Dale Cunningham, The
Solos Y Soledades
Some of My Best Friends Are
Some of These Days
Something Close to Heaven
Song of the Loon
Sordid Lives
Sospiro d'amore nell'attesa
Soufflé
Sparky's Shoes
Special Day, A
   (aka: Una Giornata particolare)
Special Guest Star
Speedway Junky
Speedy Boys
Spent
Spin the Bottle
Split World, The
Spokes
Sprinter, The
Squeeze
Staircase
Star is Porn, A
Star Maps
Stargaze
Stephen
Story of a Bad Boy, The
Straight in the Face
Straightman
Strange Life and Death of Dr
   Turing, The
Strange Love Affair, A

Strange One, The (aka: End as a Man)
Strawberry and Chocolate
   (aka: Fresa y Chocolate)
Strip Jack Naked: Nighthawks II
'Sucker
Suddenly, Last Summer (1959)
Sum of Us, The
Summer Dress, A
   (aka: Une Robe d'été)
Summer in My Veins (Director's Cut)
Summer Vacation 1999
   (aka: 1999 Nen No Natsu Yasumi)
Super 8 1/2
Surviving Sabu
Swimming Prohibited (aka: Yuei Kinshi)
Swoon
TABU V (about which one cannot speak)
Take Out
Talk of the Town (aka: Stadtgespräch)
Talk to Me like the Rain
Tanaka
Tangible Fathers
Tarch Trip
Taste of Honey, A
Taxi to Cairo
   (aka: Taxi nach Kairo)
Taxi to the Toilet
   (aka: Taxi zum Klo)
Tea and Sympathy
Tell Me No Lies
Tell Me the Truth About Love
Tell Me Why: The Epistemology of Disco
Tenebrae Lessons
   (aka: Leçons de Ténèbres)
Teorema (aka: Theorem)
Terence Davies Trilogy, The
Terry and Julian (Vol. 1 and 2)
That Certain Summer
Theme: Murder
There is no Pain in Paradise (aka:
   En el Paraiso no Existe el Dolor)
Third Sex, The
   (aka: Anders als du und ich)
This I Wish and Nothing More
   (aka: Nincsen Nekem Vagyam Semmi)
This Special Friendship
   (aka: Les Amitiés Particulières)
Three Bewildered People (aka:
   Three Bewildered People in the Night)
Threesome
Thug
Tidy Endings

Tim Miller: Loud and Queer
Time Being, The
Time Off
Time Piece
Time Regained
   (aka: Le Temps retrouvé)
Time Zones
To an Unknown God
   (aka: A un Dios Desconocido)
To Die for (aka: Heaven's a Drag)
To Forget Venice
   (aka: Dimenticare Venezia)
To Play or to Die
   (aka: Spelen of sterven)
Toc Storee
Together Alone
Together and Apart
Toilers and the Wayfarers, The
Token of Love
Tom
Tom Clay Jesus
Tongues Untied
Too Much Sun
Too Young (aka: Ye Maque)
Torch Song Trilogy
Total Eclipse
Total Loss
Tour Abroad (aka: Auslandstournee)
Toxic Queen
Trials of Oscar Wilde, The
Triche, La (aka: The Cheat)
Trick
Trip, The
True Faith
Truth About Gay Sex, The
Truth Game, The
Twice a Man
Twilight of the Gods
Twilight of the Golds, The
Twinkle (aka: Kira Kira Hikaru)
Twinkle Toes
Twisted
Two Brothers
Two Men
Two of Us (aka: Mates)
Two Point Five
Unconditional Love
Uncut
Under Heat
Unknown Cyclist, The
Urbania
Valentino

Vanished
Vaudeville
Very Funny
Very Natural Thing, A
Via Appia
Victim
Villain
Violet's Visit
Virgin Larry, The
Virus Knows No Morals, A
   (aka: Ein Virus kennt keine Moral)
Vive l'Amour (aka: Aiqing Wansui)
Waiting
Waiting 'round Wynyard
Walking On Water
Wallowitch & Ross: This Moment
Waves (aka: Bølgene)
We Think the World of You
We Were One Man
   (aka: Nous étions un Seul Homme)
Webcam Boys
Wedding Banquet, The (aka: Hsi yen)
Wedding Video, The
Weekend, The
Weiner Brut
Weiningers Nacht
Well Lit Shadows
West Fickt Ost (aka: West Fucks East)
Westler: East of the Wall
What is the Relationship between
   Rosa von Praunheim and the
   Male Strippers of San Francisco?
What Kind of Music!
   (aka: Ma Che Musica!)
When Boys Fly
When the Party's Over
Where Is My Love?
   (aka: Qiangpo Puguang)
Where Lies the Homo?
Where the Sun Beats Down
   (aka: Onde Bate o Sol)
Who Killed Pasolini?
   (aka: Pasolini, an Italian Crime;
   Pasolini, un delitto Italiano)
Wild Life
Wild Reeds, The
   (aka: Les Roseaux Sauvages)
Wilde (aka: Oscar Wilde)
Wittgenstein
Wolves of Kromer, The
Women in Love
World and Time Enough

Wrong Son, The
Yearning for Sodom
Yellow Fever
You Are Not Alone (aka: Du er ikke alene)
You Taste American
Young Soul Rebels
Your Brother, My Tidda
Zero de Conduite
   (aka: Zero for Conduct)
Zero Patience
Zippers & Tits (aka: Fasuna to Chibusa)
Zorro, the Gay Blade

Lesbian

10 Violent Women
101 Reykjavik
17 Rooms
   (or What Do Lesbians Do in Bed?)
2 or 3 Things But Nothing for Sure
27 Pieces of Me
301 - 302
4pm
99 Women
   (aka: Isle of Lost Women; 99 mujeres)
Acquiring a Taste for Raffaella
After the Break (1992)
After the Break (1998)
After the Game
Afternoon Breezes
   (aka: Kaze tachi No Gogo)
Age 12: Love with a Little L
Aileen Wuornos: The Selling of a
   Serial Killer
Aimée and Jaguar
Airport
Alicia was Fainting
All Fall Down
All Girl Action: The History of
   Lesbian Erotica
All Over Me
Alles Wird Gut
   (aka: Everything Will Be Fine)
Almost the Cocktail Hour
Älskande par (aka: Loving Couples)
Alternative Conceptions
Amelia Rose Towers
Amor Maldito
Amorosa
And/Or=One
Anna und Edith
Anna und Elisabeth

Anne Trister
Another Way (aka: Egymásra Nézve)
Antonia's Line
Apartments
Are You Greedy?
Ashley 22
Atomic Sake
B. D. Women
B.U.C.K.L.E.
B/side
Bad Brownies
Badass Supermama
Baise-moi (aka: Fuck Me; Rape Me)
Balcony, The
Bar Girls
Bargain Lingerie
Basement Girl, The
Basic Instinct
Basic Necessities
Because the Dawn
bed
Beguines, The
   (aka: Le Rampart des Beguines)
Being John Malkovich
Belle
Below the Belt
Berlin Affair, The (aka: Interno Berlinese)
Bete Noire
Better than Chocolate
Between the Lines
Between Two Women
Biches, Les (aka: The Does)
Bilitis
Bird in the Hand
Bisexual Kingdom, The
Bitter Moon
Bitter Tears of Petra von Kant, The
   (aka: Die Bitteren Tränen der
   Petra von Kant)
Bittersweet
Black Sheep
Black Sunday
   (aka: La Maschera del Demonio)
Black Widow
Blessed are Those Who Thirst
   (aka: Salige er de som tørster)
Blind Moment, The
Blood and Roses
   (aka: Et Mourir de Plaisir)
Blood Splattered Bride, The
   (aka: La Novia Ensangrentada)
Bloodsisters: Leather Dykes and S&M
Bodies in Trouble

Body of a Poet: A Tribute to Audre
   Lorde 1934-1992, The
Boots, Boobs and Bitches: The Art
   of G. B. Jones
Border Line...Family Pictures
Born in Flames
Bound
Bounty, The
Boy Germs
Boy Girl
Boys on the Side
Breaking the Silence
Breaking up Really Sucks
Brincando el Charco: Portrait of a
   Puerto Rican
Bubbles Galore!
But I Was a Girl: The Story of
   Frieda Belinfante
Butter & Pinches
Butterfly Kiss
By Design
Caged
Caged Fury
Call Me Your Girlfriend
Came Out, It Rained, Went Back
   in Again
Can't You Take a Joke?
Cancer in Two Voices
Carmelita Tropicana: Your Kunst Is
   Your Waffen
Carmilla
Cass
Cat Nip
Cat Swallows Parakeet and Speaks!
Cats, The (aka: Kattorna)
Celine and Julie Go Boating
   (aka: Céline et Julie vont en bateau)
Certain Grace, A
Chained Girls
Chained Heat II
Change the Frame
Chastity
Chicks in White Satin
Child-Play
Children's Hour, The
Choosing Children
Chopper Chicks in Zombie Town
Chosen Family, The
Chrissy
Chutney Popcorn
Cicely
Claire of the Moon

Clips
Closer
Closets Are for Clothes
Club de Femmes
    (aka: The Women's Club; Girl's Club)
Coal Miner's Granddaughter
Coconut / Cane and Cutlass
Color Purple, The
Come and Go
Comedy in Six Unnatural Acts, A
Common Flower, A
Companions: Tales from the Closet
Complaints of a Dutiful Daughter
Conception
Confessions of a Pretty Lady
Corpo, O (aka: The Body)
Cosmic Demonstration of Sexuality, A
Costa Brava
Countess Dracula
Crimes of Passion
Crocodiles in Amsterdam
    (aka: Krokodillen in Amsterdam)
Cruel
Crueles, Las (aka: The Cruel Ones)
Cuz It's Boy
Cynara: Poetry in Motion
Dallas Doll
Damned if You Don't
Danza Macabra, La
    (aka: Castle of Blood)
Dark Habits (aka: Entre tinieblas)
Darling International
Daughter of Dykes
Daughters of Darkness
    (aka: Le Rouge aux Lévres)
Daughters of the Sun
Day in the Life of a Bull-Dyke, A
Deal, The
Dear Mom
Deccada
Depart to Arrive
    (aka: Weggehen um Anzukommen)
Desert Hearts
Desi's Looking for a New Girl
Devotion
Different Corner, A
Dirty Fingernails
Disgraceful Conduct
Do You Think We Can Talk about
    Anything but Love?
Domestic Bliss
Double Entente

Double Strength
Dozens, The
Dr T & the Women
Dracula's Daughter
Drama Queen
Dreamers of the Day
Dry Kisses Only
Dykes and Their Dogs
Dykes and Tykes
Each Other (aka: Rega'im)
Eight Million
Eileen is a Spy
Elegant Spanking, The
Ellen DeGeneres: The Beginning
Emergence
Emily and Gitta
Emmanuelle
Enchantment, The (aka: Yuwakusha)
Entre Nous (aka: Coup de Foudre)
Entwined
Erika's Passions
    (aka: Erika's Leidenschaften)
Erotica: A Journey into Female Sexuality
Erotique
Et L'Amore
Eve's Daughters
Even Cowgirls Get the Blues
Everything Relative
Execution of Wanda Jean, The
Extramuros (aka: Beyond the Walls)
Family Affair, A (1995)
Family Affair, A (2001)
Family Pack (aka: Que Faisaient les
    Femmes Pendant que L'homme
    Marchait sur la Lune?)
Family Values
Fantasy Dancer
Farewell, The (aka: Avskedet)
Farewell to Charms
Fascination
Felicity
Female Closet, The
Female Misbehavior
Female Perversions
Fiction and Other Truths: A Film
    about Jane Rule
Fingered!
Fire
First Base
First Comes Love (1997)
Fish & Elephant
    (aka: Jin Nian Xia Tian)

Flaming Ears (aka: Rote Ohren
    Fetzen Durch Asche)
Flesh and Paper
Flesh on Glass
Florida Enchantment, A
Forbidden Fruit
Forbidden Love: The Unashamed
    Stories of Lesbian Lives
Forever (1991)
Fourth Sex, The
    (aka: Le Quatrième sexe)
Fox, The
Framing Lesbian Fashion
Freebird
French Twist (aka: Gazon Maudit)
Fresh Blood: A Consideration of
    Belonging
Fresh Kill
Fried Green Tomatoes
Frisson des Vampires, Le
    (aka: Sex and the Vampire)
Fuga, La (aka: The Escape)
Fun
Fun with a Sausage (aka: L'Ingenue)
Future is Woman, The
    (aka: Il Futuro è Donna)
Gaea Girls
Gang Girls 2000
Gang of Four, The
    (aka: La Bande des Quatre)
Gay Tape: Butch and Femme
Gemini Affair, The
Gently down the Stream
Gertrude Stein and a Companion
Gertrude Stein: When You See This
    Remember Me
Get the Bowheads
Getting It On
Gia
Girl King
Girl Power
Girl, The
Girl with the Golden Eyes, The
    (aka: La Fille aux yeux d'or)
Girlfriends (1993)
Girls Can't Swim
    (aka: Les filles ne savent par nager)
Girls Who Like Girls
Gladys, A Cuban Mother
Glasses Break
Go Fish
Goblin Market

Golden Threads
Good Citizen: Betty Baker
Goodbye Emma Jo
Grapefruit
Groove on a Stanley Knife
Group
Group, The
Hand on the Pulse
Hard Love & How to Fuck in High Heels
Haunting of Morella, The
Health Status Survey
Heatwave
Heavenly Creatures
Her Urge
Hey Sailor, Hey Sister
Hide and Seek
High Art
High Tech Rice
History Lessons
History of the World According to
    a Lesbian, The
Holding
Home Movie
Home You Go
Home-Made Melodrama
How to Female Ejaculate
How to Find Your Goddess Spot
How to Have a Sex Party
How to Kill Her
Howling II: Your Sister is a Werewolf
Hunger, The
Hungry Hearts
I Became a Lesbian and So Can You
I, Eugenia
I, the Worst of All
    (aka: Yo, la Peor de Todas)
I Will Not Think about Death Anymore
I'm Starving
I've Heard the Mermaids Singing
Ice Palace, The
If She Grows Up Gay
If These Walls Could Talk 2
Images
Immacolata e Concetta - l'altra gelosia
In My Father's House
In the Best Interests of the Children
Incidental Journey
    (aka: Haijiao Tianya)
Incredibly True Adventures of Two
    Girls in Love, The
Independently Blue

Infidel
Inn Trouble
Interviews With My Next Girlfriend
Intimate Friendship, An
Intimates, The (aka: Ji Sor)
Investigator, The
Irma Vep
Is Mary Wings Coming?
Isle of Lesbos
It Wasn't Love
It's Personal
It's That Age
Janine
Jenny
Jodie: An Icon
Jodie Promo, The
Joe-Joe
Johanna, D'Arc of Mongolia
    (aka: Joan of Arc of Mongolia)
Johnny Greyeyes
Jollies
Journey to Kafiristan, The
    (aka: Die Reise nach Kafiristan)
Julie Johnson
Jumping the Gun
Jupon Rouge, Le
    (aka: Manuela's Loves)
Just Because of Who We Are
Just Desserts
Just the Two of Us
Justine's Film (aka: Le Film de Justine)
Kalin's Prayer
Kamikaze Hearts
Kate's Addiction
Keep it Up, Jack! (aka: Auntie)
Khush
Killer Nun (aka: Suor Omicidi)
Killing of Sister George, The
Kim
Kindling Point, The
Kings
Kiss Me Monster
    (aka: Bésame Monstruo)
Kiss the Boys and Make Them Die
Kore Cara Mia
L Is for the Way You Look
Labor More than Once
Lakme Takes Flight
Last Call at Maud's
Last Empress, The
    (aka: Wei dai huang hou)

Late Bloomers
Lavender Limelight: Lesbians in Films
Leave It!
Legend of Fong Sai-Yuk, The
Lesbian Avengers Eat Fire Too
Lesbian Bed Death: Myth or Epidemic
Lesbian Health Matters
Lesbian Physicians on Practice,
    Patients & Power
Lesbian Teenagers in High School
Lesbian Tongues
Lesbians Behaving Badly
Lesbians Go Mad in Lesbos
Lesbians in the Pulpit
Lesbians Olé
Let's Love Hong Kong (aka: Ho Yuk)
Let's Play Prisoners
Lez B Friends: A Biker Bitch Hate Story
Lez Be Friends
Lianna
Life is a Woman
    (aka: Zhizn-Zhenshchina)
Life's a Butch!
Lifetime Commitment: A Portrait of
    Karen Thomson
Lifetime Guarantee: Phranc's
    Adventures in Plastic
Lilith
Listen
Listening for Something
Live Nude Girls UNITE!
Living with Pride: Ruth Ellis @ 100
Long Awaited Pleasure
Long Time Comin'
Loose Ends
Losing Lois
Loss of Heat
Lost and Delirious
Love and Other Catastrophes
Love in Progress (aka: Amori in corso)
Love Story: Berlin 1942, A
Love/Juice
Low-Fat Elephants
Lune
Lust for a Vampire
    (aka: To Love a Vampire)
Luv Tale, A
M.U.F.F. Match
Macumba
Mad, Bad and Barking

Madame X: An Absolute Ruler
    (aka: Madame X: Eine Absolute
    Herrscherin)
Mädchen in Uniform
    (aka: Girls in Uniform) (1931)
Mädchen in Uniform
    (aka: Girls in Uniform) (1957)
Mafu Cage, The
    (aka: My Sister, My Love)
Mai's America
Maid of Honor
Maiden Work
Manji (aka: All Mixed Up)
Manodestra
Mark of Lilith, The
Martirio (aka: Sufferance)
Mask of Desire
    (aka: Shades of Black)
Match that Started My Fire, The
Maybe We're Talking About a
    Different God
Mayhem
Meeting Magdalene
Meeting of Two Queens
Memento Mori (aka: Yeogo Guidam II)
Memsahib Rita
Mercy (1989)
Mercy (1999)
Metalguru
Midwife's Tale, The
Minor Disturbances
Moments: The Making of Claire of
    the Moon
Monkey's Mask, The
More than Friends: The Coming
    Out of Heidi Leiter
Mujeria
Mulholland Drive
Mum's the Word
MURDER and murder
Muriel's Parents Have Had it up to Here
    (aka: Muriel fait le désespoir de
    ses parents)
Murmur of Youth
    (aka: Mei li zai chang ge)
My Babushka
My Father is Coming
My Feminism
My Femme Divine
My Girlfriend Did It
My Left Breast
My Mother is an Alien

My Two Loves
Mystère Alexina, Le
    (aka: The Mystery of Alexina)
Nadja
Naked Killer (aka: Chiklo gouyeung)
Naomi's Legacy
Naya Zamana
Need and Want
Nice Girls Don't
Nice Girls Don't Do It
Nietta's Diary
Night Visions
Nine Days
Nitrate Kisses
No Exit
No Exit (aka: Huis Clos)
Noche de Walpurgis, La
Nocturne (1990)
Not Just Passing Through
November Moon (aka: Novembermond)
Nuestra Salud: Violencia Domestica
Nun, The (aka: La Religieuse)
Odd Girl Out
Oh Baby, A Baby! (aka: Zwei
    Frauen, ein Mann und ein Baby)
Olga's Girls
Olivia (aka: The Pit of Loneliness)
On Guard
Once Is Not Enough (aka: Jacqueline
    Susann's Once Is Not Enough)
One Shadowless Hour
One Small Step
Only the Brave
Oranges Are Not the Only Fruit
Orlando
Other Mothers
Our Mom's a Dyke
Out For a Change: Homophobia in
    Women's Sports
Out in Suburbia
Out of Our Time
Out of Season
Out: The Making of a Revolutionary
Outtakes
Override
Pandora's Box
    (aka: Die Büchse der Pandora)
Paris Was a Woman
Party Favor, The
Party Safe with DiAna and Bambi
Pasajes (aka: Passages)
Passengers

Peach
Peccatum Mutum (aka: The Silent Sin)
Peony Pavilion (aka: Youyuan jingmeng)
Peony Pavilion, The
Pepi, Luci and Bom
Peppermills
Persona
Personal Best (1982)
Personals
Perverted Justice
Petals
Pixel Pose
Place Called Lovely, A
Place of Rage, A
Playing the Part
Please Don't Stop: Lesbian Tips for
    Givin' and Gettin' It
Politics of Fur, The
Portland Street Blues
Portrait of a Marriage
Portrait of a Young Girl at the End
    of the '60s in Brussels
    (aka: Portrait d'une jeune fille de
    la fin des années 60 à Bruxelles)
Potluck and the Passion, The
Prefaces
Prisonnières
Privilege
Pump
Queen Christina
Queen: Marianne Hoppe, The
    (aka: Die Königin: Marianne Hoppe)
Queen of the Night
    (aka: La Reina de la Noche)
Quest for Love
Question of Love, A
Rachel Williams Documentary
Radical Harmonies
Rainbow, The
Real Ellen Story, The
Rebel Rebel
Red Heat
Red Label
Red Rain
Red Shoe Diaries 3, The: Another
    Woman's Lipstick
Reno Finds Her Mom
Replay (aka: La Répétition)
Requiem pour un Vampire
    (aka: Vierges et Vampires)
Rescuing Desire

Residencia, La
(aka: The House that Screamed)
Return of Sarah's Daughters, The
Revoir Julie (aka: Julie and Me)
Richard's Things
Righteous Babes, The
Rosebud
Rules of the Road
Ruthie & Connie: Every Room in
the House
S.
Sabor a Mi (aka: Savour Me)
Safe is Desire
Salmonberries
Sambal Belacan in San Francisco
Sari Red
Satan's Princess (aka: Malediction)
Scent Uva Butch
Scrubbers
Seduction of Innocence
See the Sea (aka: Regarde la Mer)
Self-Destruction of Gia, The
Serving in Silence: The Marguerite
Cammermeyer Story
Set Me Free (aka: Emporte-moi)
Sex Bytes
Sex Monster, The
Shades
Shatzi is Dying
She Don't Fade
She Even Chewed Tobacco
She Must Be Seeing Things
She Wears Cufflinks
She's Real Worse than Queer
Sherlock, Louise and Mina
Shifting Positions
Shoplifting Chanel
Show Me Love (aka: Fucking Åmål)
Signed: Lino Brocka
Silences
Silent Thrush, The
(aka: Shisheng Huamei)
Simone
Sink or Swim
Siren
Sister Louise's Discovery
Sister My Sister
Sister Smile (aka: Suor Sorriso)
Sisters Lumiere, The
(aka: Sisters of Light)
Size 'Em Up

Skin Deep
Skindeep
Skud
Sleep Come Free Me
Sluts and Goddesses Video Workshop
Snatch it
Some Ground to Stand On
Some Prefer Cake
Sotto Sotto (aka: Softly, Softly;
Sotto... sotto... strapazzato da
anomala passione)
Souvenir
Spacked Out (aka: Mo yan ka sai)
Spot the Lesbian
Staceyann Chin - A Poetry Slammer
Stand on Your Man
Steers and Queers
Sticky Fingers of Time, The
Stolen Diary, The (aka: Le Cahier Volé)
Stolen Moments
Story of PuPu, The
(aka: PuPu No Monogatari)
Story So Far, The
Straight Down the Aisle: Confes-
sions of Lesbian Bridesmaids
Straight for the Money: Interviews
with Queer Sex Workers
Strange Fits of Passion
Stranger Inside
Stray Dogs
Strung Up
Such a Crime
Suddenly Last Summer (1991)
Sugar and Spice
Sugar Cookies
Sugar High, Glitter City
Sugar Sweet
Sun and Rain (aka: Taiyang Yu)
Superdyke
Susana
Sweet Boy
Swimming
Swimming Upstream: A Year in the
Life of Karen and Jenny
Switch (1999)
Switchblade Sisters
Swollen Stigma
Swordsman III: The East is Red
(aka: Dung fong bat baai 2: fung
wan joi hei)
Sync Touch

Tampon Thieves
(aka: Ladronas de tampones)
Tank Girl
Tea Leaf
Teenage Tupelo
Tender Fictions
Terms of Conception
Terror in the Crypt
(aka: La Cripta e L'Incubo)
Thank God I'm a Lesbian
That Tender Touch
Thérèse and Isabelle
Thin Ice: Passion on the Pink Rink
Things We Said Today
This Is Not a Very Blank Tape Dear
This Marching Girl Thing
Thousand Miles, A
Three (aka: Tatlo... magkasalo)
Three of Hearts
Three on a Match
Ties that Bind, The
Times Square
Tiny and Ruby: Hell Drivin' Women
Titanic 2000
To My Women Friends
Tokyo Cowboy
Touch Me (1994)
Touch Me (1997)
Toward Intimacy
Tragedy of Samantha Biggle and the
Twins, The
Transeltown
Treading Water
Treyf
Troika
True Blue Camper
True Inversions
Truth About Jane, The
Twice a Woman (aka: Twee vrouwen)
Twilight Girls, The
Twin Bracelets (aka: Shuang Cho)
Twins of Evil (aka: The Gemini Twins)
Twisted Sheets
Two Girls and a Baby
Two in Twenty
Two or Three Things I Know about Them
Two Roads
Uh-Oh!
Union in Wait, A
Unknown Friend
(aka: Fremde Freundin)

Valentine's Day
Vampire Lovers, The
Vampire Nue, La
　(aka: The Naked Vampire)
Vampyres, Daughters of Dracula
　(aka: Blood Hunger)
Vampyros Lesbos
　(aka: Lesbian Vampires; Die
　Erbin des Dracula)
Velvet Vampire, The
　(aka: The Waking Hour)
Vendetta
Vera
Veronica 4 Rose
Vicious
Village Affair, A
Viol du Vampire, Le
Virgin Machine
　(aka: Die Jungfrauenmaschine)
Visitors
Voicing the Legacy
Voleurs, Les (aka: Thieves)
Waiting for the Moon
Walk on the Wild Side
War on Lesbians
War Widow, The
Watching Lesbian Porn
Watching You
Watermelon Woman, The
Wavelengths
Wax Me
We Always Danced
We've Been Framed
Weeki Wachee Girls
Welcome to Africville
Well Sexy Women
Wellness
West Coast Crones
What Makes a Family
What You Take for Granted
When Night Is Falling
When Shirley Met Florence
Wild Side
　(aka: Donald Cammell's Wild Side)
Wildflowers
Wilma's Sacrifice
Windows
Without You I'm Nothing
Woman Accused, A
　(aka: In the Glitter Palace)

Woman like Eve, A
　(aka: Een Vrouw als Eva)
Woman to Woman
Women I Love
Women in Cages
　(aka: Women's Penitentiary III)
Women Like Us/Women Like That
Women of Gold
Women on the Roof
　(aka: Kvinnorna på taket)
Work
Working Class Dykes from Hell
Working Girls
Worthy Mothers
Wu Yen
Yes (aka: To Ingrid My Love Lisa;
　Kvinnolek)
Yo Yo Gang
Your Heart is All Mine
Your Mother Wears Combat Boots

Queer

21st Century Nuns
Absolutely Positive
After Stonewall
After the Bath
After the War You Have to Tell
　Everyone about the Dutch Gay
　Resistance Fighters
Age of Dissent
Agora
AIDS
AIDS Show: Artists Involved with
　Death and Survival, The
AIDS: Words from One to Another
All About My Mother
　(aka: Todo sobre mi madre)
All God's Children
All of Me
All Out Comedy
Alone Together: Young Adults
　Living with HIV
Ambiguous Feeling, An
American Slices
Among Good Christian Peoples
Anatomy of Desire
Andy Warhol and His Work
Anguished Love
Annie Sprinkle's Herstory of Porn:
　Reel to Real

Apostles of Civilised Vice
Aren't You Lucky You Brought Your
　Own Chair
Army of Lovers: or Revolt of the Perverts
Attack of the Giant Moussaka, The
Avenge Tampa
Ballot Measure 9
Barbarella
Bare
Because this is About Love
Before Stonewall: The Making of a
　Gay and Lesbian Community
Best of Out and Out on Tuesday, The
Betty Anderson
Beyond the Valley of the Dolls
Bill Called William, A
Bit of Scarlett, A
Bite Me Again
Black Glove, The
Black Is... Black Ain't
Black Nations/Queer Nations?
Blair Princess Project, The
Blood for Dracula
Bloody Mama
Blow Job
Blue Boys
Bolo! Bolo!
Box, The
Boy Next Door: A Profile of Boy George
Bradfords Tour America, The
Bright Eyes
Broadcast Tapes of Dr Peter, The
Broken Goddess
But, I'm a Cheerleader
By the Dawn's Early Light
Caligula
Call to Witness
Camp Lavender Hill
Can I Be Your Bratwurst, Please?
Can't Stop Dancing
Can't Stop the Music
Car Wash
Castro, The
Caught in the Crossfire
Celluloid Closet, The
Changing Our Minds: The Story of
　Dr Evelyn Hooker
Charlie
Chelsea Girls, The
China Dolls
Chocolate Babies

City of Lost Souls (aka: Stadt der Verlorenen Seelen)
Closet Space
Cockettes, The
Come As You Are
Coming Home
Coming Out, Coming Home: Asian and Pacific Islander Family Stories
Coming Out of the Iron Closet
Coming Out under Fire
Common Ground
Common Threads: Stories from the Quilt
Comrades in Arms
Criminal Lovers (aka: Les Amants Criminels)
Critical Mass: Gay Games Amsterdam
Cruising in the Channels
Dads Wanted
Dandy Dust
Danny
Darkness before Dawn
De Colores
Dear Jesse
Debutantes, The
Desire (1989)
Desperate Living
Desperate Remedies
Destiny's Children
Destroying Angel
Devil in the Holy Water, The
Diane Linkletter Story, The
Different Story, A
Ding Dong
Dirty Laundry (1995)
Divine Trash
Does Your Mother Know?
Dog's Dialogue (aka: Colloque de chiens)
Double Trouble
Dr Jekyll and Sister Hyde
Drop Dead Georgeous: The Power of HIV Positive Thinking
Drugs 'R' Us
e-male
Eagle Shooting Heroes, The (aka: Sediu yinghung tsun tsi dung sing sai tsau)
Educate Your Attitude
Endangered
Enter the Clowns (aka: Choujue Dengchang)
Escape to Life: The Erika and Klaus Mann Story

Everything in Between
Excuse Me Duckie, But Lucas Loved Me (aka: Perdona Bonita, pero Lucas me queria a mi)
Eyes of Tammy Faye, The
Fag Hag
Family Fundamentals
Family Values: An American Tragedy
Fantasm
Fantasm Comes Again (aka: Fantasm 99)
Farewell My Concubine (aka: Ba wang bie ji)
Fassbinder's Women
Feed Them to the Cannibals!
Female Trouble
Fighting Chance
First Comes Love (1991)
Flesh (aka: Andy Warhol's Flesh)
Flesh for Frankenstein
Flesh Gordon
Flowing Hearts: Thailand Fighting AIDS
For Straights Only
Forbidden Fruit: Unfinished Stories of our Lives
Forever (1994)
Fostering
Fourth Man, The (aka: Di Vierde Man)
Framed Youth (aka: Revolt of the Teenage Perverts)
Franchesca Page
Frankenstein Created Woman
Frantz Fanon: Black Skin, White Mask
Fucked in the Face
Full Blast
Gaudi Afternoon
Gay Courage: 100 Years of the Gay Movement
Gay Cuba
Gay Games
Gay & Gray in New York City
Gay Rock and Roll Years, The
Gay Sera Sera
Gay USA
Gay Youth
Gay'ze in Wonderland
Gaymes, The
Get Bruce
Get Out
Get Over It
Ghost of Roger Casement, The
God, Gays and the Gospel

Grass is Greener, The
Greetings from Out Here
Greetings from Washington
Guess Who's Coming to Dinner?
Gypsy 83
Hairspray
Hammer and Sickle (aka: Serp i molot)
Happy Gordons, The
Harlequin Exterminator
He's a Woman, She's a Man (aka: Gum gee yuk yip)
Heat
Heavy Petting (1988)
Heavy Petting (1991)
Hedwig and the Angry Inch
Hell Bento!
Hell For Leather
Heterosexual Agenda, The
Heterosexuality
Hey, Happy!
Hidden Child
High Heels (aka: Tacones lejanos)
Home Sweet Home
Homo Heights (aka: Happy Heights)
Homo Promo
Homophobia in Hollywood
Homophobia: That Painful Problem
Homosexuality: A Film for Discussion
Homosexuality and Lesbianism
Homoteens
Hotel New Hampshire, The
Hunting Season, The
I Almost Feel Like a Tourist
I Am the Camera Dying
I Exist: Voices From the Lesbian and Gay Middle Eastern Community
I.K.U
I Shot Andy Warhol
I'll Be Your Mirror
I'm the One that I Want
Imagining October
Immigration
Impromptu
Improper Conduct (aka: Mauvaise Conduite)
In Pursuit of Prince/ess Charming
Indecent Acts
Inside Monkey Zetterland
Inverted Minstrel

It's a Queer World
It's Elementary: Talking about Gay
    Issues in School
It's in the Water
It's My Life
It's Not Unusual: A Lesbian and
    Gay History
Jaundiced Eye, The
Je, tu, il, elle
Joys of Smoking, The
Julian Clary - The Mincing
    Machine Tour
Just One Time
Kamikaze Summer
Kanada
Kansas Anymore
Karen Black Like Me
Ke Kulana He Mahu: Remember-
    ing a Sense of Place
Keep Your Laws off My Body
Kenneth Anger's Hollywood
    Babylon (aka: Kenneth Anger)
Kika
Killer Condom
    (aka: Kondom des Grauens)
Labyrinth of Passion
    (aka: Laberinto de pasiones)
Laramie Project, The
Last Coming Out, The
Last Island, The
Last Song, The
Latin Queens: Unfinished Stories of
    Our Lives
Lavender Tortoise
Law of Desire (aka: La Ley del Deseo)
Let Me Die, Again
Lickerish Quartet, The
    (aka: The Erotic Quartet)
Life is Like a Cucumber
    (aka: Affengeil)
Life's Evening Hour
Live Flesh (aka: Carne Trémula)
Live to Tell: The First Gay and
    Lesbian Prom in America
Living and Dying
    (aka: Ich Lebe Gern, Ich Sterbe Gern)
Living Proof: HIV and the Pursuit
    of Happiness
Lonesome Cowboys

Long Weekend, The
    (aka: The Long Weekend (O'Despair))
Looking for a Space
Looking for Common Ground
Love and Marriage
Love Ltd.
Love Makes a Family: Gay Parents
    in the '90s
Lust and Liberation
Lust in the Dust
M Butterfly
Madam Wang's
Making of Monsters
Man in the Irony Mask, The
Man like Eva, A
    (aka: Ein, Mann wie Eva)
March on Washington, The
Mary's Place
Metrosexuality
Militia Battlefield
Mob Queen
Modesty Blaise
Moscow Does Not Believe in Queers
Most Unknowable Thing, The
Multiple Maniacs
Myra Breckinridge
Naked Lunch
Neptune's Rocking Horse
Neurosia: 50 Years of Perversity
Never Met Picasso
New Women, The
Night Porter, The
    (aka: Il Portiere di notte)
Night with Derek, A
Nightwork
No Rewind
No Sad Songs
Non, Je Ne Regrette Rien
    (aka: No Regret)
None of the Above
Not All Parents are Straight
Not Alone: A Hallowe'en Romance
Nowhere
Ode
Off the Straight and Narrow: Lesbians,
    Gays, Bisexuals and Television
Olive Tree, The
One Nation Under God
Opening Closet X: A Voice for
    Queer Youth
Orientations

Osaka Story
Our House: A Very Real Documentary
Our Private Idaho
Out At Work: America Undercover
Out in Africa
Out in Nature: Homosexual Behaviour
    in the Animal Kingdom
Out in South Africa
Out Loud
Out of the Past
Out: Stories of Lesbian and Gay
    Youth
Over Our Dead Bodies
Over the Rainbow: Parts 1 - 4
Oy Gay
Parents of Gays
Party Monster
Passion of Remembrance, The
Performance
Personal Best (1991)
Piccadilly Pickups
Pink Flamingos
Pink Pimpernel, The
Pink Triangle: A Study of Prejudice
    Against Gays & Lesbians
Pink Video: Out-Rageously Pink, The
Playing Gay
Plushies & Furries
Poisoned Blood
Polskiseks
Polyester
Pourquoi Pas Moi? (aka: Why Not Me?)
Pride Divide
Pride in Puerto Rico
Pride, Politics and Pissheads
Privates on Parade
Psycho Beach Party
Queer As Folk (1998)
Queer As Folk 2
Queer As Folk (2000)
Queer Geography: Mapping Our
    Identities
Queer Son
Queercore: A Punk-u-mentary
Rainmakers - Zimbabwe
Rape of Ganymede, The
Razor Blade Smile
Reaching Out to Lesbian, Gay and
    Bisexual Youth
Reframing AIDS
Relationships

Relax... It's Just Sex
Rendez-vous d'Anna, Les
Revolutionary Girl Utena: The Movie (aka: Shôjo kakumei Utena: Adolescence mokushiroku)
Rewriting the Script: Love Letter to Our Families
Right to be Different, The
Right Wing, Right Off, Right Hons, Right?
Rights and Reactions
Ritual Nation
Rocky Horror Picture Show, The
Rules of the Game
Running Gay: Lesbian and Gay Participation in Sport
Sacred Lies, Civil Truths
Sadness
Salivation Army
Salo (aka: The 120 Days of Sodom)
Salon Kitty (aka: Madam Kitty)
Scarecrow in a Garden of Cucumbers
Scenes from a Queer Planet
School's Out: Lesbian and Gay Youth
Scream, Teen, Scream
Search for Intimacy, The
Seashell and the Clergyman, The (aka: La Coquille et le Clergyman)
See How They Run
Sex 121 and the Gulag
Sex and Balls
Sex and the Sandinistas
Sex and the Single Gene?
Sex Wars
Sexing the Label: Love and Gender in a Queer World
Sexual Identity
Sexual Orientation: Reading Between the Labels
Shades of Gray
Shame No More
Silence=Death (aka: Die AIDS-Trilogie: Schweigen=Tod)
Silence that Silences, The
Silent Pioneers
Silver Screen: Color Me Lavender, The
Simon and I: Steps for the Future
SIS: The Perry Watkins Story
Sitcom

Some Aspect of a Shared Lifestyle
Somewhere in the City
Sonny Boy
Spartacus
Spikes and Heels
Stand Together
Stiff Sheets
Still Sane
Stonewall
Stonewall 25: Voices of Pride and Protest
Storm in a Teacup
Straight Agenda, The
Straight from the Heart: Gay and Lesbian Children
Straight from the Suburbs
Sunflowers
Superstar: The Life and Times of Andy Warhol
Surviving Friendly Fire
Sydney - Living with Difference
Symposium: Ladder of Love
Tales of the City
Tales of the City 2 (aka: More Tales of the City)
Tales of the City 3 (aka: Further Tales of the City)
Taste the Sweat
That's a Family
They Are Lost to Vision Altogether
This is Dedicated: Grieving When a Partner Dies
Those Who Love Me Can Take the Train
Three Drags and a Wedding
Thundercrack!
Tillsammans (aka: Together)
Times of Harvey Milk, The
Tomboychik
Too Outrageous!
Totally F***ed Up
Touchables, The
Traditional Family Vampires
Transformers/AIDS
Trash
Treasure Island
Treaty of Chance, The (aka: Le Traité du Hasard)
Trembling Before G-d
Trey Billings Show, The

Twin Cheeks: Who Killed the Homecoming King?
Up!
Urinal (aka: Pissoir)
Victor/Victoria
Video 28
Viktor/Viktoria
Village Voices
Vintage: Families of Value
Viva Eu!
Voices from the Front
Was Sie Nie Über Frauen Wissen Wollten (aka: All You Never Wanted to Know about Women)
Water Drops on Burning Rocks (aka: Gouttes d'Eau sur Pierres Brûlantes)
We Are Family
We Were Marked with a Big A
We're Funny that Way
What Have I Done to Deserve This? (aka: Qué he hecho yo para merecer esto?!!)
What's Cooking?
When Love Comes
When the Penny Drops
White People's Business
White to be Angry, The
Who Happen to be Gay
Who's Afraid of Project 10?
Why am I Gay?
Wigstock: The Movie (1987)
Willkommen im Dom (aka: Welcome to the Dome)
Witches, Faggots, Dykes and Poofters
Women in Revolt
Word is Out
World is Sick (sic), The
Woubi Chéri
Wrecked for Life: The Trip & Magic of Trocadero Transfer
Yang±Yin: Gender in Chinese Cinema
You've Had Worse Things in Your Mouth
Youth Outloud!
Zero Budget
Zindagi Zindabad (aka: Long Live Life)

Films Listed by Genre

Action

10 Violent Women
Ben Hur
Black Mama, White Mama
Bloody Mama
Caged Fury
Cecil B Demented
Cleopatra Jones
Hidden Assassin (aka: The Shooter)
Hired to Kill
Johanna, D'Arc of Mongolia
   (aka: Joan of Arc of Mongolia)
Killer, The
   (aka: Die Xue Shuang Xiong)
Legend of Fong Sai-Yuk, The
Love in a Women's Prison
   (aka: Diario Segreto da un
   Carcere Femminile)
Naked Killer
   (aka: Chiklo gouyeung)
Portland Street Blues
Raising Heroes
Set It Off
Siege (aka: Self Defense)
Story of PuPu, The
   (aka: PuPu No Monogatari)
Switchblade Sisters
Swordsman II (aka: Xiao ao jiang
   hu zhi dong fang bu bai)
Swordsman III: The East is Red
   (aka: Dung fong bat baai 2: fung
   wan joi hei)
Thelma and Louise
Thunderbolt and Lightfoot
Vendetta
Willie Dynamite
Woman Hunt
Women in Cages
   (aka: Women's Penitentiary III)
Yo Yo Gang

Animation

Achilles
Green Pubes
Jeffery's Hollywood Screen Trick
Kizuna Volume 1 & 2
Mujeria
Pony Glass
Revolutionary Girl Utena: The Movie
   (aka: Shôjo kakumei Utena:
   Adolescence mokushiroku)

Comedy

10 Attitudes
101 Reykjavik
17 Rooms (or What Do Lesbians
   Do in Bed?)
24 Nights
4pm
Acting on Impulse
   (aka: Eyes of a Stranger)
Adam's Rib
Addicted to Love
   (aka: Boku wa koi ni muchu)
Adventures of Priscilla, Queen of
   the Desert, The
After Hours
After the Break (1998)
Airport
Algie the Miner
All About My Mother
   (aka: Todo sobre mi madre)
All Men are Liars
   (aka: Goodnight Irene)
All Out Comedy
All Over the Guy
All the Queens Men
All the Rage
Alles Wird Gut
   (aka: Everything Will Be Fine)
American Fabulous
American Slices
Among Others
Angels!
Anniversary, The (1968)
Anniversary, The (1995)
Any Wednesday
Anything Once
Apariencias
Arabian Nights
   (aka: Il Fiore delle mille e una notte)
As Good As It Gets
Ashley 22
Atomic Sake
Attack of the Giant Moussaka, The
B.U.C.K.L.E.
Bad Brownies
Badass Supermama
Bar Girls
Barbarella
Bare
Bargain Lingerie
Beautiful Thing
Because the Dawn
Bedazzled

Bedrooms & Hallways
Being John Malkovich
Belle al Bar (aka: Belles at the Bar)
Belle époque
Below the Belt
Best In Show
Best Way, The
   (aka: La Meilleure façon de marcher)
Better than Chocolate
Beware a Holy Whore
   (aka: Warnung vor einer heiligen Nutte)
Beyond Gravity
Beyond the Valley of the Dolls
Beyond Therapy
Big Business
Billy Turner's Secret
Billy's Hollywood Screen Kiss
Biloxi Blues
Birdcage, The
Birthday Time
Bisexual Kingdom, The
Black Lizard (aka: Kurotokage)
Blair Princess Project, The
Blazing Saddles
Block Party
Blue Haven
Bound and Gagged: A Love Story
Bounty, The
Box, The
Boy Germs
Boy Next Door
Boychick
Boyfriends (1995)
Boyfriends (1999)
Boys' Night Out
Boys of Cell Block Q
Breaking up Really Sucks
Britney Baby - One More Time
Broadway Damage
Broadway Melody, The
Broken Hearts Club: A Romantic
   Comedy, The
Bubbeh Lee and Me
Bubbles Galore!
Buck House
Buckeye and Pinto
But, I'm a Cheerleader
Butch Camp
Butcher's Wife, The
Butter & Pinches
By Design
Cage aux Folles II, La

Cage aux Folles III, La
Cage aux Folles, La
Calamity Jane
California Suite
Can I Be Your Bratwurst, Please?
Can't Stop Dancing
Can't Stop the Music
Can't You Take a Joke?
Car Wash
Cat and the Canary, The
Cater Waiter
Caught Looking
Cecil B Demented
Celestial Clockwork
   (aka: Mecaniques Celestes)
Certain Grace, A
Chained Girls
Charlie
Chastity
Children of Hannibal
   (aka: Figli di Annibale)
Chocolate Babies
Chopper Chicks in Zombie Town
Chosen Family, The
Chuck and Buck
Chutney Popcorn
City of Lost Souls
   (aka: Stadt der Verlorenen Seelen)
Clancy Street Boys
Clancy's Kitchen
Clinic, The
Closet, The (aka: Le Placard)
Closets Are for Clothes
Club de Femmes
   (aka: The Women's Club; Girl's Club)
Coffee Date
Cold Footsies
Comedy in Six Unnatural Acts, A
Conception
Confessions of a Window Cleaner
Confusion of Genders
   (aka: La confusion des genres)
Coonskin (aka: Street Fight)
Costa Brava
Crazy Richard
Criminal Lovers
   (aka: Les Amants Criminels)
Crocodiles in Amsterdam
   (aka: Krokodillen in Amsterdam)
Curse of the Queerwolf
Daisies (aka: Sedmikrásky)
Dallas Doll
Danger Girl, The
Dark Habits (aka: Entre tinieblas)
Das Trio (aka: The Trio)
David Searching
Day the Fish Came Out, The
   (aka: Otan ta psaria vgikan sti steria)
Deal, The

Dear Boys (aka: Lieve Jongens)
Deathtrap
Derrière, Le (aka: From Behind)
Desperate Living
Desperate Remedies
Diane Linkletter Story, The
Different for Girls
Different Story, A
Ding Dong
Dirty Fingernails
Does Your Mother Know?
Dog's Dialogue
   (aka: Colloque de chiens)
Domestic Bliss
Dona Herlinda and Her Son
   (aka: Doña Herlinda y su hijo)
Doom Generation
Double Entente
Dr Jekyll and Ms Hyde
Dr Jekyll and Sister Hyde
Dr T & the Women
Drag Attack
Drama in Blonde
Dreaded Experimental Comedies:
   How to Lessons, Body Rhythms,
   My New Lover, The
Dyke Blend
Dykes and Their Dogs
Eagle Shooting Heroes, The
   (aka: Sediu yinghung tsun tsi
   dung sing sai tsau)
Early Frost, An (2000)
Eat the Rich
Echte Kerle (aka: Regular Guys)
Ed Wood
Edge of Seventeen (aka: Edge of 17)
Eika Katappa
Eine Tunte zum Dessert
   (aka: A Fairy for Dessert)
Englishman Abroad, An
Entertaining Mr Sloane
Escalier C
Escorte, L'
Even Cowgirls Get the Blues
Evening Dress
   (aka: Tenue de Soirée; Menage)
Excuse Me Duckie, But Lucas Loved Me
   (aka: Perdona Bonita, pero Lucas
   me queria a mi)
Fag Hag
Fairy Who Didn't Want to Be a
   Fairy, The
Family Pack (aka: Que Faisaient les
   Femmes Pendant que L'homme
   Marchait sur la Lune?)
Fanci's Persuasion
Fearless Vampire Killers, The
   (aka: Dance of the Vampires)
Female Misbehavior

Female Trouble
Fete des Peres, La (aka: Dad's Day)
Final Programme, The
   (aka: The Last Days of Man on Earth)
Finding North
Fingered!
First Comes Love (1997)
First Love and Other Pains
Fisher King, The
Flawless
Flesh (aka: Andy Warhol's Flesh)
Florida Enchantment, A
Fluffer, The
Fontvella's Box
Forms and Motifs
Four Weddings and a Funeral
Franchesca Page
Frankie and Johnny
Freebie and the Bean
Freebird
French Twist (aka: Gazon Maudit)
Friends and Family
Fucked in the Face
Full Monty, The
Fun Down There
Funny Felix (aka: Dróle de Félix;
   The Adventures of Felix)
Gang Girls 2000
Garbo Talks
Gaudi Afternoon
Gay Deceivers, The
Gentlemen Prefer Blondes
Get Over It
Get the Bowheads
Get Your Stuff
Ginger Beer
Girl in Every Port, A
Girl King
Girl Power
Girl Stroke Boy
Girlfriends (1993)
Go
Go Fish
Going West
Good Citizen: Betty Baker
Good Family, The
   (aka: Thanksgiving Day)
Goodbye Girl, The
Gotta Have Heart (aka: Ba'al Ba'al Lev)
Grapefruit
Grass is Greener, The
Grief
Gypsy 83
Gypsy Boys
Hairspray
Happy Birthday Gemini
Happy Texas
Harlequin Exterminator
He Bop!

He's a Woman, She's a Man
   (aka: Gum gee yuk yip)
He's My Girl
Heat
Heatwave
Hell For Leather
Her Life as a Man
Her Urge
Heterosexual Agenda, The
Heterosexuality
High Heels (aka: Tacones lejanos)
High Tech Rice
Hit and Runway
Home for the Holidays
Home You Go
Homo Heights (aka: Happy Heights)
Homo Promo
Hooking Up
Hotel New Hampshire, The
I Became a Lesbian and So Can You
I Think I Do
Impossible on Saturday
Impromptu
In & Out
Incredibly True Adventures of Two
   Girls in Love, The
Inn Trouble
Inside Monkey Zetterland
Inside Out
Inspecteur Lavardin
Interviews With My Next Girlfriend
Irma Vep
Iron Ladies, The (aka: Sa tree lex)
Is Mary Wings Coming?
It Wasn't Love
It's a Queer World
It's in the Water
Jeffrey
Jodie Promo, The
Joe-Joe
Joey Breaker
Joggernaught
Julian Clary - The Mincing
   Machine Tour
Just Desserts
Just like a Woman
Just One of the Girls
   (aka: Anything for Love)
Just One of the Guys
Just One Time
Justine's Film
   (aka: Le Film de Justine)
Karen Black Like Me
Keep it Up, Jack! (aka: Auntie)
Kicking On
Kika
Killer Condom
   (aka: Kondom des Grauens)
Kinsey 3, The

Kiss Me Guido
Kissing Jessica Stein
Km. 0 (aka: Kilometro cero)
Labyrinth of Passion
   (aka: Laberinto de pasiones)
Lady
Lady in Waiting, The
Ladybugs
Lakme Takes Flight
Last Married Couple in America, The
Late Bloomers
Latin Boys Go To Hell
Laura
Lavender Tortoise
Law of Desire (aka: La Ley del Deseo)
Leave It!
Lesbian Bed Death: Myth or Epidemic
Let Me Die, Again
Lez B Friends: A Biker Bitch Hate Story
Lez Be Friends
Lie Down with Dogs
Life's a Butch!
Lip Gloss
Little Bit of Lippy, A
Live Flesh (aka: Carne Trémula)
Live Nude Girls
Living End, The
Lonely without You
Lonesome Cowboys
Long Awaited Pleasure
Loose Connections
Loot
Lost in the Pershing Point Hotel
Love and Human Remains
Love and Other Catastrophes
Love in Progress (aka: Amori in corso)
Love Letter, The
Love Ltd.
Love Machine, The
Love=ME3
Love! Valour! Compassion!
Loved One, The
Loverville 2: The Honeymoon
Low-Fat Elephants
Lust in the Dust
Lycanthrophobia
M.U.F.F. Match
Ma Vie (aka: My Life)
Mad, Bad and Barking
Madagascar Skin
Madam Wang's
Made in Heaven
Magic Christian, The
Making of Monsters
Man of the Year
Manhattan
Mannequin
Match that Started My Fire, The
Meeting of Two Queens

Men Men Men
   (aka: Uomini uomini uomini)
Mi Novia El
Mirror, Mirror (aka: Lille spejl)
Modesty Blaise
Morris Loves Jack
Mr Christie
Mrs Doubtfire
Multiple Maniacs
My Addiction
My Best Friend's Wedding
My Body
My Cousin Mike
My Father is Coming
My First Suit
My Hustler
My Pal Rachid
My Summer Vacation
Myra Breckinridge
Naked in New York
Naya Zamana
Neurosia: 50 Years of Perversity
Never Met Picasso
New Women, The
Next Best Thing, The
Next Stop, Greenwich Village
Nice Girls Don't
Night Larry Kramer Kissed Me, The
Nightwork
Norman, is that You?
Not Alone: A Hallowe'en Romance
Notorious C.H.O.
Oh Baby, A Baby! (aka: Zwei
   Frauen, ein Mann und ein Baby)
Okoge
Olga's Girls
One Small Step
Only When I Laugh
Outrageous!
Override
P. S. Your Cat is Dead
Party Favor, The
Passed Away
Peccatum Mutum (aka: The Silent Sin)
Pedagogue
Peoria Babylon
Pepi, Luci and Bom
Peppermills
Peter's Friends
Pillow Talk
Pink Angels, The
Pink Flamingos
Pink Video: Out-Rageously Pink, The
Play Dead
Playing the Part
Politics of Fur, The
Polyester
Pourquoi Pas Moi? (aka: Why Not Me?)

Pretty Baby (aka: Maybe...Maybe Not; Der Bewegte Mann; The Most Desired Man)
Private Benjamin
Privates on Parade
Privilege
Psycho Beach Party
Pump
Punks
Queen's Cantonese Conversational Course, The
Queens Logic
Rape of Ganymede, The
Ray's Male Heterosexual Dance Hall
Reaching for the Moon
Red Label
Red Ribbon Blues
Relax... It's Just Sex
Rescuing Desire
Rhythm & Blues
Ritz, The
Rocky Horror Picture Show, The
Roy Cohn / Jack Smith
Safe is Desire
Salome's Last Dance
Scarecrow in a Garden of Cucumbers
Scenes from the Class Struggle in Beverly Hills
Scream, Teen, Scream
Secret Policeman's Private Parts, The
Secrets
Sex Monster, The
Shadey
Shame No More
Shantay
She Don't Fade
Shoplifting Chanel
Sister Louise's Discovery
Sitcom
Size 'Em Up
Skin and Bone
Skud
Slaves to the Underground
Sleep Come Free Me
Snatch it
Soft Hearts (aka: Pusong Mamon)
Some Like It Hot
Some Prefer Cake
Something for Everyone (aka: Black Flowers for the Bride)
Somewhere in the City
Sonny Boy
Sordid Lives
Sotto Sotto (aka: Softly, Softly; Sotto... sotto... strapazzato da anomala passione)
Special Guest Star
Sprinter, The

Staircase
Star Maps
Straight Agenda, The
Straight from the Suburbs
Straight in the Face
Such a Crime
Suddenly Last Summer (1991)
Sum of Us, The
Superdyke
Surrender Dorothy
Switch (1991)
Sylvia Scarlett
Talk of the Town (aka: Stadtgespräch)
Taste
Taxi to Cairo (aka: Taxi nach Kairo)
Taxi to the Toilet (aka: Taxi zum Klo)
Tell Me No Lies
Tell Me Why: The Epistemology of Disco
Terry and Julian (Vol. 1 and 2)
This Is Not a Very Blank Tape Dear
This Marching Girl Thing
Three of Hearts
Three on a Match
Three to Tango
Threesome
Throwback (aka: Spike of Bensonhurst)
Thunderbolt and Lightfoot
Thundercrack!
Tillsammans (aka: Together)
Titanic 2000
To Wong Foo, Thanks for Everything, Julie Newmar
Too Much Sun
Too Outrageous!
Tootsie
Torch Song Trilogy
Totally Confused
Touchables, The
Traditional Family Vampires
Tragedy of Samantha Biggle and the Twins, The
Tragic But True
Transanimals
Treasure Island
Treaty of Chance, The (aka: Le Traité du Hasard)
Trevor
Trey Billings Show, The
Trick
Trip, The
True Blue Camper
Turnabout
Twin Cheeks: Who Killed the Homecoming King?
Twinkle (aka: Kira Kira Hikaru)

Twinkle Toes
Twisted
Two Girls and a Baby
Two Point Five
Two Roads
Up!
Up the Academy
Urinal (aka: Pissoir)
Vegas in Space
Velvet Goldmine
Very Funny
Victor/Victoria
Viktor/Viktoria
Violet's Visit
Virgin Larry, The
Virus Knows No Morals, A (aka: Ein Virus kennt keine Moral)
Visitors
Waiting
Was Sie Nie Über Frauen Wissen Wollten (aka: All You Never Wanted to Know about Women)
Watching Lesbian Porn
Water Drops on Burning Rocks (aka: Gouttes d'Eau sur Pierres Brûlantes)
Wavelengths
Wax Me
We Think the World of You
Wedding Banquet, The (aka: Hsi yen)
Wedding Video, The
Weeki Wachee Girls
Weiner Brut
What Have I Done to Deserve This? (aka: Qué he hecho yo para merecer esto?!!)
What's Cooking?
When the Cat's Away (aka: Chacun Cherche Son Chat)
Who's the Woman, Who's the Man
Why Not! (aka: Pourquoi Pas!)
Willy/Milly (aka: Something Special)
Withnail and I
Without You I'm Nothing
Woman on Top
Women in Revolt
Wonder Boys, The
World According to Garp, The
Wrong Son, The
Yellow Fever
You Are Not Alone (aka: Du er ikke alene)
You've Had Worse Things in Your Mouth
Your Heart is All Mine
Zazie dans le Métro
Zero Patience
Zorro, the Gay Blade

Documentary

101 Rent Boys
2 or 3 Things But Nothing for Sure
21st Century Nuns
90 Miles
99% Woman
About Vivien
Absolutely Positive
Across the Rubicon
Actions Speak Louder than Words
Adventures in the Gender Trade
After Stonewall
After the Bath
After the Break (1992)
After the War You Have to Tell
    Everyone about the Dutch Gay
    Resistance Fighters
Age of Dissent
AIDS
AIDS Show: Artists Involved with
    Death and Survival, The
AIDS: Words from One to Another
Aileen Wuornos: The Selling of a
    Serial Killer
Alias
All about my Father
    (aka: Alt om min Far)
All Girl Action: The History of
    Lesbian Erotica
All God's Children
Alone Together: Young Adults
    Living with HIV
Alternative Conceptions
Always Walter! An Inner View of
    Walter Larrabee
Ambiguous Feeling, An
Among Good Christian Peoples
Amos Gutman, Filmmaker
    (aka: Amos Gutman, Bamay Kolnoa)
Anatomy of Desire
Andy Warhol and His Work
Annie Sprinkle's Herstory of Porn:
    Reel to Real
Apostles of Civilised Vice
Are You Greedy?
Armistead Maupin is a Man I
    Dreamt Up
Army of Lovers: or Revolt of the Perverts
Art of Cruising Men, The
Avenge Tampa
B. D. Women
Ballot Measure 9
Battle of Tuntenhaus
Be Careful What Kind of Skin You
    Pull Back, You Never Know
    What Kind of Head Will Appear

Beauty Before Age
Because this is About Love
Beefcake
Before Stonewall: The Making of a
    Gay and Lesbian Community
Benjamin Smoke
Best of Out and Out on Tuesday, The
Better Dead than Gay
Beyond the Catwalk: The Search
    for Mr Gay Australia 2000
Bigger Splash, A
Bill Called William, A
Bit of Scarlett, A
Bite Me Again
Black Is... Black Ain't
Black Nations/Queer Nations?
Black Sheep
Blank Point: What is Transsexualism?, The
Bloodsisters: Leather Dykes and S&M
Blue Boys
Body without Soul
Bolo! Bolo!
Bombay Eunuch
Boots, Boobs and Bitches: The Art
    of G. B. Jones
Border Line...Family Pictures
Boy Girl
Boy Named Sue, A
Boy Next Door? A Profile of Boy George
Boys from Brazil, The
Boys in the Backyard
Boys of Manchester, The
Bradfords Tour America, The
Brandon Teena Story, The
Breaking the Silence
Brian Epstein Story, The
Bright Eyes
Brincando el Charco: Portrait of a
    Puerto Rican
Broadcast Tapes of Dr Peter, The
But I Was a Girl: The Story of
    Frieda Belinfante
Butterflies on the Scaffold
    (aka: Mariposas en el andiamo)
By the Dawn's Early Light
Call Me Your Girlfriend
Call to Witness
Camp Lavender Hill
Cancer in Two Voices
Carmelita Tropicana: Your Kunst Is
    Your Waffen
Castro, The
Caught in the Crossfire
Celluloid Closet, The
Changing Our Minds: The Story of
    Dr Evelyn Hooker
Chicks in White Satin
Children of the Regime
China Dolls

Chinese Characters
Choosing Children
Chop Suey
Chrissy
Chuck Solomon: Coming of Age
Cinema Fouad
Close To Home
Closer
Closet Space
Closets Are Health Hazards
Cockettes, The
Come As You Are
Coming Home
Coming Out (1972)
Coming Out, Coming Home:
    Asian and Pacific Islander Family Stories
Coming Out of the Iron Closet
Coming Out under Fire
Common Threads: Stories from the Quilt
Companions: Tales from the Closet
Complaints of a Dutiful Daughter
Comrades in Arms
Confessions of a Pretty Lady
Connections: Gay Aboriginal Men
    in Sydney
Could Be Worse
Creature
Crimes of Passion
Critical Mass: Gay Games Amsterdam
Crossing, The (aka: La Traversée)
Cruising in the Channels
Daddy and the Muscle Academy
Daddy & Papa
Dads (aka: Papas)
Dads Wanted
Daisy Chain Project, The
Danny
Dark and Lovely, Soft and Free
    (aka: Nega Do Cabelo Duro)
Darker Side of Black, The
Darkness before Dawn
Daughter of Dykes
Day I Decided to be Nina, The
De Colores
Dear Jesse
Dear Rock
Deep Inside Clint Star
Desire (1989)
Destiny's Children
Destroying Angel
Devil in the Holy Water, The
Different Corner, A
Different Kind of Black Man, A
Different Shades of Pink
Dirty Laundry (1995)
Divine Trash
Double Trouble
Dragtime
Drama Queen

Dream Girls

Drop Dead Georgeous: The Power of HIV Positive Thinking

Drugs 'R' Us

Dry Kisses Only

Dykes and Tykes

Educate Your Attitude

Eileen is a Spy

Ellen DeGeneres: The Beginning

Elton John: Tantrums and Tiaras

Emergence

Erotica: A Journey into Female Sexuality

Escape to Life: The Erika and Klaus Mann Story

Execution of Wanda Jean, The

Exiles of Love

Eyes of Tammy Faye, The

F2M

Fall of Communism as Seen in Gay Pornography, The

Family Fundamentals

Family Values

Family Values: An American Tragedy

Fassbinder's Women

Fated to be Queer

Fear of Love

Feed Them to the Cannibals!

Female Closet, The

Fiction and Other Truths: A Film about Jane Rule

Fight to Be Male, The

Fighting Chance

Fighting in South-West Louisiana

Finished

Flesh and Paper

Flowing Hearts: Thailand Fighting AIDS

For Better or for Worse: A Celebration of Enduring Relationships

For Straights Only

Forbidden Fruit

Forbidden Fruit: Unfinished Stories of our Lives

Forbidden Love: The Unashamed Stories of Lesbian Lives

Fostering

Framed Youth (aka: Revolt of the Teenage Perverts)

Framing Lesbian Fashion

Francis Bacon

Frantz Fanon: Black Skin, White Mask

Freddie Mercury: The Untold Story

Fresh Blood: A Consideration of Belonging

Friends in High Places

Gaea Girls

Gay Agenda, The

Gay Bombay

Gay Courage: 100 Years of the Gay Movement

Gay Cuba

Gay Games

Gay & Gray in New York City

Gay Sera Sera

Gay Tape: Butch and Femme

Gay USA

Gay Voices, Gay Legends

Gay Voices, Gay Legends 2

Gay Youth

Gay'ze in Wonderland

Gaymes, The

Gendernauts

Georgie Girl

Gertrude Stein: When You See This Remember Me

Get Bruce

Get Out

Ghost of Roger Casement, The

Girls in Boy's Bars

Girls Who Like Girls

Gladys, A Cuban Mother

God, Gays and the Gospel

God, Sreenu & Me

Golden Threads

Got 2 B There

Greetings from Out Here

Greetings from Washington

Guess Who's Coming to Dinner?

Habit

Hallelujah!

Hand on the Pulse

Happy Gordons, The

Hard Fat

Haunted World of Edward D. Wood Jnr, The

He's Bald and Racist, He's Gay and Fascist

Heaven-6-Box (aka: Tengoku No Muttsu No Hako)

Heavy Petting (1988)

Heavy Petting (1991)

Hell Bento!

Hide and Seek

History Lessons

HIV Rollercoaster

Home Sweet Home

Homecoming Queen

Homophobia in Hollywood

Homophobia: That Painful Problem

Homosexuality: A Film for Discussion

Homosexuality and Lesbianism

Homoteens

Hope Along the Wind: The Life of Harry Hay

Horse Dreams in BBQ Country

How I Love You (aka: Shou Bhebbak)

How to Female Ejaculate

How to Find Your Goddess Spot

Hunting Season, The

I Don't Just Want You to Love Me (aka: Ich will nicht nur, daß ihr mich liebt)

I Don't Wanna Be a Boy

I Exist: Voices From the Lesbian and Gay Middle Eastern Community

I Know a Place

I Shall Not Be Removed: The Life of Marlon Riggs

I'll Be Your Mirror

I'm the One that I Want

If She Grows Up Gay

Ifti

Immigration

Improper Conduct (aka: Mauvaise Conduite)

In Bed with Madonna (aka: Madonna: Truth or Dare)

In Pursuit of Prince/ess Charming

In the Best Interests of the Children

In the Flesh (2000)

Indecent Acts

It's a Boy! Journeys from Female to Male

It's Elementary: Talking about Gay Issues in School

It's My Life

It's Not Unusual: A Lesbian and Gay History

It's Personal

Jake 'Today I Became a Man'

James Baldwin: The Price of the Ticket

Jareena: Portrait of a Hijda

Jaundiced Eye, The

Jean Cocteau: Autobiography of an Unknown

Jenny

Jim Loves Jack: The James Egan Story

Jodie: An Icon

Joey Goes to Wigstock

Journey to Kafiristan, The (aka: Die Reise nach Kafiristan)

Juggling Gender

Just a Woman

Just Because of Who We Are

Just Call Me Kade

Kalihgat Fetish (aka: Kalighat Athikatha)

Kalin's Prayer

Kamikaze Summer

Ke Kulana He Mahu: Remembering a Sense of Place

Keep the River on Your Right

Keep Your Laws off My Body

Kenneth Anger's Hollywood Babylon (aka: Kenneth Anger)

Killer in the Village

Kim

Kind of Family, A

Kings
Kipling Trilogy, The
L Is for the Way You Look
Labor More than Once
Ladies Please!
Ladyboys
Last Call at Maud's
Last Coming Out, The
Latin Queens: Unfinished Stories of
　Our Lives
Lavender Limelight: Lesbians in Films
Leather
Legacies
Lesbian Avengers Eat Fire Too
Lesbian Health Matters
Lesbian Physicians on Practice,
　Patients & Power
Lesbian Teenagers in High School
Lesbian Tongues
Lesbians Behaving Badly
Lesbians Go Mad in Lesbos
Lesbians in the Pulpit
Lesbians Olé
Licensed to Kill
Life and Death on the A-List
Life and Times of Allen Ginsberg, The
Life is Like a Cucumber
　(aka: Affengeil)
Life's Evening Hour
Lifetime Commitment: A Portrait
　of Karen Thomson
Lifetime Guarantee: Phranc's
　Adventures in Plastic
Limites
Listening for Something
Live Nude Girls UNITE!
Live to Tell: The First Gay and
　Lesbian Prom in America
Living and Dying
　(aka: Ich Lebe Gern, Ich Sterbe Gern)
Living Proof: HIV and the Pursuit
　of Happiness
Living with AIDS
Living with Pride: Ruth Ellis @ 100
Lone Star Hate
Long Time Comin'
Looking for a Space
Looking for Common Ground
Lorenza
Losing Lois
Love and Marriage
Love Makes a Family: Gay Parents
　in the '90s
Love Story: Berlin 1942, A
Lust and Liberation
Mai's America
Mama, I Have Something to Tell You
Man in the Irony Mask, The
Man Who Drove with Mandela, The

Mandragora
March on Washington, The
Markova: Comfort Gay
Mary's Place
Matt
Maybe We're Talking About a
　Different God
Mayhem
Memory Pictures
Men Like Me
Menmaniacs: The Legacy of Leather
Metamorphosis: Man into Woman
Metamorphosis: The Remarkable
　Journey of Granny Lee
Michael, a Gay Son
Militia Battlefield
Minoru and Me
Moffie Called Simon, A
Moments: The Making of Claire of
　the Moon
Montgomery Clift: The Prince
Moscow Does Not Believe in Queers
Moscow Fags
Most Unknowable Thing, The
Mum's the Word
MURDER and murder
My Babushka
My Feminism
My Femme Divine
My Friend Su
My Girlfriend Did It
My Left Breast
My Mother is an Alien
My Survival as a Deviant
Myth of Father
Nana, George and Me
Naughty Little Peeptoe
Need and Want
Nice Girls Don't Do It
Night with Derek, A
Nijinsky
　(aka: The Diaries of Vaslav Nijinsky)
Nitrate Kisses
No Backup
No Dumb Questions
No Rewind
No Sad Songs
Non, Je Ne Regrette Rien
　(aka: No Regret)
Not All Parents are Straight
Not Angels, But Angels
Not Just Passing Through
Nuestra Salud: Violencia Domestica
O Boys: Parties, Porn & Politics, The
Off the Straight and Narrow: Lesbians,
　Gays, Bisexuals and Television
Oliver
On Becoming

On Being Gay: A Conversation
　with Brian McNaughton
On the Bus
One Nation Under God
One + One
One Shadowless Hour
Opening Closet X: A Voice for
　Queer Youth
Orientations
Original Schtick
Osaka Story
Our Brothers, Our Sons
Our House: A Very Real Documentary
Our Mom's a Dyke
Our Private Idaho
Out At Work: America Undercover
Out For a Change: Homophobia in
　Women's Sports
Out in Africa
Out in Nature: Homosexual
　Behaviour in the Animal
　Kingdom
Out in South Africa
Out in Suburbia
Out in the Open
Out Loud
Out of the Closet, Off the Screen:
　The Life & Times of William
　Haines
Out of the Past
Out: Stories of Lesbian and Gay Youth
Out: The Making of a Revolutionary
Outlaw
Over Our Dead Bodies
Over the Rainbow: Parts 1 - 4
Oy Gay
P(l)ain Truth
Pansexual Public Porn (aka: The
　Adventures of Hans and Del)
Paradise Bent
　(aka: Fa'afafines in Paradise)
Paragraph 175
Parents of Gays
Paris is Burning
Paris Was a Woman
Party Monster
Party Safe with DiAna and Bambi
Paul Cadmus: Enfant Terrible at 80
Paul Monette: The Brink of
　Summer's End
Pencas de Bicuda
Personal Best (1991)
Personals
Perverted Justice
Peter Allen: The Boy from Oz
Pierre et Gilles, Love Stories
Pink Triangle: A Study of Prejudice
　Against Gays & Lesbians
Place of Rage, A

Playing Gay
Please Don't Stop: Lesbian Tips for Givin' and Gettin' It
Plushies & Furries
Poisoned Blood
Polskiseks
Portion of a Lady
Portrait of Jason
Positiv
Positive Story (aka: Sipur Hiyuvi)
Pride Divide
Pride in Puerto Rico
Pride, Politics and Pissheads
Private Wars
Queen: Marianne Hoppe, The (aka: Die Königin: Marianne Hoppe)
Queen of the Whole Wide World
Queen, The
Queens Don't Lie (aka: Tunten Lügen Nicht)
Queer Geography: Mapping Our Identities
Queer Son
Queercore: A Punk-u-mentary
Questioning Faith
Rachel Williams Documentary
Radical Harmonies
Rainmakers - Zimbabwe
Reaching Out to Lesbian, Gay and Bisexual Youth
Real Ellen Story, The
Red Rain
Reframing AIDS
Relationships
Reno Finds Her Mom
Resident Alien
Return of Sarah's Daughters, The
Revolutions Happen like Refrains in a Song
Rewriting the Script: Love Letter to Our Families
Rice and Potatoes
Right to be Different, The
Right Wing, Right Off, Right Hons, Right?
Righteous Babes, The
Rights and Reactions
Ritual Nation
Rock Hudson's Home Movies
Rock the Boat
Rough Sketch of a Spiral (aka: Rasen No Sobyo)
Rules of the Game
Running Gay: Lesbian and Gay Participation in Sport
Ruthie & Connie: Every Room in the House
Sacred Lies, Civil Truths
Sadness
Salt Mines, The

Sambal Belacan in San Francisco
Sando to Samantha: The Art of Dikvel
Sari Red
Scenes from a Queer Planet
Scent Uva Butch
School Fag
School's Out: Lesbian and Gay Youth
Scout's Honor
Search for Intimacy, The
See How They Run
Self-Destruction of Gia, The
Sex 121 and the Gulag
Sex and Balls
Sex and the Sandinistas
Sex and the Single Gene?
Sex Becomes Her: The True Life Story of Chi Chi LaRue
Sex Change: Shock! Horror! Probe!
Sex, Drugs and Democracy
Sex Is...
Sex is Sex: Conversations with Male Prostitutes
Sex Wars
Sex/Life in LA
Sexing the Label: Love and Gender in a Queer World
Sexual Identity
Sexual Orientation: Reading Between the Labels
Shades of Gray
Shatzi is Dying
She Even Chewed Tobacco
She Wears Cufflinks
She's Real Worse than Queer
Shinjuku Boys
Shooting Porn
Show Me Your Pic
Signed: Lino Brocka
Silence=Death (aka: Die AIDS-Trilogie: Schweigen=Tod)
Silent Pioneers
Silver Screen: Color Me Lavender, The
Silverlake Life: The View From Here
Simon and I: Steps for the Future
Sir: Just a Normal Guy
SIS: The Perry Watkins Story
Sissy
Sister Smile (aka: Suor Sorriso)
Skin Complex
Sleep in a Nest of Flames
Sluts and Goddesses Video Workshop
Snake Boy, The
Some Aspect of a Shared Lifestyle
Some Ground to Stand On
Soufflé
Southern Comfort
Speaking for Ourselves
Spikes and Heels
Split: Portrait of a Drag Queen (aka: Split: William to Chrysis)

Spot the Lesbian
Staceyann Chin - A Poetry Slammer
Stand Together
Star is Porn, A
Steers and Queers
Stepping Out
Stiff Sheets
Still Sane
Stolen Moments
Stonewall 25: Voices of Pride and Protest
Storm in a Teacup
Storme: The Lady of the Jewel Box
Straight Down the Aisle: Confessions of Lesbian Bridesmaids
Straight for the Money: Interviews with Queer Sex Workers
Straight from the Heart: Gay and Lesbian Children
Strange Life and Death of Dr Turing, The
Strip Jack Naked: Nighthawks II
Summer in My Veins (Director's Cut)
Sunflowers
Superstar: The Life and Times of Andy Warhol
Surviving Friendly Fire
Susana
Sweet Boy
Swimming Upstream: A Year in the Life of Karen and Jenny
Sydney - Living with Difference
Symposium: Ladder of Love
Tangible Fathers
Tell Me the Truth About Love
Tender
Terms of Conception
Thank God I'm a Lesbian
That's a Family
Theme: Murder
They Are Lost to Vision Altogether
This is Dedicated: Grieving When a Partner Dies
Three Drags and a Wedding
Ties that Bind, The
Tim Miller: Loud and Queer
Time Zones
Times of Harvey Milk, The
Tiny and Ruby: Hell Drivin' Women
To My Women Friends
Tom
Tomboychik
Tongues Untied
Toward Intimacy
Toxic Queen
Transexual Menace
Transformation, The
Transformers/AIDS
Transit: Adventures of a Boy in the Big City
Transsexual Journey, A

Trappings of Transhood
Trembling Before G-d
Treyf
True Inversions
Truth About Gay Sex, The
Two Brides and a Scalpel: Diary of
    a Lesbian Marriage
Union in Wait, A
Venus Boyz
Veronica 4 Rose
Vicious
Video 28
Village Voices
Vintage: Families of Value
Viva Eu!
Voices from the Front
Voicing the Legacy
Wallowitch & Ross: This Moment
We Are Family
We Are Transgenders
We Were Marked with a Big A
We're Funny that Way
We've Been Framed
Webcam Boys
Welcome to Africville
Well Sexy Women
Wellness
West Coast Crones
What a Pretty Sister
What is the Relationship between
    Rosa von Praunheim and the
    Male Strippers of San Francisco?
What You Take for Granted
When Boys Fly
When Shirley Met Florence
When the Penny Drops
Whether You Like It or Not: The
    Story of Hedwig
White People's Business
Who Happen to be Gay
Who's Afraid of Project 10?
Why am I Gay?
Wigstock: The Movie (1987)
Wigstock: The Movie (1995)
William Burroughs: Commissioner
    of the Sewers
Willkommen im Dom
    (aka: Welcome to the Dome)
Witches, Faggots, Dykes and
    Poofters
Woman to Woman
Women Like Us/Women Like That
Women of Gold
Word is Out
Working Class Dykes from Hell
World is Sick (sic), The
Worthy Mothers
Woubi Chéri
Wrecked for Life: The Trip &
    Magic of Trocadero Transfer

XXXY
Yang±Yin: Gender in Chinese Cinema
You Don't Know Dick: Courageous
    Hearts of Transsexual Men
Your Brother, My Tidda
Your Mother Wears Combat Boots
Youth Outloud!
Zero Budget

Drama

100 Days Before the Command
    (aka: Sto dnej do prikaza)
2 by 4 (aka: 2 x 4)
2 Seconds
    (aka: 2 secondes; Deux secondes)
27 Pieces of Me
$30
'68
99 Women (aka: Isle of Lost
    Women; 99 mujeres)
A.K.A
Abandoned (aka: Torzók)
Above the Sea
    (aka: Au essus de la Mar)
Absolution of Anthony, The
Abuse
Abysses, Les
Acla (aka: La Discesa di Aclà a
    Floristella)
Acquiring a Taste for Raffaella
Adam
Adieu Bonaparte
Adiós Roberto
Adjuster, The
Adventures of Sebastian Cole, The
Advise and Consent
Affairs of Love, The
    (aka: Las Cosas del Querer)
Affirmations
Afflicted
After the Game
Afternoon Breezes
    (aka: Kaze tachi No Gogo)
Agora
Aimée and Jaguar
Alabaster Lions
Alexander: The Other Side of Dawn
Alexandria... Why?
    (aka: Iskanderija... lih?)
Alicia was Fainting
Alive and Kicking (aka: Indian Summer)
Alkali, Iowa
All about Alice
All Fall Down
All of Me
All Over Me
All-American Story, An
Almost the Cocktail Hour

Älskande par (aka: Loving Couples)
Alternative, The
Amazing Grace (aka: Hessed Mufla)
American Beauty
American Gigolo
Amerikanos
Amic/Amat (aka: Beloved/Friend)
Amigos (aka: Friends)
Among Men
Amor Maldito
Amorosa
Anatomy of a Hate Crime
And the Band Played On
And Then Came Summer
And/Or=One
Anders als die Anderen
    (aka: Different from Others)
Angelos (aka: Angel)
Anguished Love
Animal Factory
Anita: Dances of Vice
    (aka: Anita: Tanze des Lasters)
Anna und Edith
Anna und Elisabeth
Anne Trister
Another Country
Another Way (aka: Egymásra Nézve)
Antonia's Line
Anxiety of Inexpression and the
    Otherness Machine, The
Apart From Hugh
Apartments
Aqueles Dois
Arch Brown's Top Story
Arrangement, An
As Is
Asa Branca: A Brazilian Dream
Astragale, L'
At Home
Audit
Away with Words (aka: Kujaku)
baba-It (aka: At Home)
Baby Steps
Bad News Bachelors
Balcony, The
Ballad of Reading Gaol
Barry Lyndon
Basic Necessities
Basketball Diaries, The
Beat
Beau Travail (aka: Good Work)
Beautiful Dreamers
Becoming Colette
Bed of Lies
Beethoven's Nephew
    (aka: Le Neveu de Beethoven)
Before Night Falls
Beguines, The
    (aka: Le Rampart des Beguines)
Behind Glass

Behind Walls
Bellas de Noche
Belle
Belle de Jour
Bent
Berlin Affair, The
    (aka: Interno Berlinese)
Bertrand is Missing
    (aka: Bertrand Disparu)
Best Man, The
    (aka: Gore Vidal's The Best Man)
Bete Noire
Betsy, The
Betty Anderson
Between Two Women
Bezness
Biches, Les (aka: The Does)
Big Eden
Big House, The
Bike Boy
Bird in the Hand
Bishonen...Beauty
    (aka: Meishaonian zhi lian)
Bitter Moon
Bittersweet
Black and White (aka: Noir et Blanc)
Black Glove, The
Black Sheep Boy
Blessed Art Thou
    (aka: A Question of Faith)
Blind Fairies
    (aka: Le Fate Ignoranti)
Blind Moment, The
Blond Man, The
Blood and Concrete
Blood Money
Bloodbrothers
    (aka: A Father's Love)
Blue Hour, The
    (aka: Die Blaue Stund)
Blue Jeans
Blunt: The Fourth Man
Bob & Rose
Body of a Poet: A Tribute to Audre
    Lorde 1934-1992, The
Bombay Boys
BOMgaY
Borderline
Borstal Boy
Box, The
Boy like Many Others, A
    (aka: Un Ragazzo come Tanti)
Boys Don't Cry
Boys in the Band, The
Boys Next Door, The
Boys on the Side
Brad
Break of Day
Breaking the Code

Breaking the Surface
Bright Spell
    (aka: L'Embellie)
Broken Branches (aka: Naeil Ui
    Hyahae Hurunun Kang)
Buck House
Buddies
Bugis Street
    (aka: Yao jie huang hou)
Bungee Jumping of Their Own
    (aka: Beonjijeonpeureul hada)
Burlesk King
Burning Boy, The
Burning Secret
Burnt Money (aka: Plata quemada;
    Burning Money)
Bus Riley's Back in Town
Business of Fancydancing, The
Busting
Butley
By Hook or By Crook
c-l-o-s-e-r
Cabaret
Caged
Caligula
Came Out, It Rained, Went Back
    in Again
Campfire (aka: Kampvuur)
Cap Tourmente
Caravaggio
Caretaker, The (aka: The Guest)
Carrington
Cass
Cat on a Hot Tin Roof
Cats, The (aka: Kattorna)
Caught
Cavafy (aka: Kavafis)
Celeste
Cha-Cha for the Fugitive, A
    (aka: Gai Tao-wan-je de ChaCha)
Chaero
Chain of Desire
Chained Heat
Chained Heat II
Chanel Solitaire
Change
Change of Heart, A
Change the Frame
Changing Face
Chant d'Amour, Un
Chasing Amy
Children's Hour, The
Chill Out
Chocolate Babies
Choirboys, The
Christine Jorgensen Story, The
Cicely
Circuit
Citizen Cohn

Claire
Claire of the Moon
Clay Farmers, The
Cleopatra's Second Husband
Clinic E
Closing Numbers
Coal Miner's Granddaughter
Coconut / Cane and Cutlass
Cold Lands, The
    (aka: Les Terres Froides)
Colegas (aka: Pals)
Colonel Redl (aka: Oberst Redl)
Color Purple, The
Come and Go
Come Back to the Five and Dime,
    Jimmy Dean, Jimmy Dean
Comfort of Strangers, The
Coming of Age
Coming Out (1989)
Coming to Terms
Common Flower, A
Common Ground
Company of Strangers, The
    (aka: Strangers in Good Company)
Compromised Immunity
Confession, The
Confessions of Felix Krull, The
    (aka: Bekenntnisse des
    Hochstaplers Felix Krull)
Conformist, The
    (aka: Il Conformista)
Consenting Adult
Consequence, The
    (aka: Die Konsequenz)
Conta Pra Mim (aka: Trust Me)
Conversation Piece (aka: Gruppo di
    famiglia in un interno)
Corpo, O (aka: The Body)
Corps Ouverts, Les
    (aka: Open Bodies)
Coup de Grace (aka: Der Fangschuss)
Crash and Burn
Creation of Adam, The
    (aka: Sotvoreniye Adama)
Cruel
Cruising
Crush (1992)
Crush (2000)
Cynara: Poetry in Motion
Dadshuttle, The
Dakan
Damned, The (aka: Gotterdammer-
    ung; La Caduta degli Dei)
Danzón
Dark Sun: Bright Shade
Darling
Darling International
Daughters of the Sun
Day for Night
    (aka: La Nuit Américaine)

Days (aka: Giorni)
Dead Boys' Club, The
Debutantes, The
Deaf Heaven
Death in the Family, A
Death in Venice
   (aka: Morte a Venezia)
Death in Venice, CA
Deathwatch
Defying Gravity
Deliverance
Delta, The
Demons
Depart to Arrive
   (aka: Weggehen um Anzukommen)
Desert Hearts
Deserter (aka: Lipotaktis)
Desi's Looking for a New Girl
Desire (1999)
Desperate Acquaintances
   (aka: Desperate Bekjentskaper)
Detective, The
Devil's Playground, The
Devotion
Diary of a Male Whore
Different Kind of Love, A
Dinner Guest, The
Diputado, El (aka: The Deputy)
Disco Years, The
Disgraceful Conduct
Doctors' Wives
Dog Day Afternoon
Doing Time on Maple Drive
Don't Forget You're Going to Die
   (aka: N'Oublie pas que tu vas Mourir)
Don't Tell Anyone
   (aka: No Se Lo Digas a Nadie)
Doors Cut Down
Double the Trouble, Twice the Fun
Dozens, The
Drawing Girls
Dreamers of the Day
Dress Gray
Dresser, The
Drift
Drifting (aka: Nagu'a)
Drowning Lessons
Dry Cleaning (aka: Nettoyage à sec)
Duffer
e-male
Each Other (aka: Rega'im)
Early Frost, An (1985)
East Palace West Palace
   (aka: Dong Gong Xi Gong)
Eban and Charley
Eclipse
Edward II
Einstein of Sex: The Life and Work
   of Dr Magnus Hirschfeld, The
Elegant Criminal, L' (aka: Lacenaire)

Elevation
Emily and Gitta
Empty Bed, An
Enfants Terribles, Les
   (aka: The Strange Ones)
Enter the Clowns
   (aka: Choujue Dengchang)
Entre Nous (aka: Coup de Foudre)
Entwined
Équilibristes, Les
   (aka: Walking a Tightrope)
Equus
Erika's Passions
   (aka: Erika's Leidenschaften)
Ernesto
Erotique
Et L'Amore
Eve's Daughters
Evenings, The (aka: De Avonden)
Everlasting Secret Family, The
Everything in Between
Everything Relative
Execution of Justice
Exploding Oedipus
Extramuros (aka: Beyond the Walls)
F. is a Bastard (aka: F. est un salaud)
Family Affair, A (2001)
Fantasy Dancer
Farewell My Concubine
   (aka: Ba wang bie ji)
Farewell, The (aka: Avskedet)
Female Perversions
Film for Two
Fire
First Base
First Breath
Fish & Elephant
   (aka: Jin Nian Xia Tian)
Fixing Frank
Flames of Passion
Flavor of Corn, The
   (aka: Il Sapore del Grano)
Fleeing By Night (aka: Ye Ben)
Flight of Fancy
Flirt
Flora's Garment Bursting Into Bloom
Flow
Flush
Food of Love
For a Lost Soldier
   (aka: Voor een verloren soldaat)
Forbidden Justice (aka: Short Eyes)
Forbidden Love of the Hero, The
Forbidden Passion: Oscar Wilde the Movie
Forever (1991)
Forever Mary (aka: Mery per sempre)
Forgive & Forget
Forsaken
Fortune and Men's Eyes
Forty Deuce

Fourth Sex, The
   (aka: Le Quatrième sexe)
Fox and His Friends
   (aka: Faustrecht der Freiheit)
Fox, The
Foxfire
French Dressing
   (aka: Furenchi doressingu)
Fresh Kill
Freunde: The Whiz Kids
Fried Green Tomatoes
Friend of Dorothy, A
Friends Forever
   (aka: Venner for Altid)
Frisk
From the Ashes
From the Edge of the City
   (aka: Apo tin akri tis polis)
Fruit Machine, The
   (aka: Wonderland)
Fuga, La (aka: The Escape)
Full Blast
Full Moon in New York
   (aka: Ren zai Niu Yue)
Full Speed (aka: À Toute Vitesse)
Fun
Fun with a Sausage (aka: L'Ingenue)
Funeral Parade of Roses
   (aka: Bara No Soretsu)
Future is Woman, The
   (aka: Il Futuro è Donna)
Gang of Four, The
   (aka: La Bande des Quatre)
Garden, The
Gasp
Gemini Affair, The
Genesis Children, The
Gertrude Stein and a Companion
Geschlecht in Fesseln: dei Sexualnot
   der Gefangenen (aka: Sex in Chains)
Get Real
Getting It On
Getting of Wisdom, The
Ghosts of the Civil Dead
Gia
Gilda
Girl, The
Girl Thing, A
Girl with the Golden Eyes, The
   (aka: La Fille aux yeux d'or)
Girlfriends (1978)
Girls Can't Swim (aka: Les filles ne
   savent par nager)
Glasses Break
Glen or Glenda
Glider, The (aka: Le Planeur)
Goblin Market
Godass
Gods and Monsters
Gohatto (aka: Taboo)

Gold Diggers, The
Good Father, The (aka: Fathers' Rites)
Goodbye Emma Jo
Grace of God, The
Green Plaid Shirt
Groove on a Stanley Knife
Group, The
Guardian of the Frontier
   (aka: Varuh Meje)
Half Mongrel
Hamam: The Turkish Bath
   (aka: Steam)
Hammer and Sickle (aka: Serp i molot)
Hanging Garden, The
Happily Ever After
   (aka: Além da Paixão)
Happy Birthday Gemini
Happy Together
   (aka: Cheun gwong tsa sit)
Hard God, A
Harold and Hiroshi
Hate Crime
Haunted Summer
Head On (aka: Loaded)
Health Status Survey
Hearing Voices
Heart Exposed, The
   (aka: La Coeur Découvert)
Heart's Root, The
   (aka: A Raiz Do Coração)
Heavenly Creatures
Hell's Highway
Henry and June
Hidden Child
Hidden Injuries
High Art
Higher Learning
hITCH
Hold You Tight (aka: Yue Kuai Le)
Holding
Holi: Festival of Fire
Hollow Reed
Homme Blessé, L'
   (aka: The Wounded Man)
Homme Que J'aime, L'
   (aka: The Man I Love)
Horror Vacui: The Fear of Emptiness
   (aka: Horror Vacui: Die Angst
   vor der Leere)
Hotel New Hampshire, The
Hours and Times, The
How Old is the River?
   (aka: Fuyu no Kappa)
How to Kill Her
Hu-Du-Men (aka: Stage Door)
Hubo un Tiempo en que Los
   Suenos Dieron Paso a Largas
   Noches de Insomnio
Hungry Hearts

Hush!
I Am a Camera
I Am a Man
I Am My Own Woman
   (aka: Ich Bin Meine Eigene Frau)
I Am Not What You Want
I, Eugenia
I Hate Faggy Fag Fag
I Like You, I Like You Very Much
   (aka: Anata-Ga Suki Desu, Dai
   Suki Desu)
I Love You Baby
I Love You, I'll Kill You (aka: Ich
   Liebe Dich, Ich Töte Dich)
I Shot Andy Warhol
I, the Worst of All
   (aka: Yo, la Peor de Todas)
I Vitelloni (aka: The Young and the
   Passionate)
I Want What I Want
I Will Not Think about Death Anymore
I'll Love You Forever - Tonight
I'm Starving
I've Heard the Mermaids Singing
Icarus
Ice Palace, The
If
If All Goes Well I'll Meet You on
   the Next Train
If She Only Knew
If the Family Fits
If These Walls Could Talk 2
Images
Immacolata e Concetta - l'altra gelosia
In a Year of Thirteen Moons
   (aka: In einem Jahr mit 13 Monden)
In on Earth as It Is in Heaven
In the Flesh (1997)
In the Gloaming
In This House of Brede
Incidental Journey
   (aka: Haijiao Tianya)
Infidel
Intimate Friendship, An
Intimates, The (aka: Ji Sor)
Investigator, The
Iris
It is Not the Homosexual Who is
   the Pervert but the Society in
   Which He Lives (aka: Nicht der
   Homosexuelle ist pervers,
   sondern die Situation, in der er lebt)
It's My Party
It's That Age
J'embrasse pas (aka: I Don't Kiss)
Jackson: My Life Your Fault
Je, tu, il, elle
Jerker
Jewel's Darl

Johnny Eager
Johnny Greyeyes
Johns
Journey Among Women
Journey of Jared Price, The
Joys of Smoking, The
Julia
Julie Johnson
Jumping the Gun
Jupon Rouge, Le (aka: Manuela's Loves)
Just for Fun
Just the Two of Us
Kali's Vibe
Kamikaze Hearts
Kansas Anymore
Karmarama
Kesher Ir (aka: Urban Feel)
Kevin's Room
Khush
Killing of Sister George, The
King and Country
King Girl
King of the City (aka: Club Life)
Kings of the Road
   (aka: Im Lauf der Zeit)
Kiss in the Snow, A
Kiss of the Spider Woman, The
Kiss the Boys and Make Them Die
Krámpack (aka: Nico & Dani)
Krays, The
L. I. E.
L-Shaped Room, The
Lady in Cement
Lan Yu
Laramie Project, The
Larry's Visit
Last Bus Home, The
Last Emperor, The
Last Empress, The
   (aka: Wei dai huang hou)
Last Exit to Brooklyn
Last Island, The
Last Metro, The (aka: Le Dernier métro)
Last of England, The
Last Song, The
Latin Boys Go To Hell
Laughing Policeman, The
Law of Desire (aka: La Ley del Deseo)
Lawless Heart, The
Leather Boys, The
Leather Jacket Love Story
Legal Memory
Legend of Lylah Clare, The
Let's Love Hong Kong
   (aka: Ho Yuk)
Let's Play Prisoners
Lianna
Liberace
Liberace: Behind the Music

Life (aka: Containment; Out of the Blue)
Life and Death
Life History of a Star
Life is a Woman
    (aka: Zhizn-Zhenshchina)
Life that We Dreamt, The
    (aka: Het Leven dat we Droomden)
Like Grains of Sand
    (aka: Nagisa no Shindobaddo)
Like It Is
Lilies (aka: Lilies - les Feluettes)
Lilith
Liu Awaiting Spring
Living End, The
Living Out Loud
Lola and Billy the Kid
    (aka: Lola and Bilidikid)
Lonely Lady, The
Long Day Closes, The
Long Voyage Home, The
Long Weekend, The
    (aka: The Long Weekend (O'Despair))
Longtime Companion
Looking for Angel
    (aka: Tenshi No Rakuen)
Looking for Mr Goodbar
Loose Ends
Loss of Heat
Loss of Innocence
    (aka: The Greengage Summer)
Lost and Delirious
Lost Language of Cranes, The
Lot in Sodom
Love and Death on Long Island
    (aka: Amour et mort à Long Island)
Love and Human Remains
Love is the Devil
Love Like Any Other, A
    (aka: Eine Liebe wie andere auch)
Love of a Man, The
    (aka: Amor de hombre)
Love/Juice
Ludwig
Ludwig: Requiem for a Virgin King
    (aka: Ludwig: Requiem für einen jungfräulichen König)
Lulu
Lunch with Eddie
Lune
Luster
Luv Tale, A
M Butterfly
Ma Vie en Rose (aka: My Life in Pink)
Macho Dancer
Madame Sousatzka
Mädchen in Uniform
    (aka: Girls in Uniform) (1931)
Mädchen in Uniform
    (aka: Girls in Uniform) (1957)

Madras Eyes
Magnolia
Mahogany
Maid of Honor
Maiden Work
Maids, The
Making Love
Mala Noche (aka: Bad Night)
Man in Her Life, The
    (aka: Ang lalaki sa buhay ni Selya)
Man is a Woman
    (aka: L'Homme est une femme comme les autres)
Man like Eva, A
    (aka: Ein, Mann wie Eva)
Man Man Woman Woman (aka: NanNan NuNu; Men and Women)
Man of No Importance, A
Manila: In the Claws of Darkness
    (aka: Maynila: Sa mga kuko ng liwanag)
Manji
    (aka: All Mixed Up)
Map of Sex and Love, The
    (aka: Qingse ditu)
Marble Ass
    (aka: Dupe od Mramora)
March in April
Marching into Darkness
Mare, Il (aka: The Sea)
Marlene
Martin Four
Martirio (aka: Sufferance)
Mask of Desire (aka: Shades of Black)
Mass Appeal
Maurice
Maybe I Can Give You Sex?
Me and the Girls
Meeting Magdalene
Memento Mori (aka: Yeogo Guidam II)
Men in Love
Merry Christmas, Mr Lawrence
Metalguru
Meteor and Shadow
    (aka: Meteoro kai Skia)
Metrosexuality
Midnight Cowboy
Midnight Dancers
    (aka: Sibak)
Midnight Express
Midnight in the Garden of Good and Evil
Midwife's Tale, The
Miguel/Michelle
Mikaël (aka: Chained)
Mike's Murder
Milou in May
    (aka: Milou en Mai; May Fools)
Minor Disturbances

Miracle Alley
    (aka: El Callejon de los Milagros)
Mob Queen
Montreal Main
More Love
More than Friends: The Coming Out of Heidi Leiter
Morocco
Mountain King, The
Mountains of the Moon
Mull (aka: Mullaway)
Muriel's Parents Have Had it up to Here
    (aka: Muriel fait le désespoir de ses parents)
Murmur of Youth
    (aka: Mei li zai chang ge)
Muscle
Music Lovers, The
Must be the Music
My Beautiful Laundrette
My Brother's Keeper
My Own Private Idaho
My Two Loves
Mystère Alexina, Le
    (aka: The Mystery of Alexina)
Naked Civil Servant, The
Naomi's Legacy
Nea: The Young Emmanuelle (aka: Nea)
Neptune's Rocking Horse
Nervos de Aco
    (aka: Nerves Made of Steel)
Nervous Energy
Never Look Back
Nietta's Diary
Night of Varennes, The
    (aka: La Nuit de Varennes)
Night Out
Night Porter, The
    (aka: Il Portiere di notte)
Night Trade
Night Visions
Nighthawks
Nijinsky
Nine Days
No Exit
No Exit (aka: Huis Clos)
No One Sleeps
No Ordinary Love
Nocturne (1989)
Nocturne (1990)
None of the Above
Norang Mori 2
    (aka: Running Blue; Yellow Hair 2)
North of Vortex
Not Love, Just Frenzy
    (aka: Mas Que Amor, Frenesi)
November Moon
    (aka: Novembermond)
Nowhere

Number 96
Nun, The (aka: La Religieuse)
Nunzio's Second Cousin
Object of My Affection, The
Ode
Ode to Billy Joe
Offering, The
Oi Queer
Oi! Warning
Olive Tree, The
Olivia (aka: The Pit of Loneliness)
Olivier, Olivier
On Guard
ON_LINE
Once Is Not Enough
    (aka: Jacqueline Susann's Once Is
    Not Enough)
Once upon a Time in the East
    (aka: Il était une fois dans l'est)
One of Them
One Small Step
Only the Brave
Only When I Laugh
Opposite of Sex, The
Oranges Are Not the Only Fruit
Ordinary Sinner
Orlando
Other Mothers
Other Side, The (aka: Del Otro Lado)
Other Voices, Other Rooms
Otra Historia de Amour
    (aka: Another Love Story)
Our Lady of the Assassins
    (aka: La Virgen de los sicarios)
Our Sons (aka: Too Little, Too Late)
Out of Our Time
Out of Season
Outcasts, The
    (aka: Niezi; The Outsiders)
Outtakes
Pandora's Box
    (aka: Die Büchse der Pandora)
Paper Cranes
Parallel Sons
Parting Glances
Partners
Pasajes (aka: Passages)
Passengers
Passing Resemblance
Passion of Remembrance, The
Past Caring
Peach
Peixe-Lua (aka: Moon-Fish)
Penitentiary
Peony Pavilion
    (aka: Youyuan jingmeng)
Peony Pavilion, The
Perfect Son, The
Performance
Persona

Personal Best (1982)
Petals
Peter's Friends
Phantom (aka: O Fantasma)
Phantom Pain
Philadelphia
Pianese Nunzio (aka: Fourteen in
    May; Sacred Silence)
Piccadilly Pickups
Pillow Book, The
Pixote: A Lei do Mais Fraco
Place in the Sun, A
Play It as It Lays
Pleasure Principle, The
Poetry for an Englishman
Point of Departure, A
Poison
Pool Days
Portrait of a Marriage
Portrait of a Young Girl at the End
    of the '60s in Brussels
    (aka: Portrait d'une jeune fille de
    la fin des années 60 à Bruxelles)
Possible Loves
    (aka: Amores Possiveis)
Postcards from America
Postman (aka: Youchai)
Potluck and the Passion, The
Presque Rien (aka: Come Undone;
    Almost Nothing)
Pretty Boy (aka: Smukke Dreng)
Prick Up Your Ears
Priest
Prince in Hell
    (aka: Prinz in Holleland)
Prince of Tides, The
Princesa
Prisonnières
Privilege
Public Opinion
Quai des Orfèvres (aka: Jenny Lamour)
Queen Christina
Queen of the Night
    (aka: La Reina de la Noche)
Queer As Folk (1998)
Queer As Folk 2
Queer As Folk (2000)
Queer Story, A (aka: Jilao Sishi)
Querelle
Quest for Love
Question of Attribution, A
Question of Love, A
Rachel, Rachel
Rainbow, The
Rebel Rebel
Red Dirt
Red Shoe Diaries 3, The: Another
    Woman's Lipstick
Reflections
Reflections in a Golden Eye

Reform School Girls
Relax
Rendez-vous d'Anna, Les
Replay (aka: La Répétition)
Resonance
Return to Go! (aka: Zürück Auf Los!)
Revoir Julie (aka: Julie and Me)
Richard's Things
Ritual
Rock Hudson
Rockwell
Roi Danse, Le
    (aka: The King is Dancing)
Room of Words, The
    (aka: La Stanza della parole)
Roommates
Rose, The
Rosebud
Rules of the Road
S.
Safe Journey
Safe Place, A
Sagitario
Saint
Salmonberries
Salon Kitty (aka: Madam Kitty)
Salut Victor!
Sammy and Rosie Get Laid
Sand and Blood
    (aka: De sable et de sang)
Satdee Nite
Saturday Night at the Baths
Saturn's Return
Satyricon
Sauve Qui Peut (aka: Slow Motion)
Savage Nights (aka: Les Nuits fauves)
Score
Scrubbers
Seashell and the Clergyman, The
    (aka: La Coquille et le Clergyman)
Sebastian
Sebastiane
Second Awakening of Christa
    Klages, The (aka: Das Zweite
    Erwachen der Christa Klages)
Second Serve
Second Skin (aka: Segunda Piel)
Secret Ceremony
Seduction of Innocence
Separate Peace, A
Sergeant Matlovich vs. the U.S. Air Force
Sergeant, The
Servant, The
Serving in Silence: The Marguerite
    Cammermeyer Story
Set Me Free (aka: Emporte-moi)
Seven Women
Sex Bytes
Sex Warriors and the Samurai

Sexe des étoiles, Le
  (aka: Sex of the Stars)
Shades
Shall We Dance
Shampoo Horns
  (aka: Cuernos de espuma)
Shanghai Panic (aka: Wo men hai pa)
She Must Be Seeing Things
Sherlock, Louise and Mina
Shifting Positions
Shinjuku Triad Society
  (aka: Shijuku Kuro Shakai)
Show Me Love (aka: Fucking Åmål)
Siberia
Siegfried
Sign of the Cross, The
Silence, The (aka: Tystnaden)
Silences
Silencis (aka: Silent Moments)
Silent Thrush, The
  (aka: Shisheng Huamei)
Simone
Sincerely Yours
Sink or Swim
Sister My Sister
Six Degrees of Separation
Sixth Happiness, The
Skin Deep
Skindeep
Slight Fever of a 20-Year-Old
  (aka: Hatachi No Binetsu)
Smear
Smoke
Smokers Only
  (aka: Vagón Fumador)
Sodom
Soliloquy of Dale Cunningham, The
Solos Y Soledades
Some of My Best Friends Are
Some of These Days
Something Close to Heaven
Song of the Loon
Sonny Boy
Sospiro d'amore nell'attesa
Souvenir
Spacked Out (aka: Mo yan ka sai)
Spartacus
Special Day, A
  (aka: Una Giornata particolare)
Speedway Junky
Spin the Bottle
Split World, The
Spokes
Spy Who Came, The
Squeeze
Stargaze
Stephen
Stolen Diary, The (aka: Le Cahier Volé)
Stonewall

Story of a Bad Boy, The
Story So Far, The
Straight to the Heart
  (aka: À Corps Perdu)
Straightman
Strange Fits of Passion
Strange Love Affair, A
Strange One, The (aka: End as a Man)
Stranger Inside
Strawberry and Chocolate
  (aka: Fresa y Chocolate)
Stray Dogs
Streamers
Strippers
Strung Up
Suddenly, Last Summer (1959)
Sugar and Spice
Sugar Sweet
Summer Dress, A
  (aka: Une Robe d'été)
Summer of Miss Forbes, The
  (aka: El Verano de la señora Forbes)
Summer Vacation 1999
  (aka: 1999 Nen No Natsu Yasumi)
Sun and Rain
  (aka: Taiyang Yu)
Sunday, Bloody Sunday
Surviving Sabu
Swann in Love
  (aka: Un Amour de Swann)
Sweet Thing
Swimming
Switch (1999)
Swoon
Take Out
Tales of the City
Tales of the City 2
  (aka: More Tales of the City)
Tales of the City 3
  (aka: Further Tales of the City)
Talk to Me like the Rain
Tampon Thieves
  (aka: Ladronas de tampones)
Tanaka
Taste of Honey, A
Tea and Sympathy
Tea Leaf
Teenage Tupelo
Tell Me That You Love Me, Junie Moon
Teorema (aka: Theorem)
Terence Davies Trilogy, The
That Certain Summer
That Tender Touch
Thelma
Thelma and Louise
There is no Pain in Paradise
  (aka: En el Paraiso no Existe el Dolor)
Thérèse and Isabelle
Thin Ice: Passion on the Pink Rink

Things We Said Today
Things You Can Tell Just by
  Looking at Her
Third Sex, The
  (aka: Anders als du und ich)
Thirst
  (aka: Törst; Three Strange Loves)
This I Wish and Nothing More
  (aka: Nincsen Nekem Vagyam Semmi)
This Special Friendship
  (aka: Les Amitiés Particulières)
Those Who Love Me Can Take the
  Train
Thousand Miles, A
Three (aka: Tatlo... magkasalo)
Three Bewildered People (aka:
  Three Bewildered People in the Night)
Thunderbolt and Lightfoot
Tidy Endings
Time Being, The
Time Off
Time Piece
Time Regained
  (aka: Le Temps retrouvé)
Times Square
To an Unknown God
  (aka: A un Dios Desconocido)
To Die for (aka: Heaven's a Drag)
To Forget Venice
  (aka: Dimenticare Venezia)
To Play or to Die
  (aka: Spelen of sterven)
To Ride a Cow
Toc Storee
Todd Killings, The
Together Alone
Together and Apart
Toilers and the Wayfarers, The
Token of Love
Tokyo Cowboy
Tokyo Fist (aka: Tokyo-ken)
Tom Clay Jesus
Too Young (aka: Ye Maque)
Torch Song Trilogy
Total Eclipse
Total Loss
Totally F***ed Up
Touch Me (1994)
Touch Me (1997)
Touch of Love, A (aka: Thank You
  All Very Much; The Millstone)
Tour Abroad (aka: Auslandstournee)
Transeltown
Trash
Treading Water
Trials of Oscar Wilde, The
Triple Echo
Troika
Trois

True Faith
Truth About Jane, The
Truth Game, The
Twice a Woman (aka: Twee vrouwen)
Twilight Girls, The
Twilight of the Gods
Twilight of the Golds, The
Twin Bracelets (aka: Shuang Cho)
Twinkle (aka: Kira Kira Hikaru)
Two Brothers
Two in Twenty
Two Men
Two Moon Junction
Two of Us (aka: Mates)
Unconditional Love
Uncut
Under Heat
Undercover
Unknown Cyclist, The
Unknown Friend
   (aka: Fremde Freundin)
Urbania
Valentino
Vanished
Vaudeville
Velocity of Gary, The
Vendetta
Vera
Very Natural Thing, A
Via Appia
Victim
Village Affair, A
Virgin Machine
   (aka: Die Jungfrauenmaschine)
Vive l'Amour (aka: Aiqing Wansui)
Voleurs, Les (aka: Thieves)
Waiting for the Moon
Waiting 'round Wynyard
Walk on the Wild Side
Walking On Water
War on Lesbians
War Widow, The
Watching You
Watermelon Woman, The
Waves (aka: Bølgene)
We Always Danced
We Were One Man (aka: Nous
   étions un Seul Homme)
Weekend, The
Weininger's Nacht
Well Lit Shadows
Westler: East of the Wall
What Kind of Music!
   (aka: Ma Che Musica!)
What Makes a Family
When Love Comes
When Night Is Falling
When the Party's Over
Where Is My Love?
   (aka: Qiangpo Puguang)

Where the Sun Beats Down
   (aka: Onde Bate o Sol)
Who Killed Pasolini?
   (aka: Pasolini, an Italian Crime;
   Pasolini, un delitto Italiano)
Wild Life
Wild Party, The
Wild Reeds, The
   (aka: Les Roseaux Sauvages)
Wilde (aka: Oscar Wilde)
Wildflowers
Wilma's Sacrifice
Wittgenstein
Woman Accused, A
   (aka: In the Glitter Palace)
Woman in Flames, A
   (aka: Flaming Desire; Die
   Flambierte Frau)
Woman Inside, The
Woman like Eve, A
   (aka: Een Vrouw als Eva)
Women in Love
Women of Brewster Place, The
Women on the Roof
   (aka: Kvinnorna på taket)
Wonder Boys, The
Work
Working Girls
World and Time Enough
Wrestlers, The (aka: Uttara)
Wu Yen
X Y and Zee (aka: Zee and Co.)
Y tu Mamá También
   (aka: And Your Mother Too)
Yearning for Sodom
Yentl
Yes (aka: To Ingrid My Love Lisa;
   Kvinnolek)
Young Soul Rebels
Zanjeer (aka: The Chain)
Zero de Conduite
   (aka: Zero for Conduct)
Zindagi Zindabad
   (aka: Long Live Life)
Zippers & Tits (aka: Fasuna to Chibusa)

Erotica

45 Minutes of Bondage
Alley of the Tranny Boys
Another 45 Minutes of Bondage
Backroom
Baise-moi (aka: Fuck Me; Rape Me)
Bilitis
Chained Girls
Elegant Spanking, The
Emmanuelle
Fantasm
Fantasm Comes Again (aka: Fantasm 99)
Felicity

Flesh Gordon
Hard Love & How to Fuck in High Heels
Hellion Heatwave
Hey Sailor, Hey Sister
How to Have a Sex Party
Hustler White
Kindling Point, The
Kore Cara Mia
Lickerish Quartet, The
   (aka: The Erotic Quartet)
Mirror Images II
Naked Highway
No Skin Off My Ass
Olga's Girls
Pink Narcissus
Pleasure Beach
Salo (aka: The 120 Days of Sodom)
Seduction: The Cruel Woman
   (aka: Verführung: Die grausame Frau)
Sex Flesh in Blood
Siren
Skin Flick (aka; Skin Gang)
Sugar High, Glitter City
Super 8 1/2

Experimental

7 Steps to Sticky Heaven
Age 12: Love with a Little L
Aide Mémoire
Alpsee
Amelia Rose Towers
Angelic Conversation, The
Aren't You Lucky You Brought Your
   Own Chair
As Far Away as Here
B/side
Baby
Basement Girl, The
bed
Between the Lines
Bitter Tears of Petra von Kant, The
   (aka: Die Bitteren Tränen der
   Petra von Kant)
Blonde Cobra
Blow Job
Blue
Bodies in Trouble
Broken Goddess
Camp
Casta Diva
Cat Nip
Cat Swallows Parakeet and Speaks!
Celine and Julie Go Boating
   (aka: Céline et Julie vont en bateau)
Chelsea Girls, The
Child-Play
Clips
Corps Imagé, Le
Cosmic Demonstration of Sexuality, A

Cuz It's Boy
Damned if You Don't
Dandy Dust
David & Goliath
Day in the Life of a Bull-Dyke, A
Dear Mom
Deccada
Decodings
Deflatable Man, The
Do You Think We Can Talk about
    Anything but Love?
Double Strength
Dreck (aka: Dirt)
Eight Million
Elegy in the Streets
Endangered
Faggots are for Burning
Family Affair, A (1995)
Farewell to Charms
Fireworks
First Comes Love (1991)
Flaming Creatures
Flesh on Glass
Fly Away Homo
Forever (1994)
Frostbite
Gently down the Stream
Glitterbug
Group
He's Like
Heaven, Earth and Hell
Hey, Happy!
History of the World According to
    a Lesbian, The
Hole
Home Movie
Home-Made Melodrama
Hope is a Thing With Feathers
House of Pain
I Almost Feel Like a Tourist
I Am the Camera Dying
Illegal Tender
Image in the Snow
Imagining October
In My Father's House
In the Shadow of the Sun
Inauguration of the Pleasure Dome
Independently Blue
Inverted Minstrel
Invocation of My Demon Brother
Iro Kaze (aka: Colour Wind)
It Dwells in Mirrors
Janine
Jollies
Jungle Boy, The
Lesson 9
Letters from Home
Loads
Looking for Langston
Loverfilm

Lucifer Rising
Luminous Procuress
Lysis
M! Mom, Madonna and Me
Macumba
Madame X: An Absolute Ruler
    (aka: Madame X: Eine Absolute Herrscherin)
Manodestra
Massillon
Melody for Buddy Matsumae (aka:
    Matsumae-Kun No Senritsu)
Memsahib Rita
Mercy (1989)
Naked Lunch
Odd Girl Out
Panic Bodies
Pensao Globo
Pink Pimpernel, The
Pink Ulysses
Pixel Pose
Place Between Our Bodies, The
Place Called Lovely, A
Prefaces
Protagonist, The (aka: Shujinko)
RSVP
Sabor a Mi (aka: Savour Me)
Sad Disco Fantasia
Sailor (aka: Matroos)
Salivation Army
Scorpio Rising
Sea in the Blood
Seamen
Second Coming, The
Silence that Silences, The
Sisters Lumiere, The
    (aka: Sisters of Light)
Sleepy Haven
Sparky's Shoes
Speedy Boys
Spent
Swimming Prohibited (aka: Yuei Kinshi)
Swollen Stigma
Sync Touch
TABU V (about which one cannot speak)
Tarch Trip
Taste the Sweat
Tender Fictions
Tenebrae Lessons
    (aka: Leçons de Ténèbres)
Thug
Twice a Man
Twisted Sheets
Two or Three Things I Know about Them
Uh-Oh!
West Fickt Ost (aka: West Fucks East)
Where Lies the Homo?
White to be Angry, The
Women I Love
You Taste American

Horror

Alien Prey
Black Sunday
    (aka: La Maschera del Demonio)
Blood and Roses
    (aka: Et Mourir de Plaisir)
Blood for Dracula
Blood Splattered Bride, The
    (aka: La Novia Ensangrentada)
Bloodlust
Carmilla
Cat People
Chopper Chicks in Zombie Town
Countess Dracula
Crocodile Tears
Danza Macabra, La
    (aka: Castle of Blood)
Daughters of Darkness
    (aka: Le Rouge aux Lévres)
Dracula's Daughter
Ein Toter Hing im Netz
    (aka: Girls of Spider Island)
Fascination
Flesh for Frankenstein
Frankenstein Created Woman
Frisson des Vampires, Le
    (aka: Sex and the Vampire)
Haunting of Morella, The
Haunting, The
Headhunter
Homicidal
Howling II: Your Sister is a Werewolf
Hunger, The
Interview with the Vampire
Killer Nun (aka: Suor Omicidi)
Kiss Me Monster
    (aka: Bésame Monstruo)
Lust for a Vampire
    (aka: To Love a Vampire)
Mark of Lilith, The
Nadja
Noche de Walpurgis, La
Razor Blade Smile
Reflecting Skin, The
Requiem pour un Vampire
    (aka: Vierges et Vampires)
Satan's Princess (aka: Malediction)
'Sucker
Sugar Cookies
Terror in the Crypt
    (aka: La Cripta e L'Incubo)
Thundercrack!
Twins of Evil (aka: The Gemini Twins)
Vampire Lovers, The
Vampire Nue, La
    (aka: The Naked Vampire)
Vampyres, Daughters of Dracula
    (aka: Blood Hunger)

Vampyros Lesbos (aka: Lesbian
Vampires; Die Erbin des Dracula)
Velvet Vampire, The
(aka: The Waking Hour)
Viol du Vampire, Le
Wolves of Kromer, The

Musical

Because the Dawn
Broadway Melody, The
Cabaret
Calamity Jane
Can't Stop the Music
City of Lost Souls (aka: Stadt der
Verlorenen Seelen)
Dead Dreams of Monochrome Men
Eika Katappa
Funny Lady
Gay Rock and Roll Years, The
Gentlemen Prefer Blondes
Ginger Beer
Hedwig and the Angry Inch
Isle of Lesbos
Karmen Geï
Making of Monsters
Stand on Your Man
Without You I'm Nothing
Zero Patience

Sci-Fi

Barbarella
Born in Flames
Dandy Dust
Dr Jekyll and Sister Hyde
Flaming Ears (aka: Rote Ohren
Fetzen Durch Asche)
I.K.U
Kanada
Liquid Sky
Naked Lunch
New Women, The
Sticky Fingers of Time, The
Tank Girl
Valentine's Day

Thriller

301 - 302
Acting on Impulse
(aka: Eyes of a Stranger)
Anderson Tapes, The
Angel (1983)
Apartment Zero
Basic Instinct
Being at Home with Claude

Bitter Harvest (1993)
Black Widow
Blessed are Those Who Thirst
(aka: Salige er de som tørster)
Blind Faith
Boston Strangler, The
Bound
Butterfly Kiss
Compulsion
Crueles, Las (aka: The Cruel Ones)
Cruising
Crying Game, The
Day of the Jackal, The
Deadfall
Deep End, The
Diabolique
Diaboliques, Les (aka: Diabolique)
Double Face
Dressed to Kill
Eiger Sanction, The
Empire State
Enchantment, The (aka: Yuwakusha)
Fourth Man, The (aka: Di Vierde Man)
Gonin (aka: The Five)
Hard
Internal Affairs
Kate's Addiction
Last of Sheila, The
Lightship, The
Listen
Mafu Cage, The
(aka: My Sister, My Love)
Mascara
Matter of Taste, A (aka: A Question
of Taste; Une affaire de goût)
Mercy (1999)
Mona Lisa
Monkey's Mask, The
Monsieur Hawarden
Mulholland Drive
Night Rhythms
Night Warning
No Way Out
Order to Kill
(aka: El Clan de los Immorales)
Pouvoir Intime
Rainbow Serpent, The
(aka: Haltéroflic)
Red Heat
Residencia, La
(aka: The House that Screamed)
Rites of Passage
Rope
Seducers, The (aka: Death Game)
See the Sea (aka: Regarde la Mer)
Silence of the Lambs, The
Silkwood
Sticky Fingers of Time, The

Touch of Evil
Triche, La (aka: The Cheat)
Villain
Well, The
Wild Side (aka: Donald Cammell's
Wild Side)
Wild Things
Windows

Western

Ballad of Little Jo, The
Big Sky, The
Calamity Jane
Johnny Guitar
Red River

Lists of Films by Country

Argentina

Adiós Roberto
Apariencias
Burnt Money
   (aka: Plata quemada; Burning Money)
I, the Worst of All
   (aka: Yo, la Peor de Todas)
No Exit
Otra Historia de Amour
   (aka: Another Love Story)
Scenes from a Queer Planet
Smokers Only
   (aka: Vagón Fumador)
Susana

Australia

About Vivien
Acquiring a Taste for Raffaella
Adam
Adventures of Priscilla, Queen of
   the Desert, The
AIDS
Alabaster Lions
Alias
All Men are Liars
   (aka: Goodnight Irene)
Alternative, The
Amelia Rose Towers
And/Or=One
Apartments
Bad News Bachelors
Bare
Bete Noire
Beyond the Catwalk: The Search
   for Mr Gay Australia 2000
Big House, The
Black Sheep
Blond Man, The
Bloodlust
Box, The
Brad
Break of Day
Buck House
Buckeye and Pinto
Burning Boy, The
Can't You Take a Joke?
Cass
China Dolls
Chrissy
Clinic, The
Closet Space
Cold Footsies
Come As You Are

Connections: Gay Aboriginal Men
   in Sydney
Corps Imagé, Le
Crazy Richard
Dallas Doll
Deccada
Devil's Playground, The
Different Shades of Pink
Double Trouble
Drugs 'R' Us
Dykes and Tykes
Elevation
Everlasting Secret Family, The
F2M
Faggots are for Burning
Fantasm
Fantasm Comes Again (aka: Fantasm 99)
Farewell to Charms
Feed Them to the Cannibals!
Felicity
Flesh on Glass
Flight of Fancy
Getting of Wisdom, The
Ghosts of the Civil Dead
Half Mongrel
Hard God, A
Hate Crime
Head On (aka: Loaded)
Hell Bento!
Hidden Injuries
Homecoming Queen
Homosexuality: A Film for Discussion
I Almost Feel Like a Tourist
I, Eugenia
Icarus
Independently Blue
Is Mary Wings Coming?
Jenny
Journey Among Women
Jumping the Gun
Just Desserts
Karmarama
Kicking On
Ladies Please!
Last Coming Out, The
Laura
Let Me Die, Again
Life
   (aka: Containment; Out of the Blue)
Liu Awaiting Spring
Living with AIDS
Love and Other Catastrophes
Low-Fat Elephants
Man in the Irony Mask, The

Martin Four
Mary's Place
Men Like Me
Monkey's Mask, The
Morris Loves Jack
Mull (aka: Mullaway)
My Survival as a Deviant
Night Out
Night Trade
Nightwork
Nijinsky
   (aka: The Diaries of Vaslav Nijinsky)
None of the Above
Number 96
On Becoming
On Guard
Only the Brave
Original Schtick
Paradise Bent
   (aka: Fa'afafines in Paradise)
Parents of Gays
Personals
Peter Allen: The Boy from Oz
Poetry for an Englishman
Point of Departure, A
Red Label
Resonance
Sadness
Satdee Nite
Saturn's Return
Seamen
Sex and Balls
Sexing the Label: Love and Gender
   in a Queer World
Shanghai Panic (aka: Wo men hai pa)
Show Me Your Pic
Sissy
Skindeep
Skud
Soliloquy of Dale Cunningham, The
Soufflé
Special Guest Star
Spot the Lesbian
Strange Fits of Passion
Strung Up
'Sucker
Sum of Us, The
Sweet Thing
Sydney - Living with Difference
Tanaka
Taste
This Marching Girl Thing
Three Drags and a Wedding

Thug
Touch Me (1994)
Toxic Queen
Tragic But True
True Faith
Two Girls and a Baby
Two Roads
Undercover
Violet's Visit
Visitors
Waiting 'round Wynyard
Walking On Water
Wax Me
Well Lit Shadows
Well, The
When the Penny Drops
White People's Business
Witches, Faggots, Dykes and Poofters
Woman to Woman
Your Brother, My Tidda

Austria

All the Queens Men
Dandy Dust
Drag Attack
Ein Toter Hing im Netz
    (aka: Girls of Spider Island)
Flaming Ears (aka: Rote Ohren
    Fetzen Durch Asche)
Lulu
Oh Baby, A Baby! (aka: Zwei
    Frauen, ein Mann und ein Baby)
Weiner Brut
Weininger's Nacht

Belgium

Campfire (aka: Kampvuur)
Celestial Clockwork
    (aka: Mecaniques Celestes)
Daughters of Darkness
    (aka: Le Rouge aux Lévres)
Je, tu, il, elle
Life that We Dreamt, The
    (aka: Het Leven dat we Droomden)
Lonely without You
Ma Vie en Rose (aka: My Life in Pink)
Mascara
Monsieur Hawarden
Presque Rien
    (aka: Come Undone; Almost Nothing)
Rendez-vous d'Anna, Les
S.
Sailor (aka: Matroos)
Saint
Sisters Lumiere, The
    (aka: Sisters of Light)
Total Eclipse

Brazil

Amor Maldito
Aqueles Dois
Asa Branca: A Brazilian Dream
Boys from Brazil, The
Conta Pra Mim (aka: Trust Me)
Corpo, O (aka: The Body)
Dark and Lovely, Soft and Free
    (aka: Nega Do Cabelo Duro)
Happily Ever After
    (aka: Além da Paixão)
Hunting Season, The
If All Goes Well I'll Meet You on
    the Next Train
Kiss of the Spider Woman, The
Metalguru
Nervos de Aco
    (aka: Nerves Made of Steel)
Pencas de Bicuda
Pixote: A Lei do Mais Fraco
Possible Loves (aka: Amores Possiveis)
Princesa
Vera
Viva Eu!

Bulgaria

Ambiguous Feeling, An

Canada

2 Seconds
    (aka: 2 secondes; Deux secondes)
Adjuster, The
After the Bath
Anatomy of Desire
Anne Trister
Aren't You Lucky You Brought Your
    Own Chair
Atomic Sake
Bad Brownies
Basement Girl, The
Beautiful Dreamers
bed
Beefcake
Being at Home with Claude
Below the Belt
Better than Chocolate
Bisexual Kingdom, The
Bodies in Trouble
Bolo! Bolo!
Boots, Boobs and Bitches: The Art
    of G. B. Jones
Boy Girl
Broadcast Tapes of Dr Peter, The
Bubbles Galore!
Butley
By Design

Camp
Cap Tourmente
Cat Swallows Parakeet and Speaks!
Child-Play
Chinese Characters
Chosen Family, The
Coconut / Cane and Cutlass
Come and Go
Coming Out of the Iron Closet
Coming to Terms
Company of Strangers, The
    (aka: Strangers in Good Company)
Daisy Chain Project, The
Dark Sun: Bright Shade
Day in the Life of a Bull-Dyke, A
Deep Inside Clint Star
Destiny's Children
Devil in the Holy Water, The
Dirty Laundry (1995)
Dreamers of the Day
Eclipse
Educate Your Attitude
Erotica: A Journey into Female Sexuality
Escorte, L'
Fairy Who Didn't Want to Be a
    Fairy, The
Family Pack (aka: Que Faisaient les
    Femmes Pendant que L'homme
    Marchait sur la Lune?)
Fiction and Other Truths: A Film
    about Jane Rule
Fighting Chance
Fire
First Comes Love (1997)
Flow
Forbidden Fruit: Unfinished Stories
    of our Lives
Forbidden Love: The Unashamed
    Stories of Lesbian Lives
Fortune and Men's Eyes
Fox, The
Fresh Blood: A Consideration of
    Belonging
From the Ashes
Frostbite
Full Blast
Girl King
Going West
Good Citizen: Betty Baker
Got 2 B There
Grace of God, The
Hanging Garden, The
Hard Fat
Health Status Survey
Heart Exposed, The
    (aka: La Coeur Découvert)
Heterosexual Agenda, The
Hey, Happy!
High Art
House of Pain

Hustler White
I Am the Camera Dying
I Know a Place
I Will Not Think about Death
    Anymore
I've Heard the Mermaids Singing
If the Family Fits
Interviews With My Next Girlfriend
Jim Loves Jack: The James Egan Story
Johnny Greyeyes
Jungle Boy, The
Justine's Film (aka: Le Film de Justine)
Kanada
Karmen Geï
Kind of Family, A
Kings
Kipling Trilogy, The
Kore Cara Mia
Lakme Takes Flight
Legal Memory
Letters from Home
Lez Be Friends
Life's Evening Hour
Lilies (aka: Lilies - les Feluettes)
Limites
Lip Gloss
Listening for Something
Long Time Comin'
Lost and Delirious
Love and Death on Long Island
    (aka: Amour et mort à Long Island)
Love and Human Remains
M! Mom, Madonna and Me
Ma Vie (aka: My Life)
Making of Monsters
Martirio (aka: Sufferance)
Michael, a Gay Son
Moffie Called Simon, A
Montreal Main
Moscow Does Not Believe in Queers
My Addiction
My Cousin Mike
My Feminism
My Left Breast
My Summer Vacation
Naked Lunch
Nana, George and Me
Night Visions
No Sad Songs
No Skin Off My Ass
Not Alone: A Hallowe'en Romance
Offering, The
Once upon a Time in the East
    (aka: Il était une fois dans l'est)
Orientations
Out: Stories of Lesbian and Gay Youth
Outrageous!
Panic Bodies
Passengers
Perfect Son, The

Pink Pimpernel, The
Pixel Pose
Pouvoir Intime
Psycho Beach Party
Queen's Cantonese Conversational
    Course, The
Queercore: A Punk-u-mentary
Rainmakers - Zimbabwe
Revoir Julie (aka: Julie and Me)
Rewriting the Script: Love Letter to
    Our Families
RSVP
Sabor a Mi (aka: Savour Me)
Salivation Army
Salut Victor!
School Fag
Search for Intimacy, The
Set Me Free (aka: Emporte-moi)
Sexe des étoiles, Le
    (aka: Sex of the Stars)
Siege (aka: Self Defense)
Skin Deep
Skin Flick (aka; Skin Gang)
Sparky's Shoes
Special Day, A
    (aka: Una Giornata particolare)
Spent
Stand Together
Stargaze
Still Sane
Stolen Moments
Straight Down the Aisle: Confes-
    sions of Lesbian Bridesmaids
Straight from the Suburbs
Straight in the Face
Straight to the Heart
    (aka: À Corps Perdu)
Sugar and Spice
Super 8 1/2
Switch (1999)
Symposium: Ladder of Love
Take Out
Tales of the City 2
    (aka: More Tales of the City)
Tales of the City 3
    (aka: Further Tales of the City)
Thank God I'm a Lesbian
Time Being, The
Tokyo Cowboy
Tom
Too Outrageous!
Toward Intimacy
Transit: Adventures of a Boy in the
    Big City
True Inversions
Twisted Sheets
Two Brides and a Scalpel: Diary of
    a Lesbian Marriage
Two Brothers
Uncut

Urinal (aka: Pissoir)
Valentine's Day
Watching Lesbian Porn
We're Funny that Way
Wellness
When Night Is Falling
When Shirley Met Florence
Where Lies the Homo?
Wilma's Sacrifice
Woman Inside, The
World is Sick (sic), The
Yo Yo Gang
You Taste American
Zero Patience

Chile

Amigos (aka: Friends)
Lorenza

China

Darkness before Dawn
East Palace West Palace
    (aka: Dong Gong Xi Gong)
Enter the Clowns
    (aka: Choujue Dengchang)
Farewell My Concubine
    (aka: Ba wang bie ji)
Fish & Elephant
    (aka: Jin Nian Xia Tian)
Last Emperor, The
Last Empress, The
    (aka: Wei dai huang hou)
Maiden Work
Man Man Woman Woman
    (aka: NanNan NuNu; Men and Women)
Postman (aka: Youchai)
Shanghai Panic (aka: Wo men hai
    pa)
Snake Boy, The
Sun and Rain (aka: Taiyang Yu)
Wedding Banquet, The (aka: Hsi yen)

Columbia

Our Lady of the Assassins
    (aka: La Virgen de los sicarios)
Tampon Thieves
    (aka: Ladronas de tampones)

Cuba

Butterflies on the Scaffold
    (aka: Mariposas en el andiamo)
Gay Cuba
Solos Y Soledades
Strawberry and Chocolate
    (aka: Fresa y Chocolate)

Czech Republic

Body without Soul
Daisies (aka: Sedmikrásky)
Mandragora
Not Angels, But Angels

Denmark

101 Reykjavik
By the Dawn's Early Light
Cats, The (aka: Kattorna)
Friends Forever
  (aka: Venner for Altid)
Mirror, Mirror (aka: Lille spejl)
Pretty Boy (aka: Smukke Dreng)
Show Me Love (aka: Fucking Åmål)
Tillsammans (aka: Together)
You Are Not Alone
  (aka: Du er ikke alene)

East Germany

Coming Out (1989)

Egypt

Adieu Bonaparte
Alexandria... Why?
  (aka: Iskanderija... lih?)

Finland

Daddy and the Muscle Academy
Farewell, The (aka: Avskedet)
P(l)ain Truth

France

101 Reykjavik
Above the Sea (aka: Au essus de la Mar)
Abysses, Les
AIDS: Words from One to Another
Arabian Nights (aka: Il Fiore delle
  mille e una notte)
Arrangement, An
Astragale, L'
Baise-moi (aka: Fuck Me; Rape Me)
Barbarella
Beau Travail (aka: Good Work)
Beefcake
Beethoven's Nephew
  (aka: Le Neveu de Beethoven)
Beguines, The
  (aka: Le Rampart des Beguines)
Belle de Jour
Bertrand is Missing
  (aka: Bertrand Disparu)

Best Way, The (aka: La Meilleure
  façon de marcher)
Bezness
Biches, Les (aka: The Does)
Bitter Moon
Black and White (aka: Noir et Blanc)
Black Sunday
  (aka: La Maschera del Demonio)
Blind Fairies (aka: Le Fate Ignoranti)
Blood and Roses
  (aka: Et Mourir de Plaisir)
Blood for Dracula
Blue Jeans
Bright Spell (aka: L'Embellie)
Burnt Money
  (aka: Plata quemada; Burning Money)
Cage aux Folles, La
Cage aux Folles II, La
Cage aux Folles III, La
Carrington
Cavafy (aka: Kavafis)
Cecil B Demented
Celestial Clockwork
  (aka: Mecaniques Celestes)
Celine and Julie Go Boating
  (aka: Céline et Julie vont en bateau)
Chanel Solitaire
Chant d'Amour, Un
Closet, The (aka: Le Placard)
Club de Femmes (aka: The
  Women's Club; Girl's Club)
Cold Lands, The
  (aka: Les Terres Froides)
Conformist, The
  (aka: Il Conformista)
Confusion of Genders
  (aka: La confusion des genres)
Corps Ouverts, Les (aka: Open Bodies)
Coup de Grace (aka: Der
  Fangschuss)
Criminal Lovers (aka: Les Amants
  Criminels)
Crossing, The (aka: La Traversée)
Dakan
Danza Macabra, La
  (aka: Castle of Blood)
Daughters of Darkness
  (aka: Le Rouge aux Lévres)
Day for Night
  (aka: La Nuit Américaine)
Day of the Jackal, The
Derrière, Le (aka: From Behind)
Diaboliques, Les (aka: Diabolique)
Do You Think We Can Talk about
  Anything but Love?
Dog's Dialogue
  (aka: Colloque de chiens)
Don't Forget You're Going to Die
  (aka: N'Oublie pas que tu vas Mourir)

Doom Generation
Dry Cleaning (aka: Nettoyage à sec)
Each Other (aka: Rega'im)
Early Frost, An (2000)
Elegant Criminal, L' (aka: Lacenaire)
Emmanuelle
Enfants Terribles, Les
  (aka: The Strange Ones)
Entre Nous (aka: Coup de Foudre)
Équilibristes, Les
  (aka: Walking a Tightrope)
Escalier C
Evening Dress (aka: Tenue de
  Soirée; Menage)
F. is a Bastard (aka: F. est un salaud)
Family Pack (aka: Que Faisaient les
  Femmes Pendant que L'homme
  Marchait sur la Lune?)
Fascination
Fete des Peres, La (aka: Dad's Day)
Flesh for Frankenstein
Fourth Sex, The
  (aka: Le Quatrième sexe)
French Twist (aka: Gazon Maudit)
Frisson des Vampires, Le
  (aka: Sex and the Vampire)
Full Speed (aka: À Toute Vitesse)
Funny Felix (aka: Dróle de Félix;
  The Adventures of Felix)
Gang of Four, The
  (aka: La Bande des Quatre)
Gay'ze in Wonderland
Girl, The
Girl with the Golden Eyes, The
  (aka: La Fille aux yeux d'or)
Girls Can't Swim
  (aka: Les filles ne savent par nager)
Glider, The (aka: Le Planeur)
Homme Blessé, L'
  (aka: The Wounded Man)
Homme Que J'aime, L'
  (aka: The Man I Love)
Homophobia: That Painful Problem
I, the Worst of All
  (aka: Yo, la Peor de Todas)
I Vitelloni
  (aka: The Young and the Passionate)
Impossible on Saturday
Impromptu
Improper Conduct
  (aka: Mauvaise Conduite)
Inspecteur Lavardin
Irma Vep
J'embrasse pas (aka: I Don't Kiss)
Je, tu, il, elle
Jean Cocteau: Autobiography of an
  Unknown
Jupon Rouge, Le
  (aka: Manuela's Loves)

Just a Woman

Karmen Geï

Last Metro, The
(aka: Le Dernier métro)

Live Flesh (aka: Carne Trémula)

Love is the Devil

Ludwig

Ma Vie en Rose (aka: My Life in Pink)

Man is a Woman (aka: L'Homme
est une femme comme les autres)

Mascara

Matter of Taste, A (aka: A Question
of Taste; Une affaire de goût)

Milou in May
(aka: Milou en Mai; May Fools)

Mulholland Drive

Mum's the Word

Muriel's Parents Have Had it up to Here
(aka: Muriel fait le désespoir de
ses parents)

My Pal Rachid

Mystère Alexina, Le
(aka: The Mystery of Alexina)

Nea: The Young Emmanuelle (aka: Nea)

Night of Varennes, The
(aka: La Nuit de Varennes)

No Exit (aka: Huis Clos)

Nun, The (aka: La Religieuse)

Olivia (aka: The Pit of Loneliness)

Olivier, Olivier

Our Lady of the Assassins
(aka: La Virgen de los sicarios)

Peixe-Lua (aka: Moon-Fish)

Pierre et Gilles, Love Stories

Pillow Book, The

Portrait of a Young Girl at the End
of the '60s in Brussels
(aka: Portrait d'une jeune fille de
la fin des années 60 à Bruxelles)

Pourquoi Pas Moi? (aka: Why Not Me?)

Presque Rien (aka: Come Undone;
Almost Nothing)

Prisonnières

Quai des Orfèvres (aka: Jenny Lamour)

Queen: Marianne Hoppe, The
(aka: Die Königin: Marianne Hoppe)

Rainbow Serpent, The
(aka: Haltéroflic)

Replay (aka: La Répétition)

Requiem pour un Vampire
(aka: Vierges et Vampires)

Roi Danse, Le
(aka: The King is Dancing)

Salon Kitty (aka: Madam Kitty)

Sand and Blood
(aka: De sable et de sang)

Sauve Qui Peut (aka: Slow Motion)

Savage Nights (aka: Les Nuits fauves)

Seashell and the Clergyman, The
(aka: La Coquille et le Clergyman)

See the Sea (aka: Regarde la Mer)

Set Me Free (aka: Emporte-moi)

Simone

Sitcom

Staircase

Stolen Diary, The (aka: Le Cahier Volé)

Summer Dress, A (aka: Une Robe d'été)

Swann in Love (aka: Un Amour de
Swann)

Tenebrae Lessons
(aka: Leçons de Ténèbres)

Thelma

Thérèse and Isabelle

This Special Friendship
(aka: Les Amitiés Particulières)

Those Who Love Me Can Take the
Train

Time Regained
(aka: Le Temps retrouvé)

Total Eclipse

Treaty of Chance, The
(aka: Le Traité du Hasard)

Triche, La (aka: The Cheat)

Vampire Nue, La
(aka: The Naked Vampire)

Viol du Vampire, Le

Voleurs, Les (aka: Thieves)

Water Drops on Burning Rocks
(aka: Gouttes d'Eau sur Pierres
Brûlantes)

We Were One Man
(aka: Nous étions un Seul Homme)

When the Cat's Away (aka: Chacun
Cherche Son Chat)

Why Not! (aka: Pourquoi Pas!)

Wild Reeds, The
aka: Les Roseaux Sauvages)

Woubi Chéri

Zazie dans le Métro

Zero de Conduite
(aka: Zero for Conduct)

Germany

99 Women
(aka: Isle of Lost Women; 99 mujeres)

Aide Mémoire

Aimée and Jaguar

Airport

All of Me

All the Queens Men

Alles Wird Gut
(aka: Everything Will Be Fine)

Alpsee

Among Men

Anders als die Anderen
(aka: Different from Others)

Anita: Dances of Vice
(aka: Anita: Tanze des Lasters)

Anna und Edith

Anna und Elisabeth

Army of Lovers: or Revolt of the
Perverts

Be Careful What Kind of Skin You
Pull Back, You Never Know
What Kind of Head Will Appear

Becoming Colette

Berlin Affair, The (aka: Interno Berlinese)

Beware a Holy Whore
(aka: Warnung vor einer heiligen Nutte)

Bitter Tears of Petra von Kant, The
(aka: Die Bitteren Tränen der
Petra von Kant)

Blue Hour, The
(aka: Die Blaue Stund)

Burning Secret

Can I Be Your Bratwurst, Please?

Celeste

Chained Heat

Chill Out

City of Lost Souls
(aka: Stadt der Verlorenen Seelen)

Confessions of Felix Krull, The
(aka: Bekenntnisse des
Hochstaplers Felix Krull)

Conformist, The
(aka: Il Conformista)

Consequence, The
(aka: Die Konsequenz)

Coup de Grace (aka: Der
Fangschuss)

Dads (aka: Papas)

Damned, The (aka: Gotterdammerung; La Caduta degli Dei)

Das Trio (aka: The Trio)

Daughters of Darkness
(aka: Le Rouge aux Lévres)

Depart to Arrive (aka: Weggehen
um Anzukommen)

Double Face

Dr T & the Women

Drama in Blonde

Dreck (aka: Dirt)

Echte Kerle (aka: Regular Guys)

Eika Katappa

Ein Toter Hing im Netz
(aka: Girls of Spider Island)

Eine Tunte zum Dessert
(aka: A Fairy for Dessert)

Einstein of Sex: The Life and Work
of Dr Magnus Hirschfeld, The

Erika's Passions
(aka: Erika's Leidenschaften)

Erotique

Escape to Life: The Erika and Klaus
Mann Story

Fassbinder's Women

Female Misbehavior

Flirt

Fontvella's Box

Forbidden Fruit
Fox and His Friends
  (aka: Faustrecht der Freiheit)
Freunde: The Whiz Kids
Friends in High Places
Gay Courage: 100 Years of the Gay
  Movement
Gendernauts
Geschlecht in Fesseln: dei Sexualnot
  der Gefangenen (aka: Sex in Chains)
He's Bald and Racist, He's Gay and
  Fascist
Horror Vacui: The Fear of Emptiness
  (aka: Horror Vacui: Die Angst
  vor der Leere)
I Am My Own Woman (aka: Ich
  Bin Meine Eigene Frau)
I Don't Just Want You to Love Me
  (aka: Ich will nicht nur, daß ihr
  mich liebt)
I Love You, I'll Kill You (aka: Ich
  Liebe Dich, Ich Töte Dich)
In a Year of Thirteen Moons
  (aka: In einem Jahr mit 13 Monden)
It is Not the Homosexual Who is
  the Pervert but the Society in
  Which He Lives (aka: Nicht der
  Homosexuelle ist pervers,
  sondern die Situation, in der er lebt)
Johanna, D'Arc of Mongolia
  (aka: Joan of Arc of Mongolia)
Journey to Kafiristan, The
  (aka: Die Reise nach Kafiristan)
Killer Condom
  (aka: Kondom des Grauens)
Kings of the Road
  (aka: Im Lauf der Zeit)
Kiss Me Monster
  (aka: Bésame Monstruo)
Last Exit to Brooklyn
Life is Like a Cucumber
  (aka: Affengeil)
Lola and Billy the Kid
  (aka: Lola and Bilidikid)
Loose Ends
Lorenza
Love Like Any Other, A
  (aka: Eine Liebe wie andere auch)
Loverfilm
Ludwig
Ludwig: Requiem for a Virgin King
  (aka: Ludwig: Requiem für einen
  jungfräulichen König)
Macumba
Madame X: An Absolute Ruler
  (aka: Madame X: Eine Absolute
  Herrscherin)
Mädchen in Uniform
  (aka: Girls in Uniform) (1931)

Mädchen in Uniform
  (aka: Girls in Uniform) (1957)
Man like Eva, A
  (aka: Ein, Mann wie Eva)
Marlene
Maybe I Can Give You Sex?
Menmaniacs: The Legacy of Leather
Mikaël (aka: Chained)
My Father is Coming
Neurosia: 50 Years of Perversity
No One Sleeps
No Skin Off My Ass
Noche de Walpurgis, La
November Moon
  (aka: Novembermond)
Oi! Warning
Pandora's Box
  (aka: Die Büchse der Pandora)
Paragraph 175
Pensao Globo
Positiv
Pretty Baby (aka: Maybe...Maybe
  Not; Der Bewegte Mann; The
  Most Desired Man)
Prince in Hell
  (aka: Prinz in Holleland)
Princesa
Queen: Marianne Hoppe, The (aka:
  Die Königin: Marianne Hoppe)
Queens Don't Lie
  (aka: Tunten Lügen Nicht)
Querelle
Red Heat
Return to Go! (aka: Züruck Auf Los!)
Rules of the Game
Salmonberries
Salon Kitty (aka: Madam Kitty)
Second Awakening of Christa
  Klages, The (aka: Das Zweite
  Erwachen der Christa Klages)
Seduction: The Cruel Woman
  (aka: Verführung: Die grausame Frau)
Sex/Life in LA
Skin Flick (aka; Skin Gang)
Sleepy Haven
Spokes
Sprinter, The
TABU V (about which one cannot speak)
Talk of the Town (aka: Stadtgespräch)
Taste the Sweat
Taxi to Cairo (aka: Taxi nach Kairo)
Taxi to the Toilet
  (aka: Taxi zum Klo)
Third Sex, The
  (aka: Anders als du und ich)
To My Women Friends
Tour Abroad
  (aka: Auslandstournee)
Transexual Menace

Transit: Adventures of a Boy in the
  Big City
Unknown Friend
  (aka: Fremde Freundin)
Vampyros Lesbos (aka: Lesbian
  Vampires; Die Erbin des Dracula)
Venus Boyz
Via Appia
Viktor/Viktoria
Virgin Machine
  (aka: Die Jungfrauenmaschine)
Virus Knows No Morals, A
  (aka: Ein Virus kennt keine Moral)
Was Sie Nie Über Frauen Wissen Wollten
  (aka: All You Never Wanted to
  Know about Women)
We Were Marked with a Big A
West Fickt Ost (aka: West Fucks East)
Westler: East of the Wall
Willkommen im Dom
  (aka: Welcome to the Dome)
Woman in Flames, A (aka: Flaming
  Desire; Die Flambierte Frau)
Wonder Boys, The
Yearning for Sodom
Your Heart is All Mine

Greece

Amerikanos
Angelos (aka: Angel)
Attack of the Giant Moussaka, The
Cavafy (aka: Kavafis)
Day the Fish Came Out, The
  (aka: Otan ta psaria vgikan sti steria)
Deserter (aka: Lipotaktis)
From the Edge of the City
  (aka: Apo tin akri tis polis)
Meteor and Shadow
  (aka: Meteoro kai Skia)
Tender
Thelma

Guinea

Dakan

Hong Kong

Anxiety of Inexpression and the
  Otherness Machine, The
Away with Words (aka: Kujaku)
Bishonen...Beauty
  (aka: Meishaonian zhi lian)
Eagle Shooting Heroes, The
  (aka: Sediu yinghung tsun tsi
  dung sing sai tsau)
First Love and Other Pains

Full Moon in New York
  (aka: Ren zai Niu Yue)
Happy Together
  (aka: Cheun gwong tsa sit)
He's a Woman, She's a Man
  (aka: Gum gee yuk yip)
Hold You Tight (aka: Yue Kuai Le)
Hu-Du-Men (aka: Stage Door)
I Am Not What You Want
Intimates, The (aka: Ji Sor)
Killer, The
  (aka: Die Xue Shuang Xiong)
Lan Yu
Legend of Fong Sai-Yuk, The
Let's Love Hong Kong (aka: Ho Yuk)
Map of Sex and Love, The
  (aka: Qingse ditu)
Naked Killer (aka: Chiklo gouyeung)
Peony Pavilion
  (aka: Youyuan jingmeng)
Portland Street Blues
Queer Story, A (aka: Jilao Sishi)
Spacked Out (aka: Mo yan ka sai)
Swordsman II (aka: Xiao ao jiang
  hu zhi dong fang bu bai)
Swordsman III: The East is Red
  (aka: Dung fong bat baai 2: fung
  wan joi hei)
To Ride a Cow
Toc Storee
Twin Bracelets (aka: Shuang Cho)
Two or Three Things I Know about Them
Who's the Woman, Who's the Man
Wu Yen
Yang±Yin: Gender in Chinese Cinema

Hungary

Abandoned (aka: Torzók)
All the Queens Men
Another Way
  (aka: Egymásra Nézve)
Colonel Redl (aka: Oberst Redl)
This I Wish and Nothing More
  (aka: Nincsen Nekem Vagyam Semmi)

Iceland

101 Reykjavik

India

Bombay Boys
Bombay Eunuch
BOMgaY
Fire
Holi: Festival of Fire
Kalihgat Fetish (aka: Kalighat Athikatha)

Khush
My Friend Su
Petals
Scenes from a Queer Planet
Sixth Happiness, The
Summer in My Veins (Director's Cut)
Wrestlers, The (aka: Uttara)
Zanjeer (aka: The Chain)
Zindagi Zindabad
  (aka: Long Live Life)

Iran

Daughters of the Sun
Just a Woman

Ireland

Borstal Boy
Chaero
Change
Ghost of Roger Casement, The
Happy Gordons, The
Last Bus Home, The
On Being Gay: A Conversation
  with Brian McNaughton
Silences

Israel

Afflicted
Amazing Grace (aka: Hessed Mufla)
Amos Gutman, Filmmaker
  (aka: Amos Gutman, Bamay Kolnoa)
At Home
baba-It (aka: At Home)
Drifting (aka: Nagu'a)
Each Other (aka: Rega'im)
Gay Games
Gotta Have Heart (aka: Ba'al Ba'al Lev)
Impossible on Saturday
It's That Age
Kesher Ir (aka: Urban Feel)
Positive Story (aka: Sipur Hiyuvi)
Safe Place, A
Speedway Junky
Time Off
Trembling Before G-d
Watching You

Italy

Acla (aka: La Discesa di Aclà a
  Floristella)
Arabian Nights (aka: Il Fiore delle
  mille e una notte)
Are You Greedy?
Barbarella

Beguines, The
  (aka: Le Rampart des Beguines)
Belle al Bar (aka: Belles at the Bar)
Belle de Jour
Berlin Affair, The (aka: Interno Berlinese)
Biches, Les (aka: The Does)
Black Sunday
  (aka: La Maschera del Demonio)
Blind Fairies (aka: Le Fate Ignoranti)
Blood and Roses
  (aka: Et Mourir de Plaisir)
Blood for Dracula
Boy like Many Others, A
  (aka: Un Ragazzo come Tanti)
Cage aux Folles, La
Caligula
Caravaggio
Children of Hannibal
  (aka: Figli di Annibale)
Conformist, The (aka: Il Conformista)
Conversation Piece
  (aka: Gruppo di famiglia in un interno)
Damned, The (aka: Gotterdammer-
  ung; La Caduta degli Dei)
Danza Macabra, La
  (aka: Castle of Blood)
Daughters of Darkness
  (aka: Le Rouge aux Lévres)
Day for Night
  (aka: La Nuit Américaine)
Days (aka: Giorni)
Death in Venice (aka: Morte a Venezia)
Double Face
Ernesto
Flavor of Corn, The
  (aka: Il Sapore del Grano)
Flesh for Frankenstein
Forbidden Love of the Hero, The
Forever Mary (aka: Mery per sempre)
Fuga, La (aka: The Escape)
Future is Woman, The
  (aka: Il Futuro è Donna)
Genesis Children, The
Hamam: The Turkish Bath
  (aka: Steam)
I Vitelloni
  (aka: The Young and the Passionate)
If All Goes Well I'll Meet You on
  the Next Train
Immacolata e Concetta - l'altra gelosia
Impossible on Saturday
Killer Nun (aka: Suor Omicidi)
Last Emperor, The
Love in a Women's Prison
  (aka: Diario Segreto da un
  Carcere Femminile)
Love in Progress (aka: Amori in corso)
Ludwig
Madras Eyes

Marching into Darkness
Mare, Il (aka: The Sea)
Men Men Men
    (aka: Uomini uomini uomini)
Montgomery Clift: The Prince
Nietta's Diary
Night Porter, The
    (aka: Il Portiere di notte)
Order to Kill
    (aka: El Clan de los Immorales)
Pianese Nunzio
    (aka: Fourteen in May; Sacred Silence)
Princesa
Right to be Different, The
Room of Words, The
    (aka: La Stanza della parole)
Salo (aka: The 120 Days of Sodom)
Salon Kitty (aka: Madam Kitty)
Satyricon
Sister Smile (aka: Suor Sorriso)
Sospiro d'amore nell'attesa
Sotto Sotto (aka: Softly, Softly;
    Sotto... sotto... strapazzato da
    anomala passione)
Special Day, A
    (aka: Una Giornata particolare)
Split World, The
Stolen Diary, The (aka: Le Cahier Volé)
Teorema (aka: Theorem)
Terror in the Crypt
    (aka: La Cripta e L'Incubo)
To Forget Venice
    (aka: Dimenticare Venezia)
What Kind of Music!
    (aka: Ma Che Musica!)
Who Killed Pasolini?
    (aka: Pasolini, an Italian Crime;
    Pasolini, un delitto Italiano)

Ivory Coast

Woubi Chéri

Japan

Addicted to Love
    (aka: Boku wa koi ni muchu)
Afternoon Breezes
    (aka: Kaze tachi No Gogo)
Black Lizard (aka: Kurotokage)
Closets Are for Clothes
Enchantment, The (aka: Yuwakusha)
Flirt
French Dressing
    (aka: Furenchi doressingu)
Funeral Parade of Roses
    (aka: Bara No Soretsu)
Gaea Girls

Gohatto (aka: Taboo)
Gonin (aka: The Five)
Heaven-6-Box
    (aka: Tengoku No Muttsu No Hako)
How Old is the River?
    (aka: Fuyu no Kappa)
Hush!
I.K.U
I Like You, I Like You Very Much
    (aka: Anata-Ga Suki Desu, Dai
    Suki Desu)
Iro Kaze (aka: Colour Wind)
Kizuna Volume 1 & 2
Like Grains of Sand
    (aka: Nagisa no Shindobaddo)
Looking for Angel
    (aka: Tenshi No Rakuen)
Love is the Devil
Love/Juice
Manji (aka: All Mixed Up)
Melody for Buddy Matsumae
    (aka: Matsumae-Kun No Senritsu)
Merry Christmas, Mr Lawrence
More Love
Muscle
Okoge
One Shadowless Hour
Protagonist, The (aka: Shujinko)
Revolutionary Girl Utena: The Movie
    (aka: Shôjo kakumei Utena:
    Adolescence mokushiroku)
Rough Sketch of a Spiral
    (aka: Rasen No Sobyo)
Shinjuku Triad Society
    (aka: Shijuku Kuro Shakai)
Slight Fever of a 20-Year-Old
    (aka: Hatachi No Binetsu)
Story of PuPu, The
    (aka: PuPu No Monogatari)
Sugar Sweet
Summer Vacation 1999
    (aka: 1999 Nen No Natsu Yasumi)
Swimming Prohibited
    (aka: Yuei Kinshi)
Tarch Trip
Tokyo Fist (aka: Tokyo-ken)
Twinkle (aka: Kira Kira Hikaru)
We Are Transgenders
Wonder Boys, The
Zippers & Tits (aka: Fasuna to Chibusa)

Kazakhstan

Life is a Woman
    (aka: Zhizn-Zhenshchina)

Korea

301 - 302
Broken Branches (aka: Naeil Ui
    Hyahae Hurunun Kang)
Bungee Jumping of Their Own
    (aka: Beonjijeonpeureul hada)
Memento Mori
    (aka: Yeogo Guidam II)
Norang Mori 2
    (aka: Running Blue; Yellow Hair 2)

Lebanon

Cinema Fouad
How I Love You (aka: Shou Bhebbak)

Mexico

Border Line...Family Pictures
Danzón
Dona Herlinda and Her Son
    (aka: Doña Herlinda y su hijo)
Hubo un Tiempo en que Los
    Suenos Dieron Paso a Largas
    Noches de Insomnio
Miracle Alley
    (aka: El Callejon de los Milagros)
Other Side, The
    (aka: Del Otro Lado)
Queen of the Night
    (aka: La Reina de la Noche)
There is no Pain in Paradise
    (aka: En el Paraiso no Existe el Dolor)
Y tu Mamá También
    (aka: And Your Mother Too)

Netherlands

After the War You Have to Tell
    Everyone about the Dutch Gay
    Resistance Fighters
Antonia's Line
Behind Glass
Belle
But I Was a Girl: The Story of
    Frieda Belinfante
Casta Diva
Crocodiles in Amsterdam
    (aka: Krokodillen in Amsterdam)
Day I Decided to be Nina, The
Dear Boys (aka: Lieve Jongens)
Evenings, The (aka: De Avonden)
Fear of Love
For a Lost Soldier
    (aka: Voor een verloren soldaat)

Fourth Man, The (aka: Di Vierde Man)
I Don't Wanna Be a Boy
Last Island, The
Man Who Drove with Mandela, The
Pink Ulysses
Siberia
Strange Love Affair, A
To Play or to Die (aka: Spelen of sterven)
Total Loss
Twice a Woman (aka: Twee vrouwen)
Woman like Eve, A
    (aka: Een Vrouw als Eva)

New Zealand

Beyond Gravity
Crush (1992)
Dads Wanted
Death in the Family, A
Desperate Remedies
Forever (1994)
Georgie Girl
God, Sreenu & Me
Heavenly Creatures
Jewel's Darl
Merry Christmas, Mr Lawrence
My First Suit
Naughty Little Peeptoe
Naya Zamana
One of Them
Peach
Squeeze
Twilight of the Gods
What a Pretty Sister
When Love Comes

Norway

101 Reykjavik
All About My Father
    (aka: Alt om min far)
Blessed are Those Who Thirst
    (aka: Salige er de som tørster)
c-l-o-s-e-r
Desperate Acquaintances
    (aka: Desperate Bekjentskaper)
Ice Palace, The
Kiss in the Snow, A
Life and Death
Sebastian
Waves (aka: Bølgene)

Palestine

Diary of a Male Whore

Peru

Don't Tell Anyone
    (aka: No Se Lo Digas a Nadie)
Scenes from a Queer Planet

Philippines

Burlesk King
Children of the Regime
Macho Dancer
Man in Her Life, The
    (aka: Ang lalaki sa buhay ni Selya)
Manila: In the Claws of Darkness
    (aka: Maynila: Sa mga kuko ng liwanag)
Markova: Comfort Gay
Midnight Dancers (aka: Sibak)
Miguel/Michelle
Oliver
Poisoned Blood
Private Wars
Revolutions Happen like Refrains
    in a Song
Sex Warriors and the Samurai
Soft Hearts (aka: Pusong Mamon)
Three (aka: Tatlo... magkasalo)
Woman Hunt

Poland

Siegfried

Portugal

Heart's Root, The
    (aka: A Raiz Do Coração)
Peixe-Lua (aka: Moon-Fish)
Pensao Globo
Phantom (aka: O Fantasma)
Where the Sun Beats Down
    (aka: Onde Bate o Sol)

Puerto Rico

Pride in Puerto Rico

Russia

Creation of Adam, The
    (aka: Sotvoreniye Adama)
Hammer and Sickle (aka: Serp i molot)
High Tech Rice
Moscow Fags
Scenes from a Queer Planet
To My Women Friends

Senegal

Karmen Geï

Serbia

Marble Ass (aka: Dupe od Mramora)

Singapore

Bugis Street (aka: Yao jie huang hou)

Slovenia

Guardian of the Frontier
    (aka: Varuh Meje)

South Africa

Across the Rubicon
Apostles of Civilised Vice
Dark and Lovely, Soft and Free
    (aka: Nega Do Cabelo Duro)
It's My Life
Man Who Drove with Mandela, The
Metamorphosis: The Remarkable
    Journey of Granny Lee
Quest for Love
Sando to Samantha: The Art of Dikvel
Simon and I: Steps for the Future
Stepping Out

Soviet Union

100 Days Before the Command
    (aka: Sto dnej do prikaza)

Spain

Affairs of Love, The
    (aka: Las Cosas del Querer)
All About My Mother
    (aka: Todo sobre mi madre)
Amic/Amat (aka: Beloved/Friend)
Backroom
Bargain Lingerie
Bellas de Noche
Belle époque
Blood Splattered Bride, The
    (aka: La Novia Ensangrentada)
Burnt Money (aka: Plata quemada;
    Burning Money)
Celestial Clockwork
    (aka: Mecaniques Celestes)
Colegas (aka: Pals)

Costa Brava
Crueles, Las (aka: The Cruel Ones)
Danzón
Dark Habits (aka: Entre tinieblas)
Desire (1999)
Diputado, El (aka: The Deputy)
Doors Cut Down
Excuse Me Duckie, But Lucas
    Loved Me (aka: Perdona Bonita,
    pero Lucas me queria a mi)
Extramuros (aka: Beyond the Walls)
Food of Love
Gaudi Afternoon
Gladys, A Cuban Mother
Harlequin Exterminator
High Heels (aka: Tacones lejanos)
I Love You Baby
Kika
Km. 0 (aka: Kilometro cero)
Krámpack (aka: Nico & Dani)
Labyrinth of Passion
    (aka: Laberinto de pasiones)
Law of Desire (aka: La Ley del Deseo)
Live Flesh (aka: Carne Trémula)
Love of a Man, The
    (aka: Amor de hombre)
Meeting of Two Queens
Mi Novia El
Noche de Walpurgis, La
Not Love, Just Frenzy
    (aka: Mas Que Amor, Frenesi)
Our Lady of the Assassins
    (aka: La Virgen de los sicarios)
Pasajes (aka: Passages)
Peixe-Lua (aka: Moon-Fish)
Pepi, Luci and Bom
Pourquoi Pas Moi? (aka: Why Not Me?)
Residencia, La
    (aka: The House that Screamed)
Sagitario
Second Skin (aka: Segunda Piel)
Shampoo Horns
    (aka: Cuernos de espuma)
Silencis (aka: Silent Moments)
Summer of Miss Forbes, The
    (aka: El Verano de la señora Forbes)
Terror in the Crypt
    (aka: La Cripta e L'Incubo)
To an Unknown God
    (aka: A un Dios Desconocido)
Vampyros Lesbos (aka: Lesbian
    Vampires; Die Erbin des Dracula)
What Have I Done to Deserve This?
    (aka: Qué he hecho yo para
    merecer esto?!!)

Sweden

Älskande par (aka: Loving Couples)
Amorosa
Companions: Tales from the Closet
Farewell, The (aka: Avskedet)
Persona
Show Me Love (aka: Fucking Åmål)
Silence, The (aka: Tystnaden)
Thirst (aka: Törst; Three Strange Loves)
Women on the Roof
    (aka: Kvinnorna på taket)
Yes (aka: To Ingrid My Love Lisa;
    Kvinnolek)

Switzerland

F. is a Bastard (aka: F. est un salaud)
Friends in High Places
Killer Condom
    (aka: Kondom des Grauens)
Living and Dying
    (aka: Ich Lebe Gern, Ich Sterbe Gern)
Manodestra
Peppermills
Pourquoi Pas Moi? (aka: Why Not Me?)
Set Me Free (aka: Emporte-moi)
Thelma
Venus Boyz

Taiwan

Cha-Cha for the Fugitive, A
    (aka: Gai Tao-wan-je de ChaCha)
Fleeing By Night (aka: Ye Ben)
Incidental Journey
    (aka: Haijiao Tianya)
Murmur of Youth
    (aka: Mei li zai chang ge)
Outcasts, The
    (aka: Niezi; The Outsiders)
Peony Pavilion, The
Silent Thrush, The
    (aka: Shisheng Huamei)
Too Young (aka: Ye Maque)
Twin Bracelets (aka: Shuang Cho)
Vive l'Amour (aka: Aiqing Wansui)
Wedding Banquet, The (aka: Hsi yen)
Where Is My Love?
    (aka: Qiangpo Puguang)

Thailand

Anguished Love
Flowing Hearts: Thailand Fighting AIDS
I Am a Man
Iron Ladies, The (aka: Sa tree lex)
Ladyboys
Last Song, The

Turkey

Hamam: The Turkish Bath
    (aka: Steam)

United Kingdom

17 Rooms (or What Do Lesbians
    Do in Bed?)
21st Century Nuns
4pm
99 Women
    (aka: Isle of Lost Women; 99 mujeres)
A.K.A
Achilles
Actions Speak Louder than Words
After the Break (1998)
Age of Dissent
Aileen Wuornos: The Selling of a
    Serial Killer
Alive and Kicking (aka: Indian Summer)
Andy Warhol and His Work
Angelic Conversation, The
Anniversary, The (1968)
Another Country
Apartment Zero
Armistead Maupin is a Man I
    Dreamt Up
Art of Cruising Men, The
B. D. Women
Baby
Ballad of Reading Gaol
Barry Lyndon
Battle of Tuntenhaus
Beautiful Thing
Bedazzled
Bedrooms & Hallways
Beefcake
Bent
Best of Out and Out on Tuesday, The
Better Dead than Gay
Between Two Women
Bilitis
Bill Called William, A
Bit of Scarlett, A
Bitter Moon
Blind Moment, The
Blue
Blue Boys
Blunt: The Fourth Man
Bob & Rose
Body of a Poet: A Tribute to Audre
    Lorde 1934-1992, The
Borderline
Borstal Boy
Boy Next Door? A Profile of Boy George
Boyfriends (1995)
Boyfriends (1999)
Boys from Brazil, The

Boys in the Backyard
Breaking the Code
Breaking the Silence
Brian Epstein Story, The
Bright Eyes
Burning Secret
Butley
Butterfly Kiss
Call Me Your Girlfriend
Came Out, It Rained, Went Back
  in Again
Caravaggio
Caretaker, The (aka: The Guest)
Carrington
Cat and the Canary, The
Caught Looking
Chanel Solitaire
Clancy's Kitchen
Closer
Closing Numbers
Comfort of Strangers, The
Coming Out (1972)
Compromised Immunity
Comrades in Arms
Confessions of a Pretty Lady
Confessions of a Window Cleaner
Countess Dracula
Crimes of Passion
Cruising in the Channels
Crying Game, The
Dandy Dust
Darker Side of Black, The
Darling
Day of the Jackal, The
Day the Fish Came Out, The
  (aka: Otan ta psaria vgikan sti steria)
Dead Dreams of Monochrome Men
Deadfall
Deflatable Man, The
Desire (1989)
Different Corner, A
Different for Girls
Different Kind of Love, A
Disgraceful Conduct
Does Your Mother Know?
Domestic Bliss
Double Entente
Double the Trouble, Twice the Fun
Double Trouble
Dr Jekyll and Ms Hyde
Dr Jekyll and Sister Hyde
Dream Girls
Dresser, The
Duffer
Dyke Blend
e-male
Eat the Rich
Eban and Charley
Edward II
Emergence

Empire State
Englishman Abroad, An
Entertaining Mr Sloane
Escape to Life: The Erika and Klaus
  Mann Story
Exiles of Love
Eyes of Tammy Faye, The
Fearless Vampire Killers, The
  (aka: Dance of the Vampires)
Fight to Be Male, The
Final Programme, The (aka: The
  Last Days of Man on Earth)
Flames of Passion
Flesh and Paper
Forbidden Passion: Oscar Wilde the Movie
Forever (1991)
Forgive & Forget
Fostering
Four Weddings and a Funeral
Framed Youth
  (aka: Revolt of the Teenage Perverts)
Francis Bacon
Frankenstein Created Woman
Frantz Fanon: Black Skin, White Mask
Freddie Mercury: The Untold Story
Fruit Machine, The (aka: Wonderland)
Full Monty, The
Gaea Girls
Garden, The
Gay Bombay
Gay Rock and Roll Years, The
Gay Sera Sera
Get Real
Ginger Beer
Girl Stroke Boy
Girls in Boy's Bars
Glasses Break
Glitterbug
Goblin Market
Gods and Monsters
Gold Diggers, The
Good Father, The (aka: Fathers' Rites)
Grass is Greener, The
Groove on a Stanley Knife
Guess Who's Coming to Dinner?
Hanging Garden, The
Haunting, The
Heatwave
Heavy Petting (1991)
Hell For Leather
Heterosexuality
Hollow Reed
Home Sweet Home
Home You Go
Home-Made Melodrama
Homophobia in Hollywood
Hunger, The
I Am a Camera
I Want What I Want
If

Illegal Tender
Imagining October
Immigration
Impromptu
In on Earth as It Is in Heaven
In Pursuit of Prince/ess Charming
In the Shadow of the Sun
Indecent Acts
Investigator, The
Iris
It's a Queer World
It's Not Unusual: A Lesbian and
  Gay History
Jackson: My Life Your Fault
Jodie: An Icon
Julian Clary - The Mincing
  Machine Tour
Just like a Woman
Keep it Up, Jack! (aka: Auntie)
Kenneth Anger's Hollywood
  Babylon (aka: Kenneth Anger)
Khush
Killer in the Village
Killing of Sister George, The
King and Country
King Girl
Krays, The
L-Shaped Room, The
Ladyboys
Last Emperor, The
Last of England, The
Lawless Heart, The
Leather Boys, The
Lesbian Health Matters
Lesbians Behaving Badly
Lesbians Go Mad in Lesbos
Lesbians Olé
Like It Is
Little Bit of Lippy, A
Lone Star Hate
Long Day Closes, The
Looking for Langston
Loose Connections
Loot
Loss of Heat
Loss of Innocence
  (aka: The Greengage Summer)
Lost Language of Cranes, The
Love and Death on Long Island
  (aka: Amour et mort à Long Island)
Love and Marriage
Love is the Devil
Love Story: Berlin 1942, A
Lune
Lust and Liberation
Lust for a Vampire
  (aka: To Love a Vampire)
M.U.F.F. Match
Ma Vie en Rose (aka: My Life in Pink)

Mad, Bad and Barking
Madagascar Skin
Madame Sousatzka
Magic Christian, The
Man of No Importance, A
Man Who Drove with Mandela, The
Mark of Lilith, The
Matt
Maurice
Me and the Girls
Memory Pictures
Memsahib Rita
Merry Christmas, Mr Lawrence
Metrosexuality
Midnight Express
Militia Battlefield
Minoru and Me
Modesty Blaise
Mona Lisa
Music Lovers, The
My Beautiful Laundrette
My Mother is an Alien
Naked Civil Servant, The
Naked Lunch
Nervous Energy
Nice Girls Don't
Nietta's Diary
Night with Derek, A
Nighthawks
Nijinsky
Nocturne (1990)
North of Vortex
Oi Queer
Oranges Are Not the Only Fruit
Orlando
Osaka Story
Other Voices, Other Rooms
Our Private Idaho
Out in Nature: Homosexual
    Behaviour in the Animal Kingdom
Over Our Dead Bodies
Oy Gay
Pansexual Public Porn
    (aka: The Adventures of Hans and Del)
Paragraph 175
Party Monster
Passion of Remembrance, The
Past Caring
Pedagogue
Performance
Personal Best (1991)
Perverted Justice
Peter's Friends
Piccadilly Pickups
Pillow Book, The
Pink Video: Out-Rageously Pink, The
Place in the Sun, A
Place of Rage, A
Playing Gay
Pleasure Principle, The

Polskiseks
Portion of a Lady
Portrait of a Marriage
Postcards from America
Prick Up Your Ears
Pride, Politics and Pissheads
Priest
Privates on Parade
Queer As Folk (1998)
Queer As Folk 2
Question of Attribution, A
Rachel, Rachel
Rachel Williams Documentary
Rainbow, The
Razor Blade Smile
Reflecting Skin, The
Reframing AIDS
Relax
Rhythm & Blues
Richard's Things
Right Wing, Right Off, Right
    Hons, Right?
Righteous Babes, The
Ritz, The
Rocky Horror Picture Show, The
Rosebud
Running Gay: Lesbian and Gay
    Participation in Sport
Salome's Last Dance
Sammy and Rosie Get Laid
Sari Red
Scrubbers
Sebastiane
Secret Ceremony
Secret Policeman's Private Parts, The
Servant, The
Sex 121 and the Gulag
Sex and the Sandinistas
Sex Becomes Her: The True Life
    Story of Chi Chi LaRue
Sex Change: Shock! Horror! Probe!
Sex Warriors and the Samurai
Sex Wars
Sexual Identity
Shadey
Sherlock, Louise and Mina
Shinjuku Boys
Sister My Sister
Sixth Happiness, The
Skin Complex
Sodom
Staircase
Stand on Your Man
Star is Porn, A
Stonewall
Storm in a Teacup
Story So Far, The
Strip Jack Naked: Nighthawks II
Suddenly Last Summer (1991)
Sunday, Bloody Sunday

Surviving Sabu
Swollen Stigma
Tales of the City
Taste of Honey, A
Tea Leaf
Tell Me No Lies
Tell Me the Truth About Love
Terence Davies Trilogy, The
Terry and Julian (Vol. 1 and 2)
Thin Ice: Passion on the Pink Rink
This is Dedicated: Grieving When a
    Partner Dies
Time Zones
To Die for (aka: Heaven's a Drag)
Total Eclipse
Touch of Love, A (aka: Thank You
    All Very Much; The Millstone)
Touchables, The
Trials of Oscar Wilde, The
Triple Echo
True Blue Camper
Truth About Gay Sex, The
Truth Game, The
Twins of Evil (aka: The Gemini Twins)
Two Men
Two of Us (aka: Mates)
Valentino
Vampire Lovers, The
Vampyres, Daughters of Dracula
    (aka: Blood Hunger)
Velvet Goldmine
Veronica 4 Rose
Victim
Victor/Victoria
Video 28
Village Affair, A
Village Voices
Villain
Wavelengths
We Think the World of You
We've Been Framed
Weekend, The
Well Sexy Women
What's Cooking?
Why am I Gay?
Wilde (aka: Oscar Wilde)
Wildflowers
Withnail and I
Wittgenstein
Wolves of Kromer, The
Women in Love
Women Like Us/Women Like That
Wonder Boys, The
Working Class Dykes from Hell
X Y and Zee (aka: Zee and Co.)
Yang±Yin: Gender in Chinese Cinema
Yellow Fever
Young Soul Rebels
Zero Budget

Uruguay

Burnt Money (aka: Plata quemada; Burning Money)

USA

10 Attitudes
10 Violent Women
101 Rent Boys
2 by 4 (aka: 2 x 4)
2 or 3 Things But Nothing for Sure
24 Nights
27 Pieces of Me
$30
45 Minutes of Bondage
'68
7 Steps to Sticky Heaven
90 Miles
99% Woman
Absolutely Positive
Absolution of Anthony, The
Abuse
Acting on Impulse
   (aka: Eyes of a Stranger)
Adam's Rib
Adventures in the Gender Trade
Adventures of Sebastian Cole, The
Advise and Consent
Affirmations
After Hours
After Stonewall
After the Break (1992)
After the Game
Age 12: Love with a Little L
Agora
AIDS Show: Artists Involved with
   Death and Survival, The
Alexander: The Other Side of Dawn
Algie the Miner
Alicia was Fainting
Alien Prey
Alkali, Iowa
All about Alice
All Fall Down
All Girl Action: The History of
   Lesbian Erotica
All God's Children
All Out Comedy
All Over Me
All Over the Guy
All the Queens Men
All the Rage
All-American Story, An
Alley of the Tranny Boys
Almost the Cocktail Hour
Alone Together: Young Adults
   Living with HIV
Alternative Conceptions

Always Walter! An Inner View of
   Walter Larrebee
American Beauty
American Fabulous
American Gigolo
American Slices
Amerikanos
Among Good Christian Peoples
Among Others
Anatomy of a Hate Crime
And the Band Played On
And Then Came Summer
Anderson Tapes, The
Angel (1983)
Angels!
Animal Factory
Annie Sprinkle's Herstory of Porn:
   Reel to Real
Anniversary, The (1995)
Another 45 Minutes of Bondage
Anxiety of Inexpression and the
   Otherness Machine, The
Any Wednesday
Anything Once
Apart From Hugh
Arch Brown's Top Story
As Far Away as Here
As Good As It Gets
As Is
Ashley 22
Audit
Avenge Tampa
B.U.C.K.L.E.
B/side
Baby Steps
Badass Supermama
Balcony, The
Ballad of Little Jo, The
Ballot Measure 9
Bar Girls
Basic Instinct
Basic Necessities
Basketball Diaries, The
Beat
Beauty Before Age
Because the Dawn
Because this is About Love
Becoming Colette
Bed of Lies
Before Night Falls
Before Stonewall: The Making of a
   Gay and Lesbian Community
Behind Walls
Being John Malkovich
Ben Hur
Benjamin Smoke
Best In Show
Best Man, The
   (aka: Gore Vidal's The Best Man)
Betsy, The

Betty Anderson
Between the Lines
Beyond the Valley of the Dolls
Beyond Therapy
Big Business
Big Eden
Big Sky, The
Bigger Splash, A
Bike Boy
Billy Turner's Secret
Billy's Hollywood Screen Kiss
Biloxi Blues
Bird in the Hand
Birdcage, The
Birthday Time
Bite Me Again
Bitter Harvest (1993)
Bittersweet
Black Glove, The
Black Is... Black Ain't
Black Mama, White Mama
Black Nations/Queer Nations?
Black Widow
Blair Princess Project, The
Blank Point: What is Transsexualism?, The
Blazing Saddles
Blessed Art Thou
   (aka: A Question of Faith)
Blind Faith
Block Party
Blonde Cobra
Blood and Concrete
Blood Money
Bloodbrothers (aka: A Father's Love)
Bloodsisters: Leather Dykes and S&M
Bloody Mama
Blow Job
Blue Haven
Bombay Eunuch
Border Line...Family Pictures
Born in Flames
Boston Strangler, The
Bound
Bound and Gagged: A Love Story
Bounty, The
Boy Germs
Boy Named Sue, A
Boy Next Door
Boychick
Boys Don't Cry
Boys in the Band, The
Boys Next Door, The
Boys' Night Out
Boys of Cell Block Q
Boys of Manchester, The
Boys on the Side
Bradfords Tour America, The
Brandon Teena Story, The
Breaking the Surface
Breaking up Really Sucks

Brincando el Charco: Portrait of a Puerto Rican
Britney Baby - One More Time
Broadway Damage
Broadway Melody, The
Broken Goddess
Broken Hearts Club: A Romantic Comedy, The
Bubbeh Lee and Me
Buddies
Burning Secret
Bus Riley's Back in Town
Business of Fancydancing, The
Busting
But, I'm a Cheerleader
Butch Camp
Butcher's Wife, The
Butley
Butter & Pinches
By Design
By Hook or By Crook
Cabaret
Caged
Caged Fury
Calamity Jane
California Suite
Caligula
Call to Witness
Camp Lavender Hill
Can I Be Your Bratwurst, Please?
Can't Stop Dancing
Can't Stop the Music
Cancer in Two Voices
Car Wash
Carmelita Tropicana: Your Kunst Is Your Waffen
Carmilla
Castro, The
Cat Nip
Cat on a Hot Tin Roof
Cat People
Cater Waiter
Caught
Caught in the Crossfire
Cecil B Demented
Celluloid Closet, The
Certain Grace, A
Chain of Desire
Chained Girls
Chained Heat
Chained Heat II
Change of Heart, A
Change the Frame
Changing Face
Changing Our Minds: The Story of Dr Evelyn Hooker
Charlie
Chasing Amy
Chastity
Chelsea Girls, The

Chicks in White Satin
Children's Hour, The
Chocolate Babies
Choirboys, The
Choosing Children
Chop Suey
Chopper Chicks in Zombie Town
Christine Jorgensen Story, The
Chuck and Buck
Chuck Solomon: Coming of Age
Chutney Popcorn
Cicely
Circuit
Citizen Cohn
Claire
Claire of the Moon
Clancy Street Boys
Clay Farmers, The
Cleopatra Jones
Cleopatra's Second Husband
Clinic E
Clips
Close To Home
Closets Are Health Hazards
Coal Miner's Granddaughter
Cockettes, The
Coffee Date
Color Purple, The
Come Back to the Five and Dime, Jimmy Dean, Jimmy Dean
Comedy in Six Unnatural Acts, A
Coming Home
Coming of Age
Coming Out, Coming Home: Asian and Pacific Islander Family Stories
Coming Out under Fire
Common Flower, A
Common Ground
Common Threads: Stories from the Quilt
Complaints of a Dutiful Daughter
Compulsion
Conception
Confession, The
Consenting Adult
Coonskin (aka: Street Fight)
Cosmic Demonstration of Sexuality, A
Could Be Worse
Crash and Burn
Creature
Critical Mass: Gay Games Amsterdam
Crocodile Tears
Cruel
Cruising
Crush (2000)
Curse of the Queerwolf
Cuz It's Boy
Cynara: Poetry in Motion
Daddy & Papa
Dadshuttle, The
Damned if You Don't

Danger Girl, The
Danny
Darling International
Daughter of Dykes
David & Goliath
David Searching
De Colores
Dead Boys' Club, The
Deaf Heaven
Deal, The
Dear Jesse
Dear Mom
Dear Rock
Death in Venice, CA
Deathtrap
Deathwatch
Debutantes, The
Decodings
Deep End, The
Defying Gravity
Deliverance
Delta, The
Demons
Desert Hearts
Desi's Looking for a New Girl
Desire (1999)
Desperate Living
Destroying Angel
Detective, The
Devotion
Diabolique
Diane Linkletter Story, The
Different Kind of Black Man, A
Different Story, A
Ding Dong
Dinner Guest, The
Dirty Fingernails
Disco Years, The
Divine Trash
Doctors' Wives
Dog Day Afternoon
Doing Time on Maple Drive
Doom Generation
Double Strength
Dozens, The
Dr Jekyll and Ms Hyde
Dr T & the Women
Dracula's Daughter
Dragtime
Drama Queen
Drawing Girls
Dreaded Experimental Comedies: How to Lessons, Body Rhythms, My New Lover, The
Dress Gray
Dressed to Kill
Drift
Drop Dead Georgeous: The Power of HIV Positive Thinking
Drowning Lessons

Dry Kisses Only
Dykes and Their Dogs
Early Frost, An (1985)
Eban and Charley
Ed Wood
Edge of Seventeen (aka: Edge of 17)
Eiger Sanction, The
Eight Million
Eileen is a Spy
Elegant Spanking, The
Elegy in the Streets
Ellen DeGeneres: The Beginning
Elton John: Tantrums and Tiaras
Emily and Gitta
Empty Bed, An
Endangered
Entwined
Equus
Erotique
Et L'Amore
Even Cowgirls Get the Blues
Everything in Between
Everything Relative
Execution of Justice
Execution of Wanda Jean, The
Exploding Oedipus
Eyes of Tammy Faye, The
Fag Hag
Fall of Communism as Seen in Gay
    Pornography, The
Family Affair, A (1995)
Family Affair, A (2001)
Family Fundamentals
Family Values
Family Values: An American Tragedy
Fanci's Persuasion
Fantasy Dancer
Fated to be Queer
Fearless Vampire Killers, The
    (aka: Dance of the Vampires)
Female Closet, The
Female Misbehavior
Female Perversions
Female Trouble
Fighting in South-West Louisiana
Film for Two
Finding North
Fingered!
Finished
Fireworks
First Base
First Breath
First Comes Love (1991)
Fisher King, The
Fixing Frank
Flaming Creatures
Flawless
Flesh (aka: Andy Warhol's Flesh)
Flesh for Frankenstein
Flesh Gordon

Flirt
Flora's Garment Bursting Into Bloom
Florida Enchantment, A
Flow
Flowing Hearts: Thailand Fighting AIDS
Fluffer, The
Flush
Fly Away Homo
Food of Love
For Straights Only
Forbidden Justice (aka: Short Eyes)
Forms and Motifs
Forsaken
Fortune and Men's Eyes
Forty Deuce
Fox, The
Foxfire
Framing Lesbian Fashion
Franchesca Page
Frankie and Johnny
Freebie and the Bean
Freebird
Fresh Kill
Fried Green Tomatoes
Friend of Dorothy, A
Friends and Family
Frisk
Fucked in the Face
Full Moon in New York
    (aka: Ren zai Niu Yue)
Fun
Fun Down There
Fun with a Sausage (aka: L'Ingenue)
Funny Lady
Gang Girls 2000
Garbo Talks
Gasp
Gay Agenda, The
Gay Cuba
Gay Deceivers, The
Gay & Gray in New York City
Gay Tape: Butch and Femme
Gay USA
Gay Voices, Gay Legends
Gay Voices, Gay Legends 2
Gay Youth
Gaymes, The
Gemini Affair, The
Genesis Children, The
Gentlemen Prefer Blondes
Gently down the Stream
Gertrude Stein and a Companion
Gertrude Stein: When You See This
    Remember Me
Get Bruce
Get Out
Get Over It
Get the Bowheads
Get Your Stuff
Getting It On

Gia
Gilda
Girl in Every Port, A
Girl Power
Girl, The
Girl Thing, A
Girlfriends (1978)
Girlfriends (1993)
Girls Who Like Girls
Glen or Glenda
Go
Go Fish
God, Gays and the Gospel
Godass
Gods and Monsters
Golden Threads
Good Family, The
    (aka: Thanksgiving Day)
Goodbye Emma Jo
Goodbye Girl, The
Grapefruit
Green Plaid Shirt
Green Pubes
Greetings from Out Here
Greetings from Washington
Grief
Group
Group, The
Gypsy 83
Gypsy Boys
Habit
Hairspray
Hallelujah!
Hand on the Pulse
Happy Birthday Gemini
Happy Texas
Hard
Hard Love & How to Fuck in High Heels
Harlequin Exterminator
Harold and Hiroshi
Haunted Summer
Haunted World of Edward D. Wood
    Jnr, The
Haunting of Morella, The
Haunting, The
He Bop!
He's Like
He's My Girl
Headhunter
Hearing Voices
Heat
Heaven, Earth and Hell
Heavy Petting (1988)
Hedwig and the Angry Inch
Hell's Highway
Hellion Heatwave
Henry and June
Her Life as a Man
Her Urge
Hey Sailor, Hey Sister

Hidden Assassin (aka: The Shooter)
Hidden Child
Hide and Seek
High Art
High Tech Rice
Higher Learning
Hired to Kill
History Lessons
History of the World According to a Lesbian, The
Hit and Runway
hITCH
HIV Rollercoaster
Holding
Hole
Home for the Holidays
Home Movie
Homicidal
Homo Heights (aka: Happy Heights)
Homo Promo
Homosexuality and Lesbianism
Homoteens
Hooking Up
Hope Along the Wind: The Life of Harry Hay
Hope is a Thing With Feathers
Horse Dreams in BBQ Country
Hotel New Hampshire, The
Hours and Times, The
How to Female Ejaculate
How to Find Your Goddess Spot
How to Have a Sex Party
How to Kill Her
Howling II: Your Sister is a Werewolf
Hungry Hearts
I Became a Lesbian and So Can You
I Exist: Voices From the Lesbian and Gay Middle Eastern Community
I Hate Faggy Fag Fag
I Shall Not Be Removed: The Life of Marlon Riggs
I Shot Andy Warhol
I Think I Do
I'll Be Your Mirror
I'll Love You Forever - Tonight
I'm Starving
I'm the One that I Want
If She Grows Up Gay
If She Only Knew
If These Walls Could Talk 2
Ifti
Image in the Snow
Images
In Bed with Madonna (aka: Madonna: Truth or Dare)
In My Father's House
In & Out
In the Best Interests of the Children
In the Flesh (1997)

In the Flesh (2000)
In the Gloaming
In This House of Brede
Inauguration of the Pleasure Dome
Incredibly True Adventures of Two Girls in Love, The
Infidel
Inn Trouble
Inside Monkey Zetterland
Inside Out
Internal Affairs
Interview with the Vampire
Intimate Friendship, An
Inverted Minstrel
Invocation of My Demon Brother
Iris
Isle of Lesbos
It Dwells in Mirrors
It Wasn't Love
It's a Boy! Journeys from Female to Male
It's Elementary: Talking about Gay Issues in School
It's in the Water
It's My Party
Jake 'Today I Became a Man'
James Baldwin: The Price of the Ticket
Janine
Jareena: Portrait of a Hijda
Jaundiced Eye, The
Jeffery's Hollywood Screen Trick
Jeffrey
Jerker
Jodie Promo, The
Joe-Joe
Joey Breaker
Joey Goes to Wigstock
Joggernaught
Johnny Eager
Johnny Guitar
Johns
Jollies
Journey of Jared Price, The
Joys of Smoking, The
Juggling Gender
Julia
Julie Johnson
Just Because of Who We Are
Just Call Me Kade
Just for Fun
Just One of the Girls (aka: Anything for Love)
Just One of the Guys
Just One Time
Just the Two of Us
Kali's Vibe
Kalin's Prayer
Kamikaze Hearts
Kamikaze Summer
Kansas Anymore
Karen Black Like Me
Kate's Addiction

Ke Kulana He Mahu: Remembering a Sense of Place
Keep the River on Your Right
Keep Your Laws off My Body
Kevin's Room
Kim
Kindling Point, The
King of the City (aka: Club Life)
Kinsey 3, The
Kiss Me Guido
Kiss of the Spider Woman, The
Kiss the Boys and Make Them Die
Kissing Jessica Stein
L. I. E.
L Is for the Way You Look
Labor More than Once
Lady
Lady in Cement
Lady in Waiting, The
Ladybugs
Laramie Project, The
Larry's Visit
Last Call at Maud's
Last Emperor, The
Last Exit to Brooklyn
Last Married Couple in America, The
Last of Sheila, The
Late Bloomers
Latin Boys Go To Hell
Laughing Policeman, The
Lavender Limelight: Lesbians in Films
Lavender Tortoise
Leather
Leather Jacket Love Story
Leave It!
Legacies
Legend of Lylah Clare, The
Lesbian Avengers Eat Fire Too
Lesbian Bed Death: Myth or Epidemic
Lesbian Physicians on Practice, Patients & Power
Lesbian Teenagers in High School
Lesbian Tongues
Lesbians in the Pulpit
Lesson 9
Let's Play Prisoners
Lez B Friends: A Biker Bitch Hate Story
Lianna
Liberace
Liberace: Behind the Music
Licensed to Kill
Lickerish Quartet, The (aka: The Erotic Quartet)
Lie Down with Dogs
Life and Death on the A-List
Life and Times of Allen Ginsberg, The
Life's a Butch!
Lifetime Commitment: A Portrait of Karen Thomson

Lifetime Guarantee: Phranc's
    Adventures in Plastic
Lightship, The
Lilith
Liquid Sky
Listen
Live Nude Girls
Live Nude Girls UNITE!
Live to Tell: The First Gay and
    Lesbian Prom in America
Living End, The
Living Out Loud
Living Proof: HIV and the Pursuit
    of Happiness
Living with Pride: Ruth Ellis @ 100
Loads
Lonely Lady, The
Lonesome Cowboys
Long Awaited Pleasure
Long Voyage Home, The
Long Weekend, The
    (aka: The Long Weekend (O'Despair))
Longtime Companion
Looking for a Space
Looking for Common Ground
Looking for Mr Goodbar
Losing Lois
Lost in the Pershing Point Hotel
Lot in Sodom
Love Letter, The
Love Ltd.
Love Machine, The
Love Makes a Family: Gay Parents
    in the '90s
Love=ME3
Love! Valour! Compassion!
Loved One, The
Loverville 2: The Honeymoon
Lucifer Rising
Luminous Procuress
Lunch with Eddie
Lust in the Dust
Luster
Luv Tale, A
Lycanthrophobia
Lysis
M Butterfly
Madam Wang's
Madame Sousatzka
Made in Heaven
Mafu Cage, The
    (aka: My Sister, My Love)
Magnolia
Mahogany
Mai's America
Maid of Honor
Maids, The
Making Love
Mala Noche (aka: Bad Night)
Mama, I Have Something to Tell You

Man of the Year
Manhattan
Mannequin
March in April
March on Washington, The
Mascara
Mask of Desire (aka: Shades of Black)
Mass Appeal
Massillon
Match that Started My Fire, The
Maybe We're Talking About a
    Different God
Mayhem
Meeting Magdalene
Men in Love
Mercy (1989)
Mercy (1999)
Metamorphosis: Man into Woman
Midnight Cowboy
Midnight Express
Midnight in the Garden of Good
    and Evil
Midwife's Tale, The
Mike's Murder
Minor Disturbances
Mirror Images II
Mob Queen
Moments: The Making of Claire of
    the Moon
More than Friends: The Coming
    Out of Heidi Leiter
Morocco
Most Unknowable Thing, The
Mountain King, The
Mountains of the Moon
Mr Christie
Mrs Doubtfire
Mujeria
Mulholland Drive
Multiple Maniacs
MURDER and murder
Must be the Music
My Babushka
My Best Friend's Wedding
My Body
My Brother's Keeper
My Father is Coming
My Femme Divine
My Girlfriend Did It
My Hustler
My Own Private Idaho
My Two Loves
Myra Breckinridge
Myth of Father
Nadja
Naked Highway
Naked in New York
Naomi's Legacy
Need and Want
Neptune's Rocking Horse

Never Look Back
Never Met Picasso
New Women, The
Next Best Thing, The
Next Stop, Greenwich Village
Nice Girls Don't Do It
Night Larry Kramer Kissed Me, The
Night Rhythms
Night Warning
Nine Days
Nitrate Kisses
No Backup
No Dumb Questions
No Exit
No Ordinary Love
No Rewind
No Way Out
Nocturne (1989)
Non, Je Ne Regrette Rien
    aka: No Regret)
Norman, is that You?
Not All Parents are Straight
Not Just Passing Through
Notorious C.H.O.
Nowhere
Nuestra Salud: Violencia Domestica
Nunzio's Second Cousin
O Boys: Parties, Porn & Politics, The
Object of My Affection, The
Odd Girl Out
Ode
Ode to Billy Joe
Off the Straight and Narrow:
    Lesbians, Gays, Bisexuals and
    Television
Olga's Girls
Olive Tree, The
ON_LINE
On the Bus
Once Is Not Enough
    (aka: Jacqueline Susann's Once Is
    Not Enough)
One Nation Under God
One + One
One Small Step
Only When I Laugh
Opening Closet X: A Voice for
    Queer Youth
Opposite of Sex, The
Ordinary Sinner
Other Mothers
Other Side, The (aka: Del Otro Lado)
Other Voices, Other Rooms
Our Brothers, Our Sons
Our House: A Very Real Documentary
Our Mom's a Dyke
Our Sons (aka: Too Little, Too Late)
Out At Work: America Undercover
Out in Africa
Out in South Africa

Out in Suburbia
Out in the Open
Out Loud
Out of Our Time
Out of Season
Out of the Closet, Off the Screen: The Life & Times of William Haines
Out of the Past
Out: The Making of a Revolutionary
Outlaw
Outtakes
Over the Rainbow: Parts 1 - 4
Override
P. S. Your Cat is Dead
Paper Cranes
Paragraph 175
Parallel Sons
Paris is Burning
Paris Was a Woman
Parting Glances
Partners
Party Favor, The
Party Monster
Party Safe with DiAna and Bambi
Passed Away
Passing Resemblance
Paul Cadmus: Enfant Terrible at 80
Paul Monette: The Brink of Summer's End
Peccatum Mutum (aka: The Silent Sin)
Penitentiary
Peoria Babylon
Peppermills
Personal Best (1982)
Phantom Pain
Philadelphia
Pillow Talk
Pink Angels, The
Pink Flamingos
Pink Narcissus
Pink Triangle: A Study of Prejudice Against Gays & Lesbians
Place Between Our Bodies, The
Place Called Lovely, A
Play Dead
Play It as It Lays
Playing the Part
Please Don't Stop: Lesbian Tips for Givin' and Gettin' It
Pleasure Beach
Plushies & Furries
Poison
Politics of Fur, The
Polyester
Pony Glass
Pool Days
Portrait of Jason
Postcards from America
Potluck and the Passion, The

Prefaces
Pride Divide
Pride in Puerto Rico
Prince of Tides, The
Private Benjamin
Privilege
Public Opinion
Pump
Punks
Queen Christina
Queen of the Whole Wide World
Queen, The
Queens Logic
Queer As Folk (2000)
Queer Geography: Mapping Our Identities
Queer Son
Question of Love, A
Questioning Faith
Radical Harmonies
Raising Heroes
Rape of Ganymede, The
Ray's Male Heterosexual Dance Hall
Reaching for the Moon
Reaching Out to Lesbian, Gay and Bisexual Youth
Real Ellen Story, The
Rebel Rebel
Red Dirt
Red Heat
Red Rain
Red Ribbon Blues
Red River
Red Shoe Diaries 3, The: Another Woman's Lipstick
Reflections
Reflections in a Golden Eye
Reform School Girls
Relax... It's Just Sex
Reno Finds Her Mom
Rescuing Desire
Resident Alien
Return of Sarah's Daughters, The
Rice and Potatoes
Rights and Reactions
Rites of Passage
Ritual
Ritual Nation
Rock Hudson
Rock Hudson's Home Movies
Rock the Boat
Rockwell
Rocky Horror Picture Show, The
Room of Words, The (aka: La Stanza della parole)
Roommates
Rope
Rose, The
Roy Cohn / Jack Smith
Rules of the Game

Rules of the Road
Ruthie & Connie: Every Room in the House
Sacred Lies, Civil Truths
Sad Disco Fantasia
Safe is Desire
Safe Journey
Salt Mines, The
Sambal Belacan in San Francisco
Satan's Princess (aka: Malediction)
Saturday Night at the Baths
Scarecrow in a Garden of Cucumbers
Scenes from the Class Struggle in Beverly Hills
Scent Uva Butch
School's Out: Lesbian and Gay Youth
Score
Scorpio Rising
Scout's Honor
Scream, Teen, Scream
Sea in the Blood
Second Coming, The
Second Serve
Secrets
Seducers, The (aka: Death Game)
Seduction of Innocence
See How They Run
Self-Destruction of Gia, The
Separate Peace, A
Sergeant Matlovich vs. the U.S. Air Force
Sergeant, The
Serving in Silence: The Marguerite Cammermeyer Story
Set It Off
Seven Women
Sex Bytes
Sex, Drugs and Democracy
Sex Flesh in Blood
Sex Is...
Sex is Sex: Conversations with Male Prostitutes
Sex Monster, The
Sex/Life in LA
Sexual Orientation: Reading Between the Labels
Shades
Shades of Gray
Shall We Dance
Shame No More
Shantay
Shatzi is Dying
She Don't Fade
She Even Chewed Tobacco
She Must Be Seeing Things
She Wears Cufflinks
She's Real Worse than Queer
Shifting Positions
Shooting Porn
Shoplifting Chanel
Sign of the Cross, The

Signed: Lino Brocka
Silence=Death (aka: Die AIDS-
  Trilogie: Schweigen=Tod)
Silence of the Lambs, The
Silence that Silences, The
Silent Pioneers
Silkwood
Silver Screen: Color Me Lavender, The
Silverlake Life: The View From Here
Sincerely Yours
Sink or Swim
Sir: Just a Normal Guy
Siren
SIS: The Perry Watkins Story
Sister Louise's Discovery
Six Degrees of Separation
Size 'Em Up
Skin and Bone
Slaves to the Underground
Sleep Come Free Me
Sleep in a Nest of Flames
Sluts and Goddesses Video Workshop
Smear
Smoke
Snatch it
Some Aspect of a Shared Lifestyle
Some Ground to Stand On
Some Like It Hot
Some of My Best Friends Are
Some of These Days
Some Prefer Cake
Something Close to Heaven
Something for Everyone
  (aka: Black Flowers for the Bride)
Somewhere in the City
Song of the Loon
Sonny Boy
Sordid Lives
Southern Comfort
Souvenir
Spartacus
Speaking for Ourselves
Speedway Junky
Speedy Boys
Spikes and Heels
Spin the Bottle
Split: Portrait of a Drag Queen
  (aka: Split: William to Chrysis)
Spy Who Came, The
Staceyann Chin - A Poetry Slammer
Staircase
Star Maps
Steers and Queers
Stephen
Sticky Fingers of Time, The
Stiff Sheets
Stonewall
Stonewall 25: Voices of Pride and Protest
Storme: The Lady of the Jewel Box

Story of a Bad Boy, The
Straight Agenda, The
Straight Down the Aisle: Confes-
  sions of Lesbian Bridesmaids
Straight for the Money: Interviews
  with Queer Sex Workers
Straight from the Heart: Gay and
  Lesbian Children
Straightman
Strange Life and Death of Dr
  Turing, The
Strange One, The (aka: End as a Man)
Stranger Inside
Stray Dogs
Streamers
Strippers
Such a Crime
Suddenly, Last Summer (1959)
Sugar Cookies
Sugar High, Glitter City
Summer in My Veins (Director's Cut)
Sunflowers
Superdyke
Superstar: The Life and Times of
  Andy Warhol
Surrender Dorothy
Surviving Friendly Fire
Susana
Sweet Boy
Swimming
Swimming Upstream: A Year in the
  Life of Karen and Jenny
Switch (1991)
Switchblade Sisters
Swoon
Sylvia Scarlett
Sync Touch
Tales of the City
Tales of the City 2
  (aka: More Tales of the City)
Tales of the City 3
  (aka: Further Tales of the City)
Talk to Me like the Rain
Tangible Fathers
Tank Girl
Tea and Sympathy
Teenage Tupelo
Tell Me That You Love Me, Junie Moon
Tell Me Why: The Epistemology of Disco
Tender Fictions
Terms of Conception
That Certain Summer
That Tender Touch
That's a Family
Thelma and Louise
Theme: Murder
They Are Lost to Vision Altogether
Things We Said Today

Things You Can Tell Just by
  Looking at Her
This Is Not a Very Blank Tape Dear
Thousand Miles, A
Three Bewildered People (aka: Three
  Bewildered People in the Night)
Three of Hearts
Three on a Match
Three to Tango
Threesome
Throwback (aka: Spike of Bensonhurst)
Thunderbolt and Lightfoot
Thundercrack!
Tidy Endings
Ties that Bind, The
Tim Miller: Loud and Queer
Time Piece
Times of Harvey Milk, The
Times Square
Tiny and Ruby: Hell Drivin' Women
Titanic 2000
To Ride a Cow
To Wong Foo, Thanks for Every-
  thing, Julie Newmar
Toc Storee
Todd Killings, The
Together Alone
Together and Apart
Toilers and the Wayfarers, The
Token of Love
Tom Clay Jesus
Tomboychik
Tongues Untied
Too Much Sun
Tootsie
Torch Song Trilogy
Totally Confused
Totally F***ed Up
Touch Me (1997)
Touch of Evil
Traditional Family Vampires
Tragedy of Samantha Biggle and the
  Twins, The
Transanimals
Transeltown
Transexual Menace
Transformation, The
Transformers/AIDS
Transsexual Journey, A
Trappings of Transhood
Trash
Treading Water
Treasure Island
Trembling Before G-d
Trevor
Trey Billings Show, The
Treyf
Trick
Trip, The

Troika
Trois
Truth About Jane, The
Turnabout
Twice a Man
Twilight of the Golds, The
Twin Cheeks: Who Killed the
　Homecoming King?
Twinkle Toes
Twisted
Two in Twenty
Two Moon Junction
Two Point Five
Uh-Oh!
Unconditional Love
Under Heat
Union in Wait, A
Unknown Cyclist, The
Up!
Up the Academy
Urbania
Vanished
Vaudeville
Vegas in Space
Velocity of Gary, The
Velvet Goldmine
Velvet Vampire, The
　(aka: The Waking Hour)
Vendetta
Venus Boyz
Very Funny
Very Natural Thing, A
Vicious
Vintage: Families of Value
Virgin Larry, The
Voices from the Front
Voicing the Legacy
Waiting
Waiting for the Moon
Walk on the Wild Side
Wallowitch & Ross: This Moment
War on Lesbians
War Widow, The
Watermelon Woman, The
We Always Danced
We Are Family
Webcam Boys
Wedding Banquet, The (aka: Hsi yen)
Wedding Video, The
Weekend, The
Weeki Wachee Girls
West Coast Crones
What is the Relationship between
　Rosa von Praunheim and the
　Male Strippers of San Francisco?
What Makes a Family
What You Take for Granted
What's Cooking?

When Boys Fly
When the Party's Over
Whether You Like It or Not: The
　Story of Hedwig
White to be Angry, The
Who Happen to be Gay
Who's Afraid of Project 10?
Wigstock: The Movie (1987)
Wigstock: The Movie (1995)
Wild Life
Wild Party, The
Wild Side
Wild Things
William Burroughs: Commissioner
　of the Sewers
Willie Dynamite
Willy/Milly (aka: Something Special)
Windows
Without You I'm Nothing
Woman Accused, A
　(aka: In the Glitter Palace)
Woman Hunt
Woman on Top
Women I Love
Women in Cages
　(aka: Women's Penitentiary III)
Women in Revolt
Women of Brewster Place, The
Women of Gold
Wonder Boys, The
Word is Out
Work
Working Girls
World According to Garp, The
World and Time Enough
Worthy Mothers
Wrecked for Life: The Trip &
　Magic of Trocadero Transfer
Wrong Son, The
XXXY
Y tu Mamá También
　(aka: And Your Mother Too)
Yentl
You Don't Know Dick: Courageous
　Hearts of Transsexual Men
You've Had Worse Things in Your Mouth
Your Mother Wears Combat Boots
Youth Outloud!
Zorro, the Gay Blade

Yugoslavia

Score

Zimbabwe

Forbidden Fruit

Distributors

10%
10% Productions
6165 Santa Monica Blvd
Los Angeles CA 90038
USA
P: 1 323 460 4661
F: 1 323 460 6252
www.10percent.com

16MM
Sixteen Millimetre Australia Pty Ltd
136 Canterrbury Rd
Canterbury NSW 2193
Australia
P: 61 2 9718 7800

20thCenturyFox
20th Century Fox Film Corporation (Aust)
PO Box 834
Lane Cove NSW 2066
Australia
P: 61 2 9418 3111
F: 61 2 9418 3377
www.foxmovies.com

20thCenturyFox
20th Century Fox Film Corporation (USA)
www.foxmovies.com

21stCentury
21st Century Pictures
449 Darling St
Balmain NSW 2041
Australia
P: 61 2 9555 7133
F: 61 2 9555 7322

2XTexan
2 X Texan Productions
1014 Bedford St
Los Angeles CA 90035
USA
P: 1 310 657 8170

7thArt
Seventh Art Releasing
7551 Sunset Blvd, Suite 104
Los Angeles CA 90046
USA
P: 1 323 845 1455
F: 1 323 845 4717
E: seventhart@7thart.com
www.7thart.com

ABC-US
American Broadcasting Company
500 S. Buena Vista St
Burbank CA 91521-4551
USA
P: 1 800 2255 222
www.abc.go.com

Absolute
Absolute Productions
15 Coalmeadow Close, Walsall
West Midlands W53 ZPR
United Kingdom
P: 44 192 271 2467
F: 44 121 353 5973
E: simhort@hotmail.com

Academy
Academy Pictures
Via Fratelli Ruspoli, 8
Rome 00198
Italy
P: 39 6 840 424
F: 39 6 8417 043
E: academy@politecnos.it
www.politecnos.it/academy-pict/

AchabFilm
Achab Film
Viale Gorizia 24C
Rome 00198
Italy
P: 39 06 854 7230
F: 39 06 8535 5692
E: jef.nuyts@tiscalinet.it

ACMI
Australian Centre for the Moving
  Image (ACMI) Collections
222 Park St
South Melbourne Vic 3205
Australia
P: 61 3 9929 7040
F: 61 3 9929 7027
E: collections@acmi.net.au
www.acmi.net.au

Acrobat
Acrobat Films
1 Penn St
North Balwyn Vic 3104
Australia
P: 61 3 9857 0553
F: 61 3 9857 0553
E: info@acrobat-films.com
www.acrobat-films.com

Adobe
Adobe Productions
5283 Park Ave, Suite 5
Montréal Québec H2V 4G9
Canada
P: 1 514 272 3113
F: 1 514 272 3301
E: courrier@adobeproductions.com
www.adobeproductions.com

AdVitam
Ad Vitam
6 rue de l'ecole de Medecine
Paris 75006
France
P: 33 1 4634 7574
E: cineclassic-advitam@wanadoo.fr

AFTRS
Australian Film TV & Radio School
PO Box 126
North Ryde NSW 1670
Australia
P: 61 2 9805 6455
F: 61 2 9805 6563
E: ruths@aftrs.edu.au
www.aftrs.edu.au

Alexandros

Alexandros Film
Agalianou 13
Athens 11476
Greece
P: 30 1 6421 1656
F: 30 1 6454 466
www.compulink.gr/gavafy

All-Girl-Action

All-Girl-Action-Productions
530 West 113th St, #1D
New York NY 10025
USA
P: 1 212 665 4402
F: 1 212 854 7702
E: jf295@columbia.edu

Alliance

Alliance Atlantis Communications
121 Bloor St East, Suite 1500
Toronto Ontario M4W 3M5
Canada
P: 1 416 967 1174
F: 1 416 960 0971
E: info@allianceatlantis.com
www.allianceatlantis.com

AlliedArtists

Allied Artists, Bob Poirier
105 North St, #3
Portland MA 04101
USA
P: 1 207 828 4030

Alquimia

Alquimia Cinema
Parma 8
Madrid 28043
Spain
P: 34 91 748 9040
F: 34 91 300 5909
E: iker.monfort@alquimia.com
www.alquimiacinema.com

Altermedia

Altermedia
PO Box 010 -084
St George Station
Staten Island NY 10301
USA
P: 1 718 273 8829

AMAC

Academy of Media Arts Cologne
Peter-Welter-Plate 2
Cologne 50676
Germany
P: 43 221 201 89330
F: 43 221 210 8917
E: dilger@khm.de

AmericanFilm

American Film Institute
2021 North Western Ave
Los Angeles CA 90027
USA
P: 1 323 856 7600
F: 1 323 467 4578
www.afi.com

AMIP

AMIP Multimedia
52 rue Charlot
Paris 75003
France
P: 33 1 4887 4513
F: 33 1 4887 4010
E: amip@worldnet.fr

API-PFLAG

API - PFLAG Project
PO Box 640223
San Francisco CA USA
P: 1 415 921 8850
F: 1 415 563 6658
E: apipflag@aol.com

Arrow

Arrow Entertainment
E: arrowfilms@yahoo.com

ArteFrance

Arte France
8 rue Marceau
Issy-les-Moulineaux 92785
France
P: 33 1 5500 7074
F: 33 1 5500 7396
E: a-charbonnel@paris.arte.fr
www.artefrance.fr

ArtemisInt

Artemis International
Suite 3, 24 Thorogood St
Victoria Park WA 6100
Australia
P: 61 8 9470 2936
F: 61 8 9362 5500
E: terri@artemisfilms.com
www.artemisfilms.com

ArtificialEye

Artificial Eye
12 King St
1st Floor
London WC2
United Kingdom
www.artificial-eye.com

ArtisticLicense

Artistic License Films
470 Park Ave, 9th Floor
New York NY 10016
USA
P: 1 212 779 0290
F: 1 212 696 9546
E: ArtLic@aol.com
www.artlic.com

ArtistView

Artist View Entertainment
12500 Riverside Drive, Suite 201-B
North Hollywood CA 91607
USA
P: 1 818 752 2480
F: 1 818 752 9339
E: artistview@earthlink.net

Ascanbee

Ascanbee
323 Princes Hwy
Banksia NSW 2216
Australia
P: 61 2 9556 2833
F: 61 2 9556 2844

Asparas

Asparas Film & TV Productions
2091 East 47th Ave
Vancouver British Columbia V5P 1R2
Canada
P: 1 604 299 9685
F: 1 604 299 9685
E: asparasfilm@yahoo.com

Atom

Atom Films
www.atomfilms.com

AttaGirl

Atta Girl Productions
PO Box 130874
Carlsbad CA 92013
USA
P: 1 760 603 0121
F: 1 760 603 0121
E: hlesnick@attagirlprods.com
www.attagirlprods.com

Attitude

Attitude Films
300 Mercer St, Suite 26L
New York NY 10003
USA
P: 1 212 995 9008
F: 1 212 254 5135
E: mail@attitudefilms.com
www.attitudefilms.com

AucklandUni

University of Auckland
Audio Visual Centre
Private Bag 92019
Auckland 1020
New Zealand
P: 64 9 373 7599 (ext 8918)
F: 64 9 373 7413
E: postmaster@auckland.ac.nz
www.auckland.ac.nz

Automat

Laura Nix, Automat Pictures
3255 Wilshire Blvd
Suite 615
Los Angeles CA 90010
USA
P: 1 213 351 0444
F: 1 213 351 0445
E: laura@automatpictures.com
www.automatpictures.com

Avalanche

Avalanche Home Entertainment/Lions Gate Films
www.lionsgatefilms.com

Babylegs

Babylegs Entertainment
E: Filmprodny@aol.com

BBC-Arena

BBC - Arena
London United Kingdom
P: 44 20 8895 6766
F: 44 20 8895 6974
E: lucie.prescott@bbc.co.uk
www.bbc.co.uk

BBC-Enterprises

BBC Enterprises
Woodlands
80 Wood Lane
London W12 OTT
United Kingdom
P: 44 181 576 0202
F: 44 181 749 0538
www.bbc.co.uk

BBC-Scotland

BBC Scotland
Broadcasting House
Queen Margaret Dr
Glasgow G12 8DG
United Kingdom
P: 44 141 576 7642
F: 44 141 576 8419
E: enquiries.scot@bbc.co.uk
www.bbc.co.uk/scotland

BBCTV

BBC Worldwide Television
Woodlands
80 Wood Lane
London W12 OTT
United Kingdom
P: 44 181 576 2000
F: 44 181 749 0538
www.bbc.co.uk

Behind-Walls

Behind Walls Productions
345 West 50th St, #7Z
New York NY 10019
USA
P: 1 212 581 6085
F: 1 212 956 2499
E: behindwalls@hotmail.com

bellecote

belle cote pictures
1237 North Detroit, #7
Los Angeles CA 90046
USA
P: 1 323 883 0725
E: bellecote@earthlink.net

BellMovies

Bell Movies
202-1370 Davie St
Vancouver British Columbia V6K 1K1
Canada
P: 1 604 687 2329
F: 1 604 605 8263
E: richard@bellmovies.com
www.bellmovies.com

Berkeley

Berkeley Film Group
CA USA
P: 1 510 893 1820
F: 1 510 893 0816
E: berkfilmgrp@lmi.net

Beta

Beta Film
Robert-Buerkle-Strasse 2
Ismaning 85737
Germany
P: 49 89 9956 2134
F: 49 89 9956 2703
E: DSchuerhoff@betacinema.com
www.betacinema.com

Beyond

Beyond Films
53-55 Brisbane St
Surry Hills NSW 2010
Australia
P: 61 2 8217 2000
F: 61 2 8217 2035
E: films@beyond.com.au
www.beyond.com.au

BFI

British Film Institute
21 Stephen St
London W1T 1LN
United Kingdom
P: 44 20 7255 1444
F: 44 20 7436 7950
E: booking.films@bfi.org.uk
www.bfi.org.uk

Big&Little

Big and Little Films
365 Barkly St
St Kilda Vic 3182
Australia
P: 61 3 9531 3319
F: 61 3 9531 7962

BigFilm

Big Film Shorts/Tigris Films
3727 W. Magnolia Blvd, Suite 189
Burbank CA 91510
P: 1 818 563 2633
E: info@tigrisfilms.com
www.bigfilmshorts.com

BiProduct

Bi Product Productions
1216 Tenth Ave
Seattle WA 98122
USA
P: 1 206 323 0557
F: 1 206 323 0118
E: minadog10@hotmail.com
www.biproductproductions.com

Bizarre

Bizarre Productions
2501 Oak Quarters
Smyrna GA 30080
USA
P: 1 770 319 8837
F: 1 770 805 4079
E: tellsid@aol.com

BlackCat

Black Cat Productions
6111 North Talman
Chicago IL 60659
USA
P: 1 773 274 2300
F: 1 773 274 1200
E: info@blackcatfilm.net
www.blackcatfilm.net

Blackwatch

Blackwatch Communications Inc
1410, rue Stanley Bureau 606
Montréal Québec H3A 1P8
P: 1 514 844 6655

BlowUp

Blow Up Doll Productions
3288 21st St, #149
San Francisco CA 94110-2423
USA
P: 1 617 983 3443
E: srozen@earthlink.net

BobbyRoger

BobbyRoger
105 North St, #3
Portland MA 04101
USA
P: 1 207 761 7236
F: 1 207 761 7236
E: bob@bobbyroger.com
www.bobbyroger.com

BrokenHip

Broken Hip Films
240 East 35th St, #3J
New York NY 10016
USA
E: brokenhipfilms@aol.com

Brüning

Jürgen Brüning Filmproduktion
Kottbusserdamm 32
Berlin 10467
Germany
P: 49 30 6900 1042
F: 49 30 6900 1043
E: anger@snafu.de

Budapest

Budapest Film
www.budapestfilm.hu

BuenaVista

Buena Vista (Aust)
Level 5, Como Centre
650 Chapel St
South Yarra Vic 3141
Australia
P: 61 3 9823 7800
F: 61 3 9826 0411

BuenaVista

Buena Vista International
500 S. Buena Vista St
Burbank CA 91521
USA
P: 1 818 295 3673
F: 1 818 843 6925
movies.go.com

Bulgarian

Bulgarian Gay Organisaiton
PO Box 123
Sofia 1784
Bulgaria
P: 359 2 987 6872
E: bgogemini@einet.bg
www.bgogemini.org

BustinOut

Bustin' Out Films
1011 Palm Ave #103
West Hollywood CA 90069
USA
P: 1 310 854 0304
E: cjrusso@pacbell.net

Butter&Pinches

Butter & Pinches Productions
2213 Dwight Way, # 1/2
Berkeley CA 94704
USA
P: 1 510 849 0802
E: mcmpress@yahoo.com

BuzzTaxi

Buzz Taxi
#201-1110 Yonge St
Toronto Ontario M4W 2L6
Canada
P: 1 416 920 3800
F: 1 416 920 3998
E: info@buzztaxi.com
www.buzztaxi.com

CaliforniaNewsreel

California Newsreel
500 Third St, Suite 500
San Francisco CA 94107
USA
P: 1 415 284 7800
F: 1 415 284 7801
E: contact@newsreel.org
www.newsreel.org

Cambridge

Cambridge Documentary Films
PO Box 390385
Cambridge MA 02139-0004
USA
P: 1 617 484 3993
F: 1 617 484 0754
E: cdf@shore.net
nautilus.shore.net/~cdf/testsite
    /home.html

CanadianBroadcasting

Canadian Broadcasting Corporation
PO Boz 500 Station A
Toronto Ontario M5W 1E6
Canada
P: 1 416 205 3700
www.cbc.ca

Canal+

Le Studio Canal+
17 rue Dumont D'Urville
Paris 75116
France
P: 33 1 4443 9800
F: 33 1 4720 2967
www.canal-plus.com

Canyon

Canyon Cinema
145 Ninth St, # 260
San Francisco CA 94103
USA
P: 1 415 626 2255
F: 1 415 626 2255
E: films@canyoncinema.com
www.canyoncinema.com

CargoCult

Cargo Cult Productions
243 Dearing St
Athens Georgia 30605
USA
P: 1 706 543 0652
F: 1 706 542 0226

Carlton

Carlton International
35-38 Portman Square
London W1H 6NU
United Kingdom
P: 44 20 7224 3339
F: 44 20 7486 1707
E: enquiries@carltonint.co.uk
www.carltonint.co.uk

Casper

Casper Films
70B Ranelagh
Dublin 6
Ireland
P: 353 1 497 0981
F: 353 1 497 0981

CastleHill

Castle Hill Productions, Inc.
1414 Avenue of the Americas
New York NY 10019
USA
P: 1 212 888 0080
F: 1 212 644 0956

CBS

Columbia Broadcasting Service
7800 Beverly Blvd, Suite 310
Los Angeles CA 90036
USA

Celluloid-Dreams

Celluloid Dreams
24 rue Lamartine
Paris 75009
France
P: 33 1 4970 0370
F: 33 1 4970 0371
E: pierre@celluloid-dreams.com
www.celluloid-dreams.com

CentralMotion

Central Motion Picture Corporation
Taipei Taiwan
P: 886 2 2371 5191
F: 886 2 2231 0681
E: cmpc5A@ms32.HINET.NET

CFMDC

Canadian Filmmakers' Distribution Centre
37 Hanna Ave, Suite 220
Toronto Ontario M6K 1W8
Canada
P: 1 416 588 0725
F: 1 416 588 7956
E: bookings@cfmdc.org
www.cfmdc.org

Channel4

Channel 4 Television Corporation
124 Horseferry Rd
London SW1P 2TX
United Kingdom
P: 44 171 306 8477
F: 44 171 306 8357
www.channel4.com

Chapel

Chapel Distribution
Astor Theatre
1 Chapel St
St Kilda Vic 3182
Australia
P: 61 3 9505 6253
F: 61 3 9532 7951
E: potfilms@ozemail.com.au
www.potentialfilms.com.au

Cheek2Cheek

Cheek 2 Cheek Productions
36B South Hill Park, Hampstead
London NW3 2SJ
United Kingdom
P: 44 171 431 0687
F: 44 171 833 3905
E: janetpotter@beeb.net

ChenJ

Jo-fei Chen
No. 3, Alley 20, Lane 115
Sec. 1, Pei-Yi Rd, Hsin-Dien
Taipei 231
Taiwan
P: 886 2 2911 7931
F: 886 2 2911 7931
E: jofei@ms17.hinet.net

ChenM

Michelle Chen
Panorama Studio
12 Beisanhuan Dong Lu
Beijing 100013
China
P: 86 10 8425 3498
F: 86 21 6420 7482
E: chenmm02@msn.com

Chili

Chili Films
101 Eton Rd
Lindfield NSW 2070
Australia
P: 61 2 9413 8678
F: 61 2 9413 8794
E: info@chilifilms.com.au
www.chilifilms.com.au

Chimpanzee

Chimpanzee Productions
P: 718 643 0342
F: 718 246 0184
E: taharris@ucsd.edu

Christensen

Christensen Productions
230 East 44th St, Apt 14D
New York NY 10017
USA
P: 1 212 983 1142
F: 1 212 692 9116

Cineclick

Cineclick Asia
Incline Bldg, 3F, 891-37 Daechi-dong
Gangnam-gu
Seoul 135-280
South Korea
P: 82 2 538 0211
F: 82 2 538 0479
E: yjsuh@cineclickasia.com
www.cineclick.co.kr

Cinecom

Cinecom Pictures
850 3rd Ave
New York NY 10022
USA
P: 1 212 319 5000

CineL'Mod

Cine L'Mod Inc
802 Lexington Ave
4th Floor
New York NY 10021
USA
P: 1 212 751 6483
F: 1 212 751 6974
E: giafilm@hotmail.com

CinemaEsperance

Cinema Esperance International
96 Spadina Ave, #301
Toronto Ontario M5V 2J6
Canada
P: 1 416 865 1225
F: 1 416 865 9223

CinemaGuild

Cinema Guild
130 Madison Ave
2nd Floor
New York NY 10016-7038
USA
P: 1 212 685 6242
F: 1 212 685 4717
E: info@cinemaguild.com
www.cinemaguild.com

CinemaLibre

Cinema Libre, Distribution
460 Ste-Catherine O
Suite 500
Montréal Québec H3B 1A7
Canada
P: 1 514 861 9030
F: 1 514 861 3634
E: reception@cinemalibre.com
www.cinemalibre.com

CinemaService

Cinema Service Co Ltd
5th Floor, Heung-Kuk Bldg
43-1 Jooja-Dong, Joong-Gu
Seoul 100-240
South Korea
P: 82 2 2264 4667
F: 82 2 2264 2180
E: josh@cinemaservice.com
www.cinemaservice.com

Cinemax
see HBO

Cinenova
Cinenova
113 Roman Rd
London E2 0HU
United Kingdom
P: 44 208 981 6828
F: 44 208 983 4441
E: info@cinenova.org.uk
www.cinenova.org

Cinepix
Cinepix Inc.
8275 Mayrand
Montréal Québec H4P 2C8
Canada
P: 1 514 342 2340
F: 1 514 342 1922
E: info@cinepix.com
www.cinepix.com

Cinevista
Cinevista
353 West 39th St
New York NY 10018
USA
P: 1 212 947 4373

Cinexport
Cinexport
78 avenue des Champs-Elysées
Paris 75008
France
P: 33 1 4562 4945
F: 33 1 4563 8526
E: cinexport@wanadoo.fr

Clarence
Clarence Pictures
13 Merrion Square
Dublin 2
Ireland
P: 353 1 661 4022
F: 353 1 661 4186
E: info@clarencepix.ie
www.clarencepix.com

CoffeeDate
Coffee Date Productions
842 S. Sycamore Ave
Los Angeles CA 90036
USA
P: 1 323 938 7804
F: 1 323 938 7619
E: stewartnla@aol.com

Col-Tri
Columbia TriStar International
10202 W. Washington Blvd
Culver City CA 90232-3195
USA
P: 1 310 244 4000
F: 1 310 244 1875
www.columbiatristar.net

Col-Tri
Columbia TriStar Film Distributors
10202 W. Washington Blvd
Culver City CA 90232-3195
USA
P: 1 310 244 4000
F: 1 310 244 1875

CollinsR
Rhonda Collins
879 58th St
Oakland CA 94608
USA
P: 1 510 594 2546
E: sonrevolution@excite.com

Columbia
Columbia Pictures Corporation
see Sony Pictures Entertainment
www.sonypictures.com

Constantin
Constantin Film AG
Kaiserstrasse 39
Munich 80801
Germany
P: 49 89 38 6090
F: 49 89 38 60942
E: frauke.allstadt@constantin-film.de
www.constantin-film.com (English site)

Convergence
Convergence Productions
21 Kingscote Rd
London W4 5L1
United Kingdom
F: 44 181 994 9467

CottonLover
Cotton Lover Films
1440 West Jarvis Ave
Chicago IL 60626
USA
P: 1 773 764 6648
F: 1 773 764 6170
E: crouch@sistercinema.com
www.catherinecrouch.com

Could-Be-Worse
Could Be Worse
63 Jay St
Cambridge MA 02139
USA
P: 1 617 876 9141, 1 860 535 1677
F: 1 617 876 4358
E: zack@midburb.com
www.couldbeworsethemovie.com

Cowboy
Cowboy Pictures
13 Laight St, 6th Floor
New York NY 10010
USA
P: 1 212 925 7800
F: 1 212 965 5655
E: info@cowboypictures.com
www.cowboypictures.com

Crepeau
Jeanne Crepeau
P: 1 514 288 2899
F: 1 514 288 7192
E: j.crepeau@onf.ca

Crossing-the-Line
Crossing the Line Films
Sommerville House
Church Rd
Greystones County Wicklow
United Kingdom
P: 353 1 287 2622
F: 353 1 287 2622
E: johnmurr@indigo.ie

Daddy&Papa

Daddy and Papa
PO Box 3486
Berkeley CA 94703
USA
P: 1 510 653 8763
F: 1 510 653 8783
E: info@daddyandpapa.com
www.daddyandpapa.com

Daiei

Daiei Motion Picture Co
1-1-16 Higashi-Shimbashi, Minato-ku
Tokyo 105-0021
Japan
P: 81 3 3573 8700
F: 81 3 3573 8145

Daly/Harris

Daly/Harris Productions,
Paramount Pictures
5555 Melrose Ave
Marx Bros Bldg, #208
Hollywood CA 90038
USA
P: 1 323 956 8930
F: 1 323 862 1067
E: rothstar@aol.com

DameWork

Dame Work Inc.
192 1st Ave, #1
New York NY 10009
USA
P: 1 212 654 8357
F: 1 212 505 7485
E: damework@rcn.com
www.damework.com

DanishFilm

Danish Film Institute
Feature Film Dept
Vognmagegade 10, 2
Copenhagen K DK-1120
Denmark
P: 45 3374 3400
F: 45 3374 3401

DeepFocus

DeepFocus Productions
PO Box 39548
Los Angeles CA 90039-0548
USA
P: 1 323 662 6575
F: 1 323 662 6577
E: info@deepfocusproductions.com
www.deepfocusproductions.com

Dendy

Dendy Films
19 Martin Pl
Sydney   NSW 2000
Australia
P: 61 2 9233 8558
F: 61 2 9232 3841
E: dendy@dendy.com.au
www.dendy.com.au

DesiFilms

Desi Films
1048 Manzanita St
Los Angeles CA 90029
USA
P: 1 213 666 4911
F: 1 213 935 1393

Deva

Deva Films, SL
Madrid Spain
P: 34 1 361 2161
F: 34 1 361 0028
E: pedrocosta@nexo.es

DevilBunny

Devil Bunny in Bondage
3356A 16th St
San Francisco CA 94114
USA
P: 1 415 355 0922
E: ungoy76@hotmail.com

DevilsAdvocate

Devil's Advocate
Flat 83, 25 Gresse St
London W1P 1PD
United Kingdom
P: 44 171 580 6796
F: 44 171 580 6796
E: MichaelHuls@compuserve.com

Devine

Devine Productions
256 Keen St
Lismore NSW 2480
Australia
P: 61 2 6622 7270
E: christine@nrg.com.au

DirectCinema

Direct Cinema Ltd
PO Box 69799
Los Angeles CA 900069
USA
P: 1 800 525 0000
F: 1 310 396 3233
E: directcinema@attmail.com

Discodali

Discodali Productions
437 North Stanley Ave
Los Angeles CA 90036
USA
P: 1 213 508 4477
F: 1 323 653 8649
E: discodaliprods@hotmail.com

District

District Pictures
149 Sullivan St, #5E
New York NY 10012
USA
P: 1 212 777 1148
F: 1 212 777 1474

Diversity

Diversity Productions
1202 East Pike St, Suite 885
Seattle WA 98122
USA
P: 1 206 722 9079

DMC

Dept of Mass Communications
2490 S. Gaylord St
University of Denver
Denver CO 80208
USA
P: 1 303 377 0309
F: 1 303 871 4949
E: rbuxton@qwest.net, rbuxton@du.edu

Dominant7

Dominant 7 Productions
19 rue Martel
Paris 75010
France
P: 33 1 4824 1960
F: 33 1 4824 1947
E: dominant7@free.fr

DominantPredator

Dominant Predator Productions
206 Rivington St, #4D
New York NY 10002
USA
P: 1 212 614 9491
E: aaronkrach@att.net

Domino

Domino Film & TV International
4002 Grey Ave
Montréal Québec PQ H4A 3P1
Canada
P: 1 514 484 0446
F: 1 514 484 0468
E: domino@dominofilm.ca
www.@dominofilm.ca

DoRo

DoRo Wien Film und
   Fernsehproduktion GmbH
Winckelmannstrasse 8
Wien A-1150
Austria
P: 43 1892 4444
F: 43 1892 4445
E: doro@wien.doro.net
www.doro.net

DosEspiritus

Dos Espiritus, S.C.
183A Lexington St
San Francisco CA 94110
USA
P: 1 415 778 4050
E: mcallitzin@aol.com

Drift

Drift Distribution
611 Broadway, #742
New York NY 10012
USA
P: 1 212 254 4118
F: 1 212 254 3154

Dubois

Cleo Dubois Academy of SM Arts
PO Box 2345
Menlo Park CA 94026
USA
P: 1 650 322 0124
F: 1 650 326 2639
E: cleo@cleodubois.com
www.cleodubois.com

e2Filmworks

e2 Filmworks
1635 North Cahuenga Blvd
5th Floor
Los Angeles CA 90028
USA
P: 1 323 860 1550
F: 1 323 860 1554

EAI

Electronic Arts Intermix
535 W. 22nd St, 5th Floor
New York NY 10011
USA
P: 1 212 337 0680
F: 1 212 337 0679
E: info@eai.org
www.eai.org

Eccentric

Eccentric Orbit Films
1633 North Damien St, 2nd Floor
Chicago IL 60647
USA
P: 1 773 227 6328
F: 1 312 440 0799
E: meatdog3@aol.com

Egocentric

Egocentric Productions
738 East 6th St, #2B
New York NY 10009
USA
P: 1 212 529 0935

EMA

Educational Media Australia
214 Park St
South Melbourne Vic 3205
Australia
P: 61 3 9699 7144
F: 61 3 9699 4947
E: info@ema.com.au
www.ema.com.au/tertiary

Empire

Empire Pictures
350 5th Ave, Suite 7801
New York NY 10118
USA
P: 1 212 629 3535
E: info@empirepicturesusa.com
www.empirepicturesusa.com

Englewood

Englewood Entertainment
10917 Winner Rd
Independence MO 64052
USA
P: 1 888 573 5490
www.englewd.com

Equator

Equator Films
6 Heddon St
London W1B 4BT
United Kingdom
P: 44 20 7025 7400
F: 44 20 7025 7401
E: steve.turney@equatorfilms.co.uk
www.equatorfilms.co.uk

EroSpirit

EroSpirit Institute
PO Box 3893
Oakland CA 94609
USA
P: 1 510 281 1555
F: 1 510 652 4354
E: kramer@erospirit.org
www.erospirit.org

Eureka

Eureka Street Pictures
285 Eureka St
San Francisco CA 94114
USA
P: 1 415 626 7867
F: 1 415 645 4000
E: jamesarnold@yahoo.com

Everett

Karen Everett
1603 McGee Ave
Berkeley CA 94703
USA
P: 1 415 641 5614
F: 1 415 641 7841
E: karen@kareneverett.org
www.kareneverett.org

Explore

Explore International
33 Ovington Square
London SW3 ILJ
United Kingdom
P: 44 20 7581 7100
F: 44 20 7581 7200
E: info@explore-intl.com
www.explore-intl.com

Exportfilm

Exportfilm Bischoff & Co.
Isabellastrasse 20
Munich D-80798
Germany
P: 49 89 272 9360
F: 49 89 2729 3636

Eyebite

EyeBite Productions
68 Eureka St
San Francisco CA 94114
USA
P: 1 415 551 1723
F: 1 415 551 1723
E: info@eyebite.com
www.eyebite.com

Fabulous

Fabulous Pictures
18 Dupont St
Toronto Ontario M5R 1V2
Canada
P: 1 416 323 3860
F: 1 416 964 1980
home.inforamp.net/~bglawson/
    fabpics.htm

Facets

Facets Multimedia Inc
1517 W. Fullerton Ave
Chicago IL 60614
USA
P: 1 773 281 9075
F: 1 773 929 5437
E: sales@facets.org
www.facets.org

FalconLair

Falcon Lair Films LLC
P: 323 850 2757
F: 323 850 2787
E: houston_king@hotmail.com

FallingDoor

Falling Door Films
224 East 11th St, #3
New York NY 10003
USA
P: 1 212 539 1040
F: 1 212 995 4063
E: gs226@.nyu.edu

Fanlight

Fanlight Productions
4196 Washington St, Suite 2
Boston MA 02131
USA
P: 1 617 469 4999
F: 1 617 469 3379
E: fanlight@fanlight.com
www.fanlight.com

Farallon

Farallon Films
1442A Walnut St, #50
Berkeley CA 94709
USA
P: 1 415 495 3934
F: 1 415 777 5633
E: info@farfilm.com
www.farfilm.com

FDFilms

F D Films LLC
P: 1 415 350 6870
F: 1 415 920 9061

FearlessPictures

Fearless Pictures
11225 Morrison St, #308
North Hollywood CA 91601
USA
P: 1 818 752 8115
F: 1 818 752 8115
E: fearpics1@aol.com

FearlessProd

Fearless Productions
PO Box 8928
Atlanta GA 30306-9998
USA
P: 1 404 897 5218
F: 1 404 897 5565

FeminaleEV

Feminale E. V.
Maybachstr 111
Cologne 50670
Germany
P: 49 221 130 0225
F: 49 221 130 0281
E: info@feminale.de
www.feminale.de

Fever

Fever Films
23 East 10th St, #PHG
New York NY 10003
USA
P: 1 212 539 1023
F: 1 212 475 1399
E: skj@echonyc.com

Fidelite

Fidelite Productions
13 rue Etienne Marcel
Paris 75001
France
P: 33 1 5534 9808
F: 33 1 5534 9810

FifthEstate

Fifth Estate Productions
1007 Montana Ave, #610
Santa Monica CA 90403
USA
P: 1 310 289 3900
F: 1 310 289 3909
E: amy@pissantprod.com
www.thejaundicedeye.com

FillingTheGap

Filling The Gap Productions
111 West Main St
Mesa AZ 85201
USA
P: 1 800 800 6665
F: 1 602 649 9846
E: fillingthegap@msn.com

FilmakersLibrary

Filmakers Library
124 East 40th St
New York NY 10016
USA
P: 1 212 808 4980
F: 1 212 808 4983
E: info@filmakers.com
www.filmakers.com

FilmAust

Film Australia
101 Eton Rd
Lindfield NSW 2070
Australia
P: 61 2 9413 8634
F: 61 2 9416 9401
E: sales@filmaust.com.au
www.filmaust.com.au

FilmFour

Film Four International
76-78 Charlotte St
London W1P 1LX
United Kingdom
P: 44 171 868 7700
F: 44 171 868 7766

FilmIngk

Film Ingk
1648 NE 86th St
Seattle WA 98115
USA
P: 1 206 985 8012
E: scottingk@hotmail.com

FilmmakersCoop

Filmmakers' Cooperative
175 Lexington Ave
New York NY 10003
USA
P: 1 212 889 3820
F: 1 212 889 3821
E: film6000@aol.com

FilmsInc

Films Incorporated
5547 N. Ravenswood Ave
Chicago IL 60640
USA
P: 1 312 878 2600

FilmsTransit

Films Transit International
402 East Notre-Dame, # 100
Montréal Québec H2Y 1C8
Canada
P: 1 514 844 3358
F: 1 514 844 7298
E: info@filmstransit.com
www.filmstransit.com

FineLine

Fine Line Features
888 Seventh Ave, 20th Floor
New York NY 10106
USA
P: 1 212 649 4800
F: 1 212 956 1942
E: fineline.features@newline.com
www.finelinefeatures.com

FirstFloor

First Floor Features
Czaar Peterstraat 213
Amsterdam 1018 PL
The Netherlands
P: 31 20 330 2222
F: 31 20 622 7282
E: melinda@firstfloorfeatures.com
www.firstfloorfeatures.com

FirstLook

First Look Media/Overseas Filmgroup
8800 Sunset Blvd
Los Angeles CA 90069
USA
P: 1 310 855 1199
F: 1 310 855 0152
E: info@firstlookmedia.com
www.firstlookmedia.com

FirstRelease

Distributed by Col-Tri
Level 30, 1 Market St
Sydney NSW 2000
Australia
P: 61 2 9911 3300
F: 61 2 9911 3333

FirstRun/Icarus

First Run/Icarus Films
32 Court St, 21st Floor
Brooklyn NY 11201
USA
P: 1 718 488 8900
F: 1 718 488 8642
E: mail@frif.com
www.frif.com

FirstRunFeatures

First Run Features
153 Waverly Pl
New York NY 10014
USA
P: 1 800 229 8575
F: 1 212 989 7649
E: info@firstrunfeatures.com
www.firstrunfeatures.com

FirstTime

First Time Films
3305 SE 12th St
Lower Portland OR 97202
USA
P: 1 503 221 1156
F: 1 503 294 0874
E: sarahmarcus@chickmail.com

Flickerfest

Flickerfest Short Film Bureau
PO Box 7416
Bondi Beach NSW 2026
Australia
P: 61 2 9365 6877
F: 61 2 9365 6899
E: flickerfest@bigpond.com.au
www.flickerfest.com.au

FloridaUni

Florida State University
    School of Motion Picture
A3100 University Centre
Tallahassee FL 32306
USA
P: 1 850 645 4840
F: 1 850 644 2626
E: ksb2063@garnet.acns.fsu.edu

Forefront

Forefront Films
401 Broadway
Suite 1012
New York NY 10013
USA
P: 1 917 653 8643
E: forefront.films@verizon.net
www.forefrontfilms.com

Fortissimo

Fortissimo Film Sales (Netherlands)
Cruquiusweg 40
Amsterdam 1019 AT
The Netherlands
P: 31 20 627 3215
F: 31 20 626 1155
E: info@fortissimo.nl
www.fortissimo.nl

Fortissimo

Fortissimo Film Sales (Hong Kong)
14/F, 10 Knutsford Terrace, TST
Kowloon Hong Kong
P: 852 2311 8081
F: 852 2311 8023

Fountain

Fountain Films Co
3F-1, #26, Sec.3, Jen-Ai Rd
Taipei Taiwan
P: 886 2 708 5501
F: 886 2 703 8728

Fox

Now trading as 20th Century Fox

FoxSearchlight

Fox Searchlight Pictures
USA
P: 1 310 369 5584
www.foxsearchlight.com

FPI

Flach Pyramide International
5 rue du Chevalier de Saint George
Paris 75008
France
P: 33 1 4296 0220
F: 33 1 4020 0551
E: pricher@flach-pyramide.com
www.flach-pyramide.com

Frameline

Frameline Distribution
145 Ninth St, Suite 300
San Francisco CA 94103
USA
P: 1 415 703 8650
F: 1 415 861 1404
E: distribution@frameline.org
www.frameline.org/distribution

FruitFilms

Fruit Films LLC
USA
P: 1 323 656 7415
F: 1 323 656 7215
E: clint@rewindservices.com
www.rewindservices.com

Gallant

Gallant Entertainment
15540 Valley Vista Blvd
Encino CA 91436
USA
P: 1 818 905 9848
F: 1 818 906 9965
E: gallantent@aol.com

Gassman

Allan Gassman
PO Box 29879
Los Angeles CA 90029
USA
P: 1 323 953 4742
F: 1 323 953 4742
E: gassman@aol.com

GBF

GBF Productions
6312 Hollywood Blvd, #23
Hollywood CA 90028
USA
P: 1 323 769 4344
F: 1 213 381 1305
E: GBF@pacbell.net

Gemini

Gemini Films
34 boul Sébastopol
Paris 75004
France
P: 33 1 4454 1717
F: 33 1 4454 1725
E: gemini@easynet.fr

GFC

Greek Film Centre
10, Panepistimiou Ave, 106
Athens Greece
P: 30 1 3631 733, 30 1 3634 586
F: 30 1 3614 336
E: pcoutras@otenet.gr

Gidalya

Gidalya Pictures
49 Bleecker St, 4th Floor
New York NY 10012
USA
P: 1 212 358 9620
F: 1 212 358 9426
E: gidalya@aol.com

GilProd

Gil Productions
8 Hata'asiya St
Tel Aviv 67139
Israel
P: 972 3 562 5111
F: 972 3 562 2113
E: gilprod@actcom.co.il

Gimlet

Gimlet Productions
21 Knowsley Rd
Battersea
London SW11 5BN
United Kingdom
P: 44 171 350 2878
F: 44 171 350 2878

Globe

Globe Film Co.
Level 1, 11 Waltham St
Artarmon NSW 2064
Australia
P: 61 2 9437 0613
F: 61 2 9439 7560
E: andrew@globefilm.com.au
www.globefilm.com.au

Gloria

Gloria Films
65, rue Montmartre
Paris 75002
France
P: 33 1 4221 4211
F: 33 1 4221 4331
E: mel@gloriafilms.fr

GNCTV

Grupo Novo de Cinema e TV
Rua Capitao Salomao 42
Botafogo
Rio de Janeiro - RJ 22271-040
Brasil
P: 21 2539 1538
F: 21 2266 3637
E: jvargas@gnctv.com.br

GoinBack

Goin' Back Productions
390 1/2 De Longpre Ave
Los Angeles CA 90027
USA
P: 1 323 953 8520
F: 1 801 640 3026
E: crushfilm@aol.com

GoldenHarvest

Golden Harvest Entertainment
16/F The Peninsula Office Tower
18 Middle Rd
Tsim Sha Tsui Kowloon Hong Kong
P: 852 2352 8222
F: 852 2351 1683
E: movies@goldenharvest.com
www.goldenharvest.com/first.html

Goldwyn

Goldwyn Films
10 Stephen Mews
London W1P 1PP
United Kingdom
P: 44 171 333 6466
F: 44 171 306 9029
E: info@mgm.com
www.mgm.com

GoodMachine

Good Machine International
417 Canal St, 4th Floor
New York NY 10013
USA
P: 1 212 343 9230
F: 1 212 343 9645
E: lkistner@goodmachine.com

Goodvibes

Good Vibrations
1688 15th St
San Francisco CA 94103
USA
P: 1 415 974 8985 (ext 237)
F: 1 415 975 2925
www.goodvibes.com

Gosse

Bob Gosse
E: bobgosse@ix.netcom.com

Gray-Lee

Geoff Gray-Lee
PO Box 376
Northcote Vic 3070
Australia

Greycat

Greycat Films
3829 Delaware Lane
Las Vegas NV 89109
USA
P: 1 702 737 5258
www.greycatonline.com

Grisé

Pierre Grisé Distribution
21 avenue du Maine
Paris 75015
France
P: 33 1 4544 2045
F: 33 1 4544 0040
E: pierre-grise-distribution@wanadoo.fr

GroupeIntervention

Groupe Intervention Video
5505 Blvd St Laurent, #3015
Montréal Québec H2T 1S6
Canada
P: 1 514 271 5506
F: 1 514 271 6980
www.givideo.org

Gypsy83

Gypsy 83 LLC
137 Barrow St, #5B
New York NY 10014
USA
P: 1 212 620 7645
F: 1 212 255 2585
E: Gypsy083@aol.com
www. gypsy83.com

Hammer

Barbara Hammer Films
55 Bethune St, #114G
New York NY 10014
USA
P: 1 212 645 9077
F: 1 212 645 9077
E: bjhammer@aol.com
www.barbarahammerfilms.com

Haut-et-Court

Haut et Court
38 rue des Martyrs
Paris 75009
France
P: 33 1 5531 2727
F: 33 1 5531 2728
E: info@hautetcourt.com
www.hautetcourt.com

HBO

Home Box Office
2049 Century Park East
41st Floor
Los Angeles CA 90067-3215
USA
P: 1 310 201 9536
F: 1 310 201 9552
E: reilly_anne@hbo.com
www.hbo.com/films

Heathcliff

Heathcliff Distribution
PO Box 3158
Robina Town Centre Qld 4230
Australia
P: 61 7 5575 9499
F: 61 7 5575 9488
E: info@heathcliff.com.au
www.heathcliff.com.au

HeavyBlow

Heavy Blow Productions
501 Cathedral Parkway, #2B
New York NY 10025
USA
P: 1 917 701 0372
F: 1 425 963 5723
E: heavyblow@yahoo.com

HellsBells

Hells Bells Productions
212 Berry St
Brooklyn NY 11211
USA
P: 1 718 486 5812
E: estherbell@mindspring.com
www.estherbell.com

Hemdale

Hemdale Film Corporation
7966 Beverly Blvd
Los Angeles CA 90048
USA
P: 1 213 966 3750
F: 1 213 653 5452

HeraldAce

Herald Ace/Hippon Herald Films
Tokyo Japan
P: 81 3 3248 1151
F: 81 3 3248 1170

Heure

Heure D'Ete Productions
Chemin De La Cascade
Uzes 30700
France
P: 33 4 6603 6325
F: 33 4 6603 6017
E: summertime@fnac.net

HFF

HFF "Konrad Wolf"
Marlene-Dietrich-Allee 11
Potsdam 14482
Germany
P: 49 331 620 2564
F: 49 331 620 2569
E: distribution@hff-potsdam.de

Himaphiliac

Himaphiliac Productions
PO Box 460697
San Francisco CA 94146
USA
P: 1 415 339 8411
F: 1 415 647 9658
E: himabee@hotmail.com

Hochschule

Hochschule fur Fernsehen und Film
Franuenthalestr 23
Munich 8000 BRD
Germany
P: 49 89 6800 0444
F: 49 89 6800 0436

Hollywood

Hollywood Independents
1335 North La Brea Ave, Suite 2197
Hollywood CA 90028
USA
P: 1 323 876 0975
F: 1 323 876 0975
E: jaa@inetworld.net
www.hollywoodindependents.com

Horwitz

Horwitz Productions
341 West 11th St, #1B
New York NY 10014
USA
P: 1 212 691 8030

Howard

Silas Howard
P: 1 510 594 0778
E: silas898@aol.com

Hung

Kit Hung Productions
D5/15F Lung Kee Bldg
23 Matauwai Rd
Hung Hom Hong Kong
P: 852 9740 9001
F: 852 2353 4398
E: kithung@gmx.net

Iberoamerica

Iberoamerica Films
Velazquez 12, 7th Floor
Madrid 28001
Spain

Idol

Idol Pictures
32 Main Rd
Muizenberg, Cape Town 7949
South Africa
P: 27 21 788 9163
F: 27 21 788 3973
E: idoljack@iafrica.com
idol.co.za

Ihsan

Ihsan Talkies
J.G.2 / 748-B Vikas Puri
New Delhi 110018
India
P: 91 11 561 8748
E: neerajbh@vsnl.net,
    neerajbhasin@ihsan-talkies.com
www.ihsan-talkies.com

IMA

IMA Productions
34 rue de la Pompe
Paris 75016
France
P: 33 1 4072 7244
F: 33 1 4072 7244

ImageForum

Image Forum
Fudosan, Kaikan Bldg
1, 6F 3-5, Yotsuya, Shinjuku-ku
Tokyo Japan
P: 81 3 5766 0116
F: 81 3 5466 0054
E: info@imageforum.co.jp
www.imageforum.co.jp

IMCINE

IMCINE Mexican Film Institute
Tepic 40
DF 06760
Mexico
P: 52 5574 4902
F: 52 5574 0712
E: promint@imcine.gob.mx
www.imcine.gob.mx

IMM

IMM Productions
15/12 York St
St Kilda West Vic 3182
Australia
P: 61 3 9534 8680
F: 61 3 9534 8680
E: iainmurton@yahoo.com

IN*SITE

IN*SITE
273 East 10th St, #9
New York NY 10009
USA
P: 1 212 604 4466
F: 1 212 673 1467
E: insitement@earthlink.net

In-The-Life

In the Life Media Inc
Attn: Video Sales
30 West 26th St, 7th Floor
New York NY 10010
USA
P: 1 212 255 6012 (ext 305)
E: mpeyton@inthelifetv.org
www.inthelifetv.org

Incident

Incident
Sint Annadreef 26 - 1020
Brussels Belgium
P: 32 2 4789 888
E: amarona@skynet.be

Indican

Indican Pictures
8205 Santa Monica Blvd, #200
Los Angeles CA 90046
USA
P: 1 323 650 0832
F: 1 323 650 6832
E: admin@indicanpitures.com
www.indicanpitures.com

Infected

Infected Films, Jennifer Gentile
PO Box 2004
Hollywood CA 90078
USA
P: 1 323 461 7910
E: jentile@earthlink.net

Insomnio

Insomnio Films
249 Eldridge St, #16
New York NY 10002
USA
P: 1 212 475 2736
E: delvalleo@hotmail.com

Intercinema

Intercinema Agency
15 Druzhinnikovskaya Str
Moscow 123242
Russia
P: 7 095 255 9082
F: 7 095 255 9052
E: intercin@edunet.ru
www.intercinema.ru

Intra

Intra Films
Via E. Manfredi, 15
Rome 00197
Italy
P: 39 06 807 7252
F: 39 06 807 6156
E: intraf@tin.it

IslandGirl

Island Girl Productions
4250 Wilshire Blvd
Los Angeles CA 90010
USA
P: 1 323 936 8951
F: 1 323 936 8951
E: island4475@aol.com

JourDeFete

Jour de Fête Films
5955 West 6th St
Los Angeles CA 90036
USA
P: 1 323 933 2733
F: 1 323 933 3929
E: dan@jourdefete.com,
    rialtojf@pacbell.net
www.jourdefete.com

KalisVibe

Kali's Vibe Pictures
P: 1 212 281 5926
F: 1 212 281 1774
E: kali2vibe@aol.com

Kanpaï

Kanpaï Distribution
102 rue du Fbg Poissoniere
Paris 75010
France
P: 33 1 5325 0208
F: 33 1 5325 0205
E: kanpaidistri@wanadoo.fr
kanpai.free.fr/distribution

KGB

KGB Films
607 Dunsmuir, #302
Los Angeles CA 90036
USA
P: 1 323 936 3072
E: KGBFILMS@aol.com

KillerPix

Killer Pix
1048 Manzanita St
Silver Lake CA 90029
USA
P: 1 213 666 4911
F: 1 213 935 1393

KingPix

King Pictures
815 North Occidental Blvd
Los Angeles CA 90026-2925
USA
P: 1 213 484 4443
F: 1 213 484 4482
E: worker@kingpix.com
www.kingpix.com

Kino

Kino International
333 West 39th St
Suite 503
New York NY 10018
USA
P: 1 212 629 6880
F: 1 212 714 0871
E: contact@kino.com
www.kino.com

Kinofist

Kinofist Imageworks
PO Box 1102
Columbia MO 65202-1102
USA
P: 1 573 875 7151

Kismet

Kismet Talkies
USA
P: 1 212 420 7000
F: 1 212 358 1870
E: kismet@vortexweb.net

Kitchen

The Kitchen
512 West 19th St
New York NY 10011
USA
P: 1 212 255 5793
F: 1 212 645 4258
E: info@thekitchen.org
www.thekitchen.org

KMPPC

Korean Film Commission
CPO Box 2978
Myungong Post Office
Seoul 100-629
South Korea
P: 82 17 210 7882
E: darcy@koreanfilm.org
www.koreanfilm.org

Kushner-Locke

Kushner-Locke International
11601 Wilshire Blvd
Suite 2030
Los Angeles CA 90025
USA
P: 1 310 481 2000
F: 1 310 481 2101
www.kushner-locke.com

Kwan

Kwan's Creation Workshop
No 15, 1/F Lion Rock Rd
Kowloon City Hong Kong
P: 852 2383 0267
F: 852 2794 3709

L'Altra

L'Altra Comunicazione
Piazza san Carlo, 161
Torino 10123
Italy
P: 39 011 534 888
F: 39 011 521 796

Laika

Laika Films
Zuidstraat 147, #8
Brussels 1000
Belgium
P: 32 2 502 6637
F: 32 486 46 3770
E: laika@skynet.be

Lauren

Lauren Film
E: info@laurenfilm.es
www.laurenfilm.es

LaVieEstBelle

La vie est belle Films Associes
7 rue Ganneron
Paris France
P: 33 1 4387 0042
F: 33 1 4387 3472
E: lveb@club-internet.fr

LeeC

Christopher Lee
PO Box 14354
San Francisco CA 94114
USA
P: 1 415 820 3225
E: trannyfest@aol.com

Lehmann-Moore

Lehmann-Moore Productions Inc
3301 Garfield Ave S, #3
Minneapolis MN 55408-3643
USA
P: 1 612 822 1240
F: 1 612 822 1248
E: homohts@aol.com

Leonor

Leonor Films
93 avenue Niel
Paris 75017
France
P: 33 1 4763 0033
F: 33 1 4763 0032

LesGrands

Les Grands Films Classiques
E: grands.films.classiques@wanadoo.fr

Letsou

Viví Letsou
E: info@skeletonwoman.com
www.skeletonwoman.com

Liberty

Liberty Home Video/VCI Entertainment
11333 East 60th Place
Tulsa OK 74146
USA
P: 1 918 254 6337
F: 1 918 254 6117
E: vci@vcientertainment.com
www.vcihomevideo.com

LIFS

London International Film School
24 Shelton St
London WC2H 9UB
United Kingdom
P: 44 20 7836 9642
F: 44 20 7497 3718
E: film.school@lfs.org.uk
www.lifs.org.uk

Lilliput

Lilliput Pictures
573 6th St, #1
Brooklyn NY 11215
USA
P: 1 718 369 0601, 1 212 414 7654
F: 1 718 369 0601
E: EWelthorpe@aol.com

LionsGate

Lion's Gate Films
4553 Glencoe Ave, Suite 200
Marina Del Rey CA 90292
USA
P: 1 310 314 2000
F: 1 310 392 0252
E: feedback@lgecorp.com
www.lionsgatefilms.com

LittleBelly

Little Belly Productions
1726 West Division St, #3
Chicago IL 60622
USA
P: 1 773 252 8517
E: reverie555@aol.com

LittleMore

Little More Company
Japan
P: 81 3 3401 1042
F: 81 3 3401 1052
E: info@littlemore.co.jp
www.littlemore.co.jp

Lola

Lolafilms, Laura Plotkin
4131 Shafter Ave, #12
Oakland CA 94609
USA
P: 1 510 450 0571
F: 1 510 450 0571
E: Lola3@earthlink.net
www.lolafilms.net

LolaFilms

Lola Films International, Spain
Velasquez 12, 7th Floor
Madrid 28001
Spain
P: 34 1 431 4246
F: 34 1 435 5994

Lot47

Lot 47 Films
22 West 19th St, 8th Floor
New York NY 10011
USA
P: 1 212 691 4747
F: 1 212 691 7477
E: questions@lot47.com
www.lot47.com

Luster

Luster Films
P: 1 503 449 4125
F: 1 503 289 9034
E: inquiries@lusterfilm.com
www.lusterfilm.com

M6

M6 Droits Audio Visuals
89 avenue Charles de Gaulle
Neuilly-sur-Seine
Cedex 92575
France
P: 33 1 4192 6866
F: 33 1 4192 6869
E: lmarty@m6.fr
www.m6da.com

MagyarFilmunio

Magyar Filmunio
V rosligeti fasor 38
Budapest 1068
Hungary
P: 36 1 351 7760
F: 36 1 352 6734
E: filmunio@filmunio.hu

Majnounak

Majnounak Films
PO Box 13-6676
Chouran 1102 2140
Lebanon
P: 961 1 336 820
F: 961 1 336 820
E: bpanther@cyberia.net.lb

Manga

Manga Entertainment
www.manga.com

Manmade

Manmade Multimedia
887 West 9th St
San Pedro CA 90731
USA
P: 1 310 833 2020
F: 1 310 833 2345
E: manmade@
    manmademultimedia.com
www.manmademultimedia.com

Marcom

Marcom Projects
PO Box 4215
Loganholme Qld 4129
Australia
P: 61 7 3801 5600
F: 61 7 3801 5600
E: marcom@marcom.com.au
www.marcom.com.au

Margin

Margin Films
8306 Wilshire Blvd
PMB 225
Los Angeles CA 90211
USA
P: 1 213 382 8022
F: 1 213 382 5589
E: mail@marginfilms.com

Maximum-Vacuum

Maximum Vacuum
270 Jay St, #16E
Brooklyn NY 11201
USA
P: 1 718 624 1222
F: 1 718 624 1222
E: mselditch@aol.com

MayaVision

MayaVision International
Ist Floor
43 New Oxford St
London WC1A 1BH
United Kingdom
P: 44 20 7836 1113
F: 44 20 7836 5169
E: info@mayavisionint.com
www.mayavisionint.com

MBC

MBC- Filmproduktion,
Michael Brynntrup
Hermannstr 64
Berlin 12049
Germany
P: 49 30 621 7800
F: 49 30 621 7800
E: brynntrup@mbcc.de
www.brynntrup.de

MCrown

MCrown Productions
31-22, 31st St, Apt 2
LIC NY 11106
USA
P: 1 646 391 6427
E: mcrown212@aol.com

MediaEdFound

Media Education Foundation
26 Center St
Northampton MA 01060
USA
P: 1 800 897 0089
F: 1 800 659 6882
E: info@mediaed.org
www.mediaed.org

MediaLuna

Media Luna Entertainment GmbH
Hochstadenstrasse 1-3
Cologne D-50674
Germany
P: 49 221 139 2222
F: 49 221 139 2224
E: info@medialuna-entertainment.de
www.medialuna-entertainment.de

Mediatique

Mediatique Inc
11 rue Ontario
Toronto Ontario M5A 4L7
Canada
P: 1 416 367 8464
F: 1 416 367 8466
E: mediatique@on.aibn.com

Mefistofilm

Mefistofilm
Gyldenloves Gate 41-N-0260
Oslo Norway
P: 47 2243 8260
F: 47 2255 7777
E: mefisto2@online.no

MeiAh

Mei Ah Entertainment
E: meiah@meiah.com
www.meiah.com

Merrison

Lindsey Merrison Film
Ebereschenallee 15
Berlin D-14050
Germany
P: 49 30 3061 4448
F: 49 30 3061 4447
E: merrison@aol.com
www.merrison.de

MF-Films

MF Films
23 Curran St
Herne Bay, Auckland
New Zealand
P: 64 9 376 0876
F: 64 9 376 9675
E: linda@mffilms.co.nz

MGM

Metro-Goldwyn-Mayer
www.mgmhomevideo.com

Mid-Bar

Mid-Bar Films
175 5th Ave, #2582
New York NY 10010
USA
P: 1 212 889 1704

Miller/Hildebrand

Miller/Hildebrand Films
8233 W. 4th St
Los Angeles CA 90048-4401
USA
P: 1 323 852 1269
F: 1 323 852 1269
E: divacourt@hotmail.com

Millivres

Millivres Multimedia
116-134 Bayham St
London NW1 0BA
United Kingdom
P: 44 171 482 2576
F: 44 171 284 0329
E: info@millivres.co.uk
www.millivres.co.uk/mmm/

Minotaur

Minotaur International
160 Great Portland St
London W1W 5QA
United Kingdom
P: 44 20 7299 5712
F: 44 20 7299 5777
E: general@minotaur.co.uk
www.minotaur.co.uk

MiraFilm

Mira Filmproduktion GmbH
Wielandstrasse 27
Bremen 28203
Germany
P: 49 421 70 7071
F: 49 421 70 7076

Miramax

Miramax Films
99 Hudson St
New York NY 10013
USA
P: 1 212 219 4100
F: 1 212 941 3836
www.miramax.com

Mirovision

Mirovision Inc
1-151 Shinmunro 2Ga
Chongro Gu
Seoul 110-062
South Korea
P: 82 2 737 1185
F: 82 2 737 1184
E: kyunghee@mirovision.com
www.mirovision.com

MixBrasil

Festival Mix Brasil
www.mixbrasil.com.br

MK2Diffusion

Marin Karmitz Diffusion
France
E: florence.stern@mk2.com
www.mk2.com

MollyBeGood

Molly Be Good
950 N. Kings Rd, #157
West Hollywood CA 90069
USA
P: 1 323 656 7105
E: dpbridge@aol.com

MOMA

Museum of Modern Art
Film Library
11 West 53rd St
New York NY 10019
USA
P: 1 212 708 9433
www.moma.org

Moneypenny

Moneypenny Films
Linienstr. 160
Berlin D-10115
Germany
P: 49 30 2838 4077
F: 49 30 2859 930

Mongrel

Mongrel Media
109 Melville Ave
Toronto Ontario M6G 1Y3
Canada
P: 1 416 516 9775
F: 1 416 516 0651
E: info@mongrelmedia.com
www.mongrelmedia.com

Monobrow

Monobrow Productions
30 Gordon Square
Marrickville NSW 2204
Australia
P: 61 2 9517 2529, 61 2 9569 2609
F: 61 2 9362 3558
E: yasmineclement@hotmail.com

Mosvold

Frank Mosvold
8745 Delgany Ave, Apt 104
Playa Del Ray CA 90293
USA
P: 1 310 822 0130
F: 1 310 822 0130

Moxie

Moxie Firecracker Films
180 Varick St, # 1207
New York NY 10014
USA
P: 1 212 620 7727
F: 1 212 620 0383
E: info@moxiefirecracker.com
www.moxiefirecracker.com

Multimedia

Multimedia
Sieker Lanstr. 39A
Hamburg 22143
Germany
P: 49 40 6757 4231
F: 49 40 6757 4171

MyAss

My Ass Productions
856 Erie, #A
Oakland CA 94610
USA
P: 1 510 625 8473
E: lzbash@aol.com

NBC

National Broadcasting Company
USA
www.nbc.com

Need

Need Productions
109 rue du Fort
Brussels B-1060
Belgium
P: 32 2 534 4057
F: 32 2 534 7574
E: need-prod@skynet.be
www.needproductions.com

Neofilm

Neofilm, Roger Deutsch
P: 39 06 687 2723
F: 39 06 868 5058
E: rld@attglobal.net

Nepantla

Nepantla Films
644 Dehart Rd
Kelowna British Columbia V1W 1C6
Canada
P: 1 416 486 5501
F: 1 416 486 3657
E: jorgemanzano@nepantla.co.ca
www.nepantla.com

Neter

Sydney Neter Distribution
PO Box 94385
Amsterdam 1090 GL
The Netherlands
P: 31 20 404 0707
F: 31 20 404 0708
E: sydneter@worldonline.nl

Netherlands

Netherlands Ministry of Culture
PO Box 25000
The Netherlands
P: 31 79 323 2323
F: 31 79 323 2320
E: info@minocw.nl
www.minocw.nl

NewDay

New Day Films
22-D Hollywood Ave
Hohokus NJ 07423
USA
P: 1 201 652 6590
F: 1 201 652 1973
E: curator@newday.com
www.newday.com

NewLine

New Line Home Video or Cinema
www.newline.com

NewTown

New Town Films
12/37 Nicholson St
East Balmain NSW 2041
Australia
P: 61 2 9810 9825
E: newtownfilms@ozemail.com.au

NewVague

New Vague Films
205 Mulberry St, Basement
New York NY 10012
USA
P: 1 212 274 0046
F: 1 212 274 0046
E: jk237@nyu.edu

NewVision

NewVision Film Distributors
PO Box 159
Port Melbourne Vic 3207
Australia
P: 61 3 9646 5555
F: 61 3 9646 2411
E: fwaters@newvision.com.au
www.newvision.com.au

NewVoices

New Voices Productions
11824 Oxnard St
North Hollywood CA 91606
USA
E: NewVoicesLA@aol.com
www.whenboysfly.com

NewYorker

New Yorker Films
85 Fifth Ave, 11th Floor
New York NY 10003
USA
P: 1 212 645 4600
F: 1 212 645 3030
E: info@newyorkerfilms.com
www.newyorkerfilms.com

NFBC

National Film Board of Canada
PO Box 6100
Station Centre-Ville
Montréal Québec H3C 3H5
Canada
P: 1 514 283 9000, 1 800 267 7710
F: 1 514 283 7564
E: webcustserv@nfb.ca
www.nfb.ca

NFVLS

National Film & Video Lending Service
Australian Centre for the Moving
    Image (ACMI) Collections
222 Park St
South Melbourne Vic 3205
Australia
P: 61 3 9929 7040
F: 61 3 9929 7027
E: collections@acmi.net.au
www.nla.gov.au

NJB

Nice Jewish Boy Productions
1016 North Croft Ave
Los Angeles CA 90069
USA
P: 1 323 654 8745
F: 1 323 654 8745
E: boychickmovie@aol.com

Nordisk

Nordisk Film
Mosedalvej 14
Valby DK-2500
Denmark
P: 45 3618 8200
E: nordiskfilm@nordiskfilm.dk
www.nordiskfilm.dk

NorthernArts

Northern Arts Entertainment
Williamsburg MA 01096
USA
P: 1 413 268 9301
F: 1 413 268 9309

NorwegianFilm

Norwegian Film Institute
Filmens Hus
Dronningens Gate 16
Oslo N 0105
Norway
P: 47 2247 4500
F: 47 2247 4599
E: nfi@nfi.no
www.nfi.no

NoSacrifice

No Sacrifice
5 rue Taylor
Paris 75010
France
P: 33 1 4484 9700
F: 33 1 4484 9701
E: prod@nosacrifice.com

Nu-Image

Nu Image
9145 Sunset Blvd
Los Angeles CA 90069
USA
P: 1 310 246 0240
F: 1 310 246 1655

NZFC

New Zealand Film Commission
PO Box 11-546
Wellington New Zealand
P: 64 4 4382 7680
F: 64 4 4383 9717
E: info@nzfilm.co.nz
www.nzfilm.co.nz

O-Filmproduktion

Ö-Filmproduktion
Löprich & Schlösser GmbH
Langhansstr 86
Berlin 13086
Germany
P: 49 30 446 7260
F: 49 30 446 72626
E: mail@oefilm.de
www.oefilm.de

OasisPC

Oasis P.C.
Rey Francisco 3
Madrid 28008
Spain
P: 34 1 930 3156
F: 34 1 541 3387
E: jtg2881@wanadoo.es

Oceanside

Oceanside Pictures
P: 1 212 874 6041
F: 1 212 873 9477
E: oceansidepix@aol.com

October

October Films see USA Films

OFG

Overseas Film Group
8800 Sunset Blvd
Los Angeles CA 90069
USA
P: 1 310 855 1199
F: 1 310 855 0719
E: info@ofg.com
www.ofg.com

Ognon

Ognon Pictures
14 rue Montmartre
Paris F-75001
France
P: 33 1 4026 5608
F: 33 1 4026 0209
E: ognon2@online.fr

OpenEye

Open Eye Productions
91 Seward St
San Francisco CA 94114
USA
P: 1 415 552 5735
F: 1 415 552 5173
E: openeyepix@aol.com

ORF

ORF/Austrian Broadcasting
Wurzburggasse. 30
Vienna 1136
Austria
P: 43 1 87 878 14515
F: 43 1 87 878 13726
E: elfriede.hufnagl@orf.at

Orion

Orion Pictures Corporation
1888 Century Park East
Los Angeles CA 90067
USA
www.orionpictures.com

OrionClassics

Orion Classics
www.orionpictures.com

OrionHV

Orion Home Video
www.orionpictures.com

Palace

Palace Entertainment Corporation
233 Whitehorse Rd
Balwyn Vic 3103
Australia
P: 61 3 9817 6421
F: 61 3 9817 4921
E: palace@palace.net.au
www.palace.net.au

Paramount

Paramount Pictures
5555 Melrose Ave
Hollywood CA 90038
USA
P: 1 323 956 5000
www.paramount.com

ParamountClassics

Paramount Classics
www.paramountclassics.com

ParamountHV

Paramount Home Video
www.paramount.com

PBS

Public Broadcasting Service USA
www.pbs.org

Peccadillo

Peccadillo Pictures
36B Shipton St
London E2 7RU
United Kingdom
P: 44 20 7729 5225
F: 44 20 7729 3074
E: peccadillo.pictures@virgin.net
www.peccadillopictures.com

Phaedra

Phaedra Cinema
    now Pathfinder Pictures
801 Ocean Front Walk, Suite 7
Venice CA 90291
USA
P: 1 310 664 1500
F: 1 310 664 0400
E: ghatanaka@aol.com

PictureRoom

The Picture Room
286 Spring St, Suite 203
New York NY 10013
USA
P: 1 212 414 2150
F: 1 212 414 2150
E: picture1rm@aol.com

PictureThis!

Picture This! Entertainment
PO Box 46872
Los Angeles CA 90046
USA
P: 1 323 852 1398
F: 1 323 658 7265
E: info@PictureThisEnt.com
www.PictureThisEnt.com

PieTown

Pie Town Productions
5433 Laurel Canyon Blvd
North Hollywood CA 91607
USA
P: 1 818 255 9300
F: 1 818 255 9300
E: jennifer_gold@pietown.tv
www.pietown.tv

Pilgrims4

Pilgrims 4 Corporation
173 East 64th St
New York NY 10021
USA
P: 1 212 861 0696
F: 1 212 249 5177

Pineapple

Pineapple Princess Productions
54 Station St
Newtown NSW 2042
Australia
P: 61 2 9517 1909
E: c.boreham@bigpond.com

Pinkplot

Pinkplot Productions
PO Box 8548
New York NY 10116
USA
P: 1 323 876 2748
F: 1 323 876 9743
E: sales@pinkplot.com
www.pinkplot.com

Pinq

Pinq Creations
P: 61 412 633 976
E: pkinau@yahoo.com.au
www.geocities.com/pkinau

Piranha

Piranha Productions
United House
North Rd
London N7 9DP
United Kingdom
P: 44 171 607 3355
F: 44 171 607 9980

PKProd

PK Productions
336 Central Park West
New York NY 10025
USA
P: 1 212 865 1469
F: 1 212 512 5223

PlanetOut

Planet Out Distribution
1360 Mission St, #200
San Francisco CA 94103
USA
P: 1 415 252 6285
F: 1 415 252 6287

Point-Du-Jour

Point Du Jour
38 rue Croix des Petits Champs
Paris 75001
France
P: 33 1 4703 4000
F: 33 1 4139 9459
www.pointdujour.fr

PollyTickle

Polly Tickle Productions
302 Bedford Ave, Suite 133
Brooklyn NY 11211
USA
P: 1 718 599 2644
E: inka666@earthlink.com

PolyGram

PolyGram Film International
4th Floor, Oxford House
76 Oxford St
London W1N 0HQ
United Kingdom
P: 44 171 307 1300
F: 44 171 307 1301

PolyGram

PolyGram Filmed Entertainment
9348 Civic Center
Beverly Hills CA 90210
USA

PonyCanyon

Pony Canyon
2-5 10 Toranomon, Minato-ku
Tokyo 105-8487
Japan
P: 81 3 5521 8024
F: 81 3 5521 8122
E: sakoda@ponycanyon.co.jp

Potemkin

Potemkin Productions
1300 Waterloo Court
Riverside CA 92506
USA
P: 1 310 701 9101
F: 1 562 866 3667

Potential

Potential Films
34 Halstead St
Caulfield Vic 3161
Australia
P: 61 3 9505 6253
F: 61 3 9532 7951
E: potfilms@ozemail.com.au
www.potentialfilms.com

PotentPussy

Potent Pussy Productions
8 Albemarle Row, Hotwells
Bristol B58 4LY
United Kingdom
P: 44 117 7914 1903
F: 44 117 377 0884
E: raineppp@hotmail.com

Praunheim

Rosa von Praunheim Filmproduktion
Konstanzer Strasse 56
Berlin D-10707
Germany
P: 49 30 883 5496
F: 49 30 881 2958
E: rosavp@aol.com
www.rosavonpraunheim.de

ProductionIG

Production IG LLC
Japan
P: 81 310 530 3532
F: 81 310 530 3526
E: maki@productionig.com
www.productionig.com

Prometheus

Studio Prometheus
11911 Mayfield Ave, #5
Los Angeles CA 90049
USA
P: 1 310 248 4806
F: 1 310 725 9781
E: dustin1@earthlink.net

Put-Down-the-Plow

Put Down the Plow Productions
P: 40 4622 7912
F: 40 4622 7912
E: milliet@mindspring.com
www.clairefilm.com

Pyewackett

Rick Castro
Pyewackett Productions
E: pyewackett@attbi.com
www.rickcastro.com

QueenFAD

Queen For a Day Productions
3055 W. Sunnyside Ave, #2
Chicago IL 60625
USA
P: 1 773 267 3106
E: hmajid@aol.com

Queerscreen

Queerscreen
PO Box 1081
Darlinghurst NSW 2010
Australia
P: 61 2 9332 4938
F: 61 2 9331 2988
E: info@queerscreen.com.au
www.queerscreen.com.au

R&BFilms

R&B Films
2910 Motor Ave
Los Angeles CA 90064
P: 1 310 280 0214

Ragamuff

Ragamuff Productions
USA
P: 1 415 285 9236
E: maria_breaux@hotmail.com

Rainforest

Rainforest Productions
2141 Powers Ferry Rd
Marietta GA 30067
USA
P: 1 770 960 8733
F: 1 770 960 0848
E: willpower@
   rainforestproductions.com

RaiTrade

RAI Trade
Via Novaro 18
Rome 00195
Italy
P: 39 06 3749 8469
F: 39 06 370 1343
E: filippelli@raitrade.it
www.raitrade.rai.it

Rank

Rank Organisation
c/- Carlton International Media
35-38 Portman Square
London W1H 6NU
United Kingdom
P: 44 20 7224 3339
F: 44 20 7486 1707
E: enquiries@carltonint.co.uk
www.carltonint.co.uk

Rapido

Rapido TV
14-16 Great Pulteney St
London W1F 9ND
United Kingdom
P: 44 20 7440 5700
F: 44 20 7439 2733
E: info@planetrapido.com
www.rapido.co.uk

Rattled

Rattled Productions
1633 Broadway, #15 - 111
New York NY 10019
USA
P: 1 212 708 1452
F: 1 212 708 1211
E: burkhart@interport.net

Rednavel

rednaveL fiLmworx
6418 Santa Monica Blvd
Los Angeles CA 90038
USA
P: 1 323 467 7778
F: 1 323 467 7774
E: rednavel@ix.netcom.com

RedProd

Red Production Company
United Kingdom
P: 44 161 827 2530
F: 44 161 827 2518
E: redlimited@dial.pipex.com
www.bobandrose.tv

ReelMovies

Reel Movies
Box 2581
GPO Sydney NSW 2001
Australia
P: 61 2 9552 8605
F: 61 2 9660 3213

Reilly

Life of Reilly Productions
11 Fifth Ave, Suite 9S
New York NY 10003
USA
P: 1 212 995 1367
E: nyevita@aol.com

Remstar

Remstar Corporation Inc.
85 rue Saint-Paul Ouest
Montréal Québec H2Y3V4
Canada
P: 1 514 847 1136
F: 1 514 847 1163
E: josee@remstarcorp.com
www.remstarcorp.com

Reno

Reno Co
38 N. Moore #2
New York NY 10013
USA
P: 1 212 334 8320
F: 1 212 966 8436
E: renoren@idt.net

REP

REP Film Distributors Pty Ltd
Level 2, 11 Waltham St
Artarmon NSW 2064
Australia
P: 61 2 9438 3377
F: 61 2 9439 1827

Republic

Republic Pictures Corporation
12636 Beatrice St
Los Angeles CA 90066
USA
P: 1 213 306 4040

reVision

reVision Films
2534 Fourth Ave
Los Angeles CA 90018
USA
P: 1 323 419 1983
F: 1 509 267 3096
E: mwm@reVisionfilms.com
www.reVisionfilms.com

RimFilm

Rim Film Distributors
9884 Santa Monica Blvd
Beverly Hills CA 90212
USA
P: 1 310 203 8182
F: 1 310 551 1530

Ripefilms

Ripefilms
21 West 129th St, #A
New York NY 10027
USA
P: 1 212 828 0705
E: ripefilms@yahoo.com

Riverfilms

River Films
310 West 95th St
Suite 5F
New York NY 10025
USA
P: 1 212 678 7103
F: 1 212 280 1476
E: riverflix@aol.com
www.riverfilms.net

Riveter

Riveter Productions
1639 Redesdale Ave
Los Angeles CA 90026
USA
P: 1 323 665 9211
F: 1 323 665 8211
E: westamber@aol.com

Roadshow

Roadshow
Box 2581 GPO
Sydney NSW 2001
Australia
P: 61 2 9552 8600
F: 61 2 9566 2510
E: daneille_turner@roadshow.com.au
www.roadshow.com.au

RoadshowEnt

Roadshow Entertainment
E: daneille_turner@roadshow.com.au
www.village.com.au

Roadside

Roadside Attractions
427 North Canon Drive, Suite 216
Beverly Hills CA 90210
USA
P: 1 310 860 1692
F: 1 310 860 1693
E: chadm@roadsideattractions.com
www.roadsideattractions.com

RockingHorse

Rocking Horse Productions
84 Horatio St, #2D
New York NY 10014
USA
P: 1 212 627 9538
F: 1 212 627 9538
E: jmcarlo@aol.com

Rocvale

RocVale Films (Aust)
PO Box 2040
Mount Waverley Vic 3149
Australia
P: 61 3 9888 1033
F: 61 3 9888 1066

Rocvale

Rocvale Films (New Zealand)
VM Distribution
PO Box 37-376
Parnell, Auckland New Zealand
P: 64 9 378 1394
F: 64 9 309 8790

Ronin

Ronin Films
PO Box 1005
Civic Square ACT 2608
Australia
P: 61 2 6248 0851
F: 61 2 6249 1640
E: orders@roninfilms.com.au
www.roninfilms.com.au

RoyalCollege

Royal College of Art
Film & Television,
    School of the Moving Image
Stevens Bldg, Kensington Gore
London SW7 2EU
United Kingdom
P: 44 20 7590 4444
F: 44 20 7590 4500
E: info@rca.ac.uk
www.rca.ac.uk

RVQ

RVQ Productions
P: 63 2 241 4840
F: 63 2 241 4855
E: rvqprod@the.net.ph

SACIS

SACIS
Via Teulada 66
Rome 00195
Italy
P: 39 06 370 1343

Sagittaire

Sagittaire Films
122 rue la Boétie
Paris 75008
France
P: 33 1 5669 2930
F: 33 1 5669 2940
E: desgris.sagittaire@wanadoo.fr
www.sagittairefilms.com

Salud

Nuestra Salud
464 East 19th St
Brooklyn NY 11226
USA
P: 1 331 4580 2839
F: 1 331 4580 2839
E: newman41@compuserve.com

Salzgeber

Salzgeber & Co. Medien GmbH
Friedrichstrasse 122
Berlin 10117
Germany
P: 49 30 285 290 90
F: 49 30 285 290 99
E: info@salzgeber.de
www.salzgeber.de

SamuelGoldwyn

Samuel Goldwyn Films
10203 Santa Monica Blvd
Los Angeles CA 90067
USA
P: 1 310 860 3100
F: 1 310 860 3195

Savage

Savage Productions
3229 Pillsbury Ave
South Minneapolis MN 54408
USA
P: 1 612 823 8431
F: 1 612 375 7657

Schlammtaucher

Schlammtaucher FILM
Sonnenalle 7
Berlin 12047
Germany
P: 49 30 6900 1108
F: 49 30 6900 1335
E: office@schlammtaucher.de
www.schlammtaucher.de

ScoutsHonor

Scout's Honor Documentary Project
1679A Church St
San Francisco CA 94131
USA
P: 1 415 641 5700
E: tomshepard@earthlink.net
www.scouts-honor.com

Scrine

Gil Scrine Films
44 Northcote St
East Brisbane Qld 4169
Australia
P: 61 7 3391 0124
F: 61 7 3391 0154
E: gilsfilm@cairnes.net.au
www.eg.com.au/gilscrinefilms

Seduced

Seduced and Exploited Entertainment
1832 1/2 N. Wilcox Ave
Hollywood CA 90028
USA
P: 1 323 251 3007
F: 1 323 466 4765
E: bigboy@seducedandexploited.com

Seduction

Seduction Cinema
www.seductioncinema.com

Seductor

Seductor Productions
PO Box 68420
Newton, Auckland New Zealand
P: 64 9 358 2460
F: 64 9 358 2461
E: cushla.d@clear.net.nz

Senator

Senator Entertainment AG
Kurfürstendamm 65
Berlin D-10707
Germany
P: 49 30 8809 1700
F: 49 30 8809 1723
E: info@senator.de
www.senatorfilm.de

Seng

Tai Seng
170 South Spruce Ave, #200
San Francisco CA 94080
USA
P: 1 650 871 8118
F: 1 650 871 2392
E: jonsoo@taiseng.com
www.taiseng.com

SevenArts

Seven Arts Pictures
7080 Hollywood Blvd, Suite 201
Hollywood CA 90028
USA
P: 1 323 464 0225
F: 1 323 464 8305
E: info@sevenarts.net

ShadesOfGray

Shades of Gray LLC
USA
P: 1 785 841 0859
E: timd@sunflower.com

Sharmill

Sharmill Films
Suite 4, 200 Toorak Rd
South Yarra Vic 3141
Australia
P: 61 3 9826 9077
F: 61 3 9826 1935
E: distribution@sharmillfilms.com.au
www.sharmillfilms.com.au

SheFilms

She Films
10 Sherwood Pl
North Ryde NSW 2113
Australia
P: 61 2 9870 7923
F: 61 2 9870 7924
E: imak@hardy.ocs.mq.edu.au

Shorelands

Shorelands Productions
9 Shorelands Place
Old Greenwich CT 06870
USA
P: 1 203 618 4803
F: 1 203 629 8554
E: shorelands123@aol.com

Showcase

Showcase Television
121 Bloor St East, Suite 200
Toronto Ontario M4W 3M5
Canada
P: 1 416 967 0022
F: 1 416 967 0044
www.showcase.ca

Showtime

Showtime Networks
10880 Wilshire Blvd, Suite 1600
Los Angeles CA 90024
USA
P: 1 310 234 5200
F: 1 310 234 5392
www.showtimeonline.com (USA) or
alt.sho.com

Sinister

Sinister Cinema
PO Box 4369
Medford OR 97501
USA
P: 1 541 773 6860
F: 1 541 779 8650
E: sinister@magick.net
www.sinistercinema.com

Siren

Siren Entertainment
23 Wangaratta St
Richmond Vic 3121
Australia
P: 61 3 9429 9555
F: 61 3 9429 9333
E: info@sirenent.com.au
www.sirenent.com.au

SIRVideo

S. I. R. Video Productions
3288 21st St, #94 PMB
San Francisco CA 94110
USA
P: 1 415 701 0243
F: 1 415 621 5949
E: jackie@sirvideo.com, panicstrkn@aol.com
www.sirvideo.com

Skarda

Skarda International Communications Ltd
7 Portland Mews
London W1V 3FJ
United Kingdom
P: 44 20 7734 7776
F: 44 20 7734 1360
E: martin@skarda.net
www.skarda.net

Skouras

Skouras Pictures
1040 N. Las Palmas Ave
Hollywood CA 90038
USA
P: 1 323 467 3000
F: 1 323 467 0740

Slotar

Dean Slotar
PO Box 20039
New York NY 10025
USA
P: 1 917 774 2193
F: 1 917 222 3592
E: dslotar@aol.com

SlovenianFF

Slovenian Film Fund
Miklosiceva 38
Ljubljana 1000
Slovenia
P: 386 61 433 7175
F: 386 61 430 6250
E: tanika.sajatovic@film-sklad.si
www.film-sklad.si

Smokescreen

Smokescreen Pictures
6/358 Beaconsfield Pde
St Kilda VIC 3182
Australia
P: 0407 740 897
E: annadegs@hotmail.com

SockPuppet

now trading as
Hungry Jackal Productions
7411 Hawthorn Ave
Los Angeles CA 90046
USA
P: 1 323 876 2298
E: hungryjackal@hungryjackal.com
www.sockpuppetent.com

Sogepaq

Sogepaq Distribución, S.A.
c/- Gran Via, 32-1st Floor
Madrid 28013
Spain
P: 34 1 524 7200
F: 34 1 521 0875
E: info@sogepaq.es
www.sogepaq.es

SomethingWeird

Something Weird Video
Dept. JADA
PO Box 33664
Seattle WA 98133
USA
P: 1 206 361 3759
F: 1 206 364 7526
www.somethingweird.com

SonyClassics

Sony Pictures Classics
550 Madison Ave
New York NY 10022
USA
P: 1 212 833 8846
F: 1 212 833 4190
www.sony.com

SonyPictures

Sony Pictures Entertainment
www.sonypictures.com

Souvenir

Souvenir Pictures
USA
P: 1 323 512 4677
F: 1 323 512 4679
E: info@souvenirpictures.com
www.souvenirpictures.com

Sparker

Sparker Films
4108 19th St
San Francisco CA 94114
USA
P: 1 415 860 7986
E: sparker-films@sparker.net
www.sparker.net/films

Spectrum

Spectrum Media
28 West 46th St, #3F
New York NY 10036
USA
F: 1 425 977 9953
E: sean@spectrummedia.net
www.ritualnation.com

Splendid

Splendid Choice
Hong Kong
F: 852 277 454 15

Springfield

Springfield Consulting
306A St Kilda Rd
St Kilda VIC 3182
Australia
P: 61 3 9536 8000
F: 61 3 9536 8099
E: emef@ozemail.com.au

Starfish

Starfish Films
37 Burnie St
Clovelly NSW 2031
Australia
P: 61 2 9665 9678
F: 61 2 9665 9678

Stock

Michael Stock Filmproduktion
Adalbert Strasse 75
Berlin 1000
Germany
P: 49 30 614 2379
F: 49 30 611 7603

Strand

Strand Releasing
1460 Fourth St, Suite 302
Santa Monica CA 90401
USA
P: 1 310 395 5002
F: 1 310 395 2502
E: strand@strandrel.com
www.strandrel.com

Stratosphere

Stratosphere Entertainment
767 5th Ave, Suite 4700
New York NY 10153
USA
P: 1 212 605 1010
F: 1 212 813 0300
E: stratronna@aol.com
prime.ground0.com/defunct/strat/

Suma

Suma Films
P: 351 21 315 9066
E: sumafilmes@mail.telepac.pt

Sun&Moon

Sun & Moon Vision Productions
PO Box 34235
San Diego CA 92163
USA
P: 1 619 296 3668

Swank

Swank Motion Pictures
201 S. Jefferson Ave
St Louis MI 63103-2579
USA
P: 1 800 876 5577
E: mail@swank.com
www.swank.com

SwedishFilminstitute

Swedish Filminstitute
Borgv. 5, Box 27126
Stockholm 102 52
Sweden
P: 46 8 665 1100
F: 46 8 661 1820

SweetChild

Sweet Child Films
10 Richmond Rd
Brighton BN2 3RN
United Kingdom
P: 44 1273 673 171
F: 44 1273 673 172
E: sweet@dircon.co.uk

Symbiosis

Symbiosis Films
777 West End Ave, #2B
New York NY 100125
USA
P: 1 212 666 0724
F: 1 212 666 0724
E: symbiosis@sleepinanestofflames.com
www.sleepinanestofflames.com

Telling

Telling Pictures
2261 Market St, #506
San Francisco CA 94114
USA
www.tellingpictures.com

TF1

Cinematheque de TF1 International
1 quai du point du jour
Boulogne 92656
France
P: 33 4141 1234
F: 33 4141 2133

ThirdRock

Duncan Roy, Third Rock Films
2 Seaway Cottages
Wavecrest
Whitstable, Kent CT5 1EQ
United Kingdom

TLA

TLA Releasing
235 Market St, 5th Floor
Philadelphia PA 19106
USA
P: 1 215 733 0608
F: 1 215 790 1502
E: contact@tlareleasing.com
www.tlareleasing.com

TMPPA

Thai Motion Picture Producers Association
514 Banmanangkasila Lanluang Rd
Bangkok 10300
Thailand

Tokuma

Tokuma International
1-1-16, Higashi Shimbashi
Minato-ku
Tokyo 105-0002
Japan
P: 81 3 3573 8100
F: 81 3 3573 8145

TokyoILGFF

Tokyo International Lesbian
  & Gay Film Festival
5-24-16 Nakano, #601
Nakano-ku
Tokyo 164-0001
Japan
P: 81 3 5380 5760
F: 81 3 5380 5767
E: lgff@tokyo.office.ne.jp

Tomorrow

Tomorrow Pictures
45 West 36th St, 9th Floor
New York NY 10018
USA
P: 1 212 736 6533 (ext 244)
F: 1 212 563 4891

Touchstone

Touchstone Home Video
500 S. Buena Vista St
Burbank CA 91521
USA
www.movies.go.com

Trabelsi

Trabelsi Productions
Danti St No.11, PO Box 8579
Jaffa 61084
Israel
P: 972 3 518 2182
F: 972 3 602 4927
E: tawfikabuwael@hotmail.com

Transit

Transit Films
Dachauer Strasse 35
Munich 80335
Germany
P: 49 89 599 8850
F: 49 89 5998 8520
E: transitfilm@compuserve.com

Trident

Trident Releasing
8401 Melrose Pl, 2nd Floor
Los Angeles CA 90069
USA
P: 1 323 655 8818
F: 1 323 655 0515
E: info@tridentreleasing.com
www.tridentreleasing.com

Trimark

Trimark Pictures/Lions Gate Films
4553 Glencoe Ave, Suite 200
Marina Del Rey CA 90292
USA
E: feedback@lgecorp.com
www.trimarkpictures.com

Troma

Troma Entertainment Inc
733 9th Ave
New York NY 10019
USA
P: 1 212 757 4555
F: 1 212 399 9885

TunnelVision

Lauren Himmel
  Tunnel Vision Productions
160 Moss Way
Oakland CA 94611
USA
P: 1 510 832 7860
F: 1 510 653 7807
E: email@laurenhimmel.com

TurbulentArts

Turbulent Arts
673 Oak St, #1
San Francisco CA 94117
USA
P: 1 415 552 1952
F: 1 415 552 3620
E: turbarts@sirius.com

Tutak

Tutak Films
622 East 20th St, #6H
New York NY 10009
USA
P: 1 212 228 7381
F: 1 212 228 7381
E: robert@tutakfilms.com
tutakfilms.com

Tuzi

Federica Tuzi
via Salaria 1373
Rome 00138
Italy
P: 39 06 888 219, 39 330 244 978
E: degender@libero.it

TWN

Third World Newsreel
545 Eighth Ave, 10th Floor
New York NY 10018
USA
P: 1 212 947 9277
F: 1 212 594 6417
E: twn@twn.org
www.twn.org

UA

United Artists
www.unitedartists.com

UAClassics

United Artists Classics
www.unitedartists.com

UGC

Union Générale Cinématographique
(UGC International)
2 rue des Quatre-Fils
Paris 75003
France
P: 33 1 4029 8900
F: 33 1 4029 8910
E: hernst@ugc.fr
www.ugc.fr

UIP

United International Pictures Aust
GPO Box 4040
Sydney NSW 2001
Australia
P: 61 2 9264 7444
F: 61 2 9264 2499
www.uip.com

UIP

United International Pictures USA
www.uip.com

Ulmann

Roni Ulmann
Freystrasse 19
Zurich CH8004
Switzerland
F: 41 1 241 4626
E: roniulmann@compuserve.com

UniFrance

UniFrance Film International
4 Villa Bosquet
Paris 75007
France
P: 33 1 4753 9580
F: 33 1 4705 9655
E: contact@unifrance.org
www.unifrance.org

Universal

Universal Pictures
www.universalpictures.com

Uplink

UPLINK Company
3F, 1-8-1x, Jinnan, Shibuya-ku
Tokyo 150-0041
Japan
P: 81 3 5489 0755
F: 81 3 5489 0754
E: film@uplink.co.jp
www.uplink.co.jp

USAFilms

USA Films
100 North Crescent Drive
Beverly Hills CA 90210
USA
P: 1 310 385 4400
F: 1 310 385 4408
www.octoberfilms.com

USC

University of Southern California
School of Cinema
Lusac Instructional Bldg
Room 209
Los Angeles CA 90089
USA
P: 1 213 740 2235
www.usc.edu

Vagrant

Vagrant Films
E: vagrantfilms@go.com

Valhalla

Valhalla Video Productions
PO Box 31927
San Francisco CA 94131
USA
P: 1 415 978 9938
E: scooterj33@hotmail.com

VCA

Victorian College of the Arts
School of Film & Television
234 St Kilda Rd
South Bank Vic 3006
Australia
P: 61 3 9685 9000
F: 61 3 9685 9001
E: ftv.info@vca.unimelb.edu.au
www.vca.unimelb.edu.au

VDB

Video Data Bank
c/- School of the Art Institute
   of Chicago
112 S. Michigan Ave
Chicago IL 60603
USA
P: 1 312 345 3550
F: 1 312 541 8073
E: info@vdb.org
www.vdb.org

Vega

Vega Film AG
Kraftstrasse 33 - Postfach
Zurich CH8044
Switzerland
P: 41 1 252 6000
F: 41 1 252 6635

Verging

Verging Productions
1572 Grove St
San Francisco CA 94117
USA
P: 1 415 931 6478
F: 1 415 775 0634
E: pdmiller@pclient.ml.com

Verlag

Reinery Verlag Filmproduktion GmbH
Wässigertal 16
Remagen
Germany
P: 49 2642 23011

Vicarious

Vicarious Production
31 Rosenay Cres
Battersea
London SW1 4R9
United Kingdom
P: 44 171 228 0679
F: 44 171 585 3459

VideoAmericain

Video Americain
243 Elkton Rd
Newark DE 19711
USA
P: 1 302 369 3593
F: 1 302 369 0658
www.videoamericain.com

VideoOut

Video Out Distribution
1965 Main St
Vancouver
British Columbia V5T 3C1
Canada
P: 1 604 872 8449
F: 1 604 876 1185
E: videoout@telus.net

VideoPool

Video Pool Inc
#300, 100 Arthur St
Winnipeg Manitoba R3B 1H3
Canada
P: 1 204 949 9134
F: 1 204 942 1555
E: vpdist@videopool.org
www.videopool.org

Vidiola

Vidiola
117 Burniston St
Scarborough WA 6019
Australia
E: vidiola@hotmail.com

Viva

Viva Films
334 E. Rodriquez Sr. Ave
New Manila, Quezon City Philippines
P: 63 2 414 1635
F: 63 2 415 7176
E: bgil@viv.com.ph

Volcano

Del LaGrace Volcano
P: 44 171 704 1300
E: disgrace@dircon.co.uk

VSM

Video Search of Miami
E: vsom@aol.com
www.vsom.com

VTape

V Tape
401 Richmond St West
Suite 452
Toronto Ontario M5V 3A8
Canada
P: 1 416 351 1317
F: 1 416 351 1509
E: cynthial@vtape.org
www.vtape.org

WadiaMovietone

Wadia Movietone
8AB Andromeda, 89 Worli Sea Face
Mumbai 400 025
India
P: 91 22 494 7517
F: 91 22 493 8228

WalkingIris

Walking Iris Films
831 South Dunsmuir Ave
Los Angeles CA 90036
USA
P: 1 323 936 5476
F: 1 323 936 5476
E: walkingiris@earthlink.net

Warner

Warner Home Video Aust
235 Pyrmont St
Pyrmont NSW 2009
Australia
P: 61 2 9552 8700

Warner

Warner Bros
www.warnerbros.com

WaterBearer

Water Bearer Films
20 West 20th St, 2nd Floor
New York NY 10011
USA
P: 1 212 242 8686
F: 1 212 242 4560
E: sales@waterbearerfilms.com
www.waterbearerfilms.com

WelbFilm

Welb Film Pursuits
PO Box 3011
Woodinville Washington 98072
USA
P: 1 206 686 1572
E: welb@earthlink.net
www.fallsapart.com

Wellspring

Wellspring Media
419 Park Ave South, 20th Floor
New York NY 10016
USA
P: 1 212 686 6777
F: 1 212 685 2625
E: slevine@wellspring.com
www.wellspring.com

WesternDragon

Western Dragon Productions
P: 86 21 6216 0202
F: 86 21 3225 0383
E: ausgonb@yahoo.com

WhitePeople

White People's Business
Apt 3824, 38 rue Jean Longuet
Bagneux 92220
France
P: 33 1 4223 6309
F: 33 1 684 89 8518
E: whitepeoplesbusiness@yahoo.com

Wildshot

Wildshot Pictures
707 Brouwersgracht
Amsterdam 1015 GJ
The Netherlands
P: 31 20 420 5441
F: 31 20 420 6442

Wilhelm

Bettina Wilhelm Filmproduktion
Kottbusser Damm 2
Berlin D-1000
Germany

WiseWomen

Wise Women Productions
1 Springcroft Ave
London N2 9JH
United Kingdom
P: 44 777 568 3702
F: 44 870 126 9723
E: wisewomenproductions
  @hotmail.com

WMM

Women Make Movies
462 Broadway
Suite 500E
New York NY 10013
USA
P: 1 212 925 0606
F: 1 212 925 2052
E: info@wmm.com
www.wmm.com

Wolfe

Wolfe Video
P: 1 800 438 9653
www.wolfevideo.com

WomanVision

Woman Vision
c/- Transit Media Film Library
22D Hollywood Ave
Hohokus NJ 07423
USA
P: 1 800 343 5540
F: 1 201 652 1973
E: info@woman-vision.org
www.woman-vision.org

WoMedia

Women's Educational Media
2180 Bryant St, Suite 203
San Francisco CA 94110
USA
P: 1 415 641 4616
F: 1 415 641 4632
E: wemfilms@womedia.org
www.womedia.org

Wonderphil

Wonderphil Productions
615 5th Ave
San Francisco CA 94118
USA
P: 1 415 221 9711
E: wonderphilprods@hotmail.com

WorldOfWonder

World of Wonder (USA)
6500 Hollywood Blvd, Suite 400
Hollywood CA 90028
USA
P: 1 323 603 6301
F: 1 323 603 6301
E: wow@worldofwonder.net
www.worldofwonder.net

WorldOfWonder

World of Wonder (UK)
40 Chelsea Wharf, Lots Rd
London SW10 0QJ
United Kingdom
P: 44 20 7349 9000
F: 44 20 7349 9777
E: wow@worldofwonder.co.uk
www.worldofwonder.net

WringingHands

Wringing Hands Productions
USA
P: 1 212 439 1184
E: Jay_Corcoran@Scubber.com

wtp-film

wtp-film
Bayriches Filmzentrum
Bavariafilmplatz 7
Geiselgasteig 82031
Germany
P: 49 89 6498 1112
F: 49 89 6498 1312
E: miragittner@wtpfilm.de
www.wtpfilm.de

Xingu

Xingu Films
Estate House 921A Fulham Rd
London SW6 5HU
United Kingdom
P: 44 171 736 7946
F: 44 171 371 0054

Yong

Chen Yong Productions
P: 86 1390 138 7635
E: chengyongfe@hotmail.com

Zachary

Bohdan Zachary
PO Box 460910
San Francisco CA 94146
USA
P: 1 415 621 6115
F: 1 415 552 7723

Zang

Zang Pictures
1690 Ala Moana Blvd
Honolulu HA 96815
USA
P: 1 808 945 0996
F: 1 808 949 1142
E: zangpictures@cs.com
www.zangpictures.net

ZDF

ZDF Enterprises
Spichernstrasse 75-77
Cologne 50672
Germany
P: 49 221 9488 850
F: 49 221 9499 951
E: westphal.s@zdf.de
www.zdf-enterprises.de

Zeitgeist

Zeitgeist Films
247 Centre St, 2nd Floor
New York NY 10013
USA
P: 1 212 274 1989
F: 1 212 274 1644
E: mail@zeitgeistfilm.com
www.zeitgeistfilms.com

Ziegler

Regina Ziegler Film Production
Neue Kanstrase 14
Berlin 14057
Germany
P: 49 30 32 9050
F: 49 30 322 7353

Selected Queer Film Festivals

Australia

Brisbane Queer Film Festival
Brisbane Powerhouse Centre for the Live Arts
119 Lamington St
New Farm Qld 4005
P: 61 7 3358 8622
F: 61 7 3358 8611
E: catherineo@brisbanepowerhouse.org
 www.brisbanepowerhouse.org
April

Mardi Gras Film Festival
PO Box 1081
Darlinghurst NSW 1300
P: 61 2 9332 4938
F: 61 2 9331 2988
E: info@queerscreen.com.au
 www.queerscreen.com.au
February

Melbourne Queer Film Festival
6 Claremont St
South Yarra VIC 3141
P: 61 3 9827 2022
F: 61 3 9827 1622
E: info@melbournequeerfilm.com.au
 www.melbournequeerfilm.com.au
March

Western Australian Queer Film Festival
44 Ethelwyn St
Hilton WA 6163
P: 61 8 9331 2986
F: 61 8 9331 2472
E: fanny_jacobson@yahoo.com.au
 gfd.net.au/walgff

Austria

Identities Queer Film Festival
DV8-Film
Postfach 282
Vienna A-1071
P: 43 1 524 6274
F: 43 1 522 9874
E: office@identities.at
 www.identities.at
June

Belgium

Brussels Gay & Lesbian Film Festival
Tels Quels asbl
81, rue Marché au Charbon
Brussels B-1000
E: info@fglb.org
 www.fglb.org
January

Brazil

Mix Brasil
Rua Joao Moura 2432
San Paulo CEP 105413.004
P: 55 11 3819 5116
F: 55 11 3819 5360
E: mixbrasil@uol.com.br
 www.mixbrasil.com.br

Canada

image+nation
Montréal International Queer Film & Video Festival
4067 boul St Laurent, Suite 404
Montréal Québec H2W 1Y7
P: 1 514 285 1562
E: info@image-nation.org
 www.image-nation.org
September

London Lesbian Film Festival
PO Box 46014
London Ontario N5W 3A1
E: iiff@sympatico.ca
 llff.lweb.net

Making Scenes Film & Video Festival
Arts Court
2 Daly Ave, Suite 250
Ottawa Ontario K1N 6E2
P: 1 613 566 2113
F: 1 613 233 0698
E: scenes@magma.ca
 www.makingscenes.ca
September

Toronto Lesbian & Gay Film & Video Festival

Inside Out
219-401 Richmond St
Toronto Ontario M5V 3A8
P: 1 416 977 6847
F: 1 416 977 8025
E: inside@insideout.on.ca
 www.insideout.on.ca
May

Vancouver Queer Film & Video Festival

PO Box 521
1027 Davie St
Vancouver BC V6E 4L2
P: 1 604 844 1615
F: 1 604 844 1698
E: general@outonscreen.com
 www.outonscreen.com
August

Denmark

Copenhagen Gay & Lesbian Film Festival

Det Danske Filminstitut
Gothersgade 55
Copenhagen K DK-1123
E: info@cglff.dk
 www.cglff.dk
October

Finland

Turku Lesbian & Gay Film Festival

Turun Seudun SETA ry, Vinokino Film Festival
PO Box 288
Turku FIN-20101
P: 358 2 2500 695
F: 358 2 2512 905
E: vinokino@tuseta.fi
 www.tuseta.fi
November

France

Paris Gay & Lesbian Film Festival

8, rue du Repos
Paris 75020
P: 33 1 4356 5366
F: 33 1 4356 5366
E: info@ffglp.net
 www.ffglp.net
December

Paris Lesbian Film Festival

37 avenue Pasteur
Montreuil 93100
P: 33 1 4870 7711
F: 33 1 4870 7711
E: cineffable@fr.fm
 www.dpi-europe.fr/~ebrun/cineffable/
October

Germany

Bremen Queer Film Festival

c/o Kino 46
Waller Heerstrasse 46
Bremen 28217
P: 49 421 387 6736
F: 49 421 387 6734
E: info@queerfilm.de
 www.queerfilm.de
October

Hamburg Lesbian & Gay Film Festival

Querbild e. V.
Schanzenstr. 45
Hamburg D-20357
P: 49 40 348 0670
F: 49 40 34 0522
E: mail@lsf-hamberg.de
 www.lsf-hamburg.de
October

Lesben Film Festival Berlin

Koburger Strasse 14
Berlin 10825
P: 49 30 787 18 108
F: 49 30 787 18 106
E: filmfestivalberlin@hotmail.com
 www.lesbenfilmfestival.de
October

Verzaubert International Queer Film Festival

Rosebud Entertainment
Fregestr. 36
Berlin 12161
P: 49 30 861 4532
F: 49 30 861 4539
E: rosebud_entertainment@t-online.de
www.queer-view.com/verzaubert
December

Ireland

Dublin Lesbian & Gay Film Festival

Tower One, Fumbally Court
Fumbally Lane
Dublin
P: 353 1 473 0599
F: 353 1 473 0597
E: dlgff@ireland.com
www.gcn.ie/dlgff
August

Italy

Milano International Lesbian & Gay Film Festival

MBE 209
via del Torchio 12
Milano 20123
P: 39 2 5412 2225
F: 39 2 7200 2942
E: info@cinemagaylesbico.com
www.cinemagaylesbico.com
June

Turin International Gay & Lesbian Film Festival

L'altra Comunicazione
Piazza San Carlo, 161
Torino 10123
P: 39 11 534 888
F: 39 11 535 796
E: info@turinglfilmfestival.com
www.turinglfilmfestival.com
April

Japan

Tokyo International Lesbian & Gay Film Festival

5-21-16 #601
Nakano Nakano-ku
Tokyo 164-0001
P: 81 3 5380 5760
F: 81 3 5380 5767
E: lgff@tokyo.office.ne.jp
l-gff.gender.ne.jp
August

New Zealand

Out Takes Lesbian & Gay Film Festival

Reel Queer Inc
PO Box 12-201
Wellington
P: 64 4 972 6775
F: 64 4 801 9906
E: info@outtakes.org.nz
www.outtakes.org.nz
May

Norway

Oslo Gay & Lesbian Film Festival

PO Box 6838
Oslo 0130
P: 47 22 20 1960
F: 47 22 20 1960
E: oglff@online.no
www.skeivefilmer.no
June

Portugal

Lisbon Gay & Lesbian Film Festival

Lisbon
E: lisboa.filmfest@netcabo.pt
www.lisbonfilmfest.org
September

Slovenia

Ljubljana Gay & Lesbian Film Festival

c/-Slovenian Film Fund
Miklosiceva 38
Ljubljana 1000

P: 386 1 431 2056
F: 386 1 430 6250
E: info@film-sklad.si
www.film-sklad.si

South Africa

South African Gay & Lesbian Film Festival

924-926 Groote Kerk Gebou
39 Adderley St
Cape Town 8000
P: 27 21 465 1927
F: 27 21 465 1927
E: info@oia.co.za
www.oia.co.za
November

Spain

Barcelona International Exhibition of Gay & Lesbian Films

Enric Granados 135, 1r 2A
Barcelona 08008
P: 34 93 218 6327
F: 34 93 218 6398
E: info@festivalbarcelona.com
www.festivalbarcelona.com
October

Switzerland

Pink Apple - Schwullesbisches Filmfestival

Postfach 729
Frauenfeld CH-8501
E: info@pinkapple.ch
www.pinkapple.ch
April

The Netherlands

Amsterdam Roze Filmdagen

Amsterdam Pink Filmdays
Filmhuis Cavia, Van hallstraat 52-1
Amsterdam 1051 HH
P: 31 20 6811 419
E: info@rozefilmdagen.nl
www.rozefilmdagen.nl
December

United Kingdom

London Lesbian & Gay Film Festival

National Film Theatre
Southbank, Waterloo
London SE1 8XT
P: 44 20 7255 1444
www.outuk.com/llgff
April

USA

Adam Baran Gay & Lesbian Film Festival

1877 Kalakaua Ave
Honolulu HI 96815
P: 1 808 941 0424
F: 1 808 943 1724
E: info@hglcf.org
www.hawaiiscene.com/hglcf
May

Austin Gay & Lesbian International Film Festival

1216 E. 51st
Austin TX 78723
P: 1 512 302 1088
F: 1 512 302 9889
E: kino@agliff.org
www.agliff.org
August

Frameline

San Francisco International Lesbian & Gay Film Festival
145 Ninth St, Suite 300
San Francisco CA 94103
P: 1 415 703 8650
F: 1 415 861 1404
E: info@frameline.org
www.frameline.org
June

Houston Gay & Lesbian Film Festival

803 Hawthorne
Houston TX 77006
E: hglff@cs.com
www.hglff.org/hglff
May

ImageOut

Rochester Lesbian & Gay Film & Video Festival
274 N. Goodman St
Rochester NY 14607
P: 1 716 271 2640
F: 1 716 271 3798
E: imageout@rochester.rr.com
 www.imageout.org
October

Miami Gay & Lesbian Film Festival

1521 Alton Rd, #147
Miami Beach FL 33139
P: 1 305 534 9924
F: 1 305 534 2377
E: info@miamigaylesbianfilm.com
 www.miamigaylesbianfilm.com
April

Mix NYC

New York Lesbian & Gay Experimental Film Festival
29 John St, PMB 132
New York NY 10038
P: 1 212 571 4242
E: info@mixnyc.org
 www.mixnyc.org
November

Out Far!

Phoenix International Lesbian & Gay Film Festival
619 East Vista Ave
Phoenix AZ 85020
P: 1 602 410 1074
E: outfarfilmfest@aol.com
 www.outfar.org
February

Out On Film

Atlanta Gay & Lesbian Film Festival
75 Bennett St, NW, Suite N-1
Atlanta GA 30309
P: 1 404 352 4225
F: 1 404 352 0173
E: afvf@imagefv.org
 www.outonfilm.com
November

Out Takes Dallas

The Dallas Lesbian & Gay Film Festival
3818 Cedar Springs Rd, #101-405
Dallas TX 75219
P: 1 214 528 4233
E: artistic@outtakesdallas.org
 www.outtakesdallas.org
November

Outfest

Los Angeles Gay & Lesbian Film Festival
3470 Wilshire Blvd, Suite 1022
Los Angeles CA 90010
P: 1 213 480 7088
F: 1 213 480 7099
E: outfest@outfest.org
 www.outfest.org
July

Philadelphia International Gay & Lesbian Film Festival

Philadelphia PA 19102
E: paul@phillyfests.com
 www.phillyfests.com/piglff
July

Pittsburgh International Lesbian & Gay Film Festival

PO Box 81237
Pittsburgh PA 15217
P: 1 412 232 3277
E: pilgff@aol.com
 www.pilgff.org
October

Reel Affirmations

Washington International Gay & Lesbian Film Festival
PO Box 73587
Washington DC 20056
P: 1 202 986 1119
E: info@reelaffirmations.org
 www.reelaffirmations.org
October

Reeling

Chicago Lesbian & Gay International Film Festival
5243 N. Clarke St, 2rd Floor
Chicago IL 60640
P: 1 773 293 1447
F: 1 773 293 0575
E: info@chicagofilmmakers.org
 www.chicagofilmmakers.org/navreel.htm
July

Seattle Lesbian & Gay Film Festival

1122 E. Pike St, #1313
Seattle WA 98122
P: 1 206 323 4274
F: 1 206 323 4275
E: filmfest@seattlequeerfilm.com
 www.seattlequeerfilm.com
October

Sensory Perceptions

Portland LGBT Film Festival
818 SW 3rd, #1224
Portland OR 97204
P: 1 503 289 8282
F: 1 503 289 8500
E: john@sensoryperceptions.org
 www.sensoryperceptions.org
September

Tampa International Gay & Lesbian Film Festival

PO Box 18445
Tampa FL 33679-8445
P: 1 813 879 4220
E: mmurray@pridefilmfest.com
 pridefilmfest.com
October

The New Festival Inc.

New York Lesbian & Gay Film Festival
32 Broadway, 14th Floor
New York NY 10012
P: 1 212 558 6855
F: 1 212 558 6851
E: info@newfestival.org
 www.newfestival.org
June

Tranny Fest

Transgender Film Festival
584 Castro St, #273
San Francisco CA 94114
P: 1 415 820 3223
F: 1 415 282 4536
E: trannyfest@aol.com
www.trannyfest.com

Index of Directors

Ballyot, Sylvie 135

Barassat, Philippe 291

Barbato, Randy
29, 140, 153, 313, 318, 341, 366

Barbosa, Peter 210, 313

Bardem, Miquel 301

Barreto, Bruno 192

Barriga, Cecilia 277

Bartel, Paul 266, 356

Bartell, Phillip J. 119

Bartoni, Doreen 112

Bashore, Juliet 58, 232

Bat-Adam, Michal 142

Batista, Djalma Limongl 53

Baur, Gabriel 427

Baus, Janet 247

Bautista, Pablo 157

Bava, Mario 72

Beadle-Blair, Rikki 199, 280

Beatty, Maria 71, 146, 376

Beaudin, Jean 62

Beaudine, William 106

Beaumont, Gabrielle 94, 195

Beaumont, Harry 84

Beauvois, Xavier 136

Beavan, Clare 204, 389

Beerson, Jaque 231

Beeson, Constance 202

Bega, Jessica Anna 449

Behrens, Alec 210

Beiersdorf, Dagmar 145

Beldin, Dale 441

Believeau, Lulu 436

Bell, Esther 186

Bell, Richard 421

Belliveau, Lulu 333

Bellon, Yannick 417

Bemberg, María Luisa 212

Benestad, Even 40

Benner, Richard
193, 314, 411

Bennett Clay, Stanley 348

Benning, Sadie
183, 222, 227, 326

Benveniste, Michael 163

Benvenuti, Alessandro 62

Benz, Obie 197

Beresford, Bruce 181

Bergen, Brian 363

Berggold, Craig 144

Bergman, Ingmar
321, 369, 403

Bergström, Nina 112

Berkowitz, Ben 386

Berlanti, Greg 85

Berliner, Alain 267

Bernard, Chris 254

Bernard, Lionel 205

Bernardos, Peter 302

Bernaza, Lius Felipe 89

Berrios, Javier Antonio 377

Berruti, Giulio 235

Bertolucci, Bernardo 114, 242

Bertolucci, Giuseppe 262

Bettell, Paul 128, 215

Bezalel, Ronit 439

Bezucha, Thomas 67

Bhasin, Neeraj 290

Bhave, Sumitri 454

Biasatti, John 347

Bidgood, Jim 325

Bijan, Ali 360

Binder, Mike 363

Binninger, John 385

Bird, Antonia 333

Birkin, Andrew 87

Birot, Anne-Sophie 184

Black, Dustin Lance
228, 306, 378

Black, Emma 166

Black, Noel 291

Blackman, Inge 55

Blackwood, Christian 369

Blackwood, Maureen 318

Blakemore, Michael 334

Blank, Jonathan 363

Blasco, Didier 53

Bleckner, Jeff 361

Blier, Bertrand 151

Blom, Per 214

Bocahut, Laurent 179, 449

Bociurkiw, Marusia 297

Boeken, Ludi 84

Bogart, Paul 411, 432

Bogayevicz, Yurek 404

Boisvert, Johanne 62

Bokova, Jana 282

Bolden, Oriana 327

Bolden-Kramer, Rachel 338

Böll, Christoph 382

Bolton, James 143

Bonder, Diane 126

Boorman, John 128

Boos, H. Gordon 412

Borden, Lizzie 79, 149, 448

Bordowitz, Gregg 191, 377

Boreham, Craig 358

Boschman, Lorna 80, 418

Bosko, Mark 184

Boskovich, John 444

Böttger, Fritz 145

Boullata, Peter Tyler 46

Boumans, Toni 88

Bouzid, Nouri 67

Bracewell, Charles 203

Bradley, Maureen 104

Bramer, Monte 319

Branagh, Kenneth 323

Brand, Dionne 254, 257

McCaskell, Tim 356
McCollum, Rachel 421
McCredie, Elise 386
McDougall, Charles 337
McDowell, Curt 256, 405
McEwen, Mary Anne 186
McGann, Brad 110
McGee, Debbie 413
McGehee, Scott 128
McGlone, Jennifer 83
McGrath, Joseph 269
McHenry, Bryan 124, 139
McKay, Barry 154, 209
McKibben, Kerry 247
McLaughlin, Sheila 366
McLean, Steve 330
McLennan, Don 286, 328
McLennan, Gordon 217
McLeod, Dayna 433
McMurchy, Megan 51
McNaughton, John 443
Mead, Wrik 93, 173
Meckler, Nancy 40, 372
Medak, Peter 239, 454
Mehra, Prakash 453
Mehta, Deepa 160
Mehta, Ketan 202
Meier, Pierre-Alain 401
Meieran, David 431
Melville, Jean-Pierre 148
Mendes, Sam 44
Menéndez, Jessica 312
Menkes, David 211, 301
Merrison, Lindsey 172
Mersky, Liz 240
Metzger, Alan 350
Metzger, Radley
  95, 250, 357, 401
Mew, Michael 187
Meyer, Armgard 181

Meyer, Russ 66, 423
Meynell, Kate 52
Mifsud, John 380
Mignatti, Victor 84, 159
Mikels, Ted V. 29
Mikesch, Elfi 268, 360
Milici, Jennifer 363
Millan, Lorri 125, 187
Millar, Gavin 406
Miller Adato, Peter 180
Miller, Claude 65
Miller, Courtney 181
Miller, Robert Ellis 50, 198
Miller, Sam 236
Miller, Tanya 58
Miller, Thomas 400
Miller-Monzon, John 378, 402
Milling, Bill 91
Mills, Brian 133
Milton, Keith 420
Mimouni, Patrick 415
Min, Kyu-dong 277
Minello, Gianni 80
Minerba, Giovanni 166
Minnelli, Vincente 398
Mirkin, Ekaterine 201
Mitchell, Allyson 55
Mitchell, John Cameron 198
Mitchell, Max 181
Mitchell, Roy 211
Mobley, Doug 226
Moffet, Frederic 194
Moffett, Joel 289
Mohabeer, Michelle 101, 109
Molé, Franco 349
Molinaro, Edouard 91
Monette, Jean-François
  46, 395, 440
Monger, Christopher 230
Montgomery, Jennifer 37, 418

Moodysson, Lukas 368, 406
Mooney, Shayne 256
Moorcock, Sophie 436
Moore, Sara 204
Mora, Philippe 207
Morais, Jose Alvaro 319
Moreira, Rita 208
Morel, Gaël 174
Morement, Lea 31
Moreton, David 144
Morgan, U. B. 82
Morris, Richard 432
Morrissey, Paul
  61, 68, 75, 163, 167,
  197, 268, 405, 415, 447
Morrow, Vic 127
Morse, Emily 360
Mortimer, Sarah 113
Mosbacher, Dee
  41, 108, 125, 247, 312,
  340, 386
Moses, Gilbert 443
Mosvold, Frank
  90, 167, 237, 433
Motyl, H. D. 410
Moyle, Allan 407
Mozen, Paula 299
Mueller, Eric 449
Mueller, Matthais
  43, 320, 375
Muijser, Marijn 210
Muir, Madeline 437
Muller, Clare 311
Muller, Klaus 37
Mulligan, Robert 75
Munch, Christopher 206
Mundruczo, Kornel 403
Munoz, Susana 392
Murnberger, Wolfgang 304
Murray, Karen 251

Scola, Ettore 296, 380

Scorsese, Martin 36

Scott, Cynthia 112

Scott, Margaret 52

Scott, Ridley 401

Scott, Tony 208

Sedghi, Behzad 414

Seelenmeyer, Melissa 440

Segal, Jonathan 54, 55

Seidelman, Susan 176

Seidler, Ellen 151

Seitchik, Vickie 338

Selditch, Michael 161

Sender, Katherine 303

Serikbayeva, Zhanna 251

Serra, M. M 123

Serrano, Yolanda Garcia 239

Serreau, Coline 441

Sethna, Jagu 78

Severance, Abigail 335

Shadbolt, Jane 322

Shafer, Dirk 105, 272

Shahriar, Maryam 124

Shallat, Lee 310

Shallcross, Alan 277

Shapiro, David 234

Shapiro, Laurie Gwen 234

Sharandak, Natasha 408

Sharif, Rif 385

Sharman, Jim 349

Sharp, Andrew 379

Sharp, Jan 225

Shear, Barry 409

Shear, Jon 424

Sheedy, Laura 446

Sheehan, Nick 299, 395

Sheldon, Caroline 30

Shepard, Tom 93, 357

Shepp, Brian 190

Sheridan, Peter 79

Sherman, Kenneth 406

Sherwood, Bill 317

Shils, Barry 441

Shimada, Koshi 284

Shiori, Kazama 207

Shirakawa, Koji 454

Shiva, Alexandra 78

Shore, Simon 181

Shores, Del 379

Shu, Kei 207, 338

Sichel, Alex 42

Siddiqi, Atif 267

Siegel, David 128

Siegel, Lois 253

Siegel, Robert J. 393

Sigal, David 113

Siguion-Reyna, Carlos
271, 404

Silber, Rolf 143

Siler, Megan 160, 281

Sillen, Peter 63

Silver, Scott 227

Silver, Suzie 170, 319

Silvera, Charlotte 334

Simandl, Lloyd 99

Simmons, Aishah Shahidah
216

Simo, Ana Maria 207

Simon, Frank 337

Simoneau, Yves 331

Simpson, Kelli 403, 421, 434

Singer, Leslie 226

Singleton, John 201

Sirota, Greg 422

Skeet, Brian 435

Skolimowski, Jerzy 252

Slade, Eric 205

Sloan, Brian 212, 329, 365

Slotar, Dean 33

Sluizer, George 419

Smallhorne, Jimmy 30

Smaragdis, Yannis 97

Smith, Jack 161

Smith, Jo 186

Smith, Kevin 100

Smith, Leslie L. 124

Smith, Robert 443

Smith, Sidra 266

Snee, Patrick 263

Sodo, Mario 138

Sønder, Carsten 332

Soo, Andrew 254

Soomekh, Laleh 450

Sopsits, Árpád 32

Sotile, Renee 142

Soueid, Mohammed 105

Spadola, Meema 311

Spalding, Ron 356

Spano, Massimo 274

Speck, Wieland 46, 150, 437

Spence, Richard 133

Spencer, Patricia 139

Spetsiotis, Takis 280

Spheeris, Penelope 82

Spielberg, Steven 110

Spinola, Paolo 173

Spiro, Ellen 179, 189, 318

Sport, Kathy 33

Spottiswoode, Roger 47

Sprenkel, Kenn 406

Sprinkle, Annie 49, 376

Spyke 199

Stafrace, Inka 376

Stahlberg, Michael 260

Stappen, Chris Vander 155

Starr, Steven 226

Starrett, Jack 107

Steele, Lisa 247

Steger, Lawrence 319

Stein, Peter 95

Selected Websites of Interest

www.imdb.com

The Internet Movie Database features general listings of films including comprehensive credit details such as cast, crew, production companies, distributor, year, running time etc. Also has links to external film reviews.

www.gay.com

Vast website containing information on all things queer, including a large section related to queer film.

www.planetout.com/pno/splash.html

Popcorn Q is a comprehensive gay, lesbian, bisexual and transgender film website, which features an online video shop, viewing of short films and classic film trailers, live chats and interviews; reviews and information about thousands of queer films, film festivals and distributors.

www.movies-too-gay.com

Over 1,100 film reviews of queer films from around the world.

www.queerfilm.com

Cinema Q is a comprehensive video and media resource for lesbians and gay men interested in queer film.

www.qrd.org

The Queer Resources Directory contains thousands of files about everything queer and has downloads and links to other queer film sites.

www.filmfestivals.com/index.shtml

Packed full of information about film festivals from all over the world.

www.tgwebbuilders.com/TGRL/movies.html

Listings and film reviews of titles relevant to the transgendered communities.

www.queerhorror.com

Explores the horror genre from a queer perspective.

www.cinemaweb.com

Cinema Web is a collective of independent film and video websites combining the resources of smaller companies, publications and authors.

www.qcinema.com/festivals.asp

Queer Cinema includes film reviews, profiles on queer casts and crews and hot links to queer film festivals around the world

shergoodforest.com/movies/home.html

Shergood Forest contains a wide reaching database of information on international films of gay interest.

www.sexuality.org/l/lesbigay/glbfilm.html

Sexuality.Org contains a large listing of queer film, and other information relevant to the queer community.

www.allmovie.com

Database of general films including what's on and where, film finder, reviews and essays.

www.advocate.com

Major US gay and lesbian lifestyle and news magazine, features regular features and articles on queer film, as well as gay arts and media archives.